A CONCORDANCE TO BRONTË'S *JANE EYRE*

GARLAND REFERENCE LIBRARY
OF THE HUMANITIES
(VOL. 290)

A CONCORDANCE TO BRONTË'S *JANE EYRE*

C. Ruth Sabol
Todd K. Bender

GARLAND PUBLISHING, INC. • NEW YORK & LONDON
1981

Library of Congress Cataloging in Publication Data

Sabol, C. Ruth.
  A concordance to Brontë's Jane Eyre.

  (Garland reference library of the humanities;
v. 290)
  Includes bibliographical references and index.
  1. Brontë, Charlotte, 1816–1855. Jane Eyre—
Concordances. I. Bender, Todd K. II. Brontë,
Charlotte, 1816–1855. Jane Eyre. III. Title.
IV. Series.
PR4167.J5S2 1981   823′.8   81-47016
ISBN 0-8240-9339-9   AACR2

Printed on acid-free, 250-year-life paper
Manufactured in the United States of America

CONTENTS

PREFATORY NOTE
The Concordance as a Tool in Literary Scholarship

Simple as it may sound, the study of any work of imaginative literature must begin with an understanding of the words of the text, word by word. But literary scholars cannot stop there; they must push on to unravel the strands of words which are shot through a text in order to reveal precisely how any writer creates his effects and how those effects contribute to the meaning of the whole. However, just as we view the task of illuminating the text as being squarely within the domain of the literary scholar, only the most narrowly conceived understanding of the nature of that task would deny the scholar the technological tools whereby his work, although not made significantly simpler, can be made significantly more precise. Computer technology, which has been refined and has become available to us only within the last fifty years, has given scholarship an additional tool with which to conduct research. We now have the means to display and study the words of massive texts (or the complete works of a writer) unchained from the syntagmatic structures into which they were originally fixed by a writer. Computers, too, can perform arithmetical and statistical calculations which in themselves may appear to be as meaningless as did counting the streaks of the tulip to Dr. Johnson 200 years ago. However, in our computer-generated prose concordances, the literary scholar has at his disposal basic information which can be used in a wide range of research endeavors. For example, in one part of our study of style in natural languages, we examined the Word Frequency Tables of *A Concordance to Ford Madox Ford's "The Good Soldier"* (Garland, 1981) and *A Concordance to Conrad's "Lord Jim"* (Garland, 1976). What would not be perceivable from an ever-so-scrupulous reading of *The Good Soldier (TGS)* and *Lord Jim (LJ)* by the most diligent of scholars became immediately evident: the much shorter *TGS* text contained many more occurrences of *that* (2230 in all) than did *LJ* (1481). It is not too much to say, I think, that the tokens of *that* in these two novels would hardly arrest the spontaneous critical attention of even the most diligent reader. And it would be dull work indeed to pore through 224,000 words in order to strain out even 3710 tokens of *that*, should anyone be able to conjure a reason for doing so. But when we analyzed these occurrences, each of which is found in the Verbal Index and located in the Field of Reference in the concordances, we learned that *that* functions as a powerful style marker revealing a fundamentally different fictive world in *TGS* than in *LJ*. We also learned that a semantic analysis of one type of *that*, the nominal complement *that*-clause complementizer, could be used to lend refinement and linguistic verifica-

tion to Booth's notion of reliable and unreliable narration. From this, we formulated a linguistically verifiable means for determining whether narration in any work of prose fiction is reliable or unreliable.[1]

Certainly the study of style has a long-established tradition, ranging from Plato to Susan Sontag. The literature on style is replete with citations from poets and novelists, philosophers, literary critics, and linguists, either defining style or tracing the history of the study of style. Currently, as a linguistic problem, style is often viewed either as a manipulation of the grammar of a natural language or as a reimposed grammar.[2] As a literary problem it has been seen either as norms or universal, generic designations (reflecting a reader's choice of classifications) as in the high, middle, and low style of classic rhetorical doctrine, or as manifestations of deviation from a norm (reflecting a writer's conscious or unconscious choice) as in the concept of stylistics advanced by Enkvist. Individual writing styles have been characterized by such ingenious yet appropriate metaphors as *tough, sweet, stuffy, tumbling, pelting, energetik* [*sic*], and *blanket-tasting*. Style has been conceptualized aphoristically as in Buffon's "*Le style, c'est l'homme même*" and transcendentally as in Goethe's expression of style as an irreducible essence made visible.[3] More recently (1971), Roland Barthes has envisioned style, not as an expression of some irreducible essence, but as a number of textual elements residing in literary language.[4] In all these varying perspectives on style, Michael Riffaterre has been quick to find weakness. Riffaterre is critical of many of the traditional methods of appraising style because the process has relied heavily on the scholar's intuitive value judgments, rather than on encoded potentialities or stylistic constants in a text. He asserts that intuitive judgments are contingent upon psychological processes and cultural conditioning.[5] Style, then, becomes not a quality of text, but a quality of the mind of the reader. In practice, literary scholars and critics, relying on learned intuition, have often based their studies of style on those spectacular content words and images which have garnered their attention in the works of writers, while often ignoring the less psychologically striking function words. In fact, F.R. Leavis finds fault with Conrad for overusing the words *inscrutable, inconceivable*, and *unspeakable* in *Heart of Darkness*, although *inscrutable* appears only four, *inconceivable* six, and *unspeakable* three times in the entire novel.[6] As a corrective to this sort of impressionistic over-reading, the literary scholar now has the prose concordance at his disposal as an indispensable tool in verifying his intuitive judgments.

In the extensive studies of prose style, methodology has been as varied as the many aspects of the problem of style and the professed aims of those writing on style. Stephen Ullmann, in *Style in the French Novel* (1957), bases his study on a number of recurrent stylistic features which he categorizes and discusses. He works from the effect of a particular device on the reader (e.g., the use of foreign milieu which he categorizes as linguistic local color in the French novel of the Romantic period), its variations and diffusion. His method is first to count and discuss the instances of (let us say) the Italian milieu in Stendhal's *La Chartreuse de Parme* or the Spanish milieu in Mérimée's *Carmen*, then to draw some tentative conclusions about what he views as distinct traits of the Romantic movement and the effect of those traits on French literary tradition.

It is not too much to say that the American tradition in stylistic analysis begins with Richard Ohmann's *Shaw: The Style and the Man* (1962). In this analysis of Shaw's

non-dramatic prose, Ohmann specifies certain modes of expression in order to judge their semantic importance in the search for a connection between style (rhetoric) and thought (conceptual scheme). His method involves counting the occurrences (in a sample of running text, say two pages) of what he judges to be some of Shaw's favorite syntactic usages, discussing their semantic significance and associating them with Shavian habits of thought.

Louis T. Milic, in *A Quantitative Approach to the Style of Jonathan Swift* (1967), works from an extensive analysis of syntactic categories (e.g., connectives) and discusses Swift's style in terms of these categories. Milic's method involves counting the occurrences of words (in a 63,000-word sample taken from a number of Swift's writings) which fall into specific word classes (e.g., noun, determiner, and the like), then discussing the consistency of Swift's style based upon these word classes as measured against a sample corpus from other writers (such as Addison, Defoe, and Dryden).

Seymour Chatman, in *The Later Style of Henry James* (1972), is concerned, like Ullmann, with working from effect to specific devices available for producing the effect, in this case, the specific effect of abstractness encountered in the reading of James. Chatman's method is to count the occurrences of items in semantic categories (e.g., logical terms, psychological verbs, and so on) within a given sample (say 200 running sentences from *The Wings of the Dove*), and to discuss how they contribute to the effect of abstractness.

Recently, John Russell, in *Style in Modern British Fiction* (1978), works from his more-or-less impressionistic interpretations of specific works (two each from Joyce, Lawrence, Forster, Lewis, and Green) to show that style is a means of discovering meaning in the works. His method involves culling sentences from the novels, supplying sporadic data (e.g., the incidents of *what*-clauses in the works selected), then discussing a number of examples of style markers which contribute to character, situation, and theme—the meaning of the work as a whole. Russell asserts that he offers "conclusions about style that, in context, seem self-evident enough not to require statistical verification."[7]

In spite of the clear temperamental differences between such scholars as Milic, who holds to the necessity of quantitative data in the analysis of style, and Russell, who reverts to self-evident conclusions which require no statistical verification, solid scholarly research must be based upon intelligent, finely honed intuition in conjunction with rigorously produced quantitative evidence. Self-evident conclusions tend (in fact) to be learned conclusions, while quantitative counts tend to lend an aura of scientific infallibility to what (in fact) is based upon intuition, the decision about what to count. Prose concordances can provide important data basic to many types of scholarly research studies, such as those mentioned.

We are currently embarking on an extensive examination of style in natural language as found in the works of the Brontës. This index to Charlotte Brontë's *Jane Eyre* is a first step in amassing the basic information necessary to continue our studies.

CRS

NOTES

1. C. Ruth Sabol, "Lexical Selection in Ford Madox Ford's *The Good Soldier*: Structure, Style, and Motif," Diss. Univ. of Wisconsin-Madison, 1980, pp. 101–63.

2. Samuel R. Levin, "Poetry and Grammaticalness," in H.G. Lunt, ed., *Proceedings of the Ninth International Congress of Linguistics* (The Hague, 1964), cited in William M. Russell, "Some Style Rules for a Transformational Grammar," *Linguistics*, 157 (August 1, 1975), p. 91; Roman Jakobson, "Linguistics and Poetics," in Thomas A. Sebeok, ed., *Style in Language* (Cambridge, Mass.: M.I.T. Press, 1960), pp. 351–77; and Edward Stankiewicz, "Poetic and Non-Poetic Language in Their Interrelation," in D. Davie et al., eds., *Poetics* (The Hague: Mouton, 1961), cited in William M. Russell, p. 92.

3. Goethe, "Einfache Nachamung, Manier, Stil" (1788), in *Samtliche Werke*, Jubilaumsausgabe, ed. Eduard von der Hellen (Stuttgart, 1903), cited by René Wellek, "Stylistics, Poetics, and Criticism," in *Literary Style*, ed. Seymour Chatman (London: Oxford Univ. Press., 1971), pp. 74–5.

4. Roland Barthes, "Style and Its Image," in Chatman, p. 10.

5. Michael Riffaterre, "Criteria for Style Analysis," *Word*, 15 (1959), pp. 162–3.

6. F.R. Leavis, *The Great Tradition* (1948; rpt. New York: New York Univ. Press., 1967), p. 177; Sybil C. Jacobson, "Structure of *Heart of Darkness*," Diss. Univ. of Wisconsin-Madison, 1972, p. 129.

7. John Russell, *Style in Modern British Fiction* (Baltimore: Johns Hopkins Press, 1978), p. 8.

TECHNICAL NOTE

The publication of this set of indexes to *Jane Eyre* initiates what we hope will be a series of publications on the Brontes comparable to our series of concordances and verbal indexes to the complete works of Joseph Conrad in the Garland Reference Library of the Humanities. Users of this volume should be familiar with the selected bibliography and outlines of uses for verbal indexes and concordances given in the preface to our *A Concordance to Conrad's "Almayer's Folly"* (Garland, 1978). It would be redundant to state again here the details of our indexing system as it has evolved through the Conrad series. Users can see, for example, that our alphabetical sequence begins with the ampersand, followed by apostrophe, followed by Arabic numerals, and then the letters *a* through *z*, so such details hardly need elaboration here. If a reader wants to know how often Bronte uses a word, he looks to the Word Frequency Table to discover if the word occurs in the text and how often it is found. He can then turn to the Verbal Index for the page and line numbers of each occurrence. Finally, he can turn to the Field of Reference to locate the context of each word in its page and line of the prose text.

The Field of Reference reproduces exactly the pagination, lineation, spelling, and punctuation of the second edition of the novel, *Jane Eyre: An Autobiography*, by Currer Bell (London: Smith, Elder and Co., 1848), but it does not preserve italics, the ligature œ, acute and grave accents, dieresis, cedilla, or other diacritics. Parentheses have been marked by the virgule (/). All Roman numerals have been converted to Arabic to maintain their necessary distinction from letters. Creation of a verbal index to this edition reveals a number of anomalies of spelling and punctuation in the second edition, which we keep intact in our field of reference; for example, *back-stairs/ backstairs, banisters/bannisters, bason, bazars, bedroom/bed-room, bedrooms/bed-rooms, cheese-cake/cheesecake, develop/develope, Elliot/Elliott, eye-brows/eyebrows, filip/fillip, fire-side/ fireside, gentleman-like/gentlemanlike, gray/grey, help-meet/helpmeet, house-maids/housemaids, pastile/pastille, school-room/schoolroom, secrecy/secresy, steelly/steely, teased/teazed, way-side/ wayside, wood-land/woodland.* Even such apparent typesetting errors as *due* when the context seems certainly to call for *dew,* or *Thornhill* for *Thornfield,* have been retained. We elaborate the reasons for not normalizing such variations in the preface to our *Concordance to Conrad's "The Shadow Line" and "Youth"* (Garland, 1980). Briefly stated, we believe that it is important to describe the actual state of each printed document, not to speculate or to interpret it in such a way as to mislead users. Variations in spelling may be of particular importance to the scholar who is interested in distinguishing the work of one typesetter from another, or one state of composition of the

text from another. To normalize what appear to be "errors" would cripple the serious research uses of the index. Likewise, our current practice is not to separate homographs in the index since such separation—for example, of *will* (the verb) from *will* (the noun)—leads inevitably to cases of dubious interpretation of the text, rather than rigorous description of it.

The best short outline of our work is to be found in my "Literary Texts in Electronic Storage: The Editorial Potential" (*Computers and the Humanities*, 1976, pp. 193–99). The thrust of our inquiry involves the examination of style in natural languages. In the course of our work, we frequently must produce verbal indexes or concordances to massive literary texts such as *Jane Eyre*. We do not set out to produce concordances, but once we have created them for our own investigations, we come under great pressure to make the data available to scholars who are unable to work directly with our electronic archive. We have therefore a problem of economy. How can we make available information of the widest possible use at the lowest possible cost? Our plan has been to issue first a set of verbal indexes and word frequency tables along with a field of reference, exactly as provided in this volume. If user interest continues to demand further information, we are able to follow with a context-citation concordance to the low-frequency words in the text, as we have done with our *Concordance to Conrad's "Heart of Darkness"* (Garland, 1979) and the microfiche tables issued by Southern Illinois University Press (1973). This appears to us to be the most economical way to make the maximum data available, but we insist that the "real" research tool is the electronic archive of computer-readable texts which we are constructing at the University of Wisconsin and which is capable of providing configurations of information about the text far more powerful than traditional concordances. Interested scholars are invited to contact us about potential research applications requiring direct use of our archive.

A word in our work is defined as a set of letters between two spaces. *Jane Eyre* has 186,129 words in the running text. These words fall into 13,510 distinct vocabulary items. The words or tokens were sorted into their types, making up the index and the word frequency table, in approximately eight minutes of execution time using the Madison Academic Computing Center's Sperry Univac 1100/82 and its peripheral equipment.

We express our gratitude to the Research Tools Division of the National Endowment for the Humanities. They support the Wisconsin Old Spanish Dictionary Project, whose software and peripheral equipment were used in the production of these indexes. We particularly wish to thank Professor John Nitti, Professor Lloyd Kasten, and Mrs. Jean Anderson for their generous help with this publication.

TKB

VERBAL INDEX

&c	014.15	035.12	055.16	077.22	096.06
010.05	014.21	035.15	055.21	077.23	096.07
029.07	015.01	035.22	055.24	077.28	096.12
029.07	015.15	035.22	055.24	078.04	096.19
049.12	015.17	035.25	055.25	078.06	097.02
086.22	015.21	036.03	055.26	078.07	097.09
097.11	015.24	036.20	055.27	078.18	097.11
098.10	016.01	036.21	056.04	079.01	098.11
098.10	016.01	036.25	056.06	079.03	099.04
099.08	016.02	037.01	056.06	079.05	099.15
115.26	016.07	037.03	056.09	079.10	099.16
202.18	016.10	037.05	056.21	079.15	099.18
238.28	016.11	037.08	056.22	080.02	099.21
280.02	016.13	037.10	057.05	080.04	099.22
288.26	016.17	037.13	057.17	080.07	099.25
306.06	016.19	038.19	057.20	080.17	099.26
331.16	016.22	038.20	057.26	080.22	100.07
333.15	017.01	038.23	058.06	080.23	100.15
365.21	017.05	039.02	058.12	080.24	100.18
376.22	017.11	039.13	058.22	080.28	100.23
459.13	017.21	039.13	058.25	081.01	100.25
482.20	017.24	039.15	058.26	081.09	100.26
482.20	018.07	039.21	059.09	081.16	101.04
555.10	018.13	040.12	059.18	081.19	101.10
844.20	018.14	040.15	059.22	081.23	101.18
889.07	018.20	040.19	059.26	082.01	102.01
'at's	018.20	040.24	060.04	082.03	102.02
681.02	018.20	040.25	060.08	082.05	102.21
'em	019.26	040.27	060.11	082.09	102.23
696.26	020.06	041.02	060.11	082.12	102.24
'only	020.11	041.07	060.17	082.13	103.01
873.16	020.12	041.10	060.19	082.13	103.02
'rageous	020.14	041.11	060.26	082.17	103.14
600.02	020.16	041.12	061.03	082.19	103.17
-church	020.19	041.16	061.05	082.27	104.08
593.14	021.12	041.18	061.05	083.02	105.04
-street	021.20	041.20	061.15	083.08	105.07
592.19	021.22	042.05	062.16	083.10	105.17
1	022.03	042.05	063.15	083.17	105.20
098.14	022.04	042.11	063.27	083.24	105.23
151	022.04	042.13	064.07	084.07	106.15
173.04	022.08	042.15	064.07	084.09	106.18
19th	022.13	042.19	064.12	084.10	106.25
071.03	022.25	043.16	064.16	084.12	107.02
2000	023.06	043.21	064.16	084.14	108.10
777.02	023.07	043.23	065.03	084.23	108.15
20th	023.12	044.05	065.08	084.24	109.14
593.07	023.12	044.07	065.09	085.01	109.14
301	023.16	044.20	065.20	085.10	109.14
266.09	023.18	045.02	066.02	085.13	109.22
516	023.27	045.03	066.12	085.20	109.27
089.16	024.05	045.04	066.17	085.24	109.27
a	024.05	045.06	066.20	085.25	110.01
001.03	024.09	046.05	066.20	085.28	112.06
001.09	025.07	046.08	066.24	086.05	112.11
001.14	025.09	046.17	066.27	086.06	112.14
002.03	025.16	046.23	067.19	086.09	113.03
002.08	026.03	046.24	067.20	086.09	113.17
002.12	026.03	046.24	068.01	086.11	113.20
002.13	026.04	047.09	068.07	086.14	113.24
002.22	026.06	047.09	068.16	086.17	113.25
002.25	026.07	047.20	068.19	086.20	113.25
002.27	026.11	047.22	068.24	087.01	113.26
003.01	026.14	047.26	069.10	087.06	113.27
003.04	026.19	048.01	069.23	087.08	114.02
003.13	026.20	048.13	071.03	087.10	114.09
003.14	027.01	048.14	071.08	087.19	114.11
003.16	027.01	048.22	071.10	087.20	114.21
003.22	027.03	048.24	071.16	087.23	115.01
004.22	027.08	048.28	071.17	087.25	115.05
004.23	027.14	049.03	071.20	087.26	115.06
004.25	028.13	049.04	072.02	088.07	115.08
005.02	028.23	049.07	072.25	088.15	115.14
005.05	029.06	049.07	072.26	088.20	115.21
005.11	029.15	049.11	073.01	089.04	116.04
005.11	029.23	049.22	073.06	089.09	116.10
005.12	029.26	049.25	073.16	089.09	116.21
005.13	030.09	050.02	073.28	089.21	116.24
005.25	030.11	050.11	074.06	089.23	117.01
006.27	030.12	050.16	074.09	089.25	117.02
007.01	030.14	051.06	074.15	089.25	117.23
007.03	030.17	051.08	074.15	089.26	118.12
007.05	030.17	051.10	074.16	089.28	118.13
007.08	030.19	051.11	074.19	090.02	118.20
007.11	030.21	051.26	075.07	090.07	118.21
008.19	030.25	052.08	075.09	090.07	119.16
008.21	031.06	052.10	075.13	090.11	119.22
009.08	031.07	052.10	075.13	090.11	120.19
009.15	031.10	052.13	075.16	090.13	121.01
009.21	031.11	052.17	075.24	090.15	121.03
010.01	031.23	052.20	075.25	090.19	121.15
010.01	032.08	052.24	076.01	091.07	121.21
010.13	032.14	052.27	076.03	091.18	121.27
010.13	032.16	052.28	076.04	092.07	122.06
010.14	032.16	053.10	076.05	092.14	122.08
010.14	032.19	053.14	076.06	092.15	122.09
010.26	032.21	053.17	076.06	092.16	122.16
011.01	032.26	053.28	076.13	092.16	123.05
012.02	033.01	054.01	076.16	092.28	123.14
012.03	033.02	054.02	076.17	093.01	123.17
012.06	033.10	054.02	076.19	093.02	124.01
012.08	033.19	054.04	076.20	093.12	124.04
012.12	033.21	054.05	076.21	094.03	124.09
012.16	033.21	054.10	076.25	094.07	124.09
012.19	033.22	054.15	077.03	094.17	124.16
012.20	033.27	054.19	077.12	094.19	124.17
013.05	034.17	054.19	077.15	094.21	124.18
013.06	034.21	054.20		095.05	125.03
013.11	034.26	054.21		095.10	125.05
013.14	035.01	054.21		095.13	125.07
014.03	035.03	054.25		095.13	
	035.10	055.07			
		055.07			

125.12	149.22	172.15	190.22	208.26	227.26
125.13	150.10	172.16	190.23	209.02	228.05
125.15	150.13	172.17	190.23	209.04	228.10
125.16	150.16	172.21	191.01	209.06	228.10
125.27	150.20	173.01	191.07	209.10	228.18
125.27	151.10	173.02	191.20	209.16	228.19
126.01	151.16	173.13	191.23	209.22	228.25
126.03	151.17	173.22	191.26	210.03	229.05
127.09	151.18	173.27	191.26	210.06	229.06
127.13	151.20	173.27	192.18	210.06	229.08
127.14	151.25	174.05	192.20	210.07	229.08
127.17	151.26	174.21	192.25	210.11	229.08
127.17	152.01	174.22	192.26	211.03	229.10
127.18	152.02	174.26	193.01	211.09	229.14
127.20	152.07	174.27	193.12	211.09	229.16
127.25	152.10	174.28	193.14	211.11	229.17
128.01	152.26	175.09	193.14	211.12	230.08
128.05	153.15	175.09	193.15	211.13	230.09
129.05	153.16	175.13	193.15	211.14	230.09
130.17	153.16	175.14	193.16	211.20	230.20
130.17	153.17	175.20	193.17	213.02	231.04
130.26	154.23	175.26	193.23	213.04	231.06
130.27	154.23	176.20	194.01	213.07	231.10
131.11	154.28	176.27	194.02	213.09	231.14
131.12	155.01	177.05	194.03	214.02	231.16
131.19	155.11	177.06	194.05	214.06	231.21
132.11	155.12	177.10	194.07	214.16	231.24
132.12	155.18	177.17	194.09	214.17	232.05
132.21	155.22	177.21	194.17	214.19	232.14
133.03	156.22	177.23	194.19	214.19	232.20
133.06	157.02	178.02	194.23	214.25	233.09
133.15	157.10	178.04	194.28	215.05	233.10
133.16	158.01	178.15	195.09	216.01	233.14
133.17	158.03	178.18	195.23	216.02	233.15
133.23	158.21	178.18	196.04	216.09	233.16
133.25	159.12	178.25	196.08	216.16	233.16
134.05	159.15	178.26	196.16	216.18	233.19
134.06	159.20	179.04	196.21	216.19	234.01
134.08	159.20	179.12	196.28	217.09	234.06
134.19	160.05	179.23	197.04	217.10	234.10
135.06	160.09	179.27	197.05	217.10	234.18
135.14	160.09	179.27	197.06	217.13	234.22
136.06	160.19	179.28	197.10	217.14	235.13
136.08	161.05	180.01	197.18	217.19	235.14
136.17	161.09	180.12	197.22	217.19	236.02
136.26	161.09	180.13	197.27	217.27	236.14
137.02	161.13	180.15	197.28	218.05	236.15
137.10	161.23	180.18	198.03	218.05	236.16
137.16	162.03	180.26	198.06	218.11	236.18
137.19	162.04	181.02	198.08	218.13	236.27
137.26	162.05	181.02	198.24	218.14	236.28
138.07	162.20	181.02	198.24	218.17	237.14
138.09	162.21	181.03	198.27	218.22	238.05
138.10	162.22	181.05	198.27	218.22	238.10
138.11	162.27	181.07	199.02	218.25	238.15
138.16	163.06	181.09	199.07	219.07	239.08
138.25	163.10	181.11	199.07	219.08	239.10
138.26	163.24	182.10	199.11	219.10	239.14
139.06	164.03	182.11	199.12	219.12	239.25
139.18	164.04	182.13	199.13	219.14	240.01
139.19	164.10	182.17	199.15	219.25	240.09
139.24	164.25	183.01	199.16	219.25	240.10
139.24	164.27	183.11	199.18	219.28	240.15
140.01	165.16	183.13	199.26	220.01	240.24
140.02	165.18	183.18	200.06	220.03	241.01
140.13	165.21	183.21	200.11	220.12	241.09
140.14	165.22	183.24	200.16	220.14	241.13
140.15	165.26	184.06	200.17	220.15	241.19
140.23	165.28	184.12	200.22	220.24	242.02
140.26	166.06	184.18	201.11	220.26	242.07
140.26	166.09	184.24	201.28	220.26	242.10
140.27	166.13	184.27	202.18	220.28	243.03
141.04	166.26	185.01	202.26	220.28	243.05
141.05	167.02	185.06	202.28	221.01	243.12
141.08	167.03	185.10	203.05	221.05	243.21
141.12	167.05	185.12	203.06	221.13	243.24
141.14	167.05	185.13	203.14	221.18	243.27
141.17	167.09	185.13	203.16	221.18	244.02
141.26	167.15	185.14	203.18	221.24	244.06
142.08	167.20	185.16	203.19	221.26	244.19
142.11	167.21	185.18	203.22	221.27	245.02
142.17	167.23	185.19	203.23	222.01	245.07
142.18	168.04	185.22	203.27	222.02	245.13
143.11	168.09	185.25	204.02	222.06	245.15
143.15	168.12	185.27	204.03	222.06	245.17
143.16	168.17	186.04	204.04	222.13	245.18
144.13	168.19	186.06	204.07	222.15	245.26
144.14	168.20	186.06	204.07	222.15	247.21
145.06	168.20	186.13	204.09	222.17	247.25
145.10	168.25	186.16	204.10	222.21	247.27
145.10	169.09	186.16	204.28	223.13	248.01
145.11	169.10	186.23	205.05	223.15	248.03
145.20	169.13	187.06	205.18	223.20	248.07
145.22	169.16	187.06	205.25	224.04	248.08
145.26	169.18	187.08	205.25	224.09	248.12
146.07	169.26	187.17	206.08	224.13	248.13
146.14	170.07	187.18	206.13	224.14	248.15
146.16	170.08	187.23	206.18	224.19	248.18
146.16	170.09	188.08	206.18	224.23	248.21
146.18	170.26	188.25	206.21	224.25	248.23
147.12	171.02	188.27	207.07	225.20	248.28
148.11	171.09	189.01	207.17	225.26	248.28
148.12	171.11	189.03	207.17	226.01	249.03
148.28	171.12	189.09	207.20	226.14	249.03
149.01	171.22	189.11	208.03	226.17	249.07
149.02	172.01	189.18	208.06	226.17	249.07
149.06	172.03	189.20	208.14	226.19	249.13
149.09	172.05	189.20	208.14	227.01	249.14
149.13	172.07	189.24	208.23	227.05	249.25
149.16	172.12	190.07	208.25	227.09	250.16
	172.14		208.25	227.13	

250.18	275.06	296.01	324.08	345.26	370.09
250.23	275.10	296.03	324.09	346.11	370.16
251.09	275.20	296.05	324.11	346.12	370.17
251.13	275.20	296.15	324.13	346.13	370.24
251.22	275.28	296.26	324.19	346.15	370.27
252.08	276.01	297.06	324.20	346.18	372.07
252.14	276.01	297.07	325.01	346.21	372.15
252.28	276.11	297.09	325.07	347.06	372.16
253.03	276.14	297.10	325.15	347.10	372.24
253.11	276.18	297.16	325.26	347.11	372.25
253.12	276.20	297.21	325.27	347.16	373.01
253.21	276.20	298.21	326.07	347.18	373.05
254.08	276.22	298.27	326.12	347.18	373.12
254.17	276.25	299.02	326.13	347.19	373.16
254.17	277.02	299.02	327.06	348.07	373.26
255.07	277.05	299.10	328.16	348.12	374.17
255.11	277.25	299.27	328.25	349.03	375.13
255.21	278.03	299.27	328.27	349.04	375.16
255.28	278.04	300.08	329.01	349.11	375.28
256.11	279.02	300.10	329.01	349.20	376.08
256.22	279.07	301.01	329.04	349.21	376.19
256.26	279.09	301.04	329.05	349.22	376.21
256.27	279.11	301.10	329.13	351.17	377.02
256.27	280.01	301.11	329.15	351.20	377.03
257.05	280.02	302.09	329.20	352.12	377.13
257.12	280.06	302.19	330.09	352.15	377.20
257.25	280.12	302.21	330.19	352.16	377.23
258.01	280.18	302.23	330.24	352.17	377.23
258.08	280.19	302.26	331.23	352.23	377.23
258.09	280.26	305.09	331.24	353.04	377.24
258.13	280.27	305.19	331.26	353.14	377.25
258.23	281.01	306.01	332.10	353.21	378.22
259.07	281.02	306.07	332.27	353.22	378.25
259.23	281.03	306.17	333.19	354.09	379.10
260.01	281.12	306.17	333.26	354.23	379.12
260.02	281.21	306.18	333.28	354.27	379.18
260.03	281.22	307.01	333.28	355.01	379.19
260.07	281.27	307.18	334.05	355.13	379.20
260.15	282.01	307.25	334.16	355.18	379.25
260.21	282.02	307.25	334.20	355.19	380.03
260.26	282.04	308.11	335.01	355.27	380.04
261.04	282.12	308.12	335.01	356.18	380.18
261.07	282.13	308.13	335.02	356.25	380.18
261.12	282.18	308.14	335.02	356.27	380.20
261.13	282.23	308.19	335.03	357.17	381.05
261.17	283.04	308.19	335.17	357.28	381.07
261.19	283.13	308.20	335.19	358.01	381.08
261.20	283.16	308.21	335.21	358.15	381.20
261.26	283.24	309.03	335.22	358.16	382.02
262.13	283.25	310.07	336.08	358.20	382.07
263.01	284.01	310.10	336.10	358.21	382.17
263.03	284.09	310.12	336.11	358.23	382.20
263.08	284.16	310.14	336.20	359.08	383.04
263.15	284.23	310.15	336.25	359.18	383.05
263.26	285.02	310.17	337.04	359.22	383.05
264.11	285.02	310.22	337.05	359.26	383.09
264.12	285.12	310.23	337.06	360.02	383.10
264.21	285.13	311.04	337.08	360.03	383.20
264.25	285.18	311.06	337.08	360.05	383.21
264.27	285.21	311.06	337.09	360.06	383.21
265.04	286.05	311.27	337.15	360.06	383.25
265.09	286.10	312.21	338.04	360.13	383.28
265.09	286.16	312.21	338.16	360.17	384.12
265.13	286.16	312.22	339.01	360.21	384.21
265.18	286.16	312.24	339.11	360.24	384.24
265.19	286.23	313.14	340.01	360.26	384.27
265.21	286.24	313.25	340.06	361.03	385.07
266.02	287.02	313.26	341.02	361.11	385.25
266.22	287.02	314.14	341.09	361.11	386.03
266.25	287.23	314.28	341.11	361.13	386.12
266.27	287.27	315.04	341.13	361.20	386.13
267.06	288.01	315.12	341.14	361.25	386.14
267.08	288.02	315.24	341.15	362.13	386.15
267.16	288.12	316.06	341.16	362.23	386.19
267.23	288.22	316.13	341.16	362.24	386.20
268.10	288.26	316.18	341.24	363.01	387.02
268.10	288.28	316.26	341.25	363.03	387.12
268.10	289.01	317.11	341.25	363.06	387.16
268.16	289.05	317.12	341.26	364.11	387.21
268.23	289.06	317.27	341.28	364.12	388.02
269.05	289.06	317.28	342.04	365.05	388.04
269.11	289.07	318.10	342.08	365.10	388.14
269.15	289.12	318.12	342.09	365.22	388.19
269.27	289.13	318.24	342.09	366.20	388.24
270.07	289.14	318.26	342.13	366.24	388.25
270.16	289.21	319.01	342.15	366.24	388.25
270.21	289.26	319.03	342.17	366.25	389.04
270.26	290.01	319.05	342.23	366.27	389.09
271.20	290.09	319.06	342.27	367.03	389.14
271.24	290.10	319.17	342.28	367.05	389.14
271.26	290.22	319.20	343.05	367.06	389.22
272.01	291.01	320.04	343.12	367.11	390.01
272.01	291.02	320.11	343.15	367.13	390.03
272.02	291.04	320.19	343.17	367.19	390.10
272.03	291.11	320.21	343.20	367.20	390.13
272.13	291.17	320.25	343.22	367.24	390.24
272.19	292.12	320.26	343.23	367.25	391.03
272.21	292.23	321.01	344.09	368.06	392.13
272.22	292.23	321.07	344.14	368.09	393.05
273.01	293.01	321.07	344.14	368.12	394.05
273.02	293.19	321.08	344.15	368.16	394.06
273.07	293.19	321.08	344.18	369.01	394.06
273.08	293.27	321.19	344.19	369.16	394.07
273.23	294.10	322.02	344.20	369.18	394.10
273.25	294.23	322.04	344.24	369.20	394.11
273.28	294.25	322.14	344.24	369.21	394.15
274.03	294.27	323.02	344.26	369.22	394.17
274.11	295.13	323.10	345.03	369.22	395.04
274.19	295.17	323.12	345.16	369.24	395.06
274.25	295.21	323.24	345.19	370.02	395.08
275.01	295.21	324.02	345.24	370.05	395.11

395.19	423.01	451.15	472.17	496.16	522.02
395.20	423.17	451.17	472.25	496.25	522.05
395.20	423.20	451.25	472.26	497.01	522.07
396.02	423.21	452.05	472.28	497.01	522.16
396.03	424.01	452.06	473.02	497.02	523.05
396.24	424.09	452.10	473.03	497.04	523.06
396.25	424.09	452.15	473.12	497.06	523.07
397.07	424.11	452.17	473.12	497.12	523.21
397.12	424.20	452.28	473.26	497.19	524.03
397.17	424.20	453.05	474.06	497.23	524.10
397.24	425.07	454.06	474.06	497.25	524.12
397.25	425.22	454.11	474.07	498.19	524.12
398.07	425.23	454.12	474.11	498.21	524.18
398.08	425.23	454.17	474.13	498.22	524.21
398.17	425.27	454.23	474.14	498.23	525.08
399.01	425.27	454.25	474.15	498.27	525.10
399.01	426.27	455.01	474.28	499.03	525.10
399.03	427.21	455.13	475.07	499.08	525.16
399.15	427.22	455.25	475.08	499.17	525.23
400.01	427.23	456.14	475.10	499.26	525.26
400.01	428.03	457.10	475.25	499.27	525.26
400.11	428.06	457.18	476.08	501.02	526.01
400.14	429.05	457.24	476.12	501.05	526.12
400.19	429.18	458.08	476.16	501.06	527.01
400.28	429.22	458.13	476.19	502.05	527.11
401.04	429.26	458.23	476.20	502.10	527.12
401.04	430.19	458.23	476.24	502.13	527.21
401.18	430.22	458.26	478.09	502.14	527.22
401.25	430.28	459.01	478.11	502.16	528.04
401.26	431.01	459.03	478.23	502.20	528.11
402.02	431.04	459.03	478.25	502.22	528.20
402.04	431.04	459.05	478.27	502.23	528.24
402.08	431.09	459.17	479.01	502.24	529.11
403.06	431.11	459.18	479.02	502.25	529.11
403.07	431.12	459.19	479.03	502.26	529.19
403.16	431.14	459.19	479.12	503.07	529.23
403.23	431.20	459.25	480.11	503.15	530.02
404.15	432.24	460.21	480.18	503.16	530.08
404.27	433.17	460.24	480.20	503.16	530.09
405.03	434.07	460.25	481.01	504.01	530.13
405.10	434.13	460.27	481.03	504.02	530.14
406.08	434.14	460.27	481.12	504.04	530.14
407.01	434.16	461.05	481.13	504.05	530.17
407.02	434.19	461.18	481.19	504.12	530.24
407.04	434.26	461.24	482.05	504.24	530.25
407.04	434.28	461.24	482.16	504.25	531.06
407.13	435.04	462.01	482.25	505.03	531.13
407.17	435.06	462.06	483.12	505.04	531.16
407.23	435.11	462.07	483.19	505.11	531.18
408.09	435.12	462.08	483.26	505.15	531.22
408.24	435.20	462.14	484.06	505.18	531.23
409.05	435.27	463.12	484.12	505.27	532.02
409.07	435.28	463.26	484.19	506.04	532.04
409.18	436.01	464.02	484.20	506.08	532.05
409.19	436.13	464.03	485.27	506.18	532.20
409.21	436.15	464.03	486.03	506.19	532.20
409.23	436.21	464.08	486.04	506.25	533.07
410.02	437.02	464.09	486.05	507.15	533.08
410.02	437.25	464.09	486.07	507.19	533.12
410.13	438.09	464.20	486.10	508.04	533.17
410.22	438.13	464.24	486.11	508.09	533.22
411.08	438.22	464.27	486.14	508.12	534.08
411.11	439.01	464.28	487.03	508.12	535.02
411.27	439.02	465.07	487.20	508.18	535.04
412.12	439.03	465.12	488.09	508.19	535.05
413.04	439.05	465.13	488.27	508.23	535.16
414.14	439.08	466.17	489.03	509.01	535.24
414.16	439.27	466.20	489.03	509.02	536.05
414.16	440.08	466.24	489.05	509.05	537.10
414.16	440.11	467.07	489.07	509.23	537.11
415.04	440.16	467.12	489.15	509.28	537.16
415.09	440.19	467.19	489.23	510.15	537.17
415.10	441.01	467.25	490.02	510.22	538.06
415.11	441.02	468.04	490.11	510.25	538.28
415.19	441.03	468.06	490.11	510.26	539.15
416.03	441.12	468.07	490.14	511.01	539.19
416.17	441.23	468.11	490.14	511.03	539.26
417.02	442.02	468.15	490.17	511.20	539.28
417.06	442.05	469.01	490.22	511.24	540.08
417.11	442.23	469.01	491.04	512.04	540.14
417.18	442.25	469.05	491.05	512.15	540.24
417.20	442.25	469.28	491.18	512.28	540.26
418.06	444.15	470.01	491.21	513.22	540.27
418.11	444.18	470.02	492.03	513.23	541.06
418.20	444.19	470.06	492.14	513.27	541.06
418.27	445.01	470.08	492.15	514.04	541.07
419.09	445.08	470.18	492.18	514.08	541.08
419.13	445.09	470.21	492.26	514.14	541.08
419.17	445.12	470.25	492.28	514.15	541.27
419.18	445.13	470.26	493.05	514.22	542.03
419.26	445.14	471.03	493.05	514.24	542.03
420.04	445.27	471.04	493.07	515.14	542.04
420.07	446.02	471.05	493.19	515.24	542.04
420.11	446.03	471.06	493.21	515.25	542.05
420.15	446.05	471.07	493.21	516.02	542.10
420.16	446.13	471.08	493.28	516.03	542.10
420.18	447.01	471.10	494.04	516.11	542.16
420.18	447.06	471.11	494.07	516.15	542.19
420.20	448.07	471.12	494.08	516.16	542.27
420.21	449.18	471.13	494.09	516.27	542.28
420.26	449.24	471.14	494.10	518.11	543.06
421.02	449.25	471.15	494.28	519.05	543.08
421.03	449.28	471.20	495.05	519.06	543.13
421.05	450.01	471.21	495.06	519.07	543.16
421.14	450.07	471.22	495.09	519.07	543.24
421.26	450.15	471.23	495.09	519.07	543.26
421.27	450.17	472.07	495.14	519.28	543.27
422.19	450.20	472.08	495.20	520.06	544.06
422.21	450.24	472.13	495.21	521.03	544.07
422.27	450.25	472.15	495.23	521.17	544.08
422.28	451.12		496.02	521.20	

544.09	572.17	599.14	624.13	644.09	665.06
544.09	572.21	599.20	624.14	644.09	665.13
544.12	572.22	599.21	624.14	644.17	665.14
544.13	572.25	600.03	624.17	644.18	665.14
544.14	573.15	600.08	624.19	644.19	665.21
544.16	573.16	600.09	624.22	644.26	665.22
544.18	574.14	601.05	624.25	645.05	665.23
544.20	574.23	601.10	624.28	645.07	665.25
544.27	574.25	601.13	625.11	645.09	666.05
545.01	575.02	601.15	625.13	645.20	666.06
545.02	575.04	601.19	625.28	645.23	666.06
545.06	575.04	602.03	625.28	646.09	666.10
545.15	575.05	602.03	626.01	646.11	666.14
545.15	575.10	602.12	626.06	646.16	666.24
545.16	575.10	603.06	626.19	646.18	667.03
545.25	575.12	603.10	626.19	647.01	667.06
546.07	575.19	604.07	626.23	647.07	667.09
546.09	575.20	604.19	626.25	647.10	667.10
546.13	575.24	605.01	627.12	647.10	667.11
546.17	576.06	605.06	627.18	647.12	667.17
546.22	576.10	605.07	627.18	647.13	667.18
546.24	576.13	605.20	627.23	648.13	667.19
547.08	576.15	605.22	627.25	648.23	667.20
547.20	577.11	605.23	628.06	648.28	667.21
548.10	578.01	606.01	628.10	649.04	667.23
548.25	578.01	606.08	628.24	649.11	667.25
548.25	578.02	606.15	629.19	649.17	668.01
549.05	579.05	606.16	630.01	650.24	668.06
549.16	579.18	607.13	630.03	650.28	668.07
549.26	579.20	607.16	630.07	651.22	668.11
549.26	579.20	607.16	630.09	652.10	668.16
550.12	579.21	607.21	630.15	652.11	668.24
550.19	581.04	609.12	630.19	652.12	668.25
551.09	581.07	609.16	630.22	652.13	668.27
551.18	581.10	610.16	630.22	652.26	669.02
552.19	581.13	610.17	630.24	652.27	669.07
552.23	581.19	610.21	630.27	652.28	669.18
552.25	581.20	611.06	630.28	653.03	669.22
553.01	581.20	611.11	631.03	653.14	670.03
553.06	582.04	611.15	631.14	653.17	670.08
553.08	583.02	611.17	631.16	653.22	670.12
553.11	585.08	611.19	631.18	653.22	670.22
553.13	585.13	611.20	631.23	653.26	670.27
553.23	585.15	611.23	631.24	654.12	671.10
554.05	585.16	611.25	632.18	654.12	671.10
554.24	586.04	611.25	632.26	654.19	671.14
555.11	586.09	611.26	632.27	654.23	671.15
555.11	587.10	612.02	633.03	654.23	671.16
555.12	587.10	612.15	633.03	654.25	671.18
555.12	587.12	612.23	633.17	655.02	671.19
557.08	587.15	612.27	633.18	655.09	671.22
557.12	587.25	613.05	634.15	655.14	671.22
558.15	588.09	614.02	634.19	656.02	672.03
559.02	588.09	614.05	634.20	656.18	672.06
559.04	589.04	614.06	635.08	656.28	672.06
559.10	589.10	614.07	635.13	657.02	672.07
559.23	589.15	614.09	635.14	657.02	672.07
560.08	589.17	614.18	636.04	658.02	672.10
560.22	589.21	614.26	636.07	658.03	672.12
561.03	590.10	614.26	636.08	658.06	672.13
561.09	590.13	615.01	636.08	658.12	672.16
561.17	590.17	615.03	636.08	658.13	673.02
561.18	590.23	615.03	636.28	658.14	673.05
562.04	591.08	615.13	637.03	658.20	673.06
562.05	591.14	615.21	637.05	659.08	673.14
562.13	591.19	615.27	637.09	659.14	673.17
562.18	592.03	616.05	637.10	659.15	673.18
563.01	592.04	616.06	637.12	659.17	673.22
563.03	592.15	616.10	637.18	659.18	673.22
563.04	592.19	616.13	637.21	659.21	673.25
563.16	592.21	616.14	637.22	659.24	674.08
564.02	593.04	616.14	637.23	659.25	674.12
564.02	593.05	616.18	638.16	660.02	674.15
564.03	593.14	617.16	638.16	660.04	674.15
564.04	593.17	617.17	638.21	660.05	674.18
564.07	593.19	617.26	638.23	660.06	674.21
564.17	594.01	618.05	638.25	660.06	675.04
564.17	594.08	618.05	638.26	660.15	675.10
565.04	594.13	618.10	639.07	660.18	675.11
565.18	594.16	618.13	639.10	660.24	675.12
565.18	594.17	618.13	639.14	661.06	675.13
565.20	594.17	618.14	639.25	661.07	675.13
566.05	594.19	618.16	639.28	661.07	675.20
566.08	595.01	618.17	640.03	661.10	675.21
566.10	595.10	618.24	640.06	661.17	675.22
566.13	595.21	619.02	640.10	661.19	675.23
566.24	595.22	619.08	640.11	661.19	675.23
566.25	596.11	619.08	640.17	661.24	675.24
567.02	596.14	619.10	640.24	661.28	675.27
567.03	596.21	619.18	640.24	662.05	676.04
567.04	596.23	619.24	640.26	662.16	676.05
567.10	597.07	619.27	641.07	663.06	676.13
568.02	597.09	620.18	641.16	663.06	676.14
568.21	597.10	620.21	641.18	663.09	676.14
569.07	597.12	621.10	641.19	663.09	676.16
569.23	597.13	621.27	641.19	663.13	676.17
570.03	597.15	622.04	641.26	663.13	676.17
570.07	597.17	622.09	642.02	663.27	676.22
570.16	597.18	622.14	642.06	664.02	676.24
570.17	597.24	622.15	642.10	664.06	676.28
571.04	598.01	622.16	642.10	664.07	677.01
571.06	598.07	622.24	642.22	664.08	677.03
571.08	598.07	623.01	643.01	664.12	677.05
571.14	598.08	623.09	643.07	664.12	677.07
571.15	599.09	623.15	643.08	664.14	677.10
571.19	599.09	623.24	643.09	664.18	677.15
572.02	599.09	624.02	643.11	664.24	677.16
572.07	599.10	624.09	643.11	664.26	677.17
572.09	599.10	624.12	644.03	664.27	677.20
572.13	599.11	624.12	644.08	665.04	677.23
572.15	599.13				

678.01	697.14	717.13	735.21	754.19	776.18
678.05	697.25	717.22	735.23	754.25	776.21
678.07	697.26	717.24	735.24	755.04	776.24
678.15	697.26	717.26	736.04	755.16	776.24
678.16	697.28	718.03	736.10	755.18	777.07
678.18	698.02	718.05	736.11	756.09	777.08
678.23	698.05	718.21	736.13	756.19	777.10
678.24	698.12	718.25	736.25	756.21	777.17
679.05	698.12	719.05	736.25	757.03	777.25
679.13	698.17	719.06	737.06	757.18	778.05
679.24	698.18	720.05	737.07	757.22	778.17
679.24	698.21	720.06	737.12	757.27	778.19
679.25	698.22	720.09	737.14	758.21	778.21
680.01	698.26	720.26	737.14	758.27	778.28
680.04	698.27	721.02	737.17	759.01	779.03
680.05	699.06	721.07	737.18	759.03	779.22
680.06	699.10	721.14	737.19	759.05	779.22
680.10	699.16	721.20	738.01	759.06	779.25
680.13	699.23	721.20	738.02	759.15	780.05
680.15	699.24	721.21	738.13	759.15	780.12
680.19	700.02	721.23	738.15	759.15	780.13
680.20	700.03	721.25	738.22	759.16	780.15
680.24	700.10	721.27	738.24	759.17	780.16
680.24	700.28	722.08	738.28	759.21	781.07
680.25	701.03	722.13	739.08	760.03	781.15
681.01	701.06	722.14	739.19	760.07	781.19
681.11	701.07	722.22	739.28	760.13	781.20
681.12	701.09	723.05	740.01	760.24	781.21
682.02	701.12	723.05	740.10	760.25	782.04
682.05	701.13	724.07	740.11	761.03	782.04
682.06	701.14	724.10	740.15	761.10	782.08
682.12	701.21	724.17	740.16	761.11	782.17
682.14	701.21	725.04	740.17	761.14	782.18
682.15	701.24	725.06	740.26	761.15	782.21
682.17	701.25	725.07	741.01	761.16	783.01
682.18	701.28	725.11	741.01	761.17	783.02
682.19	702.06	725.16	741.04	761.17	783.06
682.28	702.08	725.22	741.06	761.24	783.15
683.07	702.08	725.27	741.06	762.06	783.17
683.14	702.09	726.07	741.11	762.06	784.03
683.18	702.16	726.08	741.14	762.10	784.16
683.19	702.23	726.10	741.16	762.15	785.01
683.27	702.25	726.16	741.21	762.15	785.05
683.28	703.05	727.03	742.11	762.16	785.10
684.07	703.24	727.11	742.12	762.24	785.12
684.08	703.24	727.21	742.17	763.18	785.16
684.13	704.05	727.22	743.10	763.19	785.17
684.15	704.06	727.25	743.18	763.21	785.18
684.16	704.08	727.26	744.01	763.28	785.22
684.20	704.13	728.04	744.16	764.07	786.01
684.23	704.20	729.02	744.21	764.09	786.07
684.26	705.04	729.03	744.21	765.04	786.20
685.02	705.05	729.03	744.27	765.07	786.26
685.17	705.11	729.04	745.09	765.10	786.27
685.20	705.21	729.05	745.21	765.19	787.12
685.23	705.23	729.05	746.08	766.04	787.22
685.26	705.27	729.05	746.20	766.24	787.28
686.13	706.05	729.06	746.27	766.25	788.03
687.06	706.09	729.07	747.11	766.27	788.13
687.15	706.10	729.08	747.13	767.01	789.08
687.18	706.15	729.16	747.14	767.06	789.14
687.19	706.17	729.19	747.15	767.17	789.15
687.23	706.18	729.19	747.26	767.26	790.02
688.04	706.20	730.02	748.12	768.16	790.06
688.08	706.20	730.05	748.16	768.16	790.14
688.09	706.26	730.05	748.19	768.24	790.19
688.11	706.26	730.22	748.22	769.13	790.20
689.06	706.27	730.24	748.23	769.22	791.08
689.06	707.06	731.02	749.01	769.25	791.19
689.08	707.07	731.04	749.03	769.25	792.04
689.19	707.08	731.05	749.04	770.02	792.13
690.02	707.08	731.07	749.05	770.05	792.13
690.16	707.12	731.14	749.11	770.08	792.19
690.20	707.17	731.15	749.12	770.11	793.09
690.27	707.26	731.18	749.14	770.12	793.14
691.06	708.17	731.26	749.14	770.19	794.01
691.06	708.18	731.26	749.20	770.21	794.02
691.07	709.09	732.01	749.20	770.28	794.06
691.07	709.11	732.02	749.22	771.01	794.08
691.16	709.11	732.06	749.24	771.02	794.22
692.14	709.16	732.07	749.26	771.08	794.26
692.21	709.26	732.13	749.26	771.11	795.01
692.22	709.26	733.04	750.02	771.11	795.17
692.25	709.27	733.06	750.03	771.13	795.22
693.01	709.27	733.07	750.07	771.15	795.24
693.02	711.03	733.12	750.09	771.19	795.25
693.05	711.09	733.14	750.11	771.24	796.03
693.11	711.09	733.15	750.11	771.24	796.11
693.24	712.01	734.02	750.12	771.25	796.16
693.26	712.07	734.03	750.12	772.06	796.24
693.27	712.08	734.03	750.15	772.08	796.26
694.01	712.09	734.05	750.18	772.09	796.27
694.04	712.11	734.05	751.01	773.01	797.02
694.08	713.09	734.06	751.01	773.12	797.09
694.20	713.09	734.06	751.06	773.25	797.11
694.26	713.15	734.11	751.12	774.06	797.22
695.03	713.17	734.27	751.13	774.07	797.24
695.15	714.03	735.01	751.14	774.08	798.01
695.18	714.11	735.02	751.15	775.03	798.02
696.05	714.23	735.07	751.22	775.08	798.05
696.07	714.24	735.10	751.24	775.08	798.20
696.14	714.24	735.11	752.03	775.09	798.20
696.16	715.01	735.14	752.09	775.10	798.21
696.21	715.05	735.16	752.10	775.11	798.23
696.22	715.05	735.17	752.11	775.19	799.05
696.24	715.20	735.17	752.21	775.20	799.17
696.28	716.16	735.17	752.22	775.23	799.19
697.06	716.20	735.18	752.23	776.02	800.01
697.09	716.26	735.18	753.17	776.04	800.14
697.10	717.09		753.28	776.12	801.01
697.13	717.12		754.03	776.16	801.10

801.11
801.26
802.24
803.02
803.15
803.19
803.22
803.27
804.02
804.15
804.16
804.17
804.17
804.22
804.23
804.26
805.01
805.04
805.24
806.01
806.05
806.12
806.15
806.16
806.19
806.23
806.28
807.03
807.09
807.13
807.19
807.27
807.28
808.03
808.19
808.24
808.25
808.26
808.27
808.27
809.15
809.18
809.19
809.22
809.23
809.23
809.26
810.09
810.14
810.27
811.04
811.07
811.09
811.15
811.21
812.14
812.15
812.16
812.20
812.21
812.22
812.22
812.27
813.01
813.11
813.12
813.13
814.15
815.04
815.05
815.13
815.16
815.25
815.26
816.10
816.11
816.17
817.04
817.18
817.23
817.26
818.08
818.08
818.17
818.19
818.20
818.22
818.23
819.05
820.10
820.12
820.13
820.14
820.23
820.23
821.01
821.05
821.17
821.22
821.23
822.12
822.12
822.13
822.13
822.14
822.14
822.15
823.05
823.07
823.24
824.09

824.21
825.18
826.02
826.10
826.11
826.13
826.14
826.20
826.20
826.25
826.26
827.01
827.02
827.03
827.04
828.03
828.04
828.10
828.15
828.19
828.21
829.06
829.09
829.10
829.12
830.02
831.04
831.05
831.05
831.11
831.13
832.08
832.13
832.16
832.16
832.19
832.20
832.24
833.04
833.16
834.07
834.09
834.20
835.07
836.03
836.05
836.15
836.18
836.24
836.26
837.03
837.14
837.18
837.19
838.06
838.20
839.06
839.14
839.22
839.22
839.23
840.02
840.18
841.13
841.14
841.23
842.01
842.12
842.13
842.21
842.25
843.01
843.02
843.02
843.28
844.01
844.25
844.25
845.10
845.12
845.15
845.24
845.26
845.28
846.02
846.09
846.19
846.20
846.21
847.06
847.07
847.17
847.19
847.22
847.28
849.11
849.20
849.20
850.18
850.20
850.22
851.06
851.08
851.12
852.15
852.16
852.27
852.28
853.07
853.19
853.22

854.18
854.19
854.26
854.27
855.01
855.06
855.13
856.04
856.10
856.20
856.22
857.03
857.12
857.25
857.25
857.26
857.26
857.27
857.28
858.05
858.05
858.06
858.11
858.17
858.18
858.24
858.25
858.26
859.04
859.04
859.09
859.11
859.12
860.15
860.16
860.16
860.22
861.16
861.18
861.19
861.24
862.02
862.04
862.05
862.05
862.11
862.15
862.15
862.16
862.22
862.23
863.04
863.05
863.13
863.19
863.21
863.21
863.22
863.23
863.24
863.27
864.07
864.10
864.15
864.17
864.20
864.22
864.23
864.25
865.01
865.03
865.05
865.06
865.08
865.09
865.10
865.22
865.23
866.02
866.20
867.04
867.12
867.13
867.17
867.19
867.19
867.24
867.26
867.27
868.04
868.04
869.02
869.04
869.20
870.06
870.13
870.20
870.20
870.23
870.24
870.24
870.25
870.27
870.27
871.05
871.06
871.06
871.10
871.13

871.14
871.14
871.21
872.03
872.11
872.13
872.21
873.05
873.14
873.18
874.04
874.11
874.12
874.23
875.04
875.04
875.19
875.26
876.08
877.02
877.06
878.03
878.14
878.16
878.21
879.07
880.08
880.09
880.21
881.01
881.06
881.06
881.13
881.14
881.15
881.15
881.24
881.26
881.27
881.27
882.02
882.11
882.14
883.04
883.07
883.12
883.12
883.13
883.19
883.24
883.25
884.04
884.14
884.17
884.21
884.22
884.28
885.11
885.14
885.27
886.10
886.12
886.14
886.18
886.26
886.27
886.28
887.08
887.11
887.12
887.12
887.21
887.21
887.22
887.22
888.05
888.27
889.16
889.18
889.18
889.22
889.23
890.08
890.14
890.20
890.21
891.10
891.11
891.13
891.14
891.14
891.20
891.21
892.05
892.12
892.17
892.26
893.07
893.18
893.25
894.12
894.23
894.24
894.24
895.05
895.08
895.14
895.22
896.08
896.08
896.14

896.22
897.01
897.14
897.17
897.24
897.25
897.26
897.27
898.08
898.19
898.22
899.14
899.20
900.14
900.22
901.08
901.09
902.04
902.07
902.13
902.16
903.05
903.14
903.26
904.02
905.03
905.12
905.15
905.18
906.03
906.17
907.16
907.27
908.04
908.04
908.11
908.12
908.13
909.10
910.01
910.09
910.11
910.13
910.14
910.24
910.25
911.01
911.08
911.08
911.08
911.09
911.09
911.16
911.21
912.03
912.14
912.21
a´most
  680.27
  681.03
a-begging
  693.22
a-tete
  549.16
abandon
  784.23
  819.19
  828.08
abandoned
  045.05
  129.12
  165.17
  288.11
  535.06
  728.06
  877.14
abandonment
  656.02
abate
  130.20
abbot
  010.24
  012.04
  012.12
  013.09
  013.11
  013.22
  014.17
  015.04
  017.05
  023.25
  023.28
  024.09
  024.17
  025.11
  027.09
  030.05
  037.07
  040.08
  040.15
  041.06
  041.07
  041.15
  042.04
abbot´s
  040.18
abbott
  444.17
abhor
  024.26
  109.18

283.05
626.03
abhorred
  283.03
  483.03
  623.10
  638.24
  656.09
abide
  514.21
  897.09
abigail
  013.26
abigails
  334.24
  365.22
abilities
  317.02
able
  029.02
  105.23
  142.06
  143.10
  147.17
  154.04
  184.11
  202.23
  323.23
  330.07
  384.05
  421.28
  442.17
  555.24
  619.21
  635.02
  691.13
  699.18
  788.10
  863.20
  890.06
  890.07
abode
  022.20
  148.24
  155.04
  489.02
  495.16
  593.03
  795.26
  908.09
abodes
  668.15
abominable
  083.06
  627.05
aboon
  698.01
about
  002.04
  005.20
  014.01
  034.07
  037.21
  042.19
  043.25
  047.18
  048.05
  048.17
  051.03
  056.09
  059.27
  062.07
  069.15
  074.19
  075.22
  077.17
  083.17
  084.10
  088.10
  086.21
  090.09
  090.22
  090.23
  090.26
  097.08
  098.15
  113.09
  115.25
  127.22
  141.26
  143.08
  152.27
  153.04
  153.08
  157.06
  159.11
  163.17
  167.12
  168.01
  168.09
  173.29
  176.05
  180.16
  185.14
  199.26
  214.10
  217.26
  219.26
  232.25
  240.03
  242.09

244.21
244.25
251.01
252.04
252.13
257.13
259.22
260.07
261.23
264.01
268.09
276.13
276.25
280.17
281.26
298.23
300.17
306.14
310.17
320.03
325.22
327.28
328.28
334.27
335.07
336.04
336.20
342.21
343.16
359.21
362.25
368.14
369.12
381.27
384.03
386.22
391.07
391.13
392.26
395.13
398.01
400.09
401.20
401.22
403.13
406.23
408.21
409.02
411.02
412.14
412.16
416.26
417.02
418.18
418.22
432.17
436.04
444.18
446.18
447.20
448.05
457.01
457.26
458.11
462.21
473.22
475.20
477.17
478.10
488.15
492.14
508.12
524.21
539.06
541.27
542.04
565.11
568.24
569.22
571.02
579.23
581.03
596.24
598.18
615.09
616.05
617.05
617.10
617.10
618.15
618.27
619.18
622.08
624.23
655.26
644.12
652.06
659.26
664.23
665.05
668.24
671.04
672.06
676.21
681.20
682.22
683.11
684.22
684.23
689.02
692.03

693.18
695.06
696.19
697.23
699.01
700.13
702.10
705.13
707.16
717.20
751.25
753.28
760.14
767.21
768.26
769.03
774.16
775.15
777.22
777.25
778.06
783.11
784.26
795.04
799.17
801.14
809.07
811.11
824.25
833.12
852.20
853.23
854.08
859.08
861.19
862.22
863.08
863.14
864.01
864.04
865.01
867.27
870.03
871.12
873.09
880.07
880.19
881.07
884.17
892.11
894.01
896.18
897.04
897.15
above
004.13
042.03
052.17
056.22
057.05
084.16
093.15
141.27
171.25
213.19
220.11
248.14
249.11
250.20
294.01
296.27
333.22
367.23
380.09
401.16
415.09
415.21
418.05
423.20
460.16
471.26
478.11
494.25
608.10
658.18
660.25
675.20
704.15
708.14
708.24
729.07
731.25
746.11
858.11
865.16
865.21
abridge
287.20
abroad
563.23
572.10
836.26
862.14
abrupt
049.16
251.21
261.02
265.10
324.09
461.24
497.11

783.25
abruptly
025.13
064.22
183.15
250.29
284.20
363.13
abruptness
754.17
absence
115.01
167.23
362.10
374.02
377.21
380.06
450.14
487.03
490.08
491.15
569.09
716.16
734.03
851.06
absences
715.03
absent
293.22
325.25
379.09
495.22
559.09
820.01
828.15
853.19
absolute
216.19
220.16
307.14
374.24
494.16
811.26
absolutely
271.12
273.27
286.19
310.24
390.01
458.24
463.14
512.07
540.12
634.27
640.23
641.15
645.12
658.11
703.18
734.02
748.09
784.24
785.10
787.28
792.10
820.01
822.16
862.09
895.21
909.02
absolved
132.02
230.20
663.19
absorbed
101.17
147.10
249.20
256.17
306.25
359.20
371.13
472.12
678.03
752.13
803.26
absorbing
347.22
abstain
889.07
703.06
832.05
abstained
853.28
abstract
357.27
817.23
abstracted
101.17
434.06
715.05
767.26
879.05
abstraction
115.07
284.25
640.21
718.24
774.05
absurd
046.26
264.15

476.08
626.28
665.20
819.08
879.26
absurdity
408.04
836.24
abundance
120.15
abundant
094.07
202.25
518.11
750.19
abuse
008.05
008.25
112.07
274.05
274.07
633.09
abused
038.27
083.14
652.01
abut
461.28
abyss
109.15
272.01
378.09
acceded
665.22
accelerated
065.02
335.06
accent
110.02
198.04
346.11
381.24
406.18
518.07
621.01
643.08
690.13
730.01
accents
119.24
130.12
210.15
333.20
337.13
716.11
737.06
902.23
accept
376.05
458.06
516.10
517.13
581.22
628.19
635.03
645.02
652.28
719.04
721.01
722.20
747.11
823.05
823.07
acceptable
755.07
806.26
acceptance
239.24
accepted
290.23
536.02
665.11
accepting
453.10
570.25
744.19
accession
545.07
889.07
accident
123.27
232.15
563.14
639.04
725.22
accidental
118.10
accommodate
149.11
458.24
825.12
accommodated
182.01
873.26
accommodation
015.19
854.24
869.12
accommodations
059.05
161.03

733.23
accompanied
211.05
223.14
285.02
318.24
459.14
459.15
462.02
750.08
823.14
accompanies
274.24
accompaniment
112.16
361.06
550.08
accompaniments
799.13
accompany
255.10
338.23
339.26
475.12
534.10
538.22
550.15
603.23
718.19
795.17
810.02
820.25
836.25
841.02
841.26
accompanying
170.12
357.07
accomplish
488.03
804.13
814.08
817.07
852.03
accomplished
149.09
174.25
319.10
322.23
346.26
403.08
713.01
890.09
accomplishing
585.03
accomplishment
810.08
accomplishments
039.05
168.28
200.11
318.23
625.05
717.18
722.26
892.10
accord
123.21
134.28
524.21
530.09
773.19
894.20
accorded
218.09
345.05
854.12
according
043.06
086.01
322.10
350.03
378.21
423.23
658.17
854.10
accordingly
072.12
168.10
173.13
173.26
253.24
264.05
309.23
389.06
615.07
accost
238.03
368.26
872.15
accosted
886.24
accosting
376.02
account
007.11
015.19
060.06
116.23
142.02
206.10

217.07
232.06
249.24
300.17
306.15
311.15
333.12
368.02
385.15
454.28
478.19
543.18
555.16
593.01
672.03
686.25
687.05
698.27
763.02
793.15
account-book
476.05
accounted
751.12
accounts
039.01
049.03
117.22
474.19
accrued
784.11
accumulation
004.11
accuracy
049.03
accurate
755.04
accursed
321.15
615.17
646.25
accusation
357.06
accuse
614.14
752.27
accused
018.15
065.10
134.15
135.06
accusing
311.25
accustom
118.08
614.14
accustomed
008.25
030.11
088.19
097.04
168.18
193.21
199.23
251.23
538.08
548.21
691.08
705.24
744.23
763.14
796.13
achan
615.18
ache
819.25
ached
019.12
390.28
achieve
019.22
172.26
762.03
762.27
achieved
201.05
625.14
aching
459.25
acknowledge
288.14
525.16
816.06
818.03
818.25
900.15
901.15
acknowledged
288.12
374.22
622.24
802.17
911.01
acknowledges
325.09
acknowledging
254.16
acknowledgment
178.27
240.11
301.02

acquaintance 907.01
097.22
150.05
213.05
215.11
240.06
254.12
381.22
399.08
401.08
439.27
624.15
652.14
642.09
667.26
734.05
748.25
864.24
acquaintances
647.15
acquaintances´
269.22
acquainted
195.24
300.15
364.17
537.05
603.06
acquiesced
854.09
acquire
002.12
acquired
159.18
198.06
506.06
717.17
806.19
acquirements
162.16
171.08
317.02
acquiring
744.04
acquistion
803.23
acquitted
097.18
371.17
acrid
018.20
478.21
601.19
acrimony
373.22
across
023.13
053.27
061.25
169.28
170.11
185.25
271.18
277.01
277.13
318.16
325.19
363.14
391.08
418.26
494.05
611.06
742.21
855.11
act
009.20
105.18
154.19
168.10
170.12
173.09
290.14
368.16
377.09
377.09
406.12
407.23
407.25
459.10
477.18
484.02
552.21
547.05
547.18
614.19
614.21
625.16
800.09
831.08
856.04
acted
031.06
217.14
291.16
369.03
406.11
478.13
529.05
632.12
800.17
849.04

acting
043.06
171.23
370.13
376.24
784.28
832.10
action
067.16
077.23
102.24
216.08
274.15
508.03
664.05
692.08
854.11
actions
125.23
273.07
312.24
581.11
689.05
active
059.05
088.10
166.27
228.23
328.15
425.17
485.24
700.06
735.13
791.03
791.03
689.26
actively
471.17
743.03
activity
749.08
849.05
actor
097.03
actors
371.11
379.06
actress
025.08
acts
107.19
257.16
actual
216.05
398.21
570.10
642.24
775.15
actually
314.10
324.12
462.08
490.03
499.15
535.21
579.15
757.14
776.17
899.06
acumen
497.09
708.20
acute
349.20
462.24
511.13
acutely
061.15
759.11
acuteness
507.04
ad
089.12
406.09
593.08
adage
383.11
725.24
adapted
374.08
496.26
add
086.08
135.11
214.24
725.25
752.10
added
014.25
035.09
039.21
076.26
087.13
104.03
138.03
173.20
221.13
277.18
292.03
308.10

336.20
338.13
388.18
417.06
428.13
434.04
461.27
463.12
488.24
493.17
495.22
497.04
499.02
513.18
517.12
517.25
523.20
553.14
632.19
651.19
691.07
691.22
700.17
724.12
739.28
778.05
799.35
830.01
833.09
860.24
876.21
addicted
060.08
adding
020.16
053.19
212.03
232.22
823.01
addition
104.04
113.26
221.24
353.26
456.14
498.13
additional
013.13
236.06
236.10
address
062.14
087.01
118.20
122.20
136.21
169.01
171.15
306.14
376.06
420.26
463.03
482.12
525.08
557.13
706.01
814.07
addressed
030.08
042.12
053.06
168.07
173.13
198.12
203.16
225.06
264.08
419.28
461.22
464.07
602.14
641.18
747.04
756.19
803.01
843.14
859.10
addresses
513.13
addressing
014.05
027.19
098.01
197.13
272.18
310.28
595.11
adds
738.04
adduced
605.10
adela
189.19
197.08
197.18
198.09
232.13
adele
199.28
201.03
202.10

211.26
212.01
214.27
215.14
218.05
218.06
218.18
231.18
233.08
234.03
235.03
236.27
237.03
239.01
239.04
239.07
240.01
240.05
240.13
240.25
241.01
243.04
245.23
246.10
246.21
251.02
251.04
251.17
254.11
255.12
255.18
256.10
257.12
257.18
258.17
263.15
264.22
274.27
276.05
276.10
279.05
284.15
287.16
288.05
288.27
289.13
313.12
313.19
314.10
320.05
327.21
328.15
331.16
332.16
333.09
334.01
334.09
335.25
336.16
337.04
337.18
338.20
340.06
341.12
341.17
341.19
341.24
347.03
352.26
353.14
362.11
363.12
366.28
373.18
380.12
381.11
453.28
454.06
455.16
493.09
498.06
498.19
499.02
501.15
506.09
507.25
508.03
520.13
522.22
538.10
538.16
538.22
539.16
539.23
540.10
540.19
540.22
541.05
541.10
541.19
541.26
543.05
548.11
549.11
582.06
583.18
583.23
598.16
610.24
615.12
615.14

615.27
618.09
618.12
618.16
622.03
639.24
639.27
653.11
748.21
864.23
907.20
adele´s
214.16
255.13
276.28
288.13
305.14
326.17
547.18
582.09
615.02
adequate
174.06
793.20
793.24
adhere
834.26
835.05
adhered
732.04
adherence
412.20
adhering
412.12
adhesion
561.04
732.19
adhesiveness
506.05
adjoined
002.25
adjoining
341.08
771.02
adjourned
094.11
adjusted
126.26
193.02
340.15
administering
431.09
admiration
030.21
177.28
287.11
359.11
369.03
374.25
473.05
744.01
781.12
787.08
admire
346.27
346.28
504.03
625.06
825.11
838.05
admired
131.12
176.19
318.21
374.22
451.16
476.21
738.12
admirers
449.16
admires
338.11
admiring
085.21
206.25
admission
605.10
admit
056.19
104.04
155.04
254.08
255.17
271.24
314.17
530.21
755.06
786.03
845.02
admittance
704.06
admitted
050.08
076.04
138.27
140.19
312.11
339.09
546.20
599.03
633.13

653.12
802.22
901.02
admitting
684.28
752.15
admonition
604.07
ado
417.02
527.15
643.18
adopt
038.09
134.27
482.17
544.26
762.17
819.14
adopted
040.07
126.12
485.25
499.01
525.18
817.27
821.07
821.08
821.10
adoption
377.07
808.09
adored
385.22
584.06
adorned
341.05
adrift
182.19
adult
062.15
748.24
advance
264.21
283.10
871.24
advanced
145.26
155.19
163.22
203.07
337.01
347.06
368.10
407.08
416.17
427.14
461.21
472.20
523.05
557.04
598.17
600.15
668.23
798.17
805.22
812.13
818.12
857.16
872.16
advancement
824.15
advances
741.08
858.10
advancing
193.26
306.16
589.17
674.12
advantage
043.19
197.26
238.12
390.17
531.03
554.11
633.23
753.21
797.19
797.23
advantageous
490.01
advantages
162.07
266.02
312.18
377.04
738.09
advent
628.20
adventitious
263.04
adventure
005.24
182.23
745.16
adventurous
735.07
adverse
268.16

adverted
473.17
772.17
advertise
167.27
167.27
184.20
454.20
454.23
455.12
508.05
advertised
171.07
242.25
advertisement
168.03
168.15
242.26
advertisements
325.21
772.07
774.07
advertising
168.01
advice
428.25
477.10
669.06
727.06
770.14
910.19
advisable
309.15
536.17
advise
403.15
603.22
646.26
advised
387.25
448.18
783.08
advisedly
591.24
advocate
058.28
756.04
762.18
823.06
advocated
373.12
aerial
221.03
522.21
525.12
afar
003.13
215.03
755.27
affability
254.19
affable
195.05
196.20
750.22
affair
173.10
306.16
307.25
775.14
768.08
affairs
173.16
300.18
378.27
487.10
736.10
affect
257.03
784.02
affectation
267.16
858.01
affected
200.24
748.13
affection
007.20
020.11
046.22
107.08
129.16
132.08
214.04
375.21
404.28
498.21
506.11
521.16
533.23
537.12
607.05
626.04
713.24
715.22
725.09
748.23
761.25
762.21
761.11
787.07

789.12
834.04
842.17
affectionate
880.09
affections
724.06
781.21
819.17
affirm
062.28
362.28
593.07
affirmations
786.20
affirmative
053.16
798.10
affirmed
007.12
288.06
391.22
483.05
493.14
555.18
698.01
749.04
826.28
affix
557.17
affixed
557.18
807.28
afflicted
555.03
901.13
afflicting
726.04
affliction
474.28
affluence
713.12
782.23
793.05
afford
353.19
405.10
789.08
afforded
159.11
affrighted
294.25
afoot
169.17
afore
693.22
695.25
afraid
035.26
036.06
068.25
069.01
073.17
106.23
123.27
134.13
177.25
186.22
211.08
225.23
227.08
227.09
227.16
244.22
275.01
275.05
275.06
315.20
393.05
435.23
435.24
480.27
481.01
511.02
533.09
565.08
619.26
641.16
800.12
833.07
838.09
875.01
afresh
142.12
296.22
674.24
787.17
after
007.19
022.01
025.15
027.26
035.23
035.26
036.20
040.10
040.24
054.06
065.11
067.09
073.07

075.08
090.07
094.11
095.12
111.10
112.14
114.27
115.10
123.15
131.09
135.27
137.26
141.18
151.18
151.20
152.26
157.02
159.19
161.24
163.11
168.09
169.04
173.17
182.11
185.15
189.14
191.07
198.13
199.12
200.18
201.22
202.10
208.18
220.03
251.17
252.27
255.10
267.24
282.01
285.26
288.10
290.04
292.03
293.26
299.08
305.14
332.07
332.21
335.15
336.01
336.14
338.23
339.17
339.23
340.07
348.27
360.04
379.06
379.26
382.10
390.26
399.13
402.03
413.04
415.27
417.13
418.02
432.02
439.25
455.23
457.13
470.07
473.22
474.03
474.13
477.18
479.13
481.23
486.07
487.05
488.20
490.11
492.12
499.05
507.18
516.04
518.13
525.11
526.12
527.21
539.19
541.10
554.13
555.27
558.02
567.21
570.07
572.06
573.21
581.01
585.07
590.09
597.14
598.11
602.04
644.03
644.26
652.19
652.21
655.08
662.28

663.01
679.23
682.18
687.06
691.07
692.22
694.04
698.13
719.27
728.03
735.02
735.18
735.21
737.16
739.03
742.19
745.09
750.23
751.23
752.14
756.25
759.05
760.03
765.08
770.15
771.27
772.02
774.20
785.09
786.13
790.07
794.02
796.20
799.17
799.27
800.28
802.04
803.02
809.16
824.03
826.03
829.13
829.21
829.25
833.01
836.15
845.01
852.18
854.14
862.28
863.26
864.18
867.16
877.06
878.20
882.14
882.24
886.28
888.03
892.19
902.07
906.03
906.20
907.12
911.28
after-dinner-mood
258.26
after-flavour
065.19
after-occurrences
040.04
afternon
899.10
afternoon
003.12
019.27
021.01
068.14
069.28
075.01
094.14
097.09
105.13
105.16
113.01
115.04
163.21
165.14
218.04
218.17
235.01
254.04
279.04
328.12
331.12
379.17
445.26
457.02
457.25
473.09
478.27
609.02
638.23
668.23
730.21
739.01
752.01
804.28
854.27

afternoon-school
141.18
afternoons
001.12
145.02
151.05
afterwards
045.20
065.06
077.25
080.14
082.11
086.13
087.14
155.17
159.12
170.23
180.12
319.07
322.04
343.02
366.02
458.03
478.17
549.10
578.16
727.10
791.28
803.01
848.09
866.11
866.12
884.15
again
024.04
027.23
027.27
031.09
031.09
033.28
035.01
035.03
036.07
036.26
038.22
061.25
062.22
066.25
069.02
078.25
080.01
080.10
081.28
083.09
085.05
089.17
090.27
106.26
106.28
109.04
119.09
120.16
120.16
127.25
130.07
130.12
136.23
158.08
158.13
167.04
167.22
180.18
184.20
185.10
202.08
210.09
210.21
223.10
223.27
224.04
226.24
229.07
229.09
229.26
244.12
247.13
261.08
271.22
272.18
285.07
287.17
293.18
294.05
294.20
295.09
301.20
301.25
305.05
306.10
308.01
309.01
309.24
314.23
320.03
324.07
348.01
358.01
361.05
365.26
367.20
368.24

369.10
369.15
377.26
382.11
388.07
389.11
392.06
392.06
396.21
404.01
406.22
406.24
407.05
418.19
419.28
422.14
423.10
423.10
426.09
426.09
426.10
426.10
430.06
430.24
430.24
430.28
434.09
440.22
442.14
445.12
447.24
459.23
461.25
466.01
466.10
470.11
475.21
484.26
485.16
489.28
493.16
495.26
498.02
499.02
509.23
509.26
515.01
515.07
515.15
518.11
518.11
518.12
518.13
521.05
527.17
527.24
527.25
527.25
530.03
533.14
534.03
534.07
543.04
543.08
546.06
561.16
561.20
563.15
565.07
567.09
576.18
595.07
605.21
613.13
615.04
617.05
619.13
622.20
631.22
640.08
646.21
653.21
653.21
656.24
662.24
667.04
667.08
667.08
668.20
668.20
669.27
670.05
670.06
670.13
671.27
671.27
672.21
675.02
675.22
676.04
679.01
680.14
680.24
694.18
696.16
697.02
719.05
720.23
723.13
726.25
731.19

740.20	647.18	491.17	688.07	296.03	021.09
745.17	648.10	533.18	693.01	335.26	023.01
745.17	649.27	535.24	705.22	639.27	023.12
753.05	649.28	542.05	709.17	akin	024.12
753.17	674.21	569.08	710.02	057.21	024.14
754.23	690.01	593.23	711.07	351.12	025.06
755.23	692.16	597.04	722.02	510.18	026.08
760.23	725.02	651.28	751.25	alabaster	027.26
766.12	733.03	653.01	777.24	542.22	029.04
769.22	735.09	664.11	816.20	alacrity	030.04
771.14	766.12	698.21	837.21	437.21	031.17
773.23	770.14	718.10	885.20	alarm	032.05
777.05	780.18	721.17	aidea	009.21	035.26
777.26	791.09	727.05	161.16	480.19	042.17
780.13	815.23	734.04	245.26	alarmed	044.02
780.17	827.17	735.10	639.11	399.14	044.24
782.11	865.25	768.25	639.12	766.10	044.26
783.11	874.25	770.01	aids	alarming	047.21
786.17	agate	770.11	366.11	884.20	048.19
787.01	683.11	854.19	ailed	alarum	049.24
791.26	age	887.04	223.23	474.01	050.08
794.12	007.03	agonies	518.26	alas	053.12
802.11	014.04	325.12	854.03	017.15	055.06
805.24	035.04	627.17	ailing	370.21	056.22
805.25	053.02	agonized	027.13	500.12	057.22
809.19	062.15	657.14	680.21	683.24	058.16
810.21	078.08	agonizing	ailment	752.26	058.24
813.09	105.24	019.19	029.25	819.19	058.28
813.10	111.02	agony	aim	871.21	066.21
818.20	111.03	063.09	118.16	886.19	066.27
862.23	130.06	136.04	273.21	albion	069.08
836.28	165.01	349.22	791.20	501.08	069.19
857.10	168.24	493.21	791.22	737.21	073.28
857.12	171.13	610.07	810.05	album	078.06
841.19	201.04	625.16	840.06	353.02	079.06
842.06	201.13	644.25	883.02	472.26	080.11
842.06	224.17	655.19	aims	alert	080.20
843.09	244.23	867.05	822.09	406.26	080.22
852.25	245.02	agree	912.03	427.03	083.04
855.19	252.27	265.08	air	alias	083.14
858.10	264.20	266.04	039.20	686.19	084.04
861.01	268.17	266.21	075.23	708.05	084.08
866.28	319.21	266.26	077.20	774.11	084.14
875.14	344.09	369.11	084.19	alice	085.06
875.24	381.27	623.20	086.10	535.20	087.09
876.23	468.21	784.26	087.22	739.20	088.04
879.07	486.10	agreeable	111.15	773.02	088.08
880.23	629.13	014.24	139.01	alien	091.08
883.26	629.15	106.10	144.07	022.06	091.12
884.13	704.08	186.04	145.22	125.17	092.10
896.01	752.25	189.26	155.04	626.14	092.11
896.23	836.25	690.19	190.23	719.24	092.12
906.02	863.09	699.04	194.25	786.27	093.26
906.22	907.28	740.06	205.27	alienated	094.25
907.24	aged	787.11	204.22	833.14	096.09
910.28	711.18	agreeably	207.02	alienates	097.16
against	agent	030.15	209.17	293.16	098.04
008.01	125.05	agreed	218.27	alienation	101.17
008.03	180.15	014.02	219.13	444.10	102.13
009.23	235.06	041.11	235.10	alight	102.25
019.15	287.19	712.28	259.23	194.07	103.27
026.14	368.09	797.01	262.13	549.09	105.02
040.20	agents	806.11	280.15	alighted	106.19
043.10	703.27	agrees	281.04	074.11	106.22
050.13	ages	136.11	284.01	185.22	108.14
056.22	536.19	ah	295.25	281.20	108.23
066.17	816.14	198.18	327.27	381.05	109.13
074.17	aghast	226.22	346.03	854.20	113.28
088.20	776.23	232.20	347.10	alights	115.10
100.27	853.07	241.09	359.10	504.05	115.28
124.05	agile	246.01	361.09	alike	119.28
124.25	564.15	256.21	368.19	029.11	120.22
125.18	agitate	259.21	433.20	220.22	121.12
135.20	422.12	264.14	434.06	416.01	123.10
142.04	623.09	287.20	541.17	743.09	124.22
159.15	agitated	330.11	550.19	alive	125.02
176.21	052.03	398.04	570.05	022.10	126.05
185.11	215.19	399.07	570.18	044.13	126.28
216.11	392.10	463.05	574.19	046.27	127.11
220.07	517.01	578.12	629.06	065.08	129.03
221.28	745.13	600.06	629.23	112.06	131.16
224.22	839.17	680.08	630.13	189.21	131.28
249.05	agitating	680.28	631.03	364.15	132.25
252.21	704.21	838.09	641.10	405.08	134.11
258.19	745.16	878.09	641.14	429.19	135.16
259.03	agitation	893.22	653.02	457.15	139.11
281.17	023.15	897.01	671.25	457.16	141.22
283.07	026.07	ahasuerus	707.16	489.22	143.02
312.03	130.20	530.16	732.15	558.04	143.19
357.19	agnes	aia	798.14	771.24	145.08
351.21	117.14	010.21	800.15	841.18	146.03
371.24	ago	191.13	832.02	861.04	146.03
373.17	032.19	200.19	849.17	866.25	146.11
377.07	032.27	227.22	877.03	866.26	148.09
425.08	056.17	236.08	881.07	867.18	150.19
450.12	128.04	245.02	887.16	all	150.19
456.23	174.09	296.22	905.19	004.16	152.19
479.25	179.23	410.18	air-torrent	008.16	152.21
492.04	197.20	426.08	560.10	009.14	154.06
494.27	200.03	438.28	aire	012.02	154.18
496.24	242.07	487.13	199.05	012.11	157.07
498.15	276.13	554.09	airily	015.19	161.03
498.15	307.18	616.22	335.16	017.19	162.04
519.09	403.13	623.13	airing	017.23	162.13
552.08	447.21	638.11	327.19	018.10	163.25
582.24	451.17	668.10	airs	018.10	164.19
614.21	452.01	669.04	375.24	018.11	164.21
626.10	457.23	673.06	380.02	018.12	165.04
656.04	459.16	677.21	462.27	018.23	166.23
658.18	463.26	684.13	ajar	019.27	167.04
658.19	473.05	687.13	155.03	019.28	169.04

169.15	345.06	492.20	676.01	822.28	251.25
170.28	345.15	494.25	676.13	824.13	761.10
171.15	347.04	497.04	676.21	824.23	allowed
171.25	348.04	497.21	677.11	824.23	005.20
173.15	350.02	498.28	677.22	824.24	030.22
174.16	354.11	501.09	679.11	825.08	100.14
174.20	355.02	509.16	679.23	828.27	109.26
175.18	357.02	514.14	681.02	829.03	135.07
176.04	357.27	518.24	682.27	832.18	142.19
181.12	358.17	522.09	684.04	833.28	147.05
182.15	360.12	526.23	684.07	836.15	151.07
184.28	362.16	527.09	684.08	837.26	203.07
185.05	363.07	527.22	685.10	839.05	235.03
185.20	364.05	529.15	687.24	841.17	317.24
185.26	364.07	529.21	687.25	841.20	331.19
189.21	364.08	530.19	690.08	843.23	336.16
190.03	369.23	530.22	691.23	844.09	366.09
192.03	370.19	531.27	692.14	844.17	476.09
193.07	371.03	536.06	696.11	845.07	654.27
196.26	372.07	537.06	698.02	845.08	698.08
198.22	376.26	537.25	698.15	846.06	748.28
199.08	377.08	538.02	699.01	846.23	829.11
199.09	377.12	538.04	700.13	847.17	allowing
199.12	377.14	539.10	704.22	847.22	289.17
202.20	379.04	539.19	707.22	848.01	allows
205.11	379.06	541.17	708.14	848.24	014.20
206.10	385.26	542.27	708.24	848.24	alloy
206.26	387.06	546.05	708.28	850.03	133.12
207.15	387.08	548.20	711.04	852.24	721.06
207.26	388.02	548.26	711.06	855.28	allude
209.09	389.14	551.26	711.18	857.19	670.21
209.12	389.15	552.14	717.03	858.10	838.26
210.03	389.27	553.03	718.01	859.07	alluded
216.01	390.13	553.03	719.17	861.06	114.24
216.04	390.24	555.13	722.09	863.03	671.23
219.23	391.12	555.27	722.20	863.14	alluding
221.09	391.13	557.05	722.25	864.13	836.28
222.26	392.18	558.05	725.08	864.24	907.14
225.22	392.21	559.21	726.15	865.16	allure
227.21	395.04	562.24	726.15	867.12	375.06
228.12	395.22	565.11	730.27	867.17	allured
228.24	396.23	566.23	731.25	870.16	625.13
228.26	397.07	567.17	733.28	872.22	allusion
229.04	398.15	567.18	735.23	873.09	042.09
251.22	399.13	569.19	736.02	873.20	291.22
255.24	399.24	572.18	736.02	876.21	353.27
257.10	399.24	574.12	738.09	876.24	546.06
238.21	400.23	574.24	740.06	877.06	704.22
239.26	401.21	576.04	742.21	877.18	allusions
242.06	404.22	576.05	743.05	877.25	716.17
247.25	405.09	581.03	743.08	879.17	ally
250.20	405.16	581.07	744.22	881.18	532.16
251.08	406.19	583.17	744.28	882.17	almost
254.12	408.02	583.20	745.08	887.06	054.01
255.16	410.26	585.07	745.22	887.09	058.19
258.14	411.23	586.04	747.24	887.25	082.20
260.17	411.27	586.25	750.31	888.15	111.11
260.17	412.27	589.03	750.21	894.11	112.23
264.17	415.24	589.25	751.08	895.26	113.04
267.24	415.25	592.13	751.25	899.14	115.09
269.01	416.06	596.04	753.24	899.15	146.12
269.16	416.15	597.22	754.27	901.14	147.05
270.04	417.08	598.05	756.26	908.04	160.04
272.08	417.12	598.09	757.23	909.09	160.09
272.24	417.23	599.18	758.23	909.11	162.21
274.20	424.04	602.12	758.26	909.11	187.05
278.09	424.08	602.17	759.22	all's	205.11
280.10	426.13	603.19	761.25	417.01	208.05
282.11	427.06	605.02	763.23	417.01	262.24
284.02	427.12	605.13	765.03	all-perfect	263.19
285.09	427.23	606.08	766.04	813.28	264.16
286.05	429.15	606.09	767.23	allay	264.28
289.25	429.19	609.12	770.14	670.04	268.20
290.08	430.11	611.19	772.07	allaying	270.05
292.10	432.23	612.13	772.15	778.03	284.23
294.13	433.09	612.26	773.04	allegation	292.23
295.15	434.03	615.08	774.16	591.09	301.17
296.27	434.24	615.25	774.24	allege	311.23
297.11	435.01	617.28	775.12	505.16	319.15
297.27	437.13	619.23	775.15	alleged	333.01
298.10	437.18	620.06	776.26	142.04	335.21
298.21	438.18	622.10	778.12	609.10	344.11
299.21	439.08	623.08	778.26	allegiance	344.18
306.10	440.03	623.21	779.10	163.04	370.01
307.18	441.24	624.10	785.03	823.08	371.23
310.03	443.05	625.05	785.06	alleviate	380.28
310.18	447.21	626.03	785.09	151.02	386.14
311.07	449.16	626.09	785.27	854.04	396.23
313.10	450.02	627.17	789.02	alliance	396.26
316.21	452.09	628.25	790.07	357.05	396.27
317.17	452.12	632.05	792.10	390.02	397.24
321.19	453.13	634.18	792.17	751.11	408.10
326.27	456.10	636.14	794.25	allotted	420.18
327.11	457.25	638.02	795.06	474.05	421.12
327.25	464.01	638.15	796.04	699.13	422.16
328.06	465.14	638.18	796.25	allow	429.07
329.09	468.16	638.19	798.10	064.15	441.16
329.15	469.03	640.22	799.24	118.04	459.20
330.14	475.25	643.23	799.28	118.06	460.20
330.23	475.26	646.14	801.20	126.23	463.10
330.27	476.25	648.18	802.15	215.23	474.12
331.11	476.25	650.16	804.25	260.19	477.03
333.22	477.01	650.23	809.10	265.28	479.11
334.17	481.23	653.04	811.06	590.06	499.11
336.12	483.17	654.16	813.28	600.09	509.11
339.01	484.16	659.07	814.03	709.02	516.08
340.06	485.19	663.23	819.02	711.08	523.27
341.01	488.14	664.12	820.02	761.07	536.20
342.15	488.16	666.27	820.14	792.27	556.03
342.28	489.10	672.27	820.19	allowance	575.18
344.04	492.02	673.27	822.09	112.25	581.12

776.11
777.25
778.21
778.23
778.25
779.11
781.01
781.27
781.27
782.11
784.01
784.13
784.14
784.16
785.03
790.26
793.09
800.12
807.26
813.24
813.24
815.19
816.05
816.19
816.28
818.24
821.04
833.10
833.19
834.01
834.03
834.07
835.16
838.02
838.06
838.11
839.18
840.01
840.23
841.10
841.15
842.08
842.09
842.10
849.24
857.04
876.02
876.22
876.25
876.26
877.02
877.03
878.01
878.05
878.23
878.24
880.15
882.04
882.08
883.19
884.22
884.23
885.23
887.08
894.04
894.07
894.24
895.11
896.11
897.27
902.06
907.17
907.18
908.28
909.01
909.17
amateur
312.19
amazed
197.16
295.24
307.05
519.25
amazement
140.11
359.12
743.13
803.21
amazon's
746.10
ambassador
390.25
amber
280.19
464.22
amber-coloured
318.15
318.18
ambition
723.25
761.28
762.25
762.26
791.21
792.12
825.14
912.02
ambitions
759.23
ambitious
723.23

723.24
723.26
724.01
761.25
911.23
ambrosia
138.18
ambush
286.01
ameliorated
144.06
amen
726.17
912.25
amenable
439.11
amend
441.07
amends
317.03
amenities
796.18
amethyst
544.07
ami
234.12
amiable
047.17
184.10
238.18
743.17
748.26
amicable
498.27
amid
152.23
341.04
amidst
079.23
164.13
230.07
249.11
337.13
369.24
424.04
601.16
674.06
675.13
676.26
688.10
745.02
745.15
758.12
793.28
808.23
826.16
854.17
859.26
870.24
911.17
amie
218.24
amiss
767.24
amity
465.15
485.14
among
004.04
031.13
040.26
088.19
097.21
100.22
170.07
229.13
412.28
504.12
540.15
613.08
674.07
693.09
714.13
719.23
amongst
020.12
058.09
075.09
088.13
144.19
167.02
184.07
205.20
220.08
221.12
231.17
234.18
378.02
412.04
447.13
447.18
546.19
546.23
588.13
622.05
631.05
636.05
636.14
663.10
664.10
665.02

712.07
720.13
731.14
743.10
743.10
743.18
744.09
744.14
745.10
784.26
786.08
818.09
878.04
902.15
amounted
330.24
amphitheatre
872.22
ample
016.09
149.21
183.27
258.15
380.27
amplitude
342.16
359.07
amply
202.21
amputate
867.22
amusant
334.08
amuse
142.28
241.02
256.01
265.03
291.06
amused
336.27
640.03
amusement
218.23
470.22
amusements
365.01
amuses
400.01
amusing
150.06
257.27
amy
343.07
347.16
351.04
352.21
357.14
366.25
378.28
389.08
390.22
417.17
an
001.05
004.16
005.08
006.26
007.15
007.21
008.26
014.02
014.19
016.08
021.14
021.28
022.05
024.28
026.08
026.14
027.03
027.05
027.11
028.28
029.25
032.24
039.14
039.15
043.01
043.05
044.09
045.03
048.10
048.24
049.16
053.18
057.13
060.06
060.24
060.27
061.10
062.15
063.20
065.13
066.17
071.05
074.12
074.14
076.17
077.25
081.10

081.22
083.08
084.19
086.23
087.13
088.01
088.06
088.28
089.18
091.09
091.13
093.19
095.17
097.03
097.28
099.11
102.09
109.15
111.02
111.04
111.14
112.07
112.09
112.16
112.25
113.02
118.06
120.09
123.09
123.27
124.04
125.16
125.17
126.15
127.03
127.15
128.02
128.04
128.07
130.06
130.25
131.14
132.20
133.08
133.11
141.24
145.06
146.27
147.22
152.19
154.15
155.14
155.15
159.05
161.24
162.02
162.20
165.01
167.18
169.15
170.02
171.04
171.05
171.21
171.27
172.28
173.20
174.11
174.13
174.20
178.09
180.05
180.16
181.12
181.14
181.18
182.26
183.24
186.07
192.06
194.09
195.04
195.05
195.28
196.11
199.14
200.25
201.08
201.10
201.12
202.24
202.27
205.03
210.09
210.12
210.27
214.12
218.07
219.14
222.16
224.06
225.15
227.04
228.17
228.23
228.24
229.06
229.27
229.28
230.04
232.02

232.05
232.15
233.10
234.19
239.24
239.27
240.11
243.02
248.14
248.27
249.08
253.09
254.13
256.03
257.08
260.07
261.02
261.25
262.26
264.15
264.18
264.28
264.28
266.01
268.24
268.24
271.19
271.19
271.23
279.20
280.08
280.19
281.12
281.20
281.21
285.21
286.01
286.03
286.06
286.15
286.22
287.26
288.19
289.17
289.23
294.20
296.07
300.05
301.14
302.12
312.19
318.15
318.18
319.01
319.26
322.23
323.08
323.10
323.11
326.16
332.02
332.07
335.06
335.23
337.25
343.19
344.11
346.03
348.28
349.20
350.05
350.05
352.25
353.02
354.15
356.21
356.22
357.26
358.19
359.25
360.08
361.06
361.17
367.26
368.09
368.09
368.13
370.25
370.26
371.02
372.11
373.12
377.16
379.10
381.13
381.18
382.16
382.18
382.28
383.08
384.26
390.12
394.04
394.08
397.17
399.08
403.04
403.13
403.15
404.11
405.07

417.05
417.08
417.09
418.09
418.18
421.04
422.05
423.21
424.18
424.26
424.28
425.24
427.04
430.24
431.11
431.23
434.03
438.07
438.08
439.18
440.08
440.10
440.14
445.09
451.21
451.25
457.27
458.14
459.05
459.12
459.25
461.18
463.03
463.15
468.26
471.07
472.22
474.01
475.22
476.28
477.09
478.16
481.16
481.27
483.10
485.13
486.12
490.01
490.08
490.22
492.26
494.16
495.22
497.09
497.24
498.12
499.11
499.25
504.10
505.08
505.10
506.03
506.11
507.13
508.15
510.08
511.14
512.04
512.04
512.28
514.08
514.27
517.19
523.07
525.26
527.04
528.12
531.23
536.24
537.06
537.21
541.05
544.13
544.28
545.07
545.26
546.07
546.08
546.16
547.02
547.13
548.10
549.14
555.27
556.04
556.07
560.02
560.22
563.14
564.22
565.17
567.14
567.21
567.24
569.04
570.11
572.19
573.24
575.23
579.10
588.05

590.19	744.19	378.10	014.02	030.09	045.26
590.22	748.01	analyzed	014.16	030.12	045.28
591.09	748.24	402.17	014.17	030.15	046.04
593.01	748.26	491.06	014.19	030.16	046.04
595.04	749.01	analyzing	014.22	030.20	046.08
595.19	751.11	337.12	014.23	030.21	046.11
596.10	752.04	anathemas	014.27	030.27	046.16
605.10	753.22	297.05	015.02	031.02	046.18
605.19	754.09	anathematized	015.06	031.03	046.19
607.21	755.08	354.24	015.12	031.05	046.19
611.01	756.22	anatomical	015.13	031.07	046.21
611.04	757.13	256.06	015.20	031.09	046.23
613.16	758.01	ancestors	015.26	031.11	046.27
616.02	758.20	751.14	016.05	031.14	047.01
617.19	764.04	anchor	016.06	031.15	047.02
618.20	765.09	683.26	016.11	031.19	047.05
619.19	766.23	ancient	016.14	031.20	047.11
619.27	768.19	209.05	016.17	031.21	047.12
620.26	770.20	697.26	016.18	031.25	047.13
621.01	770.26	701.10	016.22	031.26	047.16
624.04	771.26	and	016.22	031.27	047.17
625.16	772.10	001.09	017.01	032.01	047.17
627.16	773.14	001.14	017.04	032.04	047.22
629.27	774.28	001.14	017.12	032.06	047.25
632.19	775.14	001.16	017.14	032.07	047.28
633.04	777.05	001.17	017.15	032.09	048.01
635.07	777.23	002.01	017.19	032.10	048.01
635.17	783.18	002.04	017.20	032.12	048.09
636.02	783.20	002.10	017.22	032.13	048.10
637.03	783.23	002.12	017.22	032.15	048.11
637.13	785.14	002.13	018.01	032.15	048.12
639.23	788.10	002.23	018.18	032.20	048.14
640.16	789.17	003.04	018.21	033.03	048.15
641.06	791.25	003.14	018.22	033.04	048.17
642.07	792.08	003.14	018.24	033.05	048.21
642.15	792.10	003.16	019.01	033.07	049.05
645.07	793.20	003.20	019.06	033.08	049.06
647.02	794.17	003.25	019.06	033.09	049.13
649.03	799.17	004.03	019.08	033.11	049.15
649.03	800.09	004.09	019.09	033.12	049.18
649.06	800.10	004.10	019.10	033.14	049.18
650.01	804.06	004.13	019.12	033.17	049.20
650.06	805.04	004.21	019.13	033.20	049.22
655.05	806.16	004.22	019.14	033.21	049.24
664.11	807.24	004.24	019.20	034.15	049.27
667.01	808.10	005.02	019.24	034.24	049.27
667.04	809.14	005.14	019.28	035.24	050.02
667.09	810.05	005.18	020.21	035.28	050.11
669.11	810.17	005.21	021.01	036.02	050.14
670.26	810.21	005.22	021.04	036.05	050.15
670.26	811.08	005.23	021.06	036.08	050.21
671.18	813.13	005.24	021.10	036.15	051.01
672.17	813.15	005.26	021.12	036.19	051.09
672.21	813.19	006.02	021.16	036.25	051.10
674.09	813.24	006.12	021.21	036.27	051.12
676.03	814.20	006.16	021.23	037.07	051.17
676.19	817.08	006.19	021.25	037.19	051.21
678.08	818.18	006.26	021.28	038.01	051.25
680.06	818.19	006.28	022.05	038.08	051.26
681.23	818.28	007.03	022.11	038.25	052.11
682.14	823.27	007.04	022.12	038.26	052.12
684.05	824.04	007.05	022.18	038.27	052.21
685.07	828.05	007.07	022.18	038.28	052.25
686.19	829.04	007.08	022.22	039.08	052.28
687.05	835.18	007.08	022.23	039.09	053.05
688.06	836.02	007.14	023.04	039.20	053.11
690.12	841.25	007.16	023.09	040.02	053.12
691.06	842.19	007.18	023.10	040.03	053.13
696.12	847.08	007.21	023.22	040.06	053.14
697.05	847.09	007.21	023.25	040.10	053.22
699.11	848.28	007.22	024.05	040.14	053.23
700.04	849.03	007.25	024.07	040.25	053.28
700.06	851.03	008.03	024.09	040.28	054.02
701.10	852.06	008.04	024.15	041.02	054.03
701.25	853.01	008.06	024.17	041.05	054.07
701.26	858.04	008.13	025.01	041.16	054.09
702.08	859.11	008.14	025.02	041.16	054.11
702.25	861.20	008.17	025.07	042.02	054.12
705.05	863.20	008.18	025.10	042.04	054.17
706.09	864.21	008.21	025.11	042.06	054.27
706.15	869.15	008.22	025.12	042.07	055.01
708.04	872.26	009.05	025.13	042.14	055.09
713.12	877.13	009.10	025.15	042.16	055.15
715.05	878.05	009.11	026.04	043.05	055.16
715.11	878.14	009.12	026.06	043.06	055.16
715.22	878.18	009.16	026.08	043.09	055.17
716.02	879.12	009.17	026.11	043.11	055.17
716.03	880.09	009.19	026.12	043.13	055.18
716.10	880.25	009.20	026.14	043.14	055.19
716.16	881.24	009.23	026.18	043.17	055.23
716.23	885.14	009.24	027.01	044.02	056.04
719.03	887.04	009.27	027.04	044.06	056.06
719.07	888.05	010.04	027.06	044.08	056.07
719.21	890.06	010.09	027.13	044.21	056.18
719.24	890.09	010.12	027.17	044.24	056.20
720.05	893.25	010.15	027.19	044.25	056.21
721.06	894.13	010.18	027.22	044.25	057.04
722.01	895.10	010.20	027.24	044.25	057.11
722.08	899.26	010.22	027.25	044.27	057.14
723.21	906.09	010.24	027.27	045.02	057.17
727.03	909.10	011.04	028.20	045.05	057.22
729.15	910.20	011.06	029.05	045.09	057.23
734.04	analogous	012.03	029.08	045.10	057.25
734.09	771.14	012.04	029.11	045.13	058.06
735.15	analysis	012.09	029.22	045.16	058.11
735.26	036.15	013.02	029.23	045.17	058.14
739.19	149.23	013.04	029.24	045.19	058.15
740.15	823.19	013.13	030.06	045.20	058.17
742.04	analyze	013.19	030.07	045.22	058.17
742.12	036.15	013.21	030.08	045.22	058.18
744.06	219.01	013.23		045.23	

058.20	072.26	086.24	102.15	120.07	135.11
058.21	072.27	087.08	102.26	120.15	135.13
059.02	073.06	087.13	103.01	120.16	135.19
059.05	073.09	087.15	103.02	120.20	135.21
059.07	073.14	087.16	103.03	120.23	135.23
059.10	073.19	087.16	103.06	120.27	136.06
059.11	073.20	087.20	103.10	121.02	136.07
059.13	073.24	087.21	103.15	121.06	136.15
059.20	073.28	087.26	103.22	121.19	136.20
060.01	074.02	088.01	103.25	121.20	136.20
060.01	074.03	088.04	104.01	121.20	136.25
060.02	074.03	088.05	104.03	122.01	136.27
060.02	074.07	088.10	104.03	122.03	137.08
060.09	074.09	088.11	104.12	122.05	137.10
060.12	074.11	088.12	104.13	122.09	137.11
060.13	074.16	088.13	104.18	122.12	137.14
060.18	074.20	088.21	104.20	122.13	137.20
060.18	074.21	088.22	104.24	122.15	137.28
060.20	074.27	088.25	104.27	122.19	138.03
060.22	075.01	088.26	105.02	122.21	138.06
060.22	075.07	088.28	105.05	122.22	138.07
060.24	075.13	089.02	105.09	122.24	138.09
060.28	075.14	089.02	105.18	122.27	138.15
061.02	075.17	089.04	105.19	123.04	138.17
061.03	075.19	089.05	105.20	123.08	138.18
061.03	075.20	089.07	105.23	123.10	138.22
061.13	075.21	089.08	106.05	123.15	138.24
061.15	075.23	089.17	106.10	123.16	138.25
061.28	075.25	089.18	106.20	123.23	139.05
062.02	075.26	089.21	106.21	123.24	139.07
062.07	076.02	089.22	106.23	123.26	139.10
062.09	076.04	090.01	106.24	124.03	139.16
062.24	076.08	090.03	107.10	124.04	139.22
062.25	076.17	090.12	107.11	124.05	140.05
062.26	076.20	090.15	107.18	124.12	140.10
063.03	076.20	090.25	107.19	124.16	140.14
063.04	077.04	091.05	107.20	124.17	140.15
063.06	077.12	091.07	107.23	124.18	140.16
063.07	077.14	091.08	108.01	124.18	141.03
063.11	077.20	091.13	108.02	124.22	141.04
063.20	077.23	091.21	108.03	125.05	141.13
063.25	077.28	091.21	108.14	125.08	141.15
063.25	078.01	091.24	108.22	125.09	141.19
064.08	078.04	091.25	108.23	125.17	141.22
064.09	078.06	092.01	108.26	125.20	141.22
064.15	078.12	092.02	108.28	126.01	142.05
064.16	078.15	092.04	109.01	126.06	142.08
064.21	078.21	092.07	109.11	126.08	142.08
064.25	078.24	092.08	109.12	126.08	142.14
064.28	078.24	092.12	109.15	126.12	142.20
065.01	078.28	092.16	109.16	126.14	142.21
065.07	079.03	092.21	110.03	126.22	142.27
065.10	079.03	092.23	110.04	126.28	143.03
065.11	079.08	092.24	110.05	127.04	143.04
065.14	079.13	092.25	110.07	127.12	143.17
065.15	079.13	092.27	111.03	127.13	143.19
065.16	079.23	092.27	111.05	127.18	144.07
065.19	079.27	092.28	111.09	127.20	144.08
065.20	079.28	093.01	111.10	127.24	144.09
065.22	080.03	093.03	111.17	127.26	144.14
065.23	080.04	093.07	111.18	128.06	144.14
066.03	080.06	093.14	112.01	128.10	144.17
066.06	080.07	094.05	112.02	128.11	145.01
066.10	080.11	094.06	112.14	129.03	145.03
066.11	080.11	094.08	112.25	129.06	145.08
066.16	080.12	094.12	112.25	129.08	145.11
066.17	080.13	094.17	113.02	129.13	145.12
066.19	080.19	094.23	113.07	129.14	145.18
066.23	080.22	095.01	113.09	129.16	145.18
066.25	081.02	095.13	113.10	130.02	145.21
067.10	081.04	095.15	113.11	130.04	145.22
067.12	081.06	095.18	113.16	130.06	145.24
067.14	081.09	095.19	113.20	130.08	145.28
067.16	081.14	096.03	114.07	130.08	146.01
067.21	082.03	096.07	114.08	130.10	146.04
067.24	082.09	096.10	114.09	130.15	146.07
068.08	082.13	096.12	114.16	130.23	146.12
068.13	082.15	096.13	114.18	131.02	146.12
068.13	082.16	096.15	114.21	131.12	146.13
068.14	082.23	096.20	114.25	131.18	146.18
068.16	082.25	097.01	115.10	131.20	146.18
068.19	082.27	097.06	115.14	131.27	146.22
068.25	083.01	097.07	115.21	131.28	146.25
069.03	083.03	097.07	115.22	132.02	146.26
069.12	083.05	097.11	115.27	132.07	146.28
069.13	083.12	097.16	116.04	132.12	147.08
069.15	083.12	097.18	116.08	132.17	147.14
069.18	083.14	098.12	116.11	132.20	147.16
069.21	083.18	098.14	116.12	132.21	147.17
069.25	083.25	098.15	116.19	132.22	147.20
069.27	084.01	098.15	116.22	132.24	147.20
070.01	084.07	098.20	116.25	132.25	147.23
070.01	084.10	099.13	116.26	132.26	147.24
070.03	084.13	099.19	116.28	133.01	147.25
071.04	084.15	099.20	117.09	133.03	147.26
071.05	084.19	099.20	117.14	133.04	148.01
071.06	084.21	099.23	117.16	133.08	148.04
071.07	084.25	099.25	117.20	133.14	148.06
071.18	084.25	100.07	117.23	133.15	148.08
071.20	084.27	100.22	117.26	133.21	148.08
072.02	085.07	100.23	117.28	133.24	148.09
072.02	085.12	100.25	118.04	133.26	148.11
072.03	085.13	100.25	118.09	134.01	148.12
072.05	085.15	101.05	118.16	134.05	148.13
072.08	085.24	101.10	118.27	134.06	148.14
072.09	085.25	101.11	119.04	134.09	148.18
072.11	086.09	101.12	119.13	134.15	149.03
072.11	086.10	101.14	119.14	134.16	149.03
072.15	086.10	101.22	119.17	134.20	149.05
072.22	086.19	101.23	119.28	134.23	149.06
072.24	086.23	102.09	120.05	134.26	149.07

149.08	163.20	177.14	191.05	202.27	218.06
149.12	163.21	177.20	191.05	202.28	218.15
149.15	163.22	177.21	191.08	203.06	218.15
149.16	163.28	177.23	191.10	203.06	218.20
149.18	164.01	178.02	191.11	203.12	218.22
149.28	164.08	178.08	191.13	203.17	218.23
150.07	164.10	178.17	191.17	203.19	219.01
150.07	164.10	178.17	191.18	203.27	219.01
150.12	164.11	178.18	191.23	204.04	219.03
150.12	164.15	178.19	191.24	204.06	219.06
150.12	164.22	178.22	191.28	204.10	219.09
150.14	164.24	179.01	192.01	204.13	219.09
150.17	165.03	179.01	192.15	204.15	219.11
150.19	165.09	179.06	192.18	204.18	219.12
150.20	165.10	179.08	192.19	204.19	219.15
150.28	165.10	179.10	192.21	204.26	219.15
151.01	165.10	179.10	192.22	204.26	219.18
151.05	165.11	179.20	192.22	204.27	219.19
151.07	165.11	179.20	192.23	205.06	219.26
151.09	165.12	179.23	192.26	205.06	220.05
151.10	165.18	179.27	192.27	205.18	220.06
151.15	166.07	180.01	193.02	205.18	220.08
151.16	166.19	180.16	193.04	205.25	220.09
151.17	166.19	180.17	193.07	206.11	220.18
151.27	167.03	180.26	193.08	206.13	220.20
152.07	167.12	181.03	193.10	206.19	220.25
152.11	167.13	181.10	193.15	206.20	220.25
152.13	167.15	181.11	193.15	206.24	221.02
152.14	167.16	181.13	193.18	206.25	221.04
152.16	167.17	181.15	193.19	206.27	221.09
152.16	167.18	181.15	193.20	206.28	221.10
152.17	167.20	181.16	193.25	207.01	221.12
152.18	167.22	181.17	193.27	207.05	221.14
152.21	167.25	181.19	194.07	207.09	221.15
152.22	168.02	182.01	194.09	207.11	221.20
152.23	168.03	182.10	194.10	207.21	221.25
152.25	168.08	182.14	194.15	207.25	221.26
152.27	168.10	182.15	194.16	207.25	222.02
153.04	168.13	182.21	194.23	208.13	222.06
153.13	168.16	182.25	194.24	208.22	222.09
153.17	168.26	182.27	194.27	208.24	222.14
153.21	169.07	183.10	195.04	208.25	222.15
153.22	169.09	183.11	195.05	208.27	222.16
154.01	169.12	183.12	195.12	208.28	222.17
154.05	169.16	183.18	195.13	209.02	222.18
154.08	169.20	183.24	196.06	209.05	222.21
154.09	169.24	183.26	196.08	209.13	222.22
154.12	169.27	183.27	196.12	209.17	222.25
154.13	169.28	184.01	196.20	209.18	222.28
154.15	170.03	184.05	196.24	209.20	223.12
154.16	170.06	184.08	197.09	209.24	223.15
154.19	170.07	184.10	197.10	209.27	223.19
154.24	170.13	184.14	197.13	209.28	223.21
154.25	170.15	184.22	197.18	210.01	223.24
154.27	170.16	185.05	197.19	210.13	223.28
155.01	170.18	185.06	197.27	210.27	224.04
155.05	170.27	185.07	198.01	211.03	224.05
155.06	171.09	185.12	198.04	211.04	224.07
155.07	171.11	185.15	198.07	211.11	224.10
155.08	171.13	185.16	198.08	211.12	224.12
155.10	171.15	185.18	198.09	211.14	224.14
155.25	171.20	185.22	198.11	211.19	224.15
156.04	171.23	185.25	198.14	211.20	224.16
156.06	171.25	186.01	198.20	211.27	224.19
156.07	172.02	186.04	198.25	212.05	224.22
156.07	172.10	186.07	198.26	213.05	224.25
156.08	172.14	186.10	198.26	213.08	225.02
156.08	172.19	186.12	198.28	213.10	225.05
156.14	172.22	186.19	198.28	213.10	225.08
156.26	172.27	186.20	199.02	213.12	225.09
157.01	173.04	186.20	199.08	213.15	225.12
157.04	173.07	186.27	199.10	213.16	225.22
157.05	173.17	187.01	199.11	214.04	226.02
157.07	173.20	187.06	199.12	214.05	226.24
157.08	173.22	187.08	199.14	214.11	227.07
157.10	173.23	187.09	199.15	214.17	227.14
157.11	173.28	187.16	199.17	214.17	227.18
157.21	174.01	187.19	199.18	214.19	227.18
157.23	174.07	187.23	200.05	214.21	227.26
158.01	174.16	187.25	200.05	214.22	228.01
158.08	174.17	187.28	200.06	214.24	228.07
158.15	174.18	188.01	200.07	214.26	228.09
159.03	175.01	188.23	200.08	214.28	228.11
159.17	175.08	189.04	200.13	215.02	228.11
159.22	175.11	189.04	200.15	215.04	228.15
160.15	175.12	189.06	200.21	215.04	228.16
160.17	175.13	189.10	200.21	215.13	228.20
160.20	175.16	189.11	200.22	215.15	228.23
161.03	175.19	189.12	200.28	215.15	228.26
161.04	175.21	189.13	201.01	215.17	228.28
161.07	175.26	189.16	201.04	215.22	229.01
161.11	176.01	189.17	201.05	215.23	229.02
161.14	176.04	189.18	201.11	215.23	229.06
161.18	176.06	189.20	201.12	215.25	229.07
161.23	176.06	189.21	201.13	215.26	229.08
161.26	176.12	189.24	201.17	215.28	229.10
161.26	176.13	189.25	201.25	216.03	229.11
161.27	176.19	190.03	202.02	216.05	229.14
162.04	176.20	190.11	202.02	216.08	229.18
162.16	176.22	190.13	202.04	216.10	229.23
162.18	176.22	190.15	202.05	216.16	229.23
162.22	176.24	190.18	202.05	216.20	229.24
162.28	176.26	190.20	202.07	216.23	229.28
163.04	176.26	190.20	202.08	216.24	230.01
163.07	176.27	190.23	202.10	217.11	230.05
163.09	177.01	190.24	202.17	217.16	230.06
163.12	177.03	190.25	202.21	217.22	230.10
163.13	177.04	190.25	202.23	217.22	230.14
163.14	177.05	190.27	202.25	217.25	230.16
163.19	177.13	191.02	202.25	217.28	230.17
		191.03		217.28	

230.24	246.06	262.18	283.06	299.19	318.11
230.24	246.09	262.21	283.07	299.20	318.12
230.26	246.10	263.07	283.09	300.18	318.13
230.26	246.15	263.10	283.19	300.27	318.16
231.03	246.20	263.11	283.20	301.02	318.17
231.04	246.22	263.12	283.21	301.05	318.22
231.07	246.26	263.22	283.21	301.05	318.25
231.10	246.27	263.26	283.28	301.25	319.01
231.11	247.12	264.03	284.03	302.06	319.03
231.12	247.15	264.05	284.07	302.09	319.05
231.12	247.20	264.07	284.11	302.11	319.06
231.15	247.24	264.12	284.11	302.16	319.08
231.21	248.02	264.14	284.13	302.22	319.10
231.23	248.05	264.20	284.13	302.23	319.10
231.24	248.07	264.23	284.26	303.01	319.14
231.27	248.12	264.23	285.03	305.03	320.04
231.28	248.14	264.25	285.05	305.10	320.06
231.28	248.17	265.02	285.16	305.17	320.10
232.01	248.20	265.06	285.24	305.17	320.10
232.01	248.25	265.12	286.07	305.18	320.13
232.03	249.05	265.14	286.11	306.08	320.20
232.05	249.06	265.25	286.12	306.08	320.22
232.12	249.08	266.01	286.13	306.18	320.28
232.13	249.09	266.04	286.14	306.21	321.04
232.14	249.13	266.16	286.15	306.23	321.07
232.16	249.20	266.24	286.17	306.26	321.08
232.23	249.26	266.27	286.18	307.02	321.12
232.25	250.02	266.28	287.01	307.03	321.15
233.06	250.03	267.09	287.16	307.10	321.18
233.07	250.06	267.12	287.19	307.11	321.20
233.08	250.09	267.15	288.03	307.11	321.22
233.11	250.14	267.24	288.06	307.21	321.22
233.12	250.19	268.01	288.11	307.23	321.26
233.18	250.21	268.07	288.17	308.01	322.03
234.05	250.22	268.12	288.17	308.07	322.10
234.10	250.24	268.15	288.23	308.10	322.16
234.14	251.11	268.17	289.01	308.12	322.18
234.28	251.14	268.17	289.02	308.13	322.18
235.01	251.20	269.06	289.10	308.17	322.19
235.02	251.24	269.17	289.13	308.18	322.21
235.04	251.28	269.28	289.13	308.19	322.22
235.04	252.01	270.15	289.14	308.22	322.27
235.05	252.03	270.22	289.15	309.01	323.03
235.09	252.20	270.27	289.16	309.02	323.05
235.10	252.22	271.02	289.19	309.08	323.06
235.12	252.24	271.03	289.20	310.01	323.09
235.16	252.27	271.08	289.24	310.06	323.12
235.21	252.28	271.12	289.26	310.09	323.16
236.01	253.02	271.15	290.10	310.12	323.16
236.07	253.08	271.17	290.16	310.15	323.17
236.09	253.13	272.01	290.17	310.16	324.02
236.17	253.19	272.02	290.23	310.21	324.03
236.21	253.21	272.27	291.01	310.22	324.06
236.23	254.04	273.05	291.06	310.26	324.07
236.26	254.06	273.07	291.13	311.03	324.09
236.27	254.12	273.08	291.14	311.04	324.11
237.03	254.16	273.11	291.17	311.06	324.14
237.04	254.18	273.16	291.19	311.08	324.16
237.10	254.18	273.18	292.07	311.18	325.06
237.11	255.02	273.19	292.08	311.27	325.06
237.15	255.05	273.22	292.09	312.06	325.10
237.18	255.09	273.24	292.10	312.10	325.12
237.24	255.12	274.08	292.23	312.17	325.13
237.26	255.13	274.10	292.26	312.20	325.15
238.08	255.13	274.11	293.02	312.22	325.16
238.18	255.16	274.20	293.07	312.23	325.18
238.19	256.01	274.23	293.09	312.26	325.20
238.24	256.02	275.18	293.11	312.28	325.21
238.27	256.04	275.19	293.13	313.06	325.24
239.01	256.12	275.20	293.14	313.07	326.04
239.15	256.14	275.25	293.20	313.10	326.06
239.16	256.16	275.25	293.23	313.13	326.06
239.26	257.06	275.26	293.23	313.24	326.09
240.06	257.08	276.07	293.28	313.25	326.19
240.10	257.13	276.16	294.03	313.26	326.24
240.13	257.15	276.18	294.19	313.28	327.01
240.20	257.19	276.21	294.28	314.02	327.01
240.23	257.22	277.03	295.02	314.10	327.02
240.27	258.14	277.07	295.05	314.11	327.04
240.27	258.15	277.12	295.07	314.15	327.04
241.07	258.16	277.21	295.08	314.16	327.05
241.19	258.18	278.06	295.11	314.20	327.07
241.26	258.24	279.05	295.15	314.20	327.08
242.08	258.27	279.05	295.15	314.24	327.12
242.13	258.27	279.06	295.16	314.27	327.14
242.18	258.28	279.07	295.19	315.02	327.15
242.20	259.03	279.18	295.20	315.03	327.16
242.22	259.05	280.06	295.26	315.11	327.18
242.25	259.06	280.13	295.27	315.21	327.19
242.28	259.11	280.19	296.03	316.15	327.22
243.03	259.18	280.21	296.04	316.21	327.26
243.03	259.24	280.23	296.10	316.22	327.27
243.15	259.25	280.24	296.14	316.24	328.01
243.16	260.01	280.24	296.17	316.25	328.01
243.19	260.12	280.25	296.18	317.02	328.02
243.26	260.14	281.02	296.18	317.03	328.02
244.05	260.17	281.03	296.20	317.06	328.06
244.07	260.22	281.04	296.22	317.08	328.07
244.08	260.26	281.07	296.27	317.08	328.08
244.09	261.10	281.08	297.16	317.12	328.08
244.14	261.11	281.13	297.19	317.16	328.09
244.14	261.14	282.03	297.27	317.17	328.14
244.18	261.15	282.14	298.01	317.23	328.15
244.19	261.18	282.17	298.03	317.25	328.16
244.21	261.22	282.20	298.09	317.27	328.17
244.26	261.24	282.21	298.19	317.27	328.19
245.03	261.25	282.22	298.20	318.05	328.19
245.04	261.27	282.26	298.24	318.07	328.22
245.11	262.07	282.28	299.08	318.09	328.24
245.15	262.12	283.01	299.12	318.09	329.03
245.21	262.16	283.02	299.17	318.10	329.05

329.12	344.05	357.22	375.27	390.15	407.03
329.12	344.10	358.11	376.04	390.17	407.04
329.20	344.12	358.22	376.04	390.18	407.11
329.23	344.13	359.10	376.07	390.22	407.15
330.01	344.16	359.14	376.07	390.23	408.08
330.06	344.17	359.19	376.08	390.26	408.12
330.07	344.20	359.21	376.08	390.26	408.22
330.07	344.24	359.22	376.11	391.05	408.24
330.13	344.28	359.25	376.12	391.06	409.09
330.18	345.01	359.28	376.17	391.08	409.14
330.18	345.08	360.01	376.23	391.12	409.25
330.22	345.12	360.09	376.25	391.13	410.07
330.25	345.15	360.11	377.15	391.18	410.08
331.04	345.21	360.14	377.22	391.19	410.11
331.04	345.22	360.17	377.25	391.23	410.13
331.06	346.02	361.05	377.26	391.25	410.14
331.07	346.10	361.14	378.01	392.03	410.14
331.10	346.11	361.16	378.02	392.05	410.24
331.13	346.12	361.18	378.03	392.06	410.24
332.03	346.13	362.02	378.04	392.06	411.02
332.21	346.17	362.13	378.07	392.08	411.02
332.23	346.21	362.24	378.10	392.09	411.03
332.27	346.24	363.03	378.12	392.11	411.05
332.27	346.27	363.03	378.13	392.12	411.05
333.03	347.07	363.04	378.16	392.14	411.07
333.06	347.09	363.05	378.16	392.17	411.07
333.09	347.10	363.11	378.19	392.22	411.11
333.10	347.15	363.13	378.24	392.26	411.14
333.20	347.16	364.03	378.26	393.02	411.14
333.21	347.19	364.04	379.01	393.03	411.17
333.24	347.21	364.15	379.01	393.06	411.20
333.26	347.23	364.15	379.02	394.03	411.21
333.27	347.24	364.16	379.05	394.06	411.23
333.27	347.26	364.19	379.07	394.10	411.25
333.28	348.06	365.02	379.08	394.16	411.27
333.28	348.07	365.11	379.11	395.01	412.03
334.03	348.10	365.13	379.16	395.05	412.03
334.13	348.15	365.17	379.24	395.07	412.04
334.15	348.18	365.18	379.28	395.09	412.05
334.18	348.24	365.19	380.02	395.10	412.12
334.18	348.26	365.23	380.02	395.20	412.15
334.19	348.28	365.27	380.05	395.20	412.23
334.21	349.01	366.03	380.06	396.03	412.24
334.23	349.03	366.11	380.07	396.04	412.25
335.02	349.06	366.20	380.10	396.07	413.01
335.03	349.09	366.25	380.15	396.09	413.03
335.04	349.12	366.26	380.16	396.15	413.07
335.09	349.15	367.06	380.24	396.22	414.03
335.13	349.18	367.08	380.27	397.10	414.05
335.16	349.19	367.09	381.03	397.15	414.08
336.07	349.25	367.14	381.05	397.19	414.11
336.10	349.28	367.17	381.12	397.19	414.12
336.14	350.07	367.24	381.14	397.21	414.20
336.15	350.10	367.28	381.21	398.02	415.08
336.16	350.12	368.01	381.22	398.19	415.11
336.19	350.18	368.03	381.28	398.20	415.13
336.19	350.23	368.07	382.06	398.25	415.14
336.25	351.01	368.07	382.14	399.04	415.15
336.27	351.02	368.18	382.15	399.16	415.21
336.26	351.03	368.18	382.18	399.21	415.22
336.26	351.13	368.20	382.21	399.24	415.28
337.04	351.14	368.23	382.25	400.06	416.01
337.07	351.15	368.28	383.01	400.08	416.02
337.08	351.15	369.02	383.05	400.11	416.08
337.12	351.27	369.03	383.06	400.12	416.16
337.14	351.28	369.03	383.13	400.13	416.17
337.21	352.03	369.05	383.16	400.13	416.26
337.22	352.03	369.06	383.21	400.14	417.04
338.01	352.07	369.07	383.22	400.17	417.10
338.02	352.08	369.08	383.23	400.20	417.17
338.13	352.10	369.19	383.25	400.21	417.22
338.21	352.12	369.25	383.28	400.21	417.22
338.23	352.14	369.25	383.28	400.22	418.01
339.02	352.17	370.02	384.01	400.23	418.02
339.04	352.18	370.07	384.06	401.06	418.08
339.05	352.19	370.26	384.09	401.14	418.13
339.09	352.21	371.04	384.11	401.23	418.13
339.18	352.22	371.06	384.12	402.04	418.16
339.25	352.27	371.07	384.15	402.06	418.17
340.06	354.01	371.10	384.17	402.12	418.18
340.12	354.07	371.16	384.20	402.13	418.20
340.14	354.08	371.21	384.27	402.18	418.23
340.20	354.10	371.23	385.04	402.20	418.25
340.24	354.11	371.26	385.06	402.22	419.05
341.03	354.18	372.05	385.16	403.01	419.11
341.16	354.22	372.10	385.20	403.04	419.14
341.24	355.01	372.17	386.03	403.08	419.14
341.25	355.15	372.19	386.09	403.20	419.16
342.03	355.16	373.14	386.09	403.28	419.22
342.07	355.16	373.15	386.26	404.08	419.24
342.10	355.20	373.21	387.06	404.18	419.28
342.15	355.21	373.21	387.09	404.18	420.05
342.16	355.22	373.27	387.13	404.25	420.08
342.22	355.26	374.06	387.16	404.28	420.10
342.25	355.27	374.07	387.21	404.28	420.14
342.26	355.28	374.10	387.26	405.04	420.20
342.27	355.28	374.11	388.05	405.05	420.23
343.02	356.04	374.14	388.07	405.12	420.27
343.04	356.05	374.14	388.15	405.12	421.01
343.06	356.09	374.16	388.20	405.13	421.09
343.08	356.12	374.18	389.02	405.15	421.11
343.08	356.14	374.20	389.08	405.18	421.14
343.09	356.15	374.21	389.09	405.19	421.17
343.10	356.17	374.23	389.15	405.25	421.18
343.11	356.24	374.24	389.16	405.28	421.21
343.15	356.26	375.03	389.18	406.02	422.09
343.19	357.04	375.04	389.26	406.19	422.10
343.23	357.05	375.05	390.05	406.22	422.12
343.25	357.07	375.07	390.07	406.23	422.18
344.02	357.16	375.12	390.11	406.24	422.23
344.03	357.21	375.15	390.13	406.26	422.27

422.27	437.28	456.25	468.18	483.06	496.17
423.08	438.19	456.27	468.18	483.09	496.21
423.10	438.19	457.04	468.19	483.12	496.23
423.11	438.21	457.07	468.23	483.22	497.04
423.11	438.24	457.08	468.26	483.24	497.13
423.15	438.24	457.09	469.03	483.26	497.18
423.16	439.02	457.09	469.04	483.26	497.23
423.21	439.07	457.14	469.09	484.03	497.26
423.23	439.19	457.16	469.13	484.10	498.02
423.27	439.21	457.16	469.15	484.11	498.08
423.28	439.24	457.22	469.27	484.13	498.12
424.01	439.25	457.25	470.01	484.15	498.17
424.11	440.01	457.27	470.08	484.15	498.18
424.14	440.02	458.01	470.12	484.16	498.18
424.16	440.03	458.02	470.15	484.21	498.19
424.19	440.03	458.04	470.17	484.26	498.21
424.20	440.07	458.05	470.20	484.28	498.25
424.22	440.14	458.06	470.23	485.01	499.02
424.24	440.16	458.13	470.25	485.05	499.06
425.01	440.23	458.13	470.27	485.06	499.10
425.08	440.24	458.17	471.04	485.12	499.17
425.09	440.27	458.22	471.05	485.21	499.18
425.25	441.03	458.23	471.06	485.24	499.20
426.01	441.04	458.26	471.13	485.25	499.21
426.03	441.06	458.26	471.14	485.26	499.25
426.07	441.07	459.01	471.15	485.28	500.07
426.08	441.13	459.02	471.21	486.01	500.08
426.09	441.17	459.04	471.24	486.04	500.12
426.10	441.25	459.06	471.25	486.11	501.07
426.15	441.25	459.06	472.02	486.13	501.10
426.15	441.26	459.09	472.03	486.13	501.10
426.16	442.04	459.14	472.05	487.09	501.12
427.01	442.20	459.19	472.06	487.14	501.12
427.06	442.26	459.20	472.09	487.15	501.18
427.13	443.01	459.22	472.12	487.16	502.01
427.13	443.03	459.24	472.16	487.18	502.02
428.13	444.02	459.27	472.24	487.18	502.06
428.18	444.03	459.28	473.07	488.03	502.07
428.19	444.03	460.02	473.09	488.08	502.08
428.24	444.13	460.15	473.11	488.10	502.09
428.27	444.18	460.15	473.12	488.14	502.10
429.09	445.06	460.21	473.16	488.16	502.19
429.14	445.14	460.26	473.21	488.19	502.25
429.19	445.15	460.27	473.24	488.21	503.03
429.20	445.21	461.02	474.05	488.24	503.09
429.24	445.22	461.05	474.09	488.25	503.10
429.26	445.26	461.07	474.18	488.27	503.14
429.27	446.04	461.08	474.22	488.28	503.19
429.28	446.11	461.11	474.27	489.04	503.22
430.02	446.15	461.14	475.02	489.07	503.25
430.12	446.19	461.14	475.03	489.10	503.26
430.13	446.20	461.16	475.04	489.11	504.06
430.15	446.21	461.17	475.09	489.24	504.08
430.22	446.28	461.20	475.10	489.25	504.19
430.24	447.05	461.22	475.13	490.03	504.22
430.25	447.09	461.24	475.17	490.03	504.25
431.03	447.13	461.26	475.21	490.05	505.01
431.04	447.14	461.28	475.21	490.12	505.04
431.06	447.15	462.01	475.28	490.14	505.10
431.16	447.17	462.04	476.02	490.15	505.17
431.21	447.21	462.18	476.05	490.25	505.19
432.01	447.24	462.24	476.08	490.26	505.23
432.13	448.03	462.24	476.12	490.28	505.25
432.17	448.03	463.09	476.19	491.03	505.26
432.18	448.05	463.10	476.22	491.05	506.04
432.19	448.10	463.11	476.25	491.06	506.07
432.21	448.11	463.13	477.04	491.07	506.10
432.24	448.13	463.17	477.10	491.24	506.13
432.25	448.18	463.17	477.13	492.04	506.15
432.27	448.18	463.19	477.13	492.05	506.15
433.01	448.20	463.21	477.14	492.07	506.19
433.11	448.22	463.22	477.16	492.11	507.08
433.16	449.03	464.04	477.21	492.14	507.23
433.27	449.03	464.11	477.28	492.16	507.23
433.28	449.04	464.14	478.01	492.19	507.25
433.28	449.05	464.24	478.07	492.20	508.04
434.02	449.13	465.02	478.13	492.23	508.05
434.04	449.15	465.06	478.14	492.23	508.13
434.06	449.21	465.09	478.14	492.24	508.15
434.11	449.23	465.10	478.16	492.27	509.04
434.18	449.27	465.11	478.17	493.03	509.07
434.20	450.03	465.11	478.25	493.06	509.08
434.21	450.06	465.13	478.27	493.08	509.11
434.22	450.08	465.15	479.07	493.09	509.15
434.24	450.09	465.18	479.16	493.11	509.16
434.27	450.27	465.20	479.19	493.17	509.17
434.28	451.07	465.21	479.23	493.20	509.18
435.03	451.09	465.22	480.08	493.20	509.19
435.05	451.09	465.23	480.09	493.23	509.21
435.08	451.14	465.23	480.10	493.23	509.21
435.08	451.19	466.02	480.18	493.26	509.24
435.09	451.19	466.08	480.23	494.01	510.04
435.13	451.23	466.13	480.24	494.01	510.07
435.16	452.01	466.19	480.24	494.05	510.14
435.18	452.14	466.19	481.03	494.07	510.15
435.22	452.24	466.21	481.06	494.08	510.26
436.14	453.02	466.26	481.07	494.19	510.28
436.25	453.06	466.27	481.13	494.20	511.01
436.28	454.07	467.06	481.24	494.24	511.03
437.04	454.12	467.09	481.25	494.25	511.12
437.09	454.13	467.20	482.05	494.27	511.19
437.12	454.15	467.21	482.09	495.03	511.19
437.15	454.15	467.22	482.12	495.04	511.20
437.16	454.26	467.23	482.14	495.05	511.21
437.16	454.27	468.01	482.16	495.06	511.22
437.17	455.12	468.07	482.17	495.16	511.25
437.21	455.16	468.07	482.18	495.23	511.28
437.23	455.25	468.10	482.24	495.28	512.01
437.23	455.28	468.10	483.04	496.05	512.02
437.25	456.12	468.13		496.08	512.06
437.27	456.13			496.11	
	456.20				

512.06	524.01	540.10	554.02	573.02	591.17
512.08	524.04	540.14	554.06	573.03	591.24
512.15	524.14	540.16	554.08	573.04	591.25
512.23	524.25	540.17	554.09	573.06	592.09
513.01	524.28	540.21	554.15	573.08	592.12
513.02	525.03	540.21	554.16	573.10	592.16
513.04	525.04	540.27	554.17	573.13	592.21
513.05	525.06	541.01	554.20	573.15	593.05
513.06	525.07	541.07	554.22	573.25	593.07
513.07	525.10	541.17	554.23	574.02	593.10
513.08	525.12	541.20	554.24	574.09	593.14
513.15	525.13	541.22	554.27	574.24	594.15
513.21	525.21	541.23	555.01	575.01	594.18
513.23	525.21	541.24	555.03	575.04	594.19
513.26	525.22	542.01	555.07	575.11	594.20
514.03	525.24	542.03	555.19	575.12	594.24
514.07	525.24	542.04	555.19	575.18	595.20
514.10	526.01	542.04	555.23	576.03	595.23
514.12	526.07	542.05	556.02	576.10	596.02
514.13	526.11	542.09	556.04	576.12	596.06
514.18	526.14	542.13	556.05	576.16	596.09
514.21	526.15	542.14	557.05	576.18	596.14
514.25	526.16	542.14	557.10	576.21	596.17
515.03	526.17	542.16	558.03	576.24	596.19
515.05	526.20	542.17	558.08	577.11	596.25
515.06	526.21	542.20	558.19	577.12	597.06
515.08	526.22	542.22	559.04	577.14	597.10
515.14	526.27	542.28	559.15	577.19	597.11
515.16	527.01	543.02	559.18	577.20	597.13
515.18	527.04	543.02	559.22	577.21	597.23
515.28	527.12	543.03	559.25	577.23	597.23
516.04	527.13	543.03	560.01	577.24	597.25
516.06	527.14	543.15	560.16	578.03	598.01
516.09	527.14	543.17	560.20	578.07	598.05
516.09	527.22	543.19	561.01	578.14	598.05
516.10	527.24	544.07	561.02	578.17	598.08
516.13	527.25	544.09	561.02	578.22	598.17
517.01	527.25	544.14	561.06	578.24	598.22
517.02	528.04	544.18	561.08	579.05	598.23
517.03	528.05	544.20	561.13	579.07	599.04
517.06	528.06	544.21	561.15	579.09	599.06
517.06	528.07	544.22	561.18	579.17	599.10
517.08	528.08	544.23	561.20	580.01	599.10
517.10	528.09	544.26	561.21	580.08	599.15
517.12	528.10	545.05	562.01	580.11	599.18
517.19	528.17	545.06	562.07	580.12	599.20
517.25	528.18	545.09	562.09	580.17	599.21
518.01	528.19	545.12	562.14	580.23	599.23
518.02	528.22	545.14	562.19	581.05	600.05
518.05	528.23	545.14	562.23	581.10	600.13
518.07	529.02	545.16	562.24	581.11	600.18
518.11	529.09	545.17	563.04	581.18	601.03
518.12	529.17	545.18	563.07	581.20	601.04
518.12	529.19	545.26	563.17	581.24	601.07
518.15	529.22	546.01	563.19	582.04	601.13
518.15	531.01	546.05	563.25	582.09	601.17
518.16	531.04	546.11	564.08	582.13	601.19
518.17	531.04	546.14	564.09	582.16	601.24
518.18	531.04	546.15	564.12	582.20	602.01
518.24	531.05	546.20	564.18	582.21	602.04
518.26	531.08	546.21	565.02	582.23	602.08
518.27	531.11	547.19	565.03	583.03	602.09
518.28	531.21	547.19	565.06	583.11	603.01
519.04	531.28	547.21	565.12	583.12	603.08
519.07	532.01	547.24	565.17	583.12	603.12
519.07	532.05	547.26	565.19	583.13	603.19
519.08	532.08	548.04	566.01	583.20	604.04
519.11	532.15	548.06	566.02	583.21	604.14
519.14	532.20	548.23	566.03	583.22	604.16
519.21	532.24	548.27	566.04	584.01	604.19
519.25	533.03	549.03	566.06	584.02	604.20
519.26	534.01	549.04	566.18	584.05	604.20
520.03	534.05	549.10	567.02	585.13	604.22
520.04	534.09	549.11	567.08	585.16	605.13
520.05	534.11	549.19	567.10	586.02	605.16
520.07	534.14	549.23	567.14	586.05	606.01
520.10	534.17	549.25	567.19	586.06	606.04
520.10	534.19	549.27	567.20	586.15	606.05
520.16	534.21	550.06	568.03	586.16	606.06
521.02	534.26	550.07	568.14	586.22	606.11
521.03	535.04	550.12	568.17	587.01	606.16
521.05	535.06	550.15	569.02	587.01	607.01
521.06	535.08	550.17	569.03	587.02	607.11
521.08	535.14	550.18	569.07	587.07	607.12
521.09	535.18	550.18	569.17	587.11	607.13
521.10	535.18	551.03	569.17	587.17	607.14
521.11	535.24	551.07	569.19	587.22	607.17
521.16	536.07	551.09	570.02	587.25	607.23
521.17	536.17	551.11	570.03	588.01	608.03
521.18	536.18	551.11	570.05	588.07	608.10
522.04	536.25	551.20	570.08	588.12	609.02
522.05	537.01	551.23	570.12	588.14	609.03
522.07	537.04	551.27	570.18	588.17	609.12
522.09	537.07	552.03	570.21	588.18	609.12
522.09	537.13	552.07	571.01	588.23	609.13
522.13	537.14	552.13	571.02	588.23	609.17
522.16	537.18	552.13	571.07	589.01	610.02
522.19	537.22	552.14	571.11	589.06	610.05
522.21	537.22	552.15	571.12	589.12	610.13
522.21	537.23	552.15	571.21	589.20	610.19
523.02	537.26	552.15	571.23	589.21	610.21
523.02	537.27	552.18	572.02	589.23	610.28
523.04	538.06	552.26	572.04	590.11	611.02
523.05	538.16	553.08	572.05	590.12	611.08
523.07	538.19	553.11	572.15	590.17	611.10
523.10	538.21	553.14	572.16	590.21	611.12
523.10	539.01	553.19	572.22	590.24	611.13
523.14	539.03	553.19	572.23	591.05	611.20
523.15	539.04	553.25	572.24	591.12	611.26
523.23	539.15	553.26	573.01	591.14	612.03
523.27	539.22	554.01	573.01	591.14	612.03

612.08	625.08	637.27	650.08	667.05	682.26
612.11	625.21	637.28	650.23	667.06	683.01
612.12	625.27	638.02	651.07	667.08	683.15
612.17	626.02	638.18	651.16	667.11	683.15
612.20	626.06	639.05	651.26	667.17	683.16
612.22	626.08	639.06	652.02	667.19	683.19
612.23	626.10	639.07	652.04	667.20	684.01
613.01	626.16	639.10	652.11	668.04	684.04
613.02	626.23	639.10	652.13	668.05	684.06
613.15	626.23	639.11	653.06	668.18	684.09
613.18	626.27	639.12	653.07	668.19	684.12
613.21	627.03	639.14	653.20	668.20	684.15
613.24	627.08	639.18	653.21	668.24	684.20
614.07	627.09	639.25	653.23	668.27	684.22
614.09	627.10	639.27	653.25	669.03	685.01
614.10	627.12	640.03	653.26	669.04	685.01
614.12	627.13	640.06	654.08	669.08	685.03
614.14	627.17	640.08	654.10	669.10	685.08
614.15	627.19	640.09	654.12	669.21	685.17
614.16	627.20	640.16	654.13	669.24	685.22
614.17	627.24	640.18	654.15	669.25	685.26
614.22	627.25	640.19	654.19	669.27	685.28
615.06	627.25	640.20	654.21	670.06	686.01
615.06	628.06	640.24	654.26	670.06	686.03
615.06	628.26	640.26	655.04	670.25	686.06
615.08	629.01	640.28	655.08	671.04	686.07
615.10	629.02	641.08	655.08	671.04	686.11
615.11	629.04	641.09	655.16	671.12	686.12
615.12	629.05	641.10	655.17	671.13	686.17
615.16	629.07	641.13	655.18	671.17	686.20
615.28	629.08	641.14	655.18	671.21	686.27
616.03	629.11	641.16	655.19	671.23	687.01
616.09	629.11	641.19	655.23	671.26	687.03
616.14	629.12	641.20	655.27	671.27	687.04
616.15	629.23	641.22	656.06	672.15	687.13
616.17	629.25	641.24	656.09	672.26	687.14
616.20	630.01	641.25	656.16	672.28	687.16
616.22	630.05	642.01	656.19	673.04	687.19
616.25	630.05	642.02	656.23	673.04	687.22
617.09	630.20	642.04	656.23	673.08	687.24
617.10	630.21	642.05	656.24	673.12	687.27
617.12	630.25	642.06	656.27	673.13	688.01
617.14	630.26	642.08	656.28	673.14	688.01
617.15	631.01	642.09	657.01	673.16	688.02
617.22	631.02	642.18	657.03	673.19	688.11
617.23	631.03	642.20	657.08	673.19	689.02
617.25	631.05	642.24	657.14	673.22	689.05
618.03	631.06	642.28	658.05	673.26	689.06
618.04	631.06	643.13	658.10	673.29	689.08
618.07	631.08	643.14	658.15	674.03	690.01
618.09	631.09	643.15	659.01	674.05	690.14
618.12	631.12	643.16	659.04	674.08	690.15
618.13	631.14	643.17	659.06	674.10	690.15
618.17	631.15	643.19	659.07	674.17	690.16
618.18	631.17	643.23	659.08	674.20	690.17
618.27	631.22	643.23	659.09	674.20	690.18
618.28	631.26	643.24	659.12	674.22	690.25
619.02	631.28	644.03	659.14	674.22	690.26
619.02	632.05	644.04	659.20	675.05	691.02
619.08	632.06	644.11	659.24	675.06	691.06
619.09	632.09	644.12	660.07	675.08	691.17
619.09	632.10	644.13	660.14	675.15	691.26
619.11	632.13	644.15	660.22	675.18	692.01
619.14	632.17	644.23	660.27	675.21	692.02
619.15	632.18	644.26	660.28	675.21	692.07
619.19	632.20	644.26	661.05	675.26	692.08
619.20	633.01	644.28	661.09	675.27	692.10
619.24	633.11	645.01	661.10	676.09	692.11
619.25	633.12	645.03	661.19	676.11	692.15
620.04	633.19	645.11	661.26	676.11	692.19
620.06	633.21	645.12	661.28	676.16	692.19
620.13	633.22	645.13	662.04	676.19	692.21
620.15	633.25	645.21	662.09	676.26	692.21
620.20	633.26	645.24	662.17	677.02	692.22
620.22	634.09	645.27	662.23	677.03	692.25
621.04	634.10	646.02	662.25	677.10	692.26
621.15	634.17	646.02	662.27	677.11	692.27
621.18	634.19	646.05	663.04	677.12	693.02
621.18	634.19	646.19	663.04	677.14	693.04
621.19	634.23	646.20	663.05	677.17	693.10
621.21	634.24	646.24	663.08	677.23	693.12
622.01	634.26	646.26	663.13	677.26	693.12
622.03	634.27	646.28	663.19	678.04	693.18
622.05	635.01	647.05	663.21	678.05	693.25
622.12	635.02	647.09	663.23	678.06	694.17
622.13	635.03	647.17	663.24	678.16	694.22
622.16	635.08	647.18	663.28	678.22	694.26
622.17	635.08	647.19	664.02	678.23	695.04
622.22	635.10	647.20	664.03	679.08	695.08
623.03	635.13	647.26	664.05	679.13	695.10
623.03	635.14	648.06	664.07	679.15	695.17
623.05	635.18	648.07	664.09	679.17	695.23
623.06	635.21	648.09	664.11	680.10	695.24
623.07	635.24	648.14	664.12	680.15	695.24
623.16	636.01	648.16	664.13	680.22	696.01
623.24	636.02	648.24	664.14	680.25	696.01
624.04	636.06	648.25	664.14	680.26	696.13
624.09	636.13	648.28	664.17	680.28	696.20
624.15	636.19	649.01	664.19	681.01	697.03
624.16	636.21	649.05	664.20	681.03	697.07
624.18	636.23	649.07	664.21	681.09	697.09
624.18	636.24	649.10	664.22	681.10	697.12
624.19	637.01	649.12	665.01	681.12	697.17
624.25	637.03	649.13	665.08	681.13	697.18
624.27	637.06	649.13	666.15	681.17	697.19
624.28	637.07	649.24	666.19	681.19	697.21
625.02	637.10	649.25	666.21	681.22	697.23
625.04	637.18	649.25	666.23	681.27	697.26
625.05	637.20	649.25	666.28	682.02	697.28
625.06	637.24	649.27	667.03	682.03	698.05
625.07	637.25	650.05		682.15	

698.10	713.01	726.24	740.20	753.20	773.16
698.11	713.09	726.28	740.22	753.22	773.22
698.12	713.12	727.01	740.22	753.24	773.23
698.13	713.16	727.05	740.25	753.26	773.27
698.16	713.18	727.09	740.27	754.09	773.27
698.18	713.18	727.13	740.28	754.16	773.27
698.23	713.22	727.13	741.04	754.22	774.02
698.26	713.23	727.20	741.12	754.23	774.11
698.28	713.26	727.22	741.13	754.23	774.25
698.28	714.01	727.24	741.18	754.26	775.06
699.01	714.01	727.25	741.20	755.03	775.12
699.02	714.03	728.01	741.25	755.05	775.14
699.03	714.04	728.03	741.28	755.08	775.16
699.08	714.05	728.05	741.28	755.21	775.16
699.14	714.08	728.05	742.01	756.01	775.18
699.16	714.08	729.04	742.02	756.07	775.18
699.21	714.13	729.05	742.11	756.08	775.20
699.28	714.18	729.06	742.17	756.11	775.21
700.02	714.23	729.06	742.22	756.15	775.22
700.05	714.28	729.08	743.03	756.24	776.01
700.05	715.01	729.11	743.06	756.26	776.02
700.07	715.05	729.18	743.08	756.26	776.04
700.08	715.07	730.01	743.11	757.02	776.08
700.11	715.10	730.05	743.11	757.05	776.22
700.13	715.12	730.07	743.14	757.13	777.08
700.18	715.13	730.09	743.17	757.14	777.25
700.19	715.15	730.16	743.17	757.21	778.02
700.22	715.16	730.21	743.19	757.23	778.02
701.01	715.20	730.27	744.01	757.24	778.08
701.05	715.21	730.28	744.04	757.26	778.09
701.06	715.22	731.04	744.06	758.07	778.17
701.08	715.24	731.07	744.06	758.12	778.18
701.10	715.25	731.21	744.08	758.14	778.21
701.13	716.08	731.23	744.11	758.17	778.23
701.15	716.09	731.24	744.11	758.18	778.25
701.16	716.11	731.25	744.13	758.23	778.28
701.19	716.19	732.01	744.15	758.28	779.02
701.26	716.28	732.02	744.18	759.05	780.09
702.02	717.05	732.05	744.20	760.02	780.13
702.15	717.06	732.05	744.23	760.03	780.14
702.22	717.08	732.05	744.23	760.04	780.20
702.23	717.09	732.10	745.01	760.07	781.01
702.27	717.10	732.11	745.04	760.09	781.09
703.15	717.11	732.16	745.05	760.19	781.11
703.18	717.14	732.17	745.08	760.21	781.13
703.28	717.15	732.20	745.11	760.28	781.16
704.21	717.17	732.25	745.16	761.02	781.16
704.23	717.26	732.27	745.17	761.03	781.17
704.23	717.26	732.28	745.18	761.05	781.22
704.25	718.10	733.02	745.20	761.09	781.23
705.05	718.12	733.03	745.23	761.12	782.04
705.05	718.17	733.08	745.24	761.21	782.07
705.07	718.18	733.14	745.25	761.27	782.08
705.11	718.20	733.27	745.26	762.04	782.15
705.14	718.24	733.28	745.27	762.13	782.15
705.16	718.26	734.02	746.12	762.13	782.26
705.18	719.04	734.03	746.13	762.25	783.07
705.24	719.07	734.10	746.14	763.02	783.09
706.01	719.07	734.25	746.22	763.11	783.10
706.03	719.09	734.28	746.24	763.20	783.12
706.04	719.19	735.06	746.26	763.21	783.13
706.05	719.20	735.06	747.04	763.22	783.20
706.09	719.23	735.08	747.04	763.27	783.22
706.14	719.25	735.21	747.06	764.02	784.08
706.14	719.26	735.22	747.07	764.02	784.10
706.20	719.27	735.28	747.08	764.10	784.16
706.24	720.01	735.28	747.14	764.11	784.17
706.26	720.06	736.01	747.17	765.04	784.18
707.02	720.07	736.06	747.18	765.06	784.18
707.03	720.08	736.11	747.28	765.08	784.19
707.06	720.09	736.15	748.15	765.11	784.20
707.08	720.12	736.24	748.23	765.13	784.21
707.12	720.15	736.27	749.03	765.13	784.25
707.16	720.20	737.02	749.08	765.14	784.26
707.18	720.26	737.03	749.09	766.03	785.15
707.19	721.02	737.16	749.12	766.11	785.18
707.21	721.04	737.17	749.12	766.26	785.26
707.24	721.10	737.22	749.13	767.01	785.28
708.02	721.13	737.23	749.15	767.04	786.02
708.09	721.27	737.23	749.16	767.06	786.03
708.11	722.01	737.26	749.18	767.09	786.10
708.14	722.03	737.27	749.20	767.10	786.11
708.19	722.10	737.28	749.24	767.19	786.14
708.24	722.13	737.28	749.26	767.21	786.18
709.11	722.15	738.01	749.27	768.04	786.23
709.14	722.19	738.05	750.03	768.08	786.25
709.18	723.05	738.06	750.04	768.11	786.26
709.23	723.06	738.07	750.05	768.13	787.06
710.03	723.07	738.14	750.10	768.22	787.08
710.06	723.09	738.19	750.12	769.03	787.09
711.05	723.12	738.19	750.20	769.05	787.09
711.06	724.05	738.22	750.22	769.06	787.10
711.07	724.06	739.02	750.25	769.25	787.13
711.08	724.09	739.03	750.26	769.27	787.14
711.12	724.17	739.04	750.26	770.01	787.19
711.20	724.18	739.08	751.13	770.04	787.23
711.20	724.21	739.09	751.19	770.13	787.26
712.02	724.26	739.19	751.22	770.17	788.02
712.03	724.27	739.21	751.26	771.03	788.05
712.06	724.28	739.27	751.26	771.03	788.10
712.06	725.09	740.01	752.01	771.13	788.13
712.12	725.13	740.01	752.04	771.23	789.07
712.13	725.17	740.05	752.05	771.25	789.11
712.16	725.21	740.07	752.09	772.04	789.13
712.17	725.25	740.10	752.11	772.11	789.16
712.18	725.26	740.13	752.22	772.13	790.01
712.20	726.08	740.15	753.04	772.17	790.04
712.21	726.13	740.17	753.07	772.26	790.06
712.22	726.14		753.11	773.03	790.10
712.23	726.15		753.11	773.05	790.10
712.24	726.22		753.19	773.06	790.11

790.16	803.26	817.24	834.10	853.18	870.08
790.19	803.28	817.27	834.11	853.19	870.10
790.26	803.28	818.01	834.14	854.08	870.11
791.03	804.03	818.05	834.18	854.13	870.13
791.04	804.08	818.06	834.21	854.17	870.22
791.08	804.11	818.08	834.26	854.21	870.28
791.08	804.13	818.17	835.07	854.21	871.02
791.13	804.19	818.21	835.14	854.28	871.12
791.25	804.22	818.23	835.18	855.03	871.14
792.01	804.23	818.25	835.26	855.03	871.18
792.02	805.08	819.02	836.13	855.04	871.19
792.04	805.08	819.06	836.14	855.15	871.20
792.07	805.09	819.15	836.19	855.17	871.22
792.11	805.09	819.17	836.21	855.21	871.26
792.12	805.15	819.18	837.21	855.23	872.04
792.20	805.18	819.21	837.22	856.02	872.05
792.28	805.24	819.22	837.26	856.03	872.10
793.03	805.25	819.26	837.27	856.10	872.13
793.03	805.27	820.07	838.05	856.16	872.16
793.04	806.07	820.10	838.07	856.17	872.17
793.09	806.08	820.14	838.12	856.22	872.20
793.13	806.10	820.20	838.21	856.27	872.20
793.15	806.11	821.02	838.23	857.05	872.21
793.16	806.15	821.03	838.24	857.24	873.01
793.20	806.17	821.09	839.04	857.24	873.01
793.24	806.21	821.12	839.09	857.25	873.11
793.26	806.26	821.14	839.15	857.25	873.12
793.27	807.05	821.18	839.17	857.26	873.17
794.02	807.07	821.20	839.19	857.26	873.20
794.02	807.16	821.20	840.02	857.27	873.23
794.02	807.17	822.16	840.08	857.28	873.24
794.02	807.17	822.27	840.09	858.13	873.25
794.08	807.24	823.01	840.10	858.14	873.27
794.10	808.01	823.04	840.14	858.16	874.10
794.11	808.02	823.13	840.14	858.18	874.12
794.13	808.06	823.23	840.15	858.19	874.21
794.13	808.14	823.25	840.26	858.20	874.22
794.17	808.15	823.27	841.05	858.20	874.24
794.19	808.20	824.04	841.08	859.02	875.01
794.20	808.23	824.06	841.15	859.05	875.04
794.20	809.03	824.07	841.19	859.08	875.04
794.22	809.09	824.14	842.01	859.15	875.06
794.23	809.16	824.16	842.06	859.16	875.09
794.24	809.17	824.19	842.16	859.21	875.15
795.01	809.24	824.20	842.20	859.27	875.16
795.04	810.01	824.22	842.22	859.28	875.23
795.05	810.05	824.23	842.24	859.28	875.24
795.06	810.07	824.24	843.01	860.01	876.01
795.06	810.08	825.01	843.02	860.04	876.01
795.10	810.14	825.04	843.03	860.08	876.08
795.11	810.19	825.05	843.07	860.11	876.10
795.21	810.20	825.06	843.12	860.14	876.12
795.21	810.24	825.11	843.19	861.22	876.18
795.23	810.27	825.11	843.25	862.04	876.20
796.13	811.05	825.12	843.28	862.12	877.01
796.18	811.06	825.15	844.03	862.14	877.05
796.18	811.07	825.19	844.06	862.19	877.08
796.21	811.08	825.24	844.07	863.02	877.09
796.24	811.10	825.25	844.18	863.08	877.10
797.05	811.12	825.27	844.18	863.09	877.13
797.08	811.13	825.28	844.21	863.18	877.13
797.08	811.14	826.02	845.01	863.20	877.14
797.12	811.15	826.10	845.03	863.22	877.15
797.19	811.17	826.17	845.05	863.23	877.16
797.20	811.19	826.20	845.09	863.23	877.21
797.21	811.26	826.24	845.13	863.26	877.22
797.22	812.01	826.26	845.18	864.01	877.24
797.22	812.04	827.05	845.19	864.06	878.02
798.10	812.08	827.08	845.20	864.07	878.03
798.12	812.11	827.12	845.25	864.10	878.07
798.13	812.12	827.16	845.27	864.10	878.11
798.15	812.13	827.18	846.05	864.13	878.17
798.21	812.14	827.25	846.27	864.16	878.17
798.27	812.15	827.27	847.04	864.22	878.20
798.28	812.22	828.11	847.21	864.24	878.25
799.01	812.23	828.16	848.09	865.02	879.02
799.04	812.24	828.20	848.16	865.07	879.09
799.07	812.25	828.21	848.19	865.08	879.11
799.10	812.27	828.24	848.21	865.10	879.15
799.12	813.02	829.04	848.25	865.15	879.17
799.24	813.03	829.07	848.27	865.16	879.18
799.24	813.06	829.11	849.01	865.16	880.06
799.28	813.09	829.12	849.02	865.17	880.08
800.05	813.10	829.19	849.07	865.18	880.09
800.07	813.23	829.25	849.08	865.19	880.11
800.11	813.26	830.07	849.20	865.21	880.24
800.11	814.03	830.08	849.22	865.23	880.26
800.17	814.07	830.13	849.22	865.24	881.04
800.19	814.09	831.04	849.25	865.26	881.13
800.20	814.12	831.14	850.04	866.01	881.15
800.22	814.13	831.17	850.08	866.02	881.16
800.25	814.21	831.18	850.10	866.02	881.16
800.26	814.22	831.18	850.12	866.06	881.18
801.03	814.24	832.02	850.14	866.11	881.21
801.04	814.27	832.03	850.18	866.22	881.25
801.07	815.02	832.07	850.21	867.05	882.01
801.12	815.03	832.08	850.23	867.12	882.05
801.16	815.06	832.10	851.04	867.21	882.12
801.17	815.13	832.11	851.13	867.24	882.13
801.19	815.24	832.12	851.16	868.01	882.14
802.11	815.25	832.14	852.02	868.06	882.15
802.17	815.25	832.20	852.07	868.08	882.19
802.26	816.06	832.21	852.09	869.03	882.20
802.27	816.10	833.01	852.10	869.06	882.23
803.08	816.24	833.08	852.18	869.09	883.03
803.13	816.24	833.09	852.21	869.11	883.10
803.15	817.11	833.12	853.04	869.17	883.13
803.15	817.12	833.15	853.05	869.19	883.14
803.16	817.15	833.17	853.08	870.02	883.18
803.20	817.16	833.28	853.08	870.04	883.24
803.21	817.22	834.07	853.08	870.08	883.24

884.01	906.05	676.03	095.12	053.04	438.15
884.06	906.10	857.12	109.10	054.08	441.01
884.07	906.13	**angry**	117.21	054.15	478.05
884.08	906.14	234.10	124.03	073.27	499.17
884.10	906.15	333.15	133.22	085.14	518.13
884.14	906.17	381.13	134.09	092.10	576.14
884.15	906.22	468.24	146.20	098.16	582.03
885.01	906.23	620.19	149.11	098.26	586.09
885.02	906.24	756.17	152.04	105.11	651.11
885.05	906.26	833.20	154.26	141.28	652.19
885.16	907.01	**anguish**	163.22	153.02	657.05
885.21	907.04	025.12	170.12	173.14	686.17
885.23	907.04	057.19	175.16	178.05	693.26
885.26	907.15	486.03	177.22	184.13	709.22
886.04	907.17	512.06	181.10	211.01	709.28
886.08	907.19	606.17	199.01	239.24	734.22
886.08	907.21	628.18	241.15	245.08	740.16
886.19	907.22	650.22	261.08	246.22	741.15
886.22	907.25	650.27	283.19	253.16	754.04
886.27	908.02	683.23	288.25	259.18	755.01
886.27	908.05	901.11	307.11	260.07	756.10
887.14	908.06	**animadversions**	320.02	260.20	766.11
887.17	908.10	097.19	320.06	262.07	773.16
887.19	908.12	**animal**	326.19	265.07	794.21
887.21	908.13	006.10	335.15	265.18	795.16
887.24	908.14	476.08	340.27	267.12	803.03
888.02	908.16	483.10	381.03	275.13	806.12
888.02	908.20	599.19	392.16	277.21	813.22
888.07	908.22	713.12	397.02	310.04	814.27
888.09	908.25	**animals**	402.03	314.25	821.24
888.10	909.02	380.25	403.16	332.14	826.07
888.14	909.10	**animated**	403.23	354.23	826.11
888.24	909.20	150.17	415.20	376.05	830.09
889.04	909.21	411.06	415.28	422.13	835.10
889.23	909.23	437.21	430.26	428.15	836.17
889.26	909.23	690.18	443.03	429.11	837.13
890.09	910.09	886.20	446.18	434.01	846.06
890.12	910.10	909.10	453.21	440.14	852.01
890.15	910.14	**animating**	454.09	474.13	862.20
890.18	910.17	379.14	456.26	480.17	873.16
890.21	910.19	878.11	460.07	488.21	874.06
891.13	910.20	**animation**	469.25	499.13	875.18
891.15	910.28	388.07	488.13	505.08	876.02
891.15	911.03	450.02	489.22	510.20	876.25
891.20	911.03	**animosity**	491.09	515.18	889.04
892.14	911.05	108.21	492.05	529.10	896.25
892.15	911.07	**ankle**	493.11	532.27	907.11
892.18	911.08	232.16	494.16	536.16	910.13
892.23	911.10	**ann**	499.23	541.06	**answering**
892.24	911.11	149.13	508.08	589.24	008.20
893.02	911.12	150.04	514.10	591.23	051.05
893.10	911.13	151.13	515.06	595.06	236.08
894.01	911.18	151.22	519.27	609.06	268.03
894.17	911.18	**annihilated**	525.07	614.01	671.16
895.05	911.19	437.02	533.20	659.13	687.17
895.09	911.19	**annihilation**	548.15	666.20	809.13
895.10	911.22	903.15	550.01	689.15	**answers**
895.16	912.01	**announced**	555.25	695.19	093.23
895.20	912.01	073.08	574.22	703.12	098.20
895.25	912.07	140.18	610.09	705.05	168.07
895.27	912.07	142.03	619.20	714.28	218.01
896.06	912.09	225.12	628.03	738.20	571.11
896.09	912.12	289.28	629.11	766.24	605.09
896.13	912.16	596.02	635.27	772.27	635.09
896.17	912.17	620.24	636.27	773.09	641.22
896.20	912.24	636.09	637.18	809.14	687.11
896.20	**andes**	853.18	645.19	817.08	860.14
897.22	415.03	907.02	645.25	818.18	**antagonist**
897.26	**ange**	**announcement**	658.05	821.05	062.01
898.10	281.27	262.20	666.21	830.13	**antagonistic**
898.15	**angel**	523.24	683.20	832.04	811.25
898.27	055.27	534.28	697.18	850.01	**anticipate**
899.05	128.02	**announces**	700.23	859.11	527.09
899.08	271.23	912.23	709.03	859.19	527.10
899.13	271.26	**annoy**	715.04	860.07	661.01
900.10	387.28	467.15	718.23	861.12	858.12
900.15	527.01	539.12	735.04	873.07	**anticipated**
900.27	527.04	785.15	742.18	875.23	187.18
901.02	531.23	**annoyance**	750.06	883.14	189.27
901.05	589.10	238.21	755.26	891.21	912.13
901.08	644.07	309.28	757.13	**answerable**	**anticipation**
901.10	736.18	467.20	778.07	260.23	491.11
901.11	749.02	544.20	779.28	288.27	558.21
901.13	846.22	641.28	798.04	**answered**	652.07
901.14	**angel's**	804.26	803.06	014.05	**antipathetic**
901.16	851.14	**annoyed**	803.10	034.01	225.04
901.16	**angel-girl**	264.14	807.11	034.16	**antipathies**
901.23	387.26	474.22	813.11	050.22	165.11
902.01	**angelic**	620.14	817.27	053.18	466.07
902.07	214.10	**annuity**	819.12	075.17	**antipathy**
902.14	**angels**	864.21	829.07	090.07	007.21
902.17	033.09	**annum**	835.26	137.07	062.18
902.19	055.26	171.14	847.06	167.14	193.06
903.03	132.26	173.04	856.21	182.12	373.17
903.06	495.14	266.09	863.12	183.03	617.01
903.09	753.05	**anon**	866.22	197.14	627.04
903.14	847.18	325.18	870.16	210.20	**antipodes**
903.15	**anger**	423.27	880.06	223.12	636.13
903.16	067.12	424.20	886.04	242.25	861.10
903.19	099.25	804.03	886.21	267.21	**antiquated**
903.20	693.25	**another**	894.16	294.11	207.12
904.05	727.09	023.17	908.03	297.08	**antique**
904.05	835.03	024.14	**another's**	308.04	423.14
905.04	843.18	030.02	742.22	338.18	503.25
905.04	895.23	030.06	**answer**	338.26	701.07
905.07	**anglaise**	033.01	006.25	339.06	701.27
905.08	499.03	035.07	020.02	345.11	711.16
905.10	**angle**	050.22	024.23	362.06	794.18
905.15	333.08	069.03	024.27	392.21	**antiquity**
905.16	575.23	076.18	028.03	420.04	207.02
905.19	659.25	081.14	036.14	434.18	282.27

869.03
antoinetta
593.12
593.14
anxiety
116.09
191.08
408.15
544.05
555.16
760.13
809.18
854.03
anxious
049.03
059.18
252.22
252.25
559.04
572.07
604.03
632.24
686.18
718.26
anxiously
182.05
294.06
793.16
any
012.09
018.17
022.01
022.24
054.08
036.01
036.13
037.15
038.19
041.12
048.03
062.24
067.17
068.23
091.06
104.11
116.23
118.10
120.06
130.07
132.09
150.07
150.17
158.05
165.06
166.08
166.22
168.10
170.05
179.04
182.10
164.10
188.26
203.03
203.25
208.11
211.01
211.03
211.14
213.13
213.20
225.09
241.14
245.18
256.06
256.06
260.18
262.12
269.13
270.12
272.14
274.14
275.15
280.04
280.17
288.15
293.26
297.22
299.04
309.27
310.05
310.16
313.07
317.03
321.04
324.19
327.26
331.21
332.13
333.12
333.13
338.09
339.15
340.16
347.27
351.19
356.27
362.17
365.17
366.19
385.28
366.23

388.13
388.19
392.24
396.23
396.26
396.27
399.16
399.20
400.26
411.08
412.19
417.21
419.20
422.10
432.17
436.14
439.10
441.05
449.08
452.10
454.28
456.03
462.12
462.23
462.25
467.19
468.17
470.11
470.28
472.19
473.28
474.23
475.16
477.11
484.15
488.20
494.03
505.20
508.20
525.25
527.07
528.14
528.24
529.05
531.07
533.16
540.02
553.14
555.01
568.19
569.21
571.12
587.13
590.01
613.26
627.26
635.20
635.23
636.22
638.03
638.04
638.04
638.20
643.20
665.27
666.09
667.02
667.25
669.23
673.19
679.02
683.12
684.13
686.23
689.12
694.02
704.05
704.06
707.05
707.28
718.08
721.03
724.11
725.04
726.18
731.21
734.15
742.08
751.04
757.08
766.06
766.08
768.06
768.26
784.14
790.09
804.18
806.28
811.24
821.15
822.14
832.26
834.02
837.25
837.25
840.03
844.11
852.05
853.26
857.17
858.21

858.21
861.21
863.15
864.02
866.15
868.03
872.01
884.11
887.05
888.20
891.05
899.01
901.20
903.13
905.12
908.16
909.04
anybody
011.01
062.06
063.14
088.16
214.23
328.15
430.08
483.03
862.28
anything
015.08
028.07
028.11
028.24
064.04
090.26
104.13
149.22
167.08
178.10
179.16
188.03
223.10
225.02
225.03
267.08
300.01
307.17
330.07
332.09
357.18
357.23
359.22
376.15
390.16
447.19
448.17
455.10
499.13
510.18
520.11
527.06
530.02
546.09
555.15
564.21
564.23
565.07
574.06
574.16
580.19
604.01
626.17
626.17
649.10
709.22
735.16
746.08
766.08
774.16
780.15
800.22
809.08
837.03
886.08
888.04
903.04
908.08
anywhere
037.11
175.07
316.08
514.03
565.19
575.07
629.24
682.15
683.13
870.18
anzusehen
678.20
apart
338.04
346.09
397.09
470.26
502.17
887.25
apartment
013.03
028.18
052.10
064.22

134.06
154.09
190.07
203.17
233.10
236.22
341.02
347.28
415.24
420.21
425.28
460.07
523.01
558.16
677.23
689.13
888.03
apartments
204.01
207.03
208.04
apathetic
348.14
apathy
664.07
ape
525.26
621.07
aperture
023.08
286.09
676.09
754.10
apertures
492.28
apollo
279.16
891.11
apollyon
911.26
apologize
508.17
apology
265.01
apoplectic
451.21
apostle
759.16
815.07
911.27
apostles
423.19
720.21
apostrophized
553.13
apostrophizing
381.10
apothecary
027.12
034.21
040.05
appalled
726.03
appalling
039.04
423.01
appanage
359.25
apparatus
187.23
apparel
121.20
331.19
558.13
634.04
692.10
apparelling
045.16
apparent
207.13
224.11
229.09
420.15
732.27
apparently
006.06
223.22
344.08
352.09
369.11
409.20
504.14
599.12
675.14
715.01
832.10
apparition
115.24
211.14
417.09
445.16
appeal
007.28
657.13
appealed
644.23
684.17
777.25
815.10
appeals
235.06

appear
131.22
193.04
197.03
221.16
236.19
251.22
276.23
363.09
387.19
494.24
543.21
582.02
681.27
692.12
715.08
722.11
725.01
797.18
885.12
appearance
008.14
192.12
217.14
263.03
315.13
316.28
335.22
345.05
348.02
348.11
350.19
394.20
446.02
449.26
581.13
681.22
746.09
772.19
890.16
890.17
appearances
103.20
260.08
403.03
appeared
034.21
052.13
074.07
077.18
078.10
084.07
097.05
098.16
119.13
142.28
163.06
173.18
193.19
195.02
204.08
213.07
230.19
237.01
237.19
255.23
283.26
309.10
310.25
341.12
342.06
344.15
359.09
367.04
367.25
379.14
394.15
411.07
422.16
433.10
448.09
460.19
555.06
561.11
581.24
587.24
634.27
668.02
668.12
671.07
676.25
682.16
690.02
693.26
714.12
726.03
737.13
746.23
750.12
751.15
803.25
818.15
843.10
874.26
appearing
018.01
339.01
appears
108.20
202.11
234.15

319.12
327.13
381.18
613.09
633.18
727.11
appeased
661.12
appertained
558.09
appetite
074.14
118.11
315.25
355.08
566.15
702.21
703.08
appetites
112.04
138.21
appetizing
093.28
apple
434.27
828.05
909.19
apples
148.08
561.22
605.25
application
772.27
applied
052.23
421.18
apply
126.06
167.09
203.02
234.04
250.05
666.07
669.03
884.09
applying
198.03
appointed
244.18
720.17
appointing
042.14
appointment
287.26
apportion
476.27
apportioned
094.07
appparently
387.01
appreciate
289.24
appreciated
717.17
717.18
appreciating
230.02
apprehended
436.09
apprehension
116.15
apprehensions
570.05
660.07
apprehensive
074.20
275.08
566.23
574.20
apprend
334.08
apprise
115.27
632.15
apprised
778.19
approach
006.27
052.20
073.09
136.06
246.09
340.04
373.19
390.18
458.19
552.02
636.23
667.13
717.25
854.18
866.01
872.06
approached
130.12
197.11
221.07
221.15
237.21
294.24
349.05

368.23	371.14	130.28	299.01	480.25	637.23
380.26	389.12	131.06	300.14	480.25	638.13
397.09	438.08	131.20	300.16	480.26	640.22
397.21	631.18	132.15	300.26	489.20	640.23
427.16	859.25	132.23	302.01	489.25	641.11
432.27	arch-traitor	132.28	308.07	490.07	644.07
445.22	424.02	136.13	308.12	493.10	645.06
449.19	archangel	136.22	309.19	493.20	646.14
465.03	678.23	137.04	310.08	493.24	648.07
472.14	archdeacon	155.23	310.10	493.25	648.08
484.24	059.23	156.04	310.17	494.02	648.10
504.22	114.28	156.10	310.20	494.20	648.18
619.16	arched	156.17	313.05	495.03	650.10
628.24	282.05	156.18	315.21	495.16	650.12
675.11	345.22	156.18	316.20	495.19	650.16
702.22	arches	156.27	316.22	496.27	652.21
724.27	870.09	157.16	316.23	497.05	658.02
733.15	architectural	157.27	316.27	498.02	659.01
766.17	869.03	158.26	317.05	503.28	659.02
789.03	architecture	160.10	317.06	505.09	659.07
809.27	115.19	167.10	317.08	507.02	659.17
821.03	arctic	168.10	319.23	507.18	662.08
833.17	004.08	168.21	326.02	507.28	678.04
833.24	ardent	170.05	326.11	510.04	679.11
873.03	133.03	170.15	326.26	510.18	679.22
875.11	139.03	175.24	327.02	510.24	683.06
approaches	250.07	176.13	329.27	511.17	683.14
314.03	499.25	176.27	334.12	513.16	684.08
approaching	568.17	177.25	339.18	513.17	684.21
065.12	605.19	178.01	347.03	513.22	684.22
153.26	ardently	178.12	347.27	514.22	686.20
158.09	130.10	179.12	348.04	516.10	691.26
219.05	ardour	179.21	348.05	516.15	693.06
320.20	218.07	179.22	348.06	517.08	693.14
419.26	279.13	182.15	352.02	517.16	694.01
426.21	527.21	184.21	353.19	518.12	694.10
547.28	793.20	186.26	355.03	522.24	694.18
573.18	are	187.05	355.13	524.01	695.04
663.24	009.01	187.07	356.25	525.10	695.07
718.14	009.08	188.24	357.10	525.14	696.01
795.15	009.14	189.04	358.06	525.14	697.09
approbation	010.01	189.05	362.20	527.12	700.10
150.01	010.01	189.21	362.28	527.28	700.25
750.24	010.02	190.10	363.02	530.22	703.01
757.23	012.20	195.04	371.01	531.21	704.04
866.16	014.07	197.16	376.10	532.06	704.13
appropriate	015.09	203.13	386.21	532.18	705.03
058.07	023.26	204.01	389.26	532.23	708.16
061.10	024.03	204.25	396.09	533.10	709.18
appropriated	033.03	204.25	396.09	536.18	723.01
207.03	033.03	206.12	396.12	537.04	724.01
372.07	033.04	208.19	396.13	537.13	724.01
613.25	033.08	210.24	396.14	537.16	725.20
appropriateness	033.09	216.09	396.17	538.08	729.12
201.12	033.12	216.10	397.02	540.22	730.03
approval	035.25	216.14	397.05	543.03	730.04
352.12	035.26	223.04	397.07	546.18	730.07
approve	036.06	223.28	398.04	546.22	730.10
055.23	037.04	225.16	398.14	561.08	733.25
273.05	038.16	226.14	400.23	565.03	737.01
796.22	044.04	226.15	405.15	565.05	740.04
820.04	047.26	227.08	408.20	565.06	740.05
892.04	050.20	232.13	408.25	565.24	741.10
approved	051.01	239.14	409.04	566.23	741.18
132.01	053.14	239.19	411.16	566.24	741.20
555.16	055.14	239.28	411.23	567.17	742.01
711.14	056.03	241.21	416.04	568.04	742.07
892.07	058.04	243.22	417.18	568.23	742.14
907.01	058.19	244.02	419.02	568.24	752.16
approves	062.21	244.27	427.18	568.25	752.26
313.06	063.15	245.03	428.24	570.14	755.14
440.13	063.16	246.04	429.12	576.14	755.17
april	063.27	247.15	429.19	578.05	757.17
144.09	064.09	247.16	430.28	580.01	758.09
145.26	064.14	250.15	432.16	581.21	758.22
331.26	065.12	250.17	435.16	586.13	759.13
435.05	066.28	251.01	437.10	586.15	760.04
595.17	067.05	258.02	437.11	586.23	760.12
apron	067.19	259.26	437.16	587.04	761.05
186.10	067.21	260.02	438.01	590.04	761.10
306.23	068.04	261.07	438.04	590.06	762.03
325.23	068.14	261.15	438.24	592.18	766.10
650.11	068.24	262.12	439.16	595.10	766.21
apt	077.01	264.10	440.03	595.12	767.21
116.25	091.04	264.26	440.09	598.20	771.03
289.19	091.08	265.22	442.07	599.23	771.12
805.22	091.09	266.18	444.02	601.23	774.25
816.24	091.09	266.19	444.02	601.23	775.13
aquiline	092.21	267.10	444.03	602.16	775.16
382.21	093.19	267.18	446.15	611.14	775.17
arabian	093.21	267.22	446.20	613.11	776.09
066.03	095.06	268.06	446.21	614.12	777.14
480.15	098.05	269.12	446.24	614.15	777.25
arbitration	098.05	270.15	453.15	614.18	779.11
768.09	103.02	270.17	453.26	614.25	781.01
arbitress	103.13	271.08	455.06	616.27	781.04
639.02	105.06	271.12	464.14	617.04	781.06
arbour	106.13	272.09	465.26	617.04	782.05
436.07	106.18	273.22	466.06	617.09	782.10
438.08	106.19	273.24	466.07	618.18	786.02
arch	106.21	273.27	467.16	618.22	786.03
204.03	106.25	274.08	469.08	623.12	786.20
209.16	107.02	274.09	469.11	623.24	786.23
236.23	108.22	274.26	476.17	628.14	790.07
258.16	116.25	275.01	477.04	630.14	791.01
341.06	118.06	275.06	477.05	632.03	791.20
342.05	119.03	275.15	478.06	632.08	792.03
348.02	120.13	276.25	480.17	633.13	793.08
348.20	128.09	297.09	480.19	635.06	797.26
365.11	128.11	298.22	480.23	636.11	801.26
366.21				637.12	

801.28
803.04
803.04
805.13
805.17
807.20
811.04
814.07
814.09
814.13
814.17
815.15
816.03
816.26
818.04
822.05
824.12
826.22
827.02
827.08
828.04
828.24
833.19
833.21
833.25
833.27
834.02
835.13
835.17
837.05
837.07
837.17
838.09
839.01
839.17
841.05
841.17
846.11
848.10
849.28
850.02
860.22
861.16
862.03
863.10
865.07
866.13
873.13
874.10
876.11
877.04
877.27
878.03
878.13
878.19
880.18
881.05
881.09
882.09
883.07
883.08
884.22
885.21
887.02
887.03
889.27
890.11
890.15
891.16
892.05
892.10
894.08
896.16
896.17
898.12
900.10
902.08
902.14
909.06
909.12
911.03
911.04
911.05
911.13
912.04
912.07
912.21
argue
  352.08
  785.15
  824.01
argued
  172.20
argument
  315.09
  405.18
arguments
  377.06
  787.26
aria
  720.15
ariel
  440.18
arisen
  425.18
  714.08
arises
  267.01
arising
  711.11

aristocratic
  571.02
arithmetic
  086.23
  245.01
ark
  207.10
arm
  026.14
  044.21
  128.03
  132.11
  134.22
  157.01
  248.08
  262.21
  322.19
  367.04
  370.01
  410.07
  414.13
  414.19
  416.20
  421.11
  421.21
  425.28
  429.02
  432.03
  484.28
  528.21
  555.12
  567.03
  592.16
  594.21
  610.05
  611.04
  648.25
  737.10
  848.12
  872.24
  873.04
  876.17
  881.11
  881.21
arm-chair
  006.26
  053.24
  061.06
  134.08
  186.07
  298.24
  382.28
  464.24
  562.07
armful
  507.13
armfuls
  365.21
arms
  012.12
  013.22
  017.22
  066.10
  067.14
  113.22
  130.23
  133.20
  158.15
  159.07
  159.16
  180.21
  199.10
  272.15
  288.02
  292.22
  299.25
  337.21
  352.20
  368.15
  369.07
  445.10
  492.06
  513.18
  519.24
  565.20
  572.24
  575.08
  580.18
  583.18
  601.12
  604.19
  606.18
  612.24
  613.24
  617.15
  628.20
  651.16
  658.15
  733.09
  745.19
  749.27
  798.18
  815.23
  855.17
  858.16
  865.21
  871.05
  873.01
  877.17
  879.19
  887.27

  898.06
  910.26
aromatic
  065.18
arose
  078.23
  374.03
around
  081.04
  131.16
  422.26
  640.26
  712.03
  872.26
aroused
  415.25
  769.23
arousing
  167.01
arraigned
  320.15
arrange
  135.15
  238.28
  327.27
  791.27
arranged
  049.09
  079.02
  120.17
  141.09
  206.26
  233.12
  249.26
  318.12
  331.02
  340.12
  411.01
  587.01
  747.12
  795.10
arrangement
  059.03
  204.28
  420.25
  616.07
  794.18
  796.09
arrangements
  103.26
  491.19
  562.11
  567.17
  768.27
  799.03
  854.05
  873.27
arranging
  030.08
  283.24
  521.07
  851.03
array
  194.09
  342.16
  584.05
arrested
  013.06
  222.17
  283.06
  361.09
  876.12
arrival
  114.27
  170.20
  204.28
  255.20
  327.23
  425.20
  491.07
  493.07
  557.05
  563.12
  760.17
  791.09
  854.15
arrive
  328.11
  381.20
  493.28
  669.02
arrived
  112.22
  146.26
  232.11
  233.06
  257.09
  324.02
  331.12
  384.09
  409.05
  426.09
  795.08
  809.17
  861.23
arrives
  157.24
arrogance
  463.25
arrogate
  274.10

arrow-head
  656.03
arrows
  375.10
art
  395.28
  621.24
artful
  057.13
article
  174.17
  192.09
  460.08
  474.14
articles
  141.06
  430.02
  652.26
  653.03
  665.10
articulate
  595.16
artifice
  024.26
artificial
  049.06
  278.06
artist
  735.15
artist's
  249.25
  250.14
artist-delight
  749.25
arts
  376.03
as
  002.15
  003.22
  003.22
  005.16
  005.16
  005.25
  008.11
  008.11
  012.07
  013.23
  016.11
  017.26
  019.23
  020.09
  021.06
  021.23
  021.26
  021.26
  022.11
  023.14
  023.15
  025.09
  026.03
  026.06
  027.26
  028.01
  029.12
  030.07
  030.11
  031.06
  031.12
  033.24
  033.24
  033.29
  035.11
  036.21
  036.21
  037.27
  038.23
  039.12
  039.19
  040.07
  040.10
  040.13
  041.10
  041.17
  041.17
  042.05
  043.07
  043.07
  043.10
  043.16
  043.16
  043.22
  044.15
  044.21
  045.23
  045.25
  046.09
  046.09
  046.18
  046.24
  047.19
  047.26
  048.03
  048.23
  049.11
  049.27
  050.01
  051.02
  051.13
  052.07
  054.04
  057.05
  057.16

058.01
058.21
059.09
059.16
059.16
060.26
061.10
061.14
061.15
061.22
062.15
062.22
062.22
063.19
063.26
065.02
065.02
065.04
065.05
065.12
065.18
065.20
067.08
067.20
069.06
072.03
072.21
072.28
073.25
074.03
074.13
075.02
075.06
076.14
080.06
080.06
080.08
082.11
082.20
082.20
084.27
085.01
085.06
086.07
086.11
086.11
086.13
087.24
087.28
088.05
088.13
088.16
093.01
092.01
093.09
095.01
095.16
096.02
097.16
098.02
098.05
099.02
100.04
100.22
101.09
103.21
104.06
104.06
105.18
106.16
106.27
107.02
107.07
107.07
108.04
108.13
109.02
109.23
110.07
110.08
111.19
113.11
115.05
116.04
116.12
117.27
118.12
119.13
119.15
119.22
120.02
120.09
120.25
122.12
123.06
123.11
125.03
126.13
126.21
127.11
127.17
127.25
130.06
130.17
130.25
131.14
131.16
132.19
132.27
133.13
133.27

134.01
134.19
135.02
135.09
135.09
135.10
135.24
135.27
137.01
137.05
138.03
138.14
138.17
138.20
139.07
140.02
140.02
140.21
141.17
145.16
145.16
146.17
148.04
150.03
150.16
150.17
151.14
151.23
152.02
152.07
152.08
156.09
158.01
158.17
158.21
160.04
161.25
161.26
162.06
164.03
164.04
166.02
166.03
166.09
166.17
167.25
168.22
171.10
173.08
173.09
173.12
173.14
173.20
173.21
174.02
177.02
176.03
176.03
178.04
178.20
179.04
179.04
179.21
179.22
181.06
182.05
184.01
184.26
184.26
186.01
186.19
188.01
188.22
189.24
189.26
189.27
190.13
190.22
191.21
191.28
192.01
192.14
192.14
192.15
192.15
192.28
194.10
194.13
195.23
196.19
196.28
197.28
198.01
198.01
198.05
198.05
198.11
198.19
198.19
198.20
201.23
201.28
202.12
203.11
203.23
204.26
205.12
205.12
206.26
207.05
209.04

209.16	271.03	337.24	399.17	468.19	532.01
211.02	271.08	338.01	400.20	468.28	532.09
211.02	271.08	338.02	401.08	470.14	532.14
211.03	272.13	338.14	404.21	470.14	532.15
213.11	272.20	338.27	405.15	472.04	533.21
214.18	272.26	339.10	406.11	474.22	535.20
216.15	272.27	340.15	406.19	476.04	536.24
216.17	273.15	340.15	406.20	476.12	536.25
216.17	273.19	341.07	408.13	477.09	536.25
216.19	273.23	341.27	408.18	477.12	538.07
217.14	274.18	342.02	409.18	477.21	538.07
218.01	275.24	342.02	409.19	477.22	539.08
218.06	276.14	342.12	410.27	479.07	540.07
219.04	276.22	342.17	411.08	479.07	541.09
219.16	277.02	343.02	411.08	479.17	542.01
219.16	277.03	343.14	411.10	480.09	542.19
219.28	277.04	345.01	411.21	481.13	542.24
220.12	278.06	345.09	412.10	481.16	544.09
220.26	279.14	345.11	412.10	481.22	544.12
221.08	279.15	345.11	412.20	482.16	544.21
221.15	280.09	346.01	412.28	483.10	545.15
221.15	281.18	346.15	417.18	483.15	546.17
221.21	281.25	346.22	417.26	484.02	546.21
222.05	282.11	350.26	418.19	484.04	547.18
223.12	282.12	350.26	418.19	484.04	548.02
223.21	282.23	350.27	418.24	484.18	548.14
225.03	283.14	350.27	418.26	484.20	548.19
226.16	284.10	351.20	419.13	484.27	548.20
227.05	284.13	352.06	419.13	485.04	548.27
228.02	285.11	353.06	422.06	486.12	549.09
228.09	285.15	353.06	422.15	487.15	550.16
228.09	286.07	353.14	422.19	487.15	550.16
229.03	287.06	353.25	422.22	488.27	551.02
230.08	287.06	354.13	423.20	489.08	551.04
230.08	288.02	356.07	423.23	489.27	551.04
230.10	289.06	356.12	424.04	489.28	551.05
230.11	289.07	356.16	424.04	491.20	551.07
230.19	289.17	356.18	425.23	492.07	551.09
230.23	290.07	356.20	426.06	492.21	551.17
233.09	290.19	356.20	426.07	492.26	551.18
233.15	290.24	357.10	426.18	493.01	552.12
234.08	291.07	358.03	428.02	493.13	552.20
234.13	291.07	358.12	428.02	493.14	553.05
234.28	291.14	358.17	429.14	494.15	553.06
236.16	291.24	359.13	429.18	494.15	553.07
236.18	291.25	359.22	429.18	495.08	553.13
236.22	291.26	359.23	430.07	495.20	553.26
237.20	293.03	359.27	431.14	496.09	554.03
238.15	294.09	362.07	432.22	496.27	554.28
238.19	294.20	362.11	432.23	498.24	555.07
238.19	294.28	362.14	433.26	499.15	556.04
239.06	295.06	363.08	433.26	499.26	557.12
239.06	295.25	365.23	434.04	501.03	559.24
239.27	298.11	366.04	435.04	501.05	560.21
240.01	299.02	367.22	435.17	503.02	560.25
240.28	299.02	367.26	436.28	503.24	561.02
242.08	299.07	368.24	437.17	503.24	561.10
242.08	299.07	370.01	437.25	503.25	562.22
243.19	299.13	370.04	438.01	503.27	562.23
243.27	299.22	371.06	439.23	504.15	562.25
245.04	300.12	372.09	440.19	505.24	563.16
246.13	300.25	372.11	442.26	507.15	564.11
247.18	301.06	374.26	443.03	507.16	564.19
248.04	302.22	377.01	445.22	508.18	564.19
248.04	303.03	377.03	446.08	508.19	565.16
248.05	303.03	377.09	447.16	509.11	565.17
248.06	305.12	377.10	447.16	509.13	565.17
248.13	306.21	377.10	448.09	509.17	565.18
248.15	307.03	377.21	449.21	510.24	565.25
248.17	310.05	377.22	449.25	510.24	566.04
248.17	310.05	378.01	450.11	511.05	567.03
248.19	310.09	379.04	452.05	513.06	567.03
249.08	310.15	380.26	452.05	513.06	567.05
249.13	311.23	381.13	453.03	513.07	569.21
250.16	311.23	381.16	453.11	513.09	570.12
252.15	312.10	381.22	453.20	513.10	570.13
254.09	312.22	381.25	453.25	513.14	570.25
255.08	313.07	382.13	453.25	513.15	570.25
256.24	314.03	382.16	454.06	513.17	571.06
257.15	315.19	382.25	454.19	513.22	571.25
257.23	316.04	383.01	456.18	513.23	572.01
258.06	317.23	383.08	456.19	515.09	573.16
258.11	318.09	383.23	457.12	516.01	574.02
258.20	318.10	384.15	458.07	516.09	574.03
259.24	320.12	385.01	458.08	516.10	581.12
259.27	320.28	386.14	458.10	516.11	582.04
261.20	322.14	386.14	458.15	517.26	582.07
261.20	323.14	386.27	458.17	518.26	583.16
261.25	323.14	388.09	458.17	520.03	583.22
262.23	324.09	389.13	458.24	520.04	583.22
262.23	325.07	390.09	458.27	520.05	583.23
264.19	325.28	391.04	459.25	520.06	583.24
264.22	327.10	391.09	460.05	521.02	585.08
264.27	327.25	394.02	460.09	521.10	585.09
265.17	328.14	394.13	460.20	522.14	586.04
267.12	328.15	394.19	460.20	525.08	586.17
267.13	329.13	394.19	461.03	525.27	587.08
267.21	329.13	395.03	461.06	526.01	587.15
268.02	329.26	395.11	461.11	526.27	587.24
268.03	331.04	395.11	461.12	527.01	588.16
268.04	331.05	395.12	461.21	527.03	589.23
268.04	331.06	395.12	462.16	527.20	590.04
268.20	331.06	395.17	463.03	527.22	590.08
268.20	332.01	396.17	463.25	529.07	590.15
269.08	333.16	396.24	464.05	529.08	590.22
269.23	335.21	397.02	464.23	529.23	592.07
270.06	335.21	397.24	465.17	529.26	592.13
270.06	335.24	398.05	465.22	531.11	593.21
270.24	336.24	398.09	466.22	531.11	594.09
271.02	336.24	398.18	467.21	531.16	594.16
	337.24	398.19	467.26		594.19

595.01	655.25	710.06	766.04	826.19	878.23
596.14	656.14	710.06	766.18	826.19	879.04
597.09	656.16	711.07	767.08	826.23	879.06
597.09	656.24	711.07	767.11	827.16	879.14
597.13	656.24	712.25	770.23	828.19	880.08
599.21	656.25	713.13	777.14	829.01	880.25
601.09	657.07	714.07	778.08	829.09	880.26
602.03	657.12	716.01	779.01	829.10	882.21
602.15	657.14	716.08	779.06	831.02	883.03
603.08	660.08	716.08	779.08	831.18	884.02
603.20	660.09	717.02	779.08	831.18	884.02
603.23	660.28	717.11	781.01	832.06	884.10
604.10	661.03	717.15	781.10	832.11	884.10
604.17	661.23	717.18	785.02	832.22	885.17
605.14	665.02	717.26	785.12	833.06	885.26
606.05	665.02	718.02	785.13	833.13	886.05
606.07	665.14	718.05	787.14	833.14	886.05
606.09	665.21	718.10	787.27	833.17	886.10
607.13	666.01	718.11	787.28	833.23	886.10
607.23	666.01	719.08	788.01	833.25	887.11
608.03	666.22	719.09	788.03	834.02	888.05
608.04	666.27	719.15	788.08	834.07	888.07
610.17	667.19	720.04	789.06	834.28	888.23
610.22	671.05	720.23	789.06	835.17	888.27
610.27	671.19	720.25	789.18	836.17	889.22
612.02	671.20	721.06	790.04	836.27	894.01
612.28	672.03	721.06	790.05	837.09	894.02
613.19	672.04	722.04	790.23	837.12	894.13
614.06	672.04	724.27	790.23	837.24	894.14
614.25	672.16	725.01	791.03	838.06	895.05
614.26	673.14	725.05	791.03	838.12	895.05
614.26	673.15	725.05	791.19	839.08	895.10
615.02	674.01	725.13	792.08	841.02	896.01
615.21	674.03	727.03	793.09	841.13	896.07
615.23	674.14	727.22	793.09	841.18	896.20
616.19	675.07	729.08	793.23	841.18	898.01
617.12	675.16	729.12	794.10	841.27	898.01
617.12	675.24	729.15	794.26	842.02	899.20
617.17	677.12	730.04	794.27	842.12	900.01
617.18	677.12	730.04	796.23	843.08	900.01
617.19	677.15	730.08	796.24	843.10	900.14
617.19	677.22	730.08	796.28	843.10	902.04
617.21	677.22	730.10	798.23	843.27	902.13
618.25	679.11	730.11	801.10	844.01	902.23
618.27	679.11	730.16	801.20	844.05	902.24
620.01	679.17	733.07	801.26	844.13	903.03
620.05	679.25	733.17	802.01	844.14	903.05
620.05	681.03	734.02	802.01	845.17	903.15
620.13	682.03	735.05	802.20	846.01	908.10
620.13	682.07	735.05	803.14	846.09	908.28
620.13	684.09	735.07	804.15	846.17	908.28
621.06	684.21	735.08	804.18	847.05	909.08
622.09	685.15	736.25	804.18	847.05	909.08
622.13	685.15	737.06	805.04	847.26	909.08
622.26	685.28	737.12	805.10	847.28	909.08
623.23	686.18	737.20	805.22	848.11	909.17
623.23	687.21	737.20	806.03	848.13	910.08
624.11	687.22	737.21	807.07	849.04	910.27
629.14	688.05	737.22	807.07	849.04	911.14
629.14	689.08	737.27	807.11	849.04	ascend
629.15	690.17	738.11	807.21	849.05	229.21
632.04	692.03	738.18	807.27	850.05	865.27
632.22	693.09	738.19	808.05	852.26	ascendancy
632.22	693.20	738.25	808.13	852.26	808.17
632.24	693.26	739.12	808.13	853.10	850.12
632.25	694.19	739.12	808.28	853.13	ascended
633.05	694.27	739.24	808.28	853.24	185.17
633.16	697.05	739.24	809.09	854.22	333.25
634.16	697.06	740.13	810.19	854.23	598.22
634.16	697.08	740.20	811.02	857.04	ascending
634.25	697.09	740.24	812.01	859.03	050.03
635.09	697.24	741.01	812.13	859.11	230.21
636.15	697.26	741.01	812.19	859.17	283.11
637.15	697.27	741.02	814.07	859.17	298.06
637.18	698.06	741.06	814.20	861.14	459.17
638.03	698.19	741.24	815.02	862.28	594.20
638.11	698.19	742.12	815.04	863.10	782.17
638.21	698.20	742.15	815.04	863.27	ascertain
638.27	698.23	742.19	815.22	863.27	115.13
638.27	701.17	742.20	816.09	864.09	173.07
639.06	701.17	742.25	816.09	864.14	463.20
641.11	701.27	743.03	816.19	865.02	562.02
641.27	702.03	743.03	816.24	865.07	857.17
642.18	702.09	743.10	816.24	865.25	ascertained
642.18	702.15	743.19	818.08	866.05	013.20
642.19	702.23	743.19	818.13	867.15	255.14
642.20	703.26	748.21	818.17	867.19	755.28
642.20	703.27	749.04	819.08	870.14	862.02
644.24	704.27	750.04	819.09	870.14	888.03
646.16	704.27	751.14	819.11	871.04	ascetic
646.20	705.27	751.20	820.06	871.06	460.22
647.05	705.27	752.02	820.06	871.06	ascribe
647.05	706.04	754.04	820.07	871.15	389.28
647.20	706.11	754.07	820.13	871.16	606.23
647.20	706.12	754.07	820.25	871.27	ascribed
648.06	706.20	756.06	820.26	872.08	581.13
648.09	706.20	756.07	820.27	872.18	ash
648.27	707.04	756.10	821.08	873.14	146.04
649.09	707.05	756.11	821.13	873.25	ashamed
650.04	707.26	756.21	821.18	874.19	321.13
651.02	707.26	757.01	821.20	875.01	469.16
651.02	708.01	757.21	821.22	875.08	505.20
651.18	708.19	759.12	821.23	875.22	563.05
651.23	708.19	761.06	822.04	877.07	692.12
651.23	708.20	761.06	822.18	877.08	ashes
652.05	708.23	761.16	823.24	877.09	409.27
652.07	708.23	761.16	825.07	877.18	816.06
652.09	709.10	762.10	825.27	878.12	asian
653.10	709.20	762.16	826.08	878.12	825.10
653.11	709.25	763.23	826.09	878.19	aside
	710.06	763.24		878.23	009.21

246.16
503.20
578.17
600.17
613.21
667.06
676.12
714.25
732.24
767.09
794.09
890.23
896.07
ask
028.13
055.23
068.15
069.23
085.13
093.22
151.16
179.15
188.20
199.26
235.25
265.06
282.07
314.25
355.10
449.01
463.19
464.25
475.26
485.06
493.02
496.12
514.17
520.09
529.10
529.13
529.21
531.19
551.24
553.26
543.02
565.06
571.07
581.16
585.05
590.15
610.23
618.02
623.28
659.20
668.22
669.26
672.02
685.11
686.16
687.27
709.01
718.06
751.09
751.26
766.24
772.18
773.18
776.09
816.15
852.18
855.27
860.12
867.10
879.12
882.24
886.06
893.14
896.18
asked
002.19
006.22
009.02
023.06
027.15
028.02
031.05
037.04
037.18
039.26
051.15
052.06
062.13
065.22
073.11
075.17
077.01
094.27
101.20
107.28
108.09
127.21
134.11
140.12
153.17
156.01
169.04
170.05
175.13
173.17
182.10
183.02

183.19
188.06
195.07
199.21
201.16
202.01
208.02
217.25
223.04
223.10
249.19
279.07
284.21
293.16
298.03
298.15
309.09
357.23
361.28
366.07
366.16
370.20
375.20
376.05
385.02
386.06
389.20
407.09
419.01
419.02
419.18
421.17
427.18
449.10
452.27
456.23
463.01
464.08
472.14
474.08
475.11
482.23
499.12
506.21
512.11
515.25
530.01
535.22
536.28
539.10
540.10
548.02
550.03
552.21
576.13
582.07
591.20
592.18
595.02
609.04
634.11
635.21
635.24
636.17
645.02
657.01
657.04
665.26
667.21
669.11
670.12
672.08
679.03
680.22
684.11
687.12
693.20
695.20
699.08
704.03
705.02
723.16
733.10
733.20
738.18
739.08
742.14
754.12
757.07
757.16
763.26
768.05
779.17
782.02
790.14
795.15
798.09
801.01
830.08
835.09
840.12
845.15
847.24
849.11
852.27
853.21
853.28
855.10
860.05
861.12
871.09

873.21
874.14
883.13
888.09
890.26
893.24
894.01
896.24
901.11
907.21
asking
090.05
099.06
188.18
454.19
780.15
asks
062.24
063.14
260.01
271.25
820.10
aslant
675.04
711.18
asleep
028.28
040.10
075.11
079.24
143.14
154.05
155.15
159.17
163.14
307.20
323.07
413.10
424.27
478.28
501.18
535.13
731.13
858.05
863.26
asp
758.21
aspect
003.12
082.04
089.09
128.02
191.06
207.17
445.17
480.08
521.09
580.13
619.03
640.12
664.11
685.07
747.18
795.04
896.02
asperity
552.21
aspirant
747.25
aspirants
846.25
aspiration
440.17
aspirations
192.23
473.21
716.28
786.13
aspire
796.20
808.12
aspired
230.24
759.14
aspires
719.27
assassination
616.10
assemblage
084.07
assemble
317.24
assembled
081.05
142.02
316.13
assented
244.28
assert
753.03
asserted
483.06
527.04
591.05
asserting
444.09
511.20
assertion
484.03
644.01

assez
234.25
assiduity
105.03
817.28
assiduous
239.01
714.03
assiduously
478.18
757.25
assign
424.28
488.02
618.16
647.03
819.15
assigned
087.28
097.01
527.20
558.04
assimilates
351.16
assist
211.20
805.23
assistance
225.07
508.20
603.18
818.09
assistant
836.17
assisted
123.25
433.13
associate
043.28
044.04
associated
627.24
629.04
associates
273.15
association
162.26
796.06
associations
256.25
292.09
364.07
439.20
615.12
615.16
775.16
796.01
assortment
546.16
assuage
293.09
assume
619.02
686.19
850.12
assumed
081.02
308.11
331.12
340.26
498.19
818.17
assuming
119.14
174.02
201.08
438.15
770.04
assurance
173.20
assure
059.17
064.05
268.08
271.22
427.24
577.05
761.07
766.18
assured
024.25
340.20
418.06
425.14
481.05
481.18
553.18
558.03
590.04
798.10
861.02
assuredly
146.19
assuring
543.18
astir
192.03
583.21
858.27
886.04

astonished
535.10
603.07
716.14
754.17
809.15
841.10
astonishing
531.12
641.26
astonishment
298.12
369.03
asunder
145.21
736.13
asylum
146.24
334.15
508.15
625.28
706.21
722.13
at
002.08
003.10
004.25
005.25
006.01
006.16
006.16
006.20
007.07
007.10
008.11
008.16
009.12
009.18
010.11
010.26
013.25
015.17
015.28
016.18
017.21
018.03
018.23
018.27
020.04
020.17
022.11
023.05
026.20
027.16
029.08
031.16
032.22
034.27
035.04
035.17
035.18
035.24
036.01
037.06
038.12
038.15
039.23
040.23
041.12
042.11
043.15
043.23
044.02
044.21
045.11
046.18
047.23
048.04
048.28
049.05
050.16
052.13
052.13
052.14
052.16
058.02
058.16
058.21
059.09
060.15
061.01
061.18
062.01
064.08
066.22
066.27
067.20
069.19
071.11
072.22
073.05
073.18
074.15
074.23
075.10
075.14
076.04
076.14
078.05
079.20
080.08

080.21
081.06
082.05
082.06
082.12
083.04
083.20
084.21
084.21
085.09
085.11
086.07
086.10
086.27
087.04
087.10
088.03
089.04
090.17
092.14
093.25
094.01
095.08
095.09
095.20
096.14
097.03
097.04
097.13
097.22
097.24
098.26
099.07
099.16
099.24
100.04
100.09
100.11
102.13
104.08
106.25
110.06
111.02
112.14
112.22
113.01
113.18
113.24
115.03
115.05
115.19
115.23
116.06
116.12
116.17
118.24
117.15
122.13
122.28
124.06
126.16
127.02
127.24
128.02
129.15
132.13
133.02
133.27
134.11
135.05
136.15
140.07
140.17
141.25
143.06
144.17
147.03
147.12
147.19
148.23
149.08
149.12
149.17
150.19
150.22
151.10
151.16
151.21
151.24
152.22
154.10
154.13
155.21
157.09
157.15
159.14
160.13
162.11
162.19
164.28
165.04
165.21
166.04
166.06
168.06
168.08
169.15
169.23
170.06
170.09
172.17

173.03	269.07	359.06	449.20	532.02	612.14
173.17	269.10	359.16	449.21	535.23	612.16
173.22	272.08	361.23	449.26	536.04	612.25
174.13	272.24	362.14	450.19	536.07	613.15
176.01	273.11	362.16	452.09	536.25	613.26
176.02	273.22	362.23	453.11	537.18	616.21
176.12	274.04	364.02	454.13	537.27	616.22
177.23	274.22	366.03	454.22	538.06	616.24
178.05	275.27	366.25	455.05	539.09	617.17
178.07	276.23	367.13	457.01	541.19	617.19
179.24	277.15	369.04	457.24	542.10	618.28
180.19	281.18	371.08	458.22	542.12	619.05
180.20	282.16	371.27	458.28	543.05	621.11
181.05	284.16	374.13	459.08	543.24	626.23
181.19	286.09	374.15	460.12	544.10	627.18
183.05	286.21	374.28	463.02	546.13	627.20
183.28	287.13	375.07	463.03	546.27	628.10
184.03	287.15	375.12	464.01	547.10	628.14
184.13	287.27	375.26	464.24	548.17	629.15
185.07	290.07	378.04	465.24	548.23	630.13
185.21	290.26	378.09	466.04	550.22	630.21
186.01	291.26	378.19	466.11	552.11	631.18
186.14	293.14	379.25	467.13	553.16	631.27
187.27	293.19	380.17	467.28	555.08	632.28
188.26	293.26	381.02	468.21	555.13	633.09
189.07	294.13	381.18	469.03	555.20	634.08
189.18	294.28	382.02	470.16	555.22	634.21
189.21	295.02	382.08	470.21	557.06	636.21
191.08	295.03	382.11	472.11	557.09	640.04
191.10	295.23	382.13	472.11	558.14	640.04
191.17	297.02	382.25	472.23	559.01	640.07
191.25	297.05	383.13	472.27	559.04	640.19
192.06	297.20	383.14	479.02	561.04	640.25
193.01	298.21	383.18	480.02	561.11	641.10
193.05	299.26	385.20	480.18	562.17	642.01
193.13	301.07	385.26	480.21	562.25	642.02
193.16	301.17	391.01	481.15	564.22	642.03
193.17	301.23	391.07	482.14	565.13	643.09
194.11	306.01	391.20	482.18	565.14	643.10
195.02	307.06	392.13	483.11	565.24	644.24
195.12	307.26	394.05	484.02	566.07	647.04
196.03	308.17	394.17	485.05	566.10	647.23
197.02	309.01	395.08	485.06	567.10	648.11
197.03	309.28	396.07	485.16	567.15	648.19
197.17	310.24	399.23	485.21	568.16	648.27
198.08	311.09	400.23	486.05	569.08	649.10
198.13	311.20	401.03	487.07	570.17	649.19
198.14	311.21	402.24	488.09	570.19	650.05
199.07	312.20	403.09	488.12	572.04	651.16
199.08	313.06	404.09	488.23	572.10	651.25
200.22	313.11	404.21	489.13	572.11	653.18
201.01	314.19	405.10	490.03	572.12	655.17
201.13	315.12	406.27	490.22	572.13	658.03
201.20	315.15	407.04	491.07	574.01	658.07
202.24	315.19	407.05	491.15	575.10	658.14
203.05	317.05	410.10	492.07	575.18	659.03
206.07	318.02	410.18	492.10	577.17	659.11
206.20	318.16	410.21	492.20	577.18	659.15
208.06	320.15	410.23	493.19	577.20	660.23
209.08	324.07	410.27	493.27	578.20	661.03
210.01	324.11	410.28	494.04	583.17	661.07
210.10	324.15	411.23	496.02	585.02	661.13
216.25	325.08	411.28	497.12	585.10	661.21
220.25	326.01	412.03	497.19	585.13	661.21
222.08	326.06	412.28	498.26	585.17	663.10
222.27	326.13	413.04	500.03	587.11	663.16
223.25	326.25	413.10	502.06	588.03	664.12
225.11	327.03	414.08	502.23	588.21	664.24
225.14	327.12	416.16	502.26	589.02	666.15
225.17	328.12	416.22	503.04	589.11	666.15
225.19	329.17	418.27	503.27	589.14	666.27
225.22	329.28	419.16	504.05	589.24	667.09
225.27	330.03	420.01	504.12	590.20	667.10
226.14	330.25	420.23	504.19	591.16	667.12
227.18	331.18	422.11	504.21	591.19	669.02
230.03	332.03	423.02	504.23	592.09	669.05
230.13	332.20	423.21	505.06	592.10	669.10
231.23	332.27	424.09	505.08	593.14	669.21
233.16	333.13	424.17	505.11	594.15	670.10
235.03	333.17	424.25	505.14	595.15	670.19
235.07	334.28	424.26	509.18	595.18	671.10
235.27	335.11	426.18	510.11	595.21	672.05
237.02	335.18	428.09	511.22	596.04	672.09
238.03	336.12	428.14	511.25	596.14	673.26
244.07	336.14	429.15	513.15	596.22	674.07
245.04	337.18	430.16	513.26	598.02	674.19
245.05	338.03	431.02	514.10	598.03	677.09
246.20	338.06	431.10	514.16	598.11	678.01
246.21	340.01	433.16	514.17	598.16	678.15
247.02	341.01	434.11	515.02	599.14	678.15
248.15	342.20	436.17	515.04	599.17	679.16
249.27	344.07	438.01	516.21	600.13	679.21
250.02	345.06	438.13	518.19	601.12	679.24
250.20	347.05	438.24	519.06	601.15	680.01
250.28	347.09	438.24	519.17	601.19	680.03
252.07	347.26	439.17	519.25	602.02	680.23
253.11	348.19	441.20	519.28	602.02	682.04
254.10	349.05	441.21	520.14	602.05	682.13
255.07	349.11	441.22	521.07	603.02	683.11
255.19	349.11	442.12	521.13	604.05	683.27
255.27	350.10	443.06	521.14	604.10	684.07
256.04	350.13	444.06	525.01	605.23	684.11
257.28	350.23	446.10	525.18	606.13	685.02
259.09	351.03	446.21	526.12	609.07	685.10
259.10	351.18	446.24	526.21	610.15	685.12
259.12	352.22	446.26	526.22	610.16	686.08
260.04	352.25	446.27	527.03	610.25	686.10
263.06	352.27	447.01	527.08	611.07	686.13
263.21	353.01	448.13	528.08	611.19	686.15
268.17	354.09	448.19	529.21	612.04	687.05
269.03	356.14	448.21	532.01	612.08	687.15

687.26	761.21	845.18	630.04	098.22	503.17
687.27	763.08	845.19	atom	099.03	678.02
690.03	763.19	845.24	617.11	122.25	798.02
690.07	763.20	847.01	894.13	147.10	871.07
690.21	767.14	847.10	atoms	160.16	903.22
690.24	767.14	847.12	282.21	187.27	909.10
691.10	767.23	849.02	atone	201.10	audience
693.10	767.27	850.06	263.05	222.18	172.28
694.14	769.13	850.15	518.14	336.08	auditors
695.13	769.16	850.21	518.14	347.23	359.12
695.14	770.12	851.02	727.16	348.21	auditress
695.20	770.22	851.07	attach	371.12	257.15
698.25	771.07	852.05	217.17	384.05	aught
699.19	771.23	852.17	440.25	473.06	312.16
700.09	774.10	853.18	549.05	479.12	444.13
700.13	774.16	853.20	784.19	488.15	653.14
701.15	775.12	854.13	attached	524.20	855.21
701.28	775.18	854.14	013.17	533.13	906.14
703.08	776.06	855.01	357.05	639.28	augment
703.10	776.08	855.22	370.05	908.15	559.24
703.20	776.26	855.27	590.20	attentions	571.13
704.08	777.07	856.01	506.03	372.07	augmented
706.04	779.16	856.02	506.06	449.06	460.23
706.04	781.18	856.19	707.04	462.19	august
707.21	782.16	856.26	718.12	744.19	322.17
708.04	784.18	856.28	721.22	attentive	780.09
708.06	784.27	857.08	825.17	104.25	augusta
708.10	785.27	857.15	attachment	739.12	058.13
708.17	786.07	857.20	150.16	attentively	060.02
713.17	788.01	857.24	214.06	076.25	aunt
713.27	788.07	858.02	626.06	334.02	025.03
714.11	791.04	858.27	644.08	613.15	036.25
715.11	791.08	859.25	712.12	attested	036.28
716.04	793.07	860.08	786.12	114.10	037.18
717.28	793.26	860.19	attack	219.28	038.18
718.19	794.27	861.04	451.22	attesting	052.09
720.13	795.03	861.10	attain	005.03	062.22
720.24	795.11	861.11	440.09	attic	063.11
721.12	795.15	861.22	attained	049.08	464.03
722.08	795.20	861.26	039.05	209.15	465.26
722.23	796.04	861.27	102.10	209.24	465.27
723.13	796.23	862.11	attaining	215.02	466.01
723.17	796.24	862.23	166.28	attics	475.22
723.24	796.25	864.10	attainment	208.24	480.16
725.22	797.10	864.20	741.05	865.16	480.21
726.15	797.27	864.25	attainments	attire	480.22
726.17	798.03	864.28	373.05	019.06	480.23
726.18	798.17	865.13	911.10	059.04	484.10
726.28	798.19	867.07	attempt	061.04	484.23
727.02	799.17	867.15	056.24	192.09	495.12
729.02	799.19	867.26	113.14	322.21	780.25
730.01	799.23	870.05	312.04	340.17	aunt-in-law
730.26	799.28	870.19	314.27	521.19	770.26
731.27	800.28	873.02	428.19	525.20	aunts
732.10	801.12	873.16	633.28	attired	242.18
732.11	801.19	873.26	644.19	122.01	aura
732.24	801.19	874.01	772.17	175.09	234.21
732.28	801.20	874.15	792.23	340.19	auriculas
734.06	801.24	877.07	817.06	368.11	145.01
734.15	801.25	879.14	826.23	381.06	auspices
734.21	802.09	882.16	832.27	attitude	860.03
735.23	802.15	883.15	833.16	098.10	aussi
736.19	803.01	883.25	834.17	130.24	234.22
736.19	803.17	884.12	836.01	201.08	austere
736.19	803.21	884.21	838.19	262.22	275.15
737.02	804.05	885.12	875.23	737.09	740.25
737.06	804.28	885.15	attempted	attract	813.13
737.08	805.21	886.16	043.09	351.27	829.04
737.11	805.28	889.05	247.19	attracted	832.13
737.13	806.24	893.03	307.01	371.15	austerity
738.11	807.05	895.11	310.06	attraction	733.16
738.19	808.18	897.11	489.14	050.10	825.25
738.22	808.19	899.06	attempting	474.09	author
740.02	808.20	899.18	309.11	490.18	735.15
741.11	809.02	901.11	356.06	712.25	authority
741.24	809.04	902.02	783.07	796.19	061.02
742.21	810.16	902.17	810.23	attractive	117.28
743.04	811.01	902.21	attempts	002.13	189.08
743.06	814.22	905.12	217.17	039.06	639.11
743.13	817.03	905.17	425.08	090.01	700.02
744.22	817.25	905.18	662.02	350.21	700.04
745.06	823.24	907.22	attend	503.25	authors
745.13	824.04	907.24	233.05	748.24	140.10
745.18	824.06	908.21	255.07	895.13	autobiography
745.22	824.17	909.07	257.28	attractiveness	160.05
746.05	824.27	910.08	479.01	263.06	automaton
746.16	825.01	912.16	627.18	attribute	409.23
746.23	825.03	ate	attendance	269.12	512.28
747.18	825.04	047.11	631.26	606.25	742.04
749.25	825.05	094.08	898.21	636.20	autumn
750.10	825.13	285.05	910.05	attributed	066.15
750.17	825.27	315.19	910.06	326.06	169.17
753.14	827.20	522.21	attendant	attributes	189.19
753.18	828.04	612.02	147.06	571.04	193.24
753.20	828.12	613.02	197.01	au	209.09
754.07	829.25	661.10	200.20	334.05	219.09
754.16	832.07	671.21	633.04	357.02	293.23
754.17	833.13	athenian	739.19	audacious	861.17
754.23	833.18	701.25	attended	044.06	avail
755.10	836.09	athirst	117.07	audacity	033.19
755.17	836.14	877.15	405.26	403.04	674.18
755.17	836.22	athletic	834.10	569.03	853.16
755.22	837.04	237.14	attending	756.18	availed
756.13	839.13	601.09	463.13	audible	162.07
756.18	840.09	872.02	623.19	039.17	avait
758.02	841.17	atlantic	attends	281.28	334.04
758.02	841.24	004.03	092.23	333.19	543.20
758.05	843.09	631.12	attention	342.04	543.21
758.24	843.23	atmosphere	005.03	380.19	avalanche
759.01	843.25	163.27	050.09	381.14	835.02
760.26	845.12	435.18	061.09		835.07

bar
183.05
320.15
552.02
barbara
137.06
137.18
137.22
138.02
barbarism
281.07
barbed
656.03
barber
120.19
bare
153.24
156.27
191.24
368.15
662.27
730.20
749.28
786.24
795.10
bared
623.06
barefoot
149.10
barely
163.22
306.03
barest
705.19
bargain
553.23
826.12
841.15
bargaining
546.15
bargains
648.16
bark
426.21
434.23
barked
222.22
797.28
barking
223.15
barmecide
142.25
barn
771.02
barns
771.03
baroness
357.03
barred
434.05
barrel
596.05
barren
373.06
789.05
828.21
barrenly
762.20
barrier
509.05
572.18
715.04
barriers
194.14
475.10
barrister
177.05
bars
004.25
026.05
276.01
bas
277.11
base
164.24
209.03
282.16
439.20
502.26
560.16
614.07
775.20
bashaw
546.21
basin
027.01
060.07
080.09
083.03
217.09
367.26
368.05
368.23
369.19
421.14
423.10
basins
061.20
bask
067.13

basket
367.03
694.20
basking
236.26
bason
296.17
bass
053.01
319.01
361.12
bastard
597.01
618.14
basted
906.05
basting
905.13
bates
151.23
152.25
153.03
bathe
622.01
bathed
579.05
bathos
554.06
bats
574.24
battalion
612.20
battle
020.02
064.25
802.27
battled
265.12
battledore
289.14
battlemented
220.05
battlements
194.02
208.28
225.28
283.13
856.26
857.18
859.06
865.21
867.17
bauerinnen
790.10
bay
446.14
baying
223.15
bazars
546.10
be
002.08
002.23
003.01
005.06
005.18
006.17
013.08
014.07
014.20
014.23
014.27
015.11
016.15
019.24
021.10
023.01
023.03
024.19
024.25
025.04
025.05
027.20
028.04
028.17
028.21
030.22
035.05
037.08
037.09
037.11
038.10
038.19
038.25
039.13
041.05
041.11
041.13
047.03
047.17
050.23
054.12
054.22
054.23
054.23
055.27
056.11
056.20
057.24
057.26
057.28

057.28
058.08
059.12
059.18
059.26
060.15
064.05
064.11
067.24
068.02
068.07
068.25
069.01
069.13
072.11
073.24
076.23
076.27
077.15
077.17
079.18
079.28
083.11
087.07
087.09
087.12
094.10
097.17
102.05
102.09
102.21
102.28
103.01
103.05
103.07
103.15
103.26
104.11
104.22
105.01
105.09
106.19
108.18
108.21
108.23
109.04
109.08
114.16
116.12
116.18
116.25
117.07
118.01
118.14
118.17
118.21
119.14
120.14
120.17
120.19
121.13
121.23
123.02
123.04
123.27
123.28
125.10
125.10
125.14
125.17
125.25
126.20
129.14
130.27
132.03
132.07
132.27
134.08
134.19
135.13
136.12
137.16
137.25
138.26
140.19
142.06
144.14
149.08
150.18
151.02
151.21
151.23
152.10
152.11
152.12
152.12
153.05
153.08
153.14
154.03
155.17
156.01
157.05
158.11
160.05
161.15
162.08
163.18
164.05
166.14
166.21

167.12
168.07
169.22
170.18
171.11
171.26
172.17
172.21
172.24
172.25
173.03
173.12
173.24
177.05
179.13
179.21
182.04
182.13
182.21
183.14
183.22
183.28
184.11
186.17
186.24
188.24
188.26
189.04
189.22
190.09
192.00
192.11
192.12
192.19
192.24
195.10
195.24
196.02
198.08
198.21
202.12
202.16
203.04
206.04
208.07
211.15
213.06
214.08
215.18
215.26
216.07
216.14
218.14
218.17
223.03
223.17
224.18
225.19
227.02
227.21
229.09
230.12
232.03
233.09
234.17
235.09
235.21
236.12
237.26
238.02
238.18
239.23
240.09
241.12
251.26
252.15
256.08
256.21
256.26
257.06
257.16
257.28
260.22
261.11
262.18
263.10
263.21
265.09
265.12
267.26
268.09
268.24
269.04
270.20
270.21
271.23
272.22
272.27
273.16
273.25
274.12
274.15
274.16
274.18
275.10
275.23
275.24
276.27
277.04
278.01
281.28

282.10
282.20
282.21
283.19
284.09
285.17
288.07
288.13
288.24
291.11
293.14
293.21
293.22
294.13
294.15
296.15
297.23
298.21
299.02
300.22
302.05
306.04
308.06
309.10
309.14
309.15
309.28
310.04
310.16
311.01
311.09
312.11
312.12
313.03
314.21
321.12
321.17
322.19
324.04
325.06
325.08
325.13
325.16
326.18
326.24
326.27
327.02
331.16
331.22
332.15
333.15
338.21
339.07
339.08
340.07
341.10
341.12
344.05
345.23
346.06
346.22
347.28
353.03
355.08
356.03
356.27
357.12
358.05
358.09
358.12
358.14
359.09
359.27
360.01
360.02
360.06
360.09
360.20
360.25
361.03
365.28
366.04
366.16
370.22
370.25
370.27
372.18
372.25
372.28
375.07
376.12
376.13
376.20
377.06
377.21
379.15
381.27
383.03
383.04
385.02
385.10
386.02
386.18
386.19
387.10
387.25
388.11
392.01
392.19
396.27
397.03

397.09
397.16
399.14
399.27
400.24
401.06
402.28
403.06
404.24
404.26
405.09
405.24
406.06
409.03
409.07
410.23
416.14
417.13
417.25
418.10
421.26
421.28
422.01
422.11
422.24
424.14
427.03
427.09
427.22
428.16
429.09
429.28
430.06
430.13
431.13
432.08
432.16
433.25
433.25
433.26
436.24
437.02
437.20
438.06
442.15
442.17
444.13
448.25
450.21
451.26
452.03
452.08
452.10
452.12
452.17
453.26
454.16
455.06
455.15
455.16
456.19
458.07
458.21
460.06
463.09
464.09
464.16
465.14
466.20
467.20
470.03
470.04
471.11
471.19
473.27
474.26
475.08
475.15
475.23
476.10
476.15
476.19
476.20
476.21
476.21
476.21
477.15
477.21
477.24
478.11
478.12
479.27
480.10
481.04
481.07
483.25
484.05
484.09
484.14
484.22
485.06
488.04
488.08
489.04
489.08
489.22
490.12
490.15
490.20
491.26
493.08
493.18

be (continued)

494.04 495.14 495.24 495.27 497.03 498.23 499.22 499.27 502.17 506.13 506.27 507.02 508.12 509.13 509.24 510.13 510.16 511.03 512.07 512.24 514.04 514.18 514.22 514.23 515.26 516.19 517.10 517.17 521.04 521.14 522.06 523.08 523.20 524.08 524.20 525.15 525.25 526.09 526.24 527.04 527.05 527.11 527.13 527.14 529.14 530.02 530.11 531.01 531.05 531.14 531.23 532.06 532.16 534.01 534.07 535.25 536.20 537.08 537.08 537.23 538.04 538.05 538.27 538.28 541.03 544.01 544.27 545.05 545.08 545.23 546.17 546.27 547.03 547.05 547.12 547.17 547.25 549.02 551.01 551.02 552.19 552.23 553.08 553.12 553.25 553.26 554.21 555.24 555.25 557.10 558.01 558.03 558.07 560.20 560.22 561.03 562.19 563.17 566.06 572.12 572.16 574.07 574.16 579.11 580.02 580.05 582.15 582.19 586.25 587.13

589.25 590.02 590.03 591.21 593.16 596.07 596.11 598.06 598.14 602.10 602.17 602.18 603.04 603.20 603.21 604.03 607.09 607.19 607.24 608.11 608.25 609.18 610.08 610.13 611.16 613.05 613.12 615.06 616.22 617.13 617.14 617.19 618.05 618.10 619.21 620.16 621.19 621.23 622.10 622.11 622.20 622.26 624.12 624.13 626.07 626.21 628.28 629.10 632.07 633.06 634.28 635.01 635.02 635.25 639.01 639.11 643.12 643.13 643.14 645.10 645.16 645.18 646.07 646.15 647.26 647.27 648.11 648.12 649.22 650.14 652.08 652.22 653.12 653.14 654.03 654.27 654.28 655.01 655.23 655.23 655.27 657.15 658.14 659.04 659.12 660.03 660.15 660.18 660.20 661.03 662.24 663.24 664.28 665.03 665.11 665.20 665.26 666.23 667.15 667.19 668.16 669.16 670.23 670.25 670.25 670.28 672.21 672.25 673.20 673.21 674.15

676.02 677.09 679.28 680.23 681.08 681.11 682.05 682.22 683.07 684.10 684.20 690.19 691.04 691.13 691.25 697.27 698.18 699.11 699.17 700.10 700.17 700.18 701.28 702.18 703.15 704.15 707.03 707.06 708.10 708.17 708.21 708.23 708.26 709.01 709.17 709.26 709.27 709.28 714.26 715.09 715.16 718.20 719.11 719.15 719.18 719.28 721.23 722.06 722.22 722.25 723.11 724.08 724.11 724.21 725.02 725.04 725.06 725.07 725.20 727.02 727.19 729.09 730.12 731.02 731.05 731.24 731.26 732.01 732.22 734.26 735.20 736.04 738.24 739.28 740.23 741.27 745.03 745.22 746.13 747.13 751.01 751.03 753.12 754.19 755.06 755.18 755.26 756.11 756.19 756.21 759.17 760.08 760.18 761.17 763.03 764.10 767.20 766.11 768.20 768.27 770.03 771.13 772.05 772.06 775.09 776.05 777.02 777.12 778.17 779.01

781.08 782.06 782.10 782.15 782.23 782.25 782.26 783.08 784.22 784.25 785.02 786.04 786.05 786.14 786.25 787.02 787.20 789.05 790.05 790.21 791.03 791.08 791.13 791.22 792.04 792.25 793.09 793.24 793.25 793.28 794.16 796.14 796.27 796.27 798.21 799.27 800.02 801.14 801.28 802.02 802.19 803.09 804.03 804.25 806.05 807.09 807.23 811.19 814.03 814.18 815.17 815.17 815.27 816.24 818.09 818.26 818.27 819.07 819.22 820.10 820.24 821.12 821.13 822.07 822.14 822.28 823.04 823.08 824.16 824.17 824.19 825.08 825.18 825.19 825.22 825.23 826.04 826.14 826.15 826.23 827.09 827.10 827.11 828.15 828.20 828.23 829.24 830.06 833.20 835.17 837.06 837.08 837.10 837.21 838.13 838.16 838.19 839.08 840.12 841.07 841.18 842.11 842.11 842.17 844.10 844.18 844.18 846.08 846.15 846.23 846.24

846.25 847.22 848.02 848.14 850.14 852.05 853.19 853.25 854.08 855.14 855.20 856.02 856.25 856.28 857.04 857.06 858.10 860.07 861.07 861.13 861.21 862.21 864.18 866.27 868.06 871.09 872.02 873.26 873.28 876.11 876.15 876.23 877.05 877.16 878.26 878.28 879.02 879.03 879.12 879.27 880.07 880.16 880.17 881.20 884.01 885.11 886.19 886.22 887.12 887.13 888.22 891.21 892.05 893.20 894.02 895.03 895.21 895.23 895.25 898.01 898.01 898.01 898.05 898.13 898.17 898.17 898.22 898.26 899.12 899.23 900.26 900.26 901.01 903.03 903.05 903.18 904.01 906.05 906.08 907.07 909.07 909.07 909.28 911.22 911.23 911.23 912.19 912.20 912.20

821.02

beacon
676.19

bead
363.03

beads
348.24 460.27 652.27 661.09

beak
248.03 668.18

beam
023.16 033.12 867.19

beamed
675.13 887.01

beaming
136.20 382.27

beamless
248.21

beams
521.12 907.08

bear
094.26 103.04 103.05 103.07 103.08 103.26 127.07 132.07 161.27 180.25 261.13 325.24 357.18 421.27 423.02 442.18 447.05 468.23 478.11 513.01 526.13 545.01 565.01 566.08 597.08 609.08 609.13 616.21 624.08 626.26 631.24 639.08 668.09 669.26 670.20 735.27 804.16 816.15 820.21 861.09 898.10

bearded
423.25

bearing
046.12 076.22 079.01 217.13 344.12 416.27 430.24

bears
272.08

beast
424.06 599.16 872.06

beast's
633.03

beasts
222.11

beat
023.18 240.02 294.05 479.25 653.18 735.19 846.27 852.09

beaten
280.09 859.25

beating
021.03 258.19 327.16 582.24 648.16 792.04

beats
909.05

beau
256.16

beau-ideal
186.15 792.13

beaute
287.11

beauties
148.14 506.04 738.05

beautiful
037.04 039.07 148.01 179.03 199.13 199.19 203.23 240.26 281.12 313.05

317.09
319.10
320.05
335.26
350.03
350.04
363.20
403.01
414.12
507.16
512.16
649.19
741.01
741.23
758.28
825.02
895.06
906.24
beautifully
327.12
beautifully-moulded
368.14
beauty
018.22
041.12
139.16
139.19
178.04
192.16
224.25
237.08
260.06
260.12
318.22
346.24
349.26
359.23
400.12
451.17
497.07
513.08
525.08
525.10
525.11
525.17
571.09
624.25
637.05
641.26
751.21
757.16
737.19
758.10
858.13
beaver
122.03
226.18
becalmed
005.05
became
026.09
044.19
111.16
112.23
146.03
161.22
182.26
213.15
296.01
342.04
343.10
365.01
380.19
500.09
505.20
525.18
579.02
620.25
652.24
643.05
717.22
724.26
740.17
744.27
746.26
771.11
768.13
806.28
880.24
908.09
because
007.28
014.20
016.12
016.13
016.14
019.14
034.10
034.19
035.17
063.02
063.12
068.01
069.02
091.20
092.04
093.15
099.23
106.07
108.12
128.06

134.15
147.05
149.15
149.16
162.01
166.16
167.07
218.05
228.27
228.28
240.04
250.01
251.28
254.20
261.10
265.05
265.19
265.22
265.23
270.01
272.25
274.03
275.01
282.03
286.19
286.21
297.04
310.11
314.01
314.08
344.01
372.03
372.04
372.06
372.13
372.14
372.16
374.05
375.09
378.08
379.07
396.12
396.14
396.17
431.26
437.24
444.06
451.09
466.16
471.27
477.23
482.24
498.07
510.22
511.17
511.24
513.04
515.16
516.24
521.13
521.19
524.03
525.19
532.14
566.13
569.24
571.24
573.13
573.24
573.25
584.02
585.15
614.01
615.26
617.05
619.16
620.11
624.28
626.03
626.21
626.25
632.14
644.15
648.15
673.03
697.04
697.06
700.09
701.04
735.11
736.14
744.24
747.02
752.05
762.02
762.05
762.07
785.20
791.18
804.24
805.01
805.28
806.23
808.25
817.27
823.15
823.16
833.19
835.10
835.11
836.04

838.05
842.20
844.11
845.04
858.20
879.13
882.16
883.16
888.15
894.07
894.08
895.07
896.18
896.21
898.03
908.27
910.02
911.04
beck
145.12
145.20
145.20
149.08
169.20
812.21
beckon
396.18
beckoned
406.24
542.11
847.18
854.22
beckoning
598.23
becks
220.20
beclouded
021.01
become
014.15
015.01
051.22
097.03
147.22
163.02
231.16
273.04
292.02
331.24
352.06
384.17
424.23
437.25
439.13
439.20
506.02
512.27
521.19
525.01
527.23
531.10
612.28
615.07
621.05
622.09
622.21
638.05
663.11
706.26
718.11
756.05
760.21
772.06
809.01
817.18
826.10
826.11
832.15
839.02
839.06
842.22
843.26
887.13
899.01
908.01
becomes
125.13
140.14
262.13
783.24
becoming
059.19
230.02
370.22
441.25
461.11
556.01
618.25
847.16
879.16
910.17
becomingly
318.11
bed
015.21
015.28
016.07
016.10
017.07
017.12
022.12

026.18
028.09
028.27
040.10
047.10
049.08
076.27
077.05
088.01
095.19
142.24
154.02
155.10
159.10
167.01
167.22
170.23
233.03
244.22
251.03
251.18
274.27
276.06
282.15
293.11
294.04
295.02
296.09
296.20
297.27
300.18
305.20
306.11
307.19
309.21
337.21
413.04
416.13
417.28
418.24
421.02
423.16
424.27
430.05
464.22
465.03
469.20
484.26
491.10
501.17
505.05
520.12
567.16
572.06
576.11
576.19
582.10
599.04
603.10
607.15
629.22
634.01
651.23
663.16
688.09
689.07
689.07
692.01
745.25
791.27
864.04
864.11
bed-clothes
072.14
307.22
467.12
479.22
bed-fellow
079.18
bed-foot
026.20
bed-hangings
331.01
bed-head
421.05
466.24
bed-room
072.04
079.16
096.09
140.28
190.05
190.21
429.24
794.22
809.04
bed-rooms
326.27
328.27
794.10
bed-side
191.11
306.18
690.04
692.14
bed-time
140.19
165.25
445.22
807.05

bedroom
857.17
bedrooms
327.19
beds
079.20
087.27
087.28
096.10
144.15
148.05
199.01
504.12
616.24
794.13
865.17
bedside
295.03
468.26
578.20
bedstead
729.08
bedsteads
207.07
328.01
bedtime
274.27
bee
271.03
663.09
663.11
beech
279.08
502.22
beech-trunk
283.25
been
001.04
007.09
016.26
020.19
020.25
021.11
021.15
022.02
022.10
024.10
026.13
027.10
030.03
030.10
030.16
030.20
030.24
034.06
040.19
040.25
045.11
045.12
046.04
047.20
048.07
048.26
051.03
051.19
055.02
059.02
061.09
061.27
065.09
065.21
067.07
072.10
072.18
072.18
073.04
077.10
093.17
095.16
096.18
097.02
097.23
098.11
099.06
101.05
105.15
105.23
108.11
115.04
116.01
116.02
117.04
117.24
122.16
129.07
134.15
135.08
141.21
141.23
142.04
147.08
148.22
150.23
151.24
152.15
153.03
154.04
155.17
157.14

162.17
163.28
164.07
164.08
165.04
165.06
166.08
168.19
168.28
174.19
177.21
182.11
186.03
190.03
199.22
201.14
202.23
203.02
205.10
207.04
207.15
208.14
209.17
209.20
211.07
213.10
218.08
224.19
225.05
227.09
228.20
230.04
230.05
235.17
235.24
237.17
238.22
240.07
241.04
243.02
243.20
248.10
249.24
252.12
253.10
255.20
258.12
259.10
259.11
263.14
268.04
268.19
268.20
270.08
273.17
277.24
284.10
286.26
287.10
287.18
290.02
290.25
293.20
295.13
297.08
301.13
306.16
307.19
308.26
311.21
312.06
312.07
312.12
312.15
313.22
314.08
320.12
320.17
323.26
325.25
328.21
329.22
330.27
331.26
334.26
337.03
340.06
343.05
347.04
358.19
362.09
366.04
368.01
370.01
374.17
374.23
374.25
375.17
377.13
378.01
379.15
383.10
384.21
390.21
391.05
392.08
392.17
401.15
401.22
402.05
406.17

407.27	678.15	befitted	337.22	680.21	404.06
407.28	680.20	388.24	338.01	685.03	418.01
408.06	681.21	before	338.02	686.19	499.27
408.10	684.23	003.16	339.01	692.12	535.10
408.16	689.09	006.28	339.14	704.10	542.04
413.04	690.06	013.25	341.06	706.16	549.23
416.07	690.07	016.10	352.14	707.01	589.18
418.03	691.01	017.07	354.05	710.05	638.19
418.04	693.08	017.16	366.24	713.03	656.05
420.02	693.10	018.01	367.19	715.12	680.24
420.16	694.13	018.08	367.22	716.02	687.03
424.27	695.01	022.22	377.26	719.13	716.08
425.06	695.03	026.04	382.13	720.24	744.07
425.07	695.05	026.13	385.21	726.19	767.04
425.16	696.07	028.28	387.19	730.15	783.10
427.02	696.12	032.20	388.01	732.12	796.14
428.04	697.08	034.22	388.13	734.17	796.16
435.27	698.14	036.07	389.11	740.25	879.19
437.05	698.17	039.03	392.13	743.05	882.24
438.16	699.01	039.27	398.17	752.01	888.12
441.12	701.20	043.13	399.21	756.15	900.15
444.17	701.10	049.10	403.24	761.12	900.16
445.24	703.07	050.22	407.05	766.03	900.18
447.07	704.13	051.24	410.06	768.19	beggar
447.23	705.24	053.28	420.12	770.05	468.22
448.01	707.24	057.05	432.12	770.16	670.26
450.02	710.05	056.22	438.11	771.02	670.27
459.08	716.25	071.06	440.02	776.19	671.18
462.22	720.11	073.05	442.06	779.10	672.13
462.25	720.13	075.24	442.16	779.28	693.26
463.24	724.05	077.05	443.06	780.21	694.01
463.26	726.21	080.21	449.01	789.19	694.02
464.17	727.26	080.23	451.04	792.12	694.08
464.25	731.15	081.18	451.26	818.19	696.15
468.20	740.02	082.07	455.17	819.04	734.05
468.28	746.08	083.08	456.27	823.20	beggar-woman
473.01	756.03	086.17	457.03	823.23	522.07
474.28	760.17	089.14	458.22	827.16	684.23
476.04	767.01	091.11	459.23	833.11	beggarly
484.07	768.26	095.04	460.19	836.24	038.19
484.20	771.06	096.02	464.19	837.12	begged
495.12	772.03	096.12	468.27	838.14	031.07
496.13	772.03	098.10	470.10	843.21	187.02
500.02	772.07	099.07	473.01	847.06	218.05
500.06	773.12	119.12	474.03	848.17	543.28
500.11	776.16	121.21	476.04	852.18	665.20
503.10	779.24	123.16	477.04	852.26	668.07
510.01	783.25	126.01	478.09	856.08	670.28
511.15	788.05	134.05	481.14	861.23	begging
511.26	794.09	135.03	482.04	864.13	038.20
511.26	801.21	138.07	487.03	865.04	548.18
511.27	802.21	152.09	493.01	865.12	begin
520.15	805.07	152.19	512.12	867.14	398.05
521.13	808.18	154.20	514.11	868.07	524.15
529.06	821.07	155.21	515.03	869.05	531.04
530.27	828.02	168.16	519.12	877.18	622.04
533.15	829.19	170.10	519.21	877.19	793.02
534.23	830.11	171.03	520.12	886.12	838.12
535.12	831.13	173.10	528.14	890.26	860.13
535.16	833.04	177.24	529.19	891.17	beginning
536.06	833.23	183.19	534.07	891.19	137.16
537.17	843.16	183.22	534.25	891.26	151.12
540.07	847.05	187.28	553.21	897.04	164.01
548.21	847.08	191.15	555.06	903.17	191.27
553.15	847.09	193.04	558.04	909.23	235.19
560.06	848.21	195.22	560.09	912.05	280.20
562.06	849.06	199.06	563.13	befriended	324.10
565.10	853.11	200.07	564.17	027.24	331.28
565.16	853.23	200.14	566.14	671.28	406.10
568.13	859.17	202.03	567.05	beg	427.15
569.14	860.26	203.24	567.13	009.10	516.12
577.03	862.14	215.25	570.11	126.23	656.18
580.09	864.08	225.18	573.01	227.23	756.21
581.06	864.14	229.01	574.17	260.06	765.02
581.20	865.11	229.10	576.11	264.16	765.11
589.05	866.16	230.20	577.06	288.25	816.23
591.05	879.17	234.13	577.08	538.15	begins
593.20	882.25	234.16	582.20	669.27	742.08
596.19	882.25	235.25	583.04	791.04	775.19
597.20	884.25	239.23	588.08	893.27	begot
602.22	884.27	239.26	589.06	began	607.21
605.01	885.03	244.18	597.15	020.28	begrimed
605.04	885.08	247.12	613.15	022.14	369.27
605.07	885.19	247.18	615.25	032.15	beguile
605.11	885.22	249.07	619.14	054.05	380.05
605.12	885.25	251.04	625.14	063.17	beguiled
605.19	888.08	258.15	627.08	075.02	033.16
606.22	888.16	258.22	635.11	081.07	begun
607.06	889.03	259.19	644.22	082.15	080.04
607.10	889.05	259.24	647.06	083.09	477.04
610.22	894.14	277.14	649.23	119.11	632.16
610.23	901.12	283.12	660.01	125.07	693.11
611.08	905.09	283.14	660.16	129.07	behalf
611.21	908.24	284.15	660.18	144.08	179.01
614.07	912.16	285.15	660.20	144.14	312.09
618.26	bees	288.05	661.11	170.09	681.28
620.09	438.21	289.04	662.09	187.01	823.07
629.07	663.01	292.15	663.02	201.08	909.21
629.17	bees-wax	293.14	664.18	210.09	behave
629.19	791.25	300.06	667.11	223.13	495.02
633.20	befall	307.22	668.25	238.18	beheld
636.15	769.02	309.20	671.10	243.08	231.24
638.03	befallen	310.03	671.23	273.06	301.24
651.10	518.23	311.10	672.01	280.03	327.20
661.23	befalling	314.06	672.04	286.27	378.04
669.20	524.12	321.26	672.04	294.21	402.22
672.17	befell	326.14	672.28	319.28	491.04
675.05	542.05	327.20	675.19	333.16	521.11
676.10	befit	328.03	675.23	349.12	570.08
676.18	507.23	332.27	678.24	387.24	636.08
677.23		335.24	680.12	396.04	870.20

behest
358.11
412.27
behind
005.08
008.07
008.22
009.01
015.14
021.05
053.17
075.27
076.16
089.24
101.20
113.21
119.20
152.12
151.25
152.18
174.17
184.23
165.17
202.14
209.22
220.09
230.23
295.07
318.12
335.05
342.11
353.23
366.11
367.11
392.27
420.28
454.27
480.12
492.27
504.21
539.13
569.15
591.08
601.03
601.14
602.13
639.19
659.01
707.11
712.03
719.19
734.10
757.02
768.07
763.06
815.23
857.14
858.26
858.28
874.22
326.12
331.17
332.18
333.16
335.10
335.12
338.08
349.16
367.01
369.17
369.23
381.25
382.13
385.21
399.15
415.01
440.09
463.15
475.26
476.12
477.09
479.13
487.11
488.02
494.23
498.11
514.08
533.20
545.01
548.11
550.13
550.24
555.02
557.03
581.07
592.15
597.24
617.02
624.07
625.08
626.17
629.14
629.22
630.24
631.15
632.09
643.04
645.10
647.14
663.15
699.06
702.01
703.18
717.23
716.03
745.19
745.21
759.21
763.15
764.10
771.08
775.27
780.08
794.22
798.10
802.24
803.01
811.11
817.06
823.19
839.21
839.23
849.20
875.02
880.19
881.05
883.07
884.21
898.25
904.03
910.23
behold
061.15
215.16
348.25
815.07
883.25
beholding
346.19
907.24
being
005.20
031.21
034.15
038.08
040.06
040.15
047.15
050.09
054.25
059.09
059.10
060.20
079.06
082.26
085.16
097.04
099.19
100.14
109.05
115.23
143.10
150.13
151.05
154.19
174.25
187.27
197.27
222.07
223.25
225.23
246.03
250.15
255.09
255.16
262.09
266.05
272.17
287.03
301.12
310.06
310.12
being's
063.14
beings
046.21
132.15
207.26
216.06
524.09
623.11
727.02
824.23
belabour
287.05
belated
018.01
221.21
beldame
387.04
belfry
219.05
belied
213.04
belief
533.22
894.12
believe
024.18
056.15
069.07
095.09
109.10
157.18
158.03
158.06
176.25
179.21
180.01
185.06
196.18
197.19
205.18
208.13
252.17
269.14
271.19
272.20
273.15
275.14
307.04
316.13
316.26
328.14
351.10
376.12
390.01
397.27
407.27
441.13
444.07
466.16
467.19
474.20
506.23
506.24
513.25
531.25
534.16
536.01
538.05
568.05
568.06
574.16
580.04
641.23
646.20
648.14
655.09
666.07
673.03
682.01
684.01
684.22
696.17
721.01
747.10
762.13
762.14
819.18
834.01
853.01
883.09
885.23
902.20
909.09
believed
005.06
045.06
074.21
131.28
135.24
163.05
215.14
215.16
279.15
292.25
293.01
314.26
449.11
570.02
648.14
815.11
816.04
843.19
844.27
853.25
862.14
believes
130.27
180.13
believing
047.03
903.13
bell
035.12
052.04
060.26
080.02
080.10
080.28
081.13
137.05
140.18
165.22
168.17
182.28
185.12
219.04
232.04
233.17
238.27
255.11
314.13
350.27
366.20
366.28
567.08
586.08
664.08
664.08
736.25
belle
317.18
356.16
bellowed
010.20
600.12
bells
031.14
belong
038.04
092.06
belonged
089.18
190.22
195.26
205.13
206.15
639.16
697.27
751.09
807.22
859.14
belonging
027.06
037.17
belongs
009.15
895.26
beloved
139.10
507.28
895.17
below
045.21
055.27
124.19
154.24
174.28
212.01
214.01
220.06
225.22
225.27
230.24
233.18
235.05
248.07
246.19
263.16
314.13
313.17
329.09
333.06
336.19
425.01
426.22
430.08
526.11
560.17
639.17
795.05
865.16
belvidere
279.17
bemired
692.10
bemoaned
661.27
ben't
906.22
bench
073.18
089.25
121.01
438.12
510.11
benches
078.07
084.05
bend
069.25
380.28
649.13
664.22
700.05
732.26
bending
022.27
053.23
281.25
353.02
394.09
560.03
589.21
645.27
737.16
740.24
844.05
900.06
903.20
906.01
bends
504.06
528.08
858.11
858.12
beneath
031.15
040.22
145.14
204.14
364.05
373.01
395.06
472.16
502.12
591.17
802.12
872.14
benefactors
692.12
benefactress
055.03
055.05
055.05
055.06
055.07
057.28
126.11
134.24
benefactress's
012.16
beneficent
884.12
899.28
beneficial
161.06
benefit
291.08
301.21
323.15
356.18
473.14
691.13
706.08
753.27
782.20
784.20
benefited
744.24
benefits
301.15
benevolence
261.03
625.20
benevolent
161.07
257.16
benevolent-minded
091.24
benign
660.27
benign-looking
141.15
benignant
085.24
643.14
762.17
bent
089.26
259.25
264.11
269.15
276.03
292.22
313.13
342.19
342.26
354.21
359.13
368.23
369.26
396.06
423.26
424.22
505.17
564.12
575.24
576.19
587.15
599.12
608.05
644.28
649.14
654.26
677.15
685.28
725.18
734.25
807.18
808.08
824.05
833.03
852.22
910.10
bequeath
482.18
bequeathed
727.17
bequest
775.24
783.01
783.21
bereavement
655.25
berth
813.19
bertha
593.12
597.04
597.09
597.15
613.24
627.15
865.28
beset
469.14
539.05
847.05
beside
012.06
032.11
115.15
352.16
410.08
535.18
589.03
661.15
763.07
887.25
besides
002.21
015.04
036.08
037.15
039.12
052.09
069.14
101.27
102.26
109.15
131.23
132.19
132.20
148.25
175.27
188.20
198.02
199.18
216.12
238.12
261.18
262.14
270.25
274.20
280.24
285.18
297.14
300.14
336.20
373.22
397.25
408.14
428.17
451.26
481.04
541.10
547.09
547.20
571.18
571.21
601.07
612.11
614.15
629.07
633.08
642.09
665.19
668.01
668.10
670.07
671.25
700.15
715.03
731.23
734.04
744.07
747.23
766.26
775.24
779.07
784.16
785.06
788.05
802.10
855.23
859.15
878.10
882.28
besotted
625.09
790.11
bessie
001.15
002.09
002.18
005.16
010.12
012.04
013.09
013.19
013.25

014.05	**bessie's**	**betrayed**	799.26	**beulah**	360.23
014.26	017.26	220.22	800.02	302.22	**bientot**
015.07	024.06	289.20	800.11	**beverage**	218.24
017.04	024.24	307.08	804.19	137.14	**big**
023.25	039.01	373.16	821.09	705.27	352.12
023.26	047.06	606.24	843.04	**bewailing**	442.25
024.04	067.06	**better**	846.15	200.18	601.05
024.17	073.22	028.17	846.21	**beware**	865.24
024.22	074.23	043.13	855.26	269.08	**bigamist**
025.11	177.27	053.20	866.16	437.06	596.11
026.20	178.05	065.27	866.27	623.05	**bigamy**
027.07	221.17	069.17	873.05	**bewick**	596.10
027.19	222.01	076.27	880.16	005.28	**bigger**
028.02	**best**	102.22	881.24	**bewick's**	532.19
028.08	046.18	116.27	884.27	003.18	**bilberries**
028.14	047.15	136.26	884.28	460.13	661.08
028.18	058.10	143.15	895.23	**bewildered**	663.10
030.06	072.10	148.18	896.11	007.27	**bilge**
030.16	093.13	148.27	898.12	075.20	269.02
031.05	107.14	161.09	906.21	097.07	**bilious**
032.12	149.05	163.02	907.05	243.11	007.07
032.21	162.15	167.08	**bettering**	275.04	640.13
033.23	184.12	172.17	759.23	536.04	**bill**
034.01	184.13	173.19	**between**	561.14	698.04
034.12	184.16	184.07	017.11	**bewilderment**	**billiard**
034.20	189.02	188.04	040.03	026.16	580.08
035.01	205.01	189.17	042.03	576.20	**billiard-room**
035.16	216.01	190.08	042.14	**bewitched**	379.24
035.20	218.20	196.23	066.05	241.20	449.12
036.01	219.11	196.26	069.15	863.11	**billiards**
038.23	236.09	234.02	089.22	**beyond**	379.23
039.23	265.07	235.28	109.16	045.04	449.11
040.01	292.11	236.04	112.12	095.02	**billow**
040.08	310.14	245.19	112.27	095.03	004.22
040.19	326.27	247.11	138.25	111.12	**billows**
041.04	331.13	263.15	163.09	121.07	247.26
041.11	340.22	267.26	164.25	163.13	302.19
041.18	355.18	269.06	191.21	204.09	**bind**
042.03	356.24	270.14	194.23	220.20	579.24
045.02	370.15	273.18	196.24	221.14	753.03
046.04	570.26	273.19	204.18	236.24	**biography**
046.09	388.27	273.19	211.12	248.13	202.18
047.14	391.24	284.09	250.09	274.22	**bird**
047.20	396.15	285.24	252.18	274.22	030.18
048.06	400.03	293.01	271.26	302.21	031.03
049.09	433.28	313.27	272.02	315.05	050.23
049.10	458.12	315.23	284.03	341.10	248.07
050.18	487.16	330.12	310.16	359.18	275.28
050.27	489.09	339.07	320.04	360.27	424.21
051.06	514.18	343.26	325.09	379.20	470.20
051.17	518.05	352.23	329.20	406.13	514.05
067.01	525.23	358.20	344.05	447.19	514.07
067.15	532.16	375.16	347.20	479.27	635.08
067.25	554.03	385.15	356.26	494.10	661.28
067.26	554.21	388.12	360.09	497.07	709.12
068.10	555.08	409.03	381.28	528.24	872.06
068.22	651.10	430.13	383.04	586.18	**birds**
069.02	690.28	432.10	383.05	588.10	003.19
069.06	697.08	440.05	398.19	604.24	031.26
069.19	722.23	446.23	425.14	631.20	143.06
069.26	735.28	448.09	444.08	654.23	199.19
070.02	744.08	452.07	456.13	659.03	207.25
071.03	751.12	453.13	462.16	664.23	219.20
071.12	763.02	464.04	471.03	733.05	342.23
071.16	790.03	469.19	475.10	735.26	433.04
072.06	790.08	475.23	488.26	783.26	438.19
072.17	790.08	481.25	501.14	793.02	440.09
072.25	790.10	482.04	509.18	812.21	441.15
074.01	792.21	496.26	509.21	831.10	460.14
175.17	801.15	507.25	511.02	847.20	496.05
175.17	819.16	510.17	515.13	850.01	501.07
175.18	822.07	513.28	551.06	855.20	522.13
175.23	850.09	531.03	551.12	862.02	561.06
175.24	884.06	531.22	554.09	908.27	656.05
176.05	897.10	538.27	556.03	**bianca**	656.06
176.16	897.11	541.09	556.05	358.08	656.07
177.18	908.26	545.08	581.10	**bias**	662.28
177.26	**best-born**	563.23	603.25	243.07	732.13
178.13	730.11	596.13	606.05	**bible**	**birds'**
178.16	**bestow**	600.07	626.21	055.12	881.10
179.08	462.26	600.22	628.26	080.23	**birth**
180.04	545.16	603.24	641.24	081.10	739.26
180.16	**bestowed**	613.12	673.16	096.13	748.09
313.25	058.08	620.14	675.17	102.26	751.19
313.27	297.02	629.11	677.17	534.25	770.22
444.16	378.24	641.09	685.28	535.08	**biscuits**
445.03	796.06	644.07	712.06	843.24	071.20
446.15	909.11	645.10	714.08	844.06	**bit**
446.16	**bestows**	647.12	714.10	**bid**	055.16
447.10	820.22	673.19	725.26	051.13	063.03
448.12	**betake**	680.13	727.08	072.05	100.10
448.15	478.01	682.10	727.19	156.16	311.03
448.27	508.08	691.28	762.12	258.06	363.13
457.08	**bethesda**	693.15	778.09	437.19	428.05
457.13	126.22	709.28	780.12	455.25	546.06
458.01	**bethought**	711.03	784.07	498.09	599.06
458.16	182.27	713.01	802.15	523.04	680.20
459.09	280.22	716.21	802.19	846.11	680.24
459.13	302.11	720.14	805.27	896.14	**bite**
460.05	479.09	731.04	811.25	**bidden**	228.05
463.18	769.03	731.07	819.21	191.01	616.25
463.22	**betimes**	731.10	828.06	**bidding**	**bits**
464.11	624.14	731.26	832.02	388.06	866.13
464.19	**betook**	749.21	836.19	807.06	**bitter**
469.19	640.05	757.08	856.17	**bide**	017.04
470.05	**betray**	769.05	857.13	553.08	018.07
479.14	286.23	770.03	859.28	**bids**	080.06
480.20	504.11	784.04	870.03	102.27	108.03
481.09	633.07	787.16	870.07	**bien**	113.03
485.12	835.18	791.11	895.20	212.04	230.06
		797.16	900.27	277.09	271.05

439.19
478.25
533.17
608.11
611.24
621.02
638.16
640.12
646.06
655.25
661.27
704.21
723.05
758.21
781.15
800.01
810.16
874.13
bitterest
751.28
bitterly
836.12
bitterness
465.10
716.16
bitternutt
508.25
509.15
509.25
black
005.10
026.05
047.27
052.13
065.11
066.08
086.05
092.26
093.07
115.16
117.02
125.11
170.03
172.01
174.14
175.11
186.09
192.28
193.16
209.16
210.02
221.26
226.17
226.17
251.24
236.08
236.09
237.06
249.12
318.09
331.13
332.26
343.24
344.07
345.15
346.05
353.20
365.20
380.23
386.14
394.06
394.11
395.05
396.04
396.21
417.04
419.27
423.15
446.27
460.24
461.09
471.12
471.24
490.28
531.28
544.14
545.27
546.16
558.08
560.13
578.07
581.15
594.16
599.02
607.13
629.28
634.08
640.27
673.29
675.27
677.06
692.15
746.11
773.22
850.06
850.06
865.24
884.10
884.19
910.28

blackavicea
403.15
blackberries
219.09
blackened
292.24
298.01
470.02
578.03
858.25
blacker
472.06
blackness
645.09
859.12
blacksmith
891.14
blades
356.07
blame
214.23
268.15
602.17
707.04
725.16
blamed
670.23
blameless
715.07
897.26
blames
118.25
215.17
blaming
376.23
blanche
317.08
317.10
320.05
322.12
322.23
323.11
344.03
344.28
345.02
346.13
352.28
355.10
379.26
386.27
387.05
387.24
389.19
507.16
624.26
794.07
blanched
066.19
742.15
blank
003.13
003.23
249.09
287.13
382.24
456.20
535.01
655.05
763.16
769.22
782.16
872.20
910.24
blanks
292.05
blasphemous
244.04
blasphemy
351.20
blast
003.17
575.21
712.21
804.17
blasted
065.11
blaze
076.09
231.24
296.10
394.12
778.26
blazed
622.23
631.02
blazing
113.17
bleached
540.22
bleak
004.06
blear
321.15
bleared
007.08
bled
009.24
019.12
428.01
bleeding
426.07
511.04

661.25
blended
145.19
221.04
blending
204.19
blends
276.16
blent
194.20
249.26
333.21
337.05
670.21
844.25
872.12
bless
107.22
107.26
140.22
195.28
442.27
457.11
651.06
857.05
861.03
864.27
876.22
897.22
blessed
118.25
482.15
blesses
310.20
blessing
033.17
781.22
blest
877.06
908.26
908.26
blew
189.11
302.26
478.16
479.26
520.03
559.25
572.01
575.21
630.28
blight
088.04
285.25
406.04
595.01
825.26
blighted
606.20
632.03
872.03
blights
439.24
blind
008.04
023.08
100.25
128.11
263.08
315.27
321.14
427.12
493.14
551.01
607.09
719.15
856.09
867.24
872.11
874.16
874.26
878.21
882.21
891.15
895.17
897.14
909.14
blinding
765.05
blindly
784.15
blindness
625.11
blinds
015.25
blink
119.22
bliss
397.10
405.07
406.01
518.10
551.01
552.11
563.18
568.16
643.17
731.27
775.22
847.21
901.14

blissful
521.20
545.15
583.13
661.23
blistered
833.02
blither
522.13
bloated
600.15
block
655.16
880.22
blocked
735.08
818.14
blocked-up
766.06
blockhead
388.05
625.23
blond
585.07
blonde
571.06
blood
010.15
018.05
105.27
144.11
257.06
276.15
317.03
348.16
351.15
406.05
420.01
421.12
421.23
422.06
423.10
424.17
426.13
427.23
429.03
439.09
576.21
588.21
592.08
611.22
623.07
631.15
634.10
651.14
730.08
759.28
781.05
781.18
832.24
861.01
866.06
866.28
902.01
blood-bleached
761.23
blood-red
561.13
blood-shot
578.08
bloodless
139.16
249.08
685.22
836.05
bloody
422.18
422.27
594.17
612.05
630.02
bloom
148.05
405.28
642.11
643.16
712.01
745.05
bloomed
331.11
373.07
502.20
737.18
blooming
461.16
523.10
606.11
667.12
858.13
blossom
278.05
642.14
812.16
blossom-blanched
433.05
blossomed
570.17
blossoms
148.12
blot
268.23

359.26
401.08
blotted
128.07
blow
008.13
008.27
019.12
043.16
355.22
410.02
410.02
425.27
425.27
506.25
594.23
601.11
757.17
860.26
blow-up
357.08
blowing
033.11
113.03
165.17
558.18
605.25
765.08
blown
559.21
blows
572.01
blubbering
043.21
blue
041.16
145.27
164.20
191.22
209.17
220.14
230.20
248.14
295.27
343.10
364.16
423.05
461.08
463.11
492.22
492.23
495.20
502.09
549.23
560.06
564.07
702.02
702.24
803.26
805.07
812.09
832.16
887.20
890.21
910.14
blue-eyed
891.12
blue-piled
531.13
bluebeard's
210.03
bluer
631.19
blunder
260.21
275.07
324.17
612.05
641.18
blunders
352.28
blunt
035.06
062.03
260.04
blunted
082.19
bluntly
019.04
693.21
754.12
blush
016.02
632.22
807.26
838.26
blushed
094.24
524.01
606.02
blushes
392.05
boadicea
496.24
board
082.12
091.21
547.19
616.17
boarding-school
694.13

694.14
boards
129.14
276.23
boast
502.11
565.23
624.24
boasted
039.07
boastful
564.18
boat
004.23
bobby
175.27
176.06
176.07
bodies
108.26
119.06
bodily
029.13
191.07
292.06
426.12
body
118.16
125.24
334.21
391.03
396.06
411.27
594.24
648.09
696.24
790.25
825.17
853.12
867.12
bog
675.04
692.16
799.28
boh
006.04
bohemian
204.17
boil
282.16
boiled
071.18
boiling
600.01
boils
004.02
bois
287.27
boisterous
510.28
boite
255.25
255.25
255.27
257.21
bold
148.01
311.27
395.09
856.26
857.25
bolder
068.02
865.04
boldly
023.05
boldness
756.26
boles
221.01
bolsters
328.02
bolt
295.09
295.20
309.26
310.15
596.04
604.13
610.28
bolted
309.17
456.25
488.18
683.17
bolting
309.19
bombazeen
677.02
bon
347.07
498.09
bonbons
281.06
bond
063.20
619.19
bondage
736.07
759.26

bonds	book-closet	botany	753.03	bounteous	866.06
013.13	100.05	345.27	756.16	114.03	brake
546.24	book-learned	both	757.05	bountiful	656.06
bone	681.03	008.06	770.17	896.19	branched
132.10	694.10	028.26	783.14	bounty	870.08
249.08	books	029.02	788.10	734.08	branches
555.19	009.07	031.05	798.18	738.16	168.25
655.17	039.10	033.22	798.26	bourne	207.09
909.02	078.24	040.09	804.19	021.15	494.05
909.02	080.22	041.02	806.10	302.25	503.27
bones	098.12	045.01	823.12	459.22	575.16
007.25	099.14	052.07	826.24	488.16	branchy
224.04	140.07	091.11	831.14	855.08	560.04
276.17	202.13	091.13	833.03	bow	brand
616.25	233.11	097.06	840.10	237.27	116.04
673.21	235.03	101.10	843.14	251.13	845.15
849.09	240.27	130.17	847.07	254.18	brands
bonfire	243.19	133.26	858.16	426.02	108.17
674.12	244.20	140.20	868.08	742.17	brass
bonne	342.27	156.07	876.13	bow-window	084.16
196.18	355.27	159.03	887.24	185.20	231.11
218.24	373.11	161.26	892.23	bowed	284.13
bonnet	391.19	172.09	901.10	126.28	678.19
032.16	527.19	173.21	904.04	237.23	694.05
048.09	677.19	175.19	905.11	248.25	694.07
072.02	701.10	179.08	911.05	367.17	697.07
087.19	713.04	190.20	911.11	381.15	brat
174.15	749.11	204.10	bother	699.14	256.27
181.15	766.26	204.12	256.05	780.26	469.01
218.15	779.16	214.07	bothwell	bowling	brats
226.18	811.13	230.17	358.20	541.20	536.24
289.16	909.20	231.07	358.27	bowstring	brave
394.06	bookshelves	264.02	bottle	368.10	761.06
396.03	009.13	266.02	431.17	box	brazen
406.23	boon	273.24	863.23	035.11	308.28
407.07	776.04	282.08	bottom	174.10	breach
458.04	845.15	286.12	081.06	234.18	388.25
459.13	boot	296.18	085.09	276.13	647.14
462.06	283.07	301.09	097.26	432.26	838.01
463.17	boot-toe	305.03	502.23	434.26	bread
534.09	564.14	315.10	520.14	492.12	050.14
539.15	boots	331.03	580.16	570.21	050.23
544.10	111.16	336.09	631.18	855.13	071.18
558.09	182.06	337.28	664.24	boxed	087.08
653.05	766.14	343.14	737.02	045.01	087.15
686.07	booty	345.12	bottomless	boxes	092.08
759.03	335.03	346.19	630.14	587.01	095.14
873.25	border	351.01	boudoir	798.16	095.14
bonnet-strings	097.10	351.02	204.10	boy	100.10
187.02	434.28	353.26	280.14	009.27	112.13
bonnets	474.11	359.10	285.28	055.21	112.25
798.06	529.23	368.17	331.10	063.12	113.25
bonny	bordered	377.16	365.24	175.23	117.23
272.11	087.26	383.20	boudoirs	439.02	118.28
549.06	502.25	387.09	391.20	469.14	119.04
bono	636.22	404.17	bough	522.07	128.06
763.12	712.08	410.09	050.25	865.10	130.15
bonte	bordering	419.22	boughs	910.26	137.20
277.18	434.07	425.08	433.05	boys	142.27
book	borders	430.13	514.25	098.05	149.02
003.12	005.22	446.20	560.02	386.21	335.02
003.18	102.03	455.17	560.19	721.19	355.26
009.04	148.05	461.21	561.07	brace	458.12
009.20	499.23	461.22	bought	630.22	513.02
031.06	bore	466.21	116.17	701.12	612.02
031.06	089.10	470.24	244.08	bracelet	654.14
031.09	127.17	472.22	544.19	248.03	661.06
032.10	302.24	492.07	661.06	248.10	661.11
049.03	423.18	500.02	boulogne	322.20	664.25
055.15	487.14	506.12	287.27	366.05	664.26
060.04	626.07	507.25	bound	bracelets	668.07
062.07	674.01	513.14	020.10	369.02	670.02
066.02	829.11	516.05	022.03	369.07	671.06
080.22	851.10	522.08	141.13	525.03	671.12
089.26	bored	539.01	160.06	bracing	671.14
090.04	244.19	545.13	169.23	018.06	682.15
090.18	born	552.18	182.20	bracken	682.18
101.18	197.19	558.23	184.19	712.18	685.26
140.14	405.08	560.21	228.11	brackish	686.01
187.23	476.10	564.14	240.28	161.01	686.12
341.16	477.24	565.05	468.27	brahma	688.01
366.25	484.04	565.10	598.08	125.28	693.04
366.27	511.15	578.14	601.13	braided	bread-nut
390.10	524.10	587.22	627.18	121.20	055.24
394.11	558.01	589.23	631.24	255.16	breadth
395.01	647.04	592.12	632.08	681.14	176.15
474.06	782.10	597.12	644.08	brain	224.13
474.08	borne	597.16	719.26	019.27	258.13
494.07	011.06	601.19	741.04	166.27	261.17
494.20	016.28	622.12	747.24	167.02	262.24
542.03	282.22	633.22	boundary	167.15	break
590.12	612.25	637.04	164.22	271.18	013.10
596.06	752.20	637.23	bounded	325.19	102.18
635.25	borrowed	639.27	124.06	346.17	136.03
677.15	163.25	662.01	145.07	351.15	173.05
678.16	440.18	677.01	209.10	395.21	242.03
700.28	521.11	679.01	367.02	404.23	284.08
702.22	525.27	681.08	384.23	579.10	407.14
710.04	612.03	681.09	781.26	586.01	452.08
752.21	872.25	685.01	875.04	640.25	466.02
768.12	bosom	687.16	bounding	826.26	484.16
769.25	033.18	705.11	222.20	876.10	528.08
796.11	369.01	712.02	277.10	889.28	584.03
801.11	377.03	712.13	332.26	890.04	598.01
845.01	480.11	713.01	boundless	brainless	619.11
book-case	507.13	718.10	320.13	286.16	630.20
002.27	549.07	724.28	816.12	brains	648.12
202.15	bosomed	726.02	bounds	004.18	654.16
book-cases	146.17	736.26	136.03	276.16	655.04
460.12	bosoms	743.20	735.24	311.17	718.01
	909.06	744.23		541.05	718.13

breakage
296.26
breakers
282.16
breakfast
006.03
048.07
050.14
051.21
071.14
081.15
082.25
083.13
087.06
094.01
118.02
198.11
200.10
202.10
305.14
326.06
327.08
435.20
474.03
522.16
562.20
586.06
610.21
702.20
800.28
853.18
860.10
866.11
867.15
breakfast-basons
148.27
breakfast-room
002.25
040.01
051.14
051.25
052.04
066.07
460.04
breakfast-table
820.18
885.12
breakfast-time
096.14
852.19
breakfasted
302.26
316.10
breaking
087.04
235.16
361.01
443.04
481.20
855.03
857.22
breaks
725.17
breast
045.08
172.26
266.12
318.16
375.11
468.07
513.19
573.23
606.19
611.17
656.03
659.19
662.25
754.10
756.18
881.13
breasting
568.01
breath
044.18
123.16
127.12
219.13
320.26
366.12
389.09
409.21
440.19
483.23
583.23
588.04
590.13
594.23
614.13
629.06
667.23
776.18
780.20
871.19
breathe
260.14
352.03
breathed
016.27
133.15
140.26
146.24
281.03

320.26
629.06
716.10
758.12
861.01
900.03
breathing
049.21
163.28
522.05
686.04
breathings
144.09
breathless
391.14
breeches'
277.23
breeches-pocket
543.06
breeze
066.09
248.13
302.26
333.02
522.05
660.26
712.22
812.07
813.05
899.16
breezy
732.02
811.01
brevity
703.03
brewing
700.26
briar
494.04
briar-rose
565.18
bridal
557.05
634.05
820.18
888.08
bridal-path
712.05
bride
367.16
373.12
402.22
455.17
499.16
512.16
512.17
512.17
512.18
515.13
515.15
571.03
605.20
609.10
624.22
758.02
bride's
454.03
625.25
653.02
bridegroom
373.25
506.12
587.14
bridesmaids
587.06
bridewell
370.07
bridge
033.15
bridle
227.07
227.13
227.28
463.03
bridle-path
672.17
brief
051.08
090.19
118.20
140.01
171.06
301.03
307.10
321.11
526.12
605.02
687.06
703.03
724.23
851.06
900.19
908.20
briefly
198.13
298.04
825.01
briggs
592.19
593.04
597.21

602.05
772.09
772.27
774.06
774.12
774.15
774.20
775.06
777.21
780.08
809.07
810.18
bright
034.24
090.23
137.11
139.14
145.12
145.26
147.28
191.20
204.08
209.02
215.24
221.10
224.08
225.04
240.14
331.04
335.21
341.04
414.05
440.01
457.07
492.18
512.01
544.23
551.21
565.17
564.08
566.02
685.06
701.06
740.18
750.11
751.26
753.14
781.22
794.27
825.04
832.16
886.26
brighten
109.07
427.15
brightening
220.12
855.16
brighter
144.18
314.01
643.28
brightest
200.20
292.12
brightly
030.18
100.15
brightness
128.12
331.08
brilliant
020.19
139.09
204.12
248.04
250.20
281.14
287.08
315.09
346.08
351.01
359.08
373.05
473.04
522.02
544.07
712.18
877.22
910.28
brilliantly
317.15
472.07
667.12
887.18
brilliantly-lit
347.28
brim
122.05
401.16
brimstone
057.23
844.21
brine
406.06
509.17
bring
024.12
047.08
137.07
137.19

232.20
253.02
320.11
327.05
363.01
391.15
429.27
448.14
481.21
483.13
499.16
571.08
615.23
683.11
755.20
845.03
873.23
885.14
bringing
118.07
226.02
358.05
431.06
533.18
545.07
559.23
586.13
908.06
brings
178.10
720.18
brink
315.06
brisk
352.07
bristled
395.05
bristling
282.15
370.03
bristly
051.11
british
003.19
277.23
279.20
460.13
790.06
790.07
855.20
brittle
649.26
broached
718.22
broad
076.03
085.23
087.26
149.06
149.10
185.11
191.19
194.10
204.06
237.04
237.15
349.28
407.02
471.13
471.14
511.02
556.05
579.04
630.01
659.06
735.08
765.13
370.27
884.10
broad-brimmed
394.06
broad-shouldered
891.14
broadest
729.19
brobdignag
031.21
brocaded
365.19
brocklebridge
112.20
159.18
brocklehurst
053.21
056.15
056.25
057.21
058.05
058.27
059.17
059.28
060.01
060.03
060.10
061.12
064.06
064.27
083.19
089.12
089.13
091.27

092.10
092.11
102.20
114.25
115.20
115.27
117.18
119.09
119.19
121.04
121.25
122.12
122.27
123.14
124.05
124.08
124.20
126.10
126.25
131.10
131.11
133.01
134.24
148.18
161.05
161.13
173.06
173.11
180.21
243.22
244.05
460.10
706.22
706.24
brocklehurst's
057.13
124.15
137.26
brocklehurst-hall
059.22
brocklehursts
126.05
broke
019.01
023.21
123.19
171.06
220.24
222.07
253.08
284.11
326.04
384.27
398.08
424.16
468.01
631.02
645.21
650.27
652.09
661.24
678.01
686.01
735.22
850.10
856.20
861.22
864.24
865.14
876.16
883.04
887.26
901.17
broken
004.23
005.02
017.09
029.24
033.15
045.24
130.11
132.11
147.03
224.03
257.23
282.20
286.21
288.10
294.06
347.21
364.19
495.26
500.01
560.15
590.09
591.07
596.18
617.14
651.12
662.01
671.24
717.05
730.12
868.02
bronze
193.16
231.06
794.19
899.18
brooch
236.14

340.26
585.08
brood
775.22
809.05
brooded
042.10
brooding
067.07
219.02
640.13
715.05
872.04
brook
105.07
105.11
253.06
570.14
brooklet
220.02
brother
021.20
180.02
252.08
252.10
252.15
253.12
275.20
386.18
451.02
595.17
624.02
624.11
626.01
626.08
627.20
632.13
633.25
680.27
685.09
686.11
699.08
704.26
708.17
724.28
725.21
726.14
727.05
742.25
780.10
781.08
786.04
786.07
787.02
806.10
821.07
821.23
822.12
839.27
841.21
842.01
brother's
473.18
726.07
781.02
911.10
brother-in-law's
600.24
brothers
036.24
216.17
242.22
242.23
469.05
780.05
786.01
brought
001.08
005.19
014.21
030.17
050.05
057.26
071.03
082.14
087.15
124.10
130.15
137.10
165.02
174.08
187.12
187.25
196.17
202.07
227.21
232.21
234.15
246.08
271.15
287.03
292.14
296.21
297.25
315.16
325.26
341.17
347.26
365.21
385.05
385.21

425.01	brushing	814.01	797.14	023.14	131.19
445.09	327.15	826.02	bushes	024.11	132.05
446.18	brusque	burn's	219.16	028.10	133.10
448.06	260.04	159.15	bushy	029.18	133.13
451.21	brutally	burned	052.28	029.25	135.02
466.23	784.14	544.20	busied	030.13	135.11
468.25	bubbling	burneth	174.04	030.24	137.03
470.23	105.06	844.21	449.16	032.22	138.08
562.10	buckles	burning	851.02	033.25	138.14
570.20	084.16	054.12	887.14	034.24	139.07
586.12	bud	057.23	busier	035.08	139.16
634.04	745.05	076.02	473.26	035.16	139.21
666.04	budding	141.21	busies	036.07	140.10
668.08	896.14	294.02	262.16	036.14	141.09
686.27	buds	295.22	busily	036.27	144.02
692.02	019.01	296.02	505.17	037.12	146.19
694.19	build	341.02	business	037.20	148.13
694.26	878.16	384.19	009.07	038.16	150.22
702.16	building	488.19	081.07	038.27	151.06
706.17	076.01	492.26	122.18	041.09	152.28
707.14	077.28	502.05	169.27	042.09	153.10
707.19	089.05	532.20	171.28	042.11	154.11
732.09	161.09	565.06	233.05	043.10	155.13
735.12	164.16	630.18	238.21	043.20	155.20
752.21	721.21	645.09	254.04	044.05	155.26
765.04	732.27	704.20	325.17	046.04	156.08
798.16	746.14	758.20	330.08	046.09	157.16
807.18	861.23	845.16	339.13	047.28	158.13
809.17	869.02	865.16	356.21	048.16	158.22
860.09	built	burning-glasses	378.28	048.25	159.12
862.13	091.28	124.25	379.16	050.05	159.20
862.22	197.05	burnished	399.13	051.08	160.05
874.15	bulk	457.07	453.21	051.17	160.14
882.19	602.08	burns	453.23	053.10	161.05
broughton	bulky	098.02	477.02	061.28	161.16
060.02	366.21	098.05	489.23	062.05	162.01
brow	bull	098.07	543.28	063.04	162.11
060.21	132.11	098.08	559.10	063.15	163.08
119.17	660.05	098.18	559.12	064.14	163.19
139.21	bullet	098.26	637.10	065.01	164.03
163.13	288.01	099.12	638.21	065.22	164.06
180.22	596.05	100.04	667.13	066.13	166.02
224.14	bullied	100.21	667.28	067.01	166.18
249.08	007.21	101.17	671.01	068.04	166.21
260.26	bulwark	101.27	682.13	068.12	167.17
284.27	797.10	103.13	700.07	068.24	169.10
345.18	bun	104.04	718.24	069.16	169.13
349.28	047.09	107.28	734.06	073.06	169.21
367.07	326.19	110.03	741.18	074.05	171.12
405.04	bunch	124.07	775.20	074.13	172.02
405.04	099.22	127.21	778.05	076.10	172.19
423.26	187.09	128.03	800.26	076.14	176.05
471.19	bunches	129.11	810.18	079.08	176.07
485.26	385.19	130.13	819.07	080.09	176.21
525.02	bundle	134.02	835.23	082.02	176.23
578.07	099.16	134.08	839.19	082.04	177.06
652.13	bungler	136.21	874.10	082.18	177.11
702.11	550.12	139.08	bust	082.24	177.15
733.09	bunglingly	149.28	248.16	083.21	177.19
738.02	036.26	150.15	318.06	084.04	178.06
756.16	buoy	153.01	322.18	085.06	178.10
767.10	398.24	153.12	345.13	087.04	179.21
775.23	buoyancy	480.04	bustle	088.03	182.13
799.23	342.22	burns's	204.28	088.07	182.24
813.06	buoyant	099.22	305.15	088.18	183.05
825.03	302.19	141.03	569.20	090.12	184.08
872.13	642.24	burnt	793.28	093.13	184.15
877.23	buoyed	026.19	bustled	093.25	184.18
902.18	379.13	078.06	187.16	094.23	184.27
903.20	burden	080.04	693.18	095.06	187.21
brow-beaten	301.15	081.28	bustling	095.15	188.01
018.15	301.21	082.20	328.27	096.03	188.19
brown	467.19	096.15	334.27	097.14	188.28
078.12	476.15	119.05	336.20	097.24	189.05
064.09	488.28	154.15	458.11	098.22	189.11
085.24	530.24	155.15	700.13	099.12	189.14
085.28	631.24	170.28	busy	102.05	190.01
088.04	663.24	305.20	123.04	102.11	190.07
095.14	858.19	385.03	172.16	102.20	190.10
112.13	burdened	457.08	215.07	102.24	192.04
144.15	108.23	562.07	256.12	102.28	192.06
219.20	270.24	599.09	326.12	103.15	193.20
277.05	475.15	674.10	327.11	104.03	194.15
306.22	572.21	676.19	364.03	105.22	195.09
382.24	635.04	735.13	398.15	106.24	195.22
395.05	burdens	835.27	470.27	107.02	196.09
442.26	481.15	861.18	569.19	107.04	196.21
659.22	burdensome	864.03	663.09	107.11	197.24
671.19	451.09	866.12	792.25	108.07	198.13
681.13	burgh	874.24	but	108.13	200.03
702.03	169.23	burst	001.06	108.24	200.26
891.14	burglar	043.15	002.09	109.12	201.22
brownie	611.11	063.20	003.09	109.25	201.26
884.22	buried	391.07	004.18	111.13	202.06
brows	021.16	405.13	006.02	113.17	202.14
052.28	054.19	433.27	006.15	114.03	205.05
531.28	147.20	485.22	007.03	115.03	205.14
587.16	429.14	619.18	007.10	116.21	205.19
646.09	511.27	623.14	007.15	117.19	205.21
browsed	561.15	652.09	007.23	118.09	205.27
219.19	632.07	745.28	009.19	118.28	206.03
brush	661.16	756.26	010.10	119.06	206.07
051.11	724.12	876.10	010.20	119.12	206.16
692.21	869.04	bursting	013.27	120.13	207.19
794.01	902.13	257.14	014.05	122.23	209.12
brushed	burn	423.03	014.16	123.22	210.13
172.08	033.25	811.28	015.01	125.16	211.03
174.14	100.15	bush	018.04	127.11	211.06
192.27	616.24	240.03	021.11	130.16	211.23
255.13	634.01	435.13	021.18	131.04	213.11
	747.06	675.25	021.27		213.20

214.13	299.10	388.04	478.24	559.02	637.07
215.06	299.25	388.28	479.12	559.07	637.11
215.14	300.05	392.02	479.15	560.22	638.14
216.15	301.01	393.05	480.19	561.08	639.08
217.06	301.14	395.14	481.17	561.18	640.01
217.18	301.18	396.26	481.27	562.22	640.22
217.24	302.10	397.01	483.21	563.01	640.25
217.26	302.17	398.22	483.28	564.01	641.15
219.11	302.19	399.17	484.07	564.20	642.14
220.12	302.25	399.18	484.09	564.24	642.17
220.15	305.09	399.26	484.19	565.05	642.23
220.19	305.12	400.23	485.14	565.11	644.18
221.07	306.16	401.10	487.02	565.19	644.19
221.23	307.21	401.20	487.05	565.23	644.28
223.03	308.08	403.17	488.12	566.09	646.10
223.06	308.11	403.28	489.21	566.11	646.12
223.16	308.12	404.04	491.12	567.12	646.16
224.05	308.18	405.03	491.17	568.15	649.04
224.11	310.01	405.16	491.23	569.10	649.22
224.17	310.13	405.21	493.10	571.17	650.21
224.19	310.18	406.01	493.13	571.25	651.01
224.26	312.09	406.10	493.19	572.02	651.12
225.04	312.16	406.12	493.28	572.11	651.16
225.10	312.27	406.21	494.03	573.03	651.22
227.01	314.06	406.22	494.28	573.16	652.12
227.10	314.20	407.12	495.07	573.22	652.20
227.13	315.13	407.18	495.19	574.06	652.24
231.21	317.01	407.22	496.01	574.10	653.17
232.02	318.03	408.05	496.04	574.16	653.23
235.08	318.23	408.09	497.11	574.21	654.19
237.16	319.08	408.16	497.13	574.25	654.25
238.09	319.16	412.02	498.24	576.07	655.11
239.02	319.20	414.12	499.17	576.14	655.15
239.21	319.22	416.06	499.24	577.14	656.22
240.06	319.27	416.24	499.27	577.17	657.06
241.01	320.05	417.26	500.04	579.04	658.13
243.15	324.14	418.05	502.11	579.07	659.13
245.20	325.18	420.04	502.13	580.10	659.18
246.03	326.12	420.13	503.03	581.11	660.25
246.14	327.13	423.02	503.07	581.21	662.07
247.20	327.28	424.06	503.17	582.01	662.27
247.21	329.28	424.08	503.24	583.13	663.13
249.09	330.03	427.04	504.28	583.15	663.17
249.24	330.05	427.07	505.15	583.16	663.20
250.13	330.17	428.01	505.18	584.06	665.11
251.05	332.02	428.11	506.24	586.05	665.24
251.23	332.20	428.23	506.25	586.07	666.28
252.06	333.10	429.08	507.14	586.17	667.28
252.07	333.16	430.05	508.08	586.24	668.05
253.06	338.08	431.13	509.04	587.07	668.13
253.17	339.07	431.24	510.17	587.09	669.24
255.08	341.24	431.28	512.19	590.13	670.03
258.08	342.12	432.20	515.09	591.02	670.03
258.25	342.28	432.23	516.15	591.11	670.19
259.18	343.21	435.26	516.16	591.13	671.01
261.01	343.28	436.15	518.07	592.02	671.16
261.13	344.11	436.20	518.23	592.08	671.18
261.22	344.16	437.05	519.05	593.20	671.24
263.15	345.02	438.11	519.12	594.24	672.05
263.21	345.15	438.23	520.02	596.11	672.24
265.04	345.24	439.02	521.15	596.23	673.27
265.27	346.06	439.06	521.17	597.20	673.28
266.12	346.15	439.15	522.13	599.19	674.03
266.23	347.02	440.18	522.19	600.02	674.14
267.21	347.23	440.20	523.07	601.11	674.16
268.19	348.14	440.23	523.16	603.16	674.19
269.13	350.03	441.09	525.25	603.23	674.24
269.24	351.18	441.18	527.15	604.15	674.27
269.27	352.18	444.13	527.26	604.24	675.01
270.09	353.03	445.16	528.06	606.25	675.07
270.23	354.02	446.08	528.08	607.03	675.28
272.14	354.28	447.16	528.14	607.24	676.20
274.06	355.08	448.02	529.17	609.06	679.11
275.03	355.23	448.08	530.01	609.13	679.19
275.14	357.17	448.17	530.10	609.16	679.24
275.22	358.23	448.20	530.13	610.04	679.26
276.02	359.11	448.28	530.23	611.03	680.13
276.23	359.27	451.11	531.19	611.19	680.21
277.27	360.06	452.01	532.11	611.20	682.18
278.03	361.09	453.06	535.05	612.01	682.24
278.04	362.05	453.17	535.23	613.20	683.09
280.07	362.28	454.09	536.14	614.24	683.16
280.12	363.08	454.20	537.04	616.09	683.26
282.02	365.07	456.15	537.19	616.16	683.27
282.17	366.16	456.20	538.05	617.22	684.01
283.19	370.16	457.18	539.07	617.26	684.03
284.13	371.19	457.22	540.09	619.07	684.08
284.24	372.26	458.20	541.16	619.13	685.17
285.14	373.04	459.05	542.14	619.26	685.21
285.22	373.06	459.26	542.23	619.28	687.08
286.05	373.13	460.17	543.07	620.08	687.11
287.06	374.26	461.03	543.09	620.19	687.22
288.04	376.02	461.09	544.15	620.27	689.05
288.15	376.04	461.18	545.06	621.10	689.15
288.20	376.21	466.06	545.22	621.14	690.24
289.12	377.04	467.07	547.22	621.22	691.20
289.27	377.10	468.02	547.23	621.22	691.23
290.01	377.21	468.17	548.14	624.23	692.09
290.12	378.05	468.26	548.23	625.24	692.25
290.18	381.02	469.02	549.01	626.09	693.24
291.09	381.06	469.21	549.02	626.11	693.27
291.14	381.20	470.21	549.20	628.08	694.13
291.28	381.26	472.03	550.01	628.12	694.24
292.24	382.06	472.18	550.05	628.28	695.06
294.05	382.07	472.19	550.11	630.12	696.18
294.22	382.12	472.21	551.05	633.15	696.24
295.04	384.08	474.03	553.07	634.06	696.27
295.24	384.22	475.01	554.03	634.21	697.03
296.13	385.27	475.26	554.05	635.11	697.12
297.08	386.02	476.25	554.22	635.24	697.26
297.20	386.26	478.20	557.11	636.10	698.02

698.04	772.15	848.07	butler's	099.03	229.26
698.28	772.24	848.15	364.13	101.16	230.05
699.02	773.01	849.03	butter	101.18	231.06
699.10	774.09	849.06	113.27	101.19	232.21
699.28	774.12	849.11	137.20	101.26	233.02
700.10	775.11	850.09	355.26	103.14	235.16
702.19	776.03	850.19	458.13	103.20	236.09
703.20	776.13	850.23	butterflies	109.23	237.02
704.18	777.05	851.08	143.05	112.17	237.06
704.25	777.13	851.12	button	113.02	238.08
705.04	778.19	851.17	126.26	113.10	240.25
705.19	779.16	853.09	buttoned	113.20	243.08
707.09	779.17	853.27	115.20	114.07	246.23
707.17	779.28	857.02	buxom	114.09	248.13
708.10	780.18	857.03	082.06	114.13	248.22
708.18	781.10	858.15	442.26	115.25	248.22
709.01	781.24	859.04	461.20	115.26	249.24
709.02	782.08	859.14	buy	117.28	250.08
709.15	783.05	860.08	048.19	118.14	252.24
709.16	785.05	860.12	405.07	118.18	254.17
712.01	786.13	861.13	544.09	118.28	255.23
713.02	787.28	862.15	buying	119.10	259.17
713.15	789.08	862.24	637.23	122.11	259.21
713.20	790.22	863.03	buys	124.12	260.05
715.03	792.08	863.06	092.11	126.04	264.23
715.15	792.18	863.13	buzzing	126.15	266.05
715.20	793.01	863.18	629.25	127.25	266.17
715.23	795.24	863.21	by	128.05	270.13
716.05	796.16	863.25	001.15	129.07	271.27
717.07	796.21	864.04	001.16	130.05	272.04
718.10	797.01	864.11	002.03	130.06	274.06
718.22	797.10	864.17	002.10	130.07	278.08
719.21	798.01	864.20	003.25	133.23	279.19
719.25	798.14	865.08	006.20	135.17	280.15
719.27	798.24	866.23	006.27	139.06	281.01
720.09	799.10	866.26	007.27	144.07	281.12
720.13	799.13	867.18	008.03	144.10	281.23
721.15	800.04	867.20	009.16	145.04	282.22
721.24	800.08	869.08	010.24	147.10	283.25
722.12	800.14	870.10	013.03	148.21	285.02
722.13	800.23	872.03	013.04	149.08	287.11
722.21	801.24	872.14	013.18	150.28	283.14
723.06	801.25	872.26	015.09	151.03	289.02
723.26	802.06	874.04	016.28	151.05	289.03
724.04	803.03	875.08	019.19	153.26	291.03
725.01	803.26	875.19	021.05	155.10	291.04
725.11	805.27	876.09	021.16	155.13	291.16
727.03	807.02	877.05	022.01	155.19	291.22
727.13	807.13	877.12	022.03	157.11	292.18
729.17	807.23	877.19	022.16	158.11	294.25
730.04	808.06	878.19	022.19	159.20	295.04
730.28	809.09	879.14	023.13	160.17	295.18
731.12	809.16	879.19	023.15	161.17	296.22
731.24	814.11	879.26	024.25	161.19	299.15
733.04	815.06	880.05	026.07	165.07	302.23
733.23	815.14	880.13	027.12	165.28	306.18
733.26	815.18	880.17	029.11	166.08	310.07
734.09	816.05	880.21	029.22	167.01	315.02
734.18	816.07	882.04	029.23	169.19	315.24
734.25	816.15	882.08	031.23	170.02	315.28
735.04	816.26	882.26	033.16	170.12	316.20
736.07	817.21	883.04	034.16	170.18	321.07
736.09	818.26	883.22	035.07	171.23	321.17
736.19	819.05	884.21	036.19	172.18	322.11
737.19	820.03	886.15	039.05	173.23	325.01
738.24	820.08	886.22	039.08	175.20	330.02
741.05	820.15	887.05	042.15	178.13	332.17
741.16	821.13	887.13	043.11	181.12	337.16
742.12	822.06	889.28	045.03	181.13	337.25
743.09	822.13	890.01	047.09	181.17	340.12
745.03	822.28	890.05	047.24	182.21	342.22
747.11	823.15	890.13	048.26	183.12	344.06
747.21	825.02	890.25	052.17	184.23	344.18
748.07	825.04	891.01	052.19	185.22	353.07
748.08	825.05	891.17	053.18	186.06	360.19
748.09	825.18	891.19	055.22	188.01	361.19
748.10	825.27	894.16	057.04	188.18	365.22
748.13	826.09	894.24	066.09	191.04	366.13
748.17	827.01	895.09	066.15	191.06	367.07
749.01	828.01	895.17	071.07	192.02	367.28
750.13	828.12	895.23	071.10	192.11	367.28
752.06	828.18	895.24	072.26	194.08	368.04
752.27	828.27	896.07	073.11	195.24	369.06
753.10	829.15	896.26	075.10	196.03	369.18
754.03	829.21	897.01	075.15	197.01	369.22
754.06	830.07	898.15	076.11	197.27	370.27
754.22	831.17	898.19	077.20	198.03	371.13
754.27	832.15	898.22	077.26	200.23	371.26
757.04	833.10	899.02	078.09	204.06	372.07
757.16	834.02	899.27	079.12	205.19	372.10
759.17	834.12	900.01	079.14	207.06	372.28
760.11	835.08	900.02	080.01	207.14	373.06
761.07	835.20	900.12	080.14	207.20	373.09
762.15	837.11	900.19	080.25	207.27	373.16
763.02	837.12	901.25	081.11	208.25	375.13
763.17	837.14	902.05	083.20	209.06	375.26
763.24	837.17	903.01	084.10	209.10	376.03
764.06	838.06	906.01	085.01	209.23	376.20
764.09	838.20	906.04	086.05	214.04	377.05
766.16	839.07	908.01	086.21	214.09	379.26
766.21	839.22	909.10	086.24	214.25	380.05
766.24	842.07	910.23	086.26	215.27	380.12
767.14	842.09	911.24	088.07	217.15	384.06
768.21	842.12	911.27	089.08	218.19	385.26
769.08	843.02	butcher	089.12	219.28	387.21
770.05	843.09	189.12	091.22	221.09	387.23
770.07	844.19	butler	094.17	221.25	388.21
771.07	845.22	045.22	096.03	223.01	389.27
771.18	846.05	180.06	097.05	223.15	392.21
771.21	846.20	860.23	098.04	226.03	392.24
771.26	848.06				394.11

399.01	585.17	728.01	by-and-by	268.12	912.07
402.01	587.09	729.12	027.18	280.11	912.16
402.06	587.19	738.23	336.01	298.15	callers
402.09	588.18	741.07	565.11	298.17	233.10
404.15	588.19	741.21	by-paths	299.04	488.21
405.20	589.07	744.20	673.12	322.23	calling
412.05	590.06	745.21	by-play	350.21	006.08
414.16	590.09	745.28	379.05	356.12	118.25
417.05	594.23	746.08	by-the-by	393.03	154.01
417.22	595.24	754.19	142.22	418.16	callous
418.04	597.04	756.14	211.24	434.10	628.09
418.12	599.02	756.21	257.04	438.28	calls
422.01	599.10	760.06	259.26	465.28	196.19
423.01	599.11	761.03	269.09	474.02	200.19
424.15	604.16	761.20	352.11	489.04	480.22
425.17	605.09	762.03	532.09	526.02	506.19
432.19	605.11	765.05	by-the-bye	532.16	659.16
433.11	610.03	770.04	281.22	535.19	695.08
435.06	611.05	770.17	796.10	570.16	695.08
436.10	612.04	770.26	885.13	581.07	720.11
436.21	616.23	771.04	bygone	581.08	858.18
438.15	619.10	775.25	458.27	617.03	calm
443.02	621.13	778.27	c'est	649.23	030.14
445.27	622.25	779.04	197.12	677.14	109.21
447.23	623.09	779.27	234.26	696.14	194.24
448.17	624.13	783.05	256.16	735.24	213.03
454.16	627.25	785.07	277.18	746.05	216.14
459.14	627.25	786.15	c'etait	807.12	218.11
459.15	627.26	787.17	334.08	811.17	220.21
460.23	629.17	789.02	cabinet	815.08	230.07
461.22	630.04	791.13	202.26	865.28	323.06
462.02	635.12	792.04	423.17	879.26	323.24
462.12	637.11	794.04	599.04	called	351.05
464.26	637.24	795.17	633.02	010.20	395.01
456.13	637.24	795.28	cachination	019.02	493.07
463.27	638.21	806.19	211.06	027.12	494.25
469.14	638.26	806.23	cadeau	037.20	499.08
470.20	639.09	807.10	234.21	051.20	568.14
471.22	639.11	810.05	239.10	054.23	568.15
473.15	641.13	810.12	240.01	067.05	588.08
474.17	641.15	811.20	240.17	075.16	604.15
475.26	641.17	812.05	cadeaux	080.15	620.25
477.25	641.21	813.10	239.13	081.06	716.08
478.20	642.19	815.22	cadence	086.21	716.09
478.24	643.07	816.21	032.27	091.13	745.04
480.28	647.07	817.06	cadet	092.18	745.09
483.25	647.11	817.11	906.10	092.21	759.02
484.06	647.14	819.15	caffre	092.22	793.04
484.26	647.16	819.17	797.14	098.04	797.16
485.20	647.23	819.24	cage	099.03	811.06
486.10	648.04	821.14	276.01	122.24	817.17
487.06	648.05	824.19	649.18	131.01	827.28
472.11	648.06	827.27	caged	134.10	844.25
475.26	648.19	827.28	372.07	134.24	890.15
495.26	651.03	829.02	cairngorm	152.12	907.15
496.12	655.07	829.17	461.15	155.18	calmed
496.14	658.06	830.03	cake	165.23	133.10
496.11	659.09	831.14	066.16	180.12	294.18
499.17	660.03	831.19	079.10	183.02	660.08
502.26	660.16	832.09	664.26	195.19	873.14
503.05	661.12	833.10	670.12	198.28	calmer
503.07	662.23	837.06	702.16	199.14	282.23
503.07	663.19	838.16	cakes	199.17	469.23
503.07	663.28	838.17	007.14	203.12	716.22
504.05	664.17	838.21	664.25	210.16	753.20
504.14	668.21	838.28	670.02	215.18	799.15
504.16	669.20	840.02	792.06	221.18	calming
510.20	673.12	842.26	795.14	245.17	417.05
511.16	676.06	844.14	calamity	254.06	calmly
514.21	676.19	845.19	859.23	279.11	156.05
515.06	682.07	847.05	861.19	287.11	463.02
520.15	683.14	847.06	867.11	287.19	486.07
521.16	685.27	848.04	calculated	300.09	497.24
522.15	687.01	850.06	061.04	324.15	592.02
523.09	688.05	857.06	218.01	327.25	593.04
526.16	690.13	857.14	287.01	331.22	605.07
526.24	692.14	858.21	316.28	347.19	619.05
527.19	692.17	858.21	349.06	364.17	699.16
528.01	693.03	859.13	376.04	365.08	829.28
529.07	694.07	859.13	489.09	367.15	837.14
531.16	695.03	861.02	704.01	375.14	calmness
534.06	696.07	862.11	755.20	383.20	570.04
534.27	698.22	863.23	804.19	384.07	calves
535.02	699.13	869.16	809.12	472.22	390.27
535.19	702.04	870.21	815.21	500.10	calvinistic
537.01	703.03	870.24	819.16	518.09	716.17
539.24	704.22	871.23	calculating	536.08	cambridge
541.22	704.24	872.01	776.16	559.10	828.13
544.01	705.05	872.25	calculations	570.19	831.02
545.01	705.27	873.17	820.16	585.16	846.02
545.09	706.07	873.18	calcutta	591.23	906.26
545.10	707.19	880.05	841.19	627.24	came
547.14	708.09	883.04	calibre	658.03	006.02
547.18	711.10	883.13	716.03	669.20	006.19
551.16	712.17	891.20	calico	695.10	007.26
552.23	712.17	892.24	087.20	696.01	008.09
552.27	712.18	897.09	116.18	697.24	010.23
553.11	712.18	897.15	caligula	708.10	016.16
554.08	714.02	898.20	010.04	715.23	023.23
554.17	714.18	901.05	call	770.27	024.15
558.17	716.14	901.08	027.23	773.10	024.19
559.21	716.22	902.27	028.10	803.09	028.26
562.07	717.14	905.14	055.06	810.22	032.27
563.02	718.03	905.15	062.22	816.04	033.28
563.22	719.26	908.03	066.27	832.06	050.05
564.04	721.24	908.15	091.05	847.18	050.11
564.06	724.21	909.24	091.19	855.14	050.18
568.20	725.23	910.05	105.24	863.19	060.26
569.21	727.06	910.23	174.11	865.19	061.24
571.14	727.16	911.13	177.04	895.06	067.02
579.19	727.23		177.10	909.18	068.06

072.06	639.05	227.04	746.13	299.22	481.13
075.01	650.28	227.21	748.24	306.01	515.08
078.03	662.27	228.09	754.11	307.20	517.10
079.07	665.15	240.05	756.11	344.06	536.16
096.14	666.25	245.05	771.18	394.09	537.24
109.03	668.19	246.02	772.12	416.18	538.05
110.01	680.06	246.04	775.04	420.20	563.21
115.24	690.24	252.01	775.11	421.08	563.22
123.13	693.22	263.14	782.06	421.13	566.17
126.03	707.01	263.17	793.17	423.12	573.13
127.13	707.15	265.03	785.02	426.18	577.15
133.14	721.17	270.03	787.03	578.19	580.06
133.22	733.17	271.01	787.05	578.22	580.08
133.28	738.27	272.28	787.13	582.07	590.18
148.19	746.16	274.04	791.03	674.15	591.04
152.25	766.02	274.12	792.08	676.18	595.06
154.16	767.17	275.14	799.27	677.17	608.11
156.13	769.06	284.04	802.02	682.08	609.15
156.16	769.22	298.17	804.16	765.10	612.22
160.18	776.02	312.15	816.19	768.13	613.10
163.09	789.18	316.21	816.20	844.05	614.14
167.19	795.03	322.09	816.07	848.26	617.02
167.25	807.02	327.04	818.24	candle-light	626.02
169.12	812.07	332.10	819.06	185.19	634.06
169.14	819.01	375.18	819.14	576.08	642.03
179.23	825.24	380.21	820.06	candles	648.14
185.18	851.02	385.28	820.06	078.06	649.18
186.20	852.26	386.26	820.15	100.16	652.22
189.12	864.02	387.06	820.18	236.25	672.20
189.20	865.12	397.23	820.21	341.03	672.23
197.01	867.15	401.01	822.07	350.25	673.01
197.21	869.15	405.05	822.15	369.23	673.05
198.09	871.13	405.08	826.15	562.09	677.13
198.23	875.03	409.07	826.15	798.24	679.13
199.09	876.02	410.16	828.11	874.13	683.01
199.11	884.02	427.25	828.19	874.15	685.12
200.06	886.05	432.04	831.06	882.01	694.15
200.13	886.10	442.15	835.01	candlestick	705.14
211.12	889.09	442.19	836.21	170.27	707.02
212.01	900.08	448.23	842.18	300.03	716.06
221.21	900.23	449.01	855.23	candour	724.08
222.20	902.09	449.22	855.28	267.19	726.16
227.24	910.09	451.23	856.27	625.21	733.12
229.04	camel-hair	463.06	857.07	cane	735.01
231.28	322.08	467.05	858.21	120.01	754.08
232.06	camels	469.10	858.22	canine	760.18
234.17	369.09	476.15	868.07	424.10	771.06
235.16	cameo	477.26	871.09	cankering	780.01
238.27	271.09	484.17	878.16	264.27	783.05
241.07	camp	494.15	881.25	757.28	784.06
241.17	379.19	504.09	882.03	808.19	785.22
243.19	385.18	505.05	883.19	cannily	785.26
255.11	camphor	508.21	883.27	430.12	785.27
286.06	154.15	512.27	887.09	cannnot	791.18
287.17	can	513.01	891.19	375.20	797.18
295.07	002.23	514.03	894.03	cannon-ball	801.22
314.18	023.11	517.08	895.05	630.02	805.09
317.12	029.12	524.08	896.01	cannot	817.06
319.15	034.07	524.14	896.13	004.27	821.14
320.05	035.14	528.23	900.21	024.24	821.24
330.27	036.02	528.24	902.10	025.03	821.24
332.22	036.10	530.11	902.13	036.14	823.03
335.15	036.14	532.06	908.27	038.18	823.07
361.25	037.12	535.20	910.23	041.09	826.10
376.02	044.24	541.01	can't	063.04	826.22
364.09	044.25	541.18	035.04	064.17	836.20
391.06	054.09	545.01	037.09	065.03	837.08
395.07	054.18	554.05	189.06	065.04	837.17
398.12	063.03	555.22	430.18	093.08	838.16
402.03	071.15	562.18	446.23	103.07	846.08
402.26	086.11	588.07	452.24	103.25	857.04
403.19	091.11	593.07	496.27	104.19	876.09
403.25	091.28	597.18	507.14	107.26	876.11
411.27	094.26	603.25	510.17	109.09	877.05
414.06	095.09	614.11	541.16	132.06	879.24
415.07	100.02	621.18	548.09	139.23	880.17
420.27	101.25	623.25	564.13	192.03	902.05
442.04	102.05	630.15	682.18	199.05	903.11
447.20	109.15	633.19	704.15	206.04	910.21
448.06	109.17	635.23	867.03	216.08	910.22
465.11	113.06	644.06	canadian	225.14	canoe
468.10	117.13	648.17	144.10	226.13	620.02
485.19	127.11	666.22	canary	226.28	canopied
490.19	128.10	667.24	470.20	245.11	066.21
503.22	131.09	670.20	candle	258.03	cant
514.24	135.09	674.16	026.19	265.04	214.14
518.28	137.19	679.07	029.08	270.14	canter
520.08	156.01	682.21	036.03	272.24	746.07
520.13	157.16	684.01	046.12	273.25	canvass
535.23	158.01	686.15	071.04	285.25	179.10
542.08	158.04	686.23	076.10	293.07	204.21
552.13	166.24	686.25	076.24	297.18	794.24
553.07	168.08	687.07	155.15	301.11	canzonette
562.06	171.11	689.04	170.27	308.18	201.03
563.08	178.13	690.18	171.04	312.26	cap
564.03	178.14	696.24	172.22	313.03	024.16
572.04	178.22	705.15	186.01	321.18	172.02
576.20	179.08	705.18	190.15	345.23	186.09
585.02	179.10	705.25	231.21	351.24	306.23
589.20	179.11	706.06	232.05	385.27	328.23
591.25	182.21	706.12	232.20	386.23	746.10
597.10	184.20	709.20	236.02	402.15	capable
598.11	197.22	709.22	245.13	405.10	046.28
607.13	198.20	709.27	293.10	408.02	262.09
608.06	198.20	718.08	294.01	416.12	617.11
608.12	198.20	720.08	295.22	417.13	capacities
608.13	199.20	720.14	297.10	434.19	161.26
613.19	205.12	724.11	297.16	436.11	capacity
629.25	223.10	726.17	297.21	437.05	020.14
635.17	223.28	729.17	297.25	437.06	047.21
638.22	226.12	736.08	299.01	437.24	173.23

743.20
817.16
825.09
825.17
cape
  003.28
  755.17
caper
  327.28
capital
  052.18
  361.04
  459.05
  635.27
caprice
  238.09
  312.21
  354.19
  643.12
  748.26
caprices
  824.23
capricious
  048.01
  527.14
  527.28
  549.27
caps
  764.05
captain
  720.21
  813.27
  911.06
  911.12
captious
  013.20
captivated
  172.18
captivating
  372.19
captive
  276.02
  649.21
car
  183.16
  183.25
  185.21
  254.26
  472.09
carcasses
  222.11
card
  174.10
  257.02
  775.06
card-board
  750.02
  763.15
cards
  379.25
  557.13
  865.07
care
  003.01
  008.26
  041.09
  056.06
  067.11
  067.26
  073.24
  093.11
  104.20
  122.22
  134.26
  151.01
  192.06
  201.26
  213.12
  266.25
  310.02
  332.17
  340.19
  351.25
  355.14
  359.20
  360.18
  395.13
  400.09
  412.15
  433.15
  433.25
  436.08
  449.05
  471.11
  475.03
  487.24
  492.13
  543.10
  551.23
  551.25
  582.22
  595.24
  600.10
  600.11
  648.01
  696.26
  767.12
  767.23
  782.08
  789.04
  819.01
  863.19
  880.19
  880.20
  880.21
  908.07
cared
  003.20
  632.04
career
  213.02
  734.21
  735.15
  762.05
  771.10
  797.25
  628.19
careful
  327.20
  104.22
  243.03
  377.25
  408.07
  471.28
  489.07
  536.08
  538.05
  579.11
  750.03
  755.05
carefully
  057.02
  201.14
  308.21
  322.08
  403.25
  418.01
  432.28
careless
  020.20
  051.01
  103.23
  116.25
  123.14
  192.13
  372.17
  435.27
  435.21
  702.04
  767.26
carelessness
  372.19
cares
  547.27
  775.21
  619.15
  908.02
caress
  251.05
  569.25
  737.16
caressed
  232.01
  523.09
  396.05
caresses
  555.10
  613.20
caressing
  740.21
careworn
  077.22
cargo
  335.10
carlo
  714.19
  733.06
  736.28
  737.16
  740.21
  740.21
  797.28
  798.08
carmine
  752.09
carolling
  441.15
carpet
  015.27
  076.12
  181.07
  203.18
  259.26
  298.02
  368.04
  418.26
  474.13
  498.20
  580.14
  701.15
  734.03
  791.27
carpeted
  191.23
carpets
  204.11
  327.16
  330.28
  794.17
  794.25
  799.01
carriage
  018.21
  030.05
  034.11
  034.18
  039.24
  050.03
  060.12
  086.10
  122.15
  182.08
  184.05
  280.02
  281.12
  281.18
  282.01
  433.07
  491.21
  492.10
  495.05
  496.21
  526.07
  538.14
  535.18
  539.08
  544.21
  549.10
  586.10
  586.22
  593.12
carriage-road
  049.27
carriage-step
  281.25
carriages
  050.04
  332.22
  337.28
carried
  023.13
  072.25
  073.04
  074.12
  147.03
  187.15
  199.10
  233.11
  336.14
  337.21
  365.24
  367.03
  407.18
  477.20
  561.25
  575.06
  612.24
  663.25
  770.24
  788.11
carrier
  174.11
  175.01
carries
  894.23
carrion-seeking
  424.20
carry
  056.13
  086.14
  100.03
  218.16
  311.04
  540.26
  571.05
  874.17
carrying
  076.17
  099.15
  159.08
  329.06
  759.24
carte
  794.07
carter
  232.23
  427.03
  427.23
  427.25
  428.26
  429.20
  430.16
  431.12
  432.07
  433.13
  433.21
  633.11
  867.21
carthage
  442.27
carton
  255.22
carved
  052.17
  193.18
  331.06
carvings
  207.09
cas
  389.05
case
  125.06
  193.17
  240.09
  245.04
  247.21
  250.10
  266.01
  287.20
  301.21
  339.05
  437.06
  438.22
  453.28
  470.25
  507.24
  537.07
  623.25
  635.03
  644.02
  679.07
  685.02
  784.13
  785.04
  796.02
  801.27
  802.24
  819.03
  821.11
  828.22
  338.02
  842.22
  857.03
  898.25
casement
  050.13
  286.05
  381.03
  414.07
  502.15
  631.01
  640.06
  709.13
  852.09
casements
  207.06
  711.17
  859.26
cases
  082.24
  536.18
cash
  455.05
  546.12
cashmeres
  280.02
  547.16
casket
  369.01
  888.06
cast
  054.26
  108.12
  226.01
  267.22
  283.13
  364.20
  368.17
  381.12
  451.07
  451.27
  626.15
  650.24
  654.28
  671.15
  727.23
cast-off
  597.02
castaway
  125.15
  839.06
caste
  038.15
  285.17
  325.13
  509.20
  911.22
casting
  405.18
castle
  210.04
  235.15
castled
  765.12
casts
  503.05
casually
  780.16
cat
  012.13
  043.23
  176.27
  186.13
  188.23
  419.13
  677.06
catalogue
  168.27
cataract-like
  520.05
catastrophe
  400.06
  707.07
catch
  099.12
  153.23
  227.13
  441.18
  575.14
  856.14
  856.06
catching
  266.11
  812.11
catechising
  746.18
catechism
  114.07
cathedral
  770.20
catherine
  117.14
catholic
  278.07
  489.06
cats
  031.28
cattle
  143.05
  219.19
  660.02
caught
  028.28
  040.26
  115.08
  116.13
  123.26
  204.07
  227.28
  229.16
  231.15
  244.12
  259.13
  307.23
  329.23
  337.14
  383.13
  409.21
  611.04
  636.08
  654.07
  763.18
  785.21
  804.02
  906.20
cause
  063.22
  111.21
  146.14
  205.17
  311.25
  324.19
  559.02
  793.20
  793.24
  811.03
  823.05
caused
  467.21
  516.02
  867.11
causes
  255.02
causeway
  220.01
  221.05
  222.20
  229.07
  242.05
  665.04
causewayed
  219.17
caution
  285.17
cautious
  416.27
  436.24
  589.15
cavalcade
  333.07
cavalier
  285.02
cavaliers
  332.24
cave
  540.14
  542.22
cavillers
  002.20
cawed
  522.12
cawing
  194.05
  194.26
  856.20
cease
  388.05
  469.06
  495.27
  715.12
  818.06
  847.02
  879.02
  885.06
ceased
  075.04
  144.05
  150.15
  210.09
  292.03
  372.04
  418.18
  422.23
  572.14
  664.11
  736.18
ceaseless
  003.15
  020.03
  030.12
  373.26
  375.07
  569.20
  661.28
  883.24
ceases
  404.11
ceiled
  204.12
ceiling
  023.10
  074.16
  181.13
  193.17
  200.16
  203.20
  355.27
  599.11
  652.03
cela
  234.20
  277.19
  277.22
  334.08
celebrated
  045.11
celerity
  239.01
celestial
  527.06
celine
  276.22
  279.10
  279.12
  280.11
  281.15
  284.28
  286.22
  287.07
  287.22
  547.15
  547.17
  636.27
  637.27
celine's
  286.09
cell
  491.05
  633.04
  633.26
  653.05
  865.19
  902.22
cellar
  791.24
cells
  230.19
  422.26
censure
  412.17
censures
  268.13
cent
  049.01
central
  094.25
  819.26
centre
  015.24
  114.18
  209.19
  280.09
  560.14
  644.11
  652.02
  736.02
centuries
  004.12
century's
  264.21
ceremony
  096.04
  163.11
  236.06
  367.11
  456.28
  547.09
  588.19

591.07	649.02	chalk	165.18	206.13	charm
808.01	713.13	280.06	172.17	213.17	032.05
820.17	774.10	321.27	174.24	214.22	182.23
cerises	809.13	323.13	192.02	215.11	219.05
313.18	852.07	challenge	218.23	237.08	374.12
certain	ces	605.06	228.19	243.05	497.01
003.21	201.18	chamber	235.28	249.12	497.05
016.20	341.21	015.15	236.03	274.21	502.09
030.17	cessation	016.27	259.07	289.21	536.12
032.14	075.12	022.23	293.21	301.13	617.17
059.04	087.03	029.05	331.21	311.18	620.01
068.05	235.06	136.07	336.25	312.17	642.12
081.08	cetera	163.17	349.06	366.21	659.16
133.08	569.22	190.26	357.12	373.23	699.26
143.11	chafed	191.20	365.05	377.14	712.02
198.06	131.26	193.06	453.07	407.23	715.21
221.17	410.09	210.13	453.08	407.25	737.24
223.06	chagrin	290.05	476.19	491.07	793.01
246.04	404.18	294.16	485.09	507.27	796.20
256.14	chain	296.08	543.07	528.07	799.05
259.07	165.25	300.02	558.22	528.11	808.04
308.18	370.05	305.16	602.04	553.21	814.20
351.28	524.27	306.17	605.15	619.04	832.13
365.17	549.05	329.11	615.09	623.18	891.03
365.28	599.11	364.10	647.08	627.09	charmed
462.09	757.18	421.04	647.09	632.18	178.19
464.27	779.24	433.03	671.27	641.07	277.22
497.12	chained	442.13	689.11	644.20	434.19
509.26	842.12	464.10	731.07	668.02	714.01
521.04	887.11	519.28	739.28	671.04	744.23
524.16	chair	557.09	740.01	675.15	793.27
543.26	008.10	563.06	768.26	687.03	charmer
547.03	008.19	611.06	819.10	748.06	285.01
554.04	027.02	612.28	872.04	771.20	charmers
555.17	027.25	653.16	changeable	803.15	529.02
560.08	081.03	690.02	808.15	824.21	charming
565.16	097.15	729.07	changed	855.07	383.24
579.11	155.15	791.24	075.05	909.13	400.12
603.21	186.27	850.17	155.27	characteristic	597.17
621.21	189.24	851.04	207.05	139.27	746.16
623.20	200.12	858.27	233.14	characteristically	charms
624.16	218.19	864.01	406.18	437.18	169.24
638.01	230.09	864.08	441.23	characteristics	625.05
641.26	256.22	chamber-ceiling	441.24	869.16	731.22
660.20	256.27	415.09	460.17	characterized	759.11
693.27	258.01	chamber-door	467.09	291.17	800.21
700.02	258.04	294.08	481.05	characters	charnel
706.10	258.21	295.01	481.28	141.12	272.21
755.25	259.03	415.19	500.03	370.15	charred
764.10	262.21	chamber-maid	615.09	720.26	561.02
771.15	280.26	286.09	735.20	744.14	charter
775.21	286.07	chambers	736.05	744.14	546.25
785.05	306.18	015.21	746.25	810.20	547.04
795.14	340.18	190.09	769.02	811.25	charwoman
806.19	369.21	206.27	848.04	charade	328.28
808.03	385.06	327.28	changeful	370.08	329.23
810.15	386.03	331.04	251.20	371.16	330.10
827.10	390.11	335.07	343.18	charades	330.17
832.13	394.04	335.14	715.16	365.06	charwomen
838.15	404.05	337.23	changeling	charge	329.21
840.23	409.19	413.05	555.10	034.16	chase
842.21	458.26	447.02	885.16	132.28	582.22
843.12	466.24	chambre	changent	312.04	chasm
848.06	535.08	334.07	334.01	340.05	660.25
857.05	572.05	chambres	changes	353.13	chasms
862.09	601.15	334.06	162.13	404.17	405.14
863.17	611.06	chance	254.19	572.21	chasseed
879.13	613.03	015.17	519.02	589.23	277.12
881.08	646.11	068.26	664.10	599.24	chastened
883.08	666.25	105.14	674.02	616.09	139.04
889.01	680.10	322.25	795.24	632.19	chastisement
902.23	685.18	326.12	808.23	855.14	043.09
906.13	692.14	331.17	changing	charged	360.26
certainement	693.15	336.11	056.11	027.20	464.18
197.15	693.17	372.10	847.17	122.21	chastisements
certainly	717.26	386.20	channel	135.08	900.10
008.27	754.03	397.08	282.19	214.11	chastiser
021.12	757.02	403.23	320.07	307.04	103.12
106.07	783.06	550.27	511.01	469.01	chastising
107.15	791.27	642.19	570.15	568.11	403.05
215.25	862.04	643.08	855.21	615.24	chat
273.15	880.08	659.08	chanted	647.19	256.17
275.04	886.15	668.16	082.27	745.15	chatter
318.04	chair-back	745.17	chaos	charges	388.05
339.22	352.21	747.21	101.08	142.04	470.19
356.24	chairs	769.01	152.23	charitable	741.27
400.23	016.03	809.19	167.18	120.09	chattered
452.12	049.12	chanced	334.28	126.12	072.28
461.03	049.18	005.18	794.05	241.09	chattering
476.09	080.21	279.04	chapter	257.12	198.16
544.10	203.17	294.14	098.11	706.18	347.21
558.15	207.11	328.20	181.02	charity	chatters
582.03	365.10	385.01	354.08	660.18	352.22
593.04	366.14	477.23	545.23	707.27	cheat
662.07	371.10	807.09	843.22	708.24	570.24
671.02	371.15	chancel	844.27	770.22	cheated
690.06	399.21	021.04	845.07	770.24	597.25
691.09	676.18	589.18	chapters	charity-children	cheats
725.15	701.05	chances	081.10	091.08	696.18
740.11	729.04	775.13	114.08	091.19	check
748.27	751.27	chandelier	160.05	charity-school	083.22
757.08	794.13	074.15	character	091.07	218.01
778.11	chaise	263.12	056.17	charivari	306.22
796.21	163.12	change	064.07	355.27	325.23
877.04	433.13	039.13	108.12	charlatan	328.17
878.26	434.01	039.20	125.03	431.11	441.17
891.17	868.04	042.06	163.07	charles	555.23
898.08	868.05	056.05	171.10	098.14	627.12
certainty	869.19	096.06	173.22	105.19	810.18
043.01	873.23	097.06	205.22	105.25	871.22
417.20		107.01	205.23		

checked	838.24	060.08	112.05	choachman	789.02
301.19	cherished	062.16	113.21	587.02	792.06
361.17	032.02	065.03	120.15	chocolate	800.13
564.19	214.18	066.24	124.22	281.08	christmas-time
596.12	279.11	067.19	125.11	choice	317.23
763.24	302.02	068.11	140.22	190.12	chronicles
825.28	606.10	076.23	168.21	243.01	055.17
875.14	727.15	077.15	199.18	264.03	074.23
cheek	775.28	116.05	214.10	346.22	chuckled
030.02	859.27	123.19	256.23	376.21	453.03
043.03	cherishes	124.11	261.11	377.20	545.28
077.13	837.27	125.26	353.11	400.04	church
100.07	cherishing	134.19	391.18	514.21	021.14
139.15	020.17	152.07	444.18	544.11	022.21
140.27	046.24	153.22	451.11	664.01	086.15
141.23	320.17	178.04	468.22	709.23	111.13
156.07	709.11	189.20	721.17	732.07	112.21
371.24	830.10	195.28	722.23	739.19	112.22
484.24	cherries	197.04	746.16	805.26	114.07
517.26	143.07	213.09	781.01	897.07	185.11
523.14	cherry	237.25	children's	choicest	190.22
544.19	192.19	284.17	004.18	019.01	194.21
555.12	382.22	288.11	119.05	choked	196.06
565.06	434.27	347.18	161.01	130.18	209.08
563.03	504.01	425.22	childs	choler	219.04
594.18	cherry-tree	444.18	356.05	237.09	233.15
601.05	050.12	445.14	chill	choose	474.15
611.20	050.25	446.20	016.12	043.27	477.21
623.07	cherub-like	458.02	065.07	068.20	479.02
646.03	749.14	458.09	072.27	285.08	479.06
651.05	cherubs'	467.18	145.16	322.07	490.13
720.06	207.09	467.26	181.17	326.11	491.02
738.05	chest	468.17	190.23	339.15	526.11
745.20	132.13	481.22	324.11	526.08	567.22
746.12	136.25	483.19	417.20	543.27	586.14
746.23	224.13	484.01	539.02	636.03	586.17
767.10	262.24	490.11	606.12	782.09	586.24
798.07	272.15	506.09	672.26	797.24	588.17
896.09	729.08	507.19	chilled	846.15	593.17
cheeks	741.02	551.20	294.12	897.10	596.07
007.09	815.24	572.22	492.25	897.11	598.10
016.22	chested	575.06	572.05	choosing	605.03
092.22	237.15	575.17	798.13	372.17	664.08
192.16	chestnut	576.02	chilling	chopping	698.08
395.07	510.10	597.16	290.27	792.06	716.04
568.23	514.26	606.16	674.28	chord	732.27
597.06	518.26	616.14	802.14	883.01	860.04
855.14	560.12	618.13	chilly	chords	871.06
cheer	749.28	618.14	001.12	661.25	905.05
045.12	896.12	661.04	167.02	chose	906.05
432.06	chests	699.22	204.22	149.04	church-aisle
597.06	207.08	747.15	459.21	150.08	859.12
610.01	cheviot	748.22	852.09	323.01	church-floor
883.03	765.14	781.02	chime	371.17	594.22
cheered	chez	797.23	569.16	411.02	church-like
427.13	334.04	863.05	664.08	636.26	089.09
883.03	chicken	900.14	chimed	653.23	church-militant
cheerful	295.02	907.27	386.24	661.14	720.01
034.02	335.01	child's	chimera	chosen	church-spire
067.08	336.07	060.05	682.05	020.08	668.25
154.07	chickens	136.17	chimeras	059.13	church-yard
156.07	048.16	child-like	328.14	149.12	029.06
212.27	905.18	343.08	chimney	200.25	646.17
231.16	chidden	739.09	015.12	365.23	668.26
333.27	127.23	749.07	198.24	366.23	churchyard
552.05	chidings	childer	chimney-corner	788.09	004.28
550.13	301.15	680.08	386.03	814.16	159.18
714.23	chief	680.28	394.05	816.10	588.03
860.24	666.12	696.25	562.08	839.07	770.19
862.11	824.16	697.24	chimney-piece	894.28	cicatrized
887.16	chiefest	childhood	017.06	912.07	881.21
cheerfully	616.07	124.28	173.24	christ	ciel
137.03	chiefly	135.16	chimneys	107.19	256.16
413.09	253.22	201.28	172.19	423.22	cigar
cheerfulness	315.03	213.19	220.15	911.27	280.27
323.17	319.14	218.09	328.03	christendom	281.02
cheerily	492.16	221.14	859.07	297.11	502.14
561.02	chiffone	childhood's	chin	christened	503.13
cheering	343.13	465.21	060.21	175.27	cigar-case
113.14	chiffonieres	childish	098.07	779.12	548.28
292.12	240.29	090.15	237.10	christian	cinder
798.15	chilblains	639.06	344.14	058.06	385.03
817.02	111.19	childless	344.17	059.01	cinders
850.06	child	482.17	394.08	125.27	677.24
cheeringly	002.22	childlike	395.07	531.17	cinq
443.04	003.22	002.12	461.17	697.09	334.10
cheerless	014.02	children	471.22	715.10	circle
190.25	020.20	002.17	701.26	720.16	083.25
cheers	022.04	009.11	715.13	725.17	625.06
876.12	022.20	020.08	738.08	747.03	819.26
cheese	024.24	020.23	767.15	762.15	844.02
037.08	028.22	021.24	china	797.08	circled
037.15	033.06	024.26	030.18	816.02	277.06
092.08	033.10	027.14	045.23	825.14	502.26
117.24	033.14	029.12	137.11	829.10	898.20
119.04	033.18	036.14	458.12	830.07	circles
149.03	033.22	037.25	701.10	832.09	473.12
311.06	039.19	038.12	799.01	906.12	636.03
671.12	040.12	042.14	chink	christian's	circlet
cheese-cake	041.08	054.18	261.26	851.13	030.27
047.10	044.22	058.20	286.05	christianity	343.20
cheesecakes	045.06	061.01	chintz	761.23	524.28
328.06	051.01	064.11	191.22	christians	circumstance
chemises	053.15	071.15	chips	107.11	012.03
116.19	054.04	081.05	434.22	118.24	117.13
chere	054.20		chirruped	441.04	117.20
216.25	054.21		050.12	christmas	118.01
cherish	057.14		chisel	045.10	171.21
150.15	057.20		119.16	317.12	211.04
499.28	058.26		chiselled	605.22	295.24
515.16	059.09		767.08	769.14	326.07

338.05
401.07
445.01
664.01
909.15
circumstances
150.19
167.06
230.11
268.16
269.14
270.08
274.01
293.03
372.22
396.28
397.01
405.05
428.11
452.02
558.24
623.18
669.20
720.19
779.23
812.02
819.10
826.18
829.23
854.11
897.06
cities
526.17
city
199.07
199.07
717.13
845.02
city-night
281.14
civil
196.12
551.21
589.12
civilities
188.04
257.02
civility
028.12
665.15
civilized
107.11
793.04
civilly
666.05
clad
064.17
367.05
526.01
692.13
737.14
claim
240.06
264.19
265.24
288.13
477.26
508.19
539.21
613.26
666.24
668.21
704.08
706.09
706.10
761.11
815.17
817.23
879.14
claimants
112.12
claimed
228.20
354.13
532.08
639.28
845.15
848.12
910.02
claiming
511.19
claims
405.26
843.03
clammy
465.01
clamorous
210.11
clamorously
240.01
clamour
064.02
101.13
clamoured
647.21
clang
253.16
clanked
370.05
clap
493.09

clapped
073.28
683.16
781.25
840.13
clara
637.03
637.07
637.27
clashed
185.17
clasp
366.05
465.15
525.03
clasped
158.15
224.10
877.07
clasping
887.26
clasps
658.16
class
080.26
080.26
081.05
081.26
085.16
086.19
092.28
094.17
096.20
097.14
097.24
099.13
104.24
120.27
129.19
142.18
162.09
206.16
355.02
376.27
classes
079.13
080.16
081.14
085.05
086.21
147.03
789.19
807.23
classic
701.25
808.14
clatter
220.27
clattering
222.17
223.14
495.06
claws
881.10
clay
649.24
685.15
clean
056.06
099.01
117.10
117.17
169.28
193.02
199.09
200.01
266.22
288.19
327.12
329.01
429.27
457.04
521.17
628.28
676.14
676.21
685.06
692.15
692.26
694.27
701.04
733.27
751.23
791.22
791.24
794.02
cleaned
098.25
327.02
cleaning
905.07
cleanly-attired
667.17
780.11
cleansed
527.01
clear
003.08
033.12
047.28
066.27
086.09

133.04
136.13
153.11
168.13
220.09
220.26
235.13
250.19
258.14
284.27
318.08
343.01
373.28
404.10
457.08
500.06
501.14
528.06
573.15
602.06
631.20
664.16
697.13
703.24
754.26
785.10
795.09
799.23
803.11
810.27
812.11
817.18
818.15
819.23
821.06
851.14
cleared
136.12
142.06
187.22
324.17
602.16
604.12
615.08
clearer
253.17
403.17
900.01
clearest
128.09
322.07
662.11
clearing
049.22
clearly
020.05
086.11
109.16
248.09
253.06
265.20
286.12
566.17
676.13
719.14
clearness
738.03
clears
911.20
cleft
471.23
clement
360.25
clenched
369.25
620.03
clergy
777.25
clergyman
040.19
092.16
125.12
162.20
196.04
586.15
589.20
590.11
590.20
595.09
595.18
604.06
669.04
669.14
695.21
706.15
777.25
780.05
826.20
911.09
clergyman's
669.05
751.19
780.11
clerk
180.15
586.15
589.03
590.21
596.07
905.04

clever
060.27
093.14
178.12
197.10
205.27
346.06
356.07
679.11
749.02
750.28
892.05
click
449.13
click-click
677.27
client
596.19
603.05
cliffs
501.08
climate
430.20
804.20
838.08
climates
629.22
climax
009.26
140.11
683.18
778.17
climbed
183.25
215.01
575.13
clime
631.27
731.14
737.21
cling
109.13
289.03
793.19
clinging
416.25
clings
275.17
838.24
cloak
087.20
113.08
181.15
218.15
224.10
226.17
229.08
237.12
281.21
298.23
299.12
366.26
394.06
407.11
430.18
430.22
565.04
616.14
766.03
766.11
777.09
778.27
800.05
cloaked
282.02
cloaks
286.12
clock
083.24
086.26
181.20
193.17
231.02
294.07
331.06
337.18
380.10
519.18
555.05
562.14
569.17
676.17
677.25
681.15
729.05
769.22
clock-working
474.24
clod-hopping
431.01
clogged
664.07
close
003.05
033.05
061.26
076.18
088.21
089.24
100.27
113.01

113.09
152.28
155.04
155.10
157.02
169.16
221.25
249.01
255.16
281.12
295.15
382.28
390.02
392.13
399.16
445.15
477.03
485.17
498.20
510.06
519.07
563.07
567.01
573.09
578.22
580.24
596.05
641.21
684.07
718.26
737.08
769.08
774.02
786.11
815.27
815.27
862.08
878.16
884.21
908.19
909.17
912.10
close-ranked
870.06
closed
010.12
025.17
027.26
032.09
045.26
051.17
098.12
119.15
153.25
230.16
231.19
245.21
282.13
286.04
310.21
314.10
377.26
392.27
420.27
421.08
433.09
434.04
476.03
607.11
636.04
654.19
668.05
700.27
702.22
738.26
741.18
765.06
789.04
801.12
855.12
873.11
879.07
closely
030.24
104.25
120.17
198.05
209.03
373.24
379.07
727.14
754.14
754.21
793.15
closely-printed
090.24
closer
158.15
289.03
382.03
406.23
748.23
879.20
895.17
closeset
276.28
closet
042.15
071.04
558.06
558.12

576.11
576.15
closing
050.26
174.22
333.28
492.03
cloth
016.01
086.04
474.12
clothe
121.18
clothed
600.04
clothes
009.12
037.28
038.12
047.12
071.07
092.12
092.24
117.01
155.12
415.23
467.16
541.01
688.09
690.14
692.24
899.13
clothing
111.15
161.03
161.11
599.20
722.01
cloths
791.26
cloud
003.14
004.25
026.16
124.18
152.21
220.12
230.21
248.22
249.13
296.05
415.04
492.24
519.06
541.06
561.16
563.07
652.10
737.07
747.15
852.06
882.02
909.22
cloud-high
276.03
clouded
712.24
clouding
910.16
cloudless
492.21
clouds
001.08
033.12
133.23
172.19
221.04
247.24
248.25
435.16
500.06
502.04
551.21
560.04
562.25
583.04
629.28
652.04
348.17
cloudy
570.18
612.26
cloven
560.14
clump
675.14
clumsily-contrived
703.11
clung
073.23
575.17
583.23
661.02
712.02
712.10
895.16
clustered
002.02
085.28
136.19
676.07

856.19	coffee-cups	835.01	592.11	348.02	750.05
clusters	336.16	866.29	702.03	349.09	752.16
340.13	coffin	869.16	colours	362.02	760.19
clutch	016.28	877.02	178.26	380.21	766.21
650.04	148.12	883.23	247.23	381.18	767.19
clutched	477.20	895.10	column	386.05	769.08
136.04	490.27	colder	115.16	387.09	769.25
co	673.22	017.19	797.11	387.18	770.27
124.05	coffin-dust	112.22	821.01	388.18	783.13
co-operate	112.22	821.01	columnar	393.03	792.14
759.14	coffre	coldest	870.17	403.18	799.16
co-operation	704.25	509.19	columns	412.24	799.19
822.02	cognizant	coldly	583.06	415.13	807.02
coach	494.23	131.19	comb	415.18	810.11
071.10	coherently	254.16	692.21	419.07	815.01
073.08	135.15	412.03	884.19	419.10	815.02
073.18	coiffer	coldness	combats	426.05	815.06
074.10	334.07	119.14	615.11	426.06	844.08
074.25	coiled	187.19	combed	427.09	848.09
075.19	875.01	267.17	058.17	429.08	849.17
075.21	coils	373.21	084.08	430.16	849.25
164.28	285.04	389.16	460.25	432.17	853.02
174.14	coin	420.05	combination	434.13	861.07
180.20	375.22	516.05	703.28	439.25	873.15
182.03	574.04	537.01	739.25	440.05	873.21
199.12	661.08	833.07	combinations	452.09	876.03
656.28	666.06	colds	274.28	453.18	876.26
653.06	783.02	146.28	combine	455.22	877.27
653.09	coincided	collar	161.20	457.11	878.17
707.13	713.07	460.25	246.17	457.22	880.14
852.14	788.10	collared	397.08	463.09	883.16
852.17	coincidence	224.10	combined	464.14	886.02
854.15	903.02	collect	078.16	470.02	886.09
855.01	coined	078.21	253.02	473.22	887.02
855.13	234.07	081.07	426.13	479.16	892.13
coach-door	cold	collected	444.04	482.14	901.03
075.13	001.07	457.17	738.10	487.08	907.04
coach-house	004.15	481.08	combustion	490.10	911.06
598.13	004.24	592.08	334.21	490.13	911.28
coachman	021.06	619.03	come	494.20	912.24
073.20	044.19	767.06	006.25	494.22	912.25
175.26	046.19	collectedly	015.07	495.06	comer
446.09	080.06	602.02	015.11	501.06	050.08
452.16	080.13	collecting	024.06	504.19	361.15
656.03	088.22	105.02	028.20	507.01	384.07
855.15	096.14	collective	033.23	510.06	684.17
coachmen	111.18	335.22	034.03	510.11	comes
334.22	112.22	343.02	035.15	511.02	093.03
coadjutor	112.25	college	036.07	511.15	105.08
822.12	149.02	177.03	041.20	515.04	196.18
857.19	156.07	624.21	047.07	515.07	271.21
coal	156.07	698.18	053.25	515.12	346.19
305.02	167.22	911.09	054.16	515.12	403.16
305.05	186.24	colloquize	062.23	517.24	409.14
398.09	187.05	497.22	066.28	517.24	488.09
coals	191.06	colloquy	067.05	522.17	495.15
792.01	218.06	542.15	067.14	523.04	506.28
coarse	218.11	colonel	068.08	528.15	559.17
051.10	219.27	316.15	077.07	535.18	652.22
084.24	299.12	343.21	091.04	537.28	681.18
087.19	302.08	348.07	102.01	540.04	701.27
313.01	302.09	350.17	102.02	542.06	843.07
355.22	306.05	352.07	108.24	542.11	cometh
369.19	335.01	359.02	110.05	542.16	846.14
626.23	362.17	366.13	115.03	548.23	comfits
740.11	383.02	367.14	121.27	551.27	281.08
coarse-minded	394.17	367.15	122.14	558.03	comfort
267.17	395.25	369.13	123.20	563.10	022.26
coarsely	396.09	370.07	130.16	563.11	033.14
287.06	396.12	371.16	134.02	564.22	118.15
coarsely-clad	417.19	378.26	135.27	564.24	161.21
750.07	418.23	385.13	144.04	568.11	186.15
coarseness	430.20	385.24	153.23	576.06	408.09
528.05	442.11	388.13	156.10	576.09	412.09
730.27	470.16	389.02	158.10	580.20	412.10
coast	478.17	411.07	168.10	585.06	483.26
003.28	485.26	416.12	176.06	597.22	496.13
004.24	490.12	colossal	179.06	593.09	520.10
797.15	509.15	249.04	184.20	605.23	548.26
coasted	518.15	colour	186.24	607.17	570.06
857.11	523.06	016.02	188.24	610.24	580.12
coasting	540.26	041.11	195.12	611.07	626.20
629.28	570.18	139.20	197.09	611.13	632.09
coat	572.23	221.27	208.22	618.20	718.14
287.16	576.21	268.11	217.09	619.08	755.15
369.28	588.23	307.07	225.21	638.14	793.04
421.06	605.20	313.28	227.14	639.20	879.22
coax	606.16	351.07	227.23	649.27	896.23
112.10	612.28	371.04	230.24	650.02	902.22
551.04	coaxing	521.10	232.04	650.03	908.08
coaxing	417.22	568.02	232.23	650.14	comfortable
417.22	cobwebs	674.04	233.05	652.06	076.14
cobwebs	434.20	704.28	240.22	655.28	158.20
434.20	cochere	755.13	242.24	656.28	184.02
cochere	282.05	761.12	254.10	662.04	258.04
282.05	coerce	colour-box	255.19	663.01	266.25
coerce	829.09	733.14	256.21	679.27	540.28
829.09	coercion	colour-boxes	272.11	682.11	701.04
coercion	547.04	713.26	282.18	684.21	882.11
547.04	coffee	coloured	285.01	693.12	894.07
coffee	095.13	087.20	285.28	698.26	894.08
095.13	095.15	737.27	310.12	699.18	comfortably
095.15	100.10	813.05	311.02	700.17	149.11
100.10	112.15	colouring	317.26	708.02	182.01
112.15	130.15	712.16	320.20	725.25	218.18
130.15	326.05	750.04	324.04	733.11	comforted
326.05	347.26	754.26	324.08	739.03	069.28
347.26	352.05	colourless	336.21	739.27	690.23
352.05	coffee-cup	349.27	338.22	741.09	comforter
coffee-cup	352.14	461.02	339.05	741.19	527.01
352.14	832.16		339.17	742.02	650.15

655.27
comforting
269.28
comfortless
518.16
coming
001.13
017.27
023.17
031.01
039.03
073.08
074.20
101.20
115.03
116.02
130.14
151.04
155.02
221.06
221.22
232.18
288.24
305.07
311.10
314.14
326.26
332.14
358.14
398.04
416.15
432.17
432.28
435.24
495.03
498.17
503.17
522.08
550.25
555.21
562.19
563.20
689.16
746.04
750.16
763.25
797.26
797.26
849.24
862.26
873.05
902.06
command
049.16
078.26
245.10
265.21
266.06
358.08
362.23
508.11
827.23
850.16
857.20
commanded
360.28
847.19
commanding
417.23
825.03
commands
360.16
comme
277.19
277.22
313.16
313.17
334.08
commence
043.21
142.19
327.08
456.24
487.20
558.23
652.22
718.03
723.07
commenced
086.19
096.02
198.16
200.16
340.09
359.07
361.06
539.23
579.24
691.05
713.15
commencement
097.22
189.19
661.21
805.23
commencing
770.05
commendations
097.19
commended
238.23
comment
491.23
691.08
799.08
853.28
commentary
821.05
commented
121.02
850.05
commission
226.28
625.12
commissioned
132.23
196.15
commissions
169.06
commit
019.07
102.24
439.05
484.08
committed
213.12
451.20
773.22
776.21
793.13
841.25
committee
161.13
173.06
173.17
178.28
244.18
committing
462.11
838.13
commodious
733.28
common
079.06
085.01
086.06
184.27
320.14
352.01
354.07
379.20
384.04
385.17
447.06
474.07
475.14
495.07
497.14
542.18
626.15
698.10
837.05
863.21
common-place
222.12
269.16
306.26
376.20
424.22
793.18
884.04
common-places
461.27
common-sense
554.27
commotion
334.18
795.11
875.08
communicate
534.03
825.21
905.12
communicated
109.04
712.16
832.13
903.03
907.11
communicates
106.11
communicating
402.11
496.03
772.09
783.25
communication
165.07
285.19
488.19
760.27
802.05
communications
040.18
473.14
communicative
262.19
263.10
291.11
474.26
communion
398.18
511.03
512.01
813.07
communion-rails
589.14
community
560.17
compact
598.01
companion
100.23
162.19
170.26
188.25
243.03
286.15
330.19
514.18
527.22
548.11
618.10
618.13
618.16
646.19
811.01
811.18
878.28
908.14
companionable
046.05
companionless
329.13
companions
142.10
154.06
447.17
526.28
companionship
101.18
445.23
636.26
662.06
company
001.07
046.03
046.03
047.05
125.19
189.26
251.10
255.04
263.13
327.22
331.15
338.28
392.25
399.20
412.27
442.19
459.08
474.20
477.07
539.22
566.08
616.22
642.07
741.17
777.11
878.18
909.08
comparative
084.02
146.25
235.05
389.04
861.08
comparatively
047.02
291.09
377.21
692.07
714.11
818.15
compare
322.27
602.05
698.03
compared
067.06
202.22
209.16
313.23
323.13
350.14
383.02
722.14
790.11
855.04
comparing
677.19
comparison
526.18
compartment
077.26
077.27
compartments
773.25
compassion
161.21
707.26
708.23
compassionate
041.08
687.18
762.07
compel
488.03
547.08
684.05
826.01
compels
227.25
compensate
312.17
compensation
751.20
competency
171.11
482.16
788.13
competent
213.08
814.08
competitor
360.07
competitors
625.13
complacent
263.27
complacently
020.23
complain
329.27
804.24
complaint
150.27
complaints
476.02
488.06
complement
816.03
complete
018.04
039.13
079.23
086.08
172.17
186.15
263.02
280.01
306.11
416.07
425.12
524.09
557.06
567.17
615.01
626.01
779.27
794.26
820.16
completed
315.26
323.10
330.27
562.11
completely
142.06
286.28
646.05
704.04
833.08
completer
341.22
completing
752.06
811.13
complexion
047.28
077.21
086.09
175.12
318.07
368.16
370.22
382.28
437.22
complexioned
681.08
compliance
845.26
compliant
488.10
complicated
822.08
complied
769.28
860.12
complimenting
370.12
comply
647.21
complying
530.11
composed
044.19
094.24
155.26
394.19
416.15
470.08
505.19
620.17
749.02
780.21
783.08
811.05
843.10
composes
294.19
composure
308.22
495.02
compound
025.09
compounding
792.06
comprehend
090.16
103.09
152.15
273.28
484.17
506.07
523.23
559.06
712.12
722.21
743.05
767.14
775.11
782.14
784.04
791.23
802.22
comprehended
796.25
797.02
823.21
comprehension
153.11
307.14
444.12
713.14
comprehensive
169.01
comprends-tu
256.09
compressed
404.26
716.12
740.11
compressing
827.20
comprised
098.13
111.03
645.13
779.15
compromising
706.12
comrade
149.12
561.09
825.08
comrade's
827.03
con
360.15
conceal
123.06
341.28
351.23
408.15
494.28
558.12
615.24
632.24
747.02
concealed
131.20
369.18
420.16
421.03
717.05
725.03
concealing
616.12
concealment
425.04
425.06
626.12
conceited
837.09
conceive
172.07
214.12
439.04
499.28
853.01
conceived
186.17
211.16
247.22
373.17
482.09
644.10
753.22
conceives
404.23
conceiving
021.11
313.22
842.18
concentrate
348.20
384.05
concentrated
532.23
887.07
concentre
004.13
conception
006.15
concern
133.17
241.09
298.12
392.07
462.27
681.28
concerned
725.06
827.02
concerning
061.11
152.16
772.15
809.10
concession
529.18
conciliate
836.01
concisely
705.09
concluded
163.20
298.14
541.09
569.16
681.07
840.10
conclusion
039.17
126.25
403.03
661.13
905.02
conclusions
267.25
720.27
concord
909.13
condemn
216.25
645.24
condemnatory
376.15
condemned
018.16
128.05
216.09
684.08
condemning
042.16
condense
671.08
condensed
716.13
818.16
condescension
196.25
265.01
condiments
377.19
condition
025.01
041.13
054.25
065.13
124.13
130.19
173.19
256.07
591.08
632.05
722.02
conditionally
821.28
conditions
547.06
condoled
238.20
condolence
488.21
condor
415.02
conducing
797.06
conducive
554.10
conduct
012.15
065.15
107.20
177.16
331.15
474.27
483.26
488.25
555.01
555.20
607.10
632.21

647.11	285.16	376.17	780.12	consist	630.22
767.03	663.20	657.04	869.09	094.04	701.09
771.25	736.13	784.17	901.25	consisted	containing
conducted	760.12	conning	consequences	045.15	060.06
122.13	803.10	078.14	102.25	145.09	061.08
173.21	conform	conquered	422.13	consistency	089.06
186.27	120.08	528.21	439.07	058.27	202.15
256.08	120.13	531.01	632.17	058.28	653.04
293.07	conformity	725.03	732.20	059.01	729.04
334.16	059.10	conqueror	consequent	249.13	contains
908.04	205.07	649.21	357.04	consistent	131.02
conducting	376.24	conqueror's	consequently	264.15	733.13
122.16	624.21	064.28	090.01	523.26	contaminate
909.27	confound	conquerors	162.22	528.09	126.19
conductor	257.01	797.09	379.20	642.20	contamination
185.05	confounded	803.05	770.15	822.05	268.23
conductress	307.05	conquest	775.11	consisting	629.01
815.08	794.03	375.16	780.25	095.13	contemplate
confabulate	confronted	473.08	785.22	117.23	268.11
352.10	395.08	528.23	840.27	consists	786.15
confabulation	confronting	815.28	909.06	592.03	contemplating
306.07	378.20	845.10	conservatory	889.24	602.25
confer	confronts	conscience	019.02	consolation	833.23
756.28	353.07	132.01	280.21	083.15	contemplation
conference	confused	261.13	367.27	755.18	136.17
042.03	026.09	268.22	consider	879.23	256.17
823.19	084.01	405.22	186.02	consolations	contemporary
conferences	187.27	405.26	196.10	119.02	312.12
291.06	217.28	440.12	239.26	consolatory	contempt
378.17	236.07	610.02	326.11	022.28	020.18
555.03	383.17	616.07	354.06	716.16	116.11
conferred	607.13	647.18	400.20	console	594.25
546.26	783.24	650.15	400.25	882.18	625.16
706.08	807.16	700.05	466.15	consoled	628.11
confess	confusedly	725.14	506.17	631.09	contenance
173.08	416.06	785.10	546.08	consoles	548.27
270.15	confusion	785.13	613.24	240.27	contend
402.27	100.18	832.25	614.19	consort	736.10
527.20	101.13	conscience-keeper	647.24	378.17	803.10
552.05	337.13	272.10	649.15	consorting	contended
593.03	416.10	conscientious	649.15	531.17	848.16
774.08	505.20	214.16	697.10	conspicuous	contending
confessed	794.03	717.01	724.13	141.12	286.24
858.28	congealed	831.06	762.05	261.17	content
889.01	066.14	conscientiously	775.19	641.17	163.05
confesses	220.02	427.25	783.14	constancy	183.28
753.26	602.12	664.03	785.01	518.18	191.17
confession	congenial	683.09	785.10	527.27	214.07
551.04	289.23	conscientiousness	790.13	793.20	347.24
confidant	congeniality	105.21	821.16	827.03	438.27
269.21	711.11	conscious	821.18	constant	456.16
285.09	congratulate	012.07	826.16	097.28	459.07
confide	323.20	309.02	considerable	675.01	472.12
157.23	congratulation	665.25	085.20	818.05	574.10
858.05	535.05	685.07	184.24	898.21	642.04
confided	congratulations	788.05	194.01	constantly	715.09
858.21	598.19	consciousness	224.12	042.18	724.08
confidence	congregation	001.16	319.20	724.08	724.11
240.04	078.07	307.08	367.19	consternation	730.19
263.09	conjecture	308.02	421.03	019.26	734.14
290.21	023.11	374.28	554.12	766.05	793.09
357.06	089.03	572.17	754.20	constitute	880.15
399.16	234.14	578.24	760.03	888.25	895.25
530.19	253.22	608.07	795.24	constitution	898.05
530.20	312.27	668.21	830.15	060.25	contented
530.22	589.05	759.02	869.03	241.14	002.16
559.19	771.26	789.11	considerably	486.09	136.16
568.18	862.13	790.15	704.01	632.18	202.21
606.20	conjectured	820.22	888.13	804.18	582.04
653.14	235.06	882.18	considerate	constraint	contentedly
660.09	674.16	consecrated	190.12	275.17	745.12
706.10	809.10	280.15	considerateness	constricted	contentment
748.02	conjectures	717.26	285.16	486.11	290.15
754.09	325.21	821.14	consideration	constricting	437.15
761.02	328.19	consecrating	290.20	127.12	724.17
761.20	conjugal	280.17	475.16	constriction	contents
802.22	601.22	consecration	744.21	741.03	016.19
909.11	conjured	017.02	considerations	construe	090.20
909.12	641.19	712.14	822.09	140.15	096.11
confidences	connaught	consent	considered	construed	112.15
644.22	508.26	266.27	021.24	417.09	170.08
confidential	509.25	379.04	031.10	consult	171.06
473.02	connected	488.10	034.27	335.15	234.18
confidentially	004.20	541.13	040.21	387.22	246.02
336.15	037.28	546.23	069.16	395.28	255.06
confine	059.03	546.27	076.25	consultation	257.21
203.04	102.26	650.21	103.13	371.19	326.10
216.22	188.18	768.20	202.19	consulted	365.19
617.15	256.25	788.08	205.18	085.19	367.03
651.26	379.07	820.08	253.33	367.14	411.17
confined	722.03	826.08	317.18	consulting	787.15
172.25	801.15	consented	354.04	677.20	contes
254.13	connection	048.27	376.21	consumed	543.19
confinement	089.22	173.09	378.13	747.13	contest
862.08	160.11	333.17	408.18	826.03	601.08
confines	182.19	358.25	479.05	consumption	continent
459.17	196.09	448.22	534.14	150.27	197.19
confining	488.07	541.14	552.23	150.28	324.06
189.16	632.07	694.26	620.12	contact	384.22
confirm	632.24	836.08	634.28	396.13	489.02
404.19	704.04	840.24	637.04	798.06	634.17
confirmation	779.26	consenting	665.06	contagion	773.26
442.10	801.27	044.16	735.19	147.18	continual
confirmed	connections	consequence	751.10	contain	162.17
151.05	161.14	206.08	857.23	775.22	467.23
789.12	571.09	252.26	considering	contained	476.19
conflagration	connexion	260.09	603.11	002.26	615.11
311.16	629.03	260.12	691.22	015.19	779.07
859.13	911.11	365.02	considers	134.06	continually
conflict	connexions	414.04	403.10	248.11	007.24
067.10	374.06	569.09	719.24	438.09	098.01
				558.13	

105.01
141.22
157.15
257.02
303.01
345.20
352.02
375.10
468.26
469.26
757.09
760.15
802.14
826.01
840.09
863.01
continue
  134.19
  274.19
  547.18
  719.06
  821.08
  821.23
continued
  006.07
  055.10
  057.27
  062.11
  062.19
  090.09
  094.13
  097.27
  104.19
  117.09
  130.03
  130.21
  147.04
  148.13
  182.14
  176.10
  178.12
  187.12
  188.22
  195.26
  199.25
  211.21
  211.27
  227.24
  234.11
  245.22
  256.05
  256.23
  272.18
  301.22
  515.20
  360.04
  371.05
  373.17
  385.16
  397.28
  399.14
  422.02
  470.11
  489.01
  506.17
  508.13
  532.03
  536.14
  555.04
  572.14
  572.15
  581.01
  592.01
  596.09
  598.03
  612.17
  626.05
  626.26
  644.03
  667.25
  680.13
  696.20
  700.07
  704.26
  734.23
  741.10
  743.02
  754.21
  755.10
  761.21
  765.03
  807.04
  814.26
  815.12
  842.16
  845.18
  862.03
  869.17
  903.11
  909.14
continuing
  284.17
continuous
  504.19
  401.24
  560.03
continuously
  001.03
  216.03
contort
  595.22

contorted
  620.04
contour
  461.17
  471.16
  577.08
  737.15
  871.27
contracted
  181.17
  818.11
contradict
  484.03
  724.16
contradicted
  403.22
contradiction
  757.18
contradictory
  626.28
contrary
  053.17
  090.12
  109.08
  192.14
  196.23
  206.06
  238.10
  267.16
  284.24
  309.17
  325.02
  407.07
  417.28
  533.05
  577.05
  654.24
  733.21
  785.05
  792.25
  796.04
  880.23
contrast
  204.15
  226.03
  250.09
  287.15
  323.14
  383.03
  634.20
  681.26
  833.09
  891.10
contrasted
  318.19
  350.17
  501.13
contrasting
  186.01
contrasts
  641.12
  726.22
contravened
  724.14
contribute
  472.26
  908.08
contrived
  036.20
  046.23
  114.02
  307.23
  417.23
  688.08
  831.08
control
  044.17
  061.01
  349.18
  425.22
  494.25
  619.24
  621.12
  734.24
  813.26
controlled
  716.13
  807.10
  817.16
  837.13
controlling
  139.06
  275.17
controvert
  594.02
contumacy
  339.05
contumelious
  373.18
convenience
  182.06
  529.11
  648.12
convenient
  103.17
  161.09
  262.14
conveniently
  508.21
convent
  243.27

  489.23
  490.04
  491.05
convent-like
  089.03
conventional
  266.28
  275.24
  440.11
  761.01
conventionalities
  513.12
  879.08
conventionally
  259.17
conversation
  029.01
  045.25
  056.13
  061.13
  083.13
  090.11
  116.04
  138.25
  205.27
  211.26
  217.18
  272.24
  286.27
  320.06
  330.22
  341.10
  352.07
  379.13
  380.28
  383.14
  390.11
  411.05
  422.20
  459.12
  470.11
  473.02
  474.20
  477.07
  539.21
  549.16
  625.03
  626.20
  681.23
  750.22
  787.11
  842.22
  881.01
  883.05
conversational
  337.09
conversations
  473.10
converse
  109.25
  125.21
  150.10
  189.06
  285.24
  711.06
conversed
  094.15
  140.04
  180.16
  643.01
conversing
  197.28
  335.19
  338.14
  349.12
  832.05
converting
  770.04
convey
  182.09
  792.08
conveyance
  180.23
  183.13
  184.03
  863.03
conveyed
  153.07
  336.10
  456.19
  464.10
  507.27
  632.26
  719.08
conveying
  678.19
conviction
  027.03
  124.06
  178.08
  274.25
  311.24
  638.08
  831.09
  877.25
convince
  745.01
  833.08
convinced
  090.19
  377.06
  515.27

  634.23
  662.19
  838.06
  848.07
convolvuli
  030.19
convulsion
  745.27
  761.15
convulsions
  287.25
convulsive
  409.19
  594.08
  601.17
convulsively
  511.10
cooing
  699.24
cook
  068.15
  310.27
  311.12
  328.07
  334.20
  717.19
  794.02
cook's
  305.17
cooked
  094.06
cooking
  599.13
  905.07
cool
  214.06
  244.02
  254.17
  270.11
  372.21
  456.20
  502.02
  521.16
  522.19
  527.13
  532.07
  547.26
  594.25
  623.03
  748.16
  767.06
  829.06
  834.09
  840.05
cooled
  533.06
cooler
  753.20
  902.16
coolly
  069.21
  598.14
  665.22
  703.13
  710.01
  760.11
  766.12
  820.16
coolness
  306.28
  462.09
copied
  597.16
  758.05
copies
  247.04
copse
  655.06
copy
  173.27
  593.17
copying
  128.07
  749.25
coquetry
  276.15
  533.02
coquettish
  748.07
coral
  219.10
  758.06
cord
  090.13
  256.12
  511.02
  601.13
corded
  073.05
  174.10
  557.08
  888.07
cordial
  291.25
  431.10
  745.01
cordiality
  020.24
  291.04
  802.16
  830.04

cordially
  030.27
  643.16
core
  285.06
  550.22
  568.15
  612.14
  812.18
cormorant
  248.01
corn-field
  606.01
corn-fields
  031.27
  664.13
corner
  097.12
  129.06
  240.24
  255.28
  317.27
  361.18
  457.10
  464.27
  467.13
  539.26
  589.05
  677.25
  680.10
  693.19
corners
  048.24
  403.14
cornice
  575.05
coronet
  571.15
corporeal
  886.14
corpse
  155.22
  248.07
  485.28
  646.17
  877.02
corpse-like
  421.17
corpses
  606.12
corpulent
  601.07
correct
  047.26
  086.11
  100.02
  135.13
  172.07
  178.06
  273.06
  291.24
  313.03
  408.06
  589.05
  732.07
  754.26
  808.14
corrected
  064.11
  292.27
  908.11
correcting
  264.18
correctness
  198.07
correspondence
  809.06
  907.16
correspondent
  602.23
corresponding
  082.12
  204.03
  510.27
corridor
  024.16
  210.03
  215.21
  419.15
corroborate
  142.01
corroded
  638.17
corroding
  065.20
corrupt
  291.13
  832.07
corruptible
  108.26
corruption
  043.12
corsair-song
  360.13
corsairs
  360.14
coruscating
  720.06
cost
  270.27
  742.05

  803.05
costly
  121.20
  122.08
  570.25
costume
  084.17
  368.08
  370.10
costumed
  346.04
  368.05
costumes
  165.10
cottage
  036.13
  142.21
  151.17
  462.05
  672.06
  709.02
  721.21
  729.03
  732.12
  733.23
  733.27
  748.05
  791.15
  809.03
  892.12
cottagers'
  722.23
couch
  191.15
  237.01
  239.02
  246.10
  296.22
  302.17
  445.08
  480.12
  661.14
couches
  204.15
cough
  088.15
  089.23
  133.16
coughed
  133.16
  136.23
coughing
  156.23
  156.21
could
  002.10
  003.22
  004.05
  008.12
  018.16
  019.23
  020.02
  020.11
  021.18
  021.27
  022.05
  028.06
  030.14
  031.02
  033.25
  034.11
  038.07
  039.09
  039.09
  039.10
  039.11
  041.18
  041.20
  043.17
  046.28
  048.22
  052.06
  054.22
  056.13
  057.10
  057.14
  058.25
  066.04
  071.16
  077.12
  080.06
  087.07
  089.02
  089.27
  090.15
  094.08
  097.17
  099.01
  099.07
  099.08
  101.01
  103.03
  103.06
  103.09
  103.11
  105.18
  105.21
  106.02
  118.03
  120.27
  121.01

121.04
123.02
123.16
123.21
130.08
133.20
133.13
136.03
140.19
144.12
148.26
149.18
150.06
150.18
156.04
156.14
158.17
158.22
161.15
166.02
167.14
170.17
172.25
173.20
174.19
174.20
175.06
177.03
178.20
179.05
179.06
179.26
184.26
186.03
186.17
192.15
192.24
197.21
198.01
202.16
206.27
209.14
210.14
211.15
215.16
217.07
217.17
220.04
220.16
220.19
221.15
222.11
222.26
223.03
224.06
225.01
230.16
232.03
234.04
234.06
235.25
238.07
239.24
242.10
244.09
248.05
248.06
248.17
250.19
253.06
253.16
262.08
270.22
277.04
278.04
283.10
286.04
286.23
287.06
289.04
290.01
292.14
293.11
295.05
296.15
298.10
302.11
302.25
305.16
312.10
315.09
318.27
321.09
323.14
325.24
330.13
331.05
332.18
335.08
336.18
338.15
341.10
342.01
346.23
349.17
350.20
353.19
358.25
364.09
369.11
370.22

370.27
372.02
372.12
372.25
372.28
374.11
377.01
377.03
377.26
383.04
383.14
395.03
397.04
397.11
409.10
412.01
412.11
412.17
412.19
415.01
415.03
415.06
419.12
423.02
424.14
425.25
425.28
426.02
426.26
427.13
427.27
428.11
428.21
429.11
435.06
437.01
447.12
449.18
452.02
454.28
460.12
460.28
462.23
465.18
468.23
470.13
470.14
475.24
473.10
479.14
479.16
479.23
482.26
483.08
483.24
483.27
484.09
484.14
487.06
487.15
491.24
493.22
498.04
499.18
500.05
502.27
503.02
504.21
505.15
510.20
511.11
516.07
516.25
519.02
519.04
519.12
521.04
521.14
522.19
522.21
523.23
532.16
533.26
536.05
537.26
545.08
550.16
554.23
556.06
557.17
559.05
560.18
561.01
562.12
562.23
563.13
564.19
565.01
565.18
566.11
568.08
568.08
571.08
572.07
572.10
575.21
578.02
580.04
580.24
585.09
587.11

594.21
599.16
601.10
603.13
606.13
606.17
606.18
606.19
607.03
607.05
609.08
609.13
609.17
611.02
613.04
616.04
617.23
620.17
620.21
621.08
621.11
621.21
624.08
624.11
624.19
626.18
626.21
627.11
627.26
629.10
629.24
629.26
633.06
633.15
634.20
634.22
634.24
636.03
636.06
636.25
639.17
639.25
639.27
645.10
647.08
649.13
649.23
649.27
653.12
654.01
655.20
655.24
655.26
656.13
658.04
659.13
660.14
660.17
660.18
660.20
661.01
663.08
664.27
665.05
665.08
665.16
667.01
667.15
667.24
668.04
668.09
669.25
669.27
670.13
670.16
670.25
671.22
673.26
674.02
674.24
675.14
676.13
676.13
676.17
677.08
677.24
677.26
678.10
679.09
679.10
681.06
683.21
685.19
686.17
688.04
689.13
689.14
689.25
692.01
692.09
697.27
698.04
698.16
701.21
706.16
711.04
711.05
712.12
713.14
713.26
715.28

716.05
719.09
721.03
722.10
725.02
740.23
743.03
743.05
744.10
746.28
747.02
747.23
747.26
748.11
753.19
753.23
754.04
759.08
759.13
760.26
763.03
764.10
766.21
767.13
768.20
771.28
772.05
776.23
777.13
777.22
779.19
781.08
781.08
782.14
782.15
782.20
782.21
782.22
784.22
785.16
790.05
790.22
793.28
794.01
796.10
799.11
800.19
802.22
804.03
805.28
806.22
808.11
808.25
808.26
809.26
810.10
815.07
815.06
816.22
817.03
817.13
817.15
817.16
823.18
825.25
827.15
827.23
832.10
832.23
834.13
834.25
845.22
847.24
847.27
848.06
848.08
852.23
852.28
854.37
856.03
857.02
857.15
860.08
861.06
861.09
861.21
864.15
865.22
865.24
869.08
870.01
872.02
873.26
880.07
883.11
885.18
886.20
886.25
888.02
888.05
888.09
889.16
892.09
893.19
894.02
895.24
896.27
900.25
901.37
901.15
902.18

908.08
909.25
910.26
couldn't
666.11
counsel
123.26
596.01
669.08
734.18
counselling
817.02
counsels
405.27
count
157.24
284.12
648.17
counted
389.11
782.10
countenance
076.22
077.22
245.03
272.04
283.22
288.08
289.26
307.01
344.13
346.12
351.13
370.03
380.23
423.05
429.07
461.19
516.24
522.16
528.26
529.18
618.22
648.21
687.16
699.26
738.21
815.24
824.05
827.23
872.03
879.15
886.18
countenances
083.04
798.14
counter
170.11
counter-balance
267.27
counteracting
302.26
counterfeit
827.17
counterpane
016.07
counterpanes
331.02
countesses
636.05
countless
078.10
662.15
countries
140.05
country
031.18
075.05
177.22
179.27
180.03
217.26
235.28
288.19
352.13
384.10
429.12
509.28
575.13
679.02
679.05
709.16
719.24
721.05
772.03
country-made
084.15
county
089.13
161.08
162.22
172.11
378.27
499.24
593.10
658.20
801.25
county-families
317.17
couple
286.11

coupled
590.04
courage
021.06
127.27
164.12
427.21
449.17
580.12
595.14
618.24
649.17
655.04
669.08
687.17
735.28
752.27
797.20
823.27
825.11
837.04
841.11
865.08
867.12
880.25
courageous
818.05
course
033.27
045.14
059.22
096.19
124.24
135.26
195.21
226.15
230.27
233.13
245.08
258.09
268.18
269.20
281.16
281.27
282.07
286.14
305.13
318.21
323.21
330.23
345.03
353.24
366.01
386.17
387.27
414.06
454.07
454.11
467.01
471.24
472.17
473.08
475.13
475.17
520.09
532.11
622.07
629.19
637.19
662.10
702.16
715.14
721.14
727.22
734.18
746.06
747.01
755.03
772.03
772.25
775.02
776.12
778.16
779.10
803.19
809.06
819.11
834.06
856.12
860.18
861.12
889.09
890.27
897.04
900.08
907.27
court
502.21
court-lady's
526.01
court-yard
426.22
856.23
courted
476.21
624.22
courteous
378.25
courtesy
099.18

courtship
372.17
400.05
532.13
557.02
cousin
196.08
487.19
489.18
489.21
782.08
828.08
852.16
889.12
891.26
894.10
cousin's
807.22
834.14
cousins
036.25
042.18
048.07
072.09
451.12
462.16
781.04
781.06
788.01
794.07
799.06
cousinship
892.19
cover
014.04
060.11
156.28
168.04
321.12
525.22
896.14
covered
015.28
066.10
072.14
087.25
111.19
155.10
159.20
167.02
374.15
460.11
485.01
485.25
599.19
607.11
628.27
661.14
692.25
766.04
799.08
covering
220.01
342.08
474.15
571.06
616.13
700.14
751.13
coverings
204.21
794.19
coverlet
661.19
covers
761.24
869.07
covert
131.16
462.14
covet
222.11
240.19
755.12
coveted
207.20
664.26
cowardly
644.22
cower
858.26
cows
051.26
664.20
cozy
186.04
crabbed
679.25
805.03
810.20
crack
436.14
519.07
cracking
613.07
crackle
504.10
cradle
146.22
458.02
468.16

606.16
craft
600.21
crag
220.28
282.22
659.25
659.27
661.15
663.09
712.19
812.24
815.23
craggy
194.14
282.18
cramped
735.22
cramping
721.11
crape
446.05
446.28
450.01
677.02
crash
123.09
519.07
835.03
867.17
crashed
520.04
859.07
crater
540.27
697.14
crater-crust
436.13
cravat
899.19
craves
355.09
craving
477.13
785.28
808.28
cravings
142.28
668.14
703.07
crawled
669.27
crawling
656.23
crayons
323.09
creak
424.09
creaked
296.03
315.12
crease
340.20
creased
665.19
creases
692.17
create
372.22
created
132.16
157.22
216.03
606.15
creation
359.26
creator
109.02
creature
109.03
189.11
222.01
232.03
357.17
383.21
386.13
424.18
430.14
449.23
468.28
478.07
556.06
572.22
579.10
639.06
649.19
738.12
892.06
creatures
132.19
359.20
credible
135.23
credit
040.15
516.14
creditor
301.14
credulity
389.26

creed
031.21
109.10
109.15
109.18
911.22
creeping
101.14
449.23
676.07
creole
593.14
597.12
636.13
crept
146.23
154.09
167.22
349.24
576.21
692.28
crescent
005.03
249.15
366.13
crescent-destiny
292.04
crest-fallen
796.03
crevices
096.08
crew
288.04
crib
044.09
046.20
046.20
071.09
072.06
155.11
155.19
156.06
159.15
cried
006.04
010.08
012.14
013.15
034.17
041.14
044.01
063.09
064.12
072.21
073.24
078.20
083.26
098.23
134.12
165.20
175.07
175.19
198.18
239.09
276.17
277.09
284.16
296.13
297.07
335.27
347.17
358.16
358.27
383.26
385.24
386.15
387.08
391.12
415.13
416.11
417.01
426.06
538.13
539.16
576.18
584.01
585.10
594.24
598.18
601.01
610.08
620.15
623.15
684.18
750.28
777.19
797.26
815.09
849.24
876.14
878.09
cries
494.19
630.12
crime
021.12
109.17
307.04
424.13
439.09
647.19

697.10
776.22
779.02
832.26
crimes
629.02
criminal
109.16
135.06
criminality
311.24
crimped
005.22
crimson
016.01
148.06
204.15
220.09
341.06
344.24
368.12
431.21
474.12
794.23
crimsoned
704.25
cripple
867.24
crippled
896.03
897.17
crisis
505.11
619.28
630.25
745.18
811.09
847.11
criticize
260.23
crock
386.14
crocuses
145.01
crois
277.11
crone
396.02
crooned
553.16
croquant
281.07
281.08
croquer
499.03
cross
017.16
067.09
104.03
118.26
146.20
229.21
292.28
357.19
397.15
494.01
497.18
554.22
607.08
641.25
719.27
762.28
825.08
851.13
864.28
912.01
cross-examination
891.24
cross-legged
003.04
cross-questioning
309.10
cross-ways
673.12
crossed
026.05
236.22
268.02
395.18
504.15
577.07
628.11
646.09
648.24
675.10
686.26
760.23
761.02
856.22
865.05
crossing
361.21
471.04
562.25
668.25
707.17
crouched
113.21
295.04
crow-colony
208.27

crow-trees
282.28
crowd
005.11
crowded
146.25
416.08
458.10
547.14
crowding
246.12
crown
105.22
133.05
249.16
318.12
529.22
851.14
912.14
crowned
248.18
471.06
857.14
crows
673.19
857.21
crucibles
334.20
crucifix
423.21
460.27
cruel
009.27
036.02
036.03
102.12
102.13
104.03
106.21
292.28
588.05
617.01
623.10
887.27
887.28
cruelly
057.01
cruelty
062.27
483.07
627.11
627.12
872.08
crumb
130.18
crumbled
050.15
355.26
576.01
crumbling
719.18
crumbs
050.17
050.24
199.19
496.04
crumpled
516.27
crunching
380.18
crush
856.05
crushed
130.08
132.26
545.17
547.14
605.25
649.15
732.05
738.25
832.21
838.26
867.21
crushes
109.20
crushing
014.16
044.08
crust
670.03
719.23
crusted
207.23
crusty
554.22
709.25
cry
009.21
024.02
033.23
034.19
063.26
295.09
356.04
388.28
414.14
414.19
418.15
445.26
476.17

509.13
531.05
600.03
651.18
826.02
849.12
853.07
crying
002.05
028.17
034.06
034.10
844.11
crystal
832.25
crystal-clear
414.11
cudgel
541.05
cue
450.09
cui
763.12
cuirass
193.14
culinary
792.08
culpability
707.05
culpable
439.15
cultivate
088.01
790.24
cultivated
762.20
cultivation
058.09
673.11
677.11
cumber
476.09
cumberland
110.01
cumbers
630.17
cumbrous
108.27
797.11
653.12
cunning
600.20
633.22
863.27
cup
121.06
138.07
239.03
239.06
320.02
326.10
341.27
405.28
456.23
513.03
612.03
686.12
725.26
758.20
cupboard
701.09
729.05
749.09
cups
049.18
137.08
137.11
236.28
401.16
curacy
040.28
curate
770.11
825.07
837.10
837.15
890.17
curate's
735.19
curb
149.22
741.06
curbed
741.05
curbless
145.21
curdles
634.10
cure
104.17
270.20
270.21
441.14
633.19
curiosity
149.20
217.15
315.01
355.08
387.02

389.15	414.02	cyphering	danger	daresay	874.15
392.23	414.13	722.25	152.11	034.10	877.14
399.23	427.11	d	308.26	034.24	883.10
530.05	562.09	557.11	309.27	069.22	883.20
530.08	563.07	d'athlete	357.02	178.12	dark-blue
703.22	583.02	279.16	410.14	197.25	749.27
778.04	676.10	d'ye	421.24	249.25	darken
curious	curtained	461.27	427.24	330.09	423.13
104.21	185.20	da	436.09	338.11	912.18
210.07	curtainless	678.19	436.26	408.27	darkened
211.05	745.25	dabbling	437.02	446.07	027.27
275.28	curtains	445.12	530.11	537.14	088.07
276.11	008.22	dacent	532.02	596.23	344.16
383.09	015.23	697.14	592.09	770.28	896.01
450.08	076.12	dagger	647.22	899.26	darkening
453.23	155.11	124.02	703.07	daring	559.02
533.06	191.22	571.19	797.20	359.14	darkens
643.09	203.17	dahlias	881.17	440.24	289.11
804.02	258.15	148.04	905.14	552.17	439.18
curiously	296.09	daily	dangerous	641.19	darker
193.18	306.19	045.16	025.10	748.02	017.19
640.18	307.21	054.19	032.09	872.18	390.14
curl	421.03	116.02	274.03	dark	681.11
034.09	426.20	143.20	306.01	017.08	813.12
752.10	433.02	144.16	417.03	018.13	darkly
curl-paper	457.06	198.03	417.04	019.04	013.23
048.25	465.04	204.23	530.08	023.05	016.04
curled	701.15	233.09	551.07	035.23	darkness
119.27	794.17	242.28	707.03	047.27	020.01
119.28	curtesying	372.14	863.25	060.24	046.19
119.28	052.12	467.21	864.18	072.24	075.23
120.06	curtseyed	545.03	872.06	075.07	079.23
120.26	211.18	621.18	dangers	076.19	101.12
122.07	251.13	629.05	551.11	076.20	186.02
551.03	342.18	746.18	911.18	082.03	274.20
740.10	curves	800.26	daniel	084.24	299.09
741.24	169.20	808.05	055.15	085.28	314.17
curling	cushion	808.06	678.04	116.10	416.07
557.25	237.02	892.03	dank	136.07	418.23
838.10	651.04	912.23	870.22	136.20	607.12
curls	cushioned	dainty	dans	143.02	658.15
036.22	016.09	458.26	239.11	145.12	735.21
041.16	207.12	610.04	danser	185.20	766.03
049.05	677.05	daisies	277.11	191.05	870.14
086.01	cushioning	445.12	dappled	199.08	872.23
120.10	259.02	738.23	435.07	207.01	darksome
120.11	cushions	740.15	dare	220.07	229.21
122.10	496.25	dale	021.26	221.02	darling
136.20	custards	169.21	062.28	221.10	019.07
197.06	328.08	dales	063.01	224.13	041.15
200.15	custody	220.18	063.01	229.01	158.26
318.13	311.21	damaging	176.11	231.05	387.05
318.20	376.16	008.12	187.04	235.03	519.22
340.12	custom	damanded	205.26	239.16	552.24
558.17	216.27	389.22	275.27	248.02	555.07
571.23	240.07	damask	284.05	248.14	617.03
661.15	287.10	015.23	284.06	248.20	628.17
685.27	440.13	284.06	312.26	259.05	653.10
746.12	509.20	damask-covered	321.09	259.06	736.15
750.02	513.12	258.20	339.26	283.01	877.04
798.07	590.08	dame	378.07	294.02	888.09
currants	785.06	170.02	404.23	294.10	897.22
792.05	801.12	195.01	406.10	297.03	darlings
current	807.07	196.21	411.11	318.07	002.04
262.23	807.08	343.27	412.17	328.19	468.23
currently	customary	506.10	412.19	335.12	darning
143.11	245.12	damer	437.27	335.12	116.21
currents	customer	589.11	452.24	343.18	dart
220.18	665.22	860.05	478.13	345.14	062.01
curse	customers	dames	531.07	346.15	284.11
107.22	395.23	334.07	565.12	348.10	darted
442.08	cut	damn	565.15	368.06	296.09
442.09	009.24	890.23	588.21	369.19	380.15
615.26	040.23	damned	742.08	372.10	417.05
655.03	057.06	242.05	760.25	419.15	darting
cursed	120.19	430.20	855.24	432.21	746.28
270.24	121.13	damp	872.13	459.17	dash
463.12	121.23	021.08	882.09	464.21	132.12
900.06	138.16	203.28	dared	501.11	dashed
curses	182.19	364.20	017.14	544.23	282.21
627.14	187.06	539.03	019.07	563.08	513.03
630.06	217.20	616.08	028.03	563.13	594.22
cursorily	222.14	671.25	032.10	571.25	887.14
676.23	244.07	692.10	040.11	572.15	dashing
curtail	382.07	727.23	044.09	577.12	184.06
614.22	387.28	damped	105.28	577.22	332.24
curtailed	428.02	795.27	118.04	578.07	348.07
627.02	541.08	damper	131.18	599.20	359.13
663.03	546.24	217.14	224.21	624.26	400.22
curtain	610.12	131.18	258.17	640.10	643.21
003.05	611.24	damping	293.14	651.26	date
006.11	621.08	328.16	312.03	659.23	593.08
009.01	642.15	910.03	389.07	671.10	dated
155.20	659.07	damsel	390.23	674.01	482.22
155.25	671.16	461.06	422.15	675.19	daughter
167.21	736.13	danae	463.19	678.22	058.13
181.04	817.21	545.02	485.23	711.20	126.14
204.05	cuts	dance	495.18	715.22	188.15
235.11	092.23	200.05	540.01	734.10	255.28
236.23	cutting	200.07	551.13	737.28	279.09
266.02	009.24	201.21	622.23	745.26	288.06
311.16	144.05	dancer	650.07	794.17	461.15
332.16	458.12	279.10	665.18	795.04	499.01
341.06	cuyp-like	290.10	687.02	798.01	524.21
342.05	143.04	dancer's	773.08	799.27	593.13
342.10	cynical	618.14	804.24	809.25	597.14
366.12	283.20	dancing	858.17	849.26	612.02
366.20	cynosure	476.22	896.07	856.20	624.18
367.18	491.04	740.04	daren't	868.07	627.16
369.15	cypher	dandled	028.21	869.15	628.20
371.12	729.18	445.11		870.02	652.17
		dandy			
		364.12			

706.15
721.25
733.02
750.11
770.13
770.22
780.11
daughter's
769.19
daughter-in-law
632.23
daughters
317.07
343.05
343.07
344.03
454.16
467.02
485.18
508.24
677.09
722.24
744.09
daughters'
464.05
daunt
816.08
daunted
043.18
david
358.18
885.19
dawn
080.04
159.14
426.20
427.14
578.18
631.07
652.21
654.18
800.16
851.02
dawned
022.08
081.12
163.23
302.18
303.04
882.22
day
061.04
003.10
007.23
017.01
027.23
029.16
029.22
031.23
044.11
044.26
048.27
054.20
058.12
059.06
063.08
066.20
068.19
071.10
074.06
080.03
081.12
081.18
086.04
088.06
090.06
095.20
096.02
096.19
100.09
100.12
100.20
111.14
127.05
131.19
141.22
142.24
143.12
144.13
152.05
157.07
159.05
159.12
162.24
165.02
168.15
169.04
169.17
169.21
172.24
173.10
174.01
174.07
174.20
179.22
179.28
181.19
190.03
191.07
191.19
192.05

197.11
199.16
207.19
218.11
234.03
235.24
238.21
249.28
255.04
273.05
276.12
278.09
282.18
282.25
288.24
303.03
305.04
305.11
316.07
317.14
319.24
328.06
329.04
331.18
331.26
337.24
340.06
354.10
359.16
364.08
378.08
379.15
399.01
420.12
426.08
427.21
433.17
435.17
436.14
445.03
445.26
456.27
470.17
473.13
473.15
473.15
473.23
474.06
476.04
476.26
477.03
477.20
483.20
484.13
488.16
490.04
490.22
490.23
490.27
492.09
499.12
501.17
502.01
523.21
524.18
526.06
534.25
541.28
545.07
545.11
548.20
550.25
557.04
557.05
559.21
560.07
569.19
570.04
579.04
579.23
581.20
583.20
584.07
587.19
589.24
610.20
626.08
626.20
628.03
638.06
639.22
639.25
654.02
662.27
663.02
663.06
670.19
672.02
672.03
678.16
680.21
680.25
690.02
691.28
709.18
711.05
712.22
713.06
714.21
719.27
724.27

728.02
728.03
730.17
730.18
745.10
746.03
750.06
750.16
753.05
765.04
765.11
775.28
779.08
790.16
793.14
794.03
759.11
804.09
809.16
809.17
810.11
819.09
819.09
822.14
830.04
831.02
846.11
848.03
851.15
852.07
855.16
868.08
877.11
880.18
883.22
899.12
899.20
909.09
day's
081.07
094.09
209.09
325.17
733.19
day-dream
095.05
524.13
day-dreams
095.05
day-visions
640.09
daylight
020.28
036.06
085.23
199.07
224.07
316.01
427.12
542.07
576.07
580.14
674.04
850.24
851.02
days
032.18
042.07
051.28
112.19
145.27
150.01
153.13
168.27
169.10
189.17
217.06
220.03
221.09
250.04
254.02
281.06
293.24
324.03
326.23
327.10
331.27
351.17
356.02
364.02
364.03
364.20
368.20
374.24
440.05
440.08
448.07
458.16
458.27
464.19
470.10
480.14
493.19
501.06
542.06
556.06
633.08
634.05
642.22
643.20
652.28

658.02
689.02
698.06
701.08
703.06
707.01
707.17
711.03
714.05
714.06
718.17
752.25
785.01
790.09
792.02
853.13
853.20
885.23
886.14
900.21
dazzled
119.23
186.01
519.09
576.06
625.07
746.16
dazzling
322.18
de
201.09
201.18
234.12
234.23
234.23
277.17
287.27
334.01
334.07
341.21
348.12
543.19
543.20
589.11
860.05
deacon
841.23
dead
015.05
016.26
022.15
044.27
065.12
077.10
091.10
093.20
114.17
134.26
157.05
159.17
414.10
417.20
429.14
429.18
446.26
447.25
451.07
451.18
451.26
464.05
484.01
495.13
495.16
560.19
603.22
606.08
607.19
625.26
627.20
690.07
696.04
696.05
696.06
721.12
726.01
726.05
753.01
770.17
774.24
775.26
860.27
861.22
861.26
866.04
866.05
866.05
866.27
878.02
878.07
900.26
dead-weights
356.19
deadest
424.17
deadly
415.10
655.03
880.01
deaf
008.04
188.09

856.09
deal
008.15
014.22
041.11
078.05
092.17
106.18
177.17
203.06
205.25
205.26
253.01
254.09
310.17
362.13
369.20
393.06
395.24
506.04
531.22
641.16
666.14
676.17
698.12
698.22
729.08
740.11
790.07
795.23
804.22
806.17
839.14
863.22
892.26
dealings
811.24
dear
010.25
010.26
058.15
058.27
064.16
064.17
125.11
158.12
158.24
186.22
187.13
188.08
353.20
356.20
386.21
465.26
483.15
517.23
527.23
535.16
612.02
617.12
617.13
651.06
773.11
803.06
828.08
876.25
879.03
904.02
dearer
158.16
759.28
dearest
354.16
388.27
dearly
526.03
526.03
dearth
046.22
death
021.12
022.01
054.06
060.07
061.08
133.08
145.16
147.23
155.09
159.19
181.11
253.12
301.05
422.16
447.09
448.05
468.11
469.27
473.18
477.19
482.18
486.05
512.09
553.04
615.19
653.26
663.20
669.20
673.02
674.26
680.15

683.23
685.15
698.27
706.08
719.25
725.13
727.02
735.13
736.09
742.25
775.25
780.09
819.20
822.17
844.10
844.22
859.08
900.10
912.18
death's
847.20
death-like
611.10
death-struck
608.09
death-white
004.15
deathbed
445.04
480.10
deathless
596.17
deaths
244.21
debarrassed
166.11
debasement
108.26
debasing
038.01
debauchery
636.19
debt
301.11
301.20
447.15
547.25
707.26
debts
719.17
decay
088.04
561.10
663.21
896.14
decaying
021.09
870.23
decease
475.27
deceased
016.22
697.23
deceit
056.23
057.20
060.09
064.12
deceitful
062.04
063.16
064.07
deceive
481.02
634.25
644.19
653.13
730.21
deceived
634.25
december
045.09
218.03
605.23
decency
841.24
decent
189.05
217.23
238.10
323.24
429.21
495.02
692.18
790.04
885.21
905.11
decently
489.10
637.11
deception
850.07
decide
226.20
514.12
664.01
784.21
847.24
848.06
decided
052.04

```
312.19              043.11          deference       deistic         delineate       demon
395.11              108.15            383.03          762.13          322.08          424.20
471.23              111.10          deferential     deity           delineated        571.25
499.13              129.05            555.01          272.20          891.11            602.03
702.25              166.10            744.26        dejected        delineation        644.18
decidedly           222.24          deferentially     113.14          702.06        demon's
  262.06            256.02            122.11        dejection       delirious           616.15
  290.12            294.28          deferred          487.12          155.18        demon-hate
  346.07            296.11            031.01          500.09          470.12            630.08
  555.14            296.18            379.20          745.08          581.12        demoniac
  609.14            333.20            384.03        delay             656.18            294.27
  836.12            344.22            831.03          110.09          731.16        demonstration
deciphering         350.01          deferring         140.19        delirium            552.17
  805.03            361.15            361.13          147.21          303.02        demonstrations
decision            424.11          defiance          173.18          406.08            450.09
  350.02            446.04            120.06          546.11          758.17        demurely
  405.18            473.02            436.17          550.27          883.25            186.13
  722.18            502.09            605.05          585.05        deliver             200.14
  725.15            520.04          deficiencies      587.13          630.15            340.18
  851.14            561.16            138.05          588.05          715.14        demureness
  897.09            591.02            692.25          719.01          735.27            310.22
decisions           599.14            810.06          778.18        delivered         den
  058.04            608.12            898.11          899.01          088.24            424.06
decisive            608.13          deficiency      delayed           187.09            436.01
  237.07            612.09            091.21          255.20          312.23            633.03
  803.11            627.04            112.07        delays             413.01        denied
deck                640.04            213.20          801.28          461.23            113.18
  200.20            650.15            261.02        delf              691.05            270.25
declaimed           650.28          deficient         729.07          843.27            828.23
  201.10            659.03            346.15        deliberated     delivering        denominated
declaration         659.08          defied            054.15          099.11            550.12
  044.06            660.08            061.02          259.16          415.05        denominating
  405.23            661.15            900.07        deliberately      478.05            543.16
declare             677.01          define            246.15          560.09        denote
  062.05            678.22            192.04          396.08        delivery            177.28
  467.24            720.05          definite          614.09          716.08        denoted
  593.18            765.13            206.21          773.23        dell                718.24
  647.08            789.13            818.17        deliberating      712.17        denoting
  654.24            814.28          definitively      044.02        dells               237.09
  741.16            825.05            801.05        deliberation      017.27        dense
  761.15            832.22            836.14          737.12        delude              020.01
  814.22            845.09          deformed        delicacies        525.20            088.13
declared            569.04            493.21          824.24        deluding            551.23
  010.06          deep-graved       deformities     delicacy          525.19            563.07
  024.08            806.07            287.09          571.21        deluge              870.17
  151.15          deep-thrilling    deformity         677.11          655.06            910.17
  311.23            883.01            125.02          853.27        deluged           dent
  356.17          deepden            761.24        delicate            296.19            310.15
  389.06            105.08          defrauded         007.11          298.09            343.21
  390.23            105.16            598.07          030.28          757.27            345.27
  391.16          deepen           defy              112.06        delusion            345.28
  433.03            101.12            436.19          118.15          758.17            346.05
declares            559.25            515.22          138.21          852.28            347.15
  592.15          deepened           551.14          322.07          876.03            348.07
  405.11            075.06            592.13          322.19          876.05            350.17
declaring           672.16          defying           525.11          876.06            352.08
  480.28          deepening          649.16          737.26        delusive            354.21
decline             316.02          degenerate      delicious         731.27            359.02
  563.20          deeper             109.09          113.26        dem                 366.03
  603.12            031.11            270.28          138.08          678.26            366.13
  609.04            374.25          degenerated       757.28        demand              367.09
declined            398.10            270.12          785.16          044.13            367.14
  390.11            641.08          deglutition     delight           241.19            369.13
  418.22            752.11            478.26          018.23          274.01            370.07
  453.10            835.26          degradation       031.10          449.22            371.05
  660.09            888.17            038.03          032.21          564.20            371.16
  879.05            903.08            109.19          087.16          595.07            378.23
decorated         deepest            544.20          109.12          735.01            378.26
  317.15            517.25            632.10          138.18          793.14            379.28
  701.08          deeply             670.21          162.05          820.08            385.13
decoration          103.16            691.10          194.25          868.09            388.13
  798.27            109.20          degrade           209.21        demande             389.02
decree              501.12            692.28          219.11          234.23            411.07
  900.07            623.09          degraded          291.18        demanded            416.12
decreed             659.22            469.15          301.27          024.04            443.01
  725.23            723.06            730.23          369.05          024.14          dent's
dedans              759.12          degrades          402.11          051.16            366.05
  234.21            762.07            720.14          498.06          170.14          dentelles
deed                830.03          degrading         512.04          244.15            280.02
  228.22            834.14            627.17          534.01          256.18          denuded
  462.13            841.01            637.25          548.08          297.12            051.11
  484.06            845.17            665.03          643.04          369.13          deny
  832.11            848.18            720.10          715.19          416.05            293.08
  897.24          defaulters          722.17          749.18          484.26            404.15
deeds               268.14          degree            758.08          640.28            573.13
  268.10          defect             094.20          782.18          661.27            800.11
  869.27            321.28            136.02          798.09          687.04            828.17
deem                737.25            160.08          824.16          726.08            912.01
  405.25          defective          160.19          856.21          766.08          depart
  719.26            104.15            162.27          896.19          774.07            152.27
  755.09            150.13            184.10          898.03          798.16            406.24
deemed              813.26            198.06          898.08          814.24            488.15
  023.19          defects            214.06        delighted           818.19            645.14
  030.25            128.11            263.15          315.03          858.02            852.18
  046.05            267.27            403.11          373.08          861.28            884.02
  074.03            287.08            506.02          549.21          867.01          departed
  348.28            374.01            506.08          699.25          875.21            022.22
  676.10            629.03            618.24          711.14        demanding           027.23
  718.13            759.12            664.27          798.27          888.26            060.12
  756.20            908.12            685.08        delightful      demands             245.16
  902.18          defence            730.23          166.18          240.01            311.13
deeming             135.08            770.08          511.25          632.05            604.09
  154.05            552.19            824.25          749.06          879.27            654.21
  218.09          defend           degrees           794.04        demas               800.06
  274.19            135.09            021.05          882.18          817.19          departing
  381.16          defer              160.17        delightfully    demeanor            300.23
deems               449.19            794.04          319.06          200.23            575.12
  719.25            463.13            806.19        delights          263.01          department
deep ·              543.28          deigned           404.21        demolished          244.17
  015.23            628.02            264.28          405.09          819.17          departure
  016.05                                              715.28                            047.05
```

147.15
338.28
512.08
559.14
618.01
707.02
707.10
718.15
732.21
760.15
801.04
806.04
822.01
851.03
857.26
depend
059.08
356.25
441.02
553.02
579.14
dependant
009.08
196.21
266.25
321.08
396.24
508.18
706.17
dependant's
719.23
dependants
312.01
717.15
depended
255.02
dependence
014.14
653.06
887.11
dependency
266.26
dependent
020.21
507.24
708.21
886.21
depends
265.24
403.27
719.04
897.06
deportment
290.24
deposit
018.13
depraved
627.23
deprecation
526.06
depressed
294.03
362.24
362.26
363.28
depression
021.08
deprive
436.22
depth
017.18
135.12
152.22
230.26
250.22
272.25
377.27
716.26
depths
220.18
256.03
259.08
570.13
610.07
761.16
817.05
der
678.25
deranged
766.13
derive
606.18
794.11
derived
101.09
136.17
291.14
321.05
323.15
deriving
149.25
684.13
des
201.09
313.17
descend
045.17
129.05
209.25
329.03
699.21

descendants
719.22
descended
051.18
075.07
080.12
154.23
182.05
193.11
255.18
335.20
340.26
369.15
416.18
602.15
712.05
872.16
descending
164.28
200.12
210.17
318.17
560.11
597.20
812.09
870.07
descends
672.22
descrated
638.07
describe
127.11
206.02
352.12
459.07
577.10
642.03
716.05
762.10
described
146.16
391.19
608.11
644.25
844.06
887.18
describes
702.07
describing
206.13
description
182.08
292.16
322.11
345.06
345.13
473.03
629.20
723.21
890.16
descriptive
217.27
desert
418.20
663.07
795.01
854.17
884.13
deserted
533.03
533.05
deserter
887.28
deserting
362.21
837.23
desertion
200.24
838.02
deserts
825.10
deserve
596.15
827.26
deserved
107.09
141.17
280.09
286.25
412.20
864.22
design
423.18
630.26
751.14
designated
742.24
designation
194.12
designing
377.24
533.08
designs
824.22
desirable
490.17
801.23
desire
064.05
106.19
120.16

153.17
162.04
178.10
264.24
314.08
314.12
323.15
440.06
463.13
482.14
525.11
529.14
530.24
586.06
614.17
622.26
634.18
692.08
708.26
761.28
834.03
883.25
desired
042.06
165.14
192.19
215.09
216.05
431.06
458.20
481.06
636.11
641.08
850.14
desires
200.19
405.15
desiring
099.04
632.23
desirous
168.19
744.15
857.17
861.13
desist
043.13
394.14
desk
355.28
357.21
642.18
701.13
715.12
717.26
726.24
802.25
811.07
811.14
832.07
desolate
004.23
032.08
561.09
601.20
605.22
681.25
730.22
854.21
867.27
871.05
877.14
879.04
901.12
desolation
672.26
860.14
despair
249.10
372.23
374.20
594.10
628.24
630.25
647.12
647.25
651.19
683.19
707.19
735.04
745.27
747.09
781.16
856.05
888.23
despatch
603.19
859.11
despatched
257.08
463.22
529.28
desperate
010.13
023.23
043.12
165.20
270.11
370.02
459.19
654.06

670.12
681.26
732.20
872.04
desperately
777.12
desperation
012.10
306.27
514.06
773.05
despicable
179.20
despicably
478.22
despise
124.03
131.05
709.18
730.28
797.03
despised
286.19
325.16
despises
131.07
despite
267.12
741.04
748.01
despitefully
107.23
despoiled
033.20
despondent
642.23
734.01
desponding
377.24
despot
546.25
despotic
465.19
741.03
829.04
837.27
despotism
554.25
823.25
despots
846.25
dessert
236.01
336.13
dessert-dishes
328.00
dessert-service
342.08
desserts
240.05
destined
057.09
081.25
084.13
487.19
509.17
510.13
destinies
824.22
destiny
163.08
283.24
293.04
293.13
397.25
514.12
524.11
720.19
735.15
destitute
288.16
658.11
697.09
707.15
888.09
destitution
665.09
709.04
destroy
157.22
295.17
614.25
797.05
destroyed
560.18
606.21
753.08
861.21
destruction
280.06
753.07
detail
160.02
detailing
136.01
details
039.04
224.11
256.06
300.15
459.09
627.06

670.18
687.07
697.22
712.19
752.14
770.07
772.09
detained
850.11
detaining
438.25
detect
402.18
detected
350.10
382.03
406.02
829.07
detecting
402.15
402.17
detection
307.09
determination
323.06
466.20
736.09
821.25
determinations
648.18
determined
470.21
549.15
553.20
579.07
634.23
656.24
754.07
811.26
856.25
determinedly
651.02
detestable
354.10
detestation
283.15
detrimental
721.06
deuce
222.16
226.22
236.01
298.16
451.03
495.10
885.03
deutsch
679.26
devastated
859.22
devastation
160.13
develop
730.12
develope
797.18
developed
060.20
192.20
293.03
627.09
627.28
712.24
743.12
762.21
development
213.17
802.16
deviate
280.08
668.11
deviation
139.03
device
360.03
devil
271.22
295.17
358.21
402.25
409.12
416.11
454.08
528.02
595.06
596.14
600.24
devilish
423.27
devine
274.11
349.25
devious
634.17
devise
360.24
476.24
devised
555.26
571.01

718.09
devoid
060.24
devote
489.05
724.09
878.21
devoted
337.25
474.16
714.12
790.20
792.04
796.09
909.12
911.18
devotion
214.13
342.03
517.10
574.02
625.11
903.21
devotional
479.05
devotions
360.09
devour
156.22
321.21
627.03
648.26
devoured
082.16
095.14
320.22
374.21
672.15
713.03
devouring
065.09
296.23
dew
153.24
404.08
438.18
502.02
655.11
660.25
663.02
732.15
742.08
dew-beads
504.03
dewy
435.09
586.23
dexterously
763.28
diablerie
399.13
diademed
249.16
dialogue
244.13
329.20
718.04
dialogues
690.20
diametrically
287.12
diamond
322.20
524.27
diamonds
280.02
547.16
dian
345.03
diana
678.03
681.04
685.27
687.11
688.01
690.01
691.11
696.01
699.18
699.23
700.01
702.15
704.15
704.23
705.12
708.01
708.16
709.05
709.22
711.06
713.10
713.20
714.28
717.09
724.26
725.03
726.05
726.17
726.26
727.20
728.03

741.27	157.01	389.06	634.12	893.06	258.21
742.24	164.03	389.20	634.13	893.14	267.23
767.19	166.15	389.21	634.14	893.19	268.19
768.22	177.18	394.14	634.15	897.24	301.15
778.15	177.28	394.19	635.09	898.13	313.24
781.01	180.06	395.19	635.16	898.18	364.03
783.12	180.10	397.20	637.16	900.02	375.28
783.13	186.02	402.18	637.20	901.19	391.20
784.18	188.02	403.18	638.08	901.20	452.02
784.19	188.08	404.27	638.27	905.16	461.10
788.12	189.10	406.16	639.03	905.17	487.20
791.07	195.19	406.17	642.13	905.18	506.11
792.11	195.21	406.21	642.17	909.20	524.11
794.11	196.22	407.23	643.11	909.25	537.08
798.24	197.03	407.25	648.21	909.26	581.13
799.12	198.25	408.13	654.10	didn't	681.01
800.17	199.28	409.12	654.16	906.04	697.13
800.28	201.24	409.12	665.10	die	698.11
801.22	206.16	411.10	666.09	019.25	717.11
803.19	210.17	412.15	666.13	021.13	721.07
806.08	210.21	412.27	666.17	028.22	725.04
807.09	211.01	414.03	671.17	054.17	748.19
807.15	218.10	417.25	672.05	054.19	779.16
809.27	219.27	425.03	674.14	130.11	786.27
810.25	223.13	425.05	674.14	132.06	800.27
811.17	229.19	428.13	681.27	147.19	821.12
829.20	232.17	430.17	689.20	156.03	847.06
839.12	233.03	431.20	690.20	157.07	850.19
839.14	233.04	441.17	693.21	158.02	differently
840.13	239.02	445.20	698.28	158.09	288.23
840.17	239.06	450.03	699.05	441.03	difficult
843.01	239.14	460.09	701.28	468.02	036.13
843.07	242.03	462.19	702.13	476.23	097.06
845.25	245.05	464.16	702.21	481.14	166.26
853.18	246.26	465.06	705.01	527.05	192.24
853.28	247.01	467.27	707.18	552.10	245.02
907.01	247.04	467.28	708.09	553.06	473.27
907.02	249.25	468.02	714.09	573.14	528.15
911.05	249.27	468.03	715.07	646.25	643.25
diana's	250.24	471.11	715.26	646.27	664.28
681.14	252.23	472.09	723.26	656.22	693.07
713.17	253.24	473.28	731.18	672.28	703.25
727.10	254.10	475.25	738.17	673.04	718.01
778.07	254.19	482.23	739.12	673.17	778.20
803.14	255.10	485.15	746.18	678.20	814.09
911.07	258.06	486.03	746.21	678.25	862.12
diary	261.10	486.13	747.01	678.26	873.28
270.07	262.07	487.15	747.07	683.09	902.11
474.17	265.01	490.08	749.19	684.01	difficulties
dick	266.24	491.27	754.04	684.07	111.04
450.12	267.24	492.09	754.13	726.09	542.28
453.22	275.10	492.13	754.15	735.21	775.04
547.08	279.02	494.12	767.08	819.01	818.03
dickens	280.11	496.11	770.28	840.06	824.24
008.07	282.06	496.17	772.21	841.15	difficulty
dictates	284.20	505.13	772.21	842.11	059.26
405.22	285.22	506.25	772.26	died	098.17
dictation	287.14	509.13	774.22	035.27	142.13
910.09	290.27	511.13	782.01	041.02	154.14
dictionary	291.28	515.18	782.27	091.11	388.18
677.21	292.02	519.16	789.16	135.03	391.01
679.13	297.25	519.17	793.27	147.19	467.07
749.12	298.03	523.23	795.25	154.21	470.07
dictum	298.13	528.12	796.15	374.16	544.11
357.15	299.12	531.24	800.07	414.20	685.05
did	301.25	532.11	800.23	447.01	719.02
008.02	301.26	532.21	802.15	447.25	730.02
008.06	305.09	534.13	803.01	468.02	795.19
009.18	307.26	537.19	807.02	468.03	871.23
010.08	307.27	542.24	807.02	468.27	880.26
010.09	308.15	550.03	807.26	475.04	880.26
010.19	309.07	550.11	810.03	484.01	903.13
011.01	309.26	550.23	811.02	485.17	diffidence
013.25	313.07	550.27	821.18	514.27	006.23
020.09	313.27	551.03	821.19	535.17	702.27
020.10	314.12	551.14	823.22	573.05	706.05
021.15	316.09	552.27	827.21	595.01	858.01
024.07	321.14	555.17	831.02	627.21	diffident
029.19	324.03	558.01	832.05	674.23	641.14
033.07	325.23	560.24	833.10	706.16	diffuse
035.08	326.10	565.22	835.08	809.24	818.16
035.19	327.27	567.14	835.10	dies	digest
035.19	329.08	571.17	836.03	902.14	090.16
042.19	337.15	571.18	838.11	diet	digested
044.22	338.28	571.23	839.25	161.11	168.12
047.04	346.21	573.13	843.24	differ	dignified
047.22	346.23	577.16	843.25	260.08	829.24
052.21	346.28	578.12	849.15	differed	dignity
054.16	349.09	580.20	849.17	287.12	344.27
065.02	349.10	581.05	850.08	difference	digression
067.02	349.14	581.09	857.05	189.18	285.26
072.13	351.16	582.03	860.21	264.20	dilated
079.08	351.19	582.13	864.20	319.21	622.23
080.08	353.15	583.15	864.26	488.26	dilating
088.16	353.16	583.16	875.20	536.19	283.17
088.19	354.12	585.05	881.22	602.05	dilation
090.19	356.09	587.15	882.17	681.08	715.17
092.09	356.22	588.24	886.06	681.12	diligence
092.18	361.11	590.21	887.22	743.10	474.01
099.12	362.02	598.24	887.28	743.12	diligent
102.20	362.07	612.25	888.10	762.12	762.06
105.19	362.17	615.24	888.17	848.13	818.04
115.03	365.07	617.18	889.14	differences	dim
116.07	366.08	617.21	890.23	802.14	004.17
120.02	371.10	620.08	892.13	different	007.08
124.24	373.13	623.11	892.18	078.23	078.09
134.27	375.02	623.28	892.21	091.06	101.19
137.11	375.22	624.04	892.25	091.24	209.28
148.16	380.23	624.28	893.02	145.13	215.04
150.01	381.02	625.18	893.04	185.01	248.12
156.23	381.02	628.22	893.05	233.18	248.18

249.01
295.25
369.22
550.18
551.21
611.02
639.19
652.04
654.18
673.08
674.07
675.01
673.23
689.03
847.23
870.21
dimensions
190.27
729.07
diminish
252.23
674.14
diminutive
031.25
dimly
022.14
057.07
075.24
155.16
183.13
299.17
680.05
882.02
dimly-lit
080.13
dimmed
306.14
563.03
dimness
219.06
848.17
dimpled
523.14
738.08
dimples
740.18
din
221.05
dine
074.11
254.06
548.01
dined
001.07
149.05
234.28
548.06
dingy
007.04
764.07
dining
051.21
dining-room
203.26
206.23
231.09
232.14
236.21
255.23
258.11
317.14
317.22
331.09
342.06
361.24
365.08
367.23
370.11
410.23
410.26
586.03
dinner
001.06
035.13
074.13
093.26
094.01
094.11
112.24
118.05
128.05
143.16
143.26
212.05
255.04
258.12
306.09
311.01
311.16
315.20
328.12
329.04
332.07
336.02
336.06
336.12
358.23
341.01
380.12
382.10
455.23

692.03
899.06
905.07
dinner-bell
456.24
dinner-table
339.15
dinner-time
203.09
dinners
045.13
dint
209.23
417.22
544.02
dionysius
508.25
dip
423.09
dipped
421.16
610.04
686.01
dips
078.09
direct
058.08
120.23
258.08
395.09
463.03
487.09
651.07
673.07
702.14
703.04
735.08
739.08
814.15
861.14
directed
124.25
168.04
168.16
202.12
259.26
313.13
365.12
430.07
449.04
704.09
732.07
737.10
821.19
direction
085.07
085.18
171.16
225.18
229.15
326.01
332.11
372.06
505.26
557.15
654.24
664.09
852.13
870.13
directions
027.22
097.12
117.07
211.13
245.16
326.27
482.07
688.06
812.04
directly
013.10
051.13
090.03
123.09
175.23
223.09
228.01
334.17
416.19
428.28
620.09
783.13
867.22
directness
702.25
director
243.28
directs
092.02
243.23
direful
707.08
dirt
692.27
dirty
098.24
disadvantageously
641.17
disagreeable
055.07
098.24

339.12
disappear
163.13
disappeared
160.13
411.13
673.11
764.01
disappearing
344.14
disappointed
177.25
179.25
314.21
665.21
733.24
747.14
disappointment
118.11
324.13
390.15
483.28
563.04
636.18
638.17
716.27
760.04
810.13
829.03
864.17
disapprobation
829.06
disapprove
638.14
723.15
disapprovingly
083.21
disarrange
340.16
disarrangement
255.17
disaster
563.16
859.15
disasters
551.24
900.08
disavowal
571.12
disavowed
592.12
disburthen
559.15
disc
126.09
discern
434.19
607.03
discerned
075.24
137.16
137.17
233.13
756.17
discharge
161.04
161.17
479.04
722.05
815.10
discharged
162.10
169.26
discharging
730.13
disciple
762.17
disciples
118.26
discipline
083.28
323.21
disciplined
051.10
163.06
439.02
disclose
559.18
disclosed
138.11
291.21
369.17
377.27
464.01
589.25
disclosure
604.24
604.24
708.15
903.02
disclosures
116.08
861.07
discoloured
490.25
578.01
discomfort
055.03
disconnected
255.02
322.02

disconsolate
101.02
discontent
081.23
discontented
215.18
discord
020.06
828.06
discourse
042.02
122.26
139.27
274.19
345.26
378.13
383.16
687.23
716.22
760.26
800.20
discover
002.10
006.12
473.28
658.07
660.04
667.01
754.08
759.04
767.11
814.09
892.08
discovered
005.25
031.11
048.26
140.06
145.06
154.19
161.04
309.12
321.22
337.11
376.18
588.04
627.27
713.26
743.17
749.10
771.23
771.28
776.22
886.12
888.01
892.19
899.04
discoveries
404.16
406.26
626.11
discovering
505.18
discovery
161.04
163.22
196.28
356.18
686.18
708.14
777.24
781.19
862.21
889.08
discreet
488.25
537.22
760.27
discreetly
310.20
discretion
290.23
507.21
600.20
discriminate
337.13
825.14
discriminated
675.19
discuss
713.05
828.05
discussed
029.03
106.04
329.18
378.26
903.04
discussing
040.08
383.19
408.27
discussion
287.04
756.23
784.25
disdain
826.28
disdained
898.15

disdainful
722.08
disease
147.22
603.11
691.03
diseased
126.21
disembarrassed
238.05
disembodied
480.05
disembowelling
256.01
disfigured
490.25
disgrace
094.16
532.20
disgraceful
102.28
disguise
407.16
543.06
748.06
disguised
272.19
370.04
disgust
024.09
270.13
283.15
429.06
526.27
617.21
627.03
632.17
636.21
731.08
disgusted
313.23
disgusting
008.14
081.27
598.04
disgusts
109.20
dish
118.13
377.20
dished
403.17
dishes
729.06
dishevelled
581.14
622.01
dishonest
533.01
dishonour
628.27
837.22
838.01
disinclined
203.02
disinterested
614.08
818.05
disk
414.11
471.05
561.13
652.09
dislike
056.26
062.06
069.05
069.07
102.15
107.04
383.27
384.19
468.06
468.25
disliked
244.05
451.10
482.24
dislikes
102.14
108.12
131.07
463.15
disliking
107.06
dismal
018.09
dismay
081.21
137.15
425.19
486.05
dismayed
051.23
115.23
730.26
773.03
dismiss
251.11
263.22
385.26

687.14
dismissed
077.15
094.16
099.08
129.03
311.22
729.14
764.11
869.18
873.23
disobedience
040.23
disobeying
299.15
disorder
141.07
692.27
disordered
369.27
disown
107.12
242.17
260.19
404.17
808.07
disowned
289.02
687.01
770.15
disowning
468.09
disparaging
881.23
dispassionate
623.03
dispensary
148.23
dispensation
900.06
dispense
096.04
266.27
310.19
708.22
dispensed
002.06
disperse
808.25
dispersed
342.21
382.09
491.16
displaced
407.08
556.07
displayed
367.20
625.04
displeased
382.04
724.06
830.03
840.27
displeasing
322.01
displeasure
083.05
299.15
642.28
735.10
835.04
disposed
012.05
067.11
067.12
227.10
238.03
262.18
263.10
289.24
365.10
400.25
404.22
463.20
474.25
548.22
638.18
744.15
756.03
790.26
793.09
disposition
002.13
056.18
064.07
115.26
425.16
467.22
484.12
484.18
730.05
disproportionate
262.24
793.17
dispute
605.05
disqualified
621.05
disquieting
716.28

disquietude
574.19
disregard
312.26
disregarded
019.05
287.24
disregardful
192.12
dissatisfied
390.14
792.15
dissent
618.26
disseverment
655.16
dissimilar
228.26
dissipated
155.26
177.06
441.12
dissipation
656.19
800.15
810.03
dissipations
269.17
473.22
dissolution
406.03
dissolve
129.06
655.04
dissolved
026.17
049.28
736.06
dissolves
778.25
dissuage
489.14
725.14
distance
002.09
020.04
053.11
089.01
105.23
151.10
189.08
213.16
221.03
223.16
230.26
249.03
284.17
357.16
394.17
450.22
492.11
499.24
509.03
509.04
514.27
538.06
554.09
572.13
575.10
658.15
667.03
669.16
674.23
714.10
766.07
802.18
818.22
854.16
864.20
870.01
distanceclipse
247.25
distant
005.11
073.07
080.28
162.22
220.15
229.14
254.17
349.07
364.25
426.22
504.13
575.12
621.19
652.15
658.17
700.01
728.04
732.13
739.01
740.22
854.16
distantly
196.02
642.06
distasteful
527.25
527.24
806.25

distinct
210.07
210.10
221.27
226.02
580.15
590.17
716.11
distinction
350.17
681.10
708.25
distinctly
029.02
151.09
188.11
192.25
281.13
313.01
348.25
577.22
592.02
595.07
754.22
844.19
852.04
910.22
912.23
distinctness
246.05
distinguish
101.01
109.16
231.17
271.28
460.13
675.15
677.26
distinguishable
333.21
670.21
distinguished
341.10
343.28
413.06
415.15
840.02
distinguishing
684.15
distortion
429.07
454.12
647.10
distracted
856.09
distracting
111.20
distraction
783.09
distractions
357.04
distress
063.10
094.22
133.07
511.13
755.21
distressed
156.21
572.08
603.08
623.08
802.06
distresses
725.25
distressing
112.04
670.22
675.23
distributed
087.16
112.13
district
184.28
194.21
348.09
730.01
764.05
districts
800.27
distrust
271.26
538.07
682.16
distrustfully
703.20
disturb
072.08
090.28
362.07
449.17
disturbance
475.09
disturbed
018.13
027.21
036.20
101.09
398.09
463.15
530.07

569.10
689.18
755.23
796.01
884.05
disturbing
258.03
442.08
disturbs
182.25
dit
201.18
234.25
ditch
878.02
ditto
263.16
dive
264.13
diverged
284.20
divers
016.21
122.20
553.21
divert
264.25
336.08
dives
846.13
divest
013.11
divested
237.12
divided
087.27
209.06
423.18
474.04
727.19
784.07
823.07
dividing
561.24
572.18
624.09
divine
033.26
119.02
356.14
378.07
480.11
628.19
753.11
762.24
900.07
912.13
divined
391.22
diviners
371.09
divining
369.10
division
115.06
252.24
788.03
dizzy
611.01
do
006.22
006.24
007.13
009.11
009.15
013.01
027.18
028.01
043.27
044.25
047.19
054.05
054.14
055.09
055.12
057.14
062.05
063.03
063.28
066.25
066.26
068.11
069.06
091.05
091.15
091.15
091.19
092.16
093.05
093.07
093.09
093.16
095.07
102.01
102.19
104.13
105.17
106.05
106.28
107.05
107.23

107.26
116.17
121.05
129.15
130.26
131.04
134.13
135.01
138.02
157.17
167.05
167.08
167.08
168.23
173.14
174.18
176.04
176.22
178.14
184.12
186.22
186.26
193.03
195.07
201.22
205.08
205.15
205.17
208.01
216.18
216.26
222.17
222.26
223.10
224.03
225.21
225.27
226.08
227.10
227.21
230.08
239.21
241.23
242.22
245.11
246.26
250.01
255.01
257.03
257.05
258.05
259.15
260.04
260.16
265.05
265.06
265.08
265.17
269.18
270.03
270.17
271.06
271.27
271.28
275.08
275.12
283.05
285.22
288.14
291.13
297.09
298.17
300.19
301.22
310.04
310.16
323.05
325.07
330.11
335.28
339.20
351.17
351.26
354.06
354.27
356.01
356.03
357.20
358.02
359.23
361.28
361.28
365.04
370.14
376.10
386.10
387.06
388.05
389.21
390.01
394.13
395.23
399.18
399.26
399.28
400.03
400.08
401.11
403.26

403.28
405.06
406.02
406.07
407.09
408.01
410.01
410.20
410.21
411.28
412.21
420.07
422.06
427.25
428.12
431.02
431.18
432.10
432.11
433.28
434.01
435.15
435.19
437.01
437.04
437.14
437.19
437.24
438.14
438.21
446.12
446.12
447.12
449.03
450.16
450.27
450.28
451.23
452.20
455.15
455.28
456.16
461.27
467.28
468.04
469.10
477.01
477.09
489.16
494.22
496.18
497.21
506.09
510.17
510.19
511.08
512.10
512.26
512.27
513.03
513.25
515.21
517.08
517.16
517.17
517.19
518.20
519.26
523.21
527.08
527.10
527.26
528.25
530.16
530.17
532.28
535.20
536.01
537.07
538.26
539.11
540.24
541.04
541.07
543.09
545.22
546.14
547.14
548.10
548.21
549.18
555.24
557.07
564.13
568.14
568.20
573.18
573.20
573.20
574.06
578.12
579.23
580.08
581.09
581.22
582.15
590.03
592.24
593.25
595.10
602.20

609.05
609.15
609.17
609.17
613.09
614.10
614.13
614.21
615.15
616.20
617.06
617.08
617.27
618.11
618.12
618.14
618.15
618.23
619.22
621.08
621.14
621.17
622.19
623.11
623.16
628.04
628.22
634.12
634.14
635.18
643.23
643.23
644.02
644.24
645.23
645.26
645.28
646.01
646.04
646.18
646.20
646.20
647.05
647.28
649.14
649.18
654.10
657.06
660.13
660.14
666.06
666.13
666.19
666.19
667.23
670.16
672.02
672.23
673.02
679.15
679.18
682.06
682.11
682.20
682.21
682.25
682.27
682.27
684.28
686.20
687.06
687.09
687.11
687.21
694.18
694.23
694.24
696.24
697.03
697.15
703.18
704.03
704.05
704.06
705.15
705.18
705.24
705.25
706.06
708.17
708.25
708.27
709.15
709.21
709.22
721.08
721.15
722.26
723.04
723.15
727.22
727.27
730.14
734.08
734.18
734.22
737.19
739.07
739.11
739.15
741.19

741.25
742.02
753.09
753.22
756.06
760.10
761.13
762.01
767.24
774.14
774.19
780.19
783.16
785.05
785.21
786.10
786.26
788.07
790.13
791.02
791.06
791.22
792.23
792.24
793.21
800.10
806.01
806.16
807.02
808.06
810.23
814.01
814.06
816.07
816.15
816.17
816.22
816.27
818.24
818.24
819.27
819.27
821.11
821.16
821.25
822.03
822.11
822.13
823.03
823.10
824.09
824.17
825.07
826.27
826.28
828.07
828.16
831.14
834.24
834.28
834.28
838.12
838.18
841.03
841.11
846.06
848.19
849.10
852.02
855.24
866.18
872.10
872.11
874.04
877.08
878.02
878.06
880.13
882.06
888.09
888.10
893.02
894.04
895.04
895.25
897.02
898.04
898.23
899.17
906.13
906.21
909.05
doat
041.14
360.14
ooated
046.26
docile
203.01
714.03
730.05
818.04
908.14
ooctor
431.08
457.17
470.12
690.27
doctors
627.27

doctrine
103.10
107.11
480.05
doctrines
214.10
716.18
762.18
document
169.03
170.10
171.19
326.05
593.19
documents
775.07
does
002.18
067.26
092.06
092.11
092.13
098.28
107.21
108.13
120.08
153.04
158.14
166.16
177.09
177.16
184.13
184.18
198.19
211.23
260.23
262.01
267.15
293.21
310.12
321.16
352.24
385.11
386.06
401.07
408.21
441.10
447.05
450.05
450.18
469.03
494.11
494.17
504.24
506.18
524.08
528.08
528.25
529.11
542.26
582.06
593.20
602.22
666.20
679.15
685.14
694.08
757.07
769.12
775.17
778.01
790.15
799.22
803.08
814.24
618.28
824.08
840.04
840.07
840.12
842.03
867.25
879.26
889.18
689.19
890.03
895.04
900.14
907.07
doesn't
330.20
672.13
695.12
doffed
407.07
dog
176.27
221.20
221.26
222.20
223.19
228.12
229.09
231.25
232.07
237.03
237.24
383.06
420.18
564.04
572.13

668.24
677.04
687.19
696.23
733.06
736.28
874.27
899.27
dog's
740.24
dog-like
626.06
dogmas
489.07
dogmatical
344.23
dogs
018.27
683.15
doigts
313.16
doing
009.01
034.01
050.20
051.02
131.21
177.02
184.12
188.03
245.26
362.09
408.26
409.28
410.25
411.18
447.10
447.12
489.10
553.27
576.14
659.11
744.02
757.21
772.14
785.15
800.22
805.13
864.02
882.25
883.21
884.11
909.27
doit
234.20
dole
738.14
doleful
033.02
293.21
572.11
883.10
doll
032.16
046.13
046.20
218.20
353.14
545.01
doll's
049.15
domestic
186.15
786.14
792.20
797.17
800.15
dommage
336.22
don't
002.20
010.19
013.08
013.15
013.19
015.10
033.23
033.25
037.03
037.18
043.24
064.10
067.05
067.15
068.10
068.25
068.25
069.01
069.07
069.09
072.20
107.13
110.03
123.27
124.12
132.05
158.22
176.01
183.04
189.15
197.23

206.02
206.06
206.07
240.12
242.10
243.05
245.24
246.03
246.14
253.10
256.05
256.27
264.17
265.21
267.09
267.22
268.08
269.07
272.10
272.23
273.21
275.12
299.03
312.15
325.10
326.25
334.09
336.03
339.08
354.16
355.11
360.18
363.11
385.14
389.25
395.13
395.24
395.26
395.28
397.11
399.14
400.09
400.18
400.27
404.03
407.18
411.21
416.24
420.01
421.26
429.10
430.05
434.15
436.04
438.13
439.08
441.27
442.07
452.14
453.08
467.15
489.24
491.28
496.22
506.07
514.04
524.23
525.08
525.15
526.02
526.04
529.04
529.21
529.22
530.24
530.24
530.25
531.02
535.22
536.16
543.10
546.08
555.24
565.23
569.25
582.22
612.20
617.04
618.21
621.03
628.01
635.15
637.14
637.15
638.12
643.20
679.12
682.27
683.02
683.03
695.05
707.28
754.19
755.07
757.20
773.14
773.14
776.24
782.07
782.09
786.17

790.25
791.17
793.18
807.13
827.06
864.04
874.06
880.19
881.14
881.22
892.11
899.11
907.10
donc
201.18
done
002.18
064.09
065.04
087.12
106.14
133.15
152.01
152.08
169.28
228.21
230.03
240.10
241.14
242.08
245.11
246.23
251.07
267.21
269.23
272.20
288.03
297.13
354.19
360.20
366.09
380.25
391.18
422.19
425.03
427.19
428.03
428.21
429.20
433.28
434.05
434.08
437.05
439.12
470.03
481.19
495.10
508.19
604.09
621.09
632.05
637.15
638.13
648.22
664.03
679.20
684.27
706.05
707.23
716.21
719.09
734.26
749.19
750.24
763.01
782.26
788.06
790.16
798.26
799.04
822.07
827.25
828.25
837.01
839.08
889.11
895.09
903.26
906.14
906.27
908.23
909.28
donjon
765.15
donna
358.08
donner
548.26
doom
121.12
216.10
606.08
619.25
652.08
661.26
684.09
716.20
732.18
900.16
door
006.16

009.16
009.24
015.13
017.14
023.22
027.26
029.06
051.25
052.11
061.24
072.23
073.05
073.09
073.27
075.25
075.25
076.04
076.17
078.19
081.04
089.10
091.02
127.02
140.25
151.22
152.25
152.28
153.25
154.17
155.01
155.03
175.04
180.20
183.12
183.25
185.21
191.02
195.02
210.14
211.11
230.15
231.10
231.18
233.16
234.04
245.14
251.10
256.20
281.19
295.02
295.13
295.21
296.03
296.04
297.07
300.02
306.10
309.07
309.18
309.20
310.14
314.16
314.17
328.21
335.26
361.25
385.01
389.02
391.08
392.27
415.27
415.27
416.16
418.28
420.10
420.15
420.16
420.27
423.01
432.13
432.22
434.02
434.07
435.26
442.12
450.12
456.23
464.20
488.17
520.09
522.04
576.10
578.19
582.16
585.13
588.18
598.12
599.02
599.08
604.06
604.11
610.25
616.17
639.26
650.09
651.01
653.10
654.17
667.13
667.18
668.05

671.11	116.07	013.01	347.09	773.21	263.24
672.06	158.12	013.09	349.01	777.06	309.11
674.19	175.01	015.11	361.23	777.11	315.27
676.03	215.17	015.26	365.13	781.13	321.27
680.04	243.21	023.22	365.21	783.08	375.19
682.03	251.22	027.19	366.13	783.23	379.28
683.02	252.02	027.28	368.27	791.22	407.27
683.16	273.20	029.25	394.07	791.24	414.02
684.17	273.21	030.16	409.01	795.22	414.13
685.12	285.28	035.06	410.08	796.13	614.08
690.07	290.11	035.14	414.03	810.15	614.13
696.21	338.11	036.27	416.24	812.22	620.27
699.13	344.10	041.21	416.27	813.02	713.26
700.27	347.02	044.09	418.24	813.14	752.18
707.21	403.04	048.06	420.19	818.23	780.20
732.10	417.10	051.13	421.23	820.12	drawer
733.04	427.08	054.26	427.06	825.27	016.20
746.07	454.06	056.12	429.24	827.09	032.14
746.23	463.06	063.13	430.09	830.14	049.07
752.14	491.25	064.16	430.21	835.08	110.04
765.07	491.27	064.17	434.26	839.10	138.09
766.01	491.28	066.03	435.09	843.06	169.03
766.12	515.21	067.02	438.07	847.03	170.07
768.07	529.07	067.20	445.27	850.05	218.22
778.09	536.15	069.26	446.27	850.23	419.24
780.18	555.24	072.07	447.20	860.11	429.26
790.01	581.05	073.01	448.04	861.18	431.03
797.27	596.15	073.04	450.09	864.07	521.18
798.04	615.10	075.19	455.22	865.18	557.14
799.18	643.11	076.24	459.16	867.15	drawers
811.20	668.23	079.19	461.25	868.02	030.08
849.25	747.19	080.10	465.23	873.22	068.17
851.07	774.15	084.05	466.24	875.07	141.02
851.09	785.03	087.25	467.13	875.14	174.16
860.11	796.03	095.08	471.23	875.16	357.22
873.11	816.15	101.26	477.25	886.05	488.18
874.19	820.19	114.15	484.27	886.09	652.25
874.21	823.17	119.11	487.09	886.10	724.18
875.17	825.16	129.06	488.01	896.09	729.09
906.19	838.21	130.22	491.09	911.21	851.04
door-bell	838.22	134.11	495.01	downright	drawing
050.07	842.09	145.18	502.03	530.25	029.27
255.06	843.17	151.04	502.27	doze	051.22
361.05	852.07	156.27	505.25	535.16	130.02
door-handle	853.24	165.23	514.24	dozen	142.20
052.07	856.06	167.25	519.10	099.21	168.26
door-step	862.02	174.18	522.01	114.13	203.09
683.21	876.20	175.02	522.09	141.05	313.13
door-stones	880.12	176.06	526.11	354.09	332.01
964.28	902.20	178.17	532.01	543.27	470.23
doors	doubted	184.22	534.23	dozing	472.27
033.13	022.09	185.15	535.18	470.08	515.15
045.25	022.09	186.26	540.01	drab	745.11
148.02	031.22	188.23	542.02	462.04	753.16
154.25	588.17	191.10	552.01	drag	754.26
185.26	607.04	198.27	560.14	819.08	799.21
190.21	635.01	206.25	562.09	dragged	832.23
202.14	730.24	209.01	562.17	006.20	881.12
207.22	doubtful	209.15	565.24	604.23	drawing-box
210.02	053.04	214.26	566.11	627.16	322.05
317.22	403.21	217.10	567.05	675.03	drawing-master
333.28	459.24	219.24	571.05	883.20	179.04
335.09	572.11	220.04	575.07	dragging	drawing-materials
336.18	668.02	220.08	575.22	732.22	749.13
419.27	doubtfully	221.25	577.12	drain	drawing-room
423.17	013.23	222.18	585.16	429.03	002.02
558.19	doubtless	222.28	586.12	drained	002.26
639.26	083.23	223.20	586.13	808.20	042.18
701.09	088.02	223.24	604.18	drank	045.18
795.20	172.04	227.11	604.22	079.07	045.25
853.04	172.16	229.04	607.15	095.15	076.14
858.28	220.20	229.15	607.23	484.28	204.02
dormitories	255.05	232.18	610.06	579.05	204.10
122.23	368.21	233.05	610.24	612.03	235.23
417.24	376.26	234.07	612.24	875.16	331.10
dormitory	384.11	235.04	616.14	draped	337.03
039.07	556.24	235.11	620.05	366.26	338.22
146.25	603.20	236.17	620.08	draperies	339.13
154.06	628.27	238.05	630.21	231.12	340.05
159.09	730.15	245.14	639.17	365.17	340.28
dose	733.17	255.12	640.28	434.20	362.20
431.09	774.04	256.28	645.21	drapery	363.10
doth	776.04	263.19	651.03	003.07	365.24
590.05	790.18	273.14	651.23	015.27	367.22
dotted	doubts	279.07	654.09	249.12	369.17
209.04	182.15	280.14	654.16	341.07	380.13
double	328.18	280.26	655.05	369.19	394.18
003.06	539.03	293.11	658.03	752.09	408.25
065.25	856.01	294.07	659.26	798.28	455.22
113.20	885.06	294.19	661.16	draught	758.01
113.25	dove	298.24	664.05	079.05	810.26
173.03	634.09	299.22	665.21	100.10	drawing-rooms
185.27	699.24	306.09	667.06	470.06	327.01
344.14	doves	310.03	671.20	478.23	drawings
661.19	417.18	311.02	673.26	483.16	143.01
869.19	dovetailed	311.10	674.20	579.06	246.13
double-daisies	713.24	315.16	676.11	631.17	250.15
148.06	dowager	315.27	684.24	648.28	250.26
doubled	344.02	317.27	693.01	768.06	472.21
076.18	344.05	327.16	693.15	draughts	drawled
doubt	386.24	331.01	697.14	349.25	356.03
025.07	dowager's	332.09	698.03	draw	drawling
028.17	354.13	333.10	699.18	098.08	462.01
040.07	dowagers	334.13	708.02	123.16	488.06
045.04	352.09	335.22	731.12	178.23	drawn
054.26	379.24	336.12	742.20	181.03	003.04
059.20	416.26	337.04	756.14	187.11	010.05
059.20	417.19	340.10	758.04	206.17	015.25
077.04	down	340.18	758.14	217.18	042.13
104.23	005.07	341.14	765.11	256.27	080.20
108.11	010.15	342.07	767.03	258.01	123.09

160.15
221.01
230.17
281.12
310.15
349.16
382.28
421.03
433.03
483.22
635.14
673.13
708.25
720.27
768.15
779.25
788.12
857.18
891.09
912.10
draws
644.11
908.19
dread
021.18
029.11
029.12
032.09
056.26
069.04
069.05
123.24
155.22
270.17
363.05
459.28
548.11
584.06
609.07
657.15
660.02
709.03
dreaded
154.18
170.27
309.28
437.10
660.11
662.16
856.04
867.09
867.09
dreadful
001.12
023.27
126.16
589.24
672.25
820.09
859.18
861.19
dreadfully
469.13
dreading
008.13
115.02
116.01
dreads
275.06
dream
079.26
105.04
250.18
294.23
402.02
406.17
417.09
418.06
444.18
445.09
469.27
492.03
495.09
521.04
551.18
558.17
566.24
567.01
567.04
574.14
574.22
581.04
583.12
583.16
583.17
636.10
638.21
652.20
678.05
859.04
877.06
877.17
878.10
dreamed
551.01
640.09
dreamily
768.04
dreaming
105.16
308.26

308.27
406.17
444.17
525.14
535.12
dreamland
249.26
dreams
572.14
573.08
579.17
609.11
745.13
745.13
745.14
813.10
877.07
dreamt
492.02
574.22
598.06
651.25
drear
003.10
021.02
645.13
655.18
drearily
294.02
329.13
654.09
dreariness
065.15
795.02
dreary
004.09
017.02
019.27
032.06
033.05
078.01
112.19
152.12
189.02
190.10
410.11
561.15
570.16
574.23
644.05
726.16
883.20
900.28
dreg
406.01
dregs
716.26
drenched
298.01
611.18
631.05
672.23
859.26
dress
058.21
075.15
086.03
121.28
136.18
163.10
174.15
226.16
236.04
236.09
277.02
277.12
281.24
335.16
340.22
342.03
343.10
343.24
369.28
380.11
446.27
460.24
461.09
521.17
577.13
585.02
604.16
694.27
749.27
763.23
910.14
dressed
029.04
029.22
045.18
046.09
061.03
071.05
078.11
080.06
082.03
192.08
277.07
318.01
318.14
331.16
340.17

342.15
343.17
367.10
418.01
418.10
418.11
418.24
419.05
421.06
431.27
446.04
521.02
534.21
545.01
582.20
625.02
633.11
641.11
652.24
795.06
dresser
676.14
dresses
084.09
202.05
365.16
487.16
526.08
543.27
890.20
dressing
049.04
080.03
096.03
118.13
340.09
427.05
692.23
dressing-bell
382.09
dressing-case
482.05
dressing-cases
794.20
dressing-gown
297.23
545.25
dressing-room
429.25
dressing-table
558.06
576.10
dressmaker
665.27
695.03
709.26
drew
006.11
073.18
088.20
133.20
140.21
144.03
189.24
223.26
246.11
249.06
256.22
286.02
291.25
366.21
367.08
396.03
406.23
427.11
427.12
445.23
449.21
452.28
467.11
471.28
490.17
559.24
563.07
578.17
580.23
594.13
637.28
667.16
668.19
675.17
680.01
718.05
749.21
750.03
763.13
803.19
847.25
873.12
909.16
912.12
dried
631.13
663.03
899.15
dried-up
607.15
dries
858.20
drift
100.26

244.12
561.16
766.19
890.27
drifted
560.05
765.05
859.24
drifts
605.25
777.14
drilled
243.22
drink
028.06
064.01
366.28
431.22
431.25
431.25
431.25
431.25
518.10
610.20
877.15
drinking
019.24
drinks
349.25
438.17
dripping
565.04
631.04
688.08
drive
050.04
073.01
185.18
313.21
332.21
333.08
432.15
534.12
587.20
647.12
682.24
798.12
868.07
driven
148.21
223.17
263.20
355.25
364.06
559.20
623.12
666.03
709.12
driver
010.02
185.15
381.04
432.13
432.26
657.02
798.03
798.15
798.26
869.19
drives
186.23
driving
048.16
563.08
683.04
drizzling
088.07
drooped
426.07
433.06
drooping
109.22
113.07
340.13
685.28
drop
010.14
030.01
042.19
130.17
219.22
253.23
501.18
513.02
621.12
754.11
832.24
863.24
872.13
dropped
075.10
167.24
172.22
236.24
242.13
277.15
330.23
604.20
685.17
727.28
736.06

dropping
308.15
779.07
drops
431.20
858.18
dropt
412.05
486.14
dross
273.20
drove
074.01
075.19
303.01
434.02
707.07
drover
664.20
drown
297.15
drowned
248.07
362.18
drug
147.26
drunkard
597.13
dry
149.07
297.22
297.22
301.03
313.01
456.12
566.03
660.22
674.01
688.09
692.02
692.15
886.07
887.22
drying
117.01
disease
040.28
du
334.05
543.19
dubbed
234.13
dubious
499.08
dudgeon
554.14
due
152.02
189.07
191.12
453.10
631.26
762.24
889.08
duet
318.26
337.08
dug
151.27
dull
046.17
090.21
582.22
618.18
618.18
629.27
743.08
743.08
837.09
902.14
dulls
439.24
dulness
379.10
423.09
475.20
duly
549.13
dumb
222.10
264.10
264.11
367.11
626.01
684.05
747.10
768.20
859.19
dumbfoundered
310.24
dun
209.05
dungeon
329.14
434.15
476.20
817.04
dunnut
694.04
694.23

dupe
286.26
321.09
duplicate
755.05
duplicity
025.10
durable
273.15
duration
086.25
146.01
520.07
during
027.21
044.11
080.18
083.09
090.08
111.09
112.23
114.26
117.25
126.03
127.04
140.02
161.28
170.21
172.28
198.02
254.11
283.22
305.06
311.16
328.13
362.09
390.12
398.15
445.07
456.27
482.18
490.23
520.06
522.18
554.20
572.18
707.24
713.06
730.19
740.02
829.20
831.04
841.08
843.10
851.06
882.13
dusk
075.02
129.05
221.16
248.17
314.10
316.02
335.17
380.10
658.21
795.04
870.15
871.16
duskier
681.14
dusky
673.16
701.18
dust
010.18
049.12
204.21
278.03
541.22
794.02
816.06
dusting
032.12
050.27
203.21
duties
059.02
161.17
170.20
180.25
328.04
479.06
735.12
746.02
dutiful
597.16
duty
019.08
024.27
103.05
125.13
163.04
214.11
240.28
325.07
357.04
508.18
604.08
645.14
684.27

714.19
730.12
800.09
815.11
835.21
846.05
848.16
dwell
062.11
215.24
643.27
670.17
715.27
844.08
891.13
dwelling
146.17
264.26
667.16
712.04
870.10
dwelling-place
649.24
dwelt
021.17
491.05
670.23
768.04
dye
544.07
dying
063.08
152.24
152.11
153.10
157.12
423.22
426.16
479.10
479.20
420.04
465.11
552.27
553.02
761.18
848.26
e
779.15
e'en
258.16
550.06
777.15
each
005.13
041.03
074.15
078.05
078.05
079.01
079.04
079.20
080.23
081.01
082.23
085.11
085.27
086.26
087.18
088.01
091.18
094.08
097.18
113.18
116.24
121.20
123.23
138.07
138.13
138.24
144.17
149.04
152.18
180.21
214.07
219.18
246.15
247.21
249.27
250.10
257.27
258.18
355.15
356.13
371.10
371.20
375.02
378.19
391.24
411.01
412.04
418.17
423.19
444.11
461.13
472.24
473.23
474.05
476.27
477.01
477.22
489.26

510.06
541.24
550.23
550.25
557.16
560.15
560.19
560.24
561.09
568.02
580.13
592.01
616.09
641.21
659.02
661.17
675.24
677.15
699.04
716.19
717.13
726.15
727.25
730.02
781.05
782.25
784.09
784.26
788.13
796.19
801.19
801.22
807.07
809.04
821.20
832.06
882.02
909.05
909.09
eager
005.23
139.04
349.03
389.15
559.15
575.14
635.08
656.24
702.13
719.07
850.23
eagerly
441.22
465.07
551.04
686.09
753.14
798.09
879.20
912.24
eagerness
381.01
401.25
402.08
713.02
778.16
791.01
898.27
eagle
872.07
887.11
eagles'
881.09
ear
014.15
029.10
100.27
116.07
188.10
210.07
216.01
220.17
260.16
281.28
294.24
337.11
354.22
355.05
361.14
391.23
395.19
402.10
412.23
517.26
555.13
572.09
572.24
596.24
619.16
653.14
699.23
814.15
832.03
849.08
853.08
883.15
887.08
906.07
906.07
909.24

earl
005.26
earlier
370.16
earliest
168.15
early
001.07
174.13
193.24
195.04
233.03
235.27
255.07
305.06
337.27
362.21
433.01
438.21
448.24
452.22
455.21
474.02
644.20
652.22
809.14
845.24
854.28
857.01
886.03
earn
129.16
406.05
547.19
719.22
earned
191.15
786.10
earnest
002.12
152.14
206.05
342.03
391.27
517.16
573.24
805.17
805.18
824.12
845.09
earnestly
484.22
588.20
620.16
628.05
716.10
835.24
841.19
846.18
earnestness
516.13
779.06
839.05
844.26
845.16
earnings
398.26
earrings
369.03
ears
023.19
045.02
058.17
282.14
369.08
392.12
498.15
609.08
630.05
737.01
770.07
875.03
905.14
earth
022.17
094.28
132.20
216.14
231.02
332.01
459.26
476.10
477.28
543.03
560.21
587.21
662.19
663.04
759.20
824.16
844.07
845.03
849.18
887.07
898.02
899.28
903.21
908.26
910.25
912.04

earth's
031.22
earthly
479.28
514.18
738.17
907.19
earthquake
590.22
629.27
853.03
earthquake-shock
405.19
earthward
652.13
ease
149.17
184.03
225.11
230.01
263.01
263.22
291.23
382.11
413.10
433.12
433.26
481.14
483.26
641.27
828.21
882.13
882.16
eased
286.27
616.08
easel
202.28
642.18
easier
701.22
752.06
easily
389.26
436.15
766.10
787.13
east
145.17
152.06
427.15
435.07
502.08
659.05
736.16
813.19
easter
339.23
eastern
368.09
546.06
803.23
825.10
eastward
220.10
583.05
easy
026.15
104.21
155.15
177.15
206.02
230.09
234.03
260.07
367.12
394.04
397.03
452.03
462.17
547.13
555.27
701.20
714.25
785.04
808.18
827.22
854.05
easy-chair
016.09
256.04
421.04
eat
009.11
028.06
030.27
031.03
055.24
071.15
081.16
087.07
118.04
130.16
148.26
319.27
320.01
329.04
334.14
540.18
548.10
566.10

566.12
586.07
682.15
686.05
702.18
703.08
703.10
883.24
eatable
096.16
eaten
171.02
692.04
eating
019.24
079.09
671.12
ebb
255.01
810.12
ebon
193.18
283.17
423.21
ebony
460.27
ebullition
789.09
eccentric
217.04
312.20
312.20
533.10
671.18
eccentricity
238.12
ecclesiastical
807.22
echo
210.12
214.14
742.12
832.04
902.16
903.16
echoed
222.23
eclipse
439.18
556.04
economy
161.21
244.11
354.06
economy's
244.08
ecstasies
327.24
ecstasy
340.06
ecstatic
256.17
eddies
145.13
eddying
607.11
eden
640.24
eden-like
502.19
edge
044.09
082.18
540.27
554.07
763.19
edged
430.25
434.26
edging
426.20
504.10
862.03
edification
118.18
editor
168.05
edouard
234.12
eduardo
358.06
educated
706.17
720.13
743.11
890.08
educating
091.14
education
102.09
162.02
168.25
213.08
214.11
293.04
376.22
508.24
693.08
721.28
771.15

908.11
edward
252.20
252.25
253.02
517.13
517.14
517.22
517.23
573.17
593.09
609.09
773.11
849.21
861.03
862.13
862.26
866.19
867.08
871.17
906.09
906.12
911.03
edward's
860.28
909.03
edwin
478.10
eel
565.17
een
906.24
eerie
032.06
191.04
232.02
572.03
eerily
849.23
efface
221.02
effaced
191.03
220.27
520.02
760.08
effect
017.24
171.02
191.26
320.24
355.23
472.05
542.15
624.06
716.06
783.20
794.08
822.10
833.04
848.22
873.28
879.15
909.21
effected
019.24
036.16
123.02
795.23
effective
850.19
effectually
223.16
719.08
effervesce
527.18
efficiency
662.18
efficient
709.19
efficiently
822.16
effigies
207.24
effigy
808.26
effluence
127.27
effluvia
147.28
effort
023.23
082.24
083.22
106.15
152.15
217.20
227.15
227.15
228.02
415.06
417.05
481.27
485.09
514.10
535.04
573.02
573.02
613.07
620.26
656.09

684.05
731.11
742.05
763.18
806.27
809.21
814.13
853.10
872.21
effortless
607.14
efforts
052.09
057.03
142.15
167.19
172.06
214.05
216.17
223.02
374.28
379.27
426.11
476.25
571.03
743.05
785.07
824.19
effusion
165.28
egg
885.15
eggs
048.12
048.15
143.08
792.05
egotism
214.14
egotistical
628.10
egypt
454.22
606.10
eh
268.26
407.18
890.19
eight
035.05
160.09
161.25
161.28
165.14
166.23
170.18
174.08
181.21
197.04
241.11
241.12
244.26
293.20
314.20
342.12
446.10
461.04
483.19
558.02
582.21
694.14
769.23
eighteen
168.22
178.07
244.27
268.28
269.03
317.11
704.16
eighty
078.11
084.06
131.01
131.05
147.02
einer
678.20
either
006.14
008.01
043.18
043.27
072.09
091.09
091.12
111.03
119.23
131.07
206.14
224.01
242.11
253.18
263.27
282.21
288.27
306.27
313.05
316.17
326.24
327.20

333.13
376.24
388.01
388.19
422.15
426.12
444.19
456.16
462.27
470.12
470.18
473.17
475.06
485.18
489.27
490.15
492.09
504.02
525.19
537.09
537.27
549.20
571.14
588.12
590.01
603.25
604.07
636.11
655.01
665.10
679.08
680.23
702.12
728.01
752.27
753.03
790.25
806.06
821.13
826.19
837.08
837.24
882.18
ejaculated
082.01
387.13
516.12
517.12
595.18
848.10
866.19
ejaculating
759.08
ejaculation
905.15
ejaculations
392.03
415.25
elaborate
375.24
elaborately
045.19
122.07
367.21
elapsed
165.01
182.26
299.11
367.19
370.09
470.10
487.03
553.22
667.07
716.01
743.04
elastic
804.19
elate
065.01
elbow
392.13
467.12
eld
406.28
elder
086.25
122.07
252.08
252.10
392.08
461.15
626.01
elderly
082.10
126.07
171.21
171.27
172.03
186.09
308.09
676.20
677.09
elders
002.22
065.04
eldest
319.15
343.07
381.16
624.01

elected
269.21
339.24
election
059.15
716.18
electric
248.22
849.03
electrified
749.18
elegance
224.26
238.08
279.16
316.20
335.23
350.16
elegant
184.02
236.24
281.12
317.07
343.12
element
164.01
296.25
797.17
elementary
202.16
elements
479.28
679.17
702.12
744.12
804.14
805.25
elevate
571.13
elevated
744.24
848.05
elevation
808.11
eleven
154.04
156.11
337.18
409.04
461.05
900.27
eleventh
845.12
elf
471.07
495.19
523.12
555.09
639.15
elf-land
542.16
elf-locks
395.05
elfish
250.17
529.03
elicit
022.26
809.14
elicited
354.23
376.03
817.12
eliezer
369.08
eligible
403.11
719.12
elixir
800.18
eliza
001.17
002.01
006.15
010.09
010.21
018.18
043.06
045.16
048.08
048.21
048.26
460.28
462.19
463.16
470.15
470.16
472.14
473.25
475.17
476.01
478.17
479.01
485.20
486.07
487.11
489.21
490.03
491.03
eliza's
461.23

488.13
elizabeth
589.12
elle
234.24
elles
334.01
elliot
774.08
elliott
686.18
708.03
708.07
elm
146.03
elongated
461.02
eloquence
139.26
716.25
735.28
eloquent
528.06
799.07
else
017.23
036.01
037.11
048.04
061.21
064.04
134.16
159.10
225.04
250.01
301.12
327.04
336.04
392.19
422.16
433.09
456.13
476.20
477.11
488.04
533.16
604.01
731.21
757.09
759.11
791.05
800.23
840.03
867.14
868.02
elsewhere
098.05
166.24
616.02
640.01
704.24
822.20
elude
123.02
650.01
650.08
elves
031.13
297.11
elysium
717.06
747.22
emaciated
690.10
embarrass
186.19
704.01
embarrassed
778.10
879.07
embarrassment
339.11
505.13
704.23
881.01
embers
021.08
046.17
101.19
235.13
embittered
459.19
emblem
065.09
584.06
emblems
656.07
embodied
779.21
embody
247.19
emboldened
028.12
embowered
562.22
embrace
154.20
194.16
272.16
489.11
523.07

601.22
617.19
651.16
653.13
877.19
embraced
069.27
130.22
140.20
embraces
613.25
embracing
175.16
645.27
embroidered
368.13
embroideries
207.14
embroidering
216.24
embroidery
476.06
571.18
embrowned
193.25
embruted
598.08
emerald
812.14
emerged
100.05
519.16
576.15
emergencies
418.11
emerging
078.01
eminence
269.13
762.04
eminent
910.20
emir
368.09
emotion
135.17
290.13
307.08
465.12
511.18
584.02
613.17
643.05
686.05
704.23
740.28
811.02
883.02
emotions
108.20
164.02
349.04
761.08
emperors
010.02
emphasis
201.11
724.12
emphatic
044.10
736.17
emphatically
454.05
837.14
empire
418.21
employ
666.17
896.27
employed
027.14
049.11
323.16
356.18
561.24
employer
188.01
196.12
206.11
508.20
employment
088.24
329.18
423.13
508.14
666.02
667.24
669.03
671.01
671.02
717.21
718.28
719.03
791.18
800.14
810.04
emptied
296.27
672.14
empty
006.06

051.24
066.18
339.14
572.05
644.17
657.08
680.10
734.10
766.26
819.05
877.13
emptying
488.18
emulate
825.11
emulation
039.12
emulous
744.25
en
115.11
171.27
360.23
543.20
enable
785.24
enabled
154.14
706.01
727.27
780.16
enactment
114.12
enamelled
812.15
enchained
122.25
enchaining
070.02
enchantment
883.18
encircles
738.01
enclose
272.16
enclosed
166.16
417.24
870.24
enclosing
143.07
433.07
513.18
enclosure
087.23
434.23
503.04
575.03
encore
889.22
encounter
290.28
640.27
699.25
encountered
085.07
440.02
652.27
encountering
287.28
364.11
encourage
218.02
385.25
704.02
804.13
encouraged
293.04
625.12
encourageingly
747.04
encouraging
113.09
118.18
270.28
encroach
531.07
encroaches
387.25
encumber
911.22
encyclopaedic
803.20
end
074.15
078.05
085.11
088.03
099.16
108.06
109.21
123.03
154.11
162.11
166.26
169.15
170.26
184.01
210.01
269.06
299.26

331.27
332.02
335.11
391.07
400.06
414.17
414.17
416.16
434.03
440.09
442.04
532.17
532.19
538.04
545.23
554.14
558.10
574.11
599.14
627.21
655.17
669.21
716.09
728.03
769.27
771.07
771.20
793.11
793.12
794.21
809.13
816.13
822.06
824.16
828.11
840.03
910.06

endearment
820.22

endearments
406.07
601.23
792.20

endeavour
360.22
377.14
433.23
709.15
824.17
872.28

endeavoured
023.02
023.02
056.03
227.12
320.10
341.16
470.05
562.02
603.28
862.17

endeavouring
002.11
089.21

endeavours
171.26
482.15

ended
129.02
216.02

endless
552.04
619.10

endowed
374.18
400.13
490.06
738.15

endowments
815.14

ends
318.17
762.04

endurance
023.21
103.10
360.27
762.02

endure
008.27
025.04
043.02
102.23
144.12
322.16
463.27
545.08
618.02
620.22
624.11
654.06
647.05
804.20
820.19
901.16

endured
020.22
111.21
251.05
511.11
628.12

663.26
838.20
889.01
901.15

enemies
105.26
107.22
131.15

enemy
405.03
836.02

energetic
512.01
544.02
762.06

energies
062.02
734.28
793.05
820.04
822.27

energy
273.12
287.05
302.03
350.02
425.17
429.17
573.25
607.24
612.10
649.25
655.05
664.27
797.20
818.01
845.08
850.16
901.22
911.19

enervate
755.20

enfant
256.09

enfeebled
579.06
684.15

enforce
425.05

enforced
035.18
425.04

engaged
078.14
088.10
235.24
254.04
336.13
362.08
392.12
504.14
727.10
746.17
803.25
837.23

engagement
837.26

engender
372.24

engendered
051.27
748.23

engines
861.23

england
031.18
058.24
172.09
202.02
202.07
242.07
384.09
436.12
501.02
504.26
509.07
559.14
593.11
603.14
603.24
631.25
632.26
638.22
679.05
704.07
732.03
766.28
773.05
783.21
801.05
819.04
819.21
822.02
838.15
840.16
852.18
864.26
864.27
867.01
867.03
867.04

911.14

english
097.20
168.25
172.03
197.21
198.22
207.23
245.19
257.23
277.22
281.13
288.19
289.23
335.27
347.22
370.25
381.27
546.03
547.17
636.05
701.27
721.05
775.06
908.11

englishman's
290.09

engravings
352.17

enigma
196.19
408.17
536.13
559.16

enigmas
397.11

enigmatical
275.03
311.18

enjoined
311.26

enjoy
219.01
249.21
401.18
524.09
533.14
643.08
715.08
734.11
775.12
785.22
790.23
790.24
809.27

enjoyed
064.28
146.11
148.14
150.10
563.18
711.14

enjoying
152.07
194.24

enjoyment
045.14
145.07
166.18
365.01
636.22
670.18
730.14
744.19
783.02
792.27
799.16

enjoyments
314.02
796.19

enjoys
757.10

enlarge
292.05
674.15

enlarged
161.18
473.09

enlighten
534.12

enlightened
392.01
716.22
850.23

enlist
814.01
823.06

enmity
552.04

enormous
328.03

enough
009.22
037.09
038.14
040.07
040.11
042.04
054.28
066.24
067.01

076.15
088.18
091.20
093.06
093.23
132.05
137.21
139.25
139.25
146.19
147.16
149.11
165.13
166.27
172.16
177.14
178.02
193.03
194.16
201.03
211.23
222.03
226.19
245.17
250.14
254.07
261.01
261.21
265.11
286.05
290.11
294.26
298.22
323.12
326.12
327.11
330.04
354.28
394.02
394.04
398.28
428.25
438.12
456.18
474.12
493.15
497.06
505.08
536.13
538.02
541.08
558.05
566.21
571.08
582.09
596.03
605.02
614.12
616.05
619.07
627.22
635.10
638.09
661.23
664.03
678.02
679.20
686.11
691.04
697.26
698.23
699.17
701.20
703.24
726.16
730.17
733.25
743.16
749.01
751.01
760.11
780.22
781.24
782.25
784.01
800.08
803.26
808.18
827.12
834.10
850.16
852.03
852.05
854.01
863.07
877.02
901.12
908.05

enounce
409.24

enounced
036.26
815.06

enrage
287.02

enriched
545.17

enrolled
096.19

ensconced
347.20

enslaved
546.19

ensnares
514.07

ensued
281.01
389.04

ensuing
553.22
800.12
801.06

ensure
489.10

entailed
319.14
627.15

entanglement
619.11
736.11

enter
052.05
057.09
348.20
364.10
389.03
507.11
510.09
568.24
581.05
588.18
667.02
746.14
775.04
824.27
828.19
851.16
870.04
882.27

entered
016.15
023.25
033.29
076.18
078.04
080.12
081.01
121.26
141.03
152.08
166.03
186.19
229.02
232.06
232.21
236.24
255.22
277.01
284.22
286.10
310.27
342.10
345.26
347.05
352.06
381.15
394.03
427.01
43.24
445.19
446.08
457.12
458.01
485.12
498.25
505.24
549.11
554.19
589.01
641.09
657.08
664.23
665.13
689.12
699.13
718.23
722.16
725.28
750.22
799.18
837.25
854.22
904.05
911.15

entering
154.13
207.06
305.08
332.05
435.07
503.20
653.13
675.26
735.11
843.08
870.23
886.11

enterprise
814.02

enters
455.18
760.22

entertain
012.05
214.09
316.22
319.26
779.19
880.12
885.06

entertained
020.24
214.02
554.23
630.23
714.04
885.01

entertaining
211.09

entertainment
138.19
149.25
202.25
365.05

enthusiasm
712.11

enthusiastic
030.21

enticed
503.04

entire
039.14
560.23
785.06
820.03
823.08

entirely
120.19
213.12
245.25
264.04
515.22
516.19
517.24
609.14
725.02
794.23
908.25

entitle
240.11

entitled
060.05

entrails
256.07

entrance
039.15
071.06
115.13
133.08
153.26
235.17
237.18
271.25
339.12
340.27
364.14
394.14
420.22
581.11
598.16
746.21
766.13

entranced
712.26
758.09

entrapped
598.06

entreat
516.10
531.04
573.03
839.04
887.12
903.25

entreated
468.12
487.06
529.14
534.01
540.04
549.25
660.18
795.08
848.20

entreaties
544.02

entreating
386.02
620.16
809.11

entrust
048.28

entrusted
086.14
161.12
274.12

entwine
552.08

entwined
876.18

enumeration
357.01

EVER (continued)

143.10
150.15
150.17
150.22
158.16
165.06
178.03
179.16
187.28
192.14
196.23
208.04
208.09
211.03
213.13
222.08
224.23
241.23
242.12
242.19
243.12
249.22
253.10
257.17
312.15
318.14
325.18
352.02
355.13
372.09
394.19
423.08
436.23
437.03
440.26
447.19
465.17
467.26
468.20
478.15
479.04
482.25
485.10
493.20
496.01
503.02
512.08
521.19
521.20
528.09
528.11
528.12
543.22
544.28
545.18
546.25
550.21
562.11
580.06
587.14
587.17
590.09
601.22
603.13
612.06
615.03
615.03
615.23
615.25
618.04
621.14
623.28
624.04
627.24
630.09
633.13
636.15
638.03
642.26
645.10
651.20
656.25
670.23
681.26
686.18
693.22
697.08
697.28
698.14
703.03
708.20
712.08
725.05
731.19
731.24
737.21
737.22
760.06
775.27
778.04
779.01
790.22
797.05
800.01
804.03
816.04
817.09
819.07
826.15
828.21
836.28
845.16
848.21
849.19
852.18
861.27
865.09
866.20
871.27
884.10
890.03
891.21
892.13
894.02
894.21
895.03
895.28
897.24
897.25
897.25
897.26
900.11
907.17
908.17
909.01
909.02
909.06

ever-shifting
471.02

ever-torturing
374.03

ever-watchful
805.06

evergreen
219.14

every
007.24
007.25
018.24
019.08
030.09
045.14
049.02
059.02
061.14
062.17
065.25
078.08
087.24
094.09
098.17
098.21
111.14
111.21
116.09
118.28
120.07
123.09
136.13
140.17
142.07
142.13
162.25
162.26
182.19
199.16
210.12
217.20
233.15
292.16
309.20
315.07
315.08
319.24
330.02
330.13
334.02
336.12
351.21
358.04
363.10
402.07
405.17
405.18
411.04
415.26
460.08
479.07
494.09
499.12
511.28
520.02
524.19
524.20
530.10
550.28
552.15
556.04
572.12
573.01
573.06
575.20
598.18
617.11
621.02
630.10
635.08
676.27
677.13
691.01
692.22
693.18
701.14
704.04
705.11
715.09
721.18
727.18
734.19
736.06
748.11
753.25
763.22
772.02
779.26
782.17
791.27
792.02
796.05
801.27
806.06
806.27
809.03
820.22
832.04
832.11
832.11
867.14
898.15
911.06

every-day
290.11

everybody
040.14
064.08
130.27
130.28
134.16
176.19
195.24
478.06
491.23
496.19
874.07

everything
092.02
092.25
176.05
193.19
202.15
203.28
204.27
258.16
319.15
470.13
566.19
567.20
707.11
791.09
795.09
863.03

everywhere
132.22
334.27
364.08
433.02
662.07
663.07
753.12
809.02

evidence
320.16
591.05
605.10
623.23
859.22

evidences
057.18
750.19

evident
253.23
425.15
564.13
670.10

evidently
043.06
125.16
131.22
206.15
206.20
338.09
343.05
359.12
431.26
436.16
473.25
589.17
659.11
666.25
697.20
700.03
708.01
718.11
751.18
886.16

evil
102.25
102.27
125.04
500.06
505.21
505.21
564.05
639.02
657.16
808.19
808.21
885.19

evince
118.19
730.05
791.01

evinced
150.20
445.16
543.15

evincing
315.24
417.16
832.09

ewe
612.01

ewer
296.17
307.24

ewers
096.11

ex-act-ly
507.03

exact
060.27
063.14
360.08
492.08
527.06

exacted
049.02

exacting
020.20
205.03
265.10
626.28
719.07
748.19
806.16
911.23

exaction
911.26

exactly
058.26
178.01
180.10
221.28
256.28
368.08
402.23
496.23
799.04

exactness
280.08

exacts
841.09

exaggerate
135.11
280.16

exaggerated
581.15
742.25
812.25

exalted
756.02
885.02
889.26

examination
090.19
382.03
489.06

examine
030.23
259.14
308.03
504.06
685.02
701.20
753.16
871.20
884.20

examined
052.26
061.06
090.08
098.12
116.28
136.27
143.09
171.19
198.15
240.13
246.17
320.10
342.26
398.13
403.22
701.01
733.16
839.15

examining
084.22
141.01
387.01
693.18
888.03

example
107.20
113.10
125.18
126.19
357.03
417.15

examples
743.18

exasperation
619.09

exceeding
078.11

exceedingly
038.25
382.19

excel
162.04

excelled
713.10

excellence
374.23
730.09

excellences
717.16

excellent
055.03
126.17
162.02
162.21
181.14
293.05
319.02
387.10
507.15
532.18
743.20

excellently
554.23

except
062.07
079.16
111.12
147.12
148.10
184.09
204.22
236.10
236.13
259.26
329.16
388.19
566.21
605.02
626.11
707.12
748.22
848.24
853.28
864.28

excepted
328.15
477.27

exception
421.06
727.18
869.11

excesses
627.28

excessive
690.26

exchange
154.21
544.13
546.03
604.06
665.05
671.06
671.08

exchanged
143.18
400.28
805.04
812.25

exchanging
790.02

excitable
417.08

excitation
375.07

excite
030.15
359.11
373.02
470.13
659.14

excited
071.15
108.03
108.20
139.03
160.18
174.21
389.26
393.06
462.25
469.18
473.06
558.25
618.25
625.07
681.23
704.27
713.13
782.05
783.26
848.21
875.12
882.12

excitement
013.14
062.19
079.08
101.10
136.02
166.17
229.25
387.15
476.19
572.07
610.19
640.12
708.02
766.27
786.20
817.24
846.22

excitements
164.11

excites
270.13

exciting
715.15
735.14
745.18

exclaimed
023.28
058.15
073.28
080.18
100.01
195.16
203.23
210.28
255.25
256.15
285.07
300.26
333.05
347.10
359.16
370.07
380.13
381.09
386.22
388.21
454.11
457.12
469.24
517.05
536.21
546.01
563.11
564.11
580.19
600.06
613.22
672.09
678.21
736.25
741.23
764.04
778.01
781.27
807.11
826.05
840.22
849.28
866.25
902.04

exclaiming
110.01
212.02
277.16

exclamation
613.17
871.24

exclamations
305.19

exclude
002.15
087.24
125.20
401.07
530.20

excluded
045.14
330.26
511.28
721.18

excluding
684.27

exclusive
742.23

excrescence
120.21

excruciating
301.05

excursion
337.25
384.04
791.11

excursions
714.16

excusable
863.24

excuse
227.24
245.09
280.28
363.08
505.10
523.16
528.28
687.22
741.25
766.16
792.26

excused
024.11
553.12

execrations
043.14

execute
475.07
545.10

executed
039.08
065.18

execution
319.09
346.08
752.13

exercise
001.10
065.27
081.11
088.06
128.07
142.16
147.07
216.16
254.08
390.28
700.23
723.07
805.05

exercised
373.25
797.04
797.20

exercises
312.24

exert
514.09
619.10
721.15
730.16

exertion
745.10
790.14
800.10

exhaused
649.08
675.03

exhausted
155.16
156.25
667.04

exhaustion
688.11
707.19

exhibit
255.06
804.06

exhibition
200.27

exhilarating
781.22

exhilaration
799.07

exhort
814.12

exhortations
118.25

exigencies
287.24

exigency
112.18

exile
164.23
439.22
895.27

exiled
499.07

exist
158.15
249.25
399.03
444.08
558.01
730.11
821.15

existence
014.13
057.08
140.03
160.03
165.12
195.23
215.14
216.05
228.24
229.28
229.28

268.10
271.16
282.11
292.05
401.09
439.08
476.18
478.07
570.11
590.19
592.03
592.22
622.05
622.10
625.19
637.21
641.24
644.12
644.26
730.25
735.23
745.09
753.04
775.27
818.27
847.04
862.10

existent
194.18
505.21

exists
481.04
591.10
644.20

exit
361.19
604.05

exodus
055.17

exonerated
328.04

exorcised
885.19

exotics
331.11
367.28

expand
063.18
438.19

expanded
215.28
230.20
258.27
512.04
626.17
741.03
798.14

expanding
140.17

expanse
164.13
248.14

expansive
570.12
691.08
756.24

expect
059.25
196.12
211.01
239.14
280.11
316.16
325.08
326.02
349.09
363.09
428.14
527.06
537.09
668.22
687.08
722.08
730.14
780.01
851.14

expectancy
809.24

expectant
605.19
849.07
886.16

expectation
314.08
388.08
665.22
879.12
898.05

expectations
733.25
806.17
819.27

expected
038.25
094.22
108.06
178.03
187.18
192.04
194.17
210.06

222.05
281.18
284.23
305.07
306.28
328.11
351.06
395.16
409.08
419.02
475.27
479.18
491.17
563.12
611.15
619.06
638.24
667.19
670.25
674.10
733.20
739.13
766.05
768.28
792.03
795.04
806.16
811.08
827.24
829.05
892.09

expecting
098.21
116.09
182.07
314.16
718.21
760.18
767.13
829.22
870.09
883.14
883.21

expects
205.06
264.06

expediency
550.06

expedient
019.21
302.12
541.05
555.25
708.10

expel
102.21

expelled
424.14

expense
009.12
703.10

expensive
353.25

experience
065.23
164.08
215.09
230.06
239.18
264.21
265.13
265.26
282.09
324.13
482.28
528.11
597.19
632.16
670.19
734.26
759.01
888.12
900.17
908.20

experienced
153.15
422.21
459.26
466.05
490.09
520.07
572.16
594.08
688.10
716.22
766.27
802.08
832.28
852.23

experiences
404.24

experiencing
065.06
645.07

experiment
531.07
807.23
807.24

expiate
518.19

expiating
278.07

expired
361.16
426.19
506.20
535.06

explain
098.28
108.28
117.13
278.09
279.03
360.28
515.05
580.06
581.03
623.17
707.02
719.13
721.08
784.05
784.05
805.20
838.19

explained
077.09
104.26
194.11
196.20
372.28
481.08
591.21
704.12
784.03
842.06
854.07
861.01
873.19

explaining
906.27

explains
285.14

explanation
035.06
089.18
159.11
222.16
264.28
326.16
354.15
361.01
391.16
418.08
519.26
534.06
569.04
589.19
597.21
618.20
727.28
780.02

explanations
051.07
257.22
522.20
605.09

explanatory
087.13

explicit
253.19
854.08

exploits
074.22

explore
378.09

explored
017.18

explosion
605.04

expose
484.03

exposed
113.02
127.09
648.28

expostulate
614.17
714.22

expostulations
104.16

exposure
181.18
430.15

express
036.17
238.01
269.09
408.13
462.10
494.27
511.14
528.23
533.27
607.25
621.16
627.06
734.15
779.20
902.12
902.12

908.27

expressed
043.04
057.10
083.04
103.12
177.27
189.25
190.14
226.26
298.12
369.05
406.04
489.13
535.01
544.02
699.16
715.20
720.28
750.23
799.01
811.01
824.05
841.24

expresses
753.26

expressing
290.15
539.24

expression
099.27
266.12
289.28
301.25
308.03
344.11
345.21
346.16
350.20
375.28
377.24
392.06
429.06
450.04
521.16
618.21
642.21
643.06
699.28
737.19
755.13
760.23
764.04
791.23
827.24
886.20

expressive
053.18
390.15
746.26

expressly
333.14

exquisite
268.24
341.04
406.08
462.25
630.25
683.18
746.09
910.01

exquisitely
667.11
758.28

extant
357.28

extend
102.25
714.09
760.20
834.05

extended
124.18
185.06
272.15
690.21

extending
119.28
502.07
656.19

extends
109.13
527.21

extensive
507.13
546.11

extent
706.10

exterior
086.12
178.09

external
263.02
852.27

externally
323.26
496.26

externals
191.25

extinguished
079.22

293.10
369.23
394.08
460.03
533.06
578.22
872.08

extinguisher
286.22

extinguishing
296.23

extirpate
350.09

extort
566.05

extorted
224.05
391.01

extract
656.04
832.11

extracted
773.25

extraneous
405.09

extraordinary
127.15
209.12
290.08
567.24
676.24

extravagance
447.23
570.22

extreme
004.14
061.23
192.10
315.06
411.13
460.23
632.16

extremely
463.06

extremes
383.11

extremities
007.06
355.25
665.09
849.02

extremity
003.27
335.18
623.12
733.01

extricate
603.14

extricating
640.04

extrication
321.24
505.18

exult
063.18
187.21

exultant
215.27

exultation
518.07
564.20

exulted
853.10

exultingly
178.21

eye
007.08
022.13
029.10
042.11
044.19
046.07
056.21
057.13
060.24
061.18
062.11
062.17
084.27
099.23
116.09
119.22
123.10
128.01
140.25
155.08
164.19
215.24
226.16
229.15
247.18
249.09
268.01
269.08
272.14
283.12
286.08
305.06
309.02
313.02
322.13

344.20	018.01	568.03	273.10	222.05	651.04
346.16	023.04	576.07	273.27	224.14	651.14
349.26	025.08	577.07	275.12	226.26	656.21
351.01	031.24	578.03	276.07	228.24	666.04
372.10	034.23	578.08	277.24	237.04	666.04
375.15	034.23	578.23	279.18	239.16	670.05
377.26	041.16	583.09	281.07	241.17	674.19
382.06	047.27	586.06	282.07	259.27	674.21
382.14	052.27	587.18	283.24	262.23	682.17
382.24	054.26	587.21	297.12	276.08	686.02
383.28	068.12	590.12	320.25	276.14	686.27
392.24	076.20	590.24	321.25	292.11	686.28
395.08	080.02	602.06	338.23	298.11	690.16
395.20	085.06	607.10	406.14	313.01	691.20
404.07	085.22	607.11	447.06	321.12	697.19
404.07	085.24	617.25	448.14	322.09	699.25
404.19	094.25	619.01	456.09	323.12	701.23
437.15	095.06	620.23	461.23	324.07	701.24
461.16	103.14	628.14	465.25	326.08	701.27
465.17	115.07	628.26	467.16	338.16	704.20
466.13	124.24	635.07	467.17	341.28	719.08
485.25	125.22	643.22	480.26	343.08	720.25
497.04	127.14	651.15	481.03	343.12	726.07
506.03	128.10	656.12	482.12	343.23	732.24
528.06	133.03	657.11	482.21	345.16	733.16
544.05	136.21	662.14	484.01	345.16	737.10
545.12	137.11	668.01	489.18	346.16	737.18
547.02	138.11	680.11	495.03	349.02	740.12
563.03	139.17	686.14	507.07	349.17	740.26
578.21	163.05	694.15	508.04	349.28	742.15
591.17	175.11	699.24	522.17	359.26	747.05
592.11	186.02	701.18	523.19	361.26	760.24
594.16	198.16	702.02	524.25	361.26	763.22
594.17	200.15	702.24	525.25	369.27	767.07
610.12	206.18	703.23	535.11	370.19	767.16
611.20	222.04	704.24	544.25	374.15	798.05
612.10	224.15	725.18	602.22	375.15	807.18
622.23	225.18	726.03	603.04	375.28	821.01
640.11	230.17	733.02	604.01	382.04	836.22
641.19	237.24	737.27	605.17	382.20	839.16
649.05	239.16	740.19	605.19	384.11	855.06
649.05	248.20	744.25	774.04	390.14	858.07
649.15	250.17	755.22	774.06	395.03	882.22
659.09	258.24	758.04	774.07	397.21	896.07
673.05	259.05	774.02	774.23	397.28	faced
674.05	259.06	807.19	779.09	398.10	560.12
678.22	259.06	807.19	779.12	399.22	834.21
693.19	259.25	808.15	780.04	402.16	faces
701.24	262.15	810.21	780.06	403.22	084.08
712.15	264.13	811.10	787.19	406.20	113.05
715.17	282.14	818.12	865.11	406.24	120.23
723.20	284.26	823.20	876.24	407.06	165.10
738.02	292.09	825.04	876.24	421.10	167.06
738.22	301.24	827.14	876.26	421.17	239.25
740.27	308.01	829.18	886.06	423.27	246.14
745.20	317.01	836.21	891.06	424.19	359.21
746.19	318.08	840.08	894.03	437.16	399.24
747.06	321.14	844.09	eyre's	441.24	528.02
753.18	337.20	858.12	780.08	459.26	622.05
755.13	345.14	865.23	eyres	460.21	677.03
761.07	349.02	872.08	179.17	465.06	677.12
763.18	349.16	875.22	eyrie	465.16	681.10
768.04	350.01	877.23	415.05	470.02	facile
768.14	351.06	879.02	f	471.10	505.11
803.27	354.03	881.16	171.06	471.11	fact
805.07	363.02	887.10	faal	472.09	012.05
811.08	368.07	890.21	906.23	478.13	020.09
813.08	369.26	891.13	fable	479.19	030.13
821.01	371.14	903.21	201.09	480.08	067.09
824.05	372.06	910.27	302.02	480.24	151.03
832.15	373.22	912.12	fabric	481.28	166.22
844.16	389.14	eyre	344.25	490.26	195.23
849.08	389.15	012.15	571.22	494.26	196.10
855.06	392.12	015.09	facade	500.04	264.17
856.26	398.01	023.26	283.01	512.02	462.20
860.03	398.01	024.18	face	512.02	466.09
867.20	400.14	034.05	008.16	516.21	472.17
867.22	401.13	034.07	013.23	517.01	594.01
881.27	401.15	037.03	017.21	518.25	622.24
909.19	414.10	043.22	022.27	521.08	771.21
909.25	417.04	053.08	027.10	521.15	821.19
910.16	421.07	053.14	034.26	539.09	862.18
910.21	421.20	058.27	047.25	545.14	facts
eye-brows	422.27	062.28	050.21	552.14	031.10
060.23	423.06	075.16	051.09	567.05	160.18
eyebrow	434.18	133.28	052.16	568.17	633.16
283.18	449.22	142.05	053.28	577.16	faculties
465.19	461.08	179.23	060.20	578.01	026.09
eyebrows	461.25	182.11	063.26	578.01	075.22
224.15	463.11	183.07	071.07	578.02	192.01
257.05	468.15	199.04	072.14	578.22	216.16
242.14	471.26	199.04	075.14	579.05	675.08
343.10	480.24	204.24	084.28	581.15	712.26
350.01	483.12	237.22	084.28	587.12	724.14
471.18	485.03	237.26	099.02	588.21	743.07
551.10	485.18	238.02	099.26	592.11	790.23
578.07	498.14	239.11	104.09	594.13	797.18
884.07	504.20	239.14	119.13	594.18	808.07
eyelash	515.25	239.28	123.06	599.21	faculty
159.20	517.04	243.02	127.28	600.14	065.27
738.01	519.09	243.12	129.10	602.07	261.15
eyelashes	521.10	251.02	134.12	613.21	660.11
472.01	523.15	256.18	136.18	620.21	736.06
eyelid	523.16	256.28	155.13	622.01	fade
752.12	525.10	258.01	155.26	628.13	405.28
896.09	535.01	259.14	158.18	637.12	642.12
eyelids	536.11	262.11	159.15	641.20	907.08
872.20	537.02	264.10	170.16	643.05	faded
eyes	542.14	264.16	177.15	647.09	031.04
008.23	546.16	269.05	197.06	649.06	046.24
017.23	567.01	270.18	211.14	650.25	049.06

611.20
674.04
809.22
fading
130.13
542.07
fagged
544.22
803.21
fagging
030.13
679.23
tail
053.21
360.22
375.02
417.16
784.06
failed
052.05
114.20
164.05
172.06
375.09
382.05
445.17
481.28
545.10
633.23
804.06
810.23
failing
324.11
672.19
fails
505.09
850.17
failure
111.06
307.07
375.01
faim
212.04
fain
065.27
065.28
278.01
587.08
663.10
713.16
taint
082.16
229.25
248.24
422.07
427.19
607.19
614.12
665.03
faintest
229.12
852.25
fainting
420.07
667.20
faintly
165.17
594.25
850.02
taintness
420.05
672.26
tair
085.24
248.08
252.28
271.24
316.04
333.24
335.14
343.14
343.23
359.26
574.01
392.10
407.29
461.06
479.06
492.19
566.04
587.19
598.05
624.10
655.14
677.03
680.08
680.23
681.08
702.05
714.16
758.12
765.13
770.06
858.06
890.21
891.12
906.24
908.10
fairer
191.27
346.14

fairfax
171.17
172.01
173.28
184.06
184.17
186.11
186.25
188.06
188.12
191.01
193.04
195.01
196.08
197.09
198.22
199.21
203.12
203.20
204.21
206.11
208.10
208.20
209.22
210.16
210.28
211.17
213.06
214.19
214.28
215.13
218.04
218.13
229.23
231.22
232.12
232.22
234.12
235.16
236.14
236.20
237.18
237.22
238.16
239.04
240.23
242.13
242.25
243.09
244.12
246.11
246.20
251.11
251.16
253.17
255.08
257.05
257.09
257.18
263.16
286.20
293.18
295.19
296.06
298.15
298.16
302.13
308.08
311.13
312.13
317.20
322.11
324.04
325.26
326.14
327.07
328.05
331.12
332.05
333.05
338.05
338.19
339.09
361.10
365.14
384.21
386.01
420.12
426.04
433.20
433.23
449.10
491.14
491.18
492.08
493.07
496.16
498.07
498.18
499.12
506.10
519.15
522.15
524.06
534.04
536.21
555.15
569.11
571.22
576.23
587.07

593.09
598.16
610.25
624.03
633.14
640.17
640.28
653.09
773.02
809.11
849.22
864.19
871.17
fairfax's
212.06
218.19
231.20
235.01
236.08
305.16
308.07
311.15
315.14
345.05
345.12
446.01
534.22
539.02
fairies
090.22
fairly
152.04
549.03
773.21
fairy
005.24
017.25
031.12
049.18
167.23
204.07
241.19
496.27
524.12
542.16
542.26
543.10
543.13
882.04
884.21
fairy-born
885.16
fairy-like
461.05
525.04
742.20
faisait
277.19
faith
157.18
263.08
395.15
398.06
480.05
515.23
552.06
574.01
606.20
608.09
828.23
912.20
faithful
150.20
437.28
472.17
479.15
517.06
561.04
638.20
656.06
696.13
755.05
818.05
888.17
911.18
912.07
912.16
faithfully
321.27
322.21
644.28
645.01
716.06
743.03
811.27
falcon
383.05
falcon-eye
552.14
fall
019.13
033.15
035.01
035.03
035.19
054.11
079.27
105.04
108.27
114.15
154.04

232.17
240.12
351.06
425.23
535.13
677.24
685.16
742.09
835.02
863.10
fallen
066.14
272.01
363.04
408.03
425.22
478.28
575.05
582.23
603.15
692.11
731.13
859.13
860.01
867.19
fallibilities
823.21
fallible
274.08
274.10
falling
123.08
153.24
197.06
356.13
545.03
833.02
873.02
falls
015.27
765.05
902.14
false
033.16
034.16
122.09
200.22
244.11
381.12
603.17
622.28
758.22
falsehood
057.21
060.08
135.08
484.04
591.06
616.07
falter
170.09
441.04
faltering
667.21
falters
125.26
familiar
140.09
406.19
407.10
465.07
480.25
580.13
616.24
855.06
856.17
familiarly
637.25
families
717.13
family
022.06
039.02
124.21
126.27
148.18
161.14
165.06
168.20
188.16
205.10
252.05
252.06
252.22
253.08
289.05
321.07
374.04
446.21
451.19
452.19
473.19
474.28
479.15
487.10
597.10
597.15
624.27
629.12
632.18
696.09

697.26
699.06
751.01
751.04
751.06
776.03
786.13
892.22
family's
468.09
famine
082.21
670.04
898.04
famished
112.09
138.21
685.24
685.25
877.16
famous
526.16
786.11
fanatic's
630.18
fancied
186.11
314.14
640.01
677.26
825.06
839.22
910.16
fancies
221.10
fancy
041.18
172.18
181.04
247.20
302.26
319.12
319.17
319.25
322.26
345.07
345.09
409.23
438.28
470.28
472.15
481.03
509.28
535.14
546.09
597.18
671.19
690.18
757.20
777.23
859.01
867.04
fancying
375.02
858.08
fand
680.28
fang
286.20
891.02
fans
392.06
fantastic
320.27
454.13
far
008.11
016.18
027.08
033.07
036.21
054.28
073.14
073.17
075.03
076.02
081.22
093.15
102.22
103.03
112.24
120.20
129.07
135.21
140.06
150.11
151.15
151.15
162.14
163.22
183.19
184.21
184.26
185.09
205.12
209.01
210.01
219.18
220.25
230.24
250.08

258.02
261.05
263.15
282.15
294.07
308.05
315.05
337.01
345.11
349.08
349.08
359.19
375.28
381.22
396.16
406.10
426.21
427.14
459.22
492.21
498.24
507.28
526.03
539.14
541.09
557.10
561.18
562.22
564.01
572.03
608.01
619.07
632.23
638.02
650.05
654.15
656.01
659.03
664.19
668.12
669.19
673.09
673.19
674.07
674.17
679.05
687.05
691.11
705.16
711.04
713.10
716.08
717.11
725.05
732.23
745.06
751.03
752.21
753.25
756.11
760.10
769.02
772.04
775.13
788.08
802.07
802.19
802.21
826.05
834.07
835.26
840.17
847.26
855.09
870.10
883.27
884.27
888.24
899.05
900.01
900.02
far-distant
444.08
farce
514.15
fare
059.04
094.10
138.22
855.15
farewell
456.03
456.06
456.09
456.17
456.20
618.04
651.18
651.19
653.09
653.10
790.03
813.08
828.14
farm
666.14
867.26
farm-house
671.10
farmer
671.11

744.18
farmers'
722.23
744.09
farming
698.11
farms
559.11
farther
019.15
025.14
105.21
194.12
230.24
404.14
406.12
457.10
573.06
573.06
658.04
683.02
855.26
870.11
farthest
004.03
527.20
568.22
658.18
819.26
fascinated
017.17
022.13
fascinating
066.06
374.28
402.10
759.01
fascination
224.26
712.13
738.02
fashion
076.12
066.01
122.04
301.03
363.12
390.05
461.09
490.02
494.23
637.21
650.20
fashionable
251.10
316.19
473.12
717.12
fashionable-looking
581.07
fashioned
171.20
fashions
207.05
fast
065.02
100.26
153.15
199.21
218.28
226.09
229.03
267.25
316.02
421.23
426.14
458.10
467.16
485.15
497.25
498.04
542.07
551.17
555.21
560.05
560.24
563.08
564.01
598.10
613.18
618.27
627.10
655.10
656.17
656.17
674.23
680.02
758.12
770.24
782.12
853.02
847.16
848.27
852.09
856.13
863.26
873.02
874.21
877.01
fasten
209.23

236.01
295.09
309.26
476.13
477.25
582.16
587.24
826.24
899.08
fastened
084.15
183.25
190.17
191.02
259.13
310.15
341.25
369.06
422.25
432.22
435.26
466.03
604.13
719.07
870.23
899.18
fastening
366.04
427.05
585.06
faster
167.16
648.16
782.13
fastidious
205.03
549.19
fasting
118.05
fat
094.04
476.16
fatal
732.20
814.22
884.12
fatality
861.27
fate
103.07
270.10
280.10
292.28
514.20
532.08
568.10
596.11
635.26
647.03
663.20
673.05
725.23
734.28
844.23
846.13
859.13
895.27
fated
294.22
808.27
fateful
419.15
fates
771.14
father
009.09
033.17
036.23
037.17
040.19
040.25
089.15
091.10
140.13
157.10
158.06
252.21
265.12
275.20
288.15
469.03
536.07
536.20
536.22
624.04
624.22
626.08
627.21
629.12
632.13
632.21
669.21
680.20
681.05
695.24
696.04
698.05
698.21
721.12
725.20
727.05

727.06
727.15
736.08
750.07
750.21
751.16
756.01
757.02
780.13
801.18
861.01
869.06
father's
179.16
180.02
480.11
695.21
698.27
714.18
719.17
780.23
fatherland
813.14
fatherly
880.13
fathom
377.01
377.27
600.21
703.25
fathomless
230.25
fatigue
079.09
191.08
664.04
690.26
795.23
841.04
841.05
fatigued
190.13
fatuous
495.21
674.09
faugh
629.06
fault
018.24
019.07
056.22
057.20
064.12
157.15
260.16
317.04
381.13
402.24
579.15
633.18
828.02
863.21
863.21
912.15
faulties
229.27
faults
064.11
102.14
103.18
104.18
108.23
149.20
150.14
268.07
288.28
292.13
292.26
355.02
377.12
505.07
faut
276.17
faux
881.07
favour
018.18
030.28
239.08
501.04
529.11
544.13
593.01
806.02
831.10
favourable
316.06
404.26
600.04
637.12
favoured
211.07
250.04
401.23
473.03
739.23
752.26
favourite
131.15
149.06
316.26

321.01
468.08
744.27
favours
031.01
276.08
454.19
555.14
fawkes
040.16
fawn
016.02
fear
010.18
017.23
044.20
051.27
111.06
147.24
148.22
155.28
171.22
182.25
182.25
189.08
195.10
211.07
224.16
275.19
294.12
307.09
312.08
315.10
340.20
377.28
422.15
427.19
436.08
436.25
438.03
446.03
483.10
495.27
520.07
523.28
529.09
537.07
547.08
568.20
597.08
607.08
619.25
622.17
630.18
641.28
642.11
647.16
655.28
656.21
662.06
672.23
687.21
708.14
722.15
746.18
759.27
767.04
769.01
817.05
817.05
827.06
832.07
841.01
884.33
912.18
fear'd
683.10
feared
006.01
007.24
028.03
052.01
052.01
054.22
151.27
155.08
305.03
305.05
314.07
353.27
366.08
426.16
521.14
563.16
584.03
615.27
644.19
644.20
646.12
676.02
750.25
796.06
823.14
844.23
851.08
853.09
862.17
872.10
fearful
022.24
029.17

032.08
036.18
048.26
126.18
154.17
415.01
577.24
578.03
616.19
627.14
632.26
844.19
fearfulness
486.05
fearing
438.25
533.16
660.05
858.27
fearless
067.16
fears
164.11
182.15
191.17
487.13
569.22
651.27
734.17
773.03
847.14
858.20
feasible
166.25
feast
496.05
777.07
feasted
138.17
142.28
712.15
feat
149.09
feather
654.12
featherbeds
327.19
feathers
049.06
881.09
feature
043.16
099.26
209.11
368.18
405.01
726.10
855.04
features
047.28
053.11
061.07
086.09
192.22
224.14
245.03
249.07
259.05
260.18
275.18
289.26
292.24
306.26
318.08
344.13
344.15
345.18
346.13
350.01
350.28
368.07
382.05
395.12
408.16
454.12
461.07
471.17
517.03
577.21
600.15
643.17
646.09
691.27
699.27
720.26
737.20
746.24
808.13
825.02
858.11
871.28
877.05
886.17
887.01
february
111.09
189.13
fed
005.22
151.19
199.19

374.11
877.16
fee
543.19
729.14
751.24
feeble
132.18
132.19
288.02
480.12
485.02
572.23
611.02
626.04
669.09
753.07
813.26
814.04
814.06
816.10
feeble-minded
487.14
feebleness
476.13
feeblest
477.25
feebly
686.08
feed
048.10
119.06
148.26
683.01
feeding
066.18
feeds
321.21
feel
028.01
029.12
029.15
036.14
059.17
075.02
106.23
107.04
107.09
125.08
127.08
158.21
164.02
182.18
190.04
206.03
216.15
216.15
219.27
265.01
269.25
272.06
275.08
291.05
294.21
301.15
324.11
334.09
349.23
351.11
389.21
398.22
410.01
432.10
434.15
439.18
440.05
469.16
484.13
490.07
494.26
504.21
512.07
522.04
533.02
535.10
548.22
558.19
568.07
568.09
566.14
582.03
587.12
587.25
623.04
638.09
654.05
657.10
662.07
672.20
673.26
675.18
687.23
700.03
709.13
732.04
734.09
734.14
752.19
786.23
787.13
793.24

796.16
816.27
818.26
828.07
831.05
845.22
871.15
876.09
882.05
885.17
887.09
888.01
898.18
898.20
899.11
901.06

feeling
026.03
057.10
066.01
074.19
088.18
100.24
127.17
130.17
139.07
162.25
213.18
216.04
244.06
259.09
261.20
274.23
283.19
351.22
361.13
371.26
373.02
400.25
404.08
422.22
439.24
466.12
478.19
478.22
478.24
497.15
498.12
505.20
508.09
510.23
520.03
523.24
606.14
611.25
615.04
615.11
621.15
628.13
638.07
647.20
672.25
682.16
689.19
712.12
716.21
719.08
730.10
731.25
753.25
761.27
785.13
799.03
807.17
823.13
824.24
842.24
846.24
849.01
849.03
853.02
863.22

feelings
005.15
009.26
036.15
045.07
063.03
065.05
108.18
119.10
131.20
131.21
163.02
276.25
512.08
320.10
323.22
325.11
350.06
352.01
364.06
396.15
398.12
405.13
440.06
462.22
500.06
513.01
517.09
532.22

532.23
621.11
643.25
722.10
725.09
731.01
736.12
744.21
745.05
771.18
783.19
785.14
822.08
825.21
828.27
829.07
834.13
843.03
856.16
880.13

feels
102.23
189.02
204.02
204.22
422.07
620.02
649.11

fees
543.20

teet
003.03
033.03
054.27
111.19
112.01
114.20
123.26
144.06
156.27
186.14
190.04
223.13
227.17
277.07
277.16
298.25
299.18
341.18
347.05
352.25
359.22
369.05
374.15
375.12
399.10
432.04
497.19
513.15
575.16
590.23
600.05
640.26
656.24
659.03
661.16
667.08
713.17
737.14
758.03
821.03
823.24
850.22

feigned
408.15
532.13
598.07

felix
103.16

fell
009.23
021.08
028.16
028.28
049.20
066.22
079.24
121.11
122.06
143.14
152.02
168.13
176.20
180.23
199.01
232.15
307.20
323.06
342.10
367.18
372.10
375.12
403.14
415.21
471.10
502.02
502.28
520.06
560.21
561.17
576.03

587.25
591.01
594.25
606.09
611.03
651.23
656.20
660.25
674.23
675.07
699.05
735.22
740.20
752.05
770.12
770.13
806.28
809.18
823.25
843.24
850.18
855.19
862.24
862.27
867.17

felling
243.08

fellow
175.21
261.21
358.19
427.18
431.11
504.19
835.21
841.14

fellow-being
706.06

fellow-beings
665.02

fellow-creature
441.03
647.12

fellow-creatures
216.21
498.11
659.16

fellow-feeling
020.25
787.01

fellow-labourer
815.02
840.18

fellow-missionary
826.09

fellow-pupils
130.05

fellow-servants
329.09

fellow-soldier's
827.03

fellow-students
804.01

fellow-teachers
169.07

fellow-worms
813.26

felt
010.11
010.14
012.10
023.01
025.07
026.14
027.03
027.24
029.24
043.01
045.07
057.09
061.14
063.19
065.01
089.18
096.13
100.13
103.13
108.04
121.05
124.24
133.12
135.24
150.12
152.20
158.17
165.13
167.16
168.13
171.27
178.05
184.28
187.26
189.16
190.13
192.20
196.23
203.03
214.16
220.17
223.21
224.18

225.09
238.13
250.06
282.06
282.08
291.26
313.07
315.23
372.13
374.06
376.23
377.08
377.21
378.03
379.15
389.07
394.18
420.04
438.16
459.25
460.28
462.17
466.11
466.19
466.19
466.20
483.10
493.01
503.02
519.28
521.08
525.19
533.17
550.22
573.06
579.06
580.17
588.22
592.08
594.09
604.18
607.17
608.13
612.27
619.27
627.04
631.17
637.28
639.17
641.24
644.15
648.27
657.11
660.01
662.17
665.03
665.19
665.24
670.24
674.27
682.04
686.03
686.17
686.28
689.04
692.06
692.12
699.17
703.21
704.20
712.14
716.10
730.22
730.23
730.23
744.27
749.24
753.20
756.21
760.26
768.06
773.03
776.05
777.05
788.04
789.10
800.01
800.10
802.05
802.18
802.24
805.10
806.06
807.16
807.27
808.06
809.13
809.25
810.13
814.20
822.18
823.26
823.26
829.03
832.21
832.26
844.14
845.20
846.27
848.14
854.25

877.09
879.07
879.22
880.27
885.17
910.05

female
126.05
346.24
759.15
760.28
837.15

femmes
334.06

fence
194.09
502.23
502.27
505.26

fender
101.16
355.28
599.10

ferment
216.13
630.03

fern-banks
712.06

ferndean
593.10
616.03
867.26
868.07
869.02
869.10
902.12

ferny
017.27

ferocity
872.11

ferret
166.27

fertilized
693.08

fervent
041.15
287.10
644.09
663.28

fervently
006.12
848.18

fervid
139.26
502.01

fervour
374.18
527.27
746.27
778.23
793.17
799.10

festal
258.13

festive
045.12

festooned
331.01

festoons
015.26

fetch
015.12
031.07
078.27
085.16
124.08
203.11
224.01
226.28
246.01
297.10
297.16
297.21
298.19
339.05
410.22
416.03
419.22
421.27
427.02
430.22
438.19
448.14
481.09
685.21
799.20

fetched
009.05
380.03
421.14

fetid
161.01
269.02

fetter
757.18

fettered
350.07
546.22
573.04
817.05
872.05

fetters
229.27
370.06
736.05
807.28

feuille
313.16

fever
040.26
150.26
153.24
154.16
160.12
208.18
374.11
468.01
484.02
703.05
725.11
761.14

fever-room
155.18

fevered
731.27

feverish
101.11
167.19
303.03
315.22
544.22
558.18
558.21
565.05
581.12
622.02
692.05
797.03

feverishly
174.24

few
009.15
061.05
071.14
071.17
073.06
135.14
136.09
137.02
142.17
147.04
147.12
150.14
151.25
160.09
180.18
202.18
217.19
219.10
220.15
222.15
245.17
249.24
252.08
266.14
267.28
273.07
276.20
289.12
298.27
299.27
305.09
310.10
351.17
363.01
370.16
396.12
425.13
425.23
434.14
462.22
481.12
491.01
493.19
514.22
535.05
588.14
600.08
600.09
604.07
605.06
621.27
623.24
637.05
652.28
673.14
689.05
691.06
695.15
698.27
699.16
701.07
708.18
711.03
712.07
717.24
718.21
729.19
731.04
731.06
743.18
752.03

764.07
780.13
790.02
790.19
798.20
804.17
811.04
814.09
852.15
873.19
895.14
fewer
007.14
148.26
fibre
898.24
fiction
380.05
893.25
fiddler
358.18
fidelity
633.06
645.03
827.04
fidget
554.02
fie
054.20
field
064.24
066.18
164.10
192.02
209.04
213.04
216.17
219.25
493.28
541.19
541.26
564.08
668.25
736.21
737.03
742.20
747.27
757.23
856.22
909.22
fields
004.11
031.25
193.26
219.19
242.09
413.15
492.16
501.09
502.24
654.23
655.08
673.14
732.11
855.03
855.11
856.08
861.07
887.18
fiend
005.07
044.23
109.09
309.22
424.06
467.26
615.20
fiendish
066.01
fiendishly
784.15
fierce
065.01
065.28
064.24
344.20
358.24
363.05
500.04
520.04
555.14
567.25
600.03
602.04
649.06
fiercest
601.16
fiery
235.17
326.07
578.21
629.20
645.07
fifteen
091.17
091.20
159.19
389.10
433.06
535.17
593.08

597.04
598.20
fifteenth
048.05
fifth
114.07
751.22
fifty
049.01
073.15
179.25
317.16
344.05
453.06
fig
453.15
490.22
490.23
889.19
fig
358.16
fight
360.01
figments
581.16
figurative
703.24
figuratively
374.16
549.04
figure
017.21
061.06
076.21
115.08
133.26
192.20
211.13
224.09
237.14
282.01
312.28
343.12
343.23
348.26
366.21
367.05
399.22
573.20
585.14
599.15
638.26
753.16
766.04
825.06
871.13
figured
074.23
181.06
221.18
figures
344.01
399.25
588.12
677.22
777.01
777.03
file
080.11
789.19
filed
079.13
filial
661.02
filing
583.05
filip
360.02
fill
315.25
330.13
368.24
471.17
819.16
874.11
912.03
filled
023.19
074.17
075.23
079.21
080.25
093.27
145.28
146.07
148.27
230.18
257.20
258.13
281.01
292.05
295.25
296.18
332.23
337.09
371.09
401.16
411.08
415.28
431.16
561.12
610.17

613.24
630.05
631.15
633.09
663.04
729.09
741.21
810.21
819.22
852.20
912.12
fillette
286.05
filling
258.18
488.18
fillip
899.14
filthy
631.24
final
262.04
finally
170.24
180.20
190.26
223.18
457.19
find
022.02
032.05
046.23
065.28
117.22
117.26
133.28
154.14
155.08
167.15
189.26
190.27
194.18
196.16
204.27
216.09
240.13
242.10
246.26
260.16
264.07
269.20
269.23
273.04
275.24
295.27
297.18
397.02
397.03
397.04
408.03
416.12
431.05
439.28
455.13
462.17
481.13
489.08
505.15
508.07
516.26
528.02
537.26
546.22
553.19
571.17
571.19
629.24
634.19
636.07
642.26
652.25
673.25
691.16
719.16
723.27
729.02
730.13
732.17
739.12
754.09
770.03
780.17
789.14
839.02
842.01
852.07
860.08
869.08
878.27
884.03
884.20
888.02
892.09
900.25
910.23
finding
297.05
361.03
633.04
659.24
660.06

764.09
769.27
873.27
finds
858.05
858.23
fine
037.05
085.25
122.02
127.27
139.20
152.04
177.11
179.04
184.07
188.27
193.23
195.13
201.28
203.21
218.11
220.24
226.18
236.12
259.06
293.23
316.19
318.06
318.10
319.01
325.11
326.25
337.24
344.06
346.09
348.08
361.02
361.11
373.05
397.23
398.16
414.06
502.09
525.04
549.17
570.04
624.25
640.22
653.14
690.15
725.18
737.15
738.01
750.02
751.12
775.09
775.10
796.24
809.26
810.27
812.14
843.24
899.13
fine-looking
382.02
finely
192.20
finer
190.10
199.14
744.13
finest
322.07
819.25
898.24
finger
283.28
407.03
528.20
531.11
532.19
543.01
565.18
623.04
649.13
767.15
768.03
858.18
884.07
fingers
001.14
061.18
076.08
099.24
131.26
207.14
294.09
302.15
407.01
420.08
442.11
466.02
471.17
485.02
525.04
620.04
830.03
876.14
876.15
898.20

finish
246.13
394.15
628.04
773.18
885.12
finished
032.12
033.24
047.11
050.27
063.17
101.22
109.23
114.20
136.08
140.18
171.03
200.10
238.06
567.06
574.10
582.20
678.12
699.07
750.15
752.07
771.19
794.25
835.23
fir-cones
066.14
fire
016.13
026.19
029.08
033.25
046.14
054.10
057.23
071.13
073.03
076.06
085.10
113.17
134.06
137.13
138.24
139.09
141.20
175.20
181.14
185.27
186.07
186.24
187.11
204.19
216.04
225.03
231.10
231.21
233.10
236.27
237.03
240.22
258.14
259.04
259.11
263.12
276.07
292.13
296.10
297.09
298.07
302.04
307.21
334.18
334.24
341.02
342.28
382.28
384.06
385.02
387.16
388.03
394.10
394.18
396.08
396.13
398.08
404.03
405.20
406.22
411.06
416.04
424.16
436.14
457.08
461.26
479.20
484.16
490.15
492.26
528.07
540.24
540.25
562.03
562.06
567.09
586.01
592.08

596.17
599.10
599.12
612.27
619.02
648.16
651.15
678.15
680.03
680.06
685.28
688.06
693.05
700.15
740.27
745.23
747.12
765.08
766.17
769.26
778.25
798.15
826.01
832.19
844.21
861.22
862.25
863.14
864.05
865.13
873.18
874.24
881.16
881.25
881.26
883.23
905.18
fire-irons
231.12
356.01
457.07
fire-light
767.10
fire-lit
677.23
fire-place
074.15
fire-places
101.15
fire-side
074.23
256.04
456.22
fire-spirit
532.05
fireless
038.01
572.05
fires
100.14
130.14
327.18
328.03
502.01
792.02
795.04
fireside
002.03
052.20
218.20
235.12
563.22
797.11
firm
004.11
023.03
127.21
270.16
350.01
405.12
411.14
471.22
560.16
591.15
693.09
705.05
749.03
761.16
911.18
firmament
812.13
firmer
459.27
590.23
755.11
848.11
891.20
firmly
094.26
125.10
650.18
734.19
742.20
firmness
382.21
693.28
753.24
firs
675.14
711.18
719.19

850.03
first
009.18
010.10
014.12
036.18
040.17
048.23
052.14
059.01
064.26
064.28
065.18
076.19
077.06
077.19
081.26
082.07
082.18
085.16
086.19
089.22
095.20
097.04
105.19
109.17
111.02
114.26
119.11
120.22
120.27
130.25
139.14
142.20
142.21
150.05
152.14
152.17
152.18
160.03
162.08
162.09
165.02
166.10
168.06
169.27
176.06
186.01
188.17
190.16
197.03
197.21
198.13
203.05
210.10
213.03
217.03
223.12
228.11
247.15
247.24
260.20
263.18
265.08
265.15
290.26
295.03
295.08
301.09
301.24
303.17
317.17
332.28
343.04
345.04
350.11
362.14
364.04
365.05
376.18
380.01
381.02
382.02
383.14
384.17
388.11
388.23
420.23
428.14
429.23
435.12
438.21
438.23
448.19
453.11
457.02
460.04
460.10
468.14
470.16
477.10
490.23
504.22
507.08
507.21
519.17
547.05
572.11
572.18
576.19
577.17

594.04
598.25
599.17
612.25
614.12
632.15
633.27
635.27
636.26
637.17
643.15
644.05
644.24
652.10
655.02
671.03
674.09
678.18
686.09
686.10
693.11
701.01
703.08
705.23
711.10
712.06
713.16
716.03
718.03
718.22
720.20
733.19
737.06
743.04
743.08
745.23
749.11
749.17
749.22
754.03
756.28
753.27
784.28
791.03
791.22
792.18
795.08
798.04
798.06
798.25
802.04
809.19
812.20
814.18
815.21
817.09
841.27
845.17
846.06
852.03
856.15
856.24
857.24
858.02
858.14
864.05
866.21
890.04
893.03
909.14
912.03
first-born
606.09
910.25
first-rate
236.13
firstly
228.27
356.28
fish
334.18
368.01
fissure
561.12
fit
021.13
025.16
028.23
044.04
135.28
156.22
158.20
225.16
290.22
359.17
390.18
417.11
420.07
427.07
463.02
489.15
708.02
815.19
816.03
816.03
fitful
208.18
229.13
607.06
fitly
678.23

fits
290.27
883.04
fitted
713.07
779.23
822.21
822.22
822.22
869.12
fitting
058.26
193.01
663.12
840.18
fitzjames
911.12
five
026.16
054.20
071.02
083.28
094.13
095.12
100.11
101.23
121.10
129.02
170.10
175.25
426.24
432.19
453.01
453.17
455.02
455.04
455.04
457.02
473.23
477.01
503.24
535.24
566.06
611.10
629.11
692.23
734.04
776.17
782.25
783.15
784.09
784.20
878.08
892.20
five-and-twenty
536.25
five-pound
906.18
fix
068.12
245.03
349.19
445.03
805.25
824.14
858.15
fixed
034.22
095.06
249.09
346.18
371.14
437.26
461.25
467.13
535.01
544.06
619.01
631.03
634.18
701.19
702.23
733.10
761.16
788.02
796.25
801.05
805.28
815.24
fixedly
307.26
482.24
827.20
fixedness
323.17
fixing
174.01
423.08
804.01
fixity
119.14
fixture
768.19
867.04
flabby
007.09
flag
363.04
flakes
066.21
804.17

flame
249.14
281.19
296.08
307.23
385.03
404.07
406.25
460.02
502.06
533.07
644.13
766.19
817.24
826.03
861.24
flamed
578.24
flames
065.12
296.23
865.25
flaming
587.17
648.26
flang
601.03
flanked
237.15
flanking
765.16
flash
375.23
472.07
539.16
715.16
flashed
331.09
407.02
651.14
flashing
552.15
587.17
flat
312.28
flatness
528.04
flatter
214.13
261.24
267.22
269.07
270.14
526.03
526.04
flattered
279.18
321.17
476.22
553.27
625.03
flatterers
760.07
flattery
531.22
flavour
406.02
692.05
flaw
738.08
flaxen
060.25
flayed
113.04
144.06
flecked
248.02
fled
110.07
294.24
588.22
856.11
877.18
888.01
flee
503.18
607.18
652.17
fleet
551.27
fleeting
166.20
636.07
flesh
007.25
056.08
108.28
121.18
133.05
262.05
292.07
313.28
428.02
513.13
516.09
546.15
616.25
617.11
630.17
673.21
674.27

730.07
761.14
793.19
832.15
845.14
849.08
851.17
852.02
876.28
899.01
901.11
909.02
909.03
fleshless
690.16
fleshly
719.28
fleurs
341.21
flew
194.06
296.20
332.16
431.06
526.26
551.18
617.17
634.08
849.25
flexibility
201.11
flexible
404.25
flexible-looking
471.21
flicker
740.27
flickered
809.22
flickering
423.24
flickers
404.07
flight
154.26
619.25
640.15
649.27
655.18
655.25
fling
647.01
flinging
578.14
flint
273.15
485.25
592.12
flinty
553.19
flirted
378.28
flit
480.02
flitted
104.09
flittered
271.18
flitting
398.16
float
004.17
floated
088.28
746.12
floating
282.13
flock
125.16
342.23
501.07
712.09
flocked
342.13
flog
100.21
flogged
102.28
flood
282.16
297.07
607.16
620.14
757.27
flood-gates
614.15
floods
088.09
608.14
floor
095.06
101.26
129.06
191.23
419.13
457.06
578.15
611.17
648.24
676.14
729.04

751.26
766.15
778.28
flooring
415.21
florence
526.22
636.01
flour
700.14
flourishing
810.20
floury
697.17
flow
220.18
255.02
282.12
361.18
386.08
518.11
560.18
607.13
620.13
635.10
713.13
799.10
861.02
flowed
139.23
flower
318.18
341.24
435.11
503.03
503.12
642.11
750.11
812.15
812.23
900.03
flower-roots
048.17
flower-sprinkled
712.18
floweret
277.28
flowers
031.04
039.08
049.06
088.02
144.18
145.04
148.03
152.01
191.28
204.12
207.25
262.17
280.21
331.03
341.05
342.27
346.01
367.03
435.01
438.18
502.20
504.02
606.02
655.15
711.20
731.13
738.26
758.19
870.26
887.19
flowery
146.03
494.05
631.18
640.24
flowing
233.19
461.11
798.07
flown
043.23
424.25
504.26
flows
781.05
fluctuations
615.10
fluency
346.10
713.16
799.08
fluent
199.23
fluently
198.17
flung
009.22
296.26
380.04
580.18
867.16
888.28

flurried 827.13
389.17
flush 912.01
748.12
792.18
flushed
515.21
517.02
568.17
594.18
740.28
760.21
fluttered
113.08
fluttering
332.22
fly
010.26
541.18
542.25
877.18
flying
024.16
507.19
791.10
854.25
foam
248.02
282.20
509.17
foaming
820.12
foamy
551.07
foe
072.19
fog
068.08
145.19
146.22
fog-bred
146.22
foil
360.07
fois
277.17
fold
110.04
320.14
565.21
845.12
folded
013.22
047.01
049.13
141.06
251.12
292.22
299.26
552.20
492.06
661.18
704.10
726.24
753.09
768.17
815.23
872.28
folding
200.14
272.14
folding-doors
203.15
folds
003.07
249.12
353.03
402.04
652.11
foliage
050.01
209.07
675.16
676.12
870.18
folk
666.21
698.09
folk's
683.11
folks
664.23
follow
008.28
043.19
106.16
118.27
164.26
399.23
405.20
418.15
439.07
587.11
598.09
598.24
617.27
631.10
720.03
735.02
747.20
806.28

840.07
912.01
followed
010.24
029.13
030.02
040.03
069.27
076.18
085.07
138.25
140.25
185.25
188.17
190.15
197.01
206.25
208.23
222.06
230.27
232.21
305.04
307.02
332.16
334.02
337.08
367.11
371.19
419.16
433.13
435.05
445.02
450.10
464.11
471.19
485.12
492.01
504.28
505.16
564.06
566.01
604.22
648.24
663.27
713.02
714.18
746.08
796.26
809.01
809.29
848.22
850.10
859.16
870.09
873.17
875.12
889.08
891.24
901.26
follower
762.16
followers
683.12
following
087.21
098.02
134.03
291.20
333.07
445.27
538.20
550.20
560.05
572.19
647.24
672.02
845.07
follows
404.10
640.15
842.10
folly
321.04
428.19
464.05
625.09
814.04
841.03
847.12
fomented
061.16
fond
048.11
055.14
239.15
252.15
252.22
256.23
316.27
353.11
493.06
537.15
545.16
550.04
617.19
643.14
697.20
731.23
fonder
069.08

fondly
747.05
756.16
910.06
fondness
162.03
661.02
895.13
food
037.28
079.08
082.23
092.11
112.04
161.01
355.09
439.20
667.05
668.16
672.05
692.04
707.18
735.06
898.05
fool
211.09
261.04
300.16
320.25
494.16
529.19
623.15
734.02
810.09
847.07
879.18
894.24
fool's
731.26
fooled
447.19
foolish
464.02
506.09
foot
015.28
062.18
082.09
174.19
223.21
224.05
237.01
276.28
281.24
361.24
432.18
458.17
462.03
495.04
504.06
511.13
526.25
585.17
610.05
639.07
648.20
653.18
676.05
735.07
738.26
829.25
854.14
869.18
footing
488.01
590.24
683.26
footman
385.04
385.28
387.11
388.09
586.09
586.18
footmen
045.23
336.15
footstool
016.10
341.14
464.24
for
002.04
002.16
003.20
006.19
007.02
007.03
007.11
007.20
008.16
008.20
008.21
008.23
009.14
010.17
010.22
012.02
012.14
012.14
012.20

013.01
013.12
014.25
015.08
015.10
018.04
018.15
018.24
019.04
019.14
020.24
023.14
024.03
027.09
027.13
028.03
028.09
028.21
028.27
029.09
029.18
030.03
031.02
031.12
032.16
032.21
033.19
034.13
034.17
035.12
035.13
036.09
036.23
038.02
038.28
040.07
040.15
040.17
041.09
041.18
042.05
043.03
044.14
044.23
045.07
046.03
047.05
047.21
048.13
048.14
049.10
049.17
049.20
050.22
051.04
051.05
051.19
051.22
052.08
052.24
053.05
053.18
054.12
056.01
056.27
058.01
059.14
059.17
060.12
061.22
062.08
063.13
064.04
064.11
064.18
065.17
066.01
067.11
067.26
068.08
068.17
069.23
070.04
071.19
074.19
074.21
076.01
076.25
079.07
080.06
080.17
081.13
082.07
082.14
082.26
082.28
083.10
084.23
085.10
085.21
086.16
086.23
087.28
088.06
088.12
090.14
091.14
091.16
091.18
091.20
092.10

092.24
093.23
093.26
094.20
097.24
102.27
103.12
104.23
105.10
109.13
109.26
113.16
114.03
115.02
115.12
115.23
116.02
116.05
116.18
117.17
117.19
118.01
119.03
121.28
123.12
124.04
124.24
125.13
125.25
127.23
131.19
131.23
132.22
132.23
133.02
133.18
135.28
136.03
136.06
136.16
137.08
137.15
137.21
138.05
140.25
140.26
141.23
143.19
145.24
146.13
146.16
147.15
148.10
149.23
149.23
150.16
150.20
150.23
150.27
151.09
151.24
152.16
152.17
153.23
154.19
159.09
159.19
161.08
161.25
162.03
162.11
164.06
164.07
165.05
165.15
165.15
165.18
166.05
166.19
167.12
167.18
167.25
168.04
169.06
169.26
170.05
170.08
170.10
170.13
170.25
171.23
173.01
173.05
173.14
174.02
174.11
179.22
179.26
180.18
180.20
180.22
182.06
183.09
186.03
186.16
187.24
188.27
189.08
190.06
190.12
191.27

192.09
194.28
196.16
196.22
199.22
200.25
201.21
201.27
202.03
202.07
202.20
202.22
202.28
203.10
203.24
203.28
205.15
206.26
207.14
208.20
210.09
210.10
210.16
211.02
211.09
212.05
213.14
214.02
214.12
214.16
214.19
214.21
215.05
216.16
216.17
216.27
217.07
217.12
218.05
218.23
219.02
219.08
219.09
219.14
221.16
223.23
223.25
223.26
224.25
225.24
226.19
227.18
228.02
228.16
230.06
230.26
232.04
232.14
232.15
233.10
233.12
234.01
234.15
235.04
236.04
237.08
237.20
239.08
240.07
241.27
242.01
242.02
242.03
243.01
243.07
243.10
244.08
245.12
246.02
246.07
247.26
248.11
249.10
250.15
250.20
250.25
252.05
252.16
253.04
253.09
253.11
254.02
254.12
255.05
255.19
256.24
257.11
258.12
259.05
259.27
260.23
261.16
262.02
262.03
262.14
263.05
263.12
263.13
263.14
264.06
264.17

266.09	360.25	464.09	530.01	613.06	672.24
267.04	361.04	464.18	530.15	613.27	674.03
267.06	361.23	464.21	530.23	614.01	677.07
267.08	362.23	464.26	530.24	616.20	677.10
267.12	363.11	465.12	531.05	616.28	677.15
267.13	364.20	466.26	532.17	617.03	678.08
267.14	365.14	468.06	533.12	617.17	679.07
267.25	366.19	468.12	533.21	617.26	679.11
268.14	367.15	468.13	534.12	618.01	679.20
269.11	370.09	469.06	534.14	618.04	680.23
270.23	371.12	469.16	534.25	618.10	681.01
272.09	374.04	470.22	536.24	618.13	681.02
275.11	374.23	470.24	536.27	618.16	681.07
276.10	376.16	471.26	537.12	618.18	682.02
279.19	376.24	472.25	537.17	619.04	682.21
281.20	376.28	473.13	539.15	619.09	683.03
284.23	377.12	474.12	539.22	620.09	683.27
285.09	377.22	474.15	539.24	621.27	684.25
285.12	379.06	475.15	540.13	621.27	686.23
285.24	380.11	475.24	540.20	622.04	687.09
286.16	380.17	476.11	540.24	623.13	687.10
286.22	382.17	476.12	541.05	623.27	687.22
286.24	382.27	476.18	541.07	624.13	690.27
286.24	383.15	477.05	542.06	624.22	692.08
287.23	385.02	477.16	542.19	624.24	692.24
287.26	389.07	478.15	543.10	625.04	693.24
288.15	390.12	478.16	544.12	625.15	694.16
288.26	391.02	478.22	544.15	626.11	696.13
288.27	391.16	478.25	545.25	627.27	696.28
289.01	391.26	479.02	546.03	628.11	697.21
290.05	392.04	480.14	546.08	630.24	698.01
290.10	392.20	483.18	546.09	630.24	698.20
290.19	392.24	483.25	546.15	631.08	698.24
290.25	393.02	483.28	546.23	631.14	698.26
291.02	399.03	484.07	547.02	631.16	699.06
291.07	402.05	484.14	547.11	631.16	699.10
291.07	402.13	484.27	547.26	632.04	699.20
292.14	403.26	485.06	548.04	632.21	700.15
292.20	405.01	485.08	548.14	633.03	702.21
292.27	406.26	486.04	548.21	633.05	703.05
293.06	412.12	486.12	549.15	633.06	703.06
293.08	412.17	487.16	549.15	633.09	704.20
293.12	412.19	488.16	549.25	635.10	705.19
298.17	414.06	488.24	550.05	635.26	707.06
299.10	415.07	489.02	550.16	636.07	707.06
300.17	415.17	489.05	551.11	636.12	707.23
300.20	416.06	490.12	551.19	636.13	707.23
301.14	416.25	490.14	553.03	638.19	708.02
301.27	417.12	491.10	553.04	639.02	709.22
305.09	418.04	491.16	553.10	639.22	710.05
306.15	418.11	491.20	555.04	639.23	711.10
308.28	418.14	492.09	555.10	639.28	712.24
310.09	421.18	492.22	555.11	641.03	712.25
310.17	421.28	493.06	555.12	641.05	714.26
310.22	422.05	493.20	555.20	641.25	715.22
311.13	422.13	494.10	556.06	642.06	715.26
312.05	424.05	494.18	557.05	642.10	716.20
312.16	427.04	495.05	558.09	642.23	716.23
312.18	427.19	497.14	560.15	642.24	717.05
314.13	428.25	497.17	561.17	643.22	717.21
314.13	429.22	497.22	562.03	644.05	717.28
314.19	430.13	497.26	562.10	645.22	718.09
315.16	430.13	497.28	562.24	646.11	719.16
316.07	430.26	499.11	564.07	646.16	719.25
317.03	431.14	503.02	564.17	646.18	720.10
318.22	431.23	503.18	565.01	646.19	721.02
318.23	432.15	505.16	565.13	647.01	721.05
319.02	434.12	506.04	566.04	647.02	721.16
319.15	434.13	506.09	566.10	647.04	721.19
319.18	436.11	506.10	567.14	647.14	721.20
320.19	436.12	506.12	569.20	647.27	721.21
323.02	436.22	506.20	570.03	648.01	721.22
324.07	437.07	508.10	570.17	648.07	721.28
325.05	437.17	508.14	570.23	648.09	722.19
325.06	437.18	508.15	571.06	648.23	723.18
326.13	438.10	508.20	571.08	651.08	724.27
326.27	438.13	509.28	572.06	651.19	725.06
327.22	439.16	511.05	575.12	652.24	725.07
327.27	440.01	511.10	575.12	653.14	725.16
328.12	440.14	511.20	578.19	653.23	725.16
329.06	440.15	512.07	579.01	654.02	726.26
330.07	440.26	513.09	579.12	654.03	727.16
330.08	441.07	513.10	582.10	654.04	727.20
330.14	441.14	513.22	582.19	654.14	727.27
331.14	441.27	513.26	583.17	657.04	728.03
331.20	442.08	514.20	583.20	657.15	728.04
331.23	442.16	515.19	587.06	658.04	731.01
332.08	442.20	515.27	587.13	658.09	731.07
333.14	444.08	516.01	588.22	659.18	731.08
333.28	444.13	516.18	590.03	661.17	731.17
335.13	445.04	516.28	590.13	661.19	731.18
335.17	445.07	518.20	590.16	661.26	731.21
336.01	445.17	518.21	596.01	662.05	732.08
336.08	446.02	519.27	597.14	662.13	732.18
336.17	448.01	520.11	600.10	663.25	732.19
336.25	448.19	522.20	602.23	665.05	732.20
339.24	450.15	522.24	603.05	666.02	732.26
340.19	450.17	523.17	603.18	667.04	733.13
340.23	450.21	524.02	604.01	667.05	734.21
345.02	451.16	524.10	604.15	667.28	735.05
345.12	453.18	524.17	604.18	668.01	735.07
351.25	453.19	524.19	606.20	668.07	735.13
351.25	454.25	524.24	606.22	669.04	735.14
352.02	455.24	525.01	607.06	669.26	735.15
353.21	455.25	525.14	608.01	670.03	735.26
353.26	456.06	526.08	610.02	670.03	736.02
354.28	456.09	527.07	610.20	670.08	736.11
357.24	456.15	527.11	611.08	670.12	736.16
358.16	458.04	529.08	611.16	671.03	738.24
360.11	459.15	529.22	612.27	671.06	739.19
360.14	462.27	529.27		671.14	739.28

741.01	813.21	881.18	474.23	108.19	708.05
741.01	814.04	882.14	611.11	123.17	808.22
741.04	814.17	882.16	652.28	213.15	831.17
741.27	814.28	883.20	653.18	257.02	847.14
742.08	815.13	883.26	656.26	266.08	907.20
744.15	815.15	883.27	664.05	266.24	forgive
746.02	815.16	884.06	703.05	300.01	029.18
747.22	815.18	884.15	704.27	425.25	fork
747.27	815.18	884.18	709.24	425.28	335.03
748.20	815.19	885.19	818.25	429.11	forlorn
748.22	815.25	886.02	825.28	429.16	004.09
750.26	815.28	886.21	842.17	461.26	021.08
750.27	816.03	887.05	843.09	465.14	388.25
751.20	816.03	887.21	849.07	466.01	675.08
751.25	816.05	888.08	887.12	482.26	812.27
752.21	816.23	888.13	888.22	483.08	forlornness
753.15	816.26	892.05	900.09	483.24	041.08
754.07	817.08	894.19	forces	508.01	form
754.08	817.10	895.11	123.12	511.05	080.15
755.03	818.18	895.12	726.20	573.10	089.02
757.04	819.01	895.28	fore	573.12	114.16
757.13	819.22	896.06	227.17	578.02	120.22
759.20	819.22	896.26	foreboding	595.10	123.04
759.25	820.09	897.08	563.12	610.26	124.28
759.26	820.11	898.01	forefinger	623.02	155.12
759.26	823.01	898.04	077.14	623.17	168.13
759.27	826.15	898.05	forego	638.02	221.19
760.02	826.25	898.26	785.16	640.23	222.12
760.18	827.02	899.09	foregone	647.06	264.16
760.25	828.13	900.11	648.18	647.06	315.08
762.25	828.21	900.17	foreground	730.06	328.23
762.28	829.12	901.09	221.02	760.08	343.09
763.01	829.16	901.10	247.25	774.18	368.18
763.11	831.02	902.07	248.11	805.22	377.16
763.17	831.16	902.15	249.03	824.09	424.03
765.23	833.27	902.23	forehead	828.08	456.03
766.16	834.01	904.04	076.20	828.17	486.06
767.23	837.01	905.19	136.19	829.14	503.16
769.08	837.07	905.20	141.15	831.19	560.22
769.11	837.27	906.03	156.07	882.09	576.15
770.09	838.15	906.14	237.05	890.16	602.07
771.19	839.03	906.21	248.18	894.23	631.28
773.07	839.05	907.07	249.06	forgets	636.09
773.07	839.22	907.27	260.24	843.02	652.12
776.18	841.22	908.07	277.06	forgetting	670.22
777.07	841.23	908.25	306.25	191.12	684.14
779.17	842.08	909.07	382.23	377.11	684.14
782.04	842.08	909.17	383.25	495.23	737.14
782.08	842.10	909.21	398.01	738.14	737.15
784.19	842.11	909.28	405.11	forgie	778.09
785.16	842.12	910.15	405.23	696.19	785.22
785.28	842.17	911.16	471.15	forging	798.04
786.05	842.20	911.19	471.26	757.18	818.17
786.25	843.05	911.27	480.25	forgive	823.23
787.07	843.21	912.18	524.28	025.03	858.17
787.07	844.24	forage	531.11	109.17	871.26
787.12	845.10	336.09	588.22	217.12	formal
787.14	845.11	forbade	594.19	406.01	173.18
787.15	845.12	470.11	646.02	408.04	210.08
787.16	845.21	570.05	702.03	465.14	237.28
790.07	846.03	707.20	738.04	483.18	291.03
790.13	846.22	forbear	767.09	553.10	339.11
790.22	846.27	766.21	776.06	612.06	837.25
790.26	847.21	793.20	796.23	697.15	formalist
791.10	848.14	850.13	840.05	825.15	479.03
791.19	848.24	forbearance	881.16	828.01	formally
792.07	849.15	103.12	882.22	830.11	236.19
792.11	849.19	477.08	foreign	835.21	formed
792.17	849.24	forbearing	082.10	839.21	004.15
792.26	850.24	488.02	179.27	841.01	010.04
792.27	851.03	806.15	180.03	forgiven	080.11
792.28	851.18	forbid	343.24	779.01	090.05
793.20	852.18	351.19	381.26	780.12	329.21
794.09	852.23	forbidden	439.04	831.16	341.08
794.11	853.23	257.12	900.13	843.19	405.24
794.20	853.26	423.08	foreigner	forgiveness	475.02
795.14	854.06	613.20	084.25	484.11	548.13
796.08	855.14	735.05	197.18	485.06	596.02
796.19	855.21	877.15	foreigners	forgiving	738.07
797.01	858.09	forbidding	197.16	253.08	738.13
797.03	858.28	002.21	forelock	forgot	751.13
797.10	859.26	147.21	906.15	116.20	762.26
800.21	860.16	forbore	forenoon	133.16	770.18
801.01	862.09	646.10	337.27	135.28	815.15
801.05	863.03	force	foresight	141.10	842.08
801.09	863.14	323.17	104.20	142.25	842.10
802.02	863.21	351.27	507.22	496.08	842.10
803.10	863.24	361.13	forest	658.08	894.24
803.12	863.25	374.18	145.24	662.25	former
803.18	864.13	472.05	151.27	707.13	090.27
805.04	864.21	497.25	870.28	741.23	292.26
805.10	864.21	588.01	871.07	764.11	292.26
805.27	865.03	601.08	forest-aisle	765.18	312.21
806.07	865.10	649.12	870.07	883.24	425.07
807.10	866.21	691.20	forest-dell	forgotten	425.13
807.27	866.23	716.12	146.21	106.02	425.15
808.03	869.07	745.23	forest-high	150.02	458.16
808.05	869.12	791.23	031.27	175.15	461.01
808.09	871.10	808.08	foretold	219.22	464.19
808.19	872.27	833.09	327.10	226.23	773.06
808.24	873.13	841.10	609.17	263.19	806.09
809.17	873.27	847.27	forewarned	266.20	809.21
809.21	874.14	850.13	912.22	284.28	835.25
810.14	874.21	856.04	forgave	292.13	844.12
812.17	876.06	860.26	612.08	352.12	848.03
812.24	876.06	forced	612.12	364.07	formerly
812.26	880.09	019.18	830.08	414.02	377.13
812.28	880.11	112.17	forget	534.16	554.28
813.14	880.12	237.27	036.04	534.28	832.12
813.15	880.13	270.15	088.21	544.24	835.10
	881.05	323.22	103.23	588.12	

formidable	610.27	094.04	foundation	587.23	267.07
046.07	624.19	101.16	759.20	594.11	freed
825.03	727.11	125.05	foundations	629.14	291.23
forming	735.08	131.15	853.03	638.16	freedom
100.26	739.24	145.03	foundry	639.15	063.19
348.22	751.21	149.20	666.16	649.26	362.06
618.21	756.06	155.03	769.07	663.19	759.25
637.12	775.05	159.14	fount	667.20	800.16
formless	775.19	163.21	521.11	717.28	freedoms
152.21	782.04	169.17	653.26	733.03	289.18
779.25	784.11	176.24	fountain	870.28	freely
forms	785.06	176.25	757.22	880.02	083.12
100.22	789.06	203.01	fountaine	884.06	143.03
101.14	808.23	209.24	201.09	framed	270.06
243.22	837.20	212.05	four	165.18	275.22
266.28	854.23	228.07	007.02	179.01	620.13
398.20	888.26	234.17	011.05	323.05	642.11
546.05	889.07	278.02	021.01	418.09	756.20
675.15	fortune-teller	280.12	073.19	535.05	806.22
820.19	389.22	288.20	078.23	631.03	825.15
formula	fortune-tellers	288.25	080.20	689.05	826.08
223.07	408.12	289.27	080.21	frames	freer
forres	fortunes	290.19	181.19	088.14	196.27
283.27	319.13	292.21	300.21	framing	freezing
forsake	385.22	294.15	332.20	325.21	281.04
020.28	386.08	298.09	378.19	337.16	807.01
forsaken	698.24	299.21	443.07	505.09	freezingly
200.17	908.21	313.24	522.11	814.20	062.11
289.02	forty	323.25	523.21	france	french
553.02	211.13	335.25	526.09	093.03	012.07
654.05	319.22	337.15	553.22	622.14	039.10
forsakes	330.06	341.01	557.14	731.16	082.11
610.27	343.16	351.08	627.08	frank	093.04
forsaking	344.05	356.21	627.21	067.16	122.09
623.07	381.28	372.03	658.13	178.05	130.03
forsook	453.19	410.26	658.15	267.15	140.10
242.07	663.08	430.02	707.01	756.23	140.10
817.26	forty-five	432.20	729.04	franker	142.19
fort-night	147.02	441.13	769.07	002.14	143.11
427.21	forward	444.05	776.17	frankly	168.26
forte	052.02	446.02	782.24	191.14	179.07
269.24	113.11	463.22	799.23	719.12	197.17
forth	114.01	474.07	817.21	756.19	197.24
006.20	114.17	476.15	853.20	frankness	197.27
061.22	123.20	479.17	854.14	291.24	197.27
067.04	186.21	496.14	899.10	802.11	198.03
164.12	231.26	518.15	900.21	827.03	198.18
193.09	256.21	536.12	four-post	frantic	217.23
325.12	258.02	537.08	464.22	010.18	217.25
559.01	320.20	566.07	fours	025.12	277.27
651.14	358.06	570.21	599.18	514.05	279.10
652.09	367.02	571.22	fourteen	575.13	286.22
871.15	402.21	574.13	007.01	622.21	290.10
forthwith	407.03	593.16	139.24	650.06	326.08
108.01	420.21	597.13	168.21	650.16	343.13
173.24	429.25	598.12	fourth	656.09	346.09
507.26	499.22	607.25	081.03	841.03	347.13
fortitude	563.25	609.12	081.13	901.22	347.21
118.19	575.24	624.17	096.20	907.23	352.27
663.26	576.19	624.25	114.16	franz	489.23
797.21	589.21	626.14	543.01	678.04	526.14
804.25	594.06	626.18	691.28	678.05	543.16
fortnight	655.01	628.23	foxglove	fraternal	585.10
117.25	665.15	635.02	031.14	785.28	613.14
174.01	760.01	635.20	fraction	fraternity	636.05
174.05	835.08	635.23	100.09	821.10	678.09
253.11	856.14	636.14	619.10	827.04	749.11
293.19	forwarded	641.12	fractious	fraternization	749.20
320.19	173.27	641.22	540.01	786.11	889.22
323.10	forwards	644.05	fragile	fraudulent	908.12
325.26	215.22	644.06	859.05	772.17	frenzied
491.18	230.14	663.12	fragile-looking	freak	732.06
499.06	277.10	670.05	575.01	238.11	frenzy
541.27	337.01	685.12	fragment	312.21	619.21
669.22	380.15	690.06	575.05	freaks	876.07
680.25	387.04	693.02	fragmentary	213.15	900.23
809.15	538.21	697.27	088.26	frederic	frequent
828.15	591.25	707.08	383.17	201.25	017.03
846.02	599.15	712.01	fragments	202.04	097.06
851.15	656.23	717.02	079.11	801.17	114.11
fortunate	foster	717.04	123.11	802.01	147.07
147.16	406.04	718.09	fragrance	frederick	147.23
223.18	fostering	733.19	503.08	348.06	305.08
405.03	376.08	743.09	504.03	352.15	520.05
752.24	554.25	743.14	650.02	386.16	635.13
fortunately	fought	744.13	693.04	free	689.18
158.04	020.02	750.18	fragrant	146.12	715.03
171.28	064.25	772.06	137.13	165.24	715.16
197.26	802.27	781.07	148.09	223.01	716.19
201.16	foul	781.17	435.03	276.02	748.04
296.17	273.20	787.12	522.05	302.11	907.16
307.21	479.06	790.05	606.05	447.16	frequented
340.27	578.11	795.13	frail	485.05	492.17
361.20	587.20	800.26	639.13	509.12	673.18
649.03	fouler	802.04	649.10	514.08	frequently
864.12	630.09	805.06	frame	628.20	008.07
fortune	found	806.09	036.13	634.28	049.10
253.04	006.05	806.15	036.21	636.15	074.22
261.22	006.14	810.17	053.12	649.16	088.15
268.15	031.12	814.11	060.17	700.10	210.24
395.10	032.23	817.13	108.27	707.05	292.15
400.13	049.07	839.12	132.17	732.02	399.28
403.19	050.10	841.11	334.20	767.10	500.10
403.21	058.25	870.05	423.20	782.21	629.21
475.03	066.06	876.26	426.03	785.08	670.26
490.06	066.13	877.13	467.11	821.04	677.18
516.03	071.04	882.26	485.10	825.19	840.08
536.17	073.02	907.26	485.24	854.10	889.09
545.08	077.25	908.01	510.28	909.08	908.22
563.19	082.11	908.13	583.21	free-born	fresh
571.09	090.10			267.05	155.04

194.25	510.04	016.17	138.10	285.23	445.15
271.02	610.26	017.02	139.23	287.12	445.23
271.03	669.02	019.10	140.14	287.22	447.10
331.04	686.21	019.10	140.27	289.22	450.10
379.12	691.17	019.22	142.07	291.15	460.26
433.20	697.19	022.26	142.11	291.23	461.10
435.04	703.14	023.03	146.18	293.17	462.03
440.03	703.19	023.07	147.17	295.07	463.25
522.05	729.11	023.12	148.16	296.05	466.09
630.28	734.07	023.17	149.07	296.26	467.27
639.14	737.01	024.07	149.26	297.26	470.27
738.05	740.22	027.07	150.24	301.04	473.15
738.06	770.14	029.01	151.08	309.11	475.09
757.18	785.19	029.27	151.15	311.22	477.19
765.04	828.14	030.01	152.12	311.25	480.12
794.21	833.20	031.08	154.05	313.21	481.10
798.28	833.21	037.13	154.09	315.04	483.17
812.26	833.25	039.02	155.01	321.05	485.02
825.24	853.26	039.14	160.14	323.15	487.11
836.03	864.04	040.04	161.14	324.05	489.14
860.24	878.20	040.18	162.24	325.28	490.08
883.01	896.24	041.02	162.28	327.03	490.13
fresh-looking	896.25	042.02	165.27	327.04	491.14
552.13	896.26	042.02	170.01	328.04	491.23
freshened	friendship	043.14	172.21	329.02	491.24
277.26	150.21	044.10	174.09	330.23	492.13
freshening	162.16	044.21	177.21	330.25	492.21
144.16	383.09	045.14	179.16	332.11	495.04
502.23	715.04	045.27	179.28	334.15	495.15
freshens	829.16	046.19	181.13	334.26	495.15
277.25	833.16	047.23	182.19	335.07	495.23
fresher	334.15	048.19	182.22	336.21	499.07
902.17	frieze	049.09	184.04	337.02	501.06
freshest	087.20	049.16	185.19	338.04	502.15
522.06	fright	049.26	187.08	338.25	502.21
freshly	417.11	053.23	187.24	341.08	502.22
757.22	frightened	055.01	189.12	341.16	502.24
freshness	063.23	057.08	190.15	341.25	504.01
573.09	068.01	061.05	190.17	342.05	504.13
454.13	389.09	061.17	193.05	350.06	509.05
642.12	frightens	062.18	193.16	350.09	509.07
770.08	393.02	063.23	194.04	354.18	509.07
896.15	frightful	065.23	194.08	354.23	509.10
fretted	026.03	065.23	194.14	355.14	511.12
049.22	135.28	069.13	199.09	356.19	511.28
554.01	428.12	072.15	200.12	360.16	512.07
fretting	447.27	073.22	200.17	363.04	513.02
475.20	469.16	074.01	201.05	364.03	513.03
886.01	627.10	074.16	206.10	364.06	515.19
fried	866.08	075.03	207.02	368.28	516.06
865.15	frigid	076.10	207.04	369.22	518.08
friend	172.02	077.26	208.23	369.28	519.16
053.22	251.13	077.27	209.13	370.01	521.12
059.23	258.28	078.01	209.24	370.19	521.18
064.05	frigidity	078.08	213.13	372.11	530.20
072.11	802.23	078.23	216.18	373.11	533.01
072.18	frills	080.26	219.07	373.20	535.08
114.28	005.22	081.17	220.03	373.27	542.08
156.06	fringed	081.22	220.14	374.08	542.16
289.08	318.17	081.25	223.08	375.11	549.09
381.19	081.25	084.08	224.01	376.01	550.06
383.09	frivolous	084.28	224.02	376.26	554.07
410.12	090.15	087.03	225.21	377.15	554.12
412.19	286.28	089.27	225.22	379.09	558.11
437.10	475.11	091.06	226.03	380.03	559.09
437.22	fro	093.03	226.25	380.09	559.14
438.17	045.22	094.17	228.05	380.16	559.22
441.23	063.25	097.07	230.17	380.16	560.05
510.16	126.08	099.05	230.18	381.20	560.15
516.15	336.15	099.23	230.21	381.20	561.25
516.16	390.27	100.05	230.23	384.09	564.12
527.22	416.08	101.01	231.03	386.04	567.05
643.14	fro'	101.10	231.09	390.17	567.22
666.06	185.09	101.17	233.19	391.01	568.22
853.22	frock	102.01	234.17	391.06	569.05
911.10	066.11	102.02	235.04	394.18	570.23
friend's	154.08	102.17	235.05	395.05	575.15
584.18	175.21	102.21	237.24	396.07	575.15
428.15	192.28	103.20	239.07	396.14	576.02
472.09	236.01	108.27	241.07	396.16	576.15
497.19	236.03	109.06	241.07	398.08	576.17
friendless	276.14	109.09	244.20	399.06	577.18
020.21	277.05	111.16	246.08	399.26	578.13
518.15	295.19	111.21	246.13	401.07	579.02
648.02	340.14	112.06	246.17	402.03	579.19
770.25	558.08	112.17	248.25	404.13	580.12
888.28	692.15	113.05	250.02	404.14	580.16
friendliness	frocks	114.01	250.03	407.06	581.07
498.08	045.18	114.26	250.08	408.10	581.14
friendly	058.19	115.17	253.22	409.15	584.01
151.19	078.12	116.14	254.05	409.15	585.08
291.24	084.13	117.03	256.03	410.15	588.21
433.01	092.24	117.05	256.19	410.22	590.12
468.22	327.25	122.05	259.19	411.15	593.05
615.03	331.20	123.08	261.05	413.02	594.19
615.04	545.23	124.09	262.04	414.17	594.23
674.25	frolicksome	125.20	262.15	415.04	596.05
676.03	807.09	125.21	262.20	415.10	599.07
745.02	from	126.11	263.20	415.24	599.11
friends	002.06	126.11	264.20	416.18	600.13
040.21	002.09	126.18	267.01	418.05	602.16
091.17	002.16	127.01	268.13	421.15	603.10
117.15	003.10	128.01	271.09	422.28	603.15
129.16	003.27	130.17	272.02	428.07	603.25
152.03	005.24	132.02	273.05	431.17	606.19
147.16	005.26	132.08	280.08	433.08	607.01
167.09	007.14	133.02	281.24	436.28	607.01
167.10	007.15	133.05	281.25	438.03	607.04
167.11	008.19	133.23	282.01	438.04	608.01
493.06	010.15	136.12	285.04	439.02	610.19
510.01	013.05	136.17	285.07	439.06	613.08

615.25	736.06	870.22	409.20	843.25	861.21
616.07	738.22	870.25	frozen	847.23	furred
616.13	738.27	871.12	096.06	848.26	430.18
616.25	740.14	871.24	099.02	857.15	furrowed
617.20	742.23	871.24	145.19	857.28	344.16
617.21	746.22	873.03	606.01	860.25	578.07
617.28	747.02	874.18	620.21	910.01	furrowing
618.06	747.17	874.20	766.02	911.01	659.22
618.06	747.17	875.05	802.11	911.19	furs
618.07	748.01	876.16	835.03	full-blown	122.02
619.01	748.09	877.11	fruit	461.05	further
619.05	748.19	877.23	019.01	full-grown	001.09
621.06	749.15	879.11	325.24	084.17	027.22
622.08	749.25	879.19	373.08	full-leaved	076.26
623.14	750.25	880.27	503.15	501.12	102.02
624.18	760.08	881.12	503.27	fully	121.07
626.22	762.20	883.12	694.02	036.12	164.26
628.06	762.22	886.04	697.21	081.12	191.13
629.02	763.15	888.01	fruit-parterres	089.19	206.20
629.27	764.01	891.02	503.03	135.24	214.24
630.15	765.07	895.28	fruition	146.12	238.01
630.28	766.06	896.08	521.11	147.13	256.28
631.11	766.14	899.05	792.23	148.14	258.01
631.18	767.09	899.12	fruitless	162.07	296.01
632.17	768.06	900.05	838.19	392.12	309.08
632.23	768.22	901.02	fuel	462.10	325.04
633.10	769.07	901.17	479.21	553.23	337.15
638.01	771.11	902.22	fulfil	738.11	354.01
639.18	772.08	903.07	019.08	784.04	375.05
643.22	773.01	903.20	652.23	785.12	375.05
646.04	773.01	905.05	fulfilled	806.18	390.11
646.28	773.24	906.01	160.12	806.25	391.16
650.04	775.10	906.06	583.15	831.13	392.01
650.27	778.26	911.10	663.26	861.02	463.23
651.04	781.05	911.25	806.17	906.27	497.22
651.07	781.24	912.04	fulfilling	908.28	539.07
651.15	786.28	912.11	822.10	fully-understood	589.21
652.10	791.24	912.12	fulfilment	811.09	597.21
652.19	794.04	front	116.01	fulminating	599.14
653.07	794.12	050.07	full	297.04	602.13
653.20	794.13	072.23	032.14	fumbled	603.25
655.28	797.07	084.13	046.08	173.07	610.01
655.28	798.13	085.27	054.10	fume	656.05
656.10	798.17	122.09	088.02	554.02	657.07
656.11	800.18	133.04	103.02	fumes	663.20
657.12	800.19	152.25	104.10	081.24	672.20
658.16	800.24	153.25	128.12	280.21	695.05
658.18	801.05	185.18	133.06	fun	728.01
660.28	801.18	185.21	133.26	355.18	787.25
663.20	802.07	190.09	139.26	386.20	810.07
663.28	802.25	193.27	145.12	funchal	812.22
667.19	806.10	194.04	155.05	602.23	628.12
669.17	808.08	194.27	199.16	780.07	654.05
671.16	810.17	206.27	215.07	function	furtherance
673.09	810.19	209.27	237.03	669.05	532.17
673.15	812.07	244.14	237.08	723.08	furthers
673.21	812.12	318.13	243.27	functionary	824.18
675.13	812.12	327.28	250.15	048.18	furtively
675.14	814.15	364.10	277.03	fund	643.21
676.04	815.04	423.17	327.06	543.16	755.22
677.25	816.11	538.19	331.20	funds	furtune
678.05	816.20	574.25	341.27	161.12	387.03
679.03	816.21	591.16	349.03	775.06	fury
680.01	819.09	598.11	350.04	funeral	010.26
681.26	820.18	616.17	361.16	033.01	124.05
682.11	822.02	719.20	382.20	476.01	141.20
683.25	822.14	856.25	382.27	487.05	424.25
684.13	823.25	857.02	388.08	490.27	483.01
684.15	824.14	857.15	400.12	775.25	594.10
687.20	825.14	857.19	404.08	fur	617.16
687.22	827.25	857.28	411.23	224.10	634.03
689.09	828.25	859.03	414.05	430.25	634.20
689.11	832.05	871.02	416.28	furbish	648.22
689.11	832.11	front-door	434.28	327.26	650.08
690.26	832.23	852.10	471.21	358.11	732.20
692.17	832.28	871.03	485.05	furious	765.10
693.07	834.07	871.11	494.02	065.05	856.10
693.20	834.21	frost	502.19	079.27	fuses
696.21	835.24	004.10	510.21	552.03	644.13
697.19	836.13	049.25	511.20	621.23	fustian
698.15	839.21	066.08	511.25	furiously	678.25
701.22	840.17	145.15	513.07	405.14	future
702.28	841.27	282.27	552.14	furnace	057.12
704.04	843.23	592.08	559.22	502.06	089.02
705.11	844.06	605.22	564.04	649.01	102.06
706.08	844.09	674.25	580.13	furnish	158.03
707.05	845.11	frost-flowers	606.02	148.11	188.13
707.07	845.14	049.21	608.06	286.06	192.06
711.11	845.16	frosts	608.10	547.20	233.12
712.05	845.27	144.04	613.17	furnished	269.20
714.25	846.02	frosty	628.13	173.24	279.02
716.26	846.16	113.08	641.12	190.27	310.01
718.15	849.06	638.23	645.08	280.25	322.25
718.24	849.17	798.13	664.13	701.04	373.24
719.24	849.18	frown	681.10	721.24	378.12
719.28	850.10	035.24	693.04	739.17	398.26
720.27	850.22	225.10	699.26	furniture	399.19
721.18	852.06	552.03	702.24	016.17	492.22
722.01	853.28	frowned	713.04	049.15	498.15
725.04	854.18	115.17	735.25	076.12	508.22
725.15	854.27	frowning	737.15	181.07	552.26
730.17	855.09	383.27	737.28	190.10	556.01
732.13	856.11	812.26	745.14	207.03	584.07
732.18	857.14	820.11	750.20	231.13	630.19
732.22	857.19	frowningly	758.08	247.08	632.19
732.24	857.26	411.10	782.10	331.02	643.28
733.05	861.23	frowns	787.01	460.08	655.02
734.26	862.14	361.03	790.26	701.12	663.16
735.03	865.10	froze	791.23	733.24	714.26
735.24	867.16	144.11	792.27	733.28	789.16
736.04	867.18	219.28	799.06	794.06	822.03

```
gables              531.08          071.11          814.21          gaze            239.21
   871.01           869.07          073.19          gathers            259.13          254.10
gaiety           games               185.16             271.04          349.15          259.25
   045.15           088.11           194.23             351.22          395.09          400.05
   200.23           194.23           196.06          gauging            414.09          457.24
   316.21        gander              209.08             716.02          472.09          476.01
   365.03           383.05           214.26          gaunt              479.23          549.18
   411.24        ganges              230.13             032.07          480.09          746.05
   473.21           813.10           332.09             115.09          485.03          746.16
gaily            gape                432.24             578.13          545.14          771.03
   225.07           378.03           492.04          gauzy              573.25       generated
   275.21        gaping              494.02             450.01          687.18          737.23
   335.16           460.01           541.20          gave               699.24       generation
   747.04           491.02           548.02             004.21          702.26          790.16
gain                655.17           562.17             007.08          704.26       generations
   106.12           661.24           562.22             024.18          726.07          207.15
   132.08           743.15           586.18             029.15          733.09          597.11
   206.21        garb                654.19             040.15          740.14       generosity
   675.09           381.06           847.20             050.21          740.16          126.14
   872.25           458.07           860.04             065.20          742.19          734.07
gained              641.13           870.03             078.25          755.10       generous
   064.26           677.02        gateshead              084.19          858.01          138.16
   193.12        garden              021.14             089.08       gazed               466.17
   575.19           087.18           027.06             100.18          023.09          478.19
   633.15           087.23           035.18             117.16          044.21          517.06
   651.01           089.04           037.03             119.22          119.12          693.05
   731.02           111.12           037.13             120.26          191.02          729.11
   753.02           144.13           038.13             141.24          295.06          830.06
   765.07           145.09           039.03             148.07          301.17          880.10
gait                148.02           039.14             149.21          307.06       generously
   077.22           151.06           045.11             183.27          404.05          651.13
   457.15           151.21           048.04             194.03          479.22       genesis
galaxy              151.26           050.05             202.05          486.01          055.16
   155.13           155.14           068.19             207.16          577.18       genial
gate                164.17           071.10             217.28          587.20          144.14
   250.23           288.19           072.21             236.16          600.13          231.10
   502.23           438.19           074.02             238.11          631.19          258.27
   563.09           501.19           075.04             280.01          652.13          271.20
   572.06           503.25           076.14             287.22          652.14          292.10
   869.17           504.16           088.27             301.08          677.12          364.17
   902.17           631.05           115.18             317.13          678.15          376.08
gales               631.19           143.19             330.19          758.24          440.26
   145.28           667.11           165.05             333.11          781.15          523.08
   737.23           668.27           174.09             335.14          872.20          642.28
gall                711.19           176.01             342.13       gazelle-eyes        688.06
   155.21           733.05           179.23             368.28          546.04          707.25
gallant             335.12           180.24             373.16       gazer               781.21
   553.24           843.08           446.10             382.16          349.27       genially
   550.15           849.17           447.20             397.17       gazes               496.06
   570.17           349.26           448.22             409.19          858.19       genii
   579.03           852.12           450.19             447.08          858.20          090.23
   911.08        garden-beds         450.24             462.27       gazing              302.01
gallantry           870.26           450.25             471.12          017.21       genius
   224.26        garden-coat         451.13             471.16          209.20          345.23
galled              048.09           457.01             474.10          231.23          345.24
   264.26        gardener            463.27             481.21          396.07          639.02
gallery             048.17           474.16             485.14          410.10          753.02
   074.17        gardening           477.20             491.09          583.08          753.08
   170.21           810.26           487.04             522.09          617.25          756.07
   190.24        gardens             490.11             524.03          685.10          813.07
   191.06           087.28           651.26             547.16          758.04       genteel
   193.10        gardez-vous         770.27             558.14          909.20          038.26
   228.25           360.23           780.06             575.17       gedanken            178.02
   254.15        garland          gateshead-hall        580.15          678.25       gentle
   294.10           758.21           015.17             601.13       gem                 047.14
   295.12        garlands            020.06             609.06          407.04          156.02
   295.23           204.12        gather                617.24          502.10          157.08
   297.26           433.06           494.03             620.06          642.15          343.23
   298.06        garments            540.20             641.21          812.24          345.27
   299.06           169.13           551.24             649.06          832.16          351.02
   309.06           297.22           580.12             657.07       gemmed              440.18
   328.25           380.27           640.27             671.17          249.14          440.26
   333.27           558.06           663.02             688.06       gems                643.06
   335.04           576.16           735.25             705.28          248.03          657.10
   335.19        garnish          gathered               708.04          343.20          700.01
   335.26           328.09           039.01             712.09          545.17          702.06
   364.09        garret              042.04             718.12       genealogy           702.08
   415.20           209.25           062.02             724.14          730.08          725.12
   415.28        garrett's           078.24             740.13       general             729.11
   416.16           769.05           085.04             798.19          019.16          741.08
   417.21        garrulous           113.09             807.08          083.22          818.06
   419.08           799.14           224.15             819.03          085.07          827.27
   419.14        garters             277.04             832.04          127.09          847.25
   599.01           013.10           292.06             837.04          204.19          877.17
   639.24        gas-light           330.23             855.13          224.12       gentle-tempered
   640.06           280.24           342.27             866.02          261.13          623.01
gallery-wall     gasp                384.07             880.05          316.26       gentleman
   299.17           707.20           384.16             882.26          320.18          012.16
gallic           gasped              392.25             890.17          357.07          027.01
   279.19           165.15           435.12             891.01          368.19          027.10
galling             560.14           503.01             896.23          377.07          053.10
   736.07           849.14           561.22             906.11          411.05          114.25
gallop              860.27           565.20          gay                714.28          180.01
   564.04        gastronomical       661.10             148.06          745.02          206.18
   575.10           777.06           772.05             189.22          789.03          224.20
galloped         gate                845.08             191.22          795.18          252.21
   332.21           005.01           859.22             214.04          834.04          311.28
   358.03           066.17           870.15             328.15       generalities        318.24
gallows             675.23           876.18             339.01          267.09          319.17
   005.12           675.26        gathering              413.09       generally           321.07
gambles             712.05           003.03             459.08          003.20          352.13
   469.13           733.08           021.17             500.09          046.12          361.25
gambols             737.10           064.21             504.25          106.08          377.02
   602.03           742.18           075.22             544.06          113.13          381.05
game                833.18           122.26             736.25          114.01          388.14
   289.14           839.09           219.25             740.02          135.18          390.03
   328.09           850.06           335.13             748.15          205.08          400.14
   366.19           857.12           424.01             800.18          216.15          422.05
   379.25        gate-post           501.14             886.22          217.11          459.04
   449.16           858.26           513.19             909.08          217.28          459.05
   450.03        gates               669.09                             239.19          589.17
                    050.02
```

603.06
683.15
695.10
695.26
697.26
781.17
860.28
861.05
865.04

gentleman's
194.01
205.05
446.03
595.12

gentleman-highwayman
370.17

gentleman-like
348.09

gentlemanlike
254.18
890.15

gentlemen
046.08
091.25
161.17
200.06
254.05
255.06
316.23
317.16
327.05
332.25
334.23
337.22
339.17
346.26
347.26
348.03
352.05
358.26
359.27
365.12
366.14
379.21
383.12
387.09
388.16
391.15
391.27
392.09
400.18
400.27
401.14
416.01
417.14
432.27
433.10
529.05
538.07
596.17
598.11
598.24
601.01
863.09

gentlemen's
009.10
333.20
334.23

gentleness
645.20
716.17
847.26

gentler
144.09

gentlest
730.08

gently
077.13
104.13
123.25
131.26
461.05
515.02
588.24
595.11
640.09
668.05
686.06
783.07
847.26
879.19

gentry
179.21
386.08
698.06
864.24

genuine
255.28
350.18
373.04
390.01
437.14
543.16
593.19
707.25
752.23
781.11

geography
086.20
744.12

george
181.05
181.09
316.14
327.03
339.23
352.11
366.22
378.25
451.12
492.13

georgiana
001.17
002.01
010.10
010.22
018.19
041.12
041.14
043.06
045.17
049.04
049.16
062.08
176.14
176.16
176.23
448.18
451.15
461.03
461.04
461.26
462.20
463.02
463.10
470.15
470.19
472.20
472.25
475.11
475.13
475.16
475.18
476.07
478.05
478.15
478.27
485.21
487.05
487.10
488.12
488.27
490.01
491.03

georgiana's
032.16
446.14

georgy
006.08

germ
762.21

german
578.11
636.06
637.03
678.10
679.12
713.21
749.12
749.20
752.03
803.22
805.14
805.15
893.03
893.05

germinate
325.24

germs
020.17
350.10
628.01
730.09
730.12
757.27

gesture
006.27
201.12
406.19
801.10
875.19

gestures
083.18
369.06
378.20
399.28

get
037.12
040.13
042.05
049.09
068.03
101.25
102.02
102.17
158.02
166.24
167.09
169.26
176.04
177.23
179.13
183.22
184.11
227.07
232.05
234.06
247.04
270.26
270.27
271.01
271.02
297.09
297.17
297.22
308.09
309.20
316.19
327.02
334.13
375.27
417.23
429.13
430.12
432.04
448.23
449.01
454.03
466.28
467.27
469.11
475.24
477.05
481.25
482.03
487.06
490.15
498.01
504.14
505.12
508.04
509.24
527.07
527.08
527.16
541.02
541.11
541.16
544.17
545.04
546.20
565.24
620.08
637.11
641.23
649.19
657.07
660.18
666.21
667.24
671.22
679.17
684.25
700.22
731.04
733.22
735.01
760.13
766.18
783.15
787.22
787.26
791.04
840.08
865.18
867.03
885.09
899.02
907.03

gets
056.01
203.28
329.25
330.14
332.05
386.04
433.18

getting
008.22
024.25
075.03
081.16
096.02
110.07
171.24
173.02
195.10
336.11
347.24
362.13
427.06
464.21
469.08
469.18
586.10
641.03
674.02
705.17
750.05

gewichte
678.27

ghastliness
615.18

ghastly
004.24
029.10
423.05
560.14
577.24
634.02
685.08
881.14

ghost
024.05
035.23
035.25
035.27
208.06
208.08
208.12
494.09
865.01
873.14

ghostliness
211.05

ghostly
211.15
558.15

ghosts
035.26
578.05

ghoul
548.11

giacinta
637.03
637.05
637.27

giant
502.20
627.13
705.28
820.11
911.21

giants
032.06

gibberish
429.10

gibson
469.05
475.22
487.08

gibsons
480.23

giddy
523.24
741.25

gift
325.15
358.25
530.02
733.15
755.06
781.23

gifted
321.02
513.07
644.09

gifts
286.14
400.13
738.15
739.23
814.13

giggled
371.03

giggling
391.05

gild
529.26

gilding
434.20
609.03

gilt
855.17

gin
863.23
863.26

ginger
055.24

gingham
545.24

gipsies
148.16
408.12

gipsy
379.19
385.18
392.15
394.07
401.27
407.23
408.27

gipsy's
394.20

gipsy-vagabond
390.03

gipsying
032.18

girandoles
382.26

girdle
086.07
680.02
899.08

girdled
005.02

girdling
145.10
209.03
870.27

girl
014.03
019.03
047.20
052.23
053.07
054.05
056.17
059.26
060.04
062.08
068.25
075.16
077.08
082.23
089.25
090.17
094.15
094.21
095.10
097.18
098.24
100.01
103.02
107.03
109.27
119.27
120.21
123.14
124.23
125.14
125.26
126.01
126.15
127.13
130.26
134.20
138.03
139.24
149.12
162.08
171.12
175.26
184.10
185.25
189.03
189.15
196.14
197.01
250.16
268.23
285.14
317.11
347.14
387.28
439.01
444.15
461.05
461.17
509.02
523.13
533.19
546.03
598.03
602.01
605.21
672.06
672.14
677.05
678.13
699.22
737.26
740.13
749.14
757.03
771.22
826.14

girl's
120.18

girl-bride
524.06

girls
058.16
078.07
078.23
078.28
080.03
080.09
081.26
083.17
084.06
084.17
085.12
086.25
088.10
091.12
098.04
098.12
112.09
113.20
114.14
117.10
117.24
118.07
120.14
121.17
122.02
123.22
147.02
147.15
170.21
243.26
638.06
680.12
698.19
721.20
722.23
743.16
744.08
769.07
781.12
789.19
790.12
863.10

give
018.23
035.15
056.05
056.07
062.08
065.05
069.23
086.11
116.23
138.13
149.01
150.09
154.21
171.10
178.18
187.02
200.11
221.15
232.25
239.24
243.05
250.15
253.18
260.07
328.22
330.08
339.06
357.23
365.15
379.12
381.12
405.11
409.12
410.16
420.06
427.04
431.22
437.05
446.13
446.23
447.21
453.13
454.24
455.02
458.15
466.17
469.07
496.27
507.01
508.16
517.14
522.20
531.09
531.17
534.06
543.22
547.22
547.24
548.16
549.26
564.14
566.18
586.07
600.03
602.13
616.18
616.22
624.19
637.09
638.08
645.03
645.03
646.13
651.12
659.13
668.04
670.08
671.14
672.03
672.08
672.10
672.12
679.19
682.17
685.26
686.25
687.07
687.28
694.22

697.05
697.22
698.24
708.13
719.04
720.03
747.21
748.24
761.10
769.13
784.08
785.24
789.07
789.16
790.17
791.14
791.16
792.13
794.15
798.25
805.15
808.14
816.19
822.27
823.09
824.13
838.11
841.20
846.08
846.14
855.28
857.07
874.05
874.17
875.10
879.24
900.13
903.25
906.17
907.03
given
027.21
045.13
065.06
085.04
086.24
087.18
093.23
115.25
125.01
125.02
160.04
163.03
173.19
218.20
228.21
240.17
261.15
282.10
288.05
293.09
306.16
311.21
320.16
322.11
323.17
332.19
347.16
374.07
380.11
384.24
396.16
402.13
418.09
452.25
487.02
490.17
516.17
518.10
534.14
605.10
648.04
655.01
658.05
667.13
719.14
727.28
731.20
734.27
747.19
758.16
794.07
807.25
814.14
815.15
824.19
837.25
843.12
852.21
865.06
883.13
868.06
888.26
894.06
giver
898.15
gives
104.14
325.05
348.11
706.06
738.03
802.02
824.21
giving
086.20
240.08
258.09
261.17
458.14
746.17
glacier
766.04
glad
001.11
037.12
040.11
056.20
062.21
069.18
081.15
095.16
097.08
101.24
188.22
188.24
190.26
198.21
235.21
300.14
302.05
315.15
332.06
351.07
392.22
455.15
458.05
467.27
469.04
484.20
493.01
493.02
498.01
538.17
544.17
572.13
582.15
602.17
632.28
637.09
642.28
781.27
781.27
782.11
799.09
799.14
876.22
887.08
gladdening
361.05
gladly
523.05
gladsome
522.06
glamour
434.17
glance
017.17
043.03
116.10
170.13
177.27
254.17
264.12
268.03
275.27
313.10
353.28
381.13
389.14
395.11
404.16
437.21
561.15
587.25
630.02
636.08
641.21
642.28
646.13
648.26
650.24
654.28
671.15
702.14
704.09
719.07
720.06
737.18
746.28
748.11
763.19
763.21
813.03
824.04
857.07
858.15
908.20
glanced
072.25
079.20
115.18
229.14
248.08
375.11
423.24
589.16
640.07
643.10
653.11
726.12
755.22
glances
352.22
356.15
371.25
375.23
703.21
glancing
004.25
046.14
065.08
152.18
231.11
246.21
446.26
460.12
753.14
glare
026.04
026.18
101.19
283.13
398.09
glared
016.05
578.21
594.15
glaring
794.22
glass
003.09
045.23
049.05
049.23
095.18
193.22
202.14
203.19
204.17
230.15
306.13
321.26
331.08
342.08
406.20
410.22
411.15
422.08
431.04
431.16
521.08
522.04
577.22
613.14
701.09
748.12
783.17
801.20
874.12
874.20
875.12
875.16
875.27
883.12
885.14
glass-door
066.07
glasses
170.10
411.03
glassiness
249.10
glassing
718.01
glazed
004.12
179.02
222.20
423.08
605.24
612.26
673.08
glazing
485.03
gleam
023.12
146.10
207.27
226.02
247.27
423.24
492.25
551.20
576.06
652.05
676.04
gleamed
023.06
185.19
249.13
299.16
335.16
520.05
675.22
855.16
gleaming
022.14
333.03
661.09
738.07
gleams
070.04
435.05
517.03
812.12
836.21
glean
202.24
glee
337.09
411.04
498.09
750.20
799.14
882.15
886.01
gleeful
101.02
730.19
gleefully
791.16
glen
812.05
812.17
815.03
839.10
glide
328.24
746.15
glided
023.09
221.26
285.05
419.13
653.10
654.08
gliding
652.01
glimmered
060.23
654.18
glimpse
087.24
204.07
234.06
333.16
471.03
511.28
560.06
575.14
785.17
858.06
glimpses
291.12
856.17
glistened
100.07
glistening
322.21
541.24
glitter
568.03
glittering
017.22
248.05
544.16
664.14
667.14
910.11
glitters
537.07
791.26
gloaming
100.17
495.18
503.01
globe
265.15
764.05
globes
085.17
086.18
202.28
gloom
017.22
022.26
073.10
101.12
147.24
207.18
390.18
486.01
594.18
675.16
715.24
880.23
903.07
gloomy
081.19
230.18
253.15
258.23
299.20
329.07
364.07
473.19
475.28
490.12
538.17
562.04
797.11
870.03
874.23
glorify
089.15
glorious
083.10
414.09
501.07
551.19
569.23
573.16
609.11
631.13
652.13
679.26
759.23
776.05
781.19
819.14
844.27
912.10
glory
109.06
133.09
735.18
813.23
845.03
845.05
846.07
gloss
017.09
glossiest
316.13
glossily
343.18
glove
764.02
gloves
174.15
331.13
463.17
665.08
665.19
670.15
glow
182.24
230.28
231.07
326.07
594.19
648.28
688.11
704.20
740.26
746.24
799.10
881.27
887.01
glowed
139.14
148.02
204.14
532.06
glowing
152.04
215.26
606.12
641.19
676.16
768.04
gnawed
088.23
668.14
gnawing
891.02
gnome
279.20
go
009.15
012.11
014.10
015.07
024.01
024.23
028.09
034.11
035.14
035.17
036.01
037.11
037.22
038.20
038.21
039.16
039.28
041.21
043.26
046.02
048.09
051.13
052.02
054.06
054.07
061.20
068.23
072.05
083.01
102.04
110.03
111.13
140.24
151.07
152.13
153.21
154.01
158.17
164.12
166.02
168.08
169.05
172.13
175.04
202.02
217.10
221.09
225.12
227.22
234.07
236.01
238.14
244.22
245.09
245.12
255.12
260.16
267.25
276.06
284.17
289.10
293.21
295.18
300.25
300.28
302.07
302.10
302.10
314.11
315.15
321.04
324.05
329.05
333.10
335.28
336.18
338.26
339.07
339.13
339.25
359.19
363.11
385.27
387.13
387.22
388.13
388.23
390.23
390.24
392.18
392.21
406.21
412.02
412.06
412.22
417.28
419.22
428.16
429.24
430.04
443.01
448.26
450.16
452.21
453.28
454.07
455.20
457.27
460.04
477.12
479.09
482.04
485.23
492.02
494.14
496.12
497.18
505.05
508.03
509.27
512.21
512.25
513.28
514.03
519.01
519.21
534.09
534.20
538.12
538.12
538.15
538.26
539.12
540.11
541.13
542.18

GO (continued)

542.23
543.26
546.17
547.08
548.14
548.19
558.19
563.24
567.15
574.18
582.14
582.17
586.14
586.24
590.18
594.03
600.24
604.10
607.02
613.04
615.14
618.02
622.14
624.10
630.20
631.21
634.13
634.15
635.11
639.09
639.26
645.24
645.25
650.22
653.23
655.26
660.13
660.15
672.20
680.09
682.24
682.26
682.28
683.02
688.01
693.22
698.18
700.11
709.01
714.19
718.17
718.18
718.21
723.09
754.06
754.20
757.13
772.21
775.24
778.11
787.16
790.22
791.07
791.12
791.28
798.24
799.25
804.11
805.25
807.01
811.20
813.18
819.20
819.20
819.27
820.17
821.04
821.04
821.26
826.08
829.21
834.19
834.23
834.24
836.14
837.17
838.03
838.07
838.21
840.20
840.24
845.24
855.26
856.01
864.01
873.06
873.22
874.03
877.19
879.21
883.23
886.07
891.20
893.21
894.17
894.24
894.26
895.15
899.22
906.05
907.22

909.27
911.07

goaded
656.02

goblin
420.24
581.13

goblin's
633.03

goblin-laughter
295.03

goblins
032.07
222.09

god
015.04
033.13
033.22
056.05
119.01
125.01
131.11
133.04
140.21
157.19
157.20
157.20
158.04
158.05
158.06
184.17
268.09
270.16
403.11
414.14
434.03
438.06
441.10
447.25
513.07
517.28
531.27
556.06
566.09
580.19
588.08
590.06
594.25
595.24
596.16
607.21
619.10
623.13
630.20
632.06
646.20
648.04
651.06
651.07
656.13
662.06
662.17
662.23
684.01
688.10
717.03
724.14
732.06
734.07
734.26
735.26
793.13
803.12
813.21
814.15
815.12
819.03
819.14
823.04
823.06
823.09
824.13
828.18
838.11
839.04
839.07
843.27
844.08
844.18
845.05
845.09
846.07
846.14
847.19
849.14
857.05
861.03
866.07
876.03
876.22
897.22
899.28
900.16
900.28
901.11
903.17
903.18
907.18
911.01
912.05

god's
125.15
296.22
415.17
485.06
513.15
518.19
525.15
530.23
590.05
600.10
662.23
683.03
724.19
848.07

gods
274.07

goes
077.05
330.02
452.14
469.12
504.04
696.19

going
034.18
067.21
068.14
069.14
073.11
078.24
099.13
102.10
142.24
153.13
156.03
156.18
156.19
157.16
157.18
177.22
179.26
180.03
203.11
208.19
225.25
238.24
274.26
276.03
298.27
302.06
306.09
315.05
330.17
365.04
374.04
385.05
385.17
453.26
456.22
457.03
458.19
491.12
493.04
499.11
499.16
507.02
508.06
522.24
536.27
545.05
552.21
566.15
576.11
588.18
598.06
643.13
650.10
650.11
650.18
657.02
667.03
694.18
717.27
724.04
751.14
757.16
780.18
791.01
795.11
813.25
839.01
841.20
853.19
855.15
863.18

gold
086.06
146.09
248.03
277.22
278.03
322.20
331.14
349.21
368.01
474.11
529.23
529.26
537.07
542.28

544.09
545.16
680.01
781.23
786.09
910.13

gold-ringed
872.07

gold-wrought
344.25

golden
018.22
111.03
322.22
492.28
498.22
545.03
663.06
752.25
812.11

golden-eyed
145.01

goldsmith's
010.03

gone
010.23
025.15
030.04
031.18
035.21
048.06
051.17
065.22
072.07
095.07
129.03
148.21
162.25
163.22
164.04
200.04
202.08
225.08
228.16
232.14
255.11
277.26
302.16
316.08
310.11
353.23
379.21
386.02
409.08
436.10
443.06
445.08
459.13
479.01
491.19
501.17
502.03
539.11
544.01
589.20
604.03
605.13
606.25
646.14
654.03
655.07
669.17
680.19
681.02
685.27
684.24
690.08
699.10
713.16
717.09
751.24
762.08
771.28
790.15
795.22
805.02
864.10
886.27
887.03
899.06
906.05

good
002.11
005.18
014.25
034.21
039.22
047.21
047.28
053.14
054.17
054.18
054.21
059.23
063.15
068.08
068.25
073.24
077.15
089.15
092.15

092.17
093.14
095.11
101.04
102.27
103.19
106.14
106.18
106.19
107.23
129.14
134.06
134.19
158.04
168.25
172.21
175.11
188.09
199.25
206.08
206.15
215.13
215.13
230.03
230.08
237.14
242.27
254.08
257.25
267.28
268.20
269.05
272.21
272.26
273.14
278.09
289.25
301.02
301.23
302.01
310.02
315.18
315.25
317.03
319.09
321.16
329.25
329.26
330.09
346.11
351.21
354.27
357.17
362.13
373.09
374.17
377.15
389.24
389.28
393.06
414.14
427.18
428.21
431.13
432.08
439.28
440.15
451.23
453.25
458.18
462.27
466.16
472.03
472.28
486.10
489.16
490.15
495.14
497.14
506.04
510.01
513.22
522.11
530.18
533.15
533.19
534.08
549.11
549.18
549.22
553.06
554.02
562.18
568.21
570.03
571.08
582.19
594.25
614.26
624.28
633.17
634.19
637.10
639.02
641.16
644.07
644.09
649.14
659.18
660.27
663.18

666.14
678.21
678.21
679.15
690.17
692.04
706.27
727.27
730.08
734.15
736.02
739.19
740.11
741.26
749.02
750.26
751.19
753.23
756.06
756.26
757.25
759.03
769.01
789.05
790.16
792.01
796.16
796.21
796.26
804.22
820.14
822.04
824.02
831.05
832.22
833.28
841.18
843.01
843.02
846.13
864.22
860.07
873.18
881.26
884.11
884.27
885.27
889.16
889.18
892.26
895.09
897.24
897.25
901.01
911.09
912.16

good-afternoon
764.02

good-bye
059.27
059.28
072.05
072.21
156.16
435.22
455.25
489.17
793.25

good-evening
257.11
736.26
736.27
742.09
742.11

good-humoured
225.06
748.10

good-morning
059.21
197.08
307.09
307.16
523.04
599.22

good-natured
034.26
346.07
357.22
378.23
769.20
906.23

good-night
047.13
159.01
159.02
191.02
251.08
278.10
300.23
301.20
302.03
363.12
519.21
519.21
554.15
777.16
807.06
829.27
829.28
885.23

good-sized
138.11
good-tempered
903.14
good-will
456.18
743.20
goodness
104.10
106.17
157.23
215.15
257.14
264.24
284.09
284.09
417.14
441.05
482.11
530.04
594.05
630.03
657.16
734.06
845.20
889.24
gooseberry-tree
503.26
gooseberries
694.19
gooseberry
699.07
gore
423.11
gorge
154.25
820.13
gorged
607.06
766.09
gory
431.26
gospel
602.08
720.20
762.14
gossamer
542.10
gossip
150.07
576.22
576.24
got
005.21
013.03
017.14
024.06
039.19
046.14
061.24
067.02
069.10
082.19
082.27
111.17
113.17
135.03
136.27
138.09
149.08
149.24
151.19
156.06
167.20
173.04
173.26
177.03
183.18
185.15
186.20
189.13
189.17
190.04
199.12
203.06
206.10
211.24
218.28
231.28
254.10
238.26
241.16
272.25
307.21
320.09
324.16
327.14
350.05
356.21
366.06
392.02
402.03
406.21
410.02
410.02
425.27
425.27
427.27
428.06
431.10
442.03
443.05
447.14
448.02
470.14
473.07
487.11
497.23
499.01
501.09
506.18
554.15
554.18
555.10
564.17
591.21
629.22
632.28
653.16
654.13
654.13
656.26
663.04
670.14
693.14
716.03
743.11
752.04
766.25
774.02
775.19
782.03
790.13
795.19
801.21
804.28
826.05
855.13
864.07
864.18
865.17
868.06
890.28
905.05
gouvernante
197.12
234.24
governed
406.11
governess
162.18
174.03
186.17
196.16
198.11
202.20
226.21
226.22
226.23
288.26
289.06
322.02
353.21
525.09
547.18
615.02
615.13
615.27
706.27
722.14
751.01
771.14
771.27
772.18
862.23
863.08
864.12
865.05
908.01
governess's
773.19
864.08
governesses
187.21
354.08
354.16
356.26
357.27
538.09
698.20
717.12
governessing
548.16
governness
357.16
gown
024.17
058.22
172.02
186.10
306.22
331.13
541.07
544.09
577.14
604.17
742.16
grace
058.06
082.13
120.15
210.20
210.28
211.01
211.17
211.18
217.02
238.08
295.06
296.07
300.09
300.11
306.20
307.16
310.28
311.18
312.06
312.20
313.23
314.24
328.23
329.21
350.15
359.06
408.17
420.23
423.03
436.03
577.01
581.06
599.12
600.01
600.06
600.08
601.01
601.13
602.14
616.20
633.10
633.16
642.03
691.26
731.21
740.25
750.02
792.27
836.19
graceful
122.05
237.16
318.07
322.22
345.14
449.27
676.27
737.15
754.26
756.28
891.11
gracefully
353.02
368.17
746.11
graces
375.24
gracious
272.08
357.01
440.26
graciously
125.01
gradations
109.06
gradual
157.09
gradually
119.17
160.13
290.18
418.18
857.24
grafinnen
636.06
grain
664.16
grains
302.01
626.04
grammar
086.22
092.27
744.12
749.12
803.28
granby
801.15
801.17
grand
206.28
546.04
698.03
699.02
776.04
906.22
granddame's
738.16
grange
279.12
grandest
662.08
grandeur
016.25
186.18
193.21
842.21
grandfather
040.22
695.24
695.24
grandson
801.16
grange
719.18
728.06
871.12
granite
659.25
712.19
870.34
granite-hewn
259.04
grant
165.21
359.25
438.06
529.12
547.04
granted
163.15
169.08
529.27
grapes
204.13
grappled
428.09
601.04
grasp
010.11
515.19
587.10
591.14
617.16
647.04
650.01
891.20
grasped
575.16
645.08
648.25
grasping
624.05
grasps
858.19
grass
066.19
248.12
277.24
561.23
858.08
859.27
grass-grown
575.03
736.22
870.07
grass-plat
870.27
872.17
grassy
159.20
grate
231.11
329.01
457.07
479.21
677.25
751.26
768.05
874.24
grated
422.22
grateful
059.14
072.11
325.06
402.13
402.15
643.07
688.11
908.15
grates
038.01
gratification
136.19
149.20
178.11
642.08
731.08
789.13
799.02
831.15
gratified
255.21
292.02
390.07
723.06
778.17
gratify
392.23
530.04
grating
426.24
486.03
792.05
gratitude
191.09
292.09
402.16
402.18
406.05
517.10
517.12
539.24
706.09
850.21
899.27
grave
029.07
076.22
094.25
104.09
152.06
159.18
259.23
275.10
333.17
340.15
403.14
406.21
411.21
505.19
513.15
519.25
602.01
636.13
655.17
673.23
677.14
680.12
696.28
733.10
740.20
770.18
775.21
790.28
819.22
861.09
907.09
grave-mounds
588.11
graved
767.12
gravel
072.26
380.20
504.11
gravel-walk
039.24
859.01
870.27
gravely
085.12
298.11
522.17
639.05
graven
046.24
588.14
806.27
graves
022.16
208.17
gravity
231.23
285.16
347.07
441.25
808.02
gray
066.20
075.05
088.21
089.05
122.03
128.01
159.20
194.04
209.03
220.05
230.18
236.11
283.01
586.08
711.16
712.09
860.04
gray-headed
750.09
great
014.22
017.11
024.10
041.11
051.06
054.02
075.05
078.05
080.17
080.22
081.19
083.17
083.22
092.16
094.21
094.22
102.22
103.02
106.18
109.27
112.09
113.20
123.22
126.28
131.12
145.06
145.10
146.03
157.12
162.05
191.26
193.17
194.07
194.28
195.13
196.21
198.24
199.07
199.16
200.06
203.05
205.25
205.25
210.17
213.16
221.01
221.26
231.09
231.24
232.02
240.14
253.01
259.05
259.06
266.28
278.08
283.04
291.15
292.17
323.14
331.06
372.07
384.01
391.01
396.25
408.04
423.17
446.25
464.22
465.13
468.08
469.28
474.09
480.03
481.23
491.08
497.28
504.04
520.14
531.22
533.15
558.22
560.19
562.21
599.04
607.16
620.10
654.19
659.01
677.18
695.24
698.12
698.22
706.06
731.02
751.06
759.20
762.03
790.06
795.23
796.21
797.10
806.17
816.11
822.11
826.11
839.14
843.02
844.06
854.18
857.28
867.15
867.17
876.03
889.26
895.09
908.12
greater
114.26
131.17
320.25
383.04
713.28
802.19
838.16
greatest
043.19

163.15
706.06
greatheart
911.25
greatly
012.03
318.21
667.05
805.23
greatness
845.20
grecian
322.17
890.21
891.13
greek
678.10
701.24
793.23
807.18
green
146.03
193.25
199.16
209.19
242.02
242.06
248.06
277.24
277.24
265.03
350.12
501.10
523.16
541.24
551.08
561.05
568.11
596.06
640.24
664.15
673.28
808.15
812.14
855.02
870.22
887.19
896.17
greener
209.06
greenland
004.07
greenness
144.15
greet
598.17
greeted
115.13
141.04
420.22
greeting
461.23
gregarious
262.18
263.10
grew
021.05
023.18
144.15
299.11
323.06
351.01
376.07
390.14
423.28
445.21
448.20
470.07
563.08
571.25
651.03
662.19
698.18
716.12
719.06
736.23
810.07
847.28
857.24
859.28
864.16
870.02
905.11
grey
033.08
034.24
044.19
052.27
087.20
355.22
426.19
greys
355.16
grief
022.25
027.24
036.19
102.22
129.09
134.12
153.16

293.08
498.17
511.18
645.21
656.15
732.20
832.20
895.23
900.23
griefs
756.24
grieve
125.06
157.06
157.06
511.23
537.03
611.12
820.15
836.10
grieved
293.08
767.11
grieving
894.17
grievous
142.11
grilled
841.18
grim
037.24
052.16
193.14
237.09
237.11
259.02
288.08
350.02
423.18
551.23
595.22
641.25
770.20
859.12
grimace
376.07
450.08
grimaces
121.02
555.11
grimacing
228.01
grimly
228.02
587.15
grimms
678.27
grimsby
616.21
633.10
grimy
628.27
grinding
552.03
grinning
906.06
grip
283.09
409.20
gripe
649.07
grizzled
599.20
groan
222.22
424.11
groaned
421.20
422.14
518.27
683.22
groomsmen
587.05
grope
852.06
groped
675.22
682.03
873.10
876.12
groping
209.23
294.10
gropingly
372.17
gross
625.22
627.23
grotesque
084.25
ground
129.10
130.22
194.05
213.27
242.28
266.21
266.23
266.24
283.06
283.08

299.26
300.04
333.01
369.26
378.03
526.23
611.04
649.09
656.20
671.25
672.23
674.21
676.05
692.11
769.02
781.13
866.13
870.25
ground-ivy
031.15
ground-sunshine
146.08
grounded
787.07
grounds
049.24
066.10
194.07
195.14
209.01
214.25
265.11
279.05
364.18
418.13
449.09
473.01
502.18
519.11
559.02
859.02
865.02
870.11
groundwork
816.01
group
002.07
022.07
083.17
222.25
231.14
237.24
342.28
384.06
471.05
498.27
676.24
grouped
335.18
groups
100.23
113.22
143.04
411.03
grove
021.05
209.18
grovelled
599.17
grovelling
625.22
637.21
groves
193.25
606.05
grow
038.10
106.24
107.02
288.18
423.15
654.06
693.09
734.12
884.10
896.17
896.20
growing
112.05
409.26
538.10
623.08
625.24
growled
454.22
599.18
grown
037.24
062.23
150.03
176.09
314.09
533.12
585.04
689.08
711.18
744.10
782.10
881.09
growning
377.11

grows
562.16
659.07
growth
659.23
676.06
grudging
820.07
gruel
692.02
702.20
gruff
305.18
gruffly
239.13
gryce
166.06
170.25
guarantee
013.17
580.03
guard
056.22
073.20
073.25
074.12
074.24
125.18
132.24
309.16
408.10
428.16
495.15
518.16
537.06
537.19
600.18
614.20
guarded
017.02
589.10
599.10
622.17
662.24
812.27
guardedness
373.27
guardian
173.12
277.02
383.07
846.21
guardian's
367.01
633.23
231.25
guardianship
359.20
guarding
812.20
guards
911.25
guess
270.03
329.25
397.12
614.02
679.09
694.06
755.04
771.18
guessed
140.07
300.11
862.01
862.01
guessing
722.10
guest
271.24
425.06
661.03
766.06
guests
257.26
333.24
350.14
379.11
401.19
418.10
guidance
134.04
168.23
171.24
732.08
813.25
845.11
900.13
guide
060.05
075.26
272.02
599.06
761.27
821.17
904.05
guided
464.16
guides
106.16
guiding
405.20

675.28
guilt
132.02
307.08
309.13
900.04
guiltlessness
889.24
guilty
439.10
guinea
797.15
guineas
727.19
guise
639.03
gulf
152.19
628.26
847.03
gulliver
032.08
gulliver's
031.08
460.15
gulph
554.08
guns
683.15
gurgled
295.11
gurt
695.24
gush
269.02
713.16
767.17
gushed
509.12
725.18
gust
660.04
714.24
gusts
079.27
gusty
572.15
guy
040.16
gytrash
221.19
222.01
222.08
222.12
231.25
gytrash-like
229.08
ha
217.03
217.03
360.28
420.24
420.24
habergeon
284.12
habiller
334.07
habit
192.12
240.08
305.08
309.19
463.24
746.10
803.27
830.09
habitation
660.17
870.11
habits
059.06
090.12
100.03
118.08
163.01
205.06
245.12
309.22
329.17
399.05
447.17
475.08
715.07
720.11
787.09
803.16
817.14
habitual
021.07
166.07
343.01
345.21
485.09
642.21
886.17
habitually
007.06
008.09
425.17
842.01

habituated
067.17
habituating
111.04
hackneyed
269.16
390.04
770.07
had
001.04
001.08
002.06
007.10
007.13
007.20
007.24
007.28
008.23
008.26
009.25
010.03
010.04
010.05
010.12
010.22
012.08
013.03
013.04
013.20
014.11
014.15
016.12
016.26
017.02
017.05
017.13
017.16
017.24
018.07
018.19
019.13
019.13
019.15
020.07
020.19
021.10
021.15
021.20
021.22
021.25
021.26
022.10
022.15
024.06
024.10
025.16
026.03
026.03
026.12
030.01
030.16
030.20
030.22
030.24
031.09
031.16
032.05
032.12
032.20
032.21
034.25
035.01
037.11
037.22
038.08
039.03
040.19
040.20
040.25
042.08
042.12
043.12
043.15
043.18
043.22
044.17
045.11
045.12
046.02
046.04
046.09
047.11
047.22
048.01
048.07
048.13
049.07
049.28
051.03
051.17
051.19
051.27
054.01
058.12
058.21
058.24
060.19
061.03
061.09
061.10

061.11	130.01	191.01	258.08	329.22	407.04
061.14	130.02	191.02	258.12	329.23	408.09
061.15	131.14	191.16	258.21	329.26	408.09
061.27	133.10	192.09	259.06	330.23	408.14
062.01	133.21	192.21	259.10	330.27	408.14
062.18	133.24	192.23	259.11	331.17	408.16
063.17	134.04	192.25	259.16	331.21	408.18
063.20	135.15	192.27	261.19	331.26	409.03
063.20	135.26	193.01	262.06	332.19	409.09
063.23	136.08	194.17	264.28	334.02	409.18
064.07	137.07	195.21	266.19	334.26	410.27
064.25	138.28	197.26	268.04	335.04	411.01
064.26	139.12	197.26	269.02	335.23	411.13
064.27	139.15	197.28	270.10	335.24	411.22
065.04	139.17	198.02	270.16	337.03	413.04
065.06	140.04	198.06	272.06	338.16	414.02
065.14	140.08	198.14	272.15	340.06	415.23
065.17	140.13	198.28	277.02	340.12	416.01
065.21	140.18	199.22	277.05	342.15	416.18
066.06	141.02	200.10	279.11	343.05	417.07
067.07	141.21	201.14	279.12	343.22	417.27
069.15	141.22	201.27	280.05	344.13	418.02
070.04	141.27	202.12	280.09	344.19	418.03
071.02	142.03	202.19	280.18	345.07	418.03
071.05	143.12	202.23	281.15	345.28	418.04
071.06	144.04	203.02	281.18	346.02	418.07
071.13	145.13	203.05	282.03	346.12	418.09
071.19	146.28	203.07	284.20	346.17	418.20
072.10	147.08	203.24	284.28	347.09	419.16
073.04	147.09	205.27	286.17	347.12	420.15
073.07	147.22	207.04	286.18	347.15	422.19
074.14	148.03	207.15	286.26	347.17	424.04
075.08	148.04	209.17	287.09	347.19	424.23
075.11	148.22	209.22	287.28	348.27	424.24
076.27	149.16	213.10	288.03	349.04	424.28
077.09	149.22	213.16	283.05	349.04	425.06
077.10	150.02	213.20	288.10	349.05	425.07
077.17	150.23	214.11	289.15	349.19	425.14
077.23	151.12	215.08	289.23	350.07	425.16
078.03	151.14	216.05	290.04	350.08	425.18
078.15	151.15	217.04	290.06	350.19	425.20
080.01	151.16	217.16	290.07	350.25	425.28
080.03	151.23	218.04	290.13	351.17	426.09
081.12	151.27	218.05	290.22	354.09	427.02
082.07	152.03	218.08	290.24	355.25	427.26
082.19	152.15	218.13	291.01	356.17	428.18
082.25	152.26	219.22	291.17	359.05	429.02
082.27	155.14	220.02	292.13	359.22	430.01
083.15	155.17	222.19	292.27	361.10	432.02
085.03	156.14	223.24	293.03	361.16	434.08
085.04	157.13	224.13	293.10	361.17	434.10
085.08	159.10	224.17	293.13	363.05	434.24
087.06	159.14	224.19	293.25	364.05	435.26
088.01	160.12	224.23	294.01	365.26	435.26
088.16	160.15	224.24	294.09	366.04	435.28
090.04	162.02	224.26	294.17	366.05	437.04
093.28	162.13	225.01	294.23	366.23	441.19
094.15	162.16	225.05	295.13	367.01	442.27
095.12	162.17	225.07	296.15	370.01	444.06
096.06	162.26	225.17	296.27	370.16	444.17
096.09	162.27	226.23	297.01	372.01	445.01
096.17	163.02	228.16	298.04	372.03	445.06
097.02	163.03	228.20	298.05	373.05	445.08
097.23	163.24	228.20	298.07	373.11	445.08
098.13	163.25	229.01	298.08	373.17	445.24
099.06	163.25	230.24	298.09	374.06	448.01
100.11	163.26	231.15	298.14	374.13	448.02
100.11	163.27	232.04	300.25	374.14	449.10
100.20	164.05	232.15	305.10	374.17	450.02
101.04	164.07	233.08	306.02	374.19	450.13
105.15	164.08	234.01	306.15	376.04	451.04
105.15	164.12	234.13	307.01	376.19	452.07
105.22	164.27	234.15	307.02	376.28	453.07
105.27	165.03	234.15	307.19	377.12	453.15
106.01	165.04	234.19	309.05	377.13	454.23
111.14	165.05	235.17	311.20	377.18	456.27
111.16	165.06	235.28	311.23	377.18	457.13
112.05	165.07	236.04	311.26	378.01	458.16
112.09	165.07	236.10	312.06	378.02	459.08
112.20	166.03	236.15	312.14	379.15	459.16
115.02	166.08	238.21	313.22	379.18	459.18
115.04	166.26	238.21	313.25	380.01	459.24
115.16	167.23	240.09	313.28	380.03	460.11
115.17	168.12	240.24	314.01	380.10	460.18
115.23	168.15	241.16	314.22	382.15	461.15
115.28	168.18	241.19	314.26	383.08	461.17
116.02	170.21	241.20	315.28	384.17	462.15
117.04	170.26	241.23	316.06	384.21	462.20
119.10	171.01	242.08	316.10	384.22	462.22
119.22	171.03	242.13	318.10	384.23	462.25
119.25	171.22	244.16	319.04	384.24	463.12
122.03	171.28	246.17	320.09	385.03	463.24
122.14	173.01	247.02	320.12	388.12	463.25
122.16	173.15	247.17	320.17	390.16	464.02
122.23	173.20	247.21	320.19	390.21	464.10
122.27	174.05	247.22	320.22	391.05	464.17
123.03	174.08	248.04	320.25	391.17	464.24
123.05	174.14	248.10	320.27	391.17	465.10
123.07	174.19	249.17	323.10	391.19	465.20
124.10	177.20	250.01	323.16	391.21	465.28
124.14	178.26	250.10	323.17	391.22	466.02
125.04	179.01	250.14	323.20	391.23	466.04
127.07	182.11	250.27	323.22	392.08	466.22
127.18	182.12	252.07	323.24	394.05	467.10
128.04	186.02	253.07	324.08	398.13	467.18
128.07	186.11	254.20	324.19	401.11	468.03
129.07	186.23	255.04	325.25	402.01	468.06
129.14	187.28	255.04	327.10	402.05	468.19
129.17	188.06	255.05	327.11	403.23	468.25
129.18	189.14	255.20	328.13	406.16	469.19
129.19	190.06	256.11	328.21	406.18	469.21

470.04	542.24	620.20	686.19	765.06	831.03
470.10	544.24	621.02	686.26	766.05	831.13
470.22	544.28	621.12	687.15	766.13	831.16
471.14	545.06	624.02	689.19	766.17	831.17
471.27	545.17	624.17	690.07	767.06	832.08
472.08	549.14	625.02	690.21	771.03	832.12
472.14	549.22	625.19	691.01	771.23	833.04
473.01	552.26	625.25	691.16	772.01	833.14
473.03	553.01	627.08	692.02	772.03	833.23
473.04	553.06	627.13	692.04	772.03	834.10
473.06	553.07	627.28	692.05	773.04	835.07
473.06	553.23	629.07	692.06	773.08	835.23
473.08	554.13	629.12	692.10	773.10	835.25
473.25	555.06	629.17	693.10	774.08	835.27
474.01	556.07	629.18	693.11	775.26	836.06
474.05	557.02	629.19	693.26	775.28	837.24
474.28	557.06	630.09	695.20	776.07	839.06
475.01	557.15	630.25	696.14	776.16	840.10
475.03	558.03	632.13	697.07	776.19	841.25
475.13	558.07	632.21	697.13	776.21	841.27
475.14	558.24	632.27	697.27	776.22	843.11
475.14	559.04	633.04	698.13	777.24	843.12
476.04	559.05	633.08	698.14	779.24	843.15
476.10	559.06	634.12	698.15	779.28	843.17
477.06	559.07	634.23	698.16	780.04	843.18
477.22	559.10	636.15	698.20	780.10	843.19
478.08	559.21	637.02	698.21	781.07	844.16
478.28	560.06	638.02	698.25	781.11	846.13
479.15	562.06	638.28	699.01	781.15	846.18
479.17	562.09	639.07	699.12	781.17	847.01
480.14	562.11	639.13	699.23	782.03	847.05
481.09	563.12	639.15	700.03	782.08	848.14
482.04	563.14	642.05	701.20	782.19	848.15
483.07	563.18	642.24	702.19	782.19	848.21
483.11	563.19	643.01	702.27	783.06	849.05
483.11	564.02	643.18	704.27	785.14	849.18
483.22	564.07	644.16	705.26	786.01	850.10
484.01	567.02	644.18	707.07	786.01	851.11
485.10	569.08	648.22	707.11	787.16	852.21
485.22	569.16	650.07	708.05	787.26	852.23
486.14	570.20	651.01	708.18	789.09	852.25
487.02	571.06	651.03	710.04	789.14	853.02
487.08	574.12	651.28	710.06	794.05	853.04
490.09	574.13	652.19	711.03	794.05	853.05
490.10	576.09	652.24	713.03	795.08	853.11
491.14	576.11	652.28	713.06	795.21	853.23
491.16	576.19	653.02	713.20	796.01	853.25
491.20	577.06	653.04	714.07	796.04	853.26
491.24	577.13	653.13	716.02	796.05	854.19
492.08	583.05	653.23	716.21	796.08	854.26
494.28	588.21	654.10	716.25	796.16	855.13
495.22	589.05	654.25	716.26	796.19	855.26
496.08	589.06	655.10	717.02	798.02	856.09
496.13	590.11	656.10	717.04	798.03	856.12
497.08	590.12	656.11	717.04	798.05	857.11
497.12	590.23	656.15	717.20	798.24	859.04
497.21	591.01	656.21	717.21	798.25	859.07
498.05	591.14	657.03	718.11	799.02	859.10
498.18	592.07	657.06	718.28	799.04	859.13
498.19	594.12	658.05	721.17	799.26	859.16
498.20	594.17	658.09	724.23	800.02	859.17
499.01	595.02	660.02	725.01	800.09	859.24
499.12	597.14	660.10	725.05	800.21	859.27
499.14	597.17	660.10	727.13	801.09	860.07
499.17	598.01	661.05	727.21	801.11	860.11
499.28	600.22	661.06	729.17	801.17	860.13
500.01	603.15	662.12	730.24	802.09	860.15
500.02	603.24	662.19	732.18	802.12	860.26
500.05	604.11	662.28	734.04	802.19	862.13
500.10	604.17	663.01	734.11	802.21	862.14
500.12	604.21	663.13	734.17	803.20	863.15
501.06	605.01	663.16	735.11	803.27	863.19
501.17	605.03	663.17	735.26	805.01	863.24
502.01	605.06	663.20	736.18	805.07	864.03
502.03	605.11	664.01	736.20	805.26	864.08
502.09	605.12	664.02	736.22	805.28	864.09
504.13	605.15	664.11	737.05	807.04	864.10
504.20	605.19	665.04	737.07	808.09	864.12
504.20	605.22	665.06	737.09	808.18	864.14
507.25	605.24	665.07	737.13	808.22	864.15
510.25	606.15	665.17	737.26	809.01	864.23
511.15	606.17	666.24	738.13	809.07	865.02
513.07	606.22	667.07	738.15	809.09	865.03
513.14	606.23	667.13	738.21	809.12	865.08
518.06	606.24	668.06	739.02	810.11	865.09
518.23	607.06	668.28	741.03	810.13	865.11
520.02	607.10	669.19	741.25	810.18	865.24
520.15	607.18	670.13	742.24	812.23	866.17
521.03	607.13	671.19	742.25	815.04	866.23
521.05	608.03	671.27	744.09	815.06	866.26
521.11	608.04	672.17	747.24	815.21	867.09
521.12	610.04	673.09	748.02	815.26	867.09
521.19	610.20	673.11	748.05	817.18	867.10
521.20	610.20	673.12	748.08	817.19	867.16
522.03	610.22	674.04	748.26	818.14	867.19
523.02	610.23	675.17	749.19	818.15	867.22
523.15	610.25	676.10	749.26	821.09	869.04
525.18	610.26	676.18	750.24	823.14	869.06
528.11	611.13	677.11	751.09	823.15	869.20
529.06	612.01	677.22	751.27	823.16	870.13
531.03	612.03	678.12	752.01	823.16	871.05
531.19	612.25	678.13	753.21	824.03	871.16
531.23	612.28	678.15	755.28	826.05	871.23
533.27	615.05	680.16	756.03	828.25	873.05
534.13	616.05	680.20	756.14	829.13	873.14
534.16	617.26	681.11	756.14	829.16	873.19
534.23	618.26	681.21	756.19	829.16	873.20
536.12	619.06	681.23	760.24	830.03	873.23
539.05	619.23	681.24	761.01	830.06	873.24
540.07	620.09	682.10	763.18	830.11	874.08
542.06	620.10	686.11	764.08	830.14	877.07

879.08
879.10
879.13
882.10
882.25
882.25
882.26
883.16
885.18
886.12
886.22
887.01
887.05
887.06
888.01
888.04
888.06
888.08
888.23
888.28
889.01
889.03
889.05
889.06
889.10
890.14
890.28
892.12
894.11
900.24
900.24
901.12
901.20
902.01
902.26
903.13
903.16
905.03
905.20
906.10
906.27
907.01
907.05
907.21
907.23
908.17
910.13
910.15
910.16
910.19
910.26
911.01
911.15

hadn't
680.19

hag
263.25
590.08
616.19

haggard
690.16

hailed
166.10

hair
010.12
023.03
045.19
047.27
048.21
049.05
058.17
060.25
076.19
085.26
092.26
119.27
119.27
120.06
120.10
120.11
120.17
120.18
121.20
121.22
175.11
192.27
193.15
197.06
222.02
237.07
244.08
248.21
255.13
260.25
318.11
318.19
340.25
343.18
343.23
344.06
348.09
370.03
423.27
442.26
450.02
460.25
461.08
471.25
489.15
519.15
521.07

523.15
525.22
532.01
577.12
581.14
585.07
599.20
621.28
651.05
681.11
692.22
702.05
767.09
813.06
831.13
865.24
871.27
877.23
881.08
885.05

halcyon
364.16
712.22

half
014.16
015.26
017.25
017.25
028.27
045.06
045.09
065.13
071.05
089.05
089.06
095.13
095.17
096.12
099.15
112.15
114.13
114.16
127.03
141.05
145.02
155.10
165.20
174.11
175.04
175.14
175.19
175.19
192.26
183.24
185.06
193.22
203.25
220.13
222.05
226.18
236.28
241.13
241.19
256.19
265.14
268.15
272.15
275.04
326.09
348.01
354.10
362.17
390.12
395.07
398.07
403.15
412.02
414.12
427.04
431.16
469.08
470.16
485.13
489.09
498.06
499.04
501.16
502.08
503.16
510.08
520.16
526.26
530.15
530.17
535.13
539.05
543.27
548.08
561.13
567.21
581.04
581.04
583.03
583.15
604.10
639.23
644.04
644.04
670.12
699.11
722.08

731.17
732.13
770.01
781.04
782.12
798.09
808.07
808.07
809.23
813.15
819.19
823.04
839.20
875.27
888.26
890.18

half-blown
435.12

half-comprehended
004.17

half-dozen
544.03
790.03

half-effaced
166.11
207.13

half-expecting
464.27

half-fancying
046.27

half-filled
875.11

half-forgotten
681.24

half-frozen
709.11

half-hid
732.28

half-holiday
163.15

half-hour
129.02

half-insincere
488.06

half-moon
071.08

half-opened
879.06

half-past
185.14
170.18
194.19
432.19

half-reclining
664.12
342.24

half-ruined
451.19

half-scared
391.09

half-sister
597.02

half-slice
113.26

half-smothered
415.11

half-start
708.04

half-submerged
248.27

half-told
767.01
885.11

half-wild
151.18

half-worn
665.18

hall
021.05
035.18
037.03
048.04
051.24
072.22
089.13
092.14
185.25
188.27
191.04
193.12
194.27
208.26
209.19
212.02
220.05
226.14
229.21
231.02
231.05
233.17
254.14
277.01
283.12
290.17
294.07
310.06
317.25
331.05
333.19
333.24
334.22
336.26
361.21
364.14

364.14
381.14
385.20
391.09
393.02
449.04
457.04
459.15
460.06
479.16
491.16
519.14
522.02
534.05
562.14
566.01
587.08
598.12
604.06
615.17
615.23
616.16
638.24
640.17
698.03
856.07
859.13
860.18
862.12
862.23
864.25

hall-door
190.16
193.21

hall-front
229.16

haloed
022.27

halted
193.12
223.23
721.08

halves
560.15
580.16

ham
885.15

hamlet
185.14
194.19
658.12
664.12
665.04
667.02

hampered
270.24

hand
003.08
017.07
024.07
024.24
027.01
027.17
030.23
032.03
044.21
060.11
061.07
077.02
077.24
082.19
099.15
102.17
115.06
120.01
123.08
131.25
132.16
133.02
136.27
138.16
155.20
156.08
175.08
195.06
201.19
217.10
222.27
227.26
228.05
239.03
239.07
240.25
246.13
246.23
246.23
247.20
251.09
257.10
286.01
295.21
295.26
296.27
297.27
301.08
302.11
308.22
312.03
320.11
322.19
326.08

330.09
347.15
349.01
352.14
358.25
366.27
368.28
371.09
375.13
397.20
397.24
399.15
403.27
406.25
406.27
409.18
410.09
411.15
418.27
419.26
420.06
422.18
423.10
436.28
446.05
466.03
466.08
482.25
485.01
494.08
514.13
523.06
533.24
543.02
545.17
552.05
555.11
562.23
564.12
565.06
566.25
567.03
574.18
587.09
590.14
591.13
598.23
601.15
601.25
610.12
616.22
620.03
622.22
623.22
628.16
639.11
639.18
643.16
645.07
640.11
649.11
651.05
652.10
654.07
657.01
659.02
664.13
666.28
672.15
675.18
684.08
686.07
697.17
699.18
790.18
701.01
709.06
715.13
742.10
745.20
747.05
747.16
754.24
758.05
763.14
767.14
767.16
780.21
783.10
789.06
790.02
801.11
807.08
818.18
822.04
836.09
836.13
839.15
840.05
841.11
845.27
846.17
848.11
851.13
863.16
867.21
871.15
872.20
872.23
873.17
874.18

875.19
876.12
876.16
880.08
881.11
883.12
884.21
897.15
898.19
900.16
904.01
904.02
906.17
909.18
910.24
912.15

handbreadth
502.16

handed
045.24
075.18
079.04
187.26
352.05
543.07
726.13

handful
148.11
151.26
661.10
874.23

handiwork
250.09

handkerchief
100.06
120.24
306.23
368.13
394.08
478.16
529.24
611.18
665.07
665.19
670.01
670.09
670.14
671.05

handle
052.11

handled
642.11
756.21

handling
026.10
427.17
579.13

handmaid
729.16

hands
010.20
011.05
013.06
013.18
032.13
050.21
051.09
052.07
062.10
063.24
080.22
097.09
111.18
119.20
142.08
143.03
170.04
172.01
187.05
187.22
196.10
200.14
219.27
249.05
259.24
267.11
277.28
298.10
301.07
323.16
325.08
327.03
331.05
348.23
351.18
353.17
359.21
369.25
378.19
389.05
394.16
410.19
411.04
416.06
422.28
442.10
445.13
454.27
456.15
465.15
467.20

```
477.19          697.20          057.01          hard-favoured   harnessing      330.04
493.09          699.12          093.21          312.09          586.23          330.11
518.21          700.13          119.03          hard-featured   harp            336.03
530.26          700.25          142.05          034.26          045.21          339.27
545.28          702.19          157.04          217.15          885.20          347.04
546.23          718.19          249.18          hard-hearted    harsh           349.24
564.14          728.05          249.20          033.09          007.16          352.16
584.01          777.11          280.14          063.16          014.26          352.24
585.08          777.13          292.01          108.10          053.13          360.26
608.05          791.04          293.14          727.01          084.25          363.03
623.08          791.11          378.08          hard-wrung      238.09          380.25
656.23          792.04          402.22          022.03          244.06          383.26
677.20          793.27          403.06          harden          292.16          386.02
683.22          795.06          458.28          137.23          321.28          387.01
695.02          797.27          465.08          137.25          395.12          388.21
697.16          798.02          472.07          hardened        441.25          390.04
704.09          798.08          474.21          100.01          465.22          392.17
756.16          798.16          518.12          hardens         638.16          392.18
766.19          799.18          522.07          376.01          harsh-featured  401.11
781.25          799.22          542.06          harder          350.23          401.18
787.23          810.13          542.17          733.19          harshly         401.22
829.14          hannah's        566.14          hardest         043.24          402.09
830.01          682.17          568.15          064.25          284.16          403.25
839.20          hannakerchief   569.20          hardiest        harshness       409.05
840.13          328.24          583.13          712.01          292.25          416.03
875.05          hapless         597.18          hardihood       377.18          416.21
879.02          860.02          622.16          090.10          harvest         417.07
handsome        happen          643.07          hardily         202.25          417.10
020.20          039.18          706.28          596.09          242.11          426.27
048.22          183.24          713.11          hardly          406.06          429.02
061.04          477.12          732.16          071.02          861.19          429.20
176.16          669.19          739.25          088.27          harvest-day     435.22
206.27          695.02          744.06          090.09          732.11          437.04
224.19          906.21          771.05          112.08          has             439.16
224.23          happened        787.03          224.23          024.08          441.05
259.15          090.02          793.24          225.18          041.17          444.05
262.13          116.12          793.25          239.18          056.17          447.07
287.14          123.08          793.26          244.10          059.02          450.17
312.06          149.01          829.24          284.23          072.18          452.16
318.03          302.05          830.05          289.22          072.18          452.18
343.06          305.13          895.11          293.25          092.10          457.20
348.14          307.17          898.01          308.24          093.01          477.04
350.21          326.18          907.17          311.15          106.08          482.15
362.17          338.19          907.25          409.28          108.11          494.18
400.22          366.03          908.09          422.28          108.14          497.06
403.07          373.19          911.03          427.22          117.24          504.07
461.07          416.03          911.04          436.06          120.05          508.19
497.02          471.01          har             446.07          121.21          516.01
497.05          521.03          245.02          457.18          125.01          522.26
526.02          522.10          harangue        496.11          125.02          524.17
637.04          535.14          310.21          498.05          126.20          525.01
677.14          559.05          harass          535.10          132.17          526.23
691.23          563.14          252.02          566.18          133.01          533.15
713.11          569.08          harassed        587.11          137.23          533.20
748.28          580.22          022.19          591.23          139.24          535.15
750.18          603.03          111.07          665.08          143.15          535.17
794.17          634.06          551.15          691.15          153.03          535.22
823.23          766.09          832.20          697.01          158.21          535.26
841.14          805.05          harassing       697.03          176.02          536.01
863.04          861.17          543.25          725.14          177.11          536.08
865.08          862.15          633.20          734.11          182.22          541.14
868.04          873.20          882.14          796.26          200.24          541.14
890.20          happening       harbourage      802.22          202.06          543.09
handsome-featured  280.10       459.21          839.23          202.07          552.05
767.07          833.11          harboured       843.11          205.05          552.09
handsomely      happens         706.12          861.21          205.12          561.09
864.20          488.08          831.11          hardness        205.19          569.10
handsomer       831.11          hard            461.19          205.21          569.11
192.17          happier         028.25          823.25          205.25          569.13
handsomest      108.18          043.16          hardships       216.27          573.22
906.23          760.10          048.16          111.07          232.15          582.23
handwriting     800.08          049.25          144.02          235.24          591.05
774.03          887.25          066.22          690.10          239.25          592.04
handy           happiest        106.26          hardy           239.25          596.11
739.22          376.13          106.27          059.05          240.05          596.12
hang            happily         130.21          069.12          240.15          597.19
617.23          051.08          142.14          118.09          240.15          600.17
905.19          285.21          211.14          858.01          243.02          600.19
hanging         538.10          218.27          harem           247.08          602.22
161.13          766.20          228.05          546.19          251.25          603.12
228.27          happiness       261.25          harlequin's     252.02          611.17
369.28          133.09          273.03          525.26          252.06          611.21
577.12          158.10          283.08          harlot          252.07          614.07
634.08          270.25          283.20          630.09          252.11          619.07
766.11          284.08          306.25          harm            253.09          626.03
hangings        341.27          344.20          285.22          253.10          632.01
155.13          377.05          350.09          285.23          261.22          633.02
207.23          397.06          513.09          437.08          261.23          633.16
306.12          403.24          553.14          651.07          262.06          633.20
423.15          436.23          555.18          harmed          264.07          633.22
464.23          439.22          619.01          580.21          271.23          635.14
599.07          496.03          650.18          harming         272.20          649.03
864.06          498.10          696.24          437.06          272.25          658.03
hannah          517.27          702.12          harmless        276.04          678.06
679.05          524.10          734.24          375.12          277.27          684.23
679.12          573.11          743.04          harmonious      282.12          686.11
680.02          646.14          757.20          163.01          287.18          690.08
680.14          730.13          761.18          322.17          287.19          690.16
681.17          731.06          761.24          702.02          293.20          691.16
682.05          782.27          766.17          harmoniously    297.08          691.17
684.18          786.14          778.19          333.21          297.17          693.07
684.26          797.06          778.21          harmonized      301.12          696.07
685.14          803.14          787.28          237.12          307.16          698.22
685.21          806.20          793.26          harmony         310.11          703.05
685.25          happy           796.17          020.07          312.11          709.21
687.26          002.06          811.25          070.01          312.23          709.23
688.07          002.17          820.06          691.26          314.08          720.12
689.17          006.01          837.27          825.02          316.06          727.17
692.02          006.01          847.05          harnessed       319.01          729.11
693.05          030.03          863.25          432.25          319.17          734.01
693.10          047.03                                          328.05          734.27
                047.03
```

735.08
741.18
753.02
758.05
758.21
761.26
762.20
762.21
762.24
762.26
762.28
766.08
767.01
768.26
772.26
774.24
775.06
775.19
778.26
776.27
760.16
763.26
764.11
792.21
793.13
816.10
820.05
820.05
820.10
823.02
829.04
829.07
829.08
831.07
840.01
840.12
842.06
842.07
845.04
858.09
867.26
872.08
874.15
876.03
876.04
884.25
895.12
899.15
900.11
903.24
907.15
908.16
912.09
912.16
912.22

haste
073.21
228.08
433.14
516.28
566.02
575.14
811.06

hasted
563.27

hasten
443.17
493.18
519.20
603.14
824.26
855.22

hastened
072.28
163.11
251.20
258.26
513.21
527.08
591.15
449.12
464.19
522.22
538.16
565.16
668.26
798.11
843.07
856.21

hastening
140.01

hastens
912.10

hastily
046.17
057.17
301.26
361.26
436.27
436.28
530.08
560.18
613.22
747.16
773.26
801.21

hasty
048.01
093.10
102.24
264.12

335.03
748.10
764.02
778.02
871.24

nat
394.07
446.04
446.28
564.09
714.18
763.06
780.21
813.05
871.15
903.20

nat-brim
395.02

nate
034.18
064.18
107.14
107.23
289.06
465.11
465.20
468.05
485.04
485.11
526.27
552.01
574.05
616.11
617.01
617.06
617.07
626.03
636.20
637.26
730.28
835.12
835.28
898.18

hated
038.27
065.16
131.28
132.07
283.08
468.14
485.10
543.28
636.19
692.27
896.17

nateful
313.22
607.09
618.06
656.12

hating
065.16
286.18

hatred
132.26
143.17
429.06
478.08

hats
122.04

hatted
282.04

haught
450.04

haughtily
254.16
449.21

haughtiness
344.12

haughty
263.03
311.27
345.22
380.04
386.27
552.01
571.12
604.08
717.14

haughty-looking
343.16

hauled
051.07

haunt
208.07
329.08
503.02
773.06
813.07

haunted
004.27
046.16
136.07
171.22
221.20
551.09
610.16
615.24
771.04

haunting
569.22

642.10

haunts
003.24

hauteur
290.27

havannah
281.03

have
002.18
006.13
007.09
009.07
009.08
010.06
014.10
014.21
014.22
015.01
015.08
020.22
020.23
020.25
022.02
022.10
024.03
024.11
025.03
027.10
028.23
030.03
030.10
031.06
033.24
034.06
034.07
035.16
036.23
036.25
037.05
037.08
037.14
037.19
037.25
038.18
039.20
046.05
047.20
048.21
048.22
050.20
050.27
051.15
051.16
053.23
055.21
055.24
056.04
057.10
057.22
058.09
058.25
061.22
062.13
063.02
063.05
063.10
063.10
064.09
065.09
065.12
065.22
068.10
068.15
069.02
069.03
074.13
077.04
077.06
085.20
086.10
087.01
087.08
091.12
092.08
093.17
093.23
095.04
095.16
098.10
098.19
098.24
101.05
101.06
101.07
101.09
101.22
102.10
103.18
103.24
104.17
104.23
105.09
105.11
106.22
108.16
112.12
112.15
114.24
116.22
116.24
117.10

119.16
120.16
120.20
121.05
121.15
121.23
121.27
121.28
123.06
123.17
123.21
130.18
131.01
131.04
131.15
132.10
134.12
134.15
135.01
135.02
135.08
136.22
137.07
138.04
138.15
141.05
141.09
143.18
146.09
146.16
147.16
150.03
150.04
150.08
152.13
153.07
153.09
157.10
157.14
157.18
158.23
160.02
160.04
165.01
166.22
167.10
167.11
168.06
168.28
175.06
177.19
178.09
179.07
179.15
181.07
186.23
187.20
188.05
188.16
188.17
190.03
190.04
190.10
191.25
191.28
192.18
196.17
203.26
204.28
205.07
205.10
205.17
206.12
207.26
208.08
208.14
210.14
211.07
211.20
211.24
216.07
224.03
224.21
224.28
225.01
225.02
225.08
225.20
226.09
227.04
227.09
228.21
230.03
230.04
230.05
235.14
237.17
238.06
238.07
238.22
239.18
240.04
240.07
240.10
240.13
240.13
240.17
241.04
241.14
241.15
241.22

242.17
242.21
242.23
243.10
243.12
243.14
243.18
243.20
243.21
246.27
247.10
249.22
249.24
250.12
250.18
251.07
252.25
253.16
256.24
257.04
257.12
257.14
257.25
258.04
258.07
258.11
259.16
259.22
260.07
260.11
260.17
261.03
262.26
263.14
263.19
263.20
264.24
265.09
265.12
265.15
265.21
265.23
265.24
265.25
266.01
267.21
267.21
267.27
268.06
268.10
268.18
268.19
268.20
269.23
270.07
270.22
270.26
271.10
271.11
272.19
273.01
273.07
273.17
274.17
275.09
275.26
276.09
276.10
277.23
278.04
280.09
282.08
283.03
283.09
284.10
285.19
288.25
288.28
290.01
290.02
293.09
297.13
297.15
298.21
299.21
300.05
300.11
301.04
301.10
301.10
301.13
301.28
306.28
308.14
308.26
309.03
309.05
309.25
310.15
311.05
312.07
312.15
313.07
314.04
317.10
317.13
317.26
319.13
319.27
320.02
321.05

322.05
323.25
325.03
325.07
327.06
327.24
332.08
336.11
338.16
339.25
341.24
344.09
346.28
348.15
348.23
351.14
351.22
351.26
351.28
352.06
352.12
353.18
353.21
353.26
354.04
354.08
354.17
354.19
355.11
357.26
358.19
358.23
358.25
362.04
362.09
366.09
367.22
368.01
370.04
370.18
372.01
374.15
374.16
374.19
374.22
374.25
375.10
375.13
375.14
375.17
375.28
376.15
382.17
383.09
386.16
387.02
387.07
388.02
388.16
388.24
390.01
390.03
390.28
395.15
395.20
398.24
399.06
399.08
399.08
399.12
399.12
399.19
400.04
400.18
400.28
401.14
401.17
401.20
402.14
402.17
402.20
402.20
402.21
402.25
403.20
404.16
404.28
405.07
405.17
405.24
405.26
406.10
406.11
407.20
407.27
407.28
408.02
408.03
408.06
408.23
410.06
412.07
416.07
417.14
419.17
419.20
420.02
420.11
422.04
424.27
425.26

425.27	513.01	601.25	696.06	784.21	861.17
426.26	513.06	604.01	696.09	785.14	862.07
427.27	513.09	607.06	696.12	785.17	863.13
428.01	513.24	607.15	696.14	785.28	865.10
428.04	513.26	609.11	696.22	786.02	866.16
428.08	514.02	611.08	697.08	787.01	866.20
428.09	514.20	611.09	699.20	787.05	868.01
428.17	515.23	611.11	700.07	787.09	868.03
428.21	515.27	611.19	701.21	787.12	866.04
428.24	516.01	611.26	702.19	788.04	869.08
428.27	516.14	612.05	703.07	788.05	875.26
429.17	516.16	613.06	703.13	788.06	876.26
430.14	516.18	614.02	704.13	789.07	877.07
431.12	518.01	614.05	705.10	790.09	877.07
433.28	518.03	614.12	705.24	790.13	877.18
435.11	518.06	614.17	706.05	790.19	878.19
435.20	518.15	614.25	706.07	791.09	879.17
435.27	519.02	614.28	706.12	791.21	879.22
437.03	519.05	615.13	706.21	792.10	879.24
437.03	522.10	615.14	706.24	793.24	879.25
437.26	524.26	615.27	706.24	795.22	880.03
438.03	525.21	616.04	707.23	795.23	880.09
438.04	526.23	616.08	707.23	796.06	881.06
438.16	527.15	616.20	708.27	797.23	881.10
439.12	527.19	617.17	709.09	801.21	881.11
439.20	528.03	617.22	709.10	801.22	881.25
440.01	529.08	618.05	709.12	803.05	882.08
441.11	529.15	619.25	717.06	805.18	883.03
441.13	529.24	620.06	717.22	805.24	883.20
441.19	530.01	621.09	718.05	806.02	884.17
441.26	530.02	621.24	718.07	806.12	884.26
442.20	530.04	622.14	718.23	807.27	884.27
442.27	530.09	623.22	719.01	811.23	885.03
444.06	530.19	624.06	719.09	811.27	885.08
444.20	530.27	625.15	719.12	813.18	885.17
446.19	531.10	625.23	719.16	813.21	885.18
447.22	531.24	626.02	720.11	814.03	885.19
449.01	532.05	626.12	721.20	815.09	885.22
450.27	533.08	626.25	722.25	815.15	885.25
451.11	533.12	627.07	724.05	815.19	886.01
451.20	535.11	628.11	724.07	816.17	886.28
452.23	535.12	628.20	726.21	817.08	888.15
452.25	535.14	630.15	727.03	817.08	888.16
452.25	535.16	630.18	727.24	817.09	888.19
452.26	535.19	632.05	727.26	817.10	888.20
453.21	536.01	633.13	727.27	817.12	888.21
453.25	536.05	633.14	729.14	817.28	888.22
454.26	537.11	633.15	730.02	818.02	888.25
462.06	537.15	634.06	730.05	821.07	888.27
463.26	537.17	634.25	731.10	821.26	889.14
464.15	537.18	636.17	731.12	821.27	891.09
466.05	538.24	637.15	731.15	822.04	891.11
467.01	538.25	638.13	731.18	822.06	892.09
467.06	540.18	639.17	733.12	822.07	894.06
467.07	546.09	640.24	733.19	822.12	894.14
467.18	546.24	644.05	733.24	825.19	894.14
468.28	547.01	644.06	734.05	826.25	894.24
469.07	547.07	644.21	734.11	826.26	894.27
470.03	548.06	644.23	735.04	827.01	895.09
476.22	548.13	645.02	736.09	827.02	896.13
476.23	548.20	646.16	736.15	827.25	897.14
477.06	548.28	647.14	737.03	828.02	897.18
477.08	549.03	648.13	739.10	828.03	898.17
478.04	549.04	648.18	739.17	828.13	898.25
478.08	551.26	650.07	739.21	828.23	899.04
478.11	552.11	650.23	740.02	829.09	899.09
481.19	552.18	651.10	741.26	829.19	899.17
482.11	553.15	652.23	741.28	829.23	899.19
482.19	554.26	653.16	747.19	831.12	900.03
483.19	555.28	654.04	748.22	834.12	901.21
484.07	557.18	654.14	751.13	834.20	901.27
484.12	561.05	656.14	752.20	836.02	902.18
484.20	565.10	658.20	752.21	836.09	902.20
484.21	565.16	659.17	754.22	836.10	903.26
485.05	565.23	659.18	755.16	836.27	905.09
486.09	566.13	661.23	755.18	836.28	906.02
489.18	566.19	663.11	755.25	837.01	907.20
489.21	567.06	663.12	757.04	837.07	907.20
489.27	567.15	665.01	757.24	838.04	908.21
493.15	567.20	668.02	759.22	838.20	908.22
493.28	568.02	668.07	760.01	838.25	908.24
494.03	568.12	668.11	760.17	839.20	910.11
494.10	569.12	669.02	761.11	839.20	910.14
494.26	569.23	669.07	761.20	839.22	haven
495.10	570.24	671.23	762.08	840.24	191.09
495.12	573.17	674.19	766.17	840.24	haven't
498.05	574.10	674.24	766.25	840.26	187.13
503.10	577.03	674.26	766.27	840.27	547.27
506.02	580.09	674.27	768.22	841.09	having
506.03	580.22	675.05	769.07	842.16	003.04
506.06	581.06	678.23	769.08	844.20	005.19
506.11	581.08	679.21	770.18	846.26	025.11
506.17	581.20	680.02	771.19	847.07	027.21
507.04	582.12	680.15	772.07	847.08	031.13
507.14	582.20	682.10	772.08	847.08	032.13
508.02	585.11	683.01	772.10	847.09	034.27
508.19	587.09	683.10	772.17	849.10	048.18
508.21	588.12	683.14	773.12	849.15	048.25
510.01	590.16	684.26	773.18	850.11	049.08
510.01	591.23	684.27	773.20	851.12	049.12
510.22	593.20	687.12	777.01	852.16	050.15
511.24	594.01	687.21	778.11	852.17	052.25
511.26	594.05	689.07	779.16	853.16	055.02
511.26	594.16	689.09	780.01	853.24	060.12
511.27	594.21	689.09	780.19	853.24	071.17
512.02	595.03	690.06	782.07	854.11	074.22
512.05	595.07	693.14	783.21	855.24	081.17
512.12	596.19	694.17	783.25	855.25	085.14
512.17	596.23	694.24	784.13	857.23	086.17
512.19	597.01	695.05	784.16	858.02	098.11
512.21	601.10		784.20	860.25	105.10

HAVING (continued)
153.14, 155.14, 135.27, 138.06, 142.02, 154.04, 154.23, 170.09, 172.27, 174.17, 190.17, 193.06, 215.03, 218.18, 218.23, 219.24, 227.28, 255.14, 256.13, 277.13, 278.02, 281.02, 512.27, 515.26, 520.15, 520.20, 523.05, 526.18, 546.17, 553.05, 570.09, 579.26, 580.03, 596.05, 597.19, 445.02, 449.03, 453.04, 463.21, 509.27, 550.23, 652.16, 665.21, 675.10, 699.07, 722.05, 752.09, 763.06, 771.06, 789.18, 790.16, 794.07, 794.09, 809.20, 811.10, 823.25, 830.11, 845.25, 854.07, 869.16, 873.08, 905.14

haws 219.11

hawthorn 219.15

hawthorn-bloom 471.06

hay 176.05, 213.16, 217.24, 220.13, 220.20, 224.02, 225.24, 225.09, 227.02, 241.17, 242.09, 379.20, 384.04, 385.17, 493.24, 501.08, 541.28

hay-field 606.01

hay-hill 542.21

hay-lane 232.17, 501.16, 653.25

hay-makers 492.19

hazarded 802.09, 816.20

hazarding 644.22

hazardous 786.19

haze 861.28, 901.06

hazel 198.16, 219.15, 221.25, 523.15, 523.15

he
006.05, 006.05, 006.07, 006.12, 006.14, 006.26, 007.06, 007.09, 007.13, 007.21, 007.26, 007.27, 008.06, 008.10, 008.11, 008.12, 008.16, 008.17, 008.21, 009.02, 010.08, 010.10, 010.12, 010.20, 012.18, 015.05, 016.27, 016.27, 018.25, 019.02, 019.06, 021.19, 021.20, 021.22, 022.10, 027.15, 027.17, 027.19, 027.22, 027.23, 027.25, 027.26, 033.29, 033.29, 034.22, 034.25, 034.27, 035.11, 035.13, 035.14, 035.27, 037.04, 039.19, 039.20, 040.23, 043.09, 043.13, 043.20, 043.23, 044.12, 052.24, 053.05, 053.06, 053.09, 053.24, 053.26, 053.27, 054.01, 054.05, 055.23, 055.25, 055.26, 055.27, 060.12, 073.25, 074.14, 086.10, 092.04, 092.13, 092.15, 092.16, 105.21, 105.22, 107.19, 107.21, 115.03, 116.05, 116.05, 116.06, 116.07, 116.13, 117.06, 117.09, 119.11, 119.24, 119.25, 120.01, 120.02, 121.04, 121.05, 121.08, 121.09, 121.15, 122.17, 124.16, 124.21, 125.02, 131.11, 131.12, 131.13, 131.14, 134.26, 135.03, 135.07, 142.01, 153.04, 153.05, 157.11, 157.22, 158.07, 161.16, 176.22, 177.02, 177.03, 177.03, 177.06, 177.09, 177.10, 177.11, 177.17, 179.25, 179.26, 179.26, 179.28, 180.01, 180.03, 180.09, 180.10, 180.13, 183.05, 183.15, 183.17, 183.19, 183.25, 185.07, 195.17, 195.19, 196.04, 196.15, 196.16, 202.04, 202.06, 202.07, 202.08, 202.19, 205.05, 205.06, 205.08, 205.15, 205.19, 205.21, 205.24, 205.24, 205.27, 206.01, 206.03, 206.05, 206.05, 206.08, 222.14, 222.24, 222.26, 222.26, 223.03, 223.06, 223.07, 223.11, 223.12, 223.23, 224.04, 224.13, 224.16, 224.19, 225.07, 225.12, 225.17, 225.17, 225.20, 226.10, 226.12, 226.15, 226.19, 226.22, 226.25, 226.26, 226.28, 227.18, 227.20, 227.24, 227.25, 227.28, 228.02, 228.04, 232.01, 232.02, 232.04, 232.08, 232.10, 233.04, 233.04, 234.15, 234.15, 235.23, 235.24, 235.27, 237.02, 237.19, 237.20, 237.23, 237.26, 238.14, 238.15, 238.15, 238.21, 239.06, 239.13, 239.15, 240.20, 242.08, 243.24, 244.06, 244.07, 244.16, 244.16, 244.18, 245.17, 246.09, 246.15, 246.16, 246.17, 246.17, 246.20, 247.12, 247.14, 250.28, 251.06, 251.08, 251.10, 251.19, 251.20, 251.22, 251.24, 252.02, 252.06, 252.07, 252.08, 252.14, 252.20, 252.23, 252.24, 252.27, 253.03, 253.07, 253.07, 253.08, 253.09, 253.10, 253.14, 253.15, 253.15, 254.03, 254.08, 254.09, 254.15, 255.04, 255.11, 256.05, 256.22, 256.23, 257.08, 258.20, 258.26, 259.01, 259.06, 259.10, 259.14, 259.22, 260.25, 261.14, 262.06, 262.09, 262.20, 263.11, 263.28, 264.05, 264.07, 264.07, 264.11, 264.14, 264.28, 266.08, 266.08, 266.11, 268.02, 266.06, 270.15, 270.15, 272.13, 272.13, 272.15, 272.16, 272.18, 279.04, 279.07, 279.09, 279.11, 279.14, 279.14, 279.15, 279.15, 281.04, 283.05, 283.06, 283.10, 283.11, 283.13, 283.22, 284.07, 284.19, 284.16, 284.25, 285.07, 285.26, 290.02, 290.07, 290.14, 290.22, 290.27, 290.28, 291.01, 291.11, 291.18, 291.19, 291.21, 291.25, 291.26, 291.27, 292.14, 292.15, 292.19, 292.23, 292.27, 293.01, 293.12, 293.17, 293.18, 293.20, 293.21, 293.22, 296.14, 297.03, 297.07, 297.12, 297.26, 298.03, 298.11, 298.13, 299.05, 299.06, 299.19, 299.20, 299.21, 299.25, 299.27, 300.24, 300.25, 300.26, 301.08, 301.09, 301.17, 301.22, 301.25, 301.26, 302.10, 302.15, 305.08, 305.09, 305.11, 306.02, 306.04, 307.20, 307.22, 308.25, 310.12, 310.12, 310.19, 311.23, 311.26, 312.03, 312.26, 313.07, 314.19, 314.24, 314.25, 314.27, 316.09, 316.10, 316.10, 316.11, 316.18, 316.26, 316.27, 319.01, 319.18, 319.18, 321.13, 321.14, 323.01, 323.02, 324.03, 324.05, 324.08, 325.05, 325.09, 325.12, 326.23, 326.26, 332.12, 332.27, 338.11, 338.21, 338.25, 339.02, 339.09, 339.27, 346.24, 346.28, 347.14, 346.14, 348.14, 348.15, 348.19, 348.28, 349.01, 349.11, 349.24, 350.12, 351.02, 351.09, 351.10, 351.11, 351.11, 351.24, 352.26, 354.02, 354.04, 356.12, 358.23, 360.10, 361.11, 361.12, 361.28, 362.23, 362.24, 363.12, 366.01, 366.02, 366.03, 366.07, 366.08, 366.09, 366.09, 366.11, 368.08, 369.01, 369.04, 370.04, 370.19, 371.07, 372.03, 372.05, 372.13, 374.04, 374.06, 374.14, 376.05, 379.09, 379.15, 380.22, 380.23, 380.24, 380.25, 381.15, 381.19, 381.23, 382.01, 382.11, 382.18, 382.27, 383.01, 383.08, 383.21, 383.25, 384.08, 384.09, 384.11, 384.16, 384.18, 385.16, 387.12, 387.18, 388.09, 386.18, 390.09, 401.03, 401.05, 403.07, 408.20, 409.08, 409.09, 409.09, 409.10, 409.12, 409.12, 409.14, 409.17, 409.19, 409.22, 409.25, 409.25, 409.27, 409.28, 410.03, 410.08, 410.09, 410.12, 410.25, 411.02, 411.14, 411.15, 411.17, 411.17, 411.26, 412.02, 413.09

416.18	447.25	515.11	564.05	620.08	703.13
416.25	447.26	515.14	564.06	620.08	703.25
417.01	449.08	515.15	564.09	620.11	704.03
417.04	449.08	515.25	564.11	620.17	704.11
417.06	449.11	517.05	564.11	620.24	704.27
417.23	449.20	517.12	564.19	620.25	705.01
419.10	450.07	517.25	565.25	620.27	705.04
419.13	450.11	517.28	566.01	621.01	705.14
419.17	450.11	518.05	566.02	623.06	706.04
419.25	450.12	518.11	566.04	623.09	708.07
419.25	451.03	518.13	566.25	624.08	708.19
419.27	451.13	519.10	567.01	624.10	710.04
419.27	451.18	519.13	567.02	624.11	710.04
420.06	452.18	519.21	567.19	624.13	714.10
420.09	452.27	519.23	568.18	624.16	714.16
420.20	453.01	521.14	573.21	624.17	714.20
420.24	453.04	522.28	580.17	624.17	714.22
420.27	453.05	523.02	580.19	624.18	715.04
421.01	453.06	523.04	580.23	624.19	715.07
421.06	453.11	523.11	581.01	624.23	715.11
421.14	453.12	523.20	582.07	626.03	715.12
421.15	454.11	524.05	583.01	626.05	715.19
421.16	454.13	524.17	584.05	626.06	715.23
421.17	454.22	525.17	586.01	632.24	715.26
421.20	455.01	525.18	586.03	633.12	716.01
421.22	456.22	525.19	586.06	634.11	716.21
422.01	456.25	526.05	586.08	636.28	717.02
422.07	456.27	527.03	587.15	638.06	717.03
422.14	457.18	530.07	587.24	643.26	717.21
422.15	459.03	530.07	588.01	644.03	718.02
422.19	459.04	531.28	588.03	645.20	718.06
422.19	459.06	532.03	588.03	646.10	718.21
422.21	460.11	533.28	588.05	646.10	718.22
424.23	468.08	534.10	588.20	647.17	719.05
424.27	468.11	535.20	588.24	648.23	719.11
425.02	468.11	535.23	590.08	648.24	720.02
425.03	468.19	535.26	590.24	648.25	720.04
425.09	468.20	536.01	591.01	649.09	720.06
425.19	468.21	536.05	591.11	649.12	720.23
425.26	468.23	536.07	591.14	650.04	720.24
426.01	468.25	536.08	591.20	650.04	720.24
426.05	468.27	536.10	592.01	650.25	720.25
426.05	468.27	536.19	592.12	650.25	720.27
426.14	469.02	536.22	592.13	651.11	721.02
426.16	469.05	536.27	592.13	651.15	721.08
427.02	469.06	539.01	592.15	651.15	722.07
427.03	469.14	539.08	592.18	653.21	722.07
427.07	469.25	539.08	594.04	654.02	722.10
427.08	469.26	539.10	594.08	654.04	722.21
427.13	491.17	539.16	594.20	654.04	723.05
427.16	491.19	539.20	594.21	654.05	723.12
427.18	491.20	540.07	595.02	655.13	723.13
427.27	493.11	540.08	595.11	657.04	723.13
428.05	493.17	540.09	595.23	657.05	723.24
428.13	494.08	540.12	595.25	657.06	723.24
429.08	494.09	541.04	596.01	657.07	724.01
429.22	494.18	543.13	596.02	658.04	724.11
430.01	494.19	544.04	598.03	662.18	724.23
430.04	494.19	544.04	598.10	662.23	724.25
431.16	495.21	544.06	598.22	662.24	725.08
431.20	495.22	544.08	599.07	669.16	725.11
431.27	495.27	544.12	599.08	669.17	725.12
431.27	496.04	544.15	601.09	669.19	725.28
431.28	496.08	544.15	601.09	669.21	726.01
432.02	496.11	544.19	601.11	671.15	726.09
432.02	496.12	545.14	601.11	671.16	726.12
432.05	497.10	545.28	601.12	671.17	726.24
432.28	497.11	545.28	601.13	678.06	727.04
433.16	497.12	546.01	601.15	679.28	727.05
433.18	497.13	547.27	601.18	680.13	727.11
433.26	497.14	548.01	601.21	680.16	727.12
434.01	497.15	549.09	602.15	680.17	727.15
434.04	497.17	549.09	602.16	680.19	727.17
434.05	498.04	549.10	602.18	680.19	727.21
434.08	498.05	549.13	603.05	680.20	727.22
434.10	498.27	549.17	603.13	680.22	731.17
434.14	498.28	549.26	603.13	680.23	731.17
434.18	499.02	549.27	603.16	680.24	731.18
434.23	499.04	550.03	603.18	680.26	731.22
434.26	499.16	550.14	604.02	681.17	733.16
435.12	499.17	550.16	604.09	686.11	733.20
436.17	500.09	552.13	606.14	687.08	736.17
436.20	500.10	552.20	606.22	690.24	736.18
436.21	503.21	552.21	606.22	690.27	736.20
436.27	503.21	552.26	606.24	690.28	737.01
438.12	503.22	552.27	607.03	691.01	737.07
440.14	503.22	553.02	607.05	691.03	737.11
441.14	503.26	553.03	607.07	691.05	738.21
441.21	504.06	553.03	610.06	691.21	738.25
441.23	504.08	553.07	611.07	695.12	738.25
442.03	504.12	553.19	612.05	695.12	740.14
442.04	504.17	553.22	612.16	695.13	740.20
442.04	504.20	553.23	612.23	695.13	740.22
442.06	504.23	553.26	612.25	695.17	740.23
443.03	504.23	554.01	613.01	695.18	740.23
443.06	504.26	554.13	613.02	698.18	740.28
446.03	505.01	554.21	613.04	698.22	741.05
446.04	505.18	554.23	613.14	698.23	741.06
446.08	505.24	555.04	613.16	699.14	741.11
446.27	506.15	555.06	613.18	701.19	741.18
447.08	506.17	556.03	613.19	701.20	742.10
447.10	508.20	559.09	613.22	701.21	742.11
447.12	510.13	559.11	618.19	701.22	742.17
447.12	510.22	559.12	618.25	701.28	742.18
447.14	512.10	559.17	618.26	702.07	742.18
447.16	512.20	562.05	618.27	702.10	742.20
447.16	513.18	562.18	618.28	702.13	746.21
447.18	514.13	563.10	619.04	702.23	746.22
447.20	515.03	563.10	619.13	703.01	747.01
447.23	515.04	563.23	619.15	703.01	747.02
447.25		564.05	620.02		

747.06	774.20	809.10	833.14	861.14	887.24
747.07	774.22	810.03	833.17	862.03	887.26
747.21	774.24	810.06	833.22	862.20	888.19
747.23	776.21	810.24	833.23	862.28	888.22
747.24	777.10	811.02	834.06	862.28	888.23
747.26	777.17	811.03	834.21	863.02	888.24
747.26	777.22	811.06	835.09	863.11	888.25
749.01	777.25	813.01	836.12	864.14	889.01
750.12	778.08	813.05	836.12	864.15	889.16
750.13	778.10	813.06	836.15	864.16	889.22
750.15	778.20	813.08	836.22	864.17	889.26
750.16	778.23	813.09	837.12	864.17	889.27
750.22	779.05	813.14	837.13	864.18	890.01
750.23	780.10	813.15	838.09	864.18	890.03
750.25	780.13	813.16	839.03	864.19	890.03
750.25	780.18	813.23	839.09	864.20	890.06
751.06	780.20	815.11	839.10	864.21	890.20
751.10	780.26	815.12	840.01	864.23	891.11
751.11	782.02	815.21	840.02	864.23	891.20
751.12	783.08	815.21	840.04	864.26	891.22
752.17	785.07	815.22	840.04	864.27	891.26
752.22	785.08	815.24	840.07	865.01	892.01
753.17	785.08	816.01	840.10	865.02	892.04
753.18	787.23	816.09	840.12	865.03	892.07
753.21	787.24	816.10	840.12	865.04	892.08
753.25	790.28	816.11	840.15	865.06	892.08
753.28	791.16	818.17	840.20	865.07	892.13
754.01	791.17	818.18	841.01	865.08	892.24
754.04	792.15	818.21	841.09	865.15	892.25
754.04	792.17	818.21	841.14	865.15	893.04
754.04	793.14	818.24	841.24	866.10	893.05
754.16	795.13	818.28	841.25	866.19	893.06
754.17	795.15	819.01	842.03	866.23	893.16
754.25	795.20	819.06	842.05	866.25	893.19
755.01	795.21	819.13	842.07	866.26	893.21
755.10	795.22	820.01	842.07	866.26	893.22
755.11	795.25	820.03	842.20	867.01	893.24
755.11	796.02	820.03	842.23	867.01	893.27
755.12	796.04	820.04	842.24	867.03	895.03
755.12	796.06	820.05	842.27	867.07	895.03
755.22	796.12	820.06	843.02	867.07	895.04
755.22	796.16	820.09	843.02	867.07	895.05
755.23	796.17	820.13	843.06	867.09	895.06
756.05	796.17	820.20	843.07	867.13	895.07
756.06	796.20	820.22	843.10	867.15	895.09
756.07	796.22	820.27	843.11	867.18	895.10
756.14	796.26	821.02	843.12	867.23	895.12
756.14	797.02	821.05	843.14	867.23	895.13
756.17	797.04	821.10	843.17	867.25	895.17
756.19	797.05	821.24	843.19	867.25	896.01
757.07	797.07	822.18	843.21	867.26	896.03
757.12	797.16	822.28	843.27	868.01	896.06
757.13	797.21	823.02	844.01	868.02	896.07
758.11	797.24	823.05	844.05	869.08	896.12
758.13	798.17	823.15	844.09	869.13	896.23
758.16	798.19	823.16	844.13	871.15	896.24
758.25	798.22	824.03	844.17	872.16	896.27
759.10	799.09	824.10	844.18	872.18	898.27
760.24	799.11	825.23	845.01	872.19	899.24
761.05	799.15	826.07	845.08	872.19	899.28
761.21	800.04	826.11	845.10	872.23	901.21
763.06	800.06	827.07	845.14	872.24	903.19
763.07	800.06	827.20	845.15	872.25	903.21
763.09	800.08	827.21	845.15	872.26	903.24
763.13	800.08	827.21	845.19	872.28	904.01
763.16	800.09	827.22	845.23	872.28	904.04
763.18	800.09	827.25	846.17	873.04	905.04
763.19	800.24	828.10	846.17	873.10	906.08
763.24	800.24	828.18	846.18	874.06	906.10
764.03	800.26	828.25	846.22	874.07	906.11
766.10	801.04	828.25	847.25	874.08	906.13
766.12	801.12	829.03	848.11	874.14	906.15
766.14	801.14	829.09	848.11	874.15	907.11
766.15	801.20	829.10	848.12	874.16	907.12
766.16	802.06	829.13	848.13	875.03	907.15
766.18	802.12	829.13	850.15	875.05	907.17
766.18	802.14	829.21	851.07	875.09	907.23
767.03	802.19	829.22	851.08	875.09	908.28
767.05	802.25	829.25	852.12	875.10	909.04
767.08	802.26	829.28	852.14	875.13	909.18
767.13	803.12	830.02	855.21	875.14	909.19
767.15	803.17	830.03	856.28	875.16	909.19
767.23	803.22	830.08	856.28	875.19	909.27
768.03	803.24	830.09	857.01	875.20	909.28
768.06	803.25	830.09	857.08	875.21	910.02
768.08	804.06	830.10	858.06	875.24	910.04
768.14	804.11	830.13	858.07	876.12	910.04
768.15	804.16	830.14	858.09	876.14	910.05
768.17	805.03	831.02	858.10	876.24	910.09
768.21	805.20	831.03	858.10	877.24	910.15
768.21	805.21	831.03	858.11	878.07	910.16
769.12	805.22	831.03	858.12	878.09	910.17
769.13	805.22	831.04	858.15	879.05	910.19
769.23	805.24	831.08	858.16	879.05	910.19
769.26	805.28	831.12	858.17	879.06	910.20
770.01	805.28	831.14	858.18	879.06	910.21
771.18	806.12	831.16	858.19	879.07	910.22
771.21	806.16	831.17	858.20	879.09	910.23
771.23	806.18	831.18	858.21	879.11	910.26
772.13	806.19	831.18	858.22	879.14	910.28
772.13	806.23	831.19	858.22	879.20	911.14
772.14	807.01	832.04	858.23	880.23	911.14
772.26	807.03	832.05	860.05	881.12	911.15
773.04	807.06	832.06	860.12	882.21	911.15
773.08	807.08	832.10	860.23	882.21	911.16
773.12	807.20	832.14	860.27	882.24	911.19
773.16	807.25	832.28	861.01	883.03	911.20
774.02	807.28	833.06	861.04	883.05	911.21
774.06	808.10	833.09	861.08	886.12	911.22
774.12	808.12	833.10	861.09	886.15	911.23
774.17	809.08	833.11		886.21	911.23

911.27
912.08
912.13
912.22
912.23
he's
403.17
867.03
867.04
906.14
head
006.16
009.23
010.15
016.09
019.12
023.04
023.10
023.18
026.14
038.07
048.22
051.10
052.24
053.19
062.18
056.10
069.17
069.26
093.21
099.24
098.09
109.22
127.20
129.18
130.23
153.19
167.17
176.12
195.11
222.02
227.15
237.20
242.06
244.14
247.05
247.06
249.03
249.04
259.02
261.09
261.18
263.21
264.11
271.09
282.04
292.22
295.01
318.11
323.13
323.16
330.22
337.19
338.14
358.17
366.08
367.06
363.06
368.17
368.25
371.22
398.03
407.08
421.07
436.04
447.17
462.03
471.06
472.16
507.05
507.18
511.12
525.22
542.11
542.20
564.10
566.19
571.07
574.15
577.19
578.13
579.05
590.24
599.21
604.20
609.02
610.17
611.01
618.24
620.26
622.19
652.03
659.27
668.03
672.22
677.04
678.14
680.25
685.17
686.08
686.24

695.05
699.19
709.06
713.17
720.01
723.14
725.19
733.03
737.07
737.17
740.24
741.24
752.07
773.17
783.24
802.25
807.18
811.21
812.18
821.10
831.13
846.17
848.11
849.02
857.16
864.03
873.02
874.25
885.05
head-dress
122.06
head-stones
588.15
headed
366.12
headlong
010.11
619.19
647.23
heads
207.10
342.19
369.10
423.19
560.04
736.25
headstone
005.01
headstrong
018.18
312.22
493.13
heal
144.08
441.08
736.08
healed
126.20
460.02
526.28
heals
107.15
health
007.12
042.09
054.17
054.18
147.08
292.06
400.12
411.16
447.13
448.01
481.15
603.03
690.17
711.04
767.22
809.09
876.06
healthy
146.20
440.03
732.03
736.06
heap
114.21
heaps
066.16
hear
010.09
053.22
079.26
105.06
138.27
149.19
154.18
157.05
182.07
188.21
200.09
210.06
210.18
210.21
210.22
220.16
282.16
285.02
302.13
305.05
307.27

308.06
308.17
314.24
317.25
354.07
354.28
358.26
371.04
387.03
400.03
403.18
403.19
409.01
419.03
428.23
453.23
482.23
503.15
511.08
523.22
524.24
546.01
558.18
561.01
569.11
574.11
582.22
595.25
602.17
603.25
619.15
620.06
623.28
624.04
629.27
644.01
677.24
690.20
708.11
719.11
721.10
724.15
756.20
757.12
767.02
770.02
770.28
771.20
793.22
814.21
817.08
827.24
829.01
842.05
853.22
858.04
861.06
862.17
863.14
864.15
865.22
882.05
887.10
888.10
890.02
894.22
906.18
heard
002.09
008.05
010.25
021.02
022.15
025.14
026.05
028.19
032.20
039.24
041.04
043.21
061.15
066.27
075.09
078.16
083.19
085.03
088.15
095.04
097.17
103.09
105.10
108.06
121.28
128.04
131.01
135.02
137.01
140.04
140.28
152.24
156.11
156.13
177.20
179.16
187.20
189.24
195.21
198.10
208.09
210.17
211.03

215.08
217.01
217.03
217.04
221.24
229.12
234.13
276.28
291.10
295.14
297.04
298.05
299.10
299.17
300.05
300.06
302.01
305.15
307.17
308.08
308.14
308.19
309.03
310.06
311.15
314.04
314.15
319.08
324.10
330.20
332.20
361.24
366.18
378.13
380.08
383.15
384.24
385.07
389.03
390.16
391.05
392.13
395.17
399.10
411.22
413.05
413.07
415.09
418.02
418.04
420.17
420.26
422.24
424.08
424.28
425.19
426.21
434.10
443.04
444.16
445.25
447.10
447.19
490.26
491.14
499.13
508.23
509.13
513.26
521.05
534.21
535.19
540.10
553.13
564.02
571.11
573.14
575.10
576.13
591.11
595.20
596.21
604.10
604.21
607.16
611.09
620.16
629.05
630.10
636.08
639.20
656.27
664.07
678.18
680.05
685.11
706.21
706.24
716.03
718.07
730.27
735.24
736.22
744.28
745.27
750.26
765.19
768.22
775.26
776.19
799.17

815.04
845.21
848.10
848.28
849.10
849.11
849.18
851.06
852.10
852.25
854.18
861.17
862.07
863.06
865.23
865.28
869.05
871.10
873.19
879.22
886.03
886.05
887.03
901.20
902.02
902.16
hearer
903.06
hearing
044.06
056.24
153.06
197.17
200.27
222.22
286.15
293.27
340.07
357.14
553.16
589.15
594.07
628.10
708.04
715.20
745.19
775.18
hears
092.27
hearse
490.28
heart
001.14
007.15
015.08
019.28
023.18
027.27
055.01
055.23
056.04
056.07
056.07
056.11
057.06
067.13
095.08
097.05
101.08
108.17
109.19
114.07
124.01
135.12
136.05
137.27
139.24
140.21
141.25
150.18
169.13
189.23
191.10
198.03
215.26
230.28
261.19
271.25
272.21
281.16
294.05
301.27
320.09
323.19
324.12
325.15
349.03
351.15
361.14
373.06
374.14
374.21
375.14
375.27
378.05
398.15
402.06
404.24
413.10
414.18
429.04

431.22
459.19
459.25
475.18
509.16
510.21
513.07
514.13
518.18
522.14
525.11
528.21
530.21
534.19
550.21
559.04
563.24
573.20
587.21
597.07
606.15
610.13
611.21
616.06
628.15
631.13
635.11
638.10
643.01
643.16
644.10
648.16
649.28
651.11
651.18
652.16
653.17
656.08
661.24
664.07
667.19
683.20
684.04
691.12
693.07
716.13
722.20
725.17
732.03
735.17
738.12
741.03
745.06
746.20
747.10
747.11
753.19
756.04
757.19
758.08
760.08
767.18
776.05
781.20
787.14
789.06
808.20
814.24
814.26
814.26
820.02
820.11
823.09
824.13
824.14
825.19
826.26
827.01
829.01
833.04
838.23
848.27
853.08
855.18
874.20
876.09
876.22
877.08
877.16
878.13
880.09
883.02
886.23
888.17
894.09
895.26
896.10
899.27
903.10
909.05
911.01
912.13
912.19
heart's
285.06
347.24
568.15
574.09
612.14
761.03
901.17

```
heart-fire         815.03              345.02              156.08              529.10              048.03
  594.20         heaven                577.08              158.16            henceforth            048.09
heart-strings      033.21              675.06              158.24              898.18              048.10
  029.20           044.24           heights               159.02              903.26              048.20
  613.07           054.22             004.12              159.15            henceforward           048.21
heart-weary        389.16             004.13              159.17              844.23              048.23
  439.24           152.16           heir                  480.04              899.09              048.27
heart-wrung        158.01             801.17            helen's             henry                 048.28
  657.12           354.19           heir-looms            109.22              005.26              049.02
  836.07           502.08             524.17              133.19              348.06              049.04
hearth             510.09           heiress               135.19              352.24              049.05
  029.24           543.04             739.23              139.27              384.01              049.17
  076.11           549.26             774.28              141.14              388.21              049.19
  085.10           556.03             780.14            hell                henrys                052.19
  113.19           583.03           held                  054.07              698.06              053.01
  119.20           608.04             053.17              054.09            hepburn               053.01
  134.09           640.16             061.07              152.16              358.23              053.19
  231.11           646.21             080.22              273.11            her                   056.19
  329.05           653.22             123.05              594.03              002.04              056.21
  341.03           653.22             140.23              602.02              002.04              056.22
  353.06           657.13             159.07              615.20              002.10              056.27
  364.12           735.24             169.01              630.13              002.22              057.01
  457.09           747.21             170.09              753.12              005.19              057.03
  460.11           753.06             248.03              753.13              005.22              057.26
  562.05           759.21             297.27              759.27              006.15              057.27
  572.05           759.27             301.08            help                  008.06              058.13
  575.04           813.04             335.26              036.02              008.08              058.14
  676.25           815.04             376.27              068.17              010.09              059.10
  635.07           844.07             378.19              215.18              010.24              059.15
  637.20           848.20             389.02              222.27              011.04              059.16
  729.16           852.03             419.25              223.28              011.05              059.27
  758.15         heaven's             421.08              226.28              012.12              060.15
  765.09           297.17             425.12              227.01              013.21              060.21
  795.15           814.14             426.09              228.20              013.27              060.21
  797.24         heaven-bestowed      431.16              252.01              014.04              060.23
  861.25           724.14             446.05              327.14              015.05              060.24
  863.11         heavenly             497.24              407.13              015.05              060.25
  885.13           597.20             542.28              410.16              015.06              060.25
hearth-rug         655.03             566.25              415.11              015.07              060.27
  115.16         heavily-laden        576.16              415.12              015.08              060.28
hearths            664.18             577.18              415.12              016.21              061.01
  327.20         heaviness            587.09              430.17              016.22              061.01
hearthstone        680.24             590.12              548.09              018.04              061.02
  693.16         heaving              596.01              608.02              018.22              061.05
  701.03           223.14             610.03              610.09              018.22              061.06
heartier           628.16             651.15              610.11              018.24              061.07
  697.18         heavy                659.21              617.02              019.03              061.17
heartily           007.05             660.06              623.14              019.04              061.17
  266.26           133.23             677.20              639.05              019.05              061.18
  463.17           166.06             682.08              655.20              019.06              061.21
  565.14           169.12             717.13              669.05              019.07              061.22
  620.15           171.01             742.10              669.06              020.08              061.26
heartless          185.04             755.11              679.13              020.08              062.10
  287.26           207.21             774.02              705.14              020.23              062.11
  439.23           224.14             808.17              705.15              021.24              063.23
  476.07           227.26             823.16              719.15              021.26              063.24
  513.05           235.19             823.16              739.27              021.27              063.24
  743.07           308.10             874.19              748.11              021.28              063.25
hearts             337.20             904.02              759.08              022.01              064.20
  151.20           434.05           helen                 815.06              022.01              064.22
  513.05           470.03             101.28              816.21              022.06              065.24
  528.03           608.06             103.13              816.25              024.12              067.02
  569.25           630.17             103.18              827.15              024.16              067.13
  628.09           637.08             104.03              843.17              024.16              067.14
  730.11           870.28             106.01              889.17              024.19              067.18
  738.04           873.05             107.04            help-meet             024.23              068.07
  789.15           902.13             107.28              815.02              025.08              069.27
  814.16         neavy-looking        108.06            helped                025.14              070.02
hearty             743.15             110.02              035.09              027.01              070.03
  446.17         hebdomadal           110.07              072.01              027.08              071.06
  456.19           113.28             124.07              079.19              027.20              072.08
  564.17         hebrew               127.21              226.20              028.03              072.11
heat               207.10             128.03              326.18              028.19              072.12
  113.16         hebrides             129.11              356.09              028.26              072.15
  236.27           004.04             130.13              447.15              029.04              073.03
  660.23         hector               130.19              510.18              030.17              073.17
heath              266.21             130.25              539.08              031.07              073.24
  065.08         hedge                131.25              541.28              032.13              075.14
  164.22           219.21             132.07              549.09              032.17              075.27
  226.13           221.25             133.10              670.26              032.23              076.20
  263.27           228.06             134.02              719.14              032.25              076.21
  659.21           229.10             134.07              865.17              035.02              076.22
  660.22           501.12             136.21              896.28              035.04              076.24
  661.10           639.19             136.22              898.17              039.04              077.02
  661.15           656.27             136.06            helper                039.27              077.04
  663.02           667.07             138.26              818.08              040.21              077.09
  673.15           675.21             139.08            helpers               040.22              077.13
  674.01         hedge-sparrow's      140.12              167.12              040.23              077.20
  712.08           471.07             140.16              709.24              040.23              077.26
  812.08         hedges               140.23            helping               041.08              080.01
  812.24           145.05             140.24              328.06              041.15              081.02
  818.23           494.02             141.02              437.16              041.16              082.07
  823.23           541.23             141.03              477.05              042.14              082.23
heath-bell         655.08             141.08              751.23              043.03              083.18
  712.17           855.02             141.19            helpless              043.03              083.21
heathen            887.19             149.28              867.24              043.25              083.25
  125.28         heeded               150.09            helplessness          043.26              085.13
heathens           483.21             150.15              783.09              043.28              085.14
  107.10           591.11             150.19            helpmeet              044.18              085.14
  405.15         heeding              150.22              822.15              044.19              085.22
heather            357.14             153.01            hem                   044.20              085.27
  659.07           899.24             153.12              097.13              044.28              085.27
heats            heel                 154.20              372.08              045.07              085.27
  364.19           228.10             155.08              392.13              046.06              086.03
heaved             282.02             155.23              432.18              046.10              086.07
  075.05         heidelberg           156.13              541.04              046.13              086.17
  215.26           235.15             156.18            hemmed                047.07              086.19
  296.19         height               156.21              124.20              047.08              087.04
  612.23           124.15             156.23            hence                 047.24              087.10
  663.19           224.12             157.16              016.28              047.25              090.03
  741.02                              157.27              054.24              047.26              090.05
                                                                                                 090.13
```

090.25	130.23	171.12	217.13	307.12	340.12
090.27	130.23	172.01	217.15	307.13	340.13
090.28	133.18	172.05	217.18	307.26	340.14
093.02	133.20	173.01	217.26	308.01	340.14
093.08	133.20	174.03	217.26	308.21	340.16
093.11	133.24	175.06	218.19	308.28	340.17
094.27	134.06	175.07	218.20	309.13	340.18
095.02	134.10	175.17	218.20	309.14	341.15
095.03	134.22	176.19	218.24	309.23	341.17
095.04	134.26	176.20	229.24	310.04	341.25
095.04	134.27	176.20	229.25	310.21	341.27
095.05	135.03	176.26	230.22	310.22	343.05
095.07	135.16	177.15	230.24	310.25	343.07
095.08	136.15	177.16	230.27	311.19	343.09
097.23	136.18	178.18	234.10	311.22	343.10
097.28	136.18	178.27	234.11	311.24	343.18
098.01	136.18	180.18	234.15	311.26	343.23
098.03	136.19	180.22	235.17	312.02	343.24
098.18	136.19	180.24	236.22	312.02	343.25
098.22	136.27	184.11	237.23	312.04	344.02
098.26	136.28	184.19	238.04	312.05	344.06
099.01	136.28	185.25	240.08	312.09	344.06
099.02	137.01	186.14	240.14	312.12	344.07
099.15	137.05	186.27	240.24	312.13	344.09
099.19	138.24	187.08	242.13	312.23	344.09
099.21	138.25	187.22	243.05	313.13	344.12
099.26	139.01	187.23	243.10	313.13	344.21
100.04	139.02	188.03	244.03	313.24	344.22
100.06	139.05	188.04	251.03	314.28	344.25
100.06	139.06	188.09	251.12	315.13	345.02
100.07	139.10	188.19	251.17	315.19	345.03
100.21	139.12	188.23	251.17	315.27	345.05
101.18	139.12	189.20	255.13	317.06	345.08
101.21	139.13	189.24	256.11	317.20	345.15
101.25	139.14	189.25	257.05	317.22	345.16
101.26	139.17	190.12	257.13	318.10	345.16
102.16	139.22	190.12	257.15	318.15	345.20
102.16	139.22	190.15	257.19	318.16	345.21
102.17	139.28	190.15	257.19	318.18	346.06
102.18	140.13	195.04	257.20	318.19	346.06
103.09	140.14	195.08	257.21	318.20	346.08
103.12	140.15	196.16	261.24	318.22	346.09
104.09	140.21	196.17	274.27	318.23	346.16
104.11	140.24	196.18	276.11	318.25	346.16
104.16	140.25	196.19	276.13	319.06	346.18
104.18	140.25	196.22	276.14	317.09	346.27
105.04	140.27	196.24	276.15	319.13	346.28
106.02	140.27	196.25	276.16	319.17	347.09
106.04	141.06	197.01	276.17	320.16	347.15
106.09	141.24	197.07	277.02	320.20	347.16
107.26	142.06	197.13	277.06	321.17	347.19
107.28	144.18	197.23	277.06	321.18	347.24
108.16	148.22	197.24	277.12	326.14	352.17
108.19	148.24	198.10	279.06	326.18	352.27
109.24	149.19	198.11	279.08	326.19	353.07
109.25	150.02	198.12	279.14	327.08	353.15
110.07	150.02	198.12	279.19	327.23	353.16
113.08	150.03	198.15	279.20	327.25	353.18
113.09	150.10	198.22	280.01	328.05	353.22
114.11	150.16	199.20	280.12	328.07	353.22
116.07	150.27	199.22	280.14	328.24	353.24
116.08	151.04	199.26	280.15	328.25	354.14
119.12	151.08	199.26	280.17	328.26	354.22
119.12	151.08	200.10	281.23	329.04	354.26
119.13	152.28	200.11	281.23	329.06	354.27
119.15	153.03	200.11	281.24	329.06	355.01
119.17	153.04	200.12	282.02	329.06	355.02
120.10	153.09	200.14	283.28	329.07	355.06
120.21	153.12	200.14	284.15	329.09	355.23
120.24	153.17	200.15	285.28	329.10	355.24
120.25	153.21	200.15	286.14	329.16	355.24
123.18	154.20	200.19	286.26	329.18	355.25
123.20	154.21	200.19	287.10	329.19	356.06
123.26	154.22	200.19	287.22	330.04	357.15
125.01	155.26	200.20	287.23	330.08	357.18
125.03	156.01	200.20	287.23	330.13	357.21
125.05	156.06	200.23	288.08	333.19	357.21
125.18	156.06	200.24	288.11	330.22	357.22
125.18	156.06	201.04	288.15	331.13	357.26
125.19	156.07	201.13	288.28	331.13	358.16
125.20	156.08	201.25	289.01	331.14	359.07
125.20	157.01	202.20	289.02	331.19	359.09
125.22	157.02	203.04	289.03	331.19	359.10
125.22	158.17	203.05	289.06	331.20	359.10
125.23	158.18	203.06	289.07	332.28	359.12
125.23	159.03	203.08	289.13	333.01	359.24
125.24	159.14	203.08	289.15	333.06	360.26
125.24	159.16	203.10	289.16	333.10	366.18
126.11	159.18	206.11	289.17	333.11	366.27
126.12	159.19	206.17	289.21	334.20	367.01
126.13	159.22	206.18	289.24	336.08	367.02
126.13	160.07	206.25	289.25	336.24	367.04
126.16	162.15	210.17	289.26	336.25	367.06
126.18	162.16	210.22	290.03	336.27	367.07
126.18	162.20	210.24	290.10	337.07	367.07
126.18	162.25	211.21	298.17	337.19	368.14
126.20	162.28	213.14	298.18	337.20	368.14
126.24	162.28	213.15	306.15	337.21	368.17
127.03	163.01	213.19	306.22	338.03	368.17
127.04	163.10	214.01	306.22	338.09	368.18
127.14	163.10	214.04	306.24	338.12	368.18
127.22	163.27	214.17	306.24	338.14	368.24
127.24	163.28	214.19	306.25	338.16	368.25
127.28	165.06	214.20	306.26	338.18	368.26
127.28	166.02	214.22	307.03	338.22	368.27
128.01	166.07	214.28	307.03	338.24	368.28
128.03	170.03	217.04	307.04	339.03	369.04
128.04	170.04	217.05	307.07	339.05	369.06
130.14	170.06	217.08	307.10	340.10	369.07
130.23	170.10	217.09	307.10	340.11	369.08
		217.10			

370.20	406.24	470.05	489.28	593.02	637.09
371.04	406.25	470.09	489.28	595.17	637.10
371.08	408.15	470.11	490.05	595.17	637.11
371.10	408.15	470.14	490.06	595.25	640.02
371.21	408.16	470.18	490.24	597.12	640.03
371.22	408.18	470.19	490.25	597.16	640.03
372.09	414.06	472.19	490.26	600.03	649.13
372.09	414.09	472.21	491.23	600.12	649.15
372.15	414.10	472.26	492.03	600.13	651.12
372.16	417.09	472.27	492.07	600.13	652.06
373.06	422.11	473.13	493.09	600.17	652.08
373.06	428.07	473.16	496.26	600.21	653.10
373.12	428.09	473.18	498.08	600.22	653.13
373.15	428.17	473.18	498.18	601.04	659.19
373.18	429.02	473.20	498.19	601.06	661.02
373.20	429.10	473.23	499.01	601.10	661.03
373.20	429.14	474.01	499.13	601.12	661.03
373.21	429.15	474.02	499.17	601.14	662.04
374.03	433.25	474.04	501.18	601.15	665.18
374.04	433.25	474.08	501.18	602.03	665.26
374.05	433.26	474.17	508.18	605.18	666.24
374.07	436.05	474.19	508.20	605.18	667.28
374.07	442.01	474.21	508.21	605.21	668.01
374.15	442.20	474.21	513.26	605.21	668.03
374.22	442.21	474.22	516.03	610.03	669.24
374.22	445.04	474.23	516.06	610.04	669.25
374.24	447.22	475.01	516.06	610.06	671.06
375.04	448.04	475.01	518.01	616.04	671.07
375.22	448.15	475.02	518.02	616.09	672.10
375.23	448.16	475.02	518.15	616.21	672.13
378.09	449.22	475.04	518.17	616.22	676.21
379.28	449.26	475.12	519.16	616.22	678.13
380.16	450.01	475.15	519.17	616.23	678.14
380.26	450.04	475.16	519.26	616.28	678.22
381.01	450.22	475.18	522.07	617.06	679.03
381.03	450.23	475.19	522.19	617.21	680.01
381.16	450.27	475.21	524.22	618.15	680.05
383.23	450.28	475.22	525.02	623.16	680.11
385.10	451.16	475.28	525.22	623.17	680.11
385.14	451.23	476.02	532.23	623.19	681.07
385.23	451.26	476.04	533.06	624.23	681.15
385.26	452.02	476.05	534.06	624.24	684.28
385.27	452.03	476.06	534.07	624.25	685.01
386.01	452.11	476.06	534.24	624.27	685.12
386.02	452.16	476.15	534.25	625.01	685.16
386.04	454.03	477.20	534.26	625.02	685.20
386.16	454.04	478.03	534.26	625.03	685.27
387.09	454.16	478.15	534.28	625.04	686.02
387.19	457.09	478.16	535.07	625.05	686.03
387.20	457.14	479.05	535.08	625.06	686.04
387.21	458.01	479.11	536.11	625.09	686.10
387.22	458.06	479.15	537.01	625.12	686.14
387.22	458.08	479.19	538.17	625.18	686.16
387.27	458.11	479.22	538.24	625.19	686.16
388.01	458.12	480.04	538.26	625.21	687.15
388.02	458.16	480.04	539.03	625.22	687.17
388.11	458.17	480.05	539.24	626.14	687.26
388.12	458.21	480.07	540.04	626.15	687.27
388.14	458.27	480.08	540.07	626.15	687.28
388.18	459.02	480.08	540.08	626.20	689.18
388.28	459.04	480.09	540.19	626.23	690.05
389.01	459.07	480.10	540.20	626.26	690.13
389.03	459.14	480.11	540.26	626.28	690.13
389.05	459.15	480.15	540.27	627.09	690.18
389.07	460.22	480.17	541.01	627.10	691.14
389.14	461.01	481.05	541.14	627.28	691.17
389.17	461.09	481.08	541.16	628.21	691.19
390.10	461.10	481.09	542.20	629.02	691.20
390.12	461.15	481.18	543.14	629.03	691.21
390.13	461.17	481.26	543.15	629.05	693.19
390.16	461.25	481.27	546.01	629.05	693.26
390.17	461.27	481.28	547.16	629.07	694.15
390.19	463.07	482.04	549.23	629.12	695.10
390.21	463.09	482.07	550.25	629.13	697.17
391.02	463.11	482.14	550.26	629.17	697.18
392.17	463.13	482.17	550.27	629.18	697.23
392.20	463.19	482.18	552.05	630.02	698.13
394.08	463.22	483.15	553.16	630.12	698.21
395.01	464.04	484.24	555.16	631.26	699.19
395.02	464.05	484.25	558.04	632.04	699.25
395.03	464.08	484.27	561.13	632.04	699.27
395.06	464.08	484.27	563.06	632.06	699.28
395.07	464.14	484.28	563.07	632.07	699.28
395.08	465.11	485.01	571.09	632.09	700.17
395.11	465.13	485.08	577.12	632.10	707.28
395.12	465.24	485.09	577.16	632.11	708.17
396.02	466.01	485.16	577.19	632.22	709.06
396.06	466.03	485.17	578.21	632.26	709.08
396.07	466.08	485.18	578.23	632.28	713.11
396.21	466.09	485.21	581.07	633.01	713.18
396.21	466.11	485.25	581.08	633.05	713.18
396.22	466.12	485.26	581.11	633.07	713.21
397.17	466.13	485.27	581.11	633.18	713.23
397.18	466.17	486.04	581.13	633.19	721.22
397.21	466.20	486.07	581.14	633.20	721.23
398.05	466.20	486.09	581.18	633.20	722.03
398.07	466.21	486.10	582.10	633.23	722.04
398.10	466.21	486.11	582.18	633.25	722.05
399.17	467.10	487.08	583.23	633.26	725.18
402.03	467.12	487.11	583.24	634.03	725.18
403.12	467.21	487.12	583.24	634.05	725.19
403.13	467.22	487.13	584.01	634.12	726.07
403.14	467.23	487.13	584.02	635.21	726.12
403.15	467.27	487.16	584.03	635.24	726.14
403.26	467.28	487.16	585.03	636.07	737.22
404.05	468.05	488.14	585.08	636.21	738.12
405.13	468.06	488.14	587.09	636.23	738.13
406.16	468.09	488.17	593.01	636.23	738.14
406.19	468.09	488.17	593.02	637.02	738.15
406.23	468.10	489.14	593.02	637.06	738.19
406.23	469.19				738.19

739.04	863.19	098.04	561.21	082.05	hied
739.26	863.20	102.01	564.05	097.18	550.16
740.15	863.23	116.27	565.23	106.01	hieroglyphics
740.18	863.28	120.08	575.03	115.15	284.02
740.18	864.01	121.25	583.01	126.08	hierophant
740.18	864.02	126.20	599.06	134.09	827.05
740.18	864.03	129.11	603.06	137.03	hierophant's
741.21	864.06	130.07	610.22	155.25	847.13
741.23	864.07	131.13	615.22	187.03	high
742.10	864.10	132.08	616.19	187.25	016.05
742.15	864.14	153.05	619.08	188.02	017.08
742.24	864.16	154.13	634.12	200.13	049.04
746.04	864.18	156.10	650.22	241.02	064.13
746.05	864.20	165.22	656.22	253.21	074.17
746.06	864.21	166.23	659.04	320.27	084.09
746.07	865.19	172.22	659.11	327.27	087.16
746.09	865.21	177.18	660.02	329.13	087.24
746.10	865.22	182.03	661.09	353.04	094.20
746.10	865.23	182.14	663.13	356.08	101.16
746.12	865.23	183.09	667.22	359.05	114.22
746.12	866.01	187.07	669.08	371.08	124.09
746.21	866.05	188.25	675.07	375.01	145.08
747.01	873.15	189.21	678.17	375.04	160.19
747.02	873.15	195.12	680.14	380.04	180.11
747.15	873.17	196.18	682.13	385.11	185.26
747.16	873.17	197.21	682.28	387.21	190.20
747.20	874.01	198.21	683.15	390.19	193.28
747.22	874.18	204.25	684.10	394.12	211.04
748.05	876.14	205.11	693.23	408.14	250.23
748.09	876.14	207.05	695.12	446.01	345.18
748.12	876.15	208.05	695.23	473.16	359.09
748.17	876.19	215.12	696.10	474.03	375.13
748.21	876.20	219.13	700.07	474.17	411.04
749.07	876.21	227.23	700.12	475.10	435.16
749.21	876.22	236.02	704.09	481.24	492.24
749.23	877.04	236.05	707.01	491.24	502.07
749.27	877.05	237.22	709.02	526.18	502.20
749.27	877.08	242.24	709.05	535.04	504.17
749.28	877.09	256.21	718.11	540.23	512.02
749.28	883.26	263.19	724.12	561.15	562.21
750.01	884.03	271.21	752.11	563.06	572.02
750.05	886.07	272.11	766.18	633.26	575.01
750.07	887.09	281.01	773.20	641.16	599.10
750.08	894.16	284.15	775.38	691.01	652.04
750.21	897.10	287.17	776.16	741.24	659.26
751.16	897.11	288.18	791.14	863.06	661.17
751.25	898.23	293.19	812.19	863.28	663.28
756.01	899.21	297.23	843.07	867.16	675.21
757.02	905.10	300.08	847.22	hervor	702.03
757.05	907.06	307.17	848.09	676.20	751.01
757.06	907.22	310.11	855.09	hesitate	751.04
758.03	907.23	310.21	859.10	155.05	779.02
758.19	907.23	311.12	859.19	438.13	804.10
758.20	907.28	312.14	859.28	hesitatingly	827.28
758.22	907.28	317.12	871.09	682.04	859.05
758.22	908.01	330.17	876.02	896.25	874.25
759.11	908.06	332.12	876.21	hesitation	887.04
759.12	908.06	332.15	886.06	052.03	912.02
760.04	908.08	336.06	893.22	643.10	high-backed
760.08	908.09	354.21	hereafter	755.01	180.07
760.10	908.10	360.13	534.20	803.02	207.11
769.20	908.12	381.23	555.24	heterogeneous	high-born
770.14	908.13	385.18	heretofore	020.12	335.23
770.15	908.15	386.05	463.24	heures	high-hung
770.23	908.18	391.27	477.12	334.11	231.06
771.06	909.01	400.18	823.18	hew	high-piled
771.10	911.10	400.27	heritage	735.07	465.04
771.13	herald	401.06	359.25	hewers	higher
772.02	023.16	401.21	hermit	724.18	109.05
772.05	167.28	402.26	864.25	hewn	142.18
772.19	168.05	403.25	hermit's	827.09	150.11
777.14	171.08	409.05	661.12	hews	293.02
780.15	815.07	409.11	hero	797.08	440.05
780.17	heralds	411.02	127.18	911.21	441.06
791.06	332.01	411.16	370.24	hiatus	623.13
791.13	herbs	412.25	370.25	045.03	626.17
797.08	143.16	416.14	heroes	741.21	644.26
797.08	148.11	416.14	797.08	hid	720.18
797.09	435.04	421.01	heroic	155.13	761.23
797.09	hercules	422.25	038.14	221.06	792.19
801.08	529.02	423.24	747.18	235.10	highest
801.18	herd	425.01	818.06	599.21	396.15
804.16	151.18	427.27	842.21	674.20	648.23
804.18	387.20	428.04	heroic-looking	733.02	highlander's
806.09	388.01	429.02	224.20	856.24	084.12
806.10	herded	429.28	herring	hidden	highlow
806.10	088.12	430.16	429.19	158.18	890.19
807.13	here	434.23	hers	616.03	highly
807.14	006.09	436.03	062.17	659.25	104.19
810.25	006.25	438.06	131.26	673.26	750.15
839.14	009.10	439.21	355.02	721.04	hill
840.05	015.01	453.05	475.17	872.24	146.18
840.13	016.16	457.27	558.07	887.21	163.12
841.20	016.27	458.01	629.04	hideous	164.28
850.09	024.12	464.09	700.05	314.27	190.06
856.07	024.28	464.14	738.11	410.14	209.19
858.06	034.03	466.26	748.19	615.16	215.04
858.07	037.08	478.20	758.06	627.17	221.03
858.11	044.01	481.17	797.06	627.22	229.04
858.11	053.25	490.01	807.11	632.18	230.23
862.10	055.27	495.17	878.11	644.18	232.18
862.10	060.04	502.27	herself	884.23	248.12
862.14	064.19	508.07	016.18	hideously	335.22
863.01	074.18	510.10	022.02	425.08	662.25
863.02	075.17	510.10	027.13	hides	664.19
863.04	080.13	515.15	046.10	348.01	673.16
863.07	091.12	515.16	056.14	725.11	673.24
863.07	092.02	535.23	059.14	hiding	674.22
863.11	092.13	542.27	063.25	519.08	675.04
863.18	093.17	546.13	072.02	hiding-place	828.27
863.18	093.21	553.13	073.11	006.13	856.17

hill-hollow	226.09	365.27	493.20	619.22	801.20
145.11	226.20	366.04	494.13	619.24	802.06
hill-peak	227.08	366.24	496.01	620.04	802.08
502.07	232.01	368.28	496.08	620.14	802.10
hill-sent	232.12	370.04	496.08	620.16	802.18
902.16	233.07	370.13	497.21	620.28	804.25
hill-side	234.13	371.10	497.24	623.09	804.26
165.13	235.22	371.21	499.19	624.18	805.23
hill-sides	236.23	371.28	500.08	632.22	806.01
540.21	238.20	372.02	500.12	645.11	806.06
hill-top	238.22	372.13	503.24	647.19	806.15
220.11	243.26	372.16	504.14	647.25	806.25
250.24	246.18	374.06	504.22	647.25	807.06
hillo	247.12	374.08	505.16	647.25	807.06
494.19	251.04	374.12	514.11	647.26	807.15
hillocks	251.13	375.18	515.16	647.26	808.03
508.13	252.03	375.19	518.06	651.03	808.05
hills	252.21	375.21	518.08	651.19	809.01
075.05	253.13	375.21	521.06	655.20	809.11
148.01	254.07	376.02	523.09	655.22	810.09
194.12	254.13	376.06	523.17	655.24	810.10
194.16	258.10	376.10	527.03	661.27	812.06
194.21	258.22	376.19	533.25	661.27	813.16
209.09	259.12	376.24	535.19	662.02	815.05
220.19	261.16	377.02	535.22	680.14	815.23
222.23	262.26	379.08	536.01	680.23	815.26
502.22	263.06	380.21	536.02	680.28	815.28
578.02	277.15	380.24	537.28	685.05	819.08
664.10	283.09	382.11	538.07	695.25	819.11
699.01	283.09	382.16	533.15	706.03	819.25
715.21	284.15	382.26	533.20	706.04	819.27
812.05	284.19	382.27	539.06	714.09	820.04
812.17	286.16	383.02	539.07	714.15	820.15
815.03	286.19	383.13	539.17	715.04	820.16
850.01	286.20	383.20	539.27	715.12	820.18
854.16	288.01	383.22	540.01	715.18	820.26
855.03	290.02	385.07	540.02	716.03	820.26
hilly	290.10	401.07	540.10	717.24	823.15
113.02	290.14	401.08	543.18	718.25	823.17
164.16	291.06	402.14	543.22	719.08	823.26
him	291.10	402.21	543.22	720.17	825.09
005.06	291.20	403.09	543.23	724.24	825.10
006.26	291.26	410.08	544.08	725.12	825.17
007.07	292.21	412.24	544.13	725.14	827.16
007.08	292.21	412.25	544.17	725.16	829.16
007.10	293.05	413.02	545.09	727.04	829.21
007.14	293.14	413.02	545.19	727.04	829.25
007.24	293.14	413.07	549.15	727.07	830.05
008.03	293.17	416.12	549.25	727.27	830.06
008.05	294.17	416.19	552.27	732.19	830.08
008.05	296.13	416.26	553.02	732.22	831.07
008.15	296.15	416.28	553.04	733.11	831.17
009.19	297.04	420.04	553.10	737.10	832.02
010.11	298.04	420.27	553.18	737.14	832.07
010.13	298.10	420.28	553.20	738.19	832.08
010.16	299.03	421.09	554.12	741.08	832.27
010.21	301.08	422.10	555.03	741.13	833.04
019.15	307.23	422.17	555.06	741.19	833.12
021.16	309.06	424.25	555.19	742.05	833.13
027.11	311.25	424.25	556.01	742.19	833.17
027.16	312.23	424.28	559.10	745.20	834.12
027.26	314.05	425.01	559.16	745.21	836.19
034.22	314.17	425.03	559.18	746.21	837.03
040.01	314.23	425.22	561.10	747.04	839.02
040.03	314.25	426.11	562.19	747.20	840.08
040.20	315.01	426.17	563.14	749.03	840.11
041.02	315.02	427.01	563.25	750.14	840.15
043.10	315.09	427.24	564.10	753.18	840.26
043.16	315.10	423.27	564.17	753.22	840.27
043.21	316.16	430.17	566.03	753.22	841.02
043.23	316.27	432.01	566.07	753.27	841.06
053.26	317.01	432.07	566.07	754.01	841.07
055.23	319.08	432.15	566.11	756.01	841.12
059.24	321.03	432.27	566.11	756.15	841.23
105.25	321.03	433.13	568.16	756.21	841.26
105.26	325.10	433.15	580.24	758.11	842.01
105.26	325.10	433.16	582.02	758.24	842.02
115.27	326.26	434.10	582.04	763.28	842.17
156.11	332.27	436.17	582.25	768.06	842.20
152.26	338.13	436.24	589.03	768.07	842.24
152.26	338.14	436.24	592.10	769.23	842.26
157.25	338.27	436.25	594.03	770.13	843.08
157.25	339.06	436.28	594.04	770.14	843.09
158.05	339.27	437.04	594.09	772.16	843.19
158.06	348.11	437.05	594.15	772.24	845.02
177.05	348.20	437.08	594.22	773.14	845.21
177.08	348.28	438.11	598.24	773.15	845.23
177.10	349.05	438.15	601.03	773.17	845.25
180.11	349.09	440.25	601.09	776.01	845.27
183.12	349.19	441.06	601.13	778.09	845.27
183.19	350.08	443.04	602.20	778.18	847.02
195.22	350.11	443.07	602.21	780.13	847.05
198.20	350.13	447.15	603.04	781.07	847.26
200.22	350.14	447.19	603.18	793.07	848.15
202.02	351.12	447.22	604.10	795.08	850.13
202.09	351.16	449.04	606.20	795.12	850.14
204.27	351.18	449.05	606.23	795.17	852.11
205.08	351.19	449.10	606.24	795.19	853.14
205.15	351.22	453.04	607.09	796.10	855.23
205.18	352.01	453.07	609.13	796.12	855.24
205.26	352.04	456.26	612.02	796.19	855.25
206.07	352.22	458.03	612.08	796.23	857.02
221.27	352.23	459.04	612.13	797.01	857.04
222.26	352.26	468.08	613.09	797.04	857.06
223.04	353.07	468.12	613.10	797.16	860.10
223.06	354.05	469.07	613.10	797.23	860.12
223.27	355.11	469.16	613.14	798.22	861.04
224.09	356.12	469.17	615.06	799.13	862.18
224.18	356.22	469.28	616.27	799.15	863.01
224.22	361.26	483.27	619.01	799.25	863.03
225.06	362.05	493.18	619.06	801.01	865.05

865.09	505.19	021.21	234.16	298.11	379.14
865.19	510.14	021.21	235.26	298.20	381.24
865.28	525.19	022.20	237.01	299.16	381.24
866.01	544.04	027.16	237.03	299.17	381.27
866.21	550.15	029.07	237.04	299.21	381.28
866.23	557.15	033.13	237.05	299.25	382.04
867.15	564.20	033.18	237.06	301.08	382.05
867.20	591.13	034.23	237.07	301.09	382.06
867.28	594.14	034.23	237.08	301.18	382.11
868.08	596.02	035.11	237.09	301.18	382.12
871.17	603.14	037.01	237.11	302.03	382.14
871.20	607.03	038.27	237.13	302.04	383.22
871.20	636.28	038.27	237.20	302.15	384.11
871.21	650.25	040.27	237.24	305.05	384.15
872.10	654.05	043.08	238.23	305.06	384.18
872.15	715.14	043.08	239.02	305.07	384.23
872.22	719.24	043.15	240.21	305.20	386.18
872.26	719.26	043.20	244.14	307.19	388.26
873.03	720.22	048.19	244.20	307.20	401.20
874.04	733.08	052.24	245.16	311.23	402.09
875.06	742.05	053.05	246.10	312.01	402.16
875.11	748.01	053.11	250.28	312.03	402.22
876.18	750.08	053.12	251.23	312.22	403.09
877.26	753.25	053.24	251.28	312.24	403.09
879.15	796.17	054.25	252.03	312.25	407.16
882.11	797.03	056.01	252.08	313.08	409.12
882.13	800.11	060.12	252.10	313.09	409.14
882.16	805.21	074.26	252.15	313.09	409.20
882.16	816.04	074.26	252.16	316.07	409.21
882.17	818.22	105.20	252.20	316.28	410.09
882.18	827.07	105.26	253.04	317.02	412.23
882.26	841.24	107.19	253.06	317.02	412.27
882.26	842.05	107.20	253.08	324.07	415.04
883.03	842.06	109.17	253.12	325.05	416.12
884.06	855.20	114.28	254.07	325.08	416.20
886.01	860.09	114.28	254.12	326.02	417.04
886.03	864.25	114.28	254.19	329.04	418.10
886.12	865.18	115.02	256.19	332.26	419.16
886.24	877.25	118.26	256.22	332.27	419.26
887.17	886.19	118.27	258.20	333.24	420.08
887.18	888.25	119.01	258.23	339.02	420.09
887.21	911.16	119.10	258.24	339.26	420.19
887.23	912.01	119.20	258.26	346.23	420.22
888.15	912.09	119.20	259.02	348.09	421.06
888.19	hind	119.22	259.03	348.10	421.07
888.21	600.05	119.28	259.04	348.13	421.07
888.22	hind'rance	120.01	259.05	348.25	421.09
889.02	551.13	121.07	260.26	349.06	421.11
889.05	hinder	121.28	261.18	349.14	421.19
889.14	714.15	123.25	262.08	349.17	422.08
889.15	hinderances	124.21	262.20	350.07	422.09
889.17	284.12	126.26	262.21	350.14	422.23
890.02	hindering	126.27	262.22	350.18	423.26
890.23	328.07	135.07	262.23	350.28	424.02
890.24	hindostanee	136.11	262.23	351.01	425.06
890.25	805.16	141.28	262.25	351.13	425.07
890.28	805.20	148.18	262.27	351.18	425.21
891.01	810.07	152.27	263.01	351.26	425.25
891.01	893.01	157.23	263.02	351.26	425.25
892.01	893.07	157.23	264.11	351.27	426.14
892.18	893.08	161.14	265.01	352.27	426.22
893.21	893.20	161.17	266.09	354.02	427.09
893.23	hinges	161.18	266.26	360.08	428.15
893.24	675.24	176.08	268.02	360.10	429.07
895.04	hint	176.21	270.13	361.12	429.23
895.11	042.19	177.02	272.14	361.13	430.05
895.12	384.24	177.05	272.14	363.13	430.17
895.15	845.26	193.25	272.15	365.28	432.03
896.05	879.15	185.05	277.16	366.11	432.15
896.07	hinted	185.07	279.15	366.25	433.21
896.23	569.07	189.04	281.03	367.14	435.08
901.01	hints	195.11	283.06	368.06	440.22
905.03	014.13	195.23	283.07	368.06	440.27
906.06	115.25	196.07	283.07	369.01	441.07
906.11	473.07	199.10	283.12	369.25	441.24
906.21	473.09	200.23	283.17	369.25	444.11
907.06	hips	202.06	283.21	369.26	446.05
909.11	219.10	204.28	283.22	369.28	446.27
909.26	hire	205.14	284.18	370.02	446.28
909.27	668.08	205.19	284.25	370.05	447.02
909.28	hired	205.22	284.26	370.13	447.05
910.06	334.26	205.23	284.27	371.07	447.07
910.24	479.12	206.21	285.13	371.16	447.09
911.28	586.09	217.22	288.01	371.24	447.13
912.11	633.10	222.21	290.15	372.05	447.13
himalayan	721.20	222.24	290.16	372.06	447.15
797.14	hireling	223.02	290.24	372.07	447.17
himself	883.13	223.02	290.26	372.15	447.17
006.14	hireling's	223.12	291.03	373.26	447.23
006.26	898.19	223.13	291.07	373.28	450.08
007.06	hiring	223.21	291.10	374.01	450.09
035.10	637.22	224.05	291.23	374.02	450.11
059.21	his	224.09	292.01	374.07	450.26
118.25	006.08	224.15	292.10	374.07	451.07
131.13	007.03	224.22	292.11	374.14	451.19
202.08	007.10	225.18	292.13	375.12	451.21
205.16	007.11	226.16	292.17	375.14	453.02
223.01	007.20	226.26	292.21	375.14	453.04
264.08	008.01	227.27	292.22	375.15	456.22
264.19	008.01	228.01	292.22	375.26	457.10
279.14	008.10	228.03	292.24	375.27	468.20
297.05	008.11	228.04	292.25	375.28	468.21
373.25	008.19	228.10	292.25	376.12	468.25
409.11	009.18	228.12	292.26	376.18	468.26
417.05	016.27	230.12	293.08	376.21	469.03
424.02	016.28	232.02	293.12	377.12	469.15
447.08	018.10	232.15	293.13	377.14	469.27
447.26	018.11	232.16	294.15	377.26	470.01
449.06	019.02	233.05	296.17	378.12	483.28
451.19	019.04	233.06	298.08	379.11	487.09
476.15	021.17	234.13		379.11	491.20

491.22	594.11	671.20	747.06	805.05	836.22
492.06	594.16	680.24	747.07	805.26	837.13
494.08	594.18	684.02	747.08	805.26	838.10
494.14	594.21	695.13	747.17	805.27	839.08
494.19	594.23	695.21	747.17	806.04	840.07
494.20	595.01	695.23	747.24	806.17	840.09
496.06	596.02	695.28	747.27	806.18	840.12
497.12	596.19	696.01	748.02	806.18	840.17
499.05	597.06	701.01	748.02	806.20	840.19
499.06	600.24	701.18	750.10	806.21	841.02
499.07	601.04	701.19	750.24	806.27	841.11
499.16	601.05	701.23	753.16	807.05	842.07
499.18	601.25	701.28	753.19	807.07	842.18
500.10	602.23	702.01	753.19	807.08	842.21
504.07	603.03	702.02	753.24	807.08	843.04
504.15	603.03	702.03	754.23	807.10	843.05
504.21	603.11	702.10	755.22	807.18	843.06
504.23	604.08	702.11	756.07	807.18	843.13
505.22	606.19	702.11	756.08	807.19	843.15
512.20	607.01	702.14	756.15	807.24	843.16
513.18	607.01	702.22	757.02	808.14	843.23
513.19	607.08	702.24	757.14	808.16	843.24
513.19	612.02	702.26	760.23	808.17	843.26
515.19	612.03	703.27	762.16	808.24	844.02
516.12	612.03	704.09	762.17	810.22	844.16
516.13	612.05	704.11	762.17	811.07	844.18
516.14	612.09	706.06	762.17	811.14	844.26
517.01	612.10	714.09	763.06	811.14	844.28
517.25	612.11	714.12	763.18	813.02	845.07
517.26	612.12	714.14	763.24	813.05	845.08
518.07	612.24	714.17	764.02	813.06	845.18
519.24	613.03	714.17	766.04	813.06	845.20
521.06	613.21	714.18	766.11	813.08	846.13
521.15	615.05	714.19	766.13	813.14	846.17
521.16	616.09	714.22	766.14	813.22	846.19
524.17	619.05	715.03	766.19	814.16	846.20
526.05	619.13	715.06	767.03	815.08	846.21
531.26	619.16	715.07	767.04	815.11	847.03
535.25	619.17	715.12	767.05	815.23	847.04
536.07	619.18	715.13	767.07	815.24	847.28
537.16	619.26	715.13	767.09	815.24	848.03
537.18	620.02	715.17	767.09	816.12	848.11
538.08	620.03	715.19	767.14	818.13	848.12
540.01	620.24	715.23	767.14	818.18	850.21
543.15	620.26	716.02	767.14	819.26	851.07
543.19	621.11	716.04	767.15	820.08	855.23
544.05	622.22	716.22	767.15	820.10	855.25
544.11	622.22	717.25	767.16	820.16	857.07
544.25	622.23	718.02	767.16	820.17	858.05
544.26	623.06	718.23	768.01	820.25	858.12
545.14	623.07	719.08	768.03	820.26	858.18
545.16	624.07	719.24	768.03	821.01	858.19
545.17	624.09	719.28	768.04	821.01	858.22
545.23	624.12	720.04	768.15	821.02	860.06
545.28	624.15	720.17	769.19	821.10	862.04
549.06	624.16	720.18	769.24	822.18	862.15
549.13	626.03	720.28	771.24	822.19	863.09
549.17	626.04	723.13	772.26	823.06	864.04
549.19	626.05	724.19	772.27	823.07	864.16
550.03	632.23	725.08	773.07	823.20	865.02
550.05	636.07	725.11	773.07	823.21	865.09
552.14	643.22	725.15	774.15	823.25	865.18
552.14	643.24	726.24	774.24	823.27	866.21
552.24	646.09	727.06	775.27	824.05	867.12
552.26	646.09	727.07	777.08	824.05	867.13
554.25	646.25	727.16	780.02	825.01	868.01
554.26	647.22	727.16	780.10	825.03	869.06
554.26	647.22	728.02	780.10	825.04	871.15
554.27	647.23	731.17	781.01	825.05	871.26
555.05	647.23	732.07	781.02	825.06	871.27
555.22	647.26	733.02	781.18	825.07	871.27
556.06	648.22	733.08	783.10	825.08	871.28
559.13	648.26	733.09	785.07	825.11	872.02
559.14	649.05	733.09	795.26	825.12	872.02
561.10	649.06	736.09	796.13	825.13	872.03
562.07	649.06	736.17	796.24	825.25	872.06
563.12	649.09	737.01	796.27	825.26	872.10
564.04	649.12	737.01	796.28	825.27	872.18
564.09	650.04	737.02	797.06	825.27	872.19
564.09	650.08	737.07	797.13	827.05	872.20
564.12	650.08	737.10	797.17	827.20	872.23
564.20	650.17	737.10	797.17	827.23	872.25
566.01	650.25	737.13	798.18	827.27	873.01
566.25	650.27	737.18	799.09	827.28	873.02
568.17	651.04	738.21	799.20	828.27	873.10
574.19	651.04	738.21	800.05	828.27	874.25
574.20	651.05	738.26	800.10	829.02	874.27
580.16	651.14	740.10	800.10	829.02	875.03
580.23	651.15	740.11	800.25	829.13	875.15
586.05	651.16	740.12	801.02	831.03	875.19
586.06	654.05	740.13	801.04	831.10	876.12
586.08	655.15	740.14	801.11	831.13	877.22
586.21	655.21	740.22	801.19	831.17	877.23
587.02	655.23	740.25	802.11	831.19	877.23
589.02	655.23	740.26	802.13	832.03	879.06
589.13	655.27	741.02	802.13	832.07	879.12
590.12	655.27	741.02	802.17	832.14	879.14
590.12	655.27	741.21	802.22	832.15	879.15
590.12	656.01	742.15	802.23	832.16	879.19
590.13	661.26	744.18	802.25	832.22	881.04
590.15	662.07	745.19	803.12	832.25	881.12
590.23	662.08	745.19	803.13	833.04	882.20
590.24	662.10	745.20	803.22	833.05	882.22
591.15	662.11	745.20	803.24	833.16	882.22
591.16	662.11	745.22	803.25	834.15	882.22
592.10	662.12	746.17	803.27	835.14	883.02
592.11	662.18	746.23	804.01	835.21	884.05
592.16	669.20	746.24	804.11	835.24	884.07
592.17	671.12	747.03	805.01	836.09	885.19
593.05	671.17	747.05	805.03	836.13	886.02
593.14	671.19	747.05		836.21	886.15
594.07					

886.17	594.12	hollows	homeward	752.17	228.10
886.17	692.05	146.07	170.16	759.27	232.15
887.01	702.27	holly	829.02	775.28	232.17
887.11	779.25	219.14	904.06	779.01	241.20
887.23	821.07	675.25	homily	783.02	243.08
887.27	849.05	711.20	045.03	793.02	254.08
888.17	898.17	holly-bushes	honest	793.05	332.26
888.22	903.27	719.20	561.04	809.20	359.09
888.23	912.09	hollyhocks	637.07	809.24	380.23
888.26	hoar	148.03	683.15	812.27	566.01
889.24	870.08	holm	696.12	833.21	575.10
889.25	hoard	145.18	705.23	852.02	horse's
889.28	453.02	holy	709.22	856.06	227.07
890.04	hoarding	200.04	732.02	872.12	229.06
890.11	048.12	201.23	744.06	894.22	horse-chestnut
890.13	hoards	507.11	honey	901.03	502.26
890.16	048.25	843.18	271.03	912.20	505.26
890.17	hoarse	homage	663.02	hoped	520.14
890.18	569.17	224.25	honey-dew	077.14	horse-hoofs
890.19	619.17	360.08	502.28	306.04	380.19
891.26	hoary	731.20	honey-moon	353.27	horseback
892.16	066.23	home	625.26	537.23	537.27
892.22	194.27	001.13	907.04	840.14	horseman
892.23	226.02	007.10	907.07	841.27	499.26
893.10	715.22	007.15	honeyed	854.03	564.03
894.02	750.11	007.19	555.07	hopeful	horses
895.11	hob	015.01	honour	486.02	073.19
896.02	600.02	033.21	122.13	hopeless	074.10
896.07	hoist	101.04	163.16	629.16	281.13
898.27	356.19	109.14	359.03	657.14	432.25
899.06	hoisted	114.26	614.10	663.16	433.08
899.24	073.21	147.19	632.02	667.19	586.23
900.10	124.14	153.09	647.08	854.21	855.01
903.19	183.17	156.19	720.18	877.15	hose
903.20	hold	156.20	762.01	883.20	117.02
903.20	012.12	156.20	845.03	hopelessly	hospitable
903.20	013.21	162.27	honourable	743.08	798.25
904.01	024.06	207.17	317.08	818.16	hospital
904.04	099.04	225.19	745.10	hopes	146.27
906.10	107.10	225.20	771.10	164.10	147.26
906.11	109.10	229.04	771.22	170.09	150.25
906.15	139.25	242.20	honoured	314.02	hospitality
906.17	227.07	380.21	291.04	320.16	458.06
906.24	283.09	381.20	320.21	499.28	690.21
907.14	283.16	391.20	719.26	539.05	706.07
909.02	397.20	401.03	748.04	563.17	708.22
909.03	421.13	439.25	hoof	606.07	host
909.11	421.15	445.04	132.13	759.21	257.26
909.17	495.20	490.08	526.25	819.17	860.09
909.17	518.02	493.04	hoofs	907.17	860.16
909.19	549.04	493.26	229.06	hoping	871.04
909.21	560.24	495.08	564.03	485.13	hostess
909.24	620.03	496.09	hooped	655.21	136.20
909.25	648.05	496.10	365.20	hopped	hostile
910.09	649.12	497.18	hope	639.07	459.18
910.23	720.15	498.03	033.14	horizon	459.23
910.25	721.02	498.03	042.04	005.02	hostility
910.26	724.07	499.16	055.01	075.06	531.08
910.27	822.19	507.20	055.19	145.07	hot
911.10	844.02	545.04	057.08	164.18	023.18
911.20	877.01	559.09	102.05	209.10	081.21
911.24	890.28	569.05	107.01	221.03	141.22
911.25	908.26	572.04	109.13	249.02	142.26
911.26	holding	630.20	144.17	502.12	187.06
912.01	098.09	639.20	192.03	horizontal	313.19
912.02	326.14	669.17	247.10	237.06	326.06
912.10	349.01	679.27	262.02	471.18	384.10
912.13	366.27	683.26	262.03	horizontally	385.04
912.14	376.28	695.13	299.18	260.26	565.06
912.17	410.09	698.25	302.23	horn	591.14
912.19	419.09	699.03	351.24	074.27	611.16
912.19	467.16	700.09	354.26	170.03	630.01
912.20	488.19	700.24	388.25	369.22	663.06
912.20	598.10	703.16	398.24	542.21	700.15
912.21	598.23	703.18	398.27	horned	778.25
hiss	700.18	711.15	422.01	005.10	840.05
265.03	holds	714.11	426.23	horny	841.08
296.25	405.12	715.23	439.16	697.17	894.14
history	659.14	724.28	446.26	horrible	899.16
003.18	holes	725.21	454.09	301.05	hotel
010.03	117.03	729.02	457.15	646.14	199.14
086.22	holiday	729.02	499.04	horror	279.20
092.27	218.05	734.06	508.12	023.14	281.19
094.17	751.22	738.27	521.09	153.16	282.05
097.21	752.17	760.26	524.18	373.21	287.23
358.22	789.03	783.13	527.22	415.23	557.16
705.14	790.26	784.16	538.04	418.07	hothouse
706.11	holidays	786.01	550.25	423.09	018.28
744.12	145.02	791.08	556.03	424.24	hour
749.05	218.08	793.18	569.23	429.06	001.05
771.13	holland	799.05	573.17	609.12	005.03
hit	058.18	800.16	608.09	683.24	016.04
009.23	078.13	803.17	631.17	860.13	024.28
375.03	084.11	805.01	631.22	horrors	028.28
507.04	427.12	828.13	640.16	636.16	071.06
863.17	hollow	833.11	642.24	709.03	073.07
hitch	017.20	854.25	646.19	horse	078.13
619.04	026.06	856.02	646.21	132.12	081.11
hither	074.26	865.13	650.26	152.27	083.08
030.07	083.15	899.06	656.22	185.05	086.23
515.12	166.19	899.22	659.16	221.05	096.12
hitherto	230.18	907.28	671.22	221.15	097.13
030.24	249.09	908.06	672.27	221.19	101.06
097.01	659.22	homeless	675.09	221.22	111.14
119.25	673.25	655.18	684.13	222.05	127.03
122.26	712.04	709.03	719.01	222.18	128.04
160.02	742.12	homely	721.18	222.22	139.15
255.20	758.22	794.13	732.23	223.18	142.12
282.13	767.11	homes	734.14	225.16	165.22
309.25	813.02	744.17	739.10	227.09	167.18
315.26	859.25		745.21	227.27	170.21
			747.22		

174.11
174.13
180.17
182.26
183.24
185.06
219.03
219.05
225.15
228.19
233.15
289.17
323.06
329.08
332.07
340.04
371.02
379.10
380.11
390.12
402.09
403.13
413.04
416.19
422.05
427.04
431.23
445.22
457.27
457.12
466.26
470.20
474.05
476.28
476.16
481.16
484.05
485.13
493.28
501.20
505.14
506.20
510.08
515.01
543.24
547.22
556.14
559.01
560.03
564.22
567.15
567.21
568.09
605.11
626.19
651.09
639.23
643.19
657.14
664.11
667.04
672.16
682.13
683.24
692.03
649.11
714.02
724.23
731.20
736.24
741.14
741.16
741.17
744.17
746.16
752.04
757.13
765.09
770.01
782.19
799.17
813.11
813.15
816.20
816.21
818.19
839.20
845.01
845.12
845.24
847.10
848.04
851.03
861.27
873.16
883.16
887.04
902.21
912.19
hour's
045.03
065.14
095.17
769.17
houri
546.05
hourly
572.16
467.21
808.11
851.18

912.24
hours
047.04
154.03
157.24
185.07
186.03
235.27
300.21
372.05
380.06
398.15
422.06
424.17
425.23
426.26
429.19
473.02
474.10
474.16
490.24
557.03
601.24
676.04
623.27
712.23
714.05
714.17
724.10
730.20
803.18
841.08
852.15
852.19
854.26
hours'
147.12
181.18
520.07
house
009.14
021.21
037.04
037.07
049.15
050.07
059.07
069.27
076.01
078.02
089.04
091.04
092.01
092.06
093.25
105.03
120.07
150.26
151.25
154.11
154.24
167.06
172.05
174.03
180.11
185.19
189.12
189.21
190.23
194.23
199.13
201.28
206.24
225.28
226.06
230.18
241.04
265.16
293.17
294.21
299.14
310.07
310.10
314.05
327.07
329.16
333.08
356.20
356.28
364.07
365.16
380.07
384.13
390.02
396.25
399.01
401.02
417.13
418.08
420.13
424.26
433.16
434.09
434.14
446.21
455.17
457.24
459.09
467.28
469.09
475.20

488.21
489.03
494.04
494.17
505.04
506.03
519.12
537.26
549.11
561.25
562.13
563.21
565.01
572.10
581.19
586.08
596.22
597.23
602.23
604.02
616.02
624.01
630.11
639.16
649.22
655.11
667.10
668.28
669.10
669.23
671.20
674.15
675.27
676.08
681.28
683.14
685.04
686.27
694.05
694.07
695.06
695.09
697.07
697.28
707.07
716.20
721.22
721.23
722.03
722.15
723.09
734.10
739.15
751.08
751.11
751.24
770.25
794.01
795.09
795.20
798.11
800.24
844.02
848.24
849.16
856.24
858.25
860.06
862.06
864.02
864.28
866.12
867.14
869.08
869.15
870.21
871.01
873.11
873.27
878.16
885.25
906.11
house-accounts
641.01
house-front
284.02
house-keeper
117.22
house-maid's
795.16
housebreakers
683.12
housed
615.28
household
060.28
148.19
217.21
274.07
626.25
792.20
housekeeper
046.12
122.18
137.25
148.21
196.01
196.11
464.07
669.25
695.19

864.19
878.27
905.10
housekeeper's
046.11
housemaid
016.15
048.26
217.22
863.06
housemaid's
028.18
211.21
houses
031.25
076.01
143.03
184.27
195.13
199.08
666.28
668.19
683.11
housewifely
187.09
hovered
423.24
805.26
hovering
143.05
643.11
how
008.27
012.18
019.27
020.05
021.27
033.25
033.30
036.12
036.13
036.17
038.07
043.22
044.26
044.27
054.18
058.10
058.15
061.28
062.24
062.25
062.28
063.01
063.01
063.05
069.21
073.14
077.10
077.11
081.15
083.07
094.26
096.17
105.13
105.17
105.23
105.28
107.13
107.19
108.13
113.16
117.25
119.07
123.18
126.09
127.16
131.09
136.22
137.10
137.13
140.07
145.13
150.18
152.09
153.01
158.19
161.20
163.19
164.25
166.01
167.06
168.01
176.04
183.19
183.22
184.21
186.22
195.07
198.25
200.23
211.24
216.11
218.07
238.14
241.09
250.18
262.08
265.05
268.27
270.03

270.03
271.06
271.07
271.27
283.03
283.05
289.00
293.13
293.23
298.09
299.24
306.02
317.14
317.15
320.22
321.08
324.16
324.17
326.25
338.13
338.20
339.10
349.04
349.07
349.08
360.19
361.28
364.03
371.17
375.09
376.09
389.21
405.27
424.23
425.28
427.14
427.18
428.01
433.18
433.18
436.25
439.27
446.12
446.15
447.05
447.25
450.07
452.04
452.26
455.28
456.22
457.14
461.27
462.17
463.01
465.19
465.21
465.26
466.27
469.11
470.04
474.02
479.10
481.09
482.13
484.14
490.07
491.12
494.02
506.07
510.17
517.08
529.09
531.01
531.02
531.09
533.04
536.15
541.01
541.06
551.23
562.16
568.03
571.01
571.04
571.10
571.16
574.04
577.23
583.09
591.15
591.16
593.25
599.23
599.23
607.02
607.09
607.10
610.23
613.11
613.22
614.18
615.24
621.27
623.04
627.14
635.16
637.01
640.18
641.26

644.02
650.18
656.02
665.08
665.15
665.25
668.01
670.13
679.07
681.27
684.20
685.22
685.22
708.27
708.28
721.10
721.11
721.11
723.26
724.16
745.24
752.16
766.10
772.01
772.13
776.09
776.11
777.22
779.27
783.04
786.23
793.28
794.01
796.08
797.02
797.04
797.05
802.21
805.07
817.03
819.21
822.06
823.17
823.17
826.13
826.15
826.07
832.21
833.08
835.02
844.08
844.09
847.26
854.20
855.03
855.09
856.13
856.13
856.14
858.14
858.15
858.15
858.15
858.18
859.14
860.13
861.28
864.09
866.28
873.13
882.26
883.10
883.27
884.14
887.18
887.19
887.20
889.05
889.06
892.18
894.03
895.24
906.08
907.10
however
008.07
009.22
036.18
042.07
042.19
057.02
057.02
057.24
079.10
081.21
120.27
137.15
156.23
169.15
171.01
186.04
192.26
211.08
222.03
223.07
236.07
267.11
276.24
277.27
286.25
331.18

345.19	human-bred	hungry	527.21	010.03	027.24
398.09	385.17	050.11	820.11	010.05	028.03
417.28	humanities	077.04	908.28	010.06	028.03
423.04	796.18	087.07	husbands	010.10	028.04
428.23	humanity	095.17	529.07	010.11	028.09
454.09	444.04	137.16	hush	010.13	028.09
438.10	632.06	334.09	132.13	010.14	028.15
440.20	humble	336.07	207.18	010.18	028.16
446.12	014.23	671.15	220.16	010.19	028.19
449.18	058.01	702.19	294.20	010.19	028.21
452.14	481.25	703.01	333.28	010.25	028.23
463.02	589.01	882.09	529.03	011.06	028.28
476.04	639.03	899.11	611.10	012.02	029.01
477.14	677.07	hunt	620.22	012.05	029.15
489.23	698.02	360.01	684.26	012.07	029.17
509.13	717.15	hunting	758.07	012.10	029.18
526.05	722.12	545.18	758.13	012.18	029.22
529.06	724.17	hurl	850.04	013.15	029.24
544.04	730.20	009.20	hushed	013.15	030.01
559.22	738.22	hurling	022.24	013.17	030.02
560.21	816.19	628.08	294.04	013.20	030.03
575.07	humbled	hurrah	364.10	014.03	030.11
575.08	001.16	775.18	418.19	014.11	030.22
596.11	324.20	hurricane	445.10	015.03	030.27
616.13	900.11	766.02	488.06	015.07	031.02
620.12	humbler	hurricanes	575.22	015.16	031.04
650.06	165.18	384.19	677.24	016.11	031.06
660.07	humblest	629.21	hushes	017.12	031.07
663.22	709.17	hurried	465.09	017.14	031.09
667.06	720.02	077.22	hushing	017.16	031.10
674.11	humbling	229.18	080.26	017.24	031.12
749.02	532.24	232.24	husk	018.02	031.16
764.05	humbly	295.19	823.01	016.07	031.22
767.05	903.24	333.06	husky	016.08	031.23
804.28	humbug	472.16	478.25	018.14	032.03
803.17	214.15	519.10	hybrid	018.16	032.05
815.27	267.07	534.22	628.10	019.07	032.09
864.05	humid	553.08	hyena	019.08	032.10
907.13	737.22	559.01	600.04	019.08	032.20
howl	humiliation	585.08	hymn	019.13	032.22
101.11	021.07	587.10	033.01	019.14	032.23
howling	692.13	686.04	082.13	019.16	033.15
021.04	910.03	856.09	082.27	020.02	033.26
572.13	humility	858.14	hypochondria	020.03	034.01
766.03	058.05	873.15	568.12	020.04	034.10
hue	507.23	hurriedly	hypochondriac	020.05	034.15
461.09	816.01	722.07	563.11	020.06	034.16
501.13	901.12	hurry	hypocrisy	020.07	034.17
855.04	hummed	051.06	310.26	020.18	034.18
hueless	629.25	316.22	hypocrite	020.19	034.19
594.19	humming	405.13	124.04	021.02	034.19
hues	442.05	428.26	hypothesis	021.05	034.22
322.10	504.04	428.26	580.15	021.09	034.24
737.22	humour	544.23	hysteria	021.10	034.25
huge	005.18	558.20	127.20	021.11	035.06
094.02	472.28	607.04	hysterical	021.13	035.09
199.07	807.09	625.11	391.05	021.15	035.22
222.02	humoured	707.12	hysterics	021.17	035.24
770.19	756.11	719.11	287.25	021.18	035.27
hum	humph	hurrying	i	021.18	036.04
045.24	240.20	051.12	001.11	021.26	036.04
073.03	265.27	hurt	001.11	022.08	036.08
078.15	472.23	024.03	002.11	022.11	036.12
080.25	384.25	223.03	002.18	022.14	036.20
355.06	hundred	223.28	002.18	022.15	036.23
449.13	207.07	266.05	002.20	022.18	036.26
human	242.07	266.17	002.26	022.23	037.07
046.21	407.05	416.03	002.27	023.01	037.11
109.07	450.20	431.24	003.02	023.02	037.11
152.15	451.25	436.20	003.03	023.02	037.12
207.26	452.15	537.01	003.05	023.04	037.13
216.06	464.03	829.17	003.12	023.06	037.16
222.07	464.25	829.17	003.18	023.09	037.18
222.12	511.01	857.06	003.19	023.11	037.18
274.08	590.10	867.19	003.22	023.15	037.19
274.10	616.18	hurting	003.22	023.19	037.24
398.20	678.24	621.11	004.05	023.21	038.04
404.28	698.01	husband	004.15	023.22	038.07
424.11	777.08	016.22	004.27	024.05	038.07
477.26	884.28	162.20	005.05	024.05	038.11
478.25	hundreds	196.04	005.08	024.06	038.14
483.12	074.08	196.08	005.25	024.12	038.18
514.08	131.02	201.25	005.28	024.18	038.18
524.09	310.08	360.06	006.01	024.18	038.19
592.15	hung	481.09	006.11	024.19	038.22
598.02	015.22	481.21	006.11	024.26	038.22
599.16	204.04	516.11	006.12	025.02	039.06
623.11	258.15	535.17	006.19	025.03	039.12
645.09	293.06	556.01	006.19	025.05	039.16
647.13	334.20	568.21	006.22	025.07	039.27
652.12	341.06	571.09	006.25	025.14	039.27
659.15	369.18	601.06	006.27	025.16	040.04
660.17	420.13	613.23	007.02	026.02	040.10
663.13	457.05	621.06	007.02	026.03	040.15
663.13	576.12	629.08	007.24	026.05	040.17
664.20	692.15	629.10	007.28	026.09	041.14
664.21	692.24	632.04	008.09	026.12	041.18
724.06	756.16	773.10	008.12	026.13	041.20
736.13	hunger	796.26	008.14	026.17	042.04
756.25	082.18	822.13	008.15	026.17	042.06
757.21	088.23	841.13	008.18	027.03	042.08
761.24	100.12	864.03	008.25	027.04	042.10
762.23	112.18	894.27	009.03	027.10	043.01
813.25	119.02	895.03	009.05	027.11	043.15
816.16	644.26	905.10	009.18	027.15	043.15
824.22	661.11	908.03	009.19	027.16	043.17
846.04	665.04	911.07	009.20	027.20	043.18
849.20	668.17	husband's	009.23		043.21
883.07	672.25	022.01	009.27		043.25
912.12	707.19	377.05			043.27
	883.23	468.07			

044.01	059.17	069.27	090.14	105.25	125.07
044.14	059.17	071.05	090.15	105.25	125.26
044.17	059.20	071.10	090.19	105.25	126.04
044.22	059.21	071.16	090.22	106.02	126.11
044.23	059.24	072.03	090.24	106.03	126.23
045.05	060.04	072.08	090.27	106.04	127.06
045.06	060.13	072.14	091.07	106.12	127.06
045.07	060.14	072.21	091.08	106.15	127.07
045.14	061.06	072.28	091.11	106.16	127.19
045.27	061.06	073.08	092.09	106.19	127.25
046.01	061.07	073.16	093.08	106.26	127.26
046.02	061.14	073.22	093.22	107.01	128.04
046.03	061.15	073.23	093.24	107.04	129.04
046.05	061.24	074.01	094.04	107.04	129.05
046.13	061.24	074.03	094.08	107.05	129.07
046.17	061.24	074.05	094.08	107.06	129.09
046.18	061.25	074.05	094.15	107.07	129.11
046.20	061.27	074.11	094.15	107.09	129.12
046.22	061.27	074.13	094.22	107.13	129.14
046.26	062.01	074.18	094.27	107.25	129.17
046.28	062.02	074.21	094.27	107.25	129.18
047.02	062.03	074.24	094.28	107.26	130.03
047.04	062.04	075.02	095.04	108.01	130.04
047.11	062.04	075.09	095.06	108.04	130.07
047.11	062.05	075.10	095.09	108.04	130.08
047.16	062.05	075.11	095.10	108.06	130.10
047.20	062.05	075.14	095.14	108.09	130.12
047.23	062.06	075.17	095.15	108.24	130.16
047.26	062.09	075.20	095.16	109.09	130.20
048.03	062.18	075.22	096.13	109.10	130.21
049.08	062.19	075.24	096.17	109.11	130.21
049.13	062.20	075.25	096.19	109.12	130.25
049.20	062.21	076.08	097.02	109.12	131.04
049.23	062.22	076.09	097.03	109.15	131.05
049.27	062.23	076.15	097.08	109.17	131.08
050.02	062.23	077.09	097.21	109.18	131.25
050.03	062.24	077.09	098.08	109.21	132.04
050.06	062.25	077.11	098.09	109.23	132.04
050.16	063.01	077.12	098.21	111.19	132.06
050.21	063.01	077.14	098.26	111.20	132.06
050.22	063.02	077.17	098.28	112.12	132.09
050.22	063.03	077.25	099.06	112.15	132.10
050.24	063.04	077.26	099.07	113.06	132.28
050.26	063.05	078.15	099.08	114.01	133.02
050.27	063.08	079.06	099.10	114.04	133.10
051.05	063.09	079.07	099.12	114.24	133.12
051.13	063.13	079.07	099.23	115.01	133.13
051.15	063.17	079.09	100.04	115.02	133.16
051.15	063.19	079.15	100.08	115.04	133.19
051.18	063.20	079.17	100.20	115.05	133.28
051.19	064.05	079.18	100.21	115.08	134.01
051.24	064.05	079.19	100.24	115.18	134.13
051.25	064.06	079.24	100.25	115.20	134.13
051.28	064.12	079.25	101.01	115.23	134.15
052.01	064.17	079.26	101.04	115.24	134.21
052.02	064.17	080.01	101.06	115.28	135.02
052.05	064.18	080.05	101.09	116.01	135.05
052.06	064.20	080.06	101.11	116.07	135.12
052.07	064.24	080.06	101.15	116.08	135.12
052.09	064.25	080.20	101.16	116.11	135.15
052.12	064.26	081.06	101.20	116.12	135.15
052.21	064.26	081.15	101.22	116.13	135.21
052.23	064.28	081.16	101.23	116.16	135.23
052.25	065.01	081.22	101.25	116.16	135.24
053.09	065.04	082.06	101.25	116.19	135.26
053.10	065.05	082.07	101.26	116.20	135.28
053.17	065.10	082.09	102.02	116.26	136.08
053.22	065.17	082.11	102.05	116.27	136.09
053.27	065.21	082.16	102.08	116.28	136.10
054.15	065.21	082.19	102.08	117.04	136.16
054.16	065.23	082.19	102.10	117.13	136.17
054.19	065.27	082.22	102.15	117.13	136.24
054.26	066.02	083.01	102.15	117.16	137.01
055.01	066.03	083.02	102.16	117.25	137.04
055.05	066.04	083.18	102.17	117.26	137.07
055.15	066.06	084.21	102.18	118.01	137.15
055.17	066.07	085.03	103.03	118.04	137.15
055.21	066.10	085.04	103.03	120.14	138.02
055.28	066.13	085.04	103.09	120.16	138.04
056.03	066.17	085.19	103.09	120.16	138.13
056.09	066.23	085.20	103.11	120.19	139.08
056.15	066.25	085.21	103.13	120.20	139.15
056.15	066.26	086.13	103.14	121.01	139.23
056.16	066.27	087.07	103.15	121.15	140.04
056.18	067.01	087.20	103.15	121.23	141.09
056.19	067.01	087.22	103.16	122.23	141.10
056.23	067.07	087.28	103.21	122.27	141.19
056.26	067.10	088.05	103.22	123.01	142.11
056.26	067.12	088.05	103.23	123.02	142.13
057.01	067.13	088.14	103.23	123.03	142.17
057.02	067.17	088.16	103.23	123.06	142.19
057.03	067.21	088.17	103.24	123.10	142.20
057.06	067.23	088.18	103.24	123.11	142.24
057.09	068.10	088.19	103.25	123.12	142.27
057.10	068.17	088.27	103.25	123.16	142.28
057.12	068.23	088.27	104.03	123.16	143.02
057.14	068.24	089.02	104.13	123.17	143.09
057.16	068.26	089.03	104.18	123.17	143.14
057.18	069.01	089.17	104.21	123.21	143.18
057.24	069.01	089.17	104.23	123.22	145.06
057.26	069.02	089.20	104.23	123.26	145.14
058.07	069.03	089.24	105.01	123.27	146.09
058.09	069.07	089.27	105.03	124.04	146.11
058.12	069.07	089.27	105.04	124.06	146.16
058.23	069.07	090.03	105.05	124.12	146.17
058.24	069.13	090.04	105.05	124.12	148.13
058.25	069.14	090.07	105.06	124.13	149.09
058.28	069.16	090.09	105.09	124.14	149.14
059.08	069.19	090.09	105.11	124.24	149.17
059.13	069.19	090.10	105.16	125.06	149.19
059.16	069.22	090.12	105.19		

149.22	162.08	173.20	186.25	199.05	217.25
149.23	162.09	173.20	187.02	199.09	218.09
149.24	162.10	173.26	187.04	199.15	218.09
150.01	162.11	174.04	187.17	199.19	218.11
150.02	162.15	174.05	187.18	199.22	218.15
150.02	162.24	174.08	187.18	199.22	218.21
150.04	162.27	174.12	187.20	199.25	218.25
150.06	163.03	174.14	187.21	199.27	218.28
150.08	163.04	174.18	187.26	199.28	218.28
150.12	163.05	174.19	187.28	200.03	219.01
150.13	163.05	174.19	188.03	200.07	219.04
150.14	163.06	174.20	188.05	200.08	219.07
150.24	163.10	174.21	188.06	200.09	219.24
150.25	163.12	174.24	188.06	200.10	219.27
150.28	163.17	174.27	188.06	200.26	220.04
151.03	163.18	175.01	188.11	201.02	220.07
151.07	163.20	175.02	188.16	201.06	220.09
151.08	163.24	175.06	188.17	201.16	220.16
151.12	163.27	175.06	188.19	201.21	220.18
151.25	164.01	175.09	188.20	201.27	221.07
151.27	164.09	175.09	188.22	201.28	221.08
151.27	164.15	175.14	188.24	202.01	221.09
151.28	164.21	175.15	189.03	202.03	221.16
152.01	164.23	175.16	189.13	202.03	221.17
152.06	164.25	175.18	189.14	202.04	221.24
152.24	164.26	176.02	189.14	202.08	222.05
152.28	164.27	176.11	189.14	202.10	222.14
153.09	164.28	176.16	189.22	202.19	222.15
153.10	165.03	176.25	189.24	202.23	222.28
153.15	165.07	177.04	189.24	203.01	223.02
153.17	165.12	177.08	190.07	203.03	223.03
153.21	165.12	177.15	190.11	203.05	223.06
153.25	165.13	177.19	190.12	203.07	223.10
153.27	165.14	177.20	190.13	203.08	223.10
154.04	165.15	177.22	190.15	203.11	223.13
154.11	165.15	177.25	190.25	203.13	223.16
154.16	165.17	177.26	191.02	203.15	223.17
154.16	165.20	177.26	191.07	203.23	223.24
154.18	165.24	178.03	191.08	203.24	223.25
154.19	165.27	178.05	191.10	203.24	223.26
154.20	166.01	178.05	191.12	203.26	223.26
154.21	166.02	178.06	191.17	204.06	223.28
154.26	166.03	178.06	191.18	204.07	224.03
154.26	166.09	178.12	191.26	204.21	224.03
155.03	166.11	178.18	192.03	204.26	224.08
155.07	166.14	178.21	192.08	205.01	224.11
155.12	166.15	178.26	192.08	205.17	224.18
155.14	166.15	179.08	192.09	205.18	224.20
155.17	166.22	179.11	192.10	205.23	224.23
155.19	166.23	179.12	192.13	205.26	224.24
155.20	166.24	179.15	192.14	205.27	224.26
155.21	166.26	179.21	192.16	206.02	224.27
155.21	167.01	180.01	192.17	206.07	225.06
155.23	167.02	180.07	192.17	206.10	225.08
155.26	167.03	180.14	192.19	206.25	225.11
156.03	167.05	180.16	192.20	206.26	225.13
156.06	167.07	180.18	192.21	206.27	225.15
156.11	167.09	180.19	192.23	207.18	225.17
156.13	167.10	180.24	192.24	207.20	225.19
156.13	167.14	181.03	192.25	208.01	225.22
156.14	167.14	181.14	192.27	208.08	225.24
156.14	167.16	181.16	193.02	208.09	225.25
156.21	167.20	181.19	193.03	208.13	226.09
156.22	167.25	182.01	193.06	208.19	226.13
157.01	168.01	182.02	193.08	208.23	226.20
157.01	168.10	182.03	193.11	208.26	226.20
157.03	168.12	182.04	193.12	209.01	226.21
157.05	168.13	182.05	193.12	209.13	226.23
157.09	168.15	182.10	193.13	209.14	226.28
157.10	168.15	182.11	193.20	209.17	227.04
157.12	168.18	182.12	193.22	209.20	227.09
157.13	168.21	182.14	193.26	209.23	227.10
157.14	168.22	182.27	194.17	209.25	227.11
157.18	169.04	182.27	194.24	210.05	227.12
157.18	169.08	183.02	195.03	210.05	227.15
157.18	169.10	183.04	195.04	210.08	227.16
157.22	169.17	183.10	195.08	210.14	227.20
157.24	169.21	183.13	195.08	210.16	227.22
158.03	169.23	183.14	195.10	210.16	227.24
158.03	169.26	183.18	195.16	210.21	228.07
158.04	169.28	183.19	195.21	210.22	228.15
158.06	170.05	183.28	195.21	211.01	228.20
158.06	170.14	184.01	195.26	211.03	228.21
158.08	170.15	184.03	195.26	211.07	228.23
158.08	170.17	184.04	196.01	211.09	229.01
158.13	170.20	184.04	196.02	214.13	229.02
158.15	170.23	184.07	196.09	214.15	229.03
158.16	170.27	184.08	196.10	214.15	229.03
158.17	171.03	184.09	196.12	214.18	229.04
158.17	171.05	184.11	196.18	214.23	229.05
158.20	171.06	184.12	196.22	214.24	229.09
158.21	171.19	184.14	196.23	214.25	229.12
158.21	171.24	184.15	196.28	215.01	229.14
158.22	171.25	184.17	197.02	215.05	229.17
159.03	171.27	184.19	197.16	215.08	229.18
159.05	171.28	184.20	197.19	215.09	229.19
159.06	172.01	184.21	197.22	215.09	230.01
159.06	172.06	184.22	197.25	215.12	230.07
159.09	172.06	184.26	197.26	215.14	230.13
159.13	172.08	184.28	197.28	215.16	230.13
159.16	172.09	185.06	198.01	215.16	230.14
160.02	172.12	185.10	198.06	215.17	230.16
160.04	172.13	185.11	198.11	215.18	231.01
160.06	172.20	185.12	198.11	216.04	231.03
160.07	172.26	185.22	198.20	217.01	231.15
160.08	173.01	185.25	198.20	217.04	231.17
161.24	173.01	186.03	198.25	217.07	231.20
161.26	173.03	186.11	198.28	217.08	231.24
162.02	173.04	186.19	199.01	217.17	231.26
162.06	173.14	186.22		217.24	232.01
162.07	173.15	186.25			232.03

232.04	250.11	267.25	281.14	294.01	306.16
232.04	250.27	268.01	281.15	294.03	307.03
232.05	251.08	268.06	281.17	294.05	307.05
232.25	251.12	268.07	281.18	294.11	307.06
233.08	251.16	268.07	281.23	294.12	307.13
233.11	251.17	268.08	281.26	294.13	307.13
233.12	251.20	268.09	282.07	294.17	307.16
234.01	251.23	268.10	282.17	294.18	307.17
234.08	251.24	268.13	282.23	294.21	307.17
234.09	252.17	268.15	282.25	294.23	307.25
234.10	253.05	268.19	282.25	295.02	308.13
234.13	253.10	268.19	282.25	295.04	308.15
234.28	253.16	268.21	282.27	295.06	308.15
235.03	253.24	269.03	283.03	295.07	308.17
235.06	254.02	269.06	283.05	295.14	308.18
235.08	254.20	269.07	283.14	295.17	308.19
235.11	254.20	269.08	283.23	295.18	308.24
235.13	255.12	269.10	283.24	295.19	308.27
235.14	255.12	269.11	284.06	295.20	308.27
235.17	255.14	269.14	284.06	295.23	309.05
235.26	256.20	269.15	284.06	295.24	309.13
236.01	256.22	269.19	284.07	296.01	309.15
236.04	256.24	269.23	284.08	296.05	309.17
236.07	256.24	270.05	284.09	296.06	309.17
236.10	257.01	270.05	284.10	296.07	309.24
236.12	257.02	270.06	284.10	296.13	309.25
236.15	257.03	270.07	284.13	296.13	309.26
236.17	257.04	270.08	284.16	296.16	309.27
236.18	257.11	270.09	284.21	296.19	310.01
236.20	257.12	270.09	284.23	296.26	310.02
237.04	257.25	270.10	284.28	296.27	310.03
237.07	257.27	270.11	285.01	297.01	310.05
237.09	258.02	270.11	285.02	297.03	310.06
237.12	258.04	270.14	285.08	297.04	310.13
237.13	258.06	270.14	285.15	297.08	310.18
238.03	258.06	270.15	285.18	297.09	310.24
238.05	258.06	270.15	285.19	297.16	311.09
238.07	258.11	270.16	285.20	297.20	311.13
238.13	258.21	270.16	285.22	297.21	311.15
238.25	258.25	270.17	285.22	297.25	311.17
239.01	258.25	270.22	285.24	297.25	312.06
239.06	259.11	270.22	285.24	298.04	312.11
239.16	259.24	270.24	285.26	298.05	312.15
239.18	259.16	270.26	285.28	298.08	312.16
239.18	259.19	270.27	286.02	298.09	313.02
239.23	260.06	271.01	286.04	298.10	313.10
239.24	260.06	271.01	286.04	298.11	313.12
240.04	260.07	271.02	286.07	298.14	313.13
240.08	260.17	271.14	286.07	298.15	313.19
240.09	260.17	271.17	286.15	298.15	313.20
240.10	260.20	271.19	286.17	298.19	313.21
240.12	260.22	271.21	286.19	298.24	313.22
240.18	261.04	271.22	286.25	298.26	313.23
241.13	261.06	271.24	287.20	298.27	313.25
241.16	261.10	271.24	287.21	299.01	313.26
241.18	261.10	272.04	287.28	299.02	313.26
241.20	261.12	272.06	288.03	299.05	313.27
241.22	261.13	272.19	288.07	299.09	313.28
241.23	261.19	272.20	288.10	299.09	314.01
241.26	261.20	272.23	288.12	299.11	314.03
242.03	261.20	272.24	288.14	299.12	314.03
242.06	261.20	272.26	288.15	299.13	314.04
242.08	261.24	272.28	288.16	299.14	314.06
242.10	261.25	273.11	288.28	299.17	314.06
242.19	262.07	273.14	289.01	299.18	314.07
242.21	262.07	273.15	289.03	299.19	314.12
242.23	262.09	273.20	289.04	299.20	314.12
242.25	262.13	273.21	289.10	299.22	314.13
242.28	262.18	273.22	289.12	300.06	314.14
243.07	262.25	274.06	289.15	300.13	314.15
243.10	263.10	274.09	289.16	300.13	314.16
243.23	263.12	274.18	289.24	300.17	314.21
244.05	263.16	274.18	289.25	300.19	314.22
244.05	263.18	275.01	290.04	300.23	314.23
244.28	263.19	275.04	290.05	300.28	314.25
245.02	263.21	275.04	290.17	300.28	315.01
245.09	263.26	275.08	290.19	301.08	315.03
245.10	264.02	275.08	290.20	301.10	315.06
245.11	264.05	275.11	290.23	301.11	315.06
245.16	264.08	275.13	290.26	301.15	315.09
245.18	264.11	275.16	291.03	301.22	315.15
245.21	264.15	275.23	291.05	301.23	315.16
245.24	264.16	275.24	291.09	301.24	315.19
245.27	264.17	275.27	291.09	301.28	315.20
246.04	264.19	276.09	291.13	302.05	315.23
246.06	264.24	276.10	291.17	302.05	315.26
246.08	265.01	276.11	291.26	302.06	315.28
246.09	265.03	276.12	291.28	302.08	316.09
246.13	265.03	276.21	292.01	302.11	316.13
246.22	265.04	276.21	292.02	302.11	316.17
247.01	265.05	277.23	292.03	302.13	316.25
247.01	265.06	278.01	292.06	302.13	317.01
247.02	265.09	278.04	292.11	302.14	317.09
247.06	265.11	278.06	292.13	302.16	317.10
247.10	265.11	279.18	292.14	302.17	317.15
247.10	265.12	279.20	292.17	302.18	317.22
247.14	265.21	280.03	292.20	302.20	317.27
247.15	265.23	280.05	292.25	302.21	317.28
247.18	265.24	280.09	292.26	302.25	318.13
247.18	265.27	280.09	292.28	303.03	318.27
247.22	266.01	280.12	293.04	305.03	319.07
248.04	266.07	280.13	293.07	305.05	319.08
248.17	266.07	280.14	293.08	305.07	319.12
249.20	266.14	280.16	293.10	305.10	319.16
249.20	266.19	280.16	293.11	305.14	319.25
249.22	266.26	280.20	293.16	306.03	320.01
249.24	267.03	280.22	293.25	306.08	320.03
250.01	267.04	280.26	293.25	306.10	320.08
250.02	267.11	280.27	293.26	306.14	320.09
250.06	267.22	281.05	293.28	306.15	320.17
250.10	267.25	281.07	294.01	306.15	320.18

320.22	338.26	355.05	376.27	399.17	413.03
320.23	338.26	355.10	377.01	399.24	413.04
321.01	338.27	355.11	377.02	399.28	413.05
322.15	338.28	355.13	377.02	400.04	413.06
323.05	339.04	355.14	377.03	400.09	413.10
323.06	339.06	355.15	377.07	400.15	414.02
323.08	339.06	355.24	377.08	400.18	414.03
323.10	339.07	356.03	377.09	400.18	414.10
323.15	339.08	356.09	377.10	400.20	414.12
323.18	339.09	356.14	377.11	401.10	415.09
323.20	339.26	356.17	377.12	401.13	415.15
323.22	340.03	356.24	377.17	401.26	415.23
323.23	340.04	357.08	378.01	402.03	415.24
323.25	340.21	357.16	378.04	402.15	416.12
324.10	340.21	357.25	378.06	402.19	417.03
324.10	341.14	357.28	378.07	402.26	417.11
324.12	341.15	358.03	378.11	403.10	417.15
324.15	341.24	358.08	380.15	403.12	417.25
324.16	341.28	358.10	380.28	403.15	417.26
324.17	341.28	358.19	381.13	403.18	418.01
324.19	342.18	358.23	381.18	403.19	418.02
324.20	343.01	358.25	381.20	403.21	418.10
325.02	343.21	359.01	381.21	403.24	418.11
325.17	344.26	359.03	381.21	403.24	418.14
325.19	345.03	359.15	382.08	403.24	418.23
325.20	345.04	359.25	382.10	403.26	418.23
325.23	345.07	360.03	382.12	404.01	418.24
326.01	345.09	360.04	382.16	404.04	418.25
326.05	345.23	360.05	382.25	404.16	418.26
326.06	346.03	360.07	383.02	404.23	419.01
326.09	346.21	360.08	383.02	405.03	419.01
326.10	346.23	360.11	383.13	405.04	419.02
326.11	346.23	360.12	383.14	405.06	419.08
326.16	346.27	360.14	383.15	405.07	419.10
326.17	346.28	360.18	383.27	405.10	419.12
326.20	347.13	360.22	384.05	405.20	419.16
326.22	347.27	360.24	384.06	405.24	419.23
326.24	348.19	361.08	384.08	405.25	420.02
327.02	348.20	361.15	384.16	405.25	420.02
327.04	348.20	361.18	384.20	405.27	420.02
327.11	348.22	361.21	384.22	406.02	420.04
327.13	348.22	361.22	384.24	406.04	420.04
327.20	348.23	361.24	384.26	406.08	420.08
328.06	348.25	361.26	385.07	406.08	420.11
328.13	348.26	362.01	385.27	406.09	420.11
328.14	348.27	362.04	386.23	406.10	420.17
328.14	348.27	362.04	387.02	406.10	420.26
328.16	349.04	362.05	387.05	406.11	421.01
328.20	349.04	362.06	387.06	406.12	421.09
328.24	349.09	362.06	387.07	406.12	421.10
328.26	349.10	362.14	387.20	406.16	421.14
329.19	349.14	362.22	388.02	406.16	421.15
329.23	349.15	362.26	388.12	406.17	422.01
329.25	349.17	362.28	388.12	406.17	422.04
329.26	349.19	363.04	388.23	406.21	422.06
329.26	350.07	363.06	390.03	406.21	422.18
330.03	350.08	363.07	390.07	406.22	422.21
330.05	350.14	363.09	390.12	406.22	422.25
330.09	350.18	364.05	390.27	406.26	423.02
330.15	350.20	365.04	392.13	407.03	423.02
330.20	350.24	365.07	392.14	407.04	423.04
330.23	350.28	366.03	392.18	407.05	423.04
330.26	351.04	366.04	392.20	407.25	423.09
331.16	351.06	366.07	392.21	407.27	423.12
331.19	351.07	366.08	392.21	408.02	424.04
331.21	351.03	366.15	392.23	408.02	424.08
331.22	351.09	366.18	392.26	408.03	424.22
332.03	351.10	367.22	393.04	408.03	424.27
332.06	351.11	367.26	393.05	408.04	425.10
332.06	351.11	369.26	393.05	408.08	425.25
332.08	351.12	370.15	394.02	408.08	425.26
332.16	351.14	371.01	394.16	408.09	425.27
332.18	351.16	371.10	394.18	408.11	425.06
333.09	351.17	371.11	394.19	408.12	426.09
333.10	351.19	371.18	395.03	408.14	426.16
333.16	351.22	371.19	395.13	408.18	426.16
334.13	351.23	371.20	395.14	408.18	426.19
334.16	351.23	371.21	395.14	408.22	426.21
334.24	351.23	371.24	395.16	408.23	427.04
334.28	351.24	371.25	395.17	408.27	427.13
334.28	351.25	372.01	395.20	409.03	427.19
335.03	351.25	372.01	395.23	409.07	427.25
335.04	351.26	372.02	395.27	409.16	427.26
335.07	351.26	372.03	396.11	409.19	427.27
335.11	351.27	372.04	396.12	410.01	428.13
335.24	351.28	372.06	396.26	410.12	428.15
335.25	352.01	372.12	397.11	410.12	428.16
335.27	352.03	372.13	397.11	410.16	428.21
335.28	352.03	372.14	397.15	410.19	428.21
336.03	352.11	372.16	397.15	410.26	428.27
336.09	353.10	372.26	397.17	410.26	429.01
336.10	353.12	372.27	397.20	411.08	429.02
336.10	353.16	373.03	397.23	411.09	429.05
336.16	353.19	373.03	397.27	411.10	429.11
336.24	353.21	374.04	397.27	411.10	429.11
336.25	353.22	374.06	398.04	411.11	430.01
337.04	353.24	374.15	398.05	411.11	430.05
337.10	353.27	374.19	398.05	412.01	430.07
337.11	353.27	374.22	398.07	412.02	430.14
337.18	354.01	375.09	398.12	412.07	430.15
337.20	354.04	375.12	398.14	412.07	430.19
337.28	354.08	375.20	398.22	412.10	430.24
338.04	354.09	375.25	398.27	412.14	431.06
338.08	354.17	375.27	399.05	412.15	431.08
338.11	354.19	376.10	399.08	412.15	431.10
338.13	354.19	376.12	399.08	412.19	431.16
338.15	354.22	376.15	399.09	412.20	431.20
338.15	354.26	376.18	399.08	412.27	432.04
338.16	354.28	376.19	399.09	412.28	432.10
338.19	355.01	376.21	399.10	412.28	432.11
338.26	355.02	376.23	399.12	413.02	

432.15	453.07	466.01	481.05	493.02	507.08
432.20	453.08	466.04	481.07	493.04	507.16
432.22	453.10	466.11	481.08	493.08	507.20
432.26	453.18	466.13	481.11	493.21	507.21
432.28	453.20	466.19	481.11	493.22	507.24
433.17	453.21	466.19	481.12	493.28	507.26
433.28	454.01	466.19	481.13	493.28	508.01
434.08	454.09	466.23	481.14	494.01	508.02
434.10	454.09	466.23	481.14	494.03	508.05
435.19	454.17	466.24	481.18	494.03	508.06
435.23	454.18	466.26	481.19	494.04	508.06
435.24	454.20	466.26	481.20	494.06	508.07
435.26	454.23	466.27	481.21	494.07	508.07
435.26	454.23	467.04	481.25	494.09	508.07
435.27	454.26	467.05	482.03	494.10	508.08
435.28	454.26	467.05	482.04	494.11	508.12
436.08	454.27	467.08	482.07	494.12	508.14
436.11	455.10	467.17	482.16	494.13	508.16
437.01	455.11	467.18	482.17	494.14	508.17
437.03	455.15	467.24	482.19	494.15	508.21
437.03	455.16	467.27	482.20	494.15	508.23
437.05	455.24	468.02	482.23	494.16	508.26
437.05	455.25	468.03	482.23	494.17	509.11
437.06	455.27	468.06	482.24	494.22	509.13
437.07	456.07	468.12	482.26	494.22	509.14
437.09	456.13	468.14	483.07	494.23	509.18
437.12	456.23	468.14	483.08	494.26	509.21
437.14	456.23	468.28	483.10	494.28	509.23
437.14	456.26	469.03	483.11	494.28	509.25
437.19	457.01	469.05	483.15	495.01	509.27
437.24	457.03	469.07	483.15	495.12	510.15
437.27	457.11	469.08	483.18	495.18	510.17
437.28	457.12	469.10	483.21	495.25	510.20
438.11	457.13	469.16	483.23	495.28	510.22
438.15	457.13	469.16	483.24	496.02	510.24
438.16	457.14	469.18	483.24	496.08	511.02
438.25	457.14	469.18	483.27	496.11	511.04
438.27	457.15	469.19	483.27	496.12	511.06
439.08	457.23	469.25	483.28	496.14	511.10
439.09	457.27	469.27	483.28	496.17	511.10
439.22	458.05	469.28	484.05	496.25	511.11
440.14	458.05	470.02	484.07	496.25	511.11
441.01	458.06	470.03	484.13	497.04	511.12
441.11	458.08	470.08	484.16	497.21	511.13
441.11	458.10	470.10	484.19	497.23	511.15
441.13	458.19	470.14	484.20	497.25	511.23
441.13	458.21	470.14	484.21	498.01	511.23
441.16	458.26	470.21	484.24	498.04	511.24
441.20	458.28	470.22	484.25	498.14	511.24
442.01	459.02	470.26	484.27	498.15	511.26
442.12	459.04	471.10	484.27	498.19	511.26
442.15	459.04	471.11	485.05	498.22	511.27
442.16	459.06	471.12	485.13	499.03	512.02
442.17	459.07	471.13	485.17	499.10	512.03
442.17	459.14	471.27	485.21	499.12	512.03
442.19	459.16	471.28	485.28	499.27	512.05
443.03	459.17	472.01	485.28	499.28	512.07
443.04	459.18	472.02	486.13	500.03	512.08
443.06	459.24	472.04	487.04	500.05	512.17
444.05	459.25	472.04	487.04	500.07	512.20
444.06	459.26	472.06	487.13	500.08	512.20
444.07	460.07	472.08	487.15	500.12	512.21
444.15	460.09	472.11	487.17	501.17	512.23
444.16	460.12	472.11	487.18	501.18	512.25
445.06	460.12	472.12	487.18	501.18	512.25
445.09	460.25	472.15	488.01	502.13	512.25
445.18	460.28	472.17	488.02	502.15	512.26
445.20	461.04	472.23	488.04	502.16	512.28
445.21	461.21	472.26	488.09	502.16	513.04
445.24	462.16	473.07	488.12	502.17	513.05
445.25	462.16	473.26	488.23	503.02	513.06
445.27	462.17	474.02	488.24	503.02	513.08
446.01	462.20	474.07	489.01	503.12	513.10
446.07	463.01	474.08	489.02	503.13	513.21
446.08	463.06	474.20	489.04	503.14	513.25
446.09	463.08	475.11	489.05	503.14	513.26
446.11	463.09	475.25	489.08	503.15	513.27
446.12	463.09	475.26	489.08	503.18	513.27
446.23	463.11	477.10	489.11	503.18	514.02
446.23	463.12	477.15	489.13	503.19	514.07
446.26	463.13	477.16	489.15	503.20	514.08
446.26	463.16	477.17	489.18	503.22	514.09
447.10	463.18	477.17	489.20	504.08	514.10
447.19	463.19	477.18	489.21	504.08	514.13
447.27	463.21	477.19	489.24	504.09	514.15
448.15	463.23	477.21	489.27	504.10	514.17
448.22	463.25	477.24	489.28	504.13	514.23
448.23	463.26	477.26	490.08	504.14	515.01
448.25	464.02	477.28	490.09	504.15	515.07
448.26	464.04	478.07	490.10	504.15	515.08
448.27	464.05	478.08	490.19	504.20	515.09
448.28	464.07	479.09	490.24	504.21	515.10
449.03	464.08	479.17	490.25	504.22	515.11
449.06	464.11	479.17	490.27	504.27	515.11
449.10	464.13	479.21	491.03	505.13	515.18
449.12	464.16	479.23	491.04	505.15	515.18
449.18	464.17	479.27	491.05	505.16	515.19
449.19	464.19	480.03	491.10	505.20	515.25
449.21	464.19	480.06	491.12	506.06	515.27
449.23	464.24	480.14	491.13	506.07	516.01
449.26	464.26	480.15	491.13	506.08	516.02
450.14	465.03	480.16	491.14	506.11	516.04
451.09	465.03	480.17	491.28	506.21	516.06
451.24	465.06	480.24	492.01	506.21	516.06
452.02	465.07	480.27	492.02	506.22	516.08
452.06	465.10	480.27	492.03	506.23	516.10
452.07	465.11	481.01	492.08	506.23	516.12
452.12	465.22	481.02	492.09	506.24	516.18
452.24	465.23	481.03	492.10	506.25	516.24
452.25	465.28	481.05	492.13	506.27	516.28
452.26	465.28		493.01	507.01	517.08
453.07					

517.14	527.26	540.13	552.16	564.24	575.19
517.19	528.02	540.14	552.16	565.01	575.21
517.20	528.02	540.20	552.17	565.05	575.21
517.21	528.09	541.12	552.18	565.06	575.22
517.27	528.13	541.12	552.19	565.08	575.24
518.01	528.14	541.26	552.20	565.12	576.01
518.03	528.16	542.01	552.25	565.15	576.02
518.06	528.18	542.02	553.01	565.18	576.07
518.09	528.19	542.03	553.04	565.19	576.08
518.13	528.21	542.06	553.05	565.19	576.09
518.15	528.23	542.06	553.06	565.23	576.11
518.16	528.23	542.09	553.07	566.04	576.13
518.19	528.24	542.11	553.10	566.05	576.13
518.20	528.28	542.12	553.12	566.06	576.18
518.21	529.01	542.14	553.13	566.06	576.19
518.22	529.09	542.18	553.18	566.07	576.19
518.25	529.09	542.23	553.18	566.11	576.24
518.26	529.10	542.23	553.20	566.11	577.05
519.02	529.14	542.24	553.25	566.17	577.13
519.04	529.15	543.02	553.26	566.18	577.15
519.04	529.15	543.07	553.27	566.19	577.20
519.04	529.18	543.10	553.27	566.21	577.24
519.06	529.19	543.14	554.02	567.04	578.02
519.08	529.21	543.26	554.04	567.05	578.02
519.16	529.26	543.27	554.04	567.05	578.09
519.23	529.26	543.28	554.05	567.08	578.23
519.25	529.28	544.03	554.12	567.09	578.24
519.27	529.28	544.05	554.15	567.11	579.02
519.27	530.09	544.08	554.15	567.14	579.04
519.28	530.13	544.10	554.17	567.14	579.06
520.07	530.16	544.12	554.19	567.15	579.08
520.09	530.17	544.17	554.23	567.20	579.11
520.12	530.19	544.21	554.28	568.05	579.18
521.02	531.03	544.22	555.03	568.05	579.20
521.02	531.07	544.24	555.06	568.08	579.23
521.04	531.13	544.27	555.10	568.09	580.03
521.05	531.14	544.28	555.14	568.09	580.04
521.07	531.16	545.03	555.15	568.16	580.04
521.12	531.21	545.04	555.17	568.21	580.05
521.14	531.23	545.05	555.17	569.03	580.08
521.15	531.24	545.06	555.18	569.07	580.10
521.15	532.03	545.08	555.21	569.07	580.11
521.16	532.03	545.10	555.22	569.15	580.14
521.20	532.04	545.11	555.23	569.18	580.17
522.01	532.05	545.13	555.23	569.19	580.24
522.01	532.11	545.14	555.28	569.20	581.05
522.06	532.13	545.17	556.05	569.23	581.18
522.09	532.14	545.21	556.07	569.24	581.18
522.10	532.15	546.02	557.06	570.01	581.20
522.19	532.15	546.07	557.11	570.06	581.24
522.20	532.16	546.14	557.11	570.08	582.01
522.21	533.04	546.23	557.12	570.09	582.02
522.21	533.09	546.27	557.17	570.10	582.03
522.22	533.14	547.01	558.03	570.15	582.03
522.22	533.17	547.03	558.04	570.18	582.05
523.02	533.21	547.03	558.12	570.21	582.07
523.05	533.24	547.07	558.16	570.23	582.13
523.07	533.25	547.10	558.17	570.24	582.15
523.15	533.26	547.13	558.18	570.25	583.11
523.17	534.03	547.17	558.18	570.25	583.15
523.23	534.07	547.17	558.19	571.01	583.16
523.23	534.10	547.19	559.04	571.04	583.17
523.27	534.12	547.24	559.05	571.04	583.18
524.10	534.16	548.06	559.14	571.06	583.22
524.14	534.16	548.06	559.18	571.10	583.22
524.14	534.21	548.07	559.20	571.22	583.23
524.15	534.21	548.09	560.08	571.24	583.23
524.18	534.22	548.10	560.12	572.03	583.24
524.20	535.10	548.13	560.25	572.04	583.24
524.23	535.10	548.14	561.01	572.06	584.01
524.25	535.11	548.18	561.10	572.06	584.03
524.27	535.12	548.19	561.20	572.10	584.05
525.03	535.13	548.19	561.21	572.12	585.04
525.08	535.13	548.20	561.24	572.13	585.05
525.08	535.16	548.25	561.25	572.14	585.08
525.16	535.18	548.28	562.02	572.15	585.09
525.17	535.23	549.03	562.03	572.19	585.13
525.19	535.26	549.08	562.07	572.21	585.13
525.20	536.05	549.11	562.08	572.24	585.16
525.22	536.12	549.14	562.09	573.01	585.17
525.23	536.15	549.15	562.11	573.06	587.05
525.24	536.16	549.17	562.12	573.09	587.07
525.27	536.21	549.17	562.16	573.12	587.08
526.01	537.01	549.19	562.16	573.14	587.10
526.02	537.03	549.20	562.18	573.16	587.11
526.02	537.05	549.24	562.23	573.18	587.14
526.06	537.07	549.26	563.03	573.20	587.19
526.08	537.09	550.01	563.05	573.20	587.20
526.11	537.10	550.03	563.05	573.23	587.23
526.13	537.10	550.04	563.10	574.07	587.25
526.20	537.14	550.06	563.10	574.09	588.04
526.23	537.15	550.10	563.11	574.10	588.04
526.24	537.17	550.11	563.12	574.12	588.07
526.26	537.19	550.14	563.15	574.12	588.10
526.28	537.20	550.16	563.16	574.13	588.12
527.03	537.23	550.17	563.17	574.15	588.15
527.03	537.24	551.01	563.18	574.16	588.17
527.04	537.25	551.02	563.21	574.17	588.21
527.04	537.25	551.03	563.21	574.21	588.22
527.05	538.01	551.13	563.22	574.22	588.23
527.05	538.04	551.13	563.24	574.24	588.24
527.08	538.10	551.14	564.01	575.01	589.15
527.08	538.16	551.16	564.01	575.03	589.23
527.14	538.16	551.18	564.02	575.06	590.18
527.17	538.24	551.23	564.02	575.07	591.03
527.17	539.05	551.25	564.10	575.09	591.08
527.19	539.06	551.26	564.16	575.09	591.23
527.22	539.14	552.11	564.16	575.11	591.24
527.24	539.20	552.12	564.17	575.13	592.08
527.25	539.27	552.12	564.19	575.16	592.09
527.25	540.04	552.13	564.19	575.18	592.10

592.22	611.03	621.02	629.14	639.26	649.18
593.06	611.04	621.06	629.16	639.27	649.18
593.19	611.05	621.08	629.17	640.01	649.19
594.01	611.07	621.09	629.22	640.09	649.20
594.04	611.09	621.10	629.24	640.22	649.21
594.09	611.10	621.11	629.26	640.23	649.23
594.09	611.13	621.12	630.04	640.25	649.25
594.16	611.15	621.14	630.10	641.02	650.02
594.14	611.15	621.14	630.13	641.03	650.07
595.07	611.16	621.15	630.14	641.05	650.08
595.16	611.19	621.16	630.15	641.05	650.09
595.17	611.19	621.21	630.18	641.07	650.11
595.19	611.21	621.21	630.21	641.08	650.18
595.20	611.26	621.22	630.21	641.11	650.21
595.22	611.28	621.23	630.23	641.12	650.23
595.24	612.06	621.24	630.23	641.23	651.01
596.10	612.08	621.26	631.03	641.27	651.01
596.13	612.12	622.03	631.04	642.03	651.02
596.19	612.15	622.03	631.07	642.03	651.03
596.20	612.16	622.04	631.17	642.04	651.03
596.23	612.22	622.07	631.19	642.04	651.04
597.02	612.22	622.07	632.12	642.05	651.05
597.03	612.22	622.11	632.15	642.06	651.06
597.13	612.25	622.12	632.19	642.07	651.16
597.14	612.27	622.13	632.26	642.10	651.19
597.17	612.28	622.14	632.27	642.11	651.22
597.18	613.01	622.18	632.28	642.13	651.23
597.18	613.02	622.20	632.28	642.16	651.24
597.20	613.03	622.23	633.04	642.16	651.25
597.22	613.04	622.25	633.10	642.19	651.25
597.24	613.06	622.26	633.13	642.25	652.03
598.01	613.06	623.01	634.02	642.26	652.06
598.20	613.08	623.02	634.06	643.01	652.18
599.25	613.09	623.02	634.07	643.03	652.19
600.14	613.10	623.08	634.11	643.06	652.19
600.17	613.12	623.11	634.14	643.08	652.23
601.22	613.14	623.15	634.14	643.12	652.23
601.24	613.20	623.16	634.15	643.14	652.23
602.03	613.21	623.16	634.15	643.15	652.23
602.11	613.23	623.17	634.17	643.18	652.24
603.09	613.28	623.20	634.20	643.20	652.25
603.18	614.01	623.21	634.20	643.23	652.26
603.19	614.01	623.22	634.23	643.23	653.01
603.20	614.02	623.24	634.23	644.01	653.03
603.22	614.11	623.28	634.25	644.05	653.04
603.24	614.19	624.01	634.25	644.06	653.04
604.10	614.20	624.02	634.28	644.06	653.05
604.10	614.21	624.02	635.01	644.08	653.07
604.11	614.21	624.03	635.04	644.09	653.09
604.12	614.26	624.06	635.11	644.15	653.10
604.14	615.03	624.12	635.15	644.15	653.11
604.17	615.06	624.20	635.16	644.16	653.11
604.17	615.08	624.21	635.23	644.18	653.13
604.18	615.09	624.25	635.23	644.18	653.14
604.18	615.14	624.28	635.23	644.19	653.16
604.19	615.15	625.02	635.24	644.20	653.21
604.21	615.22	625.06	635.26	644.21	653.23
604.21	615.22	625.08	636.03	644.23	653.23
604.23	615.24	625.09	636.04	644.24	653.25
604.25	615.24	625.14	636.06	645.01	653.27
605.14	615.25	625.15	636.07	645.02	654.03
606.10	615.26	625.15	636.08	645.07	654.06
606.13	616.02	625.17	636.10	645.11	654.07
606.22	616.04	625.17	636.11	645.11	654.09
606.23	616.11	625.17	636.12	645.12	654.09
606.24	616.27	625.18	636.13	645.15	654.10
607.01	617.03	625.19	636.14	645.16	654.10
607.02	617.06	625.22	636.15	645.18	654.10
607.03	617.07	625.23	636.15	645.26	654.12
607.04	617.08	625.23	636.16	646.01	654.12
607.06	617.11	625.24	636.16	646.04	654.13
607.14	617.18	625.25	636.19	646.10	654.13
607.16	617.20	625.25	636.24	646.11	654.14
607.18	617.21	625.26	636.25	646.12	654.16
607.18	617.23	626.02	636.25	646.12	654.17
607.19	617.27	626.03	636.26	646.16	654.21
608.03	617.27	626.12	637.06	646.18	654.21
608.04	618.02	626.14	637.09	646.20	654.21
608.12	618.04	626.18	637.11	646.26	654.25
608.13	618.09	626.18	637.15	646.26	654.26
608.15	618.11	626.22	637.15	647.03	655.08
609.02	618.11	626.24	637.20	647.04	655.09
609.04	618.12	626.24	637.21	647.05	655.10
609.05	618.15	627.01	637.26	647.06	655.10
609.07	618.20	627.01	637.26	647.08	655.11
609.06	618.20	627.02	637.28	647.08	655.12
609.08	618.21	627.02	637.28	647.09	655.18
609.09	618.24	627.03	638.01	648.01	655.19
609.10	619.01	627.04	638.08	648.03	655.20
609.11	619.06	627.05	638.09	648.03	655.20
609.12	619.07	627.06	638.13	648.04	655.20
609.13	619.10	627.07	638.14	648.05	655.22
609.14	619.20	627.12	638.19	648.06	655.22
609.16	619.21	627.21	638.21	648.07	655.23
609.17	619.23	627.24	638.23	648.12	655.23
609.17	619.26	627.25	638.24	648.13	655.24
609.18	619.26	628.02	638.26	648.14	655.26
610.01	620.03	628.04	638.26	648.15	655.26
610.02	620.09	628.04	638.27	648.17	656.04
610.06	620.10	628.19	638.28	648.18	656.08
610.15	620.11	628.24	639.03	648.19	656.09
610.17	620.12	628.27	639.08	648.21	656.10
610.16	620.15	628.28	639.11	648.22	656.11
610.18	620.16	629.01	639.12	648.27	656.12
610.20	620.17	629.04	639.13	649.01	656.13
610.21	620.17	629.06	639.15	649.05	656.16
610.22	620.19	629.07	639.17	649.06	656.17
610.23	620.19	629.07	639.20	649.12	656.17
610.27	620.21	629.09	639.21	649.14	656.20
610.27	620.25	629.10	639.22	649.14	656.20
610.28	620.27		639.25	649.15	656.21
611.02					

656.22	665.08	674.10	686.26	704.18	717.27
656.22	665.10	674.13	686.28	704.20	718.05
656.26	665.12	674.13	687.01	705.08	718.07
656.26	665.13	674.15	687.03	705.08	718.08
656.27	665.16	674.16	687.05	705.13	718.09
656.27	665.17	674.18	687.06	705.14	718.13
656.28	665.18	674.20	687.07	705.16	718.17
657.01	665.19	674.20	687.10	705.16	718.18
657.03	665.20	674.21	687.15	705.18	718.21
657.04	665.21	674.24	687.15	705.21	718.25
657.05	665.23	674.26	687.17	705.21	719.01
657.05	665.24	674.28	687.18	705.22	719.06
657.08	665.26	675.02	687.18	705.26	719.12
657.10	665.26	675.02	687.19	705.26	719.13
658.05	666.03	675.07	687.19	706.03	719.14
658.05	666.03	675.07	687.21	706.10	719.16
658.07	666.04	675.09	687.23	706.12	719.16
658.07	666.04	675.10	687.24	706.15	719.16
658.08	666.06	675.11	688.04	706.16	719.20
658.09	666.07	675.14	688.05	706.17	720.08
658.11	666.20	675.17	688.08	706.18	720.08
658.14	666.24	675.18	688.10	706.19	720.10
658.19	666.26	675.19	689.03	706.24	720.13
658.20	666.27	675.22	689.06	706.24	720.15
659.01	666.27	675.24	689.06	706.26	720.23
659.04	667.01	676.02	689.07	706.27	721.01
659.09	667.02	676.03	689.08	706.28	721.01
659.10	667.05	676.11	689.10	707.01	721.03
659.12	667.07	676.12	689.12	707.02	721.08
659.12	667.12	676.13	689.13	707.04	721.10
659.18	667.13	676.17	689.14	707.06	721.11
659.19	667.16	676.23	689.15	707.07	721.13
659.21	667.21	677.11	689.19	707.09	721.13
659.21	667.24	677.12	690.08	707.10	721.15
659.22	667.25	677.13	690.10	707.11	721.15
659.23	667.25	677.13	690.12	707.13	721.16
659.23	667.26	677.24	690.17	707.15	721.19
659.25	668.06	677.26	690.18	707.15	721.19
660.01	668.07	677.26	690.20	707.18	721.20
660.02	668.08	678.10	690.23	707.22	722.13
660.05	668.09	678.13	691.13	707.23	722.18
660.06	668.10	678.16	691.20	707.25	722.19
660.09	668.12	678.17	691.28	708.01	722.20
660.10	668.13	678.18	692.01	708.04	723.04
660.10	668.19	678.27	692.03	708.05	723.09
660.11	668.19	679.07	692.03	708.09	723.15
660.13	668.20	679.09	692.06	708.09	723.20
660.14	668.23	679.21	692.06	708.11	723.23
660.17	668.25	679.26	692.08	708.14	723.26
660.18	668.26	680.05	692.09	708.15	723.26
660.22	668.28	680.05	692.10	708.16	723.28
660.23	669.01	681.06	692.11	708.22	724.04
660.27	669.06	681.06	692.13	708.24	724.06
660.28	669.09	681.07	692.23	708.25	724.07
660.28	669.10	681.21	692.24	708.27	724.11
661.03	669.11	681.24	692.25	708.27	724.16
661.03	669.25	682.03	692.27	708.28	724.16
661.05	669.26	682.04	692.28	709.02	724.19
661.06	669.27	682.09	693.17	709.13	724.23
661.08	669.27	682.09	693.24	709.16	725.15
661.10	670.01	682.12	693.25	709.20	727.24
661.12	670.02	682.14	693.26	709.26	728.02
661.16	670.04	682.16	694.02	709.26	729.02
661.18	670.05	682.21	694.04	709.27	729.14
661.20	670.06	682.24	694.05	709.27	729.16
662.03	670.07	682.25	694.07	709.28	729.17
662.12	670.12	683.01	694.14	710.02	730.01
662.14	670.13	683.04	694.17	710.05	730.06
662.17	670.19	683.06	694.17	710.05	730.13
662.18	670.20	683.09	694.19	711.02	730.14
662.19	670.23	683.09	694.23	711.03	730.15
662.21	670.24	683.20	694.24	711.03	730.16
662.24	670.28	683.21	694.28	711.04	730.19
663.04	671.09	683.21	695.01	711.05	730.20
663.05	671.10	683.22	695.05	711.13	730.22
663.08	671.12	683.22	695.19	711.15	730.22
663.08	671.14	683.22	695.20	711.16	730.23
663.08	671.17	683.28	696.10	712.11	730.23
663.09	671.18	684.01	696.13	712.12	730.23
663.10	671.20	684.01	696.17	712.13	730.24
663.11	671.20	684.01	696.17	712.14	730.24
663.13	671.22	684.03	696.20	713.01	730.26
663.14	671.23	684.04	696.25	713.02	730.27
663.15	671.26	684.11	696.28	713.03	731.01
663.15	672.03	684.22	697.03	713.06	731.02
663.16	672.04	684.24	697.03	713.14	731.03
663.16	672.06	684.25	697.07	713.16	731.03
663.18	672.08	684.26	697.09	713.20	731.19
663.26	672.15	684.28	697.11	713.21	731.22
663.27	672.16	685.01	697.12	713.21	731.24
664.01	672.17	685.02	697.12	713.26	731.25
664.02	672.19	685.05	697.13	714.19	731.26
664.02	672.20	685.05	697.15	714.24	732.04
664.02	672.20	685.11	697.21	714.26	732.04
664.06	672.21	685.12	699.08	715.14	732.04
664.07	672.22	685.12	699.25	715.18	732.07
664.09	672.23	685.17	700.08	716.02	732.10
664.11	672.23	685.18	700.12	716.03	732.16
664.11	672.28	685.19	701.01	716.03	732.16
664.18	673.01	685.25	702.21	716.04	732.19
664.21	673.02	685.27	703.02	716.04	732.24
664.23	673.03	685.27	703.10	716.06	732.25
664.26	673.09	686.02	703.10	716.22	733.02
664.27	673.09	686.03	703.17	716.24	733.07
665.02	673.11	686.08	703.21	716.25	733.10
665.03	673.17	686.17	703.22	717.01	733.12
665.04	673.18	686.17	704.05	717.04	733.12
665.05	673.24	686.17	704.06	717.04	733.13
665.06	673.24	686.19	704.09	717.06	733.15
665.06	673.25	686.22	704.10	717.22	733.16
665.07	674.02	686.24	704.18	717.24	733.17

733.21	750.05	764.06	779.27	791.18	807.02
733.21	750.15	764.08	780.01	791.28	807.02
733.26	750.18	764.08	780.02	792.18	807.02
733.28	750.18	764.11	780.18	792.21	807.03
734.01	750.21	765.06	780.19	792.25	807.06
734.04	750.24	765.10	780.20	792.26	807.15
734.04	750.26	765.18	780.22	792.27	807.17
734.05	751.03	765.19	781.01	793.02	807.21
734.06	751.03	765.19	781.07	793.05	807.26
734.08	751.03	766.05	781.07	793.07	807.26
734.11	751.27	766.05	781.08	793.08	807.27
734.14	752.02	766.08	781.08	793.08	807.27
734.17	752.04	766.15	781.10	793.09	808.02
734.18	752.13	766.17	781.15	793.15	808.05
734.18	752.16	766.18	781.25	793.16	808.06
734.22	752.17	766.21	781.27	793.23	808.06
734.22	752.19	766.24	781.27	793.24	808.09
734.26	752.21	766.25	781.27	793.24	808.11
735.10	752.27	766.27	782.01	793.26	808.22
735.11	753.01	767.03	782.03	793.26	809.02
735.11	753.14	767.04	782.08	793.28	809.02
735.13	753.18	767.06	782.11	794.01	809.04
735.19	753.18	767.12	782.11	794.05	809.07
735.20	753.20	767.13	782.12	794.08	809.11
736.04	753.21	767.18	782.12	794.10	809.12
736.09	753.22	767.18	782.13	794.11	809.13
736.14	753.23	767.23	782.16	794.16	809.14
736.14	753.25	767.24	782.19	794.22	809.18
736.15	753.27	768.01	782.20	794.24	809.19
736.15	754.01	768.05	782.21	794.25	809.25
736.15	754.03	768.10	782.21	795.06	809.26
736.19	754.05	768.13	783.04	795.08	810.01
736.20	754.06	768.20	783.05	795.15	810.03
737.02	754.08	768.21	783.05	795.16	810.03
737.19	754.10	768.24	783.09	795.19	810.05
733.11	754.12	769.01	783.17	795.20	810.05
738.11	754.13	769.02	783.25	795.22	810.08
738.12	754.15	769.02	784.01	795.27	810.09
738.16	754.18	769.06	784.04	796.02	810.11
738.19	754.21	769.15	784.09	796.05	810.15
738.20	754.22	769.19	784.13	796.06	810.17
736.27	754.23	769.28	784.13	796.08	810.19
739.03	754.27	770.01	784.14	796.10	810.24
739.10	755.02	770.03	784.16	796.12	811.05
739.10	755.04	770.18	784.16	796.15	811.12
739.10	755.07	770.24	784.17	796.16	811.17
739.17	755.25	770.27	784.17	796.23	811.18
739.22	755.28	770.28	784.18	796.25	811.21
739.26	756.02	771.02	784.18	796.27	811.23
739.27	756.09	771.06	784.23	797.01	811.23
743.01	756.11	771.17	785.03	797.02	811.26
743.02	756.17	771.18	785.05	797.07	812.03
740.03	756.13	771.19	785.12	797.13	812.05
743.26	757.01	771.21	785.13	797.25	813.01
740.26	757.01	772.08	785.14	797.28	813.09
741.05	757.16	772.10	785.16	798.05	813.10
741.16	757.21	772.11	785.17	798.24	813.16
741.23	757.24	772.15	785.27	799.02	813.18
741.24	758.01	772.17	785.28	799.04	813.22
742.01	758.06	772.23	786.01	799.15	813.24
742.01	758.09	773.03	786.01	799.25	813.24
7-2.07	758.11	773.08	786.02	800.12	814.06
742.08	758.12	773.10	786.04	800.21	814.07
743.02	758.17	773.15	786.09	801.17	814.20
743.03	758.19	773.17	786.17	802.04	814.21
743.05	758.22	773.19	786.22	802.05	814.26
743.09	758.24	773.20	786.22	802.08	814.28
743.09	758.25	773.26	786.25	802.09	815.04
743.11	759.01	774.02	786.26	802.10	815.07
743.14	759.04	774.07	786.28	802.16	815.07
743.17	759.07	774.08	787.01	802.18	815.08
744.06	759.08	774.08	787.03	802.21	815.09
744.07	759.13	774.15	787.05	802.21	815.10
744.08	759.14	774.27	787.05	802.22	815.17
744.11	759.27	775.26	787.05	802.24	815.19
744.13	760.01	775.28	787.05	803.01	815.19
744.16	760.03	776.01	787.06	803.02	815.19
744.27	760.10	776.05	787.11	803.08	815.24
744.27	760.13	776.07	787.13	803.08	816.05
744.28	760.15	776.11	787.13	803.09	816.06
744.28	760.17	776.13	787.20	803.11	816.07
745.12	760.25	776.16	787.21	803.21	816.08
745.17	760.26	776.19	787.25	804.04	816.15
745.23	761.01	776.22	787.26	804.05	816.17
745.24	761.11	777.05	787.26	804.09	816.17
745.25	761.12	777.11	787.27	804.22	816.19
746.01	761.12	777.14	787.28	804.23	816.19
746.16	761.13	777.15	788.07	804.24	816.20
747.08	761.13	777.19	788.11	804.28	816.22
747.08	761.14	777.25	788.13	805.01	816.23
747.10	761.15	778.01	789.03	805.02	816.27
747.10	761.17	778.05	789.09	805.04	816.28
747.26	761.19	778.06	789.14	805.05	817.02
748.01	761.22	778.09	789.15	805.05	817.02
748.05	762.01	778.12	789.16	805.09	817.06
748.20	762.04	778.13	790.01	805.10	817.08
748.21	762.05	778.15	790.09	805.11	817.08
748.27	762.07	778.18	790.22	805.15	817.09
748.28	762.11	778.19	790.22	805.18	817.10
749.02	762.13	778.19	790.23	805.18	817.12
749.03	762.13	778.21	790.24	805.28	817.13
749.19	762.15	778.23	790.26	806.01	817.15
749.21	762.17	778.25	791.03	806.02	817.18
749.21	762.18	779.03	791.03	806.08	817.23
749.22	762.18	779.05	791.08	806.13	818.03
749.24	763.11	779.11	791.10	806.15	818.04
749.24	763.14	779.14	791.10	806.17	818.07
750.02	763.25	779.16	791.14	806.22	818.13
750.03	763.29	779.18	791.17	806.25	818.19
	764.04	779.19		806.28	818.20
				807.01	

818.24	829.02	841.01	852.17	863.13	879.24
818.24	829.15	841.02	852.18	864.04	879.24
818.25	829.16	841.09	852.19	865.09	879.25
818.26	829.19	841.10	852.22	865.10	880.03
819.04	829.23	841.15	852.23	865.22	880.03
819.09	829.24	841.22	852.23	865.26	880.06
819.12	829.25	841.22	852.24	866.11	880.12
819.17	829.27	841.23	852.25	866.19	880.12
819.18	830.01	841.25	852.25	866.23	880.15
819.18	830.08	841.27	852.27	866.25	880.15
819.19	830.13	842.08	852.28	867.01	880.19
819.19	831.10	842.09	853.13	867.04	880.20
819.20	831.16	842.10	853.13	867.09	880.20
819.20	831.18	842.16	853.14	867.09	880.21
819.23	831.19	842.16	853.18	867.10	880.23
819.25	832.02	842.18	853.19	869.04	880.27
819.27	832.07	842.24	853.23	869.15	881.01
819.27	832.21	842.26	853.24	869.18	881.04
820.01	832.21	843.07	853.26	869.19	881.05
820.02	832.26	843.07	854.01	870.05	881.10
820.04	832.26	843.08	854.01	870.09	881.11
820.06	833.08	843.09	854.01	870.13	881.20
820.15	833.09	843.11	854.02	870.13	881.22
820.16	833.13	843.12	854.03	870.15	881.27
820.19	833.15	843.13	854.06	870.19	882.04
820.21	833.16	843.18	854.07	870.20	882.07
820.24	833.18	844.14	854.09	870.24	882.08
820.25	833.19	844.18	854.11	871.09	882.09
820.26	833.21	844.23	854.13	871.10	882.10
820.27	833.23	845.17	854.14	871.16	882.11
821.04	833.23	845.18	854.18	871.19	882.13
821.04	834.01	845.19	854.19	871.23	882.16
821.08	834.01	845.26	854.22	872.03	882.17
821.09	834.02	845.27	854.22	872.10	882.17
821.12	834.03	846.01	854.25	872.12	882.20
821.18	834.07	846.01	854.26	872.15	882.25
821.21	834.10	846.03	855.07	873.12	882.25
821.22	834.11	846.04	855.07	873.13	882.26
821.22	834.14	846.05	855.09	873.14	882.26
822.13	834.16	846.08	855.12	873.16	882.28
822.15	834.23	846.08	855.13	873.17	883.03
822.15	834.23	846.27	855.13	873.19	883.09
822.18	834.25	847.01	855.14	873.19	883.11
822.18	834.25	847.01	855.14	873.20	883.13
822.23	834.28	847.04	855.17	873.21	883.16
822.25	835.05	847.05	855.18	873.21	883.18
822.27	835.05	847.06	856.03	873.22	883.20
823.02	835.10	847.10	856.04	873.24	883.23
823.06	835.11	847.10	856.06	873.24	883.23
823.06	835.12	847.12	856.09	873.25	883.26
823.07	835.16	847.13	856.11	873.26	884.03
823.09	835.16	847.27	856.11	874.01	884.03
823.09	835.23	847.28	856.12	874.01	884.05
823.11	835.25	848.01	856.12	874.03	884.07
823.13	835.27	848.01	856.13	874.06	884.08
823.14	835.28	848.02	856.13	874.08	884.19
823.15	836.01	848.06	856.14	874.14	884.20
823.18	836.01	848.06	856.16	874.17	884.22
823.20	836.05	848.06	856.16	874.18	884.23
823.21	836.06	848.07	856.21	874.19	884.27
823.21	836.06	848.08	856.25	875.03	885.05
823.22	836.08	848.08	856.27	875.06	885.12
823.24	836.09	848.13	857.02	875.11	885.13
823.24	836.10	848.13	857.03	875.14	885.14
823.26	836.15	848.14	857.04	875.18	885.17
823.27	836.17	848.15	857.04	875.20	885.22
824.01	836.17	848.16	857.05	875.26	885.23
824.02	836.20	848.18	857.08	875.27	885.23
824.02	836.24	848.20	857.11	876.01	885.26
824.03	836.26	848.20	857.15	876.02	885.27
824.04	836.27	848.21	857.16	876.02	885.27
824.11	837.01	848.24	857.22	876.09	886.01
824.13	837.03	848.27	857.22	876.09	886.01
825.01	837.07	849.11	857.23	876.11	886.03
825.01	837.10	849.11	857.24	876.12	886.05
825.01	837.10	849.14	858.24	876.17	886.10
825.08	837.18	849.15	858.25	876.21	886.10
825.16	837.24	849.18	859.04	876.22	886.12
825.19	837.28	849.24	859.22	876.25	886.22
826.05	838.02	849.24	859.24	876.25	886.24
826.05	838.04	849.25	860.05	876.26	886.25
826.08	838.05	849.25	860.08	876.26	886.26
826.08	838.06	849.26	860.09	877.02	887.01
826.09	838.06	849.28	860.11	877.03	887.03
826.13	838.07	850.02	860.12	877.05	887.08
826.18	838.07	850.05	860.13	877.07	887.09
826.19	838.11	850.10	860.15	877.07	887.13
826.22	838.12	850.13	860.18	877.08	887.14
826.28	838.14	850.14	860.20	877.11	887.17
827.01	838.15	850.14	860.21	877.12	887.18
827.02	838.16	850.17	860.23	877.13	887.21
827.07	838.20	850.20	860.25	877.22	887.22
827.08	838.21	850.22	860.26	877.23	887.24
827.11	838.23	851.02	860.27	878.01	887.24
827.15	838.28	851.02	860.28	878.05	887.28
827.15	839.02	851.05	861.01	878.10	888.01
827.16	839.06	851.06	861.06	878.16	888.02
827.17	839.06	851.07	861.09	878.23	888.05
827.18	839.12	851.09	861.09	878.23	888.09
827.24	839.14	851.14	861.12	878.24	888.12
827.25	839.18	851.15	861.16	878.26	888.13
827.25	839.20	851.17	861.25	878.27	888.16
827.27	839.22	851.17	861.26	878.28	888.17
828.02	839.22	851.18	861.28	879.04	888.19
828.12	839.25	852.01	862.02	879.07	888.20
828.13	840.01	852.02	862.07	879.08	888.21
828.13	840.03	852.10	862.17	879.10	888.27
828.14	840.05	852.11	862.17	879.16	888.28
828.15	840.10	852.15	862.25	879.17	889.01
829.01	840.23	852.16	863.05	879.18	889.04
829.02	840.26	852.16	863.13	879.21	

889.04	902.04	190.05	**icily**	**if**	216.26
889.05	902.05	278.09	466.11	007.13	219.12
889.06	902.06	311.04	826.07	008.16	223.21
889.10	902.06	311.10	**icy**	013.08	223.28
889.16	902.10	323.05	612.28	014.09	225.05
890.04	902.12	339.10	**idea**	015.01	225.07
890.11	902.15	393.01	004.16	015.10	225.20
890.13	902.18	393.03	006.20	019.23	225.25
890.14	902.19	410.15	007.17	020.09	226.23
890.16	902.20	410.20	008.26	022.09	227.02
890.25	902.24	421.27	021.17	023.01	234.05
890.27	902.26	422.12	022.28	024.10	235.21
891.03	902.27	428.25	037.26	025.05	240.08
891.17	903.01	429.21	086.12	026.03	242.16
892.04	903.04	435.22	151.03	026.06	245.09
892.11	903.09	455.10	152.24	028.01	246.02
893.03	903.13	455.13	166.03	026.10	248.13
893.22	903.17	455.19	172.19	028.24	251.24
893.27	903.17	495.24	195.28	031.05	257.01
894.03	903.18	508.01	229.06	036.02	259.08
894.04	903.23	538.24	250.09	036.15	259.16
894.06	903.24	533.24	268.02	037.11	260.04
894.07	903.26	540.08	294.18	037.22	261.06
894.10	904.01	540.26	309.12	038.06	263.17
894.11	904.04	545.22	312.10	038.18	264.05
894.14	905.03	545.23	319.26	039.01	265.03
894.15	905.04	546.06	368.19	040.13	267.22
894.15	905.05	546.17	407.17	041.07	268.03
894.21	905.08	546.20	445.20	041.17	270.06
894.22	905.09	546.20	491.21	044.12	270.23
894.23	906.03	547.20	519.28	044.15	271.01
894.24	906.04	548.23	529.01	044.21	271.22
894.26	906.06	549.04	533.05	046.04	272.07
895.04	906.08	549.07	537.21	047.25	272.13
895.07	906.08	554.05	545.10	048.22	273.03
895.11	906.12	554.07	553.01	051.02	273.05
895.15	906.13	565.11	553.10	051.16	273.25
895.16	906.14	565.14	568.22	055.07	275.10
895.22	906.14	581.03	572.15	056.20	280.27
895.23	906.17	616.16	607.01	056.21	284.04
895.25	906.18	616.16	607.20	062.04	284.04
896.05	906.20	616.18	624.09	062.24	285.11
896.05	906.26	619.17	682.04	063.20	285.22
896.08	906.27	620.05	702.08	063.26	290.01
896.11	907.01	682.17	716.03	065.20	291.26
896.23	907.06	682.26	727.15	069.05	293.21
896.25	907.10	694.22	749.25	069.22	294.09
896.26	907.11	697.04	795.10	085.01	295.25
896.26	907.17	754.08	806.24	086.09	297.22
897.01	907.18	768.11	825.06	095.01	298.22
897.06	907.21	863.08	827.15	100.11	301.06
897.11	907.21	885.22	840.17	101.04	309.12
897.11	907.26	894.20	872.26	102.15	312.21
897.24	907.28	902.10	879.11	102.16	313.07
897.25	907.28	**i'm**	885.27	102.20	314.25
897.26	908.01	189.09	902.10	103.05	314.27
897.26	**908.04**	**391.11**	**ideal**	**104.13**	**320.28**
897.27	908.07	395.25	143.01	105.02	321.20
898.01	908.13	396.01	320.23	106.20	321.22
898.04	908.17	416.15	383.24	108.18	323.01
898.06	908.22	453.23	636.04	110.03	324.05
898.07	908.24	456.01	640.16	114.15	325.07
898.07	908.24	600.18	720.12	116.24	325.24
898.08	908.25	679.21	738.10	119.02	330.05
898.12	908.26	681.16	745.14	119.16	332.09
898.13	908.28	683.10	775.15	119.22	338.14
898.13	909.01	696.27	**ideas**	120.25	339.03
898.17	909.03	754.20	048.02	123.02	339.04
898.18	909.09	799.26	190.25	125.19	339.07
898.18	909.17	862.26	263.20	125.24	341.27
898.18	909.17	**i've**	291.18	127.17	346.24
898.20	909.18	014.01	376.25	130.03	347.27
898.23	909.20	068.08	617.27	130.17	358.08
899.04	909.25	175.26	647.11	131.17	359.22
899.09	909.26	175.27	783.04	131.20	359.23
899.17	910.06	190.06	884.05	131.27	360.18
899.19	910.08	395.23	885.01	132.05	360.23
899.20	910.13	410.02	**identity**	132.24	363.04
899.26	910.13	410.02	206.22	132.25	368.24
900.02	910.15	430.26	480.28	132.27	370.01
900.02	910.19	454.25	632.07	136.11	372.09
900.05	911.03	511.03	775.02	140.12	372.17
900.07	912.11	696.10	**idiocy**	149.26	372.24
900.08	912.14	697.12	477.14	150.08	373.19
900.12	912.23	863.06	**idiot**	151.28	374.13
900.13	912.24	**ice**	320.27	153.14	374.17
900.15	**i'**	004.11	626.01	153.24	375.13
900.16	670.11	062.11	650.06	156.05	375.22
900.18	679.02	096.11	730.23	158.17	378.01
900.21	681.03	220.01	**idiotic**	158.21	379.09
900.24	698.03	222.19	625.10	164.03	381.13
900.25	698.06	232.19	**idiots**	164.04	383.01
900.27	698.07	242.05	597.11	166.02	385.10
900.28	906.24	550.28	**idle**	166.26	391.09
901.01	**i'd**	605.24	417.16	168.09	392.15
901.05	177.23	615.06	487.18	171.07	393.01
901.07	410.16	615.06	**idling**	171.09	393.02
901.09	495.18	718.01	477.13	173.19	394.03
901.10	495.20	778.25	**idol**	182.10	397.04
901.11	597.08	807.21	279.14	184.09	397.13
901.12	**i'll**	835.01	556.07	184.10	398.19
901.14	009.13	**ice-cold**	645.13	184.10	402.18
901.14	035.14	485.01	717.06	184.18	403.09
901.15	064.08	**iceberg**	**idolatrous**	189.10	403.16
901.15	068.15	248.27	214.12	190.04	405.05
901.16	069.25	249.04	**idyls**	190.16	405.08
901.20	110.05	895.10	561.07	190.22	405.28
901.21	158.24	**iceland**	**ie**	199.27	408.03
901.27	183.04	004.07	803.14	202.01	409.18
902.02	187.15	**ich**	847.15	208.05	410.18
902.02	190.01	678.25		216.08	410.24

411.22	595.01	787.16	**ignorant**	842.18	724.04
411.27	595.06	793.23	106.03	**imagined**	**impatience**
412.01	597.20	795.15	267.10	121.08	281.17
412.02	602.18	798.09	271.08	163.18	283.15
412.12	611.28	801.01	356.08	250.10	563.04
412.15	613.04	801.10	377.08	268.04	574.20
417.20	613.19	802.05	437.08	315.16	586.02
422.07	614.05	803.08	625.08	563.18	654.02
422.11	614.16	804.02	628.11	660.06	768.20
422.15	615.02	804.09	730.04	691.04	770.02
432.17	615.03	804.10	772.15	746.13	**impatient**
435.28	615.28	805.11	790.10	760.24	025.12
436.22	617.06	807.27	809.10	**imagining**	155.06
437.01	617.14	809.07	**ignus**	291.19	237.28
437.19	617.15	814.17	674.09	**imbecile**	314.09
438.03	617.17	814.20	**il**	626.24	428.23
441.05	618.27	815.04	234.23	**imbecility**	585.05
442.01	619.16	815.05	276.17	528.05	719.06
448.09	620.14	818.26	334.04	**imbibed**	734.12
448.22	621.06	819.06	543.19	162.27	767.02
449.10	621.19	819.09	543.20	**imitating**	**impatiently**
449.25	621.23	819.19	**ill**	198.04	108.09
450.14	621.24	819.20	023.26	**immeasurable**	538.02
452.12	622.25	819.27	028.15	089.01	641.05
453.03	623.27	819.27	034.28	**immeasureably**	**impeded**
453.11	630.15	821.04	035.09	652.14	575.09
453.15	635.09	821.11	035.19	**immediate**	**impediment**
455.15	638.01	824.02	084.18	116.14	256.13
456.08	639.06	826.19	108.17	287.24	440.11
456.14	642.11	827.04	118.03	421.24	590.01
458.28	642.16	828.06	147.03	775.04	590.19
459.04	642.19	828.17	150.22	**immediately**	591.10
463.03	642.26	830.08	151.23	006.19	591.20
463.06	648.11	831.13	156.14	011.05	**impediments**
463.08	648.14	832.21	266.15	080.28	182.21
464.14	649.14	833.04	374.08	087.14	**impenetrability**
468.19	649.14	833.06	410.01	094.11	307.14
475.11	649.14	835.12	481.11	098.07	**imperative**
475.24	649.19	837.10	579.07	099.12	437.07
476.03	649.20	837.17	682.23	113.19	**imperfect**
476.14	649.28	841.27	683.10	123.15	005.14
477.22	653.23	842.09	685.24	298.13	126.08
477.26	660.04	842.17	691.24	394.14	207.05
483.10	660.05	842.24	691.25	445.02	263.08
484.09	661.11	846.03	766.08	487.05	**imperfection**
484.21	665.26	848.01	810.01	508.05	272.25
487.18	667.21	848.06	833.28	626.22	823.27
489.08	668.06	848.11	834.02	713.27	**imperial**
491.27	671.07	848.13	**ill-conditioned**	770.15	344.26
492.26	672.13	849.05	040.12	803.02	**imperious**
494.17	673.19	853.10	**ill-humour**	834.11	291.23
494.21	673.26	854.01	150.24	889.11	372.10
495.08	674.16	855.21	**ill-temper**	891.03	465.19
495.18	677.22	856.02	528.05	906.26	**imperiously**
495.19	679.08	857.05	**ill-treated**	**immense**	675.24
496.12	680.22	857.17	476.17	074.14	**imperturbably**
496.22	682.24	859.17	**illegal**	256.04	706.19
499.12	683.09	863.10	772.17	301.11	**impetuosity**
500.04	683.12	864.09	**illegitimate**	430.25	898.28
500.07	684.10	864.14	288.21	861.20	**impetuous**
501.05	686.15	865.02	**illness**	**immobility**	425.11
503.02	687.09	865.09	029.13	726.10	511.14
503.22	691.19	866.16	042.12	**immoderately**	551.14
504.06	693.16	868.06	060.26	703.09	571.11
505.21	697.09	871.15	157.07	**immoral**	**impetus**
510.17	705.10	872.11	468.25	356.22	619.21
510.24	705.13	872.18	473.18	**immortal**	824.18
510.28	705.19	873.14	**illuminated**	119.07	846.28
513.07	709.01	875.01	406.25	158.04	**implacable**
513.14	709.18	876.15	**illumination**	440.09	831.06
516.15	709.27	878.15	185.27	**immortality**	**implicitly**
517.08	710.01	879.06	640.11	763.04	157.22
517.19	713.09	880.16	**illumined**	**improvement**	**implied**
518.06	714.24	880.20	398.11	149.26	039.13
520.09	719.13	883.04	435.08	**immutable**	**implore**
521.03	719.14	885.04	697.18	437.25	191.12
521.10	720.25	885.18	**illustrated**	**immutably**	**implored**
524.21	723.10	886.08	369.12	788.02	603.16
525.08	724.01	887.11	**illustration**	**imp**	**imply**
528.14	730.15	895.24	383.10	017.26	496.07
529.17	735.09	897.24	858.04	**imp-like**	**import**
530.21	737.06	897.25	**image**	465.02	089.19
531.05	739.09	897.25	046.24	**impalpable**	099.12
531.16	740.22	897.26	445.21	109.01	116.14
532.02	741.02	898.08	465.07	**impart**	178.07
532.11	741.24	900.28	585.15	172.26	268.04
538.26	742.07	901.12	760.07	248.06	**importance**
539.12	746.23	901.20	**imaginable**	276.12	161.27
540.07	747.07	902.10	186.08	404.22	321.03
540.10	747.10	903.04	**imaginary**	528.19	346.10
541.12	749.05	906.22	323.11	579.08	378.14
544.27	751.11	907.06	**imagination**	632.08	389.27
545.06	753.23	**ignis**	142.25	**imparted**	390.20
545.22	754.06	495.20	216.02	127.18	481.23
546.09	754.08	**ignis-fatuus-like**	471.02	133.11	785.23
547.01	756.07	321.23	570.09	772.10	**important**
547.24	756.12	**ignoble**	581.16	**imparting**	574.16
543.04	760.13	722.17	891.12	036.20	773.21
553.26	763.24	761.14	**imagination's**	461.18	**imported**
555.24	767.05	**ignominious**	320.12	568.20	496.07
560.25	763.06	094.20	**imagine**	**imparts**	**importunate**
570.04	763.10	**ignominy**	322.09	652.05	806.23
571.07	768.21	013.13	350.20	753.26	**importune**
574.02	776.21	**ignorance**	405.16	**impassable**	618.15
580.19	777.10	020.01	439.03	111.11	666.24
586.14	779.05	150.28	524.12	675.05	**importuned**
590.01	780.15	274.25	615.21	765.06	660.19
590.22	782.09	346.06	671.17	**impassible**	**importunes**
592.13	784.03	365.07	690.10	478.17	263.22
592.23	785.03	730.26	757.20	**impassioned**	**importunity**
593.19	787.03	759.25	785.27	656.15	392.04

impose
056.25
imposing
149.21
193.20
203.25
348.04
350.22
825.06
impossibilities
841.07
impossible
053.16
107.27
174.23
275.24
295.17
513.02
429.16
429.17
437.24
464.13
511.06
553.04
537.11
595.19
681.27
689.17
763.17
778.21
808.13
819.10
847.15
849.19
873.28
impostor
565.25
697.05
impotent
057.18
099.25
661.28
impracticable
908.02
impress
465.27
551.09
impressed
077.19
656.09
651.27
702.07
759.12
850.02
impressible
702.08
870.05
impressing
909.24
impression
047.23
108.15
153.12
191.04
172.13
305.10
535.23
541.13
542.13
404.10
404.10
866.06
855.26
852.28
900.24
903.06
impressions
323.17
impressive
004.18
748.18
843.26
imprisoned
826.03
improbable
475.05
impromptu
260.07
impropriety
841.26
879.09
improved
113.17
142.16
161.22
292.06
537.13
795.26
improvement
150.04
213.14
240.16
721.16
744.15
911.20
improvements
161.10
improvised
473.15
imps
032.08

impudence
008.20
395.16
547.26
impudent
593.25
impulse
013.05
065.26
124.04
145.17
191.09
295.08
379.12
497.24
impulses
155.06
716.27
784.28
impulsive
132.15
impulsively
351.22
impure
627.23
imputation
136.13
142.07
in
001.04
001.05
001.13
002.02
002.11
002.22
002.22
002.26
003.06
003.07
004.01
004.04
004.12
004.22
005.18
006.01
006.16
006.17
006.25
007.05
007.23
007.23
008.06
008.19
008.16
008.20
008.23
009.15
009.20
010.05
010.13
010.18
011.05
012.10
013.17
013.27
014.15
014.17
014.26
015.05
015.16
015.21
015.24
015.26
016.02
016.20
016.23
016.24
016.27
016.28
017.19
017.20
017.27
018.13
018.14
019.02
019.27
019.28
020.01
020.06
020.07
020.09
020.13
020.14
020.14
021.04
021.15
021.21
022.04
022.15
022.21
022.21
022.23
022.28
023.08
023.12
023.23
024.09
024.10
024.19
024.25

024.26
025.08
025.14
026.11
026.16
026.18
027.01
027.01
027.05
027.12
027.25
028.11
028.16
028.20
029.06
029.10
029.23
030.05
030.06
030.13
030.14
030.19
030.20
030.23
030.23
031.11
031.12
031.13
031.21
032.03
032.04
032.09
032.17
032.23
033.13
033.16
033.27
034.11
034.18
034.18
035.02
035.22
035.27
036.06
036.16
036.17
036.28
038.24
039.21
040.02
040.08
040.09
040.10
041.13
042.07
042.15
042.17
042.18
043.08
043.21
044.09
044.23
044.24
045.04
045.08
045.18
045.20
046.03
046.08
046.19
046.21
046.23
047.01
047.07
047.15
047.21
048.06
048.15
048.16
048.24
048.24
049.03
049.07
049.07
049.14
049.23
050.06
050.07
050.10
051.06
051.14
051.24
051.28
052.03
052.10
052.28
053.09
053.16
053.24
054.17
054.18
054.22
054.25
056.01
056.15
056.23
057.01
057.20

057.22
057.26
058.10
058.28
059.02
059.06
059.10
059.12
059.22
060.11
060.14
061.07
061.14
062.03
062.06
062.14
062.14
063.08
064.12
065.02
066.07
066.12
066.13
066.16
067.13
067.17
068.07
068.08
068.19
069.28
070.01
071.13
071.17
071.20
072.02
072.05
072.08
073.01
074.09
074.14
074.21
074.21
074.23
074.25
075.25
076.03
076.21
077.21
077.22
078.10
078.12
078.14
079.03
079.22
079.27
079.27
080.05
080.10
080.11
080.11
080.20
080.22
081.10
082.07
082.14
082.19
082.24
083.01
083.10
083.16
083.23
083.24
083.25
083.28
084.09
084.12
084.17
085.23
085.25
085.28
086.03
086.03
086.14
086.20
086.22
087.13
087.16
088.10
088.12
089.13
089.16
090.02
091.06
091.25
091.25
093.03
094.02
094.16
094.16
094.18
094.19
094.27
095.05
095.07
096.05
096.06
096.10
096.18
097.08
097.11
097.18

097.27
098.08
098.10
099.15
099.15
100.08
100.14
100.15
101.23
102.15
103.01
103.22
104.11
104.24
105.05
106.17
107.05
107.28
108.02
108.21
108.23
108.25
109.12
109.21
110.01
110.04
111.04
111.06
111.14
112.03
112.19
112.25
112.26
113.19
113.22
113.22
113.24
114.06
114.09
114.21
115.05
115.06
115.07
115.12
115.21
116.07
116.22
117.02
117.03
117.11
117.22
118.07
119.24
120.06
120.09
120.28
121.17
121.22
122.01
122.04
122.08
122.14
123.05
124.06
124.13
125.05
125.07
126.04
126.13
127.01
127.08
127.13
127.19
128.07
130.11
130.18
130.24
131.07
131.20
131.21
132.24
133.03
133.10
133.21
133.22
133.25
134.01
134.08
135.07
135.12
135.14
135.26
136.01
136.02
136.03
136.07
136.09
136.25
138.04
138.10
139.01
139.01
139.02
139.12
139.14
139.16
141.07
141.08
141.11
141.21

142.17
142.18
142.22
142.25
143.02
143.09
144.11
144.13
145.09
145.11
145.11
145.15
146.06
146.10
146.17
147.07
147.11
148.05
148.12
148.15
149.15
150.08
150.25
150.28
151.03
151.12
151.13
151.19
151.25
151.27
152.06
152.11
153.06
153.13
153.17
153.19
153.23
153.25
153.27
154.07
154.09
154.24
155.08
155.14
155.14
155.18
156.01
156.17
157.14
157.23
158.13
158.19
159.06
159.14
159.18
160.02
160.09
160.19
161.02
161.08
161.09
161.11
161.16
161.23
161.26
162.04
162.05
162.08
162.18
162.26
163.04
163.08
163.10
163.14
163.15
163.23
163.28
164.01
164.07
164.25
164.27
165.14
166.08
166.13
167.01
167.05
167.17
167.18
167.20
167.23
167.27
168.09
168.12
168.12
168.20
168.27
169.03
169.05
170.16
170.27
171.07
171.09
171.23
171.28
172.01
172.06
172.26
173.09
173.16
173.26
174.03

174.04	210.26	240.28	285.27	314.18	349.03
174.10	210.27	241.04	286.02	315.03	349.20
174.16	211.19	241.08	286.08	315.09	349.26
174.23	211.21	241.13	286.13	315.14	350.07
174.26	211.23	241.17	286.15	316.22	350.19
175.13	212.02	242.02	286.18	316.23	350.26
175.16	212.06	242.06	287.07	316.25	351.08
175.21	214.05	242.09	287.20	317.01	351.15
176.14	214.07	243.12	287.21	317.24	351.15
176.20	214.20	243.19	288.01	317.27	351.19
177.14	214.25	243.22	288.02	317.27	352.01
177.15	215.01	244.06	288.08	318.13	352.14
177.25	215.13	245.04	288.18	318.14	352.15
177.28	215.14	245.17	289.01	318.17	353.26
178.16	215.14	247.01	289.09	318.19	354.09
178.22	215.15	247.21	289.10	319.15	354.22
178.25	215.19	247.23	289.15	319.21	354.27
178.27	215.22	248.16	289.21	320.05	355.02
179.18	215.28	249.03	289.25	320.18	355.05
179.28	216.05	249.12	289.26	320.20	355.18
180.10	216.06	249.21	290.08	321.03	355.21
180.26	216.10	249.25	290.11	321.13	355.24
181.02	216.13	250.10	290.13	321.19	356.10
181.03	216.20	250.17	290.14	321.27	356.11
181.05	217.10	250.18	290.16	322.05	356.13
181.14	217.24	250.21	290.22	322.09	356.27
182.02	218.04	250.23	290.26	322.25	357.15
182.12	218.08	251.10	291.18	323.09	357.28
182.18	218.10	251.13	291.19	323.09	358.06
183.01	218.12	251.17	291.20	323.13	358.21
183.12	218.19	252.12	292.08	324.09	359.07
183.16	218.21	253.07	292.12	324.19	359.20
183.18	218.22	254.03	292.17	326.23	360.10
184.02	219.02	254.04	292.21	327.18	360.26
184.10	219.05	254.14	292.28	327.21	361.06
184.15	219.06	254.14	293.05	327.28	361.21
185.01	219.08	255.05	293.11	328.03	362.03
185.07	219.08	255.14	293.12	328.06	363.05
185.23	219.09	256.08	294.03	328.12	363.09
186.09	219.10	256.17	294.07	328.17	364.20
186.13	219.11	257.04	294.09	328.23	365.02
186.14	219.20	257.10	294.17	328.25	365.07
188.18	219.27	257.23	295.14	329.07	365.08
188.21	220.06	258.04	295.23	329.08	365.10
189.01	220.14	258.07	296.05	329.10	365.16
189.02	220.16	258.11	296.07	329.14	365.19
189.14	220.18	258.20	296.10	329.16	365.21
189.16	220.28	258.26	296.11	330.25	366.23
190.11	221.01	258.26	296.23	331.03	366.26
190.27	221.09	259.05	297.05	331.08	366.27
191.03	221.19	259.07	297.11	331.10	367.05
191.09	221.23	261.06	297.11	331.20	367.10
191.16	221.24	261.27	297.14	331.25	367.11
191.21	222.04	262.22	297.16	332.03	367.12
192.20	222.12	262.27	297.26	332.06	367.14
193.14	222.21	263.01	298.02	332.11	368.05
194.07	222.24	263.06	298.05	332.15	368.11
196.09	223.25	263.08	298.08	333.12	368.16
196.11	224.09	263.08	298.24	333.19	369.08
196.17	224.24	264.15	299.09	334.12	369.20
197.06	224.27	264.20	299.12	334.17	370.02
198.07	225.02	264.21	299.27	334.19	370.12
198.12	225.15	265.08	300.09	334.20	370.15
198.18	225.13	265.16	300.20	334.22	371.02
198.24	225.20	266.26	300.21	335.19	371.27
198.27	226.25	267.13	300.27	335.27	372.05
199.01	227.15	267.19	301.03	337.16	372.06
199.06	228.12	267.22	301.03	337.20	372.14
199.10	228.13	267.25	301.09	337.26	372.15
199.16	228.18	269.08	301.09	337.27	372.16
199.19	229.08	269.16	301.11	337.28	372.19
200.01	229.15	269.19	301.13	339.02	372.19
200.20	229.17	270.01	301.21	339.05	372.21
200.27	230.04	270.07	301.23	339.15	372.25
201.01	230.09	272.09	301.24	339.17	373.15
201.17	230.21	272.11	302.02	340.06	374.02
202.02	230.25	272.16	302.03	340.08	375.03
202.16	231.02	273.03	302.04	340.13	375.28
202.26	231.04	273.07	302.09	340.18	376.20
203.09	231.10	275.08	302.25	341.04	376.23
203.14	231.13	275.10	305.08	341.08	376.24
203.15	232.13	275.19	305.09	341.09	377.10
203.19	232.17	275.22	305.15	341.25	377.20
203.27	233.09	276.15	305.20	342.02	377.26
203.28	233.10	276.20	306.09	342.09	378.17
204.14	233.13	277.04	306.12	342.13	378.19
204.20	233.18	277.07	306.22	342.15	379.23
205.01	234.07	277.28	306.24	342.19	379.25
205.07	234.18	279.05	306.26	342.24	380.04
205.11	234.28	279.20	307.10	342.27	380.12
205.21	235.02	280.03	307.24	342.28	380.21
206.01	235.13	280.04	307.25	343.08	381.01
206.05	235.16	280.14	308.02	343.09	381.06
206.07	235.22	281.06	308.11	343.12	381.11
206.14	235.28	281.12	308.25	343.17	381.13
206.18	236.11	281.14	309.19	344.12	381.14
207.08	236.19	281.21	310.01	344.18	381.24
207.19	236.22	281.27	310.08	344.21	382.04
207.21	236.26	282.11	311.17	344.23	382.15
208.01	237.12	282.12	311.19	346.16	382.19
208.15	237.14	282.15	311.20	346.18	382.21
208.16	237.19	283.09	311.28	346.19	382.25
209.09	237.23	283.17	312.02	346.24	384.09
209.12	237.27	284.01	312.09	347.21	384.12
209.26	237.28	284.02	313.04	347.26	385.05
210.03	238.24	284.17	313.12	347.27	385.07
210.06	239.03	284.18	314.05	347.28	385.10
210.11	240.04	285.01	314.07	348.05	385.19
210.12	240.07	285.05	314.11	348.19	385.21
210.13	240.15	285.11		348.23	
210.23	240.21	285.19		348.25	386.03

386.05	417.20	457.24	502.03	539.23	583.21
386.12	417.24	458.02	502.18	540.01	585.03
386.16	418.18	458.16	502.25	540.14	585.10
386.24	418.23	458.20	503.03	540.21	585.11
387.28	419.08	458.27	503.16	541.11	586.20
388.03	419.14	459.12	504.25	541.26	587.02
388.12	419.17	459.18	505.04	542.01	587.08
388.24	419.18	459.27	505.09	542.13	587.20
388.26	419.24	460.07	505.14	543.05	588.05
389.01	419.26	460.22	505.25	543.23	589.02
389.18	419.27	461.01	505.27	544.02	589.04
390.02	420.14	461.13	506.02	544.08	589.06
390.02	420.23	461.24	506.11	544.13	589.12
390.04	421.05	462.01	506.16	544.23	590.02
390.06	421.09	462.12	506.18	545.15	590.10
390.10	421.12	462.22	507.13	545.21	591.08
391.03	421.16	462.26	507.22	545.24	592.03
391.19	422.04	463.15	507.24	546.07	592.09
391.23	422.22	463.19	507.27	546.09	592.15
391.24	422.25	464.18	508.12	546.11	593.05
392.03	423.10	465.10	508.13	546.22	593.10
392.08	423.18	465.15	510.09	547.24	593.11
392.11	423.20	466.21	510.12	548.08	593.16
392.12	423.20	466.22	510.27	548.22	593.17
392.16	424.02	467.07	511.09	549.07	594.12
392.25	424.06	467.10	511.10	549.13	594.17
393.01	424.13	468.16	511.24	549.16	595.06
393.03	424.16	468.25	512.03	549.19	595.10
393.05	424.17	469.12	512.14	549.21	595.16
394.04	424.19	469.22	512.15	550.19	595.20
394.10	424.24	469.22	513.16	550.23	597.16
394.19	424.27	470.01	514.06	550.28	599.09
394.20	425.09	470.28	515.01	551.18	599.13
395.11	425.09	471.02	515.23	551.25	599.13
395.17	425.15	471.07	515.25	552.06	600.20
395.22	426.22	472.17	516.12	552.15	601.06
396.05	426.24	472.24	516.13	552.18	601.08
396.12	427.12	472.28	516.15	553.08	603.16
396.14	429.01	473.02	517.03	553.16	603.24
396.25	429.22	473.04	517.03	553.21	604.13
396.28	430.14	473.08	517.16	554.14	605.03
397.01	430.19	473.12	517.25	554.16	605.14
397.12	430.20	473.23	517.26	554.28	606.07
397.25	432.14	474.13	518.10	555.02	606.09
397.26	433.04	474.17	518.17	555.21	606.10
398.01	433.08	474.21	518.18	555.22	606.15
398.02	433.17	475.14	518.24	556.06	606.16
398.06	434.07	475.19	518.28	557.06	607.13
398.15	435.27	476.12	519.01	558.05	607.15
398.16	436.21	477.02	519.14	558.24	607.16
398.17	437.02	477.08	520.09	559.13	607.23
399.01	437.05	477.20	520.12	560.02	608.06
399.04	437.12	478.01	520.13	561.03	608.10
399.13	437.15	478.07	520.15	561.07	608.11
399.17	437.17	478.09	521.08	561.10	608.12
399.17	438.08	479.03	521.09	561.12	609.02
399.20	438.13	479.20	521.10	561.16	610.05
400.06	438.25	479.20	521.20	561.24	611.06
400.14	438.26	480.03	522.10	562.01	612.03
401.13	439.03	480.06	523.01	562.06	612.09
402.01	439.13	481.04	523.02	562.10	612.10
402.04	439.16	481.15	523.20	562.13	612.11
402.11	439.22	481.17	524.10	562.13	612.12
402.16	439.22	481.20	524.16	562.14	612.13
404.05	439.23	482.25	524.17	562.21	612.24
404.07	439.28	483.02	524.18	563.23	612.28
404.19	440.08	483.04	525.07	564.08	613.03
404.21	440.10	483.12	525.10	564.08	613.03
404.26	440.17	483.26	525.21	564.20	613.07
405.03	440.20	484.16	525.22	565.01	614.08
405.17	440.24	486.05	525.26	565.20	614.11
405.16	440.25	487.12	525.26	566.03	614.13
405.25	441.04	487.12	525.28	566.06	614.24
405.26	441.05	487.13	526.01	566.19	614.24
406.06	441.14	487.16	526.07	566.19	616.06
406.07	441.23	488.06	526.09	568.17	616.22
406.07	442.10	488.17	526.10	569.09	616.24
406.08	443.01	488.28	526.16	569.10	617.12
406.20	443.01	489.03	526.16	569.20	617.16
407.15	443.04	489.10	527.18	570.01	617.19
407.26	444.06	489.22	527.19	570.08	617.21
407.28	445.10	489.22	528.14	570.19	617.24
408.25	445.13	489.25	530.09	570.21	618.22
409.15	445.23	490.18	530.18	570.22	619.04
409.22	446.04	490.24	531.09	571.03	619.20
409.26	446.05	491.14	531.12	571.18	619.23
410.09	446.24	491.18	532.07	572.10	619.26
410.13	447.02	492.03	532.14	572.14	620.02
410.26	448.15	492.12	532.16	572.23	620.17
411.03	449.06	493.24	532.21	572.24	620.25
411.03	449.08	494.08	532.23	574.14	621.01
411.04	449.09	494.12	532.26	575.05	622.14
411.27	449.15	494.14	533.07	575.17	622.20
412.08	449.24	494.22	533.20	575.23	623.20
412.23	450.01	495.17	533.22	576.09	623.22
412.25	450.19	495.21	534.05	576.19	623.24
413.04	451.17	495.25	534.18	577.22	624.26
414.06	452.18	496.01	535.16	578.14	625.01
414.07	452.26	496.16	535.18	579.01	625.05
414.08	453.28	497.04	535.23	579.05	625.19
414.10	454.05	497.10	535.24	579.14	625.21
414.15	454.11	497.21	536.11	580.13	625.28
415.03	454.19	497.26	536.18	580.16	626.04
415.08	455.13	497.26	536.19	581.09	626.05
415.26	455.15	498.26	537.07	581.19	626.06
416.07	456.19	499.14	537.28	581.24	626.07
416.12	456.19	500.07	538.04	582.06	626.10
416.14	456.23	501.04	538.07	582.09	626.20
416.26	457.02	501.09	538.11	582.19	627.03
417.16	457.03	501.11	538.14	583.06	627.20
	457.10	501.16	539.01	583.18	

628.07	658.15	691.06	727.10	760.07	801.16
628.08	658.19	691.06	728.04	760.12	801.24
628.16	659.07	691.07	729.06	760.26	801.26
628.26	659.23	691.19	730.02	760.27	801.27
628.28	659.25	691.20	730.11	761.06	802.10
629.13	661.06	691.26	730.11	761.07	802.16
629.14	661.09	692.01	730.13	761.16	803.04
629.15	661.16	692.10	730.14	761.22	803.17
629.22	662.02	692.11	730.20	762.19	803.25
629.25	662.09	692.21	730.25	763.14	805.02
630.01	662.25	692.23	731.04	763.22	805.11
630.27	663.01	693.12	731.05	763.27	805.17
631.09	663.08	693.15	731.07	764.01	805.18
631.12	663.21	694.01	731.12	764.06	805.26
631.13	663.23	694.08	731.14	764.08	806.18
631.22	664.09	695.13	731.16	765.08	806.24
632.08	664.25	696.17	731.26	765.17	806.27
632.09	665.05	698.14	732.02	765.18	807.09
632.14	665.09	699.02	732.03	766.02	807.11
632.27	665.22	699.11	732.26	766.05	808.17
633.01	665.28	699.16	732.28	767.25	809.06
633.04	666.05	699.17	733.05	768.01	809.24
633.27	666.09	700.04	733.07	768.17	810.07
634.01	666.12	700.09	733.11	768.20	810.08
635.03	666.25	700.23	733.21	770.07	810.11
635.09	667.14	701.01	733.25	770.12	810.14
635.25	667.18	701.11	734.27	770.13	810.22
635.27	667.26	701.13	735.04	770.21	810.24
635.27	668.01	701.24	735.11	770.23	810.26
635.28	668.12	702.15	736.02	770.24	811.09
635.28	668.18	702.15	736.14	771.13	811.12
636.22	668.22	702.26	736.17	772.02	811.21
637.05	668.25	703.07	736.23	772.07	811.23
637.06	668.27	703.21	737.08	773.04	811.24
637.10	669.14	703.24	737.09	773.05	812.04
637.16	669.15	703.24	737.14	773.26	812.17
637.17	670.02	704.07	737.15	774.03	813.06
638.07	670.06	705.04	737.24	774.03	813.09
638.11	670.18	705.10	737.27	774.15	813.11
638.15	671.06	705.17	738.09	774.17	813.18
638.23	671.23	705.19	738.13	774.18	813.19
638.25	672.16	705.23	738.20	775.05	814.02
639.03	672.19	706.18	739.20	775.09	814.09
639.24	672.27	707.09	739.23	775.13	814.14
639.26	673.17	707.12	739.24	777.03	814.16
640.06	673.20	707.16	740.06	777.23	815.10
640.11	673.22	707.17	741.27	777.24	815.26
640.12	673.22	709.07	742.11	778.02	816.22
640.17	674.07	709.09	742.12	779.15	816.28
640.20	674.15	709.11	744.02	779.15	817.05
640.24	674.19	709.14	744.02	779.21	817.11
641.20	674.23	710.02	744.03	780.11	817.12
642.15	675.05	711.03	744.03	780.21	817.17
642.17	675.06	711.06	744.05	781.24	817.20
642.21	676.02	711.09	744.07	781.25	817.24
642.28	676.08	711.16	744.17	783.21	817.25
642.28	676.15	712.24	744.19	783.25	817.26
643.05	676.23	713.02	744.20	784.07	817.27
643.07	676.27	713.05	744.25	784.23	818.01
643.10	676.28	713.08	744.27	784.23	818.01
644.04	677.05	713.09	745.04	785.18	818.13
644.05	677.20	713.11	745.08	785.25	819.02
644.10	677.21	713.28	745.10	786.25	819.04
644.13	677.25	714.15	745.11	787.11	819.10
644.14	678.04	714.20	745.19	787.13	819.12
644.20	678.06	715.06	746.04	787.25	820.12
645.01	678.07	715.07	746.06	788.03	821.11
645.24	678.08	715.16	746.09	788.06	822.03
646.17	678.25	715.20	746.17	788.10	822.06
646.20	679.06	715.24	746.26	789.14	822.09
646.21	680.03	715.24	747.02	789.16	822.16
647.10	680.06	716.04	747.05	789.17	822.18
647.11	680.10	716.11	747.17	790.02	822.27
647.19	680.13	717.12	747.24	790.05	823.12
647.26	680.19	717.13	747.25	790.09	823.12
648.10	680.24	717.24	748.01	790.16	823.13
649.04	681.12	717.28	748.11	791.08	823.16
649.05	681.18	718.14	748.16	791.09	823.16
649.11	681.23	718.17	749.16	791.15	823.19
650.17	682.01	718.28	749.21	791.21	823.26
650.22	682.06	719.11	749.22	792.01	824.12
650.27	682.14	719.20	750.19	792.02	824.20
651.23	682.17	719.25	750.23	792.10	825.02
651.24	682.19	720.28	750.24	792.10	825.03
651.25	683.04	721.05	751.01	794.19	825.06
651.28	683.14	721.07	751.04	795.05	825.09
652.02	683.22	721.14	751.04	795.06	825.10
652.12	683.24	721.26	751.07	795.13	825.10
652.16	684.01	721.28	751.17	795.20	825.17
652.25	684.02	722.02	752.13	795.24	825.21
652.26	684.21	722.05	752.17	795.25	825.22
653.02	684.27	722.11	753.05	796.03	826.06
653.03	684.28	722.11	753.12	796.25	826.16
653.05	685.08	722.14	754.10	797.19	827.09
653.22	686.01	723.20	754.23	798.05	827.14
653.23	686.03	723.22	755.18	798.06	828.22
654.03	686.03	724.09	755.19	798.10	828.27
654.11	686.04	724.12	756.02	798.16	829.02
654.18	686.13	724.13	756.03	798.20	829.07
654.20	687.27	724.19	757.22	798.22	829.08
654.24	688.06	724.20	758.01	799.07	829.08
655.21	689.03	724.23	758.10	799.10	829.15
656.03	689.04	724.24	758.21	799.16	829.21
656.05	689.06	725.11	758.24	800.03	830.09
656.06	689.06	725.12	759.10	800.04	831.13
656.08	690.02	726.03	759.13	800.14	832.03
656.12	690.05	726.08	759.14	800.22	832.14
657.08	690.07	726.14	759.21	800.24	833.12
657.13	690.17	726.24	759.22	800.26	834.09
657.14	690.20	727.07	759.23	800.27	834.18
658.06	691.02	727.09	759.28	801.11	

835.02
855.03
855.27
856.19
856.20
856.21
856.27
857.17
857.18
858.02
858.05
858.06
858.17
859.04
859.05
859.07
840.15
840.17
840.18
841.19
841.26
842.01
842.09
842.21
842.22
842.26
843.04
843.06
843.15
843.18
843.26
844.02
844.03
844.15
844.15
844.20
844.28
845.04
845.07
845.09
845.24
845.26
846.02
846.06
846.14
847.06
847.22
847.25
849.16
849.16
849.16
849.22
850.03
850.12
850.13
850.16
850.16
850.17
850.21
851.04
851.05
852.13
852.15
852.15
852.16
852.20
852.26
852.27
853.08
853.10
854.09
855.02
855.17
856.12
856.25
857.01
857.02
857.03
857.26
858.14
858.16
859.04
859.07
859.11
859.21
859.25
860.02
860.15
860.21
861.05
861.08
861.16
862.05
862.08
862.22
862.24
862.27
862.28
863.10
863.16
863.20
864.04
864.11
864.15
865.02
865.11
867.01
867.03
867.13
867.19
869.04

869.09
869.13
870.05
870.16
870.25
870.28
871.01
871.08
871.22
871.22
871.23
872.01
872.03
872.06
872.10
872.24
873.01
873.06
873.19
874.03
874.10
874.15
874.17
874.24
875.03
875.18
875.27
876.15
876.28
876.28
877.17
878.02
878.07
878.17
879.09
879.24
881.07
881.17
882.10
882.20
882.21
883.02
883.16
883.16
883.18
883.22
884.05
884.11
885.01
885.04
885.24
886.15
887.07
887.09
887.10
887.16
887.21
887.27
888.06
888.21
888.23
888.24
888.27
889.08
889.09
889.10
889.24
889.25
889.25
892.08
894.13
895.13
896.05
896.12
896.19
897.24
898.03
898.09
898.14
898.25
899.10
900.05
900.16
900.23
901.05
901.11
901.18
902.01
902.13
902.18
902.19
902.21
903.02
903.10
903.13
903.21
903.23
905.19
906.19
907.11
907.18
908.17
908.09
908.10
908.12
908.13
908.17
908.22
909.06
909.08
909.08
909.13

910.01
910.05
911.08
912.03
in-door
365.01
in-doors
712.28
inaccuracy
267.12
inactive
062.10
162.01
inadequacy
616.13
inadequate
792.08
inadvertently
875.02
inaminate
460.16
inammorata
281.20
inanimate
382.14
inanition
081.17
610.19
735.03
inarticulate
337.17
440.21
573.05
573.14
613.16
inattention
097.25
inaudible
595.04
inborn
715.22
incapable
020.15
079.09
141.21
230.02
626.16
684.12
784.14
834.02
incapacity
360.21
incarnate
224.27
424.13
incense
281.04
503.11
incensed
574.07
827.21
incessant
841.04
incessantly
234.11
inch
171.24
213.19
280.08
403.15
546.07
incident
029.14
118.13
216.04
228.16
228.17
290.18
294.25
300.16
384.26
445.07
474.23
582.11
633.19
incidents
141.26
incivility
516.13
696.14
inclement
088.06
255.09
563.23
inclination
043.19
106.16
250.04
709.13
734.25
753.22
824.26
inclinations
786.23
817.15
incline
371.22
734.20
inclined
007.16
219.23

249.04
402.10
596.23
700.25
709.18
812.03
inclines
615.04
inclining
652.12
inclose
168.03
inclosed
423.19
include
477.01
included
014.13
115.11
255.17
389.28
including
181.09
701.14
749.13
income
469.12
incommunicative
716.01
incompetency
354.18
incomprehensible
467.22
497.09
763.20
incongruous
636.17
inconsiderateness
879.10
inconsistent
386.24
inconsistently
300.24
inconsolable
252.16
incorruptible
912.14
increase
307.07
increased
376.07
719.01
729.11
increases
503.18
increasing
490.18
incredible
659.14
707.04
incredulity
369.05
574.07
incredulous
013.23
491.26
515.19
incredulously
761.19
incubi
354.11
incumbent
196.05
709.16
721.05
incumbrance
281.22
incurred
660.20
incurring
905.13
indebted
477.05
indeed
001.04
015.16
039.16
043.15
045.07
053.22
057.16
057.20
064.20
069.19
075.03
077.24
114.25
119.06
125.24
138.26
141.07
144.04
177.19
184.14
188.15
201.13
202.21
207.27
225.25
232.12
245.27

247.17
253.13
253.23
257.18
260.12
261.17
291.09
292.14
317.07
317.10
318.22
326.23
329.19
336.03
345.26
348.07
359.14
363.02
383.10
386.26
394.20
408.09
414.20
468.20
470.16
478.24
506.06
506.24
507.28
508.21
528.14
529.14
536.21
544.27
548.18
552.25
553.06
565.03
583.16
585.03
602.18
617.08
627.09
633.14
637.16
666.24
682.05
683.05
683.20
685.17
693.10
693.26
701.26
709.05
716.08
720.24
736.08
739.18
739.21
747.01
750.28
758.27
759.08
763.10
769.01
769.10
773.16
778.02
779.14
781.20
795.10
796.06
809.25
815.22
835.28
836.10
839.05
841.22
846.19
853.26
858.26
862.01
865.15
867.24
879.10
886.13
887.02
indefatigable
081.12
499.25
911.17
indefinite
080.27
192.06
514.27
791.26
indelibly
323.18
445.02
indemnity
018.24
independence
776.04
782.22
898.14
independency
544.28
independent
330.04
464.06
476.25

477.09
514.08
641.10
708.26
722.15
837.20
853.11
878.05
878.06
878.14
878.23
indescribable
032.24
461.18
844.14
indescribably
746.25
indestructible
642.15
india
624.14
755.18
815.01
819.20
819.22
819.22
821.04
821.26
826.14
834.19
834.23
834.24
836.14
838.03
840.20
893.21
911.15
indiaman
813.19
indian
130.25
344.25
504.24
620.01
636.20
774.03
810.21
818.08
818.09
818.28
840.19
indian-rubber
261.25
262.04
indicate
261.15
746.28
indicated
013.04
384.14
702.12
703.13
indicating
795.25
indicative
691.09
indies
384.15
409.15
409.22
409.25
indifference
018.11
050.04
263.02
263.07
308.11
390.19
767.26
806.21
indifferent
048.02
094.04
178.07
266.01
indifferently
354.05
indigence
627.22
775.10
indigent
323.03
indignant
532.04
532.06
693.24
722.08
indignation
020.17
066.02
160.19
309.23
832.19
indirect
616.10
indiscretion
269.27
312.25
indiscriminately
431.13

indisposed
155.05
741.27
indissolable
406.14
indissolubly
580.24
inditing
244.21
individual
027.05
076.17
175.07
425.21
646.11
777.05
822.24
individuals
161.07
indolence
476.02
indomitable
648.01
649.11
induce
682.02
763.22
induced
553.13
452.10
inducement
667.01
inducements
739.10
indulge
067.17
150.08
621.15
785.13
910.07
indulged
018.21
213.10
320.19
396.05
439.02
748.09
indulgence
118.09
135.20
149.21
895.12
indulgent
908.05
industrious
037.26
478.18
industry
762.02
ineffable
541.26
ineffectual
426.12
ineligible
369.09
ineradicable
825.13
inertness
425.13
inestimable
059.14
inevitable
170.25
263.07
500.09
842.19
inevitably
348.26
509.22
633.07
670.27
inexcusable
855.20
inexhaustible
268.25
inexorable
485.27
616.27
725.12
742.25
inexpedient
718.13
inexperience
454.17
493.14
inexperienced
182.17
235.13
625.08
inexplicable
290.19
528.26
903.03
inexpresible
848.28
inexpressible
027.03
027.27
153.12
716.23

inexpressibly
629.09
763.20
inextricable
416.10
inextricably
510.26
infallible
813.24
infamous
627.16
632.20
infamy
127.10
infant
021.21
056.01
200.26
445.09
575.23
infantine
040.16
357.15
infatuated
644.01
infatuatedly
375.03
infection
041.02
147.02
148.22
285.20
infects
776.24
inter
029.02
inference
638.01
inferior
081.05
150.05
264.18
373.02
511.27
513.23
637.24
inferiority
001.17
292.16
325.01
inferiors
637.25
infernal
623.19
interred
013.13
821.21
infidels
828.24
infinite
544.11
545.26
infinitude
662.11
infinitum
406.10
infirm
629.15
infirmities
898.10
infirmity
686.15
inflamed
112.01
867.23
inflammatory
431.24
inflated
344.16
inflation
578.04
inflections
344.22
inflexible
683.16
829.06
inflict
043.17
360.26
462.26
831.06
836.03
688.15
inflicted
051.08
inflictions
008.01
influence
049.25
104.17
312.24
341.13
350.05
351.27
375.18
379.14
436.16
528.22
619.27
674.28

753.12
797.03
805.06
806.19
822.16
822.18
influenced
312.08
376.20
425.17
528.21
559.02
630.04
influx
015.17
inform
149.24
361.02
496.17
597.03
780.09
801.04
814.18
informality
267.03
informant
667.09
information
106.10
116.03
202.25
253.19
309.11
320.09
365.15
448.05
540.03
668.04
740.13
744.15
772.04
809.12
855.27
informed
255.08
391.25
453.25
474.14
778.15
874.01
910.15
informer
478.14
informs
727.17
infused
135.21
152.15
ing
145.18
ingenious
401.04
ingenuous
748.14
ingram
316.14
317.09
317.18
318.03
319.03
322.12
323.11
333.05
338.01
344.02
345.24
346.02
346.14
346.21
347.09
348.12
350.16
352.10
352.16
352.20
352.28
356.04
357.08
357.09
357.25
359.05
360.25
366.01
366.16
367.05
368.11
370.12
371.08
371.21
371.21
373.01
374.17
376.24
378.08
378.17
378.28
379.02
379.08
379.24
379.26
380.15

380.22
381.09
381.16
383.16
385.24
386.25
387.13
387.25
388.23
389.04
389.12
389.19
389.25
390.10
390.22
403.01
411.09
416.20
417.15
441.27
449.12
449.14
451.15
460.20
491.22
492.02
499.22
507.12
507.25
512.15
515.28
516.07
531.26
532.12
532.13
533.01
624.26
ingram's
319.14
360.16
372.26
374.27
391.04
449.20
532.22
ingratitude
126.15
ingredient
171.28
inhabit
195.01
inhabitant
147.22
inhabitants
059.07
667.15
inhabited
003.25
204.01
204.23
inhale
504.02
650.02
inherit
844.17
inherited
289.22
910.27
inhospitable
766.23
initial
171.06
initials
779.15
injudicious
203.04
213.12
injudiciously
691.18
injure
436.18
437.27
injured
223.05
647.14
647.27
656.11
831.12
injuries
465.14
injurious
826.24
injury
057.15
107.15
injustice
108.16
109.20
ink
774.03
inkling
356.21
inmate
161.24
245.12
491.05
615.28
649.22
653.19
inmates
148.10

163.03
213.05
243.16
546.19
676.01
681.28
711.02
inmost
301.27
inn
074.12
181.05
181.07
327.03
490.22
492.14
855.01
855.16
855.28
860.08
inn-passage
183.11
innate
269.27
342.03
547.27
717.16
743.19
innately
788.05
inner
099.14
420.21
435.25
633.02
680.06
790.19
innocence
132.27
357.03
646.28
innocent
132.27
583.20
622.17
748.13
900.03
innovation
117.28
innovations
794.14
inopportune
381.18
inquire
168.08
182.11
183.05
266.15
402.26
548.05
774.19
802.05
852.05
856.02
inquired
077.10
197.16
199.28
206.19
210.21
235.26
261.06
299.27
309.04
355.03
386.11
410.01
430.09
450.05
496.12
595.11
604.02
612.16
680.17
682.06
694.10
694.19
796.02
809.07
874.08
875.13
inquiries
225.09
474.07
624.17
854.06
inquiringly
583.08
inquiry
127.24
142.03
160.16
175.02
188.17
218.02
530.14
717.28
736.20
771.27
824.06
847.25

853.16
inquisitive
170.12
635.06
705.03
inquisitive-looking
052.26
inquisitiveness
749.08
inroad
748.01
insalubrious
869.09
insane
630.24
648.15
648.15
732.06
767.05
insanity
628.01
767.06
insatiable
762.01
insatiate
716.28
inscribed
004.28
159.21
803.28
inscription
089.10
658.17
inscrutable
310.26
766.19
insect
504.24
insecurity
274.24
insensible
265.01
355.22
579.02
707.24
inside
073.26
121.07
357.22
582.16
657.07
insight
680.25
insignificant
160.03
323.03
525.13
822.23
343.05
insinuation
783.09
insipid
556.19
377.22
insist
098.08
366.08
480.05
insisted
147.06
367.01
453.03
750.16
insists
385.20
insolence
267.02
267.04
357.06
insolent
018.21
264.16
615.18
insolently
494.26
insolvable
764.10
insolvency
533.06
inspection
122.22
474.07
795.18
inspector
161.19
inspectors
173.23
inspiration
271.19
796.28
853.01
inspire
109.03
480.03
inspired
007.27
127.15
214.05
781.11
856.21

672.07
672.14
680.09
680.27
684.04
685.03
685.04
688.01
694.21
697.17
698.07
700.11
700.19
712.04
726.12
743.15
745.12
750.22
756.27
759.24
768.18
770.05
774.10
779.24
782.10
793.18
798.11
803.15
812.01
817.21
820.16
824.27
829.09
835.01
837.25
847.03
849.25
849.26
851.16
855.13
857.13
857.27
860.10
864.02
871.13
873.17
878.13
880.23
881.06
882.27
886.07
887.17
891.15
898.19
899.08
905.05
906.17
909.21
910.26
912.17
intolerable
141.25
256.26
267.27
344.23
609.14
645.13
660.13
intolerably
478.21
intonation
591.02
intractable
730.04
intricate
154.04
intrinsic
263.04
introduce
265.04
314.23
826.23
introduced
052.21
100.16
117.27
161.11
228.25
331.17
338.21
401.11
460.10
828.03
introduction
186.16
213.03
558.01
669.04
introductory
003.21
004.19
intrude
051.23
604.13
741.14
intruded
022.06
intruder
592.18
intruders
605.13

671.25
intrusion
017.03
618.07
intuitive
780.02
inundation
757.23
inured
283.15
186.03
invade
661.18
invalid
112.06
invaluable
243.02
818.10
invariable
804.12
invariably
114.04
invention
418.09
893.25
inventive
166.04
invest
808.03
invested
162.09
344.25
794.16
investigation
591.04
investment
530.18
inviolate
648.11
invisible
063.20
103.14
132.21
272.17
587.23
871.21
invitation
257.08
291.03
475.22
invite
597.22
610.24
invited
030.27
040.01
117.14
138.06
263.18
487.07
inviting
021.14
081.22
668.13
795.17
invoke
160.06
794.04
invoked
843.17
involuntarily
017.17
325.20
326.09
349.17
354.01
509.11
623.14
801.08
860.03
895.16
901.17
involuntary
120.25
224.06
269.21
529.01
649.06
703.04
involved
402.04
424.24
inward
020.03
142.28
216.01
294.06
405.07
482.01
619.27
625.16
639.01
661.25
715.08
745.05
848.17
852.22
inwardly
052.06
055.05
406.12
426.06

511.04
656.18
826.02
irate
239.16
ire
021.09
043.11
466.19
834.11
836.06
ireful
224.15
ireland
508.26
508.26
509.25
509.27
510.15
514.01
514.02
irids
085.25
349.19
472.02
irked
799.14
irksome
022.02
059.19
111.04
iron
137.28
145.14
281.17
284.13
587.10
610.06
645.08
722.16
757.17
818.11
829.03
870.03
iron-foundry
721.27
ironical
525.15
ironing
700.26
ironing-table
005.19
irrational
019.15
irregular
077.28
192.22
808.13
irregularities
383.27
irregularity
322.01
irreligious
899.26
irrepressible
114.10
irresistible
372.20
irresistibly
371.15
irresolute
755.23
irrevocably
270.25
irritate
787.17
irritated
040.23
315.01
450.03
467.14
538.10
815.22
irritating
265.19
irritation
061.23
111.20
150.22
554.13
618.19
is
002.21
006.07
006.09
006.09
006.11
006.17
008.20
012.05
012.18
014.23
014.25
024.14
024.26
025.01
025.06
026.02
028.09

028.14
033.04
033.11
033.13
033.19
033.21
033.22
033.30
034.03
034.04
034.10
034.13
035.03
035.22
036.05
036.15
037.07
039.26
041.05
043.26
044.24
052.22
053.01
053.01
054.09
054.41
054.22
055.01
055.07
057.20
057.21
058.06
058.23
059.01
059.06
059.25
060.04
062.09
062.15
063.02
063.27
064.04
064.12
067.09
067.26
073.11
073.14
073.17
075.16
076.23
077.06
081.28
082.20
087.12
089.16
090.03
090.09
091.02
091.05
091.07
091.17
091.20
091.21
092.04
092.15
092.16
092.22
092.26
093.02
093.10
093.11
093.13
093.14
093.15
093.20
095.05
095.08
095.09
095.11
101.20
101.27
102.11
102.13
102.22
103.06
103.07
103.27
104.01
104.06
104.10
104.16
104.21
104.21
104.23
106.09
106.10
106.11
106.16
106.19
107.07
107.09
107.14
107.27
108.09
116.23
117.11
117.21
117.25
118.08
119.26

120.03
121.16
121.17
123.15
124.27
125.06
125.12
125.15
126.01
128.08
131.11
131.11
131.12
131.16
132.05
132.20
132.22
132.22
133.07
133.08
134.02
134.11
134.23
134.25
135.06
135.07
136.26
137.20
136.14
143.15
143.16
146.20
152.11
153.01
153.03
155.19
153.22
153.23
153.24
156.03
156.10
157.06
157.07
157.08
157.08
157.09
157.11
157.20
157.20
157.27
158.03
158.04
158.05
158.06
158.14
159.18
160.05
166.13
160.16
166.16
166.20
166.23
166.25
166.26
167.07
167.13
166.19
168.24
170.14
171.09
171.12
171.14
171.14
175.13
175.23
176.12
176.16
177.02
177.06
177.10
178.03
178.24
179.03
179.03
180.08
180.08
181.02
181.12
181.20
182.17
182.20
183.01
183.06
184.06
184.10
184.12
187.04
187.19
188.13
188.15
188.26
188.27
188.28
189.03
190.02
190.07
195.09
195.16
196.10
196.12
196.15

197.10
197.18
198.22
198.23
199.03
200.03
201.26
201.27
202.08
203.26
205.03
205.08
205.15
205.18
205.22
205.23
205.24
205.27
206.01
206.02
206.05
206.05
206.08
206.08
208.13
208.16
210.18
210.24
211.20
216.06
216.20
216.24
222.16
225.04
225.23
226.06
226.10
226.12
227.21
232.07
232.10
232.12
232.14
232.16
235.26
236.02
236.03
236.05
237.22
238.01
236.15
240.14
240.18
243.24
243.24
244.06
245.01
245.02
245.08
245.11
247.14
249.23
250.21
250.23
250.25
251.01
251.19
251.20
251.28
252.14
253.07
255.27
256.18
257.01
257.05
257.06
257.13
259.21
260.04
260.08
261.10
262.14
263.12
263.15
264.15
264.17
264.18
264.21
264.23
265.18
265.18
266.08
266.11
266.25
267.23
268.25
269.23
270.01
270.18
270.20
270.21
270.23
270.25
271.22
271.26
273.19
273.21
274.04
274.06
274.27
275.03

276.02	360.13	450.23	518.03	594.04	678.05
276.05	360.21	450.26	518.05	595.06	678.12
276.19	361.08	451.07	518.17	595.13	678.24
276.26	362.14	451.18	522.24	595.15	679.02
277.26	363.10	451.19	522.28	596.10	679.25
281.19	366.01	452.01	523.12	596.18	679.28
282.10	370.19	453.16	523.12	596.19	680.13
285.20	371.06	456.09	523.19	597.01	680.25
285.21	375.19	456.18	524.02	597.03	681.01
285.21	376.01	456.20	524.12	597.05	681.04
268.09	381.20	456.22	526.10	597.10	682.13
288.21	385.19	457.14	526.15	599.23	682.28
288.27	386.01	457.16	528.22	600.19	683.04
289.01	386.11	457.22	529.27	600.20	684.18
289.09	387.28	463.01	530.05	601.21	684.21
294.11	388.02	463.06	530.08	601.21	684.24
295.10	388.14	463.14	530.09	601.24	685.02
295.16	389.22	464.13	530.23	603.10	685.11
297.07	390.02	465.07	531.02	603.13	685.21
297.12	390.06	465.25	531.08	603.24	685.24
297.14	391.11	466.27	531.09	608.01	685.25
297.19	392.16	467.06	531.24	608.02	686.18
297.23	392.19	469.04	531.27	609.10	687.21
298.03	396.14	469.05	531.27	609.12	687.23
299.18	397.23	469.14	532.26	609.14	689.03
299.22	397.25	469.15	533.16	613.22	690.05
300.06	397.26	469.15	533.20	613.26	690.12
300.10	397.28	469.23	534.01	614.19	690.17
300.12	398.27	469.25	534.18	615.09	691.15
300.21	399.13	470.03	535.21	615.10	691.16
301.14	399.15	470.04	536.05	615.12	691.19
301.20	399.21	472.13	536.15	616.10	691.24
305.17	400.09	476.20	536.17	616.15	693.06
305.20	401.03	477.20	536.22	616.23	695.10
306.04	402.24	478.19	536.25	617.01	695.12
307.14	402.27	478.23	536.27	617.05	695.13
308.24	402.27	478.25	536.27	617.06	695.13
310.05	402.27	480.13	537.06	617.11	695.17
310.09	403.21	480.16	537.06	617.13	695.18
310.14	404.01	480.20	537.10	618.01	695.26
310.15	404.09	480.21	537.15	618.21	695.28
312.19	404.11	481.01	538.02	619.09	696.04
312.20	404.19	481.13	538.14	619.18	696.18
314.09	404.22	481.16	539.10	621.16	700.08
516.04	404.27	481.16	539.11	621.22	700.15
316.06	405.01	481.17	539.12	621.28	700.23
316.11	406.04	481.23	540.05	622.10	700.25
316.13	406.14	481.26	540.26	622.24	701.26
316.18	407.13	482.03	541.09	622.24	702.06
316.25	407.29	482.13	541.09	622.27	702.06
316.26	409.08	482.13	541.16	622.27	703.02
519.08	409.14	484.05	541.17	625.09	703.05
319.11	410.13	484.18	542.27	628.06	703.17
319.16	410.24	487.17	543.05	628.07	705.08
319.18	410.25	488.07	543.13	628.09	706.23
319.20	411.16	488.26	546.01	628.10	708.01
319.21	412.24	489.09	546.02	628.12	708.09
319.22	413.08	489.23	546.02	628.13	708.11
321.18	416.02	490.03	549.01	628.13	708.25
321.24	416.02	493.11	554.03	628.15	708.28
323.02	416.04	493.13	561.08	628.16	709.15
325.08	416.11	494.08	562.17	628.17	709.21
325.12	417.07	494.09	563.23	628.18	709.24
325.15	417.13	494.10	564.13	629.08	710.02
325.28	421.24	495.01	564.21	630.13	716.05
326.21	427.07	495.03	564.22	630.13	717.28
326.23	427.08	495.12	565.07	630.18	718.28
330.02	427.09	497.04	565.15	631.23	719.03
330.07	428.01	498.02	565.15	631.24	719.21
330.09	428.02	498.10	565.16	632.03	719.26
330.13	428.28	498.12	566.09	632.04	720.02
330.15	429.17	503.06	566.13	633.19	720.17
332.06	431.12	503.11	566.14	633.22	720.19
332.09	431.13	503.12	566.14	635.12	721.06
332.12	431.24	503.13	566.25	635.25	721.11
336.06	432.17	503.16	567.04	637.22	721.12
339.04	433.17	503.24	567.11	637.25	721.23
339.12	433.18	504.08	568.06	643.26	722.21
339.14	433.22	504.26	568.12	643.27	723.18
341.19	433.24	505.03	568.22	644.10	723.20
345.23	434.13	505.05	573.16	644.17	723.26
346.04	434.14	505.07	573.22	644.28	725.12
346.05	434.17	505.08	574.01	646.06	725.13
347.12	434.20	505.12	574.02	646.06	725.16
347.26	434.21	505.27	574.15	646.15	726.01
348.04	434.24	505.28	576.04	647.11	726.23
348.07	436.06	506.08	576.05	647.12	727.23
348.09	436.09	506.16	576.07	648.08	729.02
348.09	436.11	506.20	579.11	648.15	729.14
348.13	436.16	507.01	579.18	649.24	731.02
348.14	436.16	507.07	579.23	651.11	731.06
348.18	437.07	508.02	579.24	652.06	731.10
349.24	437.08	508.23	581.18	655.13	731.23
349.26	437.13	509.01	582.09	658.02	731.26
349.26	437.18	509.05	582.11	658.06	733.27
351.09	437.24	509.23	582.24	658.12	734.10
351.09	437.24	509.24	583.02	658.12	734.16
351.10	438.06	510.10	583.09	658.17	734.22
351.11	438.12	510.10	583.11	662.06	734.24
351.11	438.14	510.15	586.01	662.09	736.28
352.05	439.11	510.13	586.10	669.04	737.19
552.17	440.23	510.24	586.12	670.17	739.04
552.26	442.23	512.01	586.20	670.18	739.06
353.01	446.08	512.09	590.07	670.26	739.21
353.22	446.15	513.10	590.08	672.10	739.22
353.23	446.17	513.13	590.08	672.19	740.22
355.10	446.26	514.05	591.07	673.04	741.11
358.18	447.06	515.09	591.19	673.05	741.14
358.21	448.15	515.15	592.19	674.09	741.16
359.26	448.16	515.16	593.17	674.12	741.17
360.02	450.20	517.19	593.21	674.17	741.28

745.04	799.28	866.26	912.02	039.13	103.05
747.09	801.14	867.01	912.08	042.06	103.06
747.11	801.27	867.01	island	042.07	103.06
747.12	802.27	867.07	180.05	043.13	103.07
748.23	803.11	867.08	410.13	044.14	103.17
750.28	803.11	867.23	isles	044.23	104.10
752.18	804.15	867.28	003.26	046.05	104.18
753.01	804.18	868.02	004.02	046.25	104.21
754.07	813.23	873.05	isn't	046.27	104.23
754.08	813.27	873.15	093.13	047.01	105.08
754.12	814.11	874.14	682.19	047.01	105.14
754.18	814.26	874.16	isolated	047.03	105.20
754.28	814.26	875.03	668.22	047.11	106.19
755.12	815.14	875.16	704.04	048.05	106.22
755.13	816.01	875.17	776.03	048.24	106.28
755.25	816.03	875.18	isolation	048.28	107.07
755.26	816.09	875.21	088.18	049.09	107.09
756.25	816.14	875.21	329.19	050.03	107.12
756.27	817.03	875.28	683.25	050.06	107.14
757.03	818.26	875.28	israelitish	051.23	108.20
757.09	818.27	876.05	368.19	052.24	109.02
757.12	819.03	876.08	issue	053.22	109.03
757.16	819.05	876.08	335.07	054.01	109.03
757.26	819.06	876.19	405.03	054.14	109.08
758.03	819.07	876.19	633.26	054.16	109.13
758.06	819.13	876.19	871.12	054.22	109.13
758.08	819.15	876.20	issued	055.14	110.06
758.20	819.23	876.21	210.15	056.05	111.03
758.25	820.08	877.06	231.08	056.27	112.24
758.28	820.09	877.27	296.01	057.21	113.27
759.03	820.12	877.27	337.02	059.02	115.11
759.10	820.14	878.07	415.24	060.05	115.20
759.12	820.23	878.09	issuing	061.02	116.17
759.28	821.06	878.09	334.15	061.15	116.18
760.01	821.13	878.10	it	062.09	117.11
760.06	822.13	881.03	001.08	063.02	117.19
760.13	822.23	881.08	001.11	063.19	118.04
761.06	822.25	881.13	002.15	064.25	118.17
761.14	822.28	881.15	002.26	065.18	119.16
761.16	823.05	881.17	003.01	066.19	119.17
761.21	823.06	881.17	003.13	067.01	119.22
761.27	824.06	881.26	005.08	067.18	120.03
761.28	824.09	882.02	005.21	069.09	121.03
762.12	824.13	883.18	006.11	069.16	122.14
763.09	826.12	884.01	006.14	069.22	123.10
763.09	826.22	884.11	008.15	069.23	123.12
763.26	827.07	886.06	008.26	072.17	123.15
766.20	827.08	886.07	009.05	072.24	123.18
767.02	827.12	886.26	009.20	073.02	123.27
767.20	828.01	886.27	009.23	073.05	124.10
769.01	828.05	886.27	009.24	073.14	124.11
769.05	828.10	887.07	013.06	073.18	125.13
769.20	828.17	887.08	013.13	075.02	125.26
769.20	829.21	887.09	013.27	075.14	127.17
770.05	833.27	889.12	014.23	075.25	127.26
770.10	834.06	889.22	015.14	075.27	127.26
771.01	835.02	889.26	015.18	076.13	127.27
771.25	835.20	889.28	015.19	076.13	128.07
772.06	836.01	890.03	015.20	079.07	129.05
772.10	837.15	890.04	016.02	079.10	131.16
772.13	838.01	890.06	016.10	079.17	132.12
772.13	838.20	890.09	016.12	080.05	132.17
772.14	838.22	890.20	016.13	080.19	132.22
773.02	838.24	891.09	016.14	081.06	133.14
773.17	839.02	891.12	016.19	081.25	134.06
773.20	839.18	893.25	016.24	082.22	134.11
774.12	839.23	893.27	016.26	082.24	135.01
774.15	840.13	894.09	017.02	083.03	135.18
774.17	840.18	894.09	017.18	083.11	135.18
774.17	841.14	894.16	017.24	083.15	135.23
774.24	842.06	895.01	018.04	083.23	136.26
775.05	842.09	895.03	018.17	084.18	137.01
775.08	842.20	895.05	020.05	086.11	137.07
775.14	842.20	**895.09**	020.28	087.04	137.17
776.14	843.01	895.10	021.17	087.12	137.25
776.24	**843.02**	895.19	**022.02**	**088.06**	138.02
776.24	843.04	895.19	023.02	088.19	138.04
777.03	844.21	895.26	023.06	089.09	138.10
778.05	845.05	897.03	023.09	089.28	138.15
779.06	845.16	897.05	023.27	090.05	138.26
779.09	846.03	898.01	024.07	090.07	140.24
784.01	846.10	898.07	024.11	090.09	140.25
784.05	846.11	898.19	024.26	090.17	141.13
784.09	846.22	899.02	025.01	090.24	141.16
784.24	847.27	899.05	025.04	090.25	141.17
784.28	848.07	899.10	025.07	091.05	141.19
785.03	849.14	899.14	026.19	091.05	141.20
785.05	849.15	899.16	027.11	091.07	141.28
785.06	850.07	899.16	027.17	092.09	144.13
785.12	850.08	900.12	027.28	094.26	145.14
785.21	850.15	901.25	028.09	094.27	145.21
786.19	851.17	901.26	028.12	095.07	145.27
786.22	851.18	902.02	029.14	096.17	146.03
787.07	852.01	902.02	030.24	097.20	146.07
787.10	852.02	902.11	030.28	098.03	146.14
789.08	852.02	902.12	031.10	098.08	146.17
790.06	852.04	908.25	031.11	098.18	147.08
791.01	855.09	908.28	032.11	099.05	147.12
791.11	855.12	909.07	034.04	100.11	150.18
791.14	855.21	909.10	035.13	100.26	151.16
792.10	855.23	909.11	036.01	101.09	151.20
792.12	857.01	909.12	036.02	101.20	152.02
792.17	857.08	909.13	036.02	101.22	152.08
792.19	858.10	910.24	036.04	101.23	152.08
792.22	858.23	911.08	036.05	102.09	152.12
797.13	860.05	911.09	036.13	102.17	152.13
797.17	860.27	911.24	036.20	102.18	152.16
797.19	861.11	911.26	036.21	102.22	152.17
797.20	861.15		037.07	102.28	152.19
797.24	861.18		037.12	103.04	152.19
799.12	865.03		038.23	103.05	152.20

152.20	190.08	231.05	272.07	310.07	363.10
152.22	190.20	231.07	272.08	310.13	363.11
153.03	190.27	231.14	272.20	310.15	367.12
153.10	191.15	231.15	272.21	311.04	367.19
153.11	191.16	231.26	272.25	311.09	367.27
153.22	191.18	231.26	273.02	311.10	368.01
153.23	192.04	232.18	273.04	311.27	368.23
153.27	192.11	232.21	274.04	312.05	368.24
154.03	192.20	233.02	274.06	313.23	369.02
154.10	192.24	233.05	274.07	314.08	369.08
154.14	192.25	233.09	274.15	314.09	370.01
155.07	193.01	233.12	274.16	314.12	370.20
155.21	193.23	233.15	274.18	314.16	371.06
156.01	193.27	234.01	274.19	314.19	372.11
156.10	194.03	234.01	274.27	314.20	373.27
156.11	194.28	234.15	275.10	314.26	376.01
156.23	195.08	234.18	275.11	314.28	376.02
156.24	195.09	235.02	275.24	315.03	376.03
157.08	195.10	236.01	276.02	315.13	376.05
158.02	195.11	236.03	276.02	315.24	376.07
158.14	195.13	236.17	276.04	316.04	376.11
159.05	196.10	236.18	276.15	317.14	376.11
159.19	197.20	237.14	276.27	317.23	376.17
150.13	197.22	237.19	277.04	318.19	377.01
162.01	197.23	238.02	277.27	319.06	377.13
163.19	198.25	238.08	278.02	319.12	377.23
163.25	199.02	238.17	278.02	320.28	378.03
164.02	199.05	238.22	278.05	321.16	378.07
164.04	199.06	238.24	278.06	321.18	380.10
164.15	199.19	239.05	278.06	321.21	381.06
164.20	200.09	239.25	279.03	322.02	381.07
164.26	200.17	239.26	279.04	322.09	381.18
165.03	201.15	240.18	280.05	322.23	382.07
165.13	201.17	242.02	280.12	323.02	382.10
165.16	202.11	242.09	280.17	323.02	382.13
165.17	203.03	245.02	280.24	323.05	383.03
166.02	203.16	245.11	281.03	323.12	384.15
166.14	204.04	246.10	282.11	323.15	386.04
166.16	204.05	247.08	283.04	323.23	386.10
166.16	204.09	247.10	283.04	324.09	386.18
166.20	204.10	247.21	283.21	324.16	387.09
166.28	204.26	249.05	284.04	325.23	387.28
167.02	205.01	249.06	284.04	325.28	389.05
167.07	206.02	249.16	284.06	326.06	389.13
167.16	206.03	250.01	284.06	327.07	389.18
167.18	206.08	250.08	285.11	327.13	390.17
167.25	208.13	250.15	285.20	327.22	392.19
168.04	209.13	251.06	285.20	330.07	392.20
168.05	210.07	251.24	285.21	330.13	394.03
168.11	210.09	251.28	285.22	330.15	394.15
168.12	210.10	251.29	285.23	330.24	395.04
168.17	210.11	253.07	286.03	331.14	395.04
168.22	210.13	253.15	286.08	331.23	395.13
169.06	210.18	253.15	286.10	331.26	395.17
169.14	210.21	253.22	287.01	332.01	395.17
169.18	211.04	255.23	287.09	332.05	396.04
169.27	214.01	255.26	288.18	332.08	396.11
170.02	215.19	255.27	288.20	333.09	396.18
170.11	215.19	256.01	288.21	336.09	396.19
170.13	215.25	256.25	289.10	336.27	396.19
170.16	215.27	257.01	289.10	337.06	396.26
170.17	215.28	257.04	290.01	337.14	396.27
170.18	215.28	257.16	290.04	337.15	397.03
170.22	216.05	258.09	290.19	337.15	397.05
170.26	216.08	258.25	290.19	337.21	397.06
171.06	216.09	259.08	290.24	337.25	397.15
172.09	216.20	260.05	291.10	338.07	397.17
172.17	216.24	260.07	292.01	338.16	397.19
173.27	218.09	260.21	293.09	339.03	397.19
174.06	218.11	260.23	293.17	339.08	397.22
174.11	218.16	261.05	294.08	339.14	397.23
174.12	219.03	261.11	294.13	339.27	397.28
175.13	219.13	262.14	294.22	340.03	398.11
176.23	219.28	262.14	294.24	340.08	399.27
176.24	220.15	263.23	294.28	340.20	400.01
177.04	221.06	264.04	295.07	341.19	400.09
177.27	221.07	264.15	295.14	341.25	400.09
178.03	221.09	264.23	296.03	342.06	401.08
178.06	221.16	265.18	296.24	344.20	403.06
178.17	221.23	265.28	296.27	345.06	403.20
178.25	221.28	266.24	297.03	345.08	403.24
179.03	222.02	267.13	297.19	345.08	403.25
179.06	222.05	267.23	297.26	345.19	403.26
179.08	222.09	267.24	297.27	345.27	403.26
179.09	222.26	268.07	298.03	346.07	403.28
180.08	225.23	268.25	298.03	346.10	404.08
182.17	225.25	269.02	298.23	347.02	404.09
182.20	226.02	269.07	298.25	347.12	404.09
182.22	226.06	269.11	299.08	348.27	404.11
182.24	227.11	269.23	299.11	349.26	404.11
182.25	227.13	270.01	299.18	350.25	404.14
183.17	227.28	270.05	299.21	350.26	404.14
183.19	228.02	270.21	299.22	351.07	404.15
184.12	228.05	270.24	300.07	352.26	404.21
184.14	228.07	270.27	300.12	353.19	404.22
184.24	228.07	270.27	300.17	353.25	404.23
185.21	228.17	271.02	300.21	354.23	404.25
186.02	228.18	271.05	301.09	354.26	404.27
187.04	228.21	271.05	301.14	355.09	406.27
187.15	228.23	271.06	301.23	356.18	406.28
188.03	228.26	271.19	302.11	356.22	407.04
188.19	228.27	271.20	302.25	358.05	407.14
188.24	228.28	271.21	305.11	358.08	407.29
188.26	229.01	271.22	305.20	358.18	408.02
188.28	229.03	271.22	306.04	358.22	408.05
189.09	229.17	271.23	308.17	360.14	408.09
189.10	230.03	271.24	308.21	360.26	409.03
189.11	230.08	271.26	308.23	361.21	409.07
189.16	230.11	271.26	309.15	361.22	410.06
190.02	230.19	272.06	309.26	361.26	
190.07	230.21		310.04	362.05	

410.10	453.24	497.14	536.05	576.08	623.04
410.18	454.02	497.15	536.14	576.15	623.06
410.21	454.06	497.16	536.15	576.16	624.07
411.18	454.25	499.23	536.15	576.18	627.26
412.16	455.18	499.26	536.23	576.22	628.04
412.19	455.20	500.04	536.27	576.23	628.08
414.11	456.02	500.05	537.06	576.23	628.10
415.02	456.05	501.05	537.10	576.24	628.12
415.06	456.12	501.20	538.02	576.24	628.19
415.07	456.18	502.11	538.18	577.03	629.19
415.07	456.20	502.19	538.27	577.10	629.28
415.10	457.04	502.20	538.28	577.11	630.15
415.13	459.15	502.21	539.12	577.13	631.08
416.02	460.09	502.22	541.17	577.18	631.23
416.04	461.11	503.12	542.10	577.18	632.20
416.20	462.15	503.12	542.10	577.19	632.25
417.27	462.25	503.13	542.11	578.01	633.05
413.06	463.03	504.05	542.12	578.01	633.18
418.14	463.24	504.06	542.13	578.01	634.24
418.20	464.01	504.06	542.13	578.09	634.27
419.27	464.06	505.03	542.14	578.12	635.12
420.06	464.07	505.07	542.15	578.13	636.21
420.13	464.11	505.09	542.16	578.14	636.24
421.05	464.21	505.28	542.18	578.17	637.16
421.14	465.07	506.06	542.20	578.18	637.18
421.16	465.20	506.07	542.21	578.19	637.20
421.18	466.01	506.25	542.24	578.22	637.20
422.07	466.27	507.01	543.01	579.14	637.20
422.10	467.06	507.01	543.07	579.23	637.22
422.19	467.13	507.09	543.10	580.05	638.09
423.25	468.13	507.20	543.10	580.08	638.09
424.07	468.14	508.01	543.28	580.08	638.09
424.18	468.15	508.02	544.01	580.20	638.10
425.15	468.16	508.09	544.14	581.04	638.27
426.01	468.18	508.23	544.26	581.04	638.28
426.18	468.19	509.01	545.19	581.18	638.28
426.23	468.19	509.17	546.01	581.24	639.04
426.26	468.19	509.23	547.02	582.04	639.05
427.08	468.23	509.24	548.01	582.10	639.06
427.08	468.25	510.15	548.09	582.11	639.09
427.22	469.04	510.18	548.19	583.02	639.15
428.12	469.10	510.24	549.01	583.03	639.16
428.14	471.11	511.14	549.02	585.14	639.17
428.18	471.12	511.17	550.07	586.09	639.18
428.22	471.17	511.24	551.01	586.13	639.24
429.10	471.23	511.24	552.25	586.25	640.20
429.11	472.09	512.06	553.06	590.03	640.21
429.17	472.11	512.08	553.14	591.21	641.02
430.13	472.15	512.12	553.24	591.24	641.08
430.16	472.16	512.21	555.02	592.03	641.09
431.12	472.17	512.23	555.13	593.17	641.25
431.13	473.17	513.09	555.24	593.20	642.13
431.17	473.27	513.10	558.05	594.14	642.13
431.21	474.14	513.13	558.13	594.17	643.02
431.22	475.04	514.21	558.19	595.02	643.02
431.24	475.23	514.26	558.20	595.06	644.10
431.24	476.26	514.27	559.07	595.25	644.15
431.26	477.04	515.01	559.12	596.03	645.04
432.09	477.12	515.09	559.24	597.20	645.28
432.19	477.18	516.05	560.08	598.13	646.07
432.22	478.09	516.26	560.12	598.14	646.08
433.18	478.22	517.20	561.19	599.15	647.04
433.24	478.27	518.05	562.09	599.17	647.12
433.28	480.16	518.14	562.16	599.18	647.21
434.01	481.01	518.14	562.17	599.19	648.14
434.11	481.13	518.18	562.25	600.20	648.15
434.15	481.23	518.22	563.01	602.17	648.23
434.16	482.03	518.27	563.05	603.12	649.02
434.18	482.05	520.09	563.05	603.12	649.14
435.13	482.09	520.16	563.13	603.23	649.16
435.22	482.13	521.03	563.16	604.16	649.19
436.06	482.22	521.08	564.05	606.15	649.24
436.20	483.17	521.18	564.08	606.17	650.18
436.28	483.24	521.18	564.09	606.17	651.11
437.07	484.10	522.24	565.11	606.18	652.13
437.24	484.13	523.05	566.09	606.19	652.14
437.24	484.25	523.07	566.13	607.05	652.15
438.06	485.08	523.08	567.01	607.06	652.20
438.09	486.01	523.19	567.04	607.21	652.22
438.10	486.03	523.23	567.04	608.03	653.01
438.15	486.12	523.23	567.05	608.04	653.01
439.19	487.17	523.27	567.11	608.06	653.04
441.11	488.04	524.04	568.17	609.15	653.14
445.03	488.04	524.08	568.20	609.17	654.08
445.09	488.07	524.08	568.20	609.17	654.10
445.13	488.10	525.01	568.22	610.14	654.17
445.15	488.12	526.28	569.10	612.04	654.21
445.15	489.04	527.07	569.11	612.28	654.26
445.17	489.08	527.08	569.15	613.01	655.04
445.17	489.09	528.13	569.23	613.05	655.09
445.23	489.14	528.20	570.03	613.09	655.20
445.26	489.16	529.01	570.17	615.24	655.24
447.05	489.23	529.11	570.21	616.14	656.02
447.06	489.24	529.27	571.01	617.01	656.02
448.03	490.10	530.09	571.25	617.05	656.03
448.06	490.13	530.13	572.01	617.12	656.04
448.06	491.27	530.14	572.01	617.14	656.04
448.11	491.28	531.09	572.11	617.14	656.05
448.19	492.07	531.20	572.12	617.19	657.01
448.25	492.18	531.27	572.13	618.24	657.01
449.03	492.25	532.09	573.13	619.09	657.06
449.16	492.25	532.20	573.16	620.12	657.09
449.27	493.04	532.26	573.19	620.22	658.02
450.26	493.15	534.01	573.22	620.27	658.09
451.21	494.11	534.07	573.24	621.02	658.10
452.06	494.17	534.14	574.02	621.03	658.10
452.28	495.01	534.23	574.16	621.16	658.12
453.03	496.07	534.26	575.07	621.23	659.26
453.05	496.10	535.15	575.09	621.24	660.05
453.16	496.22	535.21	575.11	622.10	660.06
453.18	497.03		576.07		660.22

660.24	689.09	733.18	769.20	808.11	845.22
661.16	690.04	734.16	769.23	808.18	846.11
661.17	690.17	734.22	770.05	808.25	846.20
661.19	690.17	734.24	770.10	808.27	847.21
661.24	690.27	734.26	770.18	808.28	847.27
661.24	692.17	735.06	770.26	809.05	848.04
661.26	692.18	735.09	771.01	809.14	848.07
661.26	693.04	735.20	771.02	809.21	848.14
661.27	693.06	735.27	771.03	809.22	848.28
662.01	693.17	737.05	771.05	809.22	849.01
662.09	694.28	737.12	771.08	810.15	849.03
662.15	695.08	737.16	771.10	810.27	849.04
662.20	695.08	737.20	771.12	811.13	849.14
663.08	696.24	739.06	771.13	812.07	849.15
663.08	697.06	739.17	771.28	812.25	849.15
664.28	697.28	739.23	772.10	812.26	849.17
664.28	697.28	739.28	772.12	813.05	849.19
665.03	698.02	740.09	773.02	813.09	849.20
665.20	700.03	740.15	773.19	813.28	849.22
665.24	700.08	740.16	773.20	814.03	849.26
665.26	700.23	740.17	773.20	814.08	849.27
666.18	701.24	741.05	774.02	814.11	850.07
667.11	701.26	741.14	774.09	814.19	850.11
667.12	702.06	741.16	774.17	814.28	851.09
667.15	702.07	741.17	775.08	815.04	851.09
667.28	702.21	741.25	775.15	815.14	852.05
668.05	702.28	742.05	776.03	815.19	852.08
668.06	703.02	742.10	776.24	816.03	852.19
668.26	703.02	743.03	777.01	816.14	852.23
669.04	703.05	744.07	777.03	816.15	852.26
670.17	703.17	744.20	777.10	817.08	852.26
670.24	705.16	744.24	777.21	817.15	852.27
671.01	705.16	744.25	778.05	817.27	853.01
671.17	705.28	745.03	778.06	818.01	853.04
671.21	706.22	746.13	778.09	819.15	853.05
671.23	707.02	746.22	778.17	820.01	853.06
672.01	707.18	746.23	778.27	820.09	853.06
672.12	708.06	747.02	778.28	820.25	853.11
672.13	708.09	747.07	779.17	821.06	853.22
672.15	708.10	747.09	781.07	821.11	854.05
672.24	708.10	747.11	782.06	821.13	854.18
673.10	708.11	747.12	782.16	821.14	854.19
673.11	708.11	747.12	783.01	821.16	854.21
673.24	708.15	748.11	783.02	821.18	854.26
673.24	708.25	750.04	783.08	821.21	855.14
673.26	708.25	750.04	783.21	821.25	855.19
674.01	709.01	750.16	783.26	822.05	855.19
674.10	713.04	750.18	784.01	822.23	856.04
674.10	713.10	750.27	784.19	822.25	856.25
674.12	713.14	751.06	784.21	822.27	856.28
674.13	714.20	751.12	784.23	823.05	858.01
674.14	715.15	751.14	784.26	823.06	858.12
674.14	715.19	751.15	785.05	823.08	858.19
674.15	716.05	751.22	785.07	823.10	859.04
674.17	716.07	753.15	785.08	823.14	859.08
674.17	716.08	753.27	785.08	824.07	859.16
674.17	716.09	754.08	785.10	824.13	859.19
674.18	716.23	754.13	785.12	824.14	860.08
674.19	717.04	754.21	785.12	825.07	861.06
674.26	717.22	754.23	785.21	826.02	861.18
674.27	717.28	754.23	785.24	826.22	861.24
675.03	718.13	754.28	785.25	826.23	861.25
675.04	719.02	755.11	786.22	826.26	861.27
675.09	719.03	755.12	787.19	826.28	861.28
675.11	719.15	755.12	789.02	827.07	862.02
675.11	720.10	755.14	790.26	827.08	862.07
675.12	721.02	755.15	791.11	827.11	862.12
675.18	721.17	755.15	791.16	827.19	863.14
675.20	721.22	755.18	791.25	827.22	863.16
675.23	722.12	755.20	791.26	828.01	863.17
675.23	722.12	755.25	792.17	828.09	863.17
675.24	722.13	755.26	792.23	828.10	863.18
676.02	722.15	756.04	794.03	828.17	863.25
676.08	722.16	756.07	794.16	828.17	863.25
676.12	722.20	756.11	794.27	828.20	864.12
676.27	722.21	756.17	796.07	829.05	864.20
677.24	723.11	756.20	796.13	829.08	864.22
678.02	723.20	757.12	796.14	829.10	865.03
678.06	723.20	757.14	796.27	829.22	865.25
678.10	723.27	757.26	797.01	831.13	866.08
678.13	725.05	758.25	797.03	832.19	866.16
678.18	725.07	759.28	797.05	834.15	866.20
678.18	725.13	760.01	797.17	834.17	866.20
678.27	725.16	760.13	797.19	835.08	867.06
679.13	725.16	761.14	797.25	835.20	867.12
679.15	725.17	761.21	798.01	835.27	867.22
679.16	726.13	763.03	799.28	835.28	868.06
679.25	726.13	763.11	800.06	836.26	869.05
679.28	726.14	763.17	800.13	837.16	869.06
680.02	726.14	763.18	800.14	838.17	870.02
680.08	726.18	763.23	800.22	838.17	870.03
680.09	726.20	763.25	800.24	838.19	870.09
681.13	726.22	764.01	801.11	838.24	870.10
681.25	726.24	764.07	801.12	838.26	870.10
681.26	727.06	764.09	802.12	838.26	871.03
681.27	727.11	764.10	803.08	838.28	871.05
682.04	727.27	764.11	803.12	838.28	871.13
682.19	728.01	765.02	804.02	839.03	871.16
682.22	728.04	765.08	804.04	839.09	871.16
683.17	729.14	766.01	804.05	841.03	871.17
684.05	730.15	766.11	805.07	842.06	871.21
684.18	731.06	766.24	805.09	842.10	872.14
684.21	731.14	767.08	805.18	842.11	873.11
685.03	731.23	767.11	805.23	842.25	873.15
685.11	731.26	767.15	806.03	843.04	874.12
685.20	732.26	767.20	806.14	843.23	874.17
686.01	733.06	768.05	807.02	845.04	874.18
686.02	733.09	768.17	807.25	845.05	874.19
686.03	733.13	768.17	808.03	845.18	874.22
687.21	733.15	768.18	808.03	845.19	874.25
689.08	733.15	769.16		845.21	875.06

675.17	820.09	282.28	625.12	818.17	434.10
875.22	iteration	283.01	628.18	856.24	435.11
875.28	445.20	283.09	631.05	ivory	435.15
875.28	its	283.13	632.17	257.21	435.20
876.08	003.27	285.05	634.08	322.04	436.13
876.13	004.28	290.17	634.18	323.10	438.06
876.19	005.01	291.13	639.08	702.04	438.14
876.19	005.01	291.13	640.15	ivy	438.28
877.06	005.01	296.20	642.11	143.08	442.06
877.13	005.02	302.21	648.17	438.09	442.06
877.27	009.25	306.12	649.18	440.18	442.13
877.27	016.25	320.10	649.23	503.21	442.23
878.12	017.09	333.02	653.18	575.16	442.25
878.13	018.07	333.25	657.09	676.06	448.14
878.13	022.20	337.24	658.16	j'ai	448.14
879.26	032.03	342.06	659.23	212.04	448.21
879.27	032.04	344.22	659.24	234.25	448.21
880.01	032.24	346.03	661.13	j'y	450.11
880.16	050.23	346.19	661.24	264.22	451.24
880.26	058.09	351.02	661.25	jack	452.27
881.03	059.07	355.08	661.25	006.18	454.25
881.13	065.04	358.17	662.01	006.21	455.03
881.13	065.05	361.17	663.23	jacket	455.07
881.15	065.19	364.05	664.24	525.26	456.01
881.15	070.04	367.13	668.12	jail	456.17
881.17	073.09	367.20	674.28	017.15	458.14
882.19	073.19	368.03	675.24	447.15	465.25
882.27	073.19	369.16	676.19	jamaica	467.16
883.13	082.18	369.20	677.04	384.13	467.17
884.01	099.26	372.19	677.25	409.16	480.26
885.09	100.14	372.19	686.28	593.15	481.03
885.12	108.17	373.09	701.02	603.03	482.12
886.07	116.10	377.07	711.17	624.21	483.01
886.13	116.14	378.09	711.17	james	484.01
886.19	119.23	382.15	711.17	358.23	489.18
886.25	125.28	383.06	711.18	jane	495.03
886.28	132.13	385.03	711.19	002.20	496.21
887.08	140.11	385.03	712.13	024.18	496.25
889.19	143.19	387.19	712.15	024.21	504.18
890.14	143.19	402.06	716.33	033.23	505.24
891.01	144.05	404.01	720.25	034.03	506.23
891.17	144.05	404.18	721.16	034.03	507.08
893.19	145.24	405.01	735.12	034.05	507.17
893.27	146.01	409.24	736.07	034.06	509.06
894.03	146.02	414.15	737.17	035.15	509.26
894.09	146.03	414.15	745.22	041.05	510.01
894.16	146.06	421.03	770.22	043.22	510.19
894.21	146.07	422.26	770.25	047.14	511.08
894.22	146.08	423.20	773.25	050.19	513.20
894.23	146.25	435.16	773.26	053.08	514.01
894.23	147.23	440.19	773.27	053.14	514.04
895.26	147.25	441.25	775.15	056.24	514.22
895.27	147.25	445.13	775.16	058.26	515.05
897.03	148.02	453.03	781.24	062.28	515.09
897.04	152.14	461.09	781.24	063.27	515.12
897.05	154.17	465.22	795.12	064.04	515.17
898.18	155.11	468.13	796.19	064.10	515.21
898.19	160.12	468.16	797.05	064.14	516.18
898.20	160.14	471.05	800.27	066.28	517.05
899.08	160.15	474.05	806.20	067.19	517.13
899.08	161.02	474.24	811.02	072.16	518.12
899.09	161.24	476.27	812.18	072.20	519.03
899.10	161.25	477.02	815.26	075.16	523.10
899.16	161.27	480.01	817.05	123.27	523.19
899.19	163.13	485.25	818.02	130.28	523.20
900.04	164.08	490.18	819.15	131.06	524.02
900.07	164.12	492.22	843.26	131.24	524.03
900.12	164.14	492.24	844.06	132.14	524.24
900.13	167.19	492.27	846.28	133.28	525.03
900.22	170.08	502.01	848.28	135.05	525.21
900.26	178.07	502.09	850.19	136.13	525.25
900.28	184.24	502.09	852.24	142.05	528.16
901.06	185.11	502.23	853.05	156.01	528.25
901.23	185.12	508.02	853.06	156.10	530.13
902.02	191.28	510.11	854.23	156.26	530.23
902.06	192.01	514.05	856.25	157.04	532.05
902.11	194.04	514.06	857.12	158.22	532.25
902.25	194.22	521.09	861.02	159.01	533.11
903.01	208.07	521.10	869.09	175.15	533.22
903.17	209.04	521.16	870.22	175.28	546.28
904.02	210.02	542.11	871.01	176.09	547.07
904.03	210.26	542.14	871.08	176.01	548.25
906.08	213.05	542.17	875.15	179.03	550.08
907.12	219.05	542.20	880.01	179.12	552.24
908.17	219.12	547.06	887.05	199.04	557.12
908.25	220.06	550.22	887.13	297.12	565.05
909.15	220.14	554.08	888.06	301.16	565.22
910.18	220.16	555.25	896.14	302.10	566.08
911.16	222.06	557.02	899.05	320.25	566.14
911.22	224.11	557.05	900.04	321.25	567.07
it's	227.15	559.20	900.08	407.09	567.12
028.22	227.17	559.24	900.14	408.01	568.01
068.27	229.20	559.25	902.22	410.02	568.12
175.05	230.25	563.19	903.07	410.03	568.18
395.16	239.27	569.16	907.08	410.05	569.02
417.01	245.01	569.17	907.27	410.18	573.09
679.23	246.02	570.15	908.19	410.22	573.19
799.26	248.03	571.18	912.10	411.19	574.03
863.17	249.12	575.08	912.11	411.28	574.12
863.24	255.06	577.18	itself	421.01	576.04
italian	255.20	578.13	082.21	422.01	577.10
370.26	267.12	591.06	121.22	425.26	578.05
431.11	268.04	594.18	145.20	425.27	580.08
501.06	269.10	599.04	182.18	429.22	581.21
526.15	270.01	599.04	186.05	430.09	582.11
636.05	270.20	599.21	290.09	430.20	585.16
637.03	270.22	600.05	376.03	431.01	587.04
italy	271.12	609.04	471.02	431.14	588.06
288.11	274.23	615.20	638.26	432.11	605.17
item	282.27	618.04	743.12	432.17	605.19
820.09	282.28	620.01	779.21		611.23

611.28	883.26	285.03	684.18	851.19	jovial
612.15	884.01	286.20	685.10	852.10	793.28
613.11	884.18	372.24	685.11	868.01	joy
613.13	884.23	373.01	686.13	873.03	302.20
613.28	885.08	374.20	687.04	873.08	493.03
615.21	885.24	532.16	687.26	873.18	520.02
617.03	887.28	890.28	690.24	873.22	523.26
618.03	890.24	jeannette	691.12	876.01	551.22
618.11	892.04	218.25	691.24	879.09	564.16
619.15	894.08	jellies	695.11	889.09	583.17
620.19	894.11	214.28	695.27	889.12	688.11
621.01	894.17	jerked	695.28	889.21	781.25
621.01	894.21	035.07	697.11	890.09	799.10
621.17	895.19	jest	698.17	890.20	813.23
621.27	896.24	206.05	699.14	891.25	853.10
622.19	897.01	jests	700.28	894.10	858.24
623.01	897.08	387.16	701.17	895.02	882.22
623.20	897.11	411.23	704.16	905.07	898.23
623.28	897.20	jesus	705.03	906.06	906.15
624.07	898.10	720.21	705.11	906.09	907.23
627.05	898.23	762.16	707.28	906.16	912.13
628.01	899.02	912.25	708.18	907.10	912.17
628.06	899.13	jet	709.10	911.14	joyfully
628.12	899.17	661.09	709.23	912.08	797.28
628.19	899.26	jetty	710.01	john's	joyless
628.24	900.14	237.05	714.07	007.17	293.23
631.08	901.04	318.20	717.01	177.16	joyous
634.14	901.18	349.28	717.20	305.17	333.19
635.06	901.22	371.22	720.04	305.18	337.09
637.11	901.18	471.25	725.06	423.26	799.05
638.12	901.20	jeune	725.10	448.05	joys
639.20	902.04	889.22	725.27	449.05	792.20
640.02	902.04	jew-usurer	726.01	474.27	879.24
641.25	902.04	530.18	727.20	703.23	jubilee
642.22	902.19	jewel	727.26	740.09	522.12
643.09	902.21	502.06	733.08	799.08	judas
643.26	907.05	549.08	734.23	812.04	423.28
645.03	910.10	jewel-casket	738.17	847.28	judge
645.06	jane's	016.21	739.06	850.19	047.23
645.15	619.04	jeweller's	741.15	873.12	103.20
645.20	651.10	544.18	742.04	883.14	123.24
645.23	687.07	jewels	747.19	905.20	127.02
645.27	696.20	200.20	748.20	912.18	243.07
646.06	698.22	286.14	751.17	johnstone	246.07
646.13	janet	318.10	752.15	117.14	319.07
646.16	497.17	524.16	753.15	join	340.16
650.03	506.24	524.23	756.03	355.17	355.01
650.10	508.01	524.24	765.02	366.16	597.25
650.19	510.15	529.22	766.01	711.05	602.08
650.23	523.21	570.24	775.03	811.21	602.10
650.26	529.13	899.13	776.18	814.02	610.16
651.12	532.09	jews	779.12	819.19	706.02
656.18	534.13	126.21	779.28	832.06	848.23
708.07	545.14	jingling	780.06	837.23	judged
725.10	564.21	545.23	780.27	joined	272.04
726.28	573.12	joan	780.27	014.17	602.10
774.04	581.03	006.09	782.01	249.05	judges
774.06	582.22	job	783.18	315.19	788.09
774.07	583.09	055.18	785.20	357.15	900.01
774.08	623.22	job's	786.12	590.02	900.02
779.09	640.19	284.10	792.15	590.06	judging
780.06	676.13	john	793.07	608.05	184.04
786.04	680.17	001.17	795.08	626.10	184.23
786.13	680.20	002.01	796.15	joining	376.23
792.22	899.08	006.05	798.17	002.07	judgment
792.26	901.10	006.13	800.23	741.27	020.18
793.15	janian	007.01	801.11	joke	303.02
793.22	495.14	007.20	802.04	389.14	320.23
802.27	january	008.09	803.17	499.17	377.17
804.15	045.09	008.25	806.05	jolting	405.16
805.13	048.05	010.27	806.11	798.12	440.13
807.12	071.03	018.10	807.12	jonah	478.23
811.04	086.04	018.25	807.18	055.18	478.24
811.15	111.09	019.14	809.09	jonas	518.20
813.17	144.08	036.27	810.02	593.13	549.20
815.01	218.04	038.26	810.22	joubert	554.26
816.01	459.18	038.28	811.13	355.19	589.24
816.14	636.15	043.08	812.19	355.23	602.09
818.04	jargon	043.25	813.01	jouberts	647.10
821.16	404.09	062.07	814.25	355.17	829.06
824.12	jasmine	068.13	815.09	joues	847.09
827.10	503.09	107.26	819.11	313.17	866.21
829.20	jaw	177.01	819.19	jour	881.23
829.28	237.10	186.23	819.24	347.08	903.24
834.23	461.17	189.04	821.22	journey	911.02
839.17	jaws	217.22	822.20	039.14	judgments
840.04	395.08	232.14	823.14	071.16	244.21
840.15	jay	287.18	826.05	074.05	596.16
840.25	525.26	298.19	827.18	184.01	judicious
841.03	je	332.09	828.01	190.14	058.04
841.12	168.07	332.13	829.19	316.07	118.22
842.04	169.01	332.19	829.27	316.08	440.16
846.01	170.05	447.01	831.11	381.21	755.26
849.12	170.13	447.03	833.19	455.24	756.12
849.13	171.07	449.06	833.25	461.28	juggernaut
849.13	171.14	451.18	834.01	464.03	126.01
853.21	276.17	469.03	834.18	490.21	julia
876.19	277.11	469.04	835.05	566.14	120.03
876.24	277.11	469.13	837.05	570.06	120.05
876.24	277.17	469.15	839.19	794.06	julia's
876.25	334.05	482.21	839.23	845.28	120.11
876.26	334.06	544.25	841.06	853.19	july
877.20	341.20	545.05	843.01	854.26	560.07
877.27	jealous	565.25	844.23	855.12	652.20
878.06	372.25	586.10	846.27	journeyings	jump
878.19	372.26	596.06	847.16	499.21	328.01
879.21	532.25	598.13	848.10	journeyman	493.09
881.14	895.21	679.27	848.25	698.05	775.17
881.20	jealousy	680.22	849.11	jove	jumped
883.06	200.28	681.01	850.10	388.21	183.10
883.07	282.06	681.17	851.07		201.05

282.01
875.03
jumping
101.14
juncture
431.02
june
151.12
281.22
492.14
522.02
605.24
813.20
852.08
just
004.26
006.15
021.11
029.06
041.17
049.27
050.27
061.10
067.13
069.19
069.21
071.08
073.03
099.11
100.05
101.22
106.11
115.08
116.18
124.10
127.11
150.14
141.02
149.10
153.27
154.27
156.17
177.23
181.20
189.18
201.17
203.26
205.18
214.18
216.15
218.13
221.07
223.11
223.24
224.16
225.22
225.27
228.05
250.07
250.10
251.25
252.10
252.19
254.16
259.27
260.22
267.21
278.06
280.20
286.05
287.18
293.28
294.08
295.22
298.21
300.11
300.25
305.12
311.03
311.06
325.02
328.27
335.05
339.18
348.27
353.22
355.12
358.24
377.16
384.08
386.01
388.12
392.26
393.02
397.01
398.18
415.08
416.18
420.06
428.28
432.14
433.04
435.07
442.26
455.05
458.07
458.15
460.09
460.16
463.08
463.18

466.22
493.25
495.04
495.08
513.14
525.11
526.18
529.04
530.27
548.19
549.04
570.17
570.20
578.20
585.06
586.18
602.03
605.14
614.28
619.14
619.18
623.21
637.13
645.16
660.24
674.12
679.28
685.19
697.06
708.26
712.19
741.17
742.10
754.06
761.11
761.16
767.08
772.10
772.11
778.13
786.06
788.03
793.23
795.20
816.09
827.08
832.10
840.13
841.22
843.10
855.11
857.12
860.15
861.19
865.01
866.21
869.15
874.01
884.19
885.24
887.11
891.09
891.21
899.04
899.28
907.03
justice
048.02
378.27
762.24
782.26
784.23
785.04
785.05
785.09
817.23
900.07
justification
638.04
justified
376.23
440.10
440.24
628.07
724.17
737.24
justify
454.19
justly
273.10
juveniles
387.08
kaleidoscope
471.02
keen
096.07
112.04
155.07
291.17
375.13
377.19
641.19
681.23
702.22
763.23
765.04
805.09
821.02
824.06
keen-eyed
383.06

keener
314.02
865.04
keenest
249.22
600.01
809.18
keenly
101.06
219.28
314.12
373.24
586.04
746.18
keenness
703.28
keep
013.01
054.16
054.18
056.21
091.15
103.22
112.06
113.10
125.22
135.04
147.07
160.10
189.07
190.01
204.20
205.01
252.22
252.26
267.09
272.24
278.06
284.07
284.16
298.26
306.01
325.13
330.04
349.17
353.26
404.03
405.08
417.03
423.04
433.16
437.08
468.27
499.05
538.06
548.20
554.07
555.22
563.13
567.14
581.19
600.16
614.27
622.13
623.16
624.08
632.20
648.04
651.07
667.23
694.16
694.17
705.11
705.19
721.03
723.02
765.15
777.11
783.21
785.09
792.01
795.09
822.06
826.01
837.04
840.09
843.05
846.06
899.08
keeper
616.21
633.17
keeping
002.08
049.02
136.15
488.05
524.17
701.18
709.09
709.11
709.14
744.02
793.13
817.21
866.21
keeps
014.08
235.27
262.14
396.16

747.09
keepsake
236.16
keepsakes
391.20
ken
735.26
kennel
426.22
kept
016.24
021.25
029.27
057.28
098.21
099.14
104.04
165.27
170.02
176.11
184.14
202.06
218.21
234.04
236.21
289.16
294.01
314.28
315.28
323.08
323.16
325.18
325.20
328.21
336.19
377.13
383.01
427.09
448.10
498.16
512.24
545.09
554.21
560.16
596.25
642.17
668.15
694.17
702.28
746.04
771.05
802.13
832.19
855.14
862.05
862.08
863.22
871.22
872.24
903.09
kernel
823.01
key
023.24
190.17
335.19
341.09
419.26
420.09
422.22
426.24
429.24
435.27
444.05
599.03
633.26
654.11
654.13
790.01
791.14
791.15
key-hole
155.01
295.01
keys
187.07
187.09
233.16
863.28
kicked
431.12
kicking
132.12
kidnappers
074.21
kidnapping
074.21
kill
105.28
689.10
832.23
835.13
835.16
killed
018.27
025.05
447.26
killing
835.13
835.16

kills
841.05
kin
444.20
kind
014.14
033.09
036.25
038.06
038.08
046.04
090.15
101.05
106.20
124.01
167.23
191.01
196.20
202.05
203.03
215.10
227.02
243.03
247.08
249.25
253.09
261.19
269.27
325.06
351.10
351.26
365.17
402.02
406.08
457.25
459.10
611.15
613.18
643.04
653.09
654.01
659.17
667.25
683.25
686.04
711.09
713.25
717.23
717.26
721.07
730.10
750.13
824.25
842.19
871.10
880.03
887.04
907.15
kind-natured
213.07
kinder
376.07
500.11
833.06
834.20
kindest
047.15
kindle
321.20
886.20
kindled
139.13
550.22
552.14
562.06
631.07
674.12
740.28
859.14
864.10
kindling
073.03
229.16
296.16
644.12
817.01
kindly
014.20
022.11
186.20
238.19
347.15
459.06
466.04
626.20
660.24
699.16
854.08
kindness
030.09
063.04
126.14
139.10
191.14
214.19
292.17
374.19
484.10
498.01
643.04
651.09

721.25
729.10
744.20
848.01
867.13
908.17
kindred
033.20
292.03
518.04
626.03
727.13
786.28
kinds
215.15
744.13
king
105.26
530.16
813.27
kingdom
121.16
132.21
762.27
874.16
kingly
249.16
kings
055.17
845.02
kingston
384.14
kinsfolk
179.16
242.18
kinswoman
802.17
834.03
kinswomen
781.16
kirsteneu
695.28
kiss
069.23
069.25
154.21
195.05
216.25
251.04
347.16
484.23
523.07
552.09
553.11
555.12
579.21
613.19
613.23
614.28
798.19
807.14
807.24
807.28
813.06
872.13
877.19
888.27
kissed
047.13
136.15
142.08
156.06
159.03
457.13
465.23
519.23
583.24
651.04
746.12
798.08
807.07
807.20
829.13
845.25
877.09
877.24
896.01
kisses
073.23
807.21
807.21
807.24
kissing
175.17
539.23
564.17
646.02
kitchen
030.16
046.11
175.05
217.11
327.03
329.04
334.17
364.13
369.21
393.04
432.21
463.19
654.11

677.07
685.06
693.03
699.13
700.09
729.08
749.10
779.03
781.14
795.05
795.13
811.20
873.18
875.18
905.06
906.19
kitchen-door
274.14
669.11
kitchen-garden
116.28
474.18
kitchens
016.14
knack
047.22
knaves
447.18
knawn't
666.20
679.07
kneaded
261.23
knee
005.28
030.26
046.13
063.24
176.07
188.24
200.13
201.05
241.01
277.15
289.16
318.18
333.10
341.18
445.11
542.12
567.10
576.02
677.04
713.16
857.24
891.06
894.05
903.19
knee-deep
659.23
kneel
398.02
404.01
464.25
kneeling
101.16
361.22
369.04
478.20
569.10
701.12
kneels
126.01
knees
150.23
200.08
223.12
369.25
648.05
656.23
662.04
662.13
850.16
knell
121.11
knelt
191.10
236.28
367.09
380.12
398.07
404.04
650.21
651.03
kne-
008.12
021.19
026.17
027.04
027.11
029.19
035.13
037.20
038.22
065.23
067.01
079.02
088.27
123.10
149.18
150.12

150.24
151.20
153.10
154.11
155.17
161.20
165.12
179.13
202.03
202.04
234.09
237.04
242.27
253.06
253.22
281.23
286.15
292.17
295.07
297.03
301.22
309.13
315.01
343.02
369.26
375.12
384.20
396.24
397.05
403.24
408.12
418.14
457.11
466.19
480.14
494.18
495.25
496.19
502.16
532.15
537.20
549.17
557.12
559.06
562.03
597.20
598.03
603.05
615.28
619.08
620.11
625.14
626.08
629.09
643.23
644.15
652.25
653.14
654.09
671.04
676.16
685.27
689.06
711.02
717.16
742.05
747.01
753.18
774.08
777.22
779.27
780.15
781.10
794.11
800.14
809.08
815.11
836.06
844.23
848.01
848.13
855.07
856.12
856.16
860.13
862.11
864.09
865.09
872.19
882.17
891.26
896.05
896.26
901.08
906.09
906.12
910.04
knife
335.02
428.03
428.07
600.17
633.24
knife-grinders
740.07
knit
099.08
315.26
729.18
733.09
779.23

909.16
knitting
186.13
187.23
216.23
240.24
242.13
251.12
498.18
679.04
722.24
knitting-basket
257.09
knitting-needles
677.27
knittng
676.01
knives
905.07
905.20
knock
233.16
674.19
684.16
851.08
knocked
035.06
036.27
063.12
261.22
667.17
669.10
682.04
830.14
867.20
873.12
875.05
knocker
667.14
knocks
068.03
knoll
194.23
675.13
820.27
knot
407.13
504.02
619.08
knots
046.18
knotted
368.14
510.26
knotty
194.10
870.08
know
010.19
020.19
024.12
036.16
037.18
044.22
044.26
054.08
064.08
074.06
090.10
124.13
127.26
131.05
132.04
132.28
135.05
136.10
157.17
160.07
166.15
168.01
179.19
183.04
189.01
195.19
206.02
226.08
239.18
245.25
255.23
262.07
265.05
267.26
268.07
269.19
270.03
270.05
271.06
271.21
271.27
272.26
273.21
276.21
285.18
285.20
288.21
289.01
293.25
306.15
308.05
309.22
310.05

312.16
316.09
326.02
326.25
330.20
346.23
351.23
356.09
357.02
360.13
363.07
370.14
373.13
388.10
399.05
400.17
400.18
400.27
403.10
403.24
405.27
407.09
409.28
412.14
416.22
430.19
436.24
441.05
442.20
444.13
450.28
453.08
458.28
462.07
463.11
464.15
471.12
472.13
474.02
478.07
480.24
481.11
490.09
493.10
494.16
494.23
503.12
511.06
515.28
518.19
525.24
529.19
529.27
532.27
535.11
536.16
553.22
566.18
569.07
574.04
577.13
581.08
587.19
590.01
593.25
599.05
601.22
602.20
612.15
612.25
613.23
614.19
617.04
617.09
618.01
618.21
623.21
624.01
625.18
635.15
635.18
637.01
639.03
641.08
642.13
643.12
644.17
655.10
662.06
665.10
666.09
673.03
682.26
686.23
687.04
687.20
699.05
705.13
705.21
706.16
707.22
709.23
714.20
715.14
716.24
718.07
723.03
723.26
731.01
731.20
734.18

734.26
736.14
743.11
747.08
749.19
753.01
754.27
758.23
759.07
761.14
761.17
769.15
771.08
771.21
772.11
773.14
777.21
778.06
779.04
779.08
780.17
785.21
786.22
787.05
787.06
809.01
811.23
816.09
816.23
819.23
820.20
833.26
834.28
838.15
838.23
839.23
841.06
842.26
849.19
853.14
855.21
861.18
863.02
864.04
872.11
876.01
884.24
885.11
892.05
892.11
895.02
899.17
900.12
902.06
903.17
906.04
906.14
907.10
908.24
909.03
912.14
knowing
436.20
615.23
717.27
722.09
774.16
861.12
knowledge
140.08
164.13
495.28
615.25
633.16
713.03
759.24
known
016.15
224.28
249.22
310.09
402.27
409.09
437.03
477.22
490.18
512.05
631.23
632.14
693.06
725.05
727.04
749.05
801.22
802.20
811.24
826.22
849.20
852.04
861.28
906.10
knows
037.14
039.18
055.22
093.15
152.13
216.11
270.17
349.23
350.08

391.13
447.25
478.06
568.10
586.17
600.19
623.17
623.21
774.13
837.24
876.01
909.04
knuckles
043.17
261.24
l'essaie
276.17
l'instant
276.18
la
197.12
201.08
201.09
234.21
356.16
labors
322.03
labour
167.20
488.03
664.21
724.10
757.24
786.21
815.16
817.14
842.08
855.26
labourer
759.15
labourer's
720.16
labourers
493.25
666.14
labouring
664.19
labours
250.07
715.06
743.02
795.18
816.18
911.19
lace
005.21
322.21
340.15
343.25
365.21
465.02
525.21
529.23
lacerated
888.17
lachrymose
355.20
687.13
lack
049.20
263.05
431.23
lacked
346.16
500.08
lad
799.19
ladder
208.25
209.15
laden
073.19
503.14
503.28
ladies
038.24
039.02
039.06
046.08
046.10
068.13
081.01
091.24
121.26
122.11
124.21
137.09
179.05
200.06
257.04
316.26
317.05
317.07
317.16
317.25
318.01
318.24
327.05
331.15
333.13
334.12

335.06
335.27
356.05
337.22
338.10
338.21
339.14
340.08
342.09
347.05
348.04
349.13
352.05
365.13
365.27
378.16
379.23
385.16
385.17
387.09
388.13
388.19
401.13
407.20
416.01
416.19
417.03
417.14
442.27
443.19
460.06
460.19
461.21
462.06
472.10
524.18
656.05
676.27
680.18
681.20
683.05
685.09
688.03
694.03
699.08
699.15
703.23
885.24
892.21
906.22
ladies'
333.20
347.22
ladle
905.17
lady
048.19
069.22
076.19
077.17
082.06
082.10
085.19
086.17
091.28
092.07
092.18
099.11
122.07
126.07
126.12
134.23
168.18
171.21
171.27
173.13
178.02
179.12
186.09
186.20
188.09
189.23
193.15
195.02
195.22
197.09
197.27
199.25
200.18
206.15
242.27
261.12
262.18
285.09
313.25
313.26
315.19
319.10
322.23
332.27
337.07
336.02
343.15
344.02
347.12
347.23
352.10
352.10
354.13
354.21
360.28

366.16
372.08
372.14
381.16
381.16
385.24
385.28
386.22
387.25
389.04
392.16
400.11
403.08
450.17
450.18
451.25
498.28
534.23
616.28
665.14
669.23
671.19
691.16
721.25
721.28
773.02
862.05
862.19
862.20
862.23
863.27
895.06
lady's
173.28
226.19
323.01
364.12
534.12
592.22
701.13
lady's-maid
012.14
lady-clock
507.19
lady-like
343.22
lady-mother
356.23
ladyship
354.26
lagging
505.17
laid
011.06
027.19
035.28
079.19
145.14
159.14
173.10
204.12
209.01
227.26
238.09
246.16
273.08
293.11
310.01
330.28
369.04
369.10
374.14
397.08
403.25
412.12
458.01
469.28
484.27
485.20
491.09
517.26
541.22
601.04
607.15
610.02
614.09
646.10
684.24
719.28
747.11
752.22
756.07
756.14
757.14
758.14
759.20
765.07
770.17
794.24
846.17
851.13
lair
307.03
lake
057.23
773.27
844.20
lamb
435.28
436.01
565.20

612.01
845.05
912.06
lamb's
844.28
lamb-like
554.24
lambs
125.15
712.10
lame
719.16
891.15
lameness
144.07
lamentable
003.16
lamentations
487.15
lameter
878.21
lamp
193.16
231.06
286.10
336.26
519.18
599.11
886.18
lamplit
183.12
lamps
073.09
075.15
lances
249.01
land
125.27
199.11
205.11
205.14
247.26
302.26
439.04
445.19
501.05
511.01
530.18
606.10
751.04
819.05
860.02
landed
206.18
565.25
landing
464.12
landlord
205.19
lands
634.18
855.19
landscape
178.25
673.09
855.07
909.23
landscapes
039.07
lane
219.08
219.23
221.06
225.15
231.26
241.18
242.09
667.06
667.10
856.22
lanes
606.02
655.08
language
106.09
127.10
135.17
139.02
139.23
197.17
198.07
198.19
214.09
269.10
275.03
313.10
351.12
483.18
630.08
643.22
647.07
678.16
679.24
679.25
716.12
730.03
743.13
805.21
832.14
837.26
908.27

languid
350.15
languidly
379.03
languish
476.23
languishing
461.07
lantern
023.13
072.25
369.23
798.02
lap
257.20
348.25
524.19
575.23
677.05
726.12
770.23
lap-dog
540.08
lapland
004.06
lappets
365.21
lapse
505.10
689.10
lapsed
069.28
640.04
lapses
282.11
633.24
larder
334.28
large
007.03
007.03
015.24
040.27
053.11
054.03
054.27
060.19
060.21
074.09
076.20
077.28
085.27
089.04
092.14
094.18
139.24
141.14
141.22
149.01
172.14
174.06
181.36
186.13
190.09
198.15
199.13
203.16
204.18
206.27
221.20
248.02
258.14
283.17
310.10
319.13
341.02
343.15
366.25
367.26
382.06
421.02
472.01
472.03
474.12
503.27
504.25
577.11
622.22
677.03
702.02
707.26
714.11
717.12
729.09
737.28
738.28
741.02
750.18
756.06
776.24
800.25
843.04
855.03
910.27
largely
161.08
789.08
larger
184.25
199.13

342.14
626.18
679.05
761.10
largest
015.20
722.27
larks
352.06
lash
363.04
752.12
lashes
085.26
702.03
lass
672.12
lassitude
404.12
last
013.25
016.23
016.27
021.21
022.16
029.08
068.06
072.06
074.24
075.10
083.01
085.09
086.27
096.14
109.18
115.03
116.27
117.16
126.16
153.13
154.21
154.22
156.20
158.20
166.03
166.06
169.15
170.09
171.08
173.17
174.07
176.18
185.07
189.09
191.08
198.02
210.05
227.18
241.18
247.01
255.27
285.14
297.02
299.08
307.03
307.20
311.24
313.08
314.26
315.12
320.17
321.12
332.20
333.17
334.19
334.28
347.01
347.26
348.19
348.27
361.15
367.21
370.15
383.19
391.01
403.11
405.17
426.18
427.04
430.16
436.09
441.20
442.11
447.08
448.08
448.13
448.21
462.21
466.16
468.25
471.27
477.10
482.02
484.05
485.05
487.07
488.12
490.25
495.10
496.06
511.22

515.04
532.07
534.05
537.24
552.11
557.03
563.15
565.17
566.09
569.06
572.12
575.18
575.24
580.20
595.17
596.13
601.12
604.18
606.02
611.07
619.05
621.16
621.17
629.01
630.13
632.28
633.10
638.15
640.04
655.05
661.08
678.01
680.28
682.04
683.24
683.27
685.08
687.26
703.06
705.01
707.20
726.17
729.02
732.14
736.13
737.11
740.03
776.06
780.08
795.16
806.28
810.17
812.27
815.26
818.13
824.03
833.16
836.23
844.26
845.19
846.18
851.11
853.15
856.19
860.19
861.17
867.09
867.16
869.18
870.19
880.25
885.22
886.13
900.22
901.23
903.13
905.22
912.06
912.11
912.19
last-born
457.09
last-named
392.02
lasted
081.10
426.26
lastly
425.10
792.02
latch
766.02
777.17
777.26
870.24
latched
654.20
late
031.02
151.13
188.28
190.01
225.15
225.23
229.18
254.10
314.19
328.21
332.05
379.17
401.14

413.04	879.25	153.18	189.14	198.02	302.15
445.06	laughed	156.24	210.24	372.01	330.05
457.14	061.02	158.17	211.21	384.08	339.15
467.06	175.19	167.25	217.22	639.15	366.04
485.08	227.19	198.27	232.06	724.24	406.14
537.14	329.12	200.27	232.20	747.28	412.25
541.26	345.20	219.05	232.21	748.05	422.04
559.01	392.09	219.11	298.19	817.17	430.06
562.16	436.27	236.27	306.12	893.03	430.18
598.21	444.05	248.23	308.16	leas	433.21
603.20	527.03	260.26	314.13	316.11	439.19
654.15	555.21	268.15	315.12	317.05	449.01
655.24	680.23	287.03	329.20	324.06	450.14
738.24	704.15	294.19	329.22	326.26	469.19
750.05	776.19	296.11	329.26	least	476.27
780.07	798.08	298.10	330.12	006.01	478.01
808.16	806.10	309.23	330.18	032.22	482.19
843.16	885.26	358.10	330.22	046.02	487.03
859.23	laughing	366.24	498.08	047.23	487.04
860.23	100.23	466.03	576.23	052.13	490.11
860.25	177.26	479.10	598.17	086.11	497.24
860.27	411.20	479.18	863.06	113.18	506.22
873.16	411.26	480.09	863.07	135.05	511.17
882.27	445.14	492.16	leah's	138.18	511.23
900.14	566.25	533.21	305.17	165.21	513.09
900.15	740.13	533.24	lean	172.17	513.10
900.26	885.26	534.25	410.04	193.01	514.09
937.07	laughs	540.27	588.06	193.05	543.03
late-found	300.09	546.11	720.12	195.12	543.28
743.01	333.27	551.06	816.15	196.04	558.17
lately	352.27	557.14	896.20	201.02	567.20
101.04	laughter	565.18	leaned	206.07	582.05
157.11	404.22	570.11	066.17	223.26	596.07
260.15	411.05	575.07	184.01	252.07	600.22
295.13	420.22	606.01	466.24	259.09	604.04
359.24	740.17	606.12	591.25	260.04	609.06
379.19	launch	607.19	604.19	269.07	609.13
457.20	287.10	612.03	705.04	274.22	613.09
459.08	launched	651.23	815.22	301.07	613.10
474.15	062.02	651.25	leaning	311.22	613.10
563.18	375.03	654.23	027.02	312.20	620.08
586.06	launddress	656.20	044.01	315.15	621.26
768.23	117.09	661.16	121.01	318.02	622.03
later	laundress	672.22	142.23	326.13	630.16
005.25	122.19	673.16	208.28	331.18	632.10
154.03	laurel	674.21	227.26	344.07	642.13
356.17	518.28	689.06	262.21	354.09	650.22
490.13	laurel-walk	716.26	332.13	356.14	657.07
675.16	505.25	763.06	404.05	362.19	666.26
779.06	514.25	818.23	484.26	382.08	699.20
latin	laurels	820.27	496.24	393.05	706.28
140.13	502.25	850.23	811.07	399.23	707.11
676.09	lavish	866.02	827.16	403.09	717.10
latmos	325.14	872.26	833.17	410.21	721.13
250.24	lavishly	874.27	874.24	496.02	732.23
250.25	375.23	880.26	leans	511.25	736.15
latter	625.04	887.25	289.07	525.01	742.07
043.25	law	888.06	338.14	529.13	768.28
068.03	177.06	laying	352.20	536.07	769.25
425.12	273.23	273.14	644.11	557.06	777.15
433.16	439.11	330.02	leant	567.15	785.08
624.19	508.03	601.25	088.20	598.02	787.24
latterly	592.23	616.14	281.17	609.10	804.28
162.18	602.09	le	337.19	617.19	819.04
593.11	627.25	234.23	390.10	619.26	828.13
717.07	647.13	313.16	421.07	637.17	831.02
lattice	648.04	389.05	465.04	661.03	834.19
549.24	732.05	lea	733.03	661.21	834.23
latticed	784.23	066.23	733.08	667.09	843.07
089.08	lawful	169.24	leap	669.05	845.23
190.20	590.07	064.17	465.02	673.26	850.14
676.05	lawfully	lead	leapt	679.16	851.05
711.17	590.02	176.26	519.06	679.21	864.26
761.14	law-giver	227.08	855.18	683.27	864.27
871.02	813.27	321.22	learn	685.02	867.14
lattices	law-givers	409.18	038.20	720.13	877.10
856.27	797.08	708.15	055.25	722.08	881.24
laugh	law-less	897.14	097.05	734.21	885.10
210.06	838.24	903.26	103.20	754.07	885.22
210.07	lawn	leader	103.24	767.14	891.19
210.18	003.14	388.25	130.03	768.01	894.03
210.26	023.13	713.09	203.06	806.24	894.17
211.02	193.26	797.22	216.26	853.20	894.20
211.03	194.07	816.09	245.05	861.04	895.15
216.25	197.02	leader's	263.24	885.15	907.22
217.02	209.02	371.09	275.23	897.11	leaven
217.05	230.14	leading	526.18	902.02	175.26
275.12	235.11	240.25	658.19	leave	176.10
275.13	445.12	503.19	713.21	015.07	313.25
275.14	502.23	712.05	730.05	037.10	444.16
294.27	550.19	736.21	805.15	037.12	446.09
296.07	859.02	leads	807.25	059.24	447.28
298.05	laws	208.22	861.09	067.24	457.12
300.05	648.07	215.03	893.14	068.19	leaves
300.06	813.26	leaf	learned	069.18	003.11
306.18	lawyer	090.02	040.17	071.10	031.14
308.19	593.24	542.08	126.11	102.07	032.03
308.24	595.14	leafless	142.20	117.16	066.15
309.04	596.18	001.05	159.13	157.09	144.19
345.20	786.10	050.12	243.20	158.22	219.21
350.24	lay	219.12	399.06	169.04	248.13
350.27	002.03	leafy	624.18	173.19	441.16
389.13	016.28	434.23	625.27	180.17	561.05
396.02	047.02	494.05	learning	239.02	631.12
514.15	062.10	606.05	178.22	245.14	676.07
535.22	080.23	leagues	328.27	262.01	871.07
565.12	130.07	786.08	698.15	264.02	leaving
565.14	145.08	leah	744.03	284.21	159.09
740.17	146.21	187.05	805.14	293.17	205.14
776.19	147.03	187.25	learnt	298.27	221.07
806.22		189.03	179.07	301.01	225.14

266.02
286.03
438.10
492.12
505.16
519.24
522.22
579.20
624.09
650.12
700.27
724.27
727.16
736.06
803.27
819.04
819.21
858.17

lecture
035.15
121.28

lectured
122.19

lectures
244.19

led
021.16
040.02
076.05
077.26
153.26
190.16
198.11
209.27
219.25
243.01
253.09
361.21
370.12
456.15
502.27
604.23
626.17
654.26
656.14
663.28
675.04
675.12
700.19
871.03
887.17
898.17
904.01
910.23

ledge
575.22

lee
047.20

left
003.08
009.09
017.05
017.10
024.19
045.02
050.01
060.13
064.24
072.03
074.14
076.06
077.06
077.17
083.25
087.14
099.13
101.04
109.02
129.12
133.24
134.26
144.17
151.28
162.24
164.01
174.17
176.03
181.19
193.07
197.20
202.15
206.23
230.23
235.08
253.13
277.27
280.18
286.10
288.01
294.15
295.22
295.27
299.09
314.11
335.23
353.16
363.13
364.15
409.06
412.05
417.27

418.25
422.21
435.23
435.28
448.22
451.11
459.18
465.10
467.20
470.09
471.27
486.13
487.11
488.04
491.10
491.16
501.18
510.25
520.12
523.02
539.12
543.02
562.23
583.23
598.10
624.21
634.20
640.04
646.15
647.23
651.19
653.01
655.11
655.20
656.11
657.14
661.17
662.28
663.16
666.28
668.19
689.13
690.08
690.28
691.18
692.06
692.17
692.28
698.19
706.26
717.23
724.23
728.02
733.13
734.17
741.21
741.28
742.18
747.20
770.21
771.13
772.01
773.04
774.24
777.13
780.10
785.08
794.10
812.13
819.16
829.15
830.13
833.11
834.12
845.25
846.03
851.11
854.13
860.15
872.24
873.20
873.24
878.07
879.04
879.24
888.07
888.09
888.19
894.12
906.19
908.13
911.14

leg
013.11
223.21

legacy
775.24
783.02
787.27

legal
598.05
627.26

legalize
273.26

legends
208.11

legible
516.26

legion
615.21

legitimate
264.22
359.24
736.10

legs
123.23
769.24
777.14

leisure
034.27
147.09
378.09
601.24
724.09

leisurely
183.27
191.03
720.25

lend
013.09
090.05
482.25

lendings
407.15

length
031.16
045.04
074.07
183.28
250.03
255.19
259.11
262.25
348.16
480.02
788.01
788.08
795.03
912.17

lengths
012.11
754.21

lenient
377.11

lent
713.04
779.16

les
334.05
334.06
334.07

less
012.20
016.08
018.25
020.26
027.08
037.08
048.11
053.20
066.01
090.20
103.11
135.21
142.18
185.02
185.02
186.12
211.15
211.15
240.04
258.23
269.28
286.25
312.04
323.10
343.21
375.27
376.23
382.12
459.28
518.06
527.19
531.21
554.12
554.27
625.23
713.24
719.09
734.12
752.26
756.02
760.07
779.20
848.02
879.12
895.22
910.17

lessened
144.03

lessening
575.20

lesson
086.20
086.26
097.23
098.13
098.20
104.27
534.24
746.18

lesson-books
078.21

lessons
083.08
086.24
087.03
094.12
097.05
097.17
103.24
522.24
714.03
810.07

lest
022.24
126.18
154.17
170.27
437.28
549.07
694.27
828.22
843.05
881.22

let
024.01
024.23
025.04
049.17
064.08
077.04
086.07
089.13
117.20
123.19
127.02
127.04
130.02
132.11
132.12
140.24
148.15
158.17
179.05
184.19
184.22
185.05
200.09
203.27
215.26
221.08
227.14
235.11
236.20
237.26
251.02
256.07
266.21
274.15
274.16
285.28
298.18
320.02
321.19
322.18
338.22
339.18
359.27
359.28
368.27
386.16
387.09
397.09
405.12
409.01
410.06
414.03
416.22
427.12
432.01
433.25
433.25
433.26
436.24
441.06
455.05
458.08
464.14
467.08
469.09
483.17
484.21
506.25
513.28
515.05
516.21
538.12
538.12
538.15
538.26
540.04
562.09
565.24
569.11
569.25
604.03
610.08
610.08
620.13
625.24
628.19

630.19
632.06
638.14
645.24
649.21
671.08
682.20
683.05
684.02
684.28
685.16
687.26
688.01
694.24
708.17
709.01
714.24
719.12
730.28
731.09
753.09
758.09
767.09
768.11
780.19
780.19
784.25
784.26
812.19
813.05
820.15
821.08
821.23
824.09
833.20
863.28
868.06
869.08
873.07
878.15
881.24
883.23
887.23
888.10
899.06
904.03
911.28

lethargic
470.12
479.19

lethargy
457.25
690.25

letter
056.16
165.08
168.09
169.11
171.05
177.21
218.14
225.26
226.09
229.02
325.27
482.05
482.07
496.16
544.24
602.25
632.15
725.27
726.12
726.24
727.17
768.16
768.24
772.08
772.16
779.15
809.20
810.14
907.06
907.11
907.14
910.09
912.11

letter-press
003.19

letters
169.22
170.05
469.06
772.26
777.03
853.15
855.17
859.10

letting
019.25
462.07

leurs
334.06

Levantine
370.27

level
054.01
106.04
208.26
213.19
270.16

673.28
807.19

levelled
043.15

lever
356.19

leviathan
284.11

lexicon
679.24

liable
012.09
274.04
285.20

liaison
637.02

liaisons
356.26

liar
061.08
062.08
126.02
130.27
515.25
647.07

liars
057.22

liberal
205.19

liberal-handed
746.13

liberality
146.25

liberally
104.14
136.22
297.01

liberate
025.02

liberated
287.21

liberty
038.14
063.21
080.08
100.19
140.13
150.01
165.15
165.15
166.17
235.07
257.28
356.13
400.23
409.10
411.11
431.09
463.04
488.23
514.10
546.18
631.13
741.05
753.04
791.04
806.20

library
031.08
202.11
218.12
233.08
234.08
245.09
245.13
246.08
292.21
300.20
306.05
327.01
380.03
387.27
388.03
389.03
391.06
394.02
411.12
413.03
502.15
562.02
566.04
613.03

library-door
389.11

licence
619.20
899.02

license
147.05
700.10

licensed
100.17

lid
256.13
404.12
485.26

lids
321.15
349.18

Lie
021.16
064.16
064.17
156.27
161.15
310.03
328.01
348.25
418.24
505.22
580.15
600.03
624.25
673.26
875.07
875.02

Lied
472.17
629.12

Lies
016.23
062.09
228.06
320.28
359.01
457.24
479.26
640.25

Life
023.21
030.12
034.18
059.15
070.04
068.28
108.20
109.01
116.04
132.17
133.07
146.05
160.04
161.28
164.15
172.14
174.21
176.27
179.16
180.26
191.27
215.06
215.28
216.04
216.13
220.17
224.24
228.19
230.05
241.13
243.21
253.10
268.11
269.18
269.20
270.19
270.26
271.11
292.03
301.04
301.10
312.03
314.01
320.26
321.21
346.16
364.08
379.08
382.07
382.08
394.19
397.12
400.12
410.16
422.11
424.01
425.07
436.06
436.22
439.07
439.17
440.07
440.28
444.06
447.07
473.13
476.11
482.18
486.10
488.28
506.16
510.09
511.25
514.17
521.09
526.17
559.22
555.22
561.03
566.19
568.24
570.10
570.11
579.01
583.21
584.05
586.05
605.18
605.21
608.08
613.04
622.04
622.17
630.13
638.17
639.02
643.03
644.12
644.25
646.14
650.27
653.26
662.22
663.22
664.21
673.03
705.20
713.12
715.07
717.11
719.25
723.22
725.07
730.15
735.13
735.20
745.06
751.15
756.07
775.13
782.19
783.02
784.19
790.20
791.21
796.18
797.17
810.04
811.23
816.17
817.01
818.26
819.12
822.16
833.14
838.11
842.12
845.01
846.14
847.19
857.07
858.27
859.17
863.25
864.21
871.09
871.10
877.14
878.13
882.19
883.20
885.02
897.25
901.02
903.26
908.20
908.28

Life's
208.18
282.19

Life-giving
800.17

Life-like
607.20

Life-long
785.19
907.08

Lifeless
421.10

Lifetime
745.21
759.06

Lift
009.19
201.19
340.19
398.03
521.15

Lifted
023.04
073.25
075.18
100.25
127.14
127.20
237.20
247.27
256.14
260.25
282.22
312.02
368.24
539.23
549.10
583.01
590.11
594.21
599.07
608.03
641.18
652.03
657.01
678.13
686.07
737.16
740.14
775.09
872.19

Lifting
026.11
063.24
200.15
283.12
283.28
482.25
503.26
600.01
766.01
777.17
903.19

Lifts
858.12

Ligature
013.12

Light
023.06
023.12
024.05
029.06
060.23
067.02
071.07
072.25
073.01
075.15
076.10
076.18
078.09
079.22
085.25
089.14
103.14
113.16
122.06
127.14
133.24
154.12
154.28
166.09
181.12
196.11
202.17
207.06
211.27
229.16
236.11
236.27
247.27
258.13
259.04
271.23
289.09
299.05
299.16
308.13
333.25
342.07
344.07
350.25
351.20
369.22
382.26
394.11
398.03
416.04
419.09
420.16
423.12
426.02
426.19
435.08
435.16
458.17
464.20
495.21
502.05
503.05
521.17
551.17
576.10
576.16
594.17
615.19
640.21
643.17
651.27
662.17
674.03
674.08
675.01
675.08
675.12
675.28
676.19
682.07
714.20
722.11
735.22
755.13
786.26
798.15
804.12
817.01
844.04
845.06
858.11
870.21
882.19
909.24

Light-footed
437.20

Light-heartedness
791.17

Lighted
065.08
236.25
501.07
658.20

Lightens
845.05

Lighter
002.15

Lighting
281.02
327.18
396.04
562.10

Lightly
113.07
277.14
441.16
541.20
806.05
824.11

Lightness
067.13
342.22

Lightning
225.03
520.05
520.15
539.16
763.23

Lightning-struck
896.11
896.16

Lights
033.16
076.02
184.24
185.13
249.01
365.09
472.07

Ligue
201.08

Like
002.20
003.04
004.16
008.02
009.11
010.01
010.01
010.02
012.39
012.12
013.06
015.23
016.11
017.25
018.13
020.07
021.27
028.06
031.01
032.27
035.03
037.22
038.04
038.09
038.10
038.20
038.21
039.16
039.27
041.12
043.23
044.07
044.20
052.16
054.11
055.15
055.19
058.19
058.26
064.01
068.07
068.20
075.13
077.23
079.16
080.23
084.12
090.07
093.05
093.07
094.10
103.16
103.25
105.25
113.12
121.11
124.01
124.25
128.01
128.10
141.14
146.10
148.15
158.22
166.17
169.15
171.20
174.27
175.09
177.09
178.02
181.02
186.11
187.17
187.20
190.08
194.14
195.01
195.07
196.21
196.22
199.02
199.09
202.02
204.02
204.04
205.08
205.15
205.17
207.10
209.02
210.03
219.21
228.13
228.25
229.19
231.25
231.26
238.25
245.18
246.21
248.23
252.23
260.18
261.10
264.02
264.18
267.04
268.14
268.15
272.27
275.01
280.04
282.25
282.25
282.26
282.27
283.04
283.26
283.27
284.04
284.04
284.06
285.12
285.14
286.09
300.07
317.21
318.05
318.08
339.01
339.08
339.16
344.14
345.03
345.16
346.18
348.03
348.13
348.13
349.22
352.23
358.20
370.24
375.21
375.21
376.08
377.02
377.19
378.22
385.22
386.11
393.01
394.11
395.16
395.23
398.17
399.24
400.03
400.08
401.16
404.08
405.15
416.28
417.18
420.18
425.22
428.06
430.16
433.06
435.15
437.12
445.20
448.23
456.08
456.13
467.25
467.25
468.11
468.17
469.04
469.04
480.26
480.26
484.04
495.06
496.05
496.23
498.11
501.06
505.13
508.26
510.05
512.09
512.26
514.04
524.24
527.16
527.17
527.24
527.25
527.26
528.18
531.01
531.22
536.22
537.19
539.15
542.23
544.16
545.01
545.02
547.02
548.10
549.05
550.02
550.03
554.04
562.05
565.04
570.17
575.19
578.01
579.12
581.18
591.15
596.04
597.15
599.18
606.15
611.11
616.13
619.12
620.05
620.11
628.01
629.23
629.27
630.01
631.28
635.07
637.15
637.20
637.22
650.01
655.06
656.18
657.15
661.09
662.16
664.22
668.24
669.07
675.20
676.21
677.10
677.20
678.18
678.27
679.19
680.21
680.22
681.01
681.05
683.13
687.22
690.17
694.05

695.28	207.18	**limbs**	**linnet**	388.01	013.14
696.26	234.01	007.05	639.07	424.04	014.03
696.27	253.17	033.03	**lion**	424.05	017.20
698.09	281.06	260.17	645.23	477.16	018.27
698.11	289.18	275.19	881.06	503.14	020.10
698.14	291.11	415.24	**lion-like**	507.16	031.24
698.28	292.11	563.24	222.01	511.09	032.14
699.03	315.06	597.06	**lip**	549.01	034.21
699.23	330.05	611.02	228.04	561.19	041.10
700.04	346.01	656.19	345.22	569.05	041.15
700.10	346.24	660.16	357.26	623.25	043.07
701.06	370.15	675.03	363.13	631.08	046.27
701.24	382.12	689.16	381.03	639.27	049.03
705.10	391.24	822.19	431.18	678.03	050.11
708.21	459.04	877.05	595.23	678.06	051.27
714.05	496.12	**limit**	725.27	678.14	052.22
714.05	536.07	117.12	740.09	713.18	053.07
716.20	549.18	215.06	740.10	843.23	053.11
722.16	553.26	828.20	767.15	846.05	053.17
723.10	620.13	**limits**	768.04	858.28	054.05
739.07	635.20	111.13	836.05	875.15	054.20
739.15	635.24	164.23	838.10	**listened**	054.21
740.01	642.04	747.25	**lips**	039.12	055.16
742.04	643.06	**limped**	083.20	047.05	055.21
744.07	698.15	227.27	120.25	116.11	055.27
745.04	711.03	**limpid**	139.22	139.06	056.17
747.14	711.13	269.01	177.12	229.06	058.18
748.17	711.13	**lindeness**	258.24	298.11	060.04
748.27	713.21	003.27	281.03	299.10	064.16
749.03	744.08	**line**	301.18	314.12	067.04
750.11	748.21	042.13	360.16	314.13	067.20
754.06	748.21	113.07	396.07	337.10	068.02
754.12	751.11	117.01	396.22	379.03	068.07
754.13	768.21	140.17	402.03	433.01	068.16
754.15	789.11	274.15	402.10	459.09	069.10
754.28	863.07	322.01	409.20	640.08	069.22
755.12	890.25	465.22	422.08	653.21	074.05
755.25	**likelihood**	546.10	422.12	660.10	074.16
757.07	023.12	555.01	423.06	660.21	075.16
757.22	672.27	563.01	426.10	685.01	077.03
763.11	**likely**	637.10	475.03	731.11	077.07
767.06	153.22	655.04	484.24	845.17	077.12
767.16	178.09	678.15	513.02	846.03	081.18
769.20	180.14	678.17	513.19	850.02	082.03
771.11	198.08	678.24	513.20	903.01	084.11
777.05	210.19	809.22	523.14	**listener**	084.24
778.28	308.06	863.20	533.24	287.02	084.24
781.23	308.24	**lineament**	555.08	401.25	087.27
783.23	316.18	552.16	573.14	402.08	092.25
784.17	323.02	677.13	578.06	770.05	093.07
784.18	326.21	**lineaments**	588.23	901.20	097.04
792.09	338.07	007.04	590.15	**listening**	098.07
796.15	345.09	127.28	595.05	045.20	100.15
800.17	346.22	248.19	608.06	105.01	105.07
802.13	379.17	322.17	610.20	105.10	107.02
809.21	428.24	450.04	613.01	114.09	109.22
809.22	455.11	578.04	619.16	194.25	112.11
810.09	456.20	702.01	623.07	294.04	113.18
811.07	524.09	737.26	623.14	334.02	113.24
815.05	629.14 '	796.24	643.07	480.06	114.14
816.13	669.22	855.06	650.27	511.10	116.10
816.14	682.19	882.23	653.27	515.01	119.07
817.04	691.15	**lined**	657.15	549.21	121.01
826.20	730.10	430.25	672.05	611.08	121.27
827.04	756.01	438.08	686.02	653.15	125.15
837.05	**likeness**	**linen**	689.16	716.25	125.28
837.11	249.15	122.22	701.19	765.09	131.12
847.19	289.26	421.11	738.06	800.22	133.15
848.15	345.17	460.25	747.08	853.07	136.26
849.03	472.12	652.25	752.10	**listless**	137.12
853.01	481.03	**lines**	756.06	346.15	137.20
853.02	515.17	053.12	763.24	**listlessness**	138.15
854.25	528.16	160.10	770.09	380.04	140.23
855.06	**likes**	283.01	801.08	**lit**	143.11
863.05	214.23	397.25	827.21	071.13	148.05
863.10	352.23	398.02	835.14	089.07	148.26
864.09	757.01	691.20	843.24	127.28	152.01
864.25	757.03	720.26	872.14	231.05	153.11
865.01	**likewise**	886.16	875.15	233.10	155.27
877.02	047.03	**linger**	877.22	258.12	156.27
877.03	097.14	457.18	879.06	276.14	158.21
878.22	344.19	475.06	896.06	286.10	159.15
879.09	366.23	663.14	901.18	306.01	169.23
880.15	567.19	**lingered**	904.02	307.20	170.01
881.09	882.11	152.01	**liquid**	317.15	171.12
884.13	911.05	209.26	139.17	336.26	175.20
884.22	**liking**	220.07	431.21	342.07	175.23
889.14	214.17	224.07	432.02	492.26	175.26
890.24	278.04	230.13	**lisle**	519.18	176.15
891.18	418.22	230.13	093.03	562.03	184.09
894.21	889.17	387.11	489.03	582.07	186.09
895.10	**lilac**	426.06	**lisp**	765.10	187.06
898.19	545.24	426.07	200.28	782.18	187.18
911.21	**lilies**	485.13	256.25	795.05	188.08
liked	148.04	563.05	**list**	798.02	189.19
001.11	343.14	594.12	328.26	798.24	189.25
002.24	**lilliput**	**lingerer**	401.08	**literal**	191.06
079.05	031.21	586.01	**listen**	546.25	191.20
090.14	**lily**	**lingering**	051.06	703.24	192.21
131.13	586.05	462.05	122.23	893.27	193.21
131.14	737.22	659.11	166.20	**literally**	194.19
148.17	**lily-flower**	684.09	269.24	796.20	194.28
148.17	357.10	829.21	269.26	909.18	196.05
149.05	**limb**	832.18	272.07	**literary**	196.14
149.19	248.09	**lingerly**	285.10	735.14	196.20
149.23	262.25	032.26	319.06	**literature**	197.01
159.15	348.16	**links**	321.25	202.17	197.22
195.08	406.28	160.10	336.24	752.25	199.01
200.09	481.13	704.05	337.05	**little**	200.14
205.09	664.07	779.25	352.09	002.17	200.23
205.15	881.12		379.05	003.20	201.10

203.06	523.12	893.07	860.20	712.14	088.17
203.10	523.13	894.11	882.20	lock	100.24
203.27	527.11	895.22	882.21	011.04	151.17
210.01	527.12	898.20	livelier	023.23	194.15
213.15	529.03	899.17	050.10	190.18	194.28
214.16	532.04	907.20	191.06	419.27	210.12
218.19	532.19	908.17	738.04	422.22	218.28
219.20	533.12	live	881.01	426.25	229.22
220.02	533.19	009.10	lively	611.11	289.06
224.19	537.04	037.06	032.21	654.07	502.24
227.01	537.17	062.22	046.11	654.13	542.19
229.22	542.03	063.04	175.12	locked	638.17
231.01	542.10	064.19	213.09	017.13	659.06
234.10	546.03	091.04	316.25	025.13	732.25
234.16	549.02	092.13	352.06	063.07	732.26
236.15	550.12	109.21	352.21	075.27	742.01
239.16	552.05	118.28	365.02	136.06	752.19
245.07	553.14	132.06	400.23	169.03	781.19
245.16	557.09	140.01	401.23	202.13	877.14
254.02	557.14	140.02	437.21	328.22	878.28
255.22	561.03	176.01	748.15	557.07	lonesome
258.01	562.13	176.02	livery	654.19	680.09
259.23	570.07	200.01	746.08	726.24	859.09
260.09	572.22	201.24	lives	790.01	long
260.12	573.09	202.02	184.09	811.14	001.11
264.11	575.06	225.27	551.06	850.17	003.16
264.25	582.09	242.22	596.21	888.07	014.05
265.09	583.16	405.05	695.10	locket	026.09
266.22	583.18	436.03	866.15	652.26	029.09
268.23	583.24	436.12	889.27	locking	031.01
276.14	596.13	446.11	livid	015.13	031.23
276.28	610.24	450.18	247.24	locks	032.19
281.23	612.01	487.19	479.19	084.08	032.26
287.07	617.03	511.21	519.05	255.17	033.04
289.07	620.20	540.16	606.12	600.13	036.08
289.16	624.11	542.23	623.08	681.13	039.13
291.09	625.03	543.22	lividly	702.04	041.16
299.07	638.26	552.10	837.12	753.25	043.02
310.13	640.02	553.04	living	881.05	044.26
314.26	642.20	615.02	121.09	lodge	047.04
315.19	642.24	616.18	186.25	049.27	051.21
317.04	651.10	621.18	194.15	071.11	058.17
326.13	662.28	622.13	408.17	073.02	062.22
331.17	664.24	622.16	460.17	176.02	073.16
335.04	667.03	629.14	476.11	457.01	074.19
340.16	667.10	631.22	485.10	459.14	075.08
342.02	668.06	636.25	488.26	480.21	075.11
343.06	670.02	637.17	513.03	508.25	075.20
347.11	671.10	637.25	541.11	509.15	077.10
347.13	672.06	646.24	560.25	509.25	078.04
352.19	673.06	646.26	569.24	661.04	078.13
352.21	680.01	653.25	573.17	682.19	078.20
353.14	685.20	663.08	592.05	lodged	079.17
362.24	686.13	664.22	593.22	616.04	079.20
373.16	690.15	685.20	593.23	633.01	081.20
375.27	691.07	695.12	595.13	661.20	082.13
380.12	691.13	724.12	595.15	lodging	085.10
383.23	693.11	726.17	602.18	547.19	085.26
384.16	697.14	730.17	605.12	660.19	086.02
389.09	698.25	745.02	615.19	671.22	093.17
391.06	700.24	753.10	622.24	loft	096.09
394.10	701.28	760.02	631.15	114.15	096.12
398.18	702.16	767.19	632.09	loftier	097.06
399.01	712.07	784.17	635.26	258.16	097.10
407.03	712.10	799.22	647.16	loftiest	100.12
410.12	725.22	819.07	673.04	344.04	102.01
413.25	729.03	838.08	674.27	lofty	114.09
427.23	729.15	840.23	704.05	194.13	115.06
431.04	729.19	867.25	731.15	203.20	115.14
431.04	730.07	876.11	777.23	258.15	130.14
431.14	733.15	878.15	861.11	541.23	131.22
432.22	734.10	879.04	861.15	762.04	133.22
433.04	749.01	902.24	866.23	796.23	139.20
437.10	749.10	907.18	876.28	logical	153.05
438.17	749.14	908.25	877.04	192.26	156.20
441.23	751.23	lived	lizard	london	157.02
444.15	753.28	039.03	663.09	091.25	169.10
444.18	754.19	147.11	663.11	172.11	169.14
445.05	758.16	148.17	lizzy	176.18	170.08
446.16	760.13	151.17	006.08	179.28	170.08
455.01	766.05	184.07	lloyd	324.06	171.19
455.26	766.25	200.03	027.11	447.02	172.19
456.14	769.25	205.20	033.28	451.17	173.15
457.05	784.03	243.12	035.09	473.05	177.19
458.14	792.19	243.21	035.20	487.07	183.22
458.23	801.01	265.15	035.24	491.17	185.18
461.01	802.06	310.11	037.01	496.13	189.17
461.18	802.14	312.14	039.19	524.16	190.13
468.22	802.24	370.16	039.27	557.10	190.20
473.25	804.23	396.24	042.02	557.16	191.05
474.06	807.27	424.13	135.27	566.15	193.10
479.13	812.22	446.09	136.10	570.23	200.03
481.15	813.22	447.18	141.28	592.20	201.28
484.20	820.07	452.18	load	699.02	209.26
492.16	833.18	477.08	142.11	774.15	218.13
493.08	835.07	486.09	525.04	910.19	222.02
497.19	843.03	511.24	loaded	lone	229.24
498.06	851.12	622.25	019.16	017.27	230.06
506.09	862.04	627.07	630.22	765.14	230.10
507.25	863.04	629.10	744.18	883.11	241.09
508.20	866.19	645.10	loaf	902.19	244.19
509.12	870.20	695.23	671.17	loneliness	249.27
510.05	872.11	696.09	671.19	404.13	251.02
510.16	875.26	696.10	loathings	712.15	252.12
510.28	879.07	697.08	636.16	734.13	276.28
513.05	879.24	698.25	loaves	825.22	279.08
515.26	880.08	705.08	693.20	850.03	283.03
517.22	888.06	733.02	lobby	898.21	295.11
520.08	888.16	796.20	174.27	lonely	299.11
520.12	890.03	802.17	locality	016.24	310.22
522.07	892.12	831.18	194.18	033.07	314.08

318.06
318.17
323.20
332.10
332.20
333.02
336.24
337.10
339.16
339.20
340.14
341.18
342.09
353.04
363.08
364.08
366.20
367.05
381.21
384.16
404.03
409.03
409.09
418.11
423.26
424.09
430.15
438.12
441.20
447.22
452.01
452.04
456.22
468.16
472.02
475.06
481.11
484.22
488.17
490.08
490.11
490.14
491.13
491.13
501.04
503.10
503.21
504.16
508.09
509.01
509.23
510.15
517.28
530.24
542.05
563.01
566.06
566.06
566.10
567.03
572.25
577.12
577.19
579.06
581.14
582.05
583.06
585.03
585.04
586.02
610.22
611.08
612.15
618.28
619.10
620.05
620.13
621.27
622.13
629.14
631.14
635.26
640.03
641.12
642.06
645.19
651.28
657.02
660.15
662.25
662.28
663.01
663.03
664.02
674.28
675.28
679.28
684.16
685.27
688.07
692.07
693.02
696.09
698.26
703.10
708.21
710.06
721.12
723.17
724.06
727.05

732.17
737.17
738.01
746.11
760.17
771.09
777.15
782.16
789.09
798.12
801.23
805.07
806.03
808.28
810.16
815.25
818.27
824.10
829.12
831.18
836.18
838.08
838.20
838.25
839.22
840.02
847.01
857.19
857.25
860.09
865.24
879.04
881.04
882.14
892.18
894.13
896.13
900.24
901.12
906.13
908.16
909.09
long-absent
  444.08
long-cherished
  475.07
  828.10
long-enduring
  623.02
long-framed
  725.08
long-haired
  231.25
long-suffering
  632.01
  846.08
longed
  113.16
  164.21
  164.26
  165.28
  172.13
  215.05
  378.16
  553.03
  631.16
  636.12
  636.14
  655.23
  668.11
  735.06
  848.18
  883.26
  901.09
  901.10
longer
  024.28
  032.10
  109.24
  115.21
  125.09
  127.03
  130.04
  140.23
  144.10
  152.01
  162.24
  172.25
  180.17
  213.04
  233.15
  289.12
  293.19
  295.18
  371.11
  371.18
  376.21
  403.17
  407.06
  417.21
  431.28
  439.01
  462.15
  463.14
  485.13
  491.25
  511.11
  521.08
  525.25
  617.26
  668.06

669.22
673.06
686.28
742.08
755.11
787.16
806.22
832.15
851.12
858.20
891.05
909.25
910.24
910.25
longest
  318.13
  806.01
longing
  480.10
  607.19
  661.28
  844.25
longings
  465.08
look
  008.23
  023.04
  034.02
  043.18
  044.20
  049.23
  050.01
  051.02
  058.16
  061.21
  068.17
  077.20
  088.03
  090.02
  090.17
  105.23
  109.24
  110.06
  115.12
  117.26
  131.18
  132.07
  137.12
  156.05
  167.11
  177.09
  177.23
  178.02
  182.01
  192.14
  194.04
  220.04
  222.03
  230.22
  241.15
  246.20
  250.19
  256.19
  258.22
  262.11
  263.02
  271.07
  288.26
  293.12
  302.04
  313.09
  315.21
  317.04
  321.15
  327.24
  328.26
  333.17
  336.27
  338.13
  348.15
  350.18
  351.05
  378.09
  382.16
  388.12
  403.13
  403.16
  410.11
  411.21
  425.25
  429.01
  435.22
  437.09
  438.23
  441.06
  455.05
  460.23
  462.09
  467.09
  469.15
  472.20
  483.04
  485.21
  488.20
  496.23
  500.03
  503.13
  503.27
  504.19
  504.23
  507.18

508.14
516.21
517.07
518.07
521.13
521.14
523.10
529.17
531.10
531.14
531.16
539.01
541.19
545.21
561.02
569.02
570.19
571.10
571.19
574.03
574.04
576.01
583.01
585.10
587.11
592.10
602.05
611.27
612.12
619.06
619.18
620.21
628.02
640.13
641.09
642.22
646.09
647.22
650.05
652.03
680.03
685.14
686.13
696.27
697.14
699.21
705.06
718.24
733.06
734.20
736.19
747.07
760.01
767.07
776.23
777.12
792.19
793.02
805.05
808.19
831.19
842.21
846.19
847.10
872.08
878.20
879.02
899.06
905.16
look-out
  377.13
looked
  002.05
  017.19
  018.23
  025.09
  040.13
  052.12
  053.09
  058.20
  061.17
  063.23
  066.17
  067.20
  075.22
  076.09
  077.24
  082.06
  083.03
  084.26
  085.23
  087.10
  088.05
  089.03
  090.21
  094.21
  100.04
  100.25
  113.28
  116.27
  119.11
  134.07
  139.05
  145.13
  151.18
  155.07
  155.27
  159.06
  163.21
  164.15
  175.09

180.01
182.04
184.22
185.10
190.22
191.20
193.13
193.26
194.22
197.02
203.24
207.26
214.26
215.03
219.21
220.13
224.15
225.17
229.05
232.02
243.11
258.21
259.01
292.23
295.05
307.06
309.01
313.14
313.27
314.03
316.04
318.03
320.09
323.12
326.01
331.04
337.18
340.15
347.09
349.19
362.23
366.03
368.08
380.16
382.25
389.09
389.16
394.02
395.02
395.04
402.13
406.21
406.22
407.04
407.05
411.14
412.03
414.08
415.27
415.28
417.04
417.13
422.14
426.15
428.14
431.28
432.28
441.21
446.27
449.21
454.13
458.05
461.11
461.12
464.27
465.24
467.26
472.11
479.13
483.11
492.06
493.06
493.17
505.19
519.23
521.07
530.07
531.28
536.04
539.08
542.09
547.03
550.18
561.10
563.01
563.03
568.16
578.18
580.11
587.14
590.20
592.09
594.13
601.19
606.10
606.13
611.04
613.15
618.28
623.12
639.10

649.05
650.05
655.12
660.05
660.23
663.05
663.15
670.10
673.27
677.10
677.16
680.12
687.15
690.24
698.02
700.02
701.15
703.20
706.04
720.24
723.13
726.15
732.10
732.16
736.20
738.11
740.11
741.01
750.11
753.18
754.17
755.11
763.07
763.19
767.16
776.07
778.10
782.16
783.04
790.28
793.07
794.21
795.20
796.23
800.08
801.13
801.19
801.20
810.01
813.02
820.27
825.01
827.20
828.26
826.27
833.13
849.25
854.02
856.14
858.24
870.15
871.04
872.04
872.08
874.23
887.20
896.27
907.25
looked-for
  810.16
looking
  013.22
  016.11
  022.11
  034.26
  082.10
  084.21
  095.08
  109.21
  115.21
  115.02
  134.11
  175.11
  177.11
  186.12
  204.06
  207.08
  209.17
  209.28
  210.01
  234.05
  237.02
  250.28
  259.10
  259.11
  263.06
  295.26
  299.26
  307.26
  309.08
  332.24
  348.19
  349.01
  349.10
  349.20
  350.13
  354.05
  375.27
  382.07
  402.21
  418.12

441.21
460.09
463.01
480.18
490.12
493.16
498.25
512.09
515.02
519.06
522.15
538.20
598.03
602.02
609.03
638.13
649.16
662.13
666.27
670.18
679.03
680.01
698.07
706.03
718.05
736.18
738.22
741.10
746.22
754.23
760.21
781.13
800.28
811.07
859.13
852.11
859.05

looking-glass
017.11
017.17
701.06

looks
037.24
077.01
095.01
121.02
177.14
275.25
278.05
352.18
366.18
369.06
367.11
368.04
400.01
404.08
456.18
499.18
536.24
522.01
620.09
662.22
691.23
725.10

looped
204.05
420.14

loose
024.24
146.02
326.18
361.22
365.06
369.28
649.21
692.24
822.15
850.02

loose-principled
637.14

loosened
013.21
519.15
583.24
607.16
620.03
693.08

lord
118.25
176.20
316.14
319.13
348.12
350.16
352.20
356.03
378.28
389.19
478.10
912.17
912.25

lore
803.22

lorn
608.08

lose
105.03
116.25
494.13
603.16
834.15

847.04

loses
469.14
555.25

losing
036.18
048.27
189.08
441.24

loss
163.19
198.08
252.16
426.13
448.03
470.22
486.04
546.13
591.19
859.15

lost
091.12
118.15
151.16
162.24
220.14
252.08
296.16
333.09
426.16
427.23
534.15
539.05
576.02
578.24
608.08
659.12
668.24
698.21
717.06
753.02
780.14
810.24
819.13
855.25
864.18
865.02
866.15
867.23
870.14
883.27
899.20

lot
111.08
216.11
524.12
668.23
719.26
722.11
724.17
734.08
842.22

lot's
734.17

lotus-flowers
471.06

loud
024.21
029.05
035.12
080.02
083.11
123.18
210.18
258.18
333.22
354.28
485.22
605.05
647.20
684.16
856.20
874.21

louder
210.10

loudly
050.08
073.21
592.02

louisa
343.11
347.16
351.03
352.25
352.27
357.16
357.19
367.09
379.01
383.16
383.21
383.26
389.08
390.22
417.17

lounging
476.03

love
005.23
020.09

020.10
022.05
046.21
062.05
063.04
107.08
107.22
107.25
132.06
132.09
132.15
143.16
158.06
176.20
200.27
281.28
282.08
286.22
321.19
323.01
325.14
347.18
350.08
350.10
350.12
352.04
356.13
372.02
372.21
374.07
375.14
377.03
383.21
402.20
403.07
484.21
485.04
511.19
511.23
511.24
513.25
515.27
516.01
516.08
517.16
518.17
521.06
525.23
526.02
527.17
527.18
527.27
528.12
528.13
532.15
533.21
534.14
536.27
549.25
550.21
552.05
552.09
552.12
555.07
561.08
569.24
573.12
573.18
573.18
583.13
588.05
606.13
608.08
612.12
614.08
617.10
620.19
621.03
621.14
621.19
628.18
634.20
634.28
644.06
644.28
645.12
646.07
646.28
647.25
647.26
650.15
650.26
651.10
651.12
653.25
654.05
656.07
657.16
714.19
731.17
731.18
731.19
747.08
747.22
749.20
757.21
758.26
770.12
770.13
781.09
785.28

786.25
796.28
797.02
807.03
813.13
815.16
820.03
820.19
821.20
827.13
827.15
828.05
829.16
831.17
835.11
838.06
841.12
842.03
842.08
842.10
842.19
842.24
848.15
858.22
862.27
862.28
863.10
895.04
895.04
895.05
895.05
895.24
895.25
897.11
898.07
898.12
908.25
911.04
911.12

loved
062.05
162.36
498.11
500.12
509.22
518.06
533.25
551.02
551.02
552.12
625.09
625.17
635.01
645.01
645.10
645.11
645.11
660.28
711.15
731.18
745.21
782.19
787.06
819.05
840.04
848.13
848.14
849.21
877.09
888.24
894.12
910.04
910.06
911.13

loveliest
322.09

loveliness
359.23
748.12

lovely
323.12
435.06
442.19
505.03
583.02
644.09
655.09
732.25
737.28
738.24
750.10
763.09
858.14
887.22

lover
200.19
499.25
735.18
846.19
858.05

lover's
545.12

lovers
286.06

loves
158.07
403.09
473.16
740.21
884.01
895.04

897.10

loving
046.23
497.04
638.20
745.20
881.17
894.16

low
005.01
017.05
032.26
037.20
046.14
052.12
060.21
061.05
080.25
109.21
116.06
134.08
137.02
141.08
185.11
207.01
209.28
210.11
210.26
217.03
247.24
261.11
294.27
307.25
341.09
342.28
345.17
382.23
385.07
385.25
418.27
419.15
420.26
449.24
468.10
498.19
541.23
567.10
588.13
591.02
599.01
614.07
626.16
661.20
667.20
666.08
675.20
675.27
676.28
678.07
691.06
703.05
705.04
711.17
725.19
726.08
742.11
753.12
781.14
798.20
826.01
850.03
855.03
862.04
874.24
889.23

low-born
571.07

low-ceiled
081.19
329.10

low-gliding
219.06

low-spirited
355.20

low-spoken
592.06

lower
086.21
100.27
109.23
207.03
231.07
249.07
284.03
354.27
449.08
450.03
471.15
549.23
616.17
677.01
740.12
810.11
857.11
858.12
864.07
904.04

lowered
465.20

lowly
589.03

lowood
056.19
058.02
058.07
058.16
059.04
059.09
064.08
086.16
089.10
091.02
095.20
097.03
100.09
102.07
102.08
111.02
115.05
129.15
143.18
144.03
146.02
146.21
147.23
148.10
148.19
160.13
162.26
164.07
164.18
165.02
173.04
173.22
180.23
184.13
185.01
191.24
194.13
202.24
230.11
241.08
243.16
243.23
244.24
245.05
247.02
275.16
459.21
467.28
484.02
490.14
545.23
553.08
706.20
706.26
771.09

lowton
116.17
117.15
148.23
166.07
169.02
169.05
169.18
174.12
180.19
181.19
184.25

lozenged
676.04

lucicrous
454.13

lucid
633.08

lucre
817.19

ludicrous
342.01

luggage
183.14
187.12
234.16
586.12
587.01

lugubrious
293.28

lui
201.18

luke
423.26

lull
572.12

lulled
075.10
633.21

lulling
736.23

luminous
882.02
901.08

lump
262.01
779.25

lunar
540.25

lunatic
596.24
601.03
605.03
625.28
633.21

771.24
855.23
862.05
863.15
lunch
066.28
087.08
117.23
117.27
lungs
358.11
lure
622.18
luria
249.15
284.02
578.23
luring
845.14
lurk
465.01
lust
647.01
luster
755.18
lustre
159.17
146.11
248.24
258.12
342.07
346.16
765.17
808.16
886.20
lustres
327.18
lustrous
355.16
472.03
521.12
lusts
121.17
lusus
749.03
luxuriant
461.16
luxuries
143.20
731.15
luxury
118.08
lying
152.10
169.19
294.17
297.05
475.19
779.24
lynn
316.14
339.24
343.15
347.12
347.24
348.06
352.10
352.16
352.24
366.22
373.16
378.26
379.02
379.25
384.02
386.16
386.22
388.22
443.01
451.12
lynns
350.15
m'a
234.23
ma
197.12
218.24
218.25
234.23
255.25
255.25
277.09
341.22
ma'am
024.21
077.03
116.26
117.09
119.27
120.05
134.16
135.01
136.24
163.04
185.24
187.14
261.04
332.14
366.09
368.04
855.11

860.20
861.15
862.01
862.08
862.20
862.26
863.02
863.17
865.06
866.01
866.08
866.12
867.13
868.04
891.19
macbeth
283.26
macedonia
815.05
machine
512.28
mad
012.13
043.23
467.25
526.27
597.10
597.10
597.13
598.08
617.02
617.06
617.06
625.27
627.28
628.23
629.19
648.06
698.10
857.04
863.27
865.18
867.10
901.21
mad-woman's
616.12
madagascar
755.17
madam
006.04
058.05
059.01
059.12
059.20
060.04
118.06
119.03
121.15
137.22
143.12
238.25
257.11
355.03
358.03
361.01
381.19
454.15
482.09
482.20
602.16
madame
093.02
093.08
093.11
198.01
198.22
199.23
201.25
202.04
355.16
355.19
355.23
made
007.07
031.16
034.28
042.09
047.24
048.22
051.28
052.20
057.28
063.11
083.21
084.09
087.22
089.24
096.10
098.26
101.15
108.16
129.17
137.27
142.04
146.07
152.14
160.16
161.10
162.26
176.23
178.26

191.04
192.10
192.13
197.28
201.19
214.01
214.28
217.08
217.17
219.13
221.27
227.15
228.02
228.10
230.28
234.10
237.05
240.16
244.22
251.26
252.28
255.13
265.25
266.01
285.17
287.26
291.05
292.10
295.14
299.25
314.26
315.13
319.24
335.03
340.01
347.06
350.12
361.19
365.23
370.18
390.21
403.13
404.17
410.08
420.25
424.25
435.22
448.13
449.25
450.07
468.09
473.08
478.19
481.27
483.06
490.01
504.20
508.02
513.09
514.20
523.24
528.07
529.08
532.10
535.04
543.18
549.11
553.23
556.07
558.21
564.16
566.04
572.12
573.02
579.12
592.10
604.05
605.08
615.05
616.06
620.26
624.17
626.12
632.13
633.03
636.18
641.11
643.03
643.25
653.03
662.19
676.06
681.09
684.05
697.06
697.21
700.19
714.04
722.18
723.25
724.15
728.01
731.11
733.06
734.01
735.11
739.19
741.04
741.08
744.25
746.06

750.07
751.27
768.26
775.27
778.28
794.05
800.10
801.10
802.14
806.06
817.10
820.23
823.19
831.04
832.26
836.02
848.02
864.37
879.10
885.21
885.26
891.25
903.02
908.10
madeira
180.06
482.15
482.21
545.04
602.19
603.02
603.22
774.24
780.07
878.07
mademoiselle
198.09
199.02
201.06
234.22
234.26
239.11
313.15
334.10
341.21
538.15
540.11
540.12
540.13
540.16
541.12
543.09
543.11
543.12
madly
532.14
madness
065.11
321.19
622.08
840.22
876.04
876.05
magic
497.03
magic-lantern
398.17
magistrate
348.08
385.12
450.25
magnanimity
644.24
magnet
490.17
magnificent
342.08
367.04
369.02
magnificently
318.01
magnified
378.22
magnifies
342.17
magnifiques
341.21
magnify
342.17
magnitude
184.25
222.24
mahogany
015.22
016.04
076.12
794.23
mahomet
227.21
227.22
maid
010.24
226.19
364.12
maid-servant
185.22
maids
327.05
365.14
maimed
605.16

main
029.02
822.01
862.18
maintain
021.23
323.26
554.08
619.02
maintained
696.28
907.16
maintaining
726.09
maintenance
468.12
723.21
mais
197.15
313.17
334.10
maister
698.09
majestic
146.04
346.24
624.27
majestically
119.21
majesty
017.12
152.06
346.25
majority
267.23
mak'
698.17
mak'em
694.21
make
014.24
020.26
035.08
035.19
046.15
065.24
066.04
071.14
076.15
089.21
092.24
097.28
106.15
107.19
108.07
116.20
129.15
130.03
131.13
138.02
157.13
176.14
177.07
180.06
187.06
187.24
189.18
197.10
197.22
197.24
214.06
216.08
227.25
228.08
240.09
243.02
250.19
252.03
262.08
272.10
310.02
311.10
317.03
321.10
325.10
328.08
331.05
331.21
346.23
353.28
368.26
377.28
383.15
397.23
407.29
419.11
429.21
435.06
439.10
439.26
444.04
464.06
468.22
476.11
476.24
483.13
485.09
491.19
494.15
495.01
497.02

499.19
503.18
516.28
517.27
517.27
525.16
527.26
529.19
531.25
532.04
541.28
542.17
543.03
544.13
544.26
545.24
566.02
582.12
613.07
614.18
615.01
622.18
632.22
634.26
635.07
635.08
636.28
640.21
641.01
647.07
657.06
682.01
683.07
691.21
694.08
707.28
734.27
748.02
749.05
750.15
751.11
754.01
759.03
760.10
763.22
783.07
783.18
787.13
792.23
795.19
796.26
804.12
804.16
806.02
817.03
819.27
820.01
829.22
833.16
837.20
842.25
853.11
854.05
858.08
858.22
880.07
880.10
880.21
861.24
884.09
885.04
885.17
895.08
895.22
897.08
898.08
903.05
maker
157.21
518.19
663.17
824.15
900.18
903.23
maker's
824.15
makes
036.05
062.26
069.11
109.13
189.20
260.02
354.17
428.23
726.18
842.03
making
032.16
049.08
116.07
147.14
216.22
239.08
251.09
253.04
316.01
339.13
448.10
493.24
497.17

561.06
591.12
641.16
642.09
788.02
818.14
881.18
888.20
mal
540.28
malaay
147.21
811.09
male
237.12
760.28
malevolent
032.07
269.26
malice
833.10
malicious
555.09
malignant
292.24
309.14
553.19
653.22
nama
002.02
006.09
007.10
008.21
009.08
010.10
030.05
043.20
044.25
048.08
053.14
176.19
177.02
200.03
200.04
200.07
201.15
201.22
201.28
345.10
354.07
354.11
355.11
356.20
357.01
368.28
369.28
463.05
453.15
mama's
009.12
058.21
359.19
368.28
maman
277.19
354.04
499.03
mammon
753.02
nan
052.10
052.24
092.15
105.17
109.05
109.09
116.03
118.27
128.05
151.12
151.17
162.21
177.07
177.11
183.11
183.15
193.14
205.04
222.07
222.18
230.08
244.06
260.18
262.26
269.05
275.20
284.10
285.12
293.01
321.07
348.08
349.23
358.21
359.22
360.03
369.24
376.19
381.08
382.02
382.18
383.20

387.14
396.16
421.05
421.21
421.27
422.14
424.22
429.18
436.15
440.24
441.13
444.14
446.02
459.05
472.22
490.02
497.02
513.22
513.23
518.01
536.06
556.05
596.08
597.18
602.09
612.01
614.26
614.27
615.05
619.18
623.01
623.13
624.05
624.12
625.12
627.18
636.28
647.13
648.05
660.06
661.01
691.07
697.25
698.22
701.21
706.06
719.15
721.26
731.23
741.01
750.10
751.13
760.25
761.18
761.25
773.12
778.19
796.16
806.05
819.14
821.20
822.24
823.24
824.14
825.15
826.13
826.20
827.09
831.06
832.07
832.22
833.13
835.21
836.26
839.08
842.12
843.01
843.02
846.12
856.01
860.17
864.17
865.06
865.09
867.05
871.14
886.23
889.16
889.18
889.19
890.06
890.08
890.21
897.14
897.17
900.01
900.02
911.09
man's
483.12
513.21
770.13
822.25
826.25
manage
035.04
339.10
376.09
376.11
690.28

managed
205.07
374.13
376.12
407.20
755.13
770.03
860.19
management
161.13
manager
060.27
092.04
196.02
mandate
061.21
mane
599.21
884.19
mange
334.11
manhood
644.03
maniac
600.12
616.02
630.06
631.25
646.16
maniacs
597.11
manifestation
081.23
665.25
manifestations
270.02
373.23
775.16
manifested
715.25
789.12
manly
612.10
896.09
manna
540.20
540.22
manner
002.14
002.22
056.10
057.27
097.17
123.05
149.16
236.11
251.24
264.03
267.13
267.14
267.16
275.11
290.21
291.23
307.11
324.09
343.09
381.24
402.01
448.06
462.10
554.17
574.20
612.11
641.13
641.27
642.28
643.10
687.03
690.13
739.09
832.14
842.21
843.15
843.16
843.26
844.01
mannered
790.08
manners
038.01
038.10
625.21
700.01
744.04
890.11
890.13
manoeuvre
121.03
manoeuvres
376.04
manor
593.11
616.03
873.26
manor-house
194.02
867.26
869.02
870.01
905.06

mansion
015.21
193.27
209.03
424.14
434.16
759.21
857.16
857.28
mansion's
194.12
mantel-piece
181.08
204.16
262.22
271.09
329.02
353.08
382.27
874.26
mantelpiece
231.15
236.26
mantle
088.21
219.26
430.25
mantling
031.15
manufacture
375.24
manufacturing
040.27
172.14
770.21
manure
278.04
many
020.05
076.02
078.03
093.22
100.18
112.11
125.27
129.15
131.08
140.02
140.07
147.18
149.19
150.13
159.12
160.04
167.10
180.10
182.21
188.20
199.17
200.06
215.17
215.26
216.12
220.19
220.20
239.25
253.09
265.13
265.14
266.28
292.09
292.19
312.14
314.22
326.25
342.15
373.05
401.14
426.27
441.19
448.21
456.19
468.01
484.19
546.15
575.12
590.04
596.23
635.14
666.01
667.07
699.02
712.20
739.10
743.16
744.16
789.10
796.08
804.20
807.03
828.13
853.13
866.26
882.24
892.08
many-coloured
745.13
map
172.09
209.02

marble
017.06
119.13
125.12
159.21
231.11
262.21
329.01
341.03
367.26
369.19
434.21
575.04
589.09
591.15
726.10
754.10
767.08
807.21
808.28
832.15
859.16
860.06
marble-seeming
746.24
marbled
209.11
492.27
march
111.10
113.11
230.22
331.27
454.08
506.28
814.04
march-spirit
634.16
marched
081.14
margin
764.01
774.01
maria
086.12
marine
005.06
mark
094.25
099.07
263.16
282.17
373.01
375.03
marked
042.13
048.14
094.14
125.03
127.28
192.22
213.17
228.18
261.17
308.12
310.01
429.06
537.18
625.20
693.27
758.09
829.17
844.26
869.16
911.16
marking
185.14
306.28
886.17
marks
159.21
marmion
753.15
753.15
765.11
768.14
marriage
163.11
367.13
400.06
468.10
499.05
499.10
547.09
590.18
591.10
592.04
593.16
603.17
605.08
624.13
625.14
632.13
704.22
759.05
771.22
786.24
821.14
824.20
827.13
828.08

842.11
846.05
847.16
866.21
907.14
married
040.20
040.25
157.11
162.19
175.24
319.11
338.08
371.02
376.10
402.21
402.28
442.01
442.16
446.15
453.26
507.02
507.24
513.22
513.23
526.09
529.06
531.14
531.16
545.06
545.24
581.20
593.12
593.20
596.19
596.20
597.03
614.26
614.26
622.11
623.16
625.22
704.13
704.18
727.12
770.13
780.05
801.15
802.01
826.14
827.11
834.25
837.18
880.19
898.26
905.03
905.09
908.20
908.24
911.05
marrow
276.16
553.15
822.19
marrow-freezing
294.25
marry
321.18
360.04
372.14
374.04
515.10
515.17
516.07
517.15
517.21
524.21
531.26
535.22
536.09
536.27
538.08
552.22
634.22
635.21
635.24
636.17
644.16
754.01
757.05
760.09
783.22
786.16
786.17
786.18
786.18
821.09
821.21
826.10
834.26
835.05
835.12
840.10
840.14
840.26
848.08
848.08
863.11
880.18
893.23
893.24

894.17
895.07
897.12
899.03
912.08
marrying
376.16
491.22
571.14
827.10
marseilles
016.07
731.27
marsh
495.21
669.21
675.10
692.11
728.02
marsh-end
695.08
697.27
698.28
718.15
marsh-glen
811.21
850.01
marshal
587.06
marshalled
861.14
marshes
033.16
673.29
674.08
marston
589.11
martha
060.07
444.17
martyr
127.17
martyr-like
747.18
martyrdom
354.18
820.24
martyrs
118.24
marvel
329.17
marvelled
241.16
marvellous
032.04
mary
149.13
150.04
151.13
151.22
317.09
344.03
344.28
345.01
346.12
346.15
352.16
354.08
355.17
358.15
379.02
383.16
383.22
389.06
389.20
390.22
679.21
681.04
686.06
688.01
690.02
696.01
699.15
700.08
700.16
704.24
705.04
709.07
711.06
713.19
714.01
717.09
724.26
725.18
726.13
726.13
726.19
727.20
727.24
728.03
741.28
767.19
768.22
769.05
769.05
773.15
781.01
733.12
734.18
734.19
738.13

791.08
792.12
794.11
799.12
801.07
803.19
806.08
806.11
810.26
811.17
840.09
845.25
853.18
873.13
873.25
874.21
875.10
875.17
875.18
876.01
882.10
886.05
905.06
905.08
905.16
906.01
906.08
906.17
907.01
911.05
mary's
348.14
681.13
686.06
699.26
714.28
787.10
798.06
800.17
803.14
883.16
911.09
masculine
224.27
228.28
mask
052.17
221.28
602.07
masked
424.18
mason
384.08
384.28
409.14
409.22
409.24
410.24
411.06
411.25
412.23
413.01
413.07
421.10
421.19
421.25
425.10
427.16
428.12
429.04
431.21
431.26
432.10
433.10
435.23
436.11
436.15
436.19
437.03
438.04
443.04
581.09
593.12
593.13
593.18
594.05
594.14
594.22
594.24
595.11
595.16
597.04
597.10
597.22
599.05
600.23
602.19
602.22
603.02
603.07
603.16
603.23
604.02
613.24
624.14
624.17
624.24
627.15
mason's
425.19
426.10

430.21
595.04
633.12
masque
571.03
masquerade
408.11
mass
120.10
220.28
226.04
261.01
318.20
385.03
392.25
560.05
560.06
608.10
675.19
861.24
masse
115.11
masses
216.13
massive
015.22
259.02
349.28
591.16
677.04
765.15
massive-featured
750.09
mast
151.19
248.01
248.07
master
006.24
007.12
008.03
010.26
012.17
012.18
012.18
014.19
038.27
060.02
068.13
121.15
206.09
222.21
232.08
232.10
232.15
234.01
239.02
240.22
245.26
253.13
256.19
275.21
282.23
291.27
305.19
307.19
308.24
309.03
310.11
325.03
325.28
330.16
333.23
377.11
378.12
401.01
430.27
449.19
459.03
495.26
495.28
509.18
521.13
522.20
527.23
528.17
537.27
538.19
577.04
598.19
599.02
605.12
609.13
641.25
643.13
651.06
654.01
656.12
679.24
697.23
721.13
732.19
740.25
749.21
773.09
806.16
813.24
822.11
846.07
855.20
871.17

874.03
876.25
879.03
895.17
903.11
906.04
906.10
912.02
912.22
master's
290.21
308.08
311.22
312.13
349.27
419.03
499.10
500.04
518.25
545.12
567.10
606.14
740.26
762.27
855.18
856.27
mattered
127.19
227.28
350.05
601.12
masterful
265.09
masterhood
825.13
mastering
755.01
masterless
687.19
masters
266.14
625.17
mastery
494.11
511.19
mastiffs
031.28
mat
361.23
765.07
766.13
match
040.22
116.19
176.21
490.32
496.26
500.01
756.02
801.21
matches
319.23
mate
353.04
822.25
842.07
909.01
material
119.15
480.01
797.07
materials
293.05
397.06
470.23
763.01
792.07
maternal
770.25
mates
656.07
mathematical
791.28
matrimonial
843.13
matrimony
401.22
507.12
589.19
590.03
590.07
matron
148.23
matronly
175.10
312.10
matrons
392.04
863.22
matt
089.16
matted
193.10
419.13
matter
028.14
063.28
085.03
103.16
166.21
173.05

173.09
183.21
258.09
271.08
324.19
362.15
390.28
426.02
439.05
439.27
453.21
453.23
509.02
539.10
539.20
564.21
565.07
568.06
637.19
667.27
688.02
763.26
770.03
771.25
772.06
775.11
779.27
782.04
785.01
785.12
796.37
824.10
833.05
839.18
875.13
893.22
mattered
314.28
matters
122.24
148.20
290.11
298.09
342.03
374.27
479.03
487.20
603.09
777.25
787.26
864.09
895.20
matthew
114.06
matting
295.22
299.18
mattrasses
328.02
mattresses
016.06
matured
146.01
maturing
221.13
maxim
274.03
may
028.10
037.14
039.18
056.24
059.08
059.12
062.08
089.14
090.17
116.20
117.19
119.06
131.18
134.02
145.26
145.27
146.26
147.28
153.21
166.22
179.20
184.17
214.23
227.01
247.10
251.22
267.26
267.27
268.01
270.21
270.27
271.02
274.18
276.11
282.17
285.25
288.07
298.23
308.14
309.23
310.16
312.16
339.07

341.24
343.02
354.27
358.22
381.21
395.13
396.17
399.16
399.27
405.14
405.16
405.20
429.13
430.06
433.26
436.13
437.27
438.06
444.13
450.21
453.20
456.18
457.03
457.18
467.04
477.12
477.15
481.23
482.19
489.16
489.28
493.19
495.01
506.07
532.03
533.12
533.14
533.19
538.22
538.22
545.24
548.04
546.21
554.02
562.19
568.11
578.10
590.02
591.21
593.19
597.07
603.08
623.22
631.25
633.14
657.10
657.11
657.13
657.15
674.15
682.09
683.13
687.13
691.13
691.18
693.15
703.08
703.15
708.23
720.10
731.08
734.26
735.02
760.20
763.11
766.11
777.02
782.06
785.10
786.14
786.16
797.16
807.23
821.04
824.10
837.21
839.05
844.02
855.20
866.08
867.12
878.17
879.25
879.26
905.12
906.25
911.22
911.23
911.23
may-day
810.27
malle
218.25
284.22
me
002.06
002.08
002.16
003.10
007.21
007.22

008.06	051.13	103.20	162.06	226.12	290.28
008.11	051.15	104.12	162.08	226.23	291.02
009.15	051.18	104.14	162.17	227.01	291.05
009.23	051.22	104.17	162.23	227.08	291.23
010.09	051.23	104.19	162.27	227.14	291.25
010.11	051.24	105.06	163.09	227.24	291.25
010.20	051.28	105.15	163.23	227.25	292.15
011.06	052.05	106.10	164.05	227.27	292.18
012.02	052.06	106.16	165.02	228.05	294.01
012.05	052.14	107.06	165.05	228.16	294.18
012.08	052.20	107.07	165.07	229.02	297.13
013.03	052.21	107.08	165.21	229.11	297.15
013.05	052.26	107.28	165.23	229.17	298.08
013.07	053.06	108.06	165.27	230.03	300.25
013.09	053.10	108.21	165.27	230.19	300.27
013.14	053.18	109.11	166.08	230.20	301.04
015.21	053.27	109.20	166.19	232.01	301.06
014.02	054.09	109.20	167.14	232.01	301.13
014.06	056.12	109.24	169.23	232.20	301.17
014.12	057.01	111.07	170.06	236.16	301.23
017.05	057.06	112.17	170.17	236.21	302.15
017.07	057.09	115.01	170.20	238.02	303.01
017.21	059.24	115.12	171.22	238.07	306.01
018.03	060.01	115.17	172.13	238.09	308.03
018.06	061.12	116.04	173.05	238.11	308.17
019.14	061.16	116.10	173.07	239.04	308.28
020.09	062.24	116.14	173.18	240.02	309.01
020.24	062.25	116.17	173.19	240.11	309.10
020.26	062.26	117.10	173.25	240.17	309.11
021.20	062.27	117.21	174.08	240.25	309.12
021.23	063.06	118.06	174.26	240.26	309.15
022.08	063.07	123.10	175.15	241.17	310.25
022.11	063.07	123.19	176.05	243.01	311.12
022.23	063.12	123.23	177.25	243.03	311.13
022.26	063.12	123.23	178.17	243.07	311.26
022.27	063.13	123.24	180.06	245.23	312.14
023.20	063.14	123.25	180.18	246.01	313.23
023.26	064.18	124.03	180.25	246.21	313.28
024.01	065.02	124.15	182.04	253.18	314.11
024.01	065.14	124.16	182.09	253.23	314.19
024.07	065.20	124.19	182.25	254.15	315.04
025.03	065.25	127.13	183.15	254.20	315.11
025.04	066.05	127.16	183.19	255.03	315.16
025.09	067.20	127.17	183.27	255.08	317.26
025.13	067.26	127.25	185.26	256.05	320.02
025.14	067.27	129.09	186.01	256.26	321.04
025.04	068.06	129.12	186.21	257.13	323.25
026.10	068.12	130.02	186.27	259.14	328.05
026.11	068.15	130.03	187.17	259.15	329.16
026.11	068.17	130.13	187.26	260.14	330.18
027.02	068.22	130.17	188.07	260.16	331.24
027.09	068.25	130.18	188.23	260.19	335.05
027.19	069.15	130.22	189.14	260.23	335.06
028.10	069.18	131.05	191.01	261.06	335.23
028.12	069.23	131.09	191.15	261.23	336.06
028.14	070.02	132.06	191.21	261.23	339.27
028.20	070.03	132.11	191.27	262.02	340.20
029.09	070.04	133.10	193.05	263.13	342.20
029.27	071.04	133.20	193.20	263.17	342.22
030.08	071.17	134.10	195.28	263.18	343.25
030.11	071.19	134.17	196.01	263.23	344.15
030.20	072.01	134.20	196.10	264.06	344.20
033.07	072.09	134.23	196.16	264.12	348.01
033.19	073.25	134.23	196.24	264.25	349.02
033.21	074.06	134.26	197.03	265.06	349.10
034.07	074.13	135.04	197.13	265.09	349.11
034.23	074.14	135.09	198.10	265.22	350.04
034.27	074.21	135.25	198.15	266.09	350.06
035.07	075.12	135.27	198.23	266.21	350.12
035.09	075.22	135.28	199.10	267.21	350.13
036.03	075.24	136.06	199.18	269.04	351.05
036.10	076.05	136.08	200.05	269.13	351.09
036.27	076.06	136.13	200.09	270.10	351.16
036.28	076.25	136.15	201.19	270.26	351.25
038.02	077.15	136.15	201.20	271.10	353.28
040.15	077.18	138.06	201.26	272.18	354.17
042.11	077.19	139.28	201.27	272.21	354.28
042.12	078.10	140.23	202.01	273.03	355.11
042.14	078.18	141.08	202.05	273.20	358.05
042.15	079.09	141.24	202.05	274.20	360.07
042.16	079.19	142.08	202.07	275.01	360.09
043.01	084.23	142.08	202.21	275.15	360.18
043.02	085.08	143.13	203.12	275.24	361.01
043.04	086.14	149.12	203.16	277.26	361.10
043.07	088.05	149.17	206.24	277.27	362.02
043.09	088.17	149.19	211.09	279.05	362.18
043.14	088.19	150.06	211.11	279.07	362.23
043.25	088.21	150.20	214.02	280.12	362.25
044.04	088.22	154.14	214.05	280.28	363.13
044.07	088.23	154.16	214.21	284.26	366.03
044.08	089.24	154.18	214.23	285.10	366.09
044.09	089.24	154.27	215.17	285.12	366.15
044.17	090.01	156.16	215.20	285.23	372.04
044.21	090.06	157.01	217.04	285.25	372.08
044.26	090.08	157.08	217.12	286.01	372.10
044.27	090.18	157.10	218.07	286.12	375.25
045.01	090.19	157.11	218.08	286.23	376.17
045.02	091.01	157.25	219.02	286.28	377.01
046.25	094.19	157.26	219.26	287.05	377.06
047.08	094.28	158.07	220.06	287.06	377.19
047.12	095.01	158.16	220.11	287.13	377.28
047.13	097.01	158.21	221.22	287.14	378.25
047.15	097.05	158.22	222.02	287.15	380.12
047.18	097.07	158.23	222.26	288.05	381.02
047.18	097.11	158.25	223.08	288.09	381.12
047.24	098.10	159.03	223.16	288.14	381.25
049.11	099.04	159.06	225.02	288.24	382.13
050.09	099.05	159.07	225.06	288.26	382.19
051.07	099.08	159.08	225.11	290.06	383.17
051.11	102.16	159.14	225.12	290.22	383.18
051.12	103.19		225.17	290.26	389.25

390.05	440.18	482.04	517.17	556.04	609.16
390.17	441.22	482.11	517.24	558.09	610.02
392.13	442.01	482.13	517.24	558.21	610.08
392.27	442.06	482.14	517.28	559.01	610.09
395.08	442.08	483.01	518.01	559.17	610.24
397.02	442.14	483.02	518.10	561.01	610.26
397.04	442.18	483.03	519.10	561.14	611.04
397.13	442.18	483.06	519.23	563.15	611.12
397.14	442.27	483.11	520.13	564.07	611.14
397.20	445.15	483.12	521.19	564.13	611.26
398.13	445.16	483.13	522.15	564.14	612.07
398.14	445.18	483.18	522.26	564.16	612.20
400.02	445.28	484.10	523.04	564.22	612.21
400.10	446.02	484.21	523.24	565.13	612.24
400.26	446.07	484.23	523.25	565.24	612.24
402.01	446.13	485.04	524.03	566.01	612.26
403.12	446.18	485.04	524.12	566.02	613.02
403.20	448.24	485.10	524.16	566.04	613.06
404.03	448.26	485.11	525.08	566.08	613.15
404.03	449.21	485.28	525.20	566.21	613.15
404.04	449.25	487.02	525.24	566.22	613.19
404.14	450.10	487.06	526.04	567.13	613.20
404.19	450.17	488.13	527.07	568.06	613.27
405.06	451.03	488.20	527.10	568.18	614.06
405.08	451.06	488.23	527.16	568.20	614.06
405.08	451.07	490.17	527.17	569.02	614.15
406.13	451.10	492.04	527.17	569.03	614.22
406.14	452.06	492.05	528.01	569.11	614.25
406.19	453.05	492.07	528.04	569.25	614.27
406.24	453.06	492.10	528.14	569.25	614.28
407.06	453.17	493.01	528.17	570.09	615.01
407.09	453.25	493.06	528.17	570.11	615.04
407.13	454.13	493.17	529.10	570.17	615.05
407.24	454.19	494.18	529.13	570.19	615.09
407.27	454.24	495.17	529.20	570.24	616.01
407.29	454.27	495.17	529.22	571.16	616.08
408.01	455.01	495.23	530.12	571.24	617.05
408.24	455.02	495.23	530.21	572.06	617.10
409.01	455.05	496.05	531.01	572.08	617.12
409.02	455.09	496.16	531.25	572.20	617.17
409.17	455.13	496.22	532.01	572.21	617.17
409.18	456.01	496.27	532.10	573.01	617.23
410.04	456.16	497.01	532.15	573.12	617.24
410.05	457.20	497.02	532.28	573.18	617.26
410.06	458.08	497.09	533.05	574.01	618.15
410.08	458.10	497.12	533.15	574.03	618.16
410.10	458.16	497.16	533.21	574.05	618.28
410.15	458.20	497.18	534.05	574.05	619.14
410.20	458.23	497.22	534.07	574.06	619.28
410.22	458.25	497.24	534.10	574.06	620.12
410.24	459.06	497.25	535.03	574.07	620.16
411.09	459.13	497.26	535.15	574.11	620.28
411.16	459.23	497.26	535.18	574.12	621.03
411.28	460.05	497.27	535.19	574.21	621.05
412.03	460.19	498.05	535.20	575.18	621.08
412.05	461.22	498.07	535.23	576.20	621.13
412.09	461.22	498.07	535.26	577.06	621.18
412.13	461.26	498.09	536.04	577.09	621.19
412.25	462.03	498.16	536.10	577.24	622.08
412.28	462.15	498.21	536.14	578.09	622.09
414.06	462.20	499.20	537.12	578.21	623.03
414.09	462.22	500.10	538.05	579.09	623.06
416.24	462.27	500.11	538.12	580.07	623.14
416.24	463.12	503.23	538.12	580.18	623.20
418.04	463.21	503.25	538.15	580.24	623.24
418.06	464.01	504.05	539.03	581.09	623.26
418.14	464.08	504.07	539.08	581.24	624.03
419.26	464.26	504.11	539.24	582.14	624.09
420.06	465.20	504.24	540.04	583.23	624.14
420.12	465.24	505.01	540.16	585.02	624.22
420.20	466.09	505.09	540.17	586.03	624.23
422.19	466.11	505.12	541.28	586.04	624.27
422.26	466.12	505.22	542.02	586.04	625.01
422.28	466.12	506.26	542.05	586.06	625.04
423.03	466.15	507.17	542.09	586.07	625.06
423.08	466.16	507.21	542.12	586.16	625.13
423.14	466.26	509.18	542.13	588.06	625.13
424.12	467.08	509.21	542.17	588.08	625.13
425.14	467.15	510.14	542.21	588.25	625.17
426.25	467.21	510.19	542.24	589.15	625.24
427.19	467.25	510.24	543.25	592.10	626.07
428.05	468.27	511.05	543.26	592.15	626.10
428.06	469.04	511.19	544.09	592.17	626.15
428.18	469.06	512.06	544.16	592.21	627.08
428.23	469.26	512.13	544.19	593.01	627.15
429.22	469.26	513.08	544.26	596.12	627.16
431.24	470.18	513.10	544.26	596.13	627.25
433.20	470.21	513.10	545.03	596.15	628.26
434.06	470.23	513.18	546.06	597.08	629.09
434.12	470.24	513.19	546.08	598.03	629.13
434.16	471.16	513.28	547.08	598.10	630.16
435.13	472.11	514.07	547.22	600.09	630.20
436.06	472.14	514.10	548.01	601.03	631.07
436.12	473.03	515.02	548.22	602.08	631.09
436.19	474.14	515.11	548.23	602.15	631.10
436.20	474.25	515.14	548.26	603.18	632.19
436.22	475.19	515.16	548.26	605.16	632.22
437.07	477.11	515.17	549.09	605.16	633.09
437.08	477.25	515.21	549.13	605.16	634.01
437.16	478.08	515.23	549.26	606.21	634.27
437.17	478.10	516.01	550.17	606.24	635.03
437.17	478.11	516.11	552.01	607.04	635.07
437.17	479.23	516.12	552.02	607.06	635.12
437.23	480.18	516.14	552.10	607.07	635.14
437.27	480.20	516.17	552.13	607.12	635.24
437.27	480.22	516.21	552.20	607.15	636.04
438.01	480.25	517.05	553.19	607.21	636.13
438.04	481.02	517.07	555.04	608.01	636.18
438.11	481.06	517.13	555.16	608.07	636.18
438.24	481.09	517.14	556.01	608.10	636.21
438.24	481.16	517.17		608.14	636.23

637.05	671.17	707.21	761.17	813.15	851.11
637.13	671.26	707.22	761.26	813.28	852.04
637.13	671.28	707.23	762.12	814.01	852.26
637.20	672.02	708.12	763.01	814.21	853.15
638.03	672.08	708.27	763.17	815.01	853.25
638.06	672.09	709.01	763.20	816.08	854.01
638.11	672.10	709.02	766.03	816.14	854.03
638.14	672.19	709.23	766.16	816.14	854.10
638.14	672.24	711.08	766.19	816.28	854.16
639.01	673.06	711.10	767.11	817.27	856.05
639.05	673.07	711.14	767.16	818.10	856.08
639.08	673.16	712.20	767.25	818.11	856.10
639.09	674.18	712.24	768.19	818.24	856.21
639.16	674.22	713.03	768.21	818.26	857.07
640.26	674.24	713.04	769.02	819.02	857.21
641.07	675.04	713.10	769.24	819.03	860.15
641.23	675.18	713.21	771.12	819.04	860.22
642.01	675.19	713.23	771.20	819.07	863.12
642.02	675.23	714.02	772.11	819.11	868.07
642.16	678.02	714.08	772.12	819.14	870.04
642.19	678.08	714.25	774.06	820.03	870.15
642.25	678.19	716.07	776.02	820.04	872.05
642.26	680.08	716.24	776.02	820.10	872.11
643.10	681.23	717.07	777.18	820.11	873.07
643.22	681.25	717.08	777.21	820.13	873.08
644.13	682.07	717.20	777.22	820.15	873.13
644.16	682.10	717.21	778.01	821.01	874.17
645.03	682.20	718.02	778.12	821.03	874.18
645.04	682.24	718.06	778.24	821.19	874.21
645.11	683.01	718.20	779.03	821.23	874.22
645.21	683.05	718.24	779.16	821.26	875.05
645.21	684.02	718.27	779.21	822.02	875.10
645.24	684.15	719.04	780.17	822.03	875.12
645.27	684.28	719.12	780.19	822.15	875.20
646.07	685.03	719.18	780.19	822.20	875.24
646.17	685.10	720.03	780.21	823.16	876.01
646.24	685.18	720.24	781.11	823.16	876.04
647.01	685.26	722.11	781.17	823.24	876.04
647.01	685.28	722.21	782.18	824.05	877.01
647.06	686.01	723.13	783.01	824.07	877.01
647.07	686.08	724.14	783.07	826.11	877.09
647.09	687.08	724.25	783.07	826.13	877.10
647.16	687.20	725.14	783.08	826.15	877.19
647.18	687.22	726.27	783.17	827.10	877.20
647.19	687.22	729.15	783.27	827.20	877.28
648.06	687.22	730.06	784.20	828.01	878.07
648.26	687.24	730.15	784.21	828.17	878.15
647.12	688.05	730.17	784.24	828.25	878.22
647.17	688.10	730.25	785.12	829.03	878.25
650.04	689.09	730.28	785.16	829.09	879.12
650.05	689.10	731.09	786.03	829.15	879.13
650.12	689.15	731.18	786.03	830.08	879.14
650.22	689.18	731.19	786.25	830.13	879.20
650.24	689.19	731.19	786.28	830.14	879.26
651.04	689.20	731.23	787.11	831.04	880.06
651.09	690.01	732.07	787.15	831.09	880.08
651.12	690.22	732.18	787.17	831.16	880.12
651.23	690.24	732.26	789.11	832.01	880.14
651.26	691.21	733.06	790.01	832.02	880.25
652.14	691.22	733.10	790.11	832.04	880.27
652.28	692.02	734.01	791.07	832.05	881.08
653.23	692.06	735.12	792.04	832.06	881.13
654.03	692.08	735.27	793.10	832.14	881.22
654.04	692.24	736.19	794.07	832.18	881.24
656.02	692.28	737.03	795.13	832.21	882.03
656.03	693.12	737.12	795.17	832.23	882.24
656.04	693.18	739.01	795.27	833.08	883.05
656.14	693.19	739.05	798.08	833.20	883.13
656.19	694.01	739.08	798.26	834.13	883.14
656.27	694.22	739.28	800.21	834.15	884.01
657.05	694.24	740.09	801.19	834.16	884.01
657.07	694.26	740.21	802.13	834.19	884.11
657.15	695.06	741.13	802.20	834.22	884.13
658.03	695.06	741.25	804.07	834.26	884.14
658.04	696.14	743.07	804.11	835.11	884.15
659.02	696.16	743.12	804.13	835.12	885.04
659.10	696.19	743.13	805.06	835.13	885.09
659.15	696.21	744.08	805.27	835.13	885.17
659.16	696.27	744.18	805.28	835.28	887.03
659.17	697.01	746.05	806.16	837.04	887.05
659.18	697.05	747.09	806.20	837.16	887.23
659.27	697.05	747.09	806.24	837.16	887.27
660.04	697.12	748.04	806.24	838.11	888.10
660.27	697.22	746.17	807.04	838.12	888.22
660.28	699.14	748.26	807.08	839.03	888.24
661.04	699.17	750.07	807.15	839.19	888.26
661.19	699.19	750.13	807.20	840.12	890.23
662.27	699.26	750.23	807.25	840.18	890.26
663.05	700.19	751.23	808.05	841.01	891.19
663.18	700.19	751.25	808.10	841.20	891.20
664.04	700.21	752.01	808.11	842.08	891.21
664.18	700.27	754.08	808.17	842.24	893.13
665.02	702.13	754.17	808.19	842.25	893.21
665.05	702.14	755.16	808.24	842.26	893.24
665.16	702.16	755.23	809.01	843.12	893.26
667.16	702.24	756.05	809.17	843.14	894.01
667.24	703.20	757.07	809.23	843.19	894.03
667.28	704.05	757.20	809.26	844.13	894.09
668.01	704.10	758.03	810.01	844.16	894.12
668.04	704.24	758.04	810.02	844.24	894.12
668.06	705.17	758.05	810.14	846.05	894.17
668.15	705.19	758.07	810.14	846.28	894.19
668.26	705.24	759.03	810.16	847.25	894.19
670.08	706.01	759.04	810.19	848.12	894.23
670.10	706.04	759.10	810.22	848.12	895.04
670.24	706.05	760.09	810.23	848.13	895.07
671.02	706.07	760.18	811.02	848.19	895.10
671.03	707.04	760.25	811.16	848.20	895.12
671.08	707.07	761.07	812.03	849.24	895.13
671.14	707.11	761.10	813.01	850.11	895.24
671.15	707.14		813.12	850.14	895.28

896.01	694.08	measured	meeting	242.06	815.09
896.28	704.03	086.26	168.20	265.13	815.11
897.08	721.19	115.14	255.07	354.06	903.24
897.12	724.06	169.26	287.27	359.15	911.02
898.01	734.22	431.20	314.07	388.26	mere
898.12	754.19	462.02	495.25	441.03	105.14
898.23	782.06	564.02	505.06	447.14	166.20
899.06	784.12	660.16	643.08	527.20	196.25
899.25	792.25	737.11	745.19	536.25	263.05
899.26	822.22	825.26	871.21	537.05	264.06
900.05	831.15	measureless	902.19	597.07	338.25
900.08	838.18	230.26	meetly	625.05	391.18
900.11	860.28	560.10	065.13	629.18	396.20
900.11	866.18	measures	meets	638.18	417.02
900.23	878.06	439.14	495.17	665.08	421.26
901.06	889.18	439.15	mein	684.07	425.20
901.20	889.20	463.23	612.12	701.08	428.18
901.21	meanest	meat	meines	740.06	434.14
901.27	312.01	094.05	678.26	762.03	434.22
902.07	709.01	112.25	678.27	844.08	440.11
903.03	meaning	311.05	melancholy	846.23	530.14
903.12	139.21	610.19	004.02	846.23	531.06
903.19	197.24	mechanically	125.13	men's	531.18
903.25	249.09	539.06	189.14	666.18	566.24
905.17	250.21	604.15	404.13	menace	637.19
906.16	267.18	654.10	561.19	112.10	638.21
907.03	382.15	875.07	574.13	465.20	647.13
907.04	678.19	medals	879.03	menaced	649.11
907.12	740.16	121.10	886.02	065.13	674.03
907.24	837.10	meddle	891.02	551.15	682.05
907.24	844.01	516.01	melancholy-looking	menaces	685.23
907.28	meanness	518.03	350.24	008.01	761.14
908.15	753.13	meddling	mellow	555.22	762.10
909.12	means	244.07	361.11	mended	781.10
909.19	024.25	medes	550.19	117.04	783.01
909.20	038.08	273.23	712.19	mendicant	786.26
910.04	091.02	mediation	mellowing	687.02	822.24
910.10	162.02	178.28	664.16	menial	824.26
910.15	166.27	mediatrix	melody	722.03	833.07
911.28	207.20	173.09	032.24	mental	834.05
912.02	310.19	medical	887.06	020.02	852.27
912.15	363.07	147.06	melt	029.17	881.13
912.22	385.26	629.18	435.17	191.08	903.14
meadow	392.21	mediocrity	465.18	426.12	merely
194.08	447.22	753.09	740.27	491.27	204.09
753.05	448.16	meditated	903.15	580.02	214.15
856.17	471.22	184.03	melted	580.04	256.15
857.13	505.18	290.17	111.17	629.03	265.22
857.27	536.08	452.20	144.05	715.08	372.03
meadows	692.20	504.15	553.15	815.14	375.26
493.25	724.22	559.13	653.02	824.20	418.09
501.14	762.03	818.25	903.17	895.14	472.15
542.01	769.13	meditating	melting	mentally	514.15
meagre	786.15	196.28	066.23	166.14	523.05
036.21	816.13	meditation	111.10	267.11	615.26
452.28	828.18	109.26	757.21	351.16	699.14
meal	838.22	715.02	melts	649.01	774.23
079.12	886.01	742.23	221.04	722.17	774.25
082.15	888.20	768.18	member	754.05	meretricious
095.12	890.01	826.06	096.20	852.01	576.03
117.27	meant	mediterranean	125.16	menteur	merge
118.12	129.14	622.15	339.24	543.17	822.09
139.09	138.13	medium	407.01	mention	merged
474.04	153.10	390.25	members	056.23	759.22
490.14	269.04	434.19	217.21	109.11	merging
522.16	475.26	440.19	717.14	173.08	683.22
566.09	493.03	513.11	720.02	343.03	meridian
661.12	497.23	811.23	meme	354.16	563.19
661.19	596.10	811.24	276.18	453.20	799.16
843.10	611.28	847.11	543.20	489.28	899.05
meals	630.23	medusa	memento	621.23	merino
009.11	634.25	776.07	284.01	621.24	226.17
035.17	804.05	meed	755.19	mentioned	462.04
042.16	886.22	104.14	899.20	117.27	merit
112.27	896.26	240.18	mementoes	135.26	086.26
700.24	907.28	720.17	588.14	150.05	106.17
801.12	meantime	meek	memoirs	171.09	193.01
mean	032.17	383.05	357.27	332.08	267.23
025.10	119.19	meet	memorable	430.01	372.12
068.11	149.28	065.09	139.28	457.20	744.25
188.12	227.16	174.14	memorandum	593.21	786.10
225.27	257.22	180.23	116.21	603.04	835.19
245.09	281.09	182.04	memories	680.17	merited
260.05	300.13	186.21	221.11	738.27	901.14
267.22	359.08	200.21	memory	890.13	meriting
285.22	365.26	212.02	098.18	mentioning	191.14
291.13	378.11	229.11	135.10	451.15	merits
351.26	390.22	229.23	142.15	907.13	289.24
351.28	392.05	279.05	160.06	mentions	mermaid
372.12	418.21	305.06	207.18	772.16	565.04
373.03	470.14	315.09	228.26	mercenary	merrily
388.02	508.06	323.23	268.22	266.20	275.14
399.03	555.18	347.06	268.23	286.28	566.28
439.23	668.23	383.11	268.27	merchant	merriment
463.05	717.09	396.19	273.02	593.13	380.08
494.11	731.09	445.18	320.15	624.15	merry
525.13	774.18	492.10	371.27	780.07	352.07
528.27	812.17	545.11	439.21	merchants	356.02
534.10	833.05	562.19	445.01	740.07	364.02
539.20	851.06	563.25	638.08	merciful	389.17
543.07	851.15	564.10	741.26	762.17	411.08
552.27	860.01	564.22	men	merciless	522.14
615.15	893.02	584.05	017.01	051.08	797.22
618.11	measure	598.17	022.15	mercy	800.15
622.09	100.16	646.21	032.01	033.13	mes
635.12	191.03	658.13	033.09	063.10	277.10
635.16	403.23	684.08	089.14	063.10	277.10
645.24	734.27	703.03	132.20	305.19	mesdames
645.28	757.15	843.09	216.18	430.28	212.02
679.16	860.15	852.14	216.19	546.27	347.08
687.12	908.12	852.17	242.02	547.01	417.18

meshes
  327.21
  343.22
mesrour
  332.26
  745.09
  380.23
  564.06
mesrour's
  639.04
mess
  082.20
  094.04
  600.01
  672.07
message
  165.08
  255.11
  272.09
  314.14
  336.20
  413.01
  445.26
  610.23
  814.14
messalina's
  636.20
messenger
  022.20
  272.01
  451.01
  615.05
messenger-pigeon
  654.25
messrs
  579.02
met
  041.08
  001.24
  119.22
  174.26
  224.26
  268.02
  236.17
  290.28
  389.14
  389.15
  434.11
  522.22
  528.16
  642.19
  713.07
  745.17
  799.03
  801.24
  617.09
  318.02
  629.05
  632.27
  855.05
  872.26
  902.20
metal
  203.02
  633.05
metallic
  065.19
  220.26
metamorphosed
  331.05
meted
  403.23
method
  103.25
  477.02
mich
  661.03
  698.09
middle
  079.03
  080.10
  083.26
  087.26
  094.16
  103.01
  127.08
  149.08
  219.17
  219.24
  224.12
  224.17
  262.01
  451.03
  471.23
  668.27
middle-aged
  400.21
  750.09
  860.17
midge
  865.05
midnight
  652.21
  800.07
  850.04
  901.24
  902.25
  903.16
midnight-dark
  230.25
midnight
  567.11
midst
  015.06
  296.10

  392.11
  656.08
  745.09
  844.02
  855.02
  856.13
  903.23
midsummer
  250.04
  501.02
  605.23
midsummer-eve
  501.15
mien
  139.01
  437.15
  460.22
  627.28
might
  006.12
  015.05
  015.11
  015.16
  021.10
  022.20
  022.25
  023.02
  028.04
  028.22
  031.23
  033.24
  037.19
  041.08
  046.18
  049.23
  056.26
  056.26
  060.15
  062.14
  077.17
  103.15
  121.05
  121.22
  123.06
  125.14
  152.07
  154.03
  167.04
  169.22
  169.22
  173.14
  189.26
  215.06
  215.06
  222.10
  224.13
  229.07
  229.09
  239.04
  268.12
  268.19
  268.19
  273.09
  294.13
  300.28
  322.28
  325.24
  335.28
  336.21
  344.05
  346.06
  349.15
  349.23
  357.20
  362.04
  370.04
  372.04
  375.10
  375.12
  375.17
  375.25
  376.11
  376.12
  378.08
  381.27
  385.14
  388.24
  396.23
  396.26
  406.13
  409.23
  425.23
  426.16
  428.17
  436.21
  439.10
  444.20
  452.07
  454.04
  472.07
  478.04
  498.23
  502.16
  504.11
  521.15
  529.23
  529.26
  536.19
  537.23
  539.18

  542.22
  544.09
  544.14
  545.15
  547.04
  551.11
  552.03
  553.02
  553.04
  560.22
  575.07
  580.22
  604.13
  610.01
  625.23
  634.06
  635.02
  638.10
  641.06
  643.12
  646.17
  648.12
  649.21
  653.14
  659.09
  659.12
  660.02
  660.03
  661.23
  662.17
  663.11
  664.03
  664.04
  667.19
  674.26
  698.07
  701.28
  709.12
  715.16
  725.07
  726.21
  732.21
  736.24
  742.14
  751.11
  756.06
  759.18
  768.21
  782.15
  782.23
  784.23
  805.24
  807.27
  819.10
  820.25
  822.14
  824.01
  824.02
  847.22
  849.15
  853.24
  856.06
  858.02
  861.07
  872.08
  879.17
  900.26
  901.01
  901.13
mightily
  705.26
mighty
  031.28
  109.14
  158.11
  194.09
  608.10
  662.14
  678.23
  785.18
  816.10
  850.20
  900.10
  912.06
migrated
  587.22
mild
  033.12
  104.16
  141.14
  151.01
  331.26
  378.23
  492.23
  732.15
  855.03
mild-looking
  667.17
milder
  186.12
  346.12
mildly
  846.18
mile
  079.18
  219.07
  220.15
  229.14
  430.19
  503.16
  564.02
  654.23

  658.06
  669.19
  732.13
  865.22
  869.18
miles
  007.12
  073.15
  074.08
  092.14
  112.20
  169.09
  172.11
  179.25
  180.05
  183.21
  218.17
  316.12
  450.20
  451.25
  452.15
  464.03
  490.22
  490.23
  499.23
  511.01
  559.12
  658.18
  695.15
  739.01
  799.23
  855.11
  867.27
military
  350.16
milk
  050.15
  071.18
  142.27
  326.20
  360.17
  685.25
  686.01
  686.12
  688.01
milky-way
  662.14
millcote
  171.17
  172.07
  172.14
  180.27
  181.05
  181.20
  184.23
  194.19
  222.14
  234.17
  254.05
  255.08
  316.12
  327.03
  330.03
  332.11
  334.26
  339.25
  379.16
  401.05
  492.10
  495.04
  526.07
  534.11
  538.12
  541.21
  543.24
  654.24
  861.23
mille
  277.17
miller
  077.06
  077.16
  077.20
  078.18
  078.25
  079.13
  079.28
  080.14
  080.18
  080.26
  081.07
  082.02
  082.08
  083.16
  083.20
  083.05
  084.26
  085.12
  104.26
  114.10
  129.19
  154.01
miller's
  079.18
millions
  131.02
  131.04
  216.09
  216.10
minature
  323.11

mince
  234.25
mince-pies
  792.07
mind
  013.19
  018.13
  023.14
  029.11
  029.26
  031.17
  061.14
  065.10
  068.24
  107.01
  139.12
  152.08
  152.14
  157.09
  163.03
  163.25
  166.03
  167.26
  168.12
  177.16
  182.02
  205.13
  214.22
  221.11
  241.19
  247.17
  256.05
  258.05
  268.02
  263.21
  276.05
  276.24
  285.18
  285.21
  289.23
  291.12
  291.28
  306.03
  311.09
  313.21
  320.18
  334.21
  336.04
  358.20
  373.06
  402.26
  408.16
  429.09
  439.08
  440.27
  448.16
  467.06
  473.20
  475.02
  479.15
  481.14
  483.10
  483.17
  485.10
  485.16
  505.22
  512.05
  514.02
  524.23
  532.26
  533.08
  535.02
  538.01
  543.15
  547.13
  559.03
  559.15
  560.10
  568.19
  607.23
  609.06
  617.13
  625.21
  626.04
  626.15
  629.15
  636.12
  638.07
  638.16
  651.27
  682.27
  689.03
  695.04
  706.13
  707.13
  716.02
  716.14
  722.27
  726.20
  730.16
  735.05
  736.05
  748.19
  757.22
  770.11
  787.09
  788.02
  790.25
  805.26
  806.20
  817.03

  817.18
  825.19
  825.23
  835.19
  835.24
  837.08
  854.03
  876.05
  880.07
  884.07
  885.13
  899.13
  902.11
  903.06
  903.07
  907.19
  912.19
mind's
  215.24
  313.02
mindful
  135.19
mindless
  637.08
minds
  161.18
  500.03
  511.28
  760.28
mine
  009.14
  013.10
  019.26
  038.28
  054.02
  061.18
  062.12
  062.21
  065.06
  085.07
  104.27
  108.13
  190.06
  199.02
  206.11
  216.10
  246.14
  257.04
  287.02
  301.08
  329.27
  351.11
  366.01
  375.22
  398.11
  417.26
  418.05
  430.22
  466.04
  469.27
  485.02
  516.19
  517.26
  542.14
  543.03
  545.13
  545.18
  547.24
  549.02
  552.06
  570.03
  578.24
  612.06
  614.24
  616.10
  623.22
  626.14
  627.24
  626.17
  653.01
  657.12
  684.28
  686.02
  697.17
  721.07
  758.06
  781.21
  782.23
  784.23
  803.15
  807.19
  815.17
  818.27
  824.19
  825.23
  836.13
  836.26
  839.27
  876.13
  882.21
  894.11
  902.23
  907.09
  908.16
  908.28
  909.04
mingle
  663.21
mingled
  337.12
  435.02

630.07
mingling
231.16
333.02
miniature
016.22
046.25
276.22
345.07
752.07
minister
724.19
ministerial
715.06
ministrant
411.16
ministry
735.12
898.22
minois
343.13
minor
824.23
minute
076.26
099.15
110.05
124.03
128.11
193.12
229.05
276.05
315.07
362.23
420.20
672.03
680.20
762.21
764.09
777.19
798.05
866.02
896.08
minutely
108.14
812.15
minutes
008.10
008.23
026.16
052.02
053.05
060.14
073.06
079.22
080.17
083.28
101.23
115.10
121.10
126.03
135.14
136.09
157.02
151.26
156.11
156.25
170.11
180.10
180.18
185.15
198.15
226.25
245.17
259.10
276.13
276.20
285.06
289.12
297.21
298.27
299.27
305.10
332.15
332.19
367.15
389.10
391.07
426.24
432.02
441.19
454.14
457.23
473.23
477.01
477.01
481.12
486.08
535.24
562.20
566.06
586.07
596.01
611.10
621.27
623.28
656.20
667.07
687.28
691.22
692.23

696.28
715.01
717.24
726.26
796.08
801.01
811.04
812.04
905.19
minutes'
573.21
581.01
miracle
749.21
850.09
miraculous
310.25
mire
608.13
mirror
009.17
022.14
360.10
577.20
585.11
mirrors
016.17
049.18
204.18
327.18
794.20
mirthless
210.08
miry
321.23
misapprehension
267.18
mischief
051.03
253.01
310.16
864.02
misconstrue
520.01
misdemeanor
779.02
miserable
034.19
036.06
046.01
051.26
062.27
184.08
439.16
476.18
483.07
707.06
735.10
777.12
miseries
618.04
misery
272.07
644.04
647.22
655.28
684.04
860.16
877.06
misfortune
192.20
542.04
misfortunes
725.24
misgiving
158.05
mishap
447.07
misinterpret
761.08
836.08
misjudge
617.05
misjudged
534.07
miss
012.04
012.12
012.15
013.09
013.11
013.22
014.07
014.17
015.04
015.09
017.05
023.26
024.21
028.01
033.23
034.03
034.06
034.20
035.15
040.18
041.05
041.12
041.14
047.13
050.19

057.25
059.25
060.01
066.27
067.19
069.07
072.13
072.16
072.20
077.05
077.16
077.20
078.18
078.25
079.12
079.18
079.28
080.14
080.18
080.26
081.02
082.02
082.08
083.16
083.20
083.25
084.25
085.12
086.12
086.24
092.09
092.18
092.22
092.26
093.10
093.13
093.14
094.17
097.09
097.15
097.19
097.27
098.21
099.03
099.09
099.17
100.01
100.21
102.11
103.21
103.27
104.06
104.06
104.08
104.10
104.26
105.02
106.05
106.07
106.13
108.13
110.05
113.06
114.10
115.15
115.27
116.06
116.16
116.20
117.08
118.02
119.10
119.25
119.26
120.03
120.11
120.18
120.24
121.14
122.12
122.21
122.27
123.25
124.22
126.28
127.22
128.05
128.10
129.19
130.01
132.09
133.27
134.07
134.21
135.24
136.08
136.27
137.17
138.01
138.28
139.19
140.11
140.20
141.01
141.11
141.18
141.27
142.02
147.09
151.06
153.19

154.01
154.10
154.28
155.10
155.16
157.11
159.13
162.13
163.09
163.26
166.06
170.25
174.26
175.15
176.09
176.12
176.13
176.22
176.24
178.01
178.20
179.03
179.04
179.12
182.11
185.07
188.05
188.12
188.12
188.18
197.08
204.24
232.13
236.16
237.22
237.26
238.02
239.14
239.28
243.02
243.12
251.02
256.18
256.28
258.01
259.14
262.11
264.10
264.16
269.05
270.18
273.10
273.27
275.12
276.07
277.24
279.18
281.06
282.06
283.23
307.10
308.06
308.13
308.25
310.17
317.18
318.03
319.03
333.05
338.01
338.23
340.23
345.24
346.02
346.14
346.21
347.09
355.16
355.19
356.12
357.25
359.05
360.16
360.25
366.01
367.05
368.11
370.12
371.08
371.20
371.21
372.26
372.28
374.17
374.27
376.24
378.07
379.08
380.15
380.22
381.09
386.13
387.13
388.23
389.06
389.12
389.24
390.10
391.04
392.15
393.01

403.01
406.14
411.09
416.20
417.15
441.27
446.07
446.14
446.17
446.24
447.06
448.17
448.18
448.23
448.27
449.12
449.14
449.20
456.09
457.27
460.20
461.23
469.21
491.22
492.02
507.07
507.12
507.24
508.04
512.15
515.27
516.07
522.17
531.26
532.12
532.13
532.22
533.01
535.11
624.23
708.03
721.25
739.22
741.10
742.03
748.04
755.01
760.04
760.06
760.22
761.12
780.05
783.22
787.19
797.01
864.23
865.11
873.15
886.06
891.06
894.03
906.03
906.15
missed
570.09
762.14
809.20
misses
014.19
122.12
366.02
386.11
389.23
416.25
449.15
454.15
mission
121.17
160.12
387.19
387.28
714.19
747.27
822.11
missionary
546.18
736.03
736.04
751.14
759.17
816.17
816.18
822.26
822.27
837.18
847.24
missionary's
759.16
797.24
815.13
815.16
895.08
missis
014.01
014.02
014.20
015.02
028.24
034.11
040.11
068.13

068.18
072.05
072.17
177.14
179.19
179.24
180.11
447.21
447.22
448.28
464.13
mist
003.13
088.14
335.21
342.17
mista'en
696.17
mistake
063.27
237.11
255.20
267.03
275.11
324.18
481.01
523.17
612.04
625.27
735.11
776.25
776.26
mistaken
131.06
156.04
327.13
500.02
576.08
617.09
694.01
743.09
843.14
mistimed
118.21
mistress
039.26
257.23
459.02
466.21
597.02
615.05
622.19
622.27
637.18
637.22
696.07
697.23
698.11
722.02
722.06
731.16
739.02
787.21
846.21
858.05
862.15
876.24
888.23
mistress's
721.22
mistresses
334.25
636.26
638.15
682.09
682.20
mistrust
661.01
752.19
797.05
818.07
mistrustful
170.13
787.17
mists
145.16
misty
075.02
185.04
459.18
673.09
852.13
misunderstand
784.01
784.02
837.09
misunderstanding
691.17
misunderstandings
252.18
misunderstood
724.05
mit
678.26
mittens
170.03
340.15
mix
322.06
mixed
094.06

```
629.06              460.07          mon                 734.21          moonrise            131.22
mixes               466.05            281.27            760.19            505.06            135.17
  197.23            477.06          monday              760.20          moor                135.23
mixture             494.10            900.22            790.19            271.04            137.20
  781.15            533.07            901.23            801.24            589.11            139.11
moan                545.04            902.25            806.04            659.07            139.18
  101.02            545.16          monde               809.16            659.26            140.24
moaned              551.25            334.05            817.10            663.07            149.18
  295.11            555.05          money               840.23            675.11            161.09
  426.08            573.07            009.09            864.13            687.14            161.18
  426.15            575.20            014.22            883.21            695.09            163.01
moaning             577.20            048.13            885.18            799.24            164.06
  468.18            586.25            048.23            892.20            829.20            166.19
  572.02            590.13            091.15            907.12          moor-edge           169.16
  674.23            591.16            168.04          months'             674.06            169.21
mobile              596.14            177.17            759.06          moor-house          170.15
  404.25            602.13            252.22            792.27            711.02            174.18
mocked              612.08            330.14          mony                717.10            185.01
  515.11            619.20            398.28            696.07            741.28            185.02
mockery             628.14            448.03            696.18            781.14            186.16
  644.17            630.24            452.23          mood                784.17            187.27
  877.13            636.07            452.24            018.05            784.18            188.11
mocking             645.08            454.28            090.27            791.07            196.13
  347.10            648.23            469.07            223.25            791.24            206.19
  404.15            648.27            469.07            237.19            793.02            206.21
  424.20            658.07            470.04            254.19            793.26            207.12
  885.16            659.15            522.10            290.16            794.26            215.09
mode                663.11            536.07            445.16            809.04            215.10
  021.07            665.21            547.21            521.20            854.13            215.15
  086.04            681.21            616.20            540.01            889.06            216.20
model               683.27            624.23            558.25            906.26            216.26
  172.03            693.24            636.02            738.13          moor-side           216.26
  322.14            697.19            661.05            812.02            659.22            237.07
  368.09            725.16            679.18            900.22          moorish             242.12
  749.26            732.06            694.08          moodily             719.19            249.14
  794.26            733.07            698.22            284.07          moorland            250.13
models              736.05            776.02          moodiness           658.21            251.06
  701.27            740.10            888.04            292.25            673.13            253.18
moderate            742.12          money-speculation moods               700.24            258.27
  155.13            753.20            786.26            277.28            712.09            258.28
  329.05            764.11          monitor             806.26            850.03            262.12
  669.03            769.25            085.15          moody             moors               263.24
moderation          770.12            109.27            292.19            017.27            265.23
  214.21            774.05            110.08          moon                033.08            270.28
modern              775.09            124.10            004.24            659.01            271.27
  190.28            776.18            855.27            023.07            699.01            272.07
  526.16            780.20          monitor's           072.24            712.03            275.15
  701.12            782.04            114.22            133.24            715.26            275.26
  752.25            782.07          monitors            152.05            749.17            277.25
modes               797.28            078.20            154.13            800.15            285.23
  365.20            798.17            078.26            220.12            852.13            288.09
modest              804.07          monitress           224.08            855.05            290.03
  502.10            805.10            538.17            226.01          mope                290.25
  537.23            808.24          monkey              230.21            006.04            292.12
  597.17            811.22            381.10            231.03          moral               292.20
  729.12            811.28          monosyllabic        242.11            444.12            295.24
  790.04            816.22            217.19            342.18            670.21            296.06
  794.27            816.22          monotonous          414.05            706.14            296.06
modestly            817.04            228.19            418.21          moralists           298.12
  120.17            821.17            400.08            471.04            570.16            299.16
modesty             857.03            724.10            502.11          morality            301.11
  625.20            857.08          monotony            503.05            292.26            307.11
moi                 858.17            364.04            504.16          morally             311.19
  212.04            873.03          monsieur            518.24            509.26            313.28
  234.21            874.02            234.12            540.14            603.21            313.28
moiety              884.13            234.22            540.22          morass              314.01
  114.02            894.10            239.10            541.12            724.13            314.01
moistened           899.18            277.16            541.17          morbid              316.18
  421.17            902.07            277.20            542.19            033.26            317.28
mole-eyed           902.17            287.18            543.05          more                319.23
  625.22            904.02            380.14            543.12            002.12            320.08
molested          moment's          monster             543.23            002.13            320.26
  130.07            012.08            031.28            561.11            002.14            327.02
momemt              803.02            537.10            562.25            007.17            339.23
  725.22            883.04            632.27            563.06            008.07            343.11
moment            momentarily       monster-splinters   564.07            017.16            343.22
  018.03            133.16            560.25            583.06            019.24            346.12
  023.05            283.16          monstrous           629.28            020.23            348.16
  039.23            305.07            820.24            652.05            020.24            350.04
  054.15            471.01          month               652.09            026.12            353.25
  093.25            511.25            007.11            652.11            026.16            357.12
  116.09            552.16            041.03            833.23            030.24            363.01
  128.02            561.11            114.27            834.21            031.20            365.02
  140.13            588.22            192.06            844.02            034.02            367.21
  141.18            630.07            475.25            845.04            037.25            370.22
  209.22            653.17            487.03            901.09            041.13            374.24
  226.17          momentary           495.11          moon-light          042.13            374.26
  238.03            424.09            495.23            207.27            043.04            375.18
  239.07            727.22            508.12            248.23            058.26            376.08
  240.02          momently            535.24          moon-rise           062.13            384.25
  273.11            220.13            548.15            151.20            067.16            385.02
  273.22            390.14            557.02          moonbeams           068.03            388.08
  283.23            831.09            565.17            229.12            068.23            390.14
  286.21          momentous           717.09          moonless            074.24            390.15
  296.15            726.04            724.25            033.05            077.21            397.13
  313.11          moments             760.07          moonlight           082.05            406.27
  316.10            007.26          months              023.08            083.12            411.14
  335.17            021.21            051.19            225.23            093.16            412.07
  348.26            434.14            130.04            242.03            093.28            417.24
  349.05            490.25            142.19            280.24            095.16            419.24
  351.03            500.07            197.20            416.06            100.15            426.24
  356.27            514.22            241.05            445.25            101.11            426.26
  371.27            670.08            288.05            516.22            101.23            428.26
  385.20            670.09            364.04            532.07            103.17            436.03
  400.26            617.21            446.19            562.17            115.22            440.08
  406.09            648.09            453.15            575.02            116.23            453.10
  408.24            703.18            462.22            712.23            116.25            456.16
  436.21            718.21            527.18            848.27            118.15            456.26
  437.02            825.22            593.23          moonlit             119.24            457.16
  445.18            846.26            637.07            285.04            120.12            461.11
  449.27                              731.06                              130.09            462.23
```

462.24	721.09	757.03	856.11	most	068.05
467.18	724.11	784.22	856.20	022.02	091.10
468.20	724.24	838.14	886.03	025.06	093.20
469.07	724.26	morning	886.26	030.21	162.18
470.07	725.10	001.05	887.16	031.01	176.08
470.10	727.02	019.10	905.10	032.08	196.07
472.05	727.10	033.27	910.08	032.09	288.10
472.07	727.14	048.06	morning's	045.01	289.02
473.24	731.20	050.21	499.27	045.05	289.22
474.25	732.19	055.09	539.19	047.16	385.19
476.01	735.13	071.02	mornings	066.20	395.13
476.08	735.14	072.08	144.10	070.02	403.18
477.17	746.09	072.28	254.03	082.24	446.20
483.16	747.13	087.06	294.18	097.13	447.05
484.10	750.27	096.03	morocco	098.08	447.15
493.19	752.05	096.15	768.16	098.16	448.20
500.10	755.11	098.25	morose	101.06	451.21
502.18	756.12	100.14	082.04	104.19	461.14
502.19	756.24	104.24	292.23	107.15	468.06
503.06	761.09	112.03	moroseness	116.13	475.04
503.07	762.01	112.23	642.01	135.13	475.28
507.18	763.07	129.18	morrow	135.13	516.06
510.13	767.07	141.11	128.06	142.05	597.12
516.26	773.20	144.18	152.05	147.01	625.25
523.21	774.13	148.07	799.15	148.10	627.16
527.07	774.26	148.16	morsel	163.17	628.18
529.05	775.13	151.28	007.25	164.20	652.18
532.28	776.23	174.13	050.16	173.18	659.19
533.25	778.04	180.19	112.13	178.08	661.04
533.26	778.06	193.24	138.08	187.08	672.09
533.28	784.03	199.06	311.06	202.13	681.02
535.15	793.06	203.07	478.25	220.23	696.06
544.19	794.12	203.13	513.01	231.13	769.05
544.19	796.07	211.25	661.05	240.19	780.23
545.11	802.08	218.13	682.15	257.16	799.20
554.05	803.17	233.04	mortal	262.25	mother's
554.12	804.09	233.13	360.27	267.07	007.15
554.25	804.20	245.24	363.05	272.08	018.11
555.15	806.21	250.02	495.07	285.11	021.19
556.02	808.05	259.01	513.12	310.26	196.03
557.06	808.06	287.28	600.20	314.12	288.28
559.03	808.06	302.18	630.16	316.01	345.16
560.18	810.07	305.07	763.04	317.09	451.01
561.05	811.05	305.12	783.23	318.02	473.18
561.06	813.11	309.06	823.18	318.02	473.23
562.10	820.10	311.21	mortality	322.07	477.18
570.12	827.05	314.07	147.28	339.12	727.04
570.13	828.26	321.11	mortally	341.13	780.04
572.03	832.17	390.09	074.20	343.28	mother-in-law
574.15	833.01	401.05	227.16	344.08	508.22
580.05	833.03	409.06	679.23	346.26	moths
582.21	834.04	422.01	mortar	348.05	507.18
582.24	834.13	433.02	859.11	349.26	motion
595.16	835.09	435.06	mortgages	350.20	075.12
598.04	843.20	443.05	469.12	358.27	075.21
601.08	843.28	448.11	mortification	391.26	358.02
601.14	844.01	448.24	466.18	394.13	494.14
606.19	844.10	449.28	mortified	401.04	motionless
607.07	844.11	452.22	035.08	401.23	084.06
611.10	846.04	456.28	mortify	401.23	296.11
612.05	847.27	457.21	058.10	410.11	347.04
616.03	848.21	459.18	121.17	471.28	689.08
618.03	849.13	460.09	462.19	475.19	847.13
619.05	852.15	464.27	mortifying	478.06	motive
619.21	853.01	469.22	161.05	493.19	042.05
621.14	854.24	471.10	834.09	526.03	164.04
633.21	856.06	485.19	morton	544.06	motives
642.05	857.07	488.23	695.14	545.12	273.22
643.20	865.03	492.03	698.03	546.25	376.20
643.25	865.26	519.03	698.08	554.10	439.06
647.03	875.26	520.12	698.28	558.15	550.06
648.02	876.15	522.02	699.10	566.23	motto
648.02	877.08	523.11	716.04	601.17	360.01
648.03	879.16	524.15	718.19	609.11	mould
648.03	880.24	534.11	721.12	616.11	267.23
649.17	882.10	534.24	721.16	622.17	672.14
658.14	883.27	540.20	723.17	627.23	808.13
667.04	884.03	580.11	728.03	662.08	moulded
670.01	884.22	588.10	732.25	666.13	203.20
670.02	885.02	605.01	736.11	689.18	345.02
671.26	887.06	605.01	739.07	693.06	737.21
672.18	889.01	617.18	749.16	704.08	moulder
673.12	894.01	622.25	750.24	724.07	673.22
676.25	896.26	634.08	751.09	727.06	mouldering
679.18	898.18	654.03	789.04	740.06	711.17
681.04	900.02	655.09	790.12	741.17	mouldings
681.25	901.14	663.03	793.03	790.08	204.13
681.26	901.16	672.01	804.08	801.16	mound
686.13	906.18	672.28	805.02	819.14	159.20
686.15	908.01	689.11	809.02	836.12	mount
687.03	908.05	690.07	855.05	836.12	134.05
687.28	909.02	714.17	891.25	864.14	152.27
692.26	909.04	717.23	mosaic	884.06	163.12
694.02	909.10	729.17	235.17	887.16	225.16
696.25	911.04	730.21	mosquitoes	897.21	564.15
697.11	911.16	740.03	629.25	908.21	652.01
699.28	912.23	746.01	moss	910.01	688.08
700.01	912.24	746.06	146.07	910.01	704.20
703.22	more's	760.16	209.07	911.04	735.26
704.01	370.21	769.06	673.29	moth	762.04
707.28	moreen	791.15	712.17	504.04	mountain
709.13	003.05	800.03	799.24	504.14	164.24
709.19	moreland	800.18	moss-blackened	504.27	227.20
711.02	005.27	800.28	659.24	mother	227.22
713.01	moreoever	810.04	mossy	007.20	658.21
714.23	642.15	811.12	588.15	019.03	711.19
715.23	moreover	811.18	661.20	036.23	724.13
716.22	553.20	832.06	812.14	040.20	732.02
717.04	554.08	845.24	858.05	040.24	804.17
720.15	629.09	852.08	mossy-faced	041.01	812.23
721.03	715.18	854.28	712.10	048.28	903.16

mountains	159.06	198.26	352.24	491.16	653.24
033.04	172.14	198.27	353.05	492.05	657.03
540.25	215.27	199.10	353.10	493.16	661.26
607.17	251.09	202.01	353.28	494.07	662.13
659.02	334.03	202.03	355.03	496.01	662.22
765.14	364.08	202.11	356.11	497.08	666.15
902.15	397.08	204.24	358.02	497.28	666.17
mounted	418.18	205.03	358.27	498.25	673.03
003.02	449.25	206.17	360.10	499.15	680.22
074.26	591.12	206.17	361.10	499.26	681.01
127.06	594.10	226.07	361.27	503.13	681.17
154.27	611.09	226.08	365.11	503.20	684.18
180.24	619.24	232.10	365.26	504.05	685.09
564.06	635.09	232.23	366.14	504.28	687.04
598.25	719.06	232.24	366.22	505.14	687.26
746.08	741.07	233.02	366.26	506.13	690.24
850.17	858.21	234.06	367.07	512.05	695.11
mounting	871.11	235.07	367.17	513.17	695.23
204.05	movements	235.21	368.05	515.01	695.26
388.25	061.19	236.05	369.26	516.21	697.11
mourn	099.10	236.20	370.11	519.01	697.25
604.14	125.22	237.01	371.05	519.09	698.03
mournful	275.25	237.17	371.20	519.17	698.17
468.09	324.18	239.03	372.02	520.08	699.14
571.20	342.23	240.20	373.25	521.05	700.27
572.09	351.13	242.16	374.28	522.26	701.17
643.03	378.14	243.06	375.11	525.28	702.22
715.02	399.22	244.05	376.16	527.05	706.03
886.13	424.05	244.15	378.26	532.26	706.22
mourning	467.24	245.21	379.06	533.08	706.24
446.04	494.24	246.12	381.06	534.21	707.20
677.01	573.04	249.19	381.19	534.27	708.05
727.21	768.15	251.15	381.27	535.21	709.10
894.16	moving	252.11	383.02	536.24	710.01
mouse	017.23	252.19	383.08	537.11	714.07
299.02	041.13	252.20	384.01	537.14	717.20
mouth	208.20	252.25	384.07	538.06	719.01
054.02	503.16	253.01	384.18	538.13	721.26
060.22	563.02	253.02	384.20	538.26	722.19
119.01	mr	253.02	384.28	541.03	723.15
119.15	007.12	253.20	385.06	543.17	726.21
158.10	016.26	254.03	390.07	543.25	728.01
192.19	021.15	255.09	401.10	545.01	728.04
237.10	022.09	256.02	401.15	545.07	731.16
350.02	022.19	257.26	401.18	547.01	733.02
382.22	027.11	258.08	401.22	555.18	733.06
383.23	033.28	258.20	402.09	557.15	736.27
398.02	035.09	260.19	402.12	559.08	737.05
403.14	035.20	266.07	402.27	562.04	740.02
404.21	035.24	277.13	403.18	571.17	740.09
404.27	035.27	279.02	407.16	576.22	741.14
471.22	037.01	289.27	408.19	580.17	741.19
485.12	039.19	290.06	409.04	583.08	742.04
602.02	039.26	292.08	409.17	585.04	745.17
701.26	042.02	294.16	410.27	585.18	746.17
702.11	053.21	296.04	411.06	586.14	748.27
740.11	056.15	296.10	411.13	586.20	750.08
mouthed	056.25	297.02	412.23	587.07	751.04
344.21	057.13	299.15	413.01	587.11	751.05
mouthful	057.21	305.03	413.06	587.22	751.18
670.03	058.05	305.15	416.17	588.19	754.03
mouths	058.27	307.26	418.08	589.22	754.15
119.05	059.17	312.09	419.08	590.14	756.05
move	059.28	312.19	420.19	590.21	765.02
017.14	060.10	313.06	421.08	591.03	769.11
226.27	061.12	314.05	421.13	591.11	771.16
275.22	064.06	314.15	421.19	591.19	771.17
299.03	064.27	315.17	421.20	592.04	771.20
302.13	083.19	316.06	421.25	592.10	772.09
307.28	092.10	316.08	422.17	593.04	772.12
356.01	092.11	316.11	424.07	594.05	772.15
422.15	102.20	316.24	424.28	594.07	772.22
427.07	114.24	317.13	425.04	594.15	772.27
431.13	115.20	317.26	425.05	595.01	773.01
506.19	115.26	318.08	425.10	595.22	773.12
506.21	117.18	318.25	425.11	596.09	774.12
574.06	119.09	318.27	425.18	598.14	774.13
663.08	119.19	319.08	425.19	599.02	774.16
664.25	121.03	319.17	427.01	599.22	774.17
689.16	121.24	319.21	427.11	600.16	774.19
692.01	122.27	319.25	428.09	601.02	774.23
797.22	123.14	320.04	429.05	601.17	776.07
830.05	124.08	321.01	430.09	602.12	776.18
moved	124.15	322.14	430.21	602.19	777.08
030.07	124.20	322.26	431.26	602.22	777.21
039.11	126.10	322.28	432.01	602.22	779.01
052.22	126.25	324.02	432.10	603.01	780.07
065.01	131.09	324.18	433.11	603.01	780.08
065.19	131.11	325.25	433.15	603.04	783.06
238.16	132.28	326.20	434.04	603.07	783.27
351.08	134.24	332.07	436.15	603.16	788.09
358.17	135.27	332.25	438.03	603.23	789.18
370.04	136.10	333.14	438.09	603.25	790.14
381.03	137.26	335.28	440.22	604.02	799.20
413.25	141.28	336.03	447.03	604.05	801.15
434.06	148.18	336.21	447.28	605.09	808.22
479.23	151.23	337.14	448.05	606.17	809.07
589.04	152.25	338.03	449.07	606.21	809.08
590.22	153.03	338.09	449.24	611.05	810.17
604.22	161.05	338.20	450.06	613.08	819.05
608.06	161.13	339.18	450.06	621.26	838.27
654.07	163.08	339.26	451.01	623.15	839.01
675.23	173.06	345.10	451.06	624.14	856.02
716.27	173.10	346.22	452.20	624.17	860.23
727.02	177.16	347.12	453.20	645.16	860.28
767.18	179.23	348.08	456.06	645.18	861.03
768.03	195.11	348.18	460.10	647.03	861.03
833.15	195.16	350.23	472.18	648.21	861.11
907.24	196.07	350.28	487.02	650.20	862.13
movement	196.15	352.08	487.08	652.27	862.21
139.21	198.19	352.15		653.16	862.23

862.26	206.10	463.20	243.14	730.14	murmured
863.07	208.10	465.06	243.18	731.01	064.20
864.13	208.20	466.08	245.04	734.12	141.08
865.13	209.22	468.04	246.27	739.16	296.14
865.26	210.16	469.24	249.23	748.01	380.01
866.19	210.28	470.07	251.07	756.06	421.24
867.08	211.17	480.14	254.04	757.10	428.05
867.21	212.06	483.15	258.06	761.21	480.12
869.05	213.06	490.24	258.23	762.28	481.24
873.09	214.13	491.14	262.06	764.11	518.14
873.21	214.28	491.18	262.11	772.12	610.27
875.07	215.13	492.08	262.27	776.09	705.03
883.09	218.04	493.07	263.01	776.11	725.21
890.25	218.13	496.16	267.13	779.20	755.12
891.08	218.19	496.22	269.08	785.12	763.09
891.23	229.23	498.07	273.19	786.19	896.04
897.24	231.20	498.18	279.18	786.22	murmuring
899.04	231.22	499.12	289.20	794.10	476.03
903.01	232.12	508.25	291.07	803.09	murmurs
905.09	232.22	509.14	293.09	817.03	217.05
906.09	234.28	519.15	306.07	823.17	220.17
906.12	235.16	522.15	310.11	823.17	415.26
906.16	236.08	524.05	311.16	829.16	muscle
907.06	236.14	524.06	311.23	829.17	746.28
907.13	236.20	534.04	312.01	829.23	muscles
907.22	237.18	534.22	312.04	830.14	494.26
909.14	237.22	536.21	313.27	835.02	muscular
911.12	238.16	539.02	336.13	837.26	567.02
mrs	239.04	544.25	336.17	837.27	876.16
001.06	240.23	555.15	338.20	838.05	mused
005.21	242.13	557.15	341.23	841.17	008.14
008.04	242.25	557.18	342.13	862.28	490.27
010.22	243.09	569.11	350.26	863.24	590.01
011.03	244.12	576.23	350.27	881.18	708.18
013.04	246.10	587.07	351.25	888.27	mushrooms
014.08	246.19	595.21	355.13	892.21	031.14
016.18	251.11	595.21	359.03	892.25	music
020.08	251.16	597.23	362.28	894.13	086.24
020.21	253.17	598.16	372.22	895.25	168.26
021.22	255.08	599.22	372.23	904.03	319.02
021.24	257.09	600.15	383.04	907.24	319.08
024.15	257.13	610.25	383.15	910.22	337.02
025.11	263.15	616.18	383.28	much-excited	387.02
027.07	288.20	622.11	390.26	392.23	476.22
027.12	293.18	624.03	400.04	mucky	573.16
029.16	295.19	633.14	404.24	694.28	765.18
037.15	296.06	640.17	404.27	mud	810.26
040.03	298.15	640.28	417.02	286.17	887.05
042.10	298.16	653.09	428.01	muff	musical
044.05	302.13	770.27	435.19	174.16	074.18
044.18	305.16	771.04	439.28	181.15	522.14
044.28	308.06	809.11	447.23	183.10	737.06
046.08	308.08	863.15	451.16	219.27	musician
048.19	310.23	863.19	452.25	227.11	288.12
051.16	311.13	863.26	452.26	228.15	549.20
051.20	311.15	864.19	456.18	muffle	musing
052.19	312.13	867.16	461.10	572.09	293.26
053.18	312.28	much	462.23	muffled	408.20
053.25	315.14	007.20	462.24	017.10	541.10
055.06	317.06	014.04	463.09	026.07	musings
056.12	317.20	018.25	467.20	281.21	039.17
056.27	322.11	036.12	469.18	282.14	384.28
057.24	324.04	037.26	472.21	328.25	640.14
058.24	325.26	049.28	474.22	765.10	732.09
060.01	326.13	053.04	475.23	muffling	853.14
060.13	327.07	060.20	489.16	275.18	musk
060.15	328.05	067.11	489.24	mug	280.19
061.11	330.01	088.19	507.15	079.03	muslin
061.17	331.12	095.16	509.28	079.06	045.18
062.10	332.05	109.26	513.06	095.13	097.10
063.01	333.05	113.14	513.07	112.15	179.10
063.22	338.05	117.11	513.08	326.19	180.10
064.03	338.19	120.21	517.01	360.17	331.20
064.18	339.08	129.15	517.02	mule	343.10
064.21	343.04	131.08	527.15	221.19	must
065.10	343.21	131.22	530.05	mullioned	002.15
065.22	344.20	132.14	530.19	089.08	013.08
067.10	345.05	136.23	531.01	multiplicity	022.02
069.15	345.12	136.24	533.25	077.23	035.05
072.04	345.27	140.02	537.13	multiplied	038.19
073.16	345.28	149.25	538.14	004.14	046.21
107.25	346.05	149.26	539.20	multitudinous	047.20
108.09	347.15	151.10	550.04	375.24	052.05
115.25	347.23	157.10	563.18	mumbling	053.22
122.12	354.21	162.28	570.13	448.11	054.14
133.02	355.16	166.24	574.02	mun	054.16
134.25	355.22	172.16	575.08	666.21	056.05
136.05	361.10	172.18	613.12	696.19	061.22
137.23	365.14	174.21	614.01	munnut	061.27
137.25	366.03	177.07	614.17	697.01	061.28
165.04	366.05	178.03	616.20	murder	064.11
171.16	367.09	179.21	620.14	307.02	064.15
172.01	378.23	179.25	636.21	776.21	068.22
173.11	378.24	184.03	640.19	murdered	087.07
173.27	379.27	184.06	641.11	105.26	093.10
176.10	379.28	184.25	643.18	murderer	102.07
177.13	384.21	187.03	643.28	010.01	107.04
184.05	386.01	189.15	643.28	010.14	107.06
184.15	386.06	192.15	667.04	murderess	108.22
184.17	399.09	195.08	672.20	422.28	118.01
184.18	399.15	196.26	674.17	murmur	120.18
186.11	411.07	198.08	686.10	142.09	121.13
186.25	420.12	203.04	687.23	210.27	121.23
191.01	445.28	205.20	692.24	229.15	123.17
193.04	446.09	205.27	696.13	281.26	125.10
195.01	449.10	211.17	697.04	293.27	125.17
197.08	450.23	216.17	705.27	337.09	125.18
199.21	457.12	223.03	706.11	341.11	125.21
203.12	457.15	230.08	708.20	418.17	137.05
203.20	463.01	235.24	710.06	800.05	138.02
204.20	463.05	240.16	711.07	804.24	138.15

151.23	508.03	780.02	004.16	044.03	095.20
154.19	508.04	783.18	005.14	044.09	096.17
154.20	512.07	784.28	005.28	044.13	097.09
154.21	512.21	785.13	006.01	044.15	097.21
157.05	512.23	786.02	006.13	044.15	099.03
157.07	512.25	787.19	007.25	044.21	099.09
160.21	514.21	788.03	008.03	044.24	099.10
167.11	516.18	788.05	008.16	045.01	099.23
167.27	517.09	790.24	008.18	045.08	099.24
168.03	519.01	791.04	008.26	045.15	100.27
168.05	522.06	795.22	009.13	046.13	101.08
168.07	522.12	796.06	009.23	046.13	101.09
172.26	522.20	801.21	009.25	046.20	101.15
173.11	522.21	805.18	010.04	046.20	102.14
174.24	523.16	808.07	010.12	047.01	103.14
181.04	526.08	811.19	010.12	047.25	103.24
186.24	527.06	814.28	010.15	048.07	104.04
187.21	542.18	815.16	010.15	049.08	104.12
189.07	550.08	819.12	010.19	049.13	104.14
190.04	552.19	819.18	012.10	049.19	104.15
195.24	555.25	821.13	012.18	050.09	104.17
216.07	561.03	822.12	013.05	050.14	105.09
223.11	563.20	823.08	013.18	051.09	106.04
227.22	572.12	826.11	013.18	051.10	106.09
237.17	575.09	827.09	013.23	051.11	108.02
238.22	577.03	827.11	013.24	052.08	108.02
241.12	579.11	834.18	014.01	053.17	108.18
242.17	580.08	839.02	014.12	054.07	109.19
247.15	581.06	839.21	014.14	054.15	111.02
255.16	582.10	841.22	014.15	054.26	111.08
257.04	582.19	850.14	017.04	055.06	112.01
264.19	586.25	857.23	017.07	055.10	112.02
266.03	600.08	860.07	017.10	056.11	112.15
266.24	602.11	876.09	017.17	057.03	114.27
271.24	603.20	876.15	018.02	057.12	115.02
287.20	607.01	879.21	018.05	057.18	115.06
289.10	607.09	879.25	018.13	057.27	115.07
295.16	609.13	880.18	019.12	058.12	115.23
299.02	613.09	885.10	019.18	058.13	115.25
306.26	614.05	885.13	019.27	058.21	115.28
315.16	614.06	885.14	019.28	058.27	116.03
315.24	615.06	890.14	020.22	059.23	116.08
321.21	615.09	894.26	021.06	060.11	118.07
321.22	615.13	895.15	021.07	061.07	119.03
333.11	618.20	895.26	021.09	061.09	121.01
339.13	621.15	899.01	021.19	061.14	121.17
351.23	621.16	899.12	021.19	061.21	122.25
351.23	621.26	900.13	022.23	062.01	123.01
351.24	622.03	900.25	022.24	062.02	123.05
352.01	622.03	902.20	023.02	063.08	123.05
352.04	622.04	903.05	023.03	063.17	123.06
355.19	622.09	mustard-seed	023.04	064.12	123.07
361.02	622.20	523.12	023.04	064.28	123.08
365.01	624.12	muster	023.10	065.03	123.12
377.06	627.19	248.28	023.14	065.10	123.21
383.09	639.11	mute	023.15	065.13	123.23
385.09	639.16	590.21	023.16	065.15	124.01
387.07	640.23	618.26	023.18	065.16	124.06
387.20	643.23	740.20	023.19	065.26	124.25
387.22	645.12	766.26	024.02	066.05	125.08
390.27	648.23	814.26	024.27	066.10	125.11
392.19	650.08	814.26	025.12	066.11	125.13
397.15	654.15	859.19	026.09	067.09	125.25
403.07	656.14	873.01	026.14	067.14	126.05
406.06	658.10	903.21	026.18	068.05	127.02
407.20	659.04	mutely	027.02	069.21	127.08
409.03	660.15	701.19	027.17	071.04	127.10
415.06	660.18	mutilate	027.24	071.07	127.12
417.11	663.14	881.12	027.25	071.07	127.12
418.15	663.24	mutilated	027.27	071.09	127.20
423.04	664.21	823.05	028.21	071.14	129.10
423.04	665.12	872.24	029.15	071.20	129.13
423.09	666.06	mutinied	029.20	072.01	129.18
423.12	666.07	532.08	029.21	072.06	129.19
427.09	668.02	mutiny	029.25	072.09	130.05
428.27	672.22	012.08	030.02	072.10	130.06
429.01	675.09	357.07	030.13	072.14	130.15
430.27	676.02	546.21	030.23	072.18	130.18
431.02	683.04	648.10	030.26	072.18	130.20
438.22	683.09	812.03	031.16	072.28	131.25
439.07	684.07	muttered	031.21	073.03	131.26
442.27	684.20	126.27	031.24	073.21	132.11
451.11	685.02	208.19	032.03	074.25	132.13
452.23	691.02	394.12	033.03	075.18	133.17
454.07	694.24	595.23	033.03	075.22	133.19
454.07	696.12	754.18	033.17	075.26	133.20
454.09	698.24	811.10	034.15	076.08	134.01
455.24	700.11	861.26	034.18	077.02	134.12
455.25	700.18	muttering	036.19	077.07	134.19
456.07	702.18	404.06	036.27	077.11	134.25
458.21	703.17	mutual	037.07	077.13	135.02
464.04	707.06	149.26	038.05	079.07	135.12
464.06	709.17	301.06	038.07	080.01	135.16
469.08	719.15	357.05	039.11	080.02	135.17
471.19	724.21	371.24	039.17	081.21	136.02
476.18	730.06	498.21	040.05	082.17	136.03
476.20	730.22	554.10	040.19	084.27	136.05
476.21	735.20	713.24	040.20	085.05	136.05
476.21	735.21	718.14	040.22	085.22	137.04
476.22	750.05	727.08	040.24	087.12	137.11
481.04	750.15	782.26	041.01	087.22	137.15
482.03	759.27	803.14	042.02	088.20	138.04
485.11	766.16	mutually	042.08	088.28	139.07
496.21	773.12	069.26	042.12	089.24	140.11
503.18	773.19	714.04	042.16	090.12	140.16
506.02	775.02	my	042.17	090.21	140.22
506.21	777.15	001.16	042.17	093.20	141.07
506.21	778.06	003.03	043.12	094.23	141.21
506.23	778.14	003.07	043.16	095.14	141.23
506.24	778.17	003.11	043.18	095.15	142.02
507.01	779.07	003.18	043.19		

142.10	174.16	227.07	282.17	350.06	414.13
142.13	174.21	227.11	283.24	350.09	414.18
142.14	175.08	227.26	284.07	351.15	414.18
142.15	175.08	228.05	285.01	351.15	414.19
142.15	175.23	228.15	285.05	351.18	415.09
142.17	176.06	228.20	285.06	351.23	415.24
142.21	177.24	229.15	285.19	353.16	415.24
142.28	178.24	229.22	286.01	354.01	418.24
143.02	179.01	229.26	286.07	354.12	418.26
143.10	179.18	229.27	286.08	354.16	419.03
143.13	180.13	230.11	286.14	355.08	419.12
144.06	181.14	230.17	286.22	356.23	419.24
146.14	181.15	230.28	287.04	356.24	419.25
149.06	182.02	230.28	287.08	357.10	420.08
149.12	182.06	232.26	287.22	358.02	421.18
149.17	182.07	234.01	288.06	358.10	422.18
149.19	182.15	234.28	289.16	358.12	422.27
149.20	183.10	235.20	290.04	358.18	423.04
150.05	183.16	236.03	290.20	358.20	423.09
150.18	184.01	236.07	290.23	358.25	423.13
150.24	184.03	236.08	291.08	359.03	424.12
150.28	184.12	236.11	291.26	360.02	426.01
151.26	184.16	237.04	291.27	360.06	426.07
152.08	185.04	238.09	292.04	361.08	426.11
152.14	186.02	239.07	292.06	361.18	426.25
153.06	186.05	239.08	292.08	361.19	427.18
153.11	186.22	239.15	292.17	361.22	428.25
154.06	187.01	240.04	293.10	362.09	429.04
154.08	187.01	240.17	294.01	363.08	429.24
154.08	187.13	241.01	294.02	363.10	429.25
154.11	188.01	241.04	294.05	363.12	430.27
155.08	188.08	241.20	294.06	365.07	430.27
155.19	188.10	242.06	294.08	366.07	431.03
155.27	188.17	242.26	294.24	366.10	431.10
156.20	189.23	243.08	295.01	370.19	433.28
156.20	189.24	243.19	295.02	371.02	435.27
156.22	189.25	245.10	295.03	371.12	435.28
156.28	189.26	245.12	295.04	371.13	436.27
157.09	190.13	246.13	295.08	372.06	437.10
157.13	190.14	246.22	295.09	372.24	437.22
157.21	190.26	247.05	295.19	374.03	438.14
158.04	191.02	247.17	296.20	374.15	438.17
158.05	191.06	247.20	296.21	374.21	439.11
158.06	191.10	247.20	296.26	374.23	441.14
158.15	191.13	248.05	297.23	374.25	441.26
158.17	191.15	248.06	297.26	374.26	442.19
159.10	191.16	250.04	298.23	377.03	444.06
159.11	191.25	250.09	301.04	377.11	444.07
159.15	192.01	250.09	301.10	377.14	445.01
159.16	192.12	251.12	301.27	378.11	445.08
160.03	192.15	254.12	302.02	381.01	445.10
160.04	192.27	254.16	302.11	381.19	445.11
161.27	192.28	255.05	302.17	382.25	446.08
161.28	193.02	255.14	302.24	384.01	446.17
162.03	193.04	257.26	308.15	384.05	448.10
162.04	193.06	257.28	309.15	384.28	449.18
162.05	196.04	258.03	309.17	385.28	451.01
162.15	196.08	259.13	309.22	386.21	451.01
162.17	196.12	259.19	311.03	387.03	452.07
163.03	196.14	259.21	311.17	387.05	452.28
163.06	196.26	259.27	313.02	387.07	453.10
163.14	197.02	260.15	313.03	387.24	454.03
163.19	198.04	260.17	313.21	387.26	454.18
163.20	198.06	260.18	315.01	387.28	454.27
163.25	198.19	260.19	315.07	388.05	454.27
164.01	198.23	260.23	315.08	388.27	455.19
164.07	200.13	261.09	320.09	388.27	456.12
164.08	201.05	262.04	320.15	389.27	456.24
164.15	201.19	262.15	323.06	390.06	458.03
164.19	201.20	263.20	323.09	392.11	458.04
165.03	203.01	264.13	323.16	392.13	458.07
165.25	203.11	264.15	323.18	392.23	458.23
166.03	204.08	264.25	323.22	394.14	459.13
166.05	206.16	265.06	324.14	394.16	459.24
166.11	206.20	265.28	324.15	394.19	459.27
166.24	209.15	266.04	324.15	395.28	460.01
167.02	210.07	266.18	325.17	396.28	461.28
167.04	213.02	267.25	325.19	397.12	462.04
167.15	213.09	268.01	326.05	397.20	462.05
167.17	213.12	268.02	326.08	398.28	462.16
167.23	213.14	268.07	326.08	399.10	463.17
167.24	215.10	268.11	326.10	400.25	463.22
167.26	215.12	268.12	326.10	402.06	463.24
168.12	215.19	268.13	328.17	403.19	464.03
168.15	215.20	269.11	331.22	404.09	464.10
168.24	215.24	269.15	333.10	404.19	464.10
169.03	215.26	270.06	334.15	405.07	465.02
169.07	216.01	270.13	335.10	405.24	466.02
169.25	216.02	271.18	337.11	406.04	466.22
170.08	216.05	271.25	337.19	406.06	466.27
170.16	218.08	272.10	337.21	406.13	467.01
170.16	218.15	272.21	339.04	406.19	467.06
170.20	218.27	272.25	339.09	406.20	467.12
170.22	219.26	273.15	340.05	406.28	467.20
170.26	219.27	273.21	340.22	407.25	468.07
171.05	219.27	273.22	340.24	408.10	468.15
171.23	220.03	274.07	340.25	408.16	468.22
171.26	220.17	274.21	341.18	409.18	469.04
172.06	221.10	274.22	341.18	409.19	469.11
172.08	222.04	276.06	341.28	410.07	470.23
172.18	222.09	276.07	345.12	410.09	471.16
172.24	222.18	276.07	347.05	410.12	472.09
172.25	224.22	276.10	346.21	410.16	472.23
173.12	224.24	276.24	348.23	411.15	473.14
173.16	225.07	276.26	348.25	412.17	474.13
173.19	225.08	277.22	349.01	412.20	477.18
174.02	225.11	277.23	349.02	413.09	477.19
174.06	225.11	277.26	349.07	414.02	478.14
174.07	225.18	277.28	349.16	414.03	480.28
174.14	226.16	281.16	349.27	414.07	481.02
174.15	226.24	281.19	350.06	414.10	481.14

481.21	521.07	565.13	607.10	636.20	659.16
481.22	521.07	565.15	607.10	637.01	659.27
482.04	521.10	565.20	607.11	637.09	660.07
482.12	521.13	566.17	607.23	638.10	660.16
482.13	521.14	566.19	608.05	639.02	660.20
482.15	521.15	567.01	608.05	639.02	660.21
482.18	521.18	567.05	608.06	639.07	661.04
482.18	522.10	567.10	608.08	639.15	661.08
483.08	522.12	567.13	608.08	639.16	661.11
483.18	522.14	567.14	608.08	639.18	661.13
483.25	522.20	567.19	608.09	639.26	661.14
484.03	523.12	568.22	608.12	640.02	661.16
484.03	523.12	569.09	609.02	640.22	661.18
484.05	524.11	569.20	609.06	640.24	661.20
484.05	524.15	570.12	609.08	640.26	661.23
484.18	525.10	570.20	609.10	641.03	662.04
484.24	525.11	571.07	609.18	641.06	662.12
484.28	525.20	572.09	610.17	642.01	662.21
485.02	526.06	572.18	610.20	642.27	663.17
485.03	526.13	572.23	611.01	643.06	663.18
485.05	526.25	572.24	611.01	643.12	663.23
486.04	526.27	573.04	611.02	643.16	664.01
487.15	527.01	573.04	611.06	643.19	664.12
488.11	527.23	573.20	611.17	643.22	665.02
489.02	528.20	573.23	612.14	643.25	665.07
489.23	528.21	574.10	612.16	644.07	665.08
490.21	528.22	574.15	612.28	644.07	665.17
491.10	529.15	575.08	613.01	644.10	665.23
491.15	530.01	575.09	613.07	644.11	666.23
491.27	530.05	575.16	613.21	644.12	666.25
492.09	530.15	575.17	613.24	644.25	667.08
492.12	530.22	575.23	613.25	644.25	668.02
493.04	530.25	576.02	614.20	644.27	668.18
493.06	531.06	576.02	614.22	644.28	668.22
494.11	531.11	576.06	614.22	645.02	669.08
494.13	532.01	576.12	614.27	645.08	669.09
494.24	532.09	576.21	615.08	645.13	670.01
494.26	532.19	576.21	616.01	646.02	670.05
494.27	533.05	577.04	616.06	646.10	670.15
495.12	533.11	577.07	616.19	646.13	671.04
495.14	533.19	577.17	616.23	647.08	671.05
495.26	533.22	578.13	617.03	647.09	671.24
495.27	533.24	578.20	617.12	647.17	671.27
496.09	533.24	578.22	617.13	648.11	672.05
496.10	534.01	578.23	617.14	648.15	672.14
497.08	534.03	579.01	617.15	648.16	672.19
497.11	534.16	579.05	618.13	648.19	672.22
498.02	534.18	579.11	618.22	648.21	673.08
498.03	535.16	579.14	618.24	648.25	673.20
498.14	535.19	580.15	619.01	648.25	673.21
498.15	536.11	581.19	619.16	649.01	674.05
499.08	536.22	581.22	619.25	649.05	674.09
500.03	537.02	582.07	620.25	649.07	674.19
500.07	538.17	583.09	620.26	649.11	674.20
503.06	538.19	583.09	621.03	649.13	674.27
505.07	539.05	583.18	621.04	649.20	675.03
505.07	539.09	583.21	621.06	649.28	675.08
507.07	539.25	583.21	622.04	650.14	675.08
507.10	542.12	584.01	622.10	650.15	675.16
507.10	543.02	584.03	622.18	650.15	675.18
507.13	543.05	584.04	623.04	650.15	676.18
507.15	544.19	584.06	623.14	650.16	681.24
507.28	544.24	585.05	623.19	650.24	681.28
508.03	545.05	585.06	624.01	650.26	682.01
508.10	545.11	585.07	624.04	650.26	682.03
508.22	545.22	585.14	624.10	650.26	683.20
509.12	547.19	586.01	624.22	651.05	683.22
509.16	547.20	587.09	625.04	651.06	683.25
510.16	548.12	587.21	625.07	651.10	684.04
510.21	548.28	587.21	625.25	651.11	684.04
510.25	549.01	588.05	625.27	651.18	684.15
512.17	549.07	588.21	626.08	651.26	685.17
513.01	549.07	588.22	626.08	652.03	685.18
513.02	549.11	588.23	626.13	652.14	686.02
513.02	550.15	589.05	627.03	652.16	686.07
513.03	550.25	589.16	627.20	652.16	686.07
513.13	550.26	591.09	627.21	652.24	686.17
513.20	551.17	591.13	627.27	652.25	686.24
514.02	551.19	592.06	628.01	653.03	687.02
514.13	552.05	592.07	628.17	653.05	687.10
514.13	552.09	592.16	628.20	653.05	687.23
514.14	552.11	592.19	628.28	653.06	688.08
514.17	552.20	593.12	629.04	653.06	689.03
514.18	553.07	593.17	629.12	653.07	689.16
515.05	553.11	593.21	629.12	653.10	689.16
515.09	553.21	596.14	630.05	653.17	689.17
515.15	554.16	596.13	630.07	653.18	689.20
515.16	555.09	597.01	630.17	653.27	690.03
515.16	555.16	597.02	631.05	654.07	690.25
516.03	555.20	597.03	631.13	654.09	691.04
516.09	555.21	597.19	631.15	654.15	691.12
516.16	555.27	597.23	631.16	654.26	692.10
516.18	556.01	598.23	631.19	655.04	692.12
516.19	556.02	600.18	632.12	655.05	692.14
517.09	556.03	601.21	632.13	655.10	692.15
517.14	557.07	601.24	632.21	655.25	692.18
517.22	557.08	601.25	633.07	656.01	692.21
517.26	558.06	602.11	633.14	656.03	692.23
517.27	558.08	602.20	634.01	656.08	693.02
518.17	558.16	603.05	634.08	656.12	693.15
518.18	559.03	604.11	634.09	656.12	694.27
518.19	559.15	604.19	634.09	656.14	696.18
518.21	559.18	604.20	634.18	656.17	699.07
518.25	560.09	605.11	634.24	656.21	699.18
519.08	563.03	605.14	634.26	656.23	699.20
519.13	563.17	606.07	634.26	656.24	699.23
519.15	563.19	606.10	635.03	657.01	700.03
519.22	563.24	606.13	636.03	657.14	700.05
519.28	563.24	606.14	636.04	658.08	700.18
520.08	564.14	606.15	636.09	659.03	702.01
520.12	565.04	607.08			

702.11	743.20	787.13	828.11	876.16	911.03
702.21	744.01	787.14	828.16	876.17	912.12
703.02	744.09	787.21	828.18	876.17	912.12
703.02	745.06	787.27	828.19	876.25	912.21
703.11	745.06	788.01	828.20	876.28	mysel
703.17	745.10	788.01	829.11	877.04	696.25
704.09	745.25	788.06	829.18	877.06	myself
704.20	747.10	788.10	830.02	877.08	002.27
704.25	748.05	788.11	831.13	877.14	012.06
705.08	748.21	789.05	832.03	877.15	012.06
705.10	749.05	789.10	832.24	877.16	013.17
705.22	749.10	789.13	832.27	877.17	019.25
705.26	749.13	790.02	833.02	877.22	021.11
705.28	749.15	790.03	833.14	878.07	023.07
706.09	750.16	790.12	833.27	878.12	024.19
706.10	751.23	790.23	834.14	878.16	042.15
706.13	751.23	790.25	835.06	878.17	046.15
706.13	752.04	791.15	835.25	878.24	054.28
706.16	752.14	791.22	836.08	879.03	057.12
707.01	753.16	791.25	837.09	879.10	065.01
707.10	753.18	791.27	837.15	879.10	066.24
707.12	754.16	792.09	838.11	879.27	088.24
707.24	755.08	792.12	839.04	880.07	094.09
708.05	756.02	794.07	839.15	880.17	094.27
708.11	756.03	795.18	839.16	880.27	111.05
708.23	756.18	798.05	839.21	881.21	114.03
708.24	757.22	799.03	840.05	881.21	129.12
709.06	758.02	799.06	841.24	882.04	129.13
709.09	758.03	802.11	842.09	882.12	132.04
709.15	758.08	803.11	842.22	882.19	162.07
709.17	758.17	803.20	844.18	883.02	163.18
710.02	758.18	804.08	845.27	883.11	169.06
710.06	759.19	805.02	846.05	883.12	169.17
711.04	759.19	806.20	846.06	883.15	171.23
712.15	759.20	807.03	846.07	883.26	173.21
712.26	759.21	807.19	846.17	883.27	174.04
713.13	760.01	807.22	847.04	884.07	174.12
713.14	760.07	807.28	847.13	884.21	182.27
713.17	760.14	808.07	847.14	885.06	190.11
713.27	760.14	808.07	847.14	885.10	192.08
713.27	761.08	808.08	847.14	885.26	192.25
715.20	761.20	808.13	847.16	886.13	196.10
716.05	761.22	808.15	848.03	886.23	196.21
717.05	761.27	808.19	848.10	887.02	198.04
717.05	761.27	808.20	848.11	887.07	203.09
717.28	761.28	809.03	848.17	887.08	214.25
718.11	762.20	809.04	848.27	887.10	237.18
718.24	762.25	809.06	849.02	888.09	243.07
719.14	762.27	809.13	849.05	888.12	255.14
719.17	763.07	809.19	849.09	888.20	261.24
720.25	763.14	809.24	850.12	888.21	266.07
721.12	763.22	810.04	850.17	888.25	268.13
721.13	764.06	810.07	850.18	889.03	269.08
721.26	764.08	810.11	850.18	889.08	270.14
722.09	765.06	810.21	851.03	889.10	273.21
722.16	765.08	810.23	851.04	890.27	280.03
722.18	766.25	811.01	851.07	891.06	280.22
722.20	767.17	811.10	852.01	894.05	290.21
723.09	767.27	811.10	852.02	894.11	293.16
724.13	768.12	811.12	852.09	894.20	294.17
724.14	768.14	811.13	852.20	895.03	295.18
724.20	768.20	811.23	852.21	895.17	300.15
725.13	769.02	811.24	853.07	895.26	302.12
725.17	769.03	811.25	853.08	896.03	311.11
727.04	769.27	812.02	853.09	896.03	313.24
727.05	770.02	813.18	853.13	896.09	323.20
727.06	770.04	813.23	854.05	897.22	324.12
727.09	773.03	813.26	854.08	897.25	325.01
727.15	773.09	813.27	854.23	898.06	326.16
729.02	773.10	813.27	855.05	898.06	326.18
729.09	773.11	813.27	855.08	898.10	331.21
729.10	773.17	814.26	855.12	898.11	351.19
730.12	773.18	814.26	855.15	898.19	375.20
730.16	773.19	815.02	855.18	898.24	381.23
730.16	774.02	815.18	855.18	899.18	388.02
731.07	774.03	815.18	856.24	899.19	399.02
731.17	774.08	816.08	856.27	899.20	401.27
732.09	775.25	816.09	857.06	899.27	406.11
732.10	775.26	816.25	857.16	900.03	418.01
732.12	776.03	816.26	857.20	900.05	421.28
732.19	776.05	817.03	857.26	900.12	431.09
732.21	776.18	817.10	860.03	900.16	436.08
732.24	777.24	817.25	860.10	900.18	441.11
733.02	778.04	818.11	860.21	900.28	456.23
733.03	778.16	818.12	861.01	901.05	459.27
733.03	778.28	818.15	861.03	901.17	464.06
733.05	780.04	819.01	862.17	901.17	464.11
733.13	780.13	819.07	865.03	902.01	470.27
733.16	780.18	819.24	865.10	902.11	472.19
733.22	780.23	819.25	865.23	902.18	476.01
733.26	780.25	821.07	866.23	903.04	479.09
733.27	780.27	821.11	866.28	903.06	481.12
734.07	781.04	821.18	870.14	903.10	481.25
734.08	781.16	822.03	870.19	903.11	487.18
735.19	781.18	822.19	871.17	903.23	489.05
735.20	781.25	822.19	871.19	903.25	492.11
735.22	781.25	822.22	871.19	904.02	493.02
735.24	781.26	822.23	871.23	904.03	493.22
736.05	782.10	822.27	871.24	907.14	494.16
736.08	782.19	823.09	872.12	908.02	506.08
738.12	783.04	823.20	873.04	908.03	508.14
739.03	784.13	825.17	873.23	908.06	509.28
740.02	785.03	825.18	873.25	908.17	515.19
741.26	785.07	825.20	874.05	908.19	516.05
741.27	785.13	825.20	874.20	908.20	524.27
742.23	786.04	825.23	874.20	908.28	526.01
742.24	786.23	826.01	875.05	909.03	527.05
743.05	786.28	826.06	876.09	909.11	533.17
743.06	787.02	826.22	876.10	910.01	533.26
743.13	787.06	827.17		910.05	546.17
743.13	787.06	828.07		910.07	549.19

```
553.13              mystification    858.18         217.26        715.18       341.16
553.27              402.04           874.05         350.18        721.06       349.04
554.10              n'avons          874.10         547.26        724.13       360.07
557.17              334.11           889.09         628.09        734.25       361.20
559.07              n'est-ce         889.11         719.24        738.13       366.04
561.24              234.26           906.12         730.09        739.24       367.08
571.06              239.09           907.13         740.25        743.06       375.19
580.10              277.19           named          naturae       747.24       380.27
564.05              n'etait          366.02         749.03        749.15       383.13
604.12              234.24           430.02         natural       763.02       384.12
605.14              n'y              657.02         002.15        763.03       385.05
611.03              543.20           763.10         047.21        772.19       388.18
613.03              nacht            nameless       107.07        796.28       397.05
625.15              678.21           551.01         127.08        797.07       409.04
627.01              naiad's          552.11         164.01        808.07       409.17
627.26              471.06           namely         173.12        815.13       411.06
629.02              nail             163.23         192.26        823.20       421.05
630.15              264.27           265.11         230.10        826.01       423.16
630.23              507.04           804.07         269.15        829.04       436.01
632.25              557.13           names          275.23        831.14       445.23
634.14              616.16           140.10         288.13        836.19       449.21
638.02              nailed           343.02         301.28        848.03       464.27
639.23              050.13           656.19         333.15        850.08       470.27
643.04              174.10           770.27         373.08        882.20       474.16
646.04              nails            903.21         466.07        898.24       489.03
647.04              098.25           namesake       506.04        909.19       498.16
648.02              099.01           779.12         523.08        nature's     498.19
648.04              681.09           naomi          552.25        668.14       510.24
649.23              681.11           089.12         554.16        natures      518.26
656.09              naive            091.27         687.03        466.06       520.04
673.01              343.08           naples         709.08        478.20       542.12
667.04              739.08           526.22         725.09        552.08       562.08
690.23              naivete          636.01         743.18        713.24       566.11
692.23              201.04           narrate        750.02        718.02       567.11
694.17              naked            772.16         761.25        828.04       570.09
694.18              004.02           787.25         762.21        naught       574.03
714.27              name             narrated       803.10        669.24       580.20
718.08              027.16           005.17         825.20        680.21       590.17
720.08              034.03           141.27         853.27        696.02       594.09
721.15              053.07           216.03         870.14        698.09       594.13
723.26              077.11           narrative      naturally     naughty      608.01
724.18              083.19           031.10         104.01        019.09       608.03
730.22              086.13           041.04         119.13        024.12       613.04
731.09              089.28           047.22         120.11        054.04       616.14
731.26              093.09           061.09         120.13        054.05       623.24
732.16              098.03           135.21         142.15        060.08       652.15
732.17              101.27           149.23         167.25        067.04       660.03
733.10              104.08           217.27         275.15        095.11       664.06
738.18              159.22           290.06         275.16        nauseous     664.21
739.04              171.15           628.02         293.01        082.19       667.16
751.27              172.05           799.07         469.02        navy         668.19
758.01              182.07           888.12         471.20        911.08       668.26
761.13              183.07           903.01         509.21        nay          671.26
767.23              183.13           908.22         553.18        276.11       673.13
769.03              199.03           narrator       714.08        594.17       675.17
772.08              252.25           401.26         738.18        666.11       676.25
775.09              287.04           narrator's     738.20        666.18       683.13
779.19              297.11           770.04         787.13        669.24       684.14
784.19              297.17           narrow         887.08        670.11       685.01
785.19              391.24           052.15         nature        694.23       686.02
805.06              399.11           071.09         021.26        695.12       689.15
808.09              409.13           084.10         056.27        900.21       701.27
816.07              409.14           168.27         065.26        naze         704.18
816.24              425.20           185.13         090.12        003.28       718.05
819.19              446.08           207.06         104.15        ne           727.03
822.28              448.13           207.11         115.28        341.20       727.13
825.06              450.23           208.24         120.14        near         733.04
848.25              461.22           209.25         128.08        003.14       733.17
850.17              517.14           209.28         133.03        007.26       750.11
851.03              524.03           221.08         140.06        010.21       781.16
855.12              535.19           361.20         147.21        016.09       789.02
856.04              573.03           471.22         160.20        017.06       792.01
861.25              592.19           494.06         162.28        023.20       813.01
870.05              593.02           575.22         192.11        027.02       833.15
871.20              594.07           615.20         214.10        027.25       850.20
879.19              595.25           626.16         215.19        028.19       855.08
879.25              597.05           661.17         239.27        042.06       860.04
887.14              603.07           676.10         251.28        043.26       873.12
888.28              629.04           689.07         252.01        050.13       876.23
908.26              630.07           693.02         253.05        060.27       887.25
mysteries           631.23           709.16         253.19        071.09       892.12
271.12              632.02           721.04         267.24        078.19       892.24
408.18              636.02           764.01         269.04        089.25       895.11
727.28              643.06           845.14         291.10        105.08       901.24
mysterious          686.16           860.06         312.22        130.13       902.25
005.13              686.17           871.02         351.21        130.22       908.05
074.04              695.06           871.03         372.27        133.25       909.16
311.25              695.26           871.11         373.07        137.13       912.10
411.21              695.28           narrow-minded  378.10        148.19       nearer
442.13              705.07           216.20         439.06        154.03       168.24
596.24              706.19           narrower       444.14        154.16       172.11
902.26              708.05           115.22         466.21        155.03       187.11
mysteriously        708.07           narrowing      522.06        158.23       189.25
543.14              708.09           721.04         525.01        171.17       194.22
mystery             708.11           narrowly       591.20        179.06       315.17
253.21              708.13           100.04         603.11        181.14       355.10
330.24              719.21           nasal          625.19        184.01       383.01
330.26              733.28           166.07         626.14        194.18       383.17
378.20              751.07           593.06         627.23        196.06       490.19
388.07              751.19           nasmyth        637.24        221.23       526.14
408.17              770.12           163.09         641.15        223.26       769.26
424.16              772.18           nasty          647.24        227.15       862.04
444.04              773.19           043.22         655.13        231.14       909.01
460.03              774.11           natal          659.19        236.28       nearest
560.07              779.09           628.18         660.26        246.11       081.03
561.22              779.17           nations        673.05        256.20       211.11
748.06              780.04           107.11         690.28        256.22       220.22
764.09              780.15           140.05         700.28        295.02       247.26
mystic              808.27           265.14         702.09        300.21       308.07
422.26              828.05           native         707.09        319.21       658.16
803.22              844.28           125.27         715.06        337.22
```

014.12
032.16
039.15
042.09
045.10
050.08
056.06
057.08
059.26
069.11
075.26
089.06
089.06
091.28
107.18
111.05
123.15
127.16
142.27
148.24
152.24
161.10
165.21
166.13
167.05
167.05
167.06
167.06
167.09
169.04
172.24
173.02
174.22
180.25
180.26
181.02
181.03
186.16
192.02
193.04
202.27
211.24
228.24
228.25
233.18
245.12
273.08
273.25
273.28
280.06
288.26
291.18
291.19
291.20
292.02
306.19
308.20
323.17
325.22
327.27
334.25
353.01
381.15
384.07
459.27
474.15
478.02
479.02
491.21
503.11
508.04
524.03
538.14
541.02
544.08
553.22
568.23
568.24
569.22
577.09
615.15
622.05
622.10
631.28
639.14
641.07
684.16
693.04
705.28
708.05
739.02
752.22
756.22
769.07
770.09
775.08
776.16
792.28
794.06
794.17
794.19
798.28
844.07
844.07
894.24
908.09

new-born
493.21
new-dyed
523.17

newer
106.09
newfoundland
229.08
newly
290.16
newly-risen
005.03
news
068.08
232.22
324.02
332.13
446.23
447.24
451.20
468.10
727.24
766.08
776.17
783.26
853.22
897.03
897.05
905.13
907.10
newspaper
700.28
next
026.02
027.23
028.04
029.22
096.02
116.22
141.11
172.24
173.10
174.13
180.19
190.06
233.04
287.27
295.09
326.24
337.24
370.26
430.22
445.03
445.14
447.24
463.27
485.19
490.23
560.20
568.11
635.16
637.23
639.22
662.27
680.25
723.10
728.02
732.01
745.28
750.08
750.16
765.04
769.07
771.25
792.12
831.02
864.06
866.02
886.03
891.06
912.15
nice
041.07
047.28
189.03
383.23
459.03
747.01
752.13
nicely
739.17
739.18
nicety
193.02
niche
346.19
857.26
nichered
396.02
niece
482.12
nieces
784.08
niggard
455.01
nigh
551.24
nigher
375.27
night
019.11
026.19
027.21
028.11
029.10

036.01
036.07
040.09
055.09
072.07
075.08
079.25
082.07
085.09
096.09
142.24
144.17
147.13
148.16
154.18
167.02
170.25
185.04
189.14
189.14
191.16
200.22
233.03
234.16
241.18
250.03
254.10
255.09
280.12
290.05
294.02
294.23
300.21
305.04
306.01
307.03
307.20
309.20
311.24
313.08
314.06
320.17
321.12
362.17
414.06
414.10
414.15
413.20
422.26
424.08
424.17
426.06
429.16
435.20
436.09
442.12
442.16
444.16
445.08
445.14
445.25
466.10
468.16
469.22
485.17
490.22
491.09
492.02
505.03
518.23
520.16
522.03
532.07
534.05
537.24
540.21
559.08
559.08
559.24
563.08
563.15
567.13
569.06
572.15
575.02
580.20
583.02
583.11
606.02
606.09
616.24
618.03
629.17
629.20
633.12
639.20
651.22
651.26
652.20
661.22
662.04
662.05
663.17
671.24
672.21
683.12
684.14
684.21
687.14
690.08
696.22

712.24
740.03
745.13
745.26
765.03
766.07
772.02
777.10
798.13
800.01
800.19
809.05
829.13
833.11
846.12
851.11
853.15
861.22
861.26
864.05
865.01
873.27
877.07
882.28
883.22
900.22
900.26
901.23
902.25
903.13
night's
207.20
314.27
682.14
799.16
night-air
661.18
901.07
night-breeze
033.11
night-cap
005.22
night-dress
049.13
154.08
night-fall
660.09
night-gown
047.03
night-mare
026.03
night-rover
504.25
night-sky
662.09
night-time
633.27
678.05
night-wind
674.22
nightingale
503.15
511.08
nightingale's
514.27
nightmare
417.07
518.08
581.16
nights
144.09
445.18
460.16
652.21
689.02
707.16
nimble
061.19
429.28
nimbly
044.07
nine
016.26
035.05
048.05
078.08
083.24
153.27
251.01
252.13
252.14
276.04
336.14
446.10
454.25
459.16
483.19
484.14
558.14
745.28
800.06
nineteen
704.18
826.14
nipped
001.14
066.19
088.22
niver
680.26

no
001.03
001.07
007.28
009.07
009.08
012.20
014.26
017.15
018.25
019.07
019.13
023.08
025.07
028.08
028.17
029.13
030.01
030.14
030.15
032.10
034.09
036.07
036.23
038.04
038.14
038.28
040.07
042.09
044.17
050.26
054.04
054.13
055.20
055.21
059.20
059.20
059.26
062.21
063.02
063.05
064.03
066.04
066.13
066.18
072.06
074.14
076.10
077.04
077.09
083.22
085.03
088.16
089.02
090.23
091.15
092.09
092.14
098.26
102.08
102.09
103.24
104.23
105.11
105.21
105.28
106.07
106.15
106.16
108.11
108.17
109.09
109.10
109.24
111.08
111.16
117.26
122.23
124.07
124.13
125.02
125.09
127.04
127.10
132.04
135.01
140.19
144.10
147.08
148.28
153.22
156.21
156.21
157.09
158.12
158.24
159.11
162.24
164.06
165.07
166.18
167.07
167.10
167.11
167.18
170.15
171.28
172.25
174.17
175.01
177.19

177.28
178.01
178.04
182.12
186.18
186.18
187.04
188.16
188.16
191.16
191.17
192.09
196.21
197.21
201.22
204.21
204.21
205.17
205.21
206.08
206.12
206.20
207.20
208.03
208.04
208.08
208.11
209.11
211.04
213.12
213.16
213.17
213.17
215.17
217.16
217.24
219.13
219.19
222.12
222.27
224.03
224.18
226.09
226.11
227.06
228.17
228.17
228.18
231.21
231.21
233.14
237.11
238.09
240.15
241.14
241.25
242.19
242.23
243.13
243.21
244.01
244.02
245.27
246.12
247.02
247.26
250.13
251.22
252.02
252.06
252.17
253.13
256.24
257.18
258.04
259.19
260.11
260.20
261.12
265.18
266.23
267.16
267.23
267.26
269.01
269.26
271.10
271.22
275.09
280.16
285.28
288.07
288.13
288.27
289.27
289.28
290.11
292.09
296.05
296.06
297.08
298.16
299.25
300.03
300.16
301.15
301.20
306.20
307.07
307.07
307.27

311.03	462.27	579.04	691.03	827.12	552.06
313.02	465.12	583.02	692.26	828.10	706.07
316.17	466.01	582.11	692.27	828.12	725.16
316.22	466.17	582.21	694.02	829.08	819.15
319.07	467.26	582.24	694.05	829.16	828.19
319.16	469.07	587.05	694.05	830.05	843.26
320.01	470.20	587.05	695.04	830.06	**nobleman**
321.16	471.22	587.06	696.06	832.15	319.16
321.24	473.24	591.12	697.07	832.27	**nobleman's**
321.28	473.25	592.09	697.07	832.28	194.02
322.01	474.19	595.23	697.11	833.03	**nobleness**
322.14	474.20	596.08	699.03	833.25	644.23
322.15	476.01	596.15	701.11	833.28	**nobly**
322.15	476.03	597.21	703.13	833.28	203.20
324.02	476.10	598.04	703.21	835.05	651.12
328.13	476.11	600.17	704.19	836.09	856.26
329.17	476.14	603.16	707.04	838.01	**nobody**
329.18	476.24	604.03	708.14	838.01	020.07
329.27	476.28	604.03	709.23	838.02	102.05
331.21	477.05	605.04	709.28	840.05	102.23
336.03	477.07	605.05	711.20	841.08	196.21
336.12	477.16	605.05	713.23	842.09	216.11
338.11	479.04	605.05	714.15	843.17	306.04
339.07	479.18	605.06	717.04	844.10	307.27
339.09	481.17	605.06	719.03	845.04	330.12
340.16	481.23	607.07	719.11	846.04	339.19
344.10	483.16	607.18	720.14	846.12	680.15
347.05	484.09	607.18	721.17	850.08	696.26
349.14	488.19	607.24	723.17	851.08	782.08
350.19	488.28	608.03	723.17	853.16	663.03
351.06	490.17	608.13	723.25	853.24	863.18
353.23	491.25	610.10	726.18	854.06	864.11
354.06	492.25	610.21	726.26	854.06	**nod**
355.22	494.03	610.22	727.13	855.26	254.17
357.12	497.10	611.20	728.01	858.08	764.02
357.20	497.22	614.17	730.22	858.20	**nodded**
360.07	498.10	614.19	731.11	858.26	067.23
361.01	499.10	615.10	731.12	858.28	117.18
364.20	499.21	617.22	731.19	859.06	376.18
366.18	499.22	617.22	731.23	859.06	432.28
371.11	499.28	617.24	732.19	859.06	542.20
371.18	502.18	617.26	732.27	859.09	543.04
373.08	503.16	620.28	733.12	859.18	**noise**
377.17	503.17	621.21	733.21	861.15	023.27
382.15	503.24	624.25	736.22	861.15	075.21
382.19	504.20	625.09	737.24	861.15	154.25
382.20	505.04	625.15	737.25	862.10	211.17
382.22	506.17	626.13	741.18	864.27	220.24
382.23	508.17	626.25	747.13	866.16	282.21
384.15	509.02	628.04	747.19	869.03	299.07
385.13	510.20	629.24	751.16	869.08	299.10
386.16	511.11	630.08	752.18	870.11	306.14
392.19	512.17	630.18	753.08	870.18	415.11
393.04	512.23	632.08	753.09	870.26	418.25
395.15	513.24	633.16	753.10	870.26	419.11
396.13	514.07	636.03	754.22	871.18	424.10
397.28	514.07	638.25	757.09	871.23	432.23
399.19	515.23	638.25	759.16	876.05	504.20
401.10	518.03	638.28	760.05	876.05	683.07
401.20	518.03	639.01	760.13	876.05	733.04
403.04	518.05	640.12	762.12	878.19	765.19
405.03	520.07	641.28	763.12	879.15	770.28
406.06	521.08	642.13	766.01	879.21	**noiselessly**
406.27	521.18	642.24	766.10	879.21	335.21
407.06	525.06	643.26	768.08	879.21	**noises**
407.26	525.06	646.23	768.08	880.12	105.06
408.04	529.07	647.03	769.17	880.26	**noisy**
408.24	530.11	647.13	769.27	882.04	210.24
409.07	531.27	648.08	771.08	882.14	420.22
409.08	532.26	653.12	771.28	882.15	605.04
409.09	536.12	653.19	772.04	883.01	**nom**
415.13	536.14	654.27	772.21	883.01	234.23
417.10	536.21	656.10	772.22	884.03	**nominally**
418.17	536.22	657.03	775.04	887.05	622.12
419.11	537.13	656.04	776.26	888.04	**nonchalance**
420.04	538.24	658.12	778.01	893.11	462.10
420.05	538.24	659.04	778.08	893.15	**nonchalantly**
421.26	540.02	659.09	778.23	894.08	326.20
422.20	541.17	659.13	779.14	895.12	**none**
426.02	542.24	659.18	782.04	895.12	009.09
427.08	543.18	660.26	782.06	896.11	014.22
427.24	544.01	663.28	784.25	896.16	030.03
428.26	547.01	667.01	784.25	896.16	033.12
430.11	548.03	667.23	786.24	898.18	037.17
431.28	548.04	667.27	787.21	899.09	050.05
433.22	548.07	668.04	792.22	901.07	082.25
436.19	548.13	668.10	792.22	901.25	084.22
437.20	548.23	668.16	796.03	902.20	206.09
437.20	549.19	668.17	796.19	903.02	241.22
437.21	549.20	668.21	796.20	908.28	242.19
437.23	549.22	668.22	799.28	909.03	242.21
438.03	550.01	668.28	800.14	909.25	243.15
438.27	553.01	669.02	801.09	910.04	249.17
439.01	553.12	669.15	801.26	910.24	252.01
439.05	555.06	669.17	806.22	910.25	263.14
439.27	557.04	670.16	807.20	912.18	289.27
440.18	559.06	671.27	808.10	**noan**	360.05
442.09	560.06	673.28	811.01	185.09	383.26
446.26	560.18	674.14	811.18	906.23	451.06
451.04	564.24	676.19	811.23	**nobility**	481.03
452.12	567.15	679.06	815.07	525.02	485.14
452.16	568.08	679.24	815.19	**noble**	515.28
452.25	568.15	682.21	817.01	145.10	516.01
453.07	569.01	683.01	817.01	161.23	521.20
454.18	569.15	686.15	817.01	318.08	579.07
455.06	569.24	686.28	817.19	323.01	587.07
455.24	571.21	687.07	820.10	345.13	595.24
456.15	571.21	687.21	820.23	348.12	604.13
456.16	576.14	687.27	821.13	374.18	608.02
456.26	576.24	689.05	823.02	403.07	610.10
462.15	577.05	689.10	825.16	512.15	656.10

659.17
670.24
729.18
808.01
870.16
880.13
898.12
909.04
nonnette
259.23
nonsense
036.05
068.04
275.09
339.03
407.28
407.29
451.23
470.19
763.20
766.17
837.06
nook
339.16
362.25
502.18
752.05
noon
019.10
019.10
029.22
203.07
211.04
250.03
250.03
439.16
661.07
689.11
689.11
800.19
800.19
noontide
173.01
noose
507.11
nor
002.05
004.05
006.13
007.23
036.01
071.16
085.02
088.16
094.24
095.04
099.01
107.15
131.11
139.20
139.20
143.13
150.15
150.21
165.06
176.10
194.13
194.14
203.11
211.06
225.01
231.05
253.03
237.16
258.16
241.23
251.07
257.03
263.13
282.16
288.14
316.17
319.12
322.20
353.12
359.18
364.10
373.11
385.28
388.18
389.17
393.05
396.18
406.06
426.08
426.23
436.12
436.19
439.15
440.12
455.04
462.20
466.07
485.15
485.18
487.13
489.14
503.12
513.12
519.17
527.06

528.03
537.26
540.02
541.18
543.22
546.23
548.28
551.23
559.09
562.12
565.08
566.06
571.09
587.21
608.05
608.05
610.19
611.09
613.26
615.15
615.22
625.20
625.20
625.21
626.19
631.24
632.03
647.15
655.12
655.13
656.13
658.12
662.20
667.01
674.11
678.09
680.16
694.05
696.25
698.14
699.05
702.13
708.25
717.16
735.03
741.07
747.21
753.01
753.02
756.18
763.03
768.19
785.21
792.23
796.22
808.26
811.02
812.02
813.16
815.11
824.11
830.04
844.11
844.11
849.16
849.16
849.17
849.18
850.07
853.09
871.28
877.02
881.11
887.22
888.04
895.03
895.11
895.12
906.21
norham's
765.12
normal
042.08
north
003.28
102.02
113.04
659.06
north-east
096.08
north-midland
658.20
855.05
north-of-england
221.18
northern
004.01
249.01
northumberland
105.05
153.08
northward
560.04
norway
003.26
606.07
nose
043.15
054.02
060.22
102.18

124.16
170.03
192.18
237.07
382.21
383.23
422.09
471.20
478.16
701.25
733.08
nostril
702.10
nostrils
081.24
094.01
237.09
421.19
471.21
622.22
not
003.09
003.22
006.09
006.12
006.14
007.20
007.22
008.02
009.10
009.18
009.21
013.15
014.05
014.12
014.18
017.13
018.04
019.05
019.23
020.02
020.04
020.09
020.10
020.11
021.18
021.28
022.05
022.09
024.07
024.27
027.06
027.06
027.20
029.19
031.02
031.23
033.21
034.04
034.11
034.13
034.24
035.08
035.19
036.16
037.04
037.07
037.16
037.26
038.04
038.06
038.07
038.14
038.20
039.21
041.11
042.19
043.02
043.26
043.26
043.27
044.04
044.22
046.01
046.02
046.28
048.07
048.11
048.15
054.17
054.23
054.25
056.03
056.17
056.24
057.10
059.24
060.18
060.19
062.04
062.05
062.09
063.21
064.06
064.12
064.17
067.02
067.11
068.06
068.22
069.19

069.24
072.08
072.18
073.17
075.11
076.13
078.10
079.02
079.08
080.03
080.08
082.01
082.08
082.27
084.09
084.24
086.06
087.07
088.07
088.19
090.15
091.09
091.20
092.06
093.11
093.12
095.03
095.07
095.09
096.15
098.09
098.28
099.09
099.12
099.22
099.26
100.11
100.16
100.24
102.13
103.03
103.06
103.09
103.16
103.20
104.04
104.17
106.02
106.07
107.14
108.09
108.18
109.14
109.26
111.03
114.15
114.24
115.01
115.12
116.07
116.23
117.04
117.19
118.03
118.04
118.08
118.14
118.21
118.28
120.13
121.04
121.16
121.19
122.28
123.07
123.17
123.21
123.28
125.15
126.23
127.07
129.11
130.06
130.20
131.06
131.11
132.03
132.05
133.14
133.21
134.27
136.24
137.07
137.19
137.20
138.18
142.15
143.18
146.16
146.20
148.20
149.26
150.01
150.24
150.27
151.07
151.09
153.05
153.09
153.22

154.04
155.16
156.03
156.04
156.14
156.23
157.05
157.08
157.11
157.13
158.17
159.09
160.05
160.14
161.15
162.01
162.01
164.03
164.04
165.13
165.24
166.15
166.16
166.17
166.24
166.25
166.26
167.14
168.19
168.23
169.22
170.17
172.03
172.18
174.05
174.19
174.20
175.14
176.09
176.11
177.02
177.15
177.16
178.01
178.06
178.09
178.20
179.06
179.14
179.26
180.10
182.02
184.02
184.06
184.13
184.17
184.19
187.02
187.19
187.21
188.02
188.15
188.19
189.10
189.11
190.01
191.12
192.05
192.10
192.11
192.17
192.24
193.05
193.28
194.02
194.13
194.17
195.19
195.21
196.22
196.25
197.03
198.08
199.08
201.27
201.28
202.06
203.02
205.05
206.02
206.16
208.13
211.01
211.22
213.04
214.03
214.13
215.18
216.05
217.01
217.07
217.27
219.14
219.14
219.27
220.19
221.23
222.03
223.03
223.06
223.17

224.11
224.17
224.21
225.09
225.22
226.10
226.14
226.23
227.04
227.08
227.14
229.19
230.16
231.05
232.03
234.03
234.04
234.09
234.13
235.14
235.25
237.19
237.23
238.02
238.03
238.07
239.02
239.26
239.28
240.14
241.21
241.26
242.09
243.07
243.20
243.24
244.03
244.06
245.20
247.20
249.23
250.12
250.14
250.20
251.15
252.07
252.11
252.17
252.19
252.23
252.28
253.06
253.07
253.18
253.18
254.10
254.20
255.10
256.22
258.17
258.22
258.25
258.25
259.07
259.08
260.04
260.07
260.24
261.10
261.12
262.07
262.12
263.13
263.26
265.01
265.02
266.01
266.16
266.23
266.25
267.15
267.19
268.09
268.26
269.06
269.11
269.12
269.12
269.24
269.28
270.09
270.10
270.21
271.11
271.26
272.08
272.10
272.26
274.07
274.10
275.04
275.15
276.06
277.25
278.01
280.05
280.08
280.11
282.07
282.07
282.15

283.10	349.17	411.23	489.23	552.18	612.05
285.20	350.03	412.07	489.27	553.04	612.13
285.22	350.07	414.20	490.08	553.08	612.13
285.23	351.09	415.01	491.13	554.05	612.25
286.24	351.10	415.02	492.08	555.27	613.06
287.14	351.26	417.16	492.09	556.06	613.09
288.15	353.03	417.25	492.18	557.11	614.21
288.27	353.10	417.28	493.04	557.13	614.24
289.18	353.16	418.06	493.11	557.17	615.22
290.04	353.19	418.14	493.17	558.01	616.01
290.27	354.04	418.22	493.22	558.01	616.05
291.13	354.11	420.02	494.09	558.09	616.10
291.28	355.13	420.07	494.12	558.20	617.05
292.13	355.20	422.09	494.15	558.21	617.15
292.14	356.22	422.12	494.17	559.05	617.20
293.11	357.14	422.15	494.23	560.08	618.13
293.16	357.14	425.25	495.05	560.15	619.26
293.25	358.14	425.28	496.08	561.08	619.26
294.15	359.11	426.16	496.11	562.12	619.28
294.22	359.17	426.26	496.13	564.01	620.08
296.15	359.23	427.21	498.23	565.01	620.11
298.13	360.02	428.01	499.06	565.15	620.17
298.21	360.06	428.03	499.18	565.15	620.19
298.22	360.09	428.08	500.05	565.18	620.22
299.13	362.02	428.13	503.06	566.05	620.27
299.13	362.05	428.25	503.07	566.12	621.12
299.19	362.07	429.15	503.21	568.08	621.15
301.01	362.19	429.17	504.11	568.21	621.21
301.01	362.26	430.16	504.17	569.21	622.11
301.03	363.05	431.12	504.20	570.24	623.01
301.25	364.09	432.15	504.25	571.07	623.02
301.26	365.07	436.19	505.13	571.23	623.02
302.11	366.08	436.22	505.15	572.01	623.16
302.25	369.11	437.11	505.28	572.07	623.16
305.08	371.11	437.27	506.25	572.12	624.01
305.20	372.02	438.24	507.14	573.12	624.08
306.05	372.12	439.09	507.17	573.13	625.11
308.06	372.26	439.19	508.09	574.16	625.18
308.17	372.28	441.17	508.10	575.07	625.18
308.27	373.04	442.17	509.02	575.21	626.18
309.05	373.09	442.23	509.04	576.22	626.21
309.07	373.10	444.05	509.13	576.23	627.05
309.19	373.13	445.01	509.27	576.23	627.12
309.26	373.15	445.08	510.02	576.24	627.26
309.27	374.06	445.17	511.26	577.01	628.12
310.19	374.11	445.20	511.26	577.13	628.13
311.20	375.18	447.06	511.27	577.17	630.19
312.03	375.21	447.10	513.11	579.07	630.24
312.10	375.22	447.12	513.21	579.12	631.23
312.26	376.03	448.02	513.25	579.14	632.03
313.05	376.11	448.15	515.18	579.22	632.13
314.19	376.15	448.28	515.24	581.05	634.22
314.21	377.01	449.08	516.03	581.21	634.24
315.21	378.05	449.09	516.06	582.01	635.09
316.05	379.17	449.19	516.07	582.06	636.06
316.09	380.23	450.03	516.14	582.13	636.11
316.27	381.02	452.03	516.16	583.12	636.14
318.22	381.06	452.07	518.01	583.16	636.25
318.27	381.25	452.10	518.15	585.06	637.08
319.11	381.26	452.25	518.16	585.11	637.12
319.12	382.10	453.13	518.17	586.05	637.16
319.19	382.18	453.16	518.24	586.24	637.20
321.09	383.04	454.06	519.16	587.12	638.08
324.03	383.15	454.09	521.04	587.19	638.13
324.04	385.11	454.18	521.14	588.12	639.03
324.07	385.25	454.28	521.16	588.17	639.09
324.08	387.19	455.04	522.01	588.20	639.17
324.20	387.28	455.06	522.19	590.02	639.21
325.12	388.17	455.12	523.05	590.06	639.25
325.16	390.16	456.01	523.21	590.10	640.10
325.23	390.23	456.15	523.23	590.11	640.23
326.03	391.04	457.14	524.08	590.24	642.13
326.10	391.11	460.17	524.10	591.11	642.17
326.21	392.08	461.04	524.26	592.02	642.22
326.24	392.17	462.19	525.25	592.24	642.23
329.15	392.18	463.13	527.04	593.20	642.23
329.23	393.04	463.21	527.04	595.10	643.12
329.27	394.14	464.16	527.07	595.12	644.03
329.28	395.25	466.06	527.08	598.01	644.27
330.03	395.27	468.02	527.17	598.14	645.09
330.06	396.01	468.16	527.26	598.20	645.18
330.13	396.18	468.23	527.28	599.17	646.07
330.14	397.26	469.03	528.08	600.02	646.22
330.15	398.20	470.21	529.11	600.07	647.08
331.22	398.27	471.11	529.21	600.20	648.06
333.11	399.21	472.03	530.01	601.11	648.07
333.22	400.04	474.02	530.09	603.13	649.26
335.08	400.28	475.13	530.20	603.19	650.14
336.14	401.03	475.15	530.27	603.21	650.14
336.18	402.18	475.18	532.18	604.14	652.11
338.07	402.20	475.25	533.01	604.14	653.01
338.26	402.23	477.11	533.20	605.03	653.07
338.28	402.26	477.23	535.12	606.17	654.01
339.06	403.09	478.10	537.06	606.18	654.16
339.16	403.18	478.13	537.19	606.21	654.27
339.22	404.04	479.23	538.08	606.22	654.28
340.08	404.14	480.14	538.22	606.23	655.01
340.16	405.06	480.19	538.28	606.24	655.15
340.21	405.12	480.23	539.20	607.03	655.20
342.01	406.03	482.26	542.26	607.04	655.24
344.15	406.04	483.08	543.14	607.05	656.13
345.19	406.04	483.24	545.10	608.01	658.05
345.28	406.05	483.27	545.21	609.08	659.14
346.07	406.10	484.18	546.03	609.09	659.15
346.23	406.21	484.19	546.06	610.24	660.10
346.23	407.22	484.25	547.13	610.25	661.11
347.03	407.23	485.17	547.17	611.02	661.21
347.22	408.05	485.23	548.19	611.03	663.14
348.19	408.13	486.04	549.15	611.09	664.19
349.09	409.03	488.01	550.04	611.19	665.10
349.10	410.28	489.20	551.25	611.23	665.11

665.17	735.02	799.26	837.07	896.18	400.11
665.18	736.09	800.07	837.15	896.27	402.19
667.23	736.19	800.23	838.02	898.19	403.20
667.28	737.20	802.12	838.07	899.14	412.14
668.09	740.22	802.15	838.11	900.01	412.15
668.12	740.23	802.24	839.05	900.01	417.02
669.19	741.12	803.01	839.08	901.12	427.08
669.25	741.14	803.04	839.25	901.13	465.18
669.27	741.16	803.06	840.06	903.08	474.22
670.17	742.03	803.08	840.22	906.13	475.14
670.25	742.03	803.08	840.24	907.05	480.27
671.02	742.08	804.11	841.12	907.16	483.21
671.05	742.25	804.15	841.13	907.18	486.01
671.17	743.13	804.23	841.17	907.20	486.02
671.22	744.22	805.17	841.27	907.21	486.02
672.02	746.21	806.02	842.03	907.25	496.01
673.26	747.02	806.05	842.06	note	499.09
674.14	747.02	807.03	842.08	124.13	512.27
674.15	747.07	807.10	842.09	173.13	522.13
674.26	747.09	807.26	842.10	173.16	532.22
677.09	747.21	807.26	842.11	326.14	536.22
678.07	747.24	808.17	842.23	453.05	540.18
678.10	747.26	808.24	845.22	664.11	545.22
679.11	747.26	808.25	846.15	689.10	547.22
679.11	748.07	809.22	846.19	763.22	557.06
679.28	748.08	809.23	846.24	810.17	565.08
681.06	748.09	809.27	848.02	906.18	569.09
682.21	748.11	810.03	848.03	noted	571.22
682.22	748.13	810.10	849.03	167.21	574.25
683.06	748.17	811.11	849.15	219.08	592.12
683.06	748.28	813.24	849.17	408.15	605.15
683.10	749.08	814.01	850.07	notes	611.23
683.14	752.17	814.03	851.16	166.10	611.24
683.20	752.19	814.06	852.26	200.27	611.24
683.25	752.27	814.18	852.28	337.07	614.11
684.03	753.01	815.07	854.07	488.21	617.09
684.08	753.09	815.08	854.22	nothing	617.10
684.24	753.10	815.14	855.24	006.02	619.22
685.19	754.01	815.16	856.04	013.01	621.10
686.10	754.04	815.17	857.03	014.11	623.17
687.20	754.06	815.19	857.05	020.07	624.23
688.04	754.13	815.22	858.09	037.20	633.19
689.15	756.01	816.03	858.17	046.15	650.16
689.20	759.03	816.07	859.19	050.09	652.24
690.12	759.03	816.15	859.23	057.16	660.14
691.09	759.08	816.17	860.21	063.13	663.15
691.19	759.17	816.25	861.08	072.14	665.05
691.23	760.24	816.27	862.03	090.22	671.04
693.27	761.05	818.27	862.09	090.22	676.24
694.08	761.13	818.28	863.08	091.16	685.21
695.01	761.15	819.05	864.26	100.02	687.10
696.22	761.27	819.13	864.28	102.19	698.14
697.04	762.07	819.15	865.06	105.10	702.19
697.10	762.15	820.05	865.08	108.08	705.13
696.23	763.03	820.19	872.01	129.12	708.06
699.05	763.11	820.26	872.14	135.11	717.20
700.06	764.10	821.06	872.15	135.11	719.12
700.13	766.21	821.09	872.19	136.03	726.11
701.11	767.23	821.11	873.05	157.06	734.04
701.21	768.24	821.16	873.28	167.14	736.07
702.06	768.26	821.19	874.04	168.01	753.17
702.13	768.27	821.21	875.17	174.18	753.27
702.21	769.01	821.25	875.20	182.09	754.18
702.27	771.06	822.03	875.20	186.14	758.08
703.09	772.10	822.12	877.02	196.10	759.13
703.10	772.23	822.13	877.10	196.13	759.14
703.20	773.01	822.23	878.02	201.26	763.27
704.05	773.08	822.28	878.03	206.02	764.07
704.06	774.17	823.03	878.20	206.19	771.21
704.13	774.19	823.10	879.03	222.08	774.26
705.15	775.11	823.11	879.05	235.08	775.15
705.21	775.17	823.11	879.12	243.10	776.12
707.02	776.02	823.15	879.21	246.06	809.17
707.24	777.03	823.18	879.26	247.16	816.27
708.01	777.10	824.09	881.10	250.01	819.08
708.11	777.13	825.04	881.10	255.01	827.05
708.13	777.14	825.26	884.02	255.15	827.26
708.21	778.01	826.09	884.25	264.05	830.11
714.09	778.11	826.13	885.09	267.05	832.17
715.07	778.13	826.22	885.13	273.03	849.11
715.14	779.05	826.27	885.17	290.07	849.13
715.16	779.11	827.01	886.15	294.11	854.02
716.24	779.19	827.10	886.19	295.05	855.24
717.02	781.22	827.15	887.03	299.10	870.01
717.27	782.01	827.22	887.03	300.17	875.09
719.01	782.24	828.16	887.08	301.12	883.21
719.25	783.01	828.17	887.13	301.27	883.21
721.02	783.01	829.01	888.19	305.13	885.15
721.11	784.14	829.23	889.16	306.27	893.06
722.09	785.16	830.04	890.05	308.09	895.13
722.10	785.21	830.09	890.11	319.27	897.04
722.17	786.02	830.11	891.03	325.03	898.25
722.17	786.10	831.02	891.05	327.28	notice
722.17	786.22	831.11	891.08	341.09	043.27
723.05	786.25	831.12	892.09	346.17	059.25
723.17	786.27	831.17	892.10	350.25	088.17
723.20	787.25	832.05	893.05	351.17	097.28
723.23	789.05	833.07	894.08	357.18	123.07
724.01	789.16	833.10	894.09	358.21	179.14
725.02	790.15	833.25	894.20	362.11	197.03
726.02	790.20	833.27	894.24	362.16	237.20
727.02	790.22	834.16	895.03	362.26	256.07
727.14	792.22	834.24	895.04	362.26	287.22
730.06	792.23	834.25	895.05	370.21	288.24
730.14	792.24	834.26	895.09	372.21	339.19
730.21	795.25	835.05	895.10	373.07	372.04
730.28	796.04	835.08	895.11	386.04	468.19
734.01	796.15	835.11	895.13	394.20	470.20
734.01	797.13	835.17	895.21	397.24	476.02
734.08	797.17	836.11	896.07	399.18	497.11
734.18	799.11	836.14		400.10	508.01

642.27	043.03	210.16	371.05	507.01	641.11
719.14	044.23	214.24	371.11	509.19	642.02
806.21	046.25	219.10	371.14	510.24	643.14
840.02	049.10	219.19	372.03	513.10	644.02
894.06	051.02	220.02	376.01	513.11	644.17
noticed	051.24	221.22	377.17	514.03	644.24
046.04	054.01	222.17	377.25	514.09	645.04
079.15	054.21	223.20	380.07	515.08	645.28
289.20	057.05	223.26	384.05	517.24	646.02
329.16	059.20	224.16	384.24	521.15	648.07
355.01	061.16	226.04	386.02	523.06	648.14
402.14	064.15	228.04	387.01	524.01	650.07
406.27	065.21	228.08	387.18	526.28	653.14
441.26	066.16	230.07	387.24	527.12	654.01
468.21	068.08	232.24	388.09	528.13	654.21
537.15	069.19	233.08	389.24	529.05	654.27
581.11	069.21	235.07	389.24	529.13	655.21
588.15	069.22	236.01	390.07	530.16	658.10
654.25	071.13	236.23	394.18	531.10	659.10
676.23	075.27	237.11	398.04	531.21	660.11
708.06	079.10	240.17	406.09	531.28	663.20
841.09	081.07	242.27	406.26	532.18	663.28
881.10	081.13	243.16	407.17	534.20	666.03
noticing	081.17	244.12	408.23	534.28	667.05
526.06	082.16	244.27	410.06	535.20	668.08
notified	083.16	245.05	411.22	538.01	669.21
492.08	084.03	247.06	412.22	540.09	671.09
noting	085.06	251.08	415.09	541.19	673.13
152.06	085.23	252.07	416.26	544.01	673.25
notion	086.07	253.08	417.11	545.09	675.06
003.16	087.18	256.18	420.14	547.28	675.13
022.08	088.03	257.25	421.28	548.07	679.18
153.07	093.24	259.27	422.17	549.02	679.28
206.12	093.27	261.04	423.06	551.23	680.09
206.21	095.05	261.24	423.07	552.22	680.12
271.18	097.03	263.23	423.07	553.28	681.07
513.22	099.03	264.25	423.08	555.06	681.25
325.01	100.25	266.04	423.25	555.10	682.22
358.23	101.25	270.12	423.26	555.23	682.28
366.17	104.27	271.17	424.16	559.14	684.12
511.04	106.01	272.18	424.16	562.19	684.28
531.17	115.18	272.22	424.20	563.13	685.19
658.20	116.05	275.27	425.02	563.20	686.16
697.13	119.12	276.19	425.21	564.10	686.26
785.23	121.26	276.26	427.03	565.08	687.12
792.09	122.20	277.25	427.18	565.19	693.18
notions	123.10	278.01	427.26	565.24	695.04
004.17	126.03	278.06	429.20	569.25	697.06
165.09	127.09	280.27	430.04	571.20	697.13
222.10	127.26	282.04	430.26	572.02	697.15
236.11	129.04	282.24	431.06	573.09	698.23
456.12	129.11	287.09	431.14	574.01	698.26
notwithstanding	130.07	288.14	431.18	576.04	699.09
390.19	130.20	288.20	431.27	579.08	702.10
444.10	134.16	289.01	432.03	580.06	702.18
nought	134.23	289.10	432.11	581.02	702.22
694.23	135.05	290.24	433.10	581.21	702.26
nourishment	136.14	292.08	434.23	582.04	703.08
066.28	138.15	292.27	435.04	582.21	705.01
112.07	138.25	293.10	436.10	583.04	705.26
735.04	139.07	293.20	437.09	583.10	707.28
nous	143.18	294.20	438.17	584.05	708.03
334.11	144.12	295.18	440.23	588.07	708.17
nova	145.03	297.03	442.20	589.07	708.28
004.07	146.01	297.09	445.15	590.03	710.04
novel	146.14	297.20	445.15	592.05	711.10
181.02	148.11	297.23	446.19	593.17	718.17
380.03	148.19	298.25	449.03	594.13	720.10
473.12	152.10	300.18	449.23	594.17	721.12
479.01	153.11	302.22	452.03	595.15	721.19
642.09	153.22	312.24	453.14	597.02	723.05
770.10	159.20	313.12	453.17	597.06	724.16
novelty	160.08	313.26	457.23	600.17	725.20
291.16	163.28	314.07	459.17	602.11	731.15
794.15	164.09	316.02	459.23	603.10	732.04
november	165.12	326.01	460.01	604.11	732.21
003.10	166.07	326.13	462.03	604.21	734.05
045.09	166.23	328.16	462.04	604.21	737.04
167.13	168.02	331.24	462.15	604.25	740.01
218.03	168.27	332.02	464.01	606.06	741.09
751.22	171.05	332.08	464.21	607.08	741.19
novice	171.27	333.09	465.11	609.09	751.10
244.02	172.12	333.13	465.23	610.21	752.01
321.08	173.03	333.19	466.02	611.17	755.03
novice-eyes	174.04	334.12	469.19	612.06	755.22
204.06	174.17	335.12	470.05	613.05	756.09
novitiate	174.20	336.26	471.26	613.11	756.17
470.05	176.26	341.27	475.01	613.20	757.26
now	181.20	342.04	477.17	614.28	757.28
001.10	184.21	343.03	479.23	619.04	758.16
002.02	184.26	346.21	480.01	619.09	761.21
007.09	185.09	347.20	481.05	620.12	767.08
008.06	185.17	349.07	481.20	620.22	767.12
009.13	187.11	350.10	484.02	620.25	767.14
010.23	187.25	352.18	484.22	621.05	767.24
020.04	188.25	353.22	485.06	627.22	768.11
022.11	189.21	354.19	485.09	627.27	770.27
023.11	190.03	355.09	485.12	628.04	774.25
024.06	191.08	357.10	487.07	628.14	776.01
024.28	194.06	357.25	488.12	628.22	776.09
025.12	197.22	358.26	492.16	629.08	776.20
030.09	200.09	359.05	493.27	630.17	777.08
030.14	201.06	360.11	496.27	631.08	778.13
030.26	201.21	360.22	497.16	633.02	779.08
032.02	202.07	361.08	497.21	635.08	779.14
032.05	202.23	363.02	498.28	635.19	781.25
032.12	203.13	363.11	501.20	637.13	782.04
032.22	204.05	364.06	503.26	637.26	782.08
034.25	208.17	364.09	503.28	638.07	782.20
036.06	208.20	366.11	504.01	638.12	782.27
039.23	208.26	368.26	504.07	640.06	783.01

NOW (continued)
735.20
786.02
787.16
787.19
789.03
789.19
790.25
790.28
791.21
796.15
797.25
798.01
801.05
802.16
803.11
806.03
809.04
810.19
811.14
819.06
819.13
823.15
829.21
853.14
854.21
855.11
855.13
855.23
855.28
856.13
857.24
858.26
859.16
841.22
842.17
843.19
847.05
847.09
847.24
848.02
848.09
848.15
848.25
849.06
854.08
854.22
857.01
858.03
858.12
861.12
862.17
863.15
863.23
866.14
867.04
867.24
867.25
872.16
873.02
873.09
873.12
873.16
875.11
877.08
877.17
877.22
878.05
878.19
880.12
881.24
883.19
885.22
886.16
886.20
888.11
892.14
897.27
898.13
899.14
899.28
900.13
902.03
903.11
903.17
908.02
908.24
910.17
910.21
912.08

now-rising
503.05
nowhere
537.26
660.15
675.28
677.11
838.21
860.08
888.02
900.25
noxious
020.16
057.14
291.22
625.06
nudge
330.19
nuisance
166.09
289.06
355.13

numbed
076.08
111.18
187.05
number
078.09
131.17
160.15
184.23
342.14
365.28
491.01
729.17
791.26
814.09
900.21
numbered
557.03
759.22
828.23
numbering
153.12
789.19
numbers
080.25
numbness
181.17
674.25
numerous
243.20
278.03
nun
243.21
nun-like
460.26
nunnery
489.03
nurse
001.15
033.30
035.14
039.26
152.26
153.20
153.25
154.17
155.14
156.24
159.07
189.20
196.19
197.13
197.18
198.23
203.03
214.28
217.23
328.14
468.13
468.19
479.12
479.18
481.16
485.12
617.22
878.27
880.09
880.16
880.17
nurse-girl
709.27
nurse-maid's
067.11
nursed
696.10
nursery
016.14
020.27
024.01
026.19
028.20
029.23
033.30
040.09
042.17
044.08
045.28
047.24
050.18
051.21
052.01
059.13
061.20
064.15
071.13
072.03
221.11
314.11
456.26
522.27
582.20
582.14
653.12
nursery-door
051.18
nursery-hearth
005.20
nursery-maid
049.11
nurses
363.22

nursing
038.11
108.21
457.09
nutriment
399.03
663.12
nuts
056.01
219.09
o
347.01
o'
679.08
680.23
680.28
681.04
685.12
696.25
698.06
698.10
698.10
906.22
o'clock
021.01
028.10
048.06
071.02
094.13
097.06
100.11
129.02
153.27
156.11
181.19
219.03
235.27
251.01
314.20
409.04
457.02
485.16
492.14
537.27
558.02
558.14
664.23
740.04
745.28
800.06
854.13
899.10
900.27
o'er
033.10
033.15
551.26
o'gall
503.25
509.15
o't'
906.21
oak
146.04
190.19
193.11
193.18
207.08
207.22
221.01
231.08
425.24
oaken
329.11
oaks
194.11
oat-cake
095.19
oaten
079.10
oath
512.24
517.19
obedience
360.12
512.03
829.10
850.16
obedient
008.09
106.20
213.15
700.18
obese
060.19
obey
227.11
258.10
437.12
497.21
539.07
646.08
obeyed
057.02
100.04
110.08
120.28
140.16
222.28
240.28
398.05

419.08
421.16
431.26
458.27
482.07
539.17
564.16
596.08
613.14
685.05
850.15
obeying
245.16
object
005.09
097.28
102.10
120.01
187.27
220.06
221.27
292.11
325.11
372.11
476.03
485.28
509.03
551.03
580.13
670.27
675.22
758.27
773.07
785.15
822.03
878.26
objection
605.07
754.22
800.05
objectionable
054.16
objections
778.16
815.21
objectless
659.12
854.21
objects
046.22
164.19
339.03
369.21
460.17
522.08
676.23
793.21
oblation
823.04
obligation
238.10
301.14
301.21
785.18
838.03
obligations
547.14
756.28
obligatioons
014.08
oblige
114.18
obliged
035.17
096.04
114.04
126.17
170.17
180.17
192.08
239.23
240.18
260.02
359.03
380.28
452.08
463.09
486.24
511.12
543.25
706.28
718.25
854.22
obliging
176.28
743.17
908.14
obligingly
173.08
obliterating
057.07
oblivion
425.09
632.08
oblong
577.22
obnoxious
027.08
626.15
obscure
097.27

101.08
513.04
516.09
677.25
719.21
720.08
obscured
652.03
obscurity
316.03
423.23
572.20
676.01
720.09
828.22
910.16
observant
149.13
observation
002.10
123.02
276.08
372.12
804.02
891.07
observations
099.09
286.04
540.02
720.28
observe
107.18
124.27
379.05
381.02
399.24
519.16
709.15
754.13
observed
059.02
097.21
104.23
112.26
126.05
137.25
204.26
251.16
308.22
336.27
349.16
367.22
401.21
486.08
527.19
540.19
586.20
639.02
681.16
689.12
707.09
708.08
714.10
754.21
766.18
773.12
811.27
812.03
854.02
873.08
observer
377.25
748.17
observers
350.21
observing
206.13
366.15
obstacle
440.10
611.01
675.17
736.10
751.16
obstacles
284.08
579.19
801.26
821.15
827.09
obstinate
691.19
742.07
obstruction
630.12
obtain
439.14
717.21
obtained
048.13
172.27
347.01
706.27
889.06
907.21
obtrusive
123.09
obviating
118.16

obvious
374.01
605.15
658.14
obviously
390.16
obviousness
377.04
occasion
040.17
055.02
117.17
125.13
163.16
169.25
279.02
425.07
431.14
489.27
639.04
804.06
837.27
910.28
occasional
218.08
254.13
321.05
456.14
occasionally
022.12
046.14
219.20
276.09
352.15
479.16
635.28
640.11
occasioned
810.12
occasioning
480.27
occasions
118.21
151.07
236.13
316.24
497.13
633.28
804.25
occupant
296.20
701.02
occupants
079.21
364.17
677.08
810.24
occupation
045.26
046.10
049.20
090.13
203.03
247.02
470.22
534.27
549.14
641.01
647.02
722.04
752.06
819.13
occupations
097.01
380.17
711.06
866.26
occupied
052.19
082.08
147.13
165.26
186.13
247.14
311.17
378.15
382.28
474.03
504.08
710.05
714.04
752.04
773.17
occupy
203.09
208.03
399.20
741.19
occupying
460.14
occur
080.08
117.20
118.11
occurred
228.16
349.06
777.18
830.04
occurrence
474.23

684.13	015.22	039.04	061.12	083.26	100.07
859.23	015.23	039.07	061.16	084.03	100.09
occurrences	015.27	039.07	061.20	084.06	100.10
323.23	015.28	039.08	062.06	084.11	100.10
occurs	016.02	039.10	062.11	084.13	100.12
505.10	016.03	039.10	062.15	084.14	100.16
ocean	016.04	039.17	062.17	084.16	100.18
004.01	016.06	039.20	062.21	084.19	100.19
509.20	016.09	040.12	062.26	084.22	100.20
630.28	016.19	040.16	063.03	085.09	101.02
ocean-surges	016.22	040.21	063.18	085.11	101.15
551.08	016.23	040.27	063.19	085.16	101.18
oceans	016.25	041.03	064.24	085.20	101.19
825.09	017.02	042.04	065.03	085.21	101.24
october	017.09	042.09	065.07	085.26	102.03
181.18	017.12	042.13	065.07	085.27	102.05
218.03	017.23	043.11	065.08	085.27	102.09
593.08	017.24	043.22	065.10	085.28	102.19
801.24	017.25	043.26	065.15	086.01	103.01
oculist	017.27	044.09	065.15	086.04	103.02
910.20	018.01	044.11	065.17	086.04	103.10
odd	018.06	044.17	065.26	086.05	104.08
046.24	018.08	045.03	065.28	086.05	104.10
210.27	018.26	045.09	066.01	086.12	104.12
300.05	018.28	045.14	066.04	086.12	104.13
382.16	019.26	045.15	066.11	086.16	104.15
772.10	020.04	045.16	066.12	086.18	104.17
777.25	020.15	045.21	066.15	086.18	105.04
oddities	020.17	045.22	067.13	086.25	105.04
217.15	020.18	045.23	068.07	086.25	105.07
oddity	020.18	045.25	068.25	087.03	105.10
084.19	020.24	045.26	069.01	087.08	105.16
odious	020.24	046.07	069.03	087.10	105.16
629.09	020.26	046.07	069.08	087.17	105.22
odour	021.07	046.08	069.08	087.19	105.24
081.22	021.09	046.11	069.11	087.20	106.03
093.27	021.11	046.22	070.02	087.25	106.02
154.15	021.14	046.22	070.03	087.27	106.12
280.19	021.22	046.28	070.04	088.02	106.27
of	021.23	047.05	071.03	088.03	106.28
001.03	021.28	047.06	071.03	088.09	109.01
001.10	022.04	047.09	071.08	088.15	109.06
001.11	022.15	047.20	071.16	088.17	111.06
001.15	022.16	047.22	071.18	088.18	111.08
001.16	022.19	047.25	072.11	088.20	111.09
002.08	022.22	048.02	073.06	088.24	112.01
003.01	022.24	048.05	073.07	089.02	112.03
003.07	023.12	048.10	073.24	089.05	112.05
003.09	023.17	048.11	074.05	089.12	112.07
003.11	023.20	048.15	074.06	089.20	112.11
003.12	024.06	048.19	074.08	089.23	112.13
003.13	025.01	048.20	074.08	089.23	112.15
003.14	025.09	048.25	074.20	089.26	112.15
003.19	025.12	048.27	074.28	090.05	112.17
003.23	025.16	049.01	075.12	090.07	112.18
003.24	026.07	049.06	075.15	090.13	112.25
003.24	026.08	049.11	075.21	090.15	113.01
003.26	026.16	049.20	076.16	091.08	113.04
003.26	027.04	049.25	077.22	091.28	113.14
004.03	027.09	049.28	077.24	092.04	113.16
004.06	027.10	050.07	077.28	092.17	113.20
004.06	029.01	050.11	078.02	093.12	113.25
004.08	029.09	050.12	078.03	094.03	113.25
004.09	029.14	050.14	078.06	094.04	113.26
004.10	029.15	050.14	078.06	094.05	113.27
004.11	029.17	050.16	078.07	094.06	113.27
004.11	029.26	050.23	078.07	094.14	114.02
004.12	030.04	051.05	078.09	094.18	114.08
004.14	030.09	051.11	078.12	094.22	114.12
004.15	030.10	051.12	078.13	094.25	114.12
004.16	030.11	051.27	078.16	094.27	114.13
004.22	030.12	051.28	078.19	095.02	114.13
004.25	030.18	052.04	078.26	095.03	114.15
005.03	030.19	052.18	079.01	095.04	114.18
005.09	030.21	052.28	079.03	095.10	114.24
005.23	030.25	053.12	079.04	095.13	114.26
005.26	030.28	053.19	079.05	095.13	115.08
005.26	031.03	054.04	079.09	095.14	115.18
006.04	031.04	054.10	079.15	095.16	115.19
006.15	031.10	054.20	079.20	095.18	115.28
006.20	031.11	054.23	079.20	095.19	116.01
007.01	031.18	055.02	080.10	096.05	116.08
007.11	031.22	055.03	080.24	096.09	116.11
007.25	031.26	055.14	080.25	096.11	116.13
008.15	032.01	055.15	081.04	096.12	116.13
008.22	032.14	055.16	081.06	096.19	116.18
008.26	032.15	055.17	081.08	096.20	116.21
009.16	033.01	055.25	081.10	097.02	117.02
009.16	033.06	055.26	081.16	097.10	117.02
009.21	033.10	056.07	081.20	097.12	117.03
010.03	033.20	056.07	081.23	097.13	117.10
010.04	033.27	056.10	081.24	097.16	117.23
010.14	035.07	057.08	081.24	097.19	118.08
010.16	035.08	057.18	081.25	097.22	118.11
011.01	035.10	058.07	081.26	097.23	118.12
012.05	035.26	058.11	082.01	097.24	118.13
012.06	035.27	058.12	082.02	097.24	118.16
013.06	036.11	058.23	082.02	097.28	118.18
013.11	036.17	059.01	082.04	098.06	118.23
013.14	036.18	059.04	082.05	098.13	118.23
013.14	036.19	059.06	082.09	098.13	118.24
013.21	037.26	059.13	082.17	098.16	118.25
013.24	037.27	059.15	082.18	098.19	119.01
014.03	038.08	059.18	082.18	098.23	119.01
014.13	038.11	059.22	083.03	099.04	119.04
014.13	038.13	060.07	083.05	099.11	119.14
014.14	038.13	060.17	083.08	099.16	120.07
014.22	038.15	060.24	083.10	099.22	120.10
015.06	038.23	060.24	083.17	099.25	120.15
015.17	039.01	061.08	083.19	099.26	120.21
015.20	039.02			100.02	

120.28	140.05	161.09	181.10	204.13	227.07
121.06	140.06	161.12	181.11	204.17	227.16
121.09	140.06	161.13	181.11	204.19	227.23
121.11	140.07	161.16	181.12	204.28	228.10
121.16	140.08	161.17	181.14	205.04	228.17
121.16	140.15	161.17	181.18	205.13	228.19
121.21	140.16	161.19	182.08	205.14	228.23
121.24	141.01	161.24	182.09	205.26	228.26
121.24	141.05	162.02	182.15	206.08	229.13
121.24	141.12	162.07	182.23	206.11	229.15
122.02	141.20	162.09	182.24	206.12	229.27
122.03	141.24	162.10	182.25	206.21	229.28
122.05	142.09	162.11	183.02	206.24	230.01
122.06	142.09	162.14	183.18	206.28	230.02
122.09	142.11	162.15	183.21	207.02	230.04
122.13	142.21	162.18	184.01	207.07	230.08
122.14	142.23	162.21	184.05	207.09	230.15
122.17	142.23	162.28	184.24	207.10	230.21
122.22	142.26	163.01	184.24	207.10	231.07
122.23	143.01	163.03	184.27	207.13	231.16
122.27	143.02	163.05	185.13	207.16	231.17
123.11	143.05	163.05	185.16	207.17	231.18
123.21	143.05	163.08	185.19	207.17	231.25
123.23	143.06	163.15	185.27	207.17	232.06
124.05	143.07	163.16	186.15	207.19	233.06
124.15	143.10	163.17	187.07	207.21	233.13
124.16	143.16	163.26	187.09	207.22	233.16
124.17	144.02	164.02	187.20	207.22	234.06
124.18	144.04	164.08	187.20	207.24	234.11
124.24	144.07	164.10	187.27	207.27	235.06
124.26	144.09	164.11	188.03	208.03	235.15
125.02	144.18	164.13	188.05	208.09	235.15
125.06	145.09	164.16	188.07	208.11	236.09
125.15	145.10	164.18	188.13	208.26	236.10
125.16	145.12	164.22	188.28	209.03	236.11
125.27	145.15	164.24	189.07	209.16	236.27
126.03	145.17	165.06	189.08	209.18	237.06
126.04	145.19	165.12	189.19	209.19	237.12
126.21	145.25	165.13	190.02	209.23	237.14
126.22	145.27	165.14	190.08	209.27	237.17
126.23	146.06	165.25	190.19	210.02	237.18
126.26	146.08	165.28	190.25	210.19	237.24
127.05	146.08	166.11	190.27	210.23	238.06
127.07	146.11	166.20	191.06	211.05	238.11
127.06	146.17	166.22	191.07	211.10	238.12
127.10	146.18	166.24	191.09	211.12	238.20
127.22	146.22	166.27	191.13	213.02	239.13
127.23	147.01	167.01	191.24	213.08	239.15
127.27	147.02	167.07	191.27	213.17	239.19
127.27	147.07	167.19	192.02	213.18	239.24
128.02	147.15	168.05	192.09	213.19	240.06
128.05	147.18	168.19	192.12	214.06	240.06
128.08	147.21	168.23	192.13	214.10	240.08
128.09	147.23	168.25	192.15	214.11	240.19
128.12	147.28	168.28	193.01	214.22	241.12
129.16	148.02	169.04	193.11	215.02	241.15
130.06	148.05	169.07	193.17	215.05	241.17
131.02	148.08	169.09	193.22	215.07	241.18
132.04	148.10	169.16	193.27	215.08	242.04
132.10	148.10	169.19	193.28	215.09	242.10
132.14	148.11	169.20	194.05	215.10	242.15
132.15	148.14	169.21	194.09	215.11	242.17
132.20	148.22	169.24	194.11	215.11	243.15
132.21	148.24	169.24	194.14	215.14	243.16
132.26	149.02	169.26	194.18	215.15	243.21
133.05	149.02	170.21	194.20	215.21	243.27
133.12	149.08	170.27	194.21	215.23	244.13
133.13	149.18	171.01	194.21	216.01	244.14
134.09	150.01	171.08	194.26	216.04	244.17
134.27	150.03	171.13	194.27	216.13	244.20
135.12	150.09	171.21	195.05	217.09	245.08
135.16	150.10	171.24	195.10	217.13	245.10
135.19	150.11	171.26	195.14	217.19	245.25
135.20	150.15	172.03	195.18	217.20	247.05
135.21	150.16	172.05	195.21	217.21	247.08
135.26	150.26	172.07	195.21	217.27	247.22
136.01	151.03	172.09	196.05	218.12	247.27
136.04	151.12	172.09	196.11	218.23	248.12
136.10	151.18	172.15	196.25	219.02	248.14
136.16	151.24	172.19	197.06	219.05	248.20
137.14	151.26	172.19	197.26	219.13	248.25
137.14	152.11	172.22	197.28	219.17	248.26
137.15	152.23	172.28	198.03	220.01	248.27
137.27	153.14	173.02	198.06	220.17	248.28
138.07	153.15	173.06	198.07	220.18	249.09
138.08	153.16	173.17	199.02	220.22	249.10
138.09	154.06	173.22	199.16	220.23	249.12
138.13	154.10	173.23	199.23	220.28	249.13
138.13	154.11	173.27	200.02	221.01	249.14
138.16	154.12	174.02	200.11	221.03	249.16
138.19	154.15	174.21	200.17	221.06	249.21
138.24	154.24	175.04	200.18	221.10	249.25
138.26	154.26	175.21	200.23	221.11	250.04
139.01	155.04	176.14	200.26	221.17	250.07
139.01	155.05	177.01	200.27	221.19	250.13
139.05	155.12	177.07	200.28	221.28	250.14
139.06	155.22	177.17	201.04	222.11	250.27
139.10	156.09	177.22	201.11	222.16	251.09
139.14	156.22	177.24	201.12	222.19	251.10
139.17	158.10	178.03	201.26	223.01	251.24
139.19	158.20	178.13	202.13	224.07	251.25
139.19	160.03	178.24	202.16	224.12	252.01
139.21	160.04	178.26	202.17	224.13	252.12
139.21	160.08	178.27	202.25	224.18	252.15
139.21	160.09	180.05	202.27	225.07	252.22
139.24	160.11	180.21	202.28	225.10	252.26
139.26	160.13	180.22	203.03	225.14	252.27
139.27	160.15	180.26	203.15	225.23	253.01
140.04	160.17	181.09	203.21	226.04	253.04
140.05	160.20	181.10	204.07	226.14	253.05
140.05	160.20	181.10	204.12	226.18	253.10

253.12	274.24	299.27	325.25	344.28	367.27
253.13	274.25	300.15	326.10	345.03	368.02
253.19	275.01	300.18	326.12	345.07	368.04
253.20	275.20	300.20	326.17	345.21	368.09
254.02	275.28	301.02	326.25	346.25	368.10
254.08	275.28	301.13	327.07	347.01	368.15
254.19	276.01	301.28	327.15	347.14	368.16
255.17	276.13	302.01	327.16	347.18	368.17
255.28	276.17	302.01	327.17	347.23	368.19
256.02	276.19	302.12	327.17	348.03	368.20
256.03	276.22	302.17	327.18	348.03	369.01
256.06	276.23	302.19	327.19	348.05	369.14
256.07	277.03	302.20	327.21	348.09	369.16
256.07	277.06	302.22	327.23	348.11	369.18
256.14	277.23	305.06	328.17	348.12	370.14
256.23	278.01	305.08	328.18	348.16	370.24
256.23	278.03	305.14	328.21	348.16	370.25
257.16	278.07	305.15	328.23	348.17	371.03
257.21	279.08	305.19	329.06	348.22	371.10
257.24	279.09	306.02	329.10	348.23	371.15
257.25	279.16	306.03	329.11	349.11	371.26
257.27	279.19	306.08	329.15	349.12	372.09
258.08	280.01	306.12	329.20	349.22	372.17
258.09	280.03	306.13	329.21	349.27	372.25
258.13	280.10	306.16	329.21	350.04	372.27
258.17	280.13	306.27	329.27	350.10	373.12
258.19	280.19	307.01	330.01	350.11	373.13
259.01	280.19	307.07	330.23	350.15	373.14
259.03	280.21	307.08	331.07	350.16	373.23
259.04	281.02	307.09	331.08	350.17	373.28
259.09	281.03	308.02	331.11	350.18	374.01
259.12	281.13	308.11	331.17	350.25	374.02
259.23	281.16	308.20	331.20	350.26	374.23
260.09	281.24	309.05	331.23	351.10	376.02
260.09	281.27	309.07	331.25	351.11	376.16
260.12	281.28	309.14	331.27	351.12	376.16
260.13	282.05	309.19	331.27	351.19	376.21
260.14	282.07	310.06	331.28	351.26	376.22
260.25	282.15	310.06	332.01	352.17	377.04
261.01	282.18	310.08	332.11	352.21	377.07
261.02	282.19	310.17	332.24	352.25	377.14
261.08	282.25	310.23	332.28	352.25	377.16
261.11	282.26	311.03	333.07	353.08	378.06
261.18	283.01	311.03	333.08	353.11	378.11
261.19	283.04	311.06	333.09	353.13	378.14
261.19	283.26	311.15	333.12	353.24	378.14
262.01	283.27	311.18	333.12	354.08	378.20
262.04	284.03	311.19	333.23	354.10	378.22
262.09	284.25	311.24	333.23	354.24	379.02
262.15	285.03	311.28	334.19	355.01	379.03
262.17	285.09	312.01	334.20	355.02	379.08
262.24	285.12	312.01	335.01	355.12	379.11
262.25	285.17	312.17	335.01	355.21	379.13
263.02	285.18	312.18	335.09	356.06	379.14
263.04	286.14	312.19	335.10	356.13	379.21
263.05	286.16	312.25	335.10	356.16	379.27
263.14	286.18	312.27	335.19	356.18	380.05
263.24	286.20	313.14	335.19	356.19	380.06
263.26	287.02	314.24	335.23	356.21	380.08
264.03	287.04	315.02	336.10	356.22	380.11
264.03	287.11	315.05	336.11	357.03	380.18
264.06	287.28	315.08	336.13	357.03	380.19
264.23	288.01	315.08	337.02	357.04	381.01
265.14	288.02	316.01	337.05	357.05	382.07
265.16	288.07	316.01	337.06	357.08	382.09
265.23	288.17	316.27	337.13	357.27	382.20
265.25	288.17	317.04	337.14	357.27	382.26
266.02	288.19	317.11	338.08	358.01	383.08
266.03	288.21	317.17	338.09	358.05	383.10
266.05	288.23	317.18	338.16	358.14	383.12
267.10	289.05	317.25	339.05	358.19	383.13
267.14	289.14	318.02	339.11	358.21	383.15
267.18	289.21	318.02	339.13	358.22	383.16
267.19	289.28	318.11	340.06	358.24	383.21
267.24	290.03	318.12	340.09	358.26	383.24
268.07	290.08	318.20	340.11	359.12	383.26
268.07	290.13	318.21	341.09	359.15	384.02
268.10	290.15	318.23	341.13	359.15	384.18
268.11	290.15	319.03	341.23	359.24	384.19
268.17	290.20	319.07	341.26	359.26	384.20
268.21	290.27	319.23	341.27	360.17	384.22
268.25	291.04	319.26	342.03	361.01	384.24
269.02	291.12	320.04	342.04	361.03	384.28
269.05	291.23	320.14	342.08	361.17	385.03
269.20	292.05	320.16	342.09	361.24	385.07
269.21	292.16	320.17	342.13	363.05	385.17
269.24	292.26	320.18	342.14	363.06	385.19
269.25	292.27	320.26	342.16	364.04	386.01
269.27	292.28	321.02	342.22	364.17	386.16
269.27	293.01	321.03	342.23	365.02	386.20
270.19	293.12	321.06	342.23	365.05	386.27
270.23	294.16	321.07	342.24	365.06	387.02
270.24	294.22	321.07	343.04	365.16	387.16
270.26	295.01	321.12	343.07	365.17	387.27
271.08	295.01	321.13	343.12	365.18	388.13
271.11	296.01	322.02	343.16	365.19	388.25
271.14	296.02	322.04	343.17	365.28	388.26
271.16	296.06	322.12	343.19	365.28	389.14
271.17	296.06	322.23	343.20	366.01	389.16
271.23	296.08	322.26	343.20	366.05	389.26
271.23	296.10	323.11	343.24	366.13	390.05
272.01	296.25	323.21	343.26	366.14	390.15
272.21	296.26	324.02	343.26	366.19	390.18
272.25	297.01	324.13	344.01	366.22	390.25
273.08	297.06	324.18	344.04	367.01	391.07
273.23	297.11	325.01	344.04	367.03	391.09
274.01	298.07	325.04	344.09	367.03	391.17
274.14	298.26	325.11	344.11	367.05	391.23
274.14	299.12	325.12	344.18	367.06	391.24
274.15	299.13	325.14	344.20	367.13	391.25
274.21	299.14	325.19	344.24	367.24	392.07

392.11	423.17	450.06	474.27	498.16	528.18
392.22	423.19	450.08	474.28	498.21	528.26
392.24	423.27	450.14	475.13	498.22	529.01
394.12	423.28	450.24	475.19	498.27	529.20
395.17	424.01	450.25	475.20	499.06	529.23
396.15	424.02	451.12	475.24	499.07	530.13
396.27	424.05	451.13	475.28	499.08	530.22
397.06	424.10	451.14	475.28	499.10	531.03
397.18	424.17	451.15	476.02	499.18	531.06
397.24	424.20	451.24	476.11	499.19	531.06
398.02	424.20	453.21	476.11	499.23	531.17
398.07	424.21	453.23	476.19	500.06	532.11
398.08	424.24	454.02	476.25	501.05	532.13
398.20	424.26	454.03	476.28	501.07	532.17
398.25	425.12	454.06	477.02	501.08	532.19
398.28	425.13	454.07	477.06	501.13	532.22
399.09	425.14	454.12	477.14	501.20	533.05
399.18	425.16	454.12	477.19	502.04	533.12
399.20	425.17	454.20	477.24	502.04	534.19
400.01	425.19	454.21	478.05	502.05	534.24
400.12	425.20	454.24	478.09	502.09	535.02
400.13	426.03	455.13	478.20	502.14	535.04
400.14	426.13	455.17	478.22	502.19	535.05
400.17	426.19	456.01	479.01	503.04	536.17
400.19	426.22	457.02	479.03	503.11	536.19
400.20	427.08	457.02	479.05	503.12	537.14
400.24	427.22	457.21	479.13	504.02	537.15
400.26	429.06	457.25	479.28	504.10	537.16
401.01	429.12	458.07	480.04	504.11	537.16
401.01	429.14	458.24	480.05	504.24	537.20
401.01	429.15	459.01	480.05	505.07	539.02
401.08	429.26	459.10	480.19	505.13	539.03
401.09	430.04	459.20	480.23	505.18	539.04
401.13	430.14	459.20	480.27	505.20	539.05
401.14	431.03	459.21	481.15	505.26	539.16
401.14	431.09	459.26	481.23	506.04	539.24
401.19	431.11	459.28	482.02	506.05	539.26
401.21	431.18	460.01	482.12	506.08	540.02
401.25	431.20	460.02	482.23	506.16	540.06
401.26	432.03	460.08	483.03	506.20	540.15
402.02	432.13	460.13	483.06	507.12	540.25
402.04	432.18	460.24	483.10	507.15	540.27
402.07	432.20	460.27	483.16	507.26	541.08
402.08	433.01	460.27	483.21	507.27	541.11
402.11	433.07	461.05	483.26	508.03	541.28
403.05	433.15	461.09	484.01	508.19	542.10
403.14	433.25	461.13	484.06	508.23	542.18
403.20	434.03	461.14	484.10	508.24	542.21
403.23	434.17	461.17	485.10	508.25	543.02
404.08	434.28	461.22	485.14	508.25	543.06
404.16	435.01	462.04	485.18	509.02	543.16
404.17	435.05	462.05	485.25	509.12	543.19
404.26	435.24	462.07	485.27	509.14	544.02
405.16	435.24	462.09	486.05	509.16	544.06
405.21	436.05	462.09	486.08	509.19	544.08
405.22	436.08	462.10	486.14	509.28	544.13
405.26	436.12	462.18	487.03	510.04	544.17
405.27	436.22	462.19	488.03	510.20	544.18
405.28	436.23	464.03	488.05	510.28	544.20
406.01	437.06	464.07	488.21	511.01	544.23
406.02	438.20	464.23	489.06	511.03	544.24
406.05	438.21	464.28	489.07	511.18	545.07
406.06	439.05	465.08	489.08	511.28	545.08
406.08	439.09	465.09	489.10	512.08	545.23
406.20	439.09	465.12	489.11	512.09	545.25
406.28	439.12	465.21	490.02	512.15	545.26
407.16	439.17	466.11	490.04	513.01	545.27
407.23	439.19	466.17	490.05	513.02	546.07
408.11	439.21	466.21	490.16	513.12	546.10
408.11	439.26	467.01	490.18	513.12	546.12
408.18	439.28	467.13	490.24	514.14	546.15
408.19	440.08	467.23	490.28	514.24	546.16
409.10	440.08	467.24	491.01	514.26	547.15
409.27	440.10	468.01	491.03	514.28	547.15
410.22	440.19	468.10	491.04	516.03	547.21
411.08	440.27	469.01	491.05	518.05	548.11
411.23	440.28	469.04	491.06	518.07	548.20
412.01	442.04	469.09	491.08	518.08	548.25
412.19	442.10	469.11	491.13	518.09	549.23
414.10	442.12	469.12	491.15	518.10	549.25
414.17	442.19	469.20	491.20	519.06	550.04
415.07	442.27	470.20	491.22	519.08	550.05
416.15	443.05	470.25	492.02	519.15	550.06
416.16	444.07	470.26	492.04	519.18	550.24
416.19	444.10	471.02	492.09	520.06	551.08
417.02	444.14	471.03	492.14	520.09	551.20
417.10	444.18	471.05	492.27	520.14	551.21
417.18	444.19	471.07	492.28	520.16	552.18
417.22	445.01	471.08	493.11	521.04	552.19
419.15	445.04	471.11	493.12	521.06	552.26
419.26	445.06	471.15	493.16	521.11	553.01
420.01	445.09	471.23	494.02	522.03	553.23
420.17	445.19	471.23	494.14	522.05	554.06
420.22	445.20	472.13	494.16	522.12	554.06
420.25	445.21	472.17	494.24	522.16	554.07
421.02	445.23	472.18	494.26	523.06	554.14
421.04	445.26	473.05	495.04	524.11	554.20
421.06	446.03	473.07	495.08	524.18	555.01
421.14	446.23	473.08	495.16	524.24	555.11
421.21	448.01	473.12	495.20	525.02	555.13
422.08	448.03	473.12	496.03	525.06	556.03
422.11	448.04	473.19	496.03	525.07	556.04
422.15	448.06	473.21	496.04	525.11	556.07
422.16	449.05	474.01	496.09	526.17	557.02
422.23	449.06	474.09	497.01	526.17	557.08
422.26	449.07	474.11	497.03	527.07	557.13
423.03	449.08	474.14	497.11	527.08	558.09
423.09	449.13	474.15	497.12	527.10	558.16
423.10	449.13	474.19	497.15	528.04	558.19
423.12	449.28	474.23	497.26	528.07	558.20
423.15	450.04	474.23	498.11	528.11	558.22

559.06	589.07	616.06	635.03	658.09	677.27
559.11	589.10	616.06	635.11	658.19	678.03
559.16	589.12	616.08	635.17	659.02	678.07
559.16	589.12	616.11	635.26	659.02	678.15
559.23	589.16	616.28	636.02	659.26	678.25
559.23	589.19	617.10	636.02	660.04	679.10
560.06	589.19	617.10	636.04	660.05	680.18
560.09	589.24	617.11	636.09	660.11	680.24
560.12	589.25	617.25	636.12	660.21	681.01
560.17	590.01	617.26	636.13	660.23	681.10
561.03	590.19	617.27	636.16	661.05	681.12
561.04	591.06	617.28	636.16	661.06	681.28
561.07	591.13	618.17	636.26	661.21	682.01
561.09	591.20	618.24	636.27	661.24	682.07
561.12	592.03	618.26	637.06	662.03	682.07
561.16	592.09	619.06	637.10	662.06	682.15
562.20	592.18	619.11	637.11	662.16	682.17
562.25	592.19	619.18	637.13	662.17	683.18
563.04	592.22	619.21	637.18	662.18	683.19
563.05	593.01	619.23	637.19	662.20	683.23
563.07	593.02	619.24	637.21	662.22	683.26
563.15	593.05	619.27	637.26	662.22	683.26
563.16	593.07	620.03	637.28	662.25	684.10
564.02	593.08	621.01	638.05	663.01	684.12
564.03	593.09	621.04	638.11	663.16	684.13
565.21	593.10	621.10	638.14	663.18	685.07
566.13	593.10	621.25	638.15	663.22	685.26
566.15	593.13	622.07	638.16	664.09	686.12
566.23	593.14	622.09	638.16	664.13	686.12
568.02	593.16	622.14	638.20	664.15	686.25
568.16	593.17	622.15	638.24	664.17	686.27
568.19	593.17	623.03	638.28	664.24	687.28
568.23	594.08	623.10	639.02	664.25	688.03
568.24	594.10	623.18	639.04	664.26	688.04
569.03	595.21	623.18	639.10	664.27	688.11
569.09	595.25	623.18	639.21	665.04	689.02
569.23	595.25	623.23	639.26	665.06	689.10
570.04	596.16	623.25	640.12	665.09	689.10
570.08	596.21	624.01	640.14	665.10	690.03
570.10	597.05	624.09	640.15	665.22	690.13
570.13	597.10	624.12	640.17	666.05	690.21
570.15	597.24	624.19	640.21	666.09	690.22
571.04	598.04	624.24	640.28	666.13	690.22
571.05	598.09	624.26	641.02	666.23	690.25
571.12	598.12	624.28	641.03	667.05	690.25
571.22	599.14	625.10	641.12	667.10	691.07
571.24	599.20	625.11	641.14	667.15	691.09
572.05	600.16	625.16	641.16	667.16	691.20
572.07	602.02	625.16	641.24	667.25	691.21
572.15	602.03	625.18	642.08	668.07	691.26
572.17	602.08	625.19	642.12	668.10	692.05
572.19	602.09	626.04	642.15	668.16	692.08
572.21	602.20	626.09	642.20	668.21	692.16
573.11	602.23	626.12	642.25	668.27	692.20
573.17	603.06	626.13	642.26	669.09	692.26
574.01	603.07	626.15	642.27	669.20	692.27
574.04	603.09	626.16	643.03	669.23	693.01
574.13	603.11	626.19	643.04	669.25	693.04
574.17	603.25	626.26	643.14	669.26	693.04
574.19	604.02	626.28	643.20	670.02	693.05
574.20	604.04	627.16	643.24	670.02	693.19
574.23	604.07	627.21	644.12	670.04	693.25
574.24	604.11	627.25	644.25	670.24	694.07
575.05	605.04	627.26	645.03	670.27	694.09
575.10	605.11	628.01	645.07	671.03	694.20
575.14	605.17	628.07	645.09	671.09	695.06
575.24	606.02	628.08	645.15	671.11	695.19
576.10	606.10	628.09	645.23	671.12	695.26
576.24	606.25	628.10	646.11	671.14	696.05
577.03	607.15	628.13	647.22	671.15	696.18
577.07	607.21	628.18	647.22	671.18	696.25
577.21	608.08	628.19	648.28	671.20	697.01
578.03	609.04	628.24	649.02	671.20	697.03
578.04	609.10	628.25	649.12	671.28	697.06
578.09	609.11	628.26	649.16	672.01	697.08
578.11	610.01	629.02	649.22	672.03	697.20
579.10	610.06	629.05	649.23	672.06	697.26
579.11	610.07	629.13	649.26	672.07	698.17
580.02	611.10	629.15	650.24	672.25	698.17
580.07	611.15	629.19	651.18	672.26	698.22
580.13	611.16	629.20	651.24	672.27	698.27
581.16	611.20	629.21	652.02	673.01	699.07
581.16	611.23	630.03	652.08	673.04	699.24
581.17	612.02	630.08	652.27	673.10	699.26
581.22	612.03	630.11	653.12	673.13	701.07
582.18	612.18	630.14	653.26	673.27	701.08
582.24	612.18	630.16	653.27	673.28	701.10
583.12	612.23	630.17	654.06	674.03	701.12
583.13	612.27	630.22	654.11	674.18	701.12
583.16	613.04	630.25	654.12	674.26	701.17
583.17	613.07	630.26	654.15	675.07	701.21
583.19	613.17	631.05	654.20	675.10	702.01
584.04	613.17	631.07	654.21	675.13	702.05
584.06	613.23	631.19	655.04	675.14	702.08
585.05	613.28	632.06	655.15	675.15	702.09
585.07	614.06	632.15	655.15	675.15	702.16
585.15	614.09	632.17	655.16	675.20	702.17
585.17	614.10	632.21	655.16	675.27	703.08
586.05	614.15	633.02	655.17	676.04	703.14
586.06	614.19	633.08	655.18	676.05	703.17
586.08	614.24	633.18	655.19	676.06	703.22
587.10	614.27	633.18	655.20	676.08	703.23
587.13	615.10	633.23	655.25	676.12	703.28
588.04	615.11	633.26	656.01	676.14	705.07
588.07	615.16	633.26	656.07	676.16	705.07
588.08	615.17	633.27	656.08	676.24	705.17
588.09	615.19	634.05	656.08	677.01	705.20
588.09	615.19	634.07	656.09	677.04	705.22
588.11	615.21	634.09	657.16	677.05	706.11
588.12	615.26	634.16	658.05	677.09	706.11
588.17	615.26		658.08	677.21	

706.13	722.09	743.02	760.26	785.18	804.18
706.14	722.14	743.14	761.01	785.23	804.20
706.15	722.15	743.18	761.02	785.24	805.06
706.19	722.27	743.19	761.10	785.25	806.01
706.22	723.07	744.05	761.14	786.06	806.20
706.24	723.15	744.08	761.15	786.07	807.07
707.01	723.20	744.12	761.17	786.20	807.23
707.05	723.21	744.13	761.23	786.24	808.09
707.08	723.25	744.15	761.25	786.26	808.16
707.13	723.28	745.03	762.06	787.08	808.18
707.13	724.10	745.06	762.16	787.21	808.21
707.18	724.18	745.09	762.16	788.03	808.23
707.21	724.18	745.14	762.23	788.04	809.01
707.22	724.18	745.19	762.24	788.12	809.03
708.25	724.24	745.21	762.24	788.13	809.06
708.26	725.13	745.27	762.28	789.03	809.08
709.03	725.24	745.28	763.10	789.09	809.09
709.03	725.26	746.03	763.13	789.10	809.10
709.07	726.10	746.06	763.22	790.02	809.19
709.14	726.21	746.10	764.04	790.03	810.06
709.16	727.02	746.15	764.07	790.05	810.09
709.17	727.07	746.19	764.10	790.09	810.21
709.18	727.11	746.20	765.10	790.10	810.25
709.24	727.19	746.21	766.02	790.14	811.08
711.02	727.21	746.27	766.15	790.15	811.21
711.02	727.22	747.01	766.25	790.20	811.28
711.09	727.24	747.03	766.27	790.24	812.05
711.11	729.06	747.09	767.04	790.26	812.08
711.18	729.07	747.21	767.07	791.15	812.09
711.19	729.08	747.22	767.12	791.23	812.20
712.01	729.10	747.23	767.17	791.26	812.20
712.07	729.12	747.26	768.14	792.05	812.21
712.08	729.15	747.27	769.22	792.05	812.27
712.09	729.17	747.28	769.27	792.05	813.07
712.11	730.01	748.12	770.01	792.06	813.12
712.14	730.03	748.13	770.02	792.06	813.13
712.14	730.07	748.14	770.08	792.07	813.20
712.15	730.08	748.17	770.14	792.09	813.24
712.21	730.09	748.19	770.18	792.11	813.26
712.23	730.11	748.20	770.19	792.13	814.06
713.02	730.25	748.20	770.20	792.18	814.07
713.12	730.25	749.10	770.23	792.22	814.16
713.13	730.27	749.11	770.25	792.23	814.19
713.16	731.04	749.14	770.27	792.28	815.05
713.21	731.06	749.15	771.01	793.01	815.10
713.22	731.15	749.16	771.07	793.04	815.26
713.23	731.23	749.25	771.15	793.12	816.02
713.25	731.28	749.25	771.15	793.14	816.05
714.09	732.03	750.02	771.20	793.16	816.07
714.12	732.06	750.02	771.25	793.19	816.08
714.14	732.11	750.04	772.04	793.28	816.12
714.17	732.21	750.07	772.06	794.03	816.13
714.19	732.22	750.14	772.12	794.14	816.14
714.24	732.23	750.15	772.15	794.18	816.16
714.24	732.25	750.15	772.18	794.26	817.01
715.01	732.25	750.19	772.19	795.01	817.05
715.05	732.26	750.20	772.25	795.09	817.18
715.05	733.01	750.24	773.19	795.10	817.19
715.09	733.03	751.05	773.24	795.14	817.23
715.11	733.17	751.05	773.25	795.18	817.24
715.14	734.03	751.08	773.27	795.18	818.03
715.17	734.07	751.10	774.01	795.20	818.08
715.19	734.07	751.14	774.04	795.23	818.13
715.21	734.08	751.17	774.05	795.26	818.19
715.21	734.11	751.21	774.06	796.09	818.23
715.23	734.13	751.24	774.13	796.17	819.11
715.26	734.17	752.03	774.24	796.18	819.26
716.02	734.18	752.03	775.02	796.22	820.10
716.03	734.24	752.06	775.14	796.28	820.12
716.09	734.25	752.09	775.20	797.02	820.19
716.14	735.13	752.12	775.27	797.07	822.10
716.16	735.14	752.13	775.28	797.12	822.11
716.21	735.15	752.23	776.12	797.16	823.05
716.26	735.16	752.24	776.13	797.19	823.12
716.28	735.17	752.25	776.17	797.23	823.17
717.03	735.17	752.26	777.05	798.01	823.20
717.16	735.17	753.13	778.03	798.20	823.23
717.18	735.17	753.15	778.05	798.23	823.24
717.19	735.18	753.21	778.16	798.27	823.26
717.23	735.21	754.09	779.02	799.03	824.10
717.26	736.01	754.11	779.10	799.06	824.15
718.01	736.05	754.11	779.25	799.10	824.22
718.06	736.07	754.27	780.06	799.10	824.24
718.08	736.12	755.03	780.07	799.11	824.26
718.23	736.24	755.05	780.09	799.12	825.22
718.26	737.02	755.20	780.12	799.13	826.01
718.26	737.06	756.05	780.15	799.14	826.10
719.02	737.08	756.23	780.16	799.16	826.11
719.18	737.14	756.27	781.08	800.09	826.14
719.19	737.18	756.28	781.14	800.12	827.11
719.21	737.21	757.09	781.15	800.14	827.13
719.22	737.22	757.13	781.21	800.15	827.15
719.27	738.05	757.16	781.23	800.16	828.05
720.01	738.09	757.18	782.04	800.16	828.06
720.02	738.10	757.25	782.06	801.15	828.08
720.06	738.15	757.26	782.15	802.09	828.16
720.09	738.17	758.08	783.02	802.10	828.21
720.16	738.23	758.18	783.02	802.13	829.04
720.19	738.25	758.19	783.09	802.16	829.06
720.20	738.28	758.27	783.17	803.05	829.26
721.05	739.08	758.28	783.20	803.10	830.09
721.07	739.08	759.07	783.27	803.19	830.10
721.14	739.19	759.21	784.08	803.22	831.08
721.18	739.23	759.23	784.10	803.23	831.10
721.18	739.24	759.24	784.13	803.23	831.11
721.21	739.25	759.24	784.14	803.27	831.13
721.25	740.12	759.27	785.04	804.02	831.15
721.26	741.03	759.27	785.13	804.07	832.12
721.27	741.05	760.05	785.13	804.12	832.19
722.01	741.21		785.14	804.17	832.20
722.04	742.22		785.17		832.24

832.25	854.15	881.16	907.18	499.23	406.01
833.05	854.17	881.17	907.22	500.01	410.05
833.09	854.23	881.17	907.26	503.16	426.11
833.22	854.26	881.18	907.27	509.01	435.13
834.02	855.02	882.15	907.27	519.13	454.23
834.04	855.03	882.25	908.06	519.20	472.23
834.04	855.04	883.01	908.20	539.15	483.15
834.06	855.05	883.08	908.21	542.09	613.02
834.11	855.06	883.12	909.02	550.11	623.06
834.15	855.07	883.22	909.02	557.04	639.05
835.01	855.10	883.23	909.03	559.12	686.08
835.02	855.13	883.25	909.04	561.20	713.20
835.02	855.16	883.27	909.05	564.09	747.10
835.03	855.27	884.04	909.05	583.05	841.02
835.03	856.07	884.05	909.15	591.07	offering
835.19	856.13	884.06	909.19	596.06	027.16
835.21	856.15	884.11	909.20	602.10	090.18
835.25	856.17	884.21	909.21	604.16	224.22
836.02	856.25	884.26	909.22	610.12	360.21
836.24	857.10	885.01	909.22	630.10	453.05
836.25	857.11	885.05	909.23	652.24	615.18
836.26	857.16	885.06	909.26	654.23	755.08
837.20	857.28	885.09	909.26	657.03	offers
837.22	858.01	885.11	909.27	658.06	758.22
838.01	858.06	885.14	910.08	666.12	819.13
838.09	858.13	885.15	910.18	670.01	896.21
838.16	859.01	885.20	910.20	677.03	office
838.27	859.08	886.01	910.21	683.08	161.19
839.02	859.09	886.02	911.10	684.25	162.10
839.07	859.12	886.11	911.11	687.02	721.05
839.07	859.23	886.12	911.19	690.14	730.14
839.10	859.26	886.14	911.21	695.15	825.11
839.27	860.02	886.16	911.24	700.22	842.07
840.01	860.06	886.18	911.26	726.18	886.22
841.03	860.13	886.20	911.26	752.09	889.06
841.04	860.14	886.23	912.02	773.26	officer
841.20	860.16	887.04	912.03	778.22	911.08
841.23	860.18	887.11	912.05	783.10	officer's
841.24	861.12	887.16	912.06	791.11	286.15
842.14	861.13	887.17	912.17	799.24	officers
842.18	861.20	887.22	912.18	812.23	740.05
842.19	861.21	888.12	912.21	864.24	offices
843.03	861.22	888.14	off	865.22	722.03
843.05	861.24	888.20	013.15	867.27	official
843.13	861.26	889.06	014.09	872.27	593.06
843.15	861.27	889.07	019.01	887.14	officiated
843.17	862.07	889.08	040.24	894.19	112.21
843.22	862.10	889.09	046.10	903.19	officious
843.24	863.07	889.10	048.21	offence	223.26
843.27	863.09	889.14	050.19	335.25	offspring
844.02	863.12	889.19	061.04	offences	288.21
844.04	863.19	889.23	079.13	464.26	often
844.07	863.22	889.25	092.14	offend	005.13
844.26	863.23	890.17	099.01	008.02	014.01
844.27	863.25	890.17	103.17	093.11	030.22
845.01	863.28	890.27	108.25	254.20	031.02
845.02	864.01	890.27	108.25	537.21	032.20
845.04	864.06	890.28	114.16	647.16	047.19
845.05	864.15	891.02	120.19	offended	050.04
845.13	864.28	891.10	121.13	830.11	105.03
845.15	865.05	891.17	121.23	831.07	106.07
845.20	865.09	891.25	122.24	offending	106.11
845.23	865.17	892.04	141.19	244.15	117.20
846.04	865.19	892.07	154.09	offensive	135.02
846.07	866.13	892.09	163.25	061.22	145.22
846.09	867.04	892.15	165.19	749.08	146.11
846.13	867.23	892.22	177.23	offer	149.01
846.19	868.03	893.19	179.25	131.17	196.01
846.20	869.02	893.22	180.05	202.24	210.22
846.21	869.02	894.13	180.22	225.07	233.17
846.23	869.05	894.20	183.26	275.27	267.15
846.24	869.05	894.21	194.12	477.10	269.20
846.24	869.07	895.20	210.11	495.20	306.09
847.03	869.09	895.28	225.07	514.13	309.25
847.04	869.11	896.05	232.26	517.09	310.20
847.08	869.12	896.24	244.07	532.10	313.07
847.09	869.16	896.25	246.19	543.22	314.19
847.11	870.01	897.04	256.28	628.08	316.23
847.12	870.02	898.14	264.07	665.05	373.15
847.23	870.02	898.15	282.15	665.18	396.22
848.03	870.06	898.22	284.27	668.13	404.28
848.04	870.11	898.24	302.26	671.07	445.06
848.15	870.14	899.21	308.05	709.20	464.17
848.16	870.15	899.28	309.14	718.08	465.20
848.17	870.16	900.06	312.26	720.09	469.21
848.20	870.24	900.09	315.26	721.01	479.07
848.22	870.28	900.09	316.10	722.09	504.25
848.27	871.04	900.12	328.01	771.22	521.12
849.17	871.10	900.14	337.21	775.04	536.17
849.20	871.26	900.15	339.09	802.08	553.19
849.21	872.05	900.16	375.11	814.15	555.28
850.08	872.13	901.03	385.11	827.18	594.16
851.08	872.22	901.09	407.11	827.19	637.24
852.03	872.26	901.11	407.15	828.16	641.14
852.06	874.24	901.17	412.05	837.17	643.15
852.07	874.27	901.25	417.03	841.23	643.18
852.08	875.01	903.06	418.26	908.17	649.03
852.13	875.02	903.08	428.27	offered	654.25
852.19	875.27	903.22	430.12	003.13	675.07
853.02	876.15	903.23	443.07	162.08	715.11
853.03	877.25	904.04	448.19	171.11	752.24
853.04	877.25	905.06	449.02	188.07	756.23
853.06	878.11	905.11	450.20	191.11	756.27
853.10	878.16	905.11	451.07	191.15	757.11
853.11	878.18	905.13	451.27	192.03	770.08
853.14	879.22	905.14	456.27	287.23	773.10
853.16	879.23	905.16	458.04	291.18	777.25
853.22	881.01	905.18	463.17	373.11	797.11
854.03	881.06	905.20	469.10	377.05	825.16
854.10	881.07	906.11	487.06	392.05	842.21
854.14	881.08	906.19	488.12	405.10	853.26

863.10	754.17	631.20	005.05	102.03	192.28
865.10	773.09	636.02	005.11	105.14	193.08
869.05	776.12	669.11	005.17	108.16	193.13
889.14	777.25	677.03	005.26	108.17	193.25
892.01	781.27	678.04	007.11	109.08	193.26
894.04	785.03	679.03	007.25	112.08	194.06
906.11	815.09	680.28	008.04	115.17	196.06
908.06	817.02	681.07	008.14	116.10	196.09
909.18	819.23	685.10	008.18	116.23	196.22
oftener	823.09	695.19	013.23	117.01	196.25
195.13	825.07	695.23	014.18	117.17	196.28
635.28	847.26	697.25	015.22	118.20	197.19
745.07	849.14	698.01	016.16	119.19	198.27
ogre	849.24	704.16	021.03	121.01	199.20
548.10	860.01	714.18	021.08	121.03	200.08
oh	861.15	718.20	021.17	121.28	200.13
024.05	876.09	719.21	022.06	123.03	203.22
025.03	887.02	728.06	023.06	123.23	204.11
034.10	887.28	733.06	024.08	123.23	204.16
034.20	894.10	736.28	025.01	125.17	204.28
055.21	895.21	751.07	025.09	125.22	207.12
055.25	897.22	751.19	026.19	127.03	207.20
056.15	901.10	770.20	029.05	127.08	208.22
072.20	**oil**	794.12	030.17	127.09	208.26
092.09	654.12	794.23	030.26	127.21	210.05
115.26	791.25	796.01	032.11	128.03	211.24
119.03	**oil-lamp**	797.28	034.23	128.06	211.26
153.01	181.13	844.06	040.17	128.09	213.04
153.22	**oiled**	868.01	041.14	129.06	215.24
156.03	654.12	874.27	043.04	130.08	216.23
177.02	**old**	896.11	044.02	130.22	218.10
179.12	005.24	898.27	044.05	131.19	218.15
187.04	007.02	906.09	044.09	131.27	219.18
188.12	016.04	**old-fashioned**	046.13	132.25	219.25
205.10	019.03	186.08	046.27	133.04	220.04
205.23	031.15	435.01	047.06	133.19	220.11
217.11	034.13	701.05	047.10	133.26	220.24
235.27	035.05	**older**	047.24	133.26	221.02
240.12	043.24	005.24	048.09	133.28	221.05
244.01	054.20	007.02	049.04	134.08	222.06
255.15	077.11	107.02	049.21	135.24	222.15
266.19	089.05	149.17	049.24	137.12	222.19
284.28	126.21	265.22	050.12	138.17	223.11
289.09	156.09	624.02	050.15	138.21	225.08
315.25	164.02	897.17	050.17	138.24	226.01
316.10	170.02	**oldfashioned**	050.24	139.05	227.11
319.01	171.20	874.25	050.25	139.22	227.15
319.20	175.21	**olive**	051.09	139.27	227.26
355.27	176.02	318.07	051.23	140.28	227.27
355.22	180.16	349.27	052.15	141.12	228.15
347.10	186.19	594.18	053.20	142.23	229.07
353.23	188.27	**oliver**	054.01	142.24	229.18
355.11	194.10	666.17	054.26	143.01	230.13
356.05	194.22	721.25	054.27	144.03	230.14
357.28	195.22	721.26	056.13	144.13	231.11
359.15	197.05	733.02	056.21	145.02	231.23
370.16	207.07	739.22	056.25	145.24	232.18
388.27	207.23	741.10	058.09	147.06	235.11
388.27	240.06	741.15	058.14	149.22	235.15
372.21	252.21	746.04	061.05	149.24	235.20
400.04	253.01	748.04	061.18	151.04	236.13
406.06	253.14	750.08	061.27	151.06	236.17
409.04	256.24	751.05	062.10	151.19	236.25
410.04	257.03	751.18	062.12	152.05	236.26
416.02	261.11	755.02	064.26	152.10	236.28
425.25	261.20	758.26	065.18	152.18	237.03
425.12	265.11	760.04	066.21	153.11	238.08
436.04	280.07	760.06	066.22	154.07	238.10
436.19	282.28	760.22	066.23	155.16	238.14
440.15	290.17	761.12	068.12	155.20	238.15
446.12	319.13	769.11	069.16	156.06	238.20
452.12	356.04	783.22	069.17	157.22	238.21
467.01	381.22	788.09	071.02	158.18	240.12
469.05	383.08	797.01	071.07	159.13	240.27
483.13	383.10	801.07	072.01	160.16	241.01
496.19	385.08	801.14	072.26	162.07	241.17
508.16	385.19	**oliver's**	074.01	163.23	241.27
517.05	386.13	666.15	075.01	164.20	242.05
524.23	390.03	698.03	076.16	165.16	242.12
540.28	394.13	698.04	076.24	167.24	247.06
542.26	396.02	752.07	077.02	169.17	247.17
545.26	397.17	756.06	077.24	169.25	248.01
553.03	476.18	758.02	078.05	170.03	248.23
576.07	408.13	**omega**	078.07	170.04	250.24
577.24	423.16	901.16	078.18	170.20	254.14
580.21	438.18	**omens**	080.09	171.28	255.02
597.19	444.15	551.14	080.23	172.15	255.22
606.19	447.17	**ominous**	081.20	174.10	258.23
607.09	451.25	099.17	083.13	174.19	259.04
613.23	454.15	645.22	084.05	176.04	259.13
615.14	458.10	**ominously**	085.10	176.06	259.25
621.24	458.21	115.17	085.27	178.14	260.16
623.20	460.14	**omission**	086.18	178.28	262.17
625.15	464.23	267.01	086.22	179.10	262.21
646.06	476.01	829.17	087.05	179.13	263.03
647.21	486.10	**omit**	087.12	179.27	264.26
650.02	492.15	321.28	087.19	181.06	265.10
650.26	498.23	322.19	089.25	181.08	265.25
655.19	507.10	**omitted**	089.26	181.16	266.20
655.28	510.11	309.26	091.01	183.17	266.23
660.13	526.16	808.10	095.06	184.11	266.23
670.03	534.12	**omnipotence**	097.20	184.21	267.09
673.06	534.23	662.11	098.06	184.26	267.16
682.26	537.06	**omnipotent**	098.09	185.13	268.15
683.02	545.22	900.04	098.20	188.23	268.16
683.23	562.14	**omnipresence**	099.09	189.06	269.04
683.23	588.08	662.12	099.21	189.17	269.18
719.03	589.09	**on**	100.07	190.02	270.16
731.17	595.19	001.12	100.20	191.13	271.04
733.21	610.02	002.03	100.20	191.26	271.23
738.27	624.15	004.23	101.26	192.13	272.15

276.03	349.19	426.01	505.18	599.18	701.19
276.23	352.08	427.03	506.19	600.01	702.17
277.15	352.20	428.02	506.21	600.05	702.24
277.15	353.06	428.16	507.04	600.18	704.10
277.28	353.08	430.17	507.27	601.25	706.09
278.07	353.16	431.09	510.04	603.03	706.10
279.02	354.07	431.17	510.16	603.10	708.21
280.23	355.15	432.04	511.26	604.19	709.06
281.04	355.23	432.11	512.09	604.20	712.15
281.05	356.06	432.20	513.20	604.23	712.16
281.22	356.25	432.26	516.27	605.25	713.17
282.03	357.04	433.18	517.26	606.09	713.18
282.13	358.03	433.21	519.18	606.10	713.20
282.22	358.03	434.28	519.24	609.04	714.19
282.22	358.05	434.28	521.18	611.03	715.13
283.22	358.10	435.12	524.28	611.17	716.07
283.27	358.12	436.13	525.02	612.08	718.14
284.24	359.03	439.17	525.03	613.14	718.22
285.03	359.09	441.03	525.17	614.20	719.04
286.10	359.13	441.15	530.05	616.26	719.08
286.19	359.26	445.11	530.25	619.01	719.28
287.03	360.14	445.12	533.05	620.26	720.26
287.08	360.21	445.25	533.09	622.15	722.01
288.13	361.23	445.26	533.24	623.04	724.07
289.16	362.05	446.01	534.09	623.08	726.07
290.16	363.04	446.14	534.19	627.15	726.20
291.15	366.13	448.07	535.01	632.12	727.23
292.22	366.24	451.14	537.05	633.05	729.16
293.27	367.01	451.21	537.19	633.16	730.17
295.19	367.04	454.18	539.26	633.27	731.13
295.22	367.06	454.28	540.06	634.01	733.10
296.09	367.24	455.20	540.27	634.04	733.21
298.10	368.02	457.08	541.24	634.06	733.22
298.12	368.04	458.03	542.03	635.11	736.22
298.22	368.06	458.10	542.11	635.14	737.10
298.25	368.17	458.26	543.01	635.14	739.03
298.25	368.25	459.07	543.15	636.23	740.15
299.14	368.27	459.17	544.06	638.10	741.14
299.17	369.07	459.26	545.16	638.23	742.24
299.22	369.16	460.09	548.13	638.25	744.28
299.26	369.25	460.14	548.14	639.04	745.25
300.03	369.26	461.25	548.19	639.08	746.07
300.13	370.13	462.01	550.18	640.09	747.11
300.20	371.10	462.05	551.17	640.15	748.02
301.18	371.14	462.11	551.21	640.16	749.16
302.18	372.10	463.22	551.27	643.27	749.26
305.04	373.07	464.06	553.02	646.11	750.16
306.05	375.04	464.12	554.19	647.01	752.22
306.16	376.14	464.21	554.22	647.25	754.20
306.18	378.21	465.20	555.07	650.24	755.08
306.24	378.25	466.03	555.12	650.25	756.15
306.25	379.16	466.28	555.12	650.26	756.19
307.12	379.19	467.06	555.16	651.23	756.23
307.21	380.02	467.12	557.10	652.08	757.13
309.15	380.04	467.20	557.14	652.14	757.16
309.15	380.17	468.15	557.14	653.05	758.01
309.17	380.19	469.11	557.16	653.07	758.04
310.02	381.12	469.20	559.24	654.08	758.11
310.13	381.22	470.14	560.06	655.10	758.14
310.14	382.03	471.14	560.19	655.15	758.18
311.04	382.22	471.25	561.14	656.14	759.10
313.20	382.23	472.11	562.04	656.20	759.20
313.20	382.26	473.10	562.18	656.23	763.04
315.06	384.06	473.15	563.08	656.28	763.06
315.12	385.02	474.07	564.03	657.09	763.14
316.06	386.28	475.19	564.06	659.01	763.16
316.12	392.01	476.14	564.14	659.05	764.07
316.24	392.10	477.12	565.25	659.21	765.09
318.25	394.05	477.18	566.03	661.17	765.12
320.27	394.09	477.28	567.19	662.08	767.10
321.15	394.14	478.28	568.02	663.08	767.15
323.03	394.16	479.07	570.06	664.06	768.04
323.18	397.28	479.22	570.07	664.22	770.02
323.21	399.04	479.23	571.13	665.04	773.06
325.01	400.05	480.09	572.14	666.22	775.04
325.17	403.12	483.02	572.25	667.08	775.20
326.05	403.25	483.23	573.02	669.10	776.17
327.20	403.27	484.28	573.08	670.17	777.09
328.01	404.01	486.01	573.14	670.23	778.28
328.01	404.12	487.20	574.18	671.15	780.16
328.11	404.24	488.05	575.02	672.22	781.05
328.18	406.26	488.11	575.10	673.18	781.12
329.03	407.03	490.27	575.20	674.11	781.13
329.05	407.07	491.06	575.22	674.26	783.01
330.17	408.03	491.10	576.06	675.22	783.08
331.11	408.08	492.06	576.10	675.23	783.21
332.10	408.10	493.16	577.13	675.24	784.28
332.17	408.17	493.17	578.14	676.19	787.06
332.26	409.20	493.23	578.15	677.01	788.02
333.02	410.04	493.27	579.14	677.04	789.05
333.10	410.10	494.21	580.10	677.12	790.22
333.11	411.01	494.22	580.14	678.18	791.05
333.16	414.10	495.04	582.16	681.22	791.11
334.08	415.03	497.13	586.01	681.28	792.03
335.23	415.14	498.04	586.20	683.21	792.25
337.04	415.21	498.20	587.02	685.06	793.21
337.11	415.23	499.11	587.21	689.08	794.24
337.27	416.06	499.23	587.23	691.28	794.25
340.14	416.27	501.08	588.06	691.28	795.11
340.24	417.28	501.15	588.14	692.09	795.17
341.03	418.24	502.02	589.22	692.11	796.04
341.14	419.23	502.06	590.18	692.14	796.07
342.07	421.11	502.13	591.25	692.24	796.12
342.25	422.08	502.21	592.21	693.16	797.23
345.27	422.10	502.21	593.07	696.21	800.04
346.05	423.03	503.05	594.04	696.26	800.11
347.04	423.13	503.26	594.07	697.13	800.17
348.21	423.14	504.04	594.22	698.27	804.06
348.21	425.07	504.05	594.25	700.21	804.25
349.01	425.22	504.10	597.15	701.14	805.20
349.15	425.24	505.03	598.22	701.18	

805.28	890.19	596.04	024.10	210.01	399.16
806.06	891.06	601.08	026.10	210.13	399.21
808.27	891.14	609.07	030.01	210.23	399.22
809.12	894.05	624.02	031.23	213.19	399.26
809.13	897.06	624.03	031.26	218.04	400.19
810.16	897.06	626.06	033.02	221.28	400.28
811.07	897.18	626.23	036.01	223.11	402.02
811.19	898.02	627.18	036.23	224.01	403.22
813.12	898.07	629.07	038.11	224.24	403.26
813.19	900.04	633.21	040.09	225.03	406.01
815.21	900.08	633.24	041.08	226.04	406.01
815.24	902.08	639.13	041.09	228.19	407.26
816.15	902.25	640.04	044.11	236.09	409.08
818.23	903.06	641.10	048.03	236.10	409.23
819.09	908.04	642.03	048.27	236.10	411.04
820.02	908.26	649.10	056.06	238.17	412.05
820.25	909.11	651.17	058.06	239.26	412.05
822.19	909.24	670.01	062.24	242.04	415.10
823.07	909.25	670.01	063.03	245.12	415.13
823.22	910.14	671.26	068.07	246.23	415.19
824.05	910.28	672.05	074.09	247.27	415.27
824.14	911.15	673.12	074.10	249.21	416.19
824.16	once	686.26	074.20	252.05	419.26
826.24	006.16	686.27	077.18	255.04	420.14
828.03	007.23	687.03	077.23	257.06	421.11
829.20	008.17	690.02	080.09	257.16	421.11
830.02	037.18	690.20	082.02	260.01	422.26
831.06	043.09	690.24	082.05	261.27	425.16
832.01	066.27	691.05	083.01	263.07	428.12
832.24	074.24	692.25	083.02	264.26	430.21
833.04	079.26	701.15	083.05	265.15	432.17
833.10	117.19	708.06	083.05	265.16	433.07
835.25	133.27	715.20	083.14	265.19	434.28
836.04	138.05	715.20	084.23	267.04	435.24
837.05	151.04	721.08	084.24	267.15	436.21
838.15	169.16	735.23	085.06	268.17	439.06
838.20	184.08	741.02	086.18	269.05	441.05
839.12	189.21	743.14	087.26	271.09	442.20
839.15	191.17	747.18	088.16	272.25	442.23
839.20	194.11	748.01	091.12	272.28	443.03
842.05	207.03	751.09	092.22	274.04	444.04
843.14	220.25	756.13	092.25	277.15	444.16
844.05	222.08	763.07	092.28	278.08	445.14
844.16	227.28	766.16	093.07	279.04	445.20
845.10	244.07	773.09	097.14	280.11	445.21
846.17	244.19	774.10	099.16	280.27	445.28
848.11	261.19	775.12	100.18	283.26	446.18
849.04	264.17	784.27	101.15	285.20	446.26
849.08	271.27	793.05	104.11	285.21	449.18
850.16	274.04	795.11	104.14	288.01	450.08
851.13	277.26	796.25	108.23	291.22	451.14
852.09	279.11	798.19	109.11	296.17	455.09
853.07	285.15	802.21	115.04	299.04	455.13
854.20	292.20	814.22	116.24	301.09	456.14
854.20	294.13	819.11	117.12	306.28	456.19
854.24	299.16	824.06	120.10	307.27	460.20
854.27	312.12	824.13	124.09	308.19	461.13
854.28	312.14	824.17	125.04	310.16	461.14
855.16	320.08	824.27	125.14	310.22	462.18
855.18	324.15	828.25	127.04	312.01	464.06
856.04	329.04	833.02	130.12	315.03	467.19
856.10	329.19	833.14	131.06	318.23	471.10
856.21	346.17	833.18	134.08	319.05	472.13
857.02	350.23	835.09	136.18	321.28	472.19
857.09	364.09	836.09	138.08	322.05	474.18
858.05	364.10	837.04	138.24	329.08	474.25
858.11	372.06	843.19	147.03	329.17	476.04
858.19	374.13	843.25	147.08	329.18	476.14
859.01	375.07	847.01	149.13	329.21	476.26
863.02	377.12	847.06	151.12	330.13	477.05
864.05	377.19	849.02	151.23	331.20	477.06
864.10	385.26	850.15	152.20	331.26	477.11
864.16	388.08	852.04	154.21	332.10	478.21
864.21	395.08	854.07	154.22	332.17	479.26
865.20	397.09	854.24	157.07	335.15	480.23
865.20	406.27	855.06	157.09	336.12	481.17
866.03	410.05	856.01	157.24	337.22	481.20
866.05	411.14	856.06	158.24	340.23	484.13
866.21	416.23	856.26	164.24	342.18	487.02
867.26	417.24	857.07	165.14	354.24	488.20
869.15	419.24	859.04	166.22	355.12	488.23
869.18	428.09	860.20	169.07	361.03	488.27
870.10	438.02	864.04	170.14	366.14	489.01
870.10	462.15	870.05	171.12	367.01	489.09
871.06	464.01	877.08	174.22	368.15	490.22
871.07	465.28	877.22	175.05	370.01	491.04
871.14	466.11	879.14	178.16	374.19	495.04
872.13	467.14	880.20	178.24	376.04	499.18
872.13	467.25	892.16	179.22	376.08	499.20
872.21	472.27	894.01	182.04	377.26	500.02
873.02	473.17	901.11	182.11	378.08	502.06
873.05	474.08	901.14	185.19	379.02	502.06
874.12	483.02	908.01	189.02	379.04	502.21
874.27	485.24	909.07	189.06	379.15	502.27
875.06	493.02	910.27	189.07	384.27	504.24
875.15	499.14	911.06	189.09	385.01	505.05
879.01	503.07	once-dreaded	189.17	385.19	505.07
880.01	526.12	464.28	190.08	387.12	507.14
880.08	528.08	once-vigorous	191.27	387.23	513.23
880.23	531.13	467.10	193.13	387.23	513.24
881.11	532.28	onding	193.15	389.15	515.06
881.16	533.14	066.21	194.20	391.12	518.03
882.22	535.15	one	194.28	392.19	527.05
883.10	544.10	003.02	200.22	392.25	528.12
883.11	545.11	015.20	202.14	395.04	530.05
883.20	548.17	017.25	203.19	396.19	532.18
885.13	549.03	018.25	204.22	396.23	532.23
886.21	550.05	019.13	207.20	396.26	533.16
887.07	560.02	020.12	208.04	396.27	536.23
887.23	580.01	021.23	208.05	397.04	540.14
888.28	590.10	023.13	208.11	399.09	541.07

541.27
543.25
545.07
546.03
546.09
546.23
548.04
550.13
552.26
555.25
555.27
557.11
559.06
560.01
560.21
560.22
561.14
563.02
566.09
574.04
575.14
576.14
577.03
579.04
582.01
582.05
585.11
586.08
569.16
599.16
600.19
606.09
607.20
608.10
611.09
611.09
612.01
615.12
615.20
618.03
618.26
619.21
621.22
623.13
625.19
626.02
626.07
628.07
629.17
629.20
630.19
633.05
635.20
635.25
635.27
636.15
637.08
637.17
638.06
641.15
642.15
644.14
645.13
645.24
646.13
646.13
654.16
654.20
654.28
654.28
655.01
655.03
656.13
656.15
656.18
660.21
661.05
662.20
664.24
665.06
666.05
666.21
670.03
674.07
676.26
677.05
678.03
678.06
679.08
680.18
681.10
685.11
686.23
688.03
689.12
701.12
701.17
702.07
702.13
702.14
703.24
707.05
713.28
714.09
717.16
717.23
718.26
720.02
721.19
723.06
725.02

725.26
726.26
727.13
731.09
731.19
731.21
731.28
734.13
735.08
736.23
742.18
747.21
747.22
749.07
749.15
750.27
752.14
752.23
753.05
754.11
757.08
759.23
760.09
763.11
764.02
766.19
770.18
771.21
771.28
772.08
772.21
772.22
773.24
775.11
775.17
775.18
775.19
775.28
777.19
780.05
780.19
781.08
781.08
782.18
786.24
787.28
791.20
793.14
798.04
798.19
800.05
800.05
801.15
804.28
807.05
807.23
810.11
811.18
811.27
815.10
817.04
817.22
819.13
819.16
820.09
820.09
822.06
822.10
822.20
822.21
822.22
824.01
824.01
824.10
825.15
828.11
831.07
831.07
831.08
834.02
839.07
840.03
840.06
841.04
842.12
843.16
848.04
848.26
853.10
857.14
859.18
861.15
861.24
862.10
863.21
866.23
867.14
867.20
867.21
871.03
871.22
872.01
872.16
872.22
872.24
874.27
880.05
880.18
881.03
881.17

885.24
886.04
886.18
887.04
887.08
899.01
900.10
900.23
905.12
906.22
908.19
908.20
910.08
910.16
910.21
one's
018.17
184.12
189.08
267.13
374.01
395.01
444.19
444.20
467.24
477.07
635.11
905.14
one-fifth
330.28
one-horse
183.13
one-tenth
748.28
ones
088.11
112.11
113.18
126.09
126.18
318.03
346.02
379.03
392.10
444.07
541.02
753.07
ones'
438.20
onion
041.20
only
002.16
003.25
014.16
024.11
024.23
025.01
029.02
029.12
029.14
029.20
033.09
036.19
037.27
045.07
048.15
050.27
054.20
054.26
058.11
061.01
071.12
074.05
079.26
083.16
094.14
097.02
108.28
123.02
124.14
128.11
130.28
133.04
137.16
145.07
145.25
147.19
149.08
150.06
151.08
153.07
157.10
158.13
159.19
160.06
160.10
163.18
166.26
170.14
170.26
173.04
186.11
187.19
189.05
190.07
196.01
210.01
210.09
219.18
222.13

224.04
229.10
229.12
229.25
231.06
236.10
243.19
248.09
248.12
252.13
260.21
264.19
271.14
272.25
286.03
286.25
296.14
300.03
300.14
305.14
306.11
307.19
314.18
315.13
318.22
322.16
325.09
329.06
333.02
342.20
344.16
347.22
348.23
348.24
351.28
359.11
359.28
364.15
365.01
369.09
369.16
370.27
377.03
377.19
378.07
378.11
378.12
378.13
378.13
380.07
385.07
392.02
397.07
398.10
404.05
404.19
405.10
407.11
410.13
412.03
416.04
427.26
429.08
437.03
444.15
448.11
452.06
454.23
457.21
459.03
461.14
466.17
468.07
475.24
476.13
479.14
480.03
488.07
494.24
498.03
499.17
505.22
507.19
508.01
511.14
514.28
515.10
516.28
517.09
518.10
519.08
519.25
527.26
528.01
529.21
538.25
540.17
541.11
547.13
555.02
558.20
558.21
565.12
573.11
576.08
579.01
580.05
580.20
582.01
586.05
589.04

592.16
595.02
597.20
600.08
601.11
604.21
607.06
607.20
611.16
612.14
615.02
615.12
618.02
620.19
621.03
622.13
623.28
625.27
626.09
627.11
630.23
633.13
636.12
643.25
649.21
650.05
650.06
654.20
660.10
661.01
661.17
661.23
665.20
671.18
673.14
673.25
674.01
676.23
678.18
683.26
684.03
685.24
692.09
695.12
698.26
717.15
717.17
719.04
719.25
721.25
722.22
726.20
733.12
736.08
738.27
742.05
748.27
749.28
750.25
753.10
760.15
761.25
768.15
771.01
774.09
775.26
776.02
790.19
796.20
802.20
806.26
810.17
810.24
811.03
811.18
812.24
814.07
821.19
823.01
824.20
825.17
825.23
827.02
828.11
828.19
829.10
836.20
842.16
846.25
848.05
848.16
848.19
862.10
866.13
870.23
870.27
871.07
875.11
876.02
876.08
880.16
882.04
882.09
882.26
885.14
885.24
889.21
893.12
893.13
895.07
895.14

899.20
900.14
900.15
901.08
903.22
906.02
907.08
907.19
onslaught
911.26
onus
358.05
ony
906.21
onybody
698.06
906.24
opaque
060.25
066.20
466.13
open
050.02
075.13
087.22
090.11
094.28
111.14
119.17
152.25
170.17
175.04
183.12
193.22
202.15
203.15
216.01
231.10
245.14
280.22
286.02
291.11
294.15
295.14
306.10
314.16
317.23
321.14
326.22
332.04
332.22
346.12
366.25
385.01
389.02
391.08
420.16
422.12
429.25
431.03
432.24
433.21
462.14
482.05
502.16
505.06
522.04
528.03
534.25
576.12
604.10
604.24
605.10
615.19
631.01
635.07
668.06
671.11
684.19
689.16
707.16
721.20
723.09
785.25
797.27
825.04
852.07
852.10
883.01
887.16
901.06
opened
006.03
032.14
045.26
066.07
075.25
076.17
148.04
153.11
164.15
170.07
178.17
185.15
185.22
190.01
193.06
203.27
211.11
231.03
295.20

300.02	842.09	063.04	248.10	422.16	525.14
369.02	865.03	066.09	248.22	423.24	525.20
377.25	opinions	068.19	252.07	424.06	527.19
389.11	648.18	072.09	253.18	424.15	529.11
390.25	691.05	076.01	254.05	425.03	531.18
414.10	opponent	076.13	254.14	426.12	533.06
415.19	062.15	076.26	254.17	426.13	534.20
416.17	opportunity	073.08	256.06	426.13	537.09
420.10	036.19	080.04	257.05	429.14	541.06
421.20	112.10	082.17	258.25	429.21	543.22
432.22	118.22	084.17	260.02	431.23	545.02
454.11	168.06	090.08	260.09	432.14	548.10
463.10	309.05	090.16	261.26	433.17	548.25
464.20	392.22	090.16	263.04	436.17	551.10
465.04	453.22	091.10	263.27	436.25	557.11
549.24	716.02	091.13	265.18	439.06	557.17
564.07	785.14	091.17	265.23	439.10	559.06
599.02	oppose	094.21	266.05	439.27	559.11
599.08	756.02	095.11	266.16	441.02	560.21
614.16	821.15	097.19	266.25	444.20	567.15
629.23	opposed	097.25	267.17	445.12	568.13
631.21	020.13	103.11	267.17	446.10	569.12
644.24	468.09	106.03	268.14	448.16	570.06
654.17	736.08	107.08	268.23	449.09	571.13
667.18	810.03	108.04	271.22	450.15	571.15
669.11	opposing	108.22	275.20	451.17	571.19
680.04	630.11	112.10	275.21	454.15	572.10
682.05	opposite	118.12	275.21	456.03	577.15
694.15	053.25	119.02	275.22	457.18	587.06
729.17	154.27	119.23	278.08	457.23	587.16
759.02	188.23	120.06	280.26	457.26	587.19
757.22	353.08	127.18	282.22	458.14	590.24
773.24	365.11	130.17	283.14	458.15	591.06
795.21	414.07	131.07	284.17	462.13	592.08
798.03	423.17	131.16	287.05	462.14	594.03
859.09	535.01	131.19	288.12	462.26	594.10
863.04	558.06	132.08	286.28	462.27	595.12
870.19	638.28	132.09	291.21	463.21	595.25
871.13	700.28	132.11	293.04	464.04	596.12
872.20	opposition	132.11	293.25	464.05	598.01
873.13	784.25	132.19	295.03	464.10	599.16
874.21	815.25	135.05	296.07	464.18	603.25
902.11	oppress	136.18	299.04	465.03	604.07
opening	088.19	139.11	300.06	467.25	604.23
051.04	784.21	140.06	301.02	467.26	605.05
145.04	oppressed	142.26	306.27	469.09	605.16
154.25	022.18	144.02	307.07	469.27	605.16
174.22	023.21	145.23	307.08	470.01	610.23
286.05	484.25	145.28	307.22	470.12	611.18
287.20	oppresses	146.20	309.15	470.17	611.25
309.07	568.19	147.09	309.27	470.18	620.07
333.27	oppression	149.02	311.21	470.22	621.07
336.19	019.22	149.22	312.08	471.12	621.08
342.10	459.28	150.02	314.05	472.08	621.09
425.07	734.09	151.04	315.10	472.19	621.15
652.19	opprobrium	157.13	316.18	473.18	622.20
750.15	019.16	159.12	317.10	473.19	623.18
745.01	optics	163.26	319.16	473.28	624.01
647.20	125.07	165.08	323.08	475.06	625.21
657.13	or	167.21	326.03	475.25	626.25
658.28	002.20	169.07	327.21	476.15	626.27
670.18	003.27	169.11	328.07	476.20	636.12
openly	005.25	169.22	329.01	476.23	639.02
120.06	006.15	173.06	329.02	477.11	639.17
312.03	007.11	175.03	329.17	479.06	639.22
654.27	007.22	176.18	329.18	481.17	641.02
705.04	007.23	179.14	329.19	483.11	641.18
opens	008.01	179.28	331.28	485.04	641.28
739.06	008.05	180.14	333.13	486.02	642.25
828.18	008.19	180.15	334.23	486.02	643.13
opera	009.15	185.14	335.02	488.04	647.27
230.17	010.14	187.06	336.09	489.28	655.02
279.10	012.06	187.23	339.22	490.08	656.14
281.20	019.23	192.06	342.18	490.12	656.21
opera-girl	019.24	192.12	348.16	490.17	659.16
268.22	020.08	195.12	353.27	492.10	659.18
opera-house	020.08	196.03	356.10	492.18	660.03
281.11	020.15	197.04	357.14	493.04	660.03
opera-mistresses	021.13	199.26	364.12	493.05	660.21
265.13	022.21	200.08	368.09	493.17	663.11
operation	022.26	206.05	369.12	493.19	665.27
056.10	026.07	206.06	372.21	493.25	666.01
256.08	026.13	206.13	372.26	493.28	666.25
540.09	026.14	206.14	375.15	494.13	667.04
601.15	028.06	207.08	375.21	494.13	667.09
operations	029.13	208.11	376.24	495.09	667.13
327.09	033.16	211.15	377.23	495.19	667.28
opiate	035.05	213.18	377.24	496.08	671.07
773.06	036.23	213.20	378.20	497.01	671.28
opinion	038.12	214.14	378.20	497.01	672.18
007.16	043.18	214.27	378.25	497.06	673.03
010.04	043.27	216.25	378.27	497.25	673.18
012.04	044.10	216.26	378.27	498.24	675.12
014.01	044.22	217.09	382.04	500.02	675.25
053.17	045.21	217.10	383.12	500.04	676.06
239.27	047.08	217.27	394.06	500.06	676.10
356.18	047.08	221.01	395.07	504.03	676.10
373.12	047.09	221.20	399.27	504.13	679.16
404.19	047.18	223.25	399.28	505.11	682.14
440.25	047.18	224.01	401.06	505.21	683.07
466.11	048.02	225.03	403.09	507.08	683.13
518.22	048.24	233.16	403.17	509.03	684.11
614.05	049.01	233.16	405.10	510.08	685.15
623.21	052.08	236.02	406.01	511.01	685.24
657.12	052.10	238.07	406.16	511.15	689.12
705.10	054.20	242.09	407.28	513.22	689.16
713.07	055.24	242.11	415.19	522.11	689.20
713.07	059.22	242.11	416.24	522.11	690.02
768.01	060.16	242.23	417.03	522.14	690.22
773.15	061.21	243.20	417.09	523.06	690.22
788.11		247.25	422.05	524.18	691.10

691.25	861.16	466.23	093.19	502.22	ottomans
693.08	862.12	543.27	126.13	510.06	204.15
694.02	865.07	567.08	146.24	520.03	342.25
694.07	865.07	875.24	289.07	525.06	ou
697.05	869.12	ordering	706.15	525.07	334.10
700.25	870.11	373.20	706.21	539.26	ought
700.26	872.01	orderly	722.01	548.23	007.09
700.28	872.02	172.05	729.15	553.15	009.09
702.09	872.06	744.04	771.05	554.14	014.07
702.12	876.09	762.06	780.11	554.28	014.18
702.13	876.11	orders	orphans	555.01	029.18
704.16	880.01	024.18	091.14	560.15	030.03
705.13	881.06	043.07	orthodox	560.24	034.02
708.28	881.10	048.18	054.07	587.14	039.20
712.08	882.17	049.09	ostensible	653.03	118.13
714.16	882.18	232.25	169.25	656.16	118.17
714.19	889.19	233.03	ostler	664.01	121.27
714.24	891.22	258.09	855.10	676.07	216.06
715.13	892.16	266.04	ostler's	676.28	216.22
715.27	896.18	266.10	492.13	677.05	225.19
717.19	903.04	266.17	855.14	678.13	257.27
718.09	907.09	299.16	ostrich	679.06	260.07
719.07	907.13	437.05	122.04	679.08	260.11
719.12	910.03	602.14	other	681.11	360.25
722.06	910.22	626.28	009.26	698.09	395.14
723.05	oracles	798.25	012.09	699.02	448.26
725.03	843.27	ordinarily	025.04	699.04	453.28
726.02	oral	062.16	031.01	701.08	476.13
727.04	217.15	ordinary	032.01	703.26	477.09
728.02	orange	077.21	036.09	705.12	621.09
729.05	124.17	099.27	036.10	726.15	634.24
729.18	729.15	112.27	041.03	727.14	683.07
732.01	orange-trees	124.28	049.20	727.18	697.10
735.20	631.04	135.22	058.11	771.08	697.11
736.12	orator	190.28	082.06	775.13	707.02
736.13	735.15	196.11	082.12	780.06	730.17
737.20	736.01	213.19	089.06	784.14	754.01
740.03	orb	370.10	091.06	784.26	757.05
745.11	116.10	424.18	092.21	790.24	821.21
746.28	128.12	670.26	113.12	792.07	823.03
748.06	230.22	783.23	120.06	801.19	835.17
748.18	orchard	794.09	121.26	801.23	838.25
753.01	433.05	843.15	122.24	806.28	880.11
753.03	434.08	843.16	132.09	812.01	oui
755.15	435.09	892.10	132.18	821.16	197.15
755.17	502.18	ore	147.14	821.20	334.10
755.18	505.15	273.19	154.11	825.16	our
755.19	520.14	organ	164.19	827.12	005.23
755.26	542.01	085.20	166.09	866.15	009.07
757.10	559.20	140.16	170.24	867.22	009.12
757.18	561.21	269.09	215.15	871.18	091.17
760.28	857.01	506.05	217.21	896.27	092.11
762.06	357.11	organs	221.12	903.14	092.12
764.09	865.02	261.01	222.27	909.09	092.24
767.12	896.12	358.12	245.18	other's	092.24
767.19	ordained	389.26	246.19	214.07	094.01
770.09	724.19	oriental	247.02	461.12	096.09
771.06	ordains	322.13	247.08	730.02	096.10
772.01	441.10	368.12	257.27	others	105.08
775.11	ordeal	805.03	260.18	069.08	108.25
777.22	645.07	origin	263.04	083.04	111.12
777.22	order	160.17	263.20	097.14	111.15
778.15	030.23	253.19	267.05	113.15	111.17
782.09	049.14	444.11	268.14	120.20	111.18
782.18	059.06	original	273.16	132.05	111.19
784.02	080.12	149.15	280.04	151.15	112.21
784.15	080.19	246.03	280.10	163.05	112.26
786.01	084.01	373.10	290.18	167.11	113.05
790.25	085.04	512.04	306.20	207.22	113.07
794.03	087.17	546.02	316.12	217.07	113.11
797.06	099.11	634.24	333.13	228.27	116.25
797.14	103.23	756.13	335.18	246.16	132.26
797.18	110.04	761.05	338.10	263.09	132.27
804.10	115.12	761.22	349.11	269.25	136.11
804.10	120.26	762.20	351.20	284.12	138.20
804.17	135.14	763.01	356.14	292.19	138.21
804.17	163.04	800.21	358.04	316.15	144.11
806.07	169.05	808.08	358.11	342.19	145.09
806.22	172.26	originality	365.12	380.16	148.26
806.27	195.10	280.05	366.12	400.22	149.26
807.21	204.20	312.16	371.06	526.19	151.16
807.21	234.07	originated	371.09	670.06	158.01
814.06	255.05	210.13	373.22	700.14	170.27
816.03	306.11	630.26	377.10	716.24	183.26
816.28	322.14	861.28	378.19	730.04	184.21
817.02	324.16	ornament	379.04	762.01	199.05
819.14	325.13	236.15	384.02	796.22	233.11
821.14	343.13	340.25	412.04	817.22	244.08
824.25	357.28	367.27	421.02	845.21	251.10
826.20	387.03	460.26	425.18	otherwise	252.01
827.22	430.05	701.11	429.01	147.08	313.05
827.22	440.25	738.08	430.04	150.18	336.11
830.06	449.25	749.28	432.07	205.17	354.09
832.24	489.11	910.11	434.28	365.09	355.15
833.05	506.27	ornamental	439.10	377.08	355.26
836.10	529.28	457.05	442.03	382.01	355.26
837.09	614.08	ornaments	456.03	454.04	355.27
837.25	779.24	136.19	461.03	461.19	356.18
843.15	791.09	181.08	462.19	590.05	356.19
845.04	794.04	204.16	462.21	622.27	357.16
846.21	851.05	240.27	465.12	672.24	488.07
846.24	882.11	343.25	468.17	691.11	489.26
846.25	889.08	391.19	469.20	773.17	501.05
849.19	896.05	794.19	472.16	786.14	542.14
850.13	905.11	orphan	472.21	826.12	543.04
851.03	ordered	033.06	476.14	903.18	546.23
853.01	387.08	033.10	477.22	ottoman	551.06
853.22	167.15	033.14	478.21	017.06	551.12
855.25	241.02	033.18	481.22	352.25	552.08
857.02	332.06	033.22	491.05	758.01	554.10
857.09	417.25	091.09	495.15		567.22

589.14
598.16
599.05
700.22
700.23
700.24
708.22
713.09
713.24
720.14
726.01
726.28
734.28
734.28
735.01
736.20
740.07
752.26
775.22
780.09
781.04
784.08
800.23
803.14
803.16
804.04
821.13
824.19
828.04
894.14
899.12
907.07
907.08
909.06
909.15

ours
892.24

ourselves
151.14
477.27
665.14
727.15
727.25
775.22
794.05

out
001.10
006.10
006.14
006.19
008.11
009.16
010.21
012.06
013.14
015.23
016.04
017.27
024.01
024.08
024.25
029.09
030.05
051.16
052.27
054.11
054.16
035.07
035.28
040.02
044.01
044.17
045.16
049.23
050.02
050.17
061.20
063.09
063.21
064.12
066.11
068.14
072.22
074.11
075.16
076.15
078.20
078.28
080.15
083.01
089.21
092.23
098.06
098.23
100.25
108.01
112.11
112.22
114.15
116.02
116.23
117.24
119.01
125.03
125.20
128.07
130.11
137.22
141.02
144.19
145.14

146.08
147.02
148.02
148.07
151.13
152.25
153.24
160.18
164.16
166.27
170.28
171.05
172.23
175.05
176.24
176.25
177.24
184.18
184.22
185.10
187.16
188.03
194.04
195.03
195.10
197.24
199.01
204.27
205.13
205.14
206.17
209.01
210.14
210.16
211.12
213.06
215.03
217.09
218.26
225.23
226.02
232.25
239.09
240.09
245.17
247.05
247.21
254.08
257.22
260.03
263.24
266.03
269.23
270.26
272.25
276.13
276.19
277.12
277.23
280.06
280.12
280.23
280.27
284.25
287.10
288.17
288.26
289.12
295.09
297.18
298.26
299.21
301.08
309.08
316.09
322.27
327.02
332.13
335.15
336.14
336.25
337.26
338.04
341.15
345.08
347.17
356.05
356.21
357.18
357.22
359.06
361.25
364.18
367.16
374.21
380.24
382.07
385.03
385.05
391.09
392.24
395.05
396.03
397.18
397.20
398.28
401.09
403.05
403.16
403.27
406.15

406.25
407.16
407.18
407.28
412.01
415.04
415.07
415.28
415.28
418.12
419.07
420.17
420.27
423.03
423.28
424.16
426.18
426.22
429.12
429.26
431.04
431.16
432.08
435.24
436.05
436.11
438.20
445.01
447.15
448.01
448.14
452.28
454.03
455.17
456.11
463.18
465.02
468.01
468.13
469.01
469.28
471.07
473.01
475.24
476.17
478.15
479.13
482.05
483.09
484.16
485.20
485.22
489.01
492.05
492.28
493.06
496.14
502.21
505.12
506.19
506.14
509.13
519.06
519.15
522.15
525.28
528.02
530.25
531.19
540.25
541.01
541.08
542.03
542.18
542.28
544.17
544.18
545.25
545.27
546.11
546.17
547.21
548.20
549.10
550.18
554.17
558.15
558.19
561.04
563.01
564.01
564.11
565.21
566.25
572.12
578.18
588.04
593.05
595.14
596.04
597.13
600.16
609.11
610.02
610.11
610.28
611.07
613.04
614.16
614.27
623.03

623.10
624.21
630.06
639.26
640.07
641.03
642.26
643.16
649.16
651.16
654.17
654.21
655.13
658.08
659.05
662.03
663.26
668.06
671.20
673.10
675.18
676.03
682.03
683.20
690.08
692.18
693.25
694.20
696.22
698.09
699.05
702.15
703.17
704.27
707.13
711.05
714.19
715.27
723.27
726.25
735.07
735.23
738.24
742.10
744.26
751.14
756.07
757.14
766.02
768.15
779.22
779.25
780.17
783.27
788.12
789.19
790.26
797.12
797.28
798.05
800.09
802.10
809.24
811.20
813.25
826.13
833.17
839.02
839.10
841.20
842.14
843.05
848.15
848.26
849.17
849.26
850.21
852.11
853.06
854.27
855.13
856.27
857.27
861.22
862.20
863.28
864.01
865.14
865.17
865.19
865.19
865.22
867.03
867.14
867.18
867.20
871.13
874.18
875.01
875.19
876.26
882.26
883.23
884.04
884.19
884.26
885.05
885.09
886.01
887.17
887.26

904.01
906.04
908.04

out-door
001.09
088.06
365.03

out-house
682.14

out-line
701.24

out-manoeuvered
596.11

out-of-the-way
777.23

out-stretched
611.04

outbreaks
626.26

outcast
660.28
672.21
686.28
734.05
878.03

outer
023.24
165.08
233.19

outlandish-looking
803.27

outlawry
459.20

outlet
209.24
286.06
852.06

outline
115.09
155.12
464.28
471.15
472.25
712.15
750.03

outrage
260.14
649.20

outraged
425.06
632.02

outrivalled
142.22

outside
058.19
101.03
121.06
145.08
183.26
294.10
295.22
432.15
432.26
466.03
541.20

outward
639.28
819.26

outwardly
612.13

outworks
761.01

oval
382.20
738.05

oven
693.20
702.17

over
003.11
005.08
010.18
013.02
022.27
023.10
027.02
029.06
032.03
033.06
042.10
044.01
044.17
058.25
066.25
066.25
067.07
067.10
068.17
074.08
074.27
076.09
078.14
079.12
082.22
082.25
089.09
089.17
089.17
089.26
090.24
091.02

096.13
101.14
104.09
113.03
115.06
117.26
118.13
119.28
120.24
123.10
133.08
134.11
136.22
143.06
144.15
148.01
154.08
156.24
157.01
168.11
170.06
176.08
178.24
184.28
193.23
194.06
194.23
198.23
199.11
203.13
206.24
208.28
209.20
215.03
220.13
225.24
226.16
229.27
234.05
247.25
260.26
265.14
281.26
283.13
286.03
309.24
311.17
312.24
313.13
318.15
324.16
327.25
331.28
334.20
336.27
337.08
342.26
346.03
355.02
354.21
364.20
368.23
373.26
379.11
380.01
382.27
394.10
395.07
397.22
408.03
409.26
418.12
420.12
421.08
423.16
424.22
425.12
432.16
433.03
433.06
433.17
434.17
437.26
445.08
453.03
454.04
462.15
465.04
466.25
467.05
475.21
475.21
475.25
475.26
478.28
482.03
484.26
485.20
495.06
497.16
497.23
498.17
501.02
502.08
504.16
507.26
509.27
510.07
518.29
521.02
526.23

537.25
539.06
540.07
542.21
544.05
549.24
561.08
561.18
575.04
575.04
576.20
577.19
578.08
578.24
584.01
586.04
589.16
591.21
594.13
599.12
605.13
605.24
608.07
610.28
617.23
620.02
622.08
625.26
629.28
630.03
630.26
631.19
634.03
634.09
650.23
659.28
661.19
663.09
673.08
674.05
674.22
674.22
675.04
675.11
676.08
676.12
677.15
686.01
688.02
688.05
694.27
699.10
702.04
705.04
714.17
717.08
718.02
725.19
726.13
737.07
739.25
748.23
750.01
753.03
753.07
756.17
761.26
763.13
766.19
767.17
768.03
775.22
792.19
797.04
799.28
802.11
802.26
803.28
805.08
805.09
805.25
806.19
809.05
810.20
812.07
814.21
815.06
817.20
824.23
833.03
833.16
833.22
836.22
844.05
845.23
852.12
853.10
857.09
858.07
863.24
870.15
874.24
876.03
882.22
884.07
886.27
887.04
894.14
900.13
900.23
906.02
907.03

907.09
910.10
over-application
  007.18
over-cast
  561.13
over-excited
  007.18
  514.23
  568.13
over-fatigued
  568.13
over-modesty
  240.12
over-stimulated
  579.10
over-strained
  691.01
over-tasked
  649.07
over-worked
  084.27
overawed
  827.27
overcast
  852.09
  879.16
overclouded
  075.08
overcome
  119.10
  147.27
  421.27
  511.21
  731.03
  736.14
  736.15
  847.14
overcomes
  107.14
  813.12
overcometh
  844.17
overflow
  349.03
  401.16
overflowed
  220.02
  608.14
overflowing
  628.15
  757.23
overgrew
  673.29
overgrown
  209.06
  770.20
overhead
  415.08
  415.08
  849.18
  857.21
overheard
  329.20
  569.12
overleaped
  879.08
overleaping
  440.10
overlook
  281.07
  898.10
overlooked
  161.15
overlooking
  780.11
overlooks
  092.02
overpass
  215.06
overpersuasion
  531.02
overpowered
  079.14
  114.14
  664.04
overshadowed
  022.12
  146.10
overshadowing
  762.22
overt
  831.07
overtake
  573.02
overtaken
  498.05
overwhelm
  186.18
overwhelmed
  133.07
overwhelming
  129.09
  891.10
owd
  698.06
  698.09
owe
  029.17
  453.17
  597.20
  707.25

owed
  162.15
  453.06
ower
  679.19
owing
  007.18
  255.19
  269.14
  301.11
  633.17
owls
  574.24
own
  002.10
  004.16
  019.04
  019.07
  021.19
  021.24
  022.06
  026.18
  031.24
  042.14
  066.05
  068.07
  074.26
  092.24
  106.09
  106.22
  108.02
  109.25
  115.02
  115.23
  123.21
  125.15
  126.13
  126.18
  130.06
  132.01
  133.17
  134.27
  135.07
  137.01
  137.27
  139.12
  143.02
  153.09
  156.02
  159.14
  163.06
  163.14
  166.24
  167.12
  168.24
  171.23
  172.25
  183.26
  186.27
  187.04
  187.22
  198.12
  218.09
  229.22
  244.20
  249.24
  256.02
  257.28
  263.02
  268.07
  268.11
  271.14
  272.14
  272.28
  276.10
  285.19
  290.05
  296.20
  296.21
  300.19
  301.09
  305.18
  312.25
  314.15
  320.15
  320.20
  321.15
  321.27
  323.09
  329.07
  350.06
  354.12
  361.02
  361.12
  361.13
  373.12
  377.05
  378.15
  403.19
  406.20
  406.20
  406.28
  407.25
  410.09
  420.23
  424.12
  425.07
  431.10
  438.23
  440.27
  444.07

  451.06
  459.27
  468.20
  468.21
  469.27
  475.02
  475.17
  476.26
  479.15
  481.22
  483.08
  488.07
  488.17
  488.28
  493.23
  494.11
  497.13
  502.09
  502.10
  514.05
  516.09
  516.18
  516.19
  522.14
  543.04
  547.21
  570.12
  570.15
  577.19
  581.14
  604.11
  605.14
  609.18
  616.09
  617.12
  618.13
  628.28
  632.22
  633.18
  634.05
  636.03
  640.21
  642.18
  650.23
  650.12
  656.14
  681.24
  692.14
  695.13
  698.17
  700.24
  702.01
  703.27
  706.13
  706.13
  710.03
  710.04
  721.13
  722.03
  734.28
  741.22
  742.24
  744.17
  744.25
  748.17
  753.13
  756.04
  767.21
  768.27
  773.19
  774.03
  774.10
  785.07
  785.11
  786.03
  787.36
  788.04
  790.23
  800.10
  803.22
  803.25
  806.18
  808.16
  811.25
  814.18
  828.02
  832.25
  837.20
  843.04
  847.04
  850.19
  862.17
  864.06
  865.09
  865.23
  867.12
  878.16
  878.24
  879.14
  884.05
  894.20
  894.27
  899.24
  901.05
  910.27
  912.21
owner
  088.01
  195.18
  424.15
  860.02

owners
  686.28
ox
  143.17
pace
  640.05
paced
  210.05
  230.14
  640.08
pacify
  418.10
pacing
  390.26
  538.19
pack
  005.07
  068.18
  174.07
packed
  557.07
packing
  147.14
  456.24
  487.16
pagan
  553.01
  762.10
  762.15
  797.08
page
  066.06
  140.15
  390.13
  516.27
  655.02
  701.19
  720.26
  833.02
  844.06
pages
  003.21
  004.20
  005.26
  090.24
  678.24
  752.03
  753.15
paid
  266.16
  266.18
  266.19
  479.11
  634.01
  719.17
  855.14
pain
  009.25
  024.10
  034.08
  132.25
  136.25
  141.25
  215.20
  226.26
  283.14
  372.27
  374.03
  466.19
  486.01
  533.17
  550.26
  569.03
  617.12
  628.10
  656.08
  806.07
  836.10
  844.11
  849.22
  871.23
  888.16
painful
  014.16
  116.09
  157.08
  236.22
  252.02
  253.03
  291.23
  342.02
  481.26
  505.13
  649.07
  670.19
  731.11
  838.21
  896.01
  910.03
  911.20
painfully
  470.13
  573.23
  807.10
pains
  104.10
  198.04
  240.14
  462.23
  516.02
  531.25

  534.07
  565.13
  620.10
  663.24
paint
  179.05
  249.21
  250.23
  322.09
  327.15
  755.04
  763.11
  764.07
painted
  030.18
  041.17
  249.18
  345.07
  729.04
painting
  202.28
  246.16
  755.16
  763.15
paintings
  039.07
  143.05
  176.24
pair
  052.27
  078.06
  086.18
  169.26
  185.16
  202.28
  281.13
  286.08
  353.01
  378.22
  400.01
  403.07
  417.18
  770.16
  905.18
pairs
  013.06
pale
  003.13
  016.11
  076.20
  086.09
  088.11
  109.06
  119.13
  139.16
  143.09
  155.26
  192.21
  197.05
  204.16
  220.12
  226.02
  234.25
  247.21
  248.23
  249.15
  299.20
  343.23
  395.26
  421.09
  422.27
  431.28
  435.22
  437.23
  442.07
  458.05
  480.08
  519.25
  522.07
  523.12
  563.01
  576.05
  591.15
  594.13
  605.21
  620.20
  662.27
  677.14
  681.13
  699.21
  767.10
  767.11
  796.24
  807.27
  831.10
  837.18
  839.18
  854.02
  907.25
  910.14
pale-beaming
  219.07
paleness
  306.27
  425.26
paler
  362.13
palette
  248.05
  322.06
  752.04

763.07
palisades
675.21
palliate
268.06
pallid
207.27
461.15
690.11
pallor
411.13
palm
207.09
397.14
397.21
397.25
453.02
465.02
palmistry
393.05
palsied
578.05
palsy
125.06
paltry
270.13
pamela
005.26
pampering
118.15
550.04
pamphlet
060.11
panel
423.20
423.26
paneless
859.06
panels
294.09
295.08
423.16
panes
003.09
050.01
105.27
255.19
306.13
306.16
316.05
414.09
479.25
676.14
pang
055.07
065.07
482.02
519.26
610.21
613.05
626.16
655.25
670.04
683.16
753.26
pangs
327.17
pannels
017.10
pansies
145.02
435.02
pant
580.24
645.23
panted
655.23
panting
502.02
pantomime
357.13
pantry
364.13
papa
064.25
065.15
739.01
741.09
741.17
742.02
749.23
751.02
papa's
359.18
paper
071.20
158.10
218.22
256.15
470.26
471.14
593.05
733.14
763.13
763.17
763.28
764.06
773.26
780.16
851.08

papered
076.11
191.23
329.02
papering
181.06
papers
116.22
488.19
715.12
772.08
803.13
par
214.08
parable
441.12
paradise
030.11
030.19
518.09
707.08
731.27
747.23
paradox
373.03
paragraph
394.15
parallel
771.12
parallels
010.05
paralyze
422.17
paralyzed
112.24
123.22
414.19
724.15
847.15
paramount
283.19
parcel
138.10
653.03
653.06
656.08
707.12
733.13
parchments
016.21
pardon
065.22
136.06
260.06
264.17
361.01
373.02
403.12
464.26
517.28
540.18
553.11
693.27
parent
022.04
158.12
486.02
597.16
parent's
461.15
parentage
593.02
parental
214.14
parenthese
214.08
parentless
021.20
289.02
parents
077.07
077.09
091.13
101.05
199.27
241.21
242.17
477.24
706.16
744.17
parian
204.16
paris
255.28
280.13
288.17
526.21
635.28
parish
695.14
709.17
714.14
721.26
800.25
parishioner
604.08
parisienne's
342.02
park
199.17
209.04

357.09
499.22
park-gates
833.27
834.18
parle
234.23
parley
025.14
parleying
381.14
parlez
201.19
parlour
052.02
076.13
175.03
175.20
218.19
235.01
534.22
680.03
681.21
688.02
700.11
701.01
701.03
717.24
794.22
797.13
797.27
798.18
798.23
810.25
839.12
860.10
874.19
874.23
878.17
892.23
parlour-bell
874.02
parlours
747.28
paroxysm
290.13
811.06
paroxysms
616.23
parson
243.24
356.11
695.18
698.19
905.04
parsonage
669.01
669.12
695.20
718.19
728.05
732.28
parsonic
890.12
part
008.03
008.03
060.06
066.12
089.06
091.28
098.13
111.09
114.04
114.13
114.26
158.04
162.15
163.15
177.22
196.26
234.01
238.09
257.25
261.18
288.13
305.06
329.20
331.14
339.12
349.04
357.05
389.07
420.14
469.09
488.11
488.28
503.04
506.13
543.15
561.12
567.19
571.13
609.10
622.04
622.09
627.25
713.22
740.12
754.20
770.04
770.18
785.18

826.10
826.11
833.27
834.18
844.20
846.15
854.23
863.12
865.10
866.24
898.15
partake
522.12
partaken
188.06
parted
010.25
180.20
489.17
493.20
498.24
600.12
681.13
727.09
763.24
789.11
894.14
parterre
048.20
544.16
partial
261.21
738.13
882.27
partiality
075.04
018.12
partially
036.16
111.14
117.19
160.08
229.20
246.03
254.15
256.26
273.23
282.18
participation
330.25
particular
104.02
339.04
362.11
463.12
629.13
863.13
particularly
024.26
205.05
257.03
317.01
703.22
particulars
124.13
171.15
882.28
parties
045.13
376.22
500.02
625.01
parting
236.16
456.01
510.07
518.09
550.26
622.08
725.04
725.06
725.07
789.04
881.04
partitions
630.11
partly
065.23
065.23
076.21
091.07
149.15
149.16
251.28
252.01
343.28
633.18
867.20
partner
597.17
598.09
624.14
759.04
partout
334.05
parts
031.22
055.14
137.27
578.14
698.14
861.16
party
316.13
317.12

328.11
331.18
332.28
337.25
339.01
341.08
365.28
366.12
367.02
367.14
369.10
371.06
371.16
378.15
379.09
379.18
382.10
387.15
410.26
449.18
488.02
491.15
pas
234.24
234.26
239.10
277.19
334.11
341.20
543.20
pass
003.22
004.05
042.17
075.04
109.05
111.14
117.19
160.08
229.20
246.03
254.15
256.26
273.23
282.18
329.03
329.09
372.04
405.20
452.07
470.02
483.17
497.17
504.13
507.26
514.17
519.13
544.15
622.07
626.18
639.17
655.14
659.09
672.05
685.03
724.08
758.09
770.08
789.16
812.21
813.02
818.22
852.10
900.09
904.03
passage
023.24
076.05
077.27
077.27
154.13
159.08
183.16
209.26
328.22
361.20
432.13
610.01
680.05
693.02
794.24
800.04
829.21
849.26
passages
005.23
134.04
147.25
passed
005.08
009.25
029.04
029.10
033.01
042.08
045.10
060.14
061.11
069.15
071.11
072.03

072.22
074.08
075.26
077.26
079.25
083.08
100.24
120.24
125.09
127.13
127.18
144.12
154.17
164.19
174.05
185.16
210.11
218.03
219.04
222.02
222.14
235.02
271.11
282.04
299.06
305.12
306.09
318.15
324.02
364.05
372.09
389.01
389.10
395.06
412.28
415.07
425.14
435.20
473.22
483.19
486.12
490.05
494.04
513.14
515.03
551.16
563.19
587.08
586.16
598.22
598.25
610.20
610.28
637.26
636.27
642.19
644.04
654.17
658.02
660.01
661.07
666.27
671.10
671.26
699.15
702.15
706.19
714.05
725.27
727.08
730.20
744.16
745.10
761.01
770.16
809.15
836.22
839.09
844.12
849.02
851.09
884.07
passees
327.26
passenger
501.07
passengers
073.20
074.11
659.04
passes
220.21
536.14
passeth
717.03
passing
033.15
045.22
046.07
052.12
083.02
115.08
127.13
134.22
175.02
185.10
236.23
266.12
285.09
335.09
336.28

363.06	pastille	pauper's	peaceful	pencil	490.07
398.18	147.27	673.23	715.28	248.06	495.16
568.25	pastime	pause	796.19	313.14	508.27
619.22	402.13	036.20	peacefully	471.12	616.24
640.06	pastor	080.24	583.07	472.25	628.06
675.26	596.14	090.07	peak	494.08	666.13
745.21	846.20	125.07	248.12	494.20	677.20
758.07	pastor's	126.03	540.26	542.04	697.08
824.23	746.19	258.18	peaks	764.08	697.24
870.05	pastoral	281.01	145.18	pencil-head	709.25
884.13	714.16	360.05	164.20	749.14	756.23
906.19	855.03	388.27	peal	pencilled	790.24
passion	pastry	590.09	210.11	139.20	835.01
011.02	030.28	645.05	217.02	143.03	843.03
061.15	328.09	652.02	519.08	738.02	855.27
279.12	pasture	653.17	pear	pencilling	859.10
279.12	209.18	682.18	434.27	085.25	862.09
283.21	pasture-fields	687.06	pearl	pencils	884.27
290.09	664.13	691.07	193.16	203.12	884.28
303.02	712.07	694.04	236.15	322.08	905.11
356.16	pat	752.27	340.26	470.25	people's
374.02	261.09	760.03	343.25	713.26	058.20
512.26	patch	769.22	652.27	733.14	554.28
552.15	719.19	836.16	888.05	752.05	703.26
595.01	patchwork	892.17	899.17	pendant	per
605.04	246.04	893.18	pearl-coloured	576.17	049.01
607.06	patent	paused	558.10	pendent	171.14
610.03	525.02	006.05	pearl-grey	074.16	173.04
611.25	paternity	036.26	544.14	193.16	266.09
620.18	288.08	099.23	545.25	550.11	perceive
628.19	path	117.06	pearllike	penetrate	123.16
644.10	033.06	119.09	143.07	089.19	246.22
647.01	057.12	131.24	pearly	850.20	295.25
731.11	066.22	155.19	209.11	penetrated	454.01
745.28	067.03	283.12	peasantry	088.14	506.08
747.26	076.03	293.12	790.06	573.22	perceived
758.27	191.13	301.17	790.07	652.10	057.07
813.14	209.06	308.10	peasants	penetrating	082.19
837.13	219.17	419.28	730.07	001.09	177.26
passionate	221.08	440.14	peat	023.07	237.12
015.02	459.17	441.15	792.01	351.06	267.03
064.14	494.06	495.22	peat-fire	706.01	330.18
108.20	542.09	506.15	676.16	761.07	340.03
483.18	588.25	590.08	761.07	869.17	346.04
484.19	607.08	634.11	pebbly	penetration	361.21
545.19	631.10	708.01	076.03	274.22	426.19
611.14	713.02	719.05	504.11	641.20	607.02
613.17	732.22	720.23	712.04	penknife	610.18
passionately	735.02	724.02	peculiar	260.15	626.24
515.26	736.21	780.20	205.24	261.08	783.05
passionless	845.14	839.25	206.01	penny	890.27
563.19	848.20	872.18	213.17	661.08	perceptible
passions	911.15	891.22	250.16	682.28	379.10
025.09	pathless	pauses	251.16	683.01	737.25
355.24	551.05	858.08	266.08	727.18	876.11
405.14	606.03	pavement	285.21	751.25	perception
773.08	pathos	230.15	293.27	pennyless	780.02
passive	125.12	282.03	299.28	786.10	perceptions
106.15	650.17	432.16	465.17	888.10	702.11
228.24	patience	502.13	547.11	pensive	perch
425.16	238.23	538.20	685.02	099.26	887.12
611.27	783.27	565.25	690.16	137.02	perched
passively	800.13	570.07	714.23	726.16	381.11
458.07	815.26	770.19	736.17	747.15	894.05
673.05	patient	857.02	763.20	801.01	percursor
passport	118.10	859.01	839.27	pent	482.01
636.02	141.16	866.03	873.11	724.13	perdition
past	155.18	paving	peculiarities	826.27	846.09
021.01	426.07	273.11	205.21	penurious	pere
028.09	427.06	pay	251.25	112.26	348.12
066.16	432.06	091.15	491.06	people	peremptorily
088.28	479.18	091.17	peculiarly	031.25	024.15
116.03	484.15	091.17	058.06	037.25	peremptory
117.25	486.10	168.04	379.15	038.05	458.21
140.05	597.23	299.02	397.05	038.08	539.01
156.10	640.02	353.24	488.09	038.17	perfect
207.17	806.15	468.13	pecuniary	063.15	025.01
224.16	811.06	868.08	455.02	069.03	126.04
268.10	830.07	paying	pedestal	103.02	154.05
274.27	patient's	469.12	127.09	106.20	274.11
301.06	811.09	paymaster	peep	106.22	308.22
307.14	patiently	351.20	585.12	127.01	344.08
320.19	102.23	paynim	857.15	131.01	373.28
332.08	108.06	368.07	857.25	159.10	663.06
355.08	829.11	pays	858.27	167.08	711.11
389.01	patients	266.09	peeped	177.10	712.11
445.07	147.11	721.28	144.19	178.08	737.18
460.18	150.26	769.11	539.27	184.07	737.19
473.21	patriarchal	paysannes	peeping	189.05	749.26
497.03	368.20	790.10	281.24	206.12	755.14
565.15	patrimony	pea-chicks	335.25	216.13	779.26
582.05	719.17	016.27	peer's	217.23	792.11
584.04	patriot's	peace	524.21	241.27	795.05
630.27	513.14	030.11	peered	262.25	882.16
643.27	patron	070.01	170.06	265.16	909.13
651.08	112.21	101.09	peeress	269.22	perfection
653.10	patroness	268.21	571.04	301.28	636.11
653.16	126.17	440.27	pelisse	308.09	perfectly
655.02	patted	485.07	072.01	310.17	002.06
670.19	740.24	498.22	462.04	316.19	058.04
716.05	798.08	510.12	pelisses	326.25	640.25
812.10	875.06	633.25	092.25	336.19	641.07
813.16	pattering	663.21	124.17	339.20	713.08
863.03	871.06	676.26	pelted	344.08	827.01
883.21	pattern	706.13	572.21	389.24	837.13
paste	808.14	708.17	674.26	390.06	perfidious
697.21	paul	717.03	penalties	398.16	115.25
pasteboard	816.06	747.28	012.09	408.25	perfidy
141.12	853.03	758.10	pence	411.27	200.18
pastile	pauper	759.25	455.04	450.21	perforated
280.18	469.01	901.14	penchant	455.28	859.05
			441.27		

perform
169.06
455.11
455.28
458.28
816.11
817.13
817.15
841.10
869.27
performance
097.20
549.21
performances
114.12
performed
056.11
257.17
257.25
547.09
601.16
689.05
800.09
869.13
performers
370.10
perfume
250.18
503.17
perhaps
007.18
014.27
021.10
037.14
047.08
053.19
101.25
109.04
109.05
114.27
119.09
121.05
159.11
172.02
180.14
188.28
192.05
197.04
205.24
208.15
210.20
214.03
224.17
239.04
245.19
252.17
252.20
253.15
261.05
265.10
268.06
268.22
306.14
313.06
317.02
323.28
336.05
359.22
344.01
374.05
399.07
400.17
422.05
451.28
453.14
461.17
469.21
481.24
482.02
504.08
519.05
527.11
527.16
528.05
550.14
557.21
543.05
569.12
573.15
578.18
590.10
591.21
596.13
620.01
654.04
654.06
654.14
655.28
664.27
685.20
691.18
701.22
724.04
751.05
752.21
753.25
735.06
744.22
750.12
760.19
767.17
774.13
776.08
777.01
779.11
784.03
787.17
795.27
806.02
807.26
808.22
856.28
857.01
857.08
857.21
862.03
866.16
879.08
879.18
880.06
891.05
900.26
902.22
909.15
peri
738.22
peril
297.20
422.11
454.22
552.18
perilous
575.14
619.28
perils
164.14
period
005.25
162.19
174.02
192.07
328.13
490.05
527.20
555.21
745.06
perish
096.14
405.28
662.20
707.21
perished
684.10
perjured
022.17
permanent
452.11
493.05
663.12
712.02
761.26
806.07
824.21
permanently
022.06
195.12
475.09
691.14
721.02
721.03
797.06
permission
058.02
169.07
559.19
390.23
408.23
665.20
841.08
permit
021.27
059.24
173.07
192.16
616.01
620.27
710.07
725.14
908.05
permits
785.09
permitted
015.11
083.11
200.10
326.16
643.03
700.06
permitting
324.12
perpendicular
053.23
perpetrate
307.05
perpetrated
633.28
perpetrator
439.11
perpetual
273.02
898.22
perplex
569.03
perplexed
559.17
persecuting
356.10
perseverance
238.24
639.10
762.02
779.06
persevere
131.21
persevered
818.01
persians
273.24
persist
107.05
person
047.26
053.24
062.14
071.12
075.13
093.12
106.27
133.22
174.28
183.09
184.06
211.20
217.19
264.08
300.10
300.14
306.17
345.11
353.22
373.05
380.27
391.24
403.09
417.08
450.05
450.07
452.17
459.01
473.26
481.06
491.07
536.11
557.12
559.13
629.04
636.12
665.14
677.09
690.12
705.08
722.05
727.14
767.01
862.11
874.04
889.23
889.24
person's
476.14
personage
082.03
085.08
149.14
343.15
368.25
597.05
750.13
personal
123.01
263.05
287.08
312.18
815.14
816.08
824.26
853.16
personally
744.27
personne
234.25
persons
121.21
206.14
214.09
342.17
671.03
744.02
persuade
385.27
470.05
493.22
557.17
778.20
persuaded
263.17
484.09
544.12
806.12
817.06
persuasion
756.09
818.11
pertinaciously
545.12
894.05
perturbed
715.15
perusal
089.26
202.21
479.01
768.13
peruse
032.10
perused
031.09
061.06
326.04
701.19
713.06
726.13
pervaded
155.02
190.24
pervading
078.02
perverse
626.23
perversity
647.10
829.11
pervious
261.26
pestilence
146.22
pet
289.05
435.28
537.16
petals
504.04
petersburg
635.28
petit
239.11
255.19
petite
234.24
499.03
petition
165.19
529.15
608.03
petitioned
030.22
333.09
petitioner
530.08
petitions
392.01
petrified
049.24
119.18
283.22
511.27
petticoats
365.20
pettishness
034.14
petty
269.17
petulance
747.17
peu
234.25
540.28
peut
234.21
pewter
676.15
phantom-like
566.23
phantoms
005.06
017.25
phase
057.08
174.21
phial
431.04
431.19
654.12
philanthropist
261.07
261.13
705.17
705.21
715.10
philanthropy
762.22
834.04
philosopher
762.11
762.15
philosophers
441.04
762.13
philter
497.01
phlegmatic
307.10
352.19
889.23
905.11
phrase
153.06
635.13
832.11
phrases
098.02
165.10
198.12
266.28
373.11
548.08
phylactery
141.14
physical
001.16
111.07
670.22
706.14
824.20
physically
029.24
344.10
630.04
648.27
713.10
physician
027.14
423.25
811.07
physiognomy
237.13
259.13
262.15
355.01
382.12
690.18
691.09
piano
045.21
178.14
202.27
216.24
245.15
245.21
318.25
337.03
358.18
359.06
361.06
380.02
549.25
piano-stool
386.28
pick
123.11
353.15
353.16
673.20
694.22
picked
697.21
picking
143.06
699.07
pickings
202.23
pictorial
599.04
pictorial-looking
702.24
pictur'
681.04
picture
005.13
011.01
076.16
086.08
179.04
186.04
220.28
228.25
235.14
248.11
321.27
345.12
588.07
677.23
726.21
750.15
754.25
755.05
755.10
755.24
756.15
758.14
763.13
891.09
902.10
picture-books
049.15
pictures
003.02
032.04
193.13
246.11
246.23
247.12
247.23
249.19
291.19
322.27
327.17
701.18
737.28
749.19
picturesque
143.03
169.18
185.02
194.03
picturing
480.07
pie
149.02
piece
095.19
115.19
141.12
149.02
201.10
201.16
322.04
477.02
668.07
671.14
682.17
685.26
701.12
776.05
905.13
pieces
039.09
piecing
235.18
pierce
746.19
pierced
905.14
piercing
239.17
248.28
705.06
piercingly
259.27
807.20
pierrot
093.03
093.11
143.12
198.01
199.24
pies
694.21
697.22
piety
056.02
pig
672.13
pig-trough
672.07
pigeons
018.26
pigmies
032.07
pigmy
627.13
piled
033.08
331.03
piled-up
016.06
328.02
piles
859.26
pilgrim
272.19
pilgrim-convoy
911.25
pillar
052.13
086.20
344.15
658.13
857.15
pillars
015.22
857.13
870.04
pillow
026.14
027.02
027.25
167.24
295.04
466.25
661.20
758.20
pillows
016.06
328.02
465.05
479.20
pilot
223.20
231.27
236.27
241.03
251.06
263.14
279.06

268.09	pitch	460.14	plaid	planted	194.25
289.13	716.09	467.10	113.08	054.27	218.17
294.14	pitch-dark	475.10	175.21	planter	231.13
308.18	684.14	491.26	plain	624.15	256.24
308.18	pitched	493.05	058.16	plants	331.24
332.26	379.19	505.27	059.04	019.02	490.16
380.24	pitcher	508.23	084.08	048.18	498.10
426.21	079.03	526.10	192.09	059.13	503.24
538.20	296.26	542.19	211.14	146.05	505.27
564.06	368.16	550.15	217.13	146.09	506.18
874.27	368.24	559.07	255.16	896.17	531.02
875.02	368.27	577.18	260.06	plaster	533.22
875.12	pitchers	579.16	320.21	191.24	641.26
875.14	096.05	589.14	322.03	415.16	670.17
876.01	piteously	593.02	462.05	plate	688.04
887.25	572.24	595.10	498.08	030.18	744.16
899.05	pith	597.05	502.02	030.22	757.12
pin	350.18	614.12	513.04	031.05	798.14
427.22	pithy	614.13	516.10	217.10	843.23
pinafore	300.20	615.17	521.09	310.08	845.28
050.19	pitied	615.26	521.17	331.10	898.20
051.11	041.05	618.05	525.09	335.02	pleasantest
099.20	329.19	622.14	529.24	458.24	100.09
326.17	468.18	632.09	585.07	686.12	pleasantly
pinafores	pities	657.02	691.25	plate-closet	002.24
058.18	386.19	658.03	697.25	310.09	please
078.13	pitilessly	666.09	735.23	plateful	018.16
113.23	843.03	666.12	819.03	094.07	057.03
pinch	pity	667.26	841.15	plates	107.05
035.10	022.28	668.01	841.17	049.18	117.19
543.25	025.03	669.02	889.23	411.03	177.16
555.11	063.05	677.07	plain-work-woman	676.15	178.08
pine	105.20	680.13	665.27	729.06	192.15
292.03	105.26	698.02	709.26	platter	214.05
pine-apples	121.03	699.03	plained	121.06	245.09
631.06	131.08	700.08	661.24	plausible	257.01
pine-forests	131.09	705.07	plainly	505.11	260.24
606.07	184.12	706.28	061.15	play	263.23
pining	290.01	721.14	120.18	039.09	265.17
007.19	370.21	750.26	210.22	065.05	310.22
468.15	373.14	761.03	220.16	178.14	331.19
878.03	506.15	771.08	224.09	178.20	339.17
pinion	612.10	777.24	262.23	181.03	360.19
551.27	623.03	785.24	314.25	216.22	370.10
pinioned	628.04	788.06	397.13	245.06	382.05
601.13	628.05	789.14	477.16	245.15	392.15
pinions	628.06	797.12	507.09	245.18	395.14
662.02	628.09	798.23	571.10	314.11	398.25
pink	628.12	802.01	634.26	317.26	400.24
016.02	628.17	808.23	644.25	355.15	450.14
018.22	661.27	814.15	701.04	360.11	484.02
148.06	686.03	873.16	703.17	366.07	494.21
276.14	742.01	874.12	753.20	406.14	527.15
340.13	751.12	887.25	767.12	514.15	528.01
503.09	761.13	912.03	789.13	550.08	528.17
541.06	767.17	placed	plainness	550.16	532.12
544.07	866.23	030.26	184.05	643.13	535.26
pinnacle	380.11	032.02	460.24	850.12	548.01
248.27	881.15	052.17	703.04	play-hour	554.03
pinned	881.15	053.27	plains	100.08	566.09
141.06	pitying	059.12	526.15	144.12	582.02
653.06	486.02	080.21	540.21	played	719.14
pinning	place	081.06	plaits	045.21	784.20
005.07	014.23	086.18	121.22	178.18	808.05
pint	037.05	124.12	318.12	214.27	pleased
311.03	037.10	137.12	plan	279.06	067.18
pioneer	038.24	138.07	118.07	289.14	084.23
142.13	044.10	162.03	172.07	319.07	173.15
720.19	068.07	182.06	377.06	346.07	196.23
911.17	079.16	200.13	464.02	355.27	206.06
pioneers	080.01	257.01	554.03	371.17	228.21
720.20	085.15	281.02	596.13	379.01	343.25
pious	094.27	285.19	837.01	406.14	357.20
126.12	096.06	365.10	planet	457.10	453.03
354.21	097.23	367.24	128.10	478.09	472.21
pip	100.16	371.08	250.20	639.24	521.14
288.03	102.02	397.02	planets	882.21	532.02
356.11	102.15	458.22	662.04	players	554.26
pipe	124.11	483.26	739.25	380.08	555.28
329.05	127.24	512.12	plank	playing	713.22
396.04	129.03	552.05	199.11	216.23	713.23
396.06	137.08	562.07	415.15	309.14	723.06
396.21	158.01	611.26	planks	346.05	727.22
piquancy	167.05	633.06	191.24	365.06	750.14
794.16	167.09	658.09	planning	379.23	794.08
piquant	172.16	746.11	707.09	445.11	799.12
253.13	183.01	754.23	plans	449.11	804.26
343.09	184.24	778.09	172.25	879.18	891.21
546.02	188.03	783.06	213.14	playthings	pleases
642.09	189.01	907.23	309.23	049.17	263.23
873.12	191.21	places	405.24	240.08	730.06
piqued	194.28	698.20	405.25	plea	pleasing
266.05	195.09	placid	488.14	339.10	058.12
266.16	199.01	145.27	616.01	plead	162.05
553.05	199.16	383.28	683.10	845.21	184.15
625.13	204.07	435.18	757.26	pleaded	209.13
778.04	213.05	480.09	801.02	024.22	239.20
pirate	233.14	702.09	803.24	339.09	321.03
370.26	241.13	830.08	820.17	901.16	437.16
pis	253.14	placid-tempered	852.22	pleasant	739.09
354.26	265.08	213.07	854.08	014.27	792.28
pisa	288.25	placidity	892.04	047.17	908.13
142.23	298.25	260.15	plant	144.14	pleasurable
pished	316.12	placing	151.26	146.16	292.10
554.01	321.26	077.01	504.05	146.19	640.10
pistols	330.06	567.01	648.19	152.03	pleasure
650.22	369.20	700.21	676.07	152.12	020.16
pit	416.21	plague-cursed	plantation	169.17	030.15
054.10	438.13	797.15	066.12	188.25	046.23
054.11	451.16	plague-house		188.26	055.14
650.14	454.17	283.04		192.05	065.02

066.13
136.17
139.05
142.09
145.06
145.09
146.13
149.14
168.05
214.20
219.02
225.24
257.28
270.26
271.02
273.09
287.28
290.16
291.07
301.10
315.02
321.05
349.20
349.21
349.22
412.06
439.22
439.23
466.05
466.17
471.16
493.15
495.25
478.26
529.12
550.06
551.07
625.04
636.22
633.25
642.25
679.17
700.04
709.09
709.11
711.09
711.10
712.21
715.24
716.13
744.01
749.24
750.04
750.21
756.22
765.17
769.10
790.17
793.16
794.12
795.25
799.03
806.07
815.16
852.08
852.13
910.01
pleasure-villa
751.15
pleasures
191.28
249.22
249.23
378.16
462.24
plebeian
323.04
571.05
pledge
022.03
213.04
455.17
645.05
912.21
pledged
115.26
541.14
plenteous
470.14
738.09
plentiful
612.11
plenty
205.07
453.16
540.05
656.02
pliability
218.10
pliancy
528.18
pliant
647.28
plied
641.21
plodding
722.13
plot
355.16
626.10

plots
040.14
plotted
297.15
297.17
425.08
plotting
614.06
plough
322.05
plover
660.06
pluck
610.11
plucked
177.04
plumage
031.03
124.18
514.05
plume
343.19
plumes
122.05
332.23
525.27
pluming
375.03
plump
461.06
plums
503.28
plumy
342.23
plunge
619.17
plunges
601.17
plunging
152.23
pm
095.12
181.19
664.23
654.13
poacher
660.03
pocket
035.12
100.06
170.16
187.08
277.23
397.18
435.27
529.24
593.05
653.05
658.08
663.23
pocket-book
453.04
768.16
773.23
pocket-comb
084.17
pocket-handkerchief
093.01
pocket-handkerchiefs
126.26
pockets
058.18
084.11
poem
752.23
poet
747.25
poetry
201.07
202.18
531.12
753.01
753.08
poignant
549.21
611.24
poignantly
310.13
point
085.06
093.21
152.20
197.28
200.26
201.01
217.16
218.10
245.02
261.27
264.26
283.24
284.19
285.08
287.13
299.14
312.27
345.11
345.12
349.22
356.03
374.09

384.03
403.13
432.20
462.11
471.13
490.18
502.06
507.14
530.06
532.11
638.15
658.17
666.03
674.07
676.28
713.28
732.10
763.22
784.27
788.11
801.27
819.26
822.01
833.18
838.20
847.01
890.04
894.02
901.26
pointed
061.09
120.01
204.03
210.14
260.20
261.14
338.04
341.15
383.10
434.23
665.23
693.17
871.01
874.16
pointer
677.04
714.16
733.07
pointing
124.09
183.16
197.13
225.26
300.18
353.14
492.04
523.01
739.05
points
111.06
125.03
150.14
206.14
211.23
224.12
267.28
282.22
377.10
392.02
533.10
553.21
597.16
707.09
716.19
771.13
773.21
774.18
782.02
843.14
895.14
poise
009.19
poised
368.16
poison
270.19
271.16
320.28
530.25
571.19
757.28
poisoned
065.21
349.24
616.15
692.05
poke
098.07
polar
248.28
pole
004.13
560.05
560.05
polish
329.01
polished
016.04
231.13
331.08
434.22

751.26
890.15
polishing
308.16
327.17
906.01
polite
188.20
259.18
381.24
843.17
politely
906.15
politeness
238.06
338.25
743.19
political
374.05
politician
735.17
politics
352.08
576.27
pollard
229.10
636.27
poltical
216.12
poltroon
051.27
pomegranates
631.06
pomp
502.04
pompous
244.07
344.22
pompously
133.01
pond
199.18
ponder
103.16
775.20
pondered
764.08
803.22
903.09
pondering
089.20
152.24
311.19
325.21
334.26
480.03
852.21
ponderous
781.23
pony
151.20
446.14
746.07
pooh
037.09
421.26
pool
126.22
297.06
302.09
poole
210.20
295.16
296.07
300.09
300.11
306.20
310.28
311.18
313.23
314.24
328.23
330.01
399.09
399.15
408.17
423.03
430.01
577.02
581.36
599.12
599.22
600.15
601.13
602.14
616.18
633.10
863.20
863.26
poole's
217.02
312.28
420.23
597.23
poor
028.22
033.06
033.10
033.14
033.18
033.22

037.19
038.04
038.07
038.11
038.16
040.19
040.27
041.05
058.19
067.24
083.14
084.26
105.26
113.13
179.20
179.21
189.15
201.27
269.17
288.01
288.16
321.09
322.03
355.19
355.23
356.04
359.17
373.06
422.14
430.14
451.09
469.03
469.14
485.08
513.04
516.09
624.12
627.22
638.05
666.21
690.10
691.13
696.25
699.22
699.22
709.16
714.13
719.16
720.08
721.10
721.18
722.22
740.21
770.11
773.09
777.13
799.19
800.27
866.19
897.14
poor-house
014.10
poorly
153.02
463.06
poplars
345.01
population
031.20
659.04
714.13
800.25
populous
185.01
porcelain
257.20
794.19
porch
271.11
588.25
pored
397.21
poring
810.19
porridge
081.28
082.20
083.03
096.15
119.05
672.07
672.11
port
061.03
182.20
263.01
871.27
portal
434.11
859.03
870.23
porte
282.05
portentous
355.06
portents
328.19
porter
176.02
217.13
311.03

329.06
porter's
049.26
073.02
073.03
073.12
portfolio
203.11
246.02
246.08
250.27
251.12
255.05
portion
057.22
078.02
082.17
089.11
096.17
112.11
137.17
150.26
154.24
198.03
369.16
421.04
534.24
624.10
676.08
722.27
portions
079.01
079.04
474.05
portmanteau
556.11
576.17
portrait
181.09
247.21
322.02
323.09
472.13
749.22
750.14
754.12
763.08
portrait-cover
774.01
portraits
472.24
701.07
portray
322.20
portrayed
248.16
291.19
portraying
207.24
position
059.11
065.16
097.27
171.09
196.26
253.03
253.05
258.03
276.06
311.19
329.18
344.18
372.24
376.22
481.27
507.24
536.17
637.24
666.05
668.02
681.25
704.08
792.28
803.04
positions
342.25
349.07
positive
223.26
462.12
811.24
positively
088.07
400.09
possess
160.07
312.16
359.28
380.21
591.13
616.02
633.25
704.06
731.22
785.21
possessed
002.27
140.09
215.10
287.05
291.05

295.16
361.11
462.16
559.11
649.01
658.05
681.09
685.18
699.24
707.11
717.07
768.13
884.26

possesses
124.28
171.08

possessing
219.10

possession
126.04
252.12
335.01
352.25
593.17
663.23
755.19
775.05

possessions
514.14
624.16
727.16

possessor
649.23
756.05

possibility
001.03
143.10
537.20
842.18

possible
043.07
059.16
125.25
198.05
273.04
299.07
312.21
432.23
437.09
452.05
582.01
631.18
731.06
820.08
847.17
860.14

possibly
037.19
118.03
271.01
289.04
321.18
336.18
336.21
386.23
667.15

post
161.16
168.06
174.02
225.26
268.23
325.26
333.06
423.04
721.01
787.21
809.17

post-boy
868.07

post-chaise
163.11
380.20
381.04
432.14
432.25

post-office
168.08
169.02
169.11
170.01
229.03

posted
218.14

postman
169.12

posts
084.04

posture
026.12

pot
217.13
329.06

potatoes
082.21
094.05
142.26

potent
436.16
462.23
712.02

725.10
761.09
847.27

poultry
048.10

poundage
098.15

pounds
091.17
091.20
171.14
453.06
453.15
453.19
454.24
454.25
455.02
547.20
624.20
626.10
721.23
727.12
727.25
776.13
776.15
782.24
783.15
784.06
784.21
785.23
878.08

pounds'
310.08

pour
108.01
234.21
234.22
239.11
341.22
524.19
548.26
550.24

poured
453.02
483.09
561.18
608.07
657.12
812.11

pouring
257.22
342.07

pours
004.04

pout
747.14

poverty
037.24
037.27
038.02
448.04
697.10
720.09
730.27

powdered
193.15

power
019.20
138.04
157.23
164.05
191.13
215.05
263.04
274.11
274.13
291.05
311.28
312.02
312.23
321.02
350.07
350.18
360.26
382.19
437.26
462.15
462.26
494.14
496.03
497.03
497.06
531.06
533.27
539.06
619.27
641.20
687.16
703.18
705.23
716.06
716.14
734.27
735.18
747.01
753.02
761.26
762.25
777.24
817.19
822.11

829.08
831.14
908.17

powerful
319.05
361.12
536.13
644.13
724.07
753.05

powerless
250.11
648.27

powerlessness
886.23

powers
139.13
459.27
730.16
735.24
777.06
814.03
816.23
816.26
850.12

practical
168.13
215.09
715.10
821.15
878.09
884.04

practice
142.16
802.10
820.17

practised
390.04
499.25

practising
810.25

praise
098.22
104.14
104.18
240.19
321.13
553.17
806.20

praised
129.19

pranks
309.14

prating
363.06

prattle
214.04
256.23
289.17

pray
056.05
184.17
260.17
662.13
851.16
851.18
900.19

prayed
530.02
553.03
850.18
897.26

prayer
060.06
165.16
474.08
498.23
607.22
650.16
662.21
845.07
845.17
845.23
848.04
897.26

prayer-book
086.14
394.11

prayers
015.09
055.09
079.12
080.13
095.19
096.12
125.28
170.22
287.25
479.08
657.13
661.13
839.04
843.21
848.10
900.19

pre-cise-ly
277.21
507.03

pre-occupied
032.25

preach
271.10
546.18
716.04

preached
724.16

preacher
716.15

precaution
334.15
857.16

precautions
122.28
631.26

precede
236.21
629.21

preceded
413.02
460.05

preceding
096.07
559.08
792.02

precept
113.10
120.07

precincts
577.07

precious
030.26
112.13
218.07
349.20
864.14

preciously
259.02

precise
038.26
253.05
300.15
633.16

precisely
084.23
192.04
216.19
381.26
397.02
437.14
459.10
550.14
632.12
635.18
788.07
843.15
909.12

precision
791.28

precluded
549.14

precocious
139.02
019.19
025.08

preconceived
648.17

predecessor
337.24

predestination
716.18

predicament
222.21

predicted
277.02

prediction
583.15

predisposed
147.01

predominant
182.26

predominate
511.21

predominated
010.17

predominating
026.08

preface
576.05

prefer
240.05
289.04
456.04
747.08

preference
279.19
321.06
359.01
537.18

preferences
165.11

preferred
048.03
155.20
176.07
279.15
555.14
756.01
800.21
896.21

prefers
338.09

prejudice
644.21

prejudiced
252.20
690.01

prejudices
693.06
911.21

prelude
359.08

premature
684.09
819.20

prematurely
627.28

premise
247.15

premises
172.07

premium
360.21

prendre
341.20

prenomens
234.14

preparation
015.12
094.06
161.02
499.10
553.20
714.26

preparations
147.14
174.04
327.22
487.13
557.05

prepare
142.25
146.28
286.01
455.24
534.11
681.19
700.24

prepared
023.14
071.19
118.03
174.15
190.06
322.05
327.01
367.21
380.05
397.07
434.09
549.14
552.19
571.06
582.05
611.15
618.01
665.18
746.02
754.20
757.24
815.25
860.15
882.11
888.08

preparing
546.17
702.16
887.15

prerogative
359.24

prerogatives
105.21

presence
008.07
020.22
027.08
051.20
057.01
061.03
067.06
139.10
195.14
236.20
254.12
254.17
275.20
280.15
291.03
292.11
306.02
315.17
371.03
372.05
377.20
494.14
498.12
499.07
500.11
549.13
554.28
570.10
607.01

641.06
662.07
753.04
787.10
806.27
823.26
855.25
879.23
882.20
886.13
887.09
895.28
901.09

present
018.09
089.01
093.23
095.10
130.18
150.23
152.20
178.26
196.07
202.22
239.14
239.25
252.11
274.23
290.15
290.19
293.06
311.09
317.17
354.25
359.16
381.17
399.19
446.24
456.06
456.09
473.19
481.16
485.17
497.10
540.01
544.15
550.02
555.13
555.20
568.09
570.21
619.22
630.19
643.27
680.15
687.05
687.27
706.10
710.07
730.01
734.20
758.06
792.17
792.26
801.26
802.23
805.21
808.18
809.08
810.04
812.01
812.02
826.12
852.22
860.28
861.05
883.02
891.12
905.04

presentable
692.20

presented
099.17
170.11
186.04
340.07
391.21
431.21
516.04
871.01

presentiment
276.26
564.05
638.28

presentiments
444.02
444.06

presently
008.15
053.06
078.04
079.28
087.15
109.27
115.15
138.11
156.18
249.19
335.14
337.05
346.03

368.10
384.06
384.13
398.06
426.21
430.10
506.17
533.28
549.03
550.11
577.17
591.02
612.26
636.10
680.06
685.05
693.03
694.10
768.06
775.03
824.04
870.20
presents
045.12
254.14
259.15
257.13
preserved
343.06
preserver
502.02
presided
062.06
739.25
prespective
568.04
press
359.25
551.03
878.06
pressed
071.17
112.06
328.05
591.16
466.04
659.13
848.11
577.22
pressing
513.19
656.20
pressure
256.20
545.20
555.11
presume
040.04
196.09
372.25
381.21
531.08
755.02
836.15
presumption
356.06
prete
499.03
pretence
200.13
552.16
pretend
271.28
337.06
pretended
261.09
pretension
376.06
pretensions
869.04
pretercanine
222.04
preternatural
022.25
074.06
211.02
344.19
pretext
422.10
452.10
505.12
638.03
667.01
pretexts
234.07
prettiest
047.15
084.19
prettily
891.11
pretty
041.08
047.25
068.03
137.10
195.09
198.27
199.09
200.01
202.05
204.09
262.12
312.15
343.12
359.21
383.23
523.11
523.11
541.08
542.28
667.10
699.27
841.18
prevailed
083.28
309.24
prevalent
541.01
prevent
603.17
722.04
763.15
765.07
prevented
111.11
182.21
223.08
315.04
479.04
684.15
836.28
previous
260.13
330.28
579.17
592.04
724.24
749.05
680.27
previously
277.05
340.19
559.13
794.05
prey
033.27
424.21
809.19
price
036.15
405.10
661.05
854.23
priceless
525.23
pricked
565.19
737.01
675.02
prickly
675.21
pricks
246.01
pride
035.03
058.11
182.24
200.19
246.01
262.27
344.17
345.18
345.19
372.20
375.04
404.13
450.03
464.05
532.23
547.27
571.23
586.05
655.27
744.06
748.14
827.23
834.11
846.04
priest
244.03
589.02
602.08
610.13
735.16
747.25
prig
565.06
priggish
390.12
prim
053.13
323.23
prime
501.11
665.01
872.03
primitive
118.23
primrose
146.09
primroses
435.02
prince
181.10
princely
570.22
princess
368.20
412.14
principal
220.05
379.06
principle
046.02
109.01
120.07
278.07
344.18
656.09
732.05
787.09
820.23
831.14
833.10
834.14
847.08
principles
293.02
324.15
376.25
376.27
533.09
533.11
648.05
648.07
711.12
724.21
911.11
prints
181.09
prison
649.20
853.04
prisoned
673.22
876.13
prisoner
329.14
prisonground
164.22
private
168.20
171.22
182.14
202.20
329.07
355.05
547.09
625.03
706.27
822.24
863.22
privately
458.25
privation
118.20
privations
143.19
144.02
privilege
030.25
059.15
083.12
138.26
150.10
493.15
524.19
700.23
854.10
privileged
216.21
375.19
853.11
898.05
privileges
002.16
230.01
prize
565.15
602.11
prizes
820.13
probability
320.03
773.04
779.22
probable
258.26
probably
021.24
101.04
102.19
130.19
131.06
154.03
155.03
156.17
172.20
238.06
243.26
245.26
250.13
254.09
289.22
290.07
322.28
323.25
329.12
403.08
412.14
415.03
464.09
489.12
569.09
616.07
621.09
626.07
639.21
665.11
679.10
691.17
721.14
725.05
757.17
760.09
773.04
889.28
probation
554.20
problem
143.13
311.19
404.01
proceed
270.05
335.08
511.07
590.25
591.04
628.22
635.16
664.28
720.23
771.04
proceeded
056.13
071.14
108.01
122.20
136.21
138.16
167.03
209.24
238.27
285.26
301.26
418.04
422.18
463.23
471.17
555.15
569.18
574.21
599.01
604.14
665.09
681.19
697.22
720.24
801.04
818.17
870.19
874.11
889.04
proceedeth
119.01
proceeding
238.13
256.03
369.22
386.24
387.16
391.06
590.13
823.20
proceedings
049.19
097.02
627.26
process
036.17
163.24
223.14
250.06
276.20
280.03
340.11
692.22
905.01
procession
081.26
proclaiming
551.28
procrastinated
760.15
procure
840.18
produce
126.06
594.03
594.04
produced
037.01
161.04
171.02
187.08
369.01
453.04
472.25
716.07
768.16
773.24
833.03
producing
281.01
558.25
productions
752.23
products
048.20
professed
279.13
390.19
541.03
630.08
771.21
professes
405.04
profession
633.20
751.20
profile
890.22
891.13
profit
048.22
793.12
profitable
719.13
profiting
910.05
profligate
614.07
profound
154.07
155.01
214.03
401.04
474.28
591.01
761.09
890.09
903.05
profoundly
005.15
825.15
profusely
146.05
profusion
122.06
progress
129.17
175.08
183.26
214.02
214.17
240.19
575.09
721.19
731.07
744.05
795.14
843.06
889.10
906.10
project
376.16
475.07
projection
334.19
prolong
642.08
856.05
856.06
prolonged
029.13
053.05
165.28
390.17
810.06
prolonging
114.27
prominences
261.14
prominent
016.08
043.16
054.03
060.22
471.14
promise
021.22
021.25
033.17
068.22
115.26
116.01
135.03
213.02
356.17
400.06
410.19
442.18
452.06
455.09
455.10
455.16
481.21
521.06
566.05
567.14
582.14
645.16
710.02
755.04
802.13
836.14
837.22
837.25
838.01
promised
130.02
152.04
472.26
492.21
567.12
717.21
750.03
789.15
844.10
869.20
promises
723.21
758.22
promontories
003.25
promoted
142.18
prompt
168.02
505.08
609.07
616.01
753.09
880.10
prompted
616.23
716.11
promptings
465.09
732.06
promptly
034.17
186.20
258.10
265.27
prone
020.26
903.07
pronounce
093.08
142.06
350.22
773.14
pronounced
027.16
044.15
083.19
121.10
182.07
216.27
271.15
274.17
320.23
386.26
586.04
605.07
629.18
643.07
690.27
716.20
720.04
901.21
pronouncing
223.07
239.27
448.13
pronunciation
097.25
196.05
proof
058.12
104.15
347.01
605.12
786.20
proofs
288.07
prop
164.03
214.14
896.22
904.05
propensities
020.14
029.21
627.13
627.20
724.20
propensity
048.14
proper
171.26
242.02

329.01
829.14
property
049.19
252.12
252.24
354.14
558.05
624.08
727.07
774.25
780.10
788.03
859.17
861.20
propitiate
832.27
propitious
209.10
239.08
405.01
660.26
proportion
112.26
222.24
714.11
proportionate
142.14
214.20
360.24
proportions
193.28
proposal
721.10
722.19
879.11
proposals
654.26
771.25
propose
566.15
714.27
791.19
proposed
203.08
206.23
365.06
377.18
472.26
492.10
639.07
proposing
836.25
840.17
841.26
propound
056.09
propounded
440.22
propped
114.22
proprietor
195.14
206.16
721.27
750.20
propriety
139.02
315.06
prosecuting
356.10
prospect
075.08
061.16
087.25
145.10
173.01
194.24
327.23
545.06
566.13
668.10
673.01
866.11
prospective
505.21
prospects
057.27
059.11
459.24
473.19
473.14
566.17
605.18
605.21
651.20
760.14
765.25
prosperity
482.20
800.16
prosperous
727.10
prostrate
169.10
222.25
506.25
821.01
prostrating
426.14

prostration
672.27
protect
111.15
537.24
813.21
867.20
protected
659.27
protecting
003.09
protection
027.04
033.13
287.22
499.06
protector
074.25
898.15
protegee
288.23
325.05
protestations
287.25
protract
406.09
867.06
protracted
081.09
140.02
340.01
441.20
690.26
818.27
857.28
protruded
740.10
proud
018.11
292.15
352.09
359.06
372.15
375.14
536.06
536.06
731.23
750.13
781.08
695.25
898.14
900.12
prove
134.18
200.22
315.24
396.11
515.02
553.11
568.21
591.07
593.07
593.19
593.20
623.23
725.23
775.02
proved
045.04
201.13
290.02
633.17
647.11
797.20
817.11
836.24
836.25
853.16
proves
056.04
696.12
provide
671.01
698.24
provided
132.17
148.24
316.21
470.25
624.13
636.01
665.25
736.11
755.06
846.25
providence
243.01
310.18
310.18
482.15
570.01
596.12
634.02
673.06
732.07
816.12
providential
306.02
provision
244.17

provisions
777.07
provocation
315.05
provoked
308.28
831.05
provoking
068.27
103.27
381.09
555.09
574.05
807.16
prowess
889.25
prudence
309.24
312.08
507.22
pruning
763.02
prurience
625.10
psalm
055.25
055.26
psalms
055.19
055.22
055.26
056.03
pshawed
554.01
public
160.15
160.18
255.07
356.17
752.24
publication
752.22
publicly
130.12
publish
632.23
pudding
311.04
puddings
216.22
puddle
269.03
puerile
563.03
puffy
476.16
puis
341.20
pull
416.24
565.04
885.05
pulled
141.02
276.13
906.15
pulsation
909.05
pulse
136.28
402.07
414.18
623.04
781.25
pulses
065.03
124.06
167.17
punctual
104.01
475.08
479.04
804.05
punctuality
035.17
punctually
084.03
555.04
746.01
817.13
punctuation
201.11
pungent
010.16
150.07
377.21
554.09
punish
015.05
022.17
107.06
125.24
312.04
punished
007.22
018.25
025.04
123.28
punishment
051.28
063.11
094.19

095.02
107.09
141.17
360.24
361.04
831.05
puny
359.17
525.13
pupil
059.09
094.08
100.21
116.24
119.24
123.15
161.25
171.12
173.22
186.14
193.05
196.14
197.02
203.01
211.25
213.09
234.28
235.22
283.17
500.07
706.20
714.03
748.21
771.11
805.24
pupil's
240.19
pupils
058.07
087.01
087.28
112.08
118.03
118.18
131.18
147.01
154.01
168.23
243.15
468.02
pupils'
161.02
puppet
347.11
555.09
puppets
378.22
puppy
321.14
purchase
018.24
036.14
727.20
794.06
purchased
340.23
869.06
purchasing
491.21
pure
109.02
139.26
150.03
266.25
273.19
318.14
349.21
434.25
501.03
502.04
533.21
547.26
583.03
597.17
631.03
631.16
644.13
660.24
690.14
701.24
712.20
737.14
737.22
762.17
771.26
781.21
832.09
832.22
pure-lived
717.01
purer
293.02
440.06
735.06
903.26
purified
692.19
puritanical
461.12
807.15
purity
126.20

649.25
766.15
900.04
purloined
458.25
purple
084.26
086.04
124.17
145.01
145.18
203.17
203.21
231.12
258.14
332.28
496.25
502.05
578.06
600.14
712.03
746.10
purpose
024.08
043.20
084.14
133.28
257.12
361.23
587.13
587.15
705.23
721.21
782.18
791.21
792.10
794.09
822.10
822.22
845.20
purposeless
810.05
purposely
330.26
725.23
purposes
497.15
purse
084.12
287.23
348.22
403.10
452.28
453.02
454.27
522.10
571.14
653.03
purses
039.10
pursue
099.09
284.18
554.04
734.20
782.02
pursued
035.20
121.15
125.11
257.26
526.05
537.03
554.19
634.15
758.25
770.01
778.23
803.19
854.09
899.24
900.07
906.03
pursues
911.16
pursuing
672.17
774.18
843.04
pursuit
843.12
pursuits
273.16
808.09
purveyor
887.13
push
047.18
246.14
458.15
894.19
pushed
123.24
483.11
535.08
550.13
669.09
766.13
807.15
pushing
373.18

733.07
put
006.15
031.05
032.11
049.17
050.17
060.10
067.14
068.04
071.07
071.20
076.27
076.21
087.18
097.09
103.17
103.22
108.20
110.03
117.16
119.04
130.16
132.17
133.19
148.12
154.07
155.07
155.25
157.01
163.25
168.05
170.15
192.28
204.06
216.15
225.07
227.11
235.03
236.17
250.25
257.26
263.08
264.15
269.18
271.23
274.27
298.25
307.13
311.03
340.14
340.24
357.18
360.17
362.06
365.03
385.02
385.10
390.08
396.21
397.17
396.05
415.23
419.27
420.08
422.07
422.17
436.05
436.22
448.19
464.06
466.13
472.27
476.05
499.15
507.10
521.18
524.27
529.23
534.09
535.07
537.05
537.19
543.01
552.23
562.01
566.02
567.05
605.09
613.01
613.14
613.21
623.04
623.22
653.05
653.07
655.10
675.18
676.11
680.02
687.02
692.09
697.17
705.17
709.13
709.24
722.07
739.03
740.06
742.15
758.18

763.04
766.23
767.08
768.17
772.07
777.08
778.21
783.27
788.08
811.13
811.19
820.16
822.04
851.10
855.01
839.14
843.05
847.25
848.15
854.23
875.16
875.19
886.07
893.06
898.19
903.19
906.17
910.26

puts
392.15
494.19
676.13

putting
050.07
055.01
068.06
076.24
100.06
100.27
106.25
151.25
251.17
266.01
327.17
423.19
434.26
557.04
586.20
709.05
800.04
909.21

puzzle
282.17
437.10
569.02
619.06

puzzled
034.21
035.04
236.16
226.19
240.09
262.11
262.13
263.16
437.09
541.03
724.25
804.09

puzzles
046.25
777.21

puzzling
076.15
115.06
311.17

pyramids
424.21

pyrenees
857.09

qu'avez
201.18

qu'avez-vous
313.15

qu'elle
540.26

qu'il
234.20
239.10

qu'oui
234.26

quailed
016.08
552.16

quailings
084.02
407.14

quaint
078.12
084.07
259.23
265.13

quaintly
641.10

quaintness
207.19

quaker
255.15

quaker-like
192.28

quakeress
510.23

quakerish
525.09

quaking
353.08

qualifications
374.07
736.01

qualified
150.09
163.24
814.17

quality
737.20

qualities
157.13
224.27
263.04
440.01
762.20
781.09
813.04
823.26

quality
096.16
116.18
160.20
385.21

quang
334.04
543.20

quantity
096.16
117.02
137.24
160.20
599.20
561.20

quarrel
065.04
780.12

quarrelled
727.05

quarrelling
092.05
176.28
420.19
529.19

quarried
591.15

quarter
049.02
083.08
111.02
185.12
215.13
330.02
424.26
503.06
510.27
564.02
757.13
753.13
813.19
873.03

quarters
189.03
476.28
671.27

que
255.16
276.17
277.09
277.11
277.19
334.11

queen
318.04
496.24
793.09

queenly
359.07
387.24

queer
063.01
262.08
499.18
510.23
862.15
862.16

quel
335.22

quell
229.25

quelled
872.02

quells
250.20
465.08

quench
307.23

quenched
296.25
297.09
608.09
886.13

quenchless
596.17

queries
206.16

query
440.22

quest
154.10
455.12
704.12

question
001.10
020.03
028.13
036.13
056.09
085.13
127.22
146.20
149.24
188.11
199.26
201.20
205.15
223.04
259.17
260.01
260.07
262.08
266.03
284.24
354.14
362.04
401.20
403.06
492.01
499.15
552.23
623.10
693.25
715.28
718.05
722.07
731.09
738.18
742.15
755.27
766.23
773.09
784.07
811.02
842.14
848.15
850.13
859.18
861.14
883.14
886.05
891.21

questioned
104.27
122.18
158.13
659.12
674.13
807.19
852.25
873.25

questioner
705.12

questioners
002.20

questioning
224.21
311.20

questions
063.14
093.22
098.14
159.12
186.20
217.26
246.22
265.06
605.08
641.21
660.14
666.23
687.27
535.01
860.07
860.11
882.24
891.23

qui
380.14

quibble
401.05

quick
006.14
269.10
339.02
387.07
395.19
395.20
395.20
431.05
458.17
763.23
875.19
886.24

quickened
216.03
550.23

quickening
146.23
146.23
817.01

quickens
401.25

quicker
736.28

quickly
005.08
079.21
147.20
154.17
167.16
257.20
275.22
286.09
333.08
340.11
340.22
516.20
517.13
641.26
684.19
912.24

quiescence
238.10
374.26
746.26
808.02

quiescent
484.15
702.09

quiet
016.18
056.15
097.12
097.16
150.20
163.04
169.28
194.15
208.15
214.17
237.23
259.23
275.11
282.11
305.13
310.05
317.27
320.21
326.11
326.25
339.16
374.23
379.25
399.16
410.13
424.23
428.14
432.23
435.09
437.23
489.04
505.23
515.02
522.18
535.02
553.25
553.26
555.01
589.01
602.01
605.01
617.21
619.02
626.25
637.07
638.26
691.06
720.05
725.10
732.11
744.04
798.19
803.26
847.11
873.01
887.26
905.03

quieter
680.15
803.15

quietly
046.06
090.25
094.26
099.19
120.04
120.12
147.20
167.25
188.04
195.19
222.03
265.15
285.11
366.10
375.26
392.27

412.22
419.07
425.03
457.10
463.16
492.11
492.12
504.17
510.08
526.10
611.25
663.21
693.27
770.17
773.16
806.13
825.12
857.15

quilt
049.13
156.28
467.13

quit
022.20
325.20
331.22
463.27
480.01
534.22
538.17
547.25
750.27
851.07
894.06

quite
005.22
004.28
017.13
023.27
026.17
051.02
056.17
056.23
059.08
066.08
066.13
069.10
069.28
072.17
089.06
102.02
116.12
136.24
154.10
155.26
175.15
177.15
177.24
176.07
179.12
179.20
180.01
182.18
188.25
189.02
189.13
189.22
196.11
197.04
199.07
202.27
217.06
223.17
226.17
238.05
249.08
250.11
250.12
252.19
252.28
255.02
258.22
265.04
269.03
288.16
295.25
313.25
315.23
316.13
324.09
327.21
335.12
348.09
350.05
353.25
356.24
377.08
382.11
385.08
433.17
441.23
442.03
442.07
443.04
456.02
453.20
459.05
460.02
469.05
472.03
480.20

480.25
481.08
491.09
495.24
499.07
508.10
519.12
523.23
527.23
539.01
554.14
577.22
588.04
591.07
613.04
648.15
666.01
668.05
672.19
673.10
674.11
684.07
684.22
690.14
691.26
692.18
696.17
701.25
701.25
707.15
708.16
708.24
710.01
731.05
732.28
739.14
741.11
742.17
743.07
746.22
751.15
763.20
766.20
767.20
774.28
777.14
783.27
791.17
795.09
809.10
812.17
820.21
826.19
834.21
835.14
849.04
861.18
863.17
864.16
867.27
868.02
871.05
878.15
880.27
885.02
899.16
907.20

quitted
064.22
165.03
182.22
324.09
353.05
361.18
416.01
439.16
459.14
487.04
584.02
651.17
726.04

quitting
147.12
251.04
290.18
300.26
493.26
838.15

quiver
378.03
423.16
594.09

quivered
023.10
099.24
375.13
622.22
662.01
836.05
849.08

quivering
155.06
283.16
465.02
597.06
630.03
745.26

quiz
357.16
462.08

quote
  678.17
rabbit
  041.18
rapidly
  320.22
race
  021.28
  152.20
  208.15
  289.13
  354.24
  477.27
  551.07
  624.28
  719.22
  720.15
  759.24
  790.21
  911.20
racing
  865.07
racked
  053.13
  484.06
  808.11
racking
  717.05
racy
  065.19
  150.07
radiance
  139.21
  231.13
  343.26
  676.16
  720.06
radiant
  351.01
  501.03
  523.15
  642.14
  747.15
  749.26
rafters
  771.01
  860.01
rag
  043.24
rage
  405.14
  465.09
  526.27
ragged
  037.28
  522.06
raging
  355.24
ragout
  602.04
raight
  697.14
railing
  870.20
raillery
  387.16
rails
  281.17
  589.09
  592.01
raiment
  226.24
  558.10
  812.24
rain
  001.09
  003.15
  006.10
  021.03
  075.23
  079.27
  145.23
  169.12
  258.19
  364.19
  479.25
  519.10
  520.06
  559.23
  563.08
  565.02
  565.03
  572.20
  582.24
  611.16
  672.22
  674.23
  675.02
  683.04
  714.16
  714.25
  804.10
  852.09
  869.17
  871.07
  873.01
  886.27
rain-drops
  899.15
rain-refreshed
  541.24

rainbow
  343.26
  541.08
  551.17
rained
  189.11
  672.01
  871.16
rains
  680.02
  812.10
  859.25
rainy
  088.07
  384.20
  687.14
raise
  201.20
  462.23
raised
  026.13
  115.07
  213.18
  215.02
  217.15
  242.14
  308.01
  367.23
  395.03
  396.06
  465.19
  478.11
  484.27
  578.03
  609.02
  646.09
  656.24
  755.22
  802.25
raising
  730.25
rake
  614.07
  637.14
rakes
  493.27
raking
  542.02
rallied
  044.28
  123.12
  220.03
  552.17
  588.24
  675.08
rally
  485.16
rallying
  324.14
ramble
  148.15
rambled
  667.02
ran
  010.11
  043.14
  044.07
  083.13
  087.25
  088.10
  141.19
  142.09
  152.28
  168.17
  171.24
  175.02
  175.05
  222.26
  226.15
  284.01
  284.15
  288.11
  289.13
  327.21
  346.03
  378.22
  414.17
  415.19
  416.08
  416.19
  430.24
  445.15
  473.15
  493.23
  519.26
  522.01
  522.09
  538.11
  560.09
  561.20
  564.04
  564.13
  599.15
  640.27
  664.14
  739.04
  798.01
  829.25
  849.26
  856.14
  885.27

rancid
  094.03
rang
  035.12
  050.07
  080.11
  137.05
  168.17
  232.04
  255.11
  257.08
  381.05
  456.25
  567.08
  586.08
  874.02
  874.14
range
  113.03
  208.03
ranged
  084.05
  460.16
  557.08
  676.15
rank
  322.24
  351.13
  374.05
  400.13
  532.08
  621.04
  627.11
  912.03
ranks
  142.09
  145.25
  746.15
  790.05
  814.16
ransack
  357.21
ransacked
  365.18
rap
  260.03
  799.17
rapid
  018.07
  119.24
  220.03
  620.02
  691.04
  752.14
rapidity
  627.10
  744.04
rapidly
  073.10
  079.25
  113.07
  174.05
  415.12
  646.04
  714.06
  743.12
raps
  029.05
rapt
  742.23
rapture
  276.14
  653.26
  759.06
  871.22
rapture-giving
  775.14
raptures
  257.22
  325.11
rapturously
  175.17
rare
  204.25
  442.23
  497.13
rarely
  046.03
  275.14
  372.27
  642.07
rascals
  451.14
rash
  767.21
  770.16
rashly
  879.08
rashness
  625.11
rasselas
  089.28
  090.21
  101.20
rat
  008.24
  010.20
  010.20
  771.01
rate
  041.12

  049.01
  293.26
  313.07
  613.26
  726.18
  734.15
  852.05
  890.04
rather
  007.16
  012.06
  028.02
  028.24
  035.16
  043.24
  044.05
  055.24
  062.14
  068.04
  068.26
  069.20
  069.21
  069.24
  084.18
  093.22
  109.25
  132.06
  144.02
  161.17
  163.26
  164.04
  171.20
  183.15
  187.26
  188.27
  190.22
  195.13
  205.24
  208.14
  218.31
  236.18
  238.19
  241.15
  245.19
  247.25
  256.02
  258.07
  265.18
  267.04
  268.14
  269.14
  271.20
  276.07
  280.18
  287.01
  287.08
  291.27
  295.04
  299.27
  318.38
  343.08
  366.08
  372.18
  382.04
  394.06
  394.17
  395.07
  401.26
  402.24
  412.07
  429.14
  448.08
  454.04
  459.05
  462.01
  466.09
  468.13
  473.28
  493.25
  497.06
  504.24
  524.26
  530.19
  531.23
  533.06
  539.14
  549.27
  553.12
  554.22
  555.28
  557.11
  565.11
  574.07
  582.13
  600.02
  611.13
  612.17
  640.14
  642.14
  668.11
  673.17
  675.28
  690.17
  691.08
  691.12
  696.20
  701.03
  703.26
  722.07
  726.03
  726.20

  735.16
  740.03
  751.03
  757.03
  766.23
  772.18
  777.05
  778.10
  778.13
  778.15
  784.02
  825.18
  829.24
  830.14
  884.20
  888.27
  889.24
  889.28
  891.05
  891.10
  891.18
  896.25
ration
  113.25
rational
  104.17
  634.28
  784.01
rationally
  553.25
  553.27
rats
  201.09
  201.18
  771.04
rattled
  074.27
  777.26
rattling
  359.16
  432.15
  519.08
rave
  079.27
  406.08
  724.20
  857.08
raved
  617.15
raven
  322.12
  333.04
raven-black
  316.11
  871.28
ravenous
  082.16
ravenously
  672.15
ravens
  673.19
  673.20
ravine
  812.10
raving
  145.22
ravings
  633.07
ravished
  774.01
raw
  001.13
  061.13
  072.27
  112.02
  267.20
  459.18
  625.08
  890.17
rawness
  181.18
ray
  023.07
  071.08
  127.01
  299.08
  351.02
  617.26
  676.18
  738.05
  745.06
  856.07
rayless
  230.19
  607.23
  817.04
  877.23
rays
  250.21
  887.06
re-appeared
  388.10
re-arranged
  479.21
re-assuring
  884.06
re-enter
  276.21
re-entered
  093.26
  299.20

  370.11
  544.21
  548.02
  809.02
re-entering
  229.19
  839.12
  873.11
re-entrance
  379.11
  429.23
re-established
  223.19
re-exciting
  065.25
re-transformation
  262.04
re-transformed
  262.09
re-trodden
  526.24
reach
  162.03
  177.24
  215.07
  215.12
  274.23
  302.25
  397.06
  451.26
  494.02
  516.02
  603.22
  656.25
  660.17
  674.16
  806.11
  870.09
  895.22
reached
  073.02
  093.18
  129.18
  134.05
  140.11
  154.26
  182.21
  211.27
  215.03
  219.24
  224.17
  277.13
  312.27
  334.28
  383.18
  457.01
  505.01
  515.14
  519.28
  552.20
  603.12
  669.13
  675.24
  809.23
  812.19
reaching
  140.28
reaction
  065.07
  129.08
  690.26
read
  008.16
  010.03
  055.12
  060.05
  066.04
  077.12
  079.12
  080.14
  089.17
  093.24
  098.11
  101.19
  103.23
  105.10
  107.18
  114.09
  133.03
  140.08
  140.15
  170.22
  179.08
  189.14
  243.18
  266.03
  269.08
  292.21
  341.17
  372.14
  394.13
  482.07
  497.08
  516.24
  516.27
  536.12
  542.14
  542.14
  568.16
  571.16
  593.05

635.10
655.03
662.11
678.07
678.15
679.13
711.13
711.13
713.01
720.25
723.20
726.11
729.18
744.11
753.19
768.17
768.18
774.02
777.01
796.14
801.12
810.22
817.18
829.02
844.19
855.17
878.28
907.06
910.22
reader
085.08
150.12
165.27
181.04
182.01
217.12
247.15
292.09
347.03
350.06
372.01
372.23
523.16
555.17
586.17
612.06
651.01
657.10
669.25
670.17
672.02
696.12
702.06
745.06
775.09
780.01
796.15
808.23
823.11
834.26
837.24
844.27
845.23
858.04
872.10
902.25
905.03
907.21
readers
097.21
752.26
readily
023.11
040.07
169.08
456.07
readiness
170.14
198.07
205.01
792.11
795.07
817.20
reading
009.03
061.09
090.14
096.13
097.15
105.15
307.19
394.10
470.17
534.23
588.14
643.21
715.13
722.24
725.27
745.11
803.20
805.02
843.21
909.26
readings
244.20
ready
054.07
096.13
098.20
105.12

212.05
276.06
311.01
315.14
340.21
388.09
418.10
432.16
432.25
448.23
448.25
458.19
506.27
529.16
534.03
538.18
562.10
586.10
586.25
587.04
641.22
700.23
760.19
791.13
821.04
824.17
868.06
real
017.24
132.08
164.09
164.13
196.24
320.22
323.13
386.15
389.22
434.24
442.25
497.15
517.09
554.10
573.11
579.15
579.17
581.17
603.09
607.05
615.20
623.25
624.16
706.11
706.13
790.16
821.11
826.20
876.09
891.14
reality
017.20
078.10
398.04
521.04
581.04
828.06
832.15
877.25
realization
636.09
realize
250.11
524.14
738.10
realized
023.01
276.27
563.17
727.11
796.14
really
002.15
013.13
013.20
021.27
033.02
041.09
044.22
077.25
095.10
189.13
189.23
190.13
211.01
291.05
314.26
336.07
374.27
389.25
398.19
525.17
535.23
536.16
536.27
539.11
687.21
755.28
756.23
767.04
771.12
783.18
788.02

789.14
794.02
805.01
814.17
833.04
837.07
861.14
873.15
895.19
898.13
realm
031.27
realms
004.15
759.24
reappeared
183.05
rear
021.23
228.11
276.06
493.23
reared
045.06
126.13
249.01
439.01
762.24
770.26
rearing
741.06
reason
019.18
106.25
161.20
164.06
192.25
192.26
208.16
320.19
323.20
360.14
384.10
405.11
405.27
493.03
505.16
548.07
581.08
619.15
647.18
707.01
714.09
723.18
761.27
863.13
reasonable
214.02
476.12
555.23
620.06
622.20
834.06
reasoned
631.08
reasons
115.02
115.23
276.10
276.11
325.19
356.25
374.05
376.28
741.26
reassuring
186.16
rebecca
369.08
rebel
012.10
494.26
rebellion
848.03
900.05
rebellions
216.12
216.12
rebuff
284.23
389.16
763.21
rebuilt
089.11
rebuke
800.23
rebuking
289.18
recall
021.17
022.14
140.13
231.01
263.22
284.19
322.16
348.26
371.25
588.07
689.04
718.25

719.13
747.20
790.25
801.10
836.14
852.23
862.18
recalled
106.04
164.26
445.06
480.04
638.21
651.28
664.17
745.24
767.03
852.22
852.24
recalling
467.07
846.20
recalls
636.28
receding
674.11
receipt
727.23
receive
147.01
266.04
276.25
325.04
331.14
351.04
351.18
402.12
463.21
617.18
628.21
672.24
782.14
815.08
820.18
received
010.18
019.13
049.08
059.09
085.08
085.14
090.25
122.11
130.05
141.28
158.11
173.07
173.26
187.28
195.05
251.13
272.19
280.04
328.16
335.24
463.25
473.07
478.12
498.07
523.07
585.17
594.19
602.24
611.18
626.22
648.06
685.18
688.10
744.26
760.16
770.22
772.08
789.08
859.10
860.25
889.05
902.26
907.10
912.11
receives
330.01
receiving
059.27
259.04
266.09
291.18
832.24
recent
061.13
072.27
reception
187.18
238.05
291.04
799.14
802.03
reception-room
233.09
recess
236.24
339.23

503.21
796.14
803.26
recesses
146.06
825.22
recipient
285.17
recipients
400.24
reciprocate
150.07
reckless
101.10
636.18
773.05
857.25
recklessly
596.09
767.21
recklessness
647.24
reclaimed
673.15
reclined
002.03
236.28
recognise
132.27
246.04
367.12
592.15
736.28
recognised
115.08
133.27
175.14
237.07
281.14
367.26
421.09
600.14
773.26
817.23
839.06
871.16
recognises
592.23
recognising
286.19
recognition
460.18
617.26
642.20
recoil
193.05
616.07
621.06
recoiled
152.17
155.21
recollect
189.10
387.05
387.06
570.04
639.25
recollected
188.19
recollecting
324.14
453.11
recollection
136.04
465.21
484.06
629.08
637.26
670.22
689.02
802.09
recollections
014.12
047.25
172.08
273.08
410.14
615.11
615.16
704.21
755.20
recommence
440.06
recommenced
094.12
505.24
619.13
645.20
708.19
813.16
recommend
040.05
316.28
recommendation
040.06
172.12
600.25
recommended
242.24
449.04

recompense
056.01
reconcile
673.01
reconciled
465.14
484.22
724.21
727.09
reconcilement
900.18
reconciliation
830.05
833.01
reconciling
553.11
reconquer
834.17
record
088.26
108.17
402.07
526.16
593.15
recorded
160.02
635.25
records
092.01
recover
457.19
475.06
611.03
recovered
266.18
711.04
910.20
recovery
691.04
recreation
095.17
173.01
recriminations
727.08
recruit
603.02
recur
165.28
recurred
221.13
313.01
563.15
572.11
681.25
906.22
recurrence
445.21
580.02
red
003.05
015.23
015.27
026.04
026.18
046.17
051.02
074.17
092.22
119.27
136.01
204.17
258.14
385.04
394.05
407.11
502.05
545.19
576.03
602.06
630.01
red-haired
211.13
red-room
011.04
015.15
016.23
020.28
024.19
028.16
029.14
036.28
063.07
651.25
redd
885.21
redeem
753.11
redeemed
912.04
redeemer
655.27
720.21
903.25
redeeming
150.14
redness
492.28
676.16
redolent
094.03

reduced
447.23
544.03
redundancy
197.06
reed
001.06
001.18
006.05
006.13
006.24
007.01
008.04
010.22
011.03
013.04
014.08
014.19
014.20
016.18
016.26
020.08
020.22
021.16
021.22
021.24
022.10
024.15
025.12
027.07
027.12
029.16
056.27
057.15
037.18
038.18
038.26
040.04
040.22
042.10
044.05
044.12
044.18
044.24
044.28
046.08
048.19
051.16
052.10
052.19
053.18
055.06
056.12
056.27
057.24
058.24
060.13
060.15
061.11
061.17
062.07
063.01
063.11
063.22
064.03
064.18
064.21
065.11
067.10
069.16
073.16
107.25
108.10
115.25
124.05
133.02
134.25
136.05
165.04
173.11
176.12
176.25
177.01
177.13
184.15
184.18
446.09
448.17
450.23
450.23
450.24
450.24
451.01
451.06
451.11
451.13
451.15
451.16
454.15
457.15
463.01
463.05
463.20
465.26
456.06
468.04
468.18
459.24
470.07
480.14
480.16

483.15
490.24
544.25
649.11
770.27
771.04
780.06
847.28
reed's
005.21
008.25
018.10
022.19
035.27
038.28
051.20
053.25
062.10
065.22
072.04
179.04
344.21
465.06
485.24
reeds
030.04
178.20
179.22
471.05
reel
619.06
refectory
081.19
082.28
093.27
129.04
refer
355.11
489.27
646.17
reference
716.19
728.01
references
171.10
171.15
173.08
referred
475.27
603.18
677.18
referring
118.23
717.07
refilled
326.19
refined
007.17
086.08
139.02
529.26
641.15
720.11
760.28
832.18
885.02
refinement
625.21
730.09
refitted
802.02
reflect
183.28
300.13
388.27
634.07
780.20
reflected
037.24
038.22
135.14
312.11
408.08
555.23
610.22
666.03
673.18
763.10
797.13
reflecting
283.02
676.15
reflection
128.01
248.23
408.03
577.21
607.12
654.27
660.12
718.23
770.02
829.12
846.03
reflections
017.09
088.25
106.09
163.20
165.25

reflecton
065.14
reform
270.22
reformation
270.21
441.02
refrain
032.26
refresh
285.25
refreshed
631.12
705.27
887.20
refreshing
139.09
refreshment
087.16
268.25
629.24
664.26
refreshments
045.24
187.26
rett
732.18
refuge
331.24
798.23
812.28
refulgent
631.06
refurnished
794.23
refusal
835.09
refusals
847.14
refuse
434.22
438.15
448.28
702.21
742.06
828.20
841.11
887.23
refused
447.22
614.28
670.13
697.04
746.25
806.05
840.26
refuses
874.07
refusing
455.01
regain
664.27
683.28
770.08
833.16
regained
042.08
302.17
335.04
660.11
665.27
regaining
008.18
regaled
094.01
regard
020.11
177.27
195.22
214.21
288.28
484.10
506.09
510.23
547.24
611.26
614.06
638.06
638.20
744.21
745.02
745.03
804.14
821.22
regardais
334.06
regarded
130.19
136.08
138.20
166.08
290.23
345.03
466.10
696.16
697.05
714.20
717.15
751.18
785.02
786.25

842.01
842.12
regarding
141.16
787.26
834.07
regardlessness
858.03
regenerate
442.01
regenerates
440.04
regenerating
790.20
regeneration
161.25
440.28
631.17
regiment
740.04
region
153.14
153.15
158.10
158.14
185.01
210.06
212.01
328.18
334.17
384.20
regions
004.09
032.09
046.11
051.23
074.04
215.07
291.21
526.13
673.20
712.25
register
593.16
registering
108.22
registers
698.07
regle
171.27
regret
157.10
322.15
451.20
639.19
690.21
734.02
759.07
837.01
regretful
572.17
regretfully
896.04
regrets
192.23
717.05
717.06
regretted
002.07
101.06
192.16
272.27
regretting
163.18
regular
060.23
096.20
148.28
160.05
203.03
382.05
461.07
474.04
737.26
803.16
907.16
regularity
474.24
477.03
regularly
744.03
regulate
730.16
regulated
163.02
regulation
474.18
regulations
117.26
161.10
rehearsal
417.02
rehumanize
881.03
reign
098.13
511.22
753.11
reigned
066.09
294.20

503.01
660.08
rein
149.22
reins
405.12
357.06
reiterate
354.14
650.18
reiterated
295.07
392.06
409.25
618.19
reject
828.17
rejected
320.22
654.05
rejection
661.01
722.09
rejoicing
522.14
776.02
rejoin
796.22
rejoinder
238.26
260.03
rejoined
251.17
330.12
386.18
390.11
513.21
566.07
785.20
818.21
rejoining
901.03
relapse
090.26
relapsed
768.17
880.23
relapsing
485.15
relate
902.03
related
027.07
196.02
201.26
296.04
582.12
727.14
886.14
relation
062.21
291.26
727.03
727.18
781.18
relations
037.15
037.20
102.22
147.17
176.21
179.14
391.21
451.04
770.26
782.09
833.15
889.08
relationship
290.28
793.01
relative
122.15
349.07
659.18
775.26
relatives
038.16
252.08
444.09
454.19
491.01
587.06
625.12
647.15
relax
664.05
746.25
relaxed
147.04
302.15
382.06
607.14
released
480.02
547.05
650.04
releasing
228.04
relent
693.11

relentless
465.16
815.01
reliance
263.03
357.06
relics
066.15
207.16
relief
027.03
115.01
166.05
215.21
247.27
384.01
439.14
544.27
669.26
735.22
756.22
relieve
566.19
relieved
059.18
085.26
086.04
116.14
142.11
169.13
426.25
458.07
545.09
582.02
660.21
704.24
883.27
relieving
036.19
religieuses
243.27
religion
479.03
556.04
759.26
762.19
762.28
847.18
religious
243.22
489.03
573.24
relinquish
747.22
759.18
759.19
759.28
834.16
relinquished
082.24
173.15
872.28
relinquishing
112.14
791.20
817.22
relish
095.15
251.06
291.10
678.13
692.04
relished
459.11
relit
886.19
reluctance
719.05
910.05
reluctant
660.19
786.03
reluctantly
080.05
140.24
rely
157.22
remain
002.24
069.17
109.28
118.04
270.11
295.18
299.01
339.20
562.12
603.24
638.10
656.10
684.05
894.05
895.27
remainder
044.11
112.16
114.03
127.05
687.28
remained
130.24

REMAINED (continued)
161.24
169.03
171.04
256.16
256.07
265.27
297.26
314.17
346.18
347.02
557.13
574.25
673.25
869.10

remaining
719.17
833.16
884.15

remains
050.14
440.07
510.06
589.10
658.10
669.09
839.03

remand
529.28

remark
1 6.07
260.02
336.19
401.04
428.09
553.13

remarkable
047.22
217.24
237.06
462.06
637.15
905.13

remarkably
319.09
545.25

remarked
055.03
151.22
244.11
327.23
347.12
401.17
432.10
463.16
466.09
475.05
695.02
697.02
705.12
726.17
776.04
804.08
896.12

remarks
122.20

remedy
057.14
114.17

remember
021.18
026.02
046.26
047.26
059.28
063.05
072.09
074.05
091.11
095.09
103.14
111.20
113.06
127.26
164.16
193.14
211.18
241.23
299.03
313.08
313.08
313.09
322.12
351.24
356.01
371.01
371.18
402.15
422.20
446.07
446.12
449.26
465.06
500.05
507.08
547.14
567.12
583.22
583.24
598.10
602.09
624.03

625.24
647.23
650.21
698.04
779.14
821.26
839.03
846.10
846.13

remembered
115.24
164.09
164.28
191.07
221.17
235.14
294.13
313.10
382.17
420.11
461.04
544.22
549.17
613.20
629.07
669.01
695.19
502.21
679.16
703.24

remembering
662.15
695.24
833.13

remembers
199.27

remembrance
509.19
607.21
656.04
830.10

remercie
277.17

remind
201.20
271.14
493.03
507.20
592.22

reminded
218.07
229.17
259.09
344.20
542.23
578.09
806.24
872.05
886.18

reminder
354.23

reminding
342.21

reminds
504.23
881.03

reminiscence
491.10

reminiscences
473.21
618.06
634.05
643.24

remittent
479.12

remnant
625.25
661.06

remonstrance
539.07
627.02

remonstrate
121.14

remorse
065.07
270.17
270.18
271.15
271.16
406.02
612.09
621.11
732.01
815.12
900.17

remote
016.13
074.03

remove
054.25
147.17
187.01
347.01
542.27

616.01

removed
078.24
136.23
150.23
153.08
162.19
207.04
223.15
256.13
286.12
289.15
337.04
369.20
410.14
422.01
578.13
686.07
688.09
692.17
813.05
838.22
873.24
875.01

removing
157.08
617.28
766.11

remuneration
705.18
869.19

rencontre
254.14

rend
649.20

render
116.09
488.10
508.21
532.14
687.06
716.06
716.15
827.13

rendered
012.08
015.18
337.16
346.27
478.21
692.19
771.27

rendering
079.09
844.04

rending
029.19
514.05
613.08

renew
225.09
521.06

renewal
424.10
631.16

renewed
313.11
350.11
396.22
414.20
473.14
479.21
745.22
809.20
809.21

renewing
669.08

renews
894.22

renounce
645.12
747.27
774.11

renovation
798.27

renown
735.18
762.25

rent
414.15
578.14
683.19

rent-roll
403.17

rented
399.01

repaid
057.04
126.15
238.08
908.16

repair
117.03
163.19
174.13
340.05
413.05
618.05

repaired
236.07
315.15

562.02
728.05
771.03

repairing
446.01

repartee
260.20
554.07

repassed
209.14

repast
081.24
114.03
336.11
548.12
882.12

repaying
744.20
785.18

repeat
121.23
201.06
352.02
373.10
415.02
415.06
429.10
477.17
573.19
780.02
787.03
787.04
826.08
827.11
894.03
902.16

repeated
017.11
105.09
110.08
133.01
188.11
204.18
210.26
226.22
232.22
263.11
321.10
375.01
402.06
480.22
513.17
678.14
686.06
709.07
723.24
726.05
742.11
841.23

repeatedly
080.18
519.23

repeating
114.06

repelled
375.05
377.18
379.26
382.18
668.20

repent
015.10
055.02
827.10
846.09
848.02

repentance
270.20
627.03
829.12
900.17

repentant
440.24

repetitions
078.17
086.22
092.28

repine
734.08
753.01

repined
230.07

replace
604.16
760.18
819.12
853.17

replaced
236.08
277.04
758.13
900.23

replacing
118.14
763.28

repletion
257.14

replied
050.26
090.17
105.13
118.02

120.03
198.13
218.23
259.16
260.07
260.11
309.25
339.02
355.05
385.11
416.25
446.28
534.10
535.27
540.12
599.25
672.12
687.10
705.08
726.09
749.24
829.28
837.28
854.02
874.11
879.05
902.06
902.27

replies
168.02
882.27

reply
013.27
036.12
038.05
053.16
063.17
105.09
110.08
136.11
173.28
217.19
260.03
265.19
299.25
330.15
359.04
427.20
495.14
590.10
595.04
604.04
614.02
615.08
648.01
685.13
691.15
730.22
741.21
763.27
778.03
801.03
803.02
809.15
818.20
833.22
835.11
856.04
884.04

replying
006.26
223.08

report
600.04
750.07

reported
042.03
473.11

repose
154.07
174.20
207.20
219.12
290.22
399.16
441.01
506.20
584.04
659.20
692.08
721.06
738.04
898.07

reposed
133.21

reposing
209.09

repository
430.01

represent
368.21

representation
181.11
472.18

representative
751.10

represented
017.26
065.12
193.14
247.24

473.11

representing
470.28

repress
057.17
511.11
620.10

repressed
627.04
746.27
823.12

repressing
882.15

reprimand
030.12
141.04
464.18

reprimanded
159.09

reproach
014.14
611.23
626.13
697.06
837.04

reprobation
459.20
716.18

reproof
604.07
835.19

reproofs
122.21

reproved
019.13

republican
571.11

repudiated
629.01

repugnance
116.11

repulse
065.24
660.20

repulsed
057.04
670.24
672.04

repulsion
619.24

repulsive
025.06

request
182.13
218.06
239.08
264.15
316.24
326.16
338.23
368.26
455.02
488.13
529.27
530.10
534.03
665.17
665.23
670.08

requested
056.21
171.14
173.04
239.06
860.10

requesting
582.18

require
195.14
202.20
273.25
273.28
405.06
589.23
632.06
663.18
687.13
816.25

required
021.22
103.08
119.16
120.28
167.24
449.17
471.28
483.16
488.14
618.24
705.05
810.05
828.06
908.03

requirements
663.23

requires
772.19
821.05

requiring
810.08

requisite
  559.12
requisition
  233.09
rescind
  553.24
rescued
  706.07
rescuer
  650.15
research
  772.02
resemblance
  461.01
  642.14
  754.28
resemble
  290.02
  469.03
  787.10
resembled
  345.06
resembles
  358.27
  531.11
resent
  084.01
  708.25
resentment
  061.16
  135.20
  460.02
resentments
  108.03
reserve
  108.04
  114.02
  404.18
  703.28
  718.01
  748.02
  761.02
  802.11
reserved
  699.28
  715.05
  756.22
reservoir
  004.10
reside
  195.12
  705.01
  892.18
resided
  172.12
  771.09
residence
  384.15
  452.11
  695.22
  703.14
  750.18
  809.08
resident
  226.10
  241.04
  253.10
  293.20
  595.19
residents
  801.16
resign
  158.04
  819.02
resignation
  141.24
resist
  102.16
  107.06
  303.02
  431.27
  650.06
  734.19
  810.10
  824.02
  847.27
resistance
  623.09
  829.05
resisted
  012.02
  052.08
resisting
  588.02
  647.19
  810.09
resistless
  644.28
  740.28
resistlessly
  664.06
resists
  339.04
resolute
  276.01
  283.21
  426.03
  567.16
  597.05
  620.21
  649.16
  741.06

  747.07
  817.20
  911.16
resolutely
  498.14
resolution
  184.14
  273.06
  322.16
  475.02
  489.13
  609.18
  624.07
  631.03
  644.27
  834.27
  835.06
resolve
  019.20
  596.02
  838.14
  846.09
  850.22
resolved
  012.10
  135.12
  142.12
  263.21
  323.05
  360.05
  463.26
  466.15
  494.28
  570.23
  624.10
  628.28
  644.16
  646.12
  652.04
  686.19
  736.04
  774.10
  784.16
  788.01
  815.27
  845.09
  856.12
  867.06
resolves
  200.21
  518.18
  725.08
resounded
  449.14
resource
  167.13
  182.13
  666.05
  667.09
resources
  132.18
  365.16
  620.05
respect
  105.25
  129.16
  217.24
  315.08
  507.22
  528.14
  625.15
  642.21
  648.03
  751.06
  787.07
  827.04
respectability
  172.03
respectable
  037.26
  171.26
  189.01
  400.21
  790.04
  889.18
respectable-looking
  692.26
  860.16
respectably
  193.03
respectably-dressed
  665.14
respected
  018.19
  205.11
  405.24
  796.05
respectful
  099.18
  150.17
  325.06
  554.16
respecting
  052.23
  116.03
  123.18
  313.22
  365.15
  372.15
  570.05

  772.05
  798.25
  840.01
  908.19
respects
  757.02
respite
  891.02
resplendent
  331.09
respond
  912.24
responded
  041.07
  195.18
  321.22
  359.02
  472.15
  685.15
  691.11
  741.07
  754.05
  768.08
response
  036.22
  167.15
  360.12
  440.16
  497.11
responses
  160.07
responsibilities
  663.24
  775.24
responsibility
  059.18
  087.12
  431.10
  663.26
responsible
  116.01
  507.23
  846.22
rest
  033.21
  091.08
  093.15
  102.14
  147.12
  148.13
  152.21
  157.09
  164.19
  174.19
  185.20
  206.24
  208.16
  267.26
  272.09
  300.20
  303.03
  329.10
  337.28
  338.04
  342.27
  354.10
  360.02
  369.17
  374.23
  378.14
  399.27
  414.15
  415.06
  423.02
  439.22
  442.08
  457.26
  501.08
  524.11
  542.02
  543.19
  546.20
  620.26
  628.03
  656.26
  661.23
  664.22
  668.17
  668.17
  671.24
  676.02
  682.02
  713.17
  715.13
  760.27
  763.14
  770.09
  780.17
  792.23
  796.22
  797.10
  812.19
  826.25
  841.08
  848.25
  858.14
  886.16
  895.28
  900.28
  906.01

rest-seeking
  440.23
reste
  357.02
rested
  026.13
  130.23
  426.01
  450.11
  677.04
  758.17
resting
  133.19
  249.05
  369.25
  467.12
  692.22
  737.10
  796.22
resting-place
  493.05
  506.18
restless
  276.01
  441.12
  448.20
  558.25
  562.10
  635.08
  702.12
  719.06
  761.17
  883.05
restlessly
  467.11
  653.20
restlessness
  215.19
  724.20
  793.10
restoration
  732.23
  383.26
restore
  157.25
  685.20
restored
  146.04
  326.11
  459.13
  480.11
  703.15
restoring
  691.19
restrain
  147.09
  619.24
  686.10
  771.18
  793.16
restrained
  135.22
  627.01
  636.21
  665.26
  716.10
  825.28
restraining
  806.21
  871.23
restraint
  100.12
  216.18
  291.24
  315.10
  375.08
  538.28
  646.04
  882.15
restricted
  051.20
  641.13
restricting
  275.19
restrictive
  539.28
  617.20
rests
  858.11
result
  036.17
  078.16
  161.05
  167.19
  171.26
  196.25
  224.05
  250.06
  264.20
  312.25
  474.01
  516.05
  612.17
  638.16
  690.25
  713.25
  795.18
  807.25
  909.13
resulted
  112.07

resulting
  357.06
  404.13
results
  397.10
  439.12
  477.14
  581.16
  819.16
resume
  165.24
  246.21
  285.28
  370.10
  687.02
resumed
  084.04
  126.10
  137.01
  157.03
  242.16
  286.07
  361.17
  418.21
  447.28
  642.27
  710.04
  720.07
  768.13
  775.03
  780.22
  803.16
  811.12
  839.25
  861.02
  881.01
resurgam
  159.22
retain
  085.21
  575.09
  673.02
  747.20
  787.21
  822.16
  823.02
retained
  093.19
  161.15
  225.11
  302.10
  458.16
  891.20
retaining
  315.07
retaliation
  062.01
retire
  045.27
  190.14
  408.23
retired
  008.19
  129.05
  163.13
  170.24
  256.11
  341.15
  430.07
  554.13
  610.03
  650.09
  676.01
  848.25
  900.27
retirement
  003.06
  282.28
  475.08
  618.17
  618.17
retorted
  362.04
  512.25
retouch
  255.16
retrace
  656.13
  737.20
retraced
  419.25
retreat
  335.04
  549.23
  574.23
  616.21
  633.10
retreated
  025.11
  295.12
  417.26
  578.19
  601.02
  651.03
retreating
  422.23
  504.28
retreats
  207.19
retrospective
  018.08

return
  052.01
  058.14
  059.21
  061.20
  064.15
  102.27
  109.04
  112.24
  203.08
  214.05
  217.11
  228.09
  229.20
  251.14
  254.09
  261.06
  279.13
  294.22
  299.02
  300.19
  326.02
  326.21
  338.01
  342.19
  362.20
  366.09
  379.17
  392.04
  393.04
  416.14
  417.17
  434.09
  452.12
  490.19
  491.18
  492.09
  499.09
  503.22
  515.08
  547.24
  559.15
  565.21
  566.03
  567.22
  586.15
  586.25
  617.24
  637.22
  639.16
  645.02
  655.23
  660.09
  717.10
  716.18
  741.12
  768.11
  794.15
  799.05
  799.12
  800.07
  845.12
  846.01
  851.15
  886.27
  903.02
returned
  003.18
  009.05
  018.02
  039.23
  049.10
  058.05
  058.24
  074.24
  075.28
  082.26
  090.24
  099.10
  099.14
  113.02
  120.11
  127.24
  136.28
  137.22
  138.01
  173.14
  180.14
  187.22
  188.09
  208.09
  238.07
  243.06
  245.21
  272.06
  387.17
  388.15
  389.12
  389.24
  392.26
  397.19
  409.11
  411.11
  411.17
  413.17
  419.23
  428.12
  430.02
  430.24
  447.16
  454.26

489.20
542.26
559.09
567.19
586.18
593.23
643.26
665.01
688.04
699.12
702.14
726.14
742.13
803.12
804.04
804.22
806.08
813.03
821.22
860.09
874.06
875.09
returning
017.16
035.11
159.13
182.22
261.15
490.07
473.26
667.03
returnings
490.16
returns
371.27
381.23
422.07
802.19
reunite
782.22
819.11
rev
153.08
706.22
reveal
157.25
703.27
revealed
017.16
251.14
286.11
349.02
567.17
603.08
640.13
revealing
231.12
revelation
424.01
441.15
revelations
055.15
590.21
643.24
823.16
843.22
revelled
817.24
revels
242.12
revenge
213.24
revenge
109.18
403.25
revengeful
856.10
reverberation
029.16
reverence
224.25
347.07
512.03
reverenced
711.15
reverend
122.15
reverently
903.19
reverie
110.07
640.05
reverse
121.09
804.26
revert
273.09
320.03
322.13
revient
360.14
review
016.19
670.20
reviewed
290.06
320.08
revile
614.14
reviled
019.03

revisit
526.28
revisiting
022.17
revive
606.13
631.17
882.18
revived
100.11
166.12
290.16
350.12
426.23
465.22
579.03
613.01
692.07
revives
433.20
440.04
reviving
480.15
612.27
711.09
revolt
043.12
216.11
611.26
revolted
018.06
881.20
reward
133.06
651.08
651.11
715.09
755.03
790.13
897.22
912.14
rewarded
897.27
rewards
267.19
rhine
235.15
ribaldry
270.13
riband
093.02
ribs
510.25
874.21
rich
145.11
203.19
204.14
258.15
269.17
319.05
319.18
333.04
337.06
343.24
544.06
546.01
597.19
627.22
696.23
721.26
722.14
727.25
733.01
738.09
770.12
770.25
774.25
774.27
781.23
783.14
799.01
617.18
878.14
878.15
878.19
878.24
richard
422.10
429.09
431.22
432.08
433.18
437.07
593.18
richest
200.21
richly
317.14
343.17
richness
571.21
rio
040.12
278.01
477.06
627.26
637.11
638.15

riddle
397.12
ride
186.23
433.17
446.13
499.27
746.06
rider
222.07
229.08
741.06
riage
065.08
065.11
471.21
660.25
712.17
797.14
riaged
658.21
ridges
674.08
ridiculous
354.10
riding
224.10
riding-habit
333.01
right
003.08
017.07
037.08
059.08
072.17
073.28
103.15
105.18
105.28
115.20
186.26
240.06
265.09
265.21
268.06
268.18
269.01
270.26
271.10
273.24
274.15
274.16
274.18
295.26
325.08
356.24
357.08
357.10
371.09
391.11
401.18
401.20
405.25
408.05
417.01
417.01
437.13
437.18
448.16
453.12
453.13
476.10
489.25
496.28
499.28
511.20
538.03
538.04
551.11
552.02
553.06
555.13
560.24
562.23
598.01
598.18
610.12
610.12
622.10
630.15
631.10
664.13
666.28
668.22
669.07
671.07
705.11
708.16
710.01
725.16
727.21
732.04
732.22
785.07
797.24
814.11
816.02
825.08
827.14
848.19
852.02

872.23
881.27
896.13
906.14
909.18
righteous
897.27
rightly
273.10
614.03
rights
306.08
786.06
rigid
115.22
216.18
259.01
477.03
479.03
485.24
591.12
rigidly
035.18
rigorous
391.02
rigors
004.14
rigour
648.10
rill
233.19
ring
182.28
229.07
238.26
249.13
307.11
314.13
322.20
407.02
498.22
543.01
543.05
543.08
652.26
779.26
820.18
ringing
052.04
080.02
165.22
365.14
ringleted
045.19
461.08
ringlets
086.03
322.13
333.04
345.15
rings
242.04
306.19
369.07
525.05
543.22
727.21
riot
636.23
riots
740.05
ripe
143.07
504.01
561.24
605.24
661.08
752.10
ripened
627.09
ripening
503.15
ripple
398.08
521.12
ripplings
220.24
rise
013.05
022.22
044.10
101.13
120.22
130.09
166.05
233.04
295.08
331.28
349.18
351.07
371.12
476.13
428.27
506.19
511.21
603.13
607.18
648.10
685.03
692.01
692.09

700.19
720.03
735.25
740.26
761.28
775.21
857.09
883.11
885.13
risen
071.05
071.12
115.16
124.10
223.24
247.17
261.03
293.13
456.27
466.22
504.17
576.19
662.05
662.12
737.13
riser
195.04
rises
540.25
856.28
rising
127.20
133.23
146.18
149.07
220.11
229.11
248.15
256.19
276.23
277.18
285.03
342.04
361.25
367.20
369.16
432.20
446.08
471.04
471.07
502.10
542.21
561.03
572.08
580.10
588.08
645.23
655.12
661.16
757.22
818.21
833.22
887.06
898.28
risk
171.24
335.10
420.07
508.09
510.20
618.25
745.16
risked
727.06
824.04
risking
299.14
risks
636.16
rite
456.14
rites
476.01
792.08
rival
286.24
360.06
rivalries
625.10
riven
560.13
661.25
river
607.16
765.13
828.27
909.22
rivers
695.23
695.27
696.02
697.25
702.22
706.03
706.22
707.20
708.05
717.01
719.01
719.21
722.19

723.15
724.26
726.22
727.20
728.02
728.04
736.27
737.05
738.17
740.02
741.19
742.24
746.17
748.27
751.05
751.05
752.15
754.03
754.15
766.01
771.17
773.13
776.07
777.08
779.02
779.13
783.06
783.27
789.18
790.14
799.20
892.21
893.08
894.18
895.02
895.20
911.05
911.14
rivers'
697.28
698.05
733.07
889.09
rivet
814.23
riveted
017.05
349.15
592.16
701.23
726.07
rizzio
358.14
358.16
road
072.26
074.08
113.02
164.23
164.27
169.18
184.21
209.08
214.27
218.28
280.06
332.10
370.24
370.25
492.05
492.15
492.15
492.20
493.01
494.01
495.06
541.17
541.21
557.10
562.18
562.22
572.20
572.25
575.11
575.24
654.23
654.25
655.15
656.25
663.27
664.18
673.18
675.12
735.07
799.27
811.20
854.24
870.16
roads
111.11
185.04
501.10
658.13
659.05
854.17
roam
715.26
roamed
265.14
504.27

roaming
229.13
668.15
864.01
roar
559.25
roared
518.28
562.21
roaring
328.03
roast
041.20
142.26
906.02
roasting
905.18
rob
614.10
robber-path
551.09
robbers
310.07
416.04
robe
277.09
343.17
344.24
369.01
449.28
526.01
558.10
761.23
robed
565.13
robert
175.25
180.13
446.12
446.22
447.28
448.25
457.09
458.01
458.14
706.22
robes
200.21
271.23
359.07
372.09
robin
050.11
robing
276.20
robust
080.17
465.24
629.14
804.21
rochester
195.11
195.16
195.20
198.19
198.26
198.27
199.10
202.01
202.03
202.12
205.03
206.17
206.17
226.08
232.10
232.24
233.02
234.06
234.12
235.07
235.21
236.05
237.01
237.17
240.20
242.16
243.06
244.15
245.22
246.12
249.19
251.15
252.11
252.19
253.01
254.03
255.09
256.03
257.26
258.08
258.20
260.19
266.07
277.14
279.02
289.27
290.06
292.08
296.11
297.02

305.03
307.27
312.09
312.19
313.06
316.06
316.08
316.24
317.13
317.26
318.25
318.27
319.08
319.18
319.21
319.26
320.04
321.02
322.14
322.26
322.28
324.03
325.25
326.21
332.07
332.25
333.14
336.01
336.03
336.21
337.14
338.03
338.09
338.20
339.18
339.26
346.22
348.18
350.23
350.28
352.24
353.05
353.10
353.28
355.04
358.02
358.28
360.10
361.10
361.27
365.11
365.26
366.22
367.07
367.17
368.05
369.27
370.11
371.05
371.20
372.02
373.25
374.28
379.06
380.14
381.07
381.20
383.02
383.08
384.18
384.21
401.10
401.18
401.22
402.09
402.12
402.27
403.10
407.16
408.19
409.05
409.17
410.27
412.24
415.16
415.17
416.11
416.17
418.03
419.08
420.19
421.08
421.13
421.20
422.17
424.28
425.04
425.05
425.11
426.04
427.01
427.11
428.06
428.10
429.05
430.09
432.01
433.11
433.15
434.04
438.10

440.22
449.07
449.14
449.24
450.06
450.06
452.20
453.20
456.06
472.18
487.02
491.16
492.05
493.16
494.07
496.02
496.22
497.08
497.28
498.25
499.15
499.26
503.20
504.28
505.14
508.13
512.05
513.17
515.02
516.21
519.01
519.17
520.08
521.05
522.26
523.20
524.04
524.05
524.06
525.28
527.05
532.26
533.09
534.22
535.21
536.24
537.11
537.14
538.06
538.13
538.26
541.03
543.17
543.25
545.02
545.07
547.01
555.18
557.12
557.15
557.16
557.18
559.08
562.04
571.17
576.22
580.17
583.08
585.04
585.18
587.07
588.19
589.11
589.22
590.14
590.22
591.11
592.04
592.10
593.09
594.07
594.15
595.01
595.21
596.09
596.22
598.14
599.23
600.16
601.02
601.18
602.12
603.01
603.07
604.05
605.09
606.21
611.05
621.26
622.12
623.15
645.16
645.18
647.03
648.21
650.20
652.28
653.25
657.03
661.26
662.13

662.23
673.03
745.17
771.16
772.13
772.15
772.22
773.01
774.13
774.16
774.17
808.22
819.05
838.27
839.01
849.22
855.17
856.02
860.05
861.03
861.11
862.23
863.07
863.15
864.13
865.13
865.26
867.16
869.05
871.04
871.17
873.09
873.21
875.07
883.09
890.25
891.08
891.23
897.24
899.04
905.09
906.16
907.06
907.22
909.14
rochester's
196.07
196.15
204.24
226.07
236.20
239.03
253.20
294.16
296.04
299.15
305.16
314.05
314.15
315.17
318.09
324.18
345.10
347.13
366.26
375.11
376.16
381.27
401.15
403.19
411.13
413.06
424.07
425.18
503.13
504.05
519.09
524.06
534.27
571.23
587.12
587.22
595.22
599.02
606.18
609.09
613.08
653.16
731.16
771.20
809.08
860.23
862.21
903.01
907.13
rochesters
196.03
205.13
208.14
536.06
589.07
rock
004.22
005.11
164.22
592.11
615.06
615.06
761.16
816.14
820.12

827.17
872.13
rocking
063.24
693.17
rocking-chair
676.28
rocks
003.24
033.08
143.04
282.15
471.04
812.20
911.18
rod
100.03
102.17
rode
222.08
254.08
332.27
338.04
380.22
564.08
638.23
roll
050.03
050.16
073.07
335.01
578.03
661.06
670.08
rolled
145.18
281.10
302.20
575.15
576.02
590.23
657.09
847.19
848.18
rolling
039.24
247.24
rolls
335.22
665.06
roman
010.02
276.07
344.13
489.06
romance
228.17
549.23
749.06
romances
202.18
romantic
185.03
211.15
217.12
664.10
745.16
rome
010.03
431.11
489.11
526.21
636.01
romping
020.20
roof
043.03
045.06
208.26
333.25
364.05
459.19
459.23
615.02
618.03
652.04
671.22
704.07
707.22
711.17
715.22
733.01
802.18
859.06
865.20
865.28
roofs
194.19
rook
588.09
rookery
194.05
220.07
856.19
856.24
rooks
194.26
522.12
room
006.06
016.12

017.12
023.05
027.05
027.26
030.06
032.13
035.22
035.28
046.08
046.12
046.16
049.12
050.01
061.20
061.26
074.15
076.06
078.04
078.20
080.05
080.10
081.01
081.15
081.20
083.17
083.26
084.06
085.10
085.19
087.14
099.14
103.01
116.13
121.27
122.14
127.01
127.08
130.15
134.01
136.01
150.24
153.18
153.19
154.10
154.16
154.28
159.14
163.14
165.26
167.20
170.16
181.05
182.14
185.27
186.06
187.15
187.24
190.06
190.16
191.07
191.17
198.28
202.11
202.26
203.14
203.23
212.06
217.09
229.22
231.20
236.07
240.26
251.05
251.17
258.13
276.08
276.19
277.13
292.12
296.21
297.14
298.08
300.19
306.09
308.37
315.15
342.21
349.12
362.03
367.25
375.20
379.09
380.06
383.14
384.03
387.21
392.17
392.24
398.16
412.01
412.22
413.02
413.08
415.08
415.27
418.05
419.17
420.11
420.17
422.04
422.21

423.06	561.05	849.07	295.05	638.17	170.17
430.06	561.23	850.06	296.09	682.22	274.02
430.20	896.18	850.22	298.02	row	743.13
430.21	rope	851.02	322.18	113.20	907.26
430.28	601.14	856.19	334.24	284.03	rumbled
435.25	rosamond	903.12	342.28	557.08	629.27
436.10	742.03	903.19	351.22	719.18	rumbling
446.01	746.04	rose-coloured	365.27	rowland	664.17
450.10	750.20	277.03	367.02	252.19	798.01
464.08	750.28	rosebuds	367.06	253.02	rummage
464.17	752.06	030.20	368.13	rows	009.13
479.14	753.28	277.06	386.28	079.20	rummaging
481.17	755.28	roses	397.19	085.11	122.16
486.13	758.02	143.06	421.02	207.10	749.09
488.17	758.26	148.04	423.14	210.02	rumour
497.17	759.15	219.08	433.01	676.15	500.01
519.16	759.16	367.06	440.18	royal	507.09
534.09	801.07	494.03	446.28	358.13	516.02
538.14	801.14	525.22	458.23	887.11	862.11
540.06	895.06	529.22	467.12	rub	run
554.15	rosamond's	605.25	497.25	791.25	006.10
562.14	750.14	740.18	501.09	rubbed	010.22
572.04	751.17	rose-wood	503.14	331.03	176.23
580.12	rose	701.13	524.27	545.28	225.24
581.05	016.05	rosy	528.20	751.27	235.04
582.09	017.07	192.18	529.24	rubbing	297.24
599.03	080.05	427.14	538.19	193.19	297.25
599.09	081.26	523.14	539.27	306.13	326.12
599.14	085.01	640.24	545.03	rubbish	336.11
604.11	086.28	676.26	560.01	221.12	400.05
605.14	094.03	rotten	561.17	859.26	416.05
612.25	099.22	082.21	561.23	rubicon	430.21
613.18	115.11	284.14	564.09	125.08	562.16
613.26	126.27	roue	565.04	rubric	594.11
613.27	127.11	286.16	575.17	474.10	619.07
629.26	152.05	rouge	580.11	ruby	663.09
633.02	154.07	370.23	580.18	204.17	857.04
639.26	162.08	rouges	588.09	ruddy	864.12
641.09	168.02	313.17	588.16	077.21	rung
650.23	191.12	313.17	607.12	100.17	060.12
651.17	191.25	rough	609.03	231.08	282.03
653.08	192.08	028.04	627.26	586.10	366.28
653.22	215.25	109.27	631.07	738.06	running
655.21	220.07	221.01	641.22	881.27	019.23
676.13	223.12	230.06	663.05	rude	023.23
680.06	226.25	370.03	665.07	015.02	050.18
680.09	248.25	387.12	667.02	038.01	197.02
689.06	249.03	579.13	668.15	220.24	212.01
692.21	262.20	640.26	712.26	261.06	234.04
700.26	274.18	675.19	730.28	261.19	255.25
701.03	283.19	697.18	747.12	rudeness	287.17
701.11	294.03	712.22	765.16	462.12	335.09
703.12	295.04	730.03	796.23	531.22	336.15
704.23	303.03	rough-coated	798.18	rue	365.13
729.03	315.27	383.05	807.06	612.06	387.16
752.12	322.22	rough-looking	809.26	rued	391.08
757.13	326.08	676.20	814.01	612.05	408.16
792.02	341.25	rougher	814.20	ruffian's	437.20
796.10	342.19	735.09	815.03	370.23	445.13
803.18	347.06	roughly	818.11	ruffle	451.24
805.11	367.20	063.06	857.15	462.20	520.13
829.15	371.04	roughness	859.21	rug	646.16
845.25	388.08	225.10	870.15	052.16	736.23
847.23	388.23	round	896.21	053.27	866.28
848.26	414.12	002.02	896.06	054.27	runs
849.16	423.21	004.02	899.18	064.27	105.07
851.07	432.06	023.05	904.03	231.23	199.20
852.20	435.12	046.14	909.23	262.17	276.15
864.06	443.06	047.12	910.11	394.16	570.14
874.27	459.23	067.14	rounded	404.02	rush
882.10	461.21	075.06	407.01	460.11	018.07
886.04	463.16	076.09	567.02	rugged	026.07
886.06	469.24	078.07	roundly	553.21	221.24
886.11	503.10	078.24	083.14	715.21	509.17
901.05	515.14	079.05	612.20	ruin	559.25
room-door	521.02	085.26	rouse	474.27	604.23
006.03	537.02	086.01	168.17	560.22	614.16
rooms	549.24	086.19	299.14	560.23	660.05
051.22	551.19	088.05	582.18	574.23	673.29
122.17	552.13	089.03	877.24	579.18	745.12
147.25	570.17	095.04	roused	655.28	812.08
161.07	572.01	097.15	043.11	792.01	847.03
204.20	579.04	101.18	139.12	803.06	rushed
205.01	583.22	105.06	159.06	858.25	023.22
207.01	583.22	112.27	192.02	861.18	228.12
208.01	587.05	120.22	297.02	896.13	276.18
209.27	600.04	126.24	371.26	896.16	296.05
210.23	610.15	132.22	406.26	ruined	296.16
327.11	643.17	133.20	414.09	447.13	415.20
331.15	646.10	134.22	445.25	451.18	519.10
334.13	646.25	137.12	512.25	478.14	551.26
417.12	649.05	141.14	518.08	727.07	631.01
449.08	652.23	152.19	535.03	ruining	651.14
650.10	662.03	158.15	828.02	280.03	773.05
721.22	663.15	159.16	843.18	ruins	779.21
766.26	674.28	164.24	850.08	143.04	812.21
798.28	675.07	173.17	rousing	867.18	850.21
869.12	675.27	182.05	137.03	rule	rushing
root	680.04	185.26	routine	038.28	023.20
278.02	681.20	186.06	165.13	107.20	075.09
762.23	723.12	191.03	474.21	350.03	rushlight
893.22	732.10	194.03	rove	641.13	080.04
rooted	737.22	194.13	105.01	846.27	096.03
043.05	745.25	203.24	544.05	ruler	russell
618.28	754.23	222.25	roved	355.28	624.11
656.05	756.14	229.05	635.26	rules	626.08
roots	763.10	229.13	674.05	103.23	russet
008.12	777.08	240.26	rover	111.05	066.15
151.26	782.13	256.19	747.24	117.11	219.21
510.11	827.16	260.03	roving	147.04	rustic
560.16	845.19	277.14	067.20	164.08	438.09

677.10	sadly	127.02	314.03	474.09	635.22
746.14	505.09	127.07	315.18	475.01	635.25
789.10	867.19	130.16	316.04	475.24	647.21
rustics	sadness	131.10	321.01	480.27	649.09
743.15	027.28	131.25	321.13	481.01	650.04
rustle	032.24	134.01	324.04	481.11	650.23
219.15	133.12	134.22	325.02	482.08	651.06
rustling	621.02	136.09	325.28	483.15	653.11
024.17	716.23	137.03	326.13	483.21	657.05
552.06	886.17	137.06	326.20	483.28	661.12
441.16	safe	137.19	329.26	484.12	667.23
576.13	047.02	138.14	330.09	484.25	670.14
rusty	191.09	142.01	332.05	485.05	671.13
094.05	215.22	143.15	332.12	485.22	672.19
264.27	310.14	149.22	334.01	487.10	678.03
ruth	320.13	153.19	334.04	488.15	678.12
060.24	399.15	158.18	338.07	489.17	679.09
465.12	436.02	167.01	338.08	489.25	679.11
832.27	438.05	170.15	338.21	491.21	680.08
832.27	455.17	173.11	338.25	491.23	682.09
ruthless	475.10	174.26	345.23	493.08	682.18
375.08	520.09	175.18	346.01	497.17	684.01
594.23	644.21	175.23	347.07	497.25	684.07
610.16	662.05	177.26	354.04	497.26	685.14
ruthlessly	662.23	178.21	354.26	498.28	686.10
717.08	722.13	178.21	357.12	499.09	687.06
s	753.05	179.19	357.25	499.14	687.08
738.27	896.22	179.24	361.05	504.17	687.18
740.03	safely	183.15	361.10	504.23	687.26
749.22	274.12	185.08	362.24	505.02	689.14
794.06	616.04	185.24	366.01	506.15	690.25
801.16	633.01	186.25	370.14	507.21	691.01
801.25	905.12	187.16	376.15	509.11	693.14
802.01	safety	190.02	380.22	509.23	694.04
sa	123.01	195.03	380.26	510.22	694.28
499.03	570.06	195.09	381.19	512.21	696.17
sabbath	632.09	197.08	383.21	514.13	697.03
114.01	649.02	197.12	384.22	515.04	697.11
114.01	658.09	201.05	385.06	515.15	697.25
sable	671.28	202.03	385.28	517.25	699.03
249.07	847.21	203.14	387.12	516.05	699.21
260.25	sagacious	204.21	387.18	518.11	700.21
652.10	642.03	208.13	388.09	519.01	702.18
675.25	sagacity	211.17	388.13	519.05	703.01
sable-clad	373.27	225.17	388.24	519.20	703.13
052.15	sage	225.20	389.19	523.04	704.16
sacques	274.06	227.01	390.27	523.11	705.14
365.20	sago	227.20	391.28	524.05	706.03
sacred	311.08	228.04	393.01	527.03	708.01
507.11	said	231.27	395.11	530.08	708.07
552.07	002.01	234.20	396.08	533.28	708.16
595.10	006.16	235.23	397.23	535.24	708.27
747.12	006.20	236.14	397.27	535.26	709.05
751.19	008.21	237.22	398.05	537.10	709.10
sacrifice	009.27	237.26	398.13	538.05	709.21
406.03	013.09	239.03	401.26	539.20	710.01
503.11	013.19	239.13	402.19	540.09	717.20
725.08	013.25	240.20	405.23	541.04	718.06
742.22	014.06	240.22	408.20	542.17	718.17
747.13	015.04	242.07	409.01	542.23	719.11
756.06	019.18	242.27	409.09	543.01	720.04
806.03	021.09	243.09	409.22	543.10	720.23
817.24	023.26	245.24	410.12	543.13	721.02
820.01	033.23	246.09	410.27	544.15	722.21
820.23	033.24	246.12	411.17	545.21	725.09
823.05	033.29	246.20	416.21	546.08	726.01
898.03	034.20	250.28	419.10	547.15	726.17
898.04	034.27	251.08	420.06	547.27	726.21
898.04	035.01	251.15	420.18	549.09	727.01
898.08	035.14	256.02	421.01	549.26	736.17
898.09	037.19	257.06	421.13	558.07	738.25
sacrificed	039.19	258.11	421.15	558.18	739.06
847.22	040.08	259.14	427.03	560.22	740.21
sacrifices	041.05	259.22	427.25	560.25	746.27
880.10	044.18	261.10	428.09	562.16	750.15
sad	047.13	261.15	428.16	567.01	750.25
051.17	052.28	264.05	429.03	567.05	751.06
046.01	053.20	264.14	429.04	567.11	752.17
054.04	053.26	266.11	429.08	568.18	753.17
057.20	054.23	267.13	430.04	569.11	754.03
125.12	055.05	268.06	430.26	573.21	754.25
135.16	057.21	270.20	432.05	573.24	757.01
135.19	058.20	271.15	432.27	580.10	757.12
140.26	061.11	272.05	433.15	583.08	758.16
141.24	067.04	272.13	434.14	586.01	760.03
152.10	067.14	272.26	438.12	588.05	761.05
364.06	067.20	273.10	441.23	590.17	762.11
398.23	068.05	274.18	442.06	590.25	763.06
404.11	072.04	279.09	446.08	591.03	766.15
500.04	072.08	279.15	446.26	594.16	767.23
522.16	076.24	283.28	448.20	595.16	767.26
561.19	081.09	284.06	448.27	598.14	769.26
655.03	082.13	290.07	449.24	599.05	771.18
661.24	085.15	293.18	450.11	599.22	772.11
680.12	087.02	294.11	451.04	600.16	773.15
723.05	090.03	299.21	451.13	601.21	774.06
724.26	092.07	300.01	453.05	602.16	776.06
747.07	092.16	300.23	453.12	609.08	776.21
808.19	101.22	300.28	455.01	611.07	777.10
869.16	103.21	302.06	457.13	614.21	777.25
895.22	104.21	302.14	458.05	614.26	778.12
910.02	108.08	307.09	458.22	619.05	778.20
saddened	108.15	307.16	460.05	620.04	779.05
001.15	113.11	307.25	463.08	620.17	779.28
101.08	116.14	308.08	463.18	621.01	780.19
574.07	117.08	308.15	464.13	621.09	783.12
saddest	119.24	308.27	465.25	621.14	783.14
052.27	122.24	309.17	466.26	624.22	783.18
saddle	123.14	310.28	467.15	630.13	785.12
228.01	124.08	313.15	468.03	630.21	790.22
564.12	124.21	313.25	469.19	631.22	791.17

792.17
793.08
795.22
796.17
798.19
801.14
801.22
802.26
807.01
810.01
810.03
811.05
811.14
812.19
813.09
813.23
815.20
816.01
819.12
821.05
821.21
821.26
821.27
823.09
824.10
825.01
826.18
827.07
827.25
828.10
829.20
829.27
831.03
834.06
834.25
835.28
836.08
836.15
837.07
838.09
839.03
839.17
841.22
843.01
846.01
849.15
853.13
853.24
853.27
862.13
863.13
866.25
867.07
871.05
873.04
873.13
874.03
874.09
875.06
875.10
875.14
875.27
876.24
860.03
861.04
861.12
862.17
863.03
866.26
868.19
890.11
897.04
905.08
906.02
906.08
907.05
907.25
910.10

sail
179.28
416.28

sailed
127.01

sailing
857.21

sails
813.19

saint
823.17

saint's-day
479.02

sake
119.03
244.06
253.04
264.06
412.18
412.19
415.17
430.13
525.15
530.23
531.06
537.17
600.10
663.03
715.26
837.02
869.07

salamander
551.18

salary
171.13
173.02
266.20
267.06
267.08
325.05
351.18
452.25
721.23

salient
206.14

sallow
382.01
384.11
460.21

sallowness
007.17

salon
198.28
334.05

saloon
340.28
341.08

saloons
331.04
364.15

salt
030.01

salt-drops
887.14

salts
419.20
419.20
419.24
422.09
426.11

salubrious
269.01

salutary
787.12
891.01

salutations
745.01

salute
607.22

salvaton
125.25

sam
385.18
387.03
387.07
387.17
388.07
388.14
388.15
390.26
392.14
393.01
393.04

sam's
390.27

same
009.11
014.14
027.17
035.25
039.05
039.23
040.17
041.13
043.03
043.11
054.22
061.18
065.11
097.13
112.26
115.16
122.28
142.24
158.10
158.11
162.25
165.26
174.08
217.02
217.02
247.08
248.24
259.11
286.21
309.01
344.18
345.17
345.18
345.18
380.17
382.13
400.05
400.06
410.10
451.16
456.08
459.23
473.16
477.24
533.20
535.26
590.21
626.07

638.06
686.05
712.25
712.26
721.28
729.07
737.09
759.01
775.17
778.27
780.01
781.05
797.28
802.18
803.18
814.01
814.02
854.19
871.26
894.04
905.20

samson
529.02
872.09

samson's
619.11

samuel
055.16

sanctifies
440.12

sanction
509.12

sanctioned
648.04

sanctions
518.20

sanctity
280.20
819.02

sanctuary
618.06

sanctum
331.22
331.23
906.19

sand-traced
808.26

sandal
361.22

sandals
277.08

sanded
676.14
729.04
779.03

sandwich
187.06

sane
648.06

sang
032.17
032.25
070.03
201.03
318.24
318.26
319.05
337.07
346.08
379.01
440.20
522.13

sanguine
020.19

sanity
013.24

sank
021.06
027.27
046.17
087.04
109.22
114.21
129.10
220.09
286.22
391.14
425.09
470.08
500.08
608.12
665.24
674.20
683.21
730.24
745.07

sans
540.11
540.12

sap
560.14
639.14

sapphire
812.12

sarah
028.19
028.26
435.23

sarcasm
377.17
823.12

sarcastic
256.02
441.26
824.07
824.07

sarcastically
357.26

sardonic
292.15
375.15

sardonically
436.27
492.06

sarvant's
695.01

sash
050.16
050.23
340.14
341.26
343.10

sash-like
368.12

sashes
045.19

sat
003.03
022.11
027.01
027.25
029.23
038.24
040.09
046.13
049.04
066.03
082.09
084.06
101.26
123.03
123.23
129.06
130.22
133.21
138.24
139.22
151.10
154.18
155.14
167.01
174.18
186.08
186.13
188.22
219.24
220.11
221.08
223.24
238.05
241.27
248.01
250.02
258.20
264.05
280.14
280.26
294.03
306.21
317.27
329.12
332.03
334.23
337.04
340.18
341.14
347.20
366.13
369.24
382.25
383.12
383.17
384.12
387.01
398.10
402.09
410.08
418.11
421.05
457.08
461.25
462.16
466.24
472.24
478.17
498.24
515.02
519.02
535.18
539.27
542.02
544.22
550.17
566.11
575.22
604.18
611.05
620.08
650.27
659.25
667.06
671.20

676.28
688.05
700.28
702.10
710.06
715.11
756.14
767.03
769.24
803.17
805.02
808.19
810.19
811.06
813.14
823.24
844.01
844.05
873.18
886.15
892.24

satan
424.02

satiety
692.07

satin
032.15
277.03
277.08
286.13
322.22
331.13
340.14
340.19
343.17
343.24
365.20
525.21
544.07
544.14
545.27

satin-smooth
523.14

satirical
345.20

satisfaction
143.14
166.10
341.26
713.05
775.21
804.06

satisfactorily
546.13

satisfactory
171.10
171.22
440.16
773.20

satisfied
100.12
138.21
168.13
174.01
216.07
554.26
581.21
582.01
661.12
751.24
787.03
795.16
823.04
855.15
880.01

satisfy
134.20
517.19
778.01
819.24
819.25

saturdays
016.16

saturnine
345.19

saucepan
599.13

saucer
326.10

saul
885.18

savage
031.18
064.13
107.10
414.16
518.07
578.02
649.19
812.25
826.16
864.16
864.16

save
125.24
258.17
398.27
562.19
562.24
571.22
647.25

662.18
701.12
723.01
732.27
764.07
793.19
853.26
854.03

saved
301.04
301.10
330.04
701.16
718.02
782.19
833.14
861.22

saving
048.14

saviour
662.22

savourless
478.22

saw
008.05
009.19
010.13
014.03
024.05
028.24
035.24
036.11
043.09
043.17
050.02
057.12
075.14
079.10
079.17
080.20
081.22
082.23
083.02
086.13
089.25
090.22
094.15
104.24
109.23
123.27
143.02
151.08
152.19
155.12
155.26
163.10
172.01
172.09
175.09
180.18
183.13
183.15
185.11
185.12
217.08
223.17
229.03
229.10
239.16
242.19
247.18
254.02
254.20
257.18
283.14
285.01
292.01
300.01
301.23
302.21
306.10
306.17
313.28
317.20
317.22
317.28
318.14
328.26
348.27
350.24
350.28
353.22
362.14
372.07
374.04
375.09
377.17
376.12
382.10
392.14
403.26
407.04
411.09
420.11
421.10
425.10
429.05
456.26
473.26
488.12
490.25

492.03	044.12	595.08	038.18	322.22	543.16
494.13	044.14	596.19	055.25	343.24	schale
498.07	055.09	596.21	055.26	368.12	678.26
499.02	062.04	603.10	069.22	450.01	scheme
499.10	062.13	606.24	105.03	541.08	168.11
502.15	062.25	614.11	107.19	scarlet	759.18
531.13	069.14	614.11	125.28	003.07	828.08
534.05	069.24	615.03	137.23	045.19	828.10
536.23	072.13	615.05	153.05	634.09	843.13
537.27	072.20	618.15	240.07	scatcherd	scheming
552.13	092.13	620.06	326.23	092.26	040.14
555.15	103.06	621.09	352.19	093.10	614.25
564.07	103.18	622.27	385.18	094.17	schiller
571.10	103.25	627.07	386.03	097.20	749.11
575.19	106.08	638.12	386.09	097.27	805.03
577.21	107.21	640.22	387.19	098.22	scholar
578.01	115.01	653.24	388.16	099.17	713.23
578.18	123.17	655.22	457.17	100.01	806.09
580.14	125.06	666.11	702.19	100.21	890.10
585.13	135.03	670.18	741.09	102.11	scholars
588.16	135.10	679.17	877.12	103.21	722.22
595.16	135.15	680.17	884.01	104.01	729.17
595.22	153.04	682.10	911.28	104.07	731.07
610.02	176.11	684.25	912.22	105.02	733.22
615.25	187.04	684.26	scaffold	108.13	739.12
619.20	188.08	696.13	655.14	110.05	743.06
625.02	189.03	704.03	scalding	128.05	744.09
627.24	192.24	708.09	141.23	141.01	745.11
629.05	192.25	712.11	657.12	141.11	749.15
651.17	199.05	714.22	scale	141.18	769.04
653.01	200.05	724.04	291.15	scatcherd's	789.10
658.26	201.17	732.26	662.08	097.15	790.03
642.04	201.23	747.06	730.25	099.09	school
643.01	205.26	747.07	scaly	128.10	007.10
648.22	208.05	756.08	434.22	scathed	038.21
656.28	216.06	767.13	scandalous	561.01	038.23
659.17	216.21	767.18	532.20	605.16	038.27
659.22	245.11	768.05	scant	719.19	039.12
661.08	246.06	771.06	031.20	scattered	039.16
662.14	264.22	772.26	scantier	049.15	040.06
663.09	266.01	776.13	720.17	050.24	043.01
663.09	269.07	780.10	scantiness	165.16	056.19
664.06	270.07	782.01	453.03	184.28	058.14
664.12	287.18	782.11	scanty	491.08	064.18
664.18	292.26	787.01	037.03	496.04	064.20
668.12	300.12	804.16	112.03	714.13	067.21
668.25	300.17	807.22	202.22	782.21	077.07
671.03	301.12	814.11	729.10	800.25	084.28
672.06	308.13	814.24	733.25	866.06	087.17
673.09	310.18	816.02	scape-goat	scattering	099.07
675.10	314.22	819.18	020.26	235.18	102.21
680.05	317.20	824.07	scar	367.02	104.12
681.08	319.09	824.12	881.16	scatterings	115.11
685.28	322.28	828.14	scarce	146.10	119.21
686.02	328.27	837.10	222.11	scene	129.03
693.12	339.04	842.03	250.27	003.14	131.07
699.14	339.26	846.04	870.21	010.24	142.03
704.09	346.17	848.13	scarcely	025.17	147.20
704.22	351.17	860.19	016.08	039.20	160.16
712.13	351.25	862.02	028.03	145.13	161.12
713.22	353.22	862.27	038.22	148.14	161.22
730.27	358.22	863.05	044.13	181.03	165.04
733.07	359.01	864.03	044.14	192.02	168.17
734.18	366.18	866.08	058.25	209.12	176.12
738.19	373.03	866.20	079.15	209.18	179.25
740.26	389.20	867.13	093.28	211.06	241.08
740.26	395.16	868.02	112.05	318.01	250.16
750.26	396.23	881.23	128.04	321.11	328.04
756.16	396.26	882.09	140.18	367.21	353.18
763.16	401.01	883.06	186.17	369.12	399.01
763.28	404.23	885.15	209.14	369.24	399.19
764.06	405.04	888.17	211.15	371.20	454.01
788.01	411.11	889.22	231.15	392.12	454.07
797.07	413.07	890.03	231.16	471.01	508.03
799.15	428.25	892.13	251.05	476.19	540.08
804.24	437.04	894.04	256.10	552.17	540.11
805.28	437.06	906.27	271.17	605.02	615.14
815.24	437.18	912.15	294.24	611.15	616.12
817.15	437.23	saying	319.25	614.18	696.19
823.21	439.08	002.07	319.27	630.05	706.25
824.02	440.15	027.18	397.04	655.14	721.17
831.19	444.16	077.14	400.19	677.22	721.20
843.08	447.26	090.26	401.10	712.11	722.04
852.11	448.09	140.20	407.29	717.11	723.10
858.25	451.27	249.03	445.07	736.24	729.17
862.10	452.24	274.14	470.17	792.22	732.12
862.27	454.06	311.12	494.23	902.19	739.02
863.05	456.03	329.22	516.26	scenery	746.01
865.06	456.05	375.24	518.25	674.07	746.05
865.22	456.07	399.17	560.02	855.02	749.22
865.28	456.17	422.20	570.09	scenes	750.25
872.03	463.19	443.04	580.24	291.13	769.03
872.22	467.08	444.20	594.02	291.14	769.06
875.09	469.25	445.06	670.20	473.11	769.13
879.09	473.28	462.08	702.07	597.19	771.09
881.21	477.17	507.16	714.20	622.06	787.19
896.08	508.07	522.17	746.13	651.24	789.04
909.19	508.28	537.06	776.23	745.15	789.17
909.19	516.19	554.15	827.24	797.19	790.26
say	517.13	723.18	860.12	scent	804.08
002.18	527.17	731.25	901.15	137.14	817.13
006.24	533.26	766.22	scare	146.08	864.23
010.08	535.11	786.19	571.23	280.19	892.02
012.07	536.15	786.22	795.12	502.14	892.12
014.11	548.27	790.06	scarecrow	503.11	907.23
015.08	554.05	803.12	046.25	scents	908.04
015.16	565.12	827.16	scared	812.08	908.13
020.05	573.11	831.16	294.25	sceptic	school-discipline
021.26	588.22	says	575.23	515.26	039.01
028.19	595.03	009.08	scarf	scepticism	school-duties
040.11		037.07	318.15	537.01	165.09

school-girl
245.19
school-girl-governe-
                sses
267.20
school-habits
165.09
school-hours
205.15
school-mistress
889.07
891.25
school-room
079.17
080.13
083.09
083.24
083.28
089.07
094.12
094.18
097.12
100.13
113.19
114.18
115.14
146.25
151.08
153.26
202.13
233.12
235.02
305.09
313.12
351.23
352.03
335.08
355.25
455.12
522.23
642.18
643.02
750.20
760.22
771.14
school-rules
155.08
schoolboy
007.01
schoolmistress
302.20
schoolroom
771.02
schools
091.06
353.17
818.08
science
250.14
345.28
393.05
811.08
scintillated
856.21
scions
753.08
scissor
748.07
scissors
047.08
scold
047.18
067.15
068.22
scolded
493.12
scolding
067.27
scorched
124.26
293.01
502.02
501.02
651.14
804.08
scorches
404.03
scores
087.27
scorn
061.02
065.25
132.25
164.17
269.26
286.25
513.27
761.13
827.15
827.17
827.18
827.26
scorned
372.08
551.13
732.05
783.09
831.16
scotland
102.03

scoundrel
612.15
scoured
331.06
676.14
751.26
772.04
scourge
160.17
scourging
856.10
scowl
292.24
scowled
453.11
scowling
284.25
370.02
scracely
673.15
scrag
899.19
scrambling
771.01
scrape
113.27
171.25
scraps
029.01
383.13
scratch
421.26
scratched
516.27
scream
024.10
416.02
screamed
024.08
024.21
screaming
468.17
screams
287.24
screen
369.18
492.27
screened
332.17
502.22
676.09
737.23
scribe
513.21
scripture
081.09
089.23
534.24
scroll
847.20
scrolls
895.04
scrub
051.09
scrubbing
306.03
327.14
scruple
616.05
787.18
824.25
scrupulous
744.21
scrupulously
676.21
796.05
620.20
543.16
scrutinize
125.23
scrutinized
027.10
121.09
148.20
246.15
764.06
scrutinizing
309.02
scrutiny
053.05
122.16
226.25
404.15
720.27
scuffle
370.02
sculptor's
119.18
sea
004.22
005.05
198.24
230.20
247.25
302.19
471.03
509.05
570.13
629.26
631.19
756.27

761.17
835.03
857.10
865.11
sea-blue
808.15
sea-fowl
003.24
sea-side
810.02
seal
171.05
326.04
807.28
sealed
619.25
701.20
821.14
872.14
896.08
sealing
552.09
search
449.06
641.08
793.26
852.05
870.16
searched
206.19
239.15
searching
262.15
351.02
517.06
667.08
702.25
726.07
740.16
805.08
825.05
searchingly
804.04
seared
896.03
season
103.17
112.20
148.15
211.07
424.26
451.17
488.09
554.20
735.21
739.03
790.14
795.01
869.13
seasonable
741.14
741.16
seasons
276.16
384.20
473.05
seat
013.18
017.04
052.19
074.26
080.24
081.02
082.12
086.17
099.10
137.01
147.18
149.06
183.26
185.07
194.02
220.04
241.01
246.22
256.19
339.15
339.26
341.15
346.18
349.11
352.16
366.10
380.13
389.18
438.09
470.26
498.19
502.27
566.08
567.10
587.02
665.23
702.23
813.01
887.21
seated
002.23
005.10
078.06
085.05

116.12
134.08
198.14
218.18
237.26
256.21
341.01
359.05
368.04
394.04
410.28
432.26
510.14
887.23
seating
006.26
seats
083.27
122.13
371.08
391.14
seclusion
194.17
second
037.01
052.08
058.13
069.16
082.27
090.08
092.27
133.02
136.06
140.26
175.16
178.10
184.18
196.08
247.20
248.11
287.13
299.03
306.17
329.11
343.11
356.02
367.20
422.20
514.18
545.02
561.17
579.01
577.01
587.12
594.11
599.08
614.13
619.23
630.27
634.01
677.17
705.05
721.20
740.17
779.22
844.22
847.22
893.18
second-sight
496.15
seconded
218.06
secondly
228.28
345.06
seconds
080.24
secrecy
632.10
707.10
secresy
311.26
425.09
secret
016.20
016.23
112.17
292.17
312.24
313.04
314.28
321.19
398.24
530.14
559.18
598.05
627.03
632.20
633.02
633.07
633.24
705.08
754.09
866.22
secreted
048.23
secrets
140.06
269.22
285.18
373.10

589.25
597.15
sect
762.16
section
476.27
sections
476.26
secure
017.16
050.23
123.01
310.03
436.07
475.03
482.16
618.05
624.27
673.27
707.10
828.11
secured
250.12
256.13
336.09
472.08
475.09
782.27
securely
582.16
securing
440.27
719.02
security
027.04
230.01
372.15
706.13
885.11
sedative
396.05
470.06
seducer
272.03
see
011.01
017.15
020.05
022.05
031.24
038.07
044.24
052.09
062.23
068.06
089.15
089.28
095.07
105.21
105.23
108.12
116.10
120.20
121.01
121.04
124.23
124.27
126.11
132.26
135.27
153.03
153.17
154.20
156.13
157.17
158.08
170.23
174.16
174.28
177.20
179.24
181.05
182.08
184.26
186.03
187.15
189.05
190.16
195.03
200.07
202.06
202.08
205.12
206.22
208.27
209.14
224.08
225.15
227.20
230.16
234.05
235.25
238.14
245.01
245.18
246.11
247.06
250.24
258.03
267.15
269.06

269.07
270.09
274.04
275.13
275.27
276.22
276.26
282.14
287.19
288.07
292.11
295.05
299.13
305.03
306.28
310.09
314.06
319.20
328.20
332.09
332.10
332.18
336.05
338.08
338.15
338.18
339.18
345.04
347.02
348.20
348.24
349.14
351.04
355.02
355.24
371.19
371.20
371.21
379.19
385.22
387.24
395.03
399.04
401.10
405.03
412.24
417.12
423.12
427.14
430.22
432.14
433.18
434.18
437.14
437.14
443.07
447.06
450.07
450.17
450.21
451.25
463.06
463.12
464.03
464.14
464.28
466.27
467.08
469.16
469.28
479.10
481.02
482.06
485.14
488.21
493.09
494.06
494.07
495.18
496.21
500.04
503.14
503.19
503.23
504.25
509.26
512.08
512.10
516.05
518.25
522.02
525.27
526.15
534.07
544.16
546.01
547.11
548.07
548.23
554.23
556.06
561.06
562.05
562.18
562.23
566.17
577.16
581.18
586.14
587.23
597.24

seminary
146.27
162.14
send
015.02
033.07
059.16
059.25
064.18
064.20
120.19
168.09
171.15
177.18
363.11
365.14
415.03
448.18
463.12
469.08
475.22
482.11
495.05
510.16
524.16
529.21
548.21
555.04
613.12
654.03
656.23
690.27
777.11
800.02
874.10
sending
043.19
sends
326.26
450.21
528.20
senior
629.12
sensation
046.28
065.20
127.15
132.17
152.23
361.14
462.01
490.09
852.23
863.22
sensations
010.17
127.10
164.11
324.15
373.14
455.08
689.04
789.09
sense
017.01
026.06
050.21
063.18
066.04
065.21
100.19
139.06
211.10
225.18
257.14
263.06
274.24
275.06
275.11
289.01
303.01
320.14
322.16
324.13
351.08
354.07
361.02
374.19
383.15
454.05
459.20
466.17
476.24
489.19
489.21
498.21
509.02
528.16
539.05
544.20
561.03
572.07
614.24
619.27
621.10
639.14
640.19
671.28
672.26
694.09
703.24

715.21
734.11
734.15
745.18
762.24
816.08
821.17
821.18
837.05
senseless
287.01
611.17
senselessness
321.16
senses
155.06
481.08
625.07
685.18
758.09
797.02
822.25
849.05
865.03
sensibility
404.18
554.25
sensible
010.16
079.28
274.21
408.07
457.16
537.23
691.23
706.24
759.11
816.28
842.25
856.03
sensitive
569.13
sensual
479.23
793.04
sensualist
734.02
sent
007.14
040.06
076.23
081.22
094.18
097.11
097.26
102.08
103.01
116.22
126.20
126.21
127.15
137.23
145.22
151.24
154.19
165.05
220.14
254.12
255.05
257.11
263.12
292.20
314.19
332.08
333.14
336.01
353.18
445.04
450.17
452.16
466.26
481.09
522.26
523.25
540.08
570.23
585.05
610.23
624.21
680.23
850.01
864.19
sentence
026.04
062.03
109.23
121.11
321.25
402.02
508.10
535.06
573.22
590.09
614.23
716.20
737.08
763.25
823.13
824.03
sentenced
464.25

sentences
057.04
383.18
604.07
690.03
sententious
274.06
sentient
261.27
sentiment
004.27
043.11
058.11
063.22
099.25
150.16
322.15
373.13
554.06
715.25
827.18
sentimental
380.01
473.11
sentiments
282.09
320.16
351.23
374.02
462.11
711.11
722.27
756.24
761.26
825.24
separate
126.17
180.22
316.23
378.15
417.24
423.20
477.21
489.21
491.06
909.06
separated
151.14
194.08
422.28
separating
003.09
209.27
separation
039.14
042.13
101.07
113.05
194.14
341.07
498.16
502.24
510.04
583.12
719.28
894.15
sequel
475.28
767.02
770.02
843.13
sequestered
066.13
215.04
424.14
711.15
sera
540.28
seraglio
546.04
546.07
seraph
109.07
272.01
sere
209.05
serene
145.26
152.03
163.27
280.25
331.26
583.11
662.05
745.05
801.20
serenely
193.24
serenity
139.01
715.08
819.02
series
268.10
544.08
545.26
serious
083.18
090.16
271.07
323.02

427.08
772.06
782.03
806.26
879.05
907.15
seriously
242.08
325.09
515.03
533.14
792.18
sermon
114.09
114.19
716.05
sermonized
356.05
sermons
720.05
serried
249.02
servant
012.19
012.20
037.08
075.14
076.05
082.14
125.05
137.06
174.26
175.10
184.05
187.10
211.11
226.14
363.06
417.07
446.03
626.25
640.17
666.10
667.21
667.23
681.07
683.16
685.10
689.17
696.13
709.27
746.08
751.23
813.24
906.09
912.16
servant's
364.13
418.06
686.07
servants
006.02
020.25
027.13
135.02
189.06
208.01
210.19
280.01
300.22
307.18
308.05
310.10
317.24
334.25
336.28
365.08
386.01
399.06
469.09
479.11
491.28
569.13
586.09
862.27
863.01
865.17
898.22
servants'
018.21
035.12
311.01
334.22
385.20
433.03
449.04
serve
084.13
121.16
166.22
166.23
257.15
410.17
437.12
638.10
665.16
667.16
886.05
served
087.09
094.02

112.27
117.24
166.22
336.08
445.02
458.21
470.24
904.04
serves
729.15
service
112.23
113.01
311.22
328.05
348.28
358.13
479.02
491.02
555.08
589.18
706.06
713.27
718.08
720.09
720.14
724.19
761.21
815.18
services
112.28
224.22
392.10
488.25
910.01
910.03
servies
212.03
serving
020.15
841.23
servitude
165.21
166.13
166.21
722.15
807.03
set
018.27
038.19
061.04
069.03
072.24
112.22
123.23
142.12
149.17
154.09
177.23
180.22
183.26
211.13
218.26
225.11
248.03
265.16
316.10
335.13
337.26
364.19
398.28
413.09
417.14
418.22
427.10
430.17
468.14
489.01
512.20
514.10
518.24
564.01
594.07
637.10
658.03
658.13
663.26
676.09
677.03
678.23
680.10
701.10
729.06
761.16
765.12
780.18
791.04
794.09
800.09
810.20
854.27
863.02
863.18
864.05
870.28
875.06
setting
071.08
299.21
306.08
439.19

456.11
630.01
736.19
912.11
settle
384.03
487.09
488.01
559.13
626.25
782.14
783.22
settled
061.18
066.22
119.17
162.25
240.24
283.21
417.13
475.01
492.23
506.18
567.20
601.10
615.14
634.12
730.19
736.11
746.02
779.10
787.27
789.02
800.14
803.15
864.21
908.09
settling
117.22
seule
341.21
seulement
341.22
seven
170.19
179.22
197.04
196.02
314.19
317.10
445.17
457.26
555.05
585.02
seven-and-thirty
060.16
seventeen
122.03
704.16
seventh
114.08
seventy
172.10
seventy-and-seven
835.22
sever
351.14
652.06
several
074.09
161.07
202.17
254.02
380.17
461.27
729.18
744.09
865.26
severe
029.13
042.11
102.13
104.06
104.11
111.16
189.09
268.09
460.21
555.12
725.15
773.07
831.05
835.19
895.09
907.27
severed
074.01
361.09
579.19
severely
061.28
696.20
834.16
severity
108.19
119.18
292.18
529.07
677.16
825.03

severn	830.01	477.24	791.12	083.23	034.02
120.03	894.19	489.02	791.28	112.12	034.10
120.05	shaken	489.04	793.15	161.19	034.10
sew	023.15	489.05	803.09	263.07	034.13
077.12	511.12	489.11	811.15	360.09	035.01
211.20	576.01	489.27	813.09	782.25	035.04
244.10	654.15	494.01	815.17	shares	035.04
729.19	835.07	504.14	815.17	348.14	035.16
744.11	shaking	506.27	819.25	352.26	037.19
sewed	023.03	508.01	820.04	817.21	037.20
329.12	062.18	508.14	825.01	sharing	039.03
sewing	120.02	509.25	828.12	800.22	039.07
030.06	200.15	512.24	828.15	860.05	040.11
040.09	519.14	514.12	840.24	sharp	040.13
060.14	675.06	515.26	844.17	009.25	041.04
097.14	741.23	524.14	844.18	069.10	041.07
099.23	shall	524.20	844.20	141.04	041.17
306.19	025.02	525.21	846.01	144.07	041.17
307.12	025.05	525.25	846.12	377.13	042.12
470.17	027.18	526.07	846.15	399.07	042.19
487.16	028.09	526.09	848.23	414.16	043.02
722.24	036.04	526.11	851.14	613.05	043.26
sewn	057.24	526.13	851.18	661.11	044.07
060.11	058.08	526.15	852.05	821.25	044.20
sews	059.12	526.17	852.15	849.04	044.21
213.23	059.21	526.18	853.16	sharp-witted	044.28
300.08	059.24	526.20	856.25	743.15	045.01
sex	063.05	526.21	863.12	sharpened	045.04
216.28	066.03	526.23	879.03	142.17	046.09
748.17	066.26	526.25	882.08	sharpers	047.07
shabby	068.13	526.28	884.03	469.14	047.10
046.24	068.16	527.08	885.09	sharpish	047.11
773.25	068.20	527.15	885.12	696.27	047.13
shade	069.01	527.25	886.28	sharply	047.16
256.22	069.03	529.18	897.08	068.26	047.19
258.07	069.13	540.14	898.18	099.20	047.21
264.26	087.09	540.16	shallows	309.25	047.22
343.19	108.25	540.20	570.14	612.20	047.24
347.01	116.22	543.03	shambles	shattered	048.01
347.27	117.07	546.22	612.04	662.01	048.03
347.28	118.27	547.18	shame	859.21	048.11
354.02	123.28	547.19	012.14	shawl	048.13
495.09	134.13	547.21	012.14	029.23	048.13
503.02	134.18	548.18	094.23	072.02	048.20
599.14	134.21	548.19	127.07	076.21	048.22
668.13	136.10	548.20	132.25	093.01	048.23
674.03	136.12	552.08	280.06	122.08	049.02
681.11	157.12	559.19	283.15	167.03	049.07
752.09	157.25	567.20	360.19	187.01	049.10
903.06	158.08	568.21	406.01	295.20	051.07
shaded	158.25	578.09	505.04	298.22	052.20
122.04	183.22	580.02	532.20	344.24	052.21
207.22	184.11	582.15	665.16	519.14	053.22
345.03	188.05	586.24	684.25	575.06	056.13
464.20	189.22	589.25	732.01	653.06	057.07
shades	200.09	596.04	740.08	661.18	057.09
016.05	201.21	597.24	802.08	692.25	057.11
322.10	215.18	602.10	910.03	873.25	057.23
346.14	224.03	610.10	shame-facedness	shawls	058.01
472.06	243.07	610.10	121.19	365.16	058.15
664.15	246.06	610.11	shameful	368.06	058.20
shadiest	260.22	610.13	083.07	she	059.12
899.23	273.16	613.12	141.07	002.03	059.13
shadow	276.12	615.22	shape	002.06	059.25
145.11	276.21	616.20	052.15	002.07	060.14
226.04	282.10	616.02	113.25	002.09	060.16
230.12	289.03	622.11	125.01	002.15	060.19
398.10	298.15	622.12	163.08	005.17	060.27
475.19	298.27	622.14	177.28	005.20	061.03
504.15	300.13	622.16	224.27	005.21	061.22
504.21	300.19	622.20	237.11	006.07	062.09
518.25	310.02	627.06	248.16	006.09	062.13
556.16	311.09	628.02	249.17	006.16	063.24
752.12	314.06	646.18	249.17	008.05	063.26
864.14	326.02	647.09	262.22	010.08	064.22
896.19	327.06	648.11	344.06	010.23	067.04
900.09	339.05	672.21	360.10	013.10	067.08
shadows	339.08	679.17	365.19	013.20	067.19
398.20	357.26	682.24	382.20	013.21	067.20
423.13	360.06	682.25	424.19	013.21	067.26
562.24	360.08	694.17	471.01	013.25	068.05
569.04	360.09	703.10	512.14	014.06	068.06
663.03	360.22	709.05	512.15	014.08	071.12
677.23	360.24	709.06	577.06	014.09	071.13
836.22	385.10	709.09	763.22	015.07	071.18
shadowy	386.04	718.18	871.12	021.23	072.01
004.16	392.20	719.28	876.19	021.25	072.03
046.16	398.05	720.03	shaped	021.25	072.04
248.21	405.17	721.10	084.11	021.27	072.06
505.15	405.20	721.11	472.01	022.04	072.09
738.01	405.24	721.13	737.27	024.07	072.10
shaft	408.04	722.02	shapely	024.08	072.18
052.17	416.05	725.20	085.24	024.10	073.11
375.02	417.03	730.13	shapes	024.11	073.25
shafts	420.02	731.02	398.17	025.07	075.17
870.06	422.04	731.04	shaping	025.08	075.26
shaggy	430.12	731.19	818.18	025.15	076.06
600.12	431.08	731.22	share	027.14	076.24
684.19	433.17	733.22	045.15	028.22	076.25
shake	442.17	736.14	336.10	028.23	076.26
053.19	448.25	739.07	476.26	028.24	076.27
195.05	452.12	739.10	488.03	030.07	077.01
267.11	454.20	739.27	514.14	030.17	077.05
301.07	454.21	754.06	558.24	032.14	077.10
312.26	455.15	763.06	559.19	032.17	077.13
442.10	455.16	766.15	582.10	032.25	077.14
523.06	455.22	769.06	618.22	033.01	077.24
622.19	460.04	778.11	712.13	033.24	077.25
697.15	477.10	778.14	912.06	033.24	078.20
761.12	477.16	786.18	shared	033.26	079.18
829.14	477.18		079.11	033.30	080.14

082.08	137.02	188.02	255.21	326.04	367.03
083.03	137.03	188.02	255.23	327.10	368.11
083.21	137.05	188.07	255.25	327.24	368.21
083.23	137.06	188.15	256.11	327.25	368.23
085.09	137.19	188.22	256.15	327.27	368.24
085.11	137.22	188.22	257.05	328.04	368.27
085.23	137.23	189.16	257.13	329.03	369.03
087.02	138.03	189.26	257.19	329.09	370.12
087.05	138.09	189.27	257.23	329.12	370.14
087.12	138.14	190.02	258.17	329.24	371.03
089.25	138.15	190.14	261.09	330.01	372.09
089.27	138.22	190.16	261.23	330.02	373.01
090.02	138.23	190.18	276.12	330.04	373.03
090.07	140.12	195.03	276.15	330.05	373.04
090.08	140.18	195.07	276.18	330.09	373.04
090.25	140.21	195.09	276.18	330.11	373.09
090.26	140.23	195.18	276.19	330.11	373.09
092.10	140.24	196.15	276.21	330.14	373.10
092.11	140.26	196.18	276.22	330.18	373.11
092.23	140.27	196.19	277.01	330.20	373.12
092.26	141.01	197.03	277.05	331.17	373.13
093.03	141.02	197.11	277.09	332.12	373.15
093.15	141.05	197.12	277.12	332.13	373.16
093.15	141.15	197.20	277.14	332.28	373.17
093.15	141.20	197.21	277.18	333.06	373.19
094.21	142.05	197.22	277.22	333.11	374.11
094.22	144.03	197.23	279.06	333.15	374.13
094.23	147.11	198.09	279.09	333.17	375.06
094.25	149.01	198.10	279.15	334.03	375.09
094.26	149.15	198.13	280.18	334.04	375.09
095.01	149.16	198.14	281.15	335.26	375.18
095.01	149.18	198.16	281.25	335.27	375.19
095.05	149.21	198.18	283.25	336.07	375.20
095.08	149.22	198.21	283.28	336.09	375.22
095.09	149.23	198.23	284.01	336.17	375.22
095.11	150.06	199.20	286.25	336.17	375.25
097.25	150.09	199.27	287.09	336.20	376.01
098.01	150.23	200.03	287.11	336.22	376.09
098.20	150.25	200.10	287.12	336.24	376.11
098.23	151.09	200.12	288.06	338.13	378.08
098.26	151.22	200.16	288.08	338.13	380.26
099.01	151.24	201.05	288.09	338.14	380.26
099.05	152.26	201.08	288.10	339.03	381.01
099.05	152.27	201.09	288.16	339.04	381.02
099.06	153.07	201.13	289.01	340.07	381.03
099.17	153.10	201.19	289.18	340.10	381.12
099.18	153.13	201.26	289.19	340.12	383.22
100.05	153.18	201.26	289.23	340.15	385.10
100.05	153.19	201.27	290.01	340.17	385.11
101.19	154.20	201.27	295.16	340.17	386.02
101.22	155.17	203.02	298.17	340.20	386.04
101.23	155.25	203.14	300.09	340.20	386.06
102.13	155.27	203.14	300.10	341.18	386.08
102.13	156.01	203.21	300.12	341.26	386.09
102.16	156.03	204.03	306.21	343.05	386.09
103.12	156.04	206.19	306.23	343.22	386.11
103.15	156.05	206.23	307.04	344.10	386.27
104.04	156.08	208.20	307.06	344.13	387.01
104.12	156.24	210.19	307.09	344.19	387.11
104.14	156.25	210.22	308.01	344.21	387.18
105.02	157.01	211.20	308.03	344.26	387.18
106.01	157.02	211.23	308.04	345.11	387.25
106.04	158.16	213.06	308.08	345.19	388.04
106.11	158.18	213.11	308.10	345.25	388.10
103.07	159.03	213.14	308.20	345.26	388.16
106.07	159.07	213.16	309.01	346.01	388.21
106.11	162.17	213.20	309.04	346.01	388.24
103.12	162.19	214.01	309.08	346.02	388.28
106.14	162.24	214.21	309.10	346.04	389.06
109.23	163.26	217.06	309.12	346.07	389.07
109.24	165.06	217.08	309.13	346.08	389.07
109.26	166.06	217.08	309.22	346.09	389.13
113.11	168.24	217.16	309.23	346.10	389.13
116.21	170.06	217.18	310.21	346.17	389.15
116.23	170.07	217.27	310.26	346.25	389.16
119.14	170.11	218.05	311.20	346.26	389.17
120.05	170.15	220.13	312.02	347.06	389.22
120.08	170.28	230.23	312.10	347.20	390.04
120.26	171.01	230.23	312.11	352.18	390.13
122.09	171.02	232.21	312.14	352.22	390.16
124.03	171.09	232.24	312.15	352.23	390.18
124.27	173.05	234.03	312.16	352.23	391.11
124.28	173.08	234.04	312.23	353.01	391.12
126.20	173.10	234.05	313.14	353.02	391.13
127.14	173.12	234.07	313.15	353.03	391.17
127.25	173.15	234.09	313.19	353.04	391.22
128.06	174.01	234.11	313.26	353.06	391.24
130.01	175.13	234.13	314.26	353.07	392.17
130.15	175.18	234.18	315.20	353.16	392.18
130.16	176.18	234.20	315.27	353.22	392.18
130.22	176.25	235.23	315.28	353.23	393.02
130.24	176.26	238.18	316.04	355.06	394.03
131.24	177.18	238.19	316.04	355.10	394.05
131.26	178.19	238.23	317.11	356.08	394.09
133.11	178.21	238.26	317.12	356.20	394.12
133.13	179.01	238.26	317.21	357.17	394.13
133.15	180.11	238.27	318.05	357.17	394.14
133.20	180.17	240.01	318.10	357.19	394.15
134.01	180.22	240.02	318.14	357.19	395.01
134.02	184.09	240.05	318.18	357.22	395.03
134.10	184.10	240.07	318.21	357.23	395.11
134.11	184.18	240.14	318.23	358.16	396.03
134.22	185.26	240.14	318.25	358.17	396.06
134.27	186.12	240.15	319.04	359.09	396.21
135.01	186.27	241.02	319.05	359.12	397.17
135.04	187.02	243.08	319.07	359.16	397.18
136.09	187.08	245.24	319.12	360.04	397.19
136.15	187.11	253.20	319.22	360.25	397.20
136.21	187.15	253.21	324.04	361.05	397.23
136.28	187.17	253.23	325.28	361.06	397.28
137.01	187.22		325.28	366.18	

398.07	474.01	534.16	640.04	700.27	824.06
398.09	474.02	535.03	649.11	702.15	826.14
398.13	474.04	535.04	652.06	702.18	839.14
398.13	474.06	535.07	652.09	704.15	839.17
402.08	474.09	535.10	660.27	704.17	839.24
403.08	474.10	536.04	665.14	708.01	839.25
403.10	474.14	536.11	665.15	709.21	840.22
403.25	474.16	536.14	665.16	709.21	840.27
404.04	474.19	536.28	665.22	709.22	841.19
404.05	474.20	538.04	665.23	709.23	850.08
405.12	474.25	538.13	666.09	709.24	854.02
406.22	475.01	538.22	666.11	713.10	858.09
411.10	475.01	538.28	666.23	713.11	858.23
416.20	475.03	539.12	667.23	713.11	862.08
416.22	475.05	539.14	668.03	714.02	862.12
417.08	475.05	539.17	668.03	714.04	862.14
417.13	475.06	539.17	668.04	722.02	863.04
418.22	475.13	539.25	668.06	725.09	863.19
420.24	475.14	539.27	669.24	725.21	863.22
428.05	475.17	540.01	670.08	726.07	863.24
428.05	475.23	540.04	670.10	726.08	864.03
428.14	475.24	540.07	670.11	726.12	864.05
429.02	475.26	540.10	670.12	727.01	864.06
429.03	475.27	540.18	670.13	738.27	864.08
429.03	476.05	540.23	670.14	739.04	864.09
436.07	476.06	540.24	670.15	739.07	864.10
442.01	478.03	540.26	670.16	739.21	864.14
442.23	479.03	541.02	671.06	739.28	864.22
444.17	479.05	541.09	672.09	740.16	864.22
446.18	479.06	541.09	672.09	740.20	865.12
448.02	479.10	541.10	677.10	740.21	865.20
448.07	479.15	541.14	678.07	740.24	865.20
448.08	480.09	541.14	678.12	741.01	865.23
448.09	480.15	541.18	678.12	741.20	865.25
448.09	480.21	542.28	678.14	741.23	866.01
448.12	480.22	543.01	678.21	742.10	866.02
448.13	481.01	543.04	680.01	742.12	873.14
448.16	481.04	543.15	680.04	742.14	873.14
448.17	481.06	543.18	680.06	742.14	874.06
448.27	481.11	543.21	680.08	742.18	874.08
449.10	481.22	546.02	680.11	742.19	874.11
449.11	481.24	546.02	681.04	742.19	874.11
449.20	481.27	557.18	681.19	742.25	874.18
449.24	481.28	558.01	682.06	746.07	876.21
449.28	482.08	558.03	682.07	746.14	877.09
450.02	482.13	561.14	682.08	746.16	877.10
450.05	483.16	577.13	682.18	746.23	884.01
450.18	483.21	577.17	684.24	747.01	884.02
450.21	483.22	577.18	685.14	747.03	884.02
451.10	483.23	577.19	685.16	747.14	886.07
451.27	484.01	578.21	685.21	747.16	886.08
452.16	484.12	581.09	685.24	747.20	886.08
457.16	484.24	584.04	685.28	748.07	886.10
457.17	484.25	585.02	686.11	748.08	890.28
457.17	484.28	585.06	686.15	748.10	894.12
457.19	485.10	585.10	687.12	748.11	894.12
457.20	485.11	593.23	687.15	748.15	894.16
457.21	485.14	595.15	688.06	748.17	895.08
457.22	485.15	597.01	689.19	748.26	905.17
457.24	485.17	597.03	689.20	748.26	905.17
458.03	485.20	597.10	690.01	748.27	906.03
458.05	485.22	598.05	690.06	749.03	906.05
458.15	486.08	598.06	690.07	749.04	906.22
458.20	486.09	599.06	690.08	749.09	907.03
458.22	486.12	600.06	690.12	749.10	907.04
458.22	487.06	600.12	690.14	749.17	907.05
458.24	487.07	600.17	690.16	749.26	907.07
458.28	487.10	600.19	691.16	750.05	907.07
459.10	487.11	600.19	691.19	750.07	907.24
460.05	487.17	601.05	691.22	750.28	907.25
461.25	488.15	601.07	691.24	757.01	907.25
463.05	488.15	601.08	691.25	757.03	908.07
463.10	488.17	610.04	692.06	757.07	908.08
463.11	488.20	615.28	693.11	757.08	908.11
464.04	488.23	615.28	693.12	757.09	908.13
464.13	488.24	616.20	693.13	757.10	908.16
464.14	489.01	617.01	693.14	758.03	she'd
465.24	489.17	617.06	693.17	758.06	429.03
465.25	489.25	618.10	693.18	759.02	she'll
466.04	490.04	623.17	693.20	759.03	153.05
466.09	490.06	623.21	693.20	759.13	388.16
466.10	491.21	624.28	694.04	760.08	906.20
466.15	491.24	625.03	694.10	762.19	she's
467.11	491.24	625.13	694.15	762.21	012.12
467.13	495.15	625.26	694.19	762.23	014.02
467.15	495.17	625.27	694.26	762.26	177.15
467.21	496.17	627.08	694.26	763.03	330.05
467.24	496.23	627.13	694.28	763.09	330.06
467.26	498.07	628.23	695.02	763.09	386.15
468.02	499.01	629.10	696.16	769.20	386.09
468.03	499.12	629.13	696.17	770.13	399.15
468.03	499.14	629.15	697.01	771.07	417.08
468.07	499.14	629.19	697.11	771.11	427.19
468.09	499.18	630.02	697.17	771.13	442.23
469.18	502.11	630.06	697.21	771.15	507.13
469.21	508.19	630.09	697.22	771.23	672.13
469.22	516.01	632.04	697.24	771.28	906.23
470.06	520.01	633.02	697.25	772.01	906.24
470.11	520.02	633.08	698.01	772.05	shed
472.21	522.13	633.09	698.04	780.04	105.27
472.28	522.21	633.11	698.08	793.27	105.28
473.03	523.02	633.15	698.12	799.22	333.16
473.04	525.21	633.22	699.05	801.09	401.15
473.06	526.15	633.25	699.17	801.10	497.16
473.06	526.16	633.28	699.18	803.20	611.17
473.08	526.17	634.01	699.21	804.16	657.11
473.17	533.02	634.03	699.24	806.10	754.11
473.22	533.04	635.22	700.02	806.11	shedding
473.25	534.05	635.25	700.07	807.10	439.09
473.27	534.06	637.01	700.19	807.15	sheen
473.28	534.13	637.02	700.21	810.01	343.18

sheep	286.13	583.07	shortened	293.22	654.03
018.28	331.28	591.17	486.10	294.23	654.14
031.26	341.04	652.12	493.01	300.06	655.22
066.18	363.03	675.28	shorter	308.13	656.22
383.06	510.09	765.17	426.27	308.25	662.20
712.09	675.01	809.21	shortly	312.07	668.07
846.21	844.03	809.26	073.06	314.21	668.11
sheepishly	886.28	shook	163.11	316.17	672.28
504.27	ship	023.22	217.11	317.13	673.20
sheet	179.27	038.07	403.02	317.15	673.21
220.01	198.24	045.01	421.19	319.25	674.18
222.19	199.06	083.21	453.26	322.25	674.26
366.24	471.04	142.08	482.14	323.25	682.22
466.04	ship-money	146.02	491.25	324.04	690.12
577.15	098.15	198.09	539.21	325.20	694.28
750.02	ships	242.06	768.08	330.03	696.22
763.13	005.05	296.13	826.18	331.22	699.20
sheets	416.28	326.09	shot	338.07	715.09
296.16	shire	330.22	124.17	340.07	717.22
298.01	167.27	366.07	375.13	345.09	718.15
327.19	169.02	415.24	676.03	353.18	751.13
387.02	171.07	456.14	763.19	353.25	755.25
470.26	171.18	574.15	779.24	353.27	756.05
472.16	172.08	618.24	should	354.07	759.04
shelf	172.10	646.11	003.01	354.09	760.10
140.14	172.10	649.12	014.26	356.27	767.20
199.02	196.17	668.03	024.18	359.01	772.06
460.15	241.08	686.24	027.23	360.02	772.18
770.12	450.19	699.19	028.01	360.20	774.15
shell	450.20	723.13	028.23	366.15	776.01
823.01	593.11	765.19	030.10	374.15	782.15
shell-like	658.20	783.10	033.15	374.19	784.04
574.25	706.21	787.23	033.19	374.22	784.10
859.04	770.21	812.23	034.25	404.27	789.05
shelter	shirked	821.10	037.11	405.09	789.15
033.20	125.10	853.03	038.04	406.09	797.03
046.19	shirt	853.09	038.19	412.07	797.04
068.12	421.21	874.19	039.16	412.14	797.05
222.11	429.27	shoot	039.27	412.15	806.02
499.06	shiver	360.01	043.28	424.27	806.11
503.08	096.10	630.23	046.05	428.08	807.13
559.20	shivered	869.14	052.09	428.08	807.21
632.10	167.21	shooting	054.11	430.15	815.27
663.12	572.23	494.05	056.18	435.27	819.04
668.13	606.15	676.12	056.19	437.08	821.12
682.14	shivering	698.10	057.26	436.01	821.20
697.05	080.07	shop	062.04	441.02	825.16
707.22	088.14	169.10	068.02	448.03	825.19
850.06	385.28	544.18	077.14	456.13	828.04
sheltered	shock	664.25	094.28	463.09	828.07
027.24	029.15	665.13	095.15	463.26	828.14
361.18	153.15	670.03	101.06	464.09	828.22
502.16	276.25	670.06	102.08	466.04	834.03
722.12	282.10	shore	102.15	475.06	834.11
825.25	480.28	302.22	102.16	475.16	835.16
857.19	537.21	813.12	102.17	481.14	836.27
sheltering	849.03	shores	102.18	484.07	838.07
219.26	853.02	004.06	103.24	484.20	838.26
shepherd	shocked	384.25	105.01	486.09	841.15
435.28	119.23	622.15	106.26	488.01	842.05
565.22	451.21	shorn	106.27	488.02	843.06
shew	534.06	501.10	107.07	488.04	844.10
009.04	594.22	short	107.25	488.05	845.02
059.14	701.28	066.19	107.26	494.12	846.04
150.05	726.02	106.21	116.10	510.12	848.02
848.19	741.24	133.16	126.19	511.04	848.08
848.20	756.18	170.26	132.04	511.06	851.05
shewed	837.06	186.14	133.06	513.09	853.19
847.20	837.07	205.22	141.05	518.06	854.11
shewing	841.24	206.07	153.09	519.05	857.07
218.10	shocking	217.20	154.18	520.01	862.02
750.19	012.15	222.14	170.28	529.10	872.12
861.13	055.21	240.15	173.24	532.04	874.01
shewn	126.09	249.21	188.17	537.11	878.10
065.14	447.09	258.26	193.03	542.23	880.12
143.12	shockingly	277.03	195.11	544.01	880.20
158.01	386.13	280.03	202.12	544.10	881.22
shift	shod	301.03	205.26	547.03	884.09
177.22	430.28	331.20	211.07	548.07	887.12
495.01	shoe	344.23	224.21	549.08	887.24
shifted	098.06	355.21	224.28	551.27	888.19
563.05	shoemaker's	396.04	225.02	552.01	888.20
shifting	170.01	396.21	225.08	553.07	888.21
423.23	shoes	407.26	225.19	553.22	888.27
shilling	084.15	452.05	227.09	557.11	890.04
040.24	111.17	461.24	238.18	559.12	895.07
397.17	112.02	473.12	238.25	582.12	908.07
516.16	154.09	477.08	239.23	595.24	shoulder
658.06	169.26	482.09	239.26	602.18	010.12
shillings	330.13	490.08	240.09	607.08	077.02
453.01	418.27	507.13	245.02	607.24	133.19
455.04	652.24	569.10	247.10	609.17	141.06
522.11	655.10	580.23	247.10	611.11	159.16
653.04	692.19	605.08	251.25	613.06	227.26
657.05	shone	652.21	252.25	617.07	316.16
shimmer	086.07	687.11	253.15	617.15	337.19
558.15	133.25	687.23	253.16	617.18	371.23
shine	139.16	713.08	259.16	617.20	410.05
089.14	147.28	738.10	261.03	617.22	421.22
231.08	154.28	748.16	267.03	619.21	426.01
242.12	191.21	770.10	270.07	622.07	428.02
767.10	193.24	792.10	270.08	622.26	428.28
845.04	237.03	795.24	270.09	624.10	432.07
907.08	248.20	802.16	271.01	624.12	519.09
shines	333.04	821.25	272.27	626.12	533.25
376.14	343.18	829.08	274.10	626.24	589.16
404.08	385.04	861.05	275.11	631.16	594.14
551.22	420.17	869.20	281.28	634.28	601.25
shining	435.09	889.04	283.18	637.21	620.26
076.12	492.28	906.03	285.08	644.23	639.13
136.20	501.02		285.10	645.02	

839.15	shrewd	604.12	196.03	sighs	098.27
876.17	034.25	610.22	219.18	356.15	104.05
904.03	149.13	611.12	223.11	sight	133.21
shouldered	640.20	616.16	310.14	052.14	136.09
060.17	shrewdly	625.27	316.12	054.04	154.05
shoulders	234.08	629.19	318.16	095.07	157.02
167.03	373.24	654.17	332.17	115.08	160.09
176.13	shriek	654.21	332.27	150.24	166.01
247.06	415.01	657.08	338.03	221.23	215.23
318.06	shrieked	668.05	349.11	279.08	235.05
345.14	630.06	674.19	353.08	333.09	240.21
493.27	shrieks	683.02	366.25	333.12	256.08
720.01	391.06	696.22	367.07	362.14	284.18
746.13	905.14	718.20	368.04	382.02	294.19
750.01	shrill	733.05	371.10	420.01	389.01
890.01	414.16	741.28	375.26	503.07	389.04
shouldn't	shrine	787.20	384.02	551.19	389.18
660.14	207.17	812.17	403.26	571.24	404.26
shout	272.22	818.12	419.16	572.04	414.15
420.22	shrined	860.11	421.02	599.17	415.22
775.18	003.06	864.25	421.11	611.01	441.20
shouted	shrink	874.22	424.06	612.26	486.08
415.11	378.01	shutter	430.04	623.23	497.22
416.14	463.25	676.10	432.13	629.01	503.01
shouting	617.20	765.06	433.07	636.23	573.21
865.21	shrinking	shutters	433.21	641.04	581.01
sho-	383.01	230.15	434.28	671.20	591.01
024.27	465.03	shutting	438.14	673.10	610.16
069.09	817.05	015.13	449.20	743.08	612.17
094.22	shrivelled	154.25	464.06	755.20	645.19
107.08	595.02	335.05	469.20	839.11	660.08
206.24	shroud	336.19	502.21	867.23	684.02
324.07	577.15	shuttlecock	509.18	881.14	696.28
367.12	606.01	279.06	514.17	883.27	715.27
367.21	818.11	284.15	515.05	910.21	726.14
367.26	shrouded	289.14	515.07	sightless	741.21
377.14	015.26	shy	539.26	872.09	766.17
412.25	145.15	068.02	540.06	875.22	775.01
436.25	shrouding	574.05	541.24	880.21	795.27
437.27	415.04	641.10	550.13	903.20	803.13
464.08	shrub	741.20	560.19	sign	812.28
478.13	003.15	shyness	564.04	022.24	829.03
553.20	503.12	224.19	592.17	261.02	829.15
621.15	shrubbery	si	661.17	444.19	836.18
623.24	001.05	234.24	668.18	485.14	838.28
708.27	066.08	334.08	675.24	609.04	854.09
749.23	443.02	siberia	737.13	618.26	854.17
814.13	503.19	004.06	745.22	855.16	859.08
820.04	shrubs	sich	750.10	859.19	883.04
sho-ed	235.11	698.11	770.17	870.11	903.15
076.11	675.26	sick	770.17	sign-post	silenced
130.14	shrug	028.16	775.24	659.11	223.19
145.24	890.01	062.26	775.25	854.14	768.02
207.07	shudder	081.17	781.05	signal	silent
211.09	429.05	148.26	789.05	052.20	002.24
231.10	580.17	198.25	810.22	125.02	016.13
245.23	819.18	359.15	812.05	signed	029.27
248.27	shuddered	395.27	812.06	078.18	045.28
260.26	088.05	396.09	825.27	173.23	053.18
369.02	152.22	396.14	829.02	546.24	066.14
420.12	423.02	420.01	840.09	593.18	069.17
468.24	644.01	450.17	874.27	773.02	101.17
601.07	674.27	450.18	895.11	significance	130.24
625.01	822.18	483.06	side-aisle	004.21	133.10
631.10	866.10	603.10	588.18	350.27	210.10
641.28	895.16	612.22	side-board	significancy	217.06
673.28	shuddering	628.02	203.22	355.07	229.21
743.16	428.13	668.13	side-door	significant	233.15
748.12	612.23	671.09	231.04	306.12	283.06
767.27	shun	714.13	361.19	significantly	283.23
768.24	125.18	800.26	554.17	330.12	375.16
776.12	253.15	sick-room	654.11	signification	380.07
840.03	378.06	147.11	side-glances	089.20	387.01
842.24	611.12	473.23	462.02	signifier	404.24
843.13	614.27	479.17	side-passage	234.20	416.13
870.04	shunned	sickbed	432.21	signifies	429.09
sho-er	225.02	152.10	side-table	404.13	432.21
545.03	283.04	sickened	701.14	signify	447.27
551.20	485.03	426.08	sideboard	405.21	491.02
804.17	642.17	656.04	331.09	472.10	496.23
873.05	753.18	sickening	411.01	494.17	515.11
sho-er-bath	847.01	324.13	sides	542.27	570.18
297.01	shuns	610.18	084.05	680.21	597.15
sho-ers	253.14	685.07	132.25	803.09	643.02
435.05	shut	sickens	331.11	824.08	645.06
showing	003.07	082.21	377.14	879.27	662.10
053.13	035.22	321.04	745.01	signior	677.22
191.22	036.02	sickly	sideways	358.06	679.01
240.26	036.28	355.20	115.19	358.10	686.22
264.07	044.26	468.15	sidling	signoras	687.25
320.21	075.26	642.23	176.07	636.06	724.27
352.17	101.23	sickness	sigh	signs	740.23
360.19	183.19	155.05	055.01	094.22	756.27
597.07	207.21	606.16	137.01	444.03	753.12
shown	210.03	617.12	140.26	444.13	824.03
048.15	295.14	side	341.26	448.10	887.08
182.13	299.08	080.01	612.23	568.16	silently
321.06	314.17	087.26	649.06	silas's	085.12
626.04	395.01	093.02	715.01	853.04	211.19
644.27	423.07	098.06	sighed	silence	341.03
showy	434.01	116.06	041.04	010.05	823.14
343.21	450.13	123.23	054.27	025.05	silhouette
373.04	469.09	134.09	110.07	042.07	675.27
shrank	498.14	134.10	334.03	060.14	silk
007.25	502.21	136.16	341.26	065.14	019.06
354.01	535.08	138.24	506.15	078.02	032.15
485.02	558.12	152.18	653.21	079.23	058.22
594.24	563.06	153.26	850.03	080.19	122.01
shreds	602.11	155.19	875.09	082.01	124.17
032.15		169.19	879.06	083.26	186.10
094.05		194.20		084.02	236.09

276.14
277.07
348.24
434.20
543.26
544.06
544.14
544.17
545.26
619.07
665.07
692.15
749.27

silken
528.20
751.13

sill
050.25

silly
037.09
103.06
396.01
396.10
396.17

silver
218.21
342.07
343.24
377.15
542.22
544.09
569.16
736.25

silver-gray
340.22

silver-white
049.28
414.11

silvered
413.13
583.06

silverplate
734.03

silvery
124.18
256.14
533.20

similar
015.27
019.04
150.03
510.26
681.06
755.16
854.11

similarly
057.21

simple
059.04
226.17
259.24
502.03
506.10
642.02
656.04
744.20

simple-minded
257.03

simpleton
270.12
437.01
465.11

simplicity
192.10
214.04
739.08
843.26

simplified
155.23

simplify
822.08

simply
542.03
721.24
761.22
766.24

simulate
643.15

simulating
614.06

simultaneously
025.01
347.17
542.14
601.02

sin
106.26
466.01
625.23
824.11

sin'
650.25
676.05

since
001.06
008.21
008.24
017.01
042.12
054.21
156.12

165.01
165.03
175.25
220.03
240.10
252.09
253.12
261.23
263.20
268.18
270.25
283.14
310.07
317.11
319.28
320.17
327.21
340.24
349.06
351.17
352.05
371.02
409.06
424.07
425.23
429.19
429.23
437.03
446.11
446.19
481.13
483.20
526.26
535.17
536.15
541.27
570.24
580.06
580.08
606.04
629.18
697.28
702.20
706.26
707.23
719.03
720.08
736.09
740.05
755.28
766.24
766.26
766.24
772.11
773.18
775.27
780.14
790.09
817.09
817.28
838.25
858.17
861.08
862.16
873.20
899.19
900.21
900.25
907.17
908.16

sincere
133.03
189.25
267.15
537.12
715.10
829.10
837.01
846.25
897.26
900.20

sincerely
025.08
109.17
374.16
517.17
787.04
799.09
845.21
843.18

sincerity
046.26
516.14
709.08
785.03

sinews
819.25

sinful
440.23

sing
039.09
055.26
200.05
200.08
200.09
317.25
318.28
360.11
360.14
361.05
549.18

550.01
550.16

sing-song
014.15

singer
200.26
288.12

singers
549.18

singing
200.16
511.08
561.06
656.06
732.14
687.04

single
079.22
219.21
228.19
236.15
264.12
388.20
392.16
399.26
409.24
423.01
539.19
626.19
626.19
747.26
832.24
836.25
836.26
856.16
856.27

singly
501.04
725.25

singular
022.06
139.18
259.22
300.10
300.12
639.19
704.08
767.03
836.20
900.22

singularity
285.14

singularly
106.10
108.15
382.01
429.05
626.16
637.04
677.02

sinister
377.23
671.07

sink
133.07
554.05

sinking
004.26
248.06
669.27

sinless
646.26

sinner
269.16

sinner's
441.02

sinners
816.07

sins
278.08

sir
034.05
034.09
037.07
037.16
053.08
054.13
055.11
055.20
059.08
117.07
117.14
118.02
223.05
223.28
225.14
226.05
227.03
237.22
239.18
239.23
240.17
241.06
242.01
243.09
243.13
243.25
246.07
247.07
249.20
259.20

260.06
261.05
262.03
264.01
265.03
265.17
265.21
266.14
266.23
267.03
268.28
270.04
270.20
270.28
271.05
271.14
271.26
272.04
272.23
273.13
273.25
274.03
275.03
276.04
284.21
289.03
297.08
297.16
299.24
300.03
300.08
300.23
300.28
301.20
302.08
302.13
316.14
339.23
352.11
362.01
362.08
362.16
362.22
362.26
366.22
378.25
388.16
407.11
407.14
407.17
407.29
408.22
409.03
409.14
410.01
410.04
410.07
410.16
410.20
411.20
412.01
412.07
412.10
412.26
419.04
419.19
422.03
427.07
428.28
430.11
434.16
435.14
435.21
436.03
436.10
436.16
436.24
437.12
437.23
438.04
438.27
441.01
442.09
442.15
442.22
442.24
450.14
450.23
450.26
451.06
451.12
451.18
452.01
452.05
452.16
452.18
452.22
453.01
453.17
453.25
453.28
454.09
454.18
454.26
455.04
455.06
455.08
455.10
455.15
455.21
455.24

455.27
456.08
456.18
495.12
496.19
497.03
506.01
506.11
506.21
506.27
507.02
507.06
508.05
508.16
509.01
509.10
510.03
510.12
510.27
511.06
512.12
513.21
517.21
518.03
523.19
524.08
524.23
525.06
525.24
526.02
526.20
527.28
528.12
528.28
529.04
529.15
529.21
530.04
530.12
530.27
531.09
531.14
532.12
532.22
534.04
534.17
538.23
539.14
540.05
546.10
546.22
547.13
548.03
548.06
548.14
548.18
550.10
554.16
565.12
566.18
566.23
567.06
567.18
567.23
568.08
568.14
569.05
569.15
569.25
570.11
571.21
571.25
572.25
573.20
574.22
576.05
577.05
577.11
577.24
578.06
578.13
579.04
579.08
579.14
580.04
580.10
582.08
582.15
583.11
586.11
586.13
586.20
587.03
592.23
594.02
595.09
595.09
595.20
595.25
599.25
600.06
600.10
600.19
612.19
613.12
613.27
614.21
615.09
615.13
616.26
617.08
618.09

618.17
621.21
622.23
623.27
628.04
628.22
634.11
634.22
635.05
635.12
637.16
638.12
643.20
650.11
687.06
703.02
703.11
705.16
737.01
755.03
799.26
800.02
801.17
802.01
873.04
875.26
876.05
876.22
877.01
877.11
877.21
878.05
878.15
878.23
880.03
880.15
884.17
884.24
885.09
885.21
886.26
889.16
889.21
890.03
891.18
893.09
894.19
894.26
895.11
895.15
895.21
895.26
896.16
897.02
897.06
897.10
897.13
897.16
897.19
897.21
898.12
898.24
899.10
899.15

sister
176.26
319.13
389.20
445.05
457.10
468.07
470.18
489.28
593.12
597.05
626.06
678.14
686.15
700.17
780.23
787.14
807.13
820.25
821.08
821.11
821.23
822.14
822.14
826.20
826.22
838.06
841.02

sister's
022.20
461.10
476.02
487.09
781.01

sisterly
785.28
793.03
842.17

sisters
006.09
007.21
036.26
043.28
242.22
242.23
343.14
346.19

348.13
461.13
664.21
696.01
702.14
706.05
707.23
709.09
714.09
714.22
715.19
718.11
726.02
728.02
733.13
748.20
781.09
782.07
784.10
766.01
786.04
786.05
786.08
787.06
792.03
799.09
801.19
802.13
804.11
805.01
805.27
807.05
829.13
853.05
877.16
892.19
893.10
sisters'
018.11
708.23
sit
005.20
013.01
013.08
047.10
056.12
078.18
097.11
170.21
176.05
176.06
178.17
181.14
186.26
200.06
234.10
245.14
249.27
251.02
256.28
259.24
298.24
336.16
347.27
398.16
409.01
410.08
418.23
432.01
438.07
438.12
442.18
458.20
467.15
470.16
503.22
505.04
510.11
510.13
562.12
563.22
611.25
620.04
656.26
665.21
685.16
687.27
693.15
700.08
700.21
708.02
711.04
713.17
714.01
750.06
763.07
805.26
860.11
878.17
879.01
891.05
site
146.16
160.20
357.26
809.10
sits
400.14
405.11
sitting
026.11

061.05
075.20
089.25
115.05
189.14
190.01
218.12
230.09
231.22
292.21
306.18
347.04
375.26
394.17
399.04
399.17
402.05
471.07
494.07
518.08
535.13
545.02
613.03
638.26
664.05
671.11
676.25
701.17
729.16
745.04
765.09
777.06
803.25
805.11
823.22
901.05
sitting-room
175.03
794.10
situated
040.28
397.05
510.27
745.24
855.02
situation
095.03
161.10
168.20
171.11
173.02
219.03
454.10
455.13
508.04
616.06
706.27
717.13
situations
167.26
325.22
six
055.22
060.16
071.11
073.06
080.09
161.25
183.21
197.20
235.27
288.04
314.20
317.10
328.12
332.08
334.10
444.15
457.26
492.14
527.18
706.19
760.20
813.18
907.12
six-and-thirty
854.26
sixteen
122.03
181.17
sixth
114.08
sixty
049.01
789.19
size
053.01
117.03
368.03
869.03
876.20
skein
099.04
528.20
skeletons
145.25
146.04
skeptical
691.21
sketch
246.15

323.09
472.24
749.22
750.14
sketched
142.21
sketches
203.10
245.23
749.13
sketching
206.13
313.20
470.28
471.10
skies
501.03
737.23
skilful
758.04
skill
250.14
315.07
402.24
472.23
713.27
717.18
735.27
832.09
skin
007.04
019.04
060.24
113.05
124.26
346.14
368.07
555.19
674.24
skipped
281.25
skirt
066.11
277.04
281.24
340.19
skirted
655.08
skirts
164.18
sky
066.20
133.23
145.14
145.27
185.12
209.10
226.04
230.20
243.14
248.15
248.28
250.23
282.25
364.16
414.07
435.16
492.20
560.06
561.12
564.08
570.05
570.18
587.21
588.10
615.19
631.20
640.24
655.12
659.27
660.24
663.04
732.25
782.17
812.09
815.03
869.16
872.21
887.21
910.24
sky-blue
449.28
sky-lark
887.02
sky-line
215.04
skylight
865.27
slab
770.18
slackened
100.13
slain
589.11
slander
618.08
slanting
248.13
slate
115.05
123.05

123.07
123.12
123.20
434.21
slattern
282.13
141.13
slatternly
100.03
103.21
slaughtered
612.04
slave
010.01
012.10
018.06
127.18
545.16
637.23
731.26
slave-purchases
546.12
slavery
548.16
slaving
786.08
slavish
325.01
slay
753.03
sleek
383.04
sleep
028.01
028.20
042.15
046.28
114.14
156.14
158.22
166.01
190.11
206.01
206.18
293.11
294.05
294.23
296.12
298.18
302.18
308.05
308.10
336.18
406.16
418.20
442.17
572.07
572.19
582.06
582.13
629.26
651.22
653.19
654.01
662.25
680.26
691.03
813.10
853.06
902.21
sleeper
306.13
sleepers
415.25
sleeping
306.05
457.23
458.02
572.14
581.10
864.11
sleepless
305.04
sleeps
206.04
282.10
sleepy
355.17
398.22
sleet
145.23
sleeve
555.22
slender
639.06
701.23
slenderly
681.09
slept
015.16
029.08
191.18
293.25
583.17
663.19
688.12
692.11
707.15
858.22
slice
095.14
149.02

671.16
slices
138.16
slid
282.13
835.07
slide
896.08
sliding
222.15
slight
127.22
341.07
343.22
630.12
643.11
649.20
733.04
844.14
876.15
slightest
838.03
slightly
155.03
197.05
589.21
590.22
792.15
slim
047.26
345.02
461.04
464.28
slime
288.17
434.20
slip
123.08
229.26
339.11
361.08
479.13
492.13
504.09
725.26
764.01
773.25
780.16
851.08
slipped
002.26
063.23
169.11
222.19
229.02
232.18
259.19
363.03
392.23
554.17
589.06
741.26
slipper
328.26
slippers
419.12
653.06
slippery
193.11
565.16
slips
048.18
620.02
slope
142.22
sloping
318.06
345.13
sloth
714.26
slothful
792.24
slough
610.05
slow
217.03
434.06
818.12
832.19
slowly
051.18
052.25
082.22
085.19
185.17
186.24
219.01
328.22
389.10
395.02
505.25
640.05
675.03
768.03
844.19
871.13
872.16
slumber
174.23
294.22
445.19

583.18
651.23
813.11
slumbered
075.11
159.04
433.02
slur
507.26
sly
260.15
small
002.25
034.24
042.15
053.01
095.13
096.16
096.17
099.13
137.17
166.01
169.06
186.06
190.07
190.27
192.18
210.02
277.07
278.08
359.22
382.21
405.21
419.27
478.19
516.10
532.18
544.28
559.10
572.22
635.13
665.06
666.28
676.05
689.06
695.02
701.03
707.12
709.18
711.16
729.09
738.08
804.07
863.04
869.17
876.14
small-featured
197.05
smaller
206.03
676.06
677.19
smallest
081.04
smart
047.21
102.23
364.11
smartest
794.14
smartly
082.03
smashed
866.03
smell
296.02
298.07
smelling-bottle
421.18
smells
147.26
smelt
152.02
smile
035.24
104.09
120.26
127.25
136.19
175.14
254.18
258.23
263.27
266.11
275.21
291.02
301.25
341.28
350.24
350.26
350.28
375.25
383.28
404.11
404.28
408.21
409.20
461.24
493.07
497.12
528.25

529.17
535.04
535.06
545.15
567.24
582.04
595.22
601.19
617.24
635.07
640.20
655.15
667.18
697.18
714.23
723.06
726.16
753.06
825.13
850.06

smiled
065.01
127.24
150.01
156.09
175.05
225.05
263.26
266.07
412.02
455.26
472.11
497.12
493.08
519.25
545.14
570.25
640.18
642.02
643.13
723.05
726.10
747.04
751.19
762.01
767.23
792.15
856.12
875.18
876.23

smiles
552.18
575.22
400.14
400.24
401.14
404.09
406.07
574.05
745.02
755.14
882.21

smiling
027.17
158.03
208.10
401.13
452.27
472.06
523.10
532.01
540.09
592.14
655.12
758.05

smith
092.23
097.09
099.04
116.20
122.21
127.23

smitten
147.18
605.15

smoke
172.19
198.25
220.14
295.26
296.04
296.14
298.07
306.14
329.04
396.05
548.25

smoked
081.20
198.25

smoking
281.06
396.22

smoky
199.08

smooth
056.02
120.25
149.06
168.02
192.27

213.02
322.01
322.04
383.26
407.01
541.21
621.28
681.14
692.21
738.03
738.06

smooth-skinned
382.20

smoothed
340.25
651.05
692.18

smoothly
619.07

smote
132.25
523.27
900.11

smother
351.24

smothered
425.09
611.05

snake
285.03
286.20
891.04

snappish
600.02

snapt
511.03

snare
603.15
614.09
731.13

snarl
641.27

snarling
420.18
424.10

snatch
024.07
147.12
646.28
763.19

snatched
140.12
301.04
513.02
599.18
845.16
879.20
900.04

snatching
420.18

snaw
066.21

sneaking
008.22
019.09
180.12

sneer
462.14
513.25

sneering
525.14

sneeringly
412.04

sneers
266.12

snivel
322.15

snored
166.06

snoring
171.03

snow
004.10
111.17
145.16
189.10
204.19
606.03
640.07
765.03
765.07
766.14
766.20
769.09
775.26
804.10
804.18

snow-drift
770.23

snow-drops
144.19

snow-flakes
235.09

snow-wet
767.09

snowed
100.26

snows
111.10
144.05
859.24

snowy
016.07
113.04
186.10
204.13
235.02
359.07
639.25
738.25

snuff
035.10
548.25

snuff-box
037.01
549.01

snuffed
222.25
232.01
768.13

snug
186.06

snugly
394.04

snugness
794.27

so
001.08
001.09
005.10
007.16
009.18
013.25
014.04
016.15
016.24
021.10
021.25
024.21
025.07
027.24
032.22
033.07
033.07
034.15
036.03
036.05
037.25
038.16
040.23
041.20
044.25
047.17
047.23
048.01
049.28
051.20
052.21
053.04
054.04
055.07
059.26
063.04
064.01
068.27
069.11
069.18
072.20
073.17
076.13
081.18
086.06
087.24
089.04
090.19
094.20
094.26
094.26
102.05
102.11
104.16
104.21
105.18
106.03
106.23
106.27
108.17
109.16
109.17
115.17
118.03
120.02
120.08
126.16
126.16
129.07
129.08
129.14
129.15
129.15
131.01
131.22
133.07
133.08
136.24
138.15
140.09
149.24
150.02
151.15
152.02

152.03
152.03
152.04
155.27
156.05
156.08
157.01
166.19
166.24
166.26
169.26
170.08
172.16
176.09
176.10
177.02
179.25
180.09
182.12
183.28
184.06
184.10
185.09
186.23
187.03
188.22
188.24
190.10
191.14
191.23
192.21
192.21
192.22
192.22
193.21
194.13
194.13
194.14
194.18
196.26
197.23
198.20
198.26
198.26
199.21
200.10
201.02
201.19
201.28
203.05
203.25
203.28
204.07
205.05
208.08
210.06
218.15
220.25
220.25
223.32
225.14
227.02
227.21
231.26
235.24
239.28
241.26
245.04
247.14
247.25
250.19
251.02
251.37
251.14
251.20
251.22
251.23
252.15
258.22
260.13
260.22
260.22
262.17
262.27
263.01
263.03
265.02
268.01
269.06
270.08
270.08
271.24
272.10
273.19
274.06
274.09
278.05
279.18
280.13
280.15
281.22
283.09
286.01
286.19
292.01
292.01
292.20
300.11
300.25
301.11
301.27

308.05
308.15
310.04
311.13
311.16
312.01
312.22
313.01
314.08
314.22
314.27
315.19
316.20
316.21
316.25
316.25
318.11
325.10
325.12
327.06
332.17
335.11
336.07
337.20
339.01
339.10
340.01
341.09
344.10
345.19
345.21
349.08
351.05
353.19
353.25
356.08
356.14
357.22
353.14
359.15
359.19
359.20
362.28
363.08
364.10
364.11
375.19
375.22
375.23
375.24
376.01
376.20
380.27
381.22
382.08
383.26
383.27
384.11
384.12
384.22
390.11
391.04
395.16
397.01
398.08
401.14
402.12
402.13
403.28
405.06
406.10
407.19
411.10
417.22
421.27
425.02
425.03
426.15
426.15
428.01
428.14
428.25
429.21
431.20
431.23
434.15
436.01
438.06
441.19
444.02
444.03
447.23
448.20
448.21
448.27
449.17
449.19
451.20
454.26
455.15
455.27
456.16
459.22
461.10
461.10
461.20
462.01
462.22
462.24
464.07

464.17
466.06
466.07
466.11
467.20
468.05
474.22
475.23
478.13
481.04
481.25
484.18
486.13
487.13
488.10
489.24
493.02
493.13
493.14
495.17
495.27
496.02
498.06
498.27
499.25
500.06
500.12
501.03
501.03
502.17
504.25
505.03
505.19
505.19
509.13
510.08
511.01
513.17
513.20
513.21
513.22
514.04
516.11
519.04
519.05
521.19
521.20
522.06
522.13
522.14
522.21
523.08
523.09
524.04
529.09
534.08
535.10
536.10
536.15
537.01
537.04
537.04
537.22
537.22
538.14
539.28
544.28
546.08
546.15
547.03
553.19
557.10
560.03
563.18
570.09
570.13
571.19
575.21
580.10
580.24
581.08
582.02
582.03
582.15
583.11
583.19
583.19
583.19
585.03
585.13
585.14
586.02
587.15
587.15
590.04
600.20
602.01
606.11
609.07
609.07
610.16
610.17
611.11
612.20
614.05
616.26
617.03
617.04
619.07
620.14
620.15

620.25	777.14	sob	738.02	230.22	solve
621.10	7?7.15	057.17	752.10	250.22	536.13
622.13	7.7.15	611.09	754.25	271.07	856.01
623.09	778.18	650.28	766.20	378.17	solved
624.03	780.02	sobbed	798.06	414.12	098.17
624.07	781.15	416.09	812.14	485.28	143.13
624.28	783.15	511.10	825.05	491.02	370.08
625.09	785.14	sobbing	872.12	502.05	sombre
627.11	785.15	130.11	877.17	551.22	001.08
632.01	785.20	509.14	878.12	573.15	066.02
632.01	788.08	640.08	889.28	644.10	472.02
632.02	790.23	sober	898.22	714.23	486.04
632.03	791.11	544.13	soften	740.27	582.21
634.27	792.23	775.16	136.03	775.23	664.16
636.15	793.08	sobered	747.15	808.16	677.02
636.25	793.19	340.10	softened	824.09	741.20
637.10	793.27	sobering	351.01	843.28	some
637.15	795.24	781.24	461.18	845.17	008.10
638.01	799.07	sobriety	466.07	848.04	019.21
643.28	802.06	121.19	620.24	solemnizing	022.27
643.28	802.07	sous	716.15	341.13	023.07
647.05	803.12	022.24	882.23	792.07	023.13
648.13	805.09	025.13	888.13	solemnly	023.17
648.22	805.10	584.03	softening	052.28	024.09
649.10	805.18	605.06	108.05	388.23	025.04
649.10	805.25	810.24	260.13	577.05	026.10
652.15	806.25	811.10	371.28	solicited	027.22
652.19	808.06	sociable	softer	454.16	029.17
655.03	818.16	002.12	346.13	solicitor	031.18
655.03	818.16	social	502.08	592.19	036.11
657.13	819.08	643.01	softest	602.14	057.19
657.14	819.08	730.25	322.10	772.09	048.25
668.13	820.26	society	softly	780.08	049.14
668.14	821.22	149.14	026.02	solicitor's	050.24
668.14	821.23	150.04	154.07	594.14	050.25
669.19	822.12	162.16	155.23	solicitous	051.03
670.28	826.05	214.07	210.05	192.11	053.05
672.22	827.21	214.20	299.06	359.27	053.23
674.14	828.02	243.14	419.13	494.24	055.17
674.16	829.11	261.11	464.20	solicitude	057.18
676.02	829.12	286.18	504.09	214.16	060.13
676.09	829.17	290.12	646.02	767.27	060.16
677.24	831.14	316.25	654.18	804.12	064.01
680.09	834.16	401.19	852.20	solid	065.27
681.06	834.19	440.04	858.07	031.22	066.01
681.17	837.01	475.15	875.07	060.21	066.02
681.21	837.09	476.23	886.12	220.28	068.08
681.23	837.09	625.10	softness	261.01	070.02
691.24	840.07	627.25	259.08	775.14	070.03
692.12	840.08	629.03	375.15	775.16	071.19
692.27	840.09	636.03	441.25	779.22	074.13
692.28	841.03	641.16	529.08	soliloquized	074.20
696.13	841.15	659.15	660.26	166.14	076.03
696.18	842.20	718.12	soil	soliloquy	077.05
697.04	843.25	720.12	288.19	672.20	077.19
697.12	843.26	785.25	373.08	solitary	080.17
698.28	845.20	793.03	440.03	003.24	080.24
699.04	846.08	909.04	663.22	004.28	082.14
699.22	846.28	society's	674.01	045.28	083.20
700.25	847.01	837.21	693.07	067.21	086.25
701.27	847.10	socket	719.19	132.07	090.06
702.01	853.27	172.22	720.16	190.11	092.08
705.16	856.04	sodden	soir	191.16	097.24
705.23	857.04	072.26	498.09	221.20	097.25
705.27	859.18	686.07	sojourn	225.15	100.15
708.09	862.28	sofa	526.21	353.06	109.05
708.27	863.04	002.03	sojourned	396.24	114.13
709.15	865.08	198.27	884.26	502.10	116.22
711.03	866.08	256.11	solace	562.24	117.10
712.20	867.21	257.19	113.24	605.21	117.15
714.08	870.02	300.20	162.17	648.02	121.10
716.24	870.22	306.06	176.13	656.17	127.22
723.11	872.14	347.19	329.07	672.17	130.12
723.19	876.15	352.14	379.25	854.17	132.08
727.02	876.23	380.04	441.07	solitude	133.22
728.05	877.05	380.16	513.17	064.28	134.04
731.19	878.11	475.20	601.23	163.14	136.02
735.20	879.03	478.28	651.08	190.25	138.13
738.02	879.04	650.26	656.10	215.23	147.19
739.03	880.04	700.21	752.22	219.12	149.17
739.11	880.14	706.02	787.12	235.20	150.23
740.02	881.14	734.03	sold	329.19	151.23
741.20	881.22	sofas	048.21	341.04	155.04
741.20	882.09	342.25	670.11	364.05	156.11
741.24	883.09	399.21	soldier	404.26	156.25
742.01	883.11	soft	735.17	610.15	160.08
742.07	888.26	016.01	736.01	618.18	162.03
747.16	894.22	033.11	820.13	618.19	162.27
747.16	896.22	104.09	soldierly	618.19	164.07
748.01	898.08	145.28	348.08	618.23	166.04
748.28	898.25	220.27	soldiers	644.05	169.06
749.25	903.12	248.17	113.12	668.16	171.24
751.12	904.03	333.27	sole	668.16	173.06
752.21	908.04	342.04	083.15	724.09	175.05
752.24	909.16	357.15	215.20	734.09	177.10
757.10	909.16	404.08	238.26	754.07	182.04
757.10	910.04	471.12	244.16	812.27	182.08
757.24	910.06	473.10	340.25	859.09	191.03
757.25	911.04	486.01	439.20	909.08	193.13
758.05	912.25	492.19	502.23	solitudes	197.11
758.26	soaked	502.07	601.22	826.16	198.12
760.17	421.12	528.19	719.22	solo	198.15
760.25	soaking	551.22	721.26	337.08	200.17
762.28	088.08	552.17	822.15	solomon	201.06
766.05	soap	573.15	840.17	143.15	203.10
767.12	051.09	582.23	883.02	solus	203.21
768.13	soar	640.11	solecism	700.27	206.28
769.02	276.02	643.05	641.17	solution	207.21
769.20	soart	649.27	solemn	559.16	210.03
771.09	681.02	662.16	016.14	581.22	210.19
772.12		712.22	214.09		211.23

217.17	506.02	779.08	259.21	192.16	440.20
220.03	513.08	787.12	260.09	192.17	514.28
223.07	515.03	787.17	283.20	210.23	549.26
223.16	522.10	790.03	290.12	213.11	887.05
224.01	526.08	790.16	295.11	215.20	songs
227.18	531.12	791.11	296.03	217.08	039.08
227.27	533.10	794.06	297.18	217.25	070.04
232.18	534.06	794.14	299.19	221.20	441.17
233.06	536.25	794.18	300.07	254.06	sonorous
235.18	541.10	795.19	308.02	254.15	333.23
238.17	546.12	796.01	321.13	254.18	sont
238.25	555.21	800.17	329.22	259.08	313.17
242.17	558.02	801.01	334.13	265.10	soon
245.20	562.06	802.08	336.04	286.17	002.27
245.23	562.20	803.23	342.01	291.02	006.03
246.27	564.18	805.27	348.11	291.28	008.13
248.13	572.06	809.21	351.14	302.21	009.22
252.13	572.12	810.19	354.22	305.10	025.15
252.27	572.18	814.21	359.13	314.14	028.17
255.20	573.21	815.09	371.26	326.11	033.05
276.12	574.02	819.09	377.22	373.20	044.28
277.28	581.01	826.28	377.28	378.24	046.09
278.09	586.07	838.21	378.04	379.04	050.10
282.18	591.04	840.01	382.04	398.22	053.19
282.23	596.25	848.02	385.06	402.24	059.16
283.08	597.02	852.17	391.11	445.10	064.18
288.09	599.18	853.23	403.12	445.10	064.20
288.24	602.13	860.07	408.07	445.11	066.18
289.18	602.24	860.11	411.22	446.14	069.03
290.25	605.08	862.09	415.21	469.28	069.13
292.28	609.02	862.14	417.10	497.08	076.27
297.22	611.15	865.07	422.16	505.08	080.08
299.10	612.04	866.13	448.10	510.22	082.21
301.23	612.22	866.20	453.12	535.12	082.24
301.23	613.18	869.11	456.13	633.08	095.12
305.15	620.10	871.10	460.22	635.27	108.24
307.13	621.07	871.12	467.08	636.07	129.08
308.27	626.04	872.05	467.25	637.15	133.08
309.14	627.06	872.27	496.07	667.03	137.10
311.05	628.06	873.03	497.01	669.03	137.22
317.25	633.04	878.02	497.26	700.09	159.03
329.10	635.01	878.03	512.26	711.05	187.21
333.15	640.28	881.03	523.25	714.21	191.18
335.02	641.17	882.08	523.26	739.27	213.15
335.09	643.21	884.12	529.13	803.18	233.04
337.26	646.17	886.02	533.28	803.28	252.27
337.27	646.19	887.17	537.08	804.22	255.10
340.03	652.08	892.09	539.04	811.28	257.09
342.14	652.25	900.21	542.08	826.15	293.18
342.24	654.13	901.27	559.05	826.16	297.18
342.26	654.14	902.18	566.02	856.14	303.03
344.25	656.20	905.14	569.08	869.06	305.14
345.14	656.21	905.19	569.11	892.02	310.14
348.05	660.01	906.20	570.25	900.18	311.01
349.12	660.03	910.15	588.11	908.07	326.21
353.05	664.25	somebody	598.02	somewhat	330.08
354.20	665.01	297.17	599.13	010.16	337.15
368.02	665.01	366.27	607.23	039.04	340.24
368.19	666.14	791.05	613.02	046.01	340.25
368.26	666.20	somebody's	616.13	060.19	340.26
369.18	666.21	159.07	624.06	067.09	356.17
373.16	667.27	somehow	629.05	075.01	356.20
379.21	670.18	067.17	633.15	078.01	372.13
379.27	675.17	123.07	639.14	082.04	381.15
380.01	676.06	259.18	641.02	236.06	405.27
381.14	676.17	311.28	642.27	258.07	413.10
384.05	679.16	342.12	655.06	275.17	415.02
384.10	683.10	686.26	666.07	293.07	428.27
385.01	685.21	864.09	667.09	294.18	447.16
398.06	686.01	something	669.07	381.25	453.04
398.06	688.06	002.14	675.20	384.27	459.12
399.01	689.04	002.21	678.07	465.18	463.01
400.21	691.02	015.10	679.10	543.24	463.16
407.26	691.16	023.20	694.24	545.09	466.06
413.04	691.22	024.04	702.10	574.19	468.28
415.19	692.02	029.04	718.09	621.28	470.07
415.23	693.20	044.16	759.10	670.20	471.13
416.09	695.08	046.21	759.11	726.22	479.27
416.09	695.08	047.09	761.06	768.08	484.04
418.15	696.28	061.21	763.17	770.06	494.15
420.25	697.07	065.17	767.13	789.07	495.20
428.21	698.21	069.14	768.05	796.03	495.27
429.17	701.10	079.02	778.02	833.06	496.12
434.15	702.20	081.16	805.11	834.03	498.24
435.24	705.16	081.21	811.11	891.06	502.11
440.15	709.12	084.12	813.08	somewhere	503.21
445.28	709.19	095.02	823.11	002.23	507.06
448.02	715.01	095.03	834.12	090.14	507.07
449.17	716.01	106.08	839.18	156.18	520.02
452.23	717.23	118.14	853.14	454.10	523.20
454.14	722.10	119.23	862.07	499.05	525.27
458.04	724.21	126.27	881.06	510.25	531.09
458.25	725.12	130.16	881.23	666.07	531.17
467.05	726.26	136.10	884.09	849.12	534.21
470.25	730.03	138.28	903.14	901.23	542.12
471.24	730.13	139.04	sometimes	somwhere	543.07
471.25	734.21	139.11	005.16	397.09	583.22
472.15	736.10	151.01	019.03	son	585.09
476.14	738.28	159.10	027.12	012.17	586.18
478.20	743.04	162.28	032.24	092.01	586.24
480.28	743.14	166.13	038.11	107.26	597.09
482.01	744.05	179.15	038.23	319.15	611.03
483.13	744.08	181.02	047.06	616.21	613.02
485.14	745.18	192.05	055.13	624.01	613.12
486.08	749.13	223.22	103.25	624.12	616.08
488.05	753.23	224.07	105.04	624.18	619.13
488.16	755.01	228.21	105.19	844.18	620.16
488.26	757.17	237.27	114.20	song	632.20
489.19	760.09	250.10	140.12	032.17	641.23
502.15	773.05	253.17	144.13	032.20	642.19
505.11	774.04	259.17	189.14	200.16	643.05

643.23
647.09
651.23
652.21
655.11
655.22
656.22
665.02
665.26
669.16
671.20
674.10
680.05
683.28
686.09
688.03
688.09
698.19
704.11
708.23
710.05
716.11
717.10
725.20
733.04
734.16
743.09
744.01
747.13
750.27
764.11
765.18
768.14
783.06
798.02
798.22
802.01
816.23
832.23
834.16
839.10
839.25
854.04
854.14
870.09
872.12
882.10
886.05
886.10
886.28
901.01
901.13
907.21
908.01
908.09
sooner
030.01
059.24
121.28
257.18
349.14
427.27
506.17
549.22
768.28
801.09
soot
370.19
soot-black
770.20
soothe
030.15
550.07
647.25
896.05
soothed
901.06
soothing
027.03
260.14
271.21
315.02
341.11
715.27
752.05
soothingly
620.04
sophie
198.21
198.23
198.26
198.28
199.11
199.15
217.23
217.24
278.19
284.17
314.12
327.24
351.19
336.10
340.09
363.11
498.09
570.19
576.09
576.13
576.17
576.18
576.22

582.06
582.17
585.02
598.17
sophistical
622.27
soporific
171.02
sorceress
297.13
386.15
sordid
369.24
434.21
668.09
753.06
795.11
sore
033.03
551.28
sorely
654.15
665.24
soreness
736.07
sorrow
406.03
583.13
583.16
650.08
662.26
725.01
760.05
767.12
844.11
872.12
883.24
900.24
sorrowful
068.12
377.23
569.03
sorrows
133.17
465.22
777.15
sorry
053.22
067.24
069.20
135.01
446.23
483.28
506.13
506.23
508.16
510.16
511.17
537.03
603.10
668.03
sort
010.18
040.15
049.11
079.15
086.05
087.10
093.12
095.10
102.20
105.04
182.09
183.18
184.27
205.04
217.20
241.17
242.15
242.17
260.10
272.21
275.28
278.03
280.18
285.18
308.11
313.14
319.03
319.26
356.19
358.19
358.24
366.19
369.18
417.10
420.25
459.01
465.12
471.11
480.19
497.02
507.26
508.19
510.20
535.04
537.16
553.23
593.05
594.08

597.24
612.23
617.10
628.07
628.09
639.10
641.02
671.18
675.13
690.03
709.17
746.20
748.19
760.26
783.20
800.14
812.21
834.04
840.01
868.03
881.06
885.11
890.17
sorted
116.19
sorting
792.05
sorts
182.15
221.10
405.16
435.01
sotto
064.21
sough
220.23
sought
031.13
032.04
046.19
058.24
155.08
172.27
174.16
228.07
289.07
291.07
334.16
337.23
353.03
372.18
379.25
413.01
419.23
430.01
440.01
465.07
501.19
537.25
545.13
559.20
610.26
624.13
634.17
636.04
642.06
654.04
654.11
654.12
671.23
672.04
704.11
717.16
738.20
773.08
773.24
774.20
809.04
864.13
887.21
908.04
soul
019.26
054.21
063.17
109.07
125.24
139.22
141.21
155.06
282.09
292.17
325.15
329.16
350.09
350.26
379.08
405.07
485.27
513.06
528.07
533.22
598.18
608.12
630.17
648.09
649.01
649.03
663.18
691.13
722.16

749.01
761.15
817.23
846.22
850.21
877.15
879.27
901.10
902.22
soul's
853.05
soul-withered
439.25
souliers
277.10
soulless
513.05
souls
119.08
158.01
480.06
528.03
662.20
753.06
756.27
sound
023.19
026.06
045.21
047.06
060.26
075.10
080.27
088.15
089.23
105.03
145.22
166.16
210.05
210.08
219.13
222.15
222.23
223.22
294.04
295.06
306.07
337.02
342.04
382.09
414.16
420.18
422.23
503.07
524.08
572.03
584.03
654.17
659.13
664.09
684.12
707.03
736.24
770.06
804.19
843.25
844.15
858.08
858.21
871.07
876.06
902.13
908.11
909.24
sounded
074.26
081.13
093.25
135.23
293.28
415.26
713.19
716.20
832.03
sounding
140.17
373.10
678.18
soundly
045.01
191.18
287.05
sounds
166.18
166.19
217.08
244.03
274.03
337.12
418.02
424.08
524.25
630.14
708.11
894.22
soup
334.18
source
139.23
268.25
292.28

444.11
466.23
474.28
574.13
662.21
781.05
808.20
832.23
sources
712.21
soured
150.21
sourly
390.15
638.18
south
501.06
559.22
622.14
659.06
857.10
south-of-england
717.12
southern
003.27
145.28
731.14
southernwood
435.03
503.09
souvent
334.06
sovereign
132.16
358.10
454.24
543.06
sovereign's
815.18
sowing
057.11
sown
757.25
space
004.10
049.22
083.10
087.27
160.09
165.20
190.25
414.07
551.05
560.11
661.17
662.16
707.18
758.16
828.16
829.12
846.02
870.24
872.01
905.20
spacious
007.05
076.13
191.05
span
140.02
spangled
812.16
spaniard
346.15
spanish
086.05
384.14
409.15
429.13
624.24
spanish-town
593.15
spar
203.21
spare
015.15
357.01
454.28
546.12
612.21
613.28
655.24
782.26
794.22
spared
051.05
478.04
692.13
818.26
837.21
spark
108.28
519.06
592.12
sparkled
258.24
678.22
sparkles
249.14
sparkling
145.12

204.17
887.20
sparks
348.07
417.05
sparrow
887.12
spasm
136.04
409.21
486.11
687.24
836.05
spasmodic
594.10
spat
411.28
speak
002.24
038.09
039.27
046.01
057.25
061.27
066.26
072.11
119.11
127.04
135.07
146.17
151.07
153.21
156.04
179.08
197.09
197.21
198.18
233.07
256.18
263.25
263.28
266.12
272.23
275.22
296.13
349.09
354.12
362.02
397.13
399.08
404.27
416.22
422.09
422.11
426.17
448.15
511.13
511.22
525.07
529.17
591.24
595.14
616.28
619.06
620.08
622.23
679.12
682.09
682.20
685.19
686.16
686.17
687.24
691.11
692.01
698.16
702.13
703.22
717.27
729.19
740.23
760.11
760.25
763.24
776.12
780.19
797.21
814.06
814.14
814.28
828.02
837.18
839.25
843.11
855.24
874.04
875.24
879.06
896.06
896.24
901.19
speaker
441.21
590.20
591.25
689.15
737.09
876.08
speaking
003.20
008.17

026.06	speechless	710.02	140.07	457.06	237.05
039.21	542.15	761.06	200.02	751.25	312.28
065.28	speed	783.05	233.18	spots	349.28
116.06	539.17	820.21	238.16	128.09	471.15
133.15	707.10	831.11	272.13	146.10	474.12
155.20	spell	832.12	313.26	sprain	571.05
242.06	016.24	843.18	341.09	224.04	585.07
263.26	129.06	850.21	365.06	228.03	740.13
309.05	222.08	851.17	384.18	238.23	square-made
344.10	351.27	852.01	409.19	243.10	211.13
344.21	380.05	853.09	413.09	254.07	squareness
347.14	438.21	880.10	467.26	sprained	237.13
361.24	712.26	884.12	473.25	232.16	squarer
355.16	807.01	885.19	515.04	sprang	237.06
409.23	814.23	886.14	542.13	146.05	squares
409.27	spellbound	902.20	542.13	228.01	557.14
420.26	424.07	912.03	614.16	278.02	squire
439.09	spend	spirited	618.17	564.16	869.13
448.08	046.06	227.14	639.10	601.03	st
472.12	058.02	361.07	647.17	627.10	089.16
517.25	150.01	865.04	647.20	651.15	114.08
549.05	229.24	spirito	652.14	674.08	423.26
592.14	440.07	360.15	686.05	753.17	635.28
619.05	510.05	spirits	700.02	853.06	679.26
625.24	546.13	044.28	726.26	spray	680.22
640.17	549.15	113.11	742.04	004.23	681.01
690.13	750.17	132.21	751.05	676.12	681.17
723.28	752.02	132.23	770.01	sprays	684.18
736.16	892.21	153.14	813.15	143.09	685.09
793.23	spending	191.25	822.18	spread	685.11
827.07	752.16	252.03	832.02	016.07	686.13
832.10	883.19	294.03	833.18	033.08	687.04
832.16	spends	379.11	836.22	049.13	687.26
862.04	177.17	427.09	844.14	076.01	690.24
speaks	spent	500.08	849.22	090.23	691.12
206.04	008.10	551.12	869.05	124.17	691.24
664.11	108.21	573.08	883.15	204.11	695.11
810.28	114.08	662.22	898.27	242.04	695.26
875.28	163.14	713.12	spoken	247.12	695.28
911.27	165.04	727.23	088.16	248.14	697.11
spear	247.02	800.17	150.08	331.02	698.17
204.11	329.10	810.12	155.14	502.04	699.14
special	473.04	882.12	156.15	606.06	700.28
345.04	475.19	spiritual	224.24	661.19	701.17
554.14	490.22	118.18	261.12	662.09	703.23
559.24	500.08	261.12	265.27	674.14	704.16
770.02	543.24	247.18	268.04	694.27	705.03
804.26	634.03	480.08	383.03	735.23	705.11
specially	745.11	824.15	383.08	735.25	707.28
499.20	790.21	spite	480.14	753.12	708.18
505.12	800.14	016.24	496.09	762.19	709.10
species	887.16	018.20	514.02	762.27	709.23
025.16	sphere	299.12	524.24	777.07	710.01
219.02	404.11	328.17	587.09	spreading	714.07
524.11	568.23	466.21	605.07	277.12	717.01
697.06	569.22	497.26	796.17	359.06	717.20
712.01	709.15	635.03	814.22	594.20	720.04
specimen	797.13	747.03	834.09	663.07	725.06
200.11	sphynx	864.10	834.20	sprightly	725.10
478.09	275.02	spiteful	846.18	002.13	725.27
702.06	sphynx-like	373.17	889.14	346.26	727.20
795.01	618.21	478.08	902.15	spring	727.26
speck	spice	581.17	spokesman	013.06	733.08
559.23	148.08	spitzbergen	369.13	085.02	734.22
563.02	358.21	004.07	sponge	139.26	736.17
575.19	spices	splash	419.17	144.03	739.06
692.26	792.05	297.01	419.23	146.23	740.09
specking	spike-guarded	splashed	421.16	189.16	741.15
017.22	145.08	419.23	422.06	277.26	742.04
spectacle	spill	690.15	422.18	293.22	747.18
050.10	239.05	splashing	sponged	331.26	748.20
099.24	spilt	076.04	421.22	364.17	751.17
141.24	326.09	380.18	spontaneous	435.06	752.15
143.01	355.25	splashy	334.21	644.11	753.15
371.27	874.20	675.06	707.25	653.27	756.03
422.27	875.26	splendid	spontaneously	658.15	765.02
498.27	spine	032.15	350.11	754.09	766.01
742.22	381.01	037.10	373.07	775.18	775.03
794.14	spinster	076.13	spoonful	809.26	776.18
860.14	704.14	317.28	082.17	812.10	779.12
861.25	spire	344.09	spoonfuls	859.27	779.28
spectacles	664.12	352.17	071.18	866.02	782.01
170.03	spirit	434.16	spoonie	sprinkled	783.18
170.06	017.24	492.18	280.05	280.21	785.20
326.14	022.19	501.02	spoonies	sprinkling	788.12
534.26	025.10	splendidly	280.10	714.24	792.15
555.07	039.11	122.01	spoons	sprite	793.07
spectator	105.24	625.01	082.22	531.18	795.08
097.02	108.28	split	238.28	555.09	796.15
spectators	133.05	520.16	sport	sprung	798.16
371.13	139.28	560.13	387.10	148.03	799.08
601.16	174.28	737.07	sports	716.26	800.23
spectre	221.18	spoiled	125.20	spue	801.11
578.11	230.17	018.20	sportsman	436.14	802.04
663.23	253.06	019.06	660.03	spun	803.17
685.23	302.24	293.07	spot	815.03	806.05
850.06	355.18	spoiling	149.04	spurn	806.11
speculation	360.17	118.12	159.21	636.28	807.11
727.07	399.03	779.03	172.05	spurned	807.17
sped	402.05	spoilt	215.23	136.05	809.09
479.10	411.16	213.10	568.02	184.16	810.02
551.17	426.03	289.05	594.05	spurred	810.22
758.13	440.15	347.24	612.09	228.10	811.13
speech	472.05	748.10	618.28	282.02	812.04
267.14	480.01	spoke	638.24	spy	812.19
406.20	513.13	038.23	854.20	478.14	813.01
440.19	513.14	043.07	867.27	839.22	814.25
635.09	574.02	044.17	871.05	square	815.09
speeches	640.15	061.23	887.22	053.28	816.06
379.03	649.24	083.18	spotless	060.17	819.11
	652.14	103.04	346.20	185.25	819.19
		130.25			
		133.13			

819.24
821.22
822.20
823.14
826.05
827.18
828.01
829.19
829.27
831.11
833.19
833.25
834.01
834.18
835.05
837.05
839.19
839.23
841.06
843.01
844.23
846.27
847.16
847.27
848.10
848.25
849.11
850.10
850.19
851.06
851.19
852.10
879.09
889.09
889.12
889.21
890.09
890.20
891.24
894.10
895.02
907.10
911.14
912.08
912.18
stab
616.25
stabbed
599.06
633.12
633.25
stable
528.09
stables
379.22
453.09
443.01
449.09
stage
334.19
603.12
stage-trappings
525.28
staggered
410.03
staggering
415.14
stagnate
126.24
797.18
stagnation
216.19
229.20
staid
217.16
306.21
stain
832.25
stained
191.24
203.19
701.09
stainless
268.21
273.08
583.03
606.25
812.09
stains
329.02
764.07
773.27
stair
044.07
602.15
stair-case
021.03
stair-cases
215.01
stair-head
045.27
staircase
134.05
154.23
190.19
191.05
208.24
209.25
229.22
231.08
295.13

295.14
299.07
328.20
331.07
335.21
361.24
566.05
598.25
688.08
693.01
867.15
stairs
010.23
011.06
047.06
051.12
079.14
080.12
122.17
151.04
165.23
175.02
190.18
190.24
203.11
206.25
206.25
210.17
232.26
233.11
234.07
235.04
236.17
254.14
255.12
306.09
311.04
315.12
315.16
333.26
336.12
337.05
365.13
413.03
419.14
427.06
432.18
445.27
463.08
479.09
519.26
522.22
549.12
570.19
582.17
585.17
598.22
612.24
640.28
654.09
794.25
795.05
795.21
795.22
798.24
829.26
843.08
885.27
stale
770.07
stalled
143.16
stalwart
113.12
871.26
stamboul
546.10
stamp
323.18
909.25
stamped
415.20
433.08
525.02
526.24
766.14
835.25
stamping
223.14
415.14
stand
006.28
009.16
009.20
022.03
103.01
114.19
127.03
127.21
132.12
136.16
223.11
224.21
332.17
422.08
436.13
456.22
458.23
546.07
575.21

648.19
677.16
735.03
754.05
816.21
912.05
standard
528.15
762.28
808.12
823.06
standing
004.22
034.22
052.15
075.14
083.17
083.25
098.05
119.19
127.07
151.21
183.12
302.09
338.06
353.01
409.17
504.12
571.14
577.06
608.13
723.12
839.13
856.28
865.20
866.14
stands
080.09
352.13
353.06
353.06
515.13
602.01
644.02
stanzas
553.16
star
167.21
248.18
248.26
250.18
437.26
502.10
660.24
675.16
856.07
star-like
812.16
starched
460.25
stare
696.16
857.26
905.17
stared
342.20
412.27
672.09
stark
606.12
680.27
698.10
starlight
316.05
starry
549.23
stars
033.12
230.27
231.03
510.08
782.17
901.07
start
068.26
228.11
307.07
313.14
443.05
550.23
580.17
736.25
753.17
770.28
started
009.21
130.12
268.14
293.26
399.10
463.10
483.09
504.21
626.22
723.24
737.05
754.16
821.02
829.18
873.14

starting
285.07
startled
291.21
377.19
803.01
853.08
startling
849.04
starts
467.23
858.15
starvation
888.15
starve
119.07
540.19
735.03
starved
113.22
244.16
672.05
800.07
starving
021.11
668.24
state
016.28
030.10
030.14
039.22
042.08
058.23
117.02
126.13
127.01
139.01
158.03
298.08
300.18
320.18
332.06
340.06
470.08
473.19
483.26
502.04
581.10
603.09
623.25
626.07
630.16
630.19
647.23
690.25
736.05
761.22
792.11
809.09
835.19
895.20
898.14
stated
265.11
stateliest
015.20
stateliness
186.18
stately
086.10
186.12
192.19
193.20
203.17
236.07
347.07
389.01
400.21
574.25
781.17
858.24
statement
136.12
statesman
736.01
statesmen
797.09
stating
173.28
station
225.12
315.38
353.08
534.17
534.18
534.18
534.18
538.08
621.04
857.19
stationed
432.26
740.05
stations
367.10
statue
238.15
346.18
701.21
stature
344.04

344.28
581.15
601.06
889.23
904.04
statute
273.26
273.28
stay
024.28
114.28
130.26
158.24
179.26
180.10
184.19
276.26
316.18
339.16
340.01
363.09
408.24
409.03
417.20
452.04
452.06
453.14
464.04
466.27
467.05
487.06
488.13
491.13
497.18
503.21
506.07
512.23
512.27
526.13
559.17
600.07
604.01
615.22
615.27
655.22
669.22
696.26
709.02
709.05
721.12
721.15
723.17
733.12
740.02
742.08
754.05
773.20
787.16
804.28
840.15
874.01
878.25
880.03
stayed
035.16
151.13
151.25
199.14
209.22
244.26
254.06
289.12
293.19
488.17
503.06
602.12
604.06
750.21
803.17
851.12
871.19
staying
222.03
299.13
412.08
438.26
459.08
603.02
695.12
880.05
stays
436.07
stead
022.04
162.18
546.07
805.02
883.16
steadfast
587.16
797.09
912.21
steadfastly
560.01
steadfastness
702.26
steadied
340.11
615.08
steadily
034.23

290.05
396.07
477.18
592.02
674.11
706.02
734.21
826.12
846.06
steady
125.07
308.21
420.09
746.02
775.21
steal
379.10
495.07
stealing
688.05
steals
858.07
steam
094.03
137.13
steamed
147.26
steed
222.06
223.02
227.12
741.06
steel
224.10
282.25
steeled
620.20
steelily
836.06
steely
349.21
steep
765.12
steeple
588.09
stem
016.07
870.17
stems
221.26
step
008.19
047.06
067.02
090.11
163.10
280.23
283.07
298.06
305.09
314.05
337.04
359.18
367.24
395.17
396.19
412.22
422.23
424.09
432.08
434.06
463.08
463.18
503.06
503.17
503.20
505.17
526.25
564.13
589.15
589.21
594.05
656.13
683.21
730.24
731.02
736.22
775.03
806.12
809.13
816.12
871.03
871.14
871.19
871.24
872.16
907.02
step-mother
738.14
stepped
053.27
169.28
193.23
407.16
457.03
798.05
steps
023.23
033.10
072.26

085.22
151.13
144.18
154.26
172.24
182.06
190.18
193.11
204.06
222.15
231.07
233.17
252.27
295.12
331.07
333.25
367.23
419.25
494.06
550.27
603.17
636.27
654.27
659.01
stern
224.14
229.01
258.22
350.28
375.14
411.15
465.16
527.14
531.09
539.28
605.08
643.13
649.17
716.17
740.12
740.22
824.06
831.05
845.08
855.05
911.23
sternen
676.21
sterner
734.26
sternest
596.16
sternest-seeming
756.25
sternly
872.14
sternness
262.26
497.06
711.24
stick
227.05
250.15
261.08
355.04
stiff
052.07
075.20
112.02
237.27
693.10
798.12
894.01
stiff-necked
900.05
stiffened
066.16
145.15
672.14
674.25
stiffly
389.17
stiffness
167.19
754.19
stifle
023.02
260.20
797.04
808.07
stifled
656.16
811.10
stifling
127.12
stile
219.25
221.07
223.23
226.26
227.12
229.05
241.28
494.06
496.11
497.18
497.23
542.03
856.08
still
013.08

017.23
018.05
018.06
019.06
019.12
021.03
023.09
032.23
033.17
037.25
043.01
048.02
049.24
057.04
062.10
066.08
084.04
084.21
088.08
089.20
095.16
097.15
098.17
101.20
103.10
103.13
105.25
120.12
136.15
145.03
152.03
155.21
157.03
161.15
169.10
170.26
171.04
175.10
182.27
188.28
192.11
193.25
207.12
208.23
210.06
218.12
218.27
219.16
221.08
224.07
229.01
229.11
230.09
234.11
237.23
252.15
256.20
258.01
258.15
259.01
261.27
263.15
264.11
266.03
270.28
275.17
276.03
280.25
283.05
289.23
291.28
295.06
295.15
295.24
297.25
298.21
299.02
302.10
307.06
308.11
308.16
310.24
311.18
314.18
315.09
324.03
326.14
328.16
335.11
336.15
341.12
343.07
344.06
344.07
344.08
343.10
353.23
354.28
364.16
371.19
375.16
378.04
381.26
383.01
385.04
387.11
391.04
405.17
405.21
406.17

414.18
419.25
421.07
423.06
430.11
431.28
432.21
433.09
436.03
439.16
446.11
457.15
458.20
459.25
460.11
461.18
473.25
479.19
480.06
480.07
480.19
485.11
485.25
491.22
502.08
503.22
514.04
514.22
514.23
515.18
515.18
515.19
519.27
550.18
551.01
562.12
562.24
572.08
573.05
575.06
576.18
576.24
584.03
589.04
591.17
593.21
595.13
593.10
598.22
598.23
602.18
607.20
611.01
614.12
617.13
617.14
621.19
622.23
629.03
630.06
631.11
638.14
642.18
645.22
648.01
649.01
649.04
656.12
662.01
662.05
663.06
673.04
674.02
674.05
674.21
674.25
676.06
676.26
684.06
685.18
693.27
698.08
699.21
700.18
701.17
703.09
723.13
724.25
725.10
735.03
745.17
745.26
748.20
752.20
762.08
768.03
768.04
768.11
792.15
794.14
796.21
796.24
804.08
808.24
810.06
812.22
818.23
820.27
821.18
825.03
825.19

830.07
833.19
833.22
837.21
848.24
848.28
856.24
858.10
863.25
871.06
871.27
871.28
872.27
875.12
885.26
886.15
886.24
894.21
899.16
901.03
909.17
911.16
stiller
216.09
stillness
025.02
155.02
282.26
364.04
416.17
433.01
678.01
856.20
stilted
890.18
stimulate
104.19
550.07
stimulated
625.07
642.04
stimulating
426.11
stimulus
019.19
031.07
165.19
724.11
sting
271.05
611.25
891.01
stinginess
329.28
stinging
061.13
stingy
450.12
stinted
738.14
stipulate
547.10
stipulating
786.05
stir
013.16
030.20
067.02
230.11
333.19
340.21
359.18
386.04
396.19
494.15
546.20
680.06
683.21
793.10
813.06
814.12
stirred
023.09
043.12
062.17
123.21
155.25
219.13
219.20
398.07
406.22
462.22
511.18
535.02
567.09
594.20
643.05
692.08
768.14
858.09
stirring
111.12
164.02
185.02
194.18
430.08
570.12
745.14
stirs
816.28

stitch
099.08
stitching
474.11
stock
681.01
729.12
815.26
stocking
676.22
stocking-foot
397.18
stockings
084.15
116.26
216.23
277.07
692.19
stocks
038.24
385.10
390.08
435.01
stoic
756.25
stoicism
747.03
stole
286.07
502.14
639.14
653.07
stone
021.06
050.25
056.07
089.09
089.25
091.02
149.07
149.10
494.06
544.12
615.20
658.13
664.06
689.08
693.01
733.03
776.08
779.06
796.24
833.05
857.13
857.14
stone-blind
867.07
867.08
stone-cold
645.22
stone-dead
858.23
stones
145.12
219.16
575.15
675.20
693.09
859.12
859.28
866.05
stony
052.21
074.27
466.13
stood
013.22
015.23
026.20
050.15
051.24
052.03
052.25
064.26
064.27
066.23
073.05
076.08
085.09
086.05
088.17
089.27
094.25
097.15
115.16
116.05
152.20
155.11
162.17
166.04
175.20
193.22
194.04
194.21
203.15
203.22
224.04
231.10
236.25
255.21
256.20

262.21
270.16
283.25
295.03
299.25
306.12
310.24
334.23
335.11
335.18
342.09
361.26
366.25
367.28
369.20
374.27
394.09
394.16
411.02
411.06
414.18
419.08
419.16
432.24
434.11
438.11
449.20
460.11
464.20
469.20
477.28
513.15
514.10
519.24
523.03
542.12
551.12
552.18
556.03
560.13
576.12
587.08
589.07
590.21
591.12
600.05
604.10
610.18
613.15
639.09
656.28
666.05
667.10
668.27
674.20
675.24
685.06
689.15
691.21
701.14
737.08
740.20
757.01
758.12
758.14
766.03
779.17
779.22
779.28
780.21
790.01
798.20
807.06
813.01
827.16
829.25
833.17
847.13
848.28
854.14
865.25
870.24
871.14
871.19
872.28
873.01
875.20
887.10
903.21
stool
013.05
018.02
049.04
061.05
124.08
127.04
127.21
298.26
341.17
347.05
550.12
677.01
713.17
stools
114.23
207.12
stoop
404.04
stooped
069.26
123.11

465.23	783.05	022.28	057.06	248.21	strike
613.19	storm-beat	028.23	090.11	333.02	008.05
619.15	003.15	044.06	217.05	631.02	008.13
676.11	stormily	067.19	225.05	778.27	012.16
753.16	024.17	074.19	240.10	streaming	015.05
stooping	storms	082.10	251.23	133.25	100.26
223.21	230.04	089.02	369.06	169.13	156.11
313.19	808.26	090.01	381.08	865.25	301.26
407.03	stormy	094.05	383.19	streams	552.01
504.01	004.04	101.10	409.05	220.23	597.09
802.26	657.11	127.14	409.07	street	601.11
839.15	745.14	146.07	421.10	074.28	856.26
stoops	story	182.17	424.23	170.01	strikes
349.24	005.13	207.09	439.28	183.13	396.13
stop	135.16	207.24	440.26	495.06	512.06
153.24	207.01	207.25	480.20	664.24	771.12
365.03	207.16	207.27	496.05	666.27	striking
365.13	209.28	222.04	585.15	673.18	009.23
409.24	215.22	249.27	594.11	779.01	019.14
573.03	295.13	274.14	615.01	streets	181.20
585.10	298.06	285.06	667.26	281.10	206.03
653.19	299.03	285.08	682.12	strength	247.19
777.19	328.20	285.10	702.28	033.19	359.13
857.27	329.11	290.13	741.11	062.01	449.27
876.10	365.18	291.16	786.27	127.19	807.26
stopped	415.07	297.05	834.08	270.22	strikingly
043.23	416.19	298.03	860.22	292.07	251.15
049.19	419.16	302.03	861.16	312.17	string
050.06	422.25	302.03	stranger's	325.15	121.21
051.25	526.16	307.25	912.15	359.28	326.17
074.10	599.01	308.19	strangers	406.13	407.13
156.21	633.01	311.27	236.18	426.14	460.27
175.08	770.06	324.11	301.06	441.07	510.25
176.24	859.14	377.27	339.02	476.14	510.27
182.03	862.17	395.04	588.13	490.18	stringent
185.21	863.12	399.14	589.06	520.11	648.10
199.06	864.07	401.27	589.16	607.19	825.18
210.08	story-book	407.17	659.10	619.11	strings
226.15	143.11	411.22	669.01	649.07	046.18
229.05	218.22	413.15	719.23	654.15	087.19
261.18	stout	422.22	722.16	662.17	250.27
301.26	007.03	435.20	781.10	665.01	stringy
361.22	013.11	444.02	786.09	669.09	762.23
363.12	044.05	444.07	834.05	672.19	strip
381.04	060.19	445.21	838.04	683.02	614.09
385.05	083.05	447.08	878.04	687.10	striped
414.16	084.23	450.08	strangest	710.07	394.07
418.26	176.10	468.04	063.18	712.13	stripped
419.14	177.14	470.02	207.25	735.25	016.28
433.26	343.15	473.17	329.15	735.28	219.15
461.23	448.02	485.27	652.07	753.05	306.12
493.02	597.07	491.23	862.22	756.08	761.22
498.15	stowed	516.08	strangle	783.26	strive
508.09	074.25	517.03	416.04	793.06	323.01
542.09	539.25	524.04	strangled	800.10	647.05
566.04	straggled	524.25	493.21	824.25	664.22
578.20	194.20	552.23	575.18	845.10	731.03
588.03	stragglers	558.13	890.18	846.14	striven
609.08	812.20	559.04	strapped	867.10	430.15
618.27	straight	572.17	587.01	872.02	striving
619.14	052.14	573.22	strapper	896.03	147.27
657.01	053.28	577.01	442.25	896.21	strode
667.12	119.12	581.07	442.25	900.12	742.20
671.12	192.18	584.02	strata	903.25	818.22
672.16	193.07	599.19	492.24	strengthened	stroke
699.15	229.11	610.21	straw	012.03	190.02
779.19	324.05	614.05	087.19	strenuously	448.07
782.12	345.28	622.05	284.13	057.03	519.18
798.03	354.05	622.05	558.08	stress	569.17
851.07	412.28	639.09	653.05	227.27	676.18
854.22	429.25	641.12	strawberries	310.01	696.05
855.01	454.08	651.27	501.16	711.19	stroked
stopping	471.20	677.07	stray	stretch	532.01
442.06	507.04	678.01	033.16	403.27	strokes
653.17	577.14	690.10	289.20	659.05	099.21
stops	617.16	701.07	476.28	stretched	769.23
097.25	659.21	707.08	496.05	296.11	stroking
store	675.12	708.12	565.20	406.25	260.14
049.07	701.25	716.16	661.07	414.13	strolling
273.08	779.26	745.12	687.19	414.19	280.13
863.02	straight-skirted	754.16	strayed	485.23	strolls
store-room	460.24	758.25	434.26	564.11	503.26
187.07	strain	759.08	505.25	590.14	strong
215.01	200.17	778.05	561.21	643.16	094.03
328.06	525.07	813.13	673.09	654.24	104.15
562.01	525.18	813.13	839.10	758.01	110.01
stored	550.20	813.28	straying	871.15	150.16
003.02	560.03	836.21	320.12	872.23	153.16
016.21	563.24	839.23	588.13	883.12	194.10
stores	650.06	842.11	857.27	904.01	221.02
070.03	strained	842.19	streached	strewn	229.01
140.08	029.11	849.04	870.10	561.23	296.01
544.06	573.01	856.21	streak	strict	330.07
816.12	580.23	901.26	023.11	049.09	350.01
stories	straining	strangely	streaked	056.21	350.12
017.26	643.18	004.18	702.04	320.11	405.19
150.06	819.24	031.04	streaks	793.14	447.18
193.28	872.21	200.25	426.19	907.27	448.03
208.12	strains	361.15	427.15	strictly	465.13
221.11	166.08	423.16	stream	716.10	485.26
285.12	732.14	490.26	087.22	strictness	517.02
336.24	735.02	491.26	146.19	161.20	551.27
storm	strait	498.01	282.19	stride	559.21
248.22	570.15	568.03	664.14	115.14	560.16
520.06	stranded	825.02	812.09	515.14	567.03
605.23	004.23	844.13	813.03	587.10	575.21
621.24	strange	strangeness	813.12	777.14	591.14
631.02	012.09	852.24	820.12	872.18	594.08
761.20	017.20	stranger	878.03	strife	594.21
765.03	019.21	027.05	streamed	797.19	599.10
765.18	022.04	052.22	071.08		627.06

842.02
860.13
861.20
862.11
867.19
877.06
895.19
901.22
903.05

sucked
429.03

sudden
060.07
061.08
075.12
204.25
244.21
312.22
467.22
669.20
687.17
740.27
754.16
777.17
781.25
790.28
847.18
857.27
871.21

suddenly
003.17
044.02
097.26
098.23
119.21
139.17
198.16
259.12
265.07
290.14
326.08
337.10
378.02
443.06
456.25
476.06
512.11
610.15
613.16
618.27
623.15
763.16
802.25
817.18
848.28
851.11
856.16
877.24
879.16
883.11
864.02
867.26

suffer
063.12
119.02
216.18
216.20
253.07
360.07
396.17
404.14
428.24
477.13
477.24
516.28
533.01
654.06
760.11
762.09
816.07
825.16
878.21

suffered
020.04
109.08
354.17
355.13
372.27
428.24
441.05
537.25

sufferer
759.15

suffering
010.16
018.14
029.18
033.26
426.13
485.08
553.16
551.21
606.16
610.02
628.17
663.25
667.05
670.22
683.19
742.22
832.28

sufferings
108.02
118.23
157.12
465.13
630.16
650.24
773.07
889.03
903.07

suffice
042.04
758.07
880.11

sufficed
174.07
231.03
323.08
425.22
474.21
624.20
687.10
795.12
912.09

sufficient
112.05
214.06
263.13
361.03
370.09
637.09
733.28
751.20
757.04

sufficiently
060.22
203.01
261.16
721.24
748.14
833.07

suffocated
023.21
782.13

suffocating
063.09
731.28

suffused
231.07

suffusing
676.26

suffusion
248.20

suggest
387.06
440.15
537.20
719.13

suggested
144.16
180.07
313.04
368.19
801.07
840.28
862.25

suggesting
190.24

suggestion
004.05
166.04
167.24
272.05
454.05
507.27
632.12
769.16
856.03

suggestions
325.18
834.11

suggestive
891.09

suggests
135.10

suicide
451.20
638.14

suit
263.17
265.28
345.09
496.22
508.23
529.11
558.09
797.15
837.16
841.16
890.14
898.23

suitable
750.27
895.08

suited
084.18
315.10
368.08
374.06
554.27
636.12
713.22
713.23
759.04
882.17
909.13

suiting
057.27

suitor
403.16

suitors
529.09
760.06

suits
489.24
898.23

suivais
334.05

sulky
531.05

sullen
019.09
083.18
572.02
608.10
674.05
872.07

sullenly
629.26

sullenness
900.24

sullied
273.01
432.01
631.23
632.02
763.16
900.03

sully
647.08
766.15

sulphur-steams
629.23

sultan
545.15

sum
115.06
123.05
330.01
637.09
657.04
658.05
727.26
776.24
784.07
794.08

summer
154.12
189.16
219.08
242.11
293.22
332.01
492.18
505.28
521.17
562.03
612.27
655.09
658.02
675.07
809.27
854.20
870.17

summer-day
660.23

summit
502.02
575.19
658.16

summits
113.04
145.10

summon
222.27
515.09
641.06
853.15

summoned
048.08
086.19
138.23
236.19
257.19
291.02
347.27
365.15
365.26
379.16
384.02
445.27
464.18
549.13
768.27
849.06
867.10

summoning
882.10

summons
093.25
183.03
815.04
816.05
902.26

sumptuously
149.05

sun
066.09
191.21
193.24
209.09
219.07
220.08
335.13
376.13
428.26
432.20
435.07
436.17
439.17
501.17
502.03
526.14
556.05
583.22
609.03
655.12
663.04
663.28
736.19
756.09
812.12
818.28
845.04
357.09
887.06
899.04
899.15
912.10

sunbeam
376.09
909.22

sunday
114.06
479.07

sundays
112.19

sundered
352.02

sundry
088.11
098.14
356.15
387.02
462.02
697.22
749.15
817.11

sung
082.13
550.19

sunk
194.09
214.01
469.15
479.20
502.23
505.26
668.18
731.12
865.11
872.01

sunken
128.01

sunless
281.04
832.22

sunlit
209.18

sunny
144.13
151.05
221.03
501.13
664.17
810.27
886.26

sunny-faced
523.13

sunrise
435.15
443.06
655.09
655.21
712.23

suns
501.03
825.10

sunset
505.05
570.17
712.23
732.11
833.12

sunshine
070.05
145.27
189.17
203.28
293.23
364.16
497.15
499.07

539.11
663.07
745.04
808.25
887.09

superb
236.27
544.07

supercilious
379.27

superciliousness
462.09

superficiality
289.21

superfluity
842.25

superfluous
701.11
768.01
784.24

superintendence
244.17

superintendent
056.20
086.16
086.27
122.19
126.23
162.14
169.05
172.28
173.27

superintendent's
134.03

superior
188.01
202.27
270.08
279.13
321.17
490.04
713.09
797.22
831.15
837.08

superiority
264.19
264.23
265.24
266.02
374.24
417.16

superlatively
403.06

supernatural
903.08

superstition
018.03
759.26
850.05
901.27

superstitious
805.10
901.27

superstitiously
211.08

supervened
725.22

supped
170.23

supper
041.19
047.09
072.07
077.05
142.26
165.22
171.01
413.23
410.27
410.28
566.07
567.06
671.12
681.16
843.09
882.06
882.07
882.13
882.24

supper-trays
078.27

supple
407.01
528.08

supplicated
547.02
845.10
900.28

supplication
136.06
165.18

supplied
045.03
091.21
136.22

supply
100.15
112.03
138.04
663.15
816.12

supplying
810.06

support
358.03
487.12
646.11

supported
015.21
129.07
237.01
288.13
433.10
484.28
611.05
619.28
677.17
700.04
756.16
874.25

supporting
026.11
249.06
368.16

suppose
025.16
028.16
067.22
085.20
091.09
116.16
138.02
167.10
176.16
183.14
184.04
186.25
200.26
202.19
203.14
205.24
237.13
241.23
260.17
269.12
293.22
316.01
317.01
317.09
326.01
326.22
330.05
334.24
344.26
347.03
347.13
353.21
554.22
357.25
397.15
406.23
438.23
439.28
448.28
454.17
455.27
475.27
489.21
494.22
496.14
508.06
508.07
523.17
527.18
531.14
536.23
548.10
570.23
585.04
600.18
603.08
611.21
612.16
636.11
658.14
694.07
772.23
787.20
610.05
361.16
680.12

supposed
151.22
216.14
376.27
451.19
481.06
490.28
516.04
576.09
665.15
692.03
798.22

supposing
324.18
434.08
694.01

supposition
313.03
548.13

suppress
342.01
suppressed
061.23
294.27
suppressing
388.19
suppression
151.23
supremely
908.26
sure
005.17
015.03
017.13
041.11
046.15
073.24
075.06
102.05
106.26
117.04
131.08
155.02
151.02
157.05
157.27
158.03
172.06
175.06
188.21
188.26
189.04
189.09
193.09
196.02
206.04
241.21
258.25
262.25
267.03
272.06
305.11
315.04
325.03
333.26
351.11
356.03
372.13
377.08
379.12
306.18
391.11
397.16
412.21
417.15
432.04
432.11
435.17
442.17
444.19
443.15
448.26
454.01
460.28
491.14
493.06
499.22
509.24
521.15
543.21
554.22
563.20
575.11
576.24
625.18
655.26
657.03
662.16
670.28
679.07
661.11
661.16
690.28
700.17
708.16
717.01
724.08
742.01
749.04
753.27
757.01
749.26
803.04
807.26
809.14
818.12
833.10
834.01
839.18
840.01
854.01
855.08
864.05
864.22
906.03
910.18
912.13
912.20
surely
034.13

109.07
150.04
167.23
184.11
314.06
314.21
375.20
385.24
505.04
535.12
679.28
730.12
738.13
772.12
779.18
793.14
857.03
912.23
surer
375.13
643.28
surface
031.22
673.27
635.26
surfeited
320.27
surge
004.03
surgeon
232.14
232.23
421.28
427.02
427.16
433.11
633.11
867.21
surgeon's
151.21
233.02
surges
302.20
surging
045.07
surly
639.08
surmised
491.19
surmises
854.06
surmount
164.21
surnames
098.04
surpass
178.22
surpassed
370.27
surplice
586.21
589.02
596.06
735.19
surprise
087.11
094.23
130.20
211.10
378.20
384.16
480.18
489.13
535.02
576.20
641.28
671.15
682.07
749.17
793.07
811.01
824.06
surprised
117.21
295.23
300.24
324.05
335.10
356.14
376.17
427.13
462.17
472.23
499.20
522.01
522.15
574.20
696.16
713.28
732.17
737.09
760.23
802.24
827.22
surprises
339.27
surprising
744.06
surrendered
731.10

surround
004.13
498.22
surrounded
084.10
087.23
113.20
316.20
367.28
446.05
760.06
848.12
surrounding
005.11
016.05
749.16
770.19
surrounduing
673.11
surtout
115.21
126.26
384.12
surveillance
373.26
survey
857.22
surveyed
042.11
085.11
119.21
193.27
209.01
247.13
297.27
349.02
472.04
486.07
536.11
576.16
586.03
682.07
687.24
755.03
781.07
surveying
005.11
194.26
susceptible
404.09
550.05
suspect
489.09
suspected
103.14
153.09
234.08
309.13
408.12
633.15
641.07
820.05
863.14
suspended
061.19
379.05
441.18
534.27
599.11
905.19
suspense
562.20
808.21
suspicion
659.14
670.10
670.27
690.22
703.21
suspicions
774.08
626.24
sustain
673.06
806.27
sustained
125.10
129.12
344.17
374.11
626.21
sustenance
712.09
735.01
suttee
553.09
swallow
081.25
062.23
095.01
swallowed
100.10
112.16
320.28
327.07
411.17
432.02
564.19
692.06
705.26

swallowing
065.18
swam
066.05
610.17
685.17
swamp
797.15
swamped
757.28
swarth
368.07
swathed
204.27
swaths
542.02
sway
425.12
511.20
swayed
126.08
608.09
swear
274.06
512.23
517.20
529.18
552.04
823.11
swearing
223.06
swears
386.09
392.18
sweep
004.08
237.06
333.07
712.16
847.18
sweeping
003.15
025.15
342.16
514.24
518.28
sweet
032.22
032.23
041.16
143.05
150.01
152.02
166.18
271.02
271.03
302.22
320.28
335.19
337.07
351.02
406.07
434.24
440.21
486.02
550.19
551.25
573.16
631.11
640.14
642.12
655.03
663.01
663.10
712.21
731.20
736.25
737.20
745.04
753.28
757.03
757.23
758.03
765.16
799.06
812.08
843.25
876.04
894.13
sweet-briar
435.03
503.09
sweet-briars
148.07
sweet-tempered
383.25
sweetens
182.23
sweeter
145.04
528.22
sweetest
070.03
146.11
158.19
169.20
322.10
396.16
501.20
910.07

sweetly
103.11
143.14
738.07
858.23
sweetmeats
007.14
sweetness
879.23
sweetwilliams
435.01
swell
661.20
674.05
712.16
818.23
swelled
112.02
191.10
215.28
578.06
581.15
631.14
745.07
776.05
812.10
896.10
swelling
139.25
259.03
swells
899.27
swept
044.07
066.15
133.23
165.19
246.17
294.09
333.01
342.05
386.28
477.27
550.11
660.04
662.16
674.22
870.25
877.23
881.25
swift-darting
023.16
swim
607.12
swimming
296.02
363.03
swimmingly
149.24
swine
151.18
swing
608.06
switch
465.01
swollen
144.07
247.25
470.01
swooning
592.09
swore
406.12
610.05
sworn
495.24
552.09
762.18
sybil
391.02
394.03
394.03
syllabic
210.26
syllable
044.11
369.12
400.19
400.28
456.26
690.21
795.25
syllables
409.26
sylph
279.19
sylph's
526.25
sylvan
870.15
symmetrically
407.02
sympathetic
398.18
sympathies
301.28
444.03
444.07
444.14
724.07
sympathize
020.12

103.11
561.09
759.13
799.11
829.08
sympathizing
161.18
sympathy
090.13
131.17
225.01
269.28
350.19
373.14
477.07
487.12
513.24
598.02
641.24
644.07
660.19
686.03
754.11
761.11
802.07
syncope
651.28
synonymous
036.02
system
056.25
476.24
489.08
554.19
691.02
908.05
systematic
103.26
systems
164.08
662.16
t'
672.13
679.08
679.08
680.28
680.28
696.10
t'chamber
680.27
tabernacle
015.24
table
007.07
015.28
026.20
032.11
050.15
076.25
080.23
081.01
082.05
082.09
137.12
138.07
155.16
181.16
186.06
187.24
193.08
198.14
236.25
239.02
246.09
246.19
255.22
286.10
287.03
341.16
342.09
353.01
353.07
366.24
367.08
369.20
394.09
410.28
458.20
464.21
535.09
562.08
604.20
613.15
676.17
676.19
677.10
701.06
702.23
704.10
705.05
717.25
729.05
752.22
756.15
757.15
763.07
777.07
791.27
804.04
844.05
862.04

875.06	377.15	252.28	846.23	351.03	032.11
892.24	379.19	319.17	talented	359.08	tarts
table-drawer	385.11	346.18	316.25	401.13	335.02
749.10	389.13	347.15	751.13	407.28	336.08
tableau	403.28	352.16	842.20	411.07	task
369.14	407.11	352.24	892.05	411.20	047.18
tables	409.10	386.03	talents	429.20	078.15
078.05	417.19	392.08	157.13	451.12	097.07
078.23	418.26	409.18	213.16	457.21	097.07
080.21	419.11	411.01	240.15	513.11	113.14
081.20	429.23	416.21	737.08	553.27	146.14
083.02	429.26	417.11	793.12	614.01	189.15
086.18	431.04	433.25	tales	614.19	315.27
100.22	431.08	464.02	005.16	617.04	323.15
101.15	432.07	467.10	005.24	617.28	337.16
331.02	433.15	473.20	031.12	697.20	402.11
341.05	436.08	475.03	047.24	758.03	474.05
342.26	438.13	498.18	066.03	802.10	476.27
355.14	439.14	516.01	221.17	talks	555.27
565.09	448.23	530.09	241.19	239.13	585.03
794.13	452.10	559.07	401.21	271.17	652.23
794.20	453.09	585.11	talisman	313.04	677.21
tablet	463.23	589.14	542.27	469.21	699.07
089.09	470.06	610.20	talk	757.09	720.16
092.01	470.20	620.10	043.25	890.03	787.27
159.21	470.26	652.24	053.23	tall	790.20
655.11	475.16	655.13	083.11	053.10	804.13
808.27	475.17	671.19	101.26	060.18	806.01
taciturn	476.26	698.13	109.24	076.19	811.12
750.12	477.09	730.24	166.01	078.23	814.17
taciturn-looking	482.05	748.26	166.15	078.28	816.11
306.21	489.02	749.16	170.28	081.26	816.20
taciturnity	489.12	761.20	189.24	085.23	841.04
379.27	491.26	794.05	197.22	092.06	tasked
390.18	492.15	813.18	198.20	092.18	797.21
759.09	495.20	815.26	217.25	120.21	tasks
tack	498.26	822.14	234.11	148.03	077.24
268.17	507.12	846.15	238.18	176.09	096.20
tact	511.04	867.18	242.15	177.10	111.06
817.16	519.20	870.13	257.13	192.19	714.25
tail	526.07	884.25	263.15	222.06	744.03
232.02	526.10	888.04	264.06	227.12	753.25
737.02	531.03	889.11	264.25	237.16	taste
taille	531.24	901.01	269.24	318.06	082.18
279.16	540.13	takes	269.25	342.14	082.23
taint	543.11	566.15	275.01	345.01	083.03
230.21	566.08	626.05	275.09	348.05	090.22
439.08	575.24	taking	286.27	348.13	150.11
440.04	596.06	001.03	291.10	352.19	201.01
tak-	598.13	002.22	301.28	380.26	213.18
656.26	600.10	003.01	352.27	381.07	271.05
take	600.10	008.03	361.17	460.20	311.06
009.07	604.04	031.23	401.27	460.20	319.02
011.03	604.16	090.20	407.29	494.04	345.10
013.15	618.09	134.09	442.19	577.11	346.24
024.01	631.25	138.10	467.05	600.05	388.21
030.23	633.23	140.14	473.26	624.26	406.04
033.18	657.04	222.13	510.07	701.23	496.04
042.16	658.04	237.24	529.04	750.09	526.17
046.10	658.08	271.09	553.25	753.16	554.27
050.19	670.15	301.01	569.13	766.04	613.13
056.06	671.05	307.11	569.25	825.05	637.09
068.20	682.19	326.05	620.05	890.21	707.18
071.17	700.22	327.16	635.15	891.12	717.19
073.24	707.13	332.16	637.18	taller	735.06
083.02	714.02	340.18	641.11	176.13	758.21
088.17	714.17	341.16	643.20	343.11	890.12
093.10	733.15	353.07	679.02	839.14	890.14
117.15	754.03	402.07	679.06	tallest	901.13
118.22	756.12	411.11	688.02	344.01	tasted
118.26	763.21	426.25	707.28	talons	065.17
120.27	785.01	458.04	713.14	668.18	319.28
138.14	785.25	503.28	753.27	tame	483.22
158.25	786.24	519.13	754.02	382.08	613.01
174.12	810.15	578.19	766.25	425.02	686.08
180.24	811.15	590.23	768.10	tamely	711.10
188.04	811.20	603.17	768.21	486.01	758.19
195.11	821.12	612.24	769.03	tameness	tastes
193.04	826.13	783.04	793.08	612.17	038.28
226.23	828.15	784.14	800.20	tangible	205.06
230.09	854.16	789.04	806.22	837.03	260.08
232.26	856.12	873.17	816.28	tangled	293.02
255.22	863.19	tale	824.11	293.07	351.28
239.23	863.28	043.22	884.21	tant	571.02
241.01	866.22	063.14	890.02	354.26	626.15
245.13	873.04	108.02	909.09	tantrums	711.11
246.12	880.01	135.26	909.09	015.06	720.12
246.19	882.06	216.01	talked	tap	722.28
251.02	882.07	216.02	099.05	458.15	787.09
255.27	883.12	290.06	203.05	752.14	808.08
269.11	896.19	320.21	291.09	tape	tasting
260.27	912.01	400.01	342.28	307.12	857.07
265.20	taken	400.03	346.09	tapestried	taught
265.23	005.24	524.12	346.10	599.02	109.11
286.04	007.10	574.10	378.23	tapestry	140.14
290.27	021.20	576.05	385.17	420.13	197.27
298.23	073.22	634.26	467.25	420.14	201.15
299.01	074.10	660.20	491.20	423.14	230.05
306.05	080.01	668.03	512.02	tapped	250.22
310.02	081.18	767.01	552.26	418.27	744.12
322.04	086.17	770.02	640.03	610.25	748.23
322.06	096.06	772.10	710.06	tardy	790.08
322.27	114.16	773.18	798.21	441.21	893.08
324.20	151.05	860.16	882.13	tarried	tauntingly
329.02	153.14	885.10	talking	042.07	610.04
339.25	163.27	889.10	069.11	tarry	tawny
353.13	172.24	903.04	106.01	586.02	594.17
360.18	190.17	908.19	264.07	tart	tea
362.05	240.13	talent	276.09	030.17	068.14
362.17	240.23	762.02	300.16	031.03	068.15
377.02	246.27	834.14	307.18	031.05	082.14

113.24
117.15
129.04
137.07
138.08
138.22
169.04
232.25
235.22
238.25
240.21
311.10
315.14
315.18
319.28
355.26
458.04
458.19
498.17
563.13
570.08
699.11
700.22
702.16
705.26
710.05
739.03
750.23
795.14
799.17
tea-cake
458.13
tea-pot
315.25
tea-things
729.06
tea-time
112.14
235.26
tea-tray
458.12
teach
009.13
106.27
121.18
130.02
168.24
197.10
200.05
234.03
356.07
456.01
679.16
713.21
722.25
739.27
893.04
893.06
893.16
teachable
213.16
739.21
teacher
082.11
083.02
083.16
099.20
102.11
101.26
102.10
165.26
168.19
173.21
198.06
243.04
706.20
771.11
teacher's
175.03
teachers
056.20
057.25
062.02
062.14
084.03
084.22
086.21
087.10
092.21
093.05
113.12
115.11
115.28
124.22
125.21
126.22
131.16
142.07
147.13
162.06
170.24
240.18
243.15
teaches
092.26
093.04
106.05
teaching
091.21
325.05
362.11

638.02
722.04
789.17
teapot
137.12
tear
099.22
100.07
140.27
486.14
563.03
563.04
579.20
610.10
649.20
763.28
896.08
tear-dimmed
662.14
tearing
581.17
tearless
486.04
tears
022.23
029.27
057.18
112.17
129.13
141.22
156.22
333.15
363.02
406.05
433.27
466.14
466.22
509.12
537.02
605.06
611.16
611.20
614.15
620.09
643.21
657.12
704.27
725.18
731.28
733.17
810.19
829.18
830.05
835.02
844.09
894.14
912.12
teased
555.28
teaze
571.01
574.05
574.09
895.22
teazed
374.10
tedious
173.18
186.23
380.06
490.21
490.21
tedium
643.02
tedo
356.09
356.14
teeth
054.03
072.28
283.06
344.07
428.04
429.02
512.20
594.08
601.04
628.08
649.09
738.07
tell
004.27
006.09
010.10
014.25
034.07
036.10
038.18
054.09
063.13
091.01
110.05
116.20
120.21
120.22
125.26
133.14
134.23
135.06
139.24
149.18

150.06
167.14
176.04
180.06
220.19
226.12
232.03
247.14
262.09
282.17
285.12
339.03
339.10
345.24
346.23
355.05
362.25
385.10
385.21
386.08
388.14
390.06
392.20
408.02
408.24
410.20
410.24
432.13
436.24
438.24
441.11
463.09
467.04
477.15
477.26
482.04
482.13
483.24
485.19
496.21
496.27
499.18
512.25
520.13
535.20
536.16
537.25
545.05
565.11
568.06
568.08
572.11
574.05
577.15
578.09
579.09
581.20
586.16
596.15
599.17
612.20
634.26
635.11
635.23
644.16
647.09
647.26
665.08
667.24
670.13
678.11
679.09
679.10
681.06
682.10
683.04
683.13
685.12
688.04
689.13
695.06
697.04
703.17
705.23
706.11
706.12
706.18
719.12
722.11
734.15
745.08
755.16
763.17
772.01
772.11
772.12
773.19
774.23
779.03
783.05
783.13
783.17
784.10
791.13
791.18
796.10
799.25
805.09
805.19
820.26
822.23

823.18
827.22
836.20
839.19
857.04
863.06
863.12
874.03
880.14
881.22
881.25
883.19
889.05
896.27
902.05
902.10
telled
906.08
telling
056.12
214.15
217.12
400.01
530.27
586.06
623.16
678.05
tells
062.09
104.12
117.10
495.17
536.10
697.12
temper
018.20
048.01
251.25
259.01
458.17
467.23
626.27
818.02
temperament
020.13
temperate
737.21
temperature
144.10
tempered
911.01
tempest
522.03
630.03
765.10
tempests
560.20
640.27
tempestuously
479.26
temple
057.25
059.25
086.12
086.13
086.24
092.09
092.19
093.13
093.14
104.06
104.10
106.05
106.08
106.13
113.06
115.15
115.27
116.16
117.08
118.02
119.10
119.26
119.26
120.03
120.12
120.18
120.24
121.14
122.12
122.27
123.25
124.22
126.28
130.01
132.09
133.27
134.07
134.21
135.24
136.08
136.27
137.17
138.01
138.28
140.12
140.20
141.27
142.02
151.06
155.16

159.13
162.13
163.09
163.26
236.16
589.01
temple's
104.08
116.06
139.19
147.10
153.19
154.10
154.28
155.10
340.23
temples
085.27
167.17
249.11
368.14
460.26
471.25
758.17
temporarily
520.01
753.21
temporary
118.19
131.23
324.17
633.23
653.22
836.05
temptation
271.20
638.04
648.08
652.17
731.10
734.19
758.18
851.16
temptations
845.13
tempted
270.18
312.07
449.25
484.07
802.05
847.02
ten
007.03
052.02
053.03
078.08
079.22
126.03
160.03
171.13
185.14
198.15
244.25
276.13
316.12
324.03
332.15
332.19
336.14
452.18
453.16
454.24
457.23
470.10
476.28
526.26
562.15
586.07
596.01
633.03
635.26
658.17
679.28
681.15
687.28
771.05
812.04
817.10
908.24
tenacious
142.16
241.12
835.26
tenaciously
793.19
tenant
222.10
869.09
874.26
tenanted
221.10
367.28
tenantless
364.11
tenantry
060.28
tenants
194.06
205.19
233.06

335.15
490.28
tend
802.15
tendencies
293.02
tendency
056.23
356.22
616.10
tender
150.17
356.15
441.26
528.09
555.15
886.27
tendered
845.27
tenderer
312.07
tenderest
276.24
tenderly
026.12
433.26
888.24
tenderness
261.19
373.14
466.14
552.15
617.24
824.25
tending
021.02
105.24
tenement
480.02
tenets
489.11
tenez
277.11
tenor
061.12
723.22
tenses
142.20
tent
615.17
tenth
484.16
term
237.15
343.13
365.08
616.19
737.24
termed
019.08
287.09
344.09
346.05
terminated
081.11
210.27
637.02
853.13
terminating
420.23
502.25
termination
367.13
terms
189.07
454.18
547.11
555.07
750.23
800.11
836.27
terrible
023.01
026.04
645.08
861.24
terrified
415.26
684.11
terror
005.09
007.27
009.25
026.09
109.14
512.06
575.18
579.02
645.22
678.06
834.28
terror-struck
610.15
terrors
417.17
465.21
580.02
580.04
618.04
test
307.13

testament	270.14	673.17	722.19	048.18	124.08
107.18	271.20	673.21	732.07	053.20	124.14
testatrix	273.16	679.05	787.15	054.01	124.16
544.26	273.20	679.18	803.11	054.04	124.16
testified	275.16	681.11	846.01	054.09	125.01
806.18	275.26	681.26	903.17	054.11	125.04
testily	277.25	694.02	903.18	055.01	125.08
768.09	280.19	703.27	903.23	055.02	125.09
testimonial	284.10	704.25	906.16	056.04	125.14
173.22	284.10	709.19	thanked	056.10	126.16
173.26	286.25	713.01	190.12	056.17	127.03
testimony	287.02	713.28	688.10	056.24	127.16
161.27	288.09	714.23	thankful	057.07	127.26
594.01	289.04	715.24	037.05	057.10	128.02
tests	290.26	717.04	243.01	058.08	129.09
817.11	291.27	721.03	603.19	059.13	129.17
tete	292.12	724.11	734.01	059.18	130.24
256.27	292.20	724.24	882.04	059.25	132.05
256.27	293.03	726.04	thankfulness	059.26	132.16
549.16	293.19	726.18	214.19	060.06	132.21
texts	306.20	727.14	745.07	060.16	134.13
081.08	312.08	733.20	thankless	062.17	135.04
texture	313.27	735.09	030.12	062.17	135.06
773.26	320.25	735.16	thanks	062.26	135.12
th	323.10	737.01	082.26	062.28	135.19
740.04	325.04	745.07	191.11	063.03	135.24
th'	336.17	746.09	191.11	063.11	138.17
696.25	340.28	746.27	225.08	063.20	139.19
698.05	343.26	747.13	323.23	064.14	139.28
698.06	346.13	748.24	thanksgiving	065.24	141.04
698.06	348.16	749.21	662.21	065.28	142.01
698.07	349.16	751.04	850.22	066.01	142.03
906.23	350.04	753.21	that	068.06	142.05
than	351.20	756.03	001.03	069.17	142.12
007.02	352.23	756.24	001.09	069.28	142.24
012.20	355.10	757.08	002.09	071.10	143.12
017.20	362.13	759.28	002.11	072.10	143.13
026.12	367.21	760.07	002.22	072.16	144.16
027.09	370.23	760.10	003.01	073.07	145.06
030.02	372.18	761.09	003.12	074.06	145.20
031.12	382.12	761.11	003.21	074.07	145.24
037.08	401.27	762.01	004.10	075.03	146.21
042.13	406.28	767.08	004.17	077.09	147.28
043.04	409.27	768.28	006.02	078.02	149.12
046.15	426.26	771.08	006.27	079.10	150.17
054.19	438.04	773.17	007.13	079.16	151.16
055.22	441.06	774.13	007.17	079.28	151.18
062.15	453.10	778.04	008.16	080.12	151.22
065.28	456.17	782.13	008.20	081.03	151.24
066.01	457.17	786.15	010.09	081.11	152.23
067.16	462.23	792.19	012.07	082.01	153.07
069.08	462.25	794.13	013.20	083.10	153.10
090.20	463.14	796.07	014.07	087.08	153.12
093.16	465.12	800.08	017.01	088.18	153.13
093.28	467.19	801.09	017.19	089.14	154.06
100.14	468.20	802.19	018.03	089.18	155.17
102.24	470.10	804.20	019.23	089.28	155.27
103.03	473.27	806.21	019.26	090.20	157.05
105.21	474.26	810.12	020.11	091.01	157.24
106.09	476.03	820.11	020.19	092.01	157.27
109.05	476.09	822.20	021.12	092.06	158.01
111.07	493.11	828.24	021.19	092.18	158.14
115.22	506.18	829.24	021.20	093.25	158.20
116.24	513.28	833.02	021.21	093.28	159.13
119.25	516.27	833.04	021.23	094.15	162.11
121.07	523.26	833.06	022.09	097.13	162.26
125.27	527.08	834.04	023.11	097.27	163.21
132.06	528.22	834.13	024.18	098.10	163.23
132.18	529.05	834.20	024.27	098.21	163.25
132.19	531.21	838.17	025.02	098.23	163.26
135.18	531.22	839.14	026.10	099.01	163.28
135.22	531.23	847.27	026.12	099.10	164.09
139.11	532.19	848.21	026.17	101.07	164.10
139.18	533.25	865.04	026.18	102.10	164.27
140.23	533.26	883.27	027.05	102.11	164.28
142.18	535.15	884.28	027.09	102.17	165.13
143.16	549.24	887.06	027.20	102.21	165.19
149.17	554.05	887.25	027.22	103.13	166.14
158.16	555.28	888.17	028.21	104.16	166.20
166.09	556.02	888.27	028.23	104.21	166.21
166.19	559.03	889.01	029.09	105.06	168.22
169.24	562.11	889.25	030.14	105.20	169.21
172.11	563.24	891.20	031.17	106.03	169.22
176.13	570.12	894.01	031.23	107.07	169.27
184.25	570.14	895.23	033.19	107.10	170.08
187.28	574.07	896.11	034.01	107.14	171.21
190.08	580.06	896.26	035.03	107.15	171.23
190.23	590.05	897.17	035.08	107.22	171.27
196.23	596.13	898.13	035.28	107.23	172.04
199.13	598.04	903.14	036.03	109.10	172.12
205.17	601.08	903.26	036.05	112.19	172.18
208.14	612.06	904.04	039.26	114.25	173.11
209.07	612.18	909.01	040.04	115.02	173.13
215.09	615.21	909.04	040.17	115.09	173.14
215.11	616.04	thank	040.19	116.17	173.20
216.10	619.05	028.08	040.20	116.20	173.24
216.27	621.14	224.03	040.22	117.13	173.28
217.05	623.13	228.08	040.24	117.23	173.28
218.02	624.02	243.10	040.28	118.03	174.01
237.08	630.09	354.19	041.01	118.07	174.16
240.05	630.19	410.20	041.10	118.27	175.18
245.20	631.19	435.14	043.02	118.28	175.23
251.06	633.21	446.17	043.16	119.15	175.27
257.07	645.11	497.27	043.17	119.23	176.25
257.19	647.04	508.16	043.18	119.27	177.20
258.28	647.13	531.27	043.22	120.15	177.21
262.12	648.17	548.03	043.27	120.16	177.27
265.22	649.17	548.04	044.10	120.18	178.06
265.24	650.06	580.18	045.05	120.21	178.09
267.26	656.01	599.25	046.15	120.26	178.10
269.15	671.26	634.02	047.16	121.05	178.24

179.03	252.25	305.11	375.25	439.04	499.20
180.08	252.28	305.17	376.01	443.02	499.24
180.08	253.05	306.02	376.18	444.17	499.28
181.13	253.21	306.10	377.01	444.18	500.01
182.22	253.23	306.19	377.06	445.08	500.02
182.23	254.20	308.15	377.18	445.25	502.14
184.12	255.12	309.03	377.18	445.28	503.17
184.14	255.14	309.12	377.24	447.24	504.10
187.28	256.27	309.23	377.28	448.12	505.07
189.26	257.01	310.16	378.04	448.21	506.09
191.04	259.09	311.12	379.15	448.26	507.07
191.05	260.07	311.21	380.22	450.05	507.09
191.05	260.08	312.02	380.28	450.20	507.18
191.07	260.08	312.07	382.04	450.21	507.20
191.16	260.09	313.02	382.05	450.22	507.21
191.25	261.10	314.09	382.10	451.04	507.22
191.26	261.15	315.14	382.19	451.06	507.24
191.28	262.01	315.16	382.21	451.21	508.02
192.05	262.22	316.21	382.23	452.01	508.18
192.06	263.06	316.25	383.11	453.08	508.23
192.09	263.11	317.14	383.18	453.26	510.05
192.17	264.18	319.23	384.07	453.28	510.28
192.21	264.24	320.24	384.08	455.10	511.02
193.04	265.09	320.26	384.09	455.16	511.06
193.07	265.11	321.21	384.11	455.28	511.08
195.01	265.12	323.01	384.16	456.10	511.14
196.05	265.18	324.20	384.20	456.15	513.13
196.06	265.28	325.08	385.19	459.06	514.05
196.22	265.28	326.07	388.05	459.08	514.20
198.10	266.08	326.23	388.16	459.16	515.28
198.24	266.14	327.26	390.13	459.21	516.03
199.19	266.20	329.15	390.16	460.07	516.04
200.01	266.23	329.27	391.20	461.02	517.06
200.22	266.24	330.15	391.22	462.02	517.08
201.01	266.24	330.24	392.07	462.07	518.05
201.15	267.01	330.25	392.16	462.15	520.10
201.22	269.09	330.26	395.04	462.26	520.13
202.16	269.12	331.18	396.14	464.02	522.02
202.19	269.19	332.17	396.23	464.02	523.07
204.01	269.19	333.11	397.24	465.08	523.22
204.22	269.23	333.14	398.08	465.17	523.26
204.26	269.26	334.17	399.04	465.28	524.02
207.14	270.14	334.26	399.18	466.02	524.20
208.05	270.15	335.06	400.08	466.05	527.20
208.09	270.23	335.16	401.01	466.10	528.07
208.15	271.11	337.11	401.07	466.11	528.15
209.16	271.18	336.25	401.15	466.14	528.25
209.18	271.21	338.27	401.17	467.18	528.26
210.11	272.27	339.06	401.21	468.21	529.18
210.16	273.01	339.27	402.10	469.10	529.19
211.04	273.03	340.03	402.27	469.28	529.24
211.04	273.05	340.10	403.03	471.01	530.13
211.06	273.23	340.28	403.05	471.16	530.23
214.24	273.24	341.09	403.12	471.19	531.14
215.05	274.03	342.16	403.24	472.06	531.16
215.06	274.04	343.13	404.12	472.10	531.27
215.08	274.14	345.28	404.22	472.13	532.17
216.02	274.21	346.05	405.01	472.15	532.21
216.04	275.08	346.27	405.04	472.19	532.24
216.21	276.11	347.03	405.21	472.22	532.27
217.20	276.12	347.23	406.07	473.13	533.15
218.07	276.24	348.03	406.27	474.04	533.16
218.09	277.27	348.24	408.17	474.09	533.19
219.21	278.02	349.02	408.17	474.26	533.21
220.21	279.09	349.05	408.21	475.05	533.24
224.26	279.15	349.09	409.05	475.21	535.14
225.04	279.20	349.14	409.10	476.17	535.16
225.28	281.10	349.15	410.19	477.23	535.18
226.03	281.19	349.26	412.23	478.05	535.21
227.04	282.02	350.05	414.04	480.01	535.24
228.13	282.03	350.06	414.07	480.13	536.12
229.06	282.12	350.20	414.17	480.24	537.02
229.07	282.25	351.05	415.01	481.05	537.06
229.17	283.02	351.16	417.07	481.07	537.07
230.03	283.10	351.17	417.10	481.08	537.11
230.19	283.25	351.24	418.03	483.05	537.15
230.27	285.08	351.08	418.06	483.07	538.01
231.02	285.10	351.26	418.08	483.10	538.02
231.26	287.14	351.28	418.14	483.20	538.16
232.23	287.18	352.02	418.20	485.16	541.19
233.03	287.20	353.14	421.11	485.19	541.26
233.13	288.15	354.24	421.15	485.20	542.05
234.03	288.21	355.13	422.08	485.28	542.24
234.16	288.24	356.21	423.01	487.17	542.26
235.07	288.25	356.25	423.26	488.09	543.18
235.19	289.01	360.13	423.27	490.01	543.19
235.24	289.09	360.14	423.28	490.03	544.08
236.22	289.25	360.21	424.13	491.13	545.11
236.15	290.05	361.03	424.16	491.19	545.21
236.17	291.04	361.09	424.18	491.25	546.09
238.22	291.06	361.23	425.11	493.02	546.12
239.16	292.01	362.06	425.15	493.03	546.18
241.16	292.03	362.17	427.25	493.04	546.25
241.27	292.17	362.28	430.14	493.11	547.02
242.04	292.25	363.01	430.19	493.14	547.03
242.04	293.08	363.08	431.18	495.27	547.09
242.19	293.08	364.18	434.14	495.28	547.19
244.03	294.13	366.15	434.19	496.03	547.21
244.11	294.22	370.14	434.21	496.07	547.25
244.14	294.23	370.23	435.15	496.09	548.11
245.06	295.14	370.26	436.11	496.14	549.22
246.01	295.16	372.01	437.01	497.01	549.27
246.23	296.04	372.03	437.04	498.04	550.01
247.06	297.12	372.28	437.07	498.11	550.05
247.16	300.06	373.08	437.08	498.12	550.21
248.04	300.09	374.03	437.13	498.14	550.27
249.23	300.14	374.07	437.18	498.16	551.06
250.21	300.27	374.08	437.24	498.23	551.20
250.23	301.03	375.01	438.14	499.01	551.22
250.25	301.12	375.02	438.25	499.02	552.07
251.10	305.11	375.10	438.25	499.04	

552.23	620.24	678.12	754.04	805.22	851.16
553.02	621.04	679.02	754.10	805.23	852.04
553.04	621.05	680.25	754.18	805.26	852.16
553.08	621.21	682.04	754.27	805.27	852.22
553.19	622.17	683.11	755.06	806.06	853.19
553.20	622.24	685.06	755.16	806.11	853.25
553.28	623.02	685.25	755.19	806.20	853.28
554.09	623.18	686.26	755.25	806.24	854.02
554.24	623.21	687.12	755.28	806.25	854.07
557.04	623.22	687.13	756.01	806.27	856.01
558.05	624.01	687.20	756.05	808.06	856.05
558.05	624.02	687.28	756.18	809.03	857.03
558.09	624.04	689.04	758.16	810.15	857.24
558.21	624.06	689.07	758.25	811.11	859.09
558.25	624.12	689.19	759.02	811.19	859.23
559.08	624.18	689.19	759.03	813.16	859.24
559.16	624.20	690.01	759.04	813.28	861.03
560.07	625.09	691.15	759.05	815.27	861.06
561.04	625.16	693.25	759.13	815.27	861.09
561.12	625.23	693.25	759.18	816.02	861.26
563.18	626.18	694.05	759.28	816.04	862.05
564.13	626.20	695.15	760.16	816.09	862.11
564.21	626.24	696.12	760.24	817.11	862.23
566.05	627.07	697.07	761.08	817.24	862.26
566.15	627.08	697.08	761.15	818.25	862.26
566.25	627.27	697.15	761.23	818.26	863.15
568.01	628.09	697.19	763.21	819.01	863.17
568.19	628.12	702.18	764.05	819.06	863.18
568.21	628.25	702.27	765.16	819.23	864.02
569.07	629.10	703.05	766.04	820.09	864.04
570.02	629.21	703.17	766.06	820.11	864.08
570.10	630.17	704.03	767.07	820.14	865.05
571.07	631.09	705.16	767.16	820.20	865.11
571.19	631.09	706.14	767.20	820.22	865.20
571.23	631.28	707.14	767.27	821.19	867.21
572.25	632.04	707.18	770.06	821.27	867.23
573.12	632.05	707.20	770.23	822.10	871.11
573.22	633.01	708.28	771.07	822.13	872.04
574.22	633.12	709.21	771.21	822.28	872.04
574.24	634.01	711.04	771.23	823.11	872.09
576.04	634.03	712.08	772.05	823.14	872.12
577.01	634.23	712.26	772.27	823.22	872.13
577.20	634.28	713.23	774.22	823.23	872.22
579.06	636.11	714.10	774.24	824.09	873.19
579.07	636.19	715.08	774.25	824.15	873.21
579.09	636.20	715.08	774.25	824.18	873.27
579.11	636.22	715.15	776.05	824.21	873.28
580.03	637.17	715.18	776.05	824.27	874.04
580.07	638.01	715.19	776.08	825.09	874.14
580.19	638.02	716.05	776.14	825.10	877.09
580.21	638.10	716.24	777.23	826.22	877.10
581.05	639.01	717.02	778.01	827.11	877.24
582.11	639.11	717.22	778.17	827.24	878.10
585.04	639.15	719.14	778.19	828.02	878.11
585.14	639.16	719.16	779.10	828.15	879.11
587.12	639.20	720.01	779.11	828.17	879.14
590.01	639.21	720.14	779.12	828.22	879.15
590.04	641.02	720.15	779.20	829.13	879.17
590.09	641.14	721.06	779.21	829.17	880.11
591.02	642.11	721.12	779.21	830.04	881.06
593.07	642.13	721.13	779.24	830.09	881.08
593.17	643.03	722.02	780.10	830.10	882.28
593.19	644.15	722.14	780.14	830.13	883.08
593.20	644.16	723.20	781.10	831.04	883.27
595.24	644.18	724.06	782.13	831.09	884.01
595.25	644.20	724.13	782.16	831.11	884.08
597.01	644.27	725.02	783.06	831.12	884.08
597.03	645.10	725.03	784.06	832.01	885.04
600.14	645.21	725.22	784.09	833.07	885.11
601.21	647.20	725.24	784.11	833.13	886.14
602.04	649.15	727.06	785.17	833.15	886.20
602.07	649.25	727.07	786.19	833.26	886.21
602.07	651.22	727.15	787.15	833.27	888.03
603.05	651.26	727.17	788.01	834.04	889.11
603.21	651.27	727.17	788.06	834.27	889.18
604.13	653.01	729.11	789.04	835.20	889.28
604.15	653.18	730.06	789.10	835.25	890.26
606.13	654.01	730.06	789.11	836.04	892.11
606.14	654.20	730.09	789.15	837.01	893.25
607.02	655.03	730.13	789.16	838.06	894.12
607.07	655.15	730.23	790.06	838.08	894.15
607.24	655.28	731.02	792.03	838.22	894.23
608.11	656.22	732.04	792.18	839.05	895.01
609.07	657.14	732.26	793.16	839.26	895.05
609.09	658.08	734.16	794.09	840.13	896.13
609.11	659.03	734.25	796.05	840.17	897.06
609.13	659.17	735.16	796.26	842.06	898.07
609.16	659.28	736.04	796.26	842.10	898.15
609.17	660.02	736.15	797.01	842.22	899.14
610.01	660.03	736.22	797.21	842.25	899.22
610.05	660.08	738.18	798.21	843.10	900.25
610.05	662.06	739.02	799.03	843.28	900.26
610.18	662.11	740.09	799.04	844.10	900.28
610.20	662.19	740.26	799.06	844.15	901.02
610.22	663.11	741.26	799.08	844.17	901.14
611.10	663.17	743.20	799.11	844.27	901.15
612.01	663.17	746.12	799.13	844.28	902.02
612.02	663.19	747.09	799.19	845.17	902.18
614.11	664.04	747.11	799.19	846.02	902.21
614.26	664.07	747.24	799.27	846.11	902.26
615.05	664.26	748.19	800.02	846.15	903.06
615.10	667.16	748.22	800.21	846.19	903.12
615.15	669.01	750.08	801.04	846.20	903.15
616.15	670.11	751.07	802.07	846.28	903.23
616.19	671.02	751.07	802.16	847.21	904.02
616.28	672.03	751.08	803.23	847.26	905.11
617.18	672.08	751.09	803.26	848.07	906.19
617.27	673.19	751.10	804.07	848.19	906.25
618.26	673.21	751.12	804.24	849.01	907.03
619.16	674.09	751.16	805.18	849.21	908.08
619.20	676.10	752.18	805.20	850.05	909.05

909.15	008.27	021.04	033.15	048.21	059.06
909.16	008.28	021.05	033.16	048.26	059.06
909.16	009.01	021.08	033.18	049.05	059.14
910.04	009.04	021.13	033.22	049.07	059.22
910.06	009.05	021.13	033.25	049.12	059.23
910.06	009.11	022.04	033.26	049.12	060.05
910.15	009.14	022.11	033.27	049.13	060.07
910.17	009.16	022.14	033.27	049.14	060.20
910.21	009.16	022.16	033.30	049.17	061.07
910.26	009.16	022.17	034.11	049.18	061.08
910.28	009.17	022.17	034.16	049.21	061.08
911.01	009.19	022.18	034.18	049.21	061.12
911.22	009.22	022.19	034.21	049.23	061.18
912.14	009.24	022.21	035.06	049.24	061.20
912.15	009.24	022.21	035.11	049.25	061.20
that's	009.24	022.22	035.12	049.26	061.24
055.13	010.02	022.26	035.19	049.27	061.25
068.05	010.17	023.05	035.24	049.28	061.26
311.06	010.23	023.06	036.15	050.01	062.06
427.23	010.25	023.07	036.17	050.02	062.06
431.08	011.04	023.08	036.17	050.04	062.07
432.08	012.02	023.10	036.28	050.07	062.14
507.14	012.04	023.13	037.27	050.07	062.25
509.26	012.05	023.16	038.08	050.08	063.02
680.28	012.07	023.19	038.11	050.10	063.07
682.27	012.14	023.22	038.13	050.12	063.18
thaw	013.03	023.22	038.13	050.12	063.28
072.27	013.12	023.24	038.15	050.13	064.15
220.03	013.13	023.24	038.24	050.13	064.22
thawed	013.14	024.01	039.02	050.14	064.24
778.26	013.26	024.16	039.17	050.15	064.25
the	013.27	024.19	039.19	050.16	064.25
001.04	014.01	024.23	039.23	050.17	064.27
001.05	014.10	025.17	039.24	050.17	065.02
001.07	014.13	026.02	039.24	050.18	065.07
001.10	014.19	026.16	040.01	050.23	065.07
001.13	015.05	026.18	040.02	050.23	065.11
001.13	015.11	026.18	040.02	050.24	065.12
001.15	015.13	026.20	040.05	050.25	065.14
001.15	015.15	027.05	040.06	050.26	065.15
001.16	015.19	027.10	040.08	051.04	065.17
002.01	015.20	027.10	040.09	051.05	065.24
002.02	015.21	027.13	040.17	051.07	066.04
002.03	015.24	027.14	040.21	051.12	066.06
002.04	015.24	027.16	040.21	051.12	066.07
002.07	015.27	027.21	040.25	051.14	066.07
002.08	015.28	027.23	040.26	051.18	066.08
002.25	015.28	027.25	040.26	051.21	066.08
003.03	015.28	027.26	041.01	051.21	066.10
003.05	015.28	027.26	041.13	051.24	066.11
003.08	016.01	028.04	041.14	052.01	066.12
003.08	016.02	028.11	042.03	052.02	066.14
003.08	016.03	028.14	042.09	052.03	066.14
003.10	016.03	028.16	042.17	052.04	066.14
003.11	016.06	028.18	042.18	052.07	066.19
003.12	016.07	028.20	043.03	052.10	066.22
003.19	016.09	029.02	043.11	052.11	066.23
003.23	016.10	029.05	043.18	052.11	067.03
003.24	016.13	029.06	043.22	052.14	067.06
003.26	016.15	029.08	044.01	052.16	067.09
003.27	016.17	029.08	044.07	052.16	067.11
003.28	016.17	029.09	044.08	052.17	067.16
004.01	016.19	029.14	044.09	052.19	068.13
004.02	016.20	029.15	044.11	052.21	069.08
004.03	016.23	029.23	045.03	052.22	069.27
004.04	016.23	030.04	045.05	052.22	070.01
004.05	016.24	030.05	045.10	052.26	071.02
004.06	016.28	030.16	045.11	053.04	071.03
004.08	017.04	030.27	045.15	053.12	071.07
004.08	017.06	031.03	045.16	053.16	071.09
004.11	017.06	031.03	045.17	053.20	071.11
004.13	017.08	031.03	045.20	053.20	071.12
004.14	017.09	031.04	045.21	053.23	071.13
004.16	017.10	031.06	045.21	053.24	071.15
004.19	017.12	031.08	045.22	053.27	071.18
004.20	017.12	031.13	045.22	054.06	072.03
004.21	017.14	031.15	045.23	054.22	072.08
004.23	017.17	031.17	045.24	054.26	072.14
004.24	017.18	031.20	045.25	054.27	072.15
004.27	017.20	031.22	045.27	055.01	072.22
005.03	017.22	031.24	045.28	055.02	072.22
005.05	017.24	031.25	046.02	055.15	072.24
005.07	017.25	031.26	046.06	055.19	072.27
005.07	018.01	031.26	046.07	055.25	073.01
005.10	018.05	031.27	046.10	056.10	073.01
005.16	018.06	031.27	046.11	056.13	073.03
005.19	018.09	031.28	046.12	056.16	073.04
005.26	018.12	032.01	046.14	056.17	073.05
006.03	018.26	032.04	046.16	056.20	073.07
006.04	018.26	032.06	046.16	057.05	073.08
006.05	018.27	032.07	046.22	057.06	073.09
006.07	018.27	032.11	047.04	057.06	073.10
006.10	018.27	032.11	047.04	057.08	073.11
006.11	018.28	032.13	047.05	057.10	073.18
006.16	019.01	032.18	047.05	057.15	073.18
006.17	019.01	032.20	047.06	057.18	073.20
006.20	019.02	032.26	047.07	057.23	073.25
006.20	019.12	032.27	047.10	057.25	073.25
006.25	019.19	033.04	047.12	058.01	073.27
007.12	020.02	033.04	047.15	058.07	073.27
007.15	020.03	033.05	047.15	058.10	074.05
007.16	020.04	033.06	047.23	058.11	074.06
007.23	020.17	033.06	048.06	058.11	074.10
007.23	020.24	033.08	048.06	058.16	074.10
007.27	020.25	033.10	048.11	058.16	074.11
008.02	020.26	033.11	048.12	058.23	074.12
008.04	020.26	033.14	048.12	059.01	074.16
008.12	020.23		048.15	059.03	074.17
008.13	021.01		048.17		074.24
008.14	021.03		048.20		074.25
008.23	021.03				
	021.04				

074.27	083.02	091.21	101.05	114.26	125.06
075.05	083.03	091.28	101.07	114.28	125.07
075.06	083.04	091.28	101.11	115.07	125.08
075.08	083.05	092.05	101.12	115.10	125.09
075.10	083.09	092.21	101.13	115.14	125.11
075.11	083.13	092.22	101.15	115.16	125.16
075.12	083.13	092.23	101.16	115.17	125.26
075.15	083.15	092.25	101.18	115.24	126.05
075.15	083.16	092.27	101.19	115.26	126.07
075.19	083.16	092.28	101.19	115.27	126.08
075.21	083.19	093.05	101.26	116.01	126.12
075.21	083.22	093.07	102.03	116.02	126.15
075.23	083.24	093.07	102.05	116.12	126.21
075.28	083.25	093.13	102.19	116.13	126.22
076.01	083.26	093.15	102.21	116.16	126.23
076.05	083.28	093.23	102.26	116.18	126.26
076.09	084.02	093.25	103.01	116.18	126.28
076.10	084.03	093.26	103.11	116.19	127.01
076.11	084.05	093.26	103.16	116.21	127.02
076.14	084.06	093.27	104.08	116.26	127.04
076.16	084.06	094.01	104.11	116.28	127.05
076.16	084.10	094.04	104.12	117.01	127.07
076.19	084.13	094.12	104.27	117.01	127.08
076.23	084.19	094.14	105.03	117.03	127.08
076.24	084.22	094.15	105.06	117.03	127.16
077.06	084.23	094.16	105.06	117.09	127.19
077.17	084.24	094.18	105.11	117.10	127.19
077.18	084.25	094.18	105.14	117.11	127.21
077.19	084.28	094.19	105.19	117.11	127.23
078.01	085.03	094.25	105.22	117.17	127.23
078.02	085.05	094.28	105.22	117.20	127.26
078.03	085.07	095.06	105.24	117.22	128.01
078.09	085.08	095.18	105.24	117.24	128.03
078.09	085.09	095.18	105.27	117.25	128.06
078.13	085.09	096.02	106.03	117.26	128.08
078.15	085.10	096.04	106.10	118.01	128.09
078.16	085.11	096.05	106.21	118.02	128.09
078.19	085.16	096.05	106.27	118.03	128.12
078.19	085.16	096.06	107.18	118.11	128.12
078.20	085.18	096.07	108.02	118.12	129.02
078.21	085.18	096.08	108.06	118.12	129.04
078.24	085.19	096.10	108.19	118.13	129.06
078.25	085.21	096.11	108.24	118.13	129.06
078.27	085.26	096.12	108.28	118.15	129.09
078.28	086.01	096.15	108.28	118.16	129.10
079.03	086.03	096.16	109.01	118.16	129.13
079.04	086.04	096.16	109.02	118.17	129.18
079.05	086.07	096.19	109.03	118.18	130.13
079.06	086.08	096.19	109.06	118.19	130.14
079.08	086.12	096.20	109.07	118.22	130.22
079.12	086.13	097.02	109.08	118.23	130.25
079.13	086.16	097.05	109.16	118.23	131.02
079.16	086.18	097.06	109.17	118.24	131.04
079.16	086.19	097.08	109.18	118.24	131.07
079.20	086.20	097.12	109.21	119.01	131.16
079.22	086.21	097.13	110.08	119.14	131.22
079.25	086.25	097.13	111.03	119.20	131.28
079.26	086.25	097.16	111.06	119.21	132.10
079.27	086.26	097.19	111.07	120.01	132.14
080.02	086.27	097.20	111.10	120.08	132.16
080.05	087.01	097.21	111.11	120.14	132.20
080.09	087.03	097.22	111.12	120.17	133.04
080.10	087.10	097.22	111.14	120.21	133.11
080.10	087.14	097.23	111.16	120.22	133.12
080.10	087.15	097.24	111.17	120.23	133.23
080.12	087.16	097.24	111.20	120.25	133.24
080.12	087.17	097.26	112.01	120.26	133.26
080.21	087.17	098.02	112.02	120.27	134.03
080.23	087.18	098.03	112.03	121.02	134.09
080.25	087.21	098.06	112.04	121.06	134.23
081.01	087.22	098.12	112.08	121.06	135.02
081.02	087.23	098.12	112.09	121.06	135.12
081.03	087.28	098.13	112.10	121.09	135.16
081.04	088.03	098.13	112.12	121.11	135.20
081.04	088.09	098.19	112.15	121.17	135.21
081.06	088.09	098.19	112.16	121.18	135.26
081.07	088.10	099.02	112.17	121.21	135.26
081.10	088.12	099.12	112.23	121.24	135.27
081.11	088.13	099.13	112.26	121.26	135.28
081.12	088.15	099.13	112.27	122.02	136.01
081.13	088.20	099.14	113.01	122.02	136.04
081.13	088.22	099.20	113.01	122.05	136.07
081.18	088.22	099.21	113.03	122.07	136.17
081.19	088.24	100.03	113.04	122.12	136.25
081.24	089.01	100.05	113.05	122.13	137.06
081.24	089.02	100.07	113.08	122.14	137.08
081.24	089.03	100.08	113.12	122.15	137.11
081.25	089.04	100.08	113.14	122.17	137.12
081.25	089.06	100.08	113.16	122.18	137.13
081.26	089.06	100.09	113.18	122.18	137.13
081.26	089.07	100.10	113.19	122.19	137.14
081.27	089.09	100.10	113.21	122.22	137.14
081.28	089.20	100.12	113.24	122.22	137.14
082.02	089.22	100.12	113.26	122.22	137.24
082.05	089.22	100.13	113.27	122.23	137.25
082.06	089.23	100.14	114.03	122.26	138.03
082.07	089.26	100.16	114.06	122.28	138.07
082.09	089.28	100.17	114.07	123.04	138.18
082.09	090.05	100.17	114.07	123.11	138.18
082.10	090.10	100.18	114.12	123.12	138.19
082.12	090.11	100.20	114.13	123.15	138.21
082.12	090.16	100.20	114.15	123.19	138.23
082.14	090.17	100.22	114.16	123.22	138.24
082.15	090.18	100.24	114.17	123.24	139.03
082.18	090.20	100.27	114.18	124.01	139.03
082.22	090.20	101.01	114.18	124.06	139.04
082.24	090.24	101.01	114.19	124.11	139.09
082.28	091.01	101.02	114.22	124.15	139.09
082.28	091.02	101.03	114.24	124.28	139.09
083.01	091.12		114.26	125.01	139.14
				125.04	

139.17	151.27	163.17	174.02	187.10	198.24
139.25	152.01	163.21	174.04	187.11	198.28
139.27	152.02	163.23	174.07	187.20	199.06
140.13	152.03	163.27	174.08	187.24	199.09
140.18	152.05	164.02	174.10	187.24	199.11
140.25	152.05	164.06	174.10	187.26	199.17
140.28	152.06	164.09	174.11	187.27	199.23
140.28	152.17	164.16	174.13	188.05	199.25
141.13	152.17	164.16	174.14	188.09	200.04
141.17	152.20	164.17	174.23	188.11	200.16
141.20	152.20	164.17	174.24	188.13	200.17
141.20	152.21	164.18	174.27	188.23	200.18
141.23	152.22	164.20	175.01	189.02	200.21
141.25	152.24	164.23	175.03	189.11	200.23
141.26	152.28	164.24	175.04	189.12	200.25
142.03	153.02	164.26	175.05	189.15	200.26
142.04	153.07	165.02	175.07	189.15	200.26
142.07	153.14	165.08	175.20	189.18	200.27
142.09	153.19	165.13	175.20	189.23	200.28
142.20	153.23	165.16	175.26	190.02	201.03
142.21	153.24	165.24	176.02	190.06	201.04
142.23	153.25	165.26	176.02	190.09	201.10
142.23	153.25	165.27	176.12	190.15	201.20
142.25	153.26	166.03	176.21	190.16	201.23
143.01	153.26	166.04	177.06	190.17	202.11
143.02	154.01	166.10	177.14	190.17	202.12
143.02	154.05	166.25	177.22	190.18	202.13
143.09	154.06	166.25	178.08	190.18	202.16
144.02	154.09	166.27	178.14	190.19	202.20
144.02	154.11	167.17	178.16	190.20	202.22
144.04	154.11	167.20	178.20	190.21	202.22
144.07	154.12	167.21	178.24	190.24	203.07
144.08	154.12	167.24	178.26	191.04	203.14
144.09	154.16	167.27	178.28	191.06	203.26
144.11	154.17	168.03	179.05	191.09	203.27
144.12	154.24	168.04	179.17	191.10	204.01
144.13	155.01	168.05	179.22	191.13	204.04
144.16	155.01	168.05	179.27	191.14	204.08
144.19	155.02	168.06	180.06	191.20	204.16
145.04	155.03	168.06	180.08	191.21	204.16
145.05	155.04	168.06	180.10	191.21	204.18
145.07	155.06	168.06	180.18	191.24	204.19
145.08	155.12	168.08	180.20	191.25	204.22
145.14	155.12	168.17	180.20	191.26	205.01
145.17	155.13	168.17	180.21	192.02	205.10
145.19	155.13	168.21	180.22	192.02	205.11
145.19	155.13	168.23	180.23	192.13	205.13
145.21	155.14	168.25	180.25	192.13	205.14
145.22	155.16	169.04	180.26	193.01	205.26
145.24	155.18	169.09	181.03	193.08	206.06
146.08	155.19	169.10	181.05	193.10	206.10
146.11	155.20	169.11	181.06	193.11	206.15
146.18	155.21	169.11	181.08	193.12	206.23
146.21	155.25	169.14	181.09	193.13	206.24
146.23	156.24	169.16	181.10	193.17	206.24
146.24	157.07	169.18	181.11	193.21	206.27
146.26	157.14	169.19	181.12	193.23	206.28
147.01	157.24	169.19	181.13	193.24	207.02
147.02	158.10	169.19	181.16	193.26	207.03
147.04	158.11	169.20	181.16	193.27	207.05
147.06	158.19	169.20	181.18	194.03	207.10
147.06	159.07	169.21	181.20	194.04	207.16
147.10	159.08	169.23	182.03	194.06	207.17
147.11	159.08	169.24	182.05	194.07	207.17
147.13	159.21	169.26	182.06	194.11	207.18
147.15	159.22	170.01	182.09	194.11	207.18
147.16	160.02	170.01	182.12	194.15	207.18
147.19	160.03	170.11	182.18	194.18	207.19
147.21	160.10	170.12	182.20	194.20	207.27
147.21	160.12	170.21	182.23	194.21	208.01
147.26	160.15	170.23	182.24	194.21	208.04
147.27	160.16	170.25	182.24	194.23	208.13
147.27	160.17	170.25	182.28	194.24	208.16
148.01	160.17	171.01	183.02	194.26	208.22
148.05	160.19	171.05	183.03	194.26	208.23
148.05	160.20	171.06	183.05	194.26	208.24
148.07	160.20	171.07	183.11	194.27	208.25
148.10	161.01	171.08	183.12	195.02	208.26
148.13	161.01	171.13	183.12	195.05	208.27
148.14	161.02	171.16	183.15	195.14	208.28
148.14	161.04	171.19	183.16	195.14	209.01
148.15	161.06	171.19	183.17	195.18	209.02
148.20	161.08	171.24	183.25	195.22	209.03
148.21	161.08	171.25	184.01	196.01	209.03
148.24	161.12	171.28	184.02	196.01	209.04
148.26	161.12	172.05	184.04	196.03	209.05
149.04	161.12	172.07	184.05	196.03	209.07
149.04	161.16	172.09	184.07	196.06	209.08
149.07	161.16	172.10	184.19	196.06	209.08
149.08	161.22	172.10	184.20	196.07	209.08
149.09	162.02	172.11	184.22	196.09	209.08
149.10	162.07	172.15	184.23	196.11	209.09
149.18	162.08	172.15	184.28	196.14	209.10
150.04	162.09	172.16	185.04	196.19	209.12
150.10	162.09	172.18	185.04	196.22	209.14
150.25	162.11	172.21	185.05	196.23	209.15
150.26	162.14	172.22	185.06	196.24	209.15
150.26	162.15	172.22	185.11	196.25	209.19
151.03	162.18	172.23	185.15	196.26	209.19
151.06	162.24	172.28	185.18	196.27	209.23
151.08	162.24	172.28	185.20	197.02	209.24
151.11	163.03	173.02	185.21	197.09	209.24
151.12	163.05	173.05	185.21	197.17	209.25
151.13	163.08	173.06	185.24	197.18	209.26
151.15	163.08	173.09	186.02	197.19	209.27
151.19	163.11	173.10	186.08	197.26	209.28
151.19	163.12	173.10	186.15	198.02	210.01
151.21	163.12	173.16	186.19	198.05	210.05
151.21	163.15	173.17	186.24	198.07	210.08
151.24	163.15	173.23	187.07	198.14	210.14
151.25	163.16	174.02	187.07		210.14

210.17	222.19	234.08	247.25	259.04	278.07
210.19	222.20	234.16	247.25	259.10	279.05
210.26	222.20	235.01	247.26	259.11	279.09
211.02	222.22	235.02	248.07	259.18	279.16
211.05	222.22	235.05	248.08	259.22	279.16
211.08	222.23	235.05	248.09	259.25	279.19
211.11	222.25	235.06	248.09	260.13	280.03
211.22	222.28	235.08	248.11	260.25	280.04
211.26	223.04	235.10	248.12	261.02	280.05
211.27	223.17	235.10	248.15	261.08	280.07
212.02	223.18	235.11	248.16	261.10	280.08
213.02	223.19	235.11	248.17	261.14	280.09
213.05	223.20	235.12	248.18	261.18	280.15
213.19	223.23	235.13	248.19	261.21	280.21
214.10	223.25	235.15	248.20	261.27	280.23
214.11	224.05	235.15	248.21	262.01	280.25
214.15	224.08	235.17	248.23	262.16	281.01
214.20	224.11	235.22	248.24	262.17	281.04
214.21	225.10	235.28	248.24	262.21	281.07
214.25	225.10	236.04	248.26	263.04	281.09
214.26	225.10	236.09	248.27	263.05	281.10
214.27	225.28	236.10	248.27	263.07	281.11
215.01	226.01	236.12	249.02	263.09	281.14
215.01	226.03	236.21	249.03	263.12	281.14
215.02	226.03	236.23	249.04	263.12	281.17
215.02	226.14	236.24	249.06	263.16	281.18
215.05	226.21	236.25	249.07	263.18	281.19
215.07	226.22	236.26	249.10	264.02	281.19
215.14	226.23	236.26	249.11	264.03	281.24
215.19	226.25	237.02	249.15	264.06	281.25
215.21	227.11	237.03	249.17	264.08	281.26
215.21	227.12	237.03	249.22	264.17	281.28
215.23	227.13	237.06	250.02	264.24	282.01
215.23	227.17	237.14	250.03	265.08	282.03
215.27	227.20	237.15	250.04	265.10	282.05
216.13	227.22	237.17	250.06	265.14	282.05
216.24	227.28	237.19	250.08	265.23	282.10
217.02	228.02	237.24	250.12	265.25	282.14
217.02	228.06	237.24	250.14	266.03	282.15
217.07	228.08	237.27	250.15	266.05	282.15
217.10	228.11	237.28	250.16	266.11	282.16
217.12	228.13	238.01	250.17	266.12	282.19
217.14	228.14	238.10	250.20	266.20	282.19
217.21	228.15	238.11	250.25	266.23	282.26
217.21	228.22	238.12	250.27	267.01	282.26
217.22	228.24	238.12	250.27	267.04	283.03
217.23	228.25	238.20	251.04	267.13	283.07
218.06	229.02	238.21	251.05	267.14	283.11
218.10	229.03	238.25	251.09	267.14	283.12
218.12	229.04	238.27	251.09	267.14	283.17
218.16	229.05	238.27	252.11	267.16	283.18
218.27	229.07	238.28	252.12	267.18	283.23
218.27	229.10	239.01	252.21	267.23	283.27
219.02	229.11	239.02	252.22	267.26	284.01
219.02	229.12	239.06	252.24	266.02	284.02
219.04	229.13	239.07	252.26	268.03	284.03
219.04	229.15	240.02	252.26	268.15	284.11
219.05	229.15	240.03	253.04	268.17	284.11
219.05	229.16	240.05	253.05	268.18	284.19
219.06	229.21	240.06	253.12	269.04	284.21
219.15	229.21	240.08	253.13	269.05	284.24
219.16	229.24	240.18	253.14	269.16	284.26
219.17	229.25	240.22	253.16	269.17	285.03
219.17	229.27	240.22	253.19	269.19	285.04
219.19	230.04	240.23	253.24	269.21	285.08
219.21	230.06	240.25	254.03	269.28	285.09
219.23	230.10	240.26	254.04	270.10	285.11
219.24	230.13	240.26	254.05	270.18	285.12
219.27	230.13	240.27	254.14	270.23	285.14
220.01	230.14	241.13	254.14	271.03	285.15
220.04	230.15	241.15	255.01	271.03	285.17
220.05	230.15	242.02	255.06	271.04	285.23
220.06	230.16	242.05	255.08	271.08	285.24
220.07	230.18	242.06	255.11	271.09	285.27
220.08	230.18	242.09	255.18	271.11	286.02
220.08	230.21	242.27	255.22	271.16	286.02
220.11	230.23	243.01	255.22	271.18	286.05
220.11	230.25	243.11	256.02	271.23	286.08
220.16	231.02	243.15	256.03	272.01	286.09
220.17	231.02	243.16	256.04	272.02	286.10
220.22	231.05	243.21	256.06	272.05	286.11
220.22	231.06	244.06	256.07	272.08	286.13
220.23	231.07	244.12	256.07	272.09	286.20
220.23	231.08	244.13	256.10	272.09	286.20
220.27	231.09	244.14	256.12	272.16	286.21
220.28	231.11	244.16	256.13	272.19	287.03
221.01	231.13	244.17	256.18	272.24	287.13
221.02	231.14	244.18	256.20	273.23	287.15
221.02	231.18	245.03	256.23	274.10	287.15
221.05	231.18	245.08	257.14	274.11	287.21
221.05	231.23	245.09	257.16	274.16	287.26
221.06	231.24	245.13	257.20	274.21	287.27
221.06	231.25	245.14	257.20	274.23	287.28
221.07	231.25	245.14	257.21	274.24	288.02
221.08	231.28	245.21	257.25	275.16	288.02
221.11	232.04	246.08	257.27	275.19	288.03
221.16	232.13	246.08	258.07	275.27	288.04
221.19	232.17	246.09	258.11	275.28	288.10
221.24	232.22	246.11	258.12	276.07	288.16
221.25	232.23	246.13	258.13	276.08	288.17
221.25	233.02	246.16	258.14	276.16	288.18
221.28	233.08	246.19	258.14	276.19	288.21
222.05	233.12	247.01	258.15	276.23	289.04
222.07	233.13	247.08	258.17	276.23	289.09
222.07	233.13	247.12	258.18	277.01	289.25
222.07	233.16	247.16	258.19	277.04	290.05
222.08	233.17	247.18	258.28	277.05	290.06
222.10	233.17	247.22	259.01	277.13	290.08
222.12	233.19	247.23	259.03	277.21	290.08
222.13	234.04	247.23	259.04	278.01	290.13
222.16	234.05			278.05	

290.14	300.20	318.13	331.09	340.10	352.21
290.15	300.20	318.16	331.10	340.11	352.21
290.16	300.21	318.19	331.14	340.12	352.25
290.19	300.21	318.24	331.15	340.19	353.01
290.20	301.13	318.25	331.18	340.22	353.05
290.21	301.21	319.14	331.23	340.26	353.06
290.26	302.02	319.26	331.27	340.28	353.07
290.28	302.22	320.03	331.28	340.28	353.08
291.05	302.24	320.05	332.01	341.02	353.08
291.12	305.04	320.08	332.02	341.03	353.23
291.15	305.06	320.13	332.03	341.04	353.27
291.16	305.06	320.16	332.04	341.05	354.02
291.18	305.08	320.18	332.07	341.06	354.04
291.19	305.09	320.22	332.07	341.06	354.08
291.20	305.10	320.26	332.10	341.07	354.10
291.23	305.12	321.02	332.11	341.08	354.13
291.24	305.13	321.07	332.12	341.12	354.13
292.05	305.15	321.11	332.14	341.14	354.17
292.11	305.17	321.21	332.16	342.02	354.21
292.12	306.03	321.26	332.18	342.05	354.23
293.06	306.05	322.09	332.19	342.05	354.24
293.13	306.09	322.11	332.21	342.06	355.02
293.17	306.10	322.12	332.23	342.07	355.12
293.21	306.11	322.13	332.24	342.09	355.14
294.02	306.13	322.16	332.25	342.10	355.18
294.04	306.13	322.17	332.28	342.13	355.21
294.07	306.16	322.18	333.01	342.17	355.27
294.07	306.17	322.19	333.02	342.19	355.28
294.09	306.18	322.21	333.07	342.21	355.28
294.10	306.27	323.13	333.07	342.22	356.04
294.14	306.28	323.13	333.08	342.25	356.06
294.16	307.04	323.15	333.08	342.26	356.11
294.17	307.18	323.17	333.12	342.26	356.11
294.18	307.21	323.21	333.19	342.27	356.13
294.19	307.22	324.05	333.22	342.28	356.17
294.21	307.22	324.06	333.23	343.07	356.17
294.21	307.23	324.11	333.25	343.11	356.20
294.28	307.24	324.17	333.26	343.13	356.21
295.01	307.24	324.17	334.12	343.19	357.01
295.02	308.04	325.02	334.17	343.20	357.05
295.03	308.07	325.03	334.18	343.26	357.05
295.06	308.16	325.04	334.19	343.26	357.12
295.08	309.01	325.09	334.19	343.28	357.27
295.09	309.05	325.10	334.22	344.01	357.27
295.12	309.08	325.14	334.24	344.01	358.01
295.12	309.12	325.14	334.24	344.02	358.05
295.20	309.17	325.26	334.25	344.04	358.14
295.20	309.19	325.28	334.28	344.05	358.17
295.22	309.26	326.01	335.04	344.17	358.18
295.23	310.02	326.04	335.05	344.18	358.21
295.25	310.06	326.05	335.06	345.07	358.24
295.26	310.08	326.09	335.08	345.13	359.01
296.04	310.14	326.14	335.09	345.13	359.04
296.07	310.19	326.17	335.13	345.14	359.06
296.08	310.22	326.25	335.14	345.14	359.11
296.09	310.27	326.26	335.17	345.17	359.11
296.09	311.01	326.27	335.19	345.18	359.15
296.10	311.08	327.01	335.20	345.18	359.15
296.14	311.12	327.03	335.25	345.21	359.17
296.16	311.15	327.04	336.05	345.27	359.24
296.18	311.17	327.05	336.07	346.19	359.26
296.19	311.19	327.10	336.13	346.24	359.27
296.22	311.22	327.11	336.18	346.25	360.01
296.23	311.28	327.21	336.26	347.01	360.07
296.25	312.01	327.22	336.26	347.04	360.10
296.25	312.04	327.22	336.27	347.05	360.12
296.25	312.10	327.27	336.28	347.13	360.28
297.01	312.18	327.28	337.01	347.22	361.05
297.01	312.19	328.01	337.02	347.26	361.09
297.11	312.25	328.01	337.03	347.27	361.09
297.11	313.04	328.03	337.04	348.01	361.14
297.14	313.11	328.06	337.05	348.01	361.14
297.25	313.12	328.07	337.06	348.02	361.15
297.26	313.21	328.11	337.06	348.03	361.16
297.27	314.04	328.13	337.08	348.03	361.19
298.01	314.05	328.18	337.10	348.08	361.21
298.02	314.07	328.20	337.12	348.09	361.23
298.05	314.07	328.22	337.13	348.11	361.23
298.05	314.11	328.25	337.16	348.19	361.24
298.06	314.13	328.26	337.18	348.22	361.24
298.06	314.16	328.28	337.22	348.22	362.03
298.07	314.17	328.28	337.24	348.23	362.04
298.07	314.18	329.04	337.25	348.24	362.14
298.10	314.23	329.05	337.26	348.26	362.19
298.16	315.02	329.08	337.27	349.11	362.20
298.24	315.05	329.10	337.27	349.12	363.04
298.25	315.06	329.11	337.28	349.13	363.04
298.26	315.12	329.15	338.01	349.19	363.09
299.01	315.18	329.16	338.02	349.22	364.03
299.03	315.25	329.21	338.03	349.23	364.06
299.05	315.27	329.22	338.06	349.26	364.09
299.06	316.01	329.23	338.10	349.27	364.10
299.07	316.05	330.01	338.21	350.08	364.13
299.08	316.06	330.02	338.22	350.09	364.13
299.12	316.10	330.06	339.11	350.10	364.14
299.13	316.11	330.09	339.12	350.15	364.15
299.14	316.12	330.14	339.13	350.15	364.16
299.14	316.26	330.15	339.13	350.15	364.17
299.16	317.05	330.16	339.14	350.16	364.18
299.17	317.08	330.22	339.15	350.25	365.02
299.18	317.14	330.28	339.17	350.25	365.04
299.22	317.15	331.05	339.23	350.26	365.07
299.26	317.17	331.06	340.04	350.27	365.08
299.26	317.18	331.07	340.05	351.03	365.08
300.03	317.18	331.07	340.07	351.12	365.09
300.03	317.22	331.05	340.08	352.05	365.10
300.13	317.24	331.06	340.05	352.05	365.11
300.14	317.25	331.07	340.07	352.09	365.12
300.15	317.25	331.08	340.08	352.17	365.13
300.18	318.01	331.08	340.09	352.19	365.15
300.20	318.02				
	318.04				

365.16	376.21	385.21	399.20	412.27	423.12
365.18	376.22	385.28	399.20	413.01	423.12
365.19	376.22	386.01	399.24	413.02	423.13
365.22	376.22	386.03	399.24	413.03	423.14
365.24	377.04	386.08	399.26	413.05	423.15
365.24	377.04	386.11	399.28	413.09	423.15
365.27	377.05	386.24	400.05	414.04	423.16
366.02	377.08	386.27	400.06	414.05	423.19
366.05	377.15	386.28	400.13	414.06	423.19
366.11	377.15	387.04	400.14	414.07	423.21
366.12	377.16	387.08	400.24	414.08	423.23
366.13	377.17	387.11	400.25	414.10	423.25
366.14	377.18	387.13	400.27	414.13	423.27
366.17	377.22	387.15	401.01	414.15	423.28
366.19	377.27	387.19	401.02	414.19	424.02
366.20	378.03	387.27	401.07	415.02	424.05
366.21	378.09	387.28	401.11	415.03	424.05
366.21	378.14	388.01	401.13	415.04	424.06
366.21	378.14	388.03	401.16	415.05	424.08
366.28	378.16	388.09	401.18	415.06	424.10
367.03	378.21	388.13	401.21	415.07	424.15
367.04	378.24	388.20	401.23	415.08	424.17
367.08	379.02	388.25	401.23	415.10	424.19
367.12	379.03	388.26	401.25	415.14	424.24
367.15	379.04	389.01	401.25	415.20	424.25
367.17	379.06	389.03	401.27	415.21	424.26
367.21	379.08	389.10	402.09	415.25	425.02
367.22	379.09	389.11	402.10	415.28	425.04
367.23	379.09	389.12	402.13	416.06	425.11
367.24	379.11	389.22	402.25	416.09	425.12
367.24	379.13	389.27	403.01	416.11	425.12
367.25	379.14	390.02	403.10	416.16	425.13
367.27	379.17	390.03	403.11	416.16	425.13
368.04	379.18	390.05	404.01	416.16	425.16
368.04	379.21	390.08	404.01	416.18	425.16
368.08	379.22	390.08	404.03	416.19	425.17
368.08	379.22	390.25	404.07	416.22	425.18
368.10	379.23	390.25	404.07	416.25	425.20
368.13	379.24	390.27	404.07	416.26	425.28
368.16	379.24	390.28	404.12	417.07	426.02
368.19	380.02	391.01	404.16	417.12	426.03
368.20	380.03	391.02	404.16	417.14	426.06
368.21	380.05	391.06	404.17	417.14	426.09
368.23	380.06	391.07	404.19	417.15	426.11
368.25	380.06	391.08	404.21	417.19	426.18
368.25	380.07	391.08	404.22	417.28	426.20
368.28	380.07	391.14	404.24	418.01	426.22
369.04	380.08	391.14	404.26	418.02	426.24
369.06	380.10	391.23	405.04	418.02	426.24
369.07	380.11	391.24	405.11	418.05	427.01
369.07	380.13	391.24	405.12	418.07	427.03
369.08	380.16	391.24	405.13	418.08	427.05
369.10	380.17	391.25	405.14	418.12	427.05
369.12	380.19	391.27	405.15	418.12	427.06
369.14	380.23	392.04	405.17	418.15	427.11
369.14	380.25	392.06	405.18	418.21	427.12
369.16	380.27	392.08	405.20	418.23	427.12
369.17	380.28	392.09	405.22	418.25	427.15
369.19	381.04	392.10	405.26	418.26	427.16
369.23	381.04	392.11	405.26	418.27	427.19
369.26	381.05	392.11	405.28	419.02	427.22
369.27	381.11	392.12	406.14	419.08	427.26
369.27	381.14	392.15	406.17	419.12	428.01
370.02	381.15	392.16	406.20	419.14	428.02
370.03	381.16	392.22	406.20	419.14	428.06
370.08	382.07	392.24	406.22	419.15	428.19
370.09	382.09	392.25	406.25	419.15	428.26
370.11	382.09	392.26	406.26	419.23	428.28
370.14	382.09	392.27	406.28	419.23	429.01
370.15	382.13	393.02	407.03	419.24	429.03
370.19	382.22	393.04	407.05	419.26	429.11
370.21	382.26	393.05	407.07	419.27	429.12
370.21	382.26	394.02	407.07	420.01	429.22
370.24	382.26	394.03	407.08	420.09	429.26
370.25	382.28	394.05	407.10	420.10	430.01
370.25	383.03	394.09	407.11	420.12	430.02
371.03	383.06	394.10	407.13	420.13	430.04
371.06	383.10	394.11	407.20	420.13	430.05
371.07	383.12	394.12	407.23	420.17	430.06
371.09	383.14	394.12	408.08	420.21	430.14
371.10	383.15	394.16	408.10	420.27	430.21
371.11	383.17	394.18	408.11	421.02	431.03
371.12	383.19	394.20	408.25	421.04	431.06
371.13	383.24	395.18	408.25	421.05	431.09
371.14	384.02	396.02	408.27	421.06	431.16
371.15	384.02	396.06	409.10	421.08	431.17
371.19	384.03	396.07	409.12	421.10	431.17
371.22	384.06	396.13	409.15	421.13	431.18
371.26	384.06	396.15	409.20	421.15	431.22
371.27	384.07	396.15	409.22	421.16	432.02
372.08	384.10	396.15	409.23	421.17	432.06
372.27	384.12	397.06	409.24	421.19	432.07
372.27	384.13	397.21	409.26	421.20	432.12
373.02	384.13	397.28	409.26	421.21	432.12
373.03	384.14	398.01	410.10	422.06	432.13
373.14	384.14	398.01	410.10	422.08	432.13
373.16	384.19	398.01	410.23	422.11	432.14
373.20	384.19	398.02	410.26	422.13	432.16
373.24	384.22	398.02	410.26	422.14	432.18
374.09	384.28	398.08	410.28	422.17	432.18
374.09	385.01	398.09	411.01	422.21	432.19
374.11	385.02	398.09	411.06	422.22	432.20
374.13	385.04	398.15	411.12	422.22	432.20
374.16	385.05	398.16	411.15	422.23	432.21
374.23	385.08	398.20	411.17	422.25	432.23
374.24	385.10	398.25	412.01	423.01	432.24
374.25	385.11	398.27	412.19	423.02	432.26
374.25	385.15	399.03	412.22	423.08	432.27
375.03	385.15	399.06		423.09	433.01
376.13	385.18	399.10		423.10	
376.13	385.19	399.13		423.11	
	385.19	399.14			

433.02	447.24	461.28	477.14	491.15	505.15
433.03	447.27	462.04	477.19	491.21	505.21
433.04	448.03	462.05	477.20	491.25	505.24
433.06	448.05	462.08	477.24	492.01	505.25
433.07	448.06	462.11	477.25	492.02	505.26
433.07	448.14	462.17	477.26	492.04	506.03
433.10	448.17	462.18	477.28	492.08	506.04
433.11	448.19	462.19	478.01	492.11	506.16
433.13	449.04	462.20	478.02	492.12	506.20
433.16	449.05	462.21	478.04	492.13	506.27
433.20	449.06	463.03	478.06	492.15	507.04
433.21	449.08	463.19	478.09	492.19	507.04
434.01	449.09	463.27	478.14	492.20	507.08
434.01	449.09	464.07	478.21	492.20	507.11
434.02	449.09	464.12	478.21	492.22	507.11
434.05	449.12	464.16	478.22	492.24	507.14
434.07	449.13	464.20	478.28	493.01	507.26
434.07	449.13	464.21	478.28	493.15	507.27
434.09	449.15	464.22	479.02	493.25	508.14
434.11	449.16	464.23	479.04	493.27	508.24
434.17	449.19	464.23	479.10	494.01	508.24
434.20	449.22	464.24	479.11	494.02	509.03
434.20	449.26	464.28	479.12	494.02	509.03
434.21	450.02	465.03	479.14	494.04	509.04
434.21	450.03	465.04	479.16	494.05	509.04
434.23	450.07	465.04	479.17	494.06	509.05
434.28	450.10	465.07	479.18	494.13	509.14
435.07	450.12	465.08	479.20	494.17	509.16
435.07	451.03	465.09	479.20	494.25	509.16
435.08	451.14	465.16	479.21	495.07	509.18
435.09	451.16	465.18	479.21	495.09	509.19
435.12	451.20	465.21	479.22	495.15	509.20
435.13	452.18	466.03	479.24	495.18	509.28
435.17	452.26	466.10	479.25	495.26	510.04
435.24	453.01	466.16	479.25	495.28	510.05
435.26	453.02	466.24	479.26	496.03	510.07
435.26	453.22	466.25	479.28	496.04	510.07
436.05	454.01	467.08	480.03	496.11	510.08
436.09	454.05	467.11	480.05	496.21	510.10
436.25	454.08	467.13	480.12	497.03	510.10
437.02	454.15	467.16	480.21	497.05	510.27
437.04	454.21	467.27	480.23	497.10	511.09
438.08	454.28	468.01	480.24	497.15	511.18
438.08	455.05	468.08	481.06	497.18	512.08
438.12	455.17	468.12	481.16	497.23	512.09
438.17	455.22	468.14	481.16	498.15	512.10
438.16	455.24	468.22	481.17	498.16	512.15
438.18	456.06	468.23	481.20	498.20	512.23
438.19	456.08	468.28	481.22	498.26	513.11
438.20	456.09	469.09	482.01	498.28	513.14
438.21	456.14	469.09	482.02	499.06	514.24
439.10	456.23	469.20	482.07	499.07	514.25
439.11	456.24	469.20	482.11	499.10	514.26
439.12	456.27	469.22	482.12	499.14	514.27
439.17	456.29	470.04	483.01	499.15	514.28
439.19	457.01	470.12	483.02	499.23	514.28
439.20	457.02	470.16	483.03	500.01	516.05
439.28	457.02	470.20	483.04	500.05	516.15
440.17	457.04	470.27	483.04	500.07	516.22
440.17	457.04	471.02	483.05	501.06	517.03
440.19	457.06	471.04	483.09	501.08	517.03
440.20	457.06	471.14	483.16	501.08	518.05
440.23	457.08	471.23	483.22	501.09	518.08
440.25	457.08	471.25	484.06	501.10	518.09
441.09	457.17	471.26	484.16	501.11	518.10
441.09	457.24	471.26	484.26	501.13	518.20
441.10	457.25	471.27	485.02	501.13	518.23
441.10	458.02	471.28	485.03	501.17	518.23
441.13	458.11	472.01	485.09	501.17	518.26
441.15	458.19	472.02	485.12	501.19	518.28
441.16	458.22	472.04	485.19	501.20	519.02
441.18	459.02	472.04	485.27	501.20	519.10
441.20	459.07	472.06	486.05	502.03	519.11
441.21	459.08	472.06	486.13	502.04	519.11
442.03	459.10	472.11	487.05	502.05	519.13
442.04	459.14	472.16	487.10	502.08	519.14
442.10	459.15	472.20	488.02	502.11	519.17
442.12	459.17	473.01	488.20	502.12	519.18
442.12	459.21	473.04	489.02	502.13	519.18
442.16	459.22	473.05	489.06	502.15	519.24
442.26	459.26	473.06	489.06	502.17	519.28
443.01	459.26	473.07	489.07	502.18	520.03
443.02	459.28	473.08	489.09	502.21	520.04
443.04	460.02	473.08	489.10	502.21	520.05
443.05	460.04	473.14	489.11	502.22	520.06
444.03	460.05	473.16	489.12	502.23	520.09
444.05	460.06	473.19	489.15	502.26	520.12
444.10	460.09	473.19	489.25	502.27	520.13
444.11	460.10	474.08	490.03	503.03	520.14
444.13	460.11	474.10	490.04	503.04	520.14
444.20	460.12	474.11	490.05	503.04	520.15
445.03	460.13	474.13	490.09	503.05	521.04
445.04	460.14	474.15	490.19	503.05	521.08
445.07	460.15	474.18	490.19	503.18	521.11
445.14	460.16	474.18	490.23	503.19	521.12
445.16	460.17	474.27	490.23	503.20	522.02
445.18	460.23	474.27	490.27	503.26	522.03
445.19	460.26	475.19	490.27	503.27	522.03
445.22	460.26	475.20	490.28	504.01	522.04
445.23	461.03	475.20	490.28	504.03	522.04
445.26	461.04	475.24	491.01	504.10	522.09
445.26	461.04	475.27	491.01	504.11	522.10
445.26	461.08	475.28	491.02	504.12	522.12
446.02	461.12	476.10	491.02	504.13	522.16
446.04	461.13	476.20	491.04	504.16	522.18
446.21	461.14	477.03	491.04	504.27	522.22
446.21	461.14	477.10	491.05	505.01	522.26
446.27	461.16		491.07	505.04	523.01
447.13	461.19		491.08	505.10	
447.14	461.22		491.15		
447.18	461.26		491.15		

523.06	543.05	560.10	572.25	586.15	598.11
523.13	543.05	560.11	573.17	586.15	598.12
523.14	543.06	560.12	574.01	586.17	598.12
523.16	543.10	560.12	574.11	586.17	598.13
523.24	543.11	560.13	574.13	586.18	598.18
523.24	543.23	560.14	574.19	586.18	598.19
524.11	543.24	560.14	574.19	586.20	598.22
524.17	543.28	560.16	574.23	586.22	598.23
524.27	544.03	560.18	574.24	586.23	598.25
524.28	544.05	560.25	575.02	586.25	599.01
525.03	544.06	561.04	575.06	587.01	599.01
525.11	544.15	561.07	575.10	587.02	599.03
525.16	544.17	561.11	575.11	587.08	599.07
525.18	544.18	561.12	575.13	587.19	599.07
525.22	544.19	561.16	575.15	587.20	599.08
526.07	544.21	561.17	575.15	587.23	599.11
526.10	544.23	561.21	575.16	587.25	599.12
526.10	544.24	561.22	575.17	588.03	599.13
526.14	545.03	561.22	575.19	588.07	599.14
526.17	545.04	561.23	575.21	588.07	599.16
526.23	545.19	561.24	575.22	588.09	600.01
527.20	545.23	561.25	575.22	588.11	600.02
528.02	545.23	561.25	575.24	588.13	600.03
528.06	545.25	562.01	576.01	588.14	600.04
528.07	545.27	562.02	576.01	588.14	600.12
528.07	546.04	562.03	576.05	588.16	600.16
528.18	546.06	562.06	576.05	588.17	600.24
528.19	546.07	562.08	576.10	588.18	601.01
528.22	546.10	562.09	576.10	588.19	601.03
528.23	546.19	562.13	576.11	588.21	601.08
528.28	546.25	562.13	576.15	588.25	601.15
529.13	547.10	562.14	576.15	588.25	601.17
529.22	547.16	562.14	576.16	589.01	601.18
529.27	547.16	562.17	576.17	589.02	601.21
529.28	548.02	562.18	577.05	589.02	601.23
530.04	548.11	562.21	577.06	589.03	602.02
531.03	548.13	562.21	577.07	589.05	602.02
531.05	548.22	562.22	577.08	589.07	602.05
531.06	549.10	562.22	577.08	589.07	602.06
531.17	549.11	562.23	577.20	589.08	602.08
532.07	549.14	562.23	577.21	589.09	602.09
532.10	549.16	562.24	577.21	589.10	602.14
532.11	549.21	562.25	577.22	589.12	602.15
532.16	549.24	563.06	578.02	589.12	602.23
532.17	549.25	563.08	578.03	589.14	602.25
532.19	549.25	563.09	578.03	589.16	603.05
533.05	550.02	563.14	578.04	589.18	603.06
533.05	550.08	563.21	578.06	589.18	603.09
533.14	550.11	563.22	578.07	589.18	603.11
533.17	550.17	564.03	578.07	589.19	603.12
533.20	550.18	564.07	578.08	589.20	603.15
533.20	550.20	564.08	578.11	589.24	603.17
533.24	550.20	564.12	578.11	589.25	604.03
534.05	550.24	564.21	578.14	590.08	604.05
534.12	550.27	565.01	578.17	590.09	604.06
534.12	551.05	565.07	578.19	590.11	604.10
534.14	551.07	565.21	578.19	590.17	604.12
534.19	553.10	565.25	578.20	590.18	604.13
534.23	553.21	566.01	578.20	590.20	604.16
534.24	554.03	566.03	579.01	590.20	604.16
534.25	554.07	566.04	579.01	590.21	604.18
535.01	554.07	566.09	579.04	590.21	605.01
535.02	554.14	566.13	579.10	591.07	605.02
535.05	554.14	566.14	579.15	591.08	605.02
535.06	554.17	566.23	579.15	591.20	605.03
535.08	554.19	567.08	579.23	591.20	605.03
535.09	554.20	567.08	580.07	591.23	605.08
535.26	554.21	567.09	580.11	591.25	605.11
536.06	554.22	567.13	580.12	592.01	605.12
536.13	555.02	568.06	580.14	592.03	605.13
537.02	555.04	568.10	580.15	592.18	605.17
537.03	555.05	568.15	580.15	592.23	605.24
537.20	555.08	566.16	580.21	593.07	605.25
537.26	555.11	568.22	581.14	593.10	606.04
537.26	555.12	563.23	581.14	593.15	606.05
538.04	555.12	566.24	581.15	593.16	606.09
538.14	555.13	569.12	581.17	593.16	606.10
538.18	556.02	569.16	581.17	593.21	606.25
538.19	556.05	569.17	581.22	593.24	607.15
538.20	557.02	569.22	582.01	594.01	607.17
539.02	557.02	569.23	582.06	594.04	608.07
539.03	557.04	570.04	582.11	594.05	608.07
539.05	557.04	570.04	582.14	594.07	608.12
539.08	557.08	570.07	582.16	594.10	608.14
539.10	557.13	570.10	582.16	594.11	609.02
539.10	557.14	570.13	582.23	594.12	609.03
539.11	557.15	570.13	582.24	594.13	609.04
539.26	558.04	570.14	583.01	594.22	609.04
540.14	558.10	570.14	583.04	594.23	609.06
540.15	558.10	570.14	583.04	595.06	609.10
540.15	558.11	570.18	583.05	595.09	610.01
540.21	558.12	570.18	583.06	595.14	610.03
540.21	558.12	570.21	583.11	595.18	610.05
540.25	558.16	570.21	583.18	596.05	610.13
540.27	558.18	571.03	583.20	596.05	610.13
541.11	558.20	571.05	583.22	596.07	610.15
541.17	558.21	571.18	584.04	596.07	610.16
541.21	558.22	571.21	584.06	596.08	610.25
541.21	558.22	571.22	585.06	596.13	610.28
541.22	559.01	571.24	585.11	596.15	611.03
541.23	559.06	571.24	585.13	596.16	611.11
541.27	559.07	571.25	585.15	596.20	611.16
541.28	559.16	572.04	585.17	596.22	612.01
542.01	559.16	572.05	585.17	596.24	612.04
542.08	559.19	572.08	586.03	597.12	612.08
542.08	559.20	572.10	586.05	597.14	612.09
542.18	559.21	572.15	586.05	597.22	612.17
542.19	559.22	572.16	586.08	598.01	612.27
542.21	559.25	572.19	586.10	598.04	613.03
542.26	560.03	572.21	586.12	598.10	
543.01	560.04		586.14	598.11	
	560.09				

613.07	629.13	642.11	656.25	667.13	677.05
613.13	629.15	642.12	656.27	667.14	677.05
613.14	629.18	642.14	657.02	667.15	677.09
613.14	629.20	642.17	657.07	667.15	677.09
613.18	629.21	643.02	657.08	667.18	677.09
613.23	629.23	643.02	657.15	668.04	677.15
613.28	629.23	643.04	658.03	668.09	677.19
614.11	629.26	643.13	658.04	668.17	677.21
614.13	629.26	643.13	658.06	668.21	677.22
614.15	629.28	643.15	658.06	668.23	677.23
614.24	630.01	643.27	658.08	668.25	677.24
615.16	630.03	643.27	658.09	668.26	677.25
615.18	630.04	643.28	658.16	668.27	677.25
615.19	630.05	644.01	658.17	669.01	677.26
615.19	630.06	644.02	658.18	669.05	677.27
615.26	630.10	644.05	658.18	669.10	678.01
615.26	630.11	645.23	659.03	669.10	678.03
616.01	630.13	645.24	659.07	669.12	678.04
616.05	630.14	646.11	659.07	669.14	678.13
616.06	630.14	646.16	659.11	669.20	678.15
616.06	630.15	647.14	659.18	669.23	678.16
616.07	630.17	647.24	659.21	669.26	678.16
616.12	630.17	647.27	659.22	670.02	678.17
616.17	630.23	648.01	659.27	670.02	678.24
616.17	630.24	648.02	659.27	670.04	679.03
616.21	630.26	648.02	660.04	670.05	679.17
616.22	630.28	648.03	660.05	670.05	680.03
617.10	631.01	648.03	660.08	670.07	680.03
616.27	631.01	648.04	660.11	670.07	680.03
619.02	631.02	648.05	660.22	670.14	680.04
619.04	631.04	648.08	660.23	670.20	680.10
619.06	631.06	648.23	660.23	670.21	680.11
619.11	631.07	648.24	660.24	670.21	680.18
619.22	631.10	648.27	660.25	671.03	680.21
619.22	631.11	648.28	660.25	671.05	680.25
619.26	631.12	649.02	661.06	671.07	681.04
619.28	631.12	649.02	661.09	671.08	681.07
620.01	631.14	649.04	661.11	671.09	681.08
620.02	631.18	649.12	661.15	671.11	681.11
620.03	631.19	649.15	661.15	671.11	681.15
620.14	631.19	649.19	661.18	671.23	681.19
620.14	631.20	649.20	661.21	671.25	681.19
621.04	631.25	649.21	661.21	671.25	681.21
621.12	632.14	649.22	662.05	672.01	681.27
621.15	632.15	649.22	662.08	672.01	682.01
621.16	632.17	650.01	662.09	672.05	682.03
621.17	632.20	650.05	662.14	672.14	682.07
621.24	632.21	650.06	662.17	672.14	682.07
622.08	632.24	650.09	662.20	672.16	682.16
622.09	632.27	650.26	662.21	672.22	683.02
622.14	633.10	651.01	662.22	672.22	683.04
622.15	633.11	651.04	662.24	673.01	683.05
622.15	633.13	651.14	662.25	673.08	683.14
623.06	633.17	651.15	662.28	673.10	683.15
623.10	633.21	651.16	663.01	673.10	683.16
623.13	633.24	651.17	663.02	673.13	683.18
623.18	633.26	651.18	663.02	673.15	683.21
623.18	633.27	651.24	663.03	673.16	683.26
623.23	633.27	651.25	663.04	673.24	683.26
623.25	633.28	651.26	663.09	673.27	683.27
623.25	634.01	651.27	663.10	673.29	684.12
624.01	634.07	652.01	663.10	674.01	684.14
624.08	634.09	652.02	663.16	674.04	684.16
624.09	634.16	652.02	663.16	674.05	684.17
624.19	634.17	652.04	663.21	674.06	684.26
624.24	634.20	652.04	663.24	674.06	685.04
624.26	635.03	652.05	663.25	674.08	685.06
625.05	635.11	652.07	663.25	674.08	685.08
625.10	635.25	652.10	663.26	674.19	685.09
625.10	636.02	652.12	663.28	674.21	685.10
625.10	636.09	652.15	664.04	674.21	685.12
625.11	636.13	652.19	664.06	674.22	685.13
625.18	636.13	652.22	664.09	674.23	685.27
625.26	636.16	652.27	664.09	674.24	685.28
626.01	636.16	653.01	664.10	674.25	686.04
626.05	636.16	653.02	664.12	674.25	686.10
626.07	636.25	653.06	664.15	675.01	686.12
626.09	636.26	653.11	664.15	675.02	686.12
626.10	637.16	653.19	664.16	675.04	686.13
626.12	637.23	654.03	664.16	675.06	686.26
626.19	637.26	654.07	664.17	675.10	687.01
626.26	637.26	654.11	664.18	675.11	687.02
626.27	637.28	654.11	664.19	675.12	687.11
627.04	638.01	654.11	664.22	675.15	687.14
627.14	638.02	654.13	664.23	675.16	687.14
627.15	638.05	654.13	664.24	675.18	687.28
627.17	638.06	654.17	664.25	675.19	688.02
627.20	638.11	654.18	664.28	675.26	688.02
627.21	638.15	654.18	665.04	675.26	688.03
627.21	638.16	654.23	665.13	675.28	688.05
627.23	638.20	654.24	665.17	676.01	688.07
627.25	638.27	655.02	665.18	676.02	689.02
627.27	639.01	655.02	665.19	676.03	689.10
628.01	639.04	655.02	665.22	676.04	689.11
628.02	639.08	655.05	665.28	676.05	689.13
628.08	639.13	655.06	666.03	676.06	689.15
628.09	639.19	655.06	666.05	676.08	689.17
628.13	639.22	655.11	666.09	676.08	690.02
628.17	639.24	655.14	666.12	676.09	690.07
628.18	639.26	655.15	666.13	676.12	690.07
628.19	640.05	655.16	666.15	676.16	690.14
628.19	640.07	655.16	666.19	676.18	690.21
628.24	640.08	655.17	666.20	676.19	690.25
628.26	640.14	655.17	666.27	676.25	691.02
628.26	640.15	655.21	666.28	676.26	691.07
628.26	640.16	655.25	666.28	676.28	691.12
629.01	640.17	656.08	666.28	677.04	691.15
629.01	641.01	656.16	667.02		691.25
629.06	641.09	656.19	667.06		691.28
629.08	641.24	656.20	667.10		691.28
629.10	642.08	656.21	667.10		692.03

692.04	705.27	719.21	730.26	740.13	753.20
692.05	706.06	719.22	730.27	740.14	753.21
692.11	706.11	719.22	731.04	740.24	754.08
692.11	706.11	719.23	731.06	741.04	754.11
692.13	706.15	719.26	731.07	741.04	754.27
692.14	706.18	719.27	731.12	741.07	755.04
692.16	706.19	719.27	731.13	741.17	755.05
692.16	706.22	720.01	731.14	741.18	755.06
692.16	706.23	720.03	731.20	741.21	755.10
692.17	706.25	720.11	731.28	742.05	755.10
692.17	707.01	720.12	732.01	742.08	755.11
692.20	707.06	720.13	732.03	742.15	755.11
692.21	707.13	720.15	732.05	742.18	755.13
692.27	707.16	720.16	732.08	742.20	755.13
692.27	707.20	720.16	732.10	743.02	755.17
693.01	707.22	720.17	732.11	743.02	755.19
693.01	708.02	720.17	732.11	743.10	755.23
693.03	708.04	720.18	732.12	744.04	756.02
693.04	708.09	720.18	732.13	744.08	756.05
693.05	708.25	720.19	732.13	744.12	756.12
693.07	709.01	720.19	732.14	744.13	756.15
693.10	709.03	720.20	732.15	744.18	756.15
693.16	709.07	720.20	732.18	744.26	756.23
693.17	709.14	720.21	732.20	744.27	756.24
693.19	709.16	720.26	732.22	745.03	756.25
693.20	709.17	721.01	732.24	745.05	756.27
693.25	709.18	721.04	732.27	745.08	756.28
694.07	710.04	721.04	732.27	745.14	757.14
694.09	711.02	721.10	732.28	745.14	757.15
694.20	711.02	721.13	733.01	745.14	757.16
695.06	711.03	721.14	733.01	745.18	757.23
695.06	711.10	721.15	733.03	745.21	757.25
695.10	711.13	721.17	733.04	745.26	757.27
695.19	711.16	721.18	733.05	745.27	758.01
695.19	711.19	721.21	733.08	745.27	758.09
695.20	712.01	721.22	733.17	745.28	758.11
695.21	712.03	721.25	733.21	746.01	758.13
695.26	712.04	721.25	734.03	746.02	758.13
695.26	712.04	721.26	734.06	746.03	758.14
696.07	712.07	721.27	734.07	746.05	758.18
696.09	712.12	721.28	734.07	746.06	758.20
696.14	712.13	721.28	734.09	746.07	758.21
696.21	712.14	721.28	734.14	746.11	758.21
697.08	712.14	722.01	734.16	746.14	758.26
697.21	712.15	722.02	734.24	746.15	758.27
697.21	712.16	722.04	734.25	746.15	759.01
697.21	712.21	722.07	734.27	746.16	759.03
697.23	712.22	722.09	735.05	746.19	759.22
697.24	712.22	722.11	735.05	746.19	759.23
697.28	712.22	722.15	735.07	746.19	759.24
698.08	712.23	722.19	735.08	746.23	759.26
698.11	712.23	722.23	735.12	747.12	759.27
698.13	712.24	722.27	735.13	747.19	759.28
698.16	712.25	723.07	735.13	747.22	760.12
698.19	712.26	723.10	735.14	747.23	760.16
699.08	713.02	723.12	735.15	747.24	760.19
699.12	713.04	723.21	735.16	747.25	760.22
699.13	713.05	723.24	735.28	747.25	760.23
699.15	713.06	724.05	736.02	747.25	761.01
699.16	713.15	724.17	736.05	747.25	761.02
699.23	713.15	724.23	736.09	747.28	761.13
700.09	713.19	724.24	736.12	747.28	761.14
700.11	713.22	724.27	736.16	748.02	761.15
700.15	713.25	725.01	736.19	748.12	761.16
700.19	713.25	725.13	736.21	748.14	761.26
700.21	714.02	725.17	736.21	748.20	762.03
700.22	714.07	725.24	736.21	749.09	762.14
700.27	714.10	725.24	736.22	749.10	762.16
701.01	714.13	725.25	736.23	749.16	762.21
701.03	714.13	725.26	736.23	749.16	762.22
701.05	714.21	725.26	736.24	749.22	762.23
701.06	714.26	725.26	737.02	749.25	762.24
701.07	715.09	725.27	737.03	750.01	762.25
701.08	715.11	726.02	737.06	750.04	762.26
701.11	715.16	726.03	737.08	750.14	762.28
701.14	715.21	726.12	737.08	750.16	762.28
701.17	715.22	726.20	737.08	750.17	763.01
701.18	715.24	726.21	737.09	750.20	763.01
701.19	715.25	726.24	737.10	750.21	763.07
701.23	715.26	727.02	737.11	750.26	763.08
701.27	715.26	727.07	737.21	751.04	763.10
701.28	715.27	727.15	737.24	751.05	763.10
702.08	716.06	727.18	737.25	751.07	763.13
702.15	716.09	727.18	737.28	751.08	763.13
702.17	716.11	727.20	738.02	751.10	763.15
702.17	716.11	727.23	738.03	751.12	763.19
702.23	716.13	727.23	738.04	751.14	763.24
702.26	716.14	727.27	738.05	751.17	763.26
703.03	716.14	727.28	738.06	751.18	763.27
703.04	716.14	728.02	738.07	751.20	763.27
703.06	716.25	728.03	738.08	751.22	763.28
703.07	717.10	728.05	738.08	751.24	764.01
703.14	717.18	728.06	738.10	752.01	764.05
703.20	717.19	729.07	738.20	752.03	764.06
703.23	717.20	729.08	738.20	752.05	764.08
703.27	717.24	729.10	738.22	752.07	764.09
704.10	717.25	729.14	738.23	752.08	765.03
704.12	718.01	729.15	738.25	752.09	765.04
704.22	718.03	729.16	738.26	752.10	765.05
704.22	718.03	729.17	738.28	752.11	765.07
704.23	718.18	729.17	739.02	752.12	765.09
704.25	718.22	729.19	739.04	752.12	765.10
704.26	718.28	730.01	739.23	752.12	765.10
705.04	719.02	730.08	739.23	752.13	765.15
705.07	719.08	730.09	739.25	752.22	765.15
705.07	719.15	730.11	740.04	752.24	765.16
705.07	719.15	730.14	740.05	752.25	765.19
705.17	719.17	730.19	740.06	752.26	
705.18	719.18	730.25	740.06	753.10	
705.19	719.19	730.26	740.12	753.13	
705.22	719.20			753.14	

765.19	781.13	796.12	809.07	820.01	838.24
766.02	781.14	796.12	809.12	820.02	839.07
766.02	781.16	796.18	809.17	820.02	839.09
766.02	781.20	796.23	809.18	820.12	839.10
766.03	781.23	796.28	809.21	820.17	839.12
766.06	782.12	797.02	810.02	820.18	839.13
766.12	782.13	797.03	810.12	820.19	839.18
766.13	782.16	797.07	810.14	820.21	839.21
766.14	782.22	797.10	810.16	820.21	841.04
766.15	782.22	797.14	810.18	820.27	841.05
766.17	782.27	797.14	810.20	821.19	841.08
766.19	783.09	797.16	810.24	822.01	841.23
766.20	783.20	797.22	810.25	822.01	841.27
766.20	783.25	797.23	810.26	822.02	842.05
766.27	784.06	797.27	811.05	822.04	842.14
767.02	784.07	797.27	811.08	822.06	842.18
767.10	784.10	798.02	811.20	822.11	842.24
767.11	784.13	798.03	811.20	822.15	843.03
768.04	784.27	798.03	811.21	822.23	843.05
768.06	785.04	798.04	811.27	822.24	843.08
768.13	785.04	798.10	811.27	822.25	843.12
768.13	785.06	798.11	812.01	822.25	843.13
768.24	785.16	798.13	812.05	822.27	843.17
769.03	785.23	798.15	812.07	823.01	843.17
769.06	785.24	798.15	812.07	823.01	843.18
769.07	785.25	798.16	812.08	823.05	843.21
769.08	785.28	798.17	812.09	823.12	843.22
769.13	786.05	798.22	812.09	823.13	843.24
769.22	786.07	798.25	812.10	823.19	843.24
769.22	786.15	798.27	812.12	823.22	843.27
769.26	786.20	798.28	812.12	823.24	844.02
770.02	786.23	799.03	812.13	823.26	844.02
770.03	786.25	799.11	812.16	824.03	844.03
770.04	787.02	799.11	812.17	824.15	844.04
770.06	787.19	799.12	812.20	824.20	844.04
770.09	787.25	799.13	812.21	824.22	844.05
770.12	787.27	799.13	812.23	824.25	844.06
770.14	788.03	799.14	812.25	825.14	844.07
770.15	788.04	799.15	812.25	825.14	844.07
770.16	788.04	799.16	812.26	825.15	844.07
770.19	788.08	799.16	812.26	825.16	844.12
770.20	788.09	799.18	812.27	826.01	844.13
770.23	788.11	799.24	813.02	826.03	844.14
770.25	789.02	799.28	813.02	826.12	844.19
770.25	789.03	800.01	813.03	826.18	844.19
771.01	789.04	800.03	813.04	826.25	844.20
771.02	789.06	800.04	813.05	827.09	844.22
771.05	789.06	800.12	813.07	827.13	844.26
771.07	789.08	800.12	813.07	827.17	844.27
771.15	789.09	800.15	813.10	827.17	844.28
771.15	789.18	800.15	813.12	828.01	845.01
771.20	790.01	800.16	813.19	828.05	845.02
771.21	790.01	800.16	813.24	828.06	845.02
771.23	790.05	800.24	813.25	828.11	845.03
771.27	790.05	800.25	813.28	828.23	845.05
772.02	790.07	800.26	814.01	829.03	845.05
772.03	790.07	801.03	814.02	829.05	845.05
772.07	790.07	801.05	814.04	829.15	845.07
772.09	790.10	801.08	814.04	829.17	845.07
772.16	790.15	801.15	814.06	829.20	845.10
772.16	790.20	801.17	814.07	829.21	845.11
772.18	790.25	801.21	814.12	829.25	845.12
772.18	791.14	801.25	814.16	829.26	845.13
772.18	791.14	801.26	814.17	830.07	845.13
772.19	791.15	801.27	814.18	830.09	845.14
772.27	791.20	802.04	814.23	830.10	845.14
773.06	791.23	802.05	814.28	831.02	845.15
773.09	791.23	802.09	815.03	831.09	845.16
773.18	792.02	802.18	815.03	831.10	845.20
773.23	792.09	802.18	815.07	831.15	845.23
774.01	792.17	802.18	815.10	831.17	845.24
774.01	792.18	802.20	815.23	832.02	845.25
774.03	792.21	802.24	816.01	832.07	846.07
774.04	792.21	802.25	816.03	832.09	846.12
774.07	792.22	802.27	816.05	832.12	846.13
774.11	792.25	802.27	816.07	832.22	846.17
774.11	792.26	803.04	816.11	832.25	846.22
775.05	792.27	803.10	816.12	833.02	847.01
775.06	793.03	803.10	816.13	833.09	847.03
775.06	793.12	803.18	816.13	833.11	847.03
775.15	793.12	803.23	816.14	833.12	847.11
775.17	793.17	803.27	816.16	833.18	847.11
775.24	793.19	804.05	816.19	833.18	847.12
775.25	793.28	804.09	816.22	833.21	847.15
775.28	794.04	804.13	817.05	833.22	847.17
777.01	794.09	804.14	817.12	833.22	847.22
777.14	794.12	804.26	817.17	834.11	847.24
777.17	794.13	805.06	817.19	834.17	847.25
777.24	794.14	805.06	817.20	834.21	848.01
777.25	794.15	805.10	817.22	835.01	848.02
777.26	794.20	805.11	817.23	835.02	848.13
778.02	794.21	805.21	817.24	835.02	848.15
778.09	794.24	805.22	817.25	835.03	848.20
778.26	794.25	805.25	817.28	835.03	848.22
778.26	795.03	806.01	818.01	835.07	848.22
778.27	795.05	806.01	818.03	835.20	848.24
779.02	795.09	806.03	818.04	835.23	848.26
779.14	795.10	806.09	818.14	835.24	848.26
779.20	795.10	807.25	818.22	836.03	849.02
779.24	795.13	808.01	818.27	836.04	849.08
779.26	795.14	808.01	819.03	836.06	849.16
779.27	795.15	808.09	819.03	836.24	849.16
780.01	795.18	808.12	819.13	837.01	849.16
780.01	795.19	808.12	819.13	837.20	849.17
780.06	795.20	808.15	819.14	837.22	849.18
780.10	795.20	808.20	819.16	837.23	849.20
780.14	795.26	808.28	819.16	837.24	849.25
780.17	796.01	809.06	819.21	837.27	849.26
780.18	796.02		819.22	838.02	849.26
781.05	796.04		819.25	838.03	850.01
781.12	796.07				850.01
	796.09				

```
850.02    859.12    870.25    887.10    906.19    126.06
850.03    859.13    870.28    887.14    906.20    126.07
850.06    859.21    870.28    887.16    907.02    126.19
850.06    859.22    871.01    887.16    907.03    126.21
850.08    859.23    871.02    887.17    907.10    131.20
850.22    859.26    871.02    887.19    907.11    131.23
850.24    859.28    871.04    887.20    907.19    144.10
851.02    860.01    871.04    888.08    907.19    146.09
851.05    860.04    871.04    888.12    907.22    148.08
851.09    860.04    871.06    888.13    907.26    164.21
851.13    860.06    871.07    888.14    907.26    167.12
851.13    860.08    871.07    888.16    908.21    167.13
851.17    860.09    871.12    888.28    909.05    170.21
851.17    860.10    871.13    889.06    909.05    172.27
852.03    860.11    871.14    889.07    909.13    200.08
852.07    860.13    871.26    889.07    909.14    207.02
852.08    860.14    872.07    889.10    909.19    207.06
852.08    860.16    872.16    889.22    909.21    207.08
852.10    860.23    872.17    890.04    909.22    208.15
852.11    860.25    872.21    890.27    909.23    208.16
852.12    860.26    872.21    891.01    910.08    208.27
852.12    860.27    872.24    891.02    910.08    214.11
852.12    860.28    872.24    891.03    910.16    216.11
852.13    861.05    872.27    891.06    910.19    216.16
852.14    861.07    872.28    891.09    910.21    216.17
852.20    861.08    873.01    891.15    910.23    216.17
852.21    861.10    873.07    892.01    910.24    216.20
852.25    861.12    873.11    892.12    910.24    216.28
852.27    861.13    873.11    892.19    910.26    220.21
853.02    861.21    873.18    892.23    911.03    240.19
853.02    861.22    873.22    892.24    911.08    242.12
853.03    861.23    873.23    892.24    911.11    243.28
853.04    861.23    673.26    893.22    911.15    249.01
853.04    361.27    873.27    893.22    911.21    250.21
853.10    862.04    874.02    893.27    911.24    250.22
853.12    862.05    874.17    894.04    911.24    255.01
854.09    862.11    874.18    894.27    911.26    256.25
854.10    862.18    874.19    895.19    911.26    259.07
854.14    862.21    874.19    895.27    911.27    266.16
854.14    862.22    874.20    896.08    912.02    266.17
854.15    862.23    874.21    896.09    912.02    269.27
854.15    862.25    874.24    896.11    912.03    272.16
854.17    862.27    874.25    897.15    912.04    282.16
854.19    863.06    874.26    898.15    912.05    286.12
854.23    863.12    874.27    898.21    912.06    286.27
854.24    863.14    875.01    898.24    912.06    287.07
854.25    863.26    875.05    898.25    912.09    291.15
854.28    863.27    875.06    898.25    912.09    292.28
854.28    863.28    875.08    899.02    912.11    301.24
855.01    864.01    875.10    899.04    912.16    308.03
855.02    364.05    875.11    899.10    912.17    317.01
855.04    364.06    875.13    899.12    theatre   321.15
855.06    364.08    875.14    899.15    348.12    327.05
855.07    864.08    875.16    899.15    thee      327.06
855.10    364.11    875.18    899.16    519.03    327.23
855.11    864.12    875.27    899.19    901.09    331.15
855.13    864.14    876.08    899.22    901.10    334.12
855.13    364.15    876.11    899.23    their     334.25
855.15    864.19    876.16    899.27    002.02    335.07
855.15    864.24    876.28    900.04    008.02    335.09
855.16    364.25    877.12    900.06    013.06    335.14
855.16    864.28    877.25    900.07    015.25    335.22
855.17    864.28    877.25    900.09    018.28    337.23
855.19    865.01    879.11    900.09    020.15    341.10
855.20    865.02    879.12    900.16    020.16    342.17
855.26    865.11    879.13    900.17    020.17    342.19
855.27    865.13    879.22    900.24    020.18    342.22
855.27    865.15    879.25    901.05    022.16    343.02
856.03    865.17    880.23    901.07    022.16    349.18
856.07    865.20    880.26    901.09    029.01    350.19
856.07    865.21    881.07    901.16    030.05    350.19
856.08    865.25    881.12    901.18    036.15    350.26
856.08    865.27    881.16    901.25    038.09    350.27
856.11    865.27    881.17    901.26    038.12    351.06
856.13    866.02    881.25    902.05    038.12    351.07
856.15    866.03    881.27    902.08    044.16    351.10
856.15    866.05    882.01    902.08    048.08    352.09
856.19    866.12    882.10    902.10    057.22    352.14
856.19    866.13    883.04    902.10    058.16    354.18
856.20    867.05    883.17    902.16    058.17    359.21
856.23    867.14    883.18    902.17    058.17    359.21
856.23    867.15    883.22    902.17    058.19    359.22
856.23    867.17    883.23    902.26    061.13    360.01
856.24    867.18    884.04    902.27    061.19    364.17
856.26    867.21    884.05    903.02    064.11    365.14
857.01    867.22    884.11    903.06    074.22    365.19
857.02    367.23    884.25    903.08    078.09    365.28
857.07    868.08    885.03    903.08    078.15    367.10
857.09    869.02    885.05    903.16    078.16    369.10
857.09    869.07    885.15    903.21    080.22    369.13
857.09    869.07    885.19    903.22    083.04    370.10
857.10    869.07    885.20    903.22    083.12    371.24
857.11    869.08    885.20    903.23    084.04    371.25
857.11    869.11    885.25    904.05    084.08    375.01
857.13    869.12    886.01    905.04    084.13    376.26
857.16    869.13    886.03    905.05    085.25    376.27
857.21    869.13    886.05    905.06    088.14    377.20
857.27    869.16    886.11    905.07    089.19    377.21
857.28    869.17    886.14    905.07    097.16    378.10
858.07    369.18    886.16    905.10    098.04    378.13
858.13    869.19    886.20    905.13    106.22    378.14
858.17    870.01    886.22    905.17    111.10    378.15
859.01    870.02    886.23    905.18    112.11    378.18
859.01    870.03    886.24    905.20    113.22    378.19
859.02    870.06    886.27    906.01    113.22    378.21
859.02    870.07    887.01    906.02    114.20    379.05
859.03    870.09    887.05    906.04    118.26    380.17
859.03    870.14    887.06    906.10    119.06    383.13
859.08    870.19    887.06    906.11    119.07    385.22
859.09    870.21    887.09    906.19    120.23    386.08
859.12    370.22                        122.15    389.09
                                        124.24
```

391.04	744.02	107.23	347.20	638.01	854.10
391.09	744.03	108.25	348.05	648.12	854.12
391.20	744.05	113.21	348.13	652.11	856.13
391.22	744.17	114.17	349.15	654.20	856.18
392.04	744.17	114.19	350.07	661.10	858.28
392.07	744.20	114.20	350.21	663.15	863.22
392.07	744.21	116.25	350.24	668.19	865.17
392.10	744.25	117.03	351.04	670.16	870.05
402.11	746.26	117.12	351.09	676.23	873.19
411.03	753.04	117.16	353.26	677.12	879.07
411.04	753.04	118.04	354.10	677.14	884.09
412.15	753.04	118.08	354.20	677.17	892.07
413.05	753.07	118.09	355.14	677.19	896.18
416.01	753.11	118.19	357.02	677.21	896.21
417.24	756.04	120.26	359.13	681.02	900.21
418.21	756.24	120.28	359.27	681.06	901.22
425.15	756.27	121.04	366.16	681.22	903.09
433.08	759.23	121.18	367.11	682.01	906.03
433.20	761.03	126.07	368.15	682.02	911.07
436.21	770.18	127.15	373.24	682.11	911.13
440.20	787.07	130.24	374.17	683.05	them's
441.17	787.08	131.27	376.26	683.13	387.20
444.10	788.04	141.09	376.26	691.18	theme
448.20	789.12	144.17	378.12	691.19	135.19
449.15	789.14	147.07	384.02	694.22	378.21
460.14	789.17	147.09	385.22	694.22	400.05
462.11	791.09	147.17	391.15	694.25	400.08
462.26	793.06	151.28	391.17	696.10	401.11
462.26	794.15	152.07	391.21	698.14	473.16
466.23	798.06	166.21	391.25	698.24	526.05
466.24	798.12	170.23	395.22	699.13	718.25
472.10	798.14	172.26	397.08	703.15	themselves
472.24	798.18	173.08	397.08	703.25	004.20
489.06	798.24	176.05	397.09	706.17	113.13
491.06	798.28	176.25	398.19	711.03	121.18
493.26	799.02	184.08	399.06	711.07	167.12
493.27	799.04	187.09	399.09	711.07	179.06
493.27	799.05	189.06	400.02	712.20	216.22
498.13	799.08	189.07	400.20	712.25	266.15
500.03	799.10	190.11	400.20	713.05	269.25
501.11	800.20	199.27	401.01	714.01	342.24
503.10	802.02	200.07	405.25	717.11	371.18
504.03	804.12	200.08	405.25	718.12	386.17
504.04	808.08	205.07	410.24	723.01	398.01
510.09	810.08	205.20	411.08	727.08	408.13
528.01	812.18	207.22	412.01	730.03	669.06
529.02	814.13	214.12	412.03	731.01	698.25
529.07	814.15	214.26	412.06	731.03	743.16
529.06	814.18	216.25	412.28	731.04	779.23
538.08	825.02	216.26	417.23	737.27	779.23
557.10	825.03	220.09	423.21	743.10	783.14
558.24	832.03	221.13	425.14	743.11	821.15
560.02	835.01	223.23	429.27	743.18	then
560.04	835.02	225.03	430.03	744.11	005.28
560.19	835.04	226.18	435.06	744.14	006.05
561.12	844.09	231.01	435.10	744.24	008.06
589.08	844.20	239.19	442.16	744.25	011.03
590.07	845.03	241.24	446.24	751.09	013.21
604.05	846.26	242.03	448.18	756.28	014.27
616.24	849.05	242.10	454.20	757.28	015.06
616.25	852.22	246.14	462.12	761.09	021.06
616.25	853.27	246.17	466.23	762.18	023.14
652.14	856.14	246.19	467.04	762.19	025.02
657.05	865.17	246.20	467.07	765.16	027.19
658.07	911.12	246.26	468.24	771.19	028.09
648.10	911.20	247.01	470.27	781.10	030.09
646.13	theirs	247.13	471.07	782.14	034.02
656.07	383.09	247.18	471.27	782.21	035.20
659.08	677.12	247.19	472.01	782.22	036.26
662.10	712.27	249.21	472.01	783.13	038.08
662.28	713.28	249.27	491.09	784.10	041.01
664.20	732.23	250.02	501.08	784.11	045.02
675.15	them	250.19	506.13	786.02	046.13
677.20	003.25	252.18	510.06	787.03	047.10
681.12	013.15	255.10	522.09	787.04	049.20
681.22	014.21	257.02	524.19	787.07	050.25
685.09	014.24	262.16	524.24	789.15	051.12
690.20	015.14	265.07	524.26	789.16	053.10
696.04	017.11	268.08	546.18	789.17	055.27
698.17	020.10	273.26	557.17	790.10	056.13
696.21	020.12	274.17	557.18	790.24	059.08
698.27	020.13	283.13	560.16	792.13	059.16
699.06	030.15	287.04	561.11	793.21	061.26
703.21	031.13	287.09	561.25	801.09	068.16
704.24	034.25	287.21	562.01	801.10	072.01
707.25	036.11	292.14	573.14	802.02	075.18
709.13	037.21	292.27	577.03	803.06	076.05
711.06	037.23	296.19	578.15	805.25	076.09
711.15	038.09	298.26	580.05	806.12	076.26
712.03	039.08	310.20	588.15	807.07	077.11
712.05	045.17	317.28	598.20	814.06	077.13
712.10	046.07	318.02	601.14	814.12	078.19
713.26	055.19	321.20	601.19	814.12	081.08
715.26	058.02	322.28	604.20	814.13	082.13
717.16	058.09	329.17	607.25	814.15	086.07
717.17	058.10	331.05	609.12	814.18	089.04
717.19	062.03	332.22	611.16	815.22	091.19
717.19	069.05	333.03	611.18	816.27	092.06
718.14	071.20	333.18	613.08	823.02	095.18
720.21	078.22	335.28	615.24	823.02	095.18
724.26	078.25	336.05	616.25	823.21	099.18
724.28	080.20	336.25	619.01	829.01	100.25
725.25	083.05	337.15	620.11	831.19	101.07
726.03	084.18	342.11	620.13	843.06	102.28
730.11	084.21	342.14	626.13	844.14	103.20
732.14	087.13	342.18	627.12	844.16	105.08
735.25	089.18	342.24	628.12	851.05	106.06
735.25	098.16	343.01	632.08	853.17	106.13
743.06	104.13	343.03	632.15	853.26	107.17
743.13	107.05	347.02	636.14	854.07	107.25
744.02	107.22	347.06	636.28		108.07

112.03	300.23	504.22	726.10	235.09	199.17
114.22	301.09	507.02	726.26	296.05	199.18
115.04	302.06	509.04	729.02	324.06	202.01
121.10	302.10	511.03	736.24	332.11	202.14
122.04	302.23	512.21	739.22	340.21	202.26
123.18	307.26	514.28	740.01	357.06	206.11
123.24	308.04	517.21	744.18	361.20	208.05
126.26	308.10	522.19	745.18	420.17	217.05
127.06	308.22	522.21	745.23	449.14	217.06
130.04	309.19	525.24	745.23	502.17	219.14
133.06	315.24	526.11	745.24	629.27	219.18
134.27	318.10	527.12	745.26	768.16	220.19
136.09	321.25	527.13	747.14	theodore	221.12
136.26	328.16	527.14	749.12	060.02	222.26
137.02	329.03	529.27	749.18	355.15	225.25
139.16	330.06	530.04	749.26	356.01	228.06
139.22	333.25	537.27	750.05	theoretical	228.27
140.09	335.20	539.15	751.16	224.25	231.21
142.07	336.25	539.27	752.04	theory	231.11
145.20	337.08	544.18	753.21	022.28	233.11
148.11	339.19	548.23	763.19	there	234.17
151.09	340.10	550.08	766.16	001.03	237.27
152.14	344.11	552.16	769.18	001.06	238.02
153.16	346.25	554.13	772.21	002.21	241.10
153.16	347.19	561.24	773.03	002.26	244.26
154.27	352.01	562.01	775.04	003.21	247.26
155.19	352.18	565.10	775.12	007.26	250.23
156.16	353.13	565.15	776.01	011.05	250.25
156.25	354.27	566.03	778.23	013.01	252.17
157.27	356.05	567.10	779.05	017.07	255.15
159.11	357.12	569.05	779.18	017.21	255.21
162.09	358.05	569.18	781.04	020.07	255.27
163.13	358.10	576.20	784.24	027.05	256.18
165.20	360.13	576.21	791.13	030.04	257.19
165.26	360.18	577.19	793.02	033.12	258.23
167.03	361.09	586.06	793.05	033.19	259.21
167.15	361.18	589.20	795.14	035.22	261.08
168.12	365.22	595.11	798.04	035.28	262.27
170.07	366.28	600.10	798.07	045.28	276.02
170.17	367.04	601.18	798.08	047.02	280.16
170.22	367.15	602.08	798.21	049.16	283.25
175.24	369.01	603.14	799.28	050.20	286.13
177.04	370.24	604.18	800.06	051.16	286.14
178.17	374.21	605.12	805.20	054.12	289.17
178.22	376.02	609.16	809.11	059.10	290.07
180.17	376.28	610.08	809.22	059.26	290.12
182.24	377.25	611.21	809.24	063.08	293.05
183.18	380.02	612.20	814.28	064.04	294.11
186.19	380.07	613.02	818.28	064.24	294.17
187.01	382.11	613.06	820.08	073.01	295.10
187.11	384.01	613.14	830.01	073.18	295.21
187.25	384.08	617.09	837.16	075.16	297.07
188.15	387.21	618.03	839.03	075.27	297.08
189.05	396.03	620.27	840.07	076.09	297.20
189.18	398.24	621.03	840.15	080.07	297.22
192.24	399.13	622.26	841.12	080.08	298.09
193.11	402.17	627.01	842.16	085.10	298.24
193.20	402.25	629.08	845.18	098.14	300.08
196.19	407.12	631.03	846.02	101.16	301.20
200.13	407.15	631.27	847.07	106.16	302.01
201.09	412.05	632.26	853.07	111.17	305.18
201.24	412.06	634.03	855.21	114.19	306.21
202.23	412.17	635.08	857.05	116.05	308.02
203.08	412.25	635.27	857.06	117.01	310.07
208.08	413.03	637.18	857.25	117.21	310.10
214.24	415.13	640.06	857.26	124.12	316.13
215.05	417.11	642.02	863.23	127.06	316.14
215.08	418.10	642.13	864.06	128.09	317.05
215.20	419.07	643.18	865.13	130.28	317.06
219.01	420.15	645.02	865.19	132.20	317.08
220.09	420.24	646.15	866.01	133.11	317.16
222.25	422.20	646.22	869.10	137.20	319.20
223.13	422.25	646.24	870.20	138.14	321.23
226.10	424.12	646.28	872.18	146.13	329.12
228.11	425.18	650.21	873.17	147.24	330.24
229.23	426.20	650.27	873.24	148.25	332.09
232.24	427.16	652.11	874.11	148.27	333.26
234.06	432.03	656.23	875.03	153.15	334.28
234.09	432.28	657.10	875.06	154.13	339.08
236.17	436.12	661.13	877.28	155.11	339.18
238.23	437.22	669.08	883.06	157.06	340.27
244.27	438.28	671.03	883.24	157.27	342.01
245.13	453.11	673.04	885.05	158.03	342.12
246.06	453.18	673.24	885.14	163.14	343.04
251.24	453.27	674.12	886.06	164.16	344.11
256.16	455.20	674.16	889.04	164.17	345.15
265.08	455.25	679.17	889.12	164.17	347.28
266.03	456.05	680.15	890.06	164.18	350.19
266.04	457.27	687.08	891.24	166.13	353.23
266.20	459.07	691.22	892.14	166.15	356.20
267.24	461.25	693.15	894.19	167.10	356.25
269.01	466.19	693.19	895.14	168.08	361.14
269.11	466.19	694.16	897.10	170.05	363.02
270.11	470.08	695.21	898.08	170.14	364.07
270.28	471.19	695.26	899.02	170.15	372.21
272.14	471.21	699.04	903.09	171.04	377.06
274.09	471.22	701.02	904.01	171.12	382.19
274.18	472.25	704.01	904.03	172.13	382.22
275.25	476.18	705.23	907.04	175.27	384.17
277.15	477.11	707.15	907.05	176.19	386.02
277.18	479.23	709.01	907.14	177.20	392.16
279.09	481.25	709.02	909.17	178.16	392.19
283.28	483.19	712.07	910.15	179.14	394.19
284.18	485.04	713.04	911.03	180.21	397.07
286.04	486.11	714.02	thence	182.03	397.26
286.07	489.20	714.22	009.06	183.01	399.12
288.03	491.03	722.12	066.21	183.23	399.21
294.08	491.17	722.14	160.14	184.27	407.15
298.12	493.21	723.03	208.23	186.17	410.23
298.19	494.01	726.08	208.24	193.12	411.03
299.12	501.03	726.09	219.25	199.14	415.22

416.04	596.25	784.25	therefrom	633.28	091.15
420.15	599.09	797.17	633.27	637.28	091.19
420.24	605.04	798.23	therein	638.05	093.16
421.24	608.02	800.03	097.04	643.24	095.06
423.25	612.09	801.25	593.21	643.24	103.19
428.03	612.11	804.10	thereof	652.26	105.24
429.20	613.26	805.05	003.19	658.16	105.27
430.23	615.09	807.20	518.21	658.19	105.27
431.05	615.12	807.23	845.06	659.05	105.28
432.24	619.08	809.19	thereon	665.06	106.22
433.22	621.22	810.14	079.02	665.10	106.23
434.03	622.16	813.23	therewith	670.17	112.10
434.13	625.09	816.19	143.17	672.10	114.21
437.19	625.28	816.23	these	673.20	114.21
439.04	630.18	819.06	004.15	674.02	115.13
439.21	631.23	820.27	004.19	676.23	116.24
445.03	638.10	823.11	010.17	684.03	116.25
446.11	638.25	823.22	014.11	691.05	117.04
450.24	639.03	825.22	016.04	694.19	120.28
453.15	640.10	825.24	024.25	698.14	121.02
457.03	640.19	827.08	039.05	699.01	121.27
459.02	641.20	827.12	048.25	707.10	122.01
460.06	642.27	828.14	053.09	712.19	122.14
460.08	643.09	836.19	060.10	712.24	122.20
460.22	643.19	838.20	064.10	714.15	122.24
461.13	643.27	838.28	081.09	714.25	124.14
464.22	646.21	839.18	087.27	716.19	124.24
464.23	648.08	840.23	088.13	720.04	127.11
465.01	648.19	841.07	089.17	730.07	131.09
465.16	653.19	842.20	111.06	730.12	131.18
465.17	653.21	844.05	111.08	731.01	132.23
467.07	656.26	844.10	111.13	731.22	139.13
468.01	657.05	846.10	114.12	736.02	139.13
469.25	658.10	847.04	118.07	743.14	139.14
472.06	658.10	847.21	119.05	744.01	139.16
473.06	659.01	850.15	120.14	744.10	140.04
477.06	659.02	852.13	121.09	749.19	140.07
479.10	661.09	855.23	121.11	752.13	140.08
479.16	662.16	856.07	121.17	756.05	140.09
479.27	663.14	856.22	121.23	762.03	140.09
481.17	664.10	857.12	122.11	778.16	145.19
482.06	664.24	857.12	131.21	783.04	146.15
485.23	665.13	859.08	137.08	807.23	156.04
488.26	665.27	859.18	139.11	808.23	167.09
489.04	666.01	859.28	148.09	815.21	173.07
491.13	668.15	860.20	150.01	818.13	176.04
492.26	669.22	861.15	151.06	823.26	176.23
474.07	669.23	862.05	152.06	836.03	176.27
494.20	669.24	862.22	154.26	851.10	177.04
495.25	670.07	864.11	161.03	860.07	177.07
496.01	670.18	864.11	161.28	861.02	178.09
496.10	672.10	866.13	192.23	861.16	179.19
499.21	673.20	866.16	192.23	877.04	179.20
500.11	675.01	867.17	194.08	877.05	179.21
503.05	676.03	869.06	194.21	879.24	180.06
504.26	676.24	869.13	202.19	880.25	185.16
505.09	678.22	870.06	204.20	885.18	189.05
505.21	679.02	870.16	207.15	885.22	190.09
506.26	679.09	870.26	207.19	901.19	190.10
510.11	681.12	871.09	208.01	902.11	190.22
510.13	684.05	871.10	210.23	903.09	192.04
516.26	684.22	873.04	220.24	910.02	194.06
517.02	684.23	873.24	246.22	they	197.16
518.03	684.24	876.15	249.02	003.23	202.21
518.17	686.03	877.21	249.18	009.14	202.24
519.07	687.27	877.21	249.26	013.03	204.23
519.24	691.03	878.10	250.17	014.11	204.25
521.09	692.20	881.26	254.09	014.21	208.03
523.01	693.09	882.14	257.02	015.13	208.16
523.02	696.18	883.18	263.14	017.13	208.18
526.13	698.13	885.21	291.06	020.09	210.24
529.23	699.03	885.24	295.27	020.10	215.25
530.11	699.06	886.10	316.19	028.26	216.07
531.21	700.21	886.22	322.27	028.27	216.08
533.19	701.11	887.02	325.22	028.28	216.08
536.12	702.10	892.13	339.20	030.04	216.16
536.18	702.24	894.07	344.15	031.17	216.18
537.08	703.06	894.08	348.21	033.03	216.21
537.16	703.21	899.02	364.02	033.03	216.26
538.14	703.22	901.03	365.12	033.07	221.12
540.05	704.11	908.10	369.21	036.02	222.10
540.14	711.08	909.28	371.03	036.14	222.19
540.16	713.09	there's	372.22	036.16	223.22
541.16	713.12	064.15	373.23	037.25	224.28
541.16	715.03	329.27	376.27	037.27	230.28
542.03	715.23	427.24	383.19	038.06	232.13
543.26	716.16	443.01	384.26	038.17	239.19
546.20	719.05	454.05	392.01	038.19	243.20
550.17	732.26	799.27	411.27	039.09	245.25
553.24	734.13	thereby	423.05	039.09	246.27
557.03	737.13	048.23	423.06	039.10	247.15
557.07	737.17	065.25	447.07	039.11	247.16
561.02	740.05	440.27	459.09	040.10	247.19
561.21	743.09	therefore	473.09	041.21	250.17
564.11	744.19	058.07	489.26	044.03	253.20
564.21	752.08	160.08	490.16	044.26	255.10
564.22	752.11	213.10	491.08	053.12	259.26
565.07	757.09	263.24	493.14	054.07	269.25
574.15	758.20	267.08	525.03	055.06	273.16
575.04	761.06	270.05	525.04	058.19	273.25
576.09	762.12	337.03	544.03	058.20	273.25
576.13	763.26	513.27	555.14	058.21	273.27
580.01	771.10	555.17	558.23	077.10	273.27
580.14	771.12	621.22	562.11	078.11	275.26
582.09	771.14	678.01	573.08	078.14	285.27
582.24	773.08	678.17	580.02	083.12	286.27
586.15	775.12	821.21	602.05	083.15	287.06
587.05	776.24	843.04	602.06	084.07	287.06
595.17	778.02	891.03	607.22	088.02	291.16
596.07	778.26	906.11	621.08	089.14	291.17
596.15	784.05		626.11	091.05	293.06

308.06	496.06	713.25	890.14	252.05	844.17
308.09	503.28	715.28	890.14	260.11	846.07
310.20	508.28	717.14	892.05	272.26	846.14
316.20	510.05	717.18	896.19	272.28	851.04
316.22	517.10	718.17	896.20	285.11	892.08
323.24	521.10	718.18	896.20	288.17	903.09
325.23	522.11	723.01	900.19	329.15	907.19
325.24	523.17	723.01	902.24	355.20	think
335.17	528.02	724.28	910.27	370.26	013.02
335.20	528.03	725.01	911.06	385.15	014.18
337.26	529.06	725.04	they'll	415.05	028.09
338.07	529.07	727.08	069.05	431.12	034.25
341.01	533.12	729.19	332.15	436.05	036.04
341.09	536.12	730.01	they're	437.04	037.03
342.10	538.18	731.05	329.28	452.28	037.16
342.12	541.01	733.25	332.14	455.09	037.27
342.13	543.21	735.01	508.27	465.08	040.15
342.21	547.11	740.06	they've	468.15	044.25
344.03	557.09	743.07	176.11	469.25	047.20
347.19	557.14	743.12	696.26	472.04	063.02
348.02	559.03	744.08	thhreatened	476.16	063.15
348.04	560.21	744.22	555.19	493.22	068.10
349.18	570.20	744.26	thick	499.20	069.01
350.03	577.23	746.25	007.04	507.15	090.13
350.04	579.17	753.03	023.18	516.08	105.05
350.11	586.13	753.06	026.05	529.14	117.13
350.22	588.16	753.10	149.02	531.19	119.07
351.06	588.16	759.12	177.12	531.23	121.24
354.11	588.17	761.10	207.24	535.26	125.04
355.03	588.19	769.08	318.12	542.10	132.04
355.12	589.06	770.08	427.11	549.07	132.14
358.12	592.07	770.21	531.11	553.14	134.16
363.02	597.14	772.24	577.12	569.23	134.18
365.04	598.20	774.09	668.12	573.17	136.24
365.06	598.24	776.13	671.16	579.15	159.10
367.08	601.05	781.11	676.07	587.23	167.04
367.08	604.05	782.20	681.15	634.07	175.15
369.11	606.12	782.21	782.17	637.23	176.22
370.11	614.16	783.14	848.27	639.09	177.04
371.17	617.26	783.15	870.02	649.16	177.08
371.17	620.13	788.03	881.04	666.21	177.15
375.02	623.07	788.06	900.08	701.14	189.15
376.10	623.12	788.07	thick-falling	704.05	201.27
376.28	625.01	789.12	640.07	770.25	204.23
378.18	626.09	790.15	thick-soled	775.09	205.26
383.20	627.11	792.13	890.19	775.10	208.08
388.17	640.23	794.11	thickened	796.27	223.06
390.23	647.19	794.21	145.23	808.12	223.26
390.24	648.08	795.03	235.10	862.15	225.14
391.07	648.11	797.18	thicker	862.16	225.19
391.09	648.11	797.26	031.19	863.05	236.17
391.12	648.13	797.26	257.06	864.14	239.22
391.13	659.05	798.07	thickly	880.05	242.10
391.16	659.06	798.12	561.23	894.04	247.10
391.17	665.11	798.16	thief's	things	251.20
391.18	666.22	798.18	005.07	030.10	251.24
391.19	669.02	798.22	thimble	036.09	253.10
391.21	673.15	798.26	047.08	036.10	258.25
391.25	673.21	799.01	097.11	058.23	259.15
392.02	677.08	800.18	thin	058.28	260.22
398.19	677.08	800.19	045.18	064.10	261.06
400.04	677.10	801.22	060.11	083.15	265.21
400.23	677.14	801.24	079.10	103.13	271.18
400.24	677.15	801.28	088.11	103.22	271.24
401.15	677.15	814.14	100.07	113.13	275.23
403.06	677.18	814.17	113.27	140.04	282.11
405.15	677.18	815.15	127.28	141.07	287.14
409.01	679.02	816.26	138.08	149.19	288.22
410.23	679.06	827.09	156.08	150.11	300.06
410.26	679.07	832.01	220.17	152.07	302.13
411.02	679.09	832.03	237.15	161.03	306.03
411.18	679.11	833.03	248.25	169.16	308.25
411.21	679.17	835.18	249.05	171.25	309.07
411.22	681.20	835.19	292.04	193.07	309.26
411.23	682.21	835.20	419.12	205.07	310.13
412.03	686.08	836.04	460.21	206.15	312.07
412.12	688.03	846.23	461.14	231.01	312.15
416.07	689.13	846.24	492.24	232.26	316.17
416.08	690.03	846.25	575.13	239.20	316.28
416.08	690.21	846.26	630.11	267.07	317.16
418.04	693.09	849.06	659.04	314.22	325.23
418.05	696.06	849.07	685.22	359.17	326.11
433.12	698.15	853.21	699.22	360.19	333.12
435.04	698.16	853.24	760.13	365.23	335.28
440.03	698.16	853.24	763.13	384.26	336.04
441.17	698.19	853.25	907.25	391.13	336.13
441.18	698.20	853.27	thing	391.17	336.08
442.11	698.24	854.08	005.10	405.16	336.28
446.24	698.25	855.28	010.13	444.02	339.21
447.25	698.28	855.28	012.02	460.17	341.23
448.21	699.01	857.22	014.03	462.21	346.21
456.03	699.02	857.23	020.11	467.05	348.23
456.03	699.04	858.02	020.13	489.10	351.19
459.10	699.10	858.15	020.15	519.20	352.03
462.07	699.12	862.01	020.16	525.07	353.25
462.23	699.13	862.01	026.02	535.14	354.09
467.28	704.22	862.10	028.23	561.01	372.23
468.24	709.10	862.13	034.17	592.13	376.11
470.15	711.07	862.27	036.23	692.15	381.21
470.24	711.08	863.01	055.08	696.26	383.03
471.27	711.13	863.05	067.04	700.22	388.12
472.05	711.14	863.10	067.21	708.14	389.21
472.22	711.14	863.10	068.02	709.19	390.07
473.15	711.15	864.03	069.10	725.12	390.27
475.14	712.02	865.19	084.26	729.12	399.07
477.15	712.10	865.22	117.21	757.20	399.18
485.18	712.20	868.02	166.25	792.10	400.17
490.07	712.28	884.08	227.14	792.21	406.08
493.11	713.03	887.19	228.23	807.21	407.19
493.17	713.04	888.07	231.28	811.19	409.16
493.24	713.19	889.03	247.22	844.12	412.07

420.02	890.11	025.06	153.13	338.18	509.11
429.02	899.26	028.12	158.13	340.21	510.20
429.14	901.27	029.14	160.05	341.07	523.11
429.15	thinking	029.16	162.19	347.04	523.12
441.27	082.17	030.10	167.01	347.28	523.12
448.27	088.25	030.25	167.07	357.15	523.13
451.24	095.02	031.08	168.11	358.03	524.10
455.10	163.19	032.02	168.27	363.07	524.15
462.07	194.27	033.02	169.03	368.04	525.02
462.21	239.07	036.12	169.25	369.12	526.06
469.18	266.14	036.18	171.21	369.24	527.03
477.23	267.01	041.04	173.16	371.27	529.21
481.15	270.23	044.06	173.26	372.14	530.12
483.16	276.10	045.26	177.26	373.16	531.23
484.05	293.12	046.20	181.04	373.27	534.11
484.09	313.20	046.27	181.12	373.27	537.07
484.18	386.21	049.26	183.01	373.28	540.06
494.12	400.20	050.08	183.14	374.01	542.15
496.22	493.10	050.21	184.09	374.09	545.10
497.14	493.12	052.22	185.24	374.09	545.24
508.23	528.28	053.16	187.19	374.10	546.03
508.27	529.01	056.17	189.19	375.06	548.26
510.19	570.08	056.23	196.20	377.05	549.05
512.26	614.18	058.23	196.28	377.10	549.09
512.28	767.15	059.09	199.13	380.26	551.03
513.04	766.05	062.03	201.04	382.16	551.25
513.06	807.17	062.07	201.17	385.20	554.03
523.27	909.10	063.14	202.26	389.28	554.06
525.06	thinks	063.17	203.26	396.05	557.09
527.24	253.15	063.22	205.11	401.05	558.14
530.17	322.26	065.01	206.10	401.26	559.01
531.03	457.19	068.14	206.16	402.01	565.02
532.03	655.14	075.25	208.06	402.14	565.16
532.21	754.01	077.06	209.26	403.25	565.17
532.26	thinned	079.14	211.25	406.09	566.09
534.13	870.27	080.27	214.08	408.13	568.12
541.07	third	081.05	219.23	409.06	570.16
561.01	112.14	084.17	221.15	413.07	572.04
565.05	114.15	086.17	221.21	413.07	576.22
569.21	181.10	087.06	222.13	417.20	578.06
569.23	207.01	089.10	223.01	419.10	579.08
573.11	207.16	089.11	223.18	420.16	580.11
573.16	209.28	089.13	225.05	422.04	583.15
573.23	215.22	091.04	225.15	422.05	590.16
580.21	248.27	091.13	225.17	423.05	591.10
603.24	295.13	091.25	225.20	424.04	591.16
614.05	298.06	091.28	231.08	424.13	595.12
617.07	328.20	092.06	232.06	424.13	595.20
621.05	332.25	094.06	232.07	424.22	596.14
621.17	365.13	094.10	235.23	424.22	596.18
625.16	369.16	096.03	236.06	424.26	597.05
634.07	415.07	096.15	238.03	425.05	598.03
637.13	419.15	098.25	242.15	425.14	599.05
640.09	422.25	099.17	243.10	425.20	599.08
641.02	460.14	099.24	245.11	427.04	601.24
644.09	516.03	101.05	245.23	427.21	602.01
647.22	559.02	101.08	248.25	428.01	602.06
647.22	599.01	101.24	249.15	428.03	602.07
650.23	633.01	103.10	250.24	429.01	604.08
650.24	691.28	103.27	254.11	429.16	613.22
667.28	719.23	104.24	256.13	429.23	615.02
671.18	787.14	105.13	258.04	430.19	615.17
679.12	791.27	105.15	259.17	431.02	615.17
679.21	807.12	107.04	262.20	431.10	615.18
685.01	899.12	108.23	264.21	432.19	615.19
685.25	thirdly	108.27	264.23	434.04	616.04
695.13	345.08	109.15	264.23	434.05	617.18
697.01	thirst	109.18	269.19	435.15	618.03
697.03	119.03	109.23	270.04	435.17	619.14
708.10	644.26	110.04	271.08	437.06	621.15
715.18	thirst-perishing	111.21	272.13	438.18	622.25
720.10	349.22	112.06	273.05	439.28	624.25
723.25	thirsted	113.18	273.11	440.09	626.09
725.12	631.16	114.02	273.22	440.26	628.14
727.01	thirsty	115.19	278.09	443.05	630.13
733.13	079.07	115.24	279.12	445.06	630.13
733.21	320.01	116.01	279.19	445.07	630.16
738.17	thirteen	117.25	282.25	445.14	630.19
739.07	094.21	117.28	282.27	445.20	630.21
741.05	thirty	118.16	284.23	445.20	632.12
761.09	171.14	120.07	285.09	445.24	634.08
769.19	211.12	121.03	285.26	455.12	638.08
776.13	381.28	121.16	287.03	457.21	639.15
776.24	547.20	122.05	288.05	460.28	642.09
785.20	559.11	123.03	290.18	461.05	642.26
787.05	624.20	124.23	292.02	465.10	643.09
793.08	626.09	125.12	293.26	465.25	644.15
803.08	657.05	125.14	294.27	469.22	644.22
808.22	696.10	125.26	295.23	472.27	645.16
809.03	701.23	126.01	300.17	474.14	645.22
814.06	721.23	126.04	305.04	474.21	646.06
816.13	727.19	126.11	308.01	477.10	646.06
818.19	826.13	126.25	309.06	477.15	646.06
823.03	367.27	130.11	310.05	477.26	647.03
824.11	thirty-five	132.19	312.27	482.23	647.17
827.25	224.18	132.28	315.10	483.17	648.09
838.13	this	138.05	315.26	484.13	648.19
838.27	013.03	138.13	319.10	489.13	650.04
841.03	013.12	139.15	320.24	490.04	652.01
841.25	014.14	145.09	321.11	494.12	653.22
845.26	016.12	145.13	323.03	495.03	653.28
847.10	016.27	146.11	323.06	495.10	654.06
866.26	021.16	146.13	324.10	498.10	654.16
872.10	021.25	149.03	328.19	503.06	658.07
874.06	022.23	150.12	330.24	503.11	658.07
880.14	022.28	151.03	333.16	503.25	658.21
880.15	023.05	151.28	334.27	504.19	659.15
880.16	023.09	152.11	335.03	505.14	661.12
881.14	023.11	152.24	335.11	506.16	662.03
885.05	024.14	153.06	336.09	506.25	663.07
890.05			338.05	507.27	663.17

663.19	807.28	182.09	713.19	032.23	737.05
663.22	809.13	183.02	748.18	033.20	745.03
664.05	810.02	183.04	805.26	045.28	746.24
666.12	810.23	183.20	827.23	057.09	748.28
667.26	811.02	185.09	882.20	060.18	752.20
669.12	811.18	188.27	890.08	061.23	771.24
670.08	816.08	194.16	those	063.08	784.23
670.19	816.22	194.22	003.23	063.09	826.03
672.21	816.26	195.07	004.09	067.08	826.25
672.25	817.04	195.18	016.23	077.21	829.15
672.26	820.15	195.26	051.28	078.10	833.01
672.26	821.11	219.07	058.18	090.14	842.16
675.08	823.13	220.04	079.05	094.24	873.28
677.07	823.19	229.14	081.24	104.18	874.16
677.22	824.03	229.19	084.16	111.08	901.07
679.25	824.09	243.16	086.01	130.21	907.15
681.21	825.17	253.11	106.18	150.13	907.16
681.28	826.04	282.27	106.21	172.06	910.02
682.13	828.27	283.27	107.04	174.06	thought
683.11	832.18	293.15	107.06	174.19	006.11
683.18	832.22	311.20	107.08	177.27	010.06
683.23	832.26	324.07	118.20	178.12	016.11
683.23	833.09	325.04	121.13	182.01	017.24
683.24	833.13	325.20	128.11	184.02	018.08
683.25	834.09	327.12	130.06	194.01	021.10
685.02	834.18	329.28	132.23	203.01	021.16
686.27	835.09	330.25	139.05	204.24	022.18
689.03	836.20	333.23	142.23	207.01	023.16
690.03	837.26	340.01	144.15	208.15	024.05
695.21	839.20	438.20	145.17	210.10	029.20
696.07	846.14	481.10	147.15	210.13	030.03
702.06	847.10	490.19	150.09	214.03	032.22
706.01	850.07	491.12	161.19	218.11	033.19
706.08	851.15	492.04	164.12	219.28	034.15
706.28	852.06	492.15	164.20	222.10	036.16
707.14	854.20	493.24	164.21	227.15	036.21
711.09	855.07	496.09	167.26	228.22	039.06
712.11	857.08	501.09	168.27	237.16	040.10
713.28	857.19	505.27	194.13	256.06	043.13
714.28	857.22	506.22	207.21	261.26	057.16
716.12	858.02	509.07	214.11	262.12	062.26
718.20	859.15	511.16	221.09	273.27	098.28
719.01	860.02	511.23	224.27	275.04	100.08
719.18	862.19	511.23	230.27	281.21	101.25
720.27	862.20	524.18	262.14	288.07	105.19
722.06	863.08	541.20	281.06	293.06	109.02
724.23	863.12	547.28	283.26	293.10	123.01
725.04	863.15	561.17	331.27	297.03	124.04
727.28	864.05	565.24	337.14	310.07	130.10
729.17	867.05	567.21	356.01	310.19	143.09
730.21	867.11	607.04	383.27	316.02	144.16
732.09	868.08	609.06	387.22	316.05	152.22
732.24	869.15	615.17	472.10	316.27	156.03
736.17	870.21	615.23	488.05	331.16	156.14
737.24	870.28	616.16	496.24	333.22	160.12
738.11	873.02	617.28	529.05	346.01	168.22
738.15	873.16	622.03	534.19	351.13	169.21
738.17	873.16	631.27	556.06	369.27	175.01
739.01	874.01	632.28	573.13	372.22	177.23
739.04	874.23	634.21	592.06	385.03	182.03
739.22	875.16	638.24	600.14	403.04	184.04
740.03	875.21	654.22	610.26	403.11	187.17
740.13	875.21	854.16	616.08	404.23	188.03
741.11	876.02	854.24	627.14	415.23	190.08
742.22	876.19	856.11	628.08	420.26	191.26
743.12	876.19	860.18	628.11	460.28	193.03
745.06	876.21	861.27	629.21	468.12	195.26
745.09	877.11	873.20	630.14	477.16	201.02
745.09	877.25	888.01	634.16	492.19	204.07
753.28	878.09	896.12	636.27	492.21	205.01
754.12	878.09	thornfield-hall	640.09	494.22	206.28
756.09	881.11	207.16	642.22	495.26	214.08
756.14	881.18	208.06	643.20	505.07	223.03
757.12	883.10	213.03	669.06	506.07	236.12
758.06	884.06	224.01	670.24	510.12	237.09
758.23	884.19	226.01	691.27	526.02	239.19
759.05	887.10	233.14	730.11	538.13	239.21
759.07	889.12	310.28	737.06	542.07	241.13
760.16	891.24	364.02	739.24	545.13	241.18
760.26	894.09	414.17	752.23	551.26	241.26
762.12	894.10	418.19	752.24	552.01	246.28
763.04	894.10	459.01	758.04	555.05	250.13
763.06	895.02	499.09	782.18	560.17	262.07
763.16	895.19	566.10	786.28	562.03	262.26
767.26	899.12	574.22	790.09	567.04	264.09
769.06	899.18	577.07	790.24	579.06	266.07
770.12	899.28	579.18	803.05	616.02	268.01
771.22	901.02	593.09	814.09	617.24	273.10
772.11	902.01	595.15	828.23	617.25	279.14
775.14	905.10	595.18	834.13	629.11	280.16
776.01	906.17	595.21	834.28	630.10	283.03
776.17	908.02	772.01	845.13	633.17	283.08
781.20	908.22	772.21	854.17	639.20	285.28
781.21	912.18	855.09	859.25	652.07	286.18
782.19	912.21	855.22	872.14	668.28	288.03
784.26	thither	861.11	875.22	670.06	290.03
791.01	030.07	861.17	880.11	672.28	290.22
792.22	315.15	865.12	902.23	674.02	291.20
793.01	431.06	thornhill	902.27	678.17	293.05
794.27	446.01	172.20	907.18	685.19	293.28
795.27	464.11	thorns	908.21	690.14	295.02
796.02	654.26	191.16	911.04	696.14	295.17
796.09	732.23	192.01	912.04	696.20	296.05
796.15	860.08	thorny	thou	700.01	296.06
797.13	thorn	565.17	590.16	703.09	299.19
797.23	194.10	thoroughly	though	703.23	299.23
798.17	thorn-trees	060.28	008.06	717.27	302.17
798.26	283.01	206.06	018.26	721.03	302.20
802.04	thornfield	406.11	019.20	721.07	307.13
806.02	171.17	482.25	020.20	722.10	307.17
807.02	172.04	537.22	027.08	729.10	308.17

309.15	715.15	356.25	637.07	648.17	597.19
313.02	717.04	386.19	666.01	throe	613.18
323.03	732.16	624.20	669.19	683.19	627.17
327.11	732.24	626.09	687.24	throes	631.01
331.17	733.16	715.28	687.25	155.07	634.18
343.22	735.11	727.12	689.02	throne	635.14
344.26	739.22	727.25	696.05	016.11	638.04
346.27	751.03	776.13	696.11	272.02	653.26
351.10	752.18	776.15	698.15	360.08	654.20
353.10	753.10	776.17	703.06	912.05	655.14
356.14	753.24	777.04	703.20	throng	661.07
361.08	757.04	782.24	707.05	084.01	664.15
362.04	765.19	782.25	718.09	235.20	675.02
376.19	776.05	783.15	718.17	throttled	675.04
378.07	776.07	783.15	719.22	601.09	675.16
378.11	777.17	784.06	726.15	through	680.04
382.08	779.20	784.09	726.15	004.18	690.09
382.22	786.24	784.20	727.21	004.25	699.15
384.22	791.10	784.22	729.06	023.28	709.12
389.05	794.26	785.23	729.17	049.23	723.12
392.19	795.27	786.07	737.14	050.03	736.12
399.12	796.07	878.08	760.19	052.12	746.15
408.02	803.24	thousands	760.19	066.09	754.10
408.08	807.15	180.05	781.04	071.09	762.08
408.19	810.09	397.03	782.09	072.22	770.09
411.10	829.14	thrall	784.08	073.10	773.24
418.23	836.27	808.18	801.20	074.09	781.13
423.03	839.06	thread	806.01	075.04	782.12
425.21	840.14	099.04	806.03	075.25	795.22
425.22	843.11	116.16	317.22	076.05	805.08
428.22	846.16	134.04	840.23	096.08	805.08
429.16	852.16	244.09	854.13	098.11	820.17
437.19	853.25	308.20	869.12	105.07	828.18
460.12	855.12	384.28	885.23	109.06	839.09
463.02	855.19	474.11	888.14	127.16	844.03
466.01	857.23	threaded	905.19	133.25	847.11
472.04	858.22	308.21	three-tailed	142.09	849.01
479.27	859.24	856.22	546.21	142.13	852.11
480.03	860.21	threading	threshold	145.22	853.08
480.06	861.09	220.21	193.23	146.25	856.08
483.06	863.03	334.27	229.20	149.09	859.22
487.16	866.20	503.03	294.16	154.28	859.24
489.15	870.13	threads	395.18	159.08	865.27
490.24	881.20	348.24	497.20	162.13	870.05
491.03	885.27	threaped	519.13	169.12	899.22
496.02	886.10	699.05	611.06	169.20	900.09
497.04	891.17	threatened	653.18	185.16	909.20
504.07	894.11	390.09	686.27	204.06	throughout
509.14	894.15	474.27	707.17	208.25	716.15
509.16	895.07	threatening	761.02	214.26	throw
515.11	895.23	334.21	781.18	216.12	327.23
518.06	897.25	424.01	threw	221.16	386.19
518.10	897.25	threatens	342.24	233.19	561.14
519.04	901.21	469.26	361.12	236.24	672.07
519.06	thoughtful	469.26	398.10	242.04	751.16
519.27	642.22	three	436.28	248.08	755.07
521.02	677.16	007.22	450.09	248.19	793.17
534.16	839.13	008.10	577.19	261.26	820.02
535.23	thoughtless	029.05	630.02	265.13	838.11
536.05	216.25	051.19	650.25	275.28	throwing
544.27	741.25	056.16	726.12	280.13	249.02
545.14	749.08	080.28	737.17	286.02	751.15
554.02	757.03	097.08	798.18	286.03	797.27
556.04	thoughts	115.04	818.22	291.20	thrown
559.04	066.05	121.26	thrice	294.21	050.02
563.22	067.07	137.21	168.11	306.10	317.23
564.24	069.16	175.21	479.26	314.16	326.18
570.10	071.16	193.28	520.38	316.05	504.16
571.04	104.25	215.01	853.07	320.12	thrust
572.25	106.06	219.03	thrift	333.03	013.04
573.15	109.25	228.12	148.06	333.26	025.13
574.12	163.01	237.10	thrill	335.17	043.08
574.13	182.16	241.04	153.16	335.25	063.06
574.24	235.19	246.16	420.04	340.28	063.06
576.07	250.16	267.19	426.03	342.06	114.17
598.05	252.02	267.19	528.20	361.13	141.20
604.17	264.25	317.06	749.24	389.01	268.16
604.21	270.06	326.23	thrilled	389.12	545.19
604.25	273.06	327.10	062.19	390.25	578.21
606.23	306.25	327.13	217.04	404.10	592.21
613.06	320.10	334.23	621.02	414.08	610.06
625.08	325.22	339.22	716.14	415.15	656.05
626.09	391.23	343.28	781.26	418.07	846.28
636.08	398.14	344.04	814.27	423.07	thrusting
639.21	424.12	355.06	844.13	434.18	008.11
642.25	436.05	364.04	849.01	439.07	112.01
642.26	481.02	370.15	thrilling	443.02	600.17
651.22	491.08	383.12	775.13	460.05	684.04
651.24	497.09	391.02	844.01	492.16	thule
652.23	505.17	409.26	thriving	508.22	004.03
653.12	539.21	415.12	446.20	513.11	thumb
653.27	566.14	424.08	throat	513.14	649.13
654.06	566.18	424.09	084.11	514.17	thumped
655.01	568.22	426.13	127.12	514.25	281.16
655.16	582.21	432.01	344.14	519.11	thunder
655.19	583.01	444.03	470.01	522.04	520.04
655.20	640.01	446.19	601.04	523.25	592.07
659.17	689.05	447.08	610.01	526.26	thunder-storm
660.10	696.18	447.20	634.08	544.01	541.22
660.27	703.27	448.07	665.07	547.08	thunderbolt
662.03	722.09	453.14	throb	550.23	425.23
663.18	742.23	474.06	065.03	551.10	737.07
664.02	753.19	474.10	167.17	558.16	thundered
670.02	782.13	482.22	182.25	560.11	631.02
674.09	782.14	491.17	848.28	561.21	thundering
681.06	822.09	522.11	throbbed	575.02	560.10
684.03	841.20	559.11	607.20	576.21	631.13
687.15	896.01	593.23	throbbing	589.08	thunderloft
696.25	899.24	597.11	378.05	589.20	531.13
713.06	thousand	598.11	throbs	594.11	thursday
713.07	267.20	601.01	623.05	597.11	117.16

145.02
171.08
326.24
328.11
330.27
792.12
795.03
854.28
thus
010.06
020.03
047.14
048.13
049.22
074.01
074.02
090.10
115.13
118.15
133.22
135.22
142.11
147.22
161.22
162.13
168.17
171.23
211.26
217.01
224.21
236.19
263.11
285.01
286.11
323.22
329.03
354.13
418.07
426.02
476.07
462.09
463.09
463.23
488.10
498.24
505.05
554.19
555.03
611.28
621.11
623.09
629.15
631.08
631.21
645.11
661.20
668.18
668.24
714.04
740.28
742.05
746.14
747.20
756.19
756.20
762.20
803.01
803.25
807.17
837.21
858.19
877.09
888.12
888.19
907.01
thwarted
018.25
213.14
224.16
555.03
thy
590.16
850.07
850.07
tick
677.25
ticked
758.11
tide
361.16
550.24
tideless
857.09
tidings
447.27
535.03
726.03
810.16
tidy
049.12
693.12
tidying
032.12
tie
022.01
325.09
361.22
631.28
659.14
704.05
822.13

894.24
tied
013.08
084.12
093.01
099.16
250.27
318.16
326.17
340.14
368.12
394.07
397.19
653.05
665.07
tiens
264.22
tiens-toi
256.08
ties
719.28
786.13
793.19
tigers
374.20
tightly
283.09
510.26
tigress
428.06
till
024.19
032.05
035.15
035.23
037.13
039.11
046.13
068.23
077.28
094.13
099.08
114.19
113.05
139.15
141.16
145.19
143.16
151.23
156.14
157.24
160.14
165.25
166.07
170.28
189.13
197.20
203.09
211.27
218.28
220.08
222.22
223.17
225.15
250.03
250.03
254.10
277.13
290.04
297.21
299.01
302.18
336.14
340.08
340.21
361.15
361.16
371.22
379.17
381.23
382.10
384.23
386.04
386.28
390.27
392.18
402.03
408.02
409.11
417.12
428.17
433.16
436.11
439.19
464.04
466.27
467.05
475.25
487.06
508.07
519.03
521.05
527.05
546.24
548.07
548.07
548.09
558.01
559.17
565.15
569.15

603.25
604.21
653.26
655.08
681.21
702.14
704.26
709.02
718.14
723.01
740.04
761.01
763.04
778.11
782.19
787.21
791.26
795.09
800.07
800.18
800.19
811.04
819.24
822.17
823.15
838.21
855.14
865.22
867.14
885.10
894.10
907.05
tillage
720.16
timber
209.05
541.23
870.02
time
002.05
010.17
013.03
027.17
032.19
032.27
033.02
035.25
037.01
040.18
042.17
060.16
061.19
065.18
074.19
077.06
079.14
081.11
081.13
083.11
099.06
099.06
108.24
109.26
112.11
113.24
116.24
117.05
117.05
118.05
121.24
122.23
122.28
126.04
136.07
140.26
147.03
148.28
149.12
151.01
151.24
152.17
152.18
153.23
153.27
156.17
158.13
161.23
162.08
162.11
163.18
164.27
166.20
170.08
181.04
183.27
188.21
188.26
189.02
193.19
205.13
207.04
207.04
208.15
223.01
227.18
230.03
239.23
240.15
241.13
246.26
246.27

252.14
259.12
265.25
273.03
275.23
287.15
293.19
299.11
301.23
308.02
311.10
328.12
328.13
329.10
331.25
332.07
333.13
333.28
336.08
340.12
347.04
361.08
363.05
380.17
381.18
382.14
390.13
392.08
402.01
410.10
413.05
418.12
419.11
429.23
432.19
433.08
433.08
439.13
439.19
448.02
452.05
455.14
465.08
468.14
473.26
474.04
475.19
484.20
485.20
488.14
489.05
494.03
500.05
507.08
510.05
510.20
515.03
519.27
522.24
529.26
541.10
546.24
549.02
549.16
550.01
550.01
553.07
553.08
553.24
557.09
558.02
561.07
562.07
566.10
572.06
579.01
579.02
582.19
589.12
596.23
603.16
604.18
609.02
619.14
619.23
620.10
621.16
621.17
627.08
631.14
635.14
637.26
638.11
640.03
642.06
643.09
644.05
658.07
660.01
664.02
671.03
679.16
683.19
683.11
689.10
698.16
699.12
707.06
707.18
710.03
711.10

714.12
716.01
722.05
731.17
733.21
734.11
736.08
743.04
750.21
755.08
756.14
757.15
758.09
759.01
771.07
778.07
787.12
789.02
795.24
799.19
802.04
805.27
807.03
817.11
819.01
823.16
828.27
831.04
839.22
846.10
847.12
848.01
853.23
860.21
861.19
863.13
881.03
882.14
886.02
892.21
901.25
905.12
905.20
906.03
906.20
907.03
908.02
910.16
time-piece
562.13
569.16
time-stained
589.09
times
007.22
042.11
061.01
086.02
140.05
150.19
180.16
291.26
355.06
383.13
404.21
407.05
409.26
415.12
448.21
458.10
464.25
474.06
505.09
537.16
648.08
670.20
718.01
744.23
779.16
835.22
843.23
847.07
883.25
884.28
timid
761.05
857.24
timorous
858.24
tin-plated
094.02
tinge
249.15
752.11
tinkle
220.22
350.26
tinkled
080.28
366.20
tinkler
388.04
tint
139.14
221.04
221.04
277.25
673.28
738.05
752.08
764.08

808.15
tinted
501.12
799.01
tints
031.04
248.04
248.16
249.27
322.07
812.12
tiny
017.25
031.26
049.17
431.16
639.08
733.05
812.15
tiolettes
327.25
tip-toe
277.15
tirade
478.05
tire
563.23
tired
045.26
077.01
077.01
079.25
150.03
150.15
158.13
165.13
190.04
218.12
230.08
251.10
280.13
362.22
393.22
458.05
541.11
542.01
575.08
604.19
612.22
637.06
665.21
666.23
679.21
766.25
800.07
804.23
885.23
tiresome
019.09
040.12
381.10
tiresomely
806.23
tissue
256.15
title
089.28
090.21
478.12
titled
343.26
473.07
titter
388.19
tittered
589.08
titters
392.03
to
001.17
002.07
002.12
003.08
003.08
003.18
003.28
004.21
004.23
004.24
005.06
005.14
005.18
005.19
005.20
006.08
006.17
006.25
006.27
007.09
007.16
007.18
007.18
007.21
008.02
008.09
008.09
008.26
008.27
009.05
009.07

009.10	033.22	050.09	068.17	090.21	108.16
009.10	033.25	050.16	068.18	090.25	108.19
009.13	033.26	050.23	068.19	090.26	108.21
009.15	034.02	051.06	068.20	090.27	108.21
009.20	035.04	051.06	068.22	091.04	109.02
010.06	035.10	051.07	068.26	092.06	109.04
010.09	035.11	051.12	069.02	092.08	109.04
010.26	035.17	051.20	069.03	092.09	109.05
011.04	036.02	051.21	069.14	092.10	109.07
012.05	036.12	051.23	069.17	092.10	109.07
012.09	036.12	052.01	069.18	092.16	109.08
012.11	036.13	052.01	069.22	092.23	109.09
012.16	036.17	052.01	071.10	093.01	109.12
013.05	036.21	052.02	071.14	093.11	109.13
013.11	037.05	052.14	071.17	093.24	109.21
013.17	037.05	052.20	072.06	094.04	109.24
013.26	037.08	052.20	072.07	094.08	109.24
014.07	037.09	052.21	072.09	094.11	109.25
014.08	037.10	052.23	072.11	094.18	110.05
014.09	037.11	053.10	072.11	094.19	111.05
014.10	037.12	053.16	072.15	094.23	111.13
014.10	037.17	053.16	072.21	094.28	111.13
014.11	037.22	053.22	073.09	094.28	111.14
014.11	037.22	054.07	073.17	096.04	111.15
014.12	037.24	054.11	073.22	096.11	112.06
014.18	037.25	054.12	073.25	096.13	112.14
014.20	038.04	054.14	073.28	097.03	112.20
014.23	038.04	054.22	074.02	097.04	112.20
014.23	038.06	054.25	074.06	097.05	112.24
014.23	038.09	055.03	074.07	097.07	112.24
014.24	038.09	055.24	074.11	097.11	113.04
014.26	038.09	055.25	074.13	097.13	113.10
015.11	038.10	055.27	075.02	097.25	113.14
015.18	038.10	056.05	075.04	097.26	113.17
015.18	038.14	056.05	076.15	097.28	113.28
016.15	038.20	056.06	076.23	098.01	114.01
016.16	038.21	056.09	076.27	098.16	114.02
016.19	038.21	056.11	077.05	098.19	114.04
017.04	038.25	056.12	077.07	099.04	114.09
017.07	039.03	056.13	077.07	099.05	114.17
017.10	039.12	056.16	077.09	099.06	114.19
017.15	039.16	056.21	077.27	099.10	114.24
017.16	039.16	056.22	077.27	099.17	115.01
018.02	039.20	056.23	078.08	099.22	115.07
018.07	039.21	056.24	078.09	100.14	115.12
018.08	039.27	056.27	078.18	100.15	115.12
018.17	039.27	057.03	078.18	101.01	115.27
018.17	040.01	057.06	078.19	101.11	116.04
018.23	040.05	057.09	079.06	101.12	116.10
018.23	040.06	057.14	079.07	101.12	116.12
018.24	040.11	057.17	079.18	101.13	116.19
019.04	040.18	057.21	079.19	101.13	116.20
019.08	041.05	057.25	079.26	101.15	116.23
019.10	041.11	057.26	079.26	101.26	116.24
019.10	042.04	057.28	079.28	102.07	116.25
019.15	042.05	057.28	080.04	102.08	116.27
019.22	042.09	058.07	080.09	102.09	117.05
020.11	042.15	058.10	080.26	102.12	117.07
020.13	042.16	058.14	081.01	102.22	117.12
020.16	043.01	059.10	081.05	102.23	117.15
020.26	043.07	059.18	081.09	102.24	117.16
020.28	043.07	059.21	081.15	102.25	117.20
021.02	043.13	059.24	081.15	102.28	117.24
021.12	043.19	059.25	081.16	103.01	118.04
021.13	043.20	060.01	081.21	103.01	118.08
021.16	043.25	060.01	081.25	103.05	118.08
021.21	043.26	060.08	082.23	103.06	118.09
022.02	044.04	061.02	083.01	103.07	118.14
022.03	044.10	061.04	083.11	103.08	118.17
022.04	044.12	061.08	083.11	103.14	118.17
022.05	044.16	061.10	083.22	103.17	118.19
022.14	045.17	061.12	083.27	103.19	118.23
022.17	045.20	061.20	084.05	103.20	118.24
022.26	045.22	061.24	084.13	103.26	118.24
023.02	045.22	061.25	084.19	103.26	118.26
023.03	045.24	061.26	084.28	103.27	118.27
023.04	045.27	062.01	085.06	104.06	119.01
023.10	046.01	062.08	085.13	104.11	119.11
023.22	046.02	062.11	085.14	104.11	119.11
024.12	046.06	062.13	086.01	104.17	119.14
024.19	046.10	062.16	086.08	104.19	119.16
024.27	046.10	062.18	086.14	104.21	120.01
027.06	046.15	062.23	086.14	104.26	120.08
027.07	046.17	063.08	086.14	105.02	120.10
027.08	046.20	063.18	086.25	105.09	120.13
027.20	046.23	063.18	087.01	105.09	120.14
027.24	046.25	063.25	087.01	105.11	120.14
028.06	047.03	064.01	087.09	105.17	120.17
028.09	047.07	064.05	087.12	105.23	120.22
028.13	047.08	064.15	087.13	105.23	120.22
028.27	047.14	064.18	087.16	105.28	120.23
029.02	047.19	064.19	087.18	106.01	120.25
029.16	048.03	064.20	087.24	106.04	121.14
029.17	048.07	065.01	088.01	106.08	121.16
029.18	048.08	065.24	088.14	106.10	121.17
030.03	048.09	066.03	088.16	106.12	121.18
030.08	048.12	066.11	088.17	106.18	121.18
030.11	048.19	066.24	088.18	106.19	121.27
030.12	048.20	066.28	088.21	106.19	121.28
030.20	048.23	067.11	088.24	106.20	122.13
030.22	048.28	067.12	088.26	106.27	122.20
030.23	048.28	067.17	088.28	106.28	122.21
030.23	049.09	067.21	089.18	107.05	122.23
030.27	049.12	067.24	089.19	107.09	122.24
031.07	049.14	068.03	089.21	107.23	122.28
031.12	049.14	068.06	090.02	107.28	123.03
031.17	049.17	068.07	090.03	108.01	123.04
031.18	049.20	068.14	090.05	108.06	123.06
032.05	050.01	068.15	090.05	108.11	123.08
033.14	050.05		090.10	108.15	123.11
033.18			090.12		123.17

123.19	142.12	161.27	180.15	198.20	218.01
123.25	142.12	162.04	180.17	199.11	218.08
124.01	142.15	162.08	180.23	199.13	218.14
124.09	142.18	162.15	180.24	199.15	218.16
124.13	142.19	162.22	180.24	199.23	218.16
124.15	142.24	162.23	180.25	200.04	218.22
124.21	142.25	162.27	180.25	200.04	218.24
125.02	142.28	163.04	181.12	200.05	219.01
125.06	143.10	163.05	181.18	200.05	219.14
125.07	143.13	163.06	182.04	200.06	219.22
125.08	144.07	163.14	182.07	200.07	219.23
125.10	144.08	163.18	182.08	200.08	221.08
125.14	144.14	163.19	182.08	200.08	221.13
125.24	145.17	164.02	182.09	200.11	221.16
125.28	145.26	164.05	182.11	200.15	221.24
126.07	146.04	164.12	182.13	200.19	222.03
126.08	146.14	164.13	182.13	200.20	222.09
126.17	146.15	164.15	182.17	200.21	222.14
126.20	147.01	164.19	182.18	200.22	222.16
126.21	147.07	164.21	182.20	201.10	222.24
126.23	147.09	164.26	182.22	201.17	222.26
126.24	147.12	165.01	182.27	201.19	222.27
126.27	147.16	165.02	183.16	201.20	222.28
126.28	147.17	165.05	183.17	201.23	223.08
127.04	147.19	165.06	183.20	201.27	223.12
127.09	147.27	165.24	183.25	202.02	223.13
127.24	148.11	165.27	183.28	202.05	223.23
128.05	148.12	165.28	183.28	202.07	224.21
128.11	148.23	166.02	184.11	202.10	224.24
129.04	148.26	166.20	184.19	202.23	225.06
129.04	148.28	166.20	184.20	202.24	225.09
129.08	149.04	166.23	185.01	203.02	225.12
129.10	149.08	166.27	185.07	203.02	225.12
129.12	149.11	167.04	185.17	203.04	225.16
129.14	149.19	167.09	186.02	203.05	225.19
129.14	149.20	167.09	186.05	203.06	225.24
129.15	149.23	167.15	186.14	203.07	225.25
129.16	149.24	167.22	186.18	203.08	225.28
130.02	150.03	167.26	186.19	203.09	226.20
130.02	150.05	168.04	186.21	203.11	226.26
130.03	150.08	168.05	186.24	203.12	226.28
130.11	150.09	168.07	186.27	203.27	227.07
130.21	150.15	168.17	187.01	204.03	227.08
130.27	150.24	168.18	187.10	204.03	227.09
131.04	151.02	168.23	187.11	204.05	227.10
131.13	151.07	168.24	187.24	204.08	227.11
131.26	151.08	169.05	188.02	204.27	227.12
132.07	151.16	169.05	188.04	204.27	227.13
132.06	151.21	169.05	188.10	205.01	227.21
132.10	151.26	169.15	188.20	205.06	227.22
132.11	152.10	169.18	188.21	205.07	227.22
132.11	152.11	169.26	188.23	205.13	227.23
132.24	152.12	170.01	188.26	205.17	227.25
133.05	152.13	170.09	189.04	206.02	227.27
133.09	152.15	170.17	189.12	206.04	228.01
133.09	152.27	170.21	189.14	206.12	228.09
133.17	152.28	170.22	189.14	206.15	228.21
133.17	153.03	170.22	189.23	206.21	228.25
133.20	153.08	170.23	189.25	206.24	228.26
133.28	153.08	171.10	190.06	207.03	229.05
134.04	153.09	171.10	190.09	207.04	229.11
134.08	153.14	171.15	190.14	207.16	229.19
134.10	153.14	171.16	190.16	208.04	229.20
134.19	153.17	171.26	190.22	208.22	229.20
134.19	153.21	172.06	190.27	208.24	229.21
134.26	153.23	172.13	191.12	208.25	229.21
135.01	153.26	172.13	191.21	209.17	229.22
135.01	154.01	172.24	191.28	209.18	229.23
135.03	154.02	172.25	192.03	209.22	229.25
135.07	154.04	172.26	192.09	209.25	229.26
135.09	154.14	173.05	192.11	209.26	230.03
135.14	154.27	173.08	192.12	210.06	230.05
135.15	155.04	173.09	192.14	210.12	230.06
135.27	155.05	173.12	192.15	211.01	230.09
135.28	155.08	173.13	192.18	211.20	230.11
136.02	155.14	173.18	192.19	212.01	230.19
136.11	155.16	173.19	192.24	213.03	230.19
136.13	155.18	173.27	192.25	213.04	230.22
136.16	156.03	174.06	193.01	213.06	230.25
136.21	156.06	174.07	193.03	213.12	231.02
136.28	156.13	174.11	193.20	214.05	231.17
137.06	156.15	174.11	193.21	214.06	231.20
137.11	156.16	174.12	193.26	214.12	231.28
137.15	156.20	174.12	194.07	214.13	232.03
137.16	156.22	174.13	194.17	214.14	232.05
138.04	157.02	174.16	194.25	214.17	232.25
138.06	157.06	174.18	195.01	214.20	232.26
138.11	157.10	174.18	195.04	214.26	233.03
138.13	157.13	174.23	195.11	215.16	233.05
138.14	157.16	174.28	195.22	215.20	233.05
138.16	157.18	175.04	195.27	215.21	233.07
138.23	157.25	175.05	195.28	215.24	233.08
138.26	157.25	175.25	196.01	215.26	233.16
138.27	157.25	176.08	196.02	216.01	234.03
139.06	158.02	176.18	196.03	216.01	234.04
139.07	158.05	176.23	196.08	216.06	234.05
139.25	158.10	177.03	196.10	216.06	234.07
139.28	158.16	177.05	196.16	216.09	234.08
140.01	158.23	177.05	196.17	216.14	234.11
140.13	159.03	177.19	197.03	216.21	234.14
140.21	159.10	177.22	197.07	216.22	235.03
140.25	159.11	178.07	197.09	216.22	235.04
141.06	159.13	178.08	197.10	216.23	235.06
141.08	160.03	178.10	197.10	216.25	235.08
141.09	160.05	178.17	197.13	216.26	235.09
141.19	160.06	178.26	197.22	217.10	235.12
141.26	160.10	179.15	198.04	217.14	235.14
141.28	161.05	179.23	198.08	217.16	235.20
142.01	161.06	179.24	198.12	217.18	235.25
142.05	161.12	179.27	198.20	217.25	236.03
142.06	161.20	179.28			
		180.03			

236.07	260.03	276.26	298.08	324.06	341.12
236.12	260.07	278.04	298.26	324.06	341.15
236.18	260.07	279.04	298.27	324.08	341.15
236.19	260.07	279.07	299.03	324.11	341.17
237.19	260.11	279.13	299.13	324.12	341.17
238.01	260.19	279.16	300.18	324.16	341.28
238.02	261.09	280.06	300.19	324.19	342.03
238.03	261.14	280.06	300.25	325.03	342.16
238.14	261.15	280.08	301.13	325.04	342.18
238.17	261.18	280.09	301.27	325.08	343.01
238.18	261.21	280.10	302.05	325.13	344.15
238.22	262.05	280.14	303.03	325.14	345.04
238.26	262.08	280.20	305.03	325.23	345.09
238.28	262.08	280.22	305.05	326.02	345.12
239.01	262.18	280.23	305.05	326.07	345.23
239.04	262.24	281.03	305.11	326.08	346.09
239.23	263.02	281.26	305.13	326.11	346.17
239.25	263.05	281.28	306.01	326.16	346.22
239.27	263.10	282.09	306.03	326.18	346.28
240.09	263.21	282.10	306.04	326.19	347.02
240.11	263.22	282.18	306.07	326.21	347.03
240.11	263.23	282.21	306.08	326.27	347.06
240.18	263.24	283.08	306.09	327.02	347.19
240.22	264.04	283.09	306.11	327.02	347.24
241.01	264.06	283.13	306.14	327.08	348.15
241.02	264.08	283.16	306.15	327.14	348.20
241.19	264.13	283.26	306.19	327.23	348.23
242.24	264.18	284.08	306.28	327.24	348.24
243.01	264.24	284.08	307.03	327.26	349.03
243.03	264.24	284.09	307.05	327.26	349.06
243.04	264.25	284.17	307.13	328.07	349.09
243.05	265.01	284.18	307.23	328.09	349.10
243.10	265.03	284.19	308.01	328.11	349.17
244.22	265.07	284.19	308.03	328.14	349.24
244.22	265.09	284.27	308.06	328.17	350.03
244.23	265.12	284.28	308.07	328.20	350.04
245.02	265.21	285.02	309.06	328.22	350.08
245.10	265.24	285.06	309.10	328.28	350.09
245.14	266.01	285.10	309.11	329.01	351.03
246.10	266.04	285.12	309.15	329.03	351.04
246.11	266.07	285.13	309.22	329.13	351.05
246.14	266.08	285.17	309.26	329.17	351.06
246.19	266.15	285.20	309.28	329.27	351.07
246.26	266.21	285.22	310.02	330.02	351.09
247.19	266.27	285.28	310.03	330.04	351.09
248.16	267.05	286.06	310.04	330.05	351.12
249.21	267.08	286.06	310.14	330.06	351.16
249.21	267.09	286.07	310.15	330.08	351.17
250.01	267.22	286.12	310.18	330.11	351.18
250.05	267.23	286.27	310.25	330.24	351.19
250.11	267.27	287.01	311.12	331.08	351.27
250.15	268.03	287.05	311.26	331.14	351.27
250.16	268.08	287.10	312.07	331.15	352.12
250.22	268.11	287.18	312.17	331.15	352.26
251.02	268.13	287.19	312.22	331.18	353.03
251.03	268.15	287.23	313.01	331.19	353.13
251.04	268.16	288.11	313.04	331.19	353.14
251.06	269.02	288.13	313.21	331.21	353.18
251.11	269.04	288.16	314.11	331.22	353.26
251.13	269.12	288.20	314.13	331.24	353.28
251.16	269.12	288.24	314.16	332.02	354.21
251.22	269.13	288.26	314.16	332.09	354.28
251.23	269.14	289.03	314.22	332.09	355.11
252.02	269.15	289.06	314.22	332.12	355.12
252.15	269.18	289.17	314.23	332.16	355.14
252.19	269.19	289.20	314.24	332.17	355.15
252.22	269.24	289.23	314.25	333.06	355.17
252.23	269.24	289.24	315.07	333.10	355.25
252.26	270.08	289.25	315.13	333.11	355.27
253.02	270.10	289.27	315.15	333.16	356.03
253.07	270.15	290.02	315.17	333.17	356.04
253.21	270.18	290.04	315.27	334.14	356.07
253.23	270.20	290.10	316.11	334.17	356.12
254.06	270.26	290.20	316.18	335.07	356.19
254.08	271.10	290.21	316.22	335.08	357.03
254.09	271.10	290.22	316.28	335.28	357.16
254.12	271.25	290.23	317.12	336.04	357.28
254.13	271.28	291.03	317.24	336.08	358.11
255.01	272.07	291.05	317.25	336.10	358.17
255.04	272.13	291.11	317.26	336.13	358.20
255.06	272.14	291.11	319.06	336.15	358.25
255.07	272.16	291.11	319.06	336.16	359.03
255.12	272.23	291.26	319.17	336.18	359.09
255.15	272.27	292.03	320.01	336.25	359.11
255.17	273.01	292.03	320.03	336.27	359.18
255.19	273.02	292.04	320.03	337.05	359.23
255.23	273.04	292.11	320.11	337.12	359.27
256.10	273.06	292.16	320.23	337.21	359.28
256.11	273.09	292.18	321.03	337.25	360.07
256.19	273.20	292.18	321.08	337.25	360.22
256.20	273.26	292.20	321.11	338.05	360.25
256.26	274.04	292.21	321.16	338.09	360.26
256.26	274.07	293.09	321.17	338.19	361.08
257.05	274.19	293.14	321.18	338.19	361.14
257.06	274.20	294.05	321.19	338.20	361.22
257.06	274.27	294.14	321.22	338.21	361.26
257.08	274.27	294.16	321.25	338.23	362.02
257.11	275.09	294.21	322.11	338.27	362.07
257.13	275.13	295.08	322.14	338.28	362.20
257.13	275.17	295.09	322.26	339.10	363.02
257.15	275.21	295.14	323.01	339.10	363.09
257.19	275.23	295.18	323.09	339.25	363.09
257.28	275.24	295.19	323.17	339.25	365.03
257.28	276.06	295.24	323.18	340.04	365.04
257.28	276.06	295.26	323.20	340.05	365.15
258.05	276.07	295.27	323.21	340.07	365.24
258.09	276.08	296.17	323.23	340.07	365.28
258.21	276.09	296.20	323.23	340.16	366.04
259.17	276.12	297.15	323.26	340.16	366.09
259.27	276.23	298.04	324.05	340.19	366.10
260.02	276.25	298.06		340.27	

366.15	387.03	409.24	437.12	461.01	477.05
366.16	387.19	409.28	437.22	461.19	477.05
367.12	387.22	410.16	438.03	461.21	477.07
367.25	387.22	410.20	438.13	461.26	477.09
368.21	388.01	410.21	438.15	461.27	477.17
368.24	388.01	411.07	438.22	462.03	477.20
368.24	388.02	411.12	438.23	462.17	477.23
368.26	388.02	411.16	438.28	462.21	477.25
368.26	388.08	411.18	439.11	462.26	478.02
368.28	388.10	412.02	439.13	463.02	478.11
370.05	388.17	412.02	439.14	463.09	478.11
370.10	389.05	412.09	440.06	463.12	478.12
370.22	389.12	412.10	440.07	463.13	479.01
370.26	389.17	412.13	440.08	463.18	479.06
371.12	389.28	412.23	440.09	463.19	479.09
371.15	390.01	412.24	440.15	463.20	479.15
371.20	390.08	413.05	440.15	463.23	479.16
371.21	390.16	414.02	440.25	463.24	479.24
372.01	390.17	414.03	440.25	463.27	480.01
372.04	390.20	414.06	441.07	464.01	480.07
372.08	390.24	414.13	441.08	464.03	480.10
372.12	390.26	414.17	441.18	464.05	480.11
372.18	391.02	416.08	441.19	464.08	480.15
372.18	391.15	416.19	442.03	464.10	480.20
372.21	391.21	417.14	442.17	464.16	480.25
372.22	392.01	417.16	442.18	464.16	481.02
372.23	392.17	417.17	442.19	464.17	481.07
372.25	392.23	417.19	443.07	464.25	481.09
373.02	393.04	417.20	444.04	464.25	481.12
373.10	394.12	417.23	444.11	464.28	481.16
373.16	394.15	417.25	444.16	465.01	481.21
373.19	394.20	417.25	444.18	465.01	481.24
374.04	395.14	417.28	444.19	465.11	481.25
374.08	395.16	417.28	445.03	465.13	481.26
374.16	395.24	418.09	445.04	465.14	481.27
374.17	396.04	418.10	445.15	466.01	481.28
374.27	396.16	418.14	445.18	466.14	482.04
374.28	396.18	418.22	446.13	466.14	482.11
375.06	396.19	418.23	446.15	466.15	482.12
375.06	396.21	418.26	447.08	466.15	482.13
375.07	396.23	419.03	447.17	466.16	482.14
375.19	396.26	420.07	447.20	466.20	482.14
375.19	397.03	420.11	447.21	466.20	482.16
375.25	397.08	420.20	447.21	466.23	482.17
376.05	397.13	420.21	448.09	466.24	482.19
376.05	397.16	421.02	448.10	466.27	482.25
376.06	397.20	421.18	448.15	467.04	482.26
376.09	397.21	421.28	448.18	467.08	483.01
376.19	398.04	422.04	448.23	467.19	483.25
376.25	398.05	422.08	448.25	467.25	483.27
377.01	398.12	422.09	448.26	467.27	484.05
377.02	398.24	422.10	449.01	468.06	484.08
377.04	398.27	422.11	449.04	468.13	484.09
377.09	398.28	422.16	449.05	468.13	484.10
377.11	399.03	422.19	449.12	468.19	484.13
377.14	399.08	422.23	449.17	468.21	484.13
377.15	399.10	423.04	449.22	468.22	484.21
377.16	399.24	423.06	449.25	468.26	484.22
377.28	400.02	424.04	450.07	468.27	484.22
378.06	400.03	424.05	450.16	469.07	484.24
378.07	400.06	425.04	450.16	469.10	485.09
378.07	400.10	425.11	450.17	469.11	485.09
378.17	400.11	425.22	450.21	469.19	485.13
378.21	400.20	426.10	450.27	469.25	485.17
379.01	400.24	426.17	451.20	470.02	485.19
379.03	400.25	427.02	451.25	470.03	485.21
379.05	400.26	427.03	452.03	470.04	485.28
379.06	401.05	427.07	452.06	470.05	486.10
379.10	401.11	427.10	452.08	470.05	487.04
379.12	401.18	427.14	452.10	470.18	487.06
379.12	401.26	427.15	452.17	470.19	487.06
379.15	401.27	428.19	452.21	470.21	487.09
379.16	402.10	428.23	453.21	470.26	487.18
379.17	402.12	428.24	453.23	471.01	487.19
379.18	402.26	429.01	453.26	471.10	488.03
379.19	402.27	429.07	453.28	471.11	488.08
379.21	402.28	429.13	453.28	471.17	488.10
379.28	403.01	429.16	454.03	471.27	488.13
380.05	403.05	429.22	454.07	472.19	488.13
380.11	403.11	430.04	454.08	472.19	488.15
380.21	403.16	430.15	454.16	472.20	488.20
380.28	403.18	430.16	455.06	472.23	488.21
380.28	403.19	430.21	455.12	472.26	488.24
381.03	403.27	430.27	455.12	473.15	489.06
381.12	404.11	431.13	455.13	473.18	489.07
381.15	404.15	431.21	455.15	473.22	489.08
381.22	404.17	431.27	455.22	473.26	489.09
382.05	404.21	432.12	456.02	473.27	489.14
382.17	404.22	432.15	456.12	473.27	489.15
382.28	404.25	432.16	456.14	473.28	489.27
383.17	405.03	432.18	456.22	474.02	489.27
384.01	405.04	433.08	456.24	474.10	490.10
384.02	405.06	433.12	457.03	474.13	490.10
384.03	405.07	433.15	458.02	474.17	490.11
384.04	405.10	433.18	458.06	474.17	490.13
384.05	405.13	434.03	458.06	474.18	490.14
384.24	405.26	434.09	458.08	474.19	490.14
385.01	406.04	434.09	458.15	474.21	490.15
385.02	406.04	434.16	458.19	474.23	490.15
385.06	406.04	434.23	458.20	474.26	490.17
385.15	406.05	435.13	458.24	475.01	490.19
385.17	406.09	435.17	458.28	475.03	490.20
385.18	406.19	436.06	459.07	475.19	491.12
385.21	406.24	436.12	459.07	475.23	491.13
385.22	407.27	436.13	459.09	475.27	491.18
385.27	407.28	436.24	459.13	476.09	491.19
386.02	408.04	436.25	459.20	476.10	491.23
386.05	408.15	437.04	459.07	476.13	492.01
386.08	408.23	437.04	459.13	476.15	492.08
386.18	409.18	437.08	460.10	476.24	492.10
386.19	409.18	437.12		476.27	492.11

492.15	508.23	528.17	545.06	568.15	598.17
493.02	509.03	528.21	545.10	568.16	598.18
493.03	509.13	529.12	545.11	568.20	598.24
493.04	509.15	529.14	545.19	568.24	599.01
493.04	509.17	529.19	545.23	569.21	599.03
493.05	509.24	530.01	546.01	569.23	600.01
493.08	509.24	530.02	546.10	570.13	600.03
493.09	509.27	530.04	546.13	570.19	600.20
493.15	510.05	530.09	546.17	570.24	600.24
493.23	510.06	530.21	546.18	571.03	601.05
493.28	510.06	530.22	546.18	571.05	601.15
494.03	510.13	531.01	546.24	571.13	601.18
494.04	510.15	531.02	546.27	571.24	601.22
494.17	510.16	531.07	547.05	572.06	601.23
494.24	510.18	531.19	547.08	572.08	601.25
494.25	510.18	531.24	547.18	572.09	602.13
494.27	510.23	531.25	548.01	572.16	602.14
494.28	510.26	531.25	548.14	572.23	602.17
495.01	511.04	532.11	548.21	573.01	602.19
495.05	511.07	532.14	548.22	573.02	603.02
495.07	511.12	532.21	548.26	573.03	603.03
495.18	511.13	532.27	549.04	573.09	603.04
495.20	511.14	532.27	549.04	573.17	603.10
495.27	511.15	533.15	549.05	574.04	603.14
495.27	511.17	533.22	549.09	574.09	603.14
496.01	511.21	533.24	549.13	574.11	603.16
496.04	511.21	533.26	549.15	574.16	603.17
496.04	511.21	533.27	549.18	575.14	603.18
496.05	511.22	534.01	549.23	575.24	603.23
496.07	511.23	534.01	549.26	576.05	604.01
496.07	512.02	534.04	550.13	576.11	604.04
496.12	512.06	534.07	550.15	577.05	604.06
496.12	512.26	534.09	550.17	577.09	604.11
496.13	512.27	534.10	550.19	577.20	604.14
496.17	512.27	534.10	551.02	577.24	604.14
496.26	513.01	534.23	551.03	578.19	604.15
497.02	513.09	535.04	552.02	578.22	605.08
497.05	513.10	535.11	552.10	579.07	606.20
497.09	513.11	535.11	552.10	579.23	606.21
497.14	513.19	535.15	552.21	579.24	606.24
497.18	513.23	535.20	552.23	580.05	607.08
497.21	513.24	535.22	553.06	580.07	607.09
497.21	513.24	535.26	553.15	580.10	607.12
497.22	514.01	536.08	553.20	580.12	607.15
497.24	514.02	536.13	553.24	580.15	607.18
498.01	514.09	536.27	553.26	580.16	607.18
498.02	514.17	537.02	554.03	580.21	607.19
498.13	514.17	537.03	554.10	580.24	607.25
498.20	514.26	537.05	554.12	581.03	608.02
498.21	515.01	537.08	554.12	581.08	608.04
498.26	515.05	537.08	554.14	581.09	608.04
499.04	515.07	537.18	554.21	581.09	609.05
499.09	515.10	537.19	555.04	581.13	609.18
499.15	515.16	537.24	555.14	581.24	610.06
499.16	516.02	538.08	555.19	582.02	610.13
499.16	516.02	538.12	555.24	582.02	610.23
499.19	516.05	538.15	555.24	582.05	610.23
499.22	516.10	538.17	556.01	582.14	610.24
499.22	516.13	538.19	557.07	582.14	611.03
499.24	516.22	539.06	557.10	582.15	611.16
499.24	516.24	539.12	557.13	582.18	611.24
499.25	517.09	539.16	557.17	582.22	611.28
499.27	517.17	539.21	557.18	583.05	612.02
499.28	517.19	539.27	558.03	583.23	612.25
500.03	517.24	539.28	558.04	584.05	612.26
500.04	517.24	540.04	558.07	584.05	613.01
500.10	518.03	540.08	558.09	585.02	613.06
500.11	518.04	540.11	558.12	585.05	613.09
501.08	518.09	540.11	558.23	585.07	613.19
501.17	518.10	540.13	559.10	586.07	614.08
502.27	519.20	540.13	559.13	586.14	614.11
503.19	520.08	540.18	559.15	586.24	614.12
503.24	520.09	540.23	559.15	586.24	614.13
503.25	520.13	540.26	559.18	587.06	614.14
503.27	521.13	541.03	559.20	587.09	614.17
504.02	521.15	541.13	559.24	587.11	614.17
504.03	522.02	541.17	560.05	587.12	614.18
504.06	522.03	541.21	560.10	587.15	614.18
504.13	522.04	541.28	560.20	587.23	614.21
505.04	522.10	542.02	560.21	587.24	614.22
505.05	522.18	542.04	560.22	587.25	614.25
505.12	522.20	542.06	560.24	588.16	614.28
505.13	522.26	542.11	560.24	588.18	615.01
505.16	523.01	542.13	561.09	588.25	615.01
505.22	523.08	542.13	561.14	590.15	615.01
506.03	523.20	542.15	561.19	591.09	615.03
506.06	524.11	542.17	561.19	591.10	615.04
506.13	524.11	542.19	562.02	591.13	615.06
506.19	524.15	542.23	562.02	592.06	615.08
506.19	524.16	542.25	562.05	592.07	615.10
506.26	524.19	543.07	562.17	592.15	615.14
507.02	524.21	543.07	562.19	592.17	615.15
507.09	524.24	543.09	562.23	593.12	615.19
507.10	525.20	543.11	563.15	594.01	615.23
507.11	526.03	543.14	563.17	594.03	615.23
507.12	526.07	543.22	563.21	594.05	615.24
507.12	526.10	543.22	564.10	594.09	615.27
507.14	526.12	543.25	564.20	595.03	616.01
507.17	526.13	543.26	564.22	595.07	616.09
507.18	526.14	543.26	565.01	596.07	616.10
507.20	526.18	543.27	565.20	596.11	616.18
507.21	527.15	543.28	565.21	596.16	616.21
508.01	527.16	544.03	566.02	596.20	616.22
508.03	527.20	544.11	566.03	596.24	616.24
508.06	527.23	544.13	566.03	597.01	616.24
508.08	527.23	544.17	566.05	597.22	616.24
508.08	528.01	544.25	566.15	597.22	616.25
508.09	528.04	544.26	567.01	598.01	617.12
508.12	528.06	545.04	567.13	598.06	618.02
508.16	528.06	545.05	567.15	598.08	618.04
508.17	528.15	545.06	567.16	598.13	618.05

618.05	635.10	650.18	668.11	689.07	708.02
618.12	635.18	650.22	668.13	689.08	708.06
618.16	635.21	651.04	668.21	689.09	708.10
618.20	635.24	651.09	668.22	689.11	708.12
618.22	635.25	651.14	669.03	689.15	708.15
618.25	636.11	651.22	669.05	689.16	708.21
618.28	636.17	651.24	669.06	690.22	708.22
619.02	636.23	652.01	669.07	690.22	708.26
619.06	636.23	652.02	669.07	690.27	708.28
619.10	637.05	652.03	669.18	690.28	708.28
619.16	637.08	652.04	669.26	691.08	709.01
619.18	637.09	652.05	670.04	691.11	709.02
619.22	637.10	652.06	670.05	691.12	709.08
619.23	637.16	652.08	670.17	691.13	709.13
620.04	637.17	652.14	670.19	691.19	709.15
620.05	637.22	652.22	670.20	692.09	709.18
620.06	637.22	652.23	670.20	692.12	709.21
620.08	637.23	652.25	670.23	692.21	709.24
620.10	637.25	652.28	670.25	692.28	710.02
620.11	638.02	653.13	670.28	693.02	711.13
620.12	638.05	653.13	671.01	693.03	711.13
620.16	638.08	653.19	671.05	693.07	712.03
620.26	638.09	653.20	671.07	693.11	712.04
620.28	638.10	653.23	671.17	693.17	712.09
621.05	638.14	653.27	671.19	693.19	712.11
621.09	638.19	654.10	671.22	693.26	712.17
621.12	638.22	654.14	671.24	694.13	712.19
622.09	638.28	654.24	671.27	694.18	712.20
622.13	639.01	654.27	672.03	694.22	713.05
622.14	639.07	654.28	672.06	694.23	713.17
622.18	639.07	655.01	672.10	694.27	713.17
622.18	639.16	655.03	673.01	695.01	713.18
622.23	639.16	655.12	673.02	695.20	713.20
622.27	640.03	655.13	673.04	696.14	713.21
623.03	640.05	655.14	673.05	696.21	714.07
623.06	640.08	655.22	673.24	696.26	714.09
623.08	640.16	655.23	673.25	696.27	714.12
623.10	640.17	655.23	674.13	697.01	714.15
623.12	640.18	656.04	674.19	697.05	714.27
623.13	640.20	656.07	674.24	697.10	714.28
623.17	640.22	656.14	674.25	697.13	715.04
623.23	640.26	656.19	674.27	697.22	715.08
623.25	640.27	656.21	675.02	697.27	715.14
624.06	641.01	656.24	675.12	698.02	715.18
624.07	641.06	656.25	675.18	698.18	715.19
624.10	641.07	656.26	675.27	698.24	715.26
624.21	641.08	656.26	676.01	698.26	716.09
624.21	641.15	657.06	677.16	699.10	716.12
624.27	641.19	657.07	677.18	699.11	716.17
625.01	641.23	657.13	677.21	699.17	716.19
625.06	641.23	657.15	678.02	699.18	716.24
625.12	641.26	657.16	678.08	699.20	716.24
625.24	642.05	658.08	678.14	699.23	716.25
626.13	642.08	658.14	678.14	699.25	717.06
626.14	642.16	658.16	678.14	699.26	717.10
626.15	642.26	658.17	678.19	700.03	717.10
626.17	643.04	659.08	679.13	700.04	717.20
626.17	643.08	659.09	679.16	700.05	717.21
627.02	643.13	659.15	680.03	700.06	717.25
627.07	643.15	659.21	680.09	700.10	717.27
627.18	643.17	660.09	680.15	700.10	717.28
627.22	643.18	660.13	680.21	700.17	718.01
628.03	643.19	660.13	680.23	700.24	718.03
628.09	643.22	660.21	680.26	701.20	718.06
628.20	643.27	660.27	681.02	701.23	718.07
628.28	644.01	661.02	681.07	702.11	718.08
629.01	644.08	661.18	681.10	702.13	718.12
629.09	644.11	662.02	681.19	702.14	718.13
629.12	644.11	662.03	681.20	703.03	718.18
629.14	644.16	662.12	681.20	703.06	718.23
629.22	644.16	662.13	681.25	703.07	718.25
630.12	644.18	662.18	681.27	703.14	718.25
630.15	644.19	662.21	682.01	703.15	718.26
630.20	644.21	662.24	682.02	703.15	719.04
630.23	644.23	662.27	682.02	703.18	719.04
631.10	644.24	663.02	682.04	703.25	719.05
631.14	644.25	663.15	682.09	703.25	719.08
631.24	644.27	663.18	682.10	703.26	719.11
631.25	644.28	663.21	682.11	703.27	719.13
631.27	645.02	664.01	682.15	704.01	719.18
632.06	645.03	664.04	682.19	704.01	719.26
632.08	645.10	664.06	682.20	704.03	720.12
632.14	645.24	664.11	682.26	704.05	720.25
632.15	645.24	664.18	682.27	704.06	721.06
632.16	646.07	664.22	683.02	704.09	721.15
632.19	646.08	664.28	683.07	704.20	721.17
632.20	646.13	665.01	683.16	704.22	721.20
632.22	646.17	665.02	683.28	704.25	721.22
632.22	646.21	665.03	684.02	704.26	722.05
632.23	646.24	665.20	684.05	705.11	722.08
632.24	646.25	665.23	684.05	705.22	722.11
632.26	646.26	665.23	684.08	705.22	722.25
632.28	646.28	665.24	684.17	705.24	723.09
633.05	647.03	666.03	684.26	705.28	724.04
633.13	647.05	666.04	684.26	706.01	724.08
633.16	647.09	666.23	685.01	706.03	724.09
633.18	647.12	666.24	685.21	706.10	724.10
633.19	647.12	666.28	686.02	706.26	724.12
633.23	647.13	666.28	686.05	706.28	725.01
633.24	647.16	667.02	686.18	707.02	725.01
633.25	648.05	667.03	686.19	707.04	725.08
633.28	648.19	667.13	686.28	707.10	725.14
634.02	648.23	667.16	687.02	707.11	725.18
634.07	648.23	667.28	687.02	707.13	725.23
634.18	648.26	668.01	687.04	707.14	725.25
634.20	648.28	668.09	687.06	707.14	725.25
634.25	649.05	668.11	687.09	707.20	726.13
634.26	649.22		687.14	707.21	726.14
634.27	650.05		688.07	707.25	726.27
634.28	650.09		688.06	707.26	727.02
635.02	650.16		689.07		727.16

727.18	750.17	770.06	790.23	805.20	821.02
727.19	751.01	770.25	790.25	805.22	821.04
727.22	751.09	770.27	791.02	805.24	821.15
727.26	751.23	771.04	791.03	806.02	821.19
727.27	752.01	771.08	791.04	806.04	821.21
728.01	752.05	771.13	791.05	806.05	821.26
728.05	752.08	771.20	791.07	806.10	822.01
729.09	752.09	771.22	791.07	806.12	822.04
730.05	752.10	771.22	791.09	806.16	822.05
730.10	752.10	772.16	791.13	806.25	822.06
730.12	752.11	772.17	791.19	806.27	822.11
730.17	752.11	772.21	791.22	807.04	822.21
730.17	752.16	772.24	791.23	807.09	822.22
730.21	752.24	772.27	791.24	807.12	822.22
730.22	752.27	773.05	791.25	807.18	822.25
731.01	753.03	773.18	791.27	807.22	823.01
731.03	753.10	773.21	792.01	807.25	823.09
731.10	753.16	773.22	792.01	807.28	824.07
731.10	753.22	774.02	792.04	808.03	824.07
731.11	753.27	774.06	792.09	808.05	824.13
731.12	754.01	774.23	792.10	808.06	824.17
731.15	754.19	775.09	792.13	808.09	824.19
731.20	754.20	775.10	792.23	808.10	824.22
731.21	754.20	775.19	792.25	808.10	824.27
731.22	754.22	775.20	793.02	808.12	825.12
731.26	755.03	776.02	793.08	808.12	825.17
732.01	755.04	776.02	793.09	808.13	825.20
732.05	755.07	776.03	793.10	808.14	825.20
732.07	755.07	776.08	793.10	808.14	825.21
732.09	755.10	776.12	793.10	808.14	825.23
732.10	755.12	777.06	793.12	808.19	825.28
732.17	755.16	777.11	793.12	808.27	826.01
732.19	755.18	777.12	793.13	809.01	826.02
732.19	755.20	777.15	793.16	809.03	826.08
732.23	755.25	777.18	793.19	809.05	826.14
732.26	756.02	777.21	793.21	809.11	826.15
733.10	756.04	777.22	793.24	809.18	826.23
733.11	756.04	777.24	793.28	810.01	826.24
733.15	756.08	777.25	794.04	810.02	827.05
734.02	756.08	778.17	794.06	810.02	827.07
734.11	756.12	778.20	794.06	810.11	827.13
734.12	756.12	778.21	794.08	810.15	827.22
734.16	756.19	778.28	794.15	810.22	827.24
734.16	756.20	779.01	794.15	810.22	827.26
734.19	756.21	779.04	794.16	810.23	828.02
734.20	756.26	779.05	795.08	811.02	828.14
734.22	756.27	779.06	795.12	811.25	828.14
734.24	757.05	779.19	795.12	811.27	828.16
734.27	757.12	779.20	795.17	812.03	828.18
734.28	757.15	780.01	795.19	812.04	828.20
735.04	757.18	780.08	795.23	812.18	828.21
735.06	758.03	780.09	796.09	812.25	828.27
735.07	758.07	780.09	796.13	813.04	828.27
735.13	758.17	780.10	796.14	813.08	828.27
735.23	759.04	780.14	796.16	813.15	829.01
735.24	759.05	780.17	796.20	813.16	829.08
735.27	759.11	780.20	796.27	813.25	829.09
735.27	759.14	781.19	797.04	813.28	829.14
736.04	760.01	781.20	797.06	814.01	829.14
736.10	760.01	782.02	797.10	814.02	829.18
736.21	760.02	782.07	797.19	814.04	830.05
736.28	760.05	782.09	797.24	814.04	830.11
737.12	760.18	782.18	798.15	814.06	831.09
737.16	760.19	782.26	798.21	814.08	831.14
738.04	760.20	783.07	798.21	814.09	831.15
738.19	760.25	783.08	798.23	814.11	832.01
738.20	760.25	783.10	798.24	814.12	832.03
738.24	761.07	783.12	798.25	814.12	832.06
739.04	761.11	783.13	799.05	814.13	832.08
739.05	761.17	783.18	799.09	814.14	832.13
739.10	761.28	783.22	799.20	814.15	832.14
739.27	762.01	784.02	799.20	814.18	832.18
740.01	762.04	784.05	799.27	814.21	832.27
740.07	762.19	784.06	800.10	815.01	833.05
740.09	762.19	784.09	800.13	815.10	833.11
740.20	762.25	784.10	800.22	815.26	833.15
740.22	762.26	784.11	800.22	815.26	833.16
740.26	762.27	784.12	801.04	816.08	833.18
741.07	763.01	784.19	801.08	816.11	834.05
741.09	763.14	784.20	801.10	816.13	834.10
741.14	763.15	784.21	801.12	816.15	834.15
741.19	763.17	784.24	801.14	816.21	834.15
741.26	763.21	784.24	801.15	816.22	834.17
742.05	763.24	785.01	801.17	817.06	834.19
742.06	765.02	785.05	801.26	817.14	834.23
742.19	765.07	785.08	802.02	817.22	834.24
743.07	765.07	785.08	802.05	817.23	834.26
743.11	765.09	785.09	802.07	818.06	835.06
744.07	766.17	785.09	802.08	818.09	835.12
744.11	766.20	785.15	802.10	818.19	835.17
744.21	766.23	785.19	802.15	818.24	835.21
744.22	766.23	785.21	802.19	818.25	835.24
744.25	766.25	785.22	802.22	818.27	836.01
745.02	767.01	785.25	803.09	819.01	836.01
745.08	767.02	785.26	803.12	819.02	836.05
745.12	767.04	786.03	803.20	819.07	836.10
746.05	767.11	786.17	803.24	819.07	836.14
746.07	767.18	786.23	804.04	819.08	836.24
746.12	768.05	787.11	804.06	819.09	836.25
746.20	768.11	787.26	804.07	819.11	836.27
746.25	768.15	788.07	804.08	819.12	836.28
747.06	768.18	788.08	804.11	819.16	837.04
747.19	768.18	788.08	804.13	819.20	837.06
748.02	768.20	788.08	804.14	819.20	837.09
748.05	768.28	789.07	804.19	819.23	837.18
748.16	769.01	789.08	804.24	819.24	837.23
748.26	769.03	789.08	804.25	819.25	838.03
749.23	769.06	789.14	804.28	820.08	838.03
749.23	769.13	790.11	805.02	820.10	838.11
750.07	769.24	790.20	805.05	820.14	838.12
750.13	770.02	790.23	805.15	821.01	838.13

838.13	856.14	879.02	898.24	731.03	803.18
838.19	857.04	879.06	898.26	783.12	826.15
838.19	857.04	879.12	899.02	791.13	847.19
838.23	857.17	879.15	899.06	828.12	874.12
838.25	858.06	879.19	899.27	884.02	909.07
838.26	858.08	880.07	900.06	885.10	909.07
838.26	858.20	880.08	900.09	to-morrow's	toil
839.01	858.26	880.10	900.13	078.15	664.22
839.03	858.26	880.11	900.15	to-night	720.18
839.04	858.28	880.16	900.17	028.22	825.09
840.03	859.01	880.21	900.18	079.17	912.09
840.03	859.10	880.25	900.19	136.22	912.10
840.05	859.11	881.03	900.28	137.04	toiled
840.10	859.15	881.13	901.01	166.09	142.14
840.12	859.19	881.15	901.02	174.22	790.19
840.18	860.04	881.15	901.02	188.06	toilet
840.18	860.07	881.23	901.06	190.01	193.08
840.20	860.10	881.24	902.11	262.19	331.02
840.20	860.12	882.13	902.12	263.11	430.05
840.26	860.13	882.18	902.12	263.21	794.20
841.02	860.19	882.19	902.17	314.22	toilet-table
841.03	860.22	882.24	902.22	316.04	016.03
841.07	860.25	882.27	902.27	316.16	431.03
841.08	860.26	882.28	903.01	336.05	464.23
841.10	861.06	883.01	903.03	358.07	toilette
841.11	861.09	883.02	903.07	359.09	236.12
841.18	861.14	883.12	903.15	363.07	341.22
841.20	862.12	883.14	903.17	398.13	341.23
841.25	862.17	883.24	903.21	401.06	toilettes
841.26	862.18	883.25	903.25	428.19	334.01
841.27	862.18	884.14	903.25	463.07	toils
842.07	862.21	884.19	903.25	463.21	192.01
842.11	862.26	885.06	904.01	467.06	735.14
842.12	863.01	885.10	904.02	507.01	840.19
842.17	863.14	885.12	905.09	510.12	token
842.24	863.19	885.13	905.12	566.17	251.10
843.05	863.21	885.15	906.05	582.10	642.20
843.09	864.05	886.02	906.05	583.13	778.27
843.11	864.07	886.04	906.06	661.02	859.20
843.18	864.07	886.13	906.07	679.20	tokens
843.23	864.20	886.14	906.16	687.07	321.06
844.08	864.23	886.19	906.18	687.21	321.06
845.02	865.06	886.22	906.26	742.03	356.16
845.02	865.12	886.24	906.26	742.03	told
845.04	865.15	887.03	906.27	770.24	005.13
845.17	865.18	887.07	907.03	778.08	014.01
845.24	865.19	887.10	907.06	778.08	021.15
846.03	865.27	887.12	907.12	787.15	043.25
846.04	866.13	887.12	907.14	843.28	064.06
846.05	866.20	887.12	907.22	882.08	070.02
846.06	866.22	887.18	907.28	885.09	072.09
846.07	867.06	887.23	908.05	to-night's	099.19
846.09	867.10	888.14	908.08	300.16	134.07
846.11	867.19	888.15	908.15	toad	135.15
846.14	867.22	888.16	908.17	041.10	141.04
847.01	868.07	888.22	908.19	621.07	150.25
847.02	869.13	888.25	908.25	toast	173.01
847.02	869.15	889.02	909.01	137.14	175.06
847.07	870.04	889.05	909.07	138.09	195.08
847.08	870.09	889.27	909.07	138.15	227.10
847.11	871.03	890.01	909.09	458.24	287.13
847.26	871.12	890.04	909.09	692.03	290.06
848.02	871.15	890.11	909.12	toasting	293.13
848.08	871.20	890.23	909.26	458.13	300.25
848.14	871.20	891.12	909.27	today	309.03
848.19	871.21	891.21	909.28	314.05	312.14
848.25	872.06	892.09	910.06	toes	320.20
848.28	872.13	892.13	910.07	001.14	333.16
849.02	872.19	893.14	910.09	096.06	336.24
849.07	872.22	893.16	910.19	112.02	372.01
849.19	872.25	893.20	910.24	together	387.03
849.25	872.25	893.21	911.06	028.27	390.05
850.11	873.09	893.21	911.07	066.16	391.12
850.13	873.10	893.23	911.14	088.12	391.17
850.14	873.15	893.24	911.15	094.06	395.10
850.16	873.16	893.25	911.20	097.10	397.20
850.17	873.19	894.04	912.03	097.17	401.21
850.19	873.21	894.06	912.09	099.16	403.12
850.20	873.22	895.07	912.11	108.19	403.20
851.05	873.22	895.15	912.15	114.21	432.15
852.02	873.25	895.15	912.15	149.25	448.17
852.03	873.28	895.17	to-day	162.04	451.03
852.04	874.04	895.22	136.23	168.26	455.07
852.05	874.04	895.22	315.21	176.27	459.02
852.06	874.10	895.24	463.26	210.25	459.04
852.17	874.11	895.26	524.15	235.10	464.08
852.17	874.17	895.27	548.01	235.18	464.13
853.11	875.08	896.05	596.08	252.23	467.10
853.15	875.15	896.06	598.15	253.11	474.25
853.18	875.15	896.14	599.24	293.06	488.23
853.22	875.22	896.27	606.03	307.18	496.16
853.25	876.11	897.03	769.08	316.19	526.09
854.01	876.18	897.14	to-morrow	333.21	533.04
854.04	876.22	897.18	141.05	335.02	538.24
854.05	876.27	897.27	316.17	347.02	542.21
854.07	877.08	898.01	321.26	352.11	543.14
854.10	877.15	898.05	336.06	367.08	544.08
854.16	877.16	898.05	390.08	369.11	566.02
854.16	877.22	898.06	401.06	379.22	566.11
854.23	877.24	898.07	428.17	416.09	574.12
854.24	877.27	898.07	448.24	487.19	610.03
855.01	878.16	898.08	452.22	499.05	618.11
855.12	878.21	898.10	455.20	510.13	622.07
855.14	878.21	898.10	489.01	536.23	624.03
855.24	878.28	898.12	557.09	570.03	624.23
855.25	878.28	898.13	558.02	590.02	640.12
856.01	879.01	898.17	558.23	590.05	698.21
856.04	879.01	898.17	565.14	590.06	702.26
856.05	879.01	898.19	567.21	624.08	739.01
856.06	879.02	898.20	582.19	678.04	750.05
856.12	879.02	898.21	618.01	714.02	771.07
			723.09		

776.22
778.11
778.18
782.03
810.13
842.07
844.07
850.13
859.13
878.23
868.15
888.21
903.04
906.16
tolerable
252.14
301.13
433.12
579.25
tolerably
094.07
169.01
tolerated
356.27
567.13
tolled
219.04
tolling
165.12
tomb
569.09
tome
001.12
tomorrow
120.19
174.22
tone
043.21
062.14
087.13
158.19
202.27
210.27
237.28
245.10
256.05
261.27
299.28
306.12
313.11
343.01
354.27
357.16
373.13
388.24
409.23
441.24
452.01
452.10
463.02
517.25
569.02
612.10
630.07
631.15
636.08
652.15
688.06
691.07
705.28
709.07
715.24
739.09
796.03
798.20
825.12
827.27
834.09
843.28
894.21
toned
699.23
852.04
tones
251.16
305.18
333.20
337.06
337.16
361.09
413.09
458.21
460.07
550.19
595.16
645.06
847.25
tongue
008.11
043.08
044.15
125.25
198.13
199.23
259.19
401.26
406.21
505.07
528.06
552.20
665.17

678.09
803.23
832.16
887.07
tongues
084.03
296.08
tonnage
098.15
tons
546.15
too
006.02
019.03
026.06
028.25
029.02
030.06
031.02
034.13
034.15
041.05
047.19
047.25
051.06
059.19
077.04
079.25
080.05
084.14
088.26
090.14
093.22
097.07
108.21
109.19
109.21
112.24
113.13
115.24
116.11
117.11
117.27
120.20
121.04
132.14
132.15
132.16
134.02
137.18
143.09
145.06
148.02
148.13
161.19
165.19
166.16
174.21
176.11
185.13
187.21
187.28
188.20
192.26
202.26
203.04
211.17
216.18
216.18
217.04
220.17
228.24
229.28
230.09
231.14
231.21
232.05
233.17
235.18
236.12
240.06
247.25
252.26
255.16
258.02
259.07
260.06
262.06
266.13
267.25
268.09
269.26
275.21
275.22
275.22
277.24
281.06
289.10
292.19
297.18
303.03
311.26
315.05
318.19
320.01
325.13
326.11
330.07
331.05
331.16
334.22

336.13
341.23
344.07
345.01
345.13
353.03
355.17
357.17
362.21
364.03
366.18
368.11
372.12
372.23
373.02
373.15
380.16
382.06
397.23
405.01
411.26
414.12
421.10
429.02
437.26
441.24
446.27
447.18
448.06
448.27
451.18
454.04
457.14
460.01
460.21
461.09
467.06
476.18
478.25
482.24
485.08
492.25
493.24
497.14
504.08
506.09
507.14
514.23
525.17
526.03
526.17
536.07
538.05
538.12
539.28
554.08
555.10
563.17
572.22
573.15
574.02
579.18
583.22
588.11
594.08
598.21
599.08
603.19
604.09
604.15
613.05
615.09
618.18
620.20
626.01
627.21
643.14
652.22
654.07
654.12
654.21
655.24
662.05
670.22
674.17
677.14
686.04
686.10
687.05
697.12
700.15
705.03
711.16
726.22
729.09
731.01
732.22
734.16
736.20
738.06
740.14
743.17
750.16
750.26
752.10
753.25
767.20
769.01
777.12
782.23
783.25

786.19
786.22
787.08
797.11
803.06
804.05
807.14
810.04
819.23
822.05
822.13
837.27
837.27
841.18
841.18
845.22
851.11
852.16
852.17
864.19
871.03
373.10
876.06
876.06
876.22
877.18
877.24
879.08
881.18
881.18
882.04
382.04
882.27
888.24
888.24
891.10
902.26
903.03
903.07
907.07
907.26
907.27
took
013.14
027.17
041.01
044.20
046.20
066.02
079.05
081.02
082.11
127.20
129.08
131.13
136.27
145.03
149.14
167.20
171.05
175.08
183.10
184.14
188.23
190.15
199.12
201.26
214.24
228.15
239.06
240.21
251.12
280.26
288.16
289.16
297.26
301.09
308.20
333.10
335.01
336.25
337.20
341.25
349.11
350.06
355.14
355.23
356.13
367.10
371.07
389.18
390.10
396.06
397.18
402.10
411.15
421.14
421.16
432.03
436.27
438.10
453.01
463.17
466.08
471.12
476.01
476.06
478.15
483.24
490.03
497.10

521.17
542.03
564.09
566.01
567.10
576.15
577.17
579.16
586.03
593.04
595.24
620.03
653.06
660.09
666.26
670.01
687.11
687.17
689.10
690.05
690.14
693.17
693.20
699.18
702.23
707.21
744.01
744.07
750.02
757.14
763.06
763.18
765.10
766.19
768.15
776.18
787.24
791.16
796.12
800.13
806.20
813.01
823.27
843.28
845.23
850.22
851.09
852.12
857.22
863.23
874.18
880.24
904.02
907.28
908.07
tool
099.17
842.13
top
051.12
052.16
073.19
078.19
082.05
097.24
116.13
122.14
126.26
194.03
337.04
367.24
423.21
429.26
575.15
580.16
667.10
702.17
top-nots
121.13
topic
265.04
358.01
626.22
713.19
828.03
828.04
tops
207.13
230.23
topsy-turvy
328.27
794.01
tore
019.05
141.19
145.21
656.03
torment
484.05
615.15
784.21
tormented
250.08
901.13
tormenting
469.06
torments
118.24
torn
248.10
248.22

370.01
374.21
428.02
512.07
515.08
580.16
610.08
646.15
689.09
773.26
torpid
005.05
691.03
743.07
torpor
707.24
849.06
torrent
145.20
607.17
608.07
847.03
905.15
torrents
079.28
torture
112.01
517.05
517.07
517.10
643.22
662.03
832.18
832.19
tortured
621.10
tortures
132.26
torturing
842.19
toss
132.11
tossed
230.04
302.18
355.26
tossing
358.16
560.02
total
078.01
299.09
316.02
462.18
572.20
672.27
tottered
008.18
tottering
152.23
touch
079.08
227.09
228.10
371.23
372.08
472.08
484.25
485.02
495.18
566.21
567.04
621.06
623.23
667.14
681.27
752.09
830.02
847.13
858.17
872.25
875.20
876.11
877.01
882.28
883.05
touched
077.13
090.13
248.04
248.24
294.09
341.18
374.10
442.12
660.22
675.24
713.20
742.10
767.05
827.27
836.04
845.19
879.22
886.23
touches
757.10
touching
056.09
361.05
397.22

549.06
745.20
tough
261.25
679.23
tour
795.19
888.08
tow
619.12
towards
022.13
052.25
123.24
169.16
214.18
249.04
251.09
255.26
264.12
279.10
281.11
284.26
289.07
290.25
295.12
302.24
314.04
331.27
336.14
370.20
371.22
374.02
404.04
434.07
406.12
469.22
478.06
504.02
504.07
542.20
552.13
589.08
589.22
590.14
613.19
645.27
653.11
654.07
668.26
672.01
675.03
736.20
737.03
737.11
706.12
807.15
811.20
812.18
820.27
829.03
855.22
858.01
858.24
872.17
872.21
875.04
896.20
towel
051.10
694.27
tower
142.23
185.11
860.04
tower-like
052.28
tower-top
194.22
towers
765.15
town
040.27
172.10
172.15
172.21
181.20
199.09
200.01
243.12
339.25
364.14
409.15
429.13
451.14
475.23
491.08
526.12
624.24
658.12
658.16
661.07
738.28
770.21
837.18
909.22
towns
074.09
075.04
215.07
658.19

699.02
toy
046.27
toys
030.08
068.20
202.06
trace
100.07
242.10
461.01
611.20
662.16
675.10
691.20
692.27
767.12
835.25
traced
164.23
224.11
465.22
471.14
471.19
472.02
774.03
traces
144.18
207.13
228.12
444.11
692.16
733.17
tracing
235.13
track
169.18
280.07
575.20
675.12
736.22
799.28
812.05
812.13
828.21
852.16
870.07
tracked
085.22
tracking
856.10
trackless
320.13
tract
061.07
640.26
673.13
tractability
691.21
817.25
tractable
528.09
trade
395.22
666.12
tradesman
180.12
traditions
208.11
traffic
048.14
tragic
211.02
trail
281.03
346.06
trailing
346.05
train
248.24
288.20
617.27
713.23
808.10
884.04
trained
059.10
201.14
533.11
training
763.02
trait
289.28
403.22
461.13
traitors
647.18
traits
215.17
485.26
tramp
220.26
220.26
221.24
221.24
380.18
564.03
trample
825.26
843.06

trampled
511.26
578.15
656.15
778.28
trampling
227.17
trance-like
652.20
tranquil
164.05
182.02
209.08
214.21
229.23
374.26
394.02
520.10
583.19
646.27
660.01
721.04
746.02
834.09
tranquille
256.09
tranquillity
133.11
164.06
216.07
294.06
671.28
734.12
861.08
tranquillize
783.19
tranquillized
641.27
tranquilly
208.16
325.17
475.05
transacted
122.17
transaction
400.26
579.15
605.03
transfer
788.12
transferred
771.07
805.09
transfix
438.01
610.14
transfixed
749.17
transformed
057.12
146.26
277.01
634.14
transforming
163.24
transgress
647.13
transient
031.07
747.17
793.21
transit
127.19
transitory
019.20
067.12
228.22
438.08
642.13
translate
039.11
143.10
translation
677.21
752.03
805.04
transparent
333.03
transpired
298.04
771.26
transplanted
288.18
transported
368.02
651.24
trap-door
208.25
209.14
209.23
215.02
trat
678.20
travail
248.22
travel
074.07
430.19
452.15
452.24
526.20

631.27
640.26
799.27
854.01
travelled
164.27
205.25
654.25
traveller
222.13
223.20
223.28
225.11
227.17
237.04
384.21
659.09
traveller's
491.10
travellers
018.02
221.21
travelling
163.10
174.15
190.23
381.06
458.07
885.22
travels
031.08
202.18
460.15
510.17
traverse
364.09
494.01
813.04
852.12
traversed
078.03
144.17
154.23
233.17
763.23
traversing
193.10
229.16
462.03
tray
079.01
079.04
137.08
137.10
138.23
187.24
217.10
238.27
240.23
311.04
567.08
874.12
874.17
874.19
875.05
883.17
trays
336.16
treacherous
123.07
treachery
290.10
425.03
626.12
tread
299.18
314.15
315.12
328.25
treading
812.05
treasure
048.27
256.11
268.24
369.04
374.08
405.07
526.13
579.12
617.13
617.14
899.20
treasured
662.20
treasurer
092.04
161.16
706.23
treasures
148.09
219.10
treasury
715.19
treat
003.23
046.05
113.28
137.05
264.18
319.06

769.13
807.13
treated
022.10
062.25
062.27
130.05
131.14
291.25
433.25
459.06
483.07
642.06
treating
264.03
373.21
802.13
treatment
020.18
187.20
325.07
484.15
744.26
treats
187.17
tree
510.10
518.27
560.12
560.22
561.23
762.22
887.22
896.12
896.16
909.22
tree-tops
440.20
trees
005.01
031.25
066.14
075.09
143.03
146.04
194.10
194.20
199.17
209.07
220.08
220.14
221.28
229.13
433.05
434.27
434.27
435.09
501.11
502.19
503.14
541.23
55.18
559.25
562.21
675.14
856.16
870.06
870.19
370.22
872.22
872.27
tremble
063.28
230.28
395.24
494.12
747.06
760.21
828.22
trembled
006.19
301.18
425.28
514.25
661.26
814.21
tremblent
313.16
trembling
051.26
230.27
295.21
392.26
628.16
660.16
685.07
745.25
832.20
853.06
tremblingly
652.02
tremors
392.03
trepidation
340.03
tresses
122.06
146.02
681.14

738.09
749.28
752.11
trial
125.09
236.19
638.11
trials
253.20
tribe
355.12
tribes
107.10
826.16
tribunal
518.19
tribute
290.23
626.07
trice
429.22
546.22
trick
478.09
tricked
525.28
trickle
010.15
890.09
trickling
421.23
423.11
tricks
024.13
024.27
355.15
495.05
tried
023.04
108.19
130.21
150.22
174.13
224.05
226.26
271.06
273.03
294.05
420.03
490.20
496.05
619.02
627.02
627.08
636.18
636.25
656.04
675.02
724.28
764.08
800.12
809.27
834.16
873.09
trifle
012.06
496.25
776.12
trifles
111.08
774.19
782.02
trifling
090.21
trim
255.15
795.06
trimmed
122.08
765.08
trimming
086.05
462.05
trio
122.02
392.26
713.09
trip
432.11
tripped
742.19
tripping
067.02
277.01
333.26
trite
238.19
269.15
626.23
770.09
793.21
triumph
063.19
528.24
564.18
649.18
753.06
844.25
triumphantly
302.24

triumphed
283.20
triumphs
803.05
trivial
223.22
721.11
795.11
824.24
trivialities
289.19
triviality
127.23
528.04
trod
504.10
512.14
trodden
061.27
130.08
713.03
559.02
675.02
trode
250.07
trooping
583.04
tropes
810.20
tropical
756.09
tropics
606.06
651.07
trot
507.26
trouble
051.05
127.03
137.04
215.28
243.05
256.15
275.13
502.20
551.25
559.06
555.21
556.02
558.17
595.01
410.13
436.04
444.17
445.25
467.18
478.04
456.11
540.05
560.09
605.01
613.28
619.10
627.05
633.04
645.11
675.05
704.26
707.15
718.03
719.10
755.08
793.06
795.23
852.20
troubled
022.15
044.20
126.22
150.22
174.28
272.05
291.21
410.11
559.21
642.10
854.06
troubles
252.05
470.03
660.08
troublesome
051.01
365.08
troubling
182.15
716.27
trousers
175.22
truant
495.21
495.21
truculent
108.03
true
035.22
125.16
127.27
135.10
150.12
251.22

319.25
349.26
351.21
375.21
396.27
405.15
466.05
478.19
487.17
517.08
528.10
535.21
536.15
596.19
612.10
627.15
631.09
647.17
683.19
705.17
705.21
737.05
747.23
773.04
838.28
842.09
853.27
902.02
902.02
truest
550.21
truly
092.21
132.09
161.23
166.18
344.26
374.26
375.20
513.25
517.16
523.11
532.23
536.10
644.06
743.04
814.11
816.04
819.14
890.07
897.20
897.21
910.04
trunk
368.18
073.04
073.21
075.18
174.08
183.16
464.10
560.13
630.22
670.17
673.23
trunks
488.19
557.07
688.07
truss
328.09
trust
059.13
073.17
106.25
455.12
457.14
459.27
533.26
646.20
687.19
694.17
703.10
731.03
779.19
792.18
816.14
818.07
824.11
851.17
898.07
trusted
452.17
455.06
537.24
570.01
698.22
877.10
trusting
310.17
trusts
907.18
trustworthy
865.20
truth
031.17
046.02
063.02

150.09
214.15
217.13
272.23
302.02
313.26
373.15
399.08
404.16
527.27
574.01
581.24
591.06
605.11
606.25
608.11
622.20
637.28
682.01
691.12
712.13
722.12
725.24
733.25
796.17
836.04
876.28
888.24
893.27
911.19
truthful
649.04
894.22
try
014.23
014.26
018.17
028.05
082.23
227.07
269.18
315.07
349.20
406.13
403.04
410.21
432.05
468.21
508.01
530.03
538.06
550.10
550.11
617.17
657.06
665.12
684.02
686.05
686.06
686.15
754.08
758.18
793.10
793.16
880.21
trying
088.21
223.21
337.12
352.26
437.27
481.12
525.20
796.27
815.25
860.26
875.21
tuck
047.12
tucker
084.10
193.02
tuckers
117.11
117.17
tuesday
443.08
854.27
tuft
733.23
tufted
471.25
tug
050.22
tugging
046.18
050.16
tuition
168.18
tumble
222.17
tumult
019.28
080.17
083.10
087.03
101.02
282.20
392.11
799.14

tune
178.18
245.15
442.05
tunefully
201.03
tunes
380.02
turban
249.11
344.24
355.06
368.06
turbans
378.18
turbid
016.14
145.21
716.26
turbulent
065.26
turf
504.10
656.21
712.18
812.14
812.23
turk
003.04
turk's
546.04
turkey
203.18
turn
014.09
015.18
048.13
061.28
079.07
089.24
093.06
105.09
107.28
116.10
120.22
149.21
167.20
170.22
184.18
217.27
289.28
355.14
357.21
371.06
371.20
372.06
385.15
395.26
412.01
420.01
437.22
455.16
472.24
477.02
481.12
488.13
491.09
505.02
516.22
516.25
527.13
528.26
530.25
606.19
620.25
626.23
646.18
656.13
687.20
692.01
696.21
714.25
734.25
738.19
747.17
764.06
792.24
825.20
350.11
872.19
383.05
turned
007.15
013.11
018.12
019.15
023.24
032.03
043.04
043.10
052.07
052.11
052.24
072.15
080.17
083.10
085.06
095.07
096.10
170.16
185.07
209.13
211.26

213.06
220.10
222.15
225.18
231.03
269.02
270.11
284.26
290.20
296.14
311.12
314.16
320.06
330.18
333.08
341.28
354.02
374.16
380.15
386.28
390.13
392.14
407.02
407.06
420.09
429.22
449.20
450.06
472.10
483.02
486.13
497.25
533.24
570.18
575.23
577.20
585.13
594.15
601.18
610.03
613.16
613.21
619.01
645.21
647.18
650.25
651.03
659.24
662.21
664.09
667.06
670.05
673.24
676.03
683.09
726.27
732.24
737.11
740.15
742.12
742.19
742.21
769.24
775.08
778.08
794.01
807.27
821.01
832.01
834.21
835.14
837.12
844.16
857.12
862.20
875.07
896.07
906.06
turning
003.11
013.26
022.13
027.07
090.02
119.24
124.21
127.01
259.12
370.20
466.09
467.11
504.18
507.17
590.24
693.19
698.22
704.24
706.03
763.01
776.08
793.12
828.25
turnings
659.24
turnpike-house
873.22
turns
315.03
404.14
838.23

turret
750.12
turtle-dove
554.24
tutor
356.10
tutors
356.26
twain
414.16
twang
454.11
tweak
555.13
tweed's
765.13
twelve
028.10
086.27
190.02
423.18
423.19
431.20
485.16
490.24
519.19
537.27
569.15
606.04
759.06
885.18
900.27
twelvemonth
721.14
twentieth
813.20
twenty
078.08
084.16
264.20
266.17
391.07
440.02
494.18
499.23
536.18
653.04
657.06
656.18
727.12
729.17
738.28
770.11
776.13
776.15
777.03
782.24
784.06
784.22
785.23
863.09
897.17
twenty-eight
701.22
twenty-first
843.22
twenty-five
319.22
twenty-four
329.08
502.20
twenty-nine
077.17
589.21
twenty-six
629.16
twice
007.23
047.12
098.11
117.24
151.04
168.11
415.03
447.16
481.19
633.25
675.07
690.02
707.17
742.19
868.08
892.16
twigs
050.12
099.16
099.22
twilight
001.13
021.02
033.05
075.06
165.01
235.09
248.15
335.13
495.08
549.22
672.16
765.05
870.06

871.14
twined
592.16
twining
528.19
twinkled
052.27
660.24
twist
885.04
twisted
018.26
121.22
450.01
twisting
063.25
twittering
433.04
two
005.01
005.05
007.11
007.22
008.19
008.23
010.14
013.06
015.24
052.08
052.26
054.20
054.26
056.01
059.23
067.14
068.19
076.26
078.05
079.13
079.13
079.21
080.04
080.11
080.11
081.20
082.17
085.11
090.08
092.14
093.18
094.02
097.10
112.12
112.20
115.10
117.10
122.02
123.11
123.22
126.08
130.04
131.19
136.19
137.04
137.08
142.18
142.20
154.03
154.25
159.12
161.26
162.11
164.16
164.25
167.21
168.19
169.07
169.09
169.11
176.14
178.18
179.28
185.07
186.03
187.07
187.23
199.26
204.06
207.14
210.02
218.16
226.25
233.16
236.25
236.26
247.01
249.05
259.10
261.27
280.26
285.06
294.07
297.21
300.21
301.02
322.27
323.06
332.22
332.24
335.02
338.03

339.22
342.19
343.04
352.09
366.02
367.15
367.23
367.25
374.20
378.18
378.24
383.12
392.02
399.27
401.16
416.26
422.05
426.26
429.19
433.17
438.13
446.19
449.15
450.15
451.17
457.18
460.13
460.19
464.10
471.03
472.08
473.01
473.05
474.16
474.17
475.25
477.28
478.20
493.28
504.13
511.01
520.06
524.18
542.09
544.03
559.11
567.15
578.14
580.16
588.12
589.04
616.18
630.10
633.13
637.02
658.02
664.20
664.23
666.01
666.25
676.27
677.17
680.11
685.09
698.01
699.08
699.15
706.20
707.09
707.15
707.16
719.07
719.22
721.17
721.21
729.05
736.12
740.04
749.11
764.09
769.11
770.16
780.04
781.09
781.12
782.09
792.02
792.26
794.03
801.24
809.16
851.03
852.19
855.11
857.13
864.12
869.11
871.01
891.22
909.14
910.08
two-leaved
231.09
two-thirds
469.11
tyne
549.08
type
346.25
584.06

types
207.10
typhus
040.26
146.24
150.27
160.12
484.01
tyrannies
018.10
tyrannized
717.08
tyrant
010.14
549.02
610.03
888.25
tyrian-dyed
204.04
ugh
224.06
ugly
008.14
262.26
279.14
292.08
359.26
386.13
459.05
472.22
596.10
ultimate
649.02
732.23
ultra-marine
773.27
umbrella
181.15
183.10
227.04
un
201.18
234.21
234.25
239.10
543.17
unable
089.19
098.16
490.15
629.22
unaccountable
407.26
unaccountably
241.18
292.19
unacquainted
271.12
291.12
unalloyed
630.25
unalterable
273.23
unamiable-looking
382.18
unannounced
498.25
unapproachable
756.20
unasked
224.23
unavailing
099.25
875.22
unawares
309.11
unbecoming
842.26
unbelieving
844.20
unbend
776.06
unblighted
825.20
unblown
143.06
unbolt
432.12
unbroken
066.09
294.20
unburdening
475.18
uncalled-for
555.02
767.17
uncanny
528.26
805.12
unceremonious
702.25
unceremoniously
550.13
uncertain
076.10
171.20
182.19
230.04
873.10
uncertainty
026.08

274.23
539.04
unchangeable
466.13
801.03
unchanged
466.12
612.11
801.02
801.03
unchaste
627.19
unchildlike
483.04
unchristian
831.11
uncivil
172.03
uncle
021.19
044.12
044.24
134.25
135.02
451.01
483.26
487.08
544.25
545.05
602.17
602.20
602.24
603.09
603.21
726.01
727.03
727.10
774.23
775.26
780.27
780.27
784.08
785.07
878.07
uncle's
134.25
780.09
uncles
177.05
242.18
unclose
361.25
423.06
unclosed
052.11
080.02
299.06
415.27
421.19
590.15
752.15
unclosing
871.11
unclouded
148.01
154.12
662.09
813.04
912.19
uncomely
312.28
uncomfortably
807.16
uncommitted
464.26
unconcious
847.12
902.21
uncongenial
022.05
817.14
unconnected
021.28
unconscious
262.27
375.01
404.12
505.23
649.04
unconsciousness
025.16
unconsecrated
838.25
uncontrolled
065.05
uncovered
873.02
uncovering
599.07
uncrossed
769.23
unction
533.22
uncurtained
844.03
uncut
881.04
und
678.26
undaunted
912.20

undeceive
522.19
undeceived
636.10
undefined
088.26
undemonstrative
709.07
undeniably
781.03
under
002.08
014.08
021.13
031.14
043.02
044.18
045.06
046.07
049.11
049.25
052.27
057.13
060.23
061.01
063.27
101.14
102.18
118.12
118.19
122.05
144.08
145.05
150.19
151.10
155.01
155.12
167.06
168.04
168.21
171.13
219.04
221.25
228.04
228.06
230.11
230.12
238.09
238.11
249.06
260.13
260.15
282.04
282.27
283.17
286.22
287.04
302.20
322.02
333.25
341.12
343.19
349.18
351.07
375.07
389.06
394.08
395.06
396.02
412.12
422.27
423.15
425.02
428.11
432.07
435.10
452.10
462.17
471.08
471.19
472.09
484.15
499.06
508.10
510.25
543.06
547.04
548.26
570.21
575.16
578.23
582.18
585.08
587.16
590.23
595.25
596.25
615.02
618.03
631.04
638.03
639.18
656.27
659.26
667.06
671.22
688.06
704.06
707.22
711.19
720.18

734.12
735.19
737.18
740.09
745.05
752.12
756.08
758.19
765.08
770.17
782.20
786.20
798.05
802.18
805.06
806.28
813.25
814.01
816.18
818.28
823.06
825.09
825.18
826.18
829.23
836.02
847.13
847.25
849.18
851.09
854.11
856.07
860.03
867.18
870.08
878.02
896.08
899.19
under-jaw
060.20
under-sound
572.09
under-teacher
077.25
underfoot
088.08
undergo
528.23
820.25
undergoing
276.20
undergone
163.24
underhand
014.03
040.14
understand
064.10
103.11
106.02
107.13
197.23
199.20
206.07
243.23
272.23
333.11
351.12
363.08
365.07
397.11
484.14
515.06
618.23
635.02
645.15
679.08
689.14
689.20
694.04
791.10
791.17
816.17
880.05
880.06
893.05
understanding
005.14
534.13
717.03
730.02
understands
198.21
330.11
understood
151.28
160.14
195.23
199.22
448.12
481.07
624.06
625.25
796.27
823.15
823.21
undertake
168.23
508.24
718.08
723.03

undertaken 803.21 813.21 822.07
undertaker's 017.01
undertaking 616.27
undertakings 727.11
undertook 759.14 771.15 841.04 861.03
underwent 226.24 808.02
undeveloped 005.14
undiscoverable 884.15
undiscovered 655.26
undisturbed 570.25 825.13
undivided 360.08
undone 427.26 456.04
undoubtedly 827.12
undress 079.19 458.08
undressed 046.17 356.22
undressing 171.03
undrew 107.21 610.27
undue 373.16 349.20 817.19
undulating 285.04
une 234.24 341.20 548.27
unearthly 516.06
uneasy 272.11 315.10 525.18 537.17 664.22 853.23
uneducated 058.10 690.12
unembroidered 571.05
unemployed 476.28
unendurable 826.04
unenslaved 825.20
unequal 252.03 319.23 323.26
unexpected 204.26 324.10 384.27 392.22 402.02 463.03 654.12 891.07
unexpectedly 290.28 903.12
unexplanatory 778.03
unexplored 459.22
unexpressed 879.13
unfathomed 152.19
unfavourable 714.21 804.09
unfeeling 637.13
unfeminine 855.18
unfinished 535.07
unflagging 818.01

unfledged 261.21
unflushed 720.05
unfolded 276.15 476.05 571.01
unforced 373.08
unfortunate 616.28 835.18
unfortunately 548.27 841.09
unfostered 261.21
unfounded 660.07
unfrequently 019.05 217.01 294.15 324.08
unfriendly 456.13
unfurnished 369.11
unfurrowed 345.17
ungloved 111.18
ungovernable 062.19
ungrateful 784.15
ungrudgingly 799.02
unguarded 436.01
unguardedly 828.02
unhappy 036.08 036.08 126.15 142.01 565.09 633.19
unhealthiness 616.05
unhealthy 167.19 578.26 890.13
unheard-of 273.28 274.01
unheeded 479.11 585.14
unhoped-for 063.21 756.22
uniform 161.28 229.27 286.15 290.25 735.12
uniformly 078.11 500.06
unimparted 832.08
unimpeachable 205.23
unimportant 810.17
unimpressible 637.08
unimpressionable 466.06
uninhabited 869.10
uninitiated 792.09
unintentionally 436.20
uninvited 463.17
union 320.04 513.27 518.09 583.14 598.07 602.25 623.19 632.16 751.17 756.04 786.11 801.26 821.13 824.20 824.21 824.27 827.14 909.15
unions 636.17

unique 139.12 285.21
united 580.01 699.06
unity 444.10
universal 081.23 158.11 659.19
universally 018.21 195.23
unjust 019.18 019.18 051.27 106.21 292.18 784.15
unjustly 105.18 107.07
unkind 108.11
unkindness 057.11
unknit 531.28
unknown 022.21 074.02 180.26 321.21 488.16 572.19 575.06 584.06 678.09 884.14
unlawful 437.15
unless 015.17 046.28 195.10 246.03 333.13 339.17 826.14 834.25
unlike 191.23 235.14 585.14
unlikely 376.19 603.13 799.19
unlimited 147.05 706.09 761.28
unlocked 138.09 630.21
unloosed 099.19
unlove 372.02 372.13
unluckily 288.04
unlucky 261.22
unmannered 730.03
unmarried 482.17 820.14 641.26 912.08
unmolested 298.18 489.05
unmoved 833.21
unnatural 295.06 467.23 524.25 842.14
unnecessary 281.21 676.11 801.28 844.04 888.16
unnoticed 004.05 417.26 417.26 472.14 504.09
unreasonable 626.27

unnumbered 146.06
unobjectionable 211.22
unobserved 392.24
unobtrusive 270.01
unpleasantly 098.08
unpolished 703.11
unpolluted 268.22
unprepared 102.10 323.25
unprincipled 637.06
unproductive 673.14
unprofitable 671.08
unquiet 302.19
unreal 566.20 580.09 640.23
unreasonable 620.07
unreasonably 047.18
unreclaimed 720.15
unremittingly 375.23 338.28
unrequired 641.15
unresentful 141.16 201.12
unreservedly 262.23 318.07 381.25 439.14
unresisting 425.21 641.06 691.09
unreturned 321.20 718.12 745.15
unreverberating 789.09 902.14
unripe 561.25 740.12
unsanctioned 029.25 274.14
unsatisfied 088.23 644.04 650.17 688.11
unscared 850.23
unseasonable 665.25
unseen 366.27 402.05 502.28 639.23 871.20
unsettled 253.09 382.14 760.14
unshaken 818.02
unshared 832.08
unshod 299.18 618.06
unsmiling 740.15 897.05
unsnuffed 155.15
unsocial 801.11
unsophisticated 059.04 239.28 789.14
unsounded 610.06
unspeakable 111.05 146.13 852.24
unspeakably 535.03
unspoken 030.25 497.08 722.17
unsteady 614.22
unstrung 494.10 705.28
unsubstantiality 539.04
unsundered 560.16
unsustained 646.03
unsympathizing 786.27
untasted 032.11
untaught 107.02 743.06

untempered 478.24
unthinking 746.15
untidily 141.06
untidy 128.03
untie 187.01
until 002.09 002.23 835.21
untimely 424.26
untiring 430.27 617.23 817.28
untiringly 889.26
untouched 888.06
untrodden 606.03
untrue 835.18
untying 256.12
unused 148.23 236.18
unusual 159.05
unutterable 029.25
unuttered 607.21
unvaried 563.01
unvarnished 320.21
unveiled 414.08
unwarped 759.02
unwarranted 426.23
unwatched 146.12 479.17
unwed 826.17
unwelcome 235.19 618.06 897.05
unwholesome 007.04
unwilling 521.13
unwise 433.16
unwisely 105.18
unwittingly 167.20 879.18
unwonted 030.09
unworthy 183.19
up 002.22 003.03 004.22 005.21 008.09 010.23 011.06 014.21 017.14 017.27 018.13 019.21 023.10 026.02 026.11 029.22 030.17 031.16 033.08 033.29 035.22 036.03 036.28 038.10 039.19 039.24 043.19 044.07 044.26 047.07 048.12 052.13 053.09 057.26 061.17 061.24 061.26 062.24 063.08 063.24 064.22 071.05 071.19 073.18 073.22 074.17 075.06 076.03 078.19 079.14 080.03 080.20 080.25 085.19 088.24 089.04 090.03 095.01 096.02 098.09 101.23 110.01 110.04 110.08 113.10 114.16 114.22 115.12 115.21 116.07 116.26 120.23 122.17 122.26 123.11 124.15 127.13 127.17 127.20 127.28 130.12 130.14 136.27 137.24 137.27 138.09 140.01 146.05 147.03 147.14 148.03 151.10 151.27 152.28 153.21 154.18 159.06 160.10 163.21 167.01 167.20 168.15 172.08 176.18 176.23 181.03 183.10 183.19 186.20 188.17 190.01 190.18 191.11 193.26 194.20 195.04 196.17 197.02 202.14 203.11 204.05 204.27 206.25 208.23 209.17 214.14 220.14

222.04	489.22	766.11	423.03	138.07	266.02
222.26	494.19	766.19	431.13	138.20	270.23
224.05	497.18	774.02	460.11	138.23	299.13
227.12	498.20	775.08	508.20	140.20	422.19
228.15	510.09	787.20	534.26	140.21	454.25
229.11	519.10	789.18	539.03	148.15	474.14
230.22	519.24	791.16	551.19	149.01	476.11
231.28	519.26	791.25	578.21	149.03	614.19
232.26	522.08	792.01	715.27	184.23	627.12
233.11	522.22	792.06	733.09	185.17	703.25
235.16	528.15	793.10	733.18	199.13	757.16
241.14	528.21	795.05	757.10	212.02	823.02
246.14	529.08	795.21	757.14	212.05	838.16
249.07	529.17	798.24	773.15	214.07	884.11
251.02	531.08	799.23	779.21	231.01	893.19
251.12	531.17	801.13	797.10	237.20	899.09
252.26	535.07	801.21	803.09	244.08	used
258.18	540.26	802.02	804.01	244.16	046.10
260.25	542.08	805.15	827.13	244.19	062.16
272.24	546.20	811.27	828.20	244.22	069.02
273.08	548.16	813.02	859.16	251.11	083.12
279.07	549.12	814.12	875.02	252.01	119.25
281.01	554.12	818.14	903.12	283.12	161.02
282.20	554.15	818.22	upper	313.04	199.15
282.22	560.13	827.16	082.02	336.01	200.04
287.17	561.11	829.22	084.03	336.13	200.07
288.18	561.22	832.19	261.18	351.14	201.17
292.06	564.16	835.03	284.03	357.01	202.12
292.23	565.20	841.20	329.07	357.19	203.02
293.14	568.16	843.08	367.24	357.23	217.25
294.03	570.19	843.12	416.18	386.16	245.10
294.16	575.05	846.09	503.04	389.12	276.22
295.12	576.19	850.06	740.10	391.12	310.20
296.19	577.18	851.09	768.03	391.13	330.06
297.09	578.21	855.18	upraised	416.22	355.15
297.17	582.17	856.01	368.15	432.12	356.04
297.20	583.01	857.18	upright	464.14	356.12
297.27	585.05	858.27	231.22	481.15	357.16
299.06	587.15	864.25	uprightly	485.19	373.10
300.22	588.25	865.15	817.14	486.14	377.28
306.12	589.18	869.12	uprightness	493.22	431.13
307.06	590.20	871.03	161.22	498.26	446.13
307.11	595.02	875.01	762.23	499.05	458.08
311.04	596.18	875.03	uproar	511.02	456.15
313.14	596.22	875.03	100.17	515.05	458.24
314.14	597.08	878.16	upstairs	515.13	465.01
315.28	597.22	879.13	050.18	518.29	468.19
317.15	598.25	879.24	150.24	536.23	470.26
324.17	600.04	880.07	uptore	538.22	497.13
327.17	602.11	881.25	649.14	572.18	500.03
327.26	604.22	885.21	uptorn	579.24	527.16
330.08	607.23	885.27	819.17	588.16	535.20
332.21	610.15	886.03	upward	589.06	571.24
335.14	610.22	886.07	573.25	589.08	603.18
336.17	611.05	889.11	824.04	591.08	641.23
337.10	611.12	890.19	upwards	598.17	643.08
337.20	616.16	899.15	094.21	599.03	695.01
339.25	616.17	905.16	325.25	602.13	745.12
340.19	625.28	908.11	439.03	604.03	787.26
352.22	627.10	910.19	urge	626.21	807.12
353.15	629.19	912.01	814.12	662.09	835.17
353.16	629.22	up-hill	826.12	679.12	863.01
355.27	629.28	219.23	841.06	679.14	useful
353.11	631.14	up-rooting	urged	680.17	014.27
365.13	633.09	029.21	073.21	688.01	057.28
366.21	637.10	up-stairs	162.06	703.14	161.23
367.10	639.05	334.25	263.28	706.26	223.25
378.19	640.16	627.07	392.09	714.10	227.25
380.16	641.02	646.16	595.14	726.18	245.01
381.11	650.22	upastree	665.24	726.28	442.15
395.02	651.14	616.14	721.08	727.01	718.10
396.03	652.03	upbraid	804.11	727.17	745.09
398.25	653.03	614.18	845.15	727.17	842.13
398.28	656.22	upbraided	855.26	734.27	895.14
403.28	656.28	611.13	866.11	735.09	898.13
406.21	658.13	upbraiding	888.12	741.09	useless
412.23	660.05	627.01	urgency	780.08	018.17
413.03	662.13	831.08	772.06	780.09	020.14
419.02	663.04	upheld	urgent	780.11	148.09
419.13	664.19	026.13	632.19	784.26	274.19
419.14	666.27	upholstery	717.22	801.04	431.27
420.14	674.08	794.24	766.05	802.15	476.16
421.27	675.12	uplifted	810.08	802.19	530.24
427.09	679.03	808.12	urgently	803.17	636.17
427.12	684.25	upon	849.23	804.01	707.03
434.01	693.14	010.23	urges	804.18	724.15
441.21	698.18	011.06	820.01	812.17	636.01
442.03	706.17	013.05	urging	812.19	394.17
442.18	709.24	022.08	894.02	815.06	ushered
447.08	710.06	030.28	us	821.08	185.26
447.21	711.04	051.18	005.20	821.23	190.26
452.10	715.14	059.08	009.11	824.09	413.02
454.21	716.05	068.04	024.12	826.24	using
456.02	718.20	078.03	091.08	828.06	764.04
457.03	733.06	118.26	091.15	833.20	usual
457.24	735.09	123.10	091.19	887.25	045.12
457.26	736.21	124.11	096.10	909.07	052.19
457.27	737.17	130.24	102.27	909.16	067.08
463.08	739.04	185.18	106.28	909.16	100.22
467.15	739.27	221.21	108.27	909.23	137.24
469.09	741.10	221.22	111.16	909.23	151.14
473.20	741.21	242.28	113.10	911.07	168.25
474.02	742.01	272.06	121.21	usage	226.16
475.22	743.15	281.17	125.02	108.17	234.28
476.06	745.25	287.21	132.22	use	238.19
479.09	746.07	331.22	132.23	102.09	238.19
480.15	747.03	377.25	132.24	107.24	255.15
481.22	752.20	385.20	132.25	167.07	267.19
483.09	753.18	388.12	132.26	203.10	285.11
483.11	763.18	389.25	133.05	227.04	305.12
489.02	765.06	391.02	133.26	265.25	306.22

307.10
336.17
362.12
366.10
362.25
474.26
498.08
507.03
548.14
548.19
585.14
605.14
725.01
738.14
749.07
803.16
810.12
852.06
852.11
853.06
843.11
usually
044.19
065.06
165.06
217.20
218.21
367.27
390.06
414.03
573.05
868.09
usurious
045.28
usurped
550.14
555.11
utmost
209.25
378.27
705.22
721.16
849.05
utter
044.10
219.12
470.18
553.15
573.03
623.12
665.17
663.22
775.25
828.02
856.21
876.21
utterance
044.16
104.06
415.05
467.09
638.06
uttered
057.05
153.06
155.16
274.28
310.22
415.01
416.03
424.19
452.01
478.23
560.01
591.01
605.11
634.03
767.02
801.09
823.13
824.03
827.26
829.01
846.17
uttering
043.14
053.09
592.01
844.15
utterly
459.13
836.06
847.17
v
557.11
va
277.09
vacancy
872.26
vacant
017.12
050.09
080.23
081.03
150.15
152.22
341.02
352.06
477.06
877.02

vacate
233.08
287.23
vacated
371.07
vacation
250.02
vacations
058.01
165.03
247.01
vacillating
734.16
vagrant
682.19
687.01
734.05
vague
014.15
080.25
089.01
133.17
165.20
249.12
259.18
274.24
293.27
325.18
377.22
634.05
660.02
610.16
901.08
vain
030.28
031.13
071.17
082.07
167.19
216.06
227.16
405.16
440.16
476.08
609.12
662.02
746.10
766.18
772.03
806.28
809.24
vainly
147.27
375.02
636.14
654.04
852.26
673.09
vais
277.11
vale
220.06
542.22
696.04
712.04
732.25
736.23
749.16
766.06
vale-hall
733.01
741.11
747.23
750.17
756.02
valet
364.12
valets
327.06
valid
785.02
valley
075.07
659.33
664.12
721.28
739.04
765.05
900.09
valleys
540.15
valour
359.28
valuable
488.25
727.26
751.15
861.20
value
104.18
161.27
526.18
834.15
898.06
valued
048.27
215.12
621.04
796.02
valueless
673.02

valuing
278.01
vampyre
578.11
van
081.25
388.26
vanish
639.18
650.02
674.10
vanished
029.05
183.05
228.12
299.09
388.07
555.17
675.16
764.03
887.03
vanishing
164.25
674.06
vanity
121.22
550.05
vanquishing
355.21
vapid
217.28
vapour
248.20
296.10
492.27
808.25
vapours
652.05
vapoury
558.11
737.23
varandah
087.25
088.13
varens
188.13
188.13
188.18
189.20
276.22
279.10
284.22
288.04
547.15
547.17
636.27
varens'
236.13
variance
245.04
826.24
variation
673.28
variations
804.20
varied
164.10
265.13
365.02
664.15
varieties
146.06
variety
090.23
215.11
275.26
various
160.18
170.20
391.14
435.03
473.10
varry
679.19
906.23
vary
474.24
varying
017.09
vase
341.25
vases
203.21
331.03
331.11
799.01
vassalage
020.09
vast
004.01
004.08
194.01
203.19
416.27
423.16
624.16
vault
021.13
021.15
022.21
204.02

209.16
477.20
491.02
589.07
615.18
859.11
vault-like
190.23
vegetation
146.01
859.27
vehemence
511.18
611.14
812.01
vehement
052.03
132.16
vehemently
858.16
vehicle
180.25
183.17
434.02
657.08
798.03
854.19
vehicles
332.23
veil
249.07
333.01
367.06
489.12
490.03
495.01
525.23
542.10
558.11
570.22
571.18
576.12
577.18
578.13
580.16
580.21
581.17
585.06
737.17
823.25
858.11
veiled
585.14
veiling
050.01
veils
332.23
vein
031.11
550.23
550.28
655.17
881.01
veins
144.11
230.28
576.22
648.16
760.01
781.26
832.24
velvet
086.05
122.01
122.08
209.02
344.24
431.01
746.11
vending
048.15
venerable
207.11
venerated
834.14
veneration
085.20
140.17
846.27
846.28
vengeance
065.17
107.15
442.02
465.09
551.28
555.20
831.15
880.01
venice
526.22
venom
483.09
vent
373.16
789.08
venture
267.09
310.03
334.13
389.08

544.10
ventured
040.05
090.27
129.04
193.08
284.19
315.06
499.04
545.11
670.07
717.24
838.06
venturesome
069.12
venturing
333.12
802.07
verandah
088.20
094.16
097.22
151.11
verb
142.21
verdant
855.04
verdure
145.11
vere
478.10
verge
146.18
315.05
628.24
659.08
verging
380.10
837.05
veriest
451.14
verily
185.06
269.14
272.20
376.12
vermilion
773.27
vernacularly
346.04
vernal
277.25
verse
055.24
055.25
089.23
verses
200.05
844.27
very
007.13
008.07
010.19
014.12
014.16
015.15
018.20
027.18
027.20
032.26
032.26
034.01
034.23
034.24
036.08
037.03
037.05
038.16
046.03
047.27
053.11
060.21
062.25
066.20
068.24
072.24
074.09
074.19
075.03
076.23
079.17
082.16
085.28
093.14
093.14
097.26
103.19
103.27
105.03
106.02
106.26
117.02
120.04
123.25
124.09
129.18
137.17
138.01
140.01
144.11
149.07

151.04
151.13
151.23
153.02
156.14
157.04
157.14
164.27
174.05
175.11
176.09
176.10
176.18
177.10
180.08
180.11
180.14
182.02
182.17
184.06
184.08
189.04
189.09
190.23
192.27
193.19
195.08
197.25
199.08
199.22
201.01
201.12
204.09
206.08
208.24
210.10
210.19
214.03
216.14
218.11
221.23
230.01
235.11
237.17
243.20
244.02
244.11
251.20
252.12
252.15
253.07
258.25
259.06
262.11
263.27
265.18
265.19
266.11
266.14
268.19
270.01
271.07
271.07
271.20
271.21
274.16
275.14
277.03
280.25
281.19
283.03
294.28
296.16
298.11
299.06
299.11
299.20
300.12
300.19
300.24
301.27
310.10
311.22
312.21
316.18
316.27
317.07
319.05
319.13
331.24
332.20
333.15
333.17
337.07
342.14
343.12
343.16
343.16
344.22
344.23
344.23
346.25
348.04
348.06
348.13
352.12
352.13
359.13
362.01
368.08
369.22

372.14	699.21	vested	756.02	064.01	visiting
372.19	700.12	775.05	829.07	virgil	040.26
372.20	701.03	vestige	839.27	140.16	714.12
372.26	701.05	772.04	843.04	virgin	800.26
373.04	701.24	vestry	885.01	200.04	908.06
376.13	703.01	586.20	vigilance	201.23	visitor
377.04	703.11	698.08	633.20	virile	147.24
377.11	714.21	vex	vigils	601.07	187.17
381.21	717.27	574.06	442.07	virtually	388.11
389.10	721.24	574.09	vignettes	622.12	464.09
396.08	723.11	804.25	004.21	virtue	689.18
397.05	730.19	893.26	470.28	264.23	700.11
408.06	733.18	vexation	vigorous	280.17	766.24
408.06	733.22	619.09	139.25	555.25	visitors
408.07	734.14	830.10	223.02	625.19	015.17
430.11	739.16	vexations	351.21	649.25	050.06
455.19	739.18	626.27	426.03	889.25	121.26
438.05	741.12	vexed	512.04	virtues	137.04
439.17	741.20	641.03	567.02	816.02	363.09
440.13	741.20	vexing	713.11	virulence	413.05
440.17	746.26	315.02	741.04	160.14	600.14
445.24	748.16	725.26	826.25	virulent	visitress
447.07	748.19	vibrated	872.02	025.09	746.19
448.02	750.13	592.06	886.14	visage	visits
449.27	751.07	592.07	890.05	007.05	114.24
449.27	754.05	853.07	890.17	461.02	204.25
452.02	754.25	vibrating	vigorously	471.16	254.09
455.19	754.26	569.17	545.18	577.21	384.24
455.19	755.05	vibration	vigour	578.23	499.22
455.20	757.12	361.16	018.07	600.13	748.05
457.04	757.12	vice	146.02	634.09	vist
460.10	761.03	214.01	221.14	704.25	234.08
460.20	766.10	606.23	343.17	881.21	vital
460.20	767.06	616.09	396.22	visible	324.20
461.06	770.22	647.01	665.01	049.26	374.19
463.27	771.10	817.19	825.12	075.27	626.03
470.15	771.23	889.25	vile	082.08	826.04
472.17	773.16	vices	119.06	084.09	vitality
479.11	775.10	038.02	626.11	129.17	100.11
481.11	777.10	627.10	vileness	181.12	560.17
483.05	778.05	636.24	816.08	182.10	vitals
484.12	783.16	vicinage	villa	248.09	645.08
485.08	787.28	495.07	622.15	249.10	725.11
490.16	791.16	616.15	village	301.18	820.02
490.21	792.17	871.08	038.13	322.19	vivacious
492.12	796.09	vicinity	185.14	369.21	214.02
493.10	799.16	155.02	196.05	492.23	vivaciously
493.10	806.15	163.28	664.23	503.17	376.02
502.20	806.15	vicious	665.28	560.07	vivacity
504.15	807.16	115.28	668.09	668.10	275.26
507.07	810.27	126.19	670.05	732.26	314.01
507.15	811.11	270.12	673.10	733.18	335.20
517.01	811.28	275.16	695.15	870.12	348.16
517.01	812.18	286.17	729.17	visibly	379.13
526.06	818.06	viciously	732.13	209.06	713.16
527.01	818.06	601.04	746.15	vision	747.16
527.12	818.21	vicomte	802.20	006.15	792.19
528.02	819.03	286.16	817.12	023.17	800.23
529.04	819.23	287.26	village-school	215.05	806.24
529.06	826.18	victim	722.22	246.26	882.15
531.12	828.05	127.18	743.02	272.13	886.24
533.25	836.18	307.02	village-schoolmistr-	445.23	vivid
537.13	839.13	368.09	ess	579.08	215.15
542.07	845.24	610.13	732.01	652.01	276.01
550.04	850.20	820.03	749.04	684.15	492.03
550.10	854.02	victims	villain	737.12	519.05
552.25	854.20	160.15	269.11	819.24	781.22
553.18	855.19	victories	616.09	844.07	799.05
554.01	856.08	762.27	villains	846.17	vividly
557.02	856.27	912.06	356.05	856.13	247.17
567.23	857.23	victory	villany	877.12	313.11
568.01	857.25	018.05	116.08	896.03	726.22
569.19	859.05	064.26	vinaigarettes	903.14	vividness
569.20	859.05	067.10	392.05	909.17	221.14
572.22	862.08	374.13	vindictive	visionary	viz
574.01	862.16	802.28	311.27	017.19	217.21
575.01	863.04	victualage	484.19	105.11	419.03
575.01	863.20	335.11	617.01	573.10	vocabulary
582.15	864.22	vienna	vindictiveness	653.02	546.03
585.03	865.08	526.22	831.12	815.05	630.09
625.02	868.04	view	vine-leaves	visions	vocal
628.18	869.20	003.07	204.14	215.25	358.12
632.15	876.14	127.09	vinegar	640.22	497.11
632.20	879.27	186.05	154.15	847.23	vocalist
635.13	882.02	191.25	vines	visit	549.19
635.15	882.27	204.08	018.28	058.14	vocation
637.12	883.18	208.23	vineyards	165.07	225.09
640.02	883.25	235.13	526.14	195.13	489.15
640.20	884.24	289.09	vining	299.03	717.22
640.22	886.03	350.11	356.11	305.11	724.18
641.22	886.11	368.11	violate	335.18	759.19
647.17	889.04	607.09	547.06	391.04	808.10
659.08	889.16	675.27	violation	424.07	815.19
661.15	890.14	718.28	022.16	597.23	822.23
667.22	891.11	784.13	violence	634.02	voce
671.15	900.19	822.06	019.16	740.01	064.21
672.25	900.19	846.06	025.06	741.13	vogue
673.10	902.27	856.15	107.14	746.05	086.03
676.04	907.15	856.24	425.02	789.16	voice
677.03	908.09	886.12	484.16	804.08	006.04
682.16	909.16	viewed	619.17	892.01	014.26
682.23	909.16	145.14	violent	902.17	022.26
685.06	910.22	231.01	018.10	visitant	024.15
685.22	vessel	807.25	022.25	232.06	032.22
685.22	030.26	viewing	208.14	580.07	032.23
688.03	632.27	589.08	626.27	visitation	044.10
689.03	846.09	viewless	637.06	357.28	053.01
690.05	vessels	229.27	835.17	852.21	062.17
692.18	094.02	272.13	888.23	visited	064.13
694.12	431.07	views	violently	016.19	066.27
698.25		749.15	063.06	169.10	073.28

077.20	903.14	388.01	418.13	080.26	walnut-panelled
082.01	voices	vulgarity	434.11	081.01	203.18
087.05	026.05	691.10	446.02	163.17	walnut-wood
105.04	078.04	vulnerable	465.01	218.28	701.06
141.01	100.18	437.28	604.04	219.01	waltz
141.09	165.10	vulture	611.08	222.28	178.18
156.02	231.17	668.17	654.02	228.15	wander
175.13	233.18	waded	819.09	229.03	104.26
201.11	449.13	659.23	854.15	235.08	106.06
201.20	void	wading	886.19	287.21	439.21
255.02	364.15	149.09	906.18	367.07	502.28
275.18	609.12	waft	waiting-woman	389.17	783.24
301.18	692.04	229.12	717.19	421.01	wandered
302.03	724.10	514.24	waits	459.16	084.28
305.05	819.16	526.12	133.04	498.04	100.22
305.16	826.12	wage	396.19	502.13	145.16
307.25	849.27	678.25	wake	509.19	151.15
308.15	859.03	wages	156.24	564.01	382.14
313.04	859.25	329.25	210.12	570.07	514.26
313.09	872.23	453.09	296.13	588.24	526.23
314.05	910.25	wagged	296.13	613.18	565.21
319.01	voila	232.02	298.19	631.04	575.02
319.03	334.10	737.02	307.27	651.02	668.20
353.23	380.13	wagging	406.16	651.02	668.24
357.05	voiture	355.06	567.13	656.17	673.08
344.22	281.15	waggon	582.17	664.02	707.16
346.09	volatile	664.19	743.15	723.12	795.21
358.06	419.20	wail	849.07	782.12	813.03
361.11	volcanic	468.16	waked	829.02	860.03
365.07	611.28	561.19	306.04	856.13	902.22
366.27	volcano-tops	wailed	652.19	865.01	wanderer
395.11	540.15	572.24	wakefulness	walking	032.08
402.01	volume	wailing	029.10	078.19	272.11
405.21	003.01	445.13	waken	113.06	459.25
405.18	009.22	waist	022.25	541.26	690.11
407.10	032.02	133.20	232.10	618.26	706.11
408.15	352.18	197.07	856.21	653.20	wanderer's
413.06	473.12	368.13	wakened	833.12	441.01
415.11	474.09	592.16	105.09	852.20	wanderers
419.02	749.11	648.25	229.26	857.01	845.11
420.26	796.12	766.20	302.23	walks	wandering
424.19	volumes	876.17	609.11	001.11	001.04
449.24	202.17	waistcoat	640.18	087.26	174.27
454.12	460.13	035.11	678.06	145.03	325.19
461.24	677.18	285.05	680.26	435.10	378.01
463.12	voluntarily	430.17	731.14	wall	382.15
463.05	758.19	617.16	853.05	005.02	423.07
463.13	voluntary	waistcoats	887.01	023.06	440.23
490.27	044.13	545.26	wakening	050.13	467.09
494.13	044.14	wait	655.13	072.15	497.19
498.16	439.26	084.05	wakes	074.17	607.22
506.19	volunteered	276.05	457.25	075.24	655.18
508.10	218.15	297.21	waking	076.16	731.24
514.28	voluptuous	353.03	026.02	120.23	803.28
539.07	461.20	391.02	284.25	374.16	846.21
549.17	volvanic-looking	393.01	361.14	433.06	859.21
550.03	378.02	417.25	576.06	434.07	876.12
573.05	vos	420.20	581.10	438.08	886.04
585.16	313.16	441.19	858.07	502.20	888.14
593.17	313.16	522.20	wales	504.01	wanderings
591.08	votary	558.03	181.10	535.01	384.23
593.06	735.17	565.01	walk	557.08	634.16
609.16	vote	587.06	001.03	575.01	682.03
610.17	405.18	628.20	035.04	575.13	wane
614.22	votre	684.02	040.01	576.01	423.13
615.06	239.11	791.05	066.12	599.07	waned
619.17	277.18	811.04	112.20	609.04	075.02
620.24	vouch	849.24	169.09	652.01	want
622.22	246.02	879.01	185.05	653.20	006.22
640.16	436.11	880.08	185.24	653.20	006.24
645.22	vouchsafe	885.10	199.15	675.20	006.25
645.25	682.02	897.18	214.25	676.08	028.11
650.17	vouchsafed	898.26	215.21	692.16	052.06
667.18	533.15	902.07	218.13	782.16	093.24
667.20	752.24	906.13	229.26	857.11	134.01
672.12	810.16	907.05	230.10	859.04	166.23
673.01	vous	waited	279.07	wall-nooks	167.05
673.07	201.13	042.06	284.18	031.16	167.07
682.06	212.03	047.04	301.06	walled	167.26
684.07	234.22	227.17	379.18	489.22	192.15
691.06	234.23	361.15	419.12	walls	223.28
699.23	277.17	371.11	429.24	016.01	236.14
705.04	vow	419.25	433.12	022.12	312.18
716.09	466.02	428.17	434.26	076.11	315.18
720.05	468.27	493.06	442.04	087.24	379.14
726.08	530.09	559.14	454.04	111.12	386.06
736.16	648.08	569.15	454.21	142.22	395.10
736.25	vowed	583.20	472.28	145.09	406.03
742.11	465.28	589.02	490.11	147.25	419.10
745.19	544.04	639.02	492.11	161.24	443.15
758.03	552.07	641.05	502.24	181.06	449.23
810.23	736.15	699.20	504.08	191.23	450.05
815.01	vowing	718.21	505.14	193.13	450.14
817.02	043.14	767.13	518.28	203.18	453.08
832.03	vows	818.18	519.11	329.02	456.24
843.25	286.06	849.08	522.09	616.08	472.05
843.26	voyage	waiter	572.23	701.09	474.19
849.12	031.24	182.10	619.13	701.18	477.11
849.20	179.27	183.02	654.14	711.18	478.22
849.21	509.03	waiting	675.02	715.23	494.04
852.25	509.04	180.19	699.10	729.03	516.24
853.15	510.07	182.08	711.05	765.16	530.16
871.24	632.27	182.14	783.10	795.12	533.12
876.08	vrai	183.09	811.15	856.23	540.23
876.21	234.26	212.05	829.20	859.21	547.13
878.11	543.17	218.14	873.09	866.13	548.14
883.15	vulcan	233.07	879.01	870.23	548.25
894.21	891.14	241.26	886.28	walnut	569.04
902.05	891.13	310.13	walked	207.08	586.24
902.05	vulgar	311.13	061.25	676.15	607.07
902.06	387.20	353.03	074.18		612.22

613.09	660.21	636.15	025.15	066.12	096.13
618.12	663.14	846.11	026.10	066.19	096.15
645.15	672.10	warning	026.17	066.20	096.16
649.26	682.01	061.10	026.18	067.01	096.19
662.27	741.17	256.10	026.19	067.09	097.03
663.25	818.24	380.11	027.05	067.11	097.08
667.05	822.28	392.07	027.08	067.12	097.16
667.27	886.08	498.16	027.11	067.16	097.20
669.03	war	503.08	027.20	067.17	097.26
669.26	479.28	563.16	028.19	069.14	098.01
672.13	759.25	639.01	028.24	071.10	098.03
673.04	warbled	warnings	029.01	071.12	098.17
681.16	200.28	118.27	029.25	072.16	098.20
682.06	warbling	135.20	030.06	072.17	099.02
682.14	503.15	539.02	030.12	072.24	099.03
684.10	ward	warped	030.26	072.24	099.05
694.07	196.15	429.07	030.27	072.27	099.11
694.23	347.13	warrant	032.02	073.01	100.05
707.21	596.25	403.03	032.06	073.18	100.13
751.20	771.15	682.26	032.17	073.21	100.26
774.22	864.23	warranted	032.23	073.22	101.09
784.09	ward-robes	812.02	033.27	073.27	101.24
786.17	365.17	warrior	034.01	073.27	102.08
786.27	wardrobe	911.24	034.22	074.01	105.10
786.28	016.03	warrior-march	035.06	074.12	105.14
790.23	016.20	825.26	035.06	074.24	105.17
791.06	017.08	wars	035.11	075.13	105.20
791.08	174.06	589.12	035.13	075.14	105.24
805.15	429.26	was	035.17	075.18	106.01
810.03	547.21	001.03	035.18	075.18	106.03
811.18	729.10	001.06	035.20	075.20	109.26
816.20	851.04	001.10	035.22	075.27	111.15
822.14	ware	001.11	035.28	076.01	112.04
822.15	601.01	001.13	036.02	076.13	112.24
823.10	warehouse	002.11	036.02	076.15	112.27
824.13	543.26	003.05	038.05	076.19	113.18
827.07	544.17	003.22	036.14	076.21	113.19
827.08	warfare	005.08	036.23	076.22	113.27
841.24	747.27	005.10	039.11	077.11	114.04
842.23	warily	005.28	039.16	077.11	114.06
878.18	308.04	006.14	039.24	077.20	114.12
897.01	wark	006.25	040.07	077.25	114.17
902.12	695.01	006.27	040.10	078.13	114.19
908.07	warm	007.01	040.11	078.16	11-.25
wanted	018.05	007.02	040.23	079.01	115.01
024.11	047.02	007.17	040.28	079.10	115.05
050.22	048.09	007.27	041.01	079.16	115.11
051.13	065.19	008.04	042.09	079.17	115.20
051.15	131.27	008.26	043.20	079.18	115.20
073.06	151.05	009.03	043.23	079.21	116.04
074.13	152.03	009.18	044.05	079.22	116.05
177.05	153.26	009.22	044.13	079.25	116.06
177.19	216.28	009.25	044.23	080.02	116.07
179.15	231.06	010.16	045.05	080.05	116.27
179.24	280.12	010.21	045.14	080.07	117.01
232.05	281.22	010.23	046.01	080.09	117.04
232.05	298.22	011.06	046.03	081.03	118.02
234.09	332.03	012.05	047.01	081.06	120.28
241.01	420.08	012.07	047.02	081.07	121.03
305.05	435.17	013.05	047.19	081.11	121.07
314.23	466.10	013.20	047.21	081.15	121.25
314.25	492.25	013.27	047.24	081.17	122.07
325.16	540.23	013.27	046.03	081.19	122.21
358.12	660.22	015.15	048.05	082.08	123.10
410.18	688.09	015.20	048.06	082.13	123.22
419.01	630.04	015.28	046.08	082.24	123.27
430.06	658.13	016.08	048.11	082.25	124.06
445.28	warm-hearted	016.12	049.08	082.28	124.10
447.21	506.27	016.13	049.22	083.01	124.12
448.09	warmed	016.14	049.24	083.10	124.13
458.26	076.08	016.26	050.06	083.15	124.14
471.24	189.23	016.28	050.08	083.16	124.16
505.12	190.05	017.05	050.16	084.01	125.09
565.23	376.08	017.08	051.05	084.21	126.17
587.23	394.16	017.13	051.13	084.23	127.06
587.25	766.18	017.15	051.17	085.03	127.09
598.15	882.23	017.23	051.25	085.04	127.17
602.03	warmer	018.03	052.16	085.10	127.23
609.18	100.13	018.04	052.24	085.18	127.26
611.16	442.11	018.05	053.04	085.28	129.03
635.10	warming	018.06	053.11	086.04	129.05
644.21	181.16	018.14	053.17	086.17	129.09
666.10	warmly	018.17	054.01	086.26	129.11
666.26	129.19	018.18	054.07	087.03	130.05
667.21	warms	018.19	054.16	087.15	130.13
722.13	182.24	018.21	056.09	087.18	130.25
723.01	691.12	019.06	056.11	087.21	133.10
774.20	warmth	019.08	056.27	087.23	133.11
806.03	088.12	019.16	057.01	088.04	135.01
808.10	308.28	019.26	057.07	088.06	135.17
810.04	606.18	019.27	057.11	088.08	135.18
852.19	612.27	020.01	059.19	088.18	136.02
893.23	676.26	020.06	060.14	088.27	136.16
895.06	693.05	020.06	060.15	089.01	137.02
895.22	773.15	021.01	060.17	089.07	137.10
896.06	warn	021.02	060.21	089.11	137.13
wanting	125.14	021.09	060.24	089.19	137.15
167.08	303.02	021.12	060.26	089.20	137.25
186.14	340.16	021.13	060.27	089.28	138.19
369.09	395.14	021.13	061.13	090.12	138.26
691.26	574.17	021.19	061.23	090.26	139.07
737.25	746.20	023.06	063.08	091.27	139.08
966.22	770.06	023.08	063.22	092.18	139.27
wantonly	793.16	023.12	063.22	093.27	140.24
019.14	warned	023.14	064.25	094.02	140.25
wants	154.15	023.16	064.25	094.07	141.01
174.07	335.06	023.21	065.24	094.21	141.03
309.22	426.25	024.02	066.08	095.16	141.21
397.07	428.15	024.23		095.19	142.05
403.05	551.15	025.07		096.05	142.14
598.20	614.22				142.17

142.19	173.13	206.26	244.18	292.12	332.02
142.27	173.19	208.20	246.23	292.15	332.14
143.13	174.01	208.26	247.25	292.18	332.25
144.03	174.06	209.12	247.26	292.19	333.19
145.20	174.10	209.13	248.09	293.01	333.22
145.27	174.11	209.19	248.15	293.09	333.26
146.14	174.12	210.07	248.18	293.11	334.18
146.21	174.17	210.10	249.15	294.02	335.04
147.10	174.21	210.26	249.17	294.04	335.12
147.24	174.22	211.02	249.20	294.06	335.13
148.21	174.24	211.04	249.20	294.08	336.07
148.28	174.27	211.09	249.21	294.12	336.09
149.06	175.02	213.04	250.01	294.22	336.12
149.10	175.04	213.09	250.08	294.27	336.14
149.15	175.16	213.11	250.11	295.02	336.22
149.28	175.18	213.11	251.10	295.06	336.26
150.02	176.24	215.12	251.15	295.08	337.01
150.05	176.25	215.13	252.14	295.15	337.06
150.09	178.06	215.13	252.19	295.16	337.11
150.22	178.06	215.19	252.21	295.21	337.21
150.25	178.16	215.21	252.24	295.23	337.24
150.25	178.19	216.02	252.27	295.24	337.25
150.27	178.25	217.06	253.05	296.03	338.02
151.03	179.14	217.27	253.16	296.04	338.05
151.07	179.26	218.11	253.22	296.08	338.07
151.09	179.28	218.12	253.22	296.17	339.24
151.20	180.01	218.14	254.07	297.03	340.03
151.21	180.03	218.27	254.11	297.03	340.04
152.02	180.11	218.27	254.13	299.09	340.07
152.06	180.13	218.28	255.14	299.12	340.08
152.21	180.17	219.03	255.15	299.13	340.17
152.26	180.19	219.07	255.19	299.14	340.21
152.27	180.24	219.14	255.21	301.18	340.22
153.02	180.25	219.28	256.12	302.03	340.24
153.06	182.10	220.05	257.23	302.06	340.25
153.10	182.12	220.15	258.06	302.16	340.27
153.12	182.27	221.05	258.14	302.18	341.07
153.13	183.11	221.05	258.16	305.08	342.01
153.27	183.13	221.07	258.23	305.11	342.05
153.27	183.20	221.08	258.26	305.20	343.04
154.01	183.27	221.09	259.08	306.10	343.06
154.10	183.23	221.22	259.19	306.11	343.07
154.27	184.03	221.23	260.06	306.14	343.11
155.13	184.16	221.28	260.07	306.20	343.15
155.16	184.23	222.09	260.21	306.23	343.21
155.20	185.12	222.13	261.20	306.26	344.06
155.23	185.21	222.26	261.20	307.05	344.10
156.07	186.12	222.26	262.09	306.02	344.11
156.24	186.14	222.27	262.22	306.16	344.17
157.05	186.18	223.06	262.27	308.17	344.22
157.06	188.02	223.07	264.11	308.25	345.01
157.07	188.18	223.18	266.14	308.27	345.02
157.09	188.19	223.19	267.13	309.27	345.16
157.11	188.21	223.19	267.15	309.28	345.19
157.16	189.09	223.25	268.10	310.04	345.20
157.17	190.17	224.06	268.27	310.07	345.21
157.19	190.20	224.09	269.03	311.13	345.24
160.16	190.26	224.16	270.09	311.17	345.25
161.16	191.08	226.16	271.19	311.27	346.04
161.19	191.15	226.20	271.19	312.10	346.07
161.28	191.13	227.10	271.20	313.12	346.08
162.01	191.27	227.13	272.05	313.12	346.09
162.09	191.28	227.16	272.21	313.25	346.14
162.22	192.05	228.16	273.02	313.26	346.15
162.24	192.10	228.17	274.20	314.19	346.25
162.25	192.10	228.21	274.22	314.20	346.26
163.04	192.11	228.22	276.26	314.26	347.14
163.05	192.17	228.23	277.21	315.03	349.14
163.21	192.21	228.23	278.03	315.13	350.14
164.01	193.01	228.25	279.04	315.14	350.25
164.04	193.17	228.26	279.09	316.02	351.03
164.06	193.20	228.28	279.14	316.09	351.07
164.10	193.22	228.28	279.18	317.11	353.16
164.17	193.23	229.17	280.12	317.14	354.23
164.18	193.28	229.20	280.13	317.18	354.24
164.20	194.24	229.25	280.17	317.21	355.17
165.12	194.28	230.02	280.17	317.23	355.18
165.13	195.04	230.10	280.20	318.04	355.19
165.24	195.19	231.05	280.24	318.05	355.22
166.06	196.04	231.05	280.25	318.14	356.08
166.11	196.04	231.01	281.07	318.15	356.22
167.02	196.06	231.26	281.15	318.21	356.24
168.12	196.07	232.23	281.26	318.23	357.17
168.15	196.19	232.24	282.02	318.27	357.19
168.22	196.21	233.05	282.04	319.09	357.19
169.06	196.24	233.10	283.06	320.03	357.22
169.08	196.26	233.14	283.12	320.06	358.23
169.09	196.28	233.19	283.18	323.14	359.04
169.19	197.04	234.03	283.23	323.23	359.12
169.23	197.18	234.09	283.24	324.10	360.12
169.25	198.08	235.01	286.08	324.12	361.19
169.27	198.10	235.07	286.13	324.16	361.22
170.02	198.25	235.09	286.14	326.06	361.26
170.13	198.26	235.13	286.21	327.13	363.05
170.16	198.26	236.18	286.24	328.04	364.08
170.22	199.02	236.18	287.01	328.06	364.19
170.25	199.06	236.23	288.06	328.14	365.05
170.28	200.17	237.02	288.16	328.17	365.14
171.02	201.01	237.14	289.19	328.19	365.22
171.05	201.15	237.19	289.24	329.10	365.27
171.20	201.28	237.27	289.25	329.15	366.12
171.21	202.04	238.13	290.01	330.15	366.23
171.28	202.14	238.25	290.04	330.17	367.12
172.04	202.26	240.23	290.07	330.23	367.23
172.06	203.11	240.25	290.12	330.24	368.05
172.10	203.14	241.02	290.14	330.26	368.11
172.12	203.16	242.02	291.03	331.05	368.21
172.13	203.21	242.15	291.10	331.14	369.08
172.14	204.09	244.05	291.27	331.23	369.17
172.18	206.10	244.11	292.01	332.01	369.20
173.12	206.17	244.14	292.08		370.08

370.12	422.25	461.09	499.21	553.03	597.25
371.13	423.01	461.10	499.23	553.04	598.05
372.18	423.25	461.13	499.24	553.06	598.06
372.21	424.13	461.23	500.01	553.14	599.16
372.26	424.18	462.16	501.05	553.18	599.19
373.01	425.02	462.20	501.09	553.20	600.24
373.02	425.10	462.25	501.20	553.24	601.05
373.04	425.15	463.18	502.11	553.27	601.09
373.04	426.02	463.20	502.19	554.21	601.14
373.06	426.16	464.01	502.23	554.23	601.16
373.09	426.20	464.04	504.12	554.28	603.02
373.09	426.23	464.21	504.27	555.02	603.06
373.27	426.25	464.22	505.22	555.13	603.19
374.04	427.13	465.16	505.23	555.17	604.03
374.09	427.14	465.17	506.25	555.18	604.15
374.09	427.17	466.10	507.09	555.27	604.23
374.10	427.19	466.12	507.16	556.01	605.04
374.10	428.03	466.15	507.19	557.03	605.13
374.11	428.12	467.07	507.20	558.05	605.14
375.06	428.15	467.13	508.06	558.20	605.17
376.03	428.18	467.27	508.10	558.23	605.18
376.18	429.11	468.07	510.21	559.09	605.20
377.08	430.08	468.24	511.11	559.09	605.21
377.10	430.11	469.02	511.12	559.12	606.14
377.11	431.26	469.18	511.14	560.03	606.20
377.20	431.27	470.21	511.19	560.08	606.21
377.25	431.28	471.11	514.28	560.18	606.22
379.09	432.19	472.12	515.11	561.13	606.25
379.12	432.20	472.15	515.19	561.19	607.07
379.16	432.22	472.17	516.03	561.23	607.24
379.18	432.23	472.19	516.04	562.03	608.03
379.20	432.24	473.13	516.05	562.24	609.07
380.08	433.09	473.17	517.01	563.01	610.18
380.10	434.01	473.27	517.26	563.13	610.23
380.20	434.03	474.07	518.24	564.05	611.01
380.24	435.07	474.08	518.26	564.05	611.02
380.28	435.24	474.14	519.06	565.19	611.05
381.06	438.08	474.20	519.07	566.06	611.15
381.07	440.14	475.04	519.13	568.17	612.01
381.14	440.21	475.25	519.18	569.07	612.09
381.24	441.20	476.09	519.18	569.19	612.11
382.01	441.21	478.27	520.09	570.03	612.26
382.02	442.05	479.01	520.10	571.07	612.23
382.06	443.06	479.03	520.10	572.13	613.02
382.07	444.15	479.14	521.08	572.19	613.03
382.10	444.19	479.18	521.09	572.21	613.04
382.19	445.04	479.20	521.15	574.23	615.22
382.22	445.13	480.06	522.01	575.11	615.24
383.21	445.23	480.15	522.06	575.11	615.28
384.05	445.26	480.17	522.13	576.01	616.13
384.07	445.27	480.27	522.18	576.08	616.16
384.08	446.03	481.06	523.05	576.08	617.27
384.10	446.05	481.07	523.25	576.09	618.25
384.11	447.01	481.12	523.26	576.18	619.17
384.15	447.09	481.20	523.27	576.22	619.23
384.26	447.10	482.09	524.10	576.23	619.26
387.16	447.16	482.22	525.19	576.23	619.28
388.28	447.18	483.18	528.28	576.23	620.17
390.24	447.24	483.27	529.01	576.24	620.24
390.28	447.25	483.28	529.01	577.01	621.03
391.04	447.27	484.01	530.14	577.14	621.10
392.22	448.02	485.08	532.09	578.01	623.07
393.05	448.07	485.15	532.15	578.02	623.08
393.05	448.11	485.17	532.20	578.06	623.10
394.04	448.12	485.19	534.03	578.23	623.10
394.09	448.27	485.20	534.06	579.03	624.01
394.20	449.08	485.23	534.21	579.07	624.04
395.04	449.09	485.25	535.06	579.09	624.07
399.17	449.11	485.28	537.01	579.15	624.15
401.13	449.18	486.10	538.02	580.20	624.16
402.12	449.27	487.07	538.10	580.21	624.21
404.25	450.01	488.13	538.18	581.04	624.24
406.16	450.07	488.15	538.19	581.06	624.25
406.27	450.24	488.23	539.01	581.17	624.28
406.28	451.01	490.10	539.06	582.01	625.06
407.06	451.03	490.13	539.25	582.05	625.14
407.07	451.09	490.20	539.28	583.03	625.15
408.05	451.12	491.01	540.09	583.03	625.18
408.09	451.14	491.12	540.10	583.15	625.23
409.17	451.15	491.13	541.22	583.21	625.26
409.28	451.16	491.14	541.26	584.05	625.27
410.23	453.01	491.16	542.01	585.02	625.28
411.10	453.05	491.17	542.06	585.06	627.20
411.26	453.10	491.19	542.07	585.17	627.22
413.10	456.27	491.27	542.10	586.17	627.24
414.04	457.04	492.01	542.15	587.09	627.27
414.05	457.06	492.16	542.16	587.10	628.23
414.06	457.17	492.18	542.17	587.12	628.25
414.11	457.21	492.21	543.11	587.19	628.27
414.15	457.23	492.23	543.21	587.21	629.08
414.19	457.24	492.25	543.24	588.04	629.13
414.20	458.05	492.26	543.27	588.20	629.15
415.22	458.19	493.04	544.12	589.03	629.16
416.05	458.28	493.04	544.17	589.14	629.19
416.10	459.02	493.15	545.15	589.17	629.23
416.14	459.03	495.27	545.18	589.19	630.01
416.20	459.03	495.28	549.15	590.13	630.04
416.06	459.05	496.01	549.19	590.14	630.27
418.09	459.06	496.05	549.22	591.15	631.08
418.19	459.12	497.15	549.26	591.23	631.11
418.22	459.15	497.21	550.02	592.08	631.12
418.24	459.17	498.06	550.04	592.11	631.20
420.09	460.01	498.10	550.11	592.11	632.22
420.13	460.07	498.17	550.14	593.11	632.28
420.14	460.08	498.28	550.19	593.23	633.05
420.15	460.09	499.02	550.25	594.09	633.12
420.16	460.22	499.09	550.26	594.14	634.18
420.24	460.23	499.13	550.28	594.16	634.23
421.05	460.28	499.16	551.05	596.20	634.24
421.06	461.03	499.21	552.21	597.12	635.04
421.11	461.05		552.23	597.18	636.10

636.16	663.14	698.11	746.17	795.15	838.28
636.20	663.22	698.12	746.22	796.02	839.10
636.27	664.13	698.13	748.06	796.07	839.14
637.01	664.24	698.23	748.07	796.11	841.03
637.04	665.02	699.03	748.09	796.16	842.25
637.06	665.13	699.06	748.10	796.17	843.09
637.07	665.16	699.26	748.16	796.21	843.12
637.09	665.21	699.28	748.17	797.01	843.14
637.20	666.02	700.03	748.19	797.07	843.23
637.21	666.03	701.03	748.27	798.01	844.19
638.09	666.04	701.06	749.01	798.02	844.28
639.08	666.10	701.11	749.1	798.09	845.08
639.12	666.12	701.20	749.02	798.10	845.19
639.15	666.18	701.22	749.03	799.06	845.24
639.25	666.20	701.4	749.04	799.09	846.07
639.26	666.25	702.04	749.09	799.15	846.19
639.27	667.07	702.10	749.17	799.17	846.20
640.10	667.21	702.21	749.21	799.19	847.02
640.19	667.28	702.25	749.26	799.20	847.04
640.20	668.03	703.02	750.04	800.04	847.07
641.02	668.11	703.11	750.13	800.06	847.12
641.05	668.10	703.21	750.20	800.08	847.16
641.08	668.13	703.22	750.21	800.11	847.17
641.14	668.16	703.28	750.26	800.13	847.23
641.20	669.01	705.06	751.06	800.24	847.25
641.25	669.12	706.17	751.14	800.25	848.03
642.03	669.14	706.28	751.22	801.03	848.04
642.07	669.17	706.28	751.24	801.05	848.14
642.10	669.21	707.08	751.25	801.11	848.19
642.13	669.23	707.18	752.07	801.20	848.20
642.20	669.24	708.07	752.08	802.10	848.22
642.22	669.24	711.08	752.13	802.11	848.24
642.27	669.26	713.02	753.14	802.12	848.26
643.02	670.24	713.04	753.15	802.17	848.26
643.02	670.25	713.09	756.01	802.26	849.03
643.09	670.28	713.10	756.17	804.09	849.03
643.13	671.01	713.11	756.21	804.09	849.11
643.14	671.07	713.11	758.16	804.10	849.20
643.22	671.11	713.12	758.20	804.26	849.26
644.15	671.18	713.14	763.14	805.09	849.27
644.16	671.20	713.16	763.17	805.21	850.03
644.22	671.24	713.25	763.25	805.21	850.08
645.07	671.25	714.10	763.27	805.22	850.11
645.11	672.02	714.11	765.02	806.05	851.09
645.23	672.04	715.01	765.05	806.07	852.08
647.17	673.10	715.03	766.01	806.23	852.08
648.01	674.01	715.15	766.05	806.25	852.27
648.06	674.09	715.18	767.06	806.25	853.01
648.22	675.01	715.19	767.14	807.07	853.19
649.07	675.06	715.23	767.15	807.08	853.22
649.10	675.08	715.25	767.18	807.10	854.01
650.05	675.11	716.01	767.26	807.11	854.01
650.17	675.23	716.09	767.27	807.17	854.05
650.18	676.01	716.13	768.07	807.18	854.06
651.18	676.09	716.16	768.14	807.24	854.16
651.24	676.09	717.01	768.18	807.25	854.19
651.26	676.21	717.02	769.16	808.13	854.26
652.05	676.24	717.09	770.26	808.24	855.07
652.13	677.05	717.27	771.02	808.25	855.15
652.20	677.07	718.25	771.05	808.27	855.18
652.23	677.22	718.25	771.10	809.02	856.03
653.01	677.23	720.21	771.28	809.10	856.06
653.01	677.24	722.12	771.28	809.14	856.08
653.04	678.02	722.12	773.01	809.19	856.12
653.18	678.08	722.13	773.23	810.04	857.12
653.19	678.08	722.15	773.25	810.12	857.23
653.20	678.18	722.17	774.09	810.14	858.02
653.22	680.19	723.28	775.08	810.25	858.14
654.02	680.20	724.04	775.26	810.26	858.27
654.20	681.12	725.02	776.03	810.27	859.03
654.21	683.18	725.06	776.16	812.05	859.08
654.27	683.20	727.04	776.22	812.07	859.18
654.28	683.27	727.06	777.17	812.09	859.23
655.01	684.14	727.12	778.02	814.20	860.01
655.02	684.28	727.28	778.19	815.04	860.16
655.05	685.12	728.06	779.10	815.07	860.23
655.06	685.15	730.19	779.12	815.22	861.04
655.09	686.02	730.26	779.25	815.25	861.04
655.24	686.03	731.22	779.26	816.04	861.04
655.26	686.22	732.04	780.04	820.21	861.06
655.26	686.27	732.12	780.14	821.19	861.08
656.02	687.05	732.15	780.18	823.11	861.10
656.06	688.05	732.16	780.23	823.17	861.14
656.12	689.06	732.19	780.27	823.20	861.18
656.16	689.14	732.27	781.18	823.27	861.24
656.22	689.16	733.07	781.06	824.03	861.24
656.26	689.17	733.15	781.21	827.21	861.26
657.02	690.01	734.04	782.23	827.22	861.27
657.03	690.13	735.10	783.01	827.27	862.02
657.06	690.23	735.20	783.02	829.01	862.05
657.08	690.25	736.23	783.07	829.10	862.08
658.05	690.28	737.02	785.08	829.16	862.09
659.27	691.03	737.25	787.03	830.03	862.11
660.05	691.15	737.25	787.28	830.05	862.12
660.13	691.28	738.22	787.28	830.07	862.12
660.22	692.04	739.03	788.02	830.09	862.21
660.24	692.13	740.03	789.02	831.10	862.22
660.28	692.13	740.16	789.02	831.15	862.28
661.05	692.24	742.15	789.12	832.14	862.28
661.11	693.04	743.03	789.13	832.16	863.04
661.15	693.05	743.09	792.15	832.18	863.08
661.20	693.24	743.10	793.26	833.06	863.14
661.21	693.25	744.05	793.27	833.08	863.18
662.04	694.14	744.19	794.03	833.14	863.25
662.15	695.21	745.01	794.15	833.15	863.26
662.18	696.17	745.24	794.25	833.21	863.27
662.22	696.24	746.01	794.27	834.09	864.09
662.23	697.20	746.05	795.05	834.15	864.11
662.23	697.25	746.13	795.06	836.06	864.17
663.02	697.28		795.10	836.19	864.22
663.13	698.09			837.26	864.23

865.04	910.25	642.01	wave-wanderings	509.01	082.27
865.06	wash	652.06	220.27	509.23	091.15
865.07	099.01	652.06	waved	510.15	091.17
865.13	477.19	660.11	124.19	532.21	092.07
865.15	518.21	674.13	225.12	532.27	092.24
865.16	808.26	748.22	423.27	539.24	094.11
865.20	wash-stand	817.09	471.26	545.21	095.12
865.20	051.07	833.22	564.09	548.20	096.04
865.23	299.22	839.20	606.04	560.01	105.15
866.08	419.23	857.21	652.11	562.18	106.25
866.12	421.15	watcher	750.01	573.01	106.25
866.20	431.17	617.22	waves	575.17	106.27
866.25	washed	watches	260.25	600.16	108.22
866.28	032.13	029.09	630.01	603.03	108.25
867.05	050.20	086.06	659.02	614.27	111.13
867.09	071.06	watchful	waving	615.12	111.16
867.12	080.07	591.17	332.23	620.15	112.05
867.14	248.10	821.02	865.21	621.22	112.20
867.17	370.19	watching	wax	637.17	112.22
867.18	washing	040.13	218.20	645.24	112.22
867.20	038.12	060.15	236.25	654.09	112.23
869.02	096.05	088.25	341.03	656.17	113.01
870.06	327.15	281.09	369.23	657.02	113.16
870.11	692.20	402.06	417.03	657.09	113.17
870.16	700.26	655.21	wax-work	660.15	113.28
870.17	washy	681.22	461.06	667.14	120.13
871.03	478.23	795.13	waxed	670.11	132.24
871.05	waste	811.08	287.08	679.03	132.27
871.07	166.20	846.22	308.20	679.06	133.06
871.10	320.13	857.08	waxen	681.03	133.21
871.11	323.02	watchings	257.21	691.02	133.21
871.12	606.06	467.24	waxes	693.03	133.27
871.16	660.04	water	352.07	698.10	134.03
871.17	673.27	026.07	435.17	703.02	134.04
871.21	756.08	051.09	waxing	703.03	134.05
871.22	793.21	064.02	224.08	705.17	134.18
871.26	795.01	079.03	337.20	709.14	138.02
871.27	859.03	079.06	way	710.03	136.17
871.28	wasted	095.18	006.01	742.18	138.20
872.17	121.24	096.05	008.22	751.17	138.24
872.23	155.26	099.02	009.16	781.24	140.28
873.07	426.18	128.06	012.02	799.24	141.03
873.10	480.08	149.09	025.05	803.11	144.12
873.21	502.01	161.01	033.04	805.05	145.03
875.08	557.02	169.24	040.02	806.18	148.16
875.27	692.24	178.25	047.09	807.11	148.17
876.17	767.16	247.23	052.17	810.06	148.17
876.18	809.23	248.08	065.24	818.14	148.17
876.24	wasting	257.07	069.11	827.09	149.03
877.13	760.12	269.02	073.16	827.12	149.04
879.18	watch	296.19	087.22	834.18	149.04
880.21	033.10	297.06	091.06	843.05	149.24
880.26	086.06	298.02	101.15	847.06	151.14
882.14	092.07	298.10	102.01	850.18	151.16
882.16	125.22	307.24	106.15	850.19	151.19
882.21	132.23	360.17	106.22	852.12	151.20
882.27	147.09	421.14	108.02	862.22	157.06
883.02	174.24	422.08	142.13	864.07	158.02
883.03	250.28	423.11	151.16	867.13	159.03
883.13	331.14	426.10	154.12	867.19	170.24
884.05	336.28	431.15	157.13	870.14	170.26
884.05	371.11	431.17	167.01	870.19	175.19
886.07	374.27	445.13	169.19	872.19	180.20
886.10	400.02	483.13	172.21	873.10	183.22
886.13	411.09	483.22	176.13	875.01	183.22
886.19	423.05	484.27	180.22	875.15	183.26
886.21	424.05	513.03	185.05	884.12	184.21
887.16	426.25	519.14	185.24	885.04	184.26
887.20	442.14	561.18	188.18	888.20	184.28
887.26	596.25	579.05	190.18	894.27	185.10
889.01	639.27	612.23	201.17	899.23	185.16
889.11	680.01	654.13	202.16	910.23	185.17
889.16	714.01	685.20	206.01	911.20	198.14
889.21	757.14	724.19	209.15	way-side	199.12
891.01	758.11	736.23	219.23	145.04	199.14
891.06	758.13	783.17	225.09	ways	206.23
892.19	762.04	855.01	229.04	148.24	211.20
892.23	793.15	863.27	237.23	221.20	211.27
894.01	851.16	874.12	243.19	291.13	212.05
894.11	863.01	874.20	257.27	291.14	235.02
894.13	871.20	875.10	258.08	447.09	236.17
894.15	899.07	875.15	285.05	494.18	236.22
894.16	watch-chain	875.26	287.07	506.11	237.20
896.06	910.13	883.12	290.27	743.14	240.28
898.28	watch-guard	885.14	292.01	wayside	242.28
900.08	549.06	887.10	294.10	855.01	244.09
900.12	watched	water-colour	294.15	wayward	251.13
900.22	050.03	472.27	300.09	213.11	251.28
901.03	057.24	water-flags	300.27	we	255.17
901.05	073.09	471.05	301.23	001.04	255.22
901.06	116.08	water-jug	315.28	009.11	258.11
901.23	163.12	296.21	320.21	010.25	283.11
902.06	221.16	306.03	321.04	014.25	289.15
902.25	227.18	watered	329.01	015.07	301.06
905.06	276.09	129.13	332.10	027.18	315.24
905.17	299.05	waterfall	339.03	032.18	326.01
906.06	317.28	812.22	354.01	069.26	326.02
906.09	328.24	waters	361.13	072.03	326.06
906.10	373.22	126.24	413.07	072.21	326.11
906.13	373.23	302.21	419.10	073.02	326.12
907.14	390.12	608.12	440.08	073.02	327.06
907.25	422.19	608.14	443.03	074.01	340.26
909.01	445.11	watery	454.03	074.07	341.01
909.15	458.11	492.25	462.07	074.08	349.08
909.17	501.18	564.08	469.22	074.27	352.02
909.18	502.17	wave	474.21	075.03	355.25
910.01	544.05	282.23	475.24	075.04	356.05
910.07	583.18	371.23	489.26	075.07	356.07
910.09	604.23	wave-girt	494.12	076.03	356.09
910.17	634.03	501.05	494.17	078.02	356.12
910.17	639.22		506.16	078.03	356.14

356.16	736.24	781.20	059.22	welcoming	343.10
356.18	737.27	781.20	068.06	333.24	346.10
357.02	748.22	782.27	116.22	welkin	349.23
357.20	748.24	785.22	117.11	283.02	362.01
357.20	775.22	817.21	141.26	well	363.07
357.23	780.15	wealthy	168.09	006.11	370.04
357.26	781.06	161.07	169.14	007.13	371.01
371.02	782.24	289.05	173.27	010.19	377.10
385.14	787.23	290.09	199.15	018.14	382.07
389.02	789.07	319.16	244.19	021.26	389.19
390.01	789.11	490.02	316.18	026.17	390.08
391.05	800.13	624.13	324.02	027.15	395.10
416.05	801.19	717.14	426.27	027.18	399.07
430.12	803.15	751.08	445.07	033.24	400.17
452.16	811.03	786.09	447.01	033.30	400.20
454.24	812.13	weapon	450.15	034.01	405.23
444.13	812.14	552.19	452.06	034.06	407.09
446.19	812.19	820.14	457.18	039.18	407.18
469.08	813.15	weapons	464.09	039.18	407.21
469.11	817.09	375.16	488.14	042.05	408.20
473.01	821.19	wear	723.10	053.14	412.10
473.02	821.21	009.12	728.04	056.26	424.04
477.22	821.24	120.10	768.24	056.26	426.02
477.23	821.24	541.01	769.07	061.03	431.08
477.28	824.10	544.11	789.15	067.01	433.17
461.15	826.15	545.22	791.08	068.12	433.23
461.18	827.11	549.07	800.12	068.24	437.26
457.20	828.04	wearied	800.13	080.06	438.28
459.17	828.07	735.12	831.04	091.12	439.01
469.26	828.07	weariness	week's	093.06	446.15
498.23	833.03	079.15	016.17	105.13	446.21
498.24	833.15	114.11	487.02	106.02	447.11
505.01	833.21	909.03	week-day	106.13	447.12
505.24	833.25	wearing	871.06	108.09	450.11
510.01	833.25	084.14	week-days	111.20	452.13
510.01	833.27	555.18	479.07	115.24	452.23
510.11	834.18	681.12	weekly	117.04	453.20
510.12	840.14	wears	641.01	117.19	455.19
513.15	841.15	092.07	804.08	123.03	455.19
513.16	845.23	092.28	weeks	125.23	458.17
513.17	846.11	weary	042.08	130.05	465.06
516.24	655.08	033.03	056.16	131.21	467.04
519.01	665.24	191.17	115.04	131.25	470.14
519.12	665.28	228.23	142.17	132.04	472.01
519.12	865.28	287.02	150.23	135.05	481.14
526.09	868.04	299.11	290.25	135.09	481.19
541.19	892.24	497.19	293.20	136.16	482.03
542.22	894.14	501.15	339.22	136.01	487.15
543.03	898.25	510.17	402.06	143.15	489.18
544.21	898.26	611.27	447.21	147.04	489.28
547.28	899.01	617.25	491.17	148.13	492.22
548.02	899.02	660.16	493.19	157.14	493.10
565.23	899.22	663.19	523.21	173.21	494.09
567.09	902.20	692.22	526.09	175.13	500.12
567.20	904.05	741.03	553.22	176.04	501.13
560.01	905.03	909.20	633.09	176.11	503.13
531.19	905.05	909.26	637.05	177.01	504.15
536.24	909.05	909.26	696.05	177.02	506.27
536.25	909.06	weather	698.27	177.14	507.16
567.06	909.08	096.07	714.05	178.20	508.18
567.24	909.12	364.17	718.10	179.03	509.08
569.01	911.04	364.19	731.05	179.19	521.19
598.12	911.07	461.28	734.04	190.05	527.16
598.25	we'll	479.04	780.13	192.01	529.23
600.22	041.21	519.02	809.22	192.14	529.26
602.12	510.06	563.23	813.18	194.04	530.04
604.01	we're	714.15	weep	197.25	530.09
615.21	599.25	909.23	130.21	198.19	532.02
647.04	weak	weather-beaten	604.14	199.05	532.13
661.07	029.24	084.26	620.12	199.22	534.14
662.06	103.06	685.08	665.24	205.14	537.13
662.07	426.15	804.23	753.07	206.26	538.01
662.11	469.02	weather-proof	912.17	208.19	538.07
667.23	469.02	733.27	weeping	211.23	541.22
679.10	476.16	web	485.22	218.10	544.09
679.11	604.19	402.04	611.21	242.16	547.22
679.12	607.10	424.24	621.25	243.22	547.26
679.13	610.01	wed	656.16	245.20	550.10
679.16	644.28	257.06	732.17	246.01	550.16
679.17	668.14	513.23	weigh	251.19	555.17
679.18	687.05	597.14	125.23	254.07	562.07
679.21	819.08	906.05	256.21	256.21	563.21
680.14	841.06	wedded	262.23	262.23	564.19
682.16	851.18	590.16	783.01	266.11	567.03
683.14	weak-hearted	wedding	weighed	266.20	567.23
683.14	645.11	340.23	027.28	268.04	568.01
686.23	weakling	491.20	weighing	268.12	568.04
687.12	804.15	526.10	377.16	270.05	570.01
687.13	weakly	558.10	weighs	284.28	571.16
690.05	133.01	567.13	404.12	289.10	573.21
691.13	730.26	596.08	weight	300.12	574.04
691.18	weakness	604.16	368.03	300.20	583.08
695.07	612.18	634.04	568.19	302.15	590.04
697.19	656.18	770.16	575.08	310.09	600.14
700.09	736.13	820.17	781.24	310.15	607.02
700.22	761.13	905.03	816.16	313.10	611.07
700.23	816.16	wedding-day	welcome	315.07	611.23
700.25	900.14	899.12	069.25	315.21	613.05
703.14	wealth	wedding-dress	100.18	315.23	613.12
712.28	146.08	570.20	291.01	316.21	620.12
713.07	161.14	576.12	458.03	318.19	620.20
725.20	252.25	wedlock's	461.21	322.26	623.23
725.20	317.03	552.07	493.08	326.11	624.07
726.17	351.14	wee	530.22	331.06	635.05
726.18	496.02	549.06	564.16	332.13	635.12
727.03	509.20	weed	733.15	334.12	635.15
727.14	513.08	859.28	781.23	336.09	637.15
735.02	571.13	weeds	792.13	338.27	638.12
735.02	748.14	693.09	798.20	342.02	639.15
735.04	750.19	week	welcomed	343.02	640.22
736.21	775.10	007.23	745.01	343.06	645.01
			856.16		

645.01
646.16
647.05
651.08
657.06
672.12
673.17
679.07
684.20
690.05
691.25
693.06
696.24
699.17
700.12
701.15
701.16
701.28
703.05
704.27
712.28
717.27
720.23
723.06
723.11
724.01
724.20
750.04
751.18
753.22
754.14
755.27
756.24
759.24
740.17
741.12
742.07
742.14
742.14
742.17
743.19
744.02
751.24
751.27
752.18
753.19
754.05
755.13
758.05
761.06
763.09
764.04
767.24
768.10
772.14
773.16
774.22
776.21
777.14
777.20
779.05
779.08
783.16
789.06
790.21
790.23
792.17
797.16
798.10
804.18
811.11
816.09
817.13
819.23
822.01
822.01
826.07
826.18
826.19
827.01
829.02
841.18
850.16
854.01
856.11
859.11
859.17
863.07
863.11
866.08
866.12
870.14
871.22
878.12
878.23
880.03
881.18
883.01
888.24
889.03
890.01
890.20
891.19
906.03
908.16
well-arranged
327.12
well-brink
368.25
well-built
668.27

well-conducted
281.05
889.19
well-cut
283.22
827.20
well-defined
298.12
471.20
well-dressed
299.05
175.10
307.12
670.27
313.20
693.12
313.20
well-executed
325.17
332.12
326.05
754.25
well-informed
345.11
790.04
380.24
well-known
387.14
464.16
388.15
465.16
401.05
502.14
409.25
658.19
410.26
793.04
413.03
856.15
415.14
well-loved
420.21
523.09
426.18
well-planted
430.01
601.10
430.09
well-principled
441.15
908.15
442.03
well-regulated
443.03
556.28
443.03
well-remembered
447.24
480.07
449.06
849.21
458.02
well-smoothed
459.07
340.13
463.21
well-timed
479.06
284.24
480.15
wellfare
483.23
214.16
485.21
welsh
489.26
041.18
496.17
welshwoman
502.17
166.07
523.02
wended
525.17
904.05
539.14
went
570.19
015.13
572.06
017.15
587.24
023.27
589.22
028.18
597.18
028.26
607.22
029.09
634.17
032.18
656.17
036.22
666.27
041.21
670.06
049.14
679.08
058.13
680.26
061.24
680.27
066.11
716.09
072.22
726.25
073.08
732.10
076.03
742.18
077.13
744.28
078.28
747.03
085.14
750.18
086.22
756.07
087.05
759.10
116.28
765.02
124.01
805.20
127.25
807.01
131.27
810.15
134.03
833.17
135.24
865.15
137.22
865.18
142.01
869.06
147.19
869.13
148.17
902.07
151.25
905.05
153.25
910.19
164.15
911.15
168.11
wept
169.08
094.24
172.23
129.11
173.16
463.11
175.19
515.01
176.18
611.19
177.03
683.22
178.16
894.14
180.09
were
180.21
002.01
185.23
002.15
190.16
003.08
195.04
003.21
201.23
003.23
203.15
007.26
206.26
010.25
211.19
011.05
214.25
012.04
220.08
014.09
222.14
014.12
227.12
015.26
231.04
016.01
231.26
016.03
232.25
016.21
233.03
017.10
235.12
020.10
236.17
023.15
236.15
027.13
239.01
028.27
244.23
029.11
251.04
029.20
255.07
030.04
030.04

030.14
031.17
031.19
032.06
034.23
038.06
038.25
038.28
039.04
039.06
040.13
041.17
042.18
044.13
044.22
045.24
049.19
049.26
051.03
051.22
053.11
053.12
054.23
056.21
057.04
060.13
060.28
062.04
066.15
069.22
072.07
074.10
075.03
076.04
078.11
078.14
079.04
079.12
080.03
080.14
081.05
081.08
081.14
082.22
084.17
085.05
085.06
086.03
086.06
086.21
086.24
087.28
088.25
090.20
092.07
094.13
094.27
095.01
096.04
097.01
097.14
098.04
098.12
098.14
099.14
102.15
104.25
105.27
106.20
111.08
111.19
112.19
113.13
114.21
116.27
117.14
122.01
122.11
127.10
129.03
132.24
141.07
144.05
146.04
147.03
147.05
147.13
147.16
147.20
148.06
148.09
148.20
148.25
148.27
153.15
154.06
156.05
156.08
156.14
161.04
161.10
161.12
163.20
164.03
164.04
164.16
164.17
169.10
171.06

172.24
176.21
176.24
177.21
177.24
178.04
179.20
179.24
184.26
184.27
184.28
185.04
185.10
185.20
190.19
191.12
194.06
194.08
194.12
194.19
198.14
199.17
200.01
202.13
202.19
204.17
204.23
207.01
207.13
208.06
209.07
215.25
217.06
217.07
217.23
218.01
219.16
219.18
220.19
221.11
222.18
223.02
223.22
224.11
230.15
233.06
235.19
237.10
239.16
241.10
241.26
242.28
244.23
245.24
245.25
246.23
247.19
247.23
248.19
249.10
249.18
252.18
252.27
252.28
253.21
255.11
255.12
258.11
261.16
263.13
266.16
268.27
270.06
272.26
276.02
277.07
283.11
285.11
285.17
286.11
290.11
291.07
291.16
291.17
291.26
292.05
293.05
294.03
296.09
296.16
296.18
296.23
301.06
305.19
313.24
317.16
317.23
317.24
318.01
319.14
320.28
324.05
326.06
327.10
327.14
327.26
328.11
330.28
331.07
332.20
332.24

332.28
334.19
334.26
335.07
336.15
337.07
337.20
338.14
338.28
341.01
341.05
341.27
342.12
342.14
342.15
343.14
344.02
344.03
344.07
344.28
345.09
345.15
346.19
349.08
349.16
350.02
350.03
350.04
351.08
353.10
354.11
356.07
359.23
360.03
362.14
364.02
364.14
364.15
365.04
365.08
365.13
365.18
365.21
365.23
365.23
369.05
369.09
369.21
370.05
371.02
371.14
373.15
374.08
377.02
377.19
378.15
379.08
379.21
379.23
380.07
381.13
382.05
383.01
383.19
389.10
391.09
391.18
392.12
392.25
394.03
394.17
398.19
401.08
406.02
406.19
410.12
410.28
411.05
412.02
415.25
416.25
416.27
419.12
421.07
421.22
426.14
427.15
429.18
432.27
433.03
433.04
435.04
435.22
436.02
439.01
442.11
446.10
447.27
448.04
449.16
452.02
457.05
457.07
459.10
459.24
460.17
463.03
470.15
471.24
473.02

473.09	665.27	848.06	014.25	176.22	365.04
473.10	666.14	848.07	019.26	177.01	370.17
473.14	670.07	848.25	020.01	177.09	371.16
477.27	673.15	849.06	020.01	178.13	371.17
478.20	674.17	850.12	021.10	180.03	373.03
479.08	676.01	855.08	022.15	186.11	375.06
481.08	677.08	856.23	023.27	187.20	376.05
481.18	677.10	857.18	024.03	188.07	380.21
484.04	677.14	857.20	024.09	188.08	380.24
485.18	678.10	859.02	024.14	188.18	383.15
487.19	679.01	863.11	028.14	192.04	383.25
490.16	681.08	866.06	029.19	194.28	386.06
492.20	681.13	866.15	031.12	195.03	386.11
495.09	685.10	870.22	033.29	195.28	386.21
496.06	687.19	870.26	034.07	199.03	389.20
496.10	687.25	871.02	034.27	203.23	389.21
496.25	688.09	871.28	035.13	204.20	390.06
500.04	689.14	872.27	035.19	205.21	391.25
501.03	690.15	880.20	035.25	206.01	392.20
501.10	692.14	882.12	036.10	213.06	397.25
501.11	692.16	884.08	038.22	215.12	398.12
517.02	692.19	884.24	039.18	215.13	398.14
518.24	692.20	885.24	044.12	215.16	400.03
519.12	697.19	887.19	044.18	220.18	400.16
521.03	698.26	887.24	046.26	221.14	401.10
522.08	699.04	888.07	050.19	222.16	402.05
523.17	699.09	889.04	051.01	226.20	402.18
525.08	701.05	891.26	051.03	230.02	402.25
529.03	702.02	895.27	051.26	232.07	407.17
532.24	703.25	900.19	052.09	234.14	407.25
533.11	704.10	902.19	053.01	238.01	408.20
534.26	704.21	902.21	053.28	239.21	408.21
536.06	712.19	902.23	054.02	242.14	408.24
537.16	712.20	902.24	054.02	242.28	409.01
537.22	712.28	902.27	054.03	244.02	409.28
538.18	713.27	903.22	054.09	244.23	410.20
559.03	714.17	905.04	054.14	245.05	410.24
541.12	716.15	905.11	057.14	247.15	411.02
541.19	716.18	906.04	061.10	249.16	411.18
547.28	717.10	907.26	061.11	250.21	411.28
555.08	717.14	908.02	061.28	251.01	412.05
557.03	720.20	910.27	062.12	252.04	414.14
557.06	720.26	werke	063.27	253.03	416.02
557.07	721.13	678.26	064.08	253.04	416.03
560.15	726.19	west	064.09	253.07	416.21
560.19	727.09	152.04	066.25	253.21	418.14
560.25	732.14	220.07	066.25	258.21	424.12
563.17	733.17	384.14	067.26	260.04	424.15
567.09	736.02	409.15	068.03	260.16	424.17
569.05	738.11	409.22	068.11	262.03	424.25
570.02	744.22	409.25	068.11	262.07	425.01
572.03	749.27	440.17	068.20	263.22	427.14
572.25	751.08	492.24	069.11	263.23	428.11
573.04	756.12	504.24	069.15	264.01	430.28
574.03	767.05	583.05	072.13	265.05	433.24
575.06	767.05	624.14	073.16	266.18	436.25
575.11	770.17	659.06	077.11	267.25	437.19
577.08	771.14	737.11	077.25	269.09	439.05
577.23	771.25	812.07	079.02	270.27	439.06
578.06	773.04	west-india	079.15	271.27	439.12
579.12	774.10	630.11	082.26	273.04	440.07
579.14	776.08	west-indian	085.03	273.21	440.14
579.17	777.10	629.20	090.09	273.22	442.11
581.12	781.09	western	091.01	274.09	449.22
581.16	781.16	145.28	091.02	274.13	450.16
583.05	782.03	226.04	092.21	275.21	450.18
587.05	782.20	609.03	094.08	276.21	450.27
588.17	782.21	wet	095.08	279.11	451.23
588.20	782.24	003.14	095.09	285.18	453.27
597.14	783.04	072.26	095.10	287.11	456.07
603.20	785.15	075.01	101.27	293.16	459.01
605.15	786.09	076.04	103.07	297.13	467.10
605.16	788.12	088.09	103.18	297.19	467.28
605.22	790.15	169.09	105.10	298.03	470.03
606.03	791.10	255.09	105.20	298.04	471.11
606.08	793.23	298.26	105.24	298.08	472.09
607.11	794.11	379.18	106.11	298.16	472.19
611.02	795.04	380.19	107.17	298.17	473.28
613.20	795.04	431.18	107.19	300.26	474.08
617.06	795.06	478.27	107.21	302.07	475.26
617.14	798.12	519.12	108.15	305.19	477.12
621.07	798.26	519.20	116.13	306.15	477.17
623.07	799.07	631.05	117.28	310.25	479.05
624.16	800.18	655.11	119.26	311.24	481.14
625.07	801.02	656.21	119.26	312.21	483.21
626.11	803.08	672.02	120.28	314.24	483.27
627.11	805.02	672.16	122.24	317.20	489.21
627.14	805.11	683.21	127.10	318.05	490.10
629.28	806.21	684.20	127.14	319.03	490.13
630.05	806.26	690.15	127.15	319.23	491.23
656.03	807.28	692.17	127.25	322.13	491.24
658.01	810.16	781.13	131.04	330.11	493.03
659.21	810.24	887.17	131.09	335.26	493.13
640.01	810.24	wetting	134.18	341.19	493.13
640.02	814.14	674.24	135.15	346.04	494.11
640.10	817.26	whalebone	139.23	347.11	494.22
641.10	819.06	137.27	140.08	347.17	494.28
641.13	819.09	wharton	142.01	348.28	495.09
642.23	821.11	911.12	148.16	349.05	496.17
647.04	823.19	what	150.24	349.22	499.19
652.08	826.19	002.18	152.15	350.14	499.24
654.19	828.06	004.27	153.04	351.09	509.06
655.11	828.27	006.22	153.18	353.13	509.21
656.06	832.01	006.24	157.20	355.03	511.11
656.07	832.21	009.01	157.22	355.15	512.01
659.26	833.15	009.18	163.02	357.20	512.03
661.16	833.25	010.08	165.12	358.22	512.03
662.05	835.12	010.08	167.05	362.09	512.14
663.03	844.12	010.19	167.13	362.14	512.17
664.20	845.14	010.26	173.03	362.24	515.27
664.21	847.14	012.15	173.17	363.07	515.28

516.03	642.05	761.17	876.03	043.17	214.27
516.12	642.25	762.08	876.04	045.26	217.01
516.16	643.12	762.08	876.19	046.16	217.03
518.20	643.23	763.16	878.06	047.01	217.06
518.23	643.26	763.26	878.13	047.11	217.07
518.26	644.06	767.24	880.15	047.14	221.12
520.01	645.15	771.24	880.20	050.17	221.23
521.02	646.15	772.12	882.25	054.15	225.06
522.21	646.18	772.13	883.19	055.23	225.12
524.02	647.10	772.26	884.18	056.11	225.17
527.10	647.19	773.06	886.24	062.23	225.23
528.25	647.28	773.07	887.28	065.10	226.26
529.19	648.12	774.20	888.08	065.13	227.10
530.07	649.14	774.22	888.10	067.05	229.02
530.07	650.17	776.14	888.14	068.05	229.04
530.16	654.10	779.03	889.19	068.26	229.14
531.12	655.19	779.17	889.27	071.03	231.01
531.19	656.08	779.17	890.03	071.15	231.18
531.24	657.04	782.06	890.16	072.07	233.04
532.05	657.10	782.15	891.23	073.02	234.10
535.11	657.16	783.20	892.27	075.11	234.16
537.09	658.19	784.05	893.02	076.16	235.16
537.25	659.10	784.09	893.19	079.06	235.26
539.10	659.13	784.24	895.19	079.19	236.05
539.17	660.13	785.21	896.06	080.01	238.27
540.23	662.15	786.22	896.13	080.07	240.22
541.04	662.15	787.06	896.27	080.19	241.17
543.09	662.18	788.07	898.04	081.23	241.27
544.23	663.06	790.28	898.06	084.27	244.16
546.14	663.06	790.28	898.07	086.02	244.23
547.07	666.07	791.01	898.07	086.02	246.17
547.11	666.12	791.18	900.12	089.23	246.26
547.15	666.12	791.20	901.26	097.08	247.02
547.23	666.19	791.20	902.02	098.18	249.18
548.04	666.24	791.21	902.12	099.10	250.28
548.08	667.12	793.10	906.09	100.24	251.16
550.14	667.14	794.08	906.12	101.06	254.07
552.27	667.27	796.21	906.24	103.24	254.15
553.23	670.16	799.04	908.25	105.01	255.22
563.13	670.25	802.09	908.25	105.08	259.12
566.18	670.25	804.05	908.27	106.05	259.26
567.24	670.28	805.17	909.18	106.25	260.01
568.01	674.18	809.01	909.24	107.01	261.09
568.06	675.14	814.13	909.28	107.09	261.20
568.07	678.15	814.24	whatever	108.03	268.27
568.09	679.09	815.10	007.28	108.24	270.09
568.10	679.10	817.06	107.05	108.26	270.12
568.20	679.15	817.12	121.05	109.02	270.17
571.17	682.06	818.24	135.10	111.21	271.24
574.15	682.10	818.28	215.24	113.17	272.05
576.14	682.13	819.06	264.02	115.10	278.05
577.13	682.21	819.06	293.08	116.27	279.04
578.09	682.25	824.08	371.01	119.04	280.11
578.12	682.27	824.18	390.20	119.11	280.22
579.09	683.06	827.07	414.20	120.27	281.11
580.14	684.11	827.08	445.16	133.07	282.28
580.21	684.14	827.22	445.17	133.14	283.11
581.08	686.08	828.07	482.19	133.22	284.22
581.09	686.25	830.02	526.15	135.06	285.01
582.23	687.08	830.03	543.18	135.18	289.15
587.14	687.13	831.05	547.04	136.05	289.20
591.05	689.14	832.09	551.15	140.11	290.14
591.14	690.08	834.24	626.21	141.03	290.28
591.19	692.06	834.28	648.24	145.14	291.02
595.02	692.09	836.18	649.18	145.16	292.20
595.07	693.14	837.06	694.15	146.17	292.23
596.16	694.18	838.18	708.15	148.27	293.12
597.07	695.05	838.23	763.25	150.19	294.14
597.24	695.17	839.02	824.17	151.19	294.24
599.15	696.24	839.19	841.09	152.08	296.27
600.19	697.13	839.23	861.07	153.24	298.13
601.24	700.07	840.03	876.10	154.04	299.16
602.09	704.11	840.13	889.03	154.16	300.02
602.20	705.24	840.20	wheel	156.24	301.24
606.22	705.25	842.03	662.10	157.04	306.08
606.22	711.13	843.15	wheeled	158.02	308.09
609.04	711.13	844.23	246.10	158.08	308.25
612.25	711.14	848.09	277.14	159.05	310.12
613.22	712.20	848.14	365.09	160.12	310.20
614.10	713.06	848.19	562.08	163.20	310.26
615.28	714.25	848.22	wheeling	164.27	312.02
616.11	715.14	849.10	588.09	169.27	313.27
617.04	717.28	849.10	wheels	170.24	314.10
618.11	718.28	849.14	073.08	175.05	314.10
618.12	720.11	852.02	332.20	177.20	314.22
618.21	722.11	856.12	380.18	181.03	316.19
621.08	722.26	856.16	432.16	182.03	317.11
621.17	722.27	857.05	656.28	182.10	320.08
623.11	723.03	857.06	664.18	182.26	323.12
627.06	723.15	857.22	798.01	183.15	324.10
627.12	723.18	858.01	when	186.03	325.26
627.13	723.25	858.03	001.06	188.06	328.20
628.22	724.03	859.13	005.17	189.10	328.24
631.23	726.08	859.14	005.18	190.26	328.26
631.24	726.09	859.15	007.26	191.01	335.05
631.27	726.10	860.02	007.27	191.18	336.22
631.28	726.21	860.03	009.19	192.27	337.01
634.06	726.23	861.12	013.19	195.01	337.14
634.11	731.23	861.17	015.09	197.20	340.04
634.14	731.25	862.12	015.17	198.10	340.17
635.12	734.17	864.26	017.14	199.20	347.05
635.16	734.22	866.18	021.20	200.01	348.27
635.17	738.17	867.05	027.04	203.05	349.10
635.18	739.24	867.10	027.13	203.06	351.08
635.21	749.20	872.26	032.02	203.16	351.25
635.25	749.20	874.08	032.03	206.03	355.25
636.12	750.24	874.14	032.18	206.23	356.07
637.01	750.25	875.08	035.20	209.13	364.16
637.04	754.27	875.13	040.09	214.23	364.18
638.28	759.19	875.27	041.04	214.24	375.04
642.04	760.01	875.28	043.04	214.25	

375.09	572.13	741.18	109.03	378.18	816.26
375.19	573.09	743.11	133.14	386.28	823.22
376.06	574.10	746.17	210.14	396.19	827.02
376.10	579.03	746.21	223.24	404.11	829.05
376.18	580.01	746.22	232.04	406.16	838.23
380.12	580.10	747.03	248.09	416.05	841.05
380.23	580.11	747.20	278.02	416.11	849.15
381.02	581.19	748.11	284.19	430.17	849.19
381.19	582.17	750.22	295.27	434.13	849.28
384.26	588.23	752.14	321.23	437.01	850.02
387.17	589.24	753.06	366.01	437.28	850.15
391.16	590.08	755.17	425.18	439.27	856.25
395.23	590.17	757.17	503.22	449.19	856.27
395.13	591.01	761.11	849.19	450.16	860.01
399.10	602.18	761.12	852.25	450.18	861.14
399.28	602.24	765.02	853.06	475.08	865.20
400.11	607.02	767.23	854.19	478.12	867.01
403.21	616.23	770.08	902.05	480.20	867.25
414.05	620.02	771.26	whenever	481.03	867.25
418.11	623.12	772.01	043.09	490.04	870.04
422.07	623.21	781.10	112.09	492.01	872.17
424.27	624.20	782.03	322.25	492.22	872.27
425.19	625.15	787.02	360.04	493.05	873.18
425.26	626.14	789.07	442.15	502.03	873.22
426.05	626.18	789.11	479.14	504.13	875.20
426.05	626.24	790.14	744.28	512.10	876.08
428.06	628.22	792.13	760.21	512.12	880.26
428.16	632.28	792.18	832.02	514.01	882.25
429.12	634.07	794.25	where	522.24	884.11
429.13	634.12	795.21	004.11	522.28	885.25
430.08	635.06	796.17	004.28	539.27	894.25
435.23	636.28	800.08	006.07	541.21	901.03
437.16	639.04	802.19	015.06	541.23	902.08
442.04	639.13	802.21	016.20	542.22	902.13
442.12	640.03	802.25	017.23	576.11	902.14
442.13	640.14	804.09	031.19	589.09	905.06
444.15	641.05	804.22	033.08	604.22	907.23
445.25	641.18	806.08	035.22	605.17	909.27
446.10	641.21	806.17	036.24	605.17	whereas
449.23	643.01	806.23	039.02	605.18	031.20
452.01	643.15	807.01	040.27	611.26	346.25
452.20	643.27	807.05	040.28	616.04	778.25
457.23	646.14	807.24	049.24	621.12	whereat
458.08	647.23	809.02	052.25	625.14	175.18
459.02	648.06	809.15	054.06	634.13	wherein
463.09	648.08	809.16	064.27	634.15	118.21
463.10	648.09	809.23	066.18	645.01	186.08
463.24	655.06	810.15	066.18	646.18	221.17
469.16	655.10	813.10	066.28	652.25	287.12
474.25	656.03	813.11	071.13	654.26	630.06
475.04	656.04	814.11	074.12	657.01	851.05
475.18	656.26	819.01	076.06	657.03	whereof
480.02	660.14	824.12	082.09	658.09	013.17
480.11	660.15	826.05	088.27	658.13	whereupon
483.08	660.17	827.19	089.27	659.16	223.13
483.22	661.16	830.08	090.10	660.13	369.14
489.17	662.08	831.19	091.04	662.10	543.14
490.07	663.03	832.26	099.14	663.14	wherever
490.11	664.02	834.19	112.21	666.08	327.04
494.13	674.07	834.23	113.02	666.10	498.02
495.17	676.11	838.07	136.16	667.24	526.24
495.22	677.27	841.22	143.16	668.10	861.04
498.06	678.12	843.27	146.21	668.15	884.26
498.17	678.17	845.18	148.17	669.02	whether
498.24	679.26	846.12	149.04	670.13	017.13
498.27	680.22	846.26	149.28	673.25	022.20
499.16	680.27	847.10	151.17	673.29	044.22
500.05	681.17	851.15	152.13	674.01	077.12
500.11	687.04	852.04	152.20	674.20	094.09
501.18	687.24	860.12	157.16	679.02	095.11
505.01	689.12	863.09	157.20	679.06	099.06
505.09	689.14	863.26	158.14	681.06	099.07
505.11	690.17	865.01	160.07	682.11	146.20
506.27	691.05	865.13	168.21	682.24	173.07
507.26	692.06	865.16	171.12	682.26	179.13
508.16	693.12	869.13	171.13	686.20	182.20
509.24	695.13	869.20	172.12	686.20	206.05
510.04	695.20	874.03	172.13	695.07	206.05
510.24	696.22	874.08	173.02	699.06	223.22
511.13	698.18	875.03	174.27	699.08	238.02
519.15	699.14	877.07	180.05	700.05	241.20
519.23	700.25	878.18	191.11	705.01	245.25
519.27	700.25	881.20	194.09	705.07	255.18
522.01	703.13	881.26	206.19	706.19	258.24
522.06	707.19	882.06	219.19	711.08	261.06
527.15	708.11	883.23	220.01	711.20	262.09
528.02	708.18	883.23	221.04	716.26	266.15
528.03	711.08	884.12	225.21	716.27	266.25
532.06	713.15	884.20	226.12	717.13	275.27
532.07	714.16	886.08	234.09	720.16	293.25
533.04	714.21	887.23	241.16	731.24	300.01
534.21	715.11	887.24	242.22	733.01	315.01
535.13	716.03	388.01	245.03	745.15	326.02
535.16	716.21	888.02	247.04	745.24	330.16
537.17	718.02	889.10	250.24	751.03	345.04
537.25	718.18	894.05	255.15	757.16	345.06
539.20	719.16	894.12	256.28	764.08	345.08
539.23	719.27	894.22	261.02	767.11	345.24
540.26	720.01	898.13	270.23	771.09	403.28
542.08	721.08	898.14	274.06	772.01	448.16
547.05	721.16	900.13	282.19	772.13	459.03
548.22	723.07	903.12	299.01	774.12	462.14
549.03	729.02	905.05	302.19	783.17	463.20
549.21	732.04	906.06	325.15	796.10	493.16
553.07	734.28	906.10	341.01	797.20	496.08
555.05	735.01	907.06	347.20	799.22	496.23
559.18	736.18	908.12	348.18	801.25	535.21
562.05	736.25	910.25	353.15	801.27	562.02
562.11	737.02	911.27	367.27	812.22	572.10
565.14	737.16	whence	374.09	812.24	577.14
567.09	741.17	094.03	374.10	812.26	587.19

595.12	107.26	248.01	425.13	640.12	803.24
597.25	109.10	248.25	426.01	653.07	808.02
599.16	109.11	249.17	426.02	654.23	808.09
620.06	109.12	250.10	435.16	655.10	809.26
635.20	109.12	253.24	436.13	658.16	812.21
635.21	112.08	256.12	438.22	663.27	813.04
635.23	113.08	256.20	439.10	668.12	813.19
635.24	113.28	258.04	439.18	668.28	814.22
642.16	115.16	258.12	440.01	669.26	817.17
643.12	117.21	259.08	440.11	670.20	817.20
665.10	121.02	260.02	444.04	671.11	817.25
674.13	121.22	260.03	444.11	672.17	817.28
678.10	123.01	260.25	445.02	673.05	818.02
705.21	124.09	261.15	445.09	673.15	818.14
716.24	125.07	261.16	450.12	675.05	818.15
718.07	126.04	264.26	460.23	675.13	819.10
751.25	129.07	267.10	464.17	676.08	820.12
755.26	132.28	267.13	464.24	677.02	820.19
760.28	133.27	268.12	465.01	677.18	823.13
770.09	136.01	269.17	465.18	678.06	824.10
771.05	136.04	272.04	466.03	678.07	825.21
796.02	137.15	272.15	470.13	680.05	825.23
827.21	138.20	273.09	474.07	685.27	825.23
838.16	138.26	273.14	474.23	687.05	825.25
846.23	139.02	274.11	476.24	688.04	828.03
846.24	139.04	274.20	481.20	691.20	828.11
848.21	139.15	274.24	481.21	692.05	829.04
871.15	139.17	277.28	483.01	692.10	829.07
873.26	141.20	278.03	483.02	692.28	829.08
881.09	142.27	281.27	483.05	694.07	832.12
896.18	143.01	282.03	484.06	701.13	832.20
whetted	143.12	282.04	490.05	702.11	833.03
552.20	144.15	282.10	492.15	702.26	833.23
836.06	145.07	282.12	493.22	703.28	838.20
whey-faced	146.14	283.18	494.26	704.10	842.08
356.11	146.22	284.01	497.13	705.10	844.21
which	148.28	284.12	503.28	705.18	844.21
003.23	149.16	286.04	507.23	705.19	845.01
007.07	150.21	289.09	508.02	707.07	845.02
008.27	151.01	289.19	514.09	707.12	845.03
010.06	151.20	289.20	514.15	708.09	846.15
012.03	151.27	290.13	518.13	709.08	846.22
016.24	153.26	291.15	519.06	710.04	848.17
017.04	157.07	291.16	524.14	712.04	849.06
023.19	157.25	291.25	525.28	712.06	852.21
028.19	160.18	293.28	527.08	713.20	853.03
029.01	162.10	296.23	527.21	714.07	853.09
029.15	164.05	296.26	530.05	714.20	854.03
029.27	165.02	297.25	545.10	715.09	854.09
030.22	165.27	298.07	545.12	715.25	854.16
032.10	166.03	305.04	545.18	716.25	855.22
033.26	175.04	306.24	550.13	717.03	856.09
040.03	178.26	312.25	558.14	717.06	865.03
042.10	179.01	313.04	558.22	717.07	866.05
043.12	180.23	315.28	558.25	717.11	870.25
044.17	180.25	320.18	559.05	717.25	871.22
045.04	181.14	321.20	559.21	718.25	872.19
048.10	182.20	323.22	561.12	719.03	873.20
049.01	183.18	323.24	561.22	720.14	873.24
049.07	186.02	324.19	562.22	723.21	877.11
049.21	187.25	326.07	564.18	725.23	880.10
049.23	190.21	326.18	568.25	730.24	884.09
050.11	191.14	326.21	569.08	731.09	886.06
051.23	192.28	329.21	570.14	732.12	888.04
052.08	193.22	331.27	570.20	732.18	895.08
052.27	194.08	334.16	570.22	732.21	897.08
055.23	195.24	335.11	572.23	733.04	898.12
056.10	199.12	335.26	579.24	734.19	900.11
056.16	201.13	337.15	583.04	735.27	900.23
057.09	202.11	339.12	587.24	736.07	901.06
061.09	203.15	341.05	588.21	736.14	902.27
062.14	203.22	343.01	588.24	736.19	905.17
066.12	204.11	345.11	592.23	737.09	907.11
066.22	204.14	349.24	598.24	738.01	912.03
067.07	207.26	351.05	601.14	738.03	while
071.11	209.17	356.15	601.23	738.04	005.11
073.04	209.19	358.26	603.11	738.10	005.21
073.22	209.20	360.05	603.15	738.23	008.13
073.06	209.26	361.12	604.11	744.22	008.21
079.21	213.02	361.19	606.02	744.23	023.09
080.08	213.18	366.05	606.04	748.06	027.25
080.18	214.01	366.08	606.14	750.01	029.19
081.03	215.06	366.12	606.14	754.10	035.09
081.04	215.06	367.12	610.16	758.28	040.26
081.10	215.27	367.26	610.17	761.23	042.17
081.21	216.13	371.19	617.11	762.03	047.04
083.09	217.03	372.17	618.05	763.06	047.11
083.14	217.16	376.01	619.23	763.14	063.09
083.20	218.14	377.07	619.27	766.12	082.05
085.22	218.21	377.12	621.28	766.13	085.18
086.26	219.17	377.28	622.01	767.27	099.05
087.06	219.20	378.21	627.18	768.07	099.23
088.22	219.25	384.10	628.07	768.17	104.26
088.23	220.13	385.02	628.13	770.22	109.18
089.05	220.27	385.07	628.14	771.27	122.17
089.08	221.19	388.24	628.15	772.19	122.26
089.16	222.19	389.02	628.19	775.03	123.04
089.26	222.23	389.06	629.26	778.03	125.26
090.08	223.08	394.17	630.22	782.23	126.07
093.27	223.15	395.06	630.25	784.22	130.11
093.26	226.01	397.18	633.09	785.17	132.01
097.18	226.16	403.13	633.18	786.21	147.22
098.16	230.07	404.27	633.19	792.03	147.24
099.11	230.23	405.08	633.25	793.13	147.25
100.20	231.17	405.21	634.04	793.14	150.08
101.19	236.11	407.06	634.07	793.17	152.24
102.23	236.15	414.02	635.04	794.16	156.22
105.07	237.28	414.05	635.13	797.07	174.24
105.14	244.09	418.07	636.09	802.01	180.19
106.08	244.22	420.15	636.27	802.15	182.14
107.25	245.24	421.02	638.07	802.26	

204.15	816.10	707.14	063.14	349.23	780.05
210.05	816.28	798.13	077.18	358.14	781.17
214.27	817.16	799.23	077.23	359.05	782.18
215.27	827.21	852.13	079.05	362.05	784.01
240.25	832.10	852.17	082.04	366.28	784.02
247.14	833.22	854.15	085.08	372.08	798.09
249.26	835.23	854.27	091.23	372.09	799.20
265.15	837.18	white	091.27	380.12	807.09
269.25	843.23	016.06	091.28	381.11	815.10
276.08	846.10	016.10	092.07	383.17	816.03
279.06	846.11	017.21	092.07	385.04	816.04
285.24	849.05	022.12	092.28	387.22	819.03
295.05	857.22	029.04	104.01	388.10	828.23
295.26	866.23	136.19	105.17	390.02	829.15
307.06	873.24	142.26	106.18	392.17	831.07
307.16	887.26	149.07	106.21	396.24	837.15
315.25	894.15	155.11	106.27	399.20	842.12
326.04	whiles	164.23	107.05	409.07	845.21
326.13	458.14	193.02	107.06	412.20	846.13
334.12	whilst	204.11	107.08	416.02	850.10
336.18	626.03	204.13	114.14	427.26	855.22
339.14	whim	209.11	115.15	441.10	857.06
350.22	390.06	219.16	117.27	450.07	862.12
352.03	643.15	221.27	120.20	450.17	863.27
365.11	whimpering	231.24	122.21	450.21	867.28
367.09	468.13	249.08	123.19	451.13	875.21
376.01	whine	249.14	123.22	451.16	875.21
378.11	675.04	277.08	125.03	451.25	875.28
392.11	whining	306.23	125.14	452.14	875.28
394.15	468.15	318.14	125.28	454.03	876.20
376.07	477.13	328.23	126.12	463.02	883.19
415.14	whip	331.01	126.27	463.18	885.03
420.04	223.05	342.15	127.06	469.19	885.08
423.20	whirl	342.23	130.25	472.14	895.01
430.05	282.20	343.09	131.01	479.10	897.10
436.07	whirled	346.20	134.23	479.22	907.18
436.17	074.02	348.10	137.06	479.27	911.25
436.18	675.24	359.21	139.05	480.13	911.27
441.24	whirling	366.24	141.27	480.17	912.04
453.21	145.23	367.05	147.04	480.17	912.04
455.26	765.03	367.10	147.15	480.22	912.05
484.26	whirls	395.06	148.13	485.21	912.06
487.17	004.01	416.27	148.22	487.08	whoever
493.18	228.14	426.10	150.10	495.12	876.10
502.28	whirlwind	433.06	151.18	495.16	whole
505.05	044.08	457.06	152.13	506.03	061.12
510.06	whiskers	501.10	154.18	507.21	083.13
518.27	543.10	524.01	157.21	516.14	084.28
521.07	471.24	540.15	161.14	528.01	087.17
525.17	whisper	541.06	161.20	532.10	098.19
527.11	124.01	558.17	164.12	534.19	113.25
527.16	330.21	575.20	165.26	535.17	119.21
528.19	412.23	577.14	167.11	536.23	142.03
533.17	419.18	589.02	167.11	565.16	147.10
534.11	540.02	595.04	167.26	566.10	218.13
546.14	549.01	597.06	170.02	571.08	256.26
547.03	690.03	605.23	171.07	579.03	269.05
549.10	703.16	606.06	173.11	579.09	282.19
550.17	whispered	611.20	173.14	587.16	288.04
553.23	078.16	652.12	174.26	590.11	294.21
554.25	081.27	659.06	175.07	592.18	306.24
563.03	083.06	667.13	175.13	594.12	316.06
563.22	123.26	668.04	179.06	597.05	325.14
569.06	126.09	675.11	183.02	598.20	355.12
570.07	155.23	676.17	195.16	602.01	369.14
573.05	156.25	685.14	197.03	603.02	387.15
523.17	286.06	685.15	197.09	605.19	408.08
621.26	354.22	709.06	197.13	611.05	477.26
629.10	391.23	737.14	200.18	612.01	495.23
650.21	412.04	738.03	201.15	614.07	536.11
651.04	425.26	766.04	206.12	619.18	546.04
651.06	440.17	773.22	210.18	628.08	549.16
654.11	430.10	796.24	213.09	628.11	554.20
659.24	597.01	612.15	214.09	632.01	554.22
659.28	600.22	835.14	214.23	633.11	556.02
642.10	607.24	835.15	215.17	634.02	573.20
647.17	652.15	890.18	232.22	645.11	592.11
649.05	653.09	white-walled	239.13	647.26	608.07
653.21	660.26	622.15	241.21	647.27	612.12
656.27	845.26	white-washed	242.24	653.02	622.04
663.18	whispering	658.14	242.27	654.01	628.13
668.17	028.27	729.03	243.23	655.13	633.17
668.23	066.24	whiteness	244.12	660.28	672.01
672.21	157.03	085.26	250.22	669.02	691.02
674.21	543.13	whiter	257.09	669.03	699.25
678.14	631.11	409.27	271.17	669.06	724.24
676.22	902.08	whither	283.26	670.24	738.12
677.20	whisperings	169.23	286.23	671.03	748.05
698.26	220.25	174.12	286.26	671.04	769.13
700.22	371.24	337.03	287.07	671.05	800.12
708.17	whispers	479.28	287.13	671.19	826.12
713.14	367.14	487.07	288.06	672.24	831.04
713.15	398.25	607.02	289.05	677.08	854.23
713.19	441.17	884.14	289.07	678.13	871.04
721.02	544.02	whitish	294.11	684.11	882.19
721.15	544.08	675.22	294.14	685.11	wholesome
731.18	582.23	who	295.10	689.13	288.19
732.16	whistled	008.15	297.14	691.16	323.21
744.24	663.06	010.22	297.18	695.10	wholly
749.07	whistling	018.18	298.03	700.28	157.23
752.16	096.03	018.19	300.08	717.15	229.25
753.14	whit	018.23	307.01	723.26	314.21
758.25	427.21	027.15	308.16	724.16	337.11
759.10	515.24	037.14	314.26	729.15	444.09
771.19	532.19	039.18	318.24	754.28	473.20
783.04	637.08	040.13	321.17	759.22	475.04
798.15	840.06	040.21	334.02	760.09	544.24
798.21	whitcross	051.15	337.07	766.01	563.06
803.19	658.04	052.06	338.05	767.01	626.14
807.17	658.12	055.22	339.24	770.14	657.16
811.05	663.27	062.09	341.12	772.26	724.10

743.06	699.24	814.13	589.13	812.25	227.02
768.01	717.14	835.09	590.16	859.09	227.20
whom	720.02	840.07	592.04	864.02	232.20
050.06	750.10	866.28	592.21	864.17	236.01
052.23	760.17	887.24	593.14	872.06	239.03
064.22	769.18	891.08	593.21	887.17	242.11
094.15	781.09	893.19	595.13	902.19	243.07
124.12	803.05	894.04	597.03	wilder	246.06
130.26	837.19	907.01	597.24	031.19	247.14
132.09	853.14	912.17	601.21	wilderness	253.12
134.23	855.02	wi-	614.02	228.13	257.16
199.28	859.18	680.10	616.19	551.10	263.17
201.24	872.07	698.03	616.23	570.16	264.07
232.09	889.24	wick	621.04	663.22	265.05
242.01	902.06	172.23	622.11	712.08	265.06
279.11	908.21	wicked	622.24	wildest	266.06
286.17	whosoever	009.27	626.13	302.02	266.21
336.10	911.28	021.09	627.18	674.06	266.27
352.11	why	045.05	627.27	712.07	267.07
352.28	018.14	054.06	629.11	wildly	269.20
358.24	018.16	056.04	632.03	003.16	269.22
366.22	018.17	063.12	632.21	101.12	269.25
425.21	020.03	106.21	644.17	415.15	270.27
427.16	033.07	132.01	646.16	480.19	270.28
513.24	034.13	134.17	734.17	517.13	271.05
513.25	035.03	291.14	744.18	600.13	271.05
545.06	063.28	574.03	759.03	617.17	272.06
552.21	067.05	646.06	759.16	647.21	272.22
556.07	069.13	646.07	771.24	656.16	275.21
557.12	091.05	793.08	796.27	750.26	275.23
596.20	091.19	wickedness	815.14	849.23	275.26
597.03	092.03	013.02	815.16	858.19	276.21
610.27	098.28	314.28	820.10	wilds	276.27
625.24	102.08	884.25	820.26	321.23	280.27
626.02	120.05	wicket	821.13	wilfully	280.27
626.02	120.06	443.02	821.20	360.23	282.18
634.20	120.15	503.19	822.15	436.17	282.20
636.15	130.26	505.01	825.07	will	282.21
647.15	130.28	588.03	825.27	009.15	284.06
702.07	133.06	654.19	826.09	013.15	284.07
705.06	134.14	675.23	828.19	014.21	284.08
708.06	150.01	733.04	828.20	014.22	284.13
744.16	156.10	736.21	832.22	015.02	285.27
748.22	192.23	738.23	837.11	015.04	286.22
753.28	204.24	798.03	837.15	015.07	286.23
754.13	251.27	wide	837.19	020.04	293.17
767.01	252.17	024.16	840.12	024.27	293.21
773.10	253.15	078.04	842.18	024.28	293.24
776.19	263.12	087.23	855.23	026.04	297.10
781.12	271.01	164.10	862.21	033.05	297.16
782.19	293.16	191.04	865.18	033.17	298.19
785.06	301.03	194.27	866.22	033.21	298.25
787.01	311.20	204.03	868.01	036.01	300.17
805.24	311.26	207.21	873.12	036.07	300.22
824.01	314.27	209.04	879.12	044.16	301.02
824.01	325.19	219.18	883.14	057.22	302.07
828.14	326.08	286.05	895.08	057.24	306.05
838.07	326.09	293.26	897.01	058.01	307.13
845.13	353.21	296.18	898.01	059.14	310.04
853.23	356.26	432.24	wild	059.16	310.19
897.14	362.02	463.11	025.13	059.23	311.01
897.18	375.18	502.07	033.04	059.26	311.01
905.12	386.15	551.05	075.09	060.04	315.25
whose	395.24	675.04	136.05	062.22	320.01
030.16	395.26	687.01	145.23	062.23	322.15
054.21	395.28	694.15	146.08	062.25	326.24
071.08	424.24	772.04	219.08	063.13	327.05
072.25	425.02	888.28	228.14	064.20	334.13
092.01	425.03	widely	235.01	068.24	336.01
102.25	425.05	351.14	248.21	072.04	336.05
114.10	425.20	578.08	271.03	086.10	338.18
115.13	447.06	wider	283.18	098.09	339.06
116.03	451.08	509.20	302.21	102.04	339.07
121.16	468.04	widest-winged	327.21	102.25	339.19
126.14	480.26	415.02	346.02	107.01	339.20
126.14	482.23	widow	358.24	108.24	339.25
142.22	516.23	196.20	405.13	108.27	339.26
149.14	528.25	211.22	424.05	108.28	345.08
185.27	530.27	243.11	426.15	109.03	350.02
193.17	531.24	450.26	439.02	109.08	352.28
194.05	537.10	519.24	447.07	116.17	353.03
194.19	547.07	537.04	463.11	120.19	355.05
207.12	548.07	widow's	498.06	124.03	355.08
219.11	570.15	172.02	501.16	131.21	356.08
221.26	573.23	186.09	514.05	134.16	356.12
226.06	579.23	wie	560.08	134.20	358.22
230.01	581.18	678.20	561.19	134.22	360.07
231.09	585.05	wielded	572.02	135.06	360.11
254.18	590.02	392.05	574.04	157.11	360.19
256.23	613.28	wife	591.17	157.21	366.07
307.02	617.27	073.03	599.19	158.10	372.23
337.19	618.14	073.12	599.21	160.07	376.09
349.03	618.15	134.25	606.06	166.25	376.11
349.22	622.19	162.21	619.20	172.20	386.10
400.24	623.17	189.04	633.03	176.07	386.26
401.27	635.15	217.22	634.16	177.07	387.07
421.21	638.12	298.20	646.09	179.13	387.10
423.17	645.06	305.18	649.16	183.14	388.10
433.05	671.06	371.02	650.15	184.12	390.07
439.06	672.28	376.12	659.08	185.24	392.18
444.12	673.02	376.21	660.02	188.24	392.21
509.18	697.04	377.03	673.14	195.10	396.12
568.01	704.15	446.17	684.21	197.24	396.18
594.01	723.18	448.10	685.08	198.21	396.18
653.02	726.11	449.05	712.16	201.06	401.01
653.06	732.18	451.07	747.27	201.22	401.06
664.10	741.19	515.09	750.01	208.22	403.06
671.01	766.21	517.18	762.23	214.08	403.28
676.07	774.19	517.22	777.10	216.08	404.14
676.18	777.21	535.22	798.09	224.22	405.12
693.07	805.19	552.27	812.05	225.24	406.07

410.23	529.10	679.27	816.15	**willingly**	314.04
415.13	529.15	679.28	818.09	065.21	314.18
417.16	529.19	680.02	819.21	132.10	332.04
417.19	529.28	681.17	820.01	670.23	332.12
420.06	530.20	683.06	820.02	818.21	332.16
422.06	531.14	684.02	820.03	**willow**	336.06
422.07	531.16	685.16	820.04	229.10	341.15
422.09	531.17	687.18	820.24	636.27	380.13
422.10	533.01	691.16	820.26	**wills**	380.27
425.12	534.12	693.16	821.10	476.25	381.11
426.05	536.15	696.13	821.17	**wilson**	418.12
426.05	537.08	697.15	821.26	149.13	418.25
428.27	538.04	700.03	822.27	150.04	426.20
429.12	538.16	700.06	823.04	355.19	433.21
430.13	538.28	705.17	823.04	356.12	470.27
430.22	539.12	705.19	823.09	**wilsons**	479.24
431.05	539.20	706.11	823.11	355.16	502.15
431.18	540.05	706.18	824.12	**wilt**	522.16
431.22	540.18	706.21	824.16	590.15	599.09
431.24	540.18	708.13	824.17	**win**	629.23
432.14	540.23	709.26	824.18	018.17	664.25
433.28	540.23	709.26	824.26	129.16	676.05
435.11	541.01	709.27	829.22	323.01	715.11
436.03	542.27	718.17	834.19	374.08	725.27
436.08	545.04	718.19	834.23	528.24	781.14
436.17	546.14	718.20	834.26	762.25	796.13
436.19	546.23	719.01	835.05	817.16	839.13
436.20	547.08	719.18	835.28	**wind**	839.21
437.09	547.10	721.01	836.14	001.08	844.03
439.16	547.11	721.10	836.17	021.04	852.11
442.13	547.17	721.15	837.10	026.07	856.27
442.18	547.25	721.23	837.18	075.09	892.24
449.01	547.28	722.04	837.20	075.23	901.06
449.03	548.15	722.05	838.15	079.27	**window-blind**
451.25	549.02	722.22	839.08	096.08	414.04
452.04	550.10	722.25	840.14	101.03	**window-blinds**
452.09	558.17	722.25	840.15	101.07	857.18
452.09	558.19	722.26	841.01	101.11	**window-curtain**
454.01	561.05	723.01	843.07	113.03	348.01
454.16	562.16	723.07	844.18	113.08	353.24
455.16	562.19	723.09	846.08	133.24	578.17
457.19	563.24	723.17	847.03	165.17	**window-panes**
457.26	565.12	725.08	848.06	228.14	583.01
457.27	566.09	725.14	849.25	229.13	**window-recess**
460.06	567.14	726.28	852.03	250.23	550.17
464.15	573.12	730.12	852.04	405.19	717.25
466.22	574.09	730.15	853.14	433.22	**window-seat**
476.24	574.15	731.05	856.26	440.17	003.03
477.03	581.20	731.19	856.28	479.26	006.17
477.11	583.12	731.24	863.02	514.24	049.14
477.21	589.23	734.15	865.09	518.27	306.13
479.27	593.16	735.02	873.04	520.03	399.04
479.28	594.02	736.15	874.06	558.18	399.18
482.06	594.04	739.28	874.17	559.21	**window-sill**
482.11	596.07	741.04	875.26	560.09	050.17
485.04	598.14	741.12	876.09	561.17	**windowless**
489.15	602.17	742.07	877.11	562.21	335.12
489.22	603.13	747.13	877.12	565.02	**windows**
493.07	603.21	752.19	877.18	565.03	009.17
493.09	607.18	752.27	878.20	571.25	015.25
494.14	612.06	753.03	878.25	582.23	017.10
494.27	612.18	754.01	878.26	583.04	076.02
496.22	613.28	755.04	878.28	630.28	089.08
503.21	614.01	756.26	879.27	631.11	096.09
503.21	614.27	760.08	880.01	640.08	100.24
503.22	615.04	760.08	880.03	660.04	154.13
508.05	615.07	760.09	880.15	709.12	204.18
506.23	615.14	760.10	884.02	714.24	283.02
509.02	615.22	763.03	884.13	765.04	284.04
509.12	616.20	768.27	885.04	765.19	433.04
510.11	617.03	770.03	885.06	800.01	457.05
511.03	618.05	770.06	885.11	804.11	616.17
512.19	618.10	775.03	886.08	850.03	857.19
512.20	619.15	775.06	891.21	896.21	859.06
512.20	621.22	776.09	895.03	902.08	871.02
514.09	623.20	783.15	896.17	**winding**	**winds**
514.12	623.24	783.20	896.20	099.05	066.16
514.23	623.27	783.21	897.08	164.24	144.06
515.07	625.11	784.08	897.11	502.24	145.17
515.17	626.07	784.16	897.12	**windings**	711.19
516.19	627.05	784.17	897.14	221.06	**windy**
516.26	630.16	784.19	897.18	572.19	478.27
517.14	631.28	786.02	898.22	**window**	**wine**
517.21	645.16	786.04	899.22	009.05	065.18
517.27	645.13	786.05	899.22	021.04	180.06
518.02	646.15	786.25	901.26	049.22	258.24
518.14	646.22	787.02	907.07	049.26	262.06
518.14	647.06	787.17	907.08	050.26	410.22
518.16	647.26	787.21	907.08	051.04	613.01
518.18	647.28	791.08	911.08	061.25	613.13
519.26	648.03	791.14	912.08	071.09	705.28
522.17	648.04	791.22	912.15	101.01	758.21
524.14	648.05	792.04	912.18	115.07	865.07
524.27	649.20	792.19	912.19	133.25	**wine-glass**
525.01	649.25	793.02	912.20	151.09	411.09
525.03	649.28	793.05	912.20	164.15	**wine-merchant**
525.16	650.01	793.24	**will-o'-the-wisp**	166.04	180.13
525.20	650.01	797.21	634.15	184.22	180.15
525.22	650.14	799.25	**willing**	190.19	**wing**
527.04	650.14	800.02	147.17	191.22	194.06
527.05	651.12	801.28	265.03	193.06	288.02
527.07	652.18	805.19	265.04	203.19	639.08
527.11	653.25	807.10	402.12	203.27	**wings**
527.13	656.14	809.07	476.15	204.04	023.20
527.15	659.19	811.04	635.02	210.01	164.16
527.14	664.01	811.17	640.15	229.17	248.02
527.16	671.13	811.21	705.22	235.08	504.23
527.26	672.08	813.21	709.21	258.16	542.25
528.28	672.24	814.17	851.17	280.23	640.15
529.09	678.17	816.11	852.01	286.02	662.01
				287.21	735.25

winner
064.24
winning
785.19
winter
001.07
003.12
005.17
072.27
113.03
144.04
145.15
176.18
189.01
189.09
213.17
219.11
229.24
242.11
243.28
258.19
473.04
658.23
675.05
859.24
859.25
winter's
560.20
winters
004.12
wintry
058.04
112.19
606.07
709.12
795.01
wipe
016.16
333.17
423.11
623.22
844.09
wiped
022.23
030.01
057.17
140.27
563.05
600.11
811.10
wire
101.16
wisdom
270.10
441.04
508.02
631.09
wise
310.04
597.17
755.26
wisely
529.04
529.06
854.09
900.02
wiser
268.20
321.10
756.11
wish
037.09
044.27
046.02
055.27
056.18
057.26
059.21
064.04
092.09
094.28
102.07
116.26
123.14
130.11
177.03
178.08
189.26
199.25
206.21
225.25
250.10
251.08
264.17
268.08
270.16
275.09
284.09
329.26
335.28
338.15
339.04
348.22
362.07
363.10
387.22
397.13
406.04
406.09
410.12
427.27

429.11
452.21
454.23
463.12
467.04
468.03
468.04
469.05
482.17
489.18
492.09
496.25
505.05
507.20
511.14
517.17
530.13
530.15
539.11
542.05
554.15
563.10
563.10
567.15
568.09
572.16
576.02
580.04
580.05
614.21
621.12
622.18
630.26
635.18
645.10
646.26
659.09
659.18
665.01
669.06
680.14
691.13
708.22
716.04
716.07
730.05
755.07
767.19
779.03
797.04
814.04
817.02
817.25
822.25
828.14
833.28
834.06
838.12
840.04
851.05
872.25
893.19
895.24
897.27
900.17
906.14
wished
006.12
031.02
036.12
047.16
048.20
096.17
101.11
105.17
106.12
109.24
130.10
166.01
171.25
192.14
192.17
215.16
251.11
253.23
294.01
305.03
306.15
307.05
323.18
338.20
345.04
375.06
377.09
390.24
391.26
394.15
467.08
469.25
481.02
487.04
488.20
531.25
532.14
537.05
537.18
550.14
572.03
601.24
624.27
642.05

642.08
642.16
663.08
663.17
689.19
692.09
696.21
711.07
787.27
788.07
794.16
799.15
807.03
808.05
810.01
829.09
840.10
845.27
865.11
879.11
882.28
888.18
893.16
897.27
909.27
909.28
wishes
019.05
022.17
040.21
174.28
287.19
320.16
388.10
412.24
440.06
452.03
606.11
799.04
822.09
840.20
842.07
358.06
874.04
901.17
910.07
wishing
042.05
054.28
378.06
457.22
475.21
801.10
834.02
835.24
363.14
wistful
643.17
wistfully
612.16
wit
287.05
witch
297.13
390.02
549.27
571.16
863.27
witch's
402.23
witchcraft
850.07
witchery
528.24
with
001.08
001.14
002.04
003.02
003.15
003.26
004.08
004.20
004.28
005.23
005.28
006.22
007.03
009.10
009.21
010.12
010.19
013.22
014.02
014.04
014.19
014.21
015.22
015.25
016.01
016.02
016.07
016.10
017.08
017.21
018.03
018.06
019.12
019.16
020.08
020.11

020.12
021.17
022.01
022.27
023.01
026.02
026.05
026.06
026.20
028.14
028.17
028.20
028.21
028.26
030.05
030.17
031.09
031.24
032.21
032.25
033.17
034.11
037.28
038.02
040.08
041.15
041.20
042.02
042.11
043.03
043.20
043.28
044.04
044.20
045.11
045.19
046.06
046.12
046.13
046.26
047.27
048.17
049.03
049.06
049.21
050.04
051.09
051.10
052.07
052.22
052.26
054.01
055.14
057.23
058.01
058.13
058.16
059.03
060.05
060.10
061.23
062.19
062.27
063.10
063.18
063.28
065.04
065.25
066.11
067.06
067.10
068.15
068.21
071.15
072.01
072.14
073.19
073.20
073.23
074.15
074.18
075.07
075.20
075.21
075.26
076.02
076.06
076.19
077.13
077.15
077.18
078.05
079.01
079.14
079.21
083.18
084.08
084.11
084.16
085.22
085.24
087.10
087.19
087.24
088.09
090.11
092.22
092.25
093.02
094.15
095.15

096.04
096.14
097.10
097.12
097.17
098.20
099.18
099.21
099.24
102.17
102.26
103.09
103.11
105.03
105.20
106.13
108.19
108.23
108.27
109.15
109.18
109.25
111.04
111.19
112.04
112.16
113.26
114.05
114.14
114.22
114.28
115.05
116.09
117.15
117.22
118.14
119.20
119.27
121.02
121.06
121.19
121.20
122.04
122.08
122.15
122.18
122.22
123.04
123.09
125.12
126.25
129.10
130.19
130.23
130.26
131.04
132.18
133.05
133.07
134.02
135.08
136.11
138.08
138.14
138.16
138.20
139.08
140.10
141.04
142.08
142.16
142.27
143.08
143.19
145.15
145.19
145.23
146.02
146.23
147.13
147.26
148.03
148.06
148.24
149.03
149.19
150.02
150.13
150.26
151.13
152.05
152.25
154.22
155.07
155.11
156.28
158.17
158.24
159.21
161.20
161.21
161.21
162.05
162.09
162.10
162.20
162.25
163.27
165.08
165.27
166.10

167.03
167.04
167.19
167.22
168.15
168.20
168.26
169.12
169.13
170.21
170.23
174.08
175.11
175.14
176.19
176.20
178.28
180.11
181.05
182.25
184.08
184.11
184.15
184.16
184.19
185.26
186.02
187.05
187.13
187.22
188.19
188.25
189.06
189.14
190.13
192.08
192.10
193.05
193.15
193.18
194.17
194.20
194.25
195.05
195.24
196.18
197.05
197.23
198.01
198.04
198.08
198.10
198.15
198.23
198.24
199.08
199.18
199.19
199.28
200.03
200.28
201.04
201.10
201.23
201.25
202.02
202.22
203.17
204.04
204.11
204.13
205.28
207.08
207.22
207.22
207.23
208.26
209.04
209.07
209.07
209.11
209.16
209.20
209.28
210.02
210.24
211.14
211.24
213.05
214.06
214.11
214.28
215.10
215.11
215.28
216.04
216.07
217.09
217.24
218.06
218.22
218.25
222.01
222.04
223.20
224.14
225.01
225.08
225.24
225.28
226.03

227.27	295.21	378.28	464.22	529.22	617.20
228.08	295.25	379.01	465.12	530.12	617.23
228.18	296.19	379.04	467.05	530.17	618.09
229.06	297.13	379.07	467.15	531.18	618.13
229.24	298.10	379.22	467.18	531.19	618.19
230.19	299.07	380.24	467.21	532.15	619.21
231.23	299.25	380.25	467.28	532.15	619.22
232.03	300.15	382.26	468.08	534.03	620.09
232.08	306.05	383.02	468.24	534.05	620.21
232.09	306.14	383.03	469.01	537.05	621.18
232.10	307.04	384.15	469.06	537.28	622.04
232.24	307.12	384.18	469.27	538.17	622.26
233.07	307.20	386.01	469.28	539.17	623.19
235.22	307.24	388.18	470.01	540.16	623.20
236.01	308.11	389.14	470.06	540.22	625.03
236.08	308.21	389.15	470.11	541.11	625.23
237.04	308.22	390.03	470.15	541.13	626.20
257.13	308.27	390.28	470.23	542.02	627.05
238.20	309.01	391.01	470.25	542.10	627.07
238.22	310.19	391.27	471.06	542.18	627.09
238.24	310.22	394.07	471.17	543.09	627.24
238.28	312.04	394.17	471.20	543.23	628.11
239.16	312.13	395.08	471.23	544.01	628.14
240.14	313.14	395.24	473.03	544.05	628.15
240.24	313.19	396.22	473.20	544.11	628.16
241.02	313.24	397.15	474.11	544.20	628.27
242.14	314.11	398.12	475.15	545.02	629.03
244.09	314.14	398.16	476.12	545.19	629.04
244.19	316.21	398.25	476.16	546.10	629.06
244.20	318.19	399.09	477.02	547.02	630.03
245.13	320.11	399.23	477.02	548.01	630.05
246.13	321.01	400.12	480.18	548.06	630.07
246.20	321.02	400.13	483.01	548.19	630.08
247.18	323.13	400.19	483.05	552.03	630.16
248.02	323.24	400.28	483.07	552.06	631.15
248.02	325.03	401.11	483.12	552.09	631.25
248.03	325.17	401.23	484.10	552.10	631.26
248.04	326.19	403.04	485.01	552.21	632.07
248.12	326.26	403.16	485.25	552.27	632.10
248.18	329.06	405.08	486.01	553.02	632.27
249.14	329.09	407.01	486.08	553.04	633.09
250.06	331.10	407.20	487.11	554.04	633.24
253.08	332.04	407.22	487.14	554.06	635.03
254.04	333.02	407.24	488.20	554.21	635.13
254.07	334.15	410.10	488.26	561.08	636.01
254.13	334.25	410.13	488.27	561.10	637.02
254.18	335.03	410.24	489.25	561.22	637.17
255.01	335.13	412.06	490.02	563.11	637.20
255.03	335.16	412.08	490.06	564.04	637.25
256.01	336.15	416.17	492.06	565.02	637.27
256.05	337.06	417.11	493.18	567.13	638.04
256.11	338.06	418.25	493.20	567.24	638.06
256.25	340.03	420.13	493.26	568.10	638.17
256.27	340.05	421.03	494.06	569.24	639.09
257.14	341.05	421.06	495.02	572.02	639.10
257.20	342.06	422.04	495.08	572.16	639.24
258.13	343.12	423.09	495.10	572.21	640.02
258.24	344.17	427.01	495.12	573.17	641.03
259.24	344.26	428.03	496.26	573.20	641.09
260.16	345.03	428.09	497.09	573.24	642.02
261.24	345.05	428.18	497.12	575.13	642.04
261.27	345.27	429.21	498.06	577.11	642.10
262.16	346.03	430.03	498.07	579.03	642.20
262.20	346.10	430.17	498.09	582.04	642.21
264.12	346.11	430.25	498.22	582.06	643.08
264.26	347.07	431.01	500.08	582.10	643.11
265.08	347.10	432.22	501.13	583.17	644.08
265.13	349.02	432.25	501.15	584.02	645.20
265.15	349.12	433.12	501.27	585.07	645.21
266.27	349.21	433.19	502.05	586.02	645.22
267.11	350.14	434.06	502.20	587.21	646.15
269.09	350.17	434.08	502.25	588.24	647.16
269.17	351.05	434.26	503.14	591.02	647.19
269.26	351.13	434.27	503.28	592.16	648.15
269.27	352.01	435.02	505.06	593.01	648.26
271.12	352.20	435.16	505.14	593.01	649.02
273.06	352.26	435.23	505.17	596.01	649.12
273.09	352.27	436.16	505.22	597.06	649.13
273.11	352.28	437.17	506.13	598.02	649.17
274.11	353.22	438.09	507.03	598.07	649.17
275.23	354.15	442.01	507.21	598.19	649.18
275.25	354.20	442.07	507.22	599.03	649.24
276.07	355.06	442.14	509.11	599.19	649.27
276.16	355.13	442.18	510.23	601.10	651.05
276.19	355.18	442.26	511.13	601.14	651.27
279.06	355.28	444.14	511.27	601.19	652.07
279.13	356.13	445.09	512.01	602.06	653.25
280.07	357.15	445.12	512.02	602.07	654.02
280.13	357.19	445.24	512.03	602.07	655.11
280.20	358.17	446.05	512.03	602.09	655.19
280.26	358.25	446.09	512.06	602.10	655.22
281.16	359.01	448.03	513.08	603.04	658.21
282.15	359.06	448.24	513.24	603.06	658.21
283.24	359.23	449.11	514.08	604.08	659.24
284.15	361.26	450.02	515.14	605.02	660.23
285.16	368.02	450.27	517.06	606.03	660.25
285.19	368.06	452.11	518.01	606.08	661.02
287.26	369.18	452.14	519.02	609.18	661.07
288.03	369.24	454.11	519.04	610.05	661.10
288.10	371.12	454.18	522.16	610.21	661.27
288.12	372.08	456.22	523.13	611.14	661.28
288.24	373.18	457.05	523.26	611.26	662.01
289.12	373.21	457.28	525.05	613.16	662.03
289.13	374.18	458.12	525.23	615.11	662.14
291.10	374.20	458.23	526.19	615.15	663.20
291.12	375.21	458.25	526.20	615.20	663.21
291.25	377.15	459.09	526.27	615.28	663.23
292.02	378.05	459.19	527.01	616.14	664.25
292.22	378.05	460.21	527.27	616.19	664.26
294.12	378.15	461.07	529.02	616.28	665.03
295.17	378.23	464.04	529.18	617.01	665.15

665.16	743.07	812.15	884.01	488.18	604.04
666.04	744.16	812.16	884.27	511.19	605.15
667.11	744.18	813.03	885.03	563.06	613.05
668.14	745.01	813.07	885.08	567.21	620.01
669.05	745.07	813.07	885.14	575.03	639.19
670.10	745.07	814.04	885.27	577.07	640.25
670.16	745.16	815.01	886.24	607.20	651.11
670.21	745.22	816.06	887.15	609.16	653.17
671.02	746.10	817.04	890.18	672.12	654.16
672.25	747.07	817.15	890.21	674.17	661.04
674.04	747.08	817.17	891.13	675.21	661.05
676.14	748.04	817.20	892.18	676.05	664.28
676.15	749.07	817.25	892.21	676.13	666.05
677.13	749.17	817.28	893.21	683.17	666.06
677.19	749.18	818.02	894.09	685.06	666.06
679.24	749.24	818.12	894.09	699.12	667.26
680.11	750.01	819.27	894.27	702.12	671.16
680.24	750.23	820.07	895.12	737.13	679.13
681.15	751.06	821.24	895.27	753.26	693.27
681.28	751.11	821.26	896.14	754.18	703.18
684.16	751.17	822.02	898.10	759.05	706.04
685.05	751.24	822.03	898.27	794.27	706.12
686.28	753.10	822.10	899.27	795.12	707.17
687.16	753.24	822.10	901.10	832.07	725.20
687.18	756.07	822.24	901.22	834.13	725.21
687.21	756.09	823.04	905.17	869.20	735.23
688.07	756.15	823.23	906.04	without	738.08
691.17	756.26	823.27	907.28	008.12	748.06
692.04	757.23	824.01	908.25	008.17	753.11
692.25	757.24	825.09	911.01	025.14	778.18
693.01	757.25	825.10	911.02	036.03	786.05
693.19	758.03	825.21	912.13	040.24	794.21
694.16	758.04	826.08	withdraw	044.02	795.02
696.09	758.05	826.13	299.05	044.15	800.05
696.16	758.26	826.28	372.11	045.02	804.13
699.04	759.12	828.23	650.21	063.03	809.15
700.02	760.13	829.11	681.20	063.22	819.07
700.13	760.27	829.14	747.16	065.06	824.11
700.14	761.23	830.06	822.05	066.23	831.07
700.27	762.05	830.13	879.19	082.17	832.23
701.09	763.18	831.09	withdrawing	088.22	834.19
702.02	764.02	832.05	796.13	090.25	853.25
702.08	766.25	832.09	withdrawn	099.19	856.07
703.03	767.20	833.20	164.03	100.23	871.14
703.04	767.26	837.08	290.04	106.25	873.08
705.08	768.19	837.16	530.02	108.04	885.20
705.28	770.12	838.04	604.12	110.08	888.19
708.19	770.13	838.04	738.21	110.08	888.26
708.23	771.06	838.07	804.03	132.03	899.01
708.24	773.15	840.07	withdraws	154.08	899.24
709.24	773.17	840.08	858.09	154.14	905.13
710.04	774.20	841.07	withdrew	154.25	906.18
711.05	775.22	841.20	138.03	158.05	907.12
711.07	775.25	844.08	141.16	175.02	907.18
711.16	777.07	844.21	155.21	245.01	910.03
711.20	781.11	844.25	202.10	253.12	910.23
712.10	781.15	845.09	251.14	258.03	912.05
712.11	782.13	845.26	286.11	259.07	witness
713.02	782.17	846.05	295.20	266.05	374.28
713.05	783.14	847.02	366.11	267.01	375.06
714.23	783.15	847.16	371.07	268.23	588.18
715.04	785.10	847.17	573.06	301.01	594.01
717.04	785.12	848.12	602.12	301.01	886.13
717.24	786.09	848.16	686.11	315.09	witnessed
718.22	786.28	851.03	688.03	321.28	337.28
719.09	789.10	852.24	710.05	332.18	372.16
719.20	790.01	853.27	798.23	335.08	745.26
720.05	790.03	854.06	836.13	341.14	861.25
720.05	790.12	854.09	873.06	349.10	865.26
721.21	791.07	854.23	wither	349.15	865.26
722.03	791.12	855.04	151.28	350.13	witnesses
722.14	791.25	855.24	756.08	358.21	371.03
722.16	791.28	856.05	withered	359.19	witnessing
722.20	793.01	856.09	406.28	364.11	045.16
722.26	793.06	856.15	878.12	375.16	wits
722.27	793.07	857.16	withering	376.05	085.05
724.12	793.17	858.17	459.28	376.06	126.05
724.13	794.16	858.24	withheld	397.22	142.17
724.17	794.23	859.05	311.25	397.24	324.14
726.23	795.16	860.05	405.09	400.25	391.10
727.18	795.19	860.25	within	420.25	767.04
727.25	797.01	861.07	041.02	430.19	witty
729.03	798.06	862.27	061.16	440.03	149.15
729.05	798.07	863.10	088.23	440.04	403.08
729.08	798.09	864.24	094.09	441.11	800.20
729.09	798.12	865.23	101.02	448.07	wives
729.14	798.13	867.28	111.13	452.24	352.09
729.19	798.27	869.11	124.16	456.25	911.13
731.16	798.28	869.19	139.13	461.24	woe
731.27	799.18	872.12	140.01	462.08	133.13
731.28	800.11	872.21	147.25	462.11	551.11
732.12	802.18	874.12	162.03	478.23	573.10
733.08	803.17	874.13	164.21	489.20	609.10
733.09	804.01	874.25	197.20	497.23	650.16
733.16	805.11	875.04	204.10	504.17	849.22
733.22	805.24	875.11	215.12	512.28	872.07
736.10	807.19	875.19	247.09	526.05	woes
736.13	808.02	875.22	268.11	533.16	473.16
737.11	808.03	878.15	279.08	539.07	486.04
738.02	808.24	878.25	285.05	546.11	628.10
738.12	809.07	879.01	296.08	559.22	682.02
738.15	809.12	879.01	321.20	560.08	woke
738.26	811.06	880.03	343.19	564.13	139.13
739.08	811.08	880.06	365.24	579.20	576.03
740.17	811.15	880.27	366.21	579.20	845.08
740.24	811.24	881.27	367.25	579.21	877.13
740.27	811.28	882.12	397.06	591.04	wolf's
740.27	812.06	882.15	398.07	592.14	436.01
741.12	812.08	882.16	420.17	592.14	wolfe
742.17	812.10	883.16	460.07	599.09	181.11
743.05		883.19	462.21		

wolfish	665.09	wood	497.23	775.25	167.18
630.12	666.17	075.07	505.11	787.02	471.13
woman	666.19	145.21	523.06	790.02	487.17
037.13	676.27	146.18	541.15	792.08	554.12
044.05	701.08	148.15	568.01	798.20	666.15
047.27	744.10	149.04	579.21	801.08	793.27
052.10	790.05	151.14	590.05	810.23	834.12
060.17	818.09	151.19	591.02	813.13	workhouse
063.15	won	209.05	592.01	818.13	673.22
108.10	375.17	284.14	596.10	828.01	722.01
137.26	743.20	501.12	611.23	831.18	working
151.17	761.03	503.16	614.24	835.17	037.26
175.09	762.19	511.09	615.03	836.03	038.17
197.11	802.28	551.10	630.10	836.08	437.17
211.12	won't	561.18	644.27	843.24	471.28
213.06	010.10	586.14	645.13	844.13	474.17
206.23	067.24	586.20	652.08	846.18	494.25
300.08	257.05	591.03	677.15	851.10	570.02
306.16	265.27	591.19	678.08	861.02	724.09
306.19	387.18	596.05	684.26	861.06	746.27
307.01	496.23	596.22	687.11	873.19	working-people
321.17	525.24	597.21	694.09	880.25	745.03
330.20	533.02	598.04	702.13	891.10	workings
343.06	538.13	602.04	720.03	901.18	402.06
344.04	613.23	616.06	723.24	901.19	444.12
344.09	619.17	664.14	724.05	902.08	489.07
359.24	763.10	668.11	741.07	902.11	517.02
359.26	773.18	671.23	746.04	902.16	734.24
372.24	840.15	724.18	779.28	902.27	works
372.25	878.15	739.20	785.01	903.22	089.15
374.18	wonder	869.04	800.02	906.20	202.17
376.13	008.15	870.03	809.23	909.21	662.08
365.08	028.24	870.25	814.22	912.21	741.18
408.14	073.16	887.05	830.07	wordy	world
425.10	095.10	887.17	831.08	905.16	022.22
479.10	103.09	899.22	834.20	wore	023.17
485.08	139.08	902.13	864.15	036.25	047.16
512.16	184.09	904.05	885.24	122.09	053.17
534.08	184.21	wood-land	896.27	128.03	062.06
553.15	199.27	664.16	908.19	141.16	108.24
571.08	241.15	wood-work	words	170.02	120.08
577.01	253.14	307.22	004.19	318.18	121.16
577.11	269.18	859.16	010.25	384.12	131.02
579.09	306.03	woodbine	014.11	445.17	131.28
581.04	319.16	896.14	016.23	449.28	132.21
581.06	330.03	wooden	036.18	485.26	132.22
581.19	330.15	182.05	044.03	677.01	149.18
590.16	349.10	woodland	044.15	809.16	152.11
593.21	389.26	146.05	052.22	work	153.13
596.20	398.12	148.02	053.09	032.25	157.14
597.09	398.14	woods	060.10	061.17	164.07
597.13	408.22	031.19	081.27	062.10	164.09
601.06	529.09	220.06	086.11	063.23	165.08
615.20	582.11	226.03	089.17	064.22	182.19
617.16	587.14	434.22	089.22	092.23	194.15
623.16	659.10	606.04	121.11	110.04	205.26
624.26	679.26	856.15	125.23	127.22	215.07
627.07	690.08	856.19	166.11	142.12	233.19
652.01	713.13	woollen	217.19	143.02	241.16
654.19	726.28	084.14	271.14	179.10	265.23
655.01	734.06	116.26	274.16	207.24	272.09
656.04	739.26	wor	282.17	211.21	282.26
658.21	753.24	680.26	301.17	235.04	285.12
665.13	769.27	681.02	310.02	272.07	291.12
667.18	857.22	681.04	313.08	278.09	321.08
669.11	859.09	697.12	337.17	306.24	377.09
670.07	903.11	698.06	344.21	330.27	391.25
671.05	wondered	word	359.10	332.03	452.26
672.10	094.09	030.09	363.01	346.23	475.11
676.20	098.26	031.06	384.13	427.10	476.20
679.03	206.20	035.02	385.08	436.22	478.01
680.04	351.04	037.27	387.20	441.10	483.04
685.03	365.04	045.02	394.12	492.20	495.15
741.02	402.04	061.14	396.12	493.26	516.15
760.24	441.16	078.26	409.24	645.25	524.10
762.07	521.03	087.01	418.03	666.18	525.16
777.13	570.15	107.20	425.13	667.27	533.20
778.21	642.25	118.28	448.14	672.04	534.14
856.25	654.26	123.17	448.17	679.23	542.18
863.19	704.11	141.13	462.08	705.18	556.02
863.20	738.11	154.22	480.04	708.28	556.02
864.22	804.04	159.22	489.26	708.28	558.04
865.24	804.05	180.08	496.06	725.19	570.16
878.05	845.18	202.06	521.06	733.19	628.27
878.14	wonderful	246.03	533.26	734.24	630.03
878.14	028.12	259.21	535.05	743.04	631.20
909.01	247.16	269.11	542.13	744.02	645.24
woman's	324.16	281.20	555.08	759.20	647.27
243.16	wonderfully	284.08	568.08	766.17	655.06
406.16	752.20	291.01	573.13	774.04	658.06
424.19	789.06	301.02	592.07	795.16	687.01
677.27	wondering	323.08	605.06	813.22	720.11
826.26	105.17	328.28	607.22	814.07	735.14
827.01	242.14	341.14	609.09	816.03	740.06
womankind	255.18	352.15	612.13	818.15	747.19
658.19	612.16	354.17	621.08	820.06	758.07
women	769.27	355.12	623.13	822.07	763.10
052.01	wonderingly	369.12	623.24	846.11	763.27
058.11	290.17	371.17	627.06	846.12	775.15
084.18	wonderment	372.28	637.28	850.08	782.10
216.14	905.16	378.25	684.03	work-bag	792.21
216.15	wondrous	405.17	686.04	084.14	792.22
261.11	403.14	425.21	691.06	work-boxes	845.13
317.09	853.02	436.22	699.16	701.13	852.27
321.19	wont	439.11	704.11	work-house	864.15
327.14	030.20	442.10	715.24	469.01	879.25
394.13	047.19	452.07	717.28	workbox	888.28
441.03	142.27	455.20	719.09	357.21	898.26
447.14	wonted	456.19	720.04	worked	901.02
528.01	554.16	462.12	774.04	167.16	907.19
		470.18	775.24	167.16	

world's	239.24	182.04	377.21	553.15	674.13
440.25	440.08	187.02	385.22	553.19	674.18
513.20	814.07	190.08	385.25	553.25	675.05
worldly	816.05	192.16	386.19	553.26	680.22
058.11	829.01	192.24	389.13	554.26	684.10
441.12	911.11	193.05	389.13	555.28	685.20
worlds	wot	199.26	396.27	557.10	687.20
662.10	268.09	202.01	397.03	558.01	689.09
858.09	would	202.20	403.03	558.03	690.03
worm	006.13	203.04	403.15	560.20	690.06
596.17	007.13	204.23	404.23	562.05	690.18
wormwood	008.13	207.26	405.28	563.10	690.28
135.22	008.15	208.05	406.12	563.10	691.04
worn	008.27	208.06	411.28	564.24	691.25
219.16	012.07	216.19	412.06	566.05	698.18
236.12	013.10	217.09	416.07	568.09	698.20
277.05	014.09	218.17	418.24	570.24	699.11
340.24	015.01	222.05	427.27	571.01	703.07
445.01	015.06	223.17	431.02	571.04	707.03
521.20	020.22	225.03	431.12	571.10	707.03
604.17	020.23	227.14	434.03	574.07	708.15
662.03	020.25	230.03	437.01	579.08	708.21
663.20	021.23	230.08	437.20	581.18	708.22
685.21	021.26	230.11	437.22	582.13	709.10
690.15	022.10	233.09	437.23	584.03	710.07
701.15	023.01	234.17	437.25	586.07	711.08
779.07	024.06	235.21	438.16	587.08	712.01
899.19	024.11	235.22	441.19	587.13	714.01
worn-out	027.09	238.06	442.01	592.13	714.02
490.02	028.06	238.14	448.28	592.21	714.16
worried	031.06	238.15	451.06	592.22	714.22
424.12	035.16	241.14	451.24	596.15	714.22
428.05	037.22	243.27	453.14	601.11	714.26
633.13	038.21	247.20	454.19	601.11	715.12
worries	039.13	251.06	456.15	603.22	716.21
109.19	041.13	253.18	457.11	606.23	719.15
worse	043.02	254.15	457.22	606.24	722.11
046.15	044.12	256.25	463.08	607.04	724.05
106.24	045.27	258.06	463.13	607.07	725.05
106.24	047.07	261.05	463.18	610.06	725.11
111.07	047.10	262.26	464.02	611.13	727.15
125.27	047.12	263.14	465.28	612.05	727.24
196.22	047.17	263.23	466.16	613.05	727.26
299.19	048.21	264.22	467.19	614.02	727.27
427.22	051.15	265.02	468.11	614.16	731.17
447.12	051.16	265.28	468.16	615.27	731.18
551.27	055.23	266.15	468.21	616.01	734.19
615.21	063.26	267.05	468.28	616.08	740.23
650.19	064.01	267.20	469.06	617.13	741.06
650.05	065.09	269.07	470.16	617.14	745.22
656.01	065.12	270.07	470.19	617.16	746.07
726.18	065.21	273.03	475.07	617.19	746.14
794.03	065.27	273.05	475.08	618.12	746.23
828.24	068.06	273.07	475.11	619.08	747.05
836.04	069.24	275.10	475.15	619.25	747.10
867.09	088.02	276.02	475.17	620.11	747.14
worship	094.10	278.01	475.22	620.27	747.15
243.27	094.22	285.23	475.23	620.27	747.16
244.03	098.22	289.05	477.28	624.19	747.19
903.22	101.05	290.02	479.13	626.26	747.21
worshipped	101.07	293.09	484.21	627.12	747.26
243.26	101.08	298.17	484.25	633.07	749.05
645.12	102.09	301.12	487.17	636.17	749.22
worst	102.19	301.22	487.20	638.06	750.27
029.25	102.20	303.01	489.04	639.01	751.03
056.22	102.21	303.02	491.25	639.09	751.16
062.06	103.05	306.28	491.26	641.27	752.02
104.11	103.15	308.06	495.25	642.12	753.12
105.27	104.04	308.24	496.09	642.12	753.27
123.12	106.22	309.13	497.03	642.16	755.06
164.20	106.23	312.12	499.04	646.07	755.08
164.20	106.23	314.24	499.27	646.08	755.15
416.22	106.24	316.27	502.11	648.12	755.15
447.14	108.07	317.26	506.13	649.14	755.18
447.14	108.18	319.26	508.09	649.22	755.19
463.03	112.10	323.02	513.27	649.28	755.26
637.23	114.15	325.16	516.06	650.07	756.11
725.13	116.18	327.24	524.20	651.10	757.04
773.03	118.21	329.03	524.25	653.07	759.02
749.27	118.22	331.16	525.27	653.16	759.06
881.17	119.16	333.14	529.07	653.27	760.25
worsted	121.04	336.11	530.19	654.02	762.10
262.16	123.02	336.24	532.16	654.04	767.13
worth	125.04	339.01	534.19	654.04	767.19
266.24	127.07	340.21	535.25	654.05	768.21
310.08	130.18	344.08	536.23	655.04	769.08
355.21	131.15	346.22	537.21	655.22	776.04
360.02	131.17	346.27	538.27	657.04	777.11
530.23	132.03	349.18	539.14	657.06	778.13
648.13	132.06	349.19	541.04	659.10	778.15
648.13	132.10	350.21	541.06	659.13	782.15
678.24	135.04	350.22	541.07	659.17	782.25
776.10	135.13	353.28	541.11	661.03	782.26
776.11	143.18	357.18	541.12	661.04	783.14
787.08	149.01	357.23	543.11	662.24	784.20
796.08	151.02	358.14	543.21	663.10	784.21
899.14	151.28	360.16	544.04	664.28	785.08
worthier	152.12	361.03	544.15	665.03	785.24
046.22	153.07	362.05	544.27	665.11	785.24
644.26	157.14	363.01	546.02	665.11	785.25
worthless	166.01	363.06	546.27	665.17	786.24
150.03	166.05	366.09	547.01	665.20	788.06
269.18	168.22	370.18	547.05	665.26	790.20
755.09	168.28	370.24	547.07	668.16	794.11
worthlessly	172.17	370.25	548.27	669.16	796.22
748.08	173.03	372.05	549.27	669.21	796.26
worthy	173.05	372.11	550.06	670.08	796.27
043.26	173.07	372.13	551.01	670.15	797.15
104.13	176.14	374.25	552.18	671.05	797.23
162.21	178.21	377.02	553.10	673.17	798.22
189.23	179.13	377.09	553.12	674.10	

803.06	903.05	646.24	632.15	yearned	041.07
804.12	903.15	671.24	772.24	845.01	041.14
804.15	906.08	681.24	774.06	yearning	055.11
804.16	906.12	735.20	777.21	465.13	073.13
804.25	906.13	762.26	780.08	833.01	075.17
805.23	907.03	842.23	780.13	yearnings	092.20
806.01	907.04	wretchedly	809.11	716.28	101.22
809.14	wouldn't	104.15	809.19	years	105.26
814.03	015.08	667.20	906.26	007.02	106.15
814.22	069.23	wretchedness	907.12	007.02	115.19
816.24	683.07	029.26	wrought	009.15	120.13
816.24	667.13	029.26	019.21	016.26	153.03
818.13	wound	wring	207.23	020.05	156.20
819.02	056.27	389.05	247.29	035.05	158.27
820.13	427.05	406.05	350.09	053.03	160.25
820.15	428.03	wrist	423.14	054.20	166.25
820.20	429.01	156.08	472.06	077.19	172.09
820.24	460.01	370.05	648.22	093.18	175.25
821.12	470.01	409.19	778.16	149.17	179.08
821.25	611.28	623.06	911.17	159.19	180.08
822.28	654.09	wrists	wrung	160.04	180.10
824.19	712.06	525.04	683.22	160.09	183.08
825.07	712.25	write	810.18	161.25	183.08
825.08	755.15	077.12	wth	161.28	186.26
825.08	812.18	136.11	232.12	162.11	187.14
825.18	870.10	322.02	757.27	164.07	195.09
825.19	wounded	482.14	y	165.14	201.17
825.22	034.16	484.03	234.20	166.23	202.03
825.23	421.21	542.04	239.10	166.19	203.26
826.04	569.14	545.04	334.04	171.13	205.10
826.23	621.13	703.15	540.28	174.09	206.18
826.26	656.11	729.18	543.20	175.21	210.22
826.28	wounds	744.11	yaas	175.25	226.05
827.10	633.12	783.12	356.03	179.23	227.03
827.13	661.25	784.10	yard	188.28	230.07
829.09	woven	910.22	124.16	197.04	232.13
829.24	121.23	912.15	367.25	198.02	232.18
830.04	wraith-like	writhed	398.07	207.07	236.04
830.13	558.13	515.18	432.14	241.11	237.10
831.03	wrang	518.27	432.23	241.12	241.06
831.12	697.12	writhing	433.07	242.07	242.27
831.19	wrap	560.01	443.04	244.26	243.25
833.07	298.23	writing	449.09	252.09	246.25
834.16	wrapped	086.23	504.12	252.13	247.07
835.12	029.23	091.01	654.18	252.14	249.20
835.20	048.24	171.19	674.18	253.09	252.11
836.28	071.19	214.13	yard-gates	273.07	255.27
837.15	138.10	270.06	434.05	288.10	262.01
838.04	151.10	470.17	yards	312.14	266.19
838.07	402.01	494.08	061.03	317.11	268.05
838.17	575.05	542.06	097.10	370.16	268.06
838.19	wrappers	715.13	225.16	439.26	284.09
840.22	416.27	722.24	542.09	440.02	297.23
841.06	wrapping	910.09	872.27	444.15	300.08
841.07	072.02	written	yawned	446.11	302.09
842.11	113.22	086.13	859.03	447.08	317.22
842.22	wraps	141.27	yawns	452.18	318.22
842.23	644.12	168.16	114.10	459.16	319.20
842.25	wrapt	173.12	348.02	481.04	329.26
842.27	154.07	218.14	ye	482.22	336.11
843.11	wrath	288.08	119.02	483.19	336.25
844.08	083.22	397.26	119.03	484.14	370.21
844.09	551.11	527.19	407.15	526.26	373.24
847.08	846.09	557.15	589.23	535.17	387.08
847.09	847.28	652.08	590.02	536.19	387.08
848.09	wreath	773.21	590.03	575.12	387.08
850.11	030.19	777.03	590.03	590.11	388.04
850.14	277.06	779.15	602.10	593.08	397.01
851.08	367.06	780.16	602.10	597.04	397.06
851.12	471.08	832.01	679.08	598.21	402.09
852.14	wreathed	844.28	679.09	602.24	403.01
856.05	143.08	wrong	680.23	627.08	410.07
857.06	249.11	072.16	681.01	627.21	410.07
858.10	435.08	103.15	681.04	629.11	412.10
861.15	wreaths	264.08	694.16	633.03	412.26
861.17	295.27	268.17	694.23	635.26	415.08
863.11	wreck	437.19	ye'll	694.14	419.04
863.28	004.25	437.25	681.16	698.21	419.06
864.18	467.10	438.14	ye've	704.16	419.19
864.27	560.12	481.19	679.19	706.20	419.21
866.16	660.02	513.06	695.01	721.17	423.01
868.01	wrecked	537.20	695.02	725.06	428.22
869.08	859.17	564.23	year	770.11	435.21
872.15	wren	615.22	040.25	770.16	436.04
873.28	352.23	637.17	045.10	771.05	442.22
877.10	wrench	644.18	091.18	862.09	442.24
879.11	824.14	651.07	324.08	897.17	446.17
879.14	wrenched	682.27	463.26	908.24	447.04
880.21	228.02	695.04	489.22	909.14	448.25
881.20	629.02	731.02	529.10	910.08	449.03
883.05	wrens'	777.01	547.20	years'	449.10
884.09	143.07	833.27	581.20	264.20	452.01
885.19	wrest	836.03	616.18	yell	452.18
887.13	808.08	870.13	696.08	415.04	453.17
888.15	wrestle	879.17	696.10	yelled	453.27
888.22	283.18	900.02	698.01	866.01	455.21
888.25	601.12	wronged	706.26	yellow	456.11
891.03	wrestled	270.10	721.23	088.08	457.13
891.05	609.18	872.05	735.10	093.02	457.16
892.01	wrestling	wrongly	759.05	461.08	465.26
892.01	845.09	134.15	785.16	765.17	467.03
892.04	wrestlings	wrongs	801.06	812.16	495.04
892.05	847.15	022.19	809.23	yells	496.14
892.08	wretch	108.22	854.19	601.16	496.19
895.08	598.07	460.01	862.15	629.17	506.01
895.23	781.19	wrote	888.13	yelp	506.11
895.25	wretched	056.16	894.23	875.04	506.14
895.27	066.24	141.11	911.06	yes	508.05
896.13	144.06	284.01	year's	017.15	510.03
900.03	161.02	483.27	872.01	029.16	511.22
901.21	626.05	524.15		034.05	512.20

513.21	019.28	513.21	856.03	014.25	063.27
514.02	030.02	517.06	856.06	014.26	063.28
516.20	032.01	518.24	857.18	014.27	063.28
518.13	033.11	527.21	860.14	015.01	064.01
524.05	034.26	527.25	861.13	015.02	064.04
536.03	048.07	527.28	872.14	015.09	064.05
540.12	071.12	530.01	872.15	015.10	064.06
549.06	080.03	540.08	881.10	015.12	064.06
562.06	085.21	544.16	883.04	023.26	064.09
565.03	088.16	546.25	883.10	024.03	064.09
567.04	088.27	553.24	884.27	024.03	064.10
567.07	100.16	555.27	902.11	024.24	064.14
567.12	100.23	557.12	903.07	024.27	064.14
573.12	103.05	559.09	907.12	024.28	066.28
582.08	105.13	560.21	911.24	025.02	067.04
586.11	107.02	561.03	912.12	028.01	067.05
587.03	114.16	572.11	yew	028.01	067.05
594.14	114.24	576.05	675.25	028.06	067.19
612.19	124.27	579.22	711.20	028.06	067.21
614.04	125.05	591.17	850.06	028.08	067.24
623.27	128.02	604.15	yew-trees	028.10	068.02
650.13	137.07	605.16	719.20	028.10	068.04
651.12	150.14	607.03	yield	028.16	068.09
666.01	152.01	610.04	133.17	029.17	068.10
669.13	175.10	611.08	248.05	029.18	068.11
679.05	189.01	612.13	511.12	029.19	068.12
664.19	192.25	614.14	534.02	029.19	068.14
684.19	194.15	621.08	623.10	029.20	068.16
686.06	194.24	621.18	646.22	029.20	068.16
670.06	194.25	622.10	648.23	034.06	068.19
694.12	194.26	624.11	664.04	034.07	068.20
696.03	204.09	627.22	715.28	034.07	068.20
718.07	207.13	629.04	730.17	034.28	068.21
718.18	208.13	635.25	734.16	035.14	068.22
719.25	220.12	636.25	779.05	035.14	068.24
726.06	220.15	639.28	910.06	035.15	069.01
730.23	221.06	641.18	yielded	035.19	069.02
731.17	221.08	642.02	050.24	035.25	069.05
732.04	221.23	642.05	374.14	035.26	069.05
735.16	228.18	646.10	428.08	036.05	069.06
754.27	228.23	652.09	788.07	036.06	069.07
754.27	231.05	652.15	847.07	036.10	069.08
769.21	237.28	652.20	847.09	036.25	069.09
774.12	240.15	653.07	848.01	037.03	069.10
774.12	241.21	655.24	yielding	037.04	069.11
774.28	250.15	655.25	426.24	037.09	069.13
776.05	250.19	659.08	503.10	037.14	069.23
780.24	252.24	660.10	700.04	037.15	069.23
781.06	258.02	660.15	702.08	037.22	069.24
786.07	262.13	660.22	703.07	037.22	069.25
786.08	262.26	661.06	757.21	038.06	072.04
790.22	267.26	663.22	yoke	038.21	072.07
791.07	270.23	667.16	758.19	043.26	072.13
793.23	271.01	669.27	782.21	043.27	077.01
813.23	276.06	674.27	825.18	044.12	077.06
819.18	282.09	675.01	yond	044.25	087.05
820.06	282.10	677.12	680.09	044.26	087.07
827.18	283.02	684.24	yonder	044.27	087.07
836.17	291.27	701.04	196.05	050.20	090.17
840.21	292.13	702.07	204.02	050.20	091.01
853.22	297.21	705.13	298.23	051.02	091.04
855.07	305.05	705.22	393.16	051.02	091.07
856.20	312.11	706.01	408.25	051.02	091.09
861.26	313.03	714.10	424.06	051.03	092.18
865.15	314.20	715.07	430.14	052.23	093.05
866.26	319.11	716.10	510.10	053.14	093.07
866.26	319.25	717.02	526.11	054.06	093.09
867.07	322.17	717.20	543.04	054.09	093.10
871.10	330.06	717.21	558.06	054.11	093.17
874.15	338.17	724.25	590.22	054.14	093.19
880.05	342.12	725.05	602.06	054.18	093.21
881.27	346.20	725.12	646.17	054.19	093.22
883.26	349.07	725.17	673.17	054.23	093.23
889.13	349.20	726.17	730.20	054.23	098.05
890.25	349.24	727.22	820.13	055.02	098.07
891.27	350.20	729.09	yor	055.09	098.10
892.07	351.07	730.15	779.06	055.12	098.23
892.23	352.03	734.11	822.08	055.14	098.24
893.09	355.24	734.16	841.17	055.19	100.02
893.17	372.18	736.17	885.12	055.22	102.01
896.25	376.11	737.08	you	055.23	102.04
897.03	376.15	737.15	002.23	056.04	102.07
897.13	390.24	745.08	006.22	056.05	102.12
897.16	392.17	749.08	006.24	056.06	102.19
897.19	395.03	754.06	006.25	056.07	102.20
901.25	403.21	754.18	008.23	056.16	102.21
903.18	420.03	760.14	008.24	056.19	102.26
910.13	433.03	760.19	009.07	056.24	103.02
yesterday	434.03	766.20	009.07	059.12	103.03
034.28	436.06	771.24	009.08	059.17	103.05
068.09	436.22	772.05	009.08	059.21	103.07
153.06	437.27	801.02	009.09	062.05	103.18
447.01	444.05	804.03	009.09	062.05	103.18
448.11	452.26	805.09	009.13	062.06	103.19
448.22	457.18	806.16	009.27	062.08	103.25
451.13	459.24	819.18	010.01	062.13	104.06
569.19	459.25	820.05	010.02	062.21	104.23
570.01	465.23	826.13	010.09	062.22	104.24
572.01	469.10	831.05	012.20	062.23	104.24
604.17	473.27	831.06	012.20	062.24	104.27
605.17	480.24	835.08	013.08	062.25	105.13
606.11	481.01	841.01	013.08	062.26	106.05
766.27	485.13	841.14	013.19	062.28	106.13
767.04	485.26	842.17	014.07	063.02	106.18
774.09	487.03	843.01	014.07	063.05	106.19
801.18	490.20	846.03	014.09	063.05	107.01
yet	494.09	846.10	014.09	063.11	107.02
003.20	495.01	848.01	014.09	063.15	107.02
005.15	499.12	848.18	014.18	063.15	107.23
015.20	502.12	852.08	014.20	063.16	107.23
018.04	504.17	852.19	014.22		107.24

108.11	177.24	235.21	264.18	284.05	338.28
108.12	177.25	235.25	264.24	284.21	339.08
108.14	178.01	235.28	265.03	285.08	339.10
108.15	178.02	236.01	265.06	285.10	339.13
108.16	178.03	236.04	265.08	285.14	339.16
108.18	178.03	236.14	265.15	285.16	339.16
110.03	178.12	239.03	265.17	285.24	339.17
116.20	178.14	239.14	265.21	285.25	339.18
118.06	178.14	239.15	265.22	285.25	339.19
119.04	178.21	239.21	265.23	287.13	339.20
119.06	178.22	239.24	265.25	287.14	341.23
119.06	179.07	239.28	266.03	287.19	341.24
119.07	179.10	240.02	266.06	288.20	347.03
123.28	179.12	240.07	266.18	288.21	353.10
124.22	179.13	240.13	266.19	288.22	353.13
124.27	179.13	240.21	266.21	288.23	353.15
124.27	179.14	240.18	266.24	288.25	353.18
125.14	179.15	241.04	266.24	288.25	353.21
125.17	179.15	241.07	266.27	289.03	353.24
125.16	179.19	241.10	267.10	289.09	353.26
125.21	179.24	241.12	267.11	289.10	354.06
126.23	179.24	241.15	267.21	297.09	354.07
130.26	181.04	241.16	267.22	297.10	354.12
131.01	181.04	241.17	267.22	297.13	355.05
131.06	181.12	241.20	267.26	297.14	355.10
131.07	183.09	241.23	267.27	297.15	356.01
131.08	185.24	241.26	268.01	297.16	356.05
131.14	186.22	241.27	268.06	297.18	356.09
131.15	186.23	242.04	268.08	297.21	356.10
131.16	186.24	242.10	268.20	298.17	356.17
131.17	186.26	242.16	268.21	298.21	356.22
131.19	187.13	242.17	268.27	298.22	357.10
151.21	187.15	242.24	269.06	298.22	358.02
151.26	188.03	243.12	269.06	298.24	358.03
152.01	188.12	243.14	269.07	298.27	358.06
152.02	188.24	243.18	269.09	299.01	358.08
152.02	189.01	243.21	269.12	300.01	358.10
152.02	189.05	243.22	269.18	300.01	358.26
152.08	189.10	243.26	269.19	300.02	358.27
152.14	189.21	244.02	269.20	300.05	359.01
152.15	190.01	244.23	269.26	300.05	359.04
152.16	190.03	244.23	270.03	300.11	360.11
152.19	190.04	244.26	270.03	300.12	360.18
152.26	190.04	244.26	270.07	300.14	360.19
153.26	190.05	245.01	270.09	300.16	360.23
154.01	190.07	245.05	270.17	300.26	361.02
154.02	190.08	245.06	270.28	300.28	361.28
154.12	195.03	245.09	271.06	301.04	362.02
154.16	195.07	245.14	271.06	301.05	362.07
154.16	195.19	245.18	271.07	301.10	362.07
154.16	195.27	245.26	271.08	301.11	362.09
156.20	195.28	246.02	271.10	301.14	362.13
154.22	197.10	246.04	271.14	301.22	362.17
154.27	197.10	246.06	271.15	301.24	362.17
155.05	197.24	246.21	271.15	302.07	362.20
155.06	198.18	246.26	271.22	308.05	362.28
155.08	198.20	247.04	271.27	308.12	363.08
155.09	199.20	247.14	271.28	308.14	363.09
156.12	199.25	249.18	272.05	308.26	364.09
156.13	199.28	249.18	272.06	309.03	366.07
156.22	200.01	249.25	272.07	309.03	370.14
156.23	200.02	249.26	272.07	309.07	370.15
157.04	200.09	249.27	272.09	309.19	370.16
157.05	201.06	250.06	272.24	309.20	370.17
157.19	201.15	250.12	272.26	310.09	370.24
158.13	201.21	250.13	272.26	311.02	371.01
156.14	201.23	250.18	272.27	313.05	372.01
158.15	201.24	250.19	272.27	313.06	372.23
140.22	202.06	250.22	273.01	313.07	381.10
153.23	204.20	250.24	273.03	315.18	381.11
153.24	205.08	251.01	273.03	315.19	382.03
155.23	205.12	251.08	273.04	315.20	385.17
156.01	205.15	251.15	273.05	315.21	385.22
156.10	206.03	255.28	273.07	315.24	385.25
156.13	206.04	257.01	273.09	315.25	386.21
156.13	206.04	257.11	273.20	316.16	386.26
156.15	206.06	257.16	274.08	316.27	387.06
156.16	208.08	258.02	274.09	317.13	387.24
156.16	208.19	258.03	274.16	317.20	389.21
155.16	208.22	259.09	274.26	317.20	389.21
156.19	210.18	259.14	275.01	319.20	389.27
157.04	210.21	259.15	275.06	319.27	389.27
157.05	211.24	259.22	275.10	319.27	392.15
157.16	223.05	259.22	275.12	319.28	392.19
157.17	223.11	259.24	275.13	320.01	393.01
157.17	223.28	259.25	275.14	321.01	393.02
157.27	224.03	260.01	275.15	321.02	393.02
158.06	225.14	260.02	275.17	321.03	395.10
158.10	225.15	260.03	275.19	321.05	395.13
158.23	225.19	260.04	275.21	321.09	395.14
158.24	225.20	260.11	275.23	321.10	395.17
158.26	225.21	260.15	275.25	321.26	395.18
157.27	225.24	260.16	276.03	322.05	395.19
168.02	225.25	260.22	276.09	322.09	395.22
168.05	225.27	260.24	276.12	322.13	395.24
168.06	225.27	261.05	277.25	322.25	395.26
168.08	226.08	261.07	280.27	322.26	395.28
168.09	226.12	261.20	282.06	325.02	396.08
174.29	226.14	262.11	282.06	325.05	396.09
175.24	226.15	262.12	282.07	325.07	396.09
176.01	226.28	262.14	282.08	325.07	396.12
176.07	227.01	263.12	282.08	325.10	396.13
176.11	227.02	263.16	282.11	334.09	396.14
176.13	227.04	263.17	282.14	334.13	396.14
176.14	227.08	263.17	282.17	335.28	396.14
176.22	227.21	263.18	282.17	336.05	396.17
177.18	227.23	263.19	282.18	338.06	396.17
177.20	227.25	263.24	282.21	338.08	396.17
177.21	228.08	263.24	283.27	338.18	396.18
177.21	228.09	264.02	284.04	338.27	396.19
177.24	232.20	264.10			

396.20	428.24	448.28	480.18	512.12	529.09
396.23	429.12	449.01	480.19	512.19	529.10
396.24	429.12	449.01	480.23	512.21	529.17
397.02	429.13	450.05	480.24	512.23	529.23
397.03	429.13	450.14	480.25	512.25	529.24
397.04	429.15	450.27	480.26	512.26	530.01
397.04	429.18	450.28	481.17	512.27	530.02
397.05	429.18	451.03	481.19	512.27	530.17
397.13	429.19	451.04	481.22	513.03	530.20
397.27	429.21	451.04	482.05	513.05	530.21
398.04	429.21	451.11	482.11	513.06	530.22
398.06	430.06	451.23	482.24	513.09	530.27
398.12	430.08	451.26	482.25	513.10	531.01
398.15	430.12	451.27	483.01	513.11	531.02
398.17	430.18	451.27	483.02	513.22	531.03
398.19	430.18	452.04	483.03	513.24	531.07
398.24	430.22	452.09	483.05	513.24	531.09
398.25	430.26	452.09	483.06	513.25	531.10
398.25	430.27	452.14	483.07	513.26	531.19
399.04	430.28	452.14	483.09	513.28	531.21
399.05	431.02	452.20	483.24	514.09	531.24
399.07	431.04	452.23	483.25	514.13	531.25
399.12	431.11	452.23	484.02	514.15	532.04
399.12	431.22	452.24	484.04	514.17	532.05
399.18	431.23	452.25	484.04	514.20	532.06
399.19	432.04	452.26	484.07	514.22	532.06
399.21	432.11	453.08	484.09	515.09	532.07
399.22	432.14	453.13	484.11	515.10	532.09
399.23	433.19	453.14	484.14	515.17	532.11
399.26	434.15	453.15	484.18	515.21	532.14
400.03	434.18	453.17	484.21	515.23	532.15
400.08	434.19	453.21	484.21	515.25	532.18
400.11	435.11	453.25	484.22	515.28	532.21
400.15	435.14	453.26	485.34	516.07	532.24
400.17	435.15	454.01	485.05	516.07	532.27
400.27	435.20	454.06	487.18	516.08	532.28
400.28	435.22	454.07	488.02	516.09	533.04
401.01	435.22	454.16	488.03	516.10	533.08
401.11	435.23	454.21	488.24	516.15	533.19
401.17	436.01	454.22	488.27	516.15	534.05
401.20	436.09	454.23	488.27	516.16	534.10
402.14	436.17	455.06	489.04	516.18	534.11
402.17	436.18	455.10	489.15	516.18	534.13
402.18	436.25	455.13	489.16	516.19	534.20
402.20	437.09	455.15	489.18	516.26	535.11
402.20	437.10	455.22	489.18	517.05	535.20
402.21	437.10	455.25	489.20	517.07	535.22
402.25	437.11	456.09	489.21	517.08	535.24
403.05	437.12	457.11	489.24	517.09	536.01
403.05	437.12	457.11	489.25	517.15	536.01
403.20	437.14	457.21	491.26	517.16	536.09
403.23	437.16	457.22	491.27	517.16	536.15
403.26	437.18	457.26	493.07	517.17	536.28
403.28	437.19	457.28	493.10	517.20	537.03
407.09	437.19	460.04	493.10	517.21	537.04
407.18	437.26	462.07	493.10	518.12	537.05
407.20	437.28	462.07	493.12	519.04	537.09
407.22	438.01	463.05	493.18	519.21	537.13
407.23	438.01	463.06	493.20	522.17	537.15
407.27	438.03	463.08	494.20	522.24	537.15
407.26	438.04	463.09	494.21	523.10	537.19
408.01	438.04	464.14	495.03	523.16	537.21
408.05	438.13	464.15	495.09	523.21	537.22
408.06	438.14	465.26	495.10	524.01	537.23
408.20	438.22	466.26	495.18	524.01	537.25
409.04	438.22	466.27	495.19	524.03	537.26
409.06	438.24	467.01	495.19	525.10	537.28
409.09	438.25	467.04	496.14	525.13	538.05
409.11	438.25	467.04	496.17	525.13	538.25
410.01	439.01	467.05	496.21	525.14	538.26
410.05	439.04	467.16	496.22	525.16	539.11
410.13	439.07	468.04	496.27	525.24	539.12
410.16	439.12	469.21	496.27	525.27	539.21
410.17	439.13	472.13	497.05	526.02	540.05
410.19	439.14	476.09	497.28	526.03	540.18
410.20	439.16	476.10	498.02	526.03	541.04
411.28	439.17	476.11	498.02	526.07	541.07
412.06	439.18	476.13	506.02	526.08	541.11
412.08	439.21	476.17	506.03	526.09	541.13
412.10	439.25	476.17	506.08	526.12	541.16
412.12	439.26	476.18	506.17	526.20	541.18
412.17	439.28	476.20	506.19	526.21	541.28
412.20	440.01	476.21	506.23	526.24	542.24
416.15	440.05	476.21	506.24	527.06	543.02
417.12	440.06	476.22	507.02	527.07	543.10
417.15	440.08	476.23	507.04	527.08	543.11
417.16	440.09	476.23	507.09	527.10	545.20
417.19	441.05	476.24	507.18	527.11	545.22
417.20	441.11	476.25	507.20	527.12	545.24
419.02	441.26	477.04	507.20	527.13	546.07
419.10	441.27	477.05	507.22	527.13	546.09
419.17	442.07	477.06	507.25	527.14	546.10
419.20	442.08	477.08	507.28	527.15	546.12
420.01	442.09	477.10	508.04	527.16	546.14
421.28	442.13	477.11	508.15	527.16	546.21
422.04	442.18	477.15	508.16	527.24	546.21
422.06	442.19	477.19	508.19	527.25	546.24
422.07	442.20	477.21	509.10	527.26	547.02
422.09	443.05	477.22	509.24	527.27	547.03
422.11	446.07	477.25	509.26	527.28	547.04
427.04	446.10	477.26	510.18	528.11	547.07
427.18	446.12	478.01	510.19	528.12	547.08
428.08	446.13	478.04	510.23	528.16	547.10
428.08	446.13	478.06	510.24	528.17	547.14
428.15	446.15	478.09	511.05	528.17	547.15
428.16	446.18	478.10	511.06	528.18	547.16
428.17	446.23	478.11	511.08	528.25	547.21
428.18	447.06	478.12	511.17	528.28	547.24
428.22	448.19	478.13	512.05	529.02	547.27
428.22	448.23		512.07	529.03	548.01
428.23	448.24		512.10	529.04	548.03

548.04	578.10	614.17	631.28	645.15	696.19
548.06	579.03	614.18	632.04	645.23	696.21
548.08	579.03	614.19	632.05	645.28	696.22
548.10	579.08	614.20	632.06	646.08	697.01
548.11	579.11	614.21	632.08	646.14	697.03
548.16	579.19	614.25	634.02	646.15	697.04
548.21	579.20	614.25	634.03	646.17	697.04
548.22	580.06	614.27	634.12	646.22	697.06
549.04	580.20	614.28	634.12	646.24	697.09
549.05	581.03	614.28	634.13	646.26	697.09
549.07	581.07	615.03	634.22	646.26	697.13
550.08	581.08	615.04	634.25	646.28	697.14
554.02	581.08	615.04	635.06	647.01	697.15
554.03	581.10	615.07	635.07	647.04	699.20
554.04	581.12	615.15	635.10	647.05	699.21
554.04	581.12	615.22	635.10	647.06	700.07
554.07	581.18	615.23	635.12	647.06	700.10
554.09	581.21	615.25	635.13	647.07	700.14
554.15	581.21	615.25	635.16	647.07	700.15
555.22	581.22	616.13	635.18	647.09	700.17
558.17	582.10	616.19	635.20	647.14	702.18
559.18	582.12	616.27	635.20	647.15	702.19
560.24	582.12	616.28	635.21	647.26	703.01
561.02	582.13	617.03	635.21	647.27	703.05
561.03	582.17	617.04	635.23	647.28	703.06
561.05	582.18	617.04	636.10	649.24	703.08
561.08	582.19	617.04	637.01	649.27	703.13
561.08	582.22	617.05	637.12	649.28	703.15
561.09	583.12	617.06	637.13	650.01	705.17
564.12	585.11	617.06	637.14	650.01	704.03
564.21	586.02	617.07	637.15	650.10	704.03
564.24	586.14	617.09	637.16	650.12	704.13
565.01	587.04	617.09	637.18	650.14	704.13
565.03	589.23	617.15	638.12	650.14	705.01
565.05	590.01	617.15	638.13	650.16	705.03
565.05	592.18	617.17	638.13	650.22	705.10
565.10	592.21	617.19	639.20	651.06	705.10
565.11	592.22	617.20	639.21	651.07	705.13
565.12	592.23	617.22	639.22	651.08	705.14
565.14	593.25	617.23	639.22	651.08	705.14
565.16	594.02	617.24	639.23	651.08	705.15
565.21	595.03	617.28	639.24	653.25	705.22
565.22	595.06	618.01	639.25	653.26	705.24
565.23	595.07	618.02	640.01	657.10	705.25
566.09	595.10	618.02	640.02	657.13	706.05
566.13	595.12	618.09	640.04	657.15	706.07
566.14	596.21	618.10	640.04	657.16	706.09
566.23	596.21	618.11	640.05	667.24	706.11
566.24	596.23	618.11	640.07	671.14	706.12
567.06	597.01	618.14	640.07	672.08	706.18
567.12	597.03	618.15	640.08	678.23	706.21
567.24	597.07	618.17	640.18	673.24	707.05
568.02	597.09	618.18	640.18	679.12	707.20
568.04	597.18	618.22	640.27	679.15	708.07
568.07	597.20	618.23	641.03	679.22	708.13
568.08	597.21	619.15	641.06	680.02	708.16
568.12	597.22	619.16	641.09	680.17	708.21
568.14	597.24	620.05	641.10	682.06	708.22
568.20	598.04	620.05	641.11	682.10	708.26
568.23	598.09	620.06	641.11	682.10	709.05
568.24	599.05	620.19	641.12	682.11	709.06
568.25	599.06	620.20	641.18	682.17	709.09
569.02	599.23	621.03	641.21	682.21	709.10
569.05	599.25	621.04	641.22	682.22	709.14
569.07	600.06	621.05	641.23	682.24	709.18
569.10	600.08	621.06	641.23	682.26	709.23
569.12	602.11	621.14	641.24	682.27	709.25
569.21	602.16	621.17	641.28	683.06	710.02
569.24	602.20	621.18	642.01	683.06	718.05
569.24	603.08	621.19	642.06	683.07	718.07
570.04	603.15	621.22	642.16	683.10	718.09
570.06	603.15	621.24	642.17	683.10	718.10
570.08	603.20	621.26	642.17	683.11	718.12
570.23	603.22	621.28	642.19	683.13	718.28
571.02	603.23	622.04	642.19	684.10	719.04
571.05	603.24	622.07	642.23	684.18	719.11
571.10	603.25	622.07	642.24	684.20	719.12
571.16	610.10	622.08	642.25	684.22	719.14
571.16	610.11	622.09	642.26	684.27	719.15
571.17	610.11	622.10	642.27	685.01	720.09
571.18	610.13	622.11	643.01	686.20	720.10
571.19	611.07	622.13	643.01	686.23	721.01
572.03	611.08	622.13	643.03	686.25	721.01
572.16	611.12	622.13	643.04	687.07	721.10
572.25	611.12	622.16	643.09	687.08	722.06
573.02	611.13	622.18	643.10	687.09	722.19
573.03	611.14	622.18	643.11	687.12	722.21
573.05	611.19	622.19	643.15	687.13	722.25
573.09	611.25	622.20	643.18	687.13	722.26
573.11	611.26	622.26	644.02	687.14	723.03
573.11	611.28	622.26	644.02	687.19	723.03
573.13	612.06	623.01	644.06	687.20	723.07
573.17	612.15	623.24	644.06	687.22	723.10
573.18	613.11	623.25	644.08	691.15	723.15
573.18	613.23	623.25	644.09	693.14	723.17
573.24	613.24	623.27	644.11	693.14	723.25
574.03	613.28	623.28	644.11	693.15	723.27
574.05	614.01	624.04	644.12	693.15	724.01
574.09	614.02	626.02	644.13	693.16	724.01
574.09	614.05	627.05	644.16	693.22	724.05
574.12	614.05	628.01	644.17	693.22	724.07
574.17	614.06	628.02	644.19	694.08	724.08
575.11	614.08	628.04	644.21	694.10	724.15
575.11	614.09	628.05	644.24	694.18	725.11
575.15	614.10	628.22	644.25	694.28	726.28
575.19	614.10	628.23	644.27	695.04	733.12
575.23	614.11	631.23	645.02	696.09	733.13
576.14	614.12	631.24	645.06	696.12	733.19
577.05	614.13	631.25	645.15	696.13	733.20
577.16	614.16	631.25		696.14	734.09
578.09		631.28		696.18	734.10

734.14	774.13	792.01	826.25	846.04	881.05
734.14	774.18	792.09	826.26	846.08	881.06
734.15	774.19	792.26	827.02	846.14	881.08
734.17	774.20	792.27	827.02	846.16	881.14
734.18	774.21	793.02	827.04	847.24	881.17
734.19	774.23	793.06	827.10	848.08	881.19
734.20	774.24	793.08	827.18	848.08	881.20
737.01	774.25	793.10	827.19	849.10	881.21
737.03	774.28	793.15	827.19	849.10	881.22
738.24	775.02	793.16	827.25	849.28	881.24
739.01	775.04	793.17	828.03	850.02	881.25
739.16	776.06	793.22	828.12	851.10	882.01
739.07	776.08	793.23	828.17	851.12	882.03
739.07	776.08	799.26	828.17	851.12	882.05
739.12	776.09	800.01	828.18	851.16	882.06
739.12	776.09	800.02	828.19	851.18	882.08
739.15	776.21	800.02	828.20	852.15	882.09
739.20	776.22	802.26	828.22	855.21	882.09
739.21	776.23	803.04	829.19	855.22	883.07
739.27	776.24	803.07	829.22	855.23	883.07
740.01	777.01	804.15	833.19	855.24	883.11
741.09	777.11	805.13	833.26	855.25	883.13
741.10	777.12	805.15	833.28	855.26	883.19
741.12	777.15	805.17	834.01	855.28	884.13
741.20	777.22	805.19	834.01	855.28	884.17
741.26	777.22	806.06	834.05	860.18	884.17
741.28	777.23	807.12	834.07	860.21	884.20
742.01	778.11	807.13	834.19	860.21	884.20
742.01	778.11	807.13	834.19	861.16	884.21
742.07	778.14	808.22	834.20	861.16	884.22
742.07	778.14	811.04	834.23	862.03	884.24
742.14	778.15	811.15	834.24	863.02	884.24
745.08	778.19	811.19	834.25	863.09	884.26
747.08	779.01	811.21	834.25	863.12	884.26
747.08	779.07	813.21	834.26	864.27	884.28
747.10	779.11	813.21	834.26	865.05	885.01
752.16	779.16	814.11	834.28	865.10	885.03
752.18	780.17	815.13	835.05	866.08	885.04
752.19	780.27	815.15	835.10	866.18	885.06
752.19	781.04	815.15	835.11	866.25	885.08
752.20	782.01	815.16	835.12	868.03	885.09
752.20	782.03	815.17	835.12	868.08	885.10
752.21	782.03	816.02	835.13	868.09	885.11
753.09	782.03	816.02	835.16	870.01	885.16
753.12	782.05	816.15	835.16	872.10	885.17
754.06	782.06	816.19	835.28	872.11	885.18
754.06	782.07	816.20	836.01	872.11	885.21
754.07	782.07	816.20	836.02	873.04	885.22
754.15	782.09	816.21	836.08	873.05	885.25
754.21	783.17	816.21	836.10	873.13	886.07
755.03	783.18	816.23	836.13	873.15	886.28
755.04	783.21	816.28	836.24	874.03	887.02
755.06	783.21	817.03	836.27	874.06	887.03
755.07	783.22	817.06	837.01	874.10	888.01
755.08	783.24	817.08	837.05	875.16	888.02
755.15	783.26	817.09	837.06	875.26	888.04
755.17	783.27	817.10	837.07	876.10	888.06
756.12	784.01	817.11	837.08	876.22	889.14
757.01	784.03	817.13	837.11	876.23	889.14
757.02	784.05	817.15	837.16	876.26	890.01
757.04	784.09	817.16	837.17	876.27	890.11
757.05	784.12	817.16	837.20	877.01	890.17
757.09	784.12	817.17	837.21	877.01	890.23
757.17	784.24	817.17	837.23	877.18	890.25
759.17	784.28	817.20	838.04	877.19	891.05
759.17	785.03	817.21	838.06	877.19	891.09
760.05	785.04	817.26	838.09	877.27	891.17
760.11	785.09	817.26	838.12	877.27	891.19
760.11	785.09	817.28	838.18	878.02	891.20
760.12	785.10	818.02	838.24	878.03	891.21
760.21	785.15	818.04	838.25	878.06	891.25
761.05	785.20	818.07	838.26	878.14	891.26
761.08	785.21	821.07	838.27	878.15	892.01
761.08	785.22	821.09	839.01	878.16	892.05
761.09	785.24	821.11	839.04	878.17	892.08
761.10	785.24	821.12	839.05	878.18	892.12
761.20	785.26	821.16	839.05	878.19	892.12
762.06	785.26	821.17	839.07	878.19	892.13
762.08	785.27	821.22	839.17	878.20	892.18
762.08	786.02	821.23	839.19	878.21	893.02
762.10	786.03	821.26	839.20	878.23	893.04
762.14	786.10	821.26	839.21	878.25	893.06
763.11	786.15	821.27	840.01	878.26	893.08
766.10	786.15	822.03	840.02	878.28	893.12
766.16	786.21	822.04	840.04	879.01	893.14
766.18	787.01	822.06	840.07	879.01	893.16
766.21	787.02	822.07	840.08	879.01	893.20
766.24	787.03	822.12	840.09	879.02	893.23
766.25	787.08	822.21	840.10	879.02	894.02
767.20	787.14	822.22	840.14	879.03	894.03
767.20	787.15	822.23	840.15	879.21	894.04
767.21	787.16	823.03	840.20	879.22	894.06
767.24	787.16	823.03	840.22	879.22	894.08
768.10	787.17	823.03	840.23	879.25	894.20
768.10	787.21	823.07	840.24	879.27	894.23
768.11	790.13	823.09	840.24	880.03	894.27
768.22	790.13	824.12	841.04	880.05	895.02
768.24	790.19	824.12	841.06	880.06	895.05
768.27	791.01	824.12	841.07	880.09	895.11
768.28	791.01	824.18	841.10	880.10	895.15
770.05	791.04	824.26	841.11	880.11	895.20
770.06	791.05	826.08	841.11	880.13	895.21
770.26	791.06	826.10	841.15	880.13	895.22
770.28	791.10	826.10	841.17	880.15	895.24
771.08	791.12	826.11	842.03	880.16	895.24
771.09	791.14	826.23	842.03	880.17	895.25
772.11	791.16		842.05	880.18	895.25
772.12	791.19		843.07	880.18	895.26
772.18	791.20		846.01	880.20	
773.14	791.21		846.03	880.21	
773.18	791.22			881.04	
774.10					

895.27	312.12	098.06	282.12	488.25	598.19
896.16	317.07	098.07	285.16	488.28	599.23
896.17	332.24	098.09	287.19	495.05	602.17
896.18	347.22	098.09	288.23	495.08	602.24
896.20	348.06	098.25	297.20	496.19	602.24
896.21	354.13	100.02	298.25	497.06	603.09
896.24	359.15	101.27	300.02	497.19	603.21
897.02	388.20	102.15	300.19	497.28	610.11
897.03	392.16	102.22	301.15	498.11	610.12
897.04	400.11	103.05	301.24	498.12	610.12
897.08	400.22	103.07	309.07	507.03	611.18
897.10	438.20	104.24	309.20	507.17	611.21
897.12	448.19	104.25	315.18	507.23	614.13
897.14	460.06	106.06	321.04	509.02	614.24
897.17	460.19	107.01	321.12	510.28	617.11
897.18	462.06	107.20	321.14	512.16	617.13
897.22	472.10	107.20	321.15	513.13	617.16
897.23	524.05	107.22	321.25	514.12	617.21
898.03	536.24	108.12	321.27	514.12	617.25
898.12	536.25	108.16	322.05	514.20	618.22
898.13	537.04	110.03	322.06	515.07	620.20
898.14	572.22	110.04	322.06	515.13	620.22
899.11	602.01	117.07	322.07	515.25	621.06
899.17	643.17	125.17	322.10	516.21	621.28
899.26	667.18	125.20	325.07	516.24	622.01
900.11	676.27	125.21	325.11	517.09	622.19
900.25	683.05	125.22	325.11	517.17	622.24
900.25	685.03	132.01	325.12	519.20	622.26
901.19	691.16	132.17	325.13	524.19	623.04
901.26	694.03	132.18	336.06	524.28	623.22
902.09	697.24	133.03	339.15	524.28	628.12
902.10	701.22	133.04	341.23	525.09	628.13
902.13	703.23	134.12	355.05	525.25	628.14
902.15	706.02	134.24	356.10	526.25	628.15
902.20	737.26	135.10	358.11	527.18	628.16
903.11	740.07	136.11	361.02	528.16	628.17
903.12	740.25	136.25	361.03	529.11	632.01
903.13	744.10	156.27	363.02	529.27	632.02
906.03	746.19	168.09	370.22	530.17	632.02
906.03	751.13	179.14	371.06	530.19	632.03
906.04	751.18	179.16	389.25	530.20	634.04
906.14	757.27	180.02	395.10	530.21	635.07
906.16	771.22	183.07	395.16	531.10	635.12
906.17	781.17	183.14	395.17	531.11	637.11
907.20	790.05	187.04	395.22	531.14	639.28
907.21	862.23	187.12	397.01	531.16	640.01
910.11	880.18	187.15	397.14	532.08	640.11
910.14	895.06	188.13	398.03	533.01	640.12
you'd	younger	188.15	398.15	533.09	640.13
009.24	054.19	190.04	399.05	533.23	640.20
511.05	055.22	190.05	399.19	534.04	640.21
800.07	077.19	199.03	401.08	534.09	641.13
you'll	103.03	201.15	402.23	534.09	641.14
026.17	112.08	201.22	403.21	534.18	641.19
153.23	113.21	203.13	403.22	536.19	641.25
511.05	122.02	211.24	403.27	536.20	641.27
421.28	126.08	225.16	405.23	537.06	642.07
427.22	318.02	235.22	408.23	537.17	642.18
456.18	379.22	235.28	410.05	537.19	642.21
507.08	379.23	239.24	410.18	539.15	642.28
508.26	392.09	241.21	411.16	539.21	642.28
you're	461.16	241.27	413.08	541.05	643.03
066.01	625.28	242.04	417.12	546.19	643.05
069.18	youngest	242.20	417.17	546.24	643.06
176.09	787.14	242.22	419.11	546.27	643.07
185.06	your	245.02	419.17	547.05	643.10
507.17	008.20	245.04	420.06	547.17	643.17
you've	008.21	245.25	422.09	547.24	644.20
069.10	008.23	246.02	422.11	547.27	644.23
175.14	009.09	246.03	422.12	548.16	647.10
187.12	012.16	246.14	428.16	548.18	647.11
375.19	012.17	246.21	430.13	548.20	647.11
427.23	013.01	247.04	430.18	549.01	649.26
663.12	013.02	247.06	430.20	561.07	649.28
694.05	013.10	249.23	432.04	565.06	650.02
694.13	014.23	249.24	433.16	565.21	650.22
863.17	014.25	250.07	434.17	566.15	651.08
young	015.09	250.13	436.04	567.17	657.11
008.02	034.03	255.27	436.05	568.03	680.20
012.16	037.17	256.07	436.06	568.18	680.27
012.17	038.16	258.01	436.16	568.19	681.02
036.24	039.26	259.24	437.15	569.02	681.03
039.02	043.27	259.25	437.15	569.13	681.05
039.05	050.19	260.06	438.23	570.03	681.16
046.10	050.21	264.16	438.28	570.06	682.09
047.27	053.06	265.12	439.08	570.06	682.13
048.19	055.03	265.24	439.17	570.10	682.20
066.13	055.09	265.25	439.21	570.11	684.21
076.23	055.12	267.12	440.07	570.21	684.27
084.18	056.07	267.28	440.12	570.22	686.20
121.21	056.23	268.21	440.12	571.02	687.20
124.27	058.02	268.21	442.07	571.02	694.02
126.18	058.04	268.22	442.08	571.03	694.09
137.08	062.08	268.27	448.13	571.11	695.02
143.08	063.12	269.03	453.09	571.12	695.05
157.12	064.05	269.04	453.18	571.13	700.08
168.18	064.17	269.08	454.22	571.13	703.08
175.10	068.07	269.20	455.15	571.14	703.10
176.20	068.17	269.22	455.17	573.03	703.14
177.07	068.18	269.24	476.13	573.08	704.08
177.11	069.25	271.14	476.26	573.14	705.13
179.05	072.17	272.04	477.14	573.25	706.05
191.26	077.07	272.28	478.08	574.04	706.07
221.09	083.27	273.06	478.13	574.09	707.21
224.20	089.14	275.03	482.26	574.13	707.22
261.12	089.15	275.06	483.10	579.17	707.23
262.17	089.15	275.18	483.17	581.05	707.26
285.09	090.04	275.18	483.25	592.22	708.07
286.16	091.10	275.19	488.03	596.05	708.13
305.13	091.10	275.25	488.05	596.06	710.02
312.06	098.06	282.09	488.07	596.24	

718.12
718.14
720.11
720.12
720.12
721.05
722.22
722.26
722.27
723.08
723.18
723.20
724.08
724.09
733.19
733.23
733.23
733.24
733.24
734.15
734.20
736.28
737.03
739.02
739.12
739.15
752.17
753.13
754.09
754.20
754.22
755.19
757.19
758.04
761.06
761.07
761.21
762.05
762.14
766.15
767.21
768.27
769.16
769.25
770.07
771.14
771.18
774.23
775.02
775.05
776.06
776.22
777.15
778.27
779.05
779.08
779.11
779.15
780.22
780.27
783.19
783.24
783.26
784.10
785.01
785.06
785.11
786.04
786.05
786.06
786.13
787.09
787.10
787.11
790.13
790.16
790.21
791.17
792.03
792.28
793.05
793.13
793.19
807.12
811.19
814.03
814.24
816.16
816.20
816.23
817.14
817.21
818.09
821.05
821.08
821.17
822.04
822.11
824.13
824.14
824.14
824.16
824.19
826.09
826.09
826.19
826.22
827.14
827.15
828.01
828.08

829.20
834.03
834.06
835.16
836.14
836.17
836.25
836.28
837.02
837.08
837.10
837.11
837.17
837.19
837.22
838.23
851.13
851.14
855.19
855.25
856.01
868.06
874.03
874.10
874.10
876.05
876.06
877.18
878.17
878.26
878.27
878.27
878.28
879.23
879.23
880.07
880.16
881.08
881.09
881.15
881.16
881.23
883.15
885.01
885.05
885.13
887.04
888.03
888.07
889.12
890.01
890.11
891.10
891.12
891.13
892.04
892.09
893.27
894.09
894.21
894.27
895.28
896.18
896.19
896.21
897.06
897.09
898.01
898.14
899.07
899.08
899.17
902.22
902.23
907.09
910.12
yours
157.21
245.24
246.24
262.15
263.20
267.24
288.28
308.07
508.19
517.27
524.20
534.17
543.02
579.12
641.08
645.03
645.16
645.18
684.09
718.15
771.13
851.18
895.26
902.24
yourself
014.13
014.24
015.10
102.24
134.18
135.09
156.28
225.20
227.01

243.05
246.07
256.01
264.04
267.09
269.21
269.24
272.10
273.04
275.13
321.11
395.14
399.07
403.27
422.12
439.03
457.26
476.12
478.04
495.10
512.21
526.08
533.21
537.24
538.07
545.25
546.22
558.17
581.07
585.11
603.01
610.10
610.11
610.12
611.12
614.14
615.01
622.25
623.04
631.27
632.07
640.05
640.19
646.20
649.26
686.25
694.02
709.14
756.12
757.05
762.10
771.09
771.12
784.03
791.19
792.28
793.18
817.22
818.07
826.20
826.21
838.09
841.10
878.21
yourseln
694.16
youth
182.18
221.13
224.16
224.24
282.12
286.17
312.12
405.27
493.13
625.11
632.03
640.14
644.03
731.21
740.18
762.19
895.14
youthful
067.13
345.17
737.15
zeal
162.10
716.10
845.08
911.19
zealots
846.24
zealous
715.06
717.02
zembla
004.07
zenith
230.25
zig-zag
664.15
zone
004.09
zornes
678.26

WORD FREQUENCY TABLE

Count	Word
25	&c
1	'at's
1	'em
1	'only
1	'rageous
1	-church
1	-street
1	1
1	15l
1	19th
1	2000
1	20th
1	30l
1	516
4444	a
2	a'most
1	a-begging
1	a-tete
3	abandon
7	abandoned
1	abandonment
1	abate
25	abbot
1	abbot's
1	abbott
4	abhor
5	abhorred
2	abide
1	abigail
2	abigails
1	abilities
22	able
8	abode
1	abodes
2	abominable
1	aboon
216	about
41	above
1	abridge
4	abroad
3	abrupt
6	abruptly
1	abruptness
14	absence
1	absences
6	absent
6	absolute
26	absolutely
3	absolved
11	absorbed
1	absorbing
2	abstain
1	abstained
2	abstract
5	abstracted
5	abstraction
7	absurd
2	absurdity
1	abundance
4	abundant
6	abuse
3	abused
1	abut
3	abyss
1	acceded
2	accelerated
10	accent
8	accents
15	accept
2	acceptable
1	acceptance
3	accepted
3	accepting
2	accession
5	accident
1	accidental
3	accommodate
2	accommodated
3	accommodation
3	accommodations
9	accompanied
1	accompanies
3	accompaniment
1	accompaniments
13	accompany
2	accompanying
5	accomplish
6	accomplished
1	accomplishing
1	accomplishment
8	accomplishmen-ts
6	accord
3	accorded
6	according
9	accordingly
3	accost
1	accosted
1	accosting
26	account
1	account-book
1	accounted
4	accounts
1	accrued
1	accumulation
1	accuracy
1	accurate
3	accursed
1	accusation
2	accuse
4	accused
1	accusing
2	accustom
15	accustomed
1	achan
1	ache
2	ached
4	achieve
2	achieved
1	aching
7	acknowledge
5	acknowledged
1	acknowledges
1	acknowledging
3	acknowledgment
17	acquaintance
1	acquaintances
1	acquaintances'
5	acquainted
1	acquiesced
1	acquire
5	acquired
3	acquirements
1	acquiring
1	acquistion
2	acquitted
3	acrid
1	acrimony
18	across
25	act
11	acted
6	acting
9	action
5	actions
12	active
2	actively
2	activity
1	actor
2	actors
1	actress
2	acts
5	actual
10	actually
2	acumen
3	acute
2	acutely
1	acuteness
3	ad
2	adage
2	adapted
5	add
43	added
1	addicted
5	adding
6	addition
3	additional
16	address
19	addressed
1	addresses
7	addressing
1	adds
1	adduced
5	adela
125	adele,
9	adele's
3	adequate
2	adhere
1	adhered
1	adherence
1	adhering
2	adhesion
1	adhesiveness
1	adjoined
2	adjoining
1	adjourned
3	adjusted
1	administering
10	admiration
6	admire
7	admired
1	admirers
1	admires
2	admiring
1	admission
11	admit
1	admittance
12	admitted
2	admitting
1	admonition
3	ado
6	adopt
9	adopted
2	adoption
2	adored
1	adorned
1	adrift
2	adult
3	advance
23	advanced
1	advancement
2	advances
4	advancing
10	advantage
1	advantageous
5	advantages
1	advent
1	adventitious
3	adventure
1	adventurous
1	adverse
2	adverted
7	advertise
2	advertised
3	advertisement
3	advertisements
1	advertising
6	advice
2	advisable
3	advise
3	advised
1	advisedly
4	advocate
1	advocated
3	aerial
3	afar
1	affability
3	affable
5	affair
5	affairs
2	affect
2	affectation
2	affected
27	affection
1	affectionate
3	affections
3	affirm
1	affirmations
2	affirmative
9	affirmed
1	affix
2	affixed
2	afflicted
1	afflicting
1	affliction
3	affluence
3	afford
1	afforded
1	affrighted
1	afoot
2	afore
34	afraid
4	afresh
189	after
1	after-dinner--mood
1	after-flavour
1	after-occurre-nces
1	afternon
36	afternoon
1	afternoon-sch-ool
3	afternoons
26	afterwards
244	again
72	against
1	agate
33	age
1	aged
5	agent
1	agents
2	ages
2	aghast
1	agile
2	agitate
6	agitated
2	agitating
3	agitation
1	agnes
40	ago
2	agonies
1	agonized
1	agonizing
9	agony
7	agree
8	agreeable
1	agreeably
5	agreed
1	agrees
21	ah
1	ahasuerus
33	aid
4	aided
1	aids
3	ailed
2	ailing
1	ailment
7	aim
2	aims
57	air
1	air-torrent
1	aire
1	airily
1	airing
3	airs
4	ajar
3	akin
1	alabaster
1	alacrity
2	alarm
2	alarmed
1	alarming
1	alarum
8	alas
2	albion
1	album
2	alert
3	alias
3	alice
5	alien
1	alienated
1	alienates
1	alienation
2	alight
5	alighted
1	alights
4	alike
19	alive
636	all
2	all's
1	all-perfect
1	allay
1	allaying
1	allegation
1	allege
2	alleged
2	allegiance
2	alleviate
3	alliance
2	allotted
13	allow
3	allowance
19	allowed
1	allowing
1	allows
2	alloy
2	allude
2	alluded
2	alluding
1	allure
1	allured
5	allusion
1	allusions
1	ally
100	almost
2	aloft
73	alone
30	along
1	aloof
1	alors
12	aloud
1	alpha
1	alpine
51	already
33	also
7	altar
3	alter
1	alteration
3	alterations
1	altercation
6	altered
1	alternate
5	alternately
1	alternation
1	alternations
1	although
5	altogether
87	always
349	am
1	amateur
4	amazed
4	amazement
1	amazon's
1	ambassador
2	amber
2	amber-coloured
8	ambition
1	ambitions
6	ambitious
1	ambrosia
1	ambush
1	ameliorated
2	amen
1	amenable
1	amend
1	amends
1	amenities
1	amethyst
1	ami
5	amiable
1	amicable
2	amid
22	amidst
1	amie
1	amiss
2	amity
16	among
40	amongst
1	amounted
1	amphitheatre
5	ample
2	amplitude
1	amply
1	amputate
1	amusant
5	amuse
2	amused
2	amusement
1	amusements
1	amuses
2	amusing
10	amy
593	an
1	analogous
3	analysis
3	analyze
2	analyzed
1	analyzing
1	anathemas
1	anathematized
1	anatomical
1	ancestors
1	anchor
3	ancient

Count	Word	Count	Word	Count	Word	Count	Word
6594	and	1	apportion	64	ask	1	auditress
1	andes	1	apportioned	153	asked	5	aught
1	ange	1	appparently	5	asking	2	augment
13	angel	1	appreciate	5	asks	1	augmented
1	angel's	2	appreciated	2	aslant	2	august
1	angel-girl	1	appreciating	19	asleep	2	augusta
1	angelic	1	apprehended	1	asp	21	aunt
6	angels	1	apprehension	17	aspect	1	aunt-in-law
7	anger	2	apprehensions	1	asperity	1	aunts
1	anglaise	4	apprehensive	1	aspirant	1	aura
5	angle	1	apprend	1	aspirants	1	auriculas
7	angry	2	apprise	1	aspiration	1	auspices
10	anguish	1	apprised	4	aspirations	1	aussi
1	animadversions	16	approach	2	aspire	5	austere
5	animal	33	approached	2	aspired	2	austerity
1	animals	1	approaches	1	aspires	1	author
6	animated	12	approaching	1	assassination	6	authority
2	animating	4	approbation	1	assemblage	1	authors
2	animation	2	appropriate	1	assemble	1	autobiography
1	animosity	3	appropriated	3	assembled	3	automaton
1	ankle	1	appropriatene-ss	1	assented	8	autumn
4	ann			1	assert	3	avail
1	annihilated	1	approval	3	asserted	1	availed
1	annihilation	5	approve	2	asserting	3	avait
10	announced	5	approved	2	assertion	2	avalanche
3	announcement	2	approves	1	assez	1	avaricious
1	announces	5	april	2	assiduity	1	avenge
3	annoy	4	apron	2	assiduous	5	avenue
6	annoyance	4	apt	2	assiduously	2	average
3	annoyed	1	aquiline	5	assign	3	averred
1	annuity	2	arabian	4	assigned	1	averse
3	annum	1	arbitration	1	assimilates	5	aversion
4	anon	1	arbitress	2	assist	5	avert
112	another	2	arbour	4	assistance	3	averted
1	another's	15	arch	1	assistant	1	avidity
86	answer	1	arch-traitor	2	assisted	10	avoid
2	answerable	1	archangel	2	associate	2	avoided
75	answered	2	archdeacon	2	associated	1	avow
7	answering	2	arched	1	associates	1	avowal
10	answers	1	arches	2	association	3	awaited
1	antagonist	1	architectural	8	associations	1	awaiting
1	antagonistic	1	architecture	1	assortment	7	awake
4	anticipate	1	arctic	1	assuage	3	awakened
3	anticipated	6	ardent	3	assume	1	awaking
3	anticipation	1	ardently	6	assumed	21	aware
1	antipathetic	4	ardour	5	assuming	147	away
2	antipathies	604	are	1	assurance	5	awe
6	antipathy	3	argue	8	assure	1	awed
2	antipodes	1	argued	11	assured	10	awful
1	antiquated	2	argument	1	assuredly	1	awfully
6	antique	2	arguments	1	assuring	7	awhile
3	antiquity	1	arid	4	astir	1	awkward
2	antoinetta	1	ariel	6	astonished	6	awoke
8	anxiety	2	arisen	2	astonishing	1	awry
10	anxious	1	arises	2	astonishment	1	axe-edge
3	anxiously	1	arising	2	asunder	6	ay
210	any	1	aristocratic	6	asylum	3	aye
9	anybody	2	arithmetic	1173	at	5	azure
56	anything	1	ark	9	ate	1	azured
10	anywhere	36	arm	1	athenian	1	b
1	anzusehen	9	arm-chair	1	athirst	1	ba
6	apart	1	armful	3	athletic	1	babel
21	apartment	1	armfuls	2	atlantic	3	baby
3	apartments	54	arms	3	atmosphere	1	baby-phantom
1	apathetic	1	aromatic	2	atom	2	bachelor
1	apathy	2	arose	1	atoms	1	bachelor's
2	ape	6	around	4	atone	131	back
4	aperture	2	aroused	4	attach	1	back-door
1	apertures	1	arousing	10	attached	1	back-offices
2	apollo	1	arraigned	6	attachment	1	back-stairs
1	apollyon	4	arrange	1	attack	1	backboards
1	apologize	14	arranged	1	attain	2	background
1	apology	6	arrangement	2	attained	3	backs
1	apoplectic	8	arrangements	1	attaining	1	backstairs
3	apostle	4	arranging	1	attainment	1	backward
2	apostles	3	array	2	attainments	5	backwards
1	apostrophized	5	arrested	17	attempt	33	bad
1	apostrophizing	13	arrival	5	attempted	2	bade
3	apothecary	4	arrive	4	attempting	1	badge
1	appalled	13	arrived	3	attempts	1	badinage
2	appalling	1	arrives	5	attend	1	badly
1	appanage	1	arrogance	4	attendance	1	baffle
1	apparatus	1	arrogate	5	attendant	7	baffled
5	apparel	1	arrow-head	3	attended	1	baffling
1	apparelling	1	arrows	2	attending	1	bag
5	apparent	2	art	1	attends	1	bags
11	apparently	1	artful	24	attention	1	bah
4	apparition	4	article	4	attentions	2	bairn
2	appeal	5	articles	2	attentive	1	bairns
4	appealed	1	articulate	3	attentively	1	bake
1	appeals	1	artifice	2	attested	2	baked
19	appear	2	artificial	1	attesting	3	baking
20	appearance	1	artist	4	attic	1	balance
3	appearances	2	artist's	2	attics	1	balanced
56	appeared	1	artist-delight	8	attire	6	balcony
2	appearing	1	arts	5	attired	1	balked
9	appears	1576	as	5	attitude	4	ball
1	appeased	2	ascend	1	attract	1	ball-room
1	appertained	2	ascendancy	1	attracted	1	ballad
7	appetite	3	ascended	5	attraction	1	ballads
2	appetites	7	ascending	7	attractive	3	balls
1	appetizing	5	ascertain	1	attractiveness	4	balm
3	apple	5	ascertained	3	attribute	1	balm-like
3	apples	1	ascetic	1	attributed	2	balmy
1	application	2	ascribe	1	attributes	1	balustrade
2	applied	1	ascribed	2	au	2	ban
8	apply	1	ash	1	audacious	10	band
1	applying	5	ashamed	3	audacity	3	bandage
2	appointed	2	ashes	12	audible	2	bandaged
1	appointing	1	asian	1	audience	2	bandages
1	appointment	14	aside	1	auditors	1	bandit

1	bandit-hero	1	beclouded	1	berth	5	blight
2	bands	46	become	7	bertha	3	blighted
1	bane	4	becomes	3	beset	1	blights
1	banish	10	becoming	10	beside	23	blind
2	banished	1	becomingly	68	besides	1	blinding
2	banishment	79	bed	2	besotted	1	blindly
1	banister	4	bed-clothes	119	bessie	1	blindness
3	banisters	1	bed-fellow	12	bessie's	1	blinds
3	bank	1	bed-foot	63	best	1	blink
3	banker	1	bed-hangings	1	best-born	13	bliss
1	bankrupt	2	bed-head	2	bestow	4	blissful
3	banks	9	bed-room	5	bestowed	1	blistered
1	banned	3	bed-rooms	1	bestows	1	blither
2	banner	4	bed-side	2	betake	1	bloated
1	bannisters	4	bed-time	1	bethesda	2	block
1	baptized	1	bedroom	5	bethought	2	blocked
3	bar	1	bedrooms	1	betimes	1	blocked-up
4	barbara	13	beds	1	betook	2	blockhead
1	barbarism	3	bedside	4	betray	1	blond
1	barbed	1	bedstead	5	betrayed	1	blonde
1	barber	2	bedsteads	125	better	37	blood
9	bare	1	bedtime	1	bettering	1	blood-bleached
1	bared	3	bee	87	between	1	blood-red
1	barefoot	2	beech	1	beulah	1	blood-shot
2	barely	1	beech-trunk	2	beverage	4	bloodless
1	barest	389	been	1	bewailing	5	bloody
3	bargain	2	bees	3	beware	6	bloom
1	bargaining	1	bees-wax	1	bewick	4	bloomed
1	bargains	1	befall	2	bewick's	5	blooming
2	bark	1	befallen	7	bewildered	3	blossom
2	barked	1	befalling	2	bewilderment	1	blossom-blanc-
1	barking	1	befell	2	bewitched		hed
1	barmecide	1	befit	43	beyond	1	blossomed
1	barn	1	befitted	1	bianca	1	blossoms
7	barns	285	before	1	bias	3	blot
1	baroness	2	befriended	9	bible	1	blotted
1	barred	10	beg	10	bid	14	blow
1	barrel	53	began	1	bidden	1	blow-up
3	barren	11	beggar	2	bidding	6	blowing
1	barrenly	2	beggar-woman	1	bide	1	blown
3	barrier	1	beggarly	1	bids	1	blows
2	barriers	7	begged	3	bien	1	blubbering
1	barrister	2	begging	1	bientot	30	blue
3	bars	7	begin	4	big	1	blue-eyed
1	bas	16	beginning	1	bigamist	1	blue-piled
6	base	2	begins	1	bigamy	1	bluebeard's
1	bashaw	1	begot	1	bigger	1	bluer
11	basin	1	begrimed	2	bilberries	5	blunder
1	basins	1	beguile	1	bilge	1	blunders
1	bask	1	beguiled	2	bilious	3	blunt
2	basket	4	begun	1	bill	1	blunted
1	basking	5	behalf	1	billiard	3	bluntly
1	bason	1	behave	2	billiard-room	4	blush
2	bass	10	beheld	2	billiards	3	blushed
2	bastard	2	behest	1	billow	1	blushes
1	basted	56	behind	2	billows	1	boadicea
1	basting	5	behold	2	bind	4	board
3	bates	2	beholding	1	biography	2	boarding-scho-
1	bathe	123	being	13	bird		ol
1	bathed	1	being's	21	birds	2	boards
1	bathos	8	beings	1	birds'	3	boast
1	bats	1	belabour	4	birth	1	boasted
1	battalion	2	belated	1	biscuits	1	boastful
3	battle	1	beldame	10	bit	1	boat
1	battled	1	belfry	2	bite	3	bobby
1	battledore	1	belied	1	bits	2	bodies
1	battlemented	2	belief	25	bitter	4	bodily
7	battlements	69	believe	1	bitterest	13	body
1	bauerinnen	21	believed	1	bitterly	3	bog
1	bay	2	believes	2	bitterness	1	boh
1	baying	2	believing	3	bitternutt	1	bohemian
1	bazars	27	bell	80	black	1	boil
1727	be	2	belle	1	blackaviced	1	boiled
1	beacon	2	bellowed	1	blackberries	1	boiling
1	bead	1	bells	5	blackened	1	boils
4	beads	2	belong	1	blacker	1	bois
2	beak	10	belonged	2	blackness	1	boisterous
3	beam	2	belonging	1	blacksmith	4	boite
2	beamed	2	belongs	1	blades	5	bold
3	beaming	3	beloved	5	blame	2	bolder
1	beamless	29	below	1	blamed	1	boldly
2	beams	1	belvidere	2	blameless	1	boldness
41	bear	1	bemired	1	blames	1	boles
1	bearded	1	bemoaned	1	blaming	1	bolsters
7	bearing	1	ben't	20	blanche	7	bolt
1	bears	5	bench	2	blanched	4	bolted
3	beast	2	benches	13	blank	1	bolting
1	beast's	6	bend	1	blanks	1	bombazeen
1	beasts	14	bending	1	blasphemous	2	bon
6	beat	4	bends	1	blasphemy	1	bonbons
2	beaten	12	beneath	4	blast	2	bond
6	beating	1	benefactors	5	blasted	2	bondage
1	beats	8	benefactress	5	blaze	2	bonds
1	beau	1	benefactress's	2	blazed	6	bone
2	beau-ideal	2	beneficent	1	blazing	6	bones
1	beaute	1	beneficial	1	bleached	1	bonfire
3	beauties	10	benefit	1	bleak	1	bonne
28	beautiful	1	benefited	1	blear	25	bonnet
1	beautifully	1	benefits	1	bleared	1	bonnet-strings
1	beautifully-m-	2	benevolence	3	bled	1	bonnets
	oulded	2	benevolent	3	bleeding	2	bonny
33	beauty	1	benevolent-mi-	2	blended	1	bono
2	beaver		nded	1	blending	1	bonte
1	becalmed	1	benign	1	blends	45	book
30	became	1	benign-looking	7	blent	2	book-case
149	because	3	benignant	12	bless	1	book-cases
6	beck	36	bent	2	blessed	1	book-closet
1	beckon	1	bequeath	1	blesses	2	book-learned
4	beckoned	1	bequeathed	2	blessing	26	books
1	beckoning	3	bequest	3	blest	1	bookshelves
1	becks	1	bereavement	9	blew	2	boon

1 boot	1 bridewell	29 burns	1 caprices
1 boot-toe	1 bridge	2 burns's	4 capricious
3 boots	4 bridle	23 burnt	1 caps
1 booty	1 bridle-path	12 burst	4 captain
4 border	16 brief	3 bursting	1 captious
4 bordered	3 briefly	4 bush	1 captivated
1 bordering	15 briggs	1 bushes	1 captivating
4 borders	39 bright	1 bushy	2 captive
9 bore	2 brighten	4 busied	5 car
1 bored	2 brightening	1 busier	1 carcasses
10 born	3 brighter	1 busies	3 card
5 borne	2 brightest	1 busily	2 card-board
4 borrowed	2 brightly	40 business	3 cards
8 bosom	2 brightness	4 bust	53 care
1 bosomed	18 brilliant	4 bustle	2 cared
1 bosoms	4 brilliantly	2 bustled	7 career
1 botany	1 brilliantly-l-it	5 bustling	15 careful
135 both	2 brim	12 busy	10 carefully
1 bother	2 brimstone	1235 but	12 careless
2 bothwell	2 brine	1 butcher	1 carelessness
2 bottle	22 bring	3 butler	4 cares
9 bottom	9 bringing	1 butler's	3 caress
1 bottomless	2 brings	4 butter	3 caressed
5 boudoir	1 brink	1 butterflies	2 caresses
1 boudoirs	1 brisk	1 button	1 caressing
1 bough	1 bristled	1 buttoned	1 careworn
5 boughs	2 bristling	3 buxom	1 cargo
4 bought	1 bristly	3 buy	8 carlo
1 boulogne	7 british	1 buying	1 carmine
19 bound	1 brittle	1 buys	1 carolling
1 boundary	1 broached	1 buzzing	14 carpet
7 bounded	24 broad	637 by	1 carpeted
3 bounding	1 broad-brimmed	3 by-and-by	6 carpets
2 boundless	1 broad-shoulde-red	1 by-paths	29 carriage
2 bounds	1 broadest	1 by-play	1 carriage-road
1 bounteous	1 brobdignag	7 by-the-by	1 carriage-step
1 bountiful	1 brocaded	3 by-the-bye	3 carriages
2 bounty	2 brocklebridge	1 bygone	20 carried
5 bourne	52 brocklehurst	4 c'est	2 carrier
5 bow	3 brocklehurst's	1 c'etait	1 carries
1 bow-window	1 brocklehurst--hall	4 cabinet	1 carrion-seeki-ng
7 bowed	1 brocklehursts	1 cachination	8 carry
1 bowling	30 broke	4 cadeau	5 carrying
1 bowstring	30 broken	1 cadeaux	1 carte
9 box	4 bronze	1 cadence	13 carter
1 boxed	3 brooch	1 cadet	1 carthage
2 boxes	2 brood	1 caffre	1 carton
9 boy	1 brooded	2 cage	3 carved
3 boys	5 brooding	1 caged	1 carvings
2 brace	4 brook	1 cairngorm	1 cas
4 bracelet	1 brooklet	5 cake	33 case
3 bracelets	40 brother	5 cakes	9 casement
1 bracing	4 brother's	3 calamity	3 casements
1 bracken	1 brother-in-la-w's	13 calculated	2 cases
1 brackish	7 brothers	1 calculating	2 cash
1 brahma	68 brought	1 calculations	2 cashmeres
3 braided	1 broughton	1 calcutta	2 casket
17 brain	33 brow	1 calibre	15 cast
1 brainless	1 brow-beaten	2 calico	1 cast-off
5 brains	19 brown	1 caligula	2 castaway
1 brake	1 brownie	43 call	4 caste
1 branched	4 brows	80 called	1 casting
5 branches	1 browsed	2 callers	2 castle
1 branchy	3 brush	3 calling	1 castled
2 brand	4 brushed	1 callous	1 casts
1 brands	1 brushing	9 calls	1 casually
7 brass	1 brusque	33 calm	7 cat
2 brat	1 brutally	4 calmed	1 catalogue
1 brats	1 bubbling	5 calmer	1 cataract-like
1 brave	1 buckles	1 calming	2 catastrophe
1 brazen	1 bud	11 calmly	7 catch
3 breach	1 budding	1 calmness	2 catching
42 bread	1 buds	1 calves	1 catechising
1 bread-nut	1 build	1 calvinistic	1 catechism
5 breadth	10 building	4 cambridge	1 cathedral
20 break	2 built	173 came	1 catherine
1 breakage	1 bulk	1 camel-hair	2 catholic
1 breakers	1 bulky	1 camels	1 cats
29 breakfast	2 bull	1 cameo	3 cattle
1 breakfast-bas-ons	2 bullet	2 camp	23 caught
7 breakfast-room	1 bullied	1 camphor	11 cause
1 breakfast-tab-le	1 bulwark	231 can	3 caused
2 breakfast-time	2 bun	15 can't	1 causes
2 breakfasted	2 bunch	1 canadian	6 causeway
7 breaking	1 bunches	1 canary	1 causewayed
1 breaks	1 bundle	48 candle	1 caution
16 breast	1 bungler	2 candle-light	3 cautious
1 breasting	1 bunglingly	11 candles	1 cavalcade
20 breath	1 buoy	2 candlestick	1 cavalier
2 breathe	1 buoyancy	2 candour	1 cavaliers
11 breathed	2 buoyant	1 cane	2 cave
4 breathing	1 buoyed	1 canine	1 cavillers
1 breathings	9 burden	3 cankering	1 cawed
1 breathless	5 burdened	1 cannily	3 cawing
1 breeches'	1 burdens	1 cannnot	8 cease
1 breeches-pock-et	1 burdensome	1 cannon-ball	11 ceased
10 breeze	1 burgh	133 cannot	8 ceaseless
2 breezy	1 burglar	1 canoe	1 ceases
1 brevity	11 buried	1 canopied	1 ceiled
1 brewing	7 burn	1 cant	9 ceiling
1 briar	1 burn's	1 canter	4 cela
1 briar-rose	1 burned	3 canvass	1 celebrated
4 bridal	1 burneth	1 canzonette	1 celerity
1 bridal-path	20 burning	6 cap	1 celestial
16 bride	1 burning-glass-es	3 capable	13 celine
3 bride's	1 burnished	1 capacities	1 celine's
3 bridegroom		7 capacity	6 cell
1 bridesmaids		2 cape	1 cellar
		1 caper	2 cells
		4 capital	1 censure
		5 caprice	

Count	Word	Count	Word	Count	Word	Count	Word
1	censures	1	cheeringly	1	cities	1	co-operation
1	cent	1	cheerless	4	city	21	coach
2	central	1	cheers	1	city-night	1	coach-door
8	centre	8	cheese	3	civil	1	coach-house
1	centuries	1	cheese-cake	2	civilities	6	coachman
1	century's	1	cheesecakes	2	civility	1	coachmen
10	ceremony	1	chemises	2	civilized	2	coadjutor
1	cerises	1	chere	1	civilly	3	coal
67	certain	4	cherish	5	clad	1	coals
1	certainement	8	cherished	17	claim	8	coarse
32	certainly	1	cherishes	1	claimants	1	coarse-minded
7	certainty	5	cherishing	7	claimed	1	coarsely
2	ces	1	cherries	1	claiming	1	coarsely-clad
3	cessation	4	cherry	2	claims	2	coarseness
1	cetera	2	cherry-tree	1	clammy	3	coast
2	chafed	1	cherub-like	1	clamorous	1	coasted
1	chagrin	1	cherubs'	1	clamorously	1	coasting
7	chain	8	chest	2	clamour	3	coat
2	chained	1	chested	1	clamoured	2	coax
52	chair	6	chestnut	1	clang	1	coaxing
1	chair-back	1	chests	1	clanked	1	cobwebs
16	chairs	1	cheviot	1	clap	1	cochere
7	chaise	1	chez	4	clapped	1	coerce
5	chalk	3	chicken	3	clara	1	coercion
1	challenge	2	chickens	1	clashed	8	coffee
36	chamber	1	chidden	3	clasp	1	coffee-cup
1	chamber-ceiling	1	chidings	3	clasped	1	coffee-cups
3	chamber-door	2	chief	1	clasping	5	coffin
1	chamber-maid	1	chiefest	1	clasps	1	coffin-dust
13	chambers	4	chiefly	20	class	2	coffre
1	chambre	1	chiffone	8	classes	1	cognizant
1	chambres	1	chiffonieres	2	classic	1	coherently
23	chance	1	chilblains	1	clatter	1	coiffer
7	chanced	85	child	3	clattering	1	coiled
2	chancel	2	child's	1	claws	1	coils
1	chances	3	child-like	2	clay	5	coin
2	chandelier	4	childer	28	clean	2	coincided
41	change	12	childhood	2	cleaned	1	coincidence
1	changeable	1	childhood's	1	cleaning	1	coined
13	changed	2	childish	1	cleanly-attired	80	cold
3	changeful	1	childless	1	cleansed	4	colder
2	changeling	1	childlike	41	clear	1	coldest
1	changent	38	children	7	cleared	3	coldly
7	changes	3	children's	3	clearer	9	coldness
2	changing	1	childs	3	clearest	1	colds
5	channel	11	chill	1	clearing	1	collar
1	chanted	4	chilled	10	clearly	1	collared
5	chaos	3	chilling	1	clearness	2	collect
7	chapter	5	chilly	1	clears	5	collected
3	chapters	2	chime	1	cleft	1	collectedly
47	character	1	chimed	1	clement	1	collecting
1	characteristic	1	chimera	2	clenched	2	collective
1	characteristically	1	chimeras	1	clergy	4	college
7	characteristics	2	chimney	20	clergyman	1	colloquize
1	characterized	3	chimney-corner	3	clergyman's	1	colloquy
7	characters	2	chimney-piece	6	clerk	19	colonel
2	charade	4	chimneys	11	clever	1	colossal
1	charades	13	chin	1	click	15	colour
12	charge	6	china	1	click-click	1	colour-box
10	charged	2	chink	2	client	1	colour-boxes
1	charges	1	chintz	1	cliffs	3	coloured
5	charitable	1	chips	3	climate	3	colouring
5	charity	1	chirruped	1	climates	4	colourless
2	charity-children	1	chisel	4	climax	2	colours
1	charity-school	1	chiselled	3	climbed	3	column
1	charivari	1	choachman	3	clime	1	columnar
1	charlatan	1	chocolate	3	cling	1	columns
3	charles	15	choice	1	clinging	2	comb
23	charm	1	choicest	2	clings	1	combats
5	charmed	1	choked	23	cloak	3	combed
1	charmer	1	choler	1	cloaked	2	combination
1	charmers	14	choose	1	cloaks	1	combinations
4	charming	1	choosing	18	clock	3	combine
5	charms	1	chopping	1	clock-working	5	combined
1	charnel	1	chord	1	clod-hopping	1	combustion
1	charred	1	chords	1	clogged	223	come
2	charter	8	chose	50	close	4	comer
4	char-woman	12	chosen	1	close-ranked	15	comes
1	char-women	3	christ	37	closed	1	cometh
1	chase	1	christendom	11	closely	1	comfits
1	chasm	2	christened	1	closely-printed	23	comfort
1	chasms	17	christian	7	closer	10	comfortable
1	chasseed	1	christian's	1	closeset	3	comfortably
1	chastened	1	christianity	6	closet	2	comforted
2	chastisement	3	christians	4	closing	3	comforter
1	chastisements	7	christmas	3	cloth	1	comforting
1	chastiser	1	christmas-time	1	clothe	1	comfortless
1	chastising	2	chronicles	1	clothed	46	coming
1	chat	2	chuckled	16	clothes	11	command
3	chatter	38	church	5	clothing	2	commanded
1	chattered	1	church-aisle	1	cloths	2	commanding
2	chattering	1	church-floor	22	cloud	1	commands
1	chatters	1	church-like	1	cloud-high	5	comme
1	cheat	1	church-militant	1	clouded	9	commence
1	cheated	1	church-spire	1	clouding	11	commenced
1	cheats	3	church-yard	1	cloudless	4	commencement
10	check	4	churchyard	17	clouds	1	commencing
7	checked	1	cicatrized	2	cloudy	1	commendations
30	cheek	1	ciel	1	cloven	1	commended
8	cheeks	4	cigar	1	clump	4	comment
5	cheer	1	cigar-case	1	clumsily-contrived	1	commentary
2	cheered	1	cinder	7	clung	2	commented
13	cheerful	1	cinders	5	clustered	2	commission
2	cheerfully	1	cinq	1	clusters	2	commissioned
1	cheerfulness	4	circle	1	clutch	1	commissions
1	cheerily	3	circled	1	clutched	4	commit
5	cheering	2	circles	1	co	6	committed
		3	circlet	1	co-operate	5	committee
		13	circumstance			2	committing
		25	circumstances			1	commodious
						20	common

7 common-place	1 condoled	1 consolations	1 cooked
1 common-places	1 condolence	2 consolatory	2 cooking
1 common-sense	1 condor	1 console	19 cool
3 commotion	1 conducing	1 consoled	1 cooled
3 communicate	1 conducive	1 consoles	2 cooler
5 communicated	15 conduct	1 consort	8 coolly
1 communicates	7 conducted	1 consorting	2 coolness
4 communicating	2 conducting	3 conspicuous	2 copied
5 communication	1 conductor	4 constancy	1 copies
2 communications	1 conductress	4 constant	1 copse
4 communicative	1 confabulate	1 constantly	2 copy
4 communion	1 confabulation	1 constitute	2 copying
1 communion-rai-ls	1 confer	5 constitution	2 coquetry
1 community	2 conference	1 constraint	1 coquettish
1 compact	3 conferences	1 constricted	2 coral
18 companion	2 conferred	1 constricting	4 cord
1 companionable	7 confess	1 constriction	4 corded
1 companionless	2 confessed	1 construe	3 cordial
4 companions	1 confesses	1 construed	4 cordiality
4 companionship	1 confession	3 consult	2 cordially
27 company	2 confidant	1 consultation	5 core
5 comparative	2 confide	2 consulted	1 cormorant
6 comparatively	1 confided	1 consulting	1 corn-field
3 compare	21 confidence	2 consumed	2 corn-fields
10 compared	1 confidences	2 consumption	14 corner
1 comparing	1 confidential	2 contact	2 corners
1 comparison	1 confidentially	1 contagion	1 cornice
2 compartment	4 confine	1 contain	1 coronet
1 compartments	2 confined	8 contained	1 corporeal
3 compassion	1 confinement	6 containing	5 corpse
3 compassionate	1 confines	2 contains	1 corpse-like
4 compel	1 confining	1 contaminate	1 corpses
1 compels	1 confirm	2 contamination	1 corpulent
1 compensate	1 confirmation	2 contemplate	14 correct
1 compensation	2 confirmed	2 contemplating	3 corrected
3 competency	2 conflagration	2 contemplation	1 correcting
2 competent	6 conflict	1 contemporary	1 correctness
1 competitor	2 conform	5 contempt	2 correspondence
1 competitors	4 conformity	1 contenance	1 correspondent
1 complacent	1 confound	2 contend	3 corresponding
1 complacently	2 confounded	1 contended	4 corridor
2 complain	1 confronted	1 contending	1 corroborate
1 complaint	1 confronting	20 content	1 corroded
2 complaints	1 confronts	4 contented	1 corroding
1 complement	9 confused	1 contentedly	2 corrupt
19 complete	1 confusedly	3 contentment	1 corruptible
4 completed	6 confusion	15 contents	1 corruption
5 completely	3 congealed	1 contes	1 corsair-song
1 completer	1 congenial	1 contest	1 corsairs
2 completing	1 congeniality	6 continent	1 coruscating
9 complexion	1 congratulate	5 continual	3 cost
1 complexioned	1 congratulation	18 continually	3 costly
1 compliance	1 congratulatio-ns	6 continue	3 costume
1 compliant	1 congregation	76 continued	2 costumed
1 complicated	8 conjecture	1 continuing	1 costumes
2 complied	3 conjectured	3 continuous	15 cottage
1 complimenting	2 conjectures	2 continuously	1 cottagers'
1 comply	1 conjugal	1 contort	9 couch
1 complying	1 conjured	1 contorted	1 couches
13 composed	2 connaught	5 contour	3 cough
1 composes	9 connected	2 contracted	2 coughed
2 composure	10 connection	2 contradict	2 coughing
1 compound	2 connections	1 contradicted	503 could
1 compounding	2 connexion	1 contradiction	1 couldn't
17 comprehend	4 connexions	1 contradictory	4 counsel
3 comprehended	1 conning	21 contrary	1 counselling
4 comprehension	3 conquered	10 contrast	1 counsels
1 comprehensive	1 conqueror	3 contrasted	3 count
1 comprends-tu	1 conqueror's	1 contrasting	2 counted
3 compressed	2 conquerors	2 contrasts	31 countenance
1 compressing	5 conquest	1 contravened	2 countenances
4 comprised	15 conscience	2 contribute	1 counter
1 compromising	1 conscience-ke-eper	7 contrived	1 counter-balan-ce
3 comrade	3 conscientious	9 control	1 counteracting
1 comrade's	3 conscientious-ly	4 controlled	1 counterfeit
1 con	1 conscientious-ness	2 controlling	1 counterpane
9 conceal	5 conscious	1 controvert	1 counterpanes
6 concealed	13 consciousness	1 contumacy	1 countesses
1 concealing	3 consecrated	1 contumelious	2 countless
3 concealment	1 consecrating	3 convenience	1 countries
1 conceited	2 consecration	3 convenient	19 country
5 conceive	11 consent	1 conveniently	1 country-made
7 conceived	9 consented	4 convent	9 county
1 conceives	1 consenting	1 convent-like	1 county-famili-es
3 conceiving	10 consequence	4 conventional	1 couple
2 concentrate	5 consequences	2 conventionali-ties	1 coupled
2 concentrated	1 consequent	1 conventionally	22 courage
1 concentre	9 consequently	38 conversation	1 courageous
1 conception	3 conservatory	1 conversational	68 course
6 concern	26 consider	1 conversations	1 court
2 concerned	13 considerable	6 converse	1 court-lady's
4 concerning	2 considerably	4 conversed	2 court-yard
1 concession	1 considerate	5 conversing	2 courted
1 conciliate	1 consideratene-ss	1 converting	1 courteous
1 concisely	3 consideration	2 convey	1 courtesy
6 concluded	1 considerations	4 conveyance	4 courtship
5 conclusion	25 considered	7 conveyed	10 cousin
2 conclusions	2 considering	1 conveying	2 cousin's
1 concord	2 considers	8 conviction	11 cousins
2 condemn	1 consist	1 convince	1 cousinship
1 condemnatory	2 consisted	7 convinced	7 cover
4 condemned	4 consistency	1 convolvuli	19 covered
1 condemning	5 consistent	2 convulsion	7 covering
1 condense	1 consisting	1 convulsions	2 coverings
2 condensed	2 consists	3 convulsive	1 coverlet
2 condescension	3 consolation	1 convulsively	2 covers
1 condiments		1 cooing	2 covert
11 condition		7 cook	3 covet
1 conditionally		1 cook's	2 coveted
1 conditions			

1 cowardly
1 cower
2 cows
1 cozy
3 crabbed
2 crack
1 cracking
1 crackle
4 cradle
1 craft
9 crag
2 craggy
1 cramped
1 cramping
4 crape
4 crash
2 crashed
2 crater
1 crater-crust
1 cravat
1 craves
3 craving
5 cravings
1 crawled
1 crawling
1 crayons
1 creak
2 creaked
1 crease
1 creased
1 creases
1 create
4 created
1 creation
1 creator
19 creature
2 creatures
1 credible
2 credit
1 creditor
1 credulity
5 creed
3 creeping
3 creole
6 crept
3 crescent
1 crescent-dest-
    iny
1 crest-fallen
1 crevices
1 crew
9 crib
57 cried
2 cries
10 crime
1 crimes
2 criminal
1 criminality
1 crimped
13 crimson
1 crimsoned
1 cripple
2 crippled
6 crisis
1 criticize
1 crock
1 crocuses
1 crois
1 crone
1 crooned
2 croquant
1 croquer
20 cross
1 cross-examina-
    tion
1 cross-legged
1 cross-questio-
    ning
1 cross-ways
15 crossed
5 crossing
2 crouched
1 crow-colony
1 crow-trees
1 crowd
4 crowded
1 crowding
7 crown
3 crowned
2 crows
1 crucibles
2 crucifix
13 cruel
1 cruelly
5 cruelty
1 crumb
3 crumbled
1 crumbling
4 crumbs
1 crumpled
1 crunching
1 crush
11 crushed
1 crushes
2 crushing
2 crust
1 crusted
2 crusty
20 cry
5 crying
1 crystal

1 crystal-clear
1 cudgel
1 cue
1 cui
1 cuirass
1 culinary
1 culpability
1 culpable
2 cultivate
1 cultivated
3 cultivation
1 cumber
1 cumberland
1 cumbers
3 cumbrous
3 cunning
14 cup
3 cupboard
5 cups
1 curacy
5 curate
1 curate's
2 curb
1 curbed
1 curbless
1 curdles
6 cure
12 curiosity
11 curious
2 curiously
2 curl
1 curl-paper
9 curled
2 curling
20 curls
1 currants
1 current
1 currently
1 currents
5 curse
3 cursed
2 curses
1 cursorily
1 curtail
2 curtailed
28 curtain
1 curtained
1 curtainless
17 curtains
1 curtesying
3 curtseyed
1 curves
2 cushion
3 cushioned
1 cushioning
1 cushions
1 custard
2 custody
11 custom
1 customary
1 customer
1 customers
25 cut
1 cuts
3 cutting
1 cuyp-like
1 cynical
1 cynosure
1 cypher
1 cyphering
1 d
1 d'athlete
1 d'ye
1 da
1 dabbling
1 dacent
2 dagger
1 dahlias
20 daily
2 dainty
3 daisies
1 dale
1 dales
1 damaging
1 damanded
1 damask
1 damask-covered
5 dame
2 damer
1 dames
1 damn
2 damned
8 damp
1 damped
1 damper
2 damping
1 damsel
1 danae
3 dance
2 dancer
1 dancer's
2 dancing
1 dandled
1 dandy
18 danger
12 dangerous
2 dangers
2 daniel
1 dank
1 dans
1 danser

1 dappled
31 dare
29 dared
1 daren't
14 daresay
6 daring
92 dark
1 dark-blue
2 darken
4 darkened
1 darkening
2 darkens
4 darker
2 darkly
17 darkness
1 darksome
14 darling
2 darlings
1 darning
2 dart
3 darted
1 darting
1 dash
4 dashed
6 dashing
1 date
1 dated
23 daughter
1 daughter's
1 daughter-in-l-
    aw
11 daughters
1 daughters'
1 daunt
1 daunted
2 david
10 dawn
6 dawned
209 day
5 day's
2 day-dream
1 day-dreams
1 day-visions
13 daylight
65 days
6 dazzled
1 dazzling
15 de
1 deacon
52 dead
1 dead-weights
1 deadest
3 deadly
3 deaf
33 deal
1 dealings
30 dear
2 dearer
2 dearest
2 dearly
1 dearth
50 death
1 death's
1 death-like
1 death-struck
1 death-white
2 deathbed
1 deathless
1 deaths
1 debarrassed
1 debasement
1 debasing
1 debauchery
5 debt
1 debts
4 decay
2 decaying
1 decease
2 deceased
4 deceit
3 deceitful
5 deceive
1 deceived
3 december
1 decency
10 decent
2 decently
1 deception
6 decide
6 decided
6 decidedly
1 deciphering
6 decision
1 decisions
2 decisive
1 deck
1 declaimed
2 declaration
8 declare
9 declared
2 declares
1 declaring
3 decline
5 declined
2 decorated
1 decoration
1 decree
1 decreed
1 dedans
5 deed
2 deeds

3 deem
9 deemed
4 deeming
1 deems
45 deep
1 deep-graved
1 deep-thrilling
2 deepen
2 deepen
2 deepened
1 deepening
8 deeper
1 deepest
13 deeply
1 defaulters
2 defect
3 defective
7 defects
2 defence
1 defend
4 defer
1 deference
2 deferential
1 deferentially
4 deferred
1 deferring
3 defiance
4 deficiencies
4 deficiency
1 deficient
2 defied
1 define
2 definite
2 definitively
1 deformed
1 deformities
2 deformity
1 defrauded
4 defy
1 defying
2 degenerate
1 degenerated
1 deglutition
6 degradation
1 degrade
2 degraded
1 degrades
5 degrading
18 degree
4 degrees
1 deigned
1 deistic
1 deity
1 dejected
3 dejection
12 delay
1 delayed
1 delays
1 delf
2 deliberated
4 deliberately
1 deliberating
1 deliberation
1 delicacies
3 delicacy
9 delicate
4 delicious
29 delight
6 delighted
5 delightful
1 delightfully
3 delights
1 delineate
1 delineated
1 delineation
5 delirious
4 delirium
3 deliver
7 delivered
4 delivering
1 delivery
1 dell
1 dells
1 delude
1 deluding
1 deluge
3 deluged
5 delusion
1 delusive
1 dem
10 demand
1 demande
23 demanded
1 demanding
3 demands
1 demas
2 demeanor
1 demolished
4 demon
1 demon's
1 demon-hate
1 demoniac
1 demonstration
1 demonstrations
3 demurely
1 demureness
3 den
3 denied
1 denominated
1 denominating
1 denote

Col1	Col2	Col3	Col4
1 denoted	4 detected	14 direct	4 dispense
1 denoting	2 detecting	13 directed	1 dispensed
6 dense	1 detection	14 direction	1 disperse
28 dent	4 determination	9 directions	3 dispersed
1 dent's	1 determinations	13 directly	2 displaced
1 dentelles	9 determined	1 directness	2 displayed
1 denuded	1 determinedly	1 director	4 displeased
6 deny	1 detestable	2 directs	1 displeasing
6 depart	1 detestation	1 direful	5 displeasure
8 departed	1 detrimental	1 dirt	19 disposed
2 departing	7 deuce	1 dirty	9 disposition
1 department	1 deutsch	1 disadvantageo-	2 disproportion-
16 departure	1 devastated	usly	ate
5 depend	1 devastation	3 disagreeable	1 dispute
7 dependant	1 develop	1 disappear	1 disqualified
1 dependant's	1 develope	4 disappeared	1 disquieting
2 dependants	9 developed	1 disappearing	1 disquietude
1 depended	2 development	6 disappointed	1 disregard
3 dependence	2 deviate	12 disappointment	2 disregarded
1 dependency	1 deviation	1 disapprobation	1 disregardful
4 dependent	1 device	2 disapprove	2 dissatisfied
4 depends	11 devil	1 disapprovingly	1 dissent
1 deportment	1 devilish	1 disarrange	1 disseverment
1 deposit	2 devine	1 disarrangement	1 dissimilar
1 depraved	1 devious	2 disaster	3 dissipated
1 deprecation	2 devise	2 disasters	3 dissipation
4 depressed	3 devised	1 disavowal	2 dissipations
1 depression	1 devoid	1 disavowed	1 dissolution
1 deprive	3 devote	1 disburthen	2 dissolve
6 depth	8 devoted	1 disc	3 dissolved
7 depths	6 devotion	2 discern	1 dissolves
1 der	1 devotional	5 discerned	2 dissuade
1 deranged	1 devotions	4 discharge	36 distance
2 derive	4 devour	2 discharged	1 distanceclipse
5 derived	6 devoured	1 discharging	21 distant
2 deriving	2 devouring	1 disciple	2 distantly
2 des	9 dew	1 disciples	3 distasteful
5 descend	1 dew-beads	2 discipline	7 distinct
1 descendants	2 dewy	3 disciplined	3 distinction
14 descended	1 dexterously	1 disclose	15 distinctly
8 descending	1 diablerie	6 disclosed	1 distinctness
1 descends	1 diademed	4 disclosure	7 distinguish
1 descrated	3 dialogue	2 disclosures	2 distinguishab-
8 describe	1 dialogues	2 discoloured	le
6 described	1 diametrically	1 discomfort	5 distinguished
1 describes	2 diamond	2 disconnected	1 distinguishing
1 describing	2 diamonds	1 disconsolate	3 distortion
9 description	1 dian	1 discontent	1 distracted
1 descriptive	70 diana	1 discontented	1 distracting
5 desert	6 diana's	2 discord	1 distraction
2 deserted	2 diary	11 discourse	1 distractions
1 deserter	3 dick	11 discover	5 distress
2 deserting	1 dickens	23 discovered	5 distressed
2 desertion	1 dictates	3 discoveries	1 distresses
1 deserts	1 dictation	1 discovering	3 distressing
2 deserve	3 dictionary	10 discovery	2 distributed
6 deserved	1 dictum	3 discreet	5 district
3 design	393 did	1 discreetly	1 districts
1 designated	1 didn't	3 discretion	3 distrust
1 designation	38 die	2 discriminate	1 distrustfully
2 designing	24 died	1 discriminated	4 disturb
1 designs	1 dies	2 discuss	1 disturbance
2 desirable	1 diet	5 discussed	12 disturbed
25 desire	1 differ	3 discussing	2 disturbing
11 desired	1 differed	3 discussion	1 disturbs
2 desires	12 difference	1 disdain	2 dit
2 desiring	1 differences	1 disdained	1 ditch
4 desirous	34 different	1 disdainful	1 ditto
2 desist	1 differently	3 disease	1 dive
11 desk	17 difficult	1 diseased	1 diverged
13 desolate	5 difficulties	1 disembarrassed	3 divers
2 desolation	17 difficulty	1 disembodied	2 divert
17 despair	4 diffidence	1 disembowelling	1 dives
2 despatch	1 diffident	1 disfigured	1 divest
3 despatched	1 diffuse	2 disgrace	1 divested
12 desperate	1 digest	1 disgraceful	7 divided
1 desperately	1 digested	3 disguise	3 dividing
4 desperation	1 dignified	2 disguised	10 divine
1 despicable	1 dignity	10 disgust	1 divined
1 despicably	1 digression	1 disgusted	1 diviners
5 despise	1 dilated	3 disgusting	1 divining
2 despised	1 dilating	3 disgusts	3 division
1 despises	1 dilation	2 dish	1 dizzy
3 despite	1 diligence	1 dished	466 do
1 despitefully	2 diligent	1 dishes	2 doat
1 despoiled	24 dim	2 dishevelled	1 doated
2 despondent	2 dimensions	1 dishonest	5 docile
1 desponding	2 diminish	3 dishonour	4 doctor
1 despot	1 diminutive	1 disinclined	1 doctors
4 despotic	8 dimly	2 disinterested	3 doctrine
2 despotism	1 dimly-lit	4 disk	3 doctrines
1 despots	2 dimmed	10 dislike	5 document
1 dessert	2 dimness	3 disliked	1 documents
1 dessert-dishes	2 dimpled	4 dislikes	72 does
1 dessert-servi-	1 dimples	1 disliking	3 doesn't
ce	1 din	1 dismal	1 doffed
1 desserts	3 dine	4 dismay	23 dog
6 destined	4 dined	4 dismayed	1 dog's
1 destinies	2 dingy	4 dismiss	1 dog-like
9 destiny	1 dining	9 dismissed	1 dogmas
5 destitute	18 dining-room	1 disobedience	1 dogmatical
2 destitution	32 dinner	1 disobeying	2 dogs
3 destroy	1 dinner-bell	2 disorder	1 doigts
4 destroyed	1 dinner-table	1 disordered	31 doing
2 destruction	1 dinner-time	5 disown	1 doit
2 detail	1 dinners	3 disowned	1 dole
1 detailing	3 dint	1 disowning	4 doleful
13 details	1 dionysius	1 disparaging	6 doll
1 detained	1 dip	1 dispassionate	1 doll's
1 detaining	3 dipped	1 dispensary	5 domestic
1 detect	1 dips	1 dispensation	1 dommage

155	don't	10	driver	1	economy's	4	embarrassment

155 don't
1 donc
76 done
1 donjon
1 gonna
1 donner
10 doom
152 door
3 door-bell
1 door-handle
1 door-step
1 door-stones
21 doors
2 dormitories
4 dormitory
1 dose
1 doth
1 dotted
9 double
1 double-daisies
1 doubled
60 doubt
7 doubted
5 doubtful
1 doubtfully
17 doubtless
5 doubts
2 dove
1 doves
1 dovetailed
3 dowager
1 dowager's
4 dowagers
264 down
1 downright
1 doze
5 dozen
1 dozing
1 drab
1 drag
5 dragged
1 dragging
1 drain
1 drained
6 drank
1 draped
3 draperies
7 drapery
9 draught
1 draughts
24 draw
13 drawer
13 drawers
17 drawing
1 drawing-box
1 drawing-master
1 drawing-materials
26 drawing-room
1 drawing-rooms
5 drawings
1 drawled
2 drawling
26 drawn
2 draws
16 dread
9 dreaded
6 dreadful
1 dreadfully
3 dreading
1 dreads
33 dream
2 dreamed
1 dreamily
7 dreaming
1 dreamland
9 dreams
4 dreamt
4 drear
3 drearily
2 dreariness
18 dreary
1 dreg
1 dregs
5 drenched
31 dress
35 dressed
1 dresser
7 dresses
7 dressing
1 dressing-bell
1 dressing-case
1 dressing-cases
2 dressing-gown
1 dressing-room
2 dressing-table
3 dressmaker
44 drew
3 dried
1 dried-up
1 dries
5 drift
3 drifted
2 drifts
1 drilled
10 drink
1 drinking
2 drinks
3 dripping
13 drive
9 driven

10 driver
1 drives
3 driving
1 drizzling
2 drooped
4 drooping
13 drop
11 dropped
2 dropping
2 drops
2 dropt
1 dross
5 drove
1 drover
1 drown
2 drowned
1 drug
1 drunkard
14 dry
1 drying
1 dsease
2 du
1 dubbed
1 dubious
1 dudgeon
7 due
2 duet
1 dug
10 dull
1 dulls
3 dulness
1 duly
9 dumb
1 dumbfoundered
1 dun
4 dungeon
2 dunnut
2 dupe
1 duplicate
1 duplicity
1 durable
3 duration
42 during
12 dusk
1 duskier
2 dusky
7 dust
3 dusting
8 duties
1 dutiful
20 duty
7 dwell
5 dwelling
1 dwelling-place
4 dwelt
1 dye
15 dying
1 e
3 e'en
97 each
11 eager
8 eagerly
7 eagerness
2 eagle
1 eagles'
36 ear
1 earl
1 earlier
1 earliest
23 early
4 earn
2 earned
11 earnest
8 earnestly
5 earnestness
1 earnings
1 earrings
13 ears
26 earth
1 earth's
4 earthly
3 earthquake
1 earthquake-shock
1 earthward
17 ease
2 eased
2 easel
2 easier
4 easily
8 east
1 easter
4 eastern
2 eastward
21 easy
3 easy-chair
26 eat
1 eatable
2 eaten
3 eating
2 ebb
3 ebon
1 ebony
1 ebullition
5 eccentric
1 eccentricity
1 ecclesiastical
6 echo
2 echoed
2 eclipse
3 economy

1 economy's
1 ecstasies
1 ecstasy
1 ecstatic
1 eddies
1 eddying
1 eden
1 eden-like
5 edge
2 edged
3 edging
1 edification
1 editor
1 edouard
1 eduardo
4 educated
1 educating
12 education
21 edward
2 edward's
1 edwin
1 eel
1 een
4 eerie
1 eerily
1 efface
4 effaced
17 effect
4 effected
1 effective
2 effectually
1 effervesce
1 efficiency
1 efficient
1 efficiently
1 effigies
1 effigy
1 effluence
1 effluvia
29 effort
1 effortless
16 efforts
1 effusion
1 egg
4 eggs
1 egotism
1 egotistical
2 egypt
3 en
23 eight
7 eighteen
5 eighty
1 einer
65 either
7 ejaculated
1 ejaculating
1 ejaculation
2 ejaculations
1 elaborate
3 elaborately
11 elapsed
1 elastic
1 elate
2 elbow
1 eld
7 elder
9 elderly
2 elders
4 eldest
2 elected
2 election
2 electric
1 electrified
6 elegance
5 elegant
3 element
1 elementary
6 elements
1 elevate
2 elevated
1 elevation
6 eleven
1 eleventh
5 elf
1 elf-land
1 elf-locks
2 elfish
2 elicit
3 elicited
1 eliezer
2 eligible
1 elixir
28 eliza
2 eliza's
1 elizabeth
1 elle
1 elles
1 elliot
3 elliott
1 elm
1 elongated
3 eloquence
2 eloquent
30 else
6 elsewhere
3 elude
2 elves
2 elysium
1 emaciated
2 embarrass
2 embarrassed

4 embarrassment
4 embers
1 embittered
2 emblem
1 emblems
1 embodied
1 embody
1 emboldened
1 embowered
10 embrace
3 embraced
1 embraces
2 embracing
1 embroidered
1 embroideries
1 embroidering
2 embroidery
1 embrowned
1 embruted
1 emerald
3 emerged
1 emergencies
1 emerging
2 eminence
1 eminent
1 emir
13 emotion
4 emotions
1 emperors
2 emphasis
2 emphatic
2 emphatically
1 empire
2 employ
5 employed
4 employer
15 employment
2 emptied
12 empty
1 emptying
1 emulate
1 emulation
1 emulous
4 en
1 enable
4 enabled
1 enactment
1 enamelled
1 enchained
1 enchaining
1 enchantment
1 encircles
1 enclose
3 enclosed
3 enclosing
4 enclosure
1 encore
3 encounter
3 encountered
2 encountering
4 encourage
2 encouraged
1 encouragingly
3 encouraging
1 encroach
1 encroaches
1 encumber
1 encyclopaedic
54 end
1 endearment
3 endearments
6 endeavour
10 endeavoured
2 endeavouring
2 endeavours
2 ended
2 endless
4 endowed
1 endowments
2 ends
4 endurance
16 endure
9 endured
3 enemies
2 enemy
3 energetic
5 energies
18 energy
1 enervate
1 enfant
2 enfeebled
1 enforce
2 enforced
12 engaged
1 engagement
1 engender
2 engendered
1 engines
37 england
23 english
1 englishman's
1 engravings
4 enigma
1 enigmas
2 enigmatical
1 enjoined
13 enjoy
6 enjoyed
2 enjoying
11 enjoyment
2 enjoyments

1	enjoys	2	est-ce	1	excusable	1	extremes
2	enlarge	2	established	11	excuse	4	extremities
2	enlarged	6	establishment	2	excused	4	extremity
1	enlighten	10	estate	1	execrations	1	extricate
3	enlightened	1	estates	2	execute	1	extricating
2	enlist	2	esteem	2	executed	2	extrication
1	enmity	2	esteemed	3	execution	2	exult
1	enormous	2	estimable	13	exercise	1	exultant
107	enough	3	estranged	3	exercised	2	exultation
1	enounce	2	estrangement	1	exercises	1	exulted
2	enounced	15	et	4	exert	1	exultingly
1	enrage	4	eternal	3	exertion	118	eye
1	enriched	4	eternity	2	exhaused	1	eye-brows
1	enrolled	1	etes	3	exhausted	2	eyebrow
1	ensconced	1	etiolated	2	exhaustion	9	eyebrows
1	enslaved	2	etre	2	exhibit	2	eyelash
1	ensnares	1	etymology	1	exhibition	1	eyelashes
2	ensued	1	eulogiums	1	exhilarating	2	eyelid
3	ensuing	7	europe	1	exhilaration	1	eyelids
1	ensure	1	eutychus	1	exhort	184	eyes
2	entailed	1	ev'n	1	exhortations	96	eyre
2	entanglement	1	evacuated	1	exigencies	1	eyre's
18	enter	1	evade	1	exigency	1	eyres
54	entered	1	evaded	3	exile	1	eyrie
12	entering	2	evangelical	1	exiled	1	f
1	enterprise	2	evasive	7	exist	1	faal
2	enters	3	eve	38	existence	2	fable
7	entertain	120	even	2	existent	2	fabric
6	entertained	1	even-tide	3	exists	1	facade
1	entertaining	86	evening	2	exit	190	face
4	entertainment	2	evenings	1	exodus	2	faced
1	enthusiasm	18	event	1	exonerated	14	faces
1	enthusiastic	2	eventful	1	exorcised	1	facile
1	enticed	2	eventide	2	exotics	17	fact
5	entire	5	events	2	expand	3	facts
11	entirely	1	eventually	7	expanded	11	faculties
1	entitle	158	ever	1	expanding	4	faculty
1	entitled	1	ever-shifting	2	expanse	3	fade
1	entrails	1	ever-torturing	3	expansive	6	faded
17	entrance	1	ever-watchful	19	expect	2	fading
2	entranced	1	evergreen	1	expectancy	2	fagged
1	entrapped	104	every	3	expectant	2	fagging
6	entreat	1	every-day	5	expectation	5	fail
9	entreated	11	everybody	3	expectations	12	failed
1	entreaties	16	everything	39	expected	2	failing
3	entreating	8	everywhere	11	expecting	2	fails
1	entrust	5	evidence	2	expects	3	failure
3	entrusted	2	evidences	1	expediency	1	faim
1	entwine	4	evident	5	expedient	6	fain
1	entwined	20	evidently	1	expel	8	faint
1	enumeration	12	evil	1	expelled	2	faintest
1	enunciated	3	evince	2	expense	2	fainting
1	enunciation	3	evinced	1	expensive	3	faintly
5	enveloped	3	evincing	20	experience	2	faintness
1	envelopes	1	ewe	14	experienced	35	fair
1	envious	2	ewer	1	experiences	2	fairer
1	environed	1	ewers	2	experiencing	123	fairfax
2	environs	1	ex-act-ly	3	experiment	14	fairfax's
3	envy	5	exact	1	expiate	1	fairies
1	epicure	1	exacted	1	expiating	3	fairly
1	episode	8	exacting	4	expired	15	fairy
1	epistles	1	exaction	17	explain	1	fairy-born
2	epithet	9	exactly	13	explained	3	fairy-like
10	equal	1	exactness	1	explaining	1	faisait
6	equality	1	exacts	1	explains	12	faith
1	equalling	2	exaggerate	18	explanation	15	faithful
15	equally	3	exaggerated	4	explanations	7	faithfully
1	equals	3	exalted	1	explanatory	1	falcon
1	equestrian	3	examination	2	explicit	1	falcon-eye
1	equestrians	9	examine	1	exploits	21	fall
1	equilibrium	18	examined	1	explore	14	fallen
1	equipages	5	examining	1	explored	1	fallibilities
1	equipped	6	example	1	explosion	2	fallible
1	equitable	1	examples	1	expose	7	falling
1	equity	1	exasperation	3	exposed	3	falls
3	equivalent	1	exceeding	2	expostulate	9	false
2	equivocal	2	exceedingly	1	expostulations	6	falsehood
2	era	1	excel	2	exposure	2	falter
2	eradicate	1	excelled	17	express	1	faltering
2	eradicated	2	excellence	22	expressed	1	falters
1	erase	1	excellences	1	expresses	9	familiar
41	ere	11	excellent	2	expressing	1	familiarly
10	erect	1	excellently	26	expression	1	families
1	erected	20	except	3	expressive	38	family
1	erection	2	excepted	1	expressly	1	family's
1	erectness	3	exception	8	exquisite	3	famine
1	erewhile	1	excesses	2	exquisitely	5	famished
1	ermine	1	excessive	1	extant	2	famous
6	err	7	exchange	4	extend	1	fanatic's
7	errand	4	exchanged	4	extended	7	fancied
1	erred	1	exchanging	3	extending	1	fancies
2	erring	1	excitable	2	extends	26	fancy
10	error	1	excitation	2	extensive	2	fancying
1	errors	5	excite	2	extent	1	fand
6	escape	22	excited	2	exterior	2	fang
3	escaped	17	excitement	2	external	1	fans
1	escaping	1	excitements	2	externally	2	fantastic
1	eschew	1	excites	1	externals	116	far
2	eschewed	3	exciting	8	extinguished	1	far-distant
27	eshton	44	exclaimed	1	extinguisher	1	farce
2	eshton's	3	exclaiming	1	extinguishing	4	fare
1	eshtons	2	exclamation	1	extirpate	13	farewell
2	especial	1	exclamations	1	extort	2	farm
21	especially	5	exclude	2	extorted	1	farm-house
1	espouse	4	excluded	2	extract	2	farmer
1	espousing	1	excluding	1	extracted	2	farmers'
1	esq	1	exclusive	1	extraneous	1	farming
2	essay	1	excrescence	5	extraordinary	1	farms
1	essence	1	excruciating	2	extravagance	14	farther
1	essences	3	excursion	7	extreme	5	farthest
5	essential	1	excursions	1	extremely	2	fascinated

Count	Word	Count	Word	Count	Word	Count	Word
4	fascinating	7	ferndean	1	five-and-twenty	2	folding
3	fascination	1	ferny	1	five-pound	1	folding-doors
11	fashion	1	ferocity	7	fix	5	folds
4	fashionable	1	ferret	22	fixed	5	foliage
1	fashionable-l-ooking	1	fertilized	3	fixedly	2	folk
1	fashioned	4	fervent	1	fixedness	1	folk's
1	fashions	2	fervently	3	fixing	1	folks
44	fast	2	fervid	1	fixity	21	follow
10	fasten	6	fervour	2	fixture	56	followed
16	fastened	1	festal	1	flabby	1	follower
5	fastening	1	festive	1	flag	1	followers
3	faster	1	festooned	2	flakes	13	following
2	fastidious	1	festoons	15	flame	3	follows
1	fasting	25	fetch	1	flamed	7	folly
2	fat	3	fetched	3	flames	1	fomented
3	fatal	2	fetid	2	flaming	16	fond
1	fatality	1	fetter	1	flang	1	fonder
18	fate	5	fettered	1	flanked	3	fondly
2	fated	4	fetters	1	flanking	3	fondness
1	fateful	1	feuille	4	flash	15	food
1	fates	12	fever	3	flashed	12	fool
48	father	1	fever-room	2	flashing	1	fool's
6	father's	1	fevered	1	flat	1	fooled
1	fatherland	12	feverish	1	flatness	2	foolish
1	fatherly	1	feverishly	7	flatter	28	foot
4	fathom	82	few	5	flattered	3	footing
1	fathomless	2	fewer	1	flatterers	6	footman
7	fatigue	1	fibre	1	flattery	2	footmen
1	fatigued	2	fiction	2	flavour	3	footstool
2	fatuus	1	fiddler	1	flaw	1295	for
1	faugh	3	fidelity	1	flaxen	1	forage
16	fault	1	fidget	2	flayed	3	forbade
1	faulties	1	fie	1	flecked	3	forbear
14	faults	20	field	6	fled	2	forbearance
1	faut	18	fields	3	flee	2	forbearing
1	faux	7	fiend	1	fleet	1	forbid
9	favour	1	fiendish	2	fleeting	5	forbidden
4	favourable	1	fiendishly	30	flesh	2	forbidding
6	favoured	13	fierce	1	fleshless	1	forbore
6	favourite	1	fiercest	1	fleshly	20	force
4	favours	5	fiery	1	fleurs	22	forced
1	fawkes	9	fifteen	9	flew	2	forces
1	fawn	1	fifteenth	1	flexibility	1	fore
62	fear	2	fifth	1	flexible	1	foreboding
1	fear'd	10	fifty	1	flexible-looking	1	forefinger
30	feared	1	fig	1	flicker	1	forego
14	fearful	1	fight	1	flickered	1	foregone
1	fearfulness	1	figments	1	flickering	4	foreground
4	fearing	1	figurative	1	flickers	31	forehead
1	fearless	2	figuratively	6	flight	7	foreign
13	tears	25	figure	1	fling	2	foreigner
1	feasible	3	figured	1	flinging	1	foreigners
2	feast	6	figures	3	flint	1	forelock
3	feasted	2	file	1	flinty	1	forenoon
1	feat	1	filed	1	flirted	2	foresight
1	feather	1	filial	1	flit	4	forest
1	featherbeds	1	filing	1	flitted	1	forest-aisle
2	feathers	1	filip	1	flittered	1	forest-dell
7	feature	7	fill	1	flitting	1	forest-high
45	features	36	filled	1	float	2	foretold
2	february	1	fillette	2	floated	1	forewarned
5	fed	2	filling	1	floating	3	forgave
3	fee	1	fillip	4	flock	45	forget
14	feeble	1	filthy	1	flocked	1	forgets
1	feeble-minded	1	final	1	flog	4	forgetting
1	feebleness	5	finally	1	flogged	1	forgie
1	feeblest	76	find	5	flood	1	forging
1	feebly	8	finding	1	flood-gates	16	forgive
4	feed	2	finds	2	floods	4	forgiven
1	feeding	57	fine	14	floor	2	forgiveness
1	feeds	1	fine-looking	1	flooring	1	forgiving
88	feel	1	finely	2	florence	13	forgot
65	feeling	3	finer	1	flour	21	forgotten
46	feelings	3	finest	1	flourishing	1	forigve
7	feels	13	finger	1	floury	1	fork
1	fees	20	fingers	13	flow	5	forlorn
42	feet	5	finish	1	flowed	1	forlornness
3	feigned	23	finished	10	flower	38	form
1	felix	1	fir-cones	1	flower-roots	6	formal
56	fell	115	fire	1	flower-sprinkled	1	formalist
1	felling	3	fire-irons	1	floweret	1	formally
8	fellow	1	fire-light	30	flowers	20	formed
1	fellow-being	1	fire-lit	4	flowery	16	former
1	fellow-beings	1	fire-place	3	flowing	4	formerly
2	fellow-creature	1	fire-places	3	flown	2	formidable
3	fellow-creatures	3	fire-side	1	flows	4	forming
2	fellow-feeling	1	fire-spirit	1	fluctuations	2	formless
2	fellow-labourer	2	fireless	3	fluency	8	forms
1	fellow-missionary	7	fires	1	fluent	1	formula
1	fellow-pupils	6	fireside	1	fluently	1	forres
1	fellow-servants	15	firm	6	flung	1	forsake
1	fellow-soldier's	1	firmament	1	flurried	4	forsaken
1	fellow-students	5	firmer	2	flush	1	forsakes
1	fellow-teachers	5	firmly	6	flushed	1	forsaking
1	fellow-worms	3	firmness	1	fluttered	2	forsook
160	felt	4	firs	1	fluttering	1	fort-night
5	female	180	first	4	fly	1	forte
1	femmes	2	first-born	4	flying	10	forth
4	fence	1	first-rate	3	foam	3	forthwith
3	fender	2	firstly	1	foaming	4	fortitude
2	ferment	2	fish	1	foamy	17	fortnight
1	fern-banks	1	fissure	1	foe	4	fortunate
		20	fit	3	fog	10	fortunately
		3	fitful	1	fog-bred	32	fortune
		1	fitly	1	foil	1	fortune-teller
		2	fits	1	fois	1	fortune-tellers
		6	fitted	4	fold	5	fortunes
		4	fitting	16	folded	8	forty
		1	fitzjames			1	forty-five
		36	five			27	forward

1 forwarded	3 froze	79 gave	5 glances
10 forwards	8 frozen	17 gay	9 glancing
1 foster	7 fruit	21 gaze	5 glare
2 fostering	1 fruit-parterr-es	21 gazed	3 glared
3 fought	2 fruition	1 gazelle-eyes	1 glaring
4 foul	1 fruitless	1 gazer	35 glass
1 fouler	1 fuel	2 gazes	1 glass-door
124 found	2 fulfil	10 gazing	2 glasses
1 foundation	4 fulfilled	1 gedanken	1 glassiness
1 foundations	1 fulfilling	5 gem	1 glassing
2 foundry	1 fulfilment	1 gemmed	7 glazed
2 fount	80 full	3 gems	1 glazing
1 fountain	1 full-blown	1 genealogy	11 gleam
1 fountaine	1 full-grown	18 general	8 gleamed
33 four	1 full-leaved	1 generalities	4 gleaming
1 four-post	20 fully	21 generally	5 gleams
1 fours	1 fully-underst-ood	1 generated	1 glean
3 fourteen	1 fulminating	1 generation	7 glee
6 fourth	1 fumbled	2 generations	2 gleeful
1 foxglove	2 fume	2 generosity	1 gleefully
2 fraction	2 fumes	8 generous	4 glen
1 fractious	2 fun	1 generously	2 glide
1 fragile	2 funchal	1 genesis	6 glided
1 fragile-looki-ng	2 function	13 genial	1 gliding
1 fragment	1 functionary	1 genially	2 glimmered
2 fragmentary	1 fund	2 genii	10 glimpse
2 fragments	2 funds	7 genius	2 glimpses
4 fragrance	5 funeral	2 genteel	1 glistened
5 fragrant	2 fur	20 gentle	2 glistening
2 frail	2 furbish	1 gentle-temper-ed	1 glitter
27 frame	4 furious	33 gentleman	6 glittering
7 framed	1 furiously	4 gentleman's	2 glitters
1 frames	2 furnace	1 gentleman-hig-hwayman	3 gloaming
4 framing	3 furnish	1 gentleman-like	2 globe
3 france	6 furnished	2 gentlemanlike	3 globes
4 frank	15 furniture	42 gentlemen	13 gloom
1 franker	1 furred	3 gentlemen's	15 gloomy
3 frankly	2 furrowed	3 gentleness	1 glorify
3 frankness	1 furrowing	1 gentler	16 glorious
11 frantic	1 furs	1 gentlest	7 glory
2 franz	42 further	14 gently	1 gloss
1 fraternal	1 furtherance	4 gentry	1 glossiest
2 fraternity	1 furthers	10 genuine	1 glossily
1 fraternization	2 furtively	2 geography	1 glove
1 fraudulent	1 furtune	10 george	6 gloves
2 freak	14 fury	42 georgiana	13 glow
1 freaks	1 fuses	2 georgiana's	4 glowed
4 frederic	1 fustian	1 georgy	6 glowing
3 frederick	29 future	1 germ	2 gnawed
23 free	1 gables	14 german	1 gnawing
2 free-born	6 gaiety	1 germinate	1 gnome
1 freed	4 gaily	6 germs	249 go
4 freedom	5 gain	5 gesture	1 goaded
1 freedoms	8 gained	4 gestures	2 goblin
10 freely	2 gait	92 get	1 goblin's
1 freer	1 galaxy	7 gets	1 goblin-laught-er
2 freezing	6 gale	21 getting	2 goblins
1 freezingly	2 gales	1 gewichte	95 god
41 french	1 gall	1 ghastliness	14 god's
1 frenzied	5 gallant	8 ghastly	1 gods
3 frenzy	1 gallantry	10 ghost	6 goes
14 frequent	1 galled	1 ghostliness	71 going
2 frequented	29 gallery	2 ghostly	20 gold
14 frequently	1 gallery-wall	2 ghosts	1 gold-ringed
23 fresh	1 gallic	1 ghoul	1 gold-wrought
1 fresh-looking	1 galling	3 giacinta	9 golden
1 freshened	2 gallop	5 giant	1 golden-eyed
2 freshening	2 galloped	1 giants	1 goldsmith's
1 freshens	1 gallows	1 gibberish	66 gone
1 fresher	1 gambles	3 gibson	186 good
1 freshest	1 gambols	1 gibsons	1 good-afternoon
1 freshly	8 game	2 giddy	9 good-bye
5 freshness	1 games	6 gift	5 good-evening
2 fretted	1 gander	3 gifted	2 good-humoured
2 fretting	1 ganges	5 gifts	6 good-morning
1 fried	1 gape	1 giggled	6 good-natured
24 friend	5 gaping	1 giggling	18 good-night
4 friend's	4 garb	1 gild	1 good-sized
5 friendless	28 garden	2 gilding	1 good-tempered
1 friendliness	1 garden-beds	1 gilt	2 good-will
9 friendly	1 garden-coat	2 gin	18 goodness
35 friends	1 gardener	1 ginger	1 gooseberry-tree
7 friendship	1 gardening	1 gingham	1 gooseberries
1 frieze	1 gardens	2 gipsies	1 gooseberry
1 fright	1 gardez-vous	7 gipsy	1 gore
3 frightened	1 garland	1 gipsy's	2 gorge
1 frightens	2 garlands	1 gipsy-vagabond	2 gorged
7 frightful	5 garments	1 gipsying	1 gory
3 frigid	1 garnish	1 girandoles	3 gospel
1 frigidity	1 garret	3 girdle	1 gossamer
1 frills	1 garrett's	1 girdled	3 gossip
1 fringed	1 garrulous	3 girdling	101 got
3 frivolous	1 garters	76 girl	2 gouvernante
6 fro	1 gas-light	1 girl's	1 governed
1 fro'	1 gasp	1 girl-bride	29 governess
12 frock	4 gasped	42 girls	2 governess's
8 frocks	1 gastronomical	129 give	8 governesses
1 frolicksome	12 gate	63 given	1 governessing
717 from	1 gate-post	1 giver	1 governness
34 front	22 gates	7 gives	11 gown
3 front-door	41 gateshead	6 giving	49 grace
8 frost	2 gateshead-hall	1 glacier	11 graceful
1 frost-flowers	7 gather	44 glad	3 gracefully
1 frosts	24 gathered	1 gladdening	1 graces
3 frosty	12 gathering	1 gladly	3 gracious
3 frown	2 gathers	1 gladsome	1 graciously
1 frowned	1 gauging	1 glamour	1 gradations
3 frowning	3 gaunt	41 glance	1 gradual
1 frowningly	1 gauzy	13 glanced	5 gradually
1 frowns			1 grafinnen

1 grain	12 grown	1 handle	17 hay
2 grains	1 growning	2 handled	1 hay-field
5 grammar	2 grows	3 handling	1 hay-hill
2 granby	2 growth	1 handmaid	3 hay-lane
6 grand	1 grudging	78 hands	1 hay-makers
1 granddame's	2 gruel	35 handsome	2 hazarded
1 grande	1 gruff	1 handsome-feat-	1 hazarding
1 grandest	1 gruffly	ured	1 hazardous
4 grandeur	2 gryce	1 handsomely	2 haze
3 grandfather	2 guarantee	1 handsomer	5 hazel
1 grandson	16 guard	1 handsomest	1890 he
3 grange	6 guarded	1 handwriting	4 he's
3 granite	1 guardedness	1 handy	129 head
1 granite-hewn	4 guardian	2 hang	1 head-dress
5 grant	2 guardian's	6 hanging	1 head-stones
3 granted	1 guardianship	7 hangings	1 headed
1 grapes	1 guarding	38 hannah	3 headlong
2 grappled	1 guards	1 hannah's	6 heads
8 grasp	8 guess	1 handkerchief	1 headstone
3 grasped	4 guessed	1 hapless	3 headstrong
1 grasping	1 guessing	6 happen	3 heal
1 grasps	4 guest	27 happened	3 healed
6 grass	6 guests	2 happening	1 heals
3 grass-grown	7 guidance	1 happens	17 health
2 grass-plat	7 guide	4 happier	4 healthy
1 grassy	1 guided	1 happiest	1 heap
6 grate	1 guides	4 happily	1 heaps
1 grated	2 guiding	23 happiness	88 hear
8 grateful	4 guilt	54 happy	180 heard
1 grates	1 guiltlessness	1 har	1 hearer
3 gratification	1 guilty	1 harangue	18 hearing
5 gratified	1 guinea	1 harass	1 hears
2 gratify	1 guineas	4 harassed	1 hearse
3 grating	1 guise	3 harassing	162 heart
11 gratitude	3 gulf	1 harbourage	7 heart's
31 grave	1 gulliver	2 harboured	1 heart-fire
1 grave-mounds	2 gulliver's	42 hard	2 heart-strings
1 graved	1 gulph	1 hard-favoured	1 heart-weary
3 gravel	1 guns	2 hard-featured	2 heart-wrung
3 gravel-walk	1 gurgled	4 hard-hearted	27 hearth
4 gravely	1 gurt	1 hard-wrung	1 hearth-rug
3 graven	3 gush	2 harden	1 hearths
2 graves	2 gushed	1 hardened	2 hearthstone
5 gravity	2 gust	1 hardens	1 heartier
17 gray	1 gusts	1 harder	4 heartily
1 gray-headed	1 gusty	1 hardest	5 heartless
117 great	1 guy	1 hardiest	9 hearts
7 greater	5 gytrash	1 hardihood	3 hearty
3 greatest	1 gytrash-like	1 hardily	3 heat
1 greatheart	5 ha	36 hardly	16 heath
4 greatly	1 habergeon	2 hardness	1 heath-bell
1 greatness	1 habiller	3 hardships	1 heathen
3 grecian	8 habit	4 hardy	2 heathens
4 greek	2 habitation	1 harem	1 heather
27 green	17 habits	1 harlequin's	1 heats
1 greener	7 habitual	1 harlot	7 heaved
1 greenland	4 habitually	4 harm	30 heaven
1 greenness	1 habituated	1 harmed	2 heaven's
1 greet	1 habituating	1 harming	1 heaven-bestow-
3 greeted	3 hackneyed	1 harmless	ed
1 greeting	1467 had	3 harmonious	2 heavenly
2 gregarious	1 hadn't	1 harmoniously	1 heavily-laden
27 grew	3 hag	1 harmonized	1 heaviness
7 grey	1 haggard	4 harmony	2 heaving
1 greys	1 hailed	1 harnessed	20 heavy
16 grief	103 half	1 harnessing	1 heavy-looking
1 griefs	1 half-blown	2 harp	1 hebdomadal
3 grieve	1 half-comprehe-	12 harsh	1 hebrew
2 grieved	nded	1 harsh-featured	1 hebrides
1 grieving	2 half-dozen	2 harshly	1 hector
1 grievous	2 half-effaced	2 harshness	9 hedge
1 grilled	1 half-expecting	4 harvest	1 hedge-sparrow-
14 grim	1 half-fancying	1 harvest-day	's
2 grimace	1 half-filled	243 has	6 hedges
2 grimaces	1 half-forgotten	7 haste	2 heeded
1 grimacing	1 half-frozen	1 hasted	2 heeding
2 grimly	1 half-hid	6 hasten	2 heel
1 grimms	1 half-holiday	16 hastened	1 heidelberg
2 grimsby	1 half-hour	1 hastening	5 height
1 grimy	1 half-insincere	1 hastens	2 heights
1 grinding	1 half-moon	12 hastily	1 heir
1 grinning	1 half-opened	9 hasty	1 heir-looms
2 grip	2 half-past	10 hat	3 heiress
1 gripe	1 half-reclining	1 hat-brim	44 held
1 grizzled	1 half-ruined	24 hate	58 helen
2 groan	1 half-scared	11 hated	5 helen's
4 groaned	1 half-sister	4 hateful	11 hell
1 groomsmen	1 half-slice	2 hating	39 help
1 grope	1 half-smothered	4 hatred	1 help-meet
4 groped	1 half-start	1 hats	16 helped
2 groping	1 half-submerged	1 hatted	1 helper
1 gropingly	2 half-told	1 haught	2 helpers
2 gross	1 half-wild	2 haughtily	4 helping
1 grotesque	1 half-worn	1 haughtiness	1 helpless
26 ground	67 hall	9 haughty	1 helplessness
1 ground-ivy	2 hall-door	1 haughty-looki-	1 helpmeet
1 ground-sunshi-	1 hall-front	ng	5 hem
ne	1 haloed	1 hauled	1 hemmed
1 grounded	3 halted	5 haunt	3 hence
13 grounds	2 halves	9 haunted	2 henceforth
1 groundwork	1 ham	2 haunting	2 henceforward
11 group	6 hamlet	1 haunts	5 henry
1 grouped	1 hampered	1 hauteur	1 henrys
4 groups	161 hand	1 havannah	1 hepburn
2 grove	1 handbreadth	1074 have	1714 her
1 grovelled	2 handbreadth	1 haven	5 herald
2 grovelling	7 handed	2 haven't	1 heralds
2 groves	4 handful	84 having	3 herbs
11 grow	1 handiwork	1 haws	1 hercules
5 growing	14 handkerchief	1 hawthorn	3 herd
2 growled		1 hawthorn-bloom	1 herded

193	here	1	homily	11	hurry	8	impatience
2	hereafter	8	honest	1	hurrying	9	impatient
3	heretofore	2	honey	13	hurt	3	impatiently
1	heritage	1	honey-dew	1	hurting	1	impeded
1	hermit	3	honey-moon	29	husband	6	impediment
1	hermit's	1	honeyed	6	husband's	1	impediments
3	hero	9	honour	1	husbands	1	impenetrabili-
1	heroes	4	honourable	12	hush		ty
4	heroic	3	honoured	8	hushed	1	imperative
1	heroic-looking	2	hoof	1	hushes	4	imperfect
1	herring	2	hoofs	1	hushing	2	imperfection
13	hers	1	hooped	1	husk	1	imperial
57	herself	74	hope	1	husky	3	imperious
1	hervor	7	hoped	1	hybrid	1	imperiously
2	hesitate	1	hopeful	1	hyena	1	imperturbably
2	hesitatingly	7	hopeless	3	hymn	1	impetuosity
4	hesitation	2	hopelessly	1	hypochondria	4	impetuous
1	heterogeneous	11	hopes	2	hypochondriac	3	impetus
1	heures	2	hoping	1	hypocrisy	1	implacable
1	hew	1	hopped	1	hypocrite	1	implicitly
1	hewers	8	horizon	1	hypothesis	1	implied
1	hewn	2	horizontal	1	hysteria	1	implore
2	hews	1	horizontally	1	hysterical	1	implored
2	hiatus	4	horn	1	hysterics	1	imply
7	hid	1	horned	7129	i	5	import
7	hidden	1	horny	7	i'	8	importance
8	hideous	2	horrible	5	i'd	2	important
1	hideously	11	horror	64	i'll	1	imported
2	hides	2	horrors	15	i'm	1	importunate
1	hiding	25	horse	14	i've	2	importune
1	hiding-place	2	horse's	15	ice	1	importuned
1	hied	3	horse-chestnut	1	ice-cold	1	importunes
1	hieroglyphics	1	horse-hoofs	3	iceberg	1	importunity
1	hierophant	1	horseback	1	iceland	1	impose
1	hierophant's	2	horseman	1	ich	6	imposing
49	high	7	horses	2	icily	1	impossibiliti-
2	high-backed	1	hose	1	icy		es
1	high-born	1	hospitable	50	idea	23	impossible
1	high-hung	3	hospital	9	ideal	2	impostor
1	high-piled	4	hospitality	10	ideas	3	impotent
12	higher	4	host	4	identity	1	impracticable
2	highest	1	hostess	1	idiocy	2	impress
1	highlander's	2	hostile	4	idiot	6	impressed
1	highlow	1	hostility	1	idiotic	2	impressible
2	highly	20	hot	1	idiots	1	impressing
20	hill	6	hotel	2	idle	16	impression
1	hill-hollow	1	hothouse	1	idling	1	impressions
1	hill-peak	121	hour	4	idol	3	impressive
1	hill-sent	4	hour's	1	idolatrous	1	imprisoned
1	hill-side	1	houri	1	idyls	1	improbable
1	hill-sides	5	hourly	2	ie	1	impromptu
2	hill-top	33	hours	535	if	2	impropriety
1	hillo	3	hours'	1	ignis	6	improved
1	hillocks	153	house	1	ignis-fatuus--	6	improvement
19	hills	1	house-accounts		like	1	improvements
2	hilly	1	house-front	2	ignoble	1	improvised
710	him	1	house-keeper	1	ignominious	1	imps
1	himalayan	1	house-maid's	1	ignominy	3	impudence
67	himself	1	housebreakers	7	ignorance	1	impudent
1	hind	1	housed	12	ignorant	8	impulse
1	hind'rance	6	household	1	ignus	3	impulses
1	hinder	12	housekeeper	5	il	1	impulsive
1	hinderances	1	housekeeper's	26	ill	1	impulsively
1	hindering	4	housemaid	1	ill-condition-	1	impure
7	hindostanee	2	housemaid's		ed	2	imputation
1	hinges	9	houses	1	ill-humour	2750	in
4	hint	1	housewifely	1	ill-temper	1	in-door
1	hinted	2	hovered	1	ill-treated	1	in-doors
4	hints	2	hovering	1	illegal	1	inaccuracy
1	hips	274	how	1	illegitimate	2	inactive
1	hire	65	however	6	illness	1	inadequacy
5	hired	1	howl	1	illuminated	1	inadequate
1	hireling	3	howling	2	illumination	1	inadvertently
1	hireling's	3	hue	3	illumined	1	inaminate
1	hiring	1	hueless	1	illustrated	1	inammorata
1203	his	2	hues	2	illustration	1	inanimate
2	hiss	4	huge	5	image	3	inanition
12	history	6	hum	1	imaginable	5	inarticulate
4	hit	43	human	1	imaginary	1	inattention
1	hitch	1	human-bred	6	imagination	1	inaudible
2	hither	1	humanities	1	imagination's	1	inborn
18	hitherto	2	humanity	11	imagine	8	incapable
1	hoar	13	humble	10	imagined	1	incapacity
1	hoard	3	humbled	1	imagining	2	incarnate
1	hoarding	1	humbler	1	imbecile	2	incense
1	hoards	2	humblest	1	imbecility	2	incensed
2	hoarse	1	humbling	1	imbibed	1	incessant
5	hoary	1	humbly	1	imitating	1	incessantly
1	hob	2	humbug	1	immeasurable	5	inch
1	hoist	1	humid	1	immeasureably	13	incident
3	hoisted	3	humiliation	4	immediate	1	incidents
28	hold	4	humility	22	immediately	2	incivility
12	holding	1	hummed	5	immense	3	inclement
2	holds	2	humming	1	immobility	7	inclination
1	holes	3	humour	1	immoderately	2	inclinations
5	holiday	1	humoured	1	immoral	2	incline
2	holidays	4	humph	3	immortal	8	inclined
4	holland	15	hundred	1	immortality	1	inclines
15	hollow	3	hundreds	1	immprovement	1	inclining
1	hollows	13	hung	1	immutable	1	inclose
3	holly	12	hunger	1	immutably	1	inclosed
1	holly-bushes	12	hungry	1	imp	1	include
1	hollyhocks	1	hunt	1	imp-like	4	included
1	holm	1	hunting	1	impalpable	3	including
4	holy	1	hurl	7	impart	1	income
3	homage	1	hurling	3	imparted	1	incommunicati-
81	home	1	hurrah	3	imparting		ve
2	homeless	1	hurricane	2	imparts	1	incompetency
1	homely	2	hurricanes	3	impassable	3	incomprehensi-
1	homes	16	hurried	1	impassible		ble
3	homeward	1	hurriedly	2	impassioned	1	incongruous

1 inconsiderate-ness	1 infirmity	1 instigated	6 invited
1 inconsistent	2 inflamed	4 instilled	4 inviting
1 inconsistently	1 inflammatory	11 instinct	2 invoke
1 inconsolable	1 inflated	1 instinctive	1 invoked
1 incorruptible	1 inflation	7 instinctively	11 involuntarily
1 increase	1 inflections	10 institution	6 involuntary
3 increased	2 inflexible	1 instruction	2 involved
1 increases	6 inflict	1 instructor	14 inward
1 increasing	2 inflicted	2 instructress	7 inwardly
2 incredible	1 inflictions	9 instrument	1 irate
2 incredulity	18 influence	3 instruments	6 ire
3 incredulous	6 influenced	2 insufferable	1 ireful
1 incredulously	1 influx	1 insufficient	7 ireland
1 incubi	7 inform	3 insult	3 irids
3 incumbent	1 informality	1 insulted	1 irked
1 incumbrance	1 informant	1 insulting	3 irksome
1 incurred	15 information	4 insuperable	12 iron
1 incurring	7 informed	4 insupportable	1 iron-foundry
1 indebted	1 informer	1 insurrection	1 ironical
114 indeed	1 informs	1 integrity	1 ironing
3 indefatigable	2 infused	3 intellect	1 ironing-table
4 indefinite	1 ing	3 intellectual	1 irrational
2 indelibly	1 ingenious	7 intelligence	3 irregular
1 indemnity	1 ingenuous	5 intelligent	1 irregularities
3 independence	63 ingram	2 intelligible	2 irregularity
1 independency	7 ingram's	1 intemperate	1 irreligious
14 independent	1 ingratitude	3 intend	1 irrepressible
3 indescribable	1 ingredient	11 intended	1 irresistible
1 indescribably	1 inhabit	2 intends	1 irresistibly
1 indestructible	1 inhabitant	3 intensely	1 irresolute
17 india	2 inhabitants	2 intensity	1 irrevocably
1 indiaman	3 inhabited	5 intent	1 irritate
11 indian	2 inhale	14 intention	6 irritated
2 indian-rubber	1 inherit	4 intentions	1 irritating
2 indicate	2 inherited	1 intercession	5 irritation
4 indicated	1 inhospitable	3 interchanged	1351 is
1 indicating	1 initial	4 intercourse	2 island
1 indicative	1 initials	32 interest	2 isles
4 indies	2 injudicious	7 interested	2 isn't
3 indifference	1 injudiciously	8 interesting	3 isolated
4 indifferent	2 injure	3 interests	3 isolation
1 indifferently	5 injured	1 interfere	1 israelitish
2 indigence	1 injuries	3 interference	4 issue
1 indigent	1 injurious	2 interim	5 issued
4 indignant	2 injury	2 interior	1 issuing
5 indignation	2 injustice	1 interjected	2386 it
1 indirect	1 ink	3 interlocutor	9 it's
2 indiscretion	1 inkling	1 interlocutor's	6 italian
1 indiscriminat-ely	6 inmate	1 interlocutrice	1 italy
2 indisposed	8 inmates	2 interloper	2 item
1 indissoluble	1 inmost	1 interlude	1 iteration
1 indissolubly	10 inn	1 interment	317 its
1 inditing	1 inn-passage	1 interminable	13 itself
7 individual	5 innate	5 interposed	4 ivory
1 individuals	1 innately	2 interpreted	6 ivy
1 indolence	6 inner	2 interpreter	2 j'ai
2 indomitable	3 innocence	1 interpreting	1 j'y
2 induce	5 innocent	1 interprets	2 jack
2 induced	1 innovation	1 interrogator	1 jacket
1 inducement	1 innovations	1 interrupt	2 jail
1 inducements	1 inopportune	15 interrupted	5 jamaica
5 indulge	10 inquire	3 interruption	1 james
2 indulged	26 inquired	12 interval	335 jane
4 indulgence	4 inquiries	14 intervals	5 jane's
1 indulgent	1 inquiringly	3 intervened	21 janet
2 industrious	13 inquiry	1 intervenes	1 janian
1 industry	3 inquisitive	1 intervening	9 january
1 ineffable	1 inquisitive-looking	4 interview	1 jargon
1 ineffectual	1 inquisitiveness	1 interweaving	1 jasmine
1 ineligible	1 inroad	1 interwoven	2 jaw
1 ineradicable	1 insalubrious	1 intimacy	1 jaws
1 inertness	5 insane	5 intimate	1 jay
1 inestimable	2 insanity	10 intimated	13 je
4 inevitable	1 insatiable	1 intimates	4 jealous
4 inevitably	1 insatiate	2 intimating	9 jealousy
1 inexcusable	3 inscribed	1 intimation	1 jeannette
1 inexhaustible	2 inscription	1 intimidated	1 jellies
4 inexorable	2 inscrutable	265 into	1 jerked
2 inexpedient	1 insect	7 intolerable	1 jest
2 inexperience	1 insecurity	1 intolerably	2 jests
3 inexperienced	4 insensible	1 intonation	3 jesus
3 inexplicable	5 inside	1 intractable	1 jet
1 inexpresible	1 insight	1 intricate	5 jetty
4 inexpressible	5 insignificant	1 intrinsic	1 jeune
2 inexpressibly	1 insinuation	3 introduce	1 jew-usurer
1 inextricable	2 insipid	10 introduced	2 jewel
1 inextricably	3 insist	4 introduction	1 jewel-casket
1 infallible	4 insisted	2 introductory	1 jeweller's
2 infamous	1 insists	3 intrude	9 jewels
1 infamy	3 insolence	1 intruded	1 jews
5 infant	3 insolent	1 intruder	1 jingling
2 infantine	1 insolently	2 intruders	1 joan
1 infatuated	1 insolvable	2 intrusion	1 job
1 infatuatedly	1 insolvency	1 intuitive	1 job's
4 infection	3 inspection	1 inundation	184 john
1 infects	1 inspector	1 inured	18 john's
1 infer	1 inspectors	1 invade	1 johnstone
1 inference	3 inspiration	1 invalid	8 join
7 inferior	2 inspire	2 invaluable	8 joined
3 inferiority	5 inspired	1 invariable	2 joining
1 inferiors	1 instal	1 invariably	2 joke
1 infernal	3 installed	2 invention	1 jolting
2 inferred	1 installing	1 inventive	1 jonah
1 infidels	13 instance	1 invest	1 jonas
2 infinite	1 instanced	3 invested	2 joubert
1 infinitude	1 instances	1 investigation	1 jouberts
1 infinitum	12 instant	1 investment	1 joues
1 infirm	24 instantly	1 inviolate	1 jour
1 infirmities	18 instead	6 invisible	19 journey
		3 invitation	1 journeyings
		2 invite	1 journeyman

1 jove	2 knives	34 laugh	1 liberated
1 jovial	4 knock	16 laughed	26 liberty
19 joy	11 knocked	8 laughing	24 library
1 joyfully	1 knocker	3 laughs	1 library-door
1 joyless	1 knocks	4 laughter	2 licence
3 joyous	3 knoll	1 launch	2 license
2 joys	3 knot	2 launched	1 licensed
1 jubilee	1 knots	1 laundress	3 lid
1 judas	2 knotted	1 laundress	2 lids
15 judge	2 knotty	1 laurel	16 lie
2 judged	225 know	3 laurel-walk	2 lied
3 judges	6 knowing	1 laurels	8 lies
3 judging	7 knowledge	1 lavish	157 life
20 judgment	24 known	2 lavishly	2 life's
2 judgments	21 knows	11 law	1 life-giving
5 judicious	2 knuckles	1 lawful	1 life-like
1 juggernaut	1 l'essaie	1 lawfully	2 life-long
2 julia	1 l'instant	1 lawgiver	1 lifeless
1 julia's	5 la	1 lawgivers	2 lifetime
2 july	1 labors	1 lawless	5 lift
3 jump	10 labour	12 lawn	29 lifted
4 jumped	1 labourer	2 laws	11 lifting
1 jumping	1 labourer's	4 lawyer	1 lifts
1 juncture	2 labourers	67 lay	1 ligature
7 june	1 labouring	4 laying	94 light
162 just	6 labours	3 le	1 light-footed
10 justice	8 lace	3 lea	1 light-hearted-ness
1 justification	1 lacerated	7 lead	4 lighted
6 justified	2 lachrymose	4 leader	1 lightens
1 justify	3 lack	1 leader's	1 lighter
1 justly	2 lacked	4 leading	4 lighting
1 juveniles	1 lad	2 leads	6 lightly
1 kaleidoscope	2 ladder	3 leaf	2 lightness
14 keen	3 laden	3 leafless	5 lightning
1 keen-eyed	76 ladies	3 leafy	2 lightning-str- uck
2 keener	2 ladies'	1 leagues	7 lights
3 keenest	1 ladle	26 leah	1 ligue
6 keenly	87 lady	1 leah's	363 like
1 keenness	7 lady's	5 lean	53 liked
72 keep	1 lady's-maid	7 leaned	2 likelihood
2 keeper	1 lady-clock	15 leaning	24 likely
13 keeping	1 lady-like	4 leans	7 likeness
5 keeps	1 lady-mother	8 leant	4 likes
1 keepsake	1 ladyship	1 leap	7 likewise
1 keepsakes	1 lagging	2 leapt	4 liking
1 ken	48 laid	19 learn	1 lilac
1 kennel	1 lair	8 learned	2 lilies
50 kept	3 lake	5 learning	1 lilliput
1 kernel	6 lamb	10 learnt	2 lily
18 key	1 lamb's	4 leas	1 lily-flower
2 key-hole	1 lamb-like	72 least	1 limb
4 keys	2 lambs	108 leave	7 limbs
1 kicked	2 lame	7 leaven	3 limit
1 kicking	1 lameness	12 leaves	3 limits
1 kidnappers	1 lamentable	22 leaving	1 limped
1 kidnapping	1 lamentations	2 lecture	1 limpid
5 kill	1 lameter	1 lectured	1 lindeness
3 killed	7 lamp	1 lectures	17 line
2 killing	1 lamplit	28 led	2 lineament
1 kills	2 lamps	1 ledge	11 lineaments
1 kin	1 lances	1 lee	2 lined
53 kind	15 land	144 left	4 linen
1 kind-natured	2 landed	2 leg	8 lines
4 kinder	1 landing	3 legacy	3 linger
1 kindest	1 landlord	2 legal	12 lingered
2 kindle	2 lands	1 legalize	1 lingerer
9 kindled	4 landscape	1 legends	5 lingering
5 kindling	1 landscapes	1 legible	1 lingerly
11 kindly	10 lane	1 legion	3 links
18 kindness	2 lanes	3 legitimate	1 linnet
6 kindred	27 language	3 legs	2 lion
2 kinds	1 languid	5 leisure	1 lion-like
3 king	1 languidly	3 leisurely	14 lip
4 kingdom	1 languish	3 lend	61 lips
1 kingly	1 languishing	1 lendings	3 liquid
2 kings	4 lantern	14 length	2 lisle
1 kingston	7 lap	2 lengths	2 lisp
2 kinsfolk	1 lap-dog	1 lenient	2 list
2 kinswoman	1 lapland	2 lent	34 listen
1 kinswomen	1 lappets	3 les	23 listened
1 kirstened	2 lapse	46 less	5 listener
24 kiss	2 lapsed	1 lessened	17 listening
19 kissed	2 lapses	1 lessening	1 listless
4 kisses	1 larder	8 lesson	1 listlessness
4 kissing	66 large	1 lesson-books	22 lit
29 kitchen	2 largely	10 lessons	3 literal
2 kitchen-door	6 larger	10 lest	2 literally
2 kitchen-garden	2 largest	133 let	1 literary
1 kitchens	1 larks	2 lethargic	2 literature
1 knack	2 lash	2 lethargy	342 little
1 knaves	2 lashes	33 letter	67 live
2 knawn't	1 lass	1 letter-press	38 lived
1 kneaded	1 lassitude	8 letters	4 livelier
24 knee	171 last	2 letting	12 lively
1 knee-deep	1 last-born	1 leurs	1 livery
3 kneel	1 last-named	1 levantine	6 lives
6 kneeling	2 lasted	7 level	5 livid
1 kneels	2 lastly	1 levelled	1 lividly
9 knees	4 latch	1 lever	36 living
1 knell	1 latched	1 leviathan	2 lizard
8 knelt	41 late	1 lexicon	1 lizzy
113 knew	1 late-found	3 liable	12 lloyd
5 knife	12 lately	1 liaison	2 load
1 knife-grinders	6 later	1 liaisons	3 loaded
6 knit	2 latin	6 liar	2 loaf
9 knitting	2 latmos	1 liars	1 loathings
1 knitting-bask- et	5 latter	1 liberal	1 loaves
1 knitting-need- les	3 latterly	1 liberal-handed	1 lobby
1 knittng	1 lattice	1 liberality	2 locality
	6 latticed	3 liberally	
	1 lattices	1 liberate	

9 lock	6 lying	6 mark	1 meditating
15 locked	20 lynn	20 marked	5 meditation
1 locket	1 lynns	3 marking	1 mediterranean
1 locking	1 m'a	1 marks	7 medium
7 locks	8 ma	4 marmion	1 medusa
12 lodge	32 ma'am	29 marriage	3 meed
3 lodged	1 macbeth	54 married	1 meek
3 lodging	1 macedonia	3 marrow	32 meet
1 loft	1 machine	1 marrow-freezi-	10 meeting
1 loftier	22 mad	ng	1 meetly
1 loftiest	1 mad-woman's	49 marry	1 meets
6 lofty	1 madagascar	4 marrying	1 mein
1 logical	21 madam	2 marseilles	2 meines
20 london	11 madame	5 marsh	9 melancholy
4 lone	163 made	4 marsh-end	1 melancholy-lo-
6 loneliness	10 madeira	2 marsh-glen	oking
22 lonely	18 mademoiselle	1 marshal	3 mellow
2 lonesome	1 madly	1 marshalled	1 mellowing
243 long	6 madness	3 marshes	2 melody
1 long-absent	1 magic	1 marston	4 melt
2 long-cherished	1 magic-lantern	2 martha	5 melted
1 long-enduring	3 magistrate	1 martyr	3 melting
1 long-framed	1 magnanimity	1 martyr-like	1 melts
1 long-haired	1 magnet	2 martyrdom	4 member
2 long-suffering	3 magnificent	1 martyrs	3 members
18 longed	1 magnificently	1 marvel	2 meme
49 longer	1 magnified	1 marvelled	3 memento
2 longest	1 magnifies	1 marvellous	1 mementoes
4 longing	1 magnifiques	85 mary	1 memoirs
1 longings	1 magnify	11 mary's	1 memorable
155 look	2 magnitude	2 masculine	1 memorandum
1 look-out	4 mahogany	3 mask	1 memories
216 looked	2 mahomet	1 masked	16 memory
1 looked-for	3 maid	56 mason	31 men
77 looking	1 maid-servant	5 mason's	1 men's
3 looking-glass	2 maids	1 masque	2 menace
22 looks	1 maimed	1 masquerade	2 menaced
2 looped	3 main	12 mass	2 menaces
10 loose	4 maintain	1 masse	1 mended
1 loose-princip-	2 maintained	1 masses	1 mendicant
led	1 maintaining	6 massive	1 menial
5 loosened	2 maintenance	1 massive-featu-	12 mental
13 lord	3 mais	red	7 mentally
1 lore	1 maister	3 mast	1 menteur
1 lorn	3 majestic	82 master	9 mention
5 lose	1 majestically	16 master's	12 mentioned
2 loses	3 majesty	4 mastered	2 mentioning
4 losing	1 majority	1 masterful	1 mentions
10 loss	1 mak'	1 masterhood	2 mercenary
31 lost	1 mak'em	1 mastering	3 merchant
9 lot	148 make	1 masterless	1 merchants
1 lot's	6 maker	2 masters	1 merciful
1 lotus-flowers	1 maker's	2 mastery	1 merciless
17 loud	10 makes	1 mastiffs	11 mercy
1 louder	21 making	3 mat	38 mere
3 loudly	1 mal	8 match	14 merely
15 louisa	2 malady	1 matches	1 meretricious
1 lounging	2 male	4 mate	1 merge
152 love	2 malevolent	3 material	1 merged
34 loved	1 malice	5 materials	1 merging
1 loveliest	1 malicious	1 maternal	3 meridian
2 loveliness	4 malignant	1 mates	2 merino
14 lovely	29 mama	1 mathematical	8 merit
5 lover	4 mama's	1 matrimonial	1 merited
1 lover's	3 maman	5 matrimony	1 meriting
1 lovers	1 mammon	1 matron	1 merits
7 loves	139 man	2 matronly	1 mermaid
6 loving	5 man's	2 matrons	2 merrily
66 low	5 manage	1 matt	1 merriment
1 low-born	7 managed	2 matted	8 merry
2 low-ceiled	1 management	42 matter	2 mes
1 low-gliding	3 manager	1 mattered	3 mesdames
1 low-spirited	1 mandate	13 matters	1 meshes
1 low-spoken	2 mane	1 matthew	3 mesrour
20 lower	1 mange	2 matting	1 mesrour's
1 lowered	1 manhood	1 mattrasses	4 mess
1 lowly	5 maniac	1 mattresses	9 message
55 lowood	1 maniacs	1 matured	1 messalina's
11 lowton	2 manifestation	1 maturing	3 messenger
1 lozenged	3 manifestations	1 maxim	1 messenger-pig-
1 ludicrous	2 manifested	142 may	eon
1 lucid	2 manly	1 may-day	1 messrs
1 lucre	2 manna	2 malle	24 met
1 ludicrous	39 manner	2047 me	2 metal
5 luggage	1 mannered	5 meadow	2 metallic
1 lugubrious	7 manners	3 meadows	1 metamorphosed
1 lui	1 manoeuvre	2 meagre	1 meted
1 luke	1 manoeuvres	13 meal	2 method
1 lull	3 manor	6 meals	2 mich
2 lulled	5 manor-house	50 mean	16 middle
1 lulling	8 mansion	2 meanest	3 middle-aged
2 luminous	1 mansion's	10 meaning	1 midge
2 lump	8 mantel-piece	1 meanness	6 midnight
1 lunar	2 mantelpiece	26 means	1 midnight-dark
9 lunatic	3 mantle	15 meant	1 midnight
4 lunch	1 mantling	26 meantime	10 midst
1 lungs	1 manufacture	7 measure	3 midsummer
1 lure	3 manufacturing	9 measured	1 midsummer-eve
5 lurid	1 manure	2 measureless	4 mien
1 luring	67 many	3 measures	160 might
1 lurk	1 many-coloured	4 meat	1 mightily
1 lust	2 map	4 mechanically	12 mighty
1 luster	22 marble	1 medals	1 migrated
9 lustre	1 marble-seeming	2 meddle	9 mild
1 lustres	2 marbled	1 meddling	1 mild-looking
3 lustrous	7 march	1 medes	2 milder
1 lusts	1 march-spirit	1 mediation	1 mildly
1 lusus	1 marched	1 mediatrix	12 mile
1 luxuriant	2 margin	2 medical	27 miles
2 luxuries	1 maria	1 mediocrity	1 military
1 luxury	1 marine	6 meditated	9 milk

Count	Word	Count	Word	Count	Word	Count	Word
1	milky-way	14	moments	19	move	1	navy
29	millcote	1	mon	25	moved	9	nay
1	mille	3	monday	19	movement	1	naze
22	miller	1	monde	14	movements	1	ne
1	miller's	29	money	5	moving	132	near
4	millions	1	money-specula-tion	543	mr	14	nearer
1	minature	5	monitor	250	mrs	6	nearest
1	mince	1	monitor's	206	much	24	nearly
1	mince-pies	2	monitors	1	much-excited	11	neat
123	mind	1	monitress	1	mucky	1	neat-handed
2	mind's	1	monkey	1	mud	1	neatest
1	mindful	1	monosyllabic	6	muff	1	nebuchadnezzar
1	mindless	3	monotonous	1	muffle	1	necessaries
4	minds	1	monotony	6	muffled	1	necessarily
76	mine	7	monsieur	1	muffling	24	necessary
1	mingle	3	monster	6	mug	12	necessity
3	mingled	1	monster-splin-ters	1	mule	20	neck
2	mingling	1	monstrous	1	mullioned	1	neck-cloth
5	miniature	16	month	1	multiplicity	1	neck-handkerc-hief
1	minister	28	months	1	multiplied	4	necklace
1	ministerial	2	months'	1	multitudinous	3	necks
1	ministrant	2	mony	1	mumbling	2	nectar
2	ministry	13	mood	2	mun	1	nectarous
1	minois	1	moodily	1	munnut	37	need
1	minor	1	moodiness	2	murder	6	needed
19	minute	2	moods	1	murdered	1	needful
2	minutely	1	moody	2	murderer	4	needle
73	minutes	42	moon	1	murderess	2	needle-factory
2	minutes'	2	moon-light	10	murmur	1	needle-maker
2	miracle	1	moon-rise	15	murmured	1	needleful
1	miraculous	1	moonbeams	1	murmuring	3	needles
1	mire	1	moonless	3	murmurs	1	needless
5	mirror	12	moonlight	1	muscle	1	needlework
5	mirrors	1	moonlit	1	muscles	3	needs
1	mirthless	1	moonrise	2	muscular	2	negative
1	miry	10	moor	4	mused	1	negatived
1	misapprehensi-on	1	moor-edge	1	mushrooms	7	neglect
4	mischief	15	moor-house	11	music	6	neglected
1	misconstrue	1	moor-side	3	musical	1	negligently
1	misdemeanor	1	moorish	2	musician	1	negociation
12	miserable	5	moorland	3	musing	1	negus
1	miseries	10	moors	5	musings	3	neighbour
7	misery	1	mope	1	musk	14	neighbourhood
2	misfortune	3	moral	6	muslin	1	neighbouring
1	misfortunes	1	moralists	309	must	1	neighbours
1	misgiving	1	morality	1	mustard-seed	57	neither
1	mishap	2	morally	1	muster	1	neophyte
2	misinterpret	1	morass	9	mute	1	neophyte's
1	misjudge	1	morbid	1	mutely	1	nephew
1	misjudged	361	more	1	mutilate	1	nero
310	miss	1	more's	2	mutilated	6	nerve
3	missed	1	moreen	1	mutinied	12	nerves
8	misses	1	moreland	5	mutiny	9	nervous
7	mission	1	moreoever	7	muttered	2	nest
11	missionary	7	moreover	1	muttering	1	nestle
5	missionary's	114	morning	11	mutual	4	nestled
19	missis	2	morning's	2	mutually	2	nestling
4	mist	3	mornings	2229	my	5	nests
1	mista'en	1	morocco	1	mysel	2	net
13	mistake	2	morose	184	myself	1	netting-needl-es
9	mistaken	1	moroseness	3	mysteries	1	nettled
1	mistimed	3	morrow	7	mysterious	1	neutralized
23	mistress	9	morsel	1	mysteriously	290	never
1	mistress's	9	mortal	13	mystery	3	nevertheless
5	mistresses	1	mortality	2	mystic	107	new
4	mistrust	3	mortally	1	mystification	1	new-born
2	mistrustful	1	mortar	1	n'avons	1	new-dyed
1	mists	1	mortgages	3	n'est-ce	1	newer
5	misty	1	mortification	1	n'etait	1	newfoundland
3	misunderstand	1	mortified	1	n'y	1	newly
1	misunderstand-ing	3	mortify	1	nacht	1	newly-risen
1	misunderstand-ings	2	mortifying	1	naiad's	17	news
1	misunderstood	25	morton	4	nail	1	newspaper
1	mit	1	mosaic	2	nailed	48	next
2	mittens	1	mosquitoes	4	nails	7	nice
1	mix	5	moss	2	naive	2	nicely
2	mixed	1	moss-blackened	1	naivete	1	nicety
1	mixes	4	mossy	1	naked	2	niche
1	mixture	1	mossy-faced	81	name	1	nichered
1	moan	98	most	4	named	1	niece
3	moaned	3	moth	2	nameless	1	nieces
3	moaning	42	mother	3	namely	1	niggard
1	mobile	12	mother's	5	names	1	nigh
1	mocked	1	mother-in-law	1	namesake	1	nigher
2	mockery	1	moths	2	naomi	146	night
4	mocking	4	motion	2	naples	4	night's
2	mode	5	motionless	2	narrate	2	night-air
5	model	2	motive	3	narrated	1	night-breeze
1	models	4	motives	13	narrative	1	night-cap
3	moderate	1	motto	1	narrator	2	night-dress
1	moderation	3	mould	1	narrator's	1	night-fall
4	modern	3	moulded	29	narrow	1	night-gown
1	modes	1	moulder	1	narrow-minded	1	night-mare
6	modest	1	mouldering	1	narrower	1	night-rover
1	modestly	1	mouldings	1	narrowing	1	night-sky
1	modesty	1	mound	1	narrowly	2	night-time
2	moi	10	mount	2	nasal	1	night-wind
1	moiety	10	mountain	1	nasmyth	2	nightingale
1	moistened	6	mountains	1	nasty	1	nightingale's
1	mole-eyed	9	mounted	1	natal	3	nightmare
1	molested	2	mounting	3	nations	6	nights
1	momemt	1	mourn	8	native	2	nimble
106	moment	6	mournful	1	naturae	1	nimbly
3	moment's	4	mourning	30	natural	19	nine
10	momentarily	1	mouse	18	naturally	2	nineteen
2	momentary	20	mouth	77	nature	3	nipped
3	momently	1	mouthed	1	nature's	1	niver
1	momentous	1	mouthful	6	natures	761	no
		1	mouths	4	naught	2	noan
				7	naughty		
				1	nauseous		

1 nobility	1 objectionable	1135 on	2 outrage
15 noble	2 objections	184 once	2 outraged
1 nobleman	2 objectless	1 once-dreaded	1 outrivalled
1 nobleman's	8 objects	1 once-vigorous	11 outside
1 nobleness	1 oblation	1 onding	2 outward
3 nobly	5 obligation	578 one	1 outwardly
15 nobody	2 obligations	12 one's	1 outworks
2 nod	1 obligatioons	1 one-fifth	2 oval
6 nodded	1 oblige	1 one-horse	2 oven
19 noise	20 obliged	1 one-tenth	256 over
1 noiselessly	3 obliging	12 ones	1 over-applicat-
1 noises	1 obligingly	1 ones'	ion
3 noisy	1 obliterating	1 onion	1 over-cast
1 nom	2 oblivion	289 only	2 over-excited
1 nominally	1 oblong	1 onslaught	1 over-fatigued
1 nonchalance	2 obnoxious	1 onus	1 over-modesty
1 nonchalantly	7 obscure	1 ony	1 over-stimulat-
43 none	1 obscured	2 onybody	ed
1 nonnette	7 obscurity	3 opaque	1 over-strained
11 nonsense	1 observant	69 open	1 over-tasked
4 nook	6 observation	62 opened	1 over-worked
13 noon	4 observations	18 opening	1 overawed
1 noontide	9 observe	4 openly	2 overcast
1 noose	30 observed	2 opens	1 overclouded
144 nor	2 observer	3 opera	8 overcome
1 norham's	1 observers	1 opera-girl	2 overcomes
1 normal	2 observing	1 opera-house	1 overcometh
4 north	5 obstacle	1 opera-mistres-	2 overflow
1 north-east	5 obstacles	ses	2 overflowed
2 north-midland	2 obstinate	4 operation	2 overflowing
1 north-of-engl-	1 obstruction	1 operations	1 overgrew
and	2 obtain	1 opiate	2 overgrown
2 northern	6 obtained	23 opinion	4 overhead
2 northumberland	1 obtrusive	2 opinions	2 overheard
1 northward	1 obviating	1 opponent	1 overleaped
2 norway	3 obvious	9 opportunity	1 overleaping
15 nose	1 obviously	2 oppose	1 overlook
1 nostril	1 obviousness	4 opposed	1 overlooked
6 nostrils	14 occasion	1 opposing	1 overlooking
1549 not	4 occasional	11 opposite	1 overlooks
10 note	8 occasionally	2 opposition	1 overpass
3 noted	1 occasioned	2 oppress	1 overpersuasion
4 notes	1 occasioning	3 oppressed	3 overpowered
166 nothing	7 occasions	1 oppresses	2 overshadowed
23 notice	2 occupant	3 oppression	1 overshadowing
17 noticed	4 occupants	1 opprobrium	1 overt
1 noticing	14 occupation	1 optics	1 overtake
1 notified	4 occupations	631 or	1 overtaken
1 noting	15 occupied	1 oracles	1 overwhelm
15 notion	4 occupy	1 oral	1 overwhelmed
5 notions	1 occupying	2 orange	2 overwhelming
2 notwithstandi-	3 occur	1 orange-trees	2 owd
ng	4 occurred	2 orator	4 owe
1 nought	3 occurrence	3 orb	2 owed
3 nourishment	1 occurrences	13 orchard	1 ower
1 nous	1 occurs	1 ordained	5 owing
1 nova	3 ocean	1 ordains	1 owls
6 novel	1 ocean-surges	1 ordeal	203 own
2 novelty	1 oceans	43 order	4 owner
5 november	4 october	9 ordered	1 owners
2 novice	1 oculist	1 ordering	1 ox
1 novice-eyes	6 odd	3 orderly	1 pace
1 novitiate	1 oddities	15 orders	3 paced
666 now	1 oddity	1 ordinarily	1 pacify
1 now-rising	1 odious	16 ordinary	2 pacing
3 nowhere	4 odour	1 ore	3 pack
4 noxious	4331 of	4 organ	1 packed
1 nuage	116 off	3 organs	3 packing
3 nuisance	1 offence	3 oriental	4 pagan
3 numbed	1 offences	3 origin	9 page
11 number	5 offend	13 original	7 pages
3 numbered	2 offended	2 originality	7 paid
2 numbering	1 offending	3 originated	25 pain
1 numbers	2 offensive	8 ornament	17 painful
2 numbness	30 offer	1 ornamental	3 painfully
3 numerous	27 offered	7 ornaments	10 pains
1 nun	7 offering	16 orphan	8 paint
1 nun-like	3 offers	1 orphans	5 painted
1 nunnery	8 office	1 orthodox	4 painting
31 nurse	1 officer	1 ostensible	3 paintings
1 nurse-girl	1 officer's	1 ostler	15 pair
1 nurse-maid's	1 officers	2 ostler's	1 pairs
1 nursed	1 offices	1 ostrich	53 pale
27 nursery	1 official	141 other	1 pale-beaming
1 nursery-door	1 officiated	3 other's	2 paleness
1 nursery-hearth	1 officious	30 others	1 paler
1 nursery-maid	1 offspring	16 otherwise	4 palette
1 nurses	68 often	3 ottoman	1 palisades
3 nursing	3 oftener	2 ottomans	1 palliate
2 nutriment	1 ogre	1 ou	3 pallid
2 nuts	118 oh	37 ought	1 pallor
1 o'	2 oil	2 oui	6 palm
13 o'	1 oil-lamp	99 our	1 palmistry
29 o'clock	1 oiled	1 ours	1 palsied
3 o'er	113 old	7 ourselves	1 palsy
2 o'gall	3 old-fashioned	401 out	1 paltry
1 o't'	7 older	3 out-door	1 pamela
9 oak	1 oldfashioned	1 out-house	1 pampering
1 oaken	3 olive	1 out-line	1 pamphlet
1 oaks	24 oliver	1 out-manoeuver-	2 panel
1 oat-cake	6 oliver's	ed	1 paneless
1 oaten	1 omega	1 out-of-the-way	3 panels
2 oath	1 omens	1 out-stretched	10 panes
4 obedience	2 ominous	1 outbreaks	11 pang
4 obedient	1 ominously	5 outcast	1 pangs
1 obese	2 omission	3 outer	1 pannels
6 obey	2 omit	1 outlandish-lo-	1 pansies
19 obeyed	2 omitted	oking	2 pant
1 obeying	1 omnipotence	1 outlawry	1 panted
22 object	1 omnipotent	3 outlet	1 panting
3 objection	1 omnipresence	7 outline	1 pantomime

1 pantry	1 patrimony	7 permission	8 pillow
3 papa	1 patriot's	9 permit	4 pillows
1 papa's	1 patron	1 permits	24 pilot
15 paper	1 patroness	6 permitted	1 pin
3 papered	3 patted	1 permitting	4 pinafore
1 papering	1 pattering	1 perpendicular	3 pinafores
5 papers	1 pattern	1 perpetrate	3 pinch
1 par	2 paul	1 perpetrated	1 pine
1 parable	1 pauper	1 perpetrator	1 pine-apples
6 paradise	1 pauper's	2 perpetual	1 pine-forests
1 paradox	23 pause	1 perplex	3 pining
1 paragraph	26 paused	1 perplexed	1 pinion
1 parallel	1 pauses	1 persecuting	1 pinioned
1 parallels	11 pavement	4 perseverance	1 pinions
1 paralyze	1 paving	1 persevere	8 pink
5 paralyzed	8 pay	1 persevered	1 pinnacle
1 paramount	1 paying	1 persians	2 pinned
6 parcel	1 paymaster	1 persist	1 pinning
1 parchments	1 paynim	47 person	1 pint
12 pardon	3 pays	1 person's	3 pioneer
4 parent	1 paysannes	7 personage	1 pioneers
1 parent's	1 pea-chicks	8 personal	2 pious
1 parentage	18 peace	1 personally	2 pip
1 parental	2 peaceful	1 personne	4 pipe
1 parenthese	1 peacefully	6 persons	1 piquancy
2 parentless	2 peak	5 persuade	5 piquant
10 parents	2 peaks	5 persuaded	5 piqued
1 parian	3 peal	2 persuasion	1 pirate
5 paris	1 pear	2 pertinaciously	1 pis
5 parish	7 pearl	1 perturbed	1 pisa
1 parishioner	1 pearl-coloured	4 perusal	1 pished
1 parisienne's	2 pearl-grey	1 peruse	1 pistols
4 park	1 pearllike	6 perused	3 pit
1 park-gates	1 pearly	2 pervaded	1 pitch
1 parle	2 peasantry	1 pervading	1 pitch-dark
1 parley	1 peasants	1 perverse	1 pitched
1 parleying	1 peat	2 perversity	5 pitcher
1 parlez	1 peat-fire	1 pervious	1 pitchers
26 parlour	3 pebbly	1 pestilence	1 piteously
1 parlour-bell	18 peculiar	3 pet	1 pith
1 parlours	3 peculiarities	1 petals	1 pithy
2 paroxysm	4 peculiarly	1 petersburg	3 pitied
1 paroxysms	1 pecuniary	2 petit	1 pities
5 parson	1 pedestal	2 petite	1 pitilessly
6 parsonage	4 peep	3 petition	31 pity
1 parsonic	2 peeped	2 petitioned	1 pitying
58 part	2 peeping	1 petitioner	103 place
1 partake	1 peer's	1 petitions	34 placed
1 partaken	1 peered	4 petrified	1 places
11 parted	1 peeress	1 petticoats	6 placid
2 parterre	2 pelisse	1 pettishness	1 placid-temper-
3 partial	2 pelisses	1 petty	ed
1 partiality	2 pelted	1 petulance	1 placidity
7 partially	1 penalties	2 peu	3 placing
1 participation	1 pence	1 peut	1 plague-cursed
6 particular	1 penchant	1 pewter	1 plague-house
5 particularly	8 pencil	1 phantom-like	2 plaid
3 particulars	1 pencil-head	2 phantoms	27 plain
4 parties	3 pencilled	2 phase	2 plain-work-wo-
11 parting	1 pencilling	3 phial	man
1 partitions	6 pencils	5 philanthropist	1 plained
11 partly	1 pendant	2 philanthropy	18 plainly
4 partner	3 pendent	2 philosopher	3 plainness
1 partout	2 penetrate	2 philosophers	2 plains
6 parts	3 penetrated	1 philter	2 plaits
24 party	6 penetrating	4 phlegmatic	8 plan
7 pas	2 penetration	3 phrase	2 planet
44 pass	2 penknife	6 phrases	2 planets
18 passage	5 penny	1 phylactery	2 plank
3 passages	2 pennyless	5 physical	1 planks
94 passed	5 pensive	5 physically	1 planning
1 passees	2 pent	3 physician	15 plans
1 passenger	1 penurious	7 physiognomy	4 plant
3 passengers	60 people	13 piano	1 plantation
2 passes	3 people's	1 piano-stool	1 planted
1 passeth	4 per	5 pick	1 planter
27 passing	5 perceive	1 picked	6 plants
26 passion	15 perceived	2 picking	2 plaster
6 passionate	3 perceptible	1 pickings	9 plate
1 passionately	1 perception	1 pictorial	1 plate-closet
1 passionless	1 perceptions	1 pictorial-loo-	1 plateful
4 passions	1 perch	king	4 plates
4 passive	2 perched	1 pictur'	1 platter
2 passively	1 percursor	25 picture	1 plausible
1 passport	1 perdition	1 picture-books	20 play
37 past	1 pere	14 pictures	2 play-hour
1 paste	1 peremptorily	4 picturesque	15 played
1 pasteboard	2 peremptory	1 picturing	1 players
1 pastile	19 perfect	1 pie	8 playing
1 pastille	1 perfection	15 piece	2 playthings
1 pastime	7 perfectly	1 pieces	1 plea
2 pastor	1 perfidious	1 piecing	1 plead
1 pastor's	1 perfidy	1 pierce	3 pleaded
2 pastoral	1 perforated	1 pierced	32 pleasant
2 pastry	9 perform	3 piercing	1 pleasantest
1 pasture	2 performance	2 piercingly	1 pleasantly
2 pasture-fields	1 performances	5 pierrot	38 please
1 pat	8 performed	2 pies	23 pleased
1 patch	1 performers	1 piety	2 pleases
1 patchwork	1 perfume	1 pig	10 pleasing
1 patent	104 perhaps	1 pig-trough	2 pleasurable
1 paternity	1 peri	1 pigeons	72 pleasure
22 path	4 peril	1 pigmies	1 pleasure-villa
2 pathless	2 perilous	1 pigmy	5 pleasures
2 pathos	1 perils	2 piled	2 plebeian
4 patience	9 period	2 piled-up	5 pledge
14 patient	4 perish	1 piles	2 pledged
1 patient's	1 perished	1 pilgrim	2 plenteous
3 patiently	1 perjured	1 pilgrim-convoy	1 plentiful
2 patients	7 permanent	5 pillar	4 plenty
1 patriarchal	7 permanently	3 pillars	1 pliability

1 pliancy	8 possession	2 presided	2 prone
1 pliant	3 possessions	1 prespective	4 pronounce
1 plied	2 possessor	3 press	18 pronounced
1 plodding	4 possibility	8 pressed	3 pronouncing
2 plot	16 possible	2 pressing	2 pronunciation
1 plots	9 possibly	3 pressure	5 proof
3 plotted	11 post	7 presume	1 proofs
1 plotting	1 post-boy	1 presumption	4 prop
1 plough	5 post-chaise	1 prete	5 propensities
1 plover	5 post-office	2 pretence	1 propensity
1 pluck	1 posted	2 pretend	4 proper
1 plucked	1 postman	1 pretended	12 property
3 plumage	1 posts	1 pretension	1 propitiate
1 plume	1 posture	1 pretensions	4 propitious
3 plumes	2 pot	1 pretercanine	3 proportion
1 pluming	3 potatoes	4 preternatural	3 proportionate
1 plump	6 potent	5 pretext	1 proportions
1 plums	1 poultry	1 pretexts	3 proposal
1 plumy	1 poundage	2 prettiest	2 proposals
1 plunge	23 pounds	1 prettily	3 propose
1 plunges	1 pounds'	23 pretty	7 proposed
1 plunging	8 pour	2 prevailed	3 proposing
4 pm	6 poured	1 prevalent	1 propound
1 poacher	2 pouring	4 prevent	1 propounded
12 pocket	1 pours	7 prevented	1 propped
3 pocket-book	1 pout	7 previous	4 proprietor
1 pocket-comb	7 poverty	4 previously	2 propriety
1 pocket-handke-	1 powdered	3 prey	1 prosecuting
rchief	47 power	4 price	12 prospect
1 pocket-handke-	6 powerful	1 priceless	1 prospective
rchiefs	2 powerless	3 pricked	11 prospects
2 pockets	1 powerlessness	1 prickly	11 prosperity
1 poem	9 powers	1 pricks	2 prosperous
1 poet	6 practical	24 pride	4 prostrate
3 poetry	3 practice	6 priest	1 prostrating
2 poignant	2 practised	1 prig	1 prostration
1 poignantly	1 practising	1 priggish	4 protect
51 point	7 praise	2 prim	1 protected
14 pointed	1 praised	3 prime	1 protecting
3 pointer	1 pranks	1 primitive	4 protection
4 pointing	1 prating	1 primrose	2 protector
21 points	3 prattle	1 primroses	2 protegee
1 poise	7 pray	1 prince	1 protestations
1 poised	4 prayed	1 princely	2 protract
6 poison	12 prayer	1 princess	7 protracted
4 poisoned	2 prayer-book	2 principal	1 protruded
1 poke	16 prayers	13 principle	14 proud
1 polar	2 pre-cise-ly	11 principles	14 prove
3 pole	1 pre-occupied	1 prints	10 proved
1 polish	3 preach	2 prison	2 proves
6 polished	1 preached	2 prisoned	2 provide
3 polishing	1 preacher	1 prisoner	10 provided
4 polite	2 precaution	1 prisonground	10 providence
1 politely	2 precautions	11 private	1 providential
3 politeness	2 precede	1 privately	1 provision
1 political	2 preceded	1 privation	1 provisions
1 politician	3 preceding	2 privations	1 provocation
2 politics	2 precept	9 privilege	1 provoked
2 pollard	1 precincts	4 privileged	6 provoking
1 poltical	5 precious	2 privileges	1 prowess
1 poltroon	1 preciously	2 prize	3 prudence
1 pomegranates	4 precise	1 prizes	1 pruning
1 pomp	13 precisely	3 probability	1 prurience
2 pompous	1 precision	1 probable	2 psalm
1 pompously	1 precluded	38 probably	4 psalms
1 pond	2 precocious	1 probation	1 pshawed
2 ponder	1 preconceived	3 problem	5 public
3 pondered	1 predecessor	10 proceed	1 publication
7 pondering	1 predestination	29 proceeded	1 publicly
1 ponderous	1 predicament	1 proceedeth	1 publish
3 pony	1 predicted	8 proceeding	1 pudding
2 pooh	1 prediction	3 proceedings	1 puddings
3 pool	1 predisposed	9 process	1 puddle
25 poole	1 predominant	1 procession	1 puerile
4 poole's	1 predominate	1 proclaiming	1 puffy
66 poor	1 predominated	1 procrastinated	1 puis
1 poor-house	1 predominating	1 procure	3 pull
2 poorly	1 preface	3 produce	3 pulled
1 poplars	4 prefer	11 produced	1 pulsation
4 population	4 preference	2 producing	5 pulse
1 populous	1 preferences	1 productions	3 pulses
2 porcelain	8 preferred	1 products	4 punctual
2 porch	1 prefers	5 professed	1 punctuality
1 pored	1 prejudice	1 professes	4 punctually
1 poring	2 prejudiced	2 profession	1 punctuation
7 porridge	2 prejudices	2 profile	4 pungent
4 port	1 prelude	2 profit	5 punish
3 portal	2 premature-	1 profitable	4 punished
1 porte	1 prematurely	1 profiting	9 punishment
1 portentous	1 premise	1 profligate	2 puny
1 portents	1 premises	9 profound	25 pupil
4 porter	1 premium	3 profoundly	1 pupil's
4 porter's	1 prendre	1 profusely	12 pupils
6 portfolio	1 prenomens	1 profusion	1 pupils'
16 portion	6 preparation	14 progress	2 puppet
3 portions	5 preparations	2 project	1 puppets
2 portmanteau	7 prepare	1 projection	1 puppy
9 portrait	25 prepared	3 prolong	4 purchase
1 portrait-cover	4 preparing	5 prolonged	2 purchased
2 portraits	1 prerogative	1 prolonging	1 purchasing
1 portray	1 prerogatives	1 prominences	28 pure
2 portrayed	42 presence	5 prominent	1 pure-lived
1 portraying	65 present	29 promise	4 purer
24 position	1 presentable	10 promised	1 purified
2 positions	8 presented	2 promises	1 puritanical
3 positive	3 presentiment	1 promontories	4 purity
2 positively	2 presentiments	1 promoted	1 purloined
10 possess	35 presently	6 prompt	16 purple
18 possessed	4 presents	2 prompted	17 purpose
2 possesses	1 preserved	2 promptings	1 purposeless
1 possessing	1 preserver	4 promptly	2 purposely

1	purposes	3	rails	9	reasons	1	refulgent
10	purse	3	raiment	1	reassuring	1	refurnished
1	purses	32	rain	1	rebecca	1	refusal
5	pursue	1	rain-drops	2	rebel	1	refusals
16	pursued	1	rain-refreshed	2	rebellion	8	refuse
1	pursues	3	rainbow	2	rebellions	7	refused
3	pursuing	3	rained	3	rebuff	1	refuses
1	pursuit	3	rains	1	rebuilt	1	refusing
2	pursuits	3	rainy	1	rebuke	4	regain
1	purveyor	2	raise	1	rebuking	5	regained
4	push	19	raised	19	recall	1	regaining
7	pushed	1	raising	11	recalled	1	regaled
2	pushing	2	rake	2	recalling	18	regard
137	put	1	rakes	1	recalls	1	regardais
3	puts	1	raking	1	receding	16	regarded
18	putting	5	rallied	1	receipt	3	regarding
4	puzzle	1	rally	15	receive	1	regardlessness
12	puzzled	1	rallying	44	received	1	regenerate
2	puzzles	1	ramble	1	receives	1	regenerates
3	puzzling	1	rambled	5	receiving	1	regenerating
1	pyramids	47	ran	2	recent	3	regeneration
1	pyrenees	1	rancid	5	reception	1	regiment
1	qu'avez	14	rang	1	reception-room	10	region
1	qu'avez-vous	2	range	5	recess	10	regions
1	qu'elle	4	ranged	2	recesses	1	register
2	qu'il	8	rank	1	recipient	1	registering
1	qu'oui	5	ranks	1	recipients	1	registers
2	quailed	1	ransack	1	reciprocate	1	regle
1	quailings	1	ransacked	4	reckless	8	regret
4	quaint	2	rap	2	recklessly	1	regretful
1	quaintly	6	rapid	1	recklessness	1	regretfully
1	quaintness	2	rapidity	1	reclaimed	3	regrets
1	quaker	8	rapidly	2	reclined	4	regretted
1	quaker-like	1	raps	5	recognise	1	regretting
1	quakeress	4	rapture	12	recognised	11	regular
1	quakerish	1	rapture-giving	1	recognises	2	regularity
1	quaking	2	raptures	1	recognising	1	regularly
2	qualifications	1	rapturously	3	recognition	1	regulate
3	qualified	3	rare	3	recoil	1	regulated
1	qualify	4	rarely	2	recoiled	1	regulation
8	qualities	1	rascals	5	recollect	2	regulations
4	quality	2	rash	1	recollected	1	rehearsal
2	quand	1	rashly	2	recollecting	1	rehumanize
6	quantity	1	rashness	8	recollection	3	reign
2	quarrel	3	rasselas	9	recollections	4	reigned
1	quarrelled	4	rat	1	recommence	1	rein
4	quarrelling	9	rate	6	recommenced	1	reins
1	quarried	124	rather	2	recommend	2	reiterate
14	quarter	1	ration	3	recommendation	4	reiterated
5	quarters	3	rational	2	recommended	1	reject
6	que	2	rationally	1	recompense	2	rejected
3	queen	3	rats	1	reconcile	2	rejection
2	queenly	2	rattled	4	reconciled	2	rejoicing
6	queer	3	rattling	1	reconcilement	1	rejoin
1	quel	4	rave	2	reconciliation	2	rejoinder
1	quell	1	raved	1	reconciling	8	rejoined
2	quelled	2	raven	1	reconquer	1	rejoining
2	quells	2	raven-black	5	record	1	relapse
1	quench	1	ravenous	2	recorded	2	relapsed
4	quenched	1	ravenously	1	records	1	relapsing
1	quenchless	2	ravens	3	recover	1	relate
1	queries	1	ravine	3	recovered	7	related
1	query	1	raving	1	recovery	5	relation
3	quest	1	ravings	2	recreation	12	relations
48	question	1	ravished	1	recriminations	2	relationship
8	questioned	8	raw	1	recruit	4	relative
1	questioner	1	rawness	1	recur	8	relatives
1	questioners	10	ray	6	recurred	2	relax
2	questioning	4	rayless	2	recurrence	4	relaxed
18	questions	2	rays	21	red	3	released
1	qui	1	re-appeared	1	red-haired	1	releasing
1	quibble	1	re-arranged	10	red-room	1	relent
12	quick	1	re-assuring	1	read	2	relentless
2	quickened	1	re-enter	1	redeem	2	reliance
3	quickening	6	re-entered	1	redeemed	2	relics
1	quickens	3	re-entering	3	redeemer	11	relief
1	quicker	2	re-entrance	1	redeeming	1	relieve
16	quickly	1	re-established	2	redness	13	relieved
4	quiescence	1	re-exciting	1	redolent	1	relieving
2	quiescent	1	re-transforma-tion	2	reduced	1	religieuses
57	quiet			1	redundancy	6	religion
2	quieter	1	re-transformed	113	reed	3	religious
34	quietly	1	re-trodden	15	reed's	5	relinquish
3	quilt	17	reach	4	reeds	3	relinquished
11	quit	25	reached	1	reel	3	relinquishing
143	quite	1	reaching	4	refectory	5	relish
13	quitted	3	reaction	3	refer	1	relished
6	quitting	68	read	2	reference	1	relit
3	quiver	38	reader	3	references	2	reluctance
7	quivered	2	readers	3	referred	2	reluctant
6	quivering	4	readily	2	referring	2	reluctantly
2	quiz	6	readiness	1	refilled	1	rely
1	quote	20	reading	9	refined	15	remain
1	rabbit	1	readings	1	refinement	5	remainder
1	rabidly	31	ready	1	refitted	15	remained
13	race	30	real	5	reflect	3	remaining
1	racing	8	reality	12	reflected	7	remains
3	racked	1	realization	2	reflecting	1	remand
1	racking	3	realize	11	reflection	6	remark
2	racy	5	realized	5	reflections	6	remarkable
5	radiance	41	really	1	reflecton	2	remarkably
6	radiant	1	realm	1	reform	17	remarked
2	rafters	2	realms	1	reformation	1	remarks
1	rag	1	reappeared	1	refrain	2	remedy
3	rage	4	rear	1	refresh	51	remember
2	ragged	6	reared	3	refreshed	20	remembered
1	raging	1	rearing	1	refreshing	3	remembering
1	ragout	24	reason	4	refreshment	1	remembers
1	raight	6	reasonable	2	refreshments	4	remembrance
1	railing	1	reasoned	1	reft	1	remercie
1	raillery			3	refuge	5	remind

9 reminded	1 reservoir	1 reverently	9 rolled
1 reminder	3 reside	2 reverie	2 rolling
1 reminding	2 resided	2 reverse	2 rolls
2 reminds	6 residence	3 revert	4 roman
1 reminiscence	5 resident	1 revient	3 romance
4 reminiscences	1 residents	2 review	1 romances
1 remittent	2 resign	2 reviewed	5 romantic
2 remnant	1 resignation	1 revile	5 rome
2 remonstrance	9 resist	1 reviled	1 romping
1 remonstrate	2 resistance	1 revisit	20 roof
11 remorse	2 resisted	1 revisiting	1 roofs
9 remote	3 resisting	3 revive	1 rook
6 remove	2 resistless	9 revived	4 rookery
22 removed	1 resistlessly	2 revives	2 rooks
3 removing	1 resists	3 reviving	188 room
2 remuneration	11 resolute	3 revolt	1 room-door
1 rencontre	1 resolutely	2 revolted	20 rooms
1 rend	11 resolution	8 reward	3 root
8 render	5 resolve	1 rewarded	3 rooted
7 rendered	25 resolved	1 rewards	7 roots
2 rendering	3 resolves	1 rhine	1 rope
3 rending	1 resounded	1 ribaldry	14 rosamond
2 rene-	4 resource	1 riband	2 rosamond's
2 renewal	3 resources	2 ribs	94 rose
9 renewed	12 respect	33 rich	1 rose-coloured
1 renewing	1 respectability	7 richard	2 rosebuds
1 renews	6 respectable	1 richest	9 roses
3 renounce	2 respectable-l-	2 richly	1 rosewood
1 renovation	ooking	1 richness	5 rosy
2 renown	1 respectably	6 rid	2 rotten
3 rent	1 respectably-d-	1 riddle	1 roue
1 rent-roll	ressed	5 ride	1 rouge
1 rented	4 respected	3 rider	2 rouges
4 repaid	4 respectful	6 ridge	12 rough
5 repair	11 respecting	1 ridged	1 rough-coated
5 repaired	1 respects	1 ridges	1 rough-looking
1 repairing	1 respite	1 ridiculous	1 rougher
2 repartee	1 resplendent	1 riding	1 roughly
1 repassed	1 respond	1 riding-habit	1 roughness
5 repast	10 responded	86 right	116 round
2 repaying	5 response	1 righteous	2 rounded
16 repeat	1 responses	2 rightly	2 roundly
21 repeated	2 responsibilit-	2 rights	4 rouse
2 repeatedly	ies	7 rigid	15 roused
1 repeating	4 responsibility	1 rigidly	1 rousing
5 repelled	3 responsible	1 rigorous	2 routine
5 repent	66 rest	1 rigors	2 rove
4 repentance	1 rest-seeking	1 rigour	2 roved
1 repentant	1 reste	1 rill	1 rover
3 repetitions	6 rested	15 ring	3 roving
2 repine	7 resting	4 ringing	4 row
1 repined	2 resting-place	2 ringleted	2 rowland
4 replace	10 restless	4 ringlets	5 rows
4 replaced	2 restlessly	6 rings	2 royal
2 replacing	3 restlessness	1 riot	1 rub
1 repletion	2 restoration	1 riots	3 rubbed
32 replied	2 restore	6 ripe	2 rubbing
2 replies	5 restored	1 ripened	2 rubbish
37 reply	1 restoring	1 ripening	1 rubicon
2 replying	5 restrain	2 ripple	1 rubric
2 report	6 restrained	1 ripplings	1 ruby
2 reported	2 restraining	32 rise	6 ruddy
14 repose	8 restraint	15 risen	5 rude
1 reposed	2 restricted	1 riser	2 rudeness
1 reposing	1 restricting	2 rises	1 rue
1 repository	2 restrictive	33 rising	1 rued
1 represent	1 rests	7 risk	1 ruffian's
2 representation	19 result	2 risked	1 ruffle
1 representative	1 resulted	1 risking	9 rug
5 represented	2 resulting	1 risks	2 rugged
1 representing	5 results	1 rite	12 ruin
3 repress	5 resume	2 rites	4 ruined
3 repressed	20 resumed	2 rival	1 ruining
1 repressing	1 resurgam	1 rivalries	2 ruins
3 reprimand	7 retain	2 riven	5 rule
1 reprimanded	6 retained	4 river	1 ruler
5 reproach	1 retaining	51 rivers	9 rules
2 reprobation	1 retaliation	4 rivers'	1 rumbled
2 reproof	3 retire	1 rivet	2 rumbling
1 reproofs	13 retired	5 riveted	1 rummage
1 reproved	5 retirement	2 rizzio	2 rummaging
1 republican	2 retorted	43 road	4 rumour
1 repudiated	1 retouch	6 roads	18 run
1 repugnance	2 retrace	1 roam	3 rung
2 repulse	1 retraced	2 roamed	21 running
3 repulsed	5 retreat	3 roaming	4 runs
1 repulsion	6 retreated	1 roar	12 rush
1 repulsive	2 retreating	2 roared	14 rushed
16 request	1 retreats	1 roaring	2 rushing
5 requested	1 retrospective	3 roast	2 rushlight
1 requesting	65 return	1 roasting	2 russell
16 require	66 returned	1 rob	2 russet
14 required	8 returning	1 robber-path	4 rustic
1 requirements	1 returnings	2 robbers	1 rustics
2 requires	4 returns	8 robe	1 rustle
1 requiring	2 reunite	1 robed	4 rustling
1 requisite	2 rev	10 robert	2 rusty
1 requisition	2 reveal	4 robes	4 ruth
1 rescind	7 revealed	1 robin	3 ruthless
1 rescued	1 revealing	1 robing	1 ruthlessly
1 rescuer	2 revelation	4 robust	7 s
1 research	5 revelations	317 rochester	1 sa
3 resemblance	1 revelled	49 rochester's	2 sabbath
3 resemble	1 revels	5 rochesters	4 sable
1 resembled	1 revenez	11 rock	1 sable-clad
2 resembles	2 revenge	2 rocking	1 sacques
1 resent	1 revengeful	1 rocking-chair	5 sacred
3 resentment	1 reverberation	7 rocks	16 sacrifice
1 resentments	3 reverence	2 rod	1 sacrificed
6 reserve	1 reverenced	7 rode	1 sacrifices
3 reserved	1 reverend	7 roll	26 sad

3 saddened	2 scare	1 second-sight	9 serene
1 saddest	1 scarecrow	1 seconded	1 serenely
2 saddle	2 scared	2 secondly	3 serenity
2 sadly	6 scarf	1 seconds	3 series
6 sadness	3 scarlet	2 secrecy	10 serious
17 safe	20 scatcherd	2 secresy	5 seriously
4 safely	3 scatcherd's	20 secret	3 sermon
7 safety	3 scathed	1 secreted	1 sermonized
1 sagacious	10 scattered	6 secrets	1 sermons
1 sagacity	2 scattering	1 sect	1 serried
1 sage	1 scatterings	1 section	33 servant
1 sago	32 scene	1 sections	3 servant's
583 said	2 scenery	12 secure	27 servants
2 sail	8 scenes	6 secured	7 servants'
1 sailed	5 scent	1 securely	11 serve
1 sailing	1 scents	2 securing	10 served
1 sails	1 sceptic	5 security	1 serves
1 saint	2 scepticism	2 sedative	18 service
1 saint's-day	1 schale	1 seducer	6 services
17 sake	5 scheme	274 see	1 servies
1 salamander	2 scheming	1 seed	2 serving
9 salary	2 schiller	1 seed-cake	5 servitude
1 salient	3 scholar	2 seeds	58 set
3 sallow	12 scholars	18 seeing	8 setting
1 sallowness	74 school	38 seek	7 settle
2 salon	1 school-discip-	4 seeking	24 settled
	line	23 seem	1 settling
2 saloon	1 school-duties	210 seemed	1 seule
2 saloons	1 school-girl	8 seeming	1 seulement
1 salt	1 school-girl-g-	4 seemingly	10 seven
1 salt-drops	overnesses	26 seems	1 seven-and-thi-
5 salts	1 school-habits	75 seen	rty
1 salubrious	1 school-hours	10 sees	2 seventeen
2 salutary	2 school-mistre-	15 seized	1 seventh
1 salutations	ss	1 seizing	1 seventy
1 salute	32 school-room	16 seldom	1 seventy-and-s-
1 salvaton	1 school-rules	2 select	even
11 sam	1 schoolboy	3 selected	2 sever
1 sam's	1 schoolmistress	1 selecting	9 several
69 same	1 schoolroom	1 selection	16 severe
2 samson	3 schools	1 selects	3 severed
1 samson's	4 science	10 self	3 severely
1 samuel	1 scintillated	1 self-abandoned	6 severity
1 sanctifies	1 scions	1 self-abandonm-	2 severn
1 sanction	1 scissor	ent	5 sew
1 sanctioned	1 scissors	1 self-approbat-	1 sewed
1 sanctions	3 scold	ion	10 sewing
2 sanctity	1 scolded	1 self-complace-	1 sewn
1 sanctuary	1 scolding	ncy	2 sews
3 sanctum	6 scorched	1 self-congratu-	2 sex
1 sand-traced	1 scorches	lation	2 shabby
1 sandal	1 scores	3 self-conscious	16 shade
1 sandals	12 scorn	2 self-control	4 shaded
3 sanded	5 scorned	2 self-denying	5 shades
1 sandwich	1 scotland	1 self-destruct-	1 shadiest
1 sane	1 scoundrel	ion	13 shadow
12 sang	4 scoured	1 self-doubt	7 shadows
1 sanguine	1 scourge	1 self-esteem	5 shadowy
1 sanity	1 scourging	1 self-indulgent	2 shaft
19 sank	1 scowl	1 self-interest	1 shafts
2 sans	1 scowled	1 self-love	2 shaggy
2 sap	2 scowling	1 self-possessi-	13 shake
1 sapphire	1 scracely	on	5 shaken
3 sarah	1 scrag	7 self-respect	7 shaking
2 sarcasm	1 scrambling	2 self-respecti-	241 shall
4 sarcastic	2 scrape	ng	1 shallows
1 sarcastically	2 scraps	1 self-satisfied	1 shambles
2 sardonic	1 scratch	1 self-willed	17 shame
2 sardonically	1 scratched	11 selfish	1 shame-facedne-
1 sarvant's	2 scream	2 sell	ss
5 sash	2 screamed	1 selling	2 shameful
1 sash-like	1 screaming	1 semi-sarcastic	23 shape
1 sashes	1 screams	1 semi-starvati-	3 shaped
106 sat	2 screen	on	1 shapely
1 satan	4 screened	3 semicircle	1 shapes
1 satiety	1 scribe	1 semicircles	1 shaping
15 satin	3 scripture	2 seminary	11 share
1 satin-smooth	1 scroll	31 send	7 shared
1 satirical	1 scrolls	1 sending	3 shares
6 satisfaction	1 scrub	3 sends	2 sharing
1 satisfactorily	2 scrubbing	1 senior	11 sharp
4 satisfactory	3 scruple	10 sensation	1 sharp-witted
15 satisfied	1 scrupulous	8 sensations	1 sharpened
5 satisfy	4 scrupulously	56 sense	1 sharpers
1 saturdays	1 scrutinize	2 senseless	1 sharpish
1 saturnine	5 scrutinized	1 senselessness	4 sharply
1 saucepan	1 scrutinizing	9 senses	2 shattered
1 saucer	5 scrutiny	2 sensibility	16 shawl
1 saul	1 scuffle	12 sensible	2 shawls
11 savage	1 sculptor's	1 sensitive	1457 she
15 save	16 sea	2 sensual	1 she'd
8 saved	1 sea-blue	1 sensualist	3 she'll
1 saving	1 sea-fowl	44 sent	15 she's
1 saviour	1 sea-side	16 sentence	8 shed
1 savourless	3 seal	1 sentenced	1 shedding
186 saw	5 sealed	4 sentences	1 sheen
200 say	1 sealing	1 sententious	6 sheep
29 saying	5 search	1 sentient	1 sheepishly
26 says	2 searched	11 sentiment	7 sheet
1 scaffold	9 searching	2 sentimental	6 sheets
2 scalding	1 searchingly	10 sentiments	4 shelf
3 scale	1 seared	10 separate	1 shell
1 scaly	13 season	3 separated	2 shell-like
1 scandalous	2 seasonable	2 separating	14 shelter
1 scant	3 seasons	12 separation	6 sheltered
1 scantier	39 seat	4 sequel	1 sheltering
1 scantiness	18 seated	4 sequestered	2 shepherd
5 scanty	1 seating	1 sera	5 shew
1 scape-goat	4 seats	2 seraglio	1 shewed
1 scar	1 seclusion	2 seraph	3 shewing
3 scarce	44 second	1 sere	3 shewn
43 scarcely			

```
  2  shift              7  sigh               1  sky-lark            1  snow-wet
  1  shifted           10  sighed             1  sky-line            1  snowed
  1  shifting           1  sighs              1  skylight            3  snows
  4  shilling          32  sight              1  slab                8  snowy
  5  shillings          4  sightless          1  slackened           2  snuff
  1  shimmer            9  sign               1  slain               2  snuff-box
  6  shine              2  sign-post          1  slander             3  snuffed
  3  shines             2  signal             1  slanting            1  snug
 10  shining            5  signed             6  slate               1  snugly
  4  ship               2  significance       1  slattern            1  snugness
  1  ship-money         1  significancy       2  slatternly        629  so
  2  ships              1  significant        1  slaughtered         1  soaked
 15  shire              1  significantly      7  slave               1  soaking
  1  shirked            1  signification      1  slave-purchas-      1  soap
  2  shirt              1  signifier                es              1  soar
  1  shiver             1  signifies          1  slavery             1  soart
  3  shivered           8  signify            1  slaving             3  sob
  3  shivering          2  signior            1  slavish             2  sobbed
  6  shock              1  signoras           1  slay                3  sobbing
 11  shocked            5  signs              1  sleek               2  sober
  4  shocking           1  silas's           37  sleep               1  sobered
  1  shockingly        61  silence            1  sleeper             1  sobering
  1  shod               2  silenced           1  sleepers            1  sobriety
  1  shoe              42  silent             6  sleeping            6  sobs
  1  shoemaker's        4  silently           1  sleepless           1  sociable
 10  shoes              1  silhouette         2  sleeps              2  social
 23  shone             20  silk               2  sleepy             25  society
 30  shook              2  silken             1  sleet               1  society's
  3  shoot              1  sill               1  sleeve              1  socket
  3  shooting           5  silly              2  slender             2  sodden
  6  shop               8  silver             1  slenderly          16  sofa
  2  shore              1  silver-gray       10  slept               2  sofas
  3  shores             2  silver-white       3  slice              37  soft
  1  shorn              2  silvered           1  slices              2  soften
 47  short              1  silverplate        2  slid                7  softened
  2  shortened          3  silvery            1  slide               3  softening
  1  shorter            7  similar            1  sliding             2  softer
 11  shortly            1  similarly          9  slight              1  softest
  5  shot               8  simple             1  slightest          14  softly
280  should             1  simple-minded      5  slightly            5  softness
 25  shoulder           3  simpleton          4  slim                8  soil
  1  shouldered         4  simplicity         2  slime               1  soir
 13  shoulders          1  simplified        12  slip                1  sojourn
  1  shouldn't          1  simplify          12  slipped             1  sojourned
  2  shout              4  simply             1  slipper            12  solace
  2  shouted            1  simulate           2  slippers            2  sold
  3  shouting           1  simulating         2  slippery            3  soldier
 22  show               4  simultaneously     2  slips               1  soldierly
 26  showed             4  sin                1  slope               1  soldiers
  4  shower             2  sin'               2  sloping            13  sole
  1  shower-bath       77  since              1  sloth               1  solecism
  1  showers           10  sincere            1  slothful           21  solemn
  2  showing            8  sincerely          1  slough              2  solemnizing
  5  shown              4  sincerity          4  slow                3  solemnly
  2  showy              1  sinews            17  slowly              1  solicited
  4  shrank             1  sinful             6  slumber             4  solicitor
  2  shreds            13  sing               3  slumbered           1  solicitor's
  3  shrewd             1  sing-song          1  slur                3  solicitous
  2  shrewdly           2  singer             1  sly                 3  solicitude
  1  shriek             1  singers           44  small               7  solid
  1  shrieked           6  singing            1  small-featured      1  soliloquized
  1  shrieks           19  single             3  smaller             1  soliloquy
  1  shrill             2  singly             1  smallest           18  solitary
  1  shrilly           10  singular           3  smart              24  solitude
  2  shrine             1  singularity        1  smartest            1  solitudes
  1  shrined            7  singularly         1  smartly             1  solo
  3  shrink             2  sinister           1  smashed             1  solomon
  3  shrinking          2  sink               2  smell               1  solus
  1  shrivelled         3  sinking            1  smelling-bott-      2  solution
  3  shroud             1  sinless                 le               2  solve
  2  shrouded           1  sinner             1  smells              3  solved
  1  shrouding          1  sinner's           1  smelt               8  sombre
  2  shrub              1  sinners           47  smile             371  some
  4  shrubbery          1  sins              29  smiled              3  somebody
  2  shrubs           316  sir               11  smiles              1  somebody's
  1  shrug             27  sister            12  smiling             7  somehow
  3  shudder            5  sister's           6  smith             136  something
  3  shuddered          3  sisterly           2  smitten            70  sometimes
  2  shuddering        45  sisters           11  smoke              29  somewhat
  5  shun               2  sisters'           2  smoked              9  somewhere
  6  shunned           60  sit                2  smoking             1  somewhere
  1  shuns              4  site               1  smoky               9  son
 47  shut               2  sits              16  smooth              7  song
  2  shutter           37  sitting            1  smooth-skinned      3  songs
  1  shutters           2  sitting-room       3  smoothed            1  sonorous
  4  shutting           5  situated           1  smoothly            1  sont
  3  shuttlecock       12  situation          3  smote             153  soon
  4  shy                2  situations         1  smother            10  sooner
  1  shyness           23  six                2  smothered           1  soot
  2  si                 1  six-and-thirty     3  snake               1  soot-black
  1  siberia            2  sixteen            1  snappish            4  soothe
  1  sich               1  sixth              1  snapt               1  soothed
 20  sick               2  sixty              3  snare               7  soothing
  3  sick-room          5  size               1  snarl               1  soothingly
  1  sickbed            2  skein              2  snarling           27  sophie
  2  sickened           2  skeletons          4  snatch              1  sophistical
  3  sickening          1  skeptical          7  snatched            1  soporific
  2  sickens            5  sketch             1  snatching           2  sorceress
  3  sickly             1  sketched           1  snaw                5  sordid
  3  sickness           3  sketches           3  sneaking            2  sore
 78  side               4  sketching          2  sneer               2  sorely
  1  side-aisle         2  skies              1  sneering            1  soreness
  1  side-board         1  skilful            1  sneeringly         13  sorrow
  4  side-door          8  skill              1  sneers              3  sorrowful
  1  side-glances       9  skin               1  snivel              3  sorrows
  1  side-passage       1  skipped            1  snored             14  sorry
  1  side-table         4  skirt              1  snoring            71  sort
  2  sideboard          1  skirted           15  snow                1  sorted
  5  sides              1  skirts             1  snow-drift          1  sorting
  1  sideways          39  sky                1  snow-drops          4  sorts
  1  sidling            1  sky-blue           1  snow-flakes         1  sotto
```

1	sough	1	spoonful	1	steadfastly	1	stranded
44	sought	1	spoonfuls	1	steadfastness	98	strange
36	soul	1	spoonie	2	steadied	11	strangely
1	soul's	1	spoonies	10	steadily	1	strangeness
1	soul-withered	2	spoons	5	steady	30	stranger
1	souliers	1	sport	2	steal	1	stranger's
1	soulless	1	sports	1	stealing	15	strangers
7	souls	1	sportsman	1	steals	5	strangest
48	sound	13	spot	2	steam	1	strangle
9	sounded	3	spotless	1	steamed	3	strangled
3	sounding	2	spots	4	steed	1	strapped
3	soundly	5	sprain	2	steel	2	strapper
12	sounds	1	sprained	1	steeled	1	strata
1	soup	10	sprang	1	steelly	4	straw
11	source	2	spray	1	steely	1	strawberries
1	sources	1	sprays	1	steep	7	stray
1	soured	23	spread	1	steeple	5	strayed
2	sourly	4	spreading	2	stem	3	straying
5	south	2	sprightly	1	stems	1	streached
1	south-of-engl-	20	spring	47	step	1	streak
	and	1	sprinkled	1	step-mother	1	streaked
3	southern	1	sprinkling	6	stepped	2	streaks
2	southernwood	2	sprite	27	steps	9	stream
1	souvent	2	sprung	21	stern	5	streamed
4	sovereign	1	spue	1	sternen	3	streaming
1	sovereign's	1	spun	1	sterner	1	streams
1	sowing	1	spurn	1	sternest	8	street
1	sown	2	spurned	1	sternest-seem-	1	streets
20	space	2	spurred		ing	42	strength
3	spacious	2	spy	1	sternly	1	strengthened
1	span	11	square	3	sternness	1	strenuously
1	spangled	1	square-made	4	stick	3	stress
1	spaniard	1	squareness	7	stiff	2	stretch
5	spanish	1	squarer	1	stiff-necked	14	stretched
1	spanish-town	1	squares	4	stiffened	1	strewn
1	spar	1	squire	1	stiffly	5	strict
9	spare	137	st	2	stiffness	1	strictly
5	spared	1	stab	4	stifle	1	strictness
3	spark	3	stabbed	2	stifled	5	stride
2	sparkled	1	stable	1	stifling	1	strife
1	sparkles	4	stables	13	stile	11	strike
3	sparkling	2	stage	245	still	3	strikes
2	sparks	1	stage-trapping-	1	stiller	8	striking
1	sparrow		gs	8	stillness	1	strikingly
5	spasm	1	staggered	1	stilted	6	string
1	spasmodic	1	staggering	2	stimulate	2	stringent
1	spat	2	stagnate	2	stimulated	3	strings
83	speak	2	stagnation	1	stimulating	1	stringy
6	speaker	2	staid	4	stimulus	1	strip
36	speaking	1	stain	3	sting	1	striped
5	speaks	3	stained	1	stinginess	4	stripped
1	spear	5	stainless	1	stinging	4	strive
5	special	3	stains	1	stingy	1	striven
2	specially	2	stair	1	stinted	1	striving
5	species	1	stair-case	1	stipulate	2	strode
4	specimen	1	stair-cases	1	stipulating	6	stroke
4	speck	1	stair-head	16	stir	1	stroked
1	specking	20	staircase	18	stirred	2	strokes
11	spectacle	56	stairs	7	stirring	1	stroking
5	spectacles	1	stale	1	stirs	1	strolling
1	spectator	1	stalled	1	stitch	1	strolls
2	spectators	2	stalwart	1	stitching	53	strong
4	spectre	1	stamboul	3	stock	1	strong-limbed
1	speculation	2	stamp	1	stocking	3	stronger
3	sped	6	stamped	1	stocking-foot	1	strongest
4	speech	2	stamping	5	stockings	6	strongly
1	speeches	26	stand	4	stocks	1	strongly-mark-
1	speechless	4	standard	1	stoic		ed
2	speed	24	standing	1	stoicism	2	strove
9	spell	7	stands	4	stole	43	struck
1	spellbound	1	stanzas	22	stone	1	structure
11	spend	9	star	2	stone-blind	12	struggle
2	spending	1	star-like	1	stone-cold	3	struggled
1	spends	1	starched	1	stone-dead	1	struggles
17	spent	3	stare	8	stones	7	struggling
5	sphere	3	stared	3	stony	1	stubble
1	sphynx	3	stark	124	stood	3	stubborn
1	sphynx-like	1	starlight	13	stool	1	stubbornness
2	spice	1	starry	2	stools	1	stuck
1	spices	6	stars	1	stoop	1	studded
1	spike-guarded	10	start	7	stooped	1	students
1	spill	15	started	6	stooping	6	studied
4	spilt	1	starting	1	stoops	5	studies
1	spine	4	startled	10	stop	1	studious
1	spinster	1	startling	46	stopped	17	study
1	spire	2	starts	2	stopping	3	studying
45	spirit	1	starvation	1	stops	9	stuff
3	spirited	3	starve	3	store	3	stumbled
1	spirito	4	starved	4	store-room	2	stump
19	spirits	2	starving	2	stored	1	stung
4	spiritual	35	state	4	stores	2	stunned
9	spite	1	stated	7	stories	1	stunner
3	spiteful	1	stateliest	9	storm	5	stupid
1	spitzbergen	1	stateliness	1	storm-beat	1	stupified
1	splash	12	stately	1	stormily	2	stupor
1	splashed	1	statement	2	storms	8	style
2	splashing	1	statesman	3	stormy	1	styled
1	splashy	1	statesmen	24	story	1	stylish
9	splendid	1	stating	2	story-book	1	suave
2	splendidly	10	station	11	stout	3	subdue
3	split	2	stationed	2	stowed	10	subdued
3	spoiled	1	stations	1	straggled	1	subduing
2	spoiling	3	statue	1	stragglers	30	subject
4	spoilt	6	stature	20	straight	1	subjected
46	spoke	2	statute	1	straight-skir-	2	subjects
23	spoken	54	stay		ted	4	subjoined
1	spokesman	17	stayed	7	strain	1	subjugation
5	sponge	8	staying	3	strained	5	sublime
1	sponged	1	stays	3	straining	1	sublunary
2	spontaneous	5	stead	3	strains	5	submission
2	spontaneously	3	steadfast	1	strait	2	submissive

10	submit
1	submitted
1	subordinate
1	subordinate's
2	subordinates
1	subscribed
1	subscribes
1	subscription
4	subsequent
2	subsequently
1	subside
3	subsided
2	subsiding
5	substance
2	substantial
1	substantiality
4	substitute
1	substituting
2	subtle
4	succeed
19	succeeded
6	succeeding
8	success
3	succession
1	successive
4	successor
1	successors
1	succour
1	succumbed
255	such
1	sucked
17	sudden
32	suddenly
19	suffer
6	suffered
1	sufferer
17	suffering
9	sufferings
3	suffice
4	sufficed
9	sufficient
6	sufficiently
2	suffocated
2	suffocating
1	suffused
1	suffusing
1	suffusion
4	suggest
7	suggested
1	suggesting
9	suggestion
2	suggestions
1	suggestive
1	suggests
2	suicide
12	suit
2	suitable
11	suited
1	suiting
1	suitor
2	suitors
2	suits
1	suivais
1	sulky
6	sullen
1	sullenly
1	sullenness
6	sullied
2	sully
1	sulphur-steams
1	sultan
10	sum
17	summer
1	summer-day
3	summit
2	summits
4	summon
17	summoned
1	summoning
5	summons
1	sumptuously
32	sun
2	sunbeam
2	sunday
1	sundays
1	sundered
8	sundry
2	sung
10	sunk
1	sunken
2	sunless
1	sunlit
7	sunny
1	sunny-faced
5	sunrise
2	suns
5	sunset
13	sunshine
2	superb
1	supercilious
1	superciliousn-ess
1	superficiality
1	superfluity
3	superfluous
1	superintenden-ce
9	superintendent
1	superintenden-t's
10	superior
6	superiority
1	superlatively
1	supernatural
4	superstition
2	superstitious
1	superstitious-ly
1	supervened
1	supped
19	supper
1	supper-trays
2	supple
3	supplicated
2	supplication
3	supplied
5	supply
1	supplying
3	support
12	supported
3	supporting
66	suppose
11	supposed
3	supposing
2	supposition
1	suppress
2	suppressed
1	suppressing
1	suppression
1	supremely
97	sure
19	surely
2	surer
3	surface
1	surfeited
1	surge
8	surgeon
2	surgeon's
1	surges
1	surging
1	surly
1	surmised
1	surmises
1	surmount
1	surnames
1	surpass
1	surpassed
4	surplice
17	surprise
21	surprised
1	surprises
1	surprising
1	surrendered
2	surround
8	surrounded
4	surrounding
1	surrounduing
3	surtout
1	surveillance
1	survey
17	surveyed
2	surveying
2	susceptible
1	suspect
9	suspected
6	suspended
2	suspense
5	suspicion
2	suspicions
2	sustain
5	sustained
2	sustenance
1	suttee
3	swallow
9	swallowed
1	swallowing
3	swam
1	swamp
1	swamped
1	swarth
1	swathed
1	swaths
2	sway
2	swayed
6	swear
1	swearing
2	swears
5	sweep
5	sweeping
42	sweet
2	sweet-briar
1	sweet-briars
1	sweet-tempered
1	sweetens
2	sweeter
8	sweetest
3	sweetly
1	sweetmeats
1	sweetness
1	sweetwilliams
4	swell
10	swelled
2	swelling
1	swells
17	swept
1	swift-darting
1	swim
2	swimming
1	swimmingly
1	swine
1	swing
1	switch
3	swollen
1	swooning
2	swore
3	sworn
3	sybil
1	syllabic
7	syllable
1	syllables
1	sylph
1	sylph's
1	sylvan
1	symmetrically
1	sympathetic
5	sympathies
6	sympathize
1	sympathizing
17	sympathy
1	syncope
1	synonymous
6	system
1	systematic
2	systems
6	t'
1	t'chamber
1	tabernacle
60	table
1	table-drawer
1	tableau
15	tables
5	tablet
1	taciturn
1	taciturn-look-ing
3	taciturnity
1	tack
1	tact
2	tail
1	taille
3	taint
1	tak'
151	take
62	taken
2	takes
34	taking
25	tale
3	talent
4	talented
5	talents
8	tales
1	talisman
63	talk
16	talked
24	talking
6	talks
38	tall
3	taller
1	tallest
1	talons
2	tame
1	tamely
1	tameness
1	tangible
1	tangled
1	tant
1	tantrums
2	tap
1	tape
1	tapestried
3	tapestry
2	tapped
1	tardy
1	tarried
1	tarry
4	tart
2	tarts
28	task
1	tasked
6	tasks
26	taste
7	tasted
12	tastes
1	tasting
10	taught
1	tauntingly
1	tawny
33	tea
1	tea-cake
1	tea-pot
1	tea-things
2	tea-time
1	tea-tray
17	teach
2	teachable
14	teacher
1	teacher's
23	teachers
3	teaches
6	teaching
1	teapot
11	tear
1	tear-dimmed
1	tearing
1	tearless
33	tears
1	teased
4	teaze
1	teazed
5	tedious
1	tedium
2	tedo
12	teeth
147	tell
1	telled
8	telling
6	tells
8	temper
1	temperament
1	temperate
1	temperature
1	tempered
3	tempest
2	tempests
1	tempestuously
56	temple
9	temple's
7	temples
2	temporarily
6	temporary
8	temptation
1	temptations
6	tempted
37	ten
3	tenacious
1	tenaciously
3	tenant
2	tenanted
1	tenantless
1	tenantry
5	tenants
1	tend
1	tendencies
3	tendency
6	tender
1	tendered
1	tenderer
1	tenderest
3	tenderly
6	tenderness
2	tending
1	tenement
1	tenets
1	tenez
2	tenor
1	tenses
1	tent
1	tenth
5	term
4	termed
4	terminated
2	terminating
1	termination
7	terms
4	terrible
2	terrified
11	terror
1	terror-struck
5	terrors
1	test
1	testament
1	testatrix
1	testified
1	testily
2	testimonial
2	testimony
1	tests
3	tete
1	texts
1	texture
1	th
6	th'
282	than
25	thank
2	thanked
5	thankful
2	thankfulness
1	thankless
5	thanks
2	thanksgiving
1647	that
10	that's
2	thaw
1	thawed
7788	the
1	theatre
3	thee
342	their
5	theirs
391	them
1	them's
8	theme
20	themselves
495	then
18	thence
3	theodore
1	theoretical
1	theory
505	there
6	there's
3	thereby
16	therefore
1	therefrom
2	therein
3	thereof
1	thereon
1	therewith
159	these
502	they
2	they'll
3	they're
2	they've
1	thhreatened
19	thick

Count	Word
1	thick-falling
1	thick-soled
2	thickened
2	thicker
1	thickly
1	thief's
2	thimble
26	thin
78	thing
63	things
217	think
25	thinking
5	thinks
1	thinned
28	third
1	thirdly
2	thirst
1	thirst-perish- ing
1	thirsted
2	thirsty
1	thirteen
14	thirty
1	thirty-five
663	this
8	thither
1	thorn
1	thorn-trees
72	thornfield
27	thornfield-ha- ll
1	thornhill
2	thorns
1	thorny
11	thoroughly
96	those
1	thou
134	though
257	thought
3	thoughtful
4	thoughtless
45	thoughts
23	thousand
2	thousands
1	thrall
7	thread
2	threaded
3	threading
1	threads
1	threaped
2	threatened
2	threatening
2	threatens
91	three
1	three-tailed
12	threshold
12	threw
4	thrice
1	thrift
5	thrill
8	thrilled
2	thrilling
1	thriving
8	throat
4	throb
1	throbbed
1	throbbing
2	throbs
1	throe
1	throes
4	throne
2	throng
1	throttled
142	through
1	throughout
9	throw
3	throwing
4	thrown
14	thrust
4	thrusting
1	thule
1	thumb
1	thumped
2	thunder
1	thunder-storm
2	thunderbolt
1	thundered
2	thundering
1	thunderloft
9	thursday
66	thus
4	thwarted
3	thy
1	tick
1	ticked
2	tide
1	tideless
4	tidings
2	tidy
1	tidying
8	tie
13	tied
1	tiens
1	tiens-toi
3	ties
1	tigers
2	tightly
1	tigress
112	till
1	tillage
3	timber
231	time
2	time-piece
1	time-stained
30	times
2	timid
1	timorous
1	tin-plated
2	tinge
2	tinkle
2	tinkled
1	tinkler
9	tint
2	tinted
6	tints
7	tiny
1	tiolettes
1	tip-toe
1	tirade
1	tire
29	tired
3	tiresome
1	tiresomely
1	tissue
3	title
2	titled
1	titter
1	tittered
1	titters
5107	to
10	to-day
25	to-morrow
1	to-morrow's
42	to-night
1	to-night's
2	toad
5	toast
1	toasting
1	today
3	toes
46	together
5	toil
2	toiled
4	toilet
3	toilet-table
3	toilette
1	toilettes
3	toils
4	token
3	tokens
81	told
4	tolerable
2	tolerably
2	tolerated
1	tolled
1	tolling
1	tomb
1	tome
2	tomorrow
43	tone
2	toned
13	tones
17	tongue
2	tongues
1	tonnage
1	tons
252	too
123	took
2	tool
18	top
1	top-nots
6	topic
2	tops
2	topsy-turvy
4	tore
3	torment
2	tormented
1	tormenting
1	torments
12	torn
3	torpid
2	torpor
5	torrent
1	torrents
8	torture
1	tortured
1	tortures
1	torturing
1	toss
3	tossed
2	tossing
6	total
1	tottered
1	tottering
12	touch
18	touched
1	touches
5	touching
2	tough
2	tour
1	tow
57	towards
2	towel
3	tower
1	tower-like
1	tower-top
1	towers
24	town
5	towns
1	toy
3	toys
10	trace
7	traced
6	traces
1	tracing
11	track
2	tracked
1	tracking
1	trackless
3	tract
2	tractability
1	tractable
2	trade
1	tradesman
1	traditions
1	traffic
1	tragic
2	trail
1	trailing
7	train
3	trained
1	training
3	trait
1	traitors
2	traits
6	tramp
2	trample
4	trampled
1	trampling
1	trance-like
14	tranquil
1	tranquille
7	tranquillity
1	tranquillize
1	tranquillized
3	tranquilly
1	transacted
3	transaction
1	transfer
2	transferred
2	transfix
1	transfixed
4	transformed
1	transforming
1	transgress
3	transient
1	transit
5	transitory
2	translate
3	translation
1	transparent
2	transpired
1	transplanted
2	transported
4	trap-door
1	trat
1	travail
9	travel
3	travelled
8	traveller
1	traveller's
2	travellers
6	travelling
4	travels
4	traverse
5	traversed
3	traversing
16	tray
1	trays
1	treacherous
3	treachery
4	tread
1	treading
11	treasure
1	treasured
3	treasurer
2	treasures
1	treasury
8	treat
10	treated
3	treating
5	treatment
1	treats
10	tree
1	tree-tops
34	trees
7	tremble
6	trembled
1	tremblent
10	trembling
1	tremblingly
1	tremors
1	trepidation
6	tresses
3	trial
1	trials
1	tribe
2	tribes
1	tribunal
2	tribute
2	trice
1	trick
1	tricked
2	trickle
2	trickling
4	tricks
26	tried
3	trifle
3	trifles
1	trifling
2	trim
2	trimmed
2	trimming
3	trio
1	trip
1	tripped
3	tripping
5	trite
6	triumph
1	triumphantly
1	triumphed
3	triumphs
4	trivial
1	trivialities
2	triviality
2	trod
5	trodden
1	trode
1	trooping
1	tropes
1	tropical
2	tropics
1	trot
38	trouble
11	troubled
3	troubles
2	troublesome
2	troubling
1	trousers
2	truant
1	truculent
38	true
1	truest
21	truly
11	trunk
3	trunks
1	truss
19	trust
6	trusted
1	trusting
1	trusts
1	trustworthy
33	truth
2	truthful
31	try
11	trying
1	tuck
2	tucker
2	tuckers
2	tuesday
1	tuft
1	tufted
1	tug
2	tugging
1	tuition
1	tumble
8	tumult
3	tune
1	tunefully
1	tunes
4	turban
1	turbans
3	turbid
1	turbulent
5	turf
1	turk
1	turk's
1	turkey
57	turn
97	turned
23	turning
1	turnings
1	turnpike-house
3	turns
1	turret
1	turtle-dove
1	tutor
1	tutors
1	twain
1	twang
1	tweak
1	tweed's
15	twelve
1	twelvemonth
1	twentieth
25	twenty
1	twenty-eight
1	twenty-first
1	twenty-five
2	twenty-four
2	twenty-nine
1	twenty-six
16	twice
3	twigs
14	twilight
1	twined
1	twining
2	twinkled
1	twist
3	twisted
1	twisting
1	twittering
193	two
1	two-leaved
1	two-thirds
1	tyne
2	type
1	types
5	typhus
1	tyrannies
1	tyrannized
4	tyrant
1	tyrian-dyed
1	ugh

Count	Word	Count	Word	Count	Word	Count	Word
9	ugly	1	unenslaved	5	unseen	3	vacations
2	ultimate	3	unequal	3	unsettled	1	vacillating
1	ultra-marine	8	unexpected	1	unshaken	3	vagrant
3	umbrella	2	unexpectedly	1	unshared	15	vague
5	un	1	unexplanatory	1	unshod	17	vain
4	unable	1	unexplored	1	unsmiling	6	vainly
1	unaccountable	1	unexpressed	2	unsnuffed	1	vais
2	unaccountably	1	unfathomed	1	unsocial	8	vale
2	unacquainted	2	unfavourable	3	unsophisticat-ed	5	vale-hall
1	unalloyed	1	unfeeling	1	unsounded	1	valet
1	unalterable	1	unfeminine	1	unspeakable	1	valets
1	unamiable-loo-king	1	unfinished	1	unspeakably	1	valid
1	unannounced	1	unflagging	1	unspoken	7	valley
1	unapproachable	3	unfolded	1	unsteady	1	valleys
1	unasked	1	unforced	2	unstrung	1	valour
2	unavailing	2	unfortunate	1	unsubstantial-ity	4	valuable
1	unawares	2	unfortunately	1	unsundered	5	value
1	unbecoming	1	unfostered	1	unsustained	4	valued
1	unbelieving	1	unfounded	1	unsympathizing	1	valueless
1	unbend	4	unfrequently	1	untasted	1	valuing
1	unblighted	1	unfriendly	2	untaught	1	vampyre
1	unblown	1	unfurnished	1	untempered	2	van
1	unbolt	1	unfurrowed	1	unthinking	3	vanish
2	unbroken	1	ungloved	1	untidily	9	vanished
1	unburdening	1	ungovernable	1	untidy	2	vanishing
2	uncalled-for	1	ungrateful	1	untie	2	vanity
2	uncanny	1	ungrudgingly	4	until	1	vanquishing
1	unceremonious	1	unguarded	1	untimely	1	vapid
1	unceremonious-ly	1	unguardedly	3	untiring	4	vapour
5	uncertain	6	unhappy	1	untiringly	1	vapours
3	uncertainty	1	unhealthiness	1	untouched	2	vapoury
2	unchangeable	1	unhealthy	1	untrodden	2	varandah
4	unchanged	2	unheard-of	1	untrue	11	varens'
1	unchaste	1	unneeded	1	untying	1	varens'
1	unchildlike	2	unhoped-for	4	unused	2	variance
1	unchristian	5	uniform	10	unusual	1	variation
1	uncivil	2	uniformly	1	unusually	1	variations
25	uncle	1	unimparted	4	unutterable	4	varied
2	uncle's	1	unimpeachable	1	unuttered	1	varieties
2	uncles	1	unimportant	1	unvaried	3	variety
2	unclose	1	unimpressible	1	unvarnished	5	various
7	unclosed	1	unimpressiona-ble	1	unveiled	2	varry
1	unclosing	1	uninhabited	1	unwarped	1	vary
5	unclouded	1	uninitiated	1	unwarranted	1	varying
1	uncomely	1	unintentional-ly	2	unwatched	1	vase
1	uncomfortably	1	uninvited	1	unwed	4	vases
1	uncommitted	18	union	3	unwelcome	1	vassalage
2	unconcious	1	unions	1	unwholesome	7	vast
2	uncongenial	2	unique	1	unwilling	10	vault
1	unconnected	2	united	1	unwise	1	vault-like
5	unconscious	1	unity	1	unwisely	1	vegetation
1	unconsciousne-ss	3	universal	1	unwittingly	2	vehemence
1	unconsecrated	2	universally	4	unwonted	2	vehement
1	uncontrolled	6	unjust	2	unworthy	1	vehemently
1	uncovered	2	unjustly	410	up	6	vehicle
1	uncovering	1	unkind	1	up-hill	1	vehicles
1	uncrossed	1	unkindness	1	up-rooting	21	veil
1	unction	1	unknit	3	up-stairs	1	veiled
1	uncurtained	10	unknown	1	upastree	1	veiling
1	uncut	1	unlawful	1	upbraid	1	veils
1	und	10	unless	1	upbraided	5	vein
1	undaunted	3	unlike	2	upbraiding	7	veins
1	undeceive	3	unlikely	1	upheld	7	velvet
1	undeceived	3	unlimited	1	upholstery	1	vending
1	undefined	2	unlocked	1	uplifted	1	venerable
1	undemonstrati-ve	1	unloosed	49	upon	1	venerated
1	undeniably	2	unlove	10	upper	4	veneration
133	under	1	unluckily	1	upraised	8	vengeance
1	under-jaw	1	unlucky	1	upright	1	venice
1	under-sound	1	unmannered	1	uprightly	1	venom
1	under-teacher	4	unmarried	2	uprightness	2	vent
1	underfoot	2	unmolested	1	uproar	5	venture
2	undergo	1	unmoved	2	upstairs	11	ventured
1	undergoing	4	unnatural	1	uptore	1	venturesome
1	undergone	5	unnecessary	1	uptorn	2	venturing
2	underhand	5	unnoticed	2	upward	4	verandah
29	understand	1	unnreasonable	3	upwards	1	verb
4	understanding	1	unnumbered	3	urge	1	verdant
2	understands	1	unobjectionab-le	12	urged	1	verdure
11	understood	1	unobserved	1	urgency	1	vere
4	undertake	1	unobtrusive	4	urgent	4	verge
3	undertaken	1	unpleasantly	1	urgently	2	verging
1	undertaker's	1	unpolished	1	urges	1	veriest
1	undertaking	1	unpolluted	1	urging	4	verily
1	undertakings	1	unprepared	123	us	1	vermilion
4	undertook	1	unprincipled	1	usage	1	vernacularly
2	underwent	1	unproductive	22	use	1	vernal
1	undeveloped	1	unprofitable	45	used	3	verse
1	undiscoverable	1	unquiet	12	useful	2	verses
1	undiscovered	3	unreal	12	useless	376	very
2	undisturbed	1	unreasonable	3	ushered	3	vessel
1	undivided	1	unreasonably	1	using	2	vessels
2	undone	1	unreclaimed	37	usual	1	vested
1	undoubtedly	1	unremittingly	10	usually	1	vestige
2	undress	1	unrequired	1	usurious	2	vestry
2	undressed	1	unresentful	2	usurped	4	vex
1	undressing	2	unreservedly	5	utmost	2	vexation
2	undrew	1	unresisting	12	utter	1	vexations
3	undue	1	unreturned	5	utterance	1	vexed
1	undulating	1	unreverberati-ng	21	uttered	2	vexing
3	une	1	unripe	4	uttering	3	vibrated
1	unearthly	1	unsanctioned	3	utterly	1	vibrating
6	uneasy	1	unsatisfied	1	v	1	vibration
2	uneducated	1	unscared	1	va	6	vice
1	unembroidered	1	unseasonable	1	vacancy	3	vices
1	unemployed			10	vacant	3	vicinage
1	unendurable			2	vacate	2	vicinity
				1	vacated	5	vicious
				1	vacation	1	viciously
						2	vicomte
						5	victim

1 victims	1 vulgarity	1 waterfall	573 when
2 victories	1 vulnerable	4 waters	19 whence
5 victory	1 vulture	2 watery	9 whenever
1 victualage	1 waded	2 wave	231 where
1 vienna	1 wading	1 wave-girt	3 whereas
19 view	3 waft	1 wave-wandering-gs	1 whereat
3 viewed	1 wage		6 wherein
1 viewing	2 wages	8 waved	1 whereof
2 viewless	2 wagged	3 waves	3 whereupon
6 views	1 wagging	2 waving	5 wherever
1 vigilance	1 waggon	5 wax	78 whether
1 vigils	2 wail	1 wax-work	2 whetted
2 vignettes	1 wailed	2 waxed	1 whey-faced
13 vigorous	1 wailing	1 waxen	593 which
1 vigorously	7 waist	2 waxes	163 while
7 vigour	4 waistcoat	2 waxing	1 whiles
2 vile	1 waistcoats	146 way	1 whilst
1 vileness	26 wait	1 way-side	2 whim
1 villa	19 waited	8 ways	1 whimpering
14 village	2 waiter	1 wayside	1 whine
2 village-school	22 waiting	1 wayward	2 whining
2 village-schoo-lmistress	1 waiting-woman	307 we	1 whip
2 villain	2 waits	2 we'll	1 whirl
1 villains	11 wake	1 we're	2 whirled
1 villany	2 waked	15 weak	2 whirling
1 vinaigarettes	1 wakefulness	1 weak-hearted	2 whirls
3 vindictive	3 waken	1 weakling	1 whirlwind
1 vindictiveness	10 wakened	2 weakly	2 whiskers
1 vine-leaves	1 wakening	6 weakness	8 whisper
1 vinegar	1 wakes	17 wealth	21 whispered
1 vines	6 waking	9 wealthy	6 whispering
1 vineyards	1 wales	2 weapon	2 whisperings
1 vining	46 walk	1 weapons	6 whispers
1 violate	33 walked	6 wear	1 whistled
1 violation	8 walking	1 wearied	1 whistling
6 violence	4 walks	3 weariness	5 whit
7 violent	30 wall	3 wearing	10 whitcross
2 violently	1 wall-nooks	2 wears	69 white
1 virgil	1 walled	17 weary	1 white-walled
2 virgin	26 walls	9 weather	2 white-washed
1 virile	2 walnut	3 weather-beaten	1 whiteness
1 virtually	1 walnut-panell-ed	1 weather-proof	1 whiter
6 virtue	1 walnut-wood	2 web	7 whither
1 virtues	1 waltz	4 wed	1 whitish
1 virulence	5 wander	1 wedded	278 who
1 virulent	17 wandered	11 wedding	1 whoever
9 visage	5 wanderer	1 wedding-day	50 whole
19 visible	1 wanderer's	2 wedding-dress	2 wholesome
1 visibly	1 wanderers	1 wedlock's	14 wholly
18 vision	18 wandering	1 wee	60 whom
5 visionary	3 wanderings	1 weed	63 whose
3 visions	1 wane	1 weeds	1 whosoever
17 visit	1 waned	30 week	102 why
2 visitant	87 want	2 week's	2 wi'
2 visitation	51 wanted	1 week-day	1 wick
2 visited	6 wanting	1 week-days	14 wicked
4 visiting	1 wantonly	2 weekly	3 wickedness
7 visitor	13 wants	26 weeks	10 wicket
7 visitors	2 war	6 weep	22 wide
1 visitress	1 warbled	5 weeping	2 widely
6 visits	1 warbling	3 weigh	1 wider
1 vist	5 ward	1 weighed	1 widest-winged
4 vital	1 ward-robes	1 weighing	6 widow
2 vitality	8 wardrobe	1 weighs	2 widow's
3 vitals	1 ware	5 weight	1 wie
1 vivacious	2 warehouse	12 welcome	1 wielded
1 vivaciously	1 warfare	2 welcomed	80 wife
12 vivacity	1 warily	1 welcoming	58 wild
6 vivid	1 wark	1 welkin	1 wilder
3 vividly	23 warm	322 well	5 wilderness
1 vividness	1 warm-hearted	1 well-arranged	3 wildest
2 viz	7 warmed	1 well-brink	12 wildly
2 vocabulary	2 warmer	1 well-built	1 wilds
2 vocal	1 warming	1 well-conducted	2 wilfully
1 vocalist	1 warmly	1 well-cut	613 will
8 vocation	2 warms	1 well-defined	1 will-o'-the-w-isp
1 voce	7 warmth	3 well-dressed	11 willing
1 vogue	8 warn	1 well-executed	4 willingly
124 voice	8 warned	1 well-informed	2 willow
7 voices	8 warning	6 well-known	1 wills
11 void	3 warnings	1 well-loved	4 wilson
2 voila	2 warped	1 well-planted	1 wilsons
1 voiture	2 warrant	1 well-principl-ed	1 wilt
1 volatile	1 warranted	1 well-regulated	7 win
1 volcanic	1 warrior	2 well-remember-ed	47 wind
1 volcano-tops	1 warrior-march	1 well-smoothed	3 winding
3 volume	1 wars	1 well-timed	2 windings
3 volumes	2525 was	1 wellfare	61 window
1 voluntarily	4 wash	1 welsh	1 window-blind
3 voluntary	5 wash-stand	1 welshwoman	1 window-blinds
1 volunteered	6 washed	1 wended	3 window-curtain
1 voluptuous	5 washing	144 went	1 window-panes
1 volcanic-look-ing	1 washy	7 wept	2 window-recess
2 vos	10 waste	621 were	6 window-seat
1 votary	9 wasted	1 werke	1 window-sill
1 vote	1 wasting	14 west	1 windowless
2 votre	31 watch	1 west-india	17 windows
2 vouch	1 watch-chain	1 west-indian	4 winds
1 vouchsafe	1 watch-guard	3 western	1 windy
3 vouchsafed	34 watched	25 wet	10 wine
5 vous	1 watcher	1 wetting	1 wine-glass
4 vow	2 watches	1 whalebone	2 wine-merchant
4 vowed	2 watchful	1 wharton	3 wing
1 vowing	11 watching	721 what	8 wings
1 vows	1 watchings	28 whatever	1 winner
6 voyage	53 water	1 wheel	1 winning
2 vrai	1 water-colour	4 wheeled	21 winter
2 vulcan	1 water-flags	1 wheeling	1 winter's
2 vulgar	2 water-jug	7 wheels	1 winters
	1 watered		5 wintry

5	wipe	1	wrang	
7	wiped	1	wrap	
1	wire	7	wrapped	
4	wisdom	1	wrappers	
3	wise	2	wrapping	
4	wisely	1	wraps	
3	wiser	1	wrapt	
106	wish	4	wrath	
70	wished	4	wreath	
19	wishes	3	wreathed	
9	wishing	1	wreaths	
1	wistful	4	wreck	
1	wistfully	1	wrecked	
1	wit	1	wren	
5	witch	1	wrench	
1	witch's	2	wrenched	
1	witchcraft	1	wrens'	
1	witchery	1	wrest	
1400	with	2	wrestle	
7	withdraw	1	wrestled	
1	withdrawing	1	wrestling	
6	withdrawn	1	wrestlings	
1	withdraws	2	wretch	
17	withdrew	10	wretched	
2	wither	2	wretchedly	
2	withered	2	wretchedness	
1	withering	2	wring	
2	withheld	4	wrist	
56	within	1	wrists	
141	without	14	write	
5	witness	2	writhed	
6	witnessed	1	writhing	
1	witnesses	11	writing	
1	witnessing	16	written	
6	wits	24	wrong	
3	witty	2	wronged	
2	wives	1	wrongly	
7	woe	3	wrongs	
4	woes	15	wrote	
4	woke	10	wrought	
1	wolf's	2	wrung	
1	wolfe	2	wtn	
1	wolfish	5	y	
85	woman	1	yaas	
6	woman's	11	yard	
1	womankind	1	yard-gates	
21	women	5	yards	
5	won	1	yawned	
13	won't	2	yawns	
35	wonder	16	ye	
16	wondered	1	ye'll	
3	wonderful	3	ye've	
2	wonderfully	25	year	
5	wondering	1	year's	
1	wonderingly	1	yearned	
1	wonderment	2	yearning	
2	wondrous	1	yearnings	
3	wont	82	years	
1	wonted	1	years'	
37	wood	1	yell	
1	wood-land	1	yelled	
2	wood-work	5	yellow	
1	woodbine	2	yells	
1	wooden	1	yelp	
2	woodland	202	yes	
7	woods	17	yesterday	
2	woollen	242	yet	
5	wor	3	yew	
83	word	1	yew-trees	
103	words	13	yield	
1	wordy	7	yielded	
12	wore	6	yielding	
51	work	3	yoke	
1	work-bag	1	yond'	
1	work-boxes	17	yonder	
1	work-house	4	yor	
1	workbox	2964	you	
9	worked	3	you'd	
2	workhouse	8	you'll	
9	working	5	you're	
1	working-people	9	you've	
5	workings	81	young	
4	works	14	younger	
76	world	1	youngest	
2	world's	676	your	
2	worldly	24	yours	
2	worlds	73	yourself	
1	worm	1	yourseln	
1	wormwood	17	youth	
14	worn	3	youthful	
1	worn-out	4	zeal	
3	worried	1	zealots	
1	worries	2	zealous	
19	worse	1	zembla	
3	worship	1	zenith	
2	worshipped	1	zig-zag	
17	worst	1	zone	
1	worsted	1	zornes	
13	worth			
2	worthier			
3	worthless			
1	worthlessly			
10	worthy			
1	wot			
664	would			
4	wouldn't			
13	wound			
5	wounded			
2	wounds			
1	woven			
1	wraith-like			

FIELD OF REFERENCE

1.01 [Jane Eyre.
1.02 Vol. 1 Chapter 1]
1.03   There was no possibility of taking a walk that
1.04 day. We had been wandering, indeed, in the
1.05 leafless shrubbery an hour in the morning;
1.06 but since dinner /Mrs. Reed, when there was
1.07 no company, dined early/ the cold winter
1.08 wind had brought with it clouds so sombre,
1.09 and a rain so penetrating, that further out--
1.10 door exercise was now out of the question.
1.11   I was glad of it: I never liked long walks,
1.12 especially on chilly afternoons: dreadful tome
1.13 was the coming home in the raw twilight,
1.14 with nipped fingers and toes, and a heart
1.15 saddened by the chidings of Bessie, the nurse,
1.16 and humbled by the consciousness of my phy-
1.17 sical inferiority to Eliza, John, and Georgiana
1.18 Reed.
2.01   The said Eliza, John, and Georgiana were
2.02 now clustered round their mama in the drawing--
2.03 room: she lay reclined on a sofa by the fire-
2.04 side, and with her darlings about her /for the
2.05 time neither quarrelling nor crying/ looked
2.06 perfectly happy. Me, she had dispensed from
2.07 joining the group; saying, "She regretted to
2.08 be under the necessity of keeping me at a
2.09 distance; but that until she heard from Bes-
2.10 sie, and could discover by her own obser-
2.11 vation that I was endeavouring in good
2.12 earnest to acquire a more sociable and child-
2.13 like disposition, a more attractive and sprightly
2.14 manner, -- something lighter, franker, more
2.15 natural as it were -- she really must exclude
2.16 me from privileges intended only for con-
2.17 tented, happy, little children."
2.18   "What does Bessie say I have done?" I
2.19 asked.
2.20   "Jane, I don't like cavillers or questioners:
2.21 besides, there is something truly forbidding
2.22 in a child taking up her elders in that manner.
2.23 Be seated somewhere; and until you can
2.24 speak pleasantly, remain silent."
2.25   A small breakfast-room adjoined the
2.26 drawing-room: I slipped in there. It con-
2.27 tained a book-case: I soon possessed myself
3.01 of a volume, taking care that it should be
3.02 one stored with pictures. I mounted into
3.03 the window-seat: gathering up my feet, I sat
3.04 cross-legged, like a Turk; and, having drawn
3.05 the red moreen curtain nearly close, I was
3.06 shrined in double retirement.
3.07   Folds of scarlet drapery shut in my view
3.08 to the right hand; to the left were the clear
3.09 panes of glass, protecting, but not separating
3.10 me from the drear November day. At in-
3.11 tervals, while turning over the leaves of my
3.12 book, I studied the aspect of that winter after-
3.13 noon. Afar it offered a pale blank of mist
3.14 and cloud; near, a scene of wet lawn and
3.15 storm-beat shrub, with ceaseless rain sweeping
3.16 away wildly before a long and lamentable
3.17 blast.
3.18   I returned to my book -- Bewick's History
3.19 of British Birds: the letter-press thereof I
3.20 cared little for, generally speaking; and yet
3.21 there were certain introductory pages that,
3.22 child as I was, I could not pass quite as a
3.23 blank. They were those which treat of the
3.24 haunts of sea-fowl; of "the solitary rocks
3.25 and promontories" by them only inhabited;
3.26 of the coast of Norway, studded with isles
3.27 from its southern extremity, the Lindeness, or
3.28 Naze, to the North Cape --
4.01   "Where the Northern Ocean, in vast whirls
4.02   Boils round the naked, melancholy isles
4.03   Of farthest Thule; and the Atlantic surge
4.04   Pours in among the stormy Hebrides."
4.05   Nor could I pass unnoticed the suggestion
4.06 of the bleak shores of Lapland, Siberia,
4.07 Spitzbergen, Nova Zembla, Iceland, Green-
4.08 land, with "the vast sweep of the Arctic
4.09 Zone, and those forlorn regions of dreary
4.10 space, -- that reservoir of frost and snow,
4.11 where firm fields of ice, the accumulation of
4.12 centuries of winters, glazed in Alpine heights
4.13 above heights, surround the pole, and con-
4.14 centre the multiplied rigors of extreme
4.15 cold." Of these death-white realms I formed
4.16 an idea of my own: shadowy, like all the
4.17 half-comprehended notions that float dim
4.18 through children's brains, but strangely im-
4.19 pressive. The words in these introductory
4.20 pages connected themselves with the succeed-
4.21 ing vignettes, and gave significance to the
4.22 rock standing up alone in a sea of billow and
4.23 spray; to the broken boat stranded on a deso-
4.24 late coast; to the cold and ghastly moon
4.25 glancing through bars of cloud at a wreck
4.26 just sinking.
4.27   I cannot tell what sentiment haunted the
4.28 quite solitary churchyard with its inscribed
5.01 headstone; its gate, its two trees, its low
5.02 horizon, girdled by a broken wall, and its
5.03 newly-risen crescent, attesting the hour of
5.04 even-tide.
5.05   The two ships becalmed on a torpid sea, I
5.06 believed to be marine phantoms.
5.07   The fiend pinning down the thief's pack
5.08 behind him, I passed over quickly: it was an
5.09 object of terror.
5.10   So was the black, horned thing seated aloof
5.11 on a rock, surveying a distant crowd surround-
5.12 ing a gallows.
5.13   Each picture told a story; mysterious often
5.14 to my undeveloped understanding and im-
5.15 perfect feelings, yet ever profoundly interest-
5.16 ing: as interesting as the tales Bessie some-
5.17 times narrated on winter evenings, when she
5.18 chanced to be in good humour; and when,
5.19 having brought her ironing-table to the
5.20 nursery-hearth, she allowed us to sit about
5.21 it, and while she got up Mrs. Reed's lace
5.22 frills, and crimped her night-cap borders, fed
5.23 our eager attention with passages of love and
5.24 adventure taken from old fairy tales and older
5.25 ballads; or /as at a later period I discovered/
5.26 from the pages of Pamela, and Henry, Earl of
5.27 Moreland.
5.28   With Bewick on my knee, I was then
6.01 happy: happy at least in my way. I feared
6.02 nothing but interruption, and that came too
6.03 soon. The breakfast room-door opened.
6.04   "Boh! Madam Mope!" cried the voice of
6.05 John Reed; then he paused: he found the
6.06 room apparently empty.
6.07   "Where the dickens is she?" he con-
6.08 tinued. "Lizzy! Georgy! /calling to his
6.09 sisters/ Joan is not here: tell mama she is
6.10 run out into the rain -- bad animal!"
6.11   "It is well I drew the curtain," thought I;
6.12 and I wished fervently he might not discover
6.13 my hiding-place: nor would John Reed have
6.14 found it out himself; he was not quick either
6.15 of vision or conception: but Eliza just put her
6.16 head in at the door and said at once: --
6.17   "She is in the window-seat, to be sure,
6.18 Jack."
6.19   And I came out immediately; for I trembled
6.20 at the idea of being dragged forth by the said
6.21 Jack.
6.22   "What do you want?" I asked, with awk-
6.23 ward diffidence.
6.24   "Say, `what do you want, Master Reed;'"
6.25 was the answer. "I want you to come here;"
6.26 and seating himself in an arm-chair, he inti-
6.27 mated by a gesture that I was to approach
6.28 and stand before him.
7.01   John Reed was a schoolboy of fourteen
7.02 years old; four years older than I, for I was
7.03 but ten; large and stout for his age, with a
7.04 dingy and unwholesome skin; thick linea-
7.05 ments in a spacious visage, heavy limbs and
7.06 large extremities. He gorged himself habi-
7.07 tually at table, which made him bilious, and
7.08 gave him a dim and bleared eye and
7.09 flabby cheeks. He ought now to have been
7.10 at school; but his mama had taken him home
7.11 for a month or two, "on account of his deli-
7.12 cate health." Mr. Miles, the master, affirmed
7.13 that he would do very well if he had
7.14 fewer cakes and sweetmeats sent him from
7.15 home; but the mother's heart turned from an
7.16 opinion so harsh, and inclined rather to the
7.17 more refined idea that John's sallowness was
7.18 owing to over-application and, perhaps, to
7.19 pining after home.
7.20   John had not much affection for his mother
7.21 and sisters, and an antipathy to me. He bul-
7.22 lied and punished me: not two or three times
7.23 in the week, nor once or twice in the day, but
7.24 continually: every nerve I had feared him,
7.25 and every morsel of flesh on my bones shrank
7.26 when he came near. There were moments
7.27 when I was bewildered by the terror he in-
7.28 spired; because I had no appeal whatever
8.01 against either his menaces or his inflictions;
8.02 the servants did not like to offend their young
8.03 master by taking my part against him, and
8.04 Mrs. Reed was blind and deaf on the subject:
8.05 she never saw him strike or heard him abuse
8.06 me; though he did both now and then in her
8.07 very presence: more frequently, however, be-
8.08 hind her back.
8.09   Habitually obedient to John, I came up to
8.10 his chair: he spent some three minutes in
8.11 thrusting out his tongue at me as far as he
8.12 could without damaging the roots: I knew he
8.13 would soon strike, and while dreading the blow,
8.14 I mused on the disgusting and ugly appearance
8.15 of him who would presently deal it. I wonder
8.16 if he read that notion in my face; for, all at
8.17 once, without speaking, he struck suddenly and
8.18 strongly. I tottered, and on regaining my equi-
8.19 librium retired back a step or two from his chair.
8.20   "That is for your impudence in answering
8.21 mama a while since," said he, "and for your
8.22 sneaking way of getting behind curtains, and
8.23 for the look you had in your eyes two minutes
8.24 since, you rat!"
8.25   Accustomed to John Reed's abuse, I never
8.26 had an idea of replying to it; my care was
8.27 how to endure the blow which would certainly
8.28 follow the insult.
9.01   "What are you doing behind the curtain?"
9.02 he asked.
9.03   "I was reading."
9.04   "Shew the book."
9.05   I returned to the window and fetched it
9.06 thence.
9.07   "You have no business to take our books:
9.08 you are a dependant, mama says; you have no
9.09 money; your father left you none; you ought

9.10 to beg, and not to live here with gentlemen's
9.11 children like us, and eat the same meals we do,
9.12 and wear clothes at our mama's expense.
9.13 Now, I'll teach you to rummage my book-
9.14 shelves: for they are mine; all the house
9.15 belongs to me or will do in a few years. Go
9.16 and stand by the door, out of the way of the
9.17 mirror and the windows."
9.18   I did so, not at first aware what was his in-
9.19 tention; but when I saw him lift and poise the
9.20 book and stand in act to hurl it, I instinc-
9.21 tively started aside with a cry of alarm: not
9.22 soon enough, however; the volume was flung,
9.23 it hit me, and I fell, striking my head against
9.24 the door and cutting it. The cut bled, the
9.25 pain was sharp: my terror had passed its
9.26 climax; other feelings succeeded.
9.27   "Wicked and cruel boy!" I said. "You
10.01 are like a murderer -- you are like a slave
10.02 driver -- you are like the Roman emperors!"
10.03 I had read Goldsmith's History of Rome,
10.04 and had formed my opinion of Nero, Caligula,
10.05 &c. Also I had drawn parallels in silence,
10.06 which I never thought thus to have declared
10.07 aloud.
10.08   "what! what!" he cried. "Did she say
10.09 that to me? Did you hear her, Eliza and
10.10 Georgiana? Won't I tell mama? but first" --
10.11   He ran headlong at me; I felt him grasp
10.12 my hair and my shoulder: he had closed with
10.13 a desperate thing. I really saw in him a
10.14 tyrant; a murderer. I felt a drop or two of
10.15 blood from my head trickle down my neck, and
10.16 was sensible of somewhat pungent suffering:
10.17 these sensations, for the time predominated
10.18 over fear, and I received him in frantic sort.
10.19 I don't very well know what I did with my
10.20 hands, but he called me "Rat! rat!" and bel-
10.21 lowed out aloud. Aid was near him: Eliza
10.22 and Georgiana had run for Mrs. Reed, who
10.23 was gone up stairs; she now came upon the
10.24 scene, followed by Bessie and her maid Abbot.
10.25 we were parted: I heard the words: --
10.26   "Dear! dear! what a fury to fly at Master
10.27 John!"
11.01   "Did ever anybody see such a picture of
11.02 passion!"
11.03   Then Mrs. Reed subjoined: --
11.04   "Take her away to the red-room, and lock
11.05 her in there." Four hands were immediately
11.06 laid upon me, and I was borne up stairs.
12.01 [Vol. 1 Chapter 2]
12.02 I resisted all the way: a new thing for me,
12.03 and a circumstance which greatly strengthened
12.04 the bad opinion Bessie and Miss Abbot were
12.05 disposed to entertain of me. The fact is, I was
12.06 a trifle beside myself; or rather out of myself,
12.07 as the French would say: I was conscious that
12.08 a moment's mutiny had already rendered me
12.09 liable to strange penalties, and like any other
12.10 rebel slave, I felt resolved, in my desperation,
12.11 to go all lengths.
12.12   "Hold her arms, Miss Abbot; she's like a
12.13 mad cat."
12.14   "For shame! for shame!" cried the lady's--
12.15 maid. "what shocking conduct, Miss Eyre,
12.16 to strike a young gentleman, your benefactress's
12.17 son! Your young master!"
12.18   "Master! How is he my master? Am I
12.19 a servant?"
12.20   "No; you are less than a servant, for you
13.01 do nothing for your keep. There, sit down,
13.02 and think over your wickedness."
13.03   They had got me by this time into the apart-
13.04 ment indicated by Mrs. Reed, and had thrust
13.05 me upon a stool: my impulse was to rise from
13.06 it like a spring; their two pairs of hands ar-
13.07 rested me instantly.
13.08   "If you don't sit still, you must be tied
13.09 down," said Bessie. "Miss Abbot, lend me
13.10 your garters; she would break mine directly."
13.11   Miss Abbot turned to divest a stout leg of
13.12 the necessary ligature. This preparation for
13.13 bonds, and the additional ignominy it inferred,
13.14 took a little of the excitement out of me.
13.15   "Don't take them off," I cried; "I will not
13.16 stir."
13.17   In guarantee whereof, I attached myself to
13.18 my seat by my hands.
13.19   "Mind you don't," said Bessie; and when
13.20 she had ascertained that I was really subsiding,
13.21 she loosened her hold of me; then she and
13.22 Miss Abbot stood with folded arms, looking
13.23 darkly and doubtfully on my face, as incre-
13.24 dulous of my sanity.
13.25   "She never did so before," at last said Bessie,
13.26 turning to the Abigail.
13.27   "But it was always in her," was the reply.
14.01   "I've told Missis often my opinion about the
14.02 child, and Missis agreed with me. She's an
14.03 underhand little thing: I never saw a girl of
14.04 her age with so much cover."
14.05   Bessie answered not; but ere long, ad-
14.06 dressing me, she said,
14.07   "You ought to be aware, Miss, that you are
14.08 under obligatioons to Mrs. Reed: she keeps
14.09 you; if she were to turn you off, you would
14.10 have to go to the poor-house."
14.11   I had nothing to say to these words: they
14.12 were not new to me: my very first recol-
14.13 lections of existence included hints of the
14.14 same kind. This reproach of my dependence
14.15 had become a vague sing-song in my ear;
14.16 very painful and crushing, but only half in-
14.17 telligible. Miss Abbot joined in: --
14.18   "And you ought not to think yourself on
14.19 an equality with the Misses Reed and Master
14.20 Reed, because Missis kindly allows you to be
14.21 brought up with them. They will have a
14.22 great deal of money, and you will have none:
14.23 it is your place to be humble, and to try to
14.24 make yourself agreeable to them."
14.25   "What we tell you, is for your good," added
14.26 Bessie, in no harsh voice: "you should try to
14.27 be useful and pleasant, then perhaps you
15.01 would have a home here; but if you become
15.02 passionate and rude, Missis will send you
15.03 away, I am sure."
15.04   "Besides," said Miss Abbot, "God will
15.05 punish her: he might strike her dead in the
15.06 midst of her tantrums, and then where would
15.07 she go? Come, Bessie, we will leave her: I
15.08 wouldn't have her heart for anything. Say
15.09 your prayers, Miss Eyre, when you are by
15.10 yourself; for if you don't repent, something
15.11 bad might be permitted to come down the
15.12 chimney, and fetch you away."
15.13   They went, shutting the door, and locking
15.14 it behind them.
15.15   The red-room was a spare chamber, very
15.16 seldom slept in; I might say never, indeed,
15.17 unless when a chance influx of visitors at Gates-
15.18 head-hall rendered it necessary to turn to
15.19 account all the accommodation it contained:
15.20 yet it was one of the largest and stateliest
15.21 chambers in the mansion. A bed supported
15.22 on massive pillars of mahogany, hung with
15.23 curtains of deep red damask, stood out like
15.24 a tabernacle in the centre; the two large
15.25 windows, with their blinds always drawn
15.26 down, were half shrouded in festoons and
15.27 falls of similar drapery; the carpet was red;
15.28 the table at the foot of the bed was covered
16.01 with a crimson cloth; the walls were a soft
16.02 fawn colour, with a blush of pink in it; the
16.03 wardrobe, the toilet-table, the chairs were of
16.04 darkly polished old mahogany. Out of these
16.05 deep surrounding shades rose high, and glared
16.06 white, the piled-up mattresses and pillows of
16.07 the bed, spread with a snowy Marseilles coun-
16.08 terpane. Scarcely less prominent was an
16.09 ample, cushioned easy-chair near the head of
16.10 the bed, also white, with a footstool before it;
16.11 and looking, as I thought, like a pale throne.
16.12   This room was chill, because it seldom had
16.13 a fire; it was silent, because remote from the
16.14 nursery and kitchens; solemn, because it was
16.15 known to be so seldom entered. The house-
16.16 maid alone came here on Saturdays, to wipe
16.17 from the mirrors and the furniture a week's
16.18 quiet dust: and Mrs. Reed herself, at far
16.19 intervals, visited it to review the contents of a
16.20 certain secret drawer in the wardrobe, where
16.21 were stored divers parchments, her jewel-casket,
16.22 and a miniature of her deceased husband; and
16.23 in those last words lies the secret of the red--
16.24 room: the spell which kept it so lonely in spite
16.25 of its grandeur.
16.26   Mr. Reed had been dead nine years: it was
16.27 in this chamber he breathed his last; here he
16.28 lay in state; hence his coffin was borne by the
17.01 undertaker's men; and, since that day, a sense
17.02 of dreary consecration had guarded it from
17.03 frequent intrusion.
17.04   My seat, to which Bessie and the bitter
17.05 Miss Abbot had left me riveted, was a low
17.06 ottoman near the marble chimney-piece; the
17.07 bed rose before me; to my right hand there
17.08 was the high, dark wardrobe, with subdued,
17.09 broken reflections varying the gloss of its
17.10 pannels; to my left were the muffled windows;
17.11 a great looking-glass between them repeated
17.12 the vacant majesty of the bed and room. I
17.13 was not quite sure whether they had locked
17.14 the door; and, when I dared move, I got up,
17.15 and went to see. Alas! yes: no jail was ever
17.16 more secure. Returning, I had to cross before
17.17 the looking-glass; my fascinated glance in-
17.18 voluntarily explored the depth it revealed.
17.19 All looked colder and darker in that visionary
17.20 hollow than in reality: and the strange little
17.21 figure there gazing at me, with a white face
17.22 and arms specking the gloom, and glittering
17.23 eyes of fear moving where all else was still,
17.24 had the effect of a real spirit: I thought it
17.25 like one of the tiny phantoms, half fairy, half
17.26 imp, Bessie's evening stories represented as
17.27 coming up out of lone, ferny dells in moors,
18.01 and appearing before the eyes of belated
18.02 travellers. I returned to my stool.
18.03   Superstition was with me at that moment;
18.04 but it was not yet her hour for complete
18.05 victory: my blood was still warm; the mood
18.06 of the revolted slave was still bracing me with
18.07 its bitter vigour; I had to stem a rapid rush
18.08 of retrospective thought before I quailed to
18.09 the dismal present.
18.10   All John Reed's violent tyrannies, all his
18.11 sisters' proud indifference, all his mother's
18.12 aversion, all the servants' partiality, turned
18.13 up in my disturbed mind like a dark deposit
18.14 in a turbid well. why was I always suffering,

18.15 always brow-beaten, always accused, for ever
18.16 condemned? why could I never please? why
18.17 why was it useless to try to win any one's
18.18 favour? Eliza, who was headstrong and
18.19 selfish, was respected. Georgiana, who had
18.20 a spoiled temper, a very acrid spite, a captious
18.21 and insolent carriage, was universally indulged.
18.22 Her beauty, her pink cheeks and golden curls,
18.23 seemed to give delight to all who looked at
18.24 her, and to purchase indemnity for every fault.
18.25 John, no one thwarted, much less punished;
18.26 though he twisted the necks of the pigeons,
18.27 killed the little pea-chicks, set the dogs at the
18.28 sheep, stripped the hothouse vines of their
19.01 fruit, and broke the buds off the choicest
19.02 plants in the conservatory: he called his
19.03 mother "old girl," too; sometimes reviled her
19.04 for her dark skin, similar to his own; bluntly
19.05 disregarded her wishes; not unfrequently tore
19.06 and spoiled her silk attire; and he was still
19.07 "her own darling." I dared commit no fault:
19.08 I strove to fulfil every duty; and I was termed
19.09 naughty and tiresome, sullen and sneaking,
19.10 from morning to noon, and from noon to
19.11 night.
19.12   My head still ached and bled with the blow
19.13 and fall I had received: no one had reproved
19.14 John for wantonly striking me; and because I
19.15 had turned against him to avert farther irra-
19.16 tional violence, I was loaded with general op-
19.17 probrium.
19.18   "Unjust! -- unjust!" said my reason, forced
19.19 by the agonizing stimulus into precocious
19.20 though transitory power; and Resolve, equally
19.21 wrought up, instigated some strange expedient
19.22 to achieve escape from insupportable oppres-
19.23 sion -- as running away, or, if that could not
19.24 be effected, never eating or drinking more, and
19.25 letting myself die.
19.26   What a consternation of soul was mine that
19.27 dreary afternoon! How all my brain was in
19.28 tumult, and all my heart in insurrection! Yet
20.01 in what darkness, what dense ignorance, was
20.02 the mental battle fought! I could not an-
20.03 swer the ceaseless inward question -- why I thus
20.04 suffered; now, at the distance of -- I will not
20.05 say how many years, I see it clearly.
20.06   I was a discord in Gateshead-hall; I was
20.07 like nobody there; I had nothing in harmony
20.08 with Mrs. Reed or her children, or her chosen
20.09 vassalage. If they did not love me, in fact, as
20.10 little did I love them. They were not bound
20.11 to regard with affection a thing that could not
20.12 sympathize with one amongst them; a hetero-
20.13 geneous thing, opposed to them in tempera-
20.14 ment, in capacity, in propensities; a useless
20.15 thing, incapable of serving their interest, or
20.16 adding to their pleasure; a noxious thing,
20.17 cherishing the germs of indignation at their
20.18 treatment, of contempt of their judgment, I
20.19 know, that had I been a sanguine, brilliant,
20.20 careless, exacting, handsome, romping child --
20.21 though equally dependent and friendless --
20.22 Mrs. Reed would have endured my presence
20.23 more complacently; her children would have
20.24 entertained for me more of the cordiality of
20.25 fellow-feeling; the servants would have been
20.26 less prone to make me the scape-goat of the
20.27 nursery.
20.28   Daylight began to forsake the red-room; it
21.01 was past four o'clock and the beclouded after-
21.02 noon was tending to drear twilight. I heard
21.03 the rain still beating continuously on the stair-
21.04 case window, and the wind howling in the
21.05 grove behind the hall; I grew by degrees
21.06 cold as stone, and then my courage sank.
21.07 My habitual mode of humiliation, self-doubt,
21.08 forlorn depression, fell damp on the embers
21.09 of my decaying ire. All said I was wicked,
21.10 and perhaps I might be so: what thought had
21.11 I been but just conceiving of starving myself
21.12 to death? That certainly was a crime: and
21.13 was I fit to die? Or was the vault under the
21.14 chancel of Gateshead church an inviting
21.15 bourne? In such vault I had been told did Mr.
21.16 Reed lie buried; and led by this thought to
21.17 recall his idea, I dwelt on it with gathering
21.18 dread. I could not remember him; but I
21.19 knew that he was my own uncle -- my mother's
21.20 brother -- that he had taken me when a parent-
21.21 less infant to his house; and that in his last mo-
21.22 ments he had required a promise of Mrs. Reed
21.23 that she would rear and maintain me as one of
21.24 her own children. Mrs. Reed probably con-
21.25 sidered she had kept this promise; and so she
21.26 had I dare say, as well as her nature would
21.27 permit her; but how could she really like
21.28 an interloper not of her race, and unconnected
22.01 with her, after her husband's death, by any tie?
22.02 It must have been most irksome to find her-
22.03 self bound by a hard-wrung pledge to stand
22.04 in the stead of a parent to a strange child she
22.05 could not love, and to see an uncongenial
22.06 alien permanently intruded on her own family
22.07 group.
22.08   A singular notion dawned upon me. I
22.09 doubted not -- never doubted -- that if Mr.
22.10 Reed had been alive he would have treated
22.11 me kindly; and now, as I sat looking at the
22.12 white bed and overshadowed walls -- occa-
22.13 sionally also turning a fascinated eye towards

22.14 the dimly gleaming mirror -- I began to recall
22.15 what I had heard of dead men, troubled in
22.16 their graves by the violation of their last
22.17 wishes, revisiting the earth to punish the per-
22.18 jured and avenge the oppressed; and I thought
22.19 Mr. Reed's spirit, harassed by the wrongs of
22.20 his sister's child, might quit its abode --
22.21 whether in the church vault or in the un-
22.22 known world of the departed -- and rise before
22.23 me in this chamber. I wiped my tears and
22.24 hushed my sobs, fearful lest any sign of
22.25 violent grief might waken a preternatural
22.26 voice to comfort me, or elicit from the gloom
22.27 some haloed face, bending over me with
22.28 strange pity. This idea, consolatory in theory,
23.01 I felt would be terrible if realized: with all
23.02 my might I endeavoured to stifle it -- I en-
23.03 deavoured to be firm. Shaking my hair from
23.04 my eyes, I lifted my head and tried to look
23.05 boldly round the dark room: at this moment
23.06 a light gleamed on the wall. Was it, I asked
23.07 myself, a ray from the moon penetrating some
23.08 aperture in the blind? No; moonlight was
23.09 still, and this stirred; while I gazed, it glided
23.10 up to the ceiling and quivered over my head.
23.11 I can now conjecture readily that this streak
23.12 of light was, in all likelihood, a gleam from a
23.13 lantern, carried by some one across the lawn:
23.14 but then, prepared as my mind was for horror,
23.15 shaken as my nerves were by agitation, I
23.16 thought the swift-darting beam was a herald
23.17 of some coming vision from another world.
23.18 My heart beat thick, my head grew hot; a
23.19 sound filled my ears, which I deemed the
23.20 rushing of wings: something seemed near me;
23.21 I was oppressed, suffocated: endurance broke
23.22 down; I rushed to the door and shook the
23.23 lock in desperate effort. Steps came running
23.24 along the outer passage; the key turned,
23.25 Bessie and Abbot entered.
23.26   "Miss Eyre are you ill?" said Bessie.
23.27   "What a dreadful noise! it went quite
23.28 through me!" exclaimed Abbot.
24.01   "Take me out! Let me go into the nur-
24.02 sery?" was my cry.
24.03   "What for? Are you hurt? Have you
24.04 seen something?" again demanded Bessie.
24.05   "Oh! I saw a light, and I thought a ghost
24.06 would come." I had now got hold of Bessie's
24.07 hand, and she did not snatch it from me.
24.08   "She has screamed out on purpose," de-
24.09 clared Abbot, in some disgust. "And what a
24.10 scream! If she had been in great pain one
24.11 would have excused it, but she only wanted
24.12 to bring us all here: I know her naughty
24.13 tricks."
24.14   "What is all this?" demanded another
24.15 voice peremptorily; and Mrs. Reed came
24.16 along the corridor, her cap flying wide, her
24.17 gown rustling stormily. "Abbot and Bessie,
24.18 I believe I gave orders that Jane Eyre should
24.19 be left in the red-room till I came to her my-
24.20 self."
24.21   "Miss Jane screamed so loud, ma'am,"
24.22 pleaded Bessie.
24.23   "Let her go;" was the only answer.
24.24 "Loose Bessie's hand, child: you cannot suc-
24.25 ceed in getting out by these means, be assured.
24.26 I abhor artifice, particularly in children; it is
24.27 my duty to show you that tricks will not an-
24.28 swer: you will now stay here an hour longer,
25.01 and it is only on condition of perfect submission
25.02 and stillness that I shall liberate you then."
25.03   "Oh aunt, have pity! Forgive me! I can-
25.04 not endure it -- let me be punished some other
25.05 way! I shall be killed if -- "
25.06   "Silence! This violence is all most repul-
25.07 sive:" and so, no doubt, she felt it. I was a
25.08 precocious actress in her eyes: she sincerely
25.09 looked on me as a compound of virulent pas-
25.10 sions, mean spirit, and dangerous duplicity.
25.11   Bessie and Abbot having retreated, Mrs.
25.12 Reed, impatient of my now frantic anguish and
25.13 wild sobs, abruptly thrust me back and locked
25.14 me in, without farther parley. I heard her
25.15 sweeping away; and soon after she was gone,
25.16 I suppose I had a species of fit: unconscious-
25.17 ness closed the scene.
26.01 [Vol. 1 Chapter 3]
26.02 The next thing I remember is, waking up with
26.03 a feeling as if I had had a frightful night-mare,
26.04 and seeing before me a terrible red glare,
26.05 crossed with thick black bars. I heard voices,
26.06 too, speaking with a hollow sound, and as if
26.07 muffled by a rush of wind or water: agitation,
26.08 uncertainty, and an all predominating sense of
26.09 terror confused my faculties. Ere long, I be-
26.10 came aware that some one was handling me;
26.11 lifting me up and supporting me in a sitting
26.12 posture: and that more tenderly than I had
26.13 ever been raised or upheld before. I rested
26.14 my head against a pillow or an arm, and felt
26.15 easy.
26.16   In five minutes more, the cloud of bewilder-
26.17 ment dissolved: I knew quite well that I was
26.18 in my own bed, and that the red glare was the
26.19 nursery fire. It was night: a candle burnt on
26.20 the table; Bessie stood at the bed-foot with a
27.01 basin in her hand, and a gentleman sat in a
27.02 chair near my pillow, leaning over me.
27.03   I felt an inexpressible relief, a soothing con-

27.04 viction of protection and security, when I knew
27.05 that there was a stranger in the room; an in-
27.06 dividual not belonging to Gateshead, and not
27.07 related to Mrs. Reed. Turning from Bessie
27.08 /though her presence was far less obnoxious to
27.09 me than that of Abbot, for instance, would
27.10 have been/, I scrutinized the face of the gen-
27.11 tleman: I knew him; it was Mr. Lloyd, an
27.12 apothecary, sometimes called in by Mrs. Reed
27.13 when the servants were ailing: for herself and
27.14 the children she employed a physician.
27.15 "Well, who am I?" he asked.
27.16 I pronounced his name, offering him at the
27.17 same time my hand: he took it, smiling and
27.18 saying, "we shall do very well by-and-by."
27.19 Then he laid me down, and addressing Bessie,
27.20 charged her to be very careful that I was not
27.21 disturbed during the night. Having given
27.22 some further directions, and intimated that he
27.23 should call again the next day, he departed;
27.24 to my grief: I felt so sheltered and befriended
27.25 while he sat in the chair near my pillow; and
27.26 as he closed the door after him, all the room
27.27 darkened and my heart again sank: inex-
27.28 pressible sadness weighed it down.
28.01 "Do you feel as if you should sleep, Miss?"
28.02 asked Bessie, rather softly.
28.03 Scarcely dared I answer her; for I feared
28.04 the next sentence might be rough. "I will
28.05 try."
28.06 "Would you like to drink, or could you eat
28.07 anything?"
28.08 "No, thank you, Bessie."
28.09 "Then I think I shall go to bed, for it is past
28.10 twelve o'clock; but you may call me if you
28.11 want anything in the night."
28.12 Wonderful civility this! It emboldened me
28.13 to ask a question.
28.14 "Bessie, what is the matter with me? Am
28.15 I ill?"
28.16 "You fell sick, I suppose, in the red-room
28.17 with crying; you'll be better soon, no doubt."
28.18 Bessie went into the housemaid's apartment
28.19 which was near. I heard her say: --
28.20 "Sarah, come and sleep with me in the nur-
28.21 sery; I daren't for my life be alone with that
28.22 poor child to-night: she might die; it's such
28.23 a strange thing she should have that fit: I
28.24 wonder if she saw anything. Missis was rather
28.25 too hard."
28.26 Sarah came back with her; they both went
28.27 to bed; they were whispering together for half
28.28 an hour before they fell asleep. I caught
29.01 scraps of their conversation, from which I was
29.02 able only too distinctly to infer the main sub-
29.03 ject discussed.
29.04 "Something passed her, all dressed in white,
29.05 and vanished" -- "Three loud raps on the chamber
29.06 door" -- "A light in the church-yard just over
29.07 his grave" -- &c. &c.
29.08 At last both slept: the fire and the candle
29.09 went out. For me, the watches of that long
29.10 night passed in ghastly wakefulness; ear, eye,
29.11 and mind were alike strained by dread: such
29.12 dread as children only can feel.
29.13 No severe or prolonged bodily illness fol-
29.14 lowed this incident of the red-room: it only
29.15 gave my nerves a shock; of which I feel the
29.16 reverberation to this day. Yes, Mrs. Reed,
29.17 to you I owe some fearful pangs of mental
29.18 suffering. But I ought to forgive you, for
29.19 you knew not what you did: while rending
29.20 my heart-strings, you thought you were only
29.21 up-rooting my bad propensities.
29.22 Next day, by noon, I was up and dressed,
29.23 and sat wrapped in a shawl by the nursery
29.24 hearth, I felt physically weak and broken
29.25 down: but my worst ailment was an un-
29.26 utterable wretchedness of mind; a wretched-
29.27 ness which kept drawing from me silent tears;
30.01 no sooner had I wiped one salt drop from
30.02 my cheek than another followed. Yet I
30.03 thought, I ought to have been happy, for none
30.04 of the Reeds were there; they were all gone
30.05 out in the carriage with their mama: Abbot,
30.06 too, was sewing in another room, and Bessie,
30.07 as she moved hither and thither, putting away
30.08 toys and arranging drawers, addressed to me
30.09 every now and then a word of unwonted kind-
30.10 ness. This state of things should have been
30.11 to me a paradise of peace, accustomed as I
30.12 was to a life of ceaseless reprimand and thank-
30.13 less fagging; but, in fact, my racked nerves
30.14 were now in such a state that no calm could
30.15 soothe, and no pleasure excite them agreeably.
30.16 Bessie had been down into the kitchen, and
30.17 she brought up with her a tart on a certain
30.18 brightly painted china plate, whose bird of
30.19 paradise, nestling in a wreath of convolvuli
30.20 and rosebuds, had been wont to stir in me
30.21 a most enthusiastic sense of admiration; and
30.22 which plate I had often petitioned to be al-
30.23 lowed to take in my hand in order to examine
30.24 it more closely, but had always hitherto been
30.25 deemed unworthy of such a privilege. This
30.26 precious vessel was now placed on my knee,
30.27 and I was cordially invited to eat the circlet
30.28 of delicate pastry upon it. Vain favour!
31.01 coming, like most other favours long deferred
31.02 and often wished for, too late! I could not
31.03 eat the tart; and the plumage of the bird, the

31.04 tints of the flowers, seemed strangely faded: I
31.05 put both plate and tart away. Bessie asked if
31.06 I would have a book: the word book acted as
31.07 a transient stimulus, and I begged her to fetch
31.08 Gulliver's Travels from the library. This
31.09 book I had again and again perused with
31.10 delight; I considered it a narrative of facts,
31.11 and discovered in it a vein of interest deeper
31.12 than what I found in fairy tales: for as to
31.13 the elves, having sought them in vain among
31.14 foxglove leaves and bells, under mushrooms
31.15 and beneath the ground-ivy mantling old
31.16 wall-nooks, I had at length made up my
31.17 mind to the sad truth that they were all
31.18 gone out of England to some savage country,
31.19 where woods were wilder and thicker,
31.20 and the population more scant; whereas,
31.21 Lilliput and Brobdignag being, in my creed,
31.22 solid parts of the earth's surface, I doubted
31.23 not that I might one day, by taking a long
31.24 voyage, see with my own eyes the little
31.25 fields, houses, and trees, the diminutive people,
31.26 the tiny cows, sheep, and birds of the one
31.27 realm; and the corn-fields forest-high, the
31.28 mighty mastiffs, the monster cats, the tower--
32.01 like men and women, of the other. Yet,
32.02 when this cherished volume was now placed
32.03 in my hand -- when I turned over its leaves,
32.04 and sought in its marvellous pictures the
32.05 charm I had, till now, never failed to find --
32.06 all was eerie and dreary; the giants were
32.07 gaunt goblins, the pigmies malevolent and
32.08 fearful imps, Gulliver a most desolate wanderer
32.09 in most dread and dangerous regions. I closed
32.10 the book, which I dared no longer peruse, and
32.11 put it on the table, beside the untasted tart.
32.12 Bessie had now finished dusting and tidy-
32.13 ing the room, and having washed her hands,
32.14 she opened a certain little drawer, full of
32.15 splendid shreds of silk and satin, and began
32.16 making a new bonnet for Georgiana's doll.
32.17 Meantime she sang: her song was --
32.18 "In the days when we went gipsying,
32.19 A long time ago."
32.20 I had often heard the song before, and
32.21 always with lively delight; for Bessie had a
32.22 sweet voice, -- at least, I thought so. But now,
32.23 though her voice was still sweet, I found in
32.24 its melody an indescribable sadness. Some-
32.25 times, pre-occupied with her work, she sang
32.26 the refrain very low, very lingerly; "A long
32.27 time ago" came out like the saddest cadence
33.01 of a funeral hymn. She passed into another
33.02 ballad, this time a really doleful one.
33.03 "My feet they are sore, and my limbs they are weary;
33.04 Long is the way, and the mountains are wild;
33.05 Soon will the twilight close moonless and dreary
33.06 Over the path of the poor orphan child.
33.07 "Why did they send me so far and so lonely,
33.08 Up where the moors spread and grey rocks are piled?
33.09 Men are hard-hearted, and kind angels only
33.10 Watch o'er the steps of a poor orphan child.
33.11 "Yet distance and soft the night-breeze is blowing,
33.12 Clouds there are none, and clear stars beam mild;
33.13 God, in His mercy, protection is showing,
33.14 Comfort and hope to the poor orphan child.
33.15 "Ev'n should I fall o'er the broken bridge passing,
33.16 Or stray in the marshes, by false lights beguiled,
33.17 Still will my Father, with promise and blessing,
33.18 Take to His bosom the poor orphan child.
33.19 "There is a thought that for strength should avail me,
33.20 Though both of shelter and kindred despoiled;
33.21 Heaven is a home, and a rest will not fail me;
33.22 God is a friend to the poor orphan child.
33.23 "Come, Miss Jane, don't cry," said Bessie,
33.24 as she finished. She might as well have said
33.25 to the fire "don't burn!" but how could
33.26 she divine the morbid suffering to which I
33.27 was a prey? In the course of the morning
33.28 Mr. Lloyd came again.
33.29 "What, already up!" said he, as he entered
33.30 the nursery. "Well, nurse, how is she?"
34.01 Bessie answered that I was doing very well.
34.02 "Then she ought to look more cheerful.
34.03 Come here, Miss Jane: your name is Jane,
34.04 is it not?"
34.05 "Yes, sir, Jane Eyre."
34.06 "Well, you have been crying, Miss Jane
34.07 Eyre, can you tell me what about? Have you
34.08 any pain?"
34.09 "No, sir."
34.10 "Oh! I daresay she is crying because she
34.11 could not go out with Missis in the carriage,"
34.12 interposed Bessie.
34.13 "Surely not! why, she is too old for such
34.14 pettishness."
34.15 I thought so too; and my self-esteem being
34.16 wounded by the false charge, I answered
34.17 promptly, "I never cried for such a thing
34.18 in my life: I hate going out in the carriage.
34.19 I cry because I am miserable."
34.20 "Oh fie, Miss!" said Bessie.
34.21 The good apothecary appeared a little puz-
34.22 zled. I was standing before him; he fixed
34.23 his eyes on me very steadily: his eyes were
34.24 small and grey; not very bright, but I daresay
34.25 I should think them shrewd now: he had
34.26 a hard-featured yet good-natured looking face.
34.27 Having considered me at leisure, he said --
34.28 "What made you ill yesterday?"
35.01 "She had a fall," said Bessie, again putting

35.02 in her word.
35.03 "Fall! why that is like a baby again!
35.04 Can't she manage to walk at her age? She
35.05 must be eight or nine years old."
35.06 "I was knocked down," was the blunt ex-
35.07 planation jerked out of me by another pang
35.08 of mortified pride: "but that did not make
35.09 me ill," I added; while Mr. Lloyd helped
35.10 himself to a pinch of snuff.
35.11 As he was returning the box to his waist-
35.12 coat pocket, a loud bell rang for the servants'
35.13 dinner; he knew what it was. "That's for
35.14 you, nurse," he said; "you can go down; I'll
35.15 give Miss Jane a lecture till you come back."
35.16 Bessie would rather have stayed; but she
35.17 was obliged to go, because punctuality at meals
35.18 was rigidly enforced at Gateshead Hall.
35.19 "The fall did not make you ill; what did,
35.20 then?" pursued Mr. Lloyd, when Bessie was
35.21 gone.
35.22 "I was shut up in a room where there is a
35.23 ghost, till after dark."
35.24 I saw Mr. Lloyd smile and frown at the
35.25 same time: "Ghost! What, you are a baby
35.26 after all! You are afraid of ghosts?"
35.27 "Of Mr. Reed's ghost I am: he died in
35.28 that room, and was laid out there. Neither
36.01 Bessie nor any one else will go into it at night,
36.02 if they can help it; and it was cruel to shut
36.03 me up alone without a candle, -- so cruel that
36.04 I think I shall never forget it."
36.05 "Nonsense! And is it that makes you so
36.06 miserable? Are you afraid now in daylight?"
36.07 "No; but night will come again before
36.08 long: and besides, I am unhappy, -- very un-
36.09 happy, for other things."
36.10 "What other things? Can you tell me
36.11 some of them?"
36.12 How much I wished to reply fully to this
36.13 question! How difficult it was to frame any
36.14 answer! Children can feel, but they cannot
36.15 analyze their feelings; and if the analysis is
36.16 partially effected in thought, they know not
36.17 how to express the result of the process in
36.18 words. Fearful, however, of losing this first
36.19 and only opportunity of relieving my grief by
36.20 imparting it, I, after a disturbed pause, con-
36.21 trived to frame a meagre, thought as far as it
36.22 went, true response.
36.23 "For one thing, I have no father or mother,
36.24 brothers or sisters."
36.25 "You have a kind aunt and cousins."
36.26 Again I paused; then bunglingly enounced:
36.27 "But John Reed knocked me down, and my
36.28 aunt shut me up in the red-room."
37.01 Mr. Lloyd a second time produced his snuff-
37.02 box.
37.03 "Don't you think Gateshead Hall a very
37.04 beautiful house?" asked he. "Are you not
37.05 very thankful to have such a fine place to
37.06 live at?"
37.07 "It is not my house, sir; and Abbot says I
37.08 have less right to be here than a servant."
37.09 "Pooh! you can't be silly enough to wish
37.10 to leave such a splendid place?"
37.11 "If I had anywhere else to go, I should be
37.12 glad to leave it; but I can never get away
37.13 from Gateshead till I am a woman."
37.14 "Perhaps you may -- who knows? Have
37.15 you any relations besides Mrs. Reed?"
37.16 "I think not, sir."
37.17 "None belonging to your father?"
37.18 "I don't know: I asked Aunt Reed once,
37.19 and she said possibly I might have some poor,
37.20 low relations called Eyre, but she knew no-
37.21 thing about them."
37.22 "If you had such, would you like to go to
37.23 them?"
37.24 I reflected. Poverty looks grim to grown
37.25 people; still more so to children: they have
37.26 not much idea of industrious, working, respect-
37.27 able poverty; they think of the word only as
37.28 connected with ragged clothes, scanty food,
38.01 fireless grates, rude manners, and debasing
38.02 vices: poverty for me was synonymous with
38.03 degradation.
38.04 "No; I should not like to belong to poor
38.05 people," was my reply.
38.06 "Not even if they were kind to you?"
38.07 I shook my head: I could not see how poor
38.08 people had the means of being kind; and then
38.09 to learn to speak like them, to adopt their
38.10 manners, to be uneducated, to grow up like
38.11 one of the poor women I saw sometimes nurs-
38.12 ing their children or washing their clothes at
38.13 the cottage doors of the village of Gateshead:
38.14 no, I was not heroic enough to purchase liberty
38.15 at the price of caste.
38.16 "But are your relatives so very poor? Are
38.17 they working people?"
38.18 "I cannot tell; Aunt Reed says if I have
38.19 any, they must be a beggarly set: I should
38.20 not like to go a begging."
38.21 "Would you like to go to school?"
38.22 Again I reflected: I scarcely knew what
38.23 school was; Bessie sometimes spoke of it as a
38.24 place where young ladies sat in the stocks,
38.25 wore backboards, and were expected to be ex-
38.26 ceedingly genteel and precise; John Reed
38.27 hated his school, and abused his master: but
38.28 John Reed's tastes were no rule for mine, and

39.01 if Bessie's accounts of school-discipline /ga-
39.02 thered from the young ladies of a family where
39.03 she had lived before coming to Gateshead/
39.04 were somewhat appalling, her details of certain
39.05 accomplishments attained by these same young
39.06 ladies were, I thought, equally attractive.
39.07 She boasted of beautiful paintings of land-
39.08 scapes and flowers by them executed; of songs
39.09 they could sing and pieces they could play,
39.10 of purses they could net, of French books
39.11 they could translate; till my spirit was moved
39.12 to emulation as I listened. Besides, school
39.13 would be a complete change: it implied a long
39.14 journey, an entire separation from Gateshead,
39.15 an entrance into a new life.
39.16 "I should indeed like to go to school," was
39.17 the audible conclusion of my musings.
39.18 "Well, well; who knows what may happen?"
39.19 said Mr. Lloyd, as he got up: "The child
39.20 ought to have change of air and scene;" he
39.21 added, speaking to himself, "nerves not in a
39.22 good state."
39.23 Bessie now returned; at the same moment
39.24 the carriage was heard rolling up the gravel--
39.25 walk.
39.26 "Is that your mistress, nurse?" asked Mr.
39.27 Lloyd: "I should like to speak to her before I
39.28 go."
40.01 Bessie invited him to walk into the break-
40.02 fast-room, and led the way out. In the inter-
40.03 view which followed between him and Mrs.
40.04 Reed, I presume, from after-occurrences, that
40.05 the apothecary ventured to recommend my
40.06 being sent to school; and the recommendation
40.07 was no doubt readily enough adopted: for as
40.08 Abbot said, in discussing the subject with Bessie
40.09 when both sat sewing in the nursery one night,
40.10 after I was in bed, and, as they thought, asleep,
40.11 "Missis was, she dared say, glad enough to get
40.12 rid of such a tiresome, ill-conditioned child,
40.13 who always looked as if she were watching
40.14 everybody, and scheming plots underhand."
40.15 Abbot, I think, gave me credit for being a sort
40.16 of infantine Guy Fawkes.
40.17 On that same occasion I learned, for the first
40.18 time, from Miss Abbot's communications to
40.19 Bessie, that my father had been a poor clergy-
40.20 man; that my mother had married him against
40.21 the wishes of her friends, who considered the
40.22 match beneath her; that my grandfather Reed
40.23 was so irritated at her disobedience, he cut her
40.24 off without a shilling; that after my mother
40.25 and father had been married a year, the latter
40.26 caught the typhus fever while visiting among the
40.27 poor of a large manufacturing town where his
40.28 curacy was situated, and where that dsease
41.01 was then prevalent; that my mother took the
41.02 infection from him, and both died within a
41.03 month of each other.
41.04 Bessie, when she heard this narrative, sighed
41.05 and said, "Poor Miss Jane is to be pitied, too,
41.06 Abbot."
41.07 "Yes," responded Abbot, "if she were a nice,
41.08 pretty child, one might compassionate her for-
41.09 lornness; but one really cannot care for such
41.10 a little toad as that."
41.11 "Not a great deal, to be sure," agreed Bessie:
41.12 "at any rate a beauty like Miss Georgiana
41.13 would be more moving in the same condition."
41.14 "Yes, I doat on Miss Georgiana!" cried the
41.15 fervent Abbot. "Little darling! -- with her
41.16 long curls and her blue eyes, and such a sweet
41.17 colour as she has; just as if she were painted!
41.18 -- Bessie, I could fancy a Welsh rabbit for
41.19 supper."
41.20 "So could I -- with a roast onion. Come,
41.21 we'll go down." They went.
42.01 [Vol. 1 Chapter 4]
42.02 From my discourse with Mr. Lloyd, and from
42.03 the above reported conference between Bessie
42.04 and Abbot, I gathered enough of hope to suf-
42.05 fice as a motive for wishing to get well: a
42.06 change seemed near, -- I desired and waited it
42.07 in silence. It tarried, however: days and
42.08 weeks passed: I had regained my normal state
42.09 of health, but no new allusion was made to the
42.10 subject over which I brooded. Mrs. Reed
42.11 surveyed me at times with a severe eye, but
42.12 seldom addressed me: since my illness, she had
42.13 drawn a more marked line of separation than
42.14 ever between me and her own children; ap-
42.15 pointing me a small closet to sleep in by myself,
42.16 condemning me to take my meals alone, and
42.17 pass all my time in the nursery while my
42.18 cousins were constantly in the drawing-room.
42.19 Not a hint, however, did she drop about send-
43.01 ing me to school: still I felt an instinctive cer-
43.02 tainty that she would not long endure me under
43.03 the same roof with her; for her glance, now
43.04 more than ever, when turned on me, expressed
43.05 an insuperable and rooted aversion.
43.06 Eliza and Georgiana, evidently acting ac-
43.07 cording to orders, spoke to me as little as pos-
43.08 sible: John thrust his tongue in his cheek
43.09 whenever he saw me, and once attempted chas-
43.10 tisement; but as I instantly turned against him,
43.11 roused by the same sentiment of deep ire and
43.12 desperate revolt which had stirred my corrup-
43.13 tion before, he thought it better to desist, and
43.14 ran from me uttering execrations, and vowing
43.15 I had burst his nose. I had indeed levelled at

43.16 that prominent feature as hard a blow as my
43.17 knuckles could inflict; and when I saw that
43.18 either that or my look daunted him, I had the
43.19 greatest inclination to follow up my advantage
43.20 to purpose; but he was already with his mama.
43.21 I heard him in a blubbering tone commence
43.22 the tale of how "that nasty Jane Eyre" had
43.23 flown at him like a mad cat: he was stopped
43.24 rather harshly --
43.25 "Don't talk to me about her, John: I told
43.26 you not to go near her; she is not worthy of
43.27 notice: I do not choose that either you or your
43.28 sisters should associate with her."
44.01 Here, leaning over the banister, I cried out
44.02 suddenly, and without at all deliberating on
44.03 my words, --
44.04 "They are not fit to associate with me."
44.05 Mrs. Reed was rather a stout woman; but, on
44.06 hearing this strange and audacious declaration,
44.07 she ran nimbly up the stair, swept me like a
44.08 whirlwind into the nursery, and crushing me
44.09 down on the edge of my crib, dared me in an
44.10 emphatic voice to rise from that place, or utter
44.11 one syllable during the remainder of the day.
44.12 "What would uncle Reed say to you, if he
44.13 were alive?" was my scarcely voluntary de-
44.14 mand. I say scarcely voluntary, for it seemed
44.15 as if my tongue pronounced words without my
44.16 will consenting to their utterance: something
44.17 spoke out of me over which I had no control.
44.18 "What?" said Mrs. Reed under her breath:
44.19 her usually cold, composed grey eye became
44.20 troubled with a look like fear, she took her
44.21 hand from my arm, and gazed at me as if she
44.22 really did not know whether I were child or
44.23 fiend. I was now in for it.
44.24 "My uncle Reed is in heaven, and can see all
44.25 you do and think; and so can papa and mama:
44.26 they know how you shut me up all day long,
44.27 and how you wish me dead."
44.28 Mrs. Reed soon rallied her spirits: she
45.01 shook me most soundly, she boxed both my
45.02 ears, and then left me without a word. Bessie
45.03 supplied the hiatus by a homily of an hour's
45.04 length, in which she proved beyond a doubt
45.05 that I was the most wicked and abandoned
45.06 child ever reared under a roof. I half believed
45.07 her; for I felt indeed only bad feelings surging
45.08 in my breast.
45.09 November, December, and half of January
45.10 passed away. Christmas and the New Year
45.11 had been celebrated at Gateshead with the
45.12 usual festive cheer; presents had been inter-
45.13 changed, dinners and evening parties given.
45.14 From every enjoyment I was, of course, ex-
45.15 cluded: my share of the gaiety consisted in
45.16 witnessing the daily apparelling of Eliza and
45.17 Georgiana, and seeing them descend to the
45.18 drawing-room, dressed out in thin muslin frocks
45.19 and scarlet sashes, with hair elaborately ring-
45.20 leted; and afterwards, in listening to the
45.21 sound of the piano or the harp played below,
45.22 to the passing to and fro of the butler and
45.23 footmen, to the jingling of glass and china as
45.24 refreshments were handed, to the broken hum
45.25 of conversation as the drawing-room doors
45.26 opened and closed. When tired of this occu-
45.27 pation, I would retire from the stair-head to
45.28 the solitary and silent nursery: there, though
46.01 somewhat sad, I was not miserable. To speak
46.02 truth, I had not the least wish to go into
46.03 company, for in company I was very rarely
46.04 noticed; and if Bessie had but been kind and
46.05 companionable, I should have deemed it a treat
46.06 to spend the evenings quietly with her, instead
46.07 of passing them under the formidable eye of
46.08 Mrs. Reed, in a room full of ladies and gentle-
46.09 men. But Bessie, as soon as she had dressed
46.10 her young ladies, used to take herself off to the
46.11 lively regions of the kitchen and housekeeper's
46.12 room, generally bearing the candle along with
46.13 her. I then sat with my doll on my knee, till
46.14 the fire got low, glancing round occasionally,
46.15 to make sure that nothing worse than myself
46.16 haunted the shadowy room; and when the
46.17 embers sank to a dull red, I undressed hastily,
46.18 tugging at knots and strings as I best might,
46.19 and sought shelter from cold and darkness in
46.20 my crib. To this crib I always took my doll:
46.21 human beings must love something; and, in
46.22 the dearth of worthier objects of affection, I
46.23 contrived to find a pleasure in loving and
46.24 cherishing a faded graven image, shabby as a
46.25 miniature scarecrow. It puzzles me now to
46.26 remember with what absurd sincerity I doated
46.27 on this little toy; half-fancying it alive and
46.28 capable of sensation. I could not sleep unless
47.01 it was folded in my night-gown; and when it
47.02 lay there safe and warm, I was comparatively
47.03 happy, believing it to be happy likewise.
47.04 Long did the hours seem while I waited the
47.05 departure of the company, and listened for the
47.06 sound of Bessie's step on the stairs: sometimes
47.07 she would come up in the interval to seek her
47.08 thimble or her scissors, or perhaps to bring me
47.09 something by way of supper -- a bun or a
47.10 cheese-cake; then she would sit on the bed
47.11 while I ate it, and when I had finished, she
47.12 would tuck the clothes round me, and twice
47.13 she kissed me, and said, "Good-night, Miss
47.14 Jane." When thus gentle, Bessie seemed to
47.15 me the best, prettiest, kindest being in the
47.16 world; and I wished most intensely that she
47.17 would always be so pleasant and amiable, and
47.18 never push me about, or scold, or task me un-
47.19 reasonably, as she was too often wont to do.
47.20 Bessie Lee must, I think, have been a girl of
47.21 good natural capacity; for she was smart in all
47.22 she did, and had a remarkable knack of narra-
47.23 tive: so, at least, I judge from the impression
47.24 made on me by her nursery tales. She was
47.25 pretty, too, if my recollections of her face and
47.26 person are correct. I remember her as a slim
47.27 young woman, with black hair, dark eyes, very
47.28 nice features, and good, clear complexion; but
48.01 she had a capricious and hasty temper, and
48.02 indifferent ideas of principle or justice: still,
48.03 such as she was, I preferred her to any one
48.04 else at Gateshead Hall.
48.05 It was the fifteenth of January, about nine
48.06 o'clock in the morning: Bessie was gone down
48.07 to breakfast; my cousins had not yet been
48.08 summoned to their mama; Eliza was putting
48.09 on her bonnet and warm garden-coat to go
48.10 and feed her poultry, an occupation of which
48.11 she was fond: and not less so of selling the
48.12 eggs to the housekeeper and hoarding up the
48.13 money she thus obtained. She had a turn for
48.14 traffic, and a marked propensity for saving;
48.15 shown not only in the vending of eggs and
48.16 chickens, but also in driving hard bargains
48.17 with the gardener about flower-roots, seeds, and
48.18 slips of plants; that functionary having orders
48.19 from Mrs. Reed to buy of his young lady all
48.20 the products of her parterre she wished to sell:
48.21 and Eliza would have sold the hair off her
48.22 head if she could have made a handsome profit
48.23 thereby. As to her money, she first secreted
48.24 it in odd corners, wrapped in a rag or an old
48.25 curl-paper; but some of these hoards having
48.26 been discovered by the housemaid, Eliza, fear-
48.27 ful of one day losing her valued treasure, con-
48.28 sented to entrust it to her mother, at a usurious
49.01 rate of interest -- fifty or sixty per cent.: which
49.02 interest she exacted every quarter, keeping her
49.03 accounts in a little book with anxious accuracy.
49.04 Georgiana sat on a high stool, dressing her
49.05 hair at the glass and interweaving her curls
49.06 with artificial flowers and faded feathers, of
49.07 which she had found a store in a drawer in the
49.08 attic. I was making my bed; having received
49.09 strict orders from Bessie to get it arranged
49.10 before she returned /for Bessie now frequently
49.11 employed me as a sort of under nursery-maid,
49.12 to tidy the room, dust the chairs, &c./. Having
49.13 spread the quilt and folded my night-dress, I
49.14 went to the window-seat to put in order some
49.15 picture-books and doll's house furniture scat-
49.16 tered there; an abrupt command from Geor-
49.17 giana to let her playthings alone /for the tiny
49.18 chairs and mirrors, the fairy plates and cups
49.19 were her property/ stopped my proceedings;
49.20 and then, for lack of other occupation, I fell to
49.21 breathing on the frost-flowers with which the
49.22 window was fretted, and thus clearing a space
49.23 in the glass through which I might look out
49.24 on the grounds, where all was still and petri-
49.25 fied under the influence of a hard frost.
49.26 From this window were visible the porter's
49.27 lodge and the carriage-road, and just as I
49.28 had dissolved so much of the silver-white
50.01 foliage veiling the panes, as left room to look
50.02 out, I saw the gates thrown open and a
50.03 carriage roll through. I watched it ascending
50.04 the drive with indifference: carriages often
50.05 came to Gateshead, but none ever brought
50.06 visitors in whom I was interested; it stopped
50.07 in front of the house, the door-bell rang
50.08 loudly, the new comer was admitted. All this
50.09 being nothing to me, my vacant attention
50.10 soon found livelier attraction in the spectacle
50.11 of a little hungry robin, which came and
50.12 chirruped on the twigs of the leafless cherry--
50.13 tree nailed against the wall near the casement.
50.14 The remains of my breakfast of bread and
50.15 milk stood on the table, and having crumbled
50.16 a morsel of roll, I was tugging at the sash to
50.17 put out the crumbs on the window-sill, when
50.18 Bessie came running upstairs into the nursery.
50.19 "Miss Jane, take off your pinafore: what
50.20 are you doing there? Have you washed
50.21 your hands and face this morning?" I gave
50.22 another tug before I answered, for I wanted
50.23 the bird to be secure of its bread: the sash
50.24 yielded; I scattered the crumbs, some on the
50.25 stone sill, some on the cherry-tree bough, then
50.26 closing the window, I replied: --
50.27 "No, Bessie; I have only just finished dust-
50.28 ing."
51.01 "Troublesome, careless child! and what are
51.02 you doing now? You look quite red as if you
51.03 had been about some mischief: what were you
51.04 opening the window for?"
51.05 I was spared the trouble of answering, for
51.06 Bessie seemed in too great a hurry to listen to
51.07 explanations; she hauled me to the wash-
51.08 stand, inflicted a merciless, but happily brief,
51.09 scrub on my face and hands with soap, water,
51.10 and a coarse towel; disciplined my head with
51.11 a bristly brush, denuded me of my pinafore,
51.12 and then hurrying me to the top of the stairs,
51.13 bid me go down directly, as I was wanted

51.14 in the breakfast-room.
51.15   I would have asked who wanted me: I
51.16 would have demanded if Mrs. Reed was there;
51.17 but Bessie was already gone, and had closed
51.18 the nursery-door upon me: I slowly descended.
51.19 For nearly three months, I had never been
51.20 called to Mrs. Reed's presence: restricted so
51.21 long to the nursery, the breakfast, dining, and
51.22 drawing rooms were become for me awful
51.23 regions, on which it dismayed me to intrude.
51.24   I now stood in the empty hall; before me
51.25 was the breakfast-room door, and I stopped,
51.26 intimidated and trembling. What a miserable
51.27 little poltroon had fear, engendered of unjust
51.28 punishment, made of me in those days! I
52.01 feared to return to the nursery; I feared to
52.02 go forward to the parlour; ten minutes I
52.03 stood in agitated hesitation: the vehement
52.04 ringing of the breakfast-room bell decided
52.05 me; I must enter.
52.06   "Who could want me?" I asked inwardly,
52.07 as with both hands I turned the stiff door--
52.08 handle which, for a second or two, resisted my
52.09 efforts. "What should I see besides aunt
52.10 Reed in the apartment? -- a man or a woman?"
52.11 The handle turned, the door unclosed, and
52.12 passing through and curtseying low, I looked
52.13 up at -- a black pillar! -- such, at least, ap-
52.14 peared to me, at first sight, the straight,
52.15 narrow, sable-clad shape standing erect on
52.16 the rug: the grim face at the top was like
52.17 a carved mask, placed above the shaft by way
52.18 of capital.
52.19   Mrs. Reed occupied her usual seat by the
52.20 fireside: she made a signal to me to approach:
52.21 I did so, and she introduced me to the stony
52.22 stranger with the words: "This is the little
52.23 girl, respecting whom I applied to you."
52.24   He, for it was a man, turned his head
52.25 slowly towards where I stood, and having
52.26 examined me with the two inquisitive-look-
52.27 ing grey eyes which twinkled under a pair
52.28 of bushy brows, said solemnly, and in a
53.01 bass voice: "Her size is small: what is her
53.02 age?"
53.03   "Ten years."
53.04   "So much?" was the doubtful answer;
53.05 and he prolonged his scrutiny for some min-
53.06 utes. Presently he addressed me: --
53.07   "Your name, little girl?"
53.08   "Jane Eyre, sir."
53.09   In uttering these words, I looked up: he
53.10 seemed to me a tall gentleman; but then I
53.11 was very little; his features were large, and
53.12 they and all the lines of his frame were equally
53.13 harsh and prim.
53.14   "Well, Jane Eyre, and are you a good
53.15 child?"
53.16   Impossible to reply to this in the affirmative:
53.17 my little world held a contrary opinion: I was
53.18 silent. Mrs. Reed answered for me by an ex-
53.19 pressive shake of the head, adding soon, "Per-
53.20 haps the less said on that subject the better,
53.21 Mr. Brocklehurst."
53.22   "Sorry indeed to hear it! she and I must
53.23 have some talk;" and bending from the per-
53.24 pendicular, he installed his person in the arm-
53.25 chair, opposite Mrs. Reed's. "Come here,"
53.26 he said.
53.27   I stepped across the rug; he placed me
53.28 square and straight before him. What a face
54.01 he had, now that it was almost on a level with
54.02 mine! what a great nose! and what a mouth!
54.03 and what large prominent teeth!
54.04   "No sight so sad as that of a naughty child,"
54.05 he began, "especially a naughty little girl. Do
54.06 you know where the wicked go after death?"
54.07   "They go to hell," was my ready and or-
54.08 thodox answer.
54.09   "And what is hell? Can you tell me that?"
54.10   "A pit full of fire."
54.11   "And should you like to fall into that pit,
54.12 and to be burning there for ever?"
54.13   "No, sir."
54.14   "What must you do to avoid it?"
54.15   I deliberated a moment; my answer, when
54.16 it did come, was objectionable: "I must keep
54.17 in good health, and not die."
54.18   "How can you keep in good health? Chil-
54.19 dren younger than you die daily. I buried a
54.20 little child of five years old only a day or two
54.21 since, -- a good little child, whose soul is now
54.22 in heaven. It is to be feared the same could
54.23 not be said of you, were you to be called
54.24 hence."
54.25   Not being in a condition to remove his
54.26 doubt, I only cast my eyes down on the two
54.27 large feet planted on the rug, and sighed;
54.28 wishing myself far enough away.
55.01   "I hope that sigh is from the heart, and
55.02 that you repent of ever having been the occa-
55.03 sion of discomfort to your excellent benefac-
55.04 tress."
55.05   "Benefactress! benefactress!" said I, in-
55.06 wardly: "they all call Mrs. Reed my bene-
55.07 factress; if so, a benefactress is a disagreeable
55.08 thing."
55.09   "Do you say your prayers night and morn-
55.10 ing?" continued my interrogator.
55.11   "Yes, sir."
55.12   "Do you read your bible?"

55.13   "Sometimes."
55.14   "With pleasure? Are you fond of it?"
55.15   "I like Revelations, and the book of Daniel,
55.16 and Genesis and Samuel, and a little bit of
55.17 Exodus, and some parts of Kings and Chroni-
55.18 cles, and Job and Jonah."
55.19   "And the Psalms? I hope you like them."
55.20   "No, sir."
55.21   "No? oh, shocking! I have a little boy,
55.22 younger than you, who knows six Psalms by
55.23 heart; and when you ask him which he would
55.24 rather have, a ginger bread-nut to eat, or a verse
55.25 of a Psalm to learn, he says: ` Oh! the verse
55.26 of a Psalm! angels sing Psalms; ` says he, ` I
55.27 wish to be a little angel here below; ` he then
56.01 gets two nuts in recompense for his infant
56.02 piety."
56.03   "Psalms are not interesting," I remarked.
56.04   "That proves you have a wicked heart; and
56.05 you must pray to God to change it: to give
56.06 you a new and a clean one: to take away
56.07 your heart of stone and give you a heart of
56.08 flesh."
56.09   I was about to propound a question, touch-
56.10 ing the manner in which that operation of
56.11 changing my heart was to be performed, when
56.12 Mrs. Reed interposed, telling me to sit down;
56.13 she then proceeded to carry on the conversa-
56.14 tion herself.
56.15   "Mr. Brocklehurst, I believe I intimated in
56.16 the letter which I wrote to you three weeks
56.17 ago, that this little girl has not quite the cha-
56.18 racter and disposition I could wish: should
56.19 you admit her into Lowood school, I should
56.20 be glad if the superintendent and teachers
56.21 were requested to keep a strict eye on her, and,
56.22 above all, to guard against her worst fault, a
56.23 tendency to deceit. I mention this in your
56.24 hearing, Jane, that you may not attempt to
56.25 impose on Mr. Brocklehurst."
56.26   Well might I dread, well might I dislike
56.27 Mrs. Reed; for it was her nature to wound
57.01 me cruelly: never was I happy in her pre-
57.02 sence: however carefully I obeyed, however
57.03 strenuously I strove to please her, my efforts
57.04 were still repulsed and repaid by such sen-
57.05 tences as the above. Now, uttered before a
57.06 stranger, the accusation cut me to the heart: I
57.07 dimly perceived that she was already oblite-
57.08 rating hope from the new phase of existence
57.09 which she destined me to enter; I felt, though
57.10 I could not have expressed the feeling, that
57.11 she was sowing aversion and unkindness along
57.12 my future path; I saw myself transformed
57.13 under Mr. Brocklehurst's eye into an artful,
57.14 noxious child, and what could I do to remedy
57.15 the injury?"
57.16   "Nothing, indeed;" thought I, as I strug-
57.17 gled to repress a sob, and hastily wiped away
57.18 some tears, the impotent evidences of my
57.19 anguish.
57.20   "Deceit is, indeed, a sad fault in a child,"
57.21 said Mr. Brocklehurst; "it is akin to false-
57.22 hood, and all liars will have their portion in
57.23 the lake burning with fire and brimstone: she
57.24 shall, however, be watched, Mrs. Reed; I will
57.25 speak to Miss Temple and the teachers."
57.26   "I should wish her to be brought up in a
57.27 manner suiting her prospects," continued my
57.28 benefactress; "to be made useful, to be kept
58.01 humble: as for the vacations, she will, with
58.02 your permission, spend them always at Lo-
58.03 wood."
58.04   "Your decisions are perfectly judicious,
58.05 madam," returned Mr. Brocklehurst. "Hu-
58.06 mility is a Christian grace, and one peculiarly
58.07 appropriate to the pupils of Lowood; I, there-
58.08 fore, direct that especial care shall be bestowed
58.09 on its cultivation amongst them. I have
58.10 studied how best to mortify in them the
58.11 worldly sentiment of pride; and only the other
58.12 day, I had a pleasing proof of my success.
58.13 My second daughter, Augusta, went with her
58.14 mama to visit the school, and on her return
58.15 she exclaimed: ` Oh, dear papa, how quiet and
58.16 plain all the girls at Lowood look! with their
58.17 hair combed behind their ears, and their long
58.18 pinafores, and those little holland pockets
58.19 outside their frocks -- they are almost like poor
58.20 people's children! and, ` said she, ` they looked
58.21 at my dress and mama's, as if they had never
58.22 seen a silk gown before. ` "
58.23   "This is the state of things I quite approve,"
58.24 returned Mrs. Reed; "had I sought all Eng-
58.25 land over, I could scarcely have found a sys-
58.26 tem more exactly fitting a child like Jane
58.27 Eyre. Consistency, my dear Mr. Brockle-
58.28 hurst; I advocate consistency in all things."
59.01   "Consistency, madam, is the first of Chris-
59.02 tian duties; and it has been observed in every
59.03 arrangement connected with the establishment
59.04 of Lowood: plain fare, simple attire; unso-
59.05 phisticated accommodations, hardy and active
59.06 habits; such is the order of the day in the
59.07 house and its inhabitants."
59.08   "Quite right, madam; I may then depend upon
59.09 this child being received as a pupil at Lowood,
59.10 and there being trained in conformity to her
59.11 position and prospects?"
59.12   "Madam, you may: she shall be placed in
59.13 that nursery of chosen plants -- and I trust she

59.14 will shew herself grateful for the inestimable
59.15 privilege of her election."
59.16 "I will send her, then, as soon as possible,
59.17 Mr. Brocklehurst; for, I assure you, I feel
59.18 anxious to be relieved of a responsibility that
59.19 was becoming too irksome."
59.20 "No doubt, no doubt, madam: and now I
59.21 wish you good-morning. I shall return to
59.22 Brocklehurst-hall in the course of a week or
59.23 two: my good friend, the Archdeacon, will
59.24 not permit me to leave him sooner. I shall
59.25 send Miss Temple notice that she is to expect
59.26 a new girl, so that there will be no difficulty
59.27 about receiving her. Good-bye."
59.28 "Good-bye, Mr. Brocklehurst; remember
60.01 me to Mrs. and Miss Brocklehurst, and to
60.02 Augusta and Theodore, and Master Broughton
60.03 Brocklehurst."
60.04 "I will madam. Little girl, here is a book
60.05 entitled the `Child's Guide;` read it with
60.06 prayer, especially that part containing `an ac-
60.07 count of the awfully sudden death of Martha
60.08 -- , a naughty child addicted to falsehood
60.09 and deceit.`"
60.10 With these words Mr. Brocklehurst put
60.11 into my hand a thin pamphlet sewn in a cover;
60.12 and having rung for his carriage, he departed.
60.13 Mrs. Reed and I were left alone: some
60.14 minutes passed in silence; she was sewing, I
60.15 was watching her. Mrs. Reed might be at
60.16 that time some six or seven-and-thirty; she
60.17 was a woman of robust frame, square shoulder-
60.18 ed and strong-limbed, not tall, and though
60.19 stout not obese; she had a somewhat large
60.20 face, the under-jaw being much developed and
60.21 very solid; her brow was low, her chin large
60.22 and prominent, mouth and nose sufficiently
60.23 regular; under her light eye-brows glimmered
60.24 an eye devoid of ruth;; her skin was dark and
60.25 opaque, her hair nearly flaxen; her constitu-
60.26 tion was sound as a bell -- illness never came
60.27 near her; she was an exact, clever manager,
60.28 her household and tenantry were thoroughly
61.01 under her control; her children, only, at times
61.02 defied her authority, and laughed it to scorn;
61.03 she dressed well, and had a presence and port
61.04 calculated to set off handsome attire.
61.05 Sitting on a low stool, a few yards from her
61.06 arm-chair, I examined her figure; I perused
61.07 her features. In my hand I held the tract,
61.08 containing the sudden death of the Liar: to
61.09 which narrative my attention had been pointed
61.10 as to an appropriate warning. What had just
61.11 passed; what Mrs. Reed had said concerning
61.12 me to Mr. Brocklehurst; the whole tenor of
61.13 their conversation, was recent, raw, and sting-
61.14 ing in my mind: I had felt every word as
61.15 acutely, as I had heard it plainly; and a pas-
61.16 sion of resentment fomented now within me.
61.17 Mrs. Reed looked up from her work; her
61.18 eye settled on mine, her fingers at the same
61.19 time suspended their nimble movements.
61.20 "Go out of the room: return to the nursery,"
61.21 was her mandate. My look or something else
61.22 must have struck her as offensive, for she
61.23 spoke with extreme, though suppressed irrita-
61.24 tion. I got up, I went to the door; I came
61.25 back again: I walked to the window, across
61.26 the room, then close up to her.
61.27 Speak I must: I had been trodden on
61.28 severely, and must turn: but how? What
62.01 strength had I to dart retaliation at my an-
62.02 tagonist? I gathered my energies and launched
62.03 them in this blunt sentence: --
62.04 "I am not deceitful: if I were, I should say
62.05 I loved you; but I declare I do not love you:
62.06 I dislike the worst of anybody in the world
62.07 except John Reed; and this book about the
62.08 liar, you may give to your girl, Georgiana, for
62.09 it is she who tells lies, and not I."
62.10 Mrs. Reed's hands still lay on her work in-
62.11 active: her eye of ice continued to dwell freez-
62.12 ingly on mine: --
62.13 "What more have you to say?" she asked,
62.14 rather in the tone in which a person might ad-
62.15 dress an opponent of adult age than such as is
62.16 ordinarily used to a child.
62.17 That eye of hers, that voice stirred every
62.18 antipathy I had. Shaking from head to foot,
62.19 thrilled with ungovernable excitement, I con-
62.20 tinued: --
62.21 "I am glad you are no relation of mine: I
62.22 will never call you aunt again as long as I live.
62.23 I will never come to see you when I am grown
62.24 up; and if any one asks me how I liked you,
62.25 and how you treated me, I will say the very
62.26 thought of you makes me sick, and that you
62.27 treated me with miserable cruelty."
62.28 "How dare you affirm that, Jane Eyre?"
63.01 "How dare I, Mrs. Reed? How dare I?
63.02 Because it is the truth. You think I have no
63.03 feelings, and that I can do without one bit of
63.04 love or kindness; but I cannot live so: and
63.05 you have no pity. I shall remember how you
63.06 thrust me back -- roughly and violently thrust
63.07 me back -- into the red-room, and locked me
63.08 up there, to my dying day; though I was in
63.09 agony; though I cried out, while suffocating
63.10 with distress, `Have mercy! Have mercy,
63.11 aunt Reed!` And that punishment you made
63.12 me suffer because your wicked boy struck me --

63.13 knocked me down for nothing. I will tell
63.14 anybody who asks me questions, this exact tale.
63.15 People think you a good woman, but you are
63.16 bad; hard-hearted. You are deceitful!"
63.17 Ere I had finished this reply, my soul began
63.18 to expand, to exult, with the strangest sense of
63.19 freedom, of triumph, I ever felt. It seemed as
63.20 if an invisible bond had burst, and that I had
63.21 struggled out into unhoped-for liberty. Not
63.22 without cause was this sentiment: Mrs. Reed
63.23 looked frightened; her work had slipped from
63.24 her knee; she was lifting up her hands, rock-
63.25 ing herself to and fro, and even twisting her
63.26 face as if she would cry.
63.27 "Jane, you are under a mistake: what is
63.28 the matter with you? Why do you tremble
64.01 so violently? Would you like to drink some
64.02 water?"
64.03 "No, Mrs. Reed."
64.04 "Is there anything else you wish for, Jane?
64.05 I assure you, I desire to be your friend."
64.06 "Not you. You told Mr. Brocklehurst I
64.07 had a bad character, a deceitful disposition;
64.08 and I'll let everybody at Lowood know what
64.09 you are, and what you have done."
64.10 "Jane, you don't understand these things:
64.11 children must be corrected for their faults."
64.12 "Deceit is not my fault!" I cried out in a
64.13 savage, high voice.
64.14 "But you are passionate, Jane, that you
64.15 must allow: and now return to the nursery --
64.16 there's a dear -- and lie down a little."
64.17 "I am not your dear; I cannot lie down:
64.18 send me to school soon, Mrs. Reed, for I hate
64.19 to live here."
64.20 "I will indeed send her to school soon," mur-
64.21 mured Mrs. Reed, sotto voce; and gathering
64.22 up her work, she abruptly quitted the apart-
64.23 ment.
64.24 I was left there alone -- winner of the field.
64.25 It was the hardest battle I had fought, and the
64.26 first victory I had gained: I stood awhile on
64.27 the rug, where Mr. Brocklehurst had stood,
64.28 and I enjoyed my conqueror's solitude. First,
65.01 I smiled to myself and felt elate; but this fierce
65.02 pleasure subsided in me as fast as did the acce-
65.03 lerated throb of my pulses. A child cannot
65.04 quarrel with its elders, as I had done; cannot
65.05 give its furious feelings uncontrolled play, as I
65.06 had given mine; without experiencing after-
65.07 wards the pang of remorse and the chill of re-
65.08 action. A ridge of lighted heath, alive, glanc-
65.09 ing, devouring, would have been a meet emblem
65.10 of my mind when I accused and menaced Mrs.
65.11 Reed: the same ridge, black and blasted after
65.12 the flames are dead, would have represented as
65.13 meetly my subsequent condition, when half an
65.14 hour's silence and reflection had shewn me the
65.15 madness of my conduct, and the dreariness of
65.16 my hated and hating position.
65.17 Something of vengeance I had tasted for the
65.18 first time; as aromatic wine it seemed, on swal-
65.19 lowing, warm and racy: its after-flavour, me-
65.20 tallic and corroding, gave me a sensation as if
65.21 I had been poisoned. Willingly would I now
65.22 have gone and asked Mrs. Reed's pardon; but
65.23 I knew, partly from experience and partly from
65.24 instinct, that was the way to make her repulse
65.25 me with double scorn, thereby re-exciting every
65.26 turbulent impulse of my nature.
65.27 I would fain exercise some better faculty
65.28 than that of fierce speaking; fain find nourish-
66.01 ment for some less fiendish feeling than that of
66.02 sombre indignation. I took a book -- some
66.03 Arabian tales; I sat down and endeavoured to
66.04 read. I could make no sense of the subject;
66.05 my own thoughts swam always between me
66.06 and the page I had usually found fascinating.
66.07 I opened the glass-door in the breakfast-room:
66.08 the shrubbery was quite still; the black frost
66.09 reigned, unbroken by sun or breeze, through
66.10 the grounds. I covered my head and arms
66.11 with the skirt of my frock, and went out to
66.12 walk in a part of the plantation which was
66.13 quite sequestered: but I found no pleasure in
66.14 the silent trees, the fallen fir-cones, the con-
66.15 gealed relics of autumn, russet leaves, swept by
66.16 past winds in heaps, and now stiffened together.
66.17 I leaned against a gate, and looked into an
66.18 empty field where no sheep were feeding, where
66.19 the short grass was nipped and blanched. It
66.20 was a very gray day; a most opaque sky,
66.21 "onding on snaw," canopied all; thence flakes
66.22 fell at intervals, which settled on the hard path
66.23 and on the hoary lea without melting. I stood,
66.24 a wretched child enough, whispering to myself
66.25 over and over again, "What shall I do? --
66.26 what shall I do?"
66.27 All at once I heard a clear voice call, "Miss
66.28 Jane! where are you? Come to lunch!"
67.01 It was Bessie, I knew well enough; but I
67.02 did not stir; her light step came tripping down
67.03 the path.
67.04 "You naughty little thing!" she said.
67.05 "Why don't you come when you are called?"
67.06 Bessie's presence, compared with the
67.07 thoughts over which I had been brooding,
67.08 seemed cheerful; even though, as usual, she
67.09 was somewhat cross. The fact is, after my
67.10 conflict with, and victory over Mrs. Reed, I
67.11 was not disposed to care much for the nurse--

67.12 maid's transitory anger; and I was disposed to
67.13 bask in her youthful lightness of heart. I just
67.14 put my two arms round her, and said, "Come,
67.15 Bessie! don't scold."
67.16 The action was more frank and fearless than
67.17 any I was habituated to indulge in: somehow
67.18 it pleased her.
67.19 "You are a strange child, Miss Jane," she
67.20 said, as she looked down at me: "a little roving,
67.21 solitary thing: and you are going to school, I
67.22 suppose?"
67.23 I nodded.
67.24 "And won't you be sorry to leave poor
67.25 Bessie?"
67.26 "What does Bessie care for me? She is
67.27 always scolding me."
68.01 "Because you're such a queer, frightened,
68.02 shy little thing. You should be bolder."
68.03 "What! to get more knocks?"
68.04 "Nonsense! But you are rather put upon,
68.05 that's certain. My mother said, when she
68.06 came to see me last week, that she would not
68.07 like a little one of her own to be in your place.
68.08 -- Now, come in, and I've some good news for
68.09 you."
68.10 "I don't think you have, Bessie."
68.11 "Child! what do you mean? what
68.12 sorrowful eyes you fix on me! well! but
68.13 Missis and the young ladies and Master John
68.14 are going out to tea this afternoon, and you
68.15 shall have tea with me. I'll ask cook to
68.16 bake you a little cake, and then you shall
68.17 help me to look over your drawers; for I
68.18 am soon to pack your trunk. Missis intends
68.19 you to leave Gateshead in a day or two, and
68.20 you shall choose what toys you like to take
68.21 with you."
68.22 "Bessie, you must promise not to scold me
68.23 any more till I go."
68.24 "Well, I will: but mind, you are a very
68.25 good girl, and don't be afraid of me. Don't
68.26 start when I chance to speak rather sharply:
68.27 it's so provoking."
69.01 "I don't think I shall ever be afraid of you
69.02 again, Bessie, because I have got used to you;
69.03 and I shall soon have another set of people to
69.04 dread."
69.05 "If you dread them, they'll dislike you."
69.06 "As you do, Bessie?"
69.07 "I don't dislike you, Miss; I believe I am
69.08 fonder of you than of all the others."
69.09 "You don't show it."
69.10 "You little sharp thing! you've got quite a
69.11 new way of talking. what makes you so
69.12 venturesome and hardy?"
69.13 "Why, I shall soon be away from you, and
69.14 besides -- --". I was going to say something
69.15 about what had passed between me and Mrs.
69.16 Reed; but on second thoughts I considered it
69.17 better to remain silent on that head.
69.18 "And so you're glad to leave me?"
69.19 "Not at all, Bessie; indeed, just now I am
69.20 rather sorry."
69.21 "Just now! and rather! How coolly my
69.22 little lady says it! I daresay now if I were to
69.23 ask you for a kiss you wouldn't give it me:
69.24 you'd say you would rather not."
69.25 "I'll kiss you and welcome: bend your
69.26 head down." Bessie stooped; we mutually
69.27 embraced, and I followed her into the house
69.28 quite comforted. That afternoon lapsed in
70.01 peace and harmony; and in the evening
70.02 Bessie told me some of her most enchaining
70.03 stores, and sang me some of her sweetest
70.04 songs. Even for me life had its gleams of
70.05 sunshine.
71.01 [Vol. 1 Chapter 5]
71.02 Five o'clock had hardly struck on the morning
71.03 of the 19th of January, when Bessie brought a
71.04 candle into my closet and found me already
71.05 up and nearly dressed. I had risen half an
71.06 hour before her entrance, and had washed
71.07 my face, and put on my clothes by the light
71.08 of a half-moon just setting, whose ray streamed
71.09 through the narrow window near my crib.
71.10 I was to leave Gateshead that day by a coach
71.11 which passed the lodge gates at six A.M.
71.12 Bessie was the only person yet risen; she
71.13 had lit a fire in the nursery, where she now
71.14 proceeded to make my breakfast. Few
71.15 children can eat when excited with the
71.16 thoughts of a journey; nor could I. Bessie,
71.17 having pressed me in vain to take a few
71.18 spoonfuls of the boiled milk and bread she
71.19 had prepared for me, wrapped up some
71.20 biscuits in a paper and put them into my
72.01 bag; then she helped me on with my pelisse
72.02 and bonnet, and wrapping herself in a shawl,
72.03 she and I left the nursery. As we passed
72.04 Mrs. Reed's bed-room, she said, "Will you
72.05 go in and bid Missis good-bye?"
72.06 "No, Bessie: she came to my crib last
72.07 night when you were gone down to supper,
72.08 and said I need not disturb her in the morning,
72.09 or my cousins either; and she told me to re-
72.10 member that she had always been my best
72.11 friend, and to speak of her and be grateful to
72.12 her accordingly."
72.13 "what did you say, Miss?"
72.14 "Nothing: I covered my face with the bed--
72.15 clothes, and turned from her to the wall."

72.16 "That was wrong, Miss Jane."
72.17 "It was quite right, Bessie: your Missis
72.18 has not been my friend; she has been my
72.19 foe."
72.20 "Oh, Miss Jane! don't say so!"
72.21 "Good-bye to Gateshead!" cried I, as we
72.22 passed through the hall and went out at the
72.23 front door.
72.24 The moon was set, and it was very dark;
72.25 Bessie carried a lantern, whose light glanced
72.26 on wet steps and gravel road sodden by a
72.27 recent thaw. Raw and chill was the winter
72.28 morning; my teeth chattered as I hastened
73.01 down the drive. There was a light in the
73.02 porter's lodge; when we reached it we found
73.03 the porter's wife just kindling her fire: my
73.04 trunk, which had been carried down the
73.05 evening before, stood corded at the door. It
73.06 wanted but a few minutes of six, and shortly
73.07 after that hour had struck, the distant roll of
73.08 wheels announced the coming coach; I went
73.09 to the door and watched its lamps approach
73.10 rapidly through the gloom.
73.11 "Is she going by herself?" asked the
73.12 porter's wife.
73.13 "Yes."
73.14 "And how far is it?"
73.15 "Fifty miles."
73.16 "what a long way! I wonder Mrs. Reed
73.17 is not afraid to trust her so far alone."
73.18 The coach drew up; there it was at the
73.19 gates with its four horses and its top laden
73.20 with passengers: the guard and coachman
73.21 loudly urged haste; my trunk was hoisted
73.22 up; I was taken from Bessie's neck, to which
73.23 I clung with kisses.
73.24 "Be sure and take good care of her," cried
73.25 she to the guard, as he lifted me into the
73.26 inside.
73.27 "Ay, ay!" was the answer: the door was
73.28 clapped to, a voice exclaimed "All right," and
74.01 on we drove. Thus was I severed from Bessie
74.02 and Gateshead: thus whirled away to un-
74.03 known, and, as I deemed, remote and
74.04 mysterious regions.
74.05 I remember but little of the journey: I only
74.06 know that the day seemed to me of a preter-
74.07 natural length, and that we appeared to travel
74.08 over hundreds of miles of road. we passed
74.09 through several towns, and in one, a very large
74.10 one, the coach stopped; the horses were taken
74.11 out, and the passengers alighted to dine. I
74.12 was carried into an inn, where the guard
74.13 wanted me to have some dinner; but, as I
74.14 had no appetite, he left me in an immense
74.15 room with a fire-place at each end, a chan-
74.16 delier pendent from the ceiling, and a little
74.17 red gallery high up against the wall filled
74.18 with musical instruments. Here I walked
74.19 about for a long time, feeling very strange,
74.20 and mortally apprehensive of some one coming
74.21 in and kidnapping me: for I believed in kid-
74.22 nappers; their exploits having frequently
74.23 figured in Bessie's fire-side chronicles. At
74.24 last the guard returned; once more I was
74.25 stowed away in the coach, my protector
74.26 mounted his own seat, sounded his hollow
74.27 horn, and away we rattled over the "stony
74.28 street" of -- .
75.01 The afternoon came on wet and somewhat
75.02 misty; as it waned into dusk, I began to feel
75.03 that we were getting very far indeed from
75.04 Gateshead: we ceased to pass through towns;
75.05 the country changed; great gray hills heaved
75.06 up round the horizon: as twilight deepened,
75.07 we descended a valley, dark with wood, and
75.08 long after night had overclouded the prospect,
75.09 I heard a wild wind rushing amongst trees.
75.10 Lulled by the sound, I at last dropped
75.11 asleep: I had not long slumbered when the
75.12 sudden cessation of motion awoke me; the
75.13 coach-door was open, and a person like a
75.14 servant was standing at it: I saw her face and
75.15 dress by the light of the lamps.
75.16 "Is there a little girl called Jane Eyre
75.17 here?" she asked. I answered "Yes," and
75.18 was then lifted out; my trunk was handed
75.19 down, and the coach instantly drove away.
75.20 I was stiff with long sitting, and bewildered
75.21 with the noise and motion of the coach:
75.22 gathering my faculties, I looked about me.
75.23 Rain, wind, and darkness filled the air; never-
75.24 theless, I dimly discerned a wall before me
75.25 and a door opened in it; through this door I
75.26 passed with my new guide: she shut and
75.27 locked it behind her. There was now visible
76.01 a house or houses -- for the building spread
76.02 far -- with many windows; and lights burning
76.03 in some; we went up a broad pebbly path,
76.04 splashing wet, and were admitted at a door;
76.05 then the servant led me through a passage
76.06 into a room with a fire, where she left me
76.07 alone.
76.08 I stood and warmed my numbed fingers
76.09 over the blaze, then I looked round; there
76.10 was no candle, but the uncertain light from
76.11 the hearth showed by intervals, papered walls,
76.12 carpet, curtains, shining mahogany furniture:
76.13 it was a parlour, not so spacious or splendid
76.14 as the drawing-room at Gateshead, but com-
76.15 fortable enough. I was puzzling to make out

76.16 the subject of a picture on the wall, when the
76.17 door opened, and an individual carrying a
76.18 light entered; another followed close behind.
76.19 The first was a tall lady with dark hair,
76.20 dark eyes, and a pale and large forehead; her
76.21 figure was partly enveloped in a shawl, her
76.22 countenance was grave, her bearing erect.
76.23 "The child is very young to be sent alone;"
76.24 said she, putting her candle down on the
76.25 table. She considered me attentively for a
76.26 minute or two, then further added: --
76.27 "She had better be put to bed soon; she
77.01 looks tired: are you tired?" she asked, placing
77.02 her hand on my shoulder.
77.03 "A little, ma'am."
77.04 "And hungry, too, no doubt: let her have
77.05 some supper before she goes to bed, Miss
77.06 Miller. Is this the first time you have left
77.07 your parents to come to school, my little
77.08 girl?"
77.09 I explained to her that I had no parents.
77.10 She inquired how long they had been dead;
77.11 then how old I was, what was my name,
77.12 whether I could read, write, and sew a little:
77.13 then she touched my cheek gently with her
77.14 forefinger, and saying, "She hoped I should
77.15 be a good child," dismissed me along with
77.16 Miss Miller.
77.17 The lady I had left might be about twenty--
77.18 nine; the one who went with me appeared
77.19 some years younger: the first impressed me
77.20 by her voice, look, and air. Miss Miller was
77.21 more ordinary; ruddy in complexion, though
77.22 of a careworn countenance; hurried in gait
77.23 and action, like one who had always a multi-
77.24 plicity of tasks on hand: she looked, indeed,
77.25 what I afterwards found she really was, an un-
77.26 der-teacher. Led by her, I passed from com-
77.27 partment to compartment, from passage to pas-
77.28 sage, of a large and irregular building; till,
78.01 emerging from the total and somewhat dreary
78.02 silence pervading that portion of the house we
78.03 had traversed, we came upon the hum of many
78.04 voices, and presently entered a wide, long room,
78.05 with great deal tables, two at each end, on each
78.06 of which burnt a pair of candles, and seated all
78.07 round on benches, a congregation of girls of
78.08 every age, from nine or ten to twenty. Seen
78.09 by the dim light of the dips, their number to
78.10 me appeared countless, though not in reality
78.11 exceeding eighty; they were uniformly dressed
78.12 in brown stuff frocks of quaint fashion, and
78.13 long holland pinafores. It was the hour of
78.14 study; they were engaged in conning over
78.15 their to-morrow's task, and the hum I had
78.16 heard was the combined result of their whis-
78.17 pered repetitions.
78.18 Miss Miller signed to me to sit on a bench
78.19 near the door, then walking up to the top of
78.20 the long room, she cried out: --
78.21 "Monitors, collect the lesson-books and put
78.22 them away!"
78.23 Four tall girls arose from different tables,
78.24 and going round, gathered the books and re-
78.25 moved them. Miss Miller again gave the
78.26 word of command: --
78.27 "Monitors, fetch the supper-trays!"
78.28 The tall girls went out and returned pre-
79.01 sently, each bearing a tray, with portions of
79.02 something, I knew not what, arranged thereon,
79.03 and a pitcher of water and mug in the middle
79.04 of each tray. The portions were handed
79.05 round; those who liked took a draught of the
79.06 water, the mug being common to all. When
79.07 it came to my turn, I drank, for I was thirsty,
79.08 but did not touch the food; excitement and
79.09 fatigue rendering me incapable of eating: I
79.10 now saw, however, that it was a thin oaten cake,
79.11 shared into fragments.
79.12 The meal over, prayers were read by Miss
79.13 Miller, and the classes filed off -- two and two,
79.14 up stairs. Overpowered by this time with
79.15 weariness, I scarcely noticed what sort of a
79.16 place the bed-room was; except that, like the
79.17 school-room, I saw it was very long. To-night
79.18 I was to be Miss Miller's bed-fellow; she
79.19 helped me to undress: when laid down I
79.20 glanced at the long rows of beds, each of
79.21 which was quickly filled with two occupants;
79.22 in ten minutes the single light was extin-
79.23 guished; amidst silence and complete darkness,
79.24 I fell asleep.
79.25 The night passed rapidly: I was too tired
79.26 even to dream; I only once awoke to hear the
79.27 wind rave in furious gusts, and the rain fall in
79.28 torrents, and to be sensible that Miss Miller
80.01 had taken her place by my side. When I again
80.02 unclosed my eyes, a loud bell was ringing: the
80.03 girls were up and dressing; day had not yet
80.04 begun to dawn, and a rushlight or two burnt
80.05 in the room. I too rose reluctantly; it was
80.06 bitter cold, and I dressed as well as I could for
80.07 shivering, and washed when there was a basin
80.08 at liberty: which did not occur soon, as there
80.09 was but one basin to six girls, on the stands
80.10 down in the middle of the room. Again the bell
80.11 rang: all formed in file, two and two, and in
80.12 that order descended the stairs and entered the
80.13 cold and dimly-lit school-room: here prayers
80.14 were read by Miss Miller; afterwards she
80.15 called out: --

80.16 "Form classes!"
80.17 A great tumult succeeded for some minutes,
80.18 during which Miss Miller repeatedly exclaimed,
80.19 "Silence!" and "Order!" when it subsided,
80.20 I saw them all drawn up in four semicircles,
80.21 before four chairs, placed at the four tables;
80.22 all held books in their hands, and a great book,
80.23 like a bible, lay on each table, before the vacant
80.24 seat. A pause of some seconds succeeded,
80.25 filled up by the low, vague hum of numbers;
80.26 Miss Miller walked from class to class, hush-
80.27 ing this indefinite sound.
80.28 A distant bell tinkled: immediately three
81.01 ladies entered the room, each walked to a table
81.02 and took her seat; Miss Miller assumed the
81.03 fourth vacant chair, which was that nearest the
81.04 door, and around which the smallest of the
81.05 children were assembled: to this inferior class
81.06 I was called, and placed at the bottom of it.
81.07 Business now began: the day's Collect was
81.08 repeated, then certain texts of scripture were
81.09 said, and to these succeeded a protracted read-
81.10 ing of chapters in the Bible, which lasted an
81.11 hour. By the time that exercise was termi-
81.12 nated, day had fully dawned. The indefati-
81.13 gable bell now sounded for the fourth time: the
81.14 classes were marshalled and marched into an-
81.15 other room to breakfast: how glad I was to be-
81.16 hold a prospect of getting something to eat! I
81.17 was now nearly sick from inanition, having
81.18 taken so little the day before.
81.19 The refectory was a great, low-ceiled gloomy
81.20 room; on two long tables smoked basins of
81.21 something hot, which, however, to my dismay,
81.22 sent forth an odour far from inviting. I saw
81.23 a universal manifestation of discontent when
81.24 the fumes of the repast met the nostrils of those
81.25 destined to swallow it: from the van of the
81.26 procession, the tall girls of the first class, rose
81.27 the whispered words: --
81.28 "Disgusting! The porridge is burnt again!"
82.01 "Silence!" ejaculated a voice; not that of
82.02 Miss Miller, but of one of the upper teachers,
82.03 a little and dark personage, smartly dressed,
82.04 but of somewhat morose aspect, who installed
82.05 herself at the top of one table, while a more
82.06 buxom lady presided at the other. I looked
82.07 in vain for her I had first seen the night be-
82.08 fore; she was not visible: Miss Miller occu-
82.09 pied the foot of the table where I sat, and a
82.10 strange foreign looking, elderly lady, the
82.11 French teacher, as I afterwards found, took
82.12 the corresponding seat at the other board. A
82.13 long grace was said and a hymn sung; then a
82.14 servant brought in some tea for the teachers
82.15 and the meal began.
82.16 Ravenous, and now very faint, I devoured
82.17 a spoonful or two of my portion without think-
82.18 ing of its taste; but the first edge of hunger
82.19 blunted, I perceived I had got in hand a nau-
82.20 seous mess: burnt porridge is almost as bad as
82.21 rotten potatoes; famine itself soon sickens
82.22 over it. The spoons were moved slowly: I
82.23 saw each girl taste her food and try to swallow
82.24 it; but in most cases the effort was soon re-
82.25 linquished. Breakfast was over, and none had
82.26 breakfasted. Thanks being returned for what
82.27 we had not got, and a second hymn chanted,
82.28 the refectory was evacuated for the school--
83.01 room. I was one of the last to go out, and in
83.02 passing the tables, I saw one teacher take a
83.03 basin of the porridge and taste it; she looked
83.04 at the others; all their countenances expressed
83.05 displeasure, and one of them, the stout one,
83.06 whispered: --
83.07 "Abominable stuff! How shameful!"
83.08 A quarter of an hour passed before lessons
83.09 again began, during which the school-room
83.10 was in a glorious tumult; for that space of
83.11 time, it seemed to be permitted to talk loud
83.12 and more freely, and they used their privilege.
83.13 The whole conversation ran on the breakfast,
83.14 which one and all abused roundly. Poor
83.15 things! it was the sole consolation they had.
83.16 Miss Miller was now the only teacher in the
83.17 room: a group of great girls standing about
83.18 her, spoke with serious and sullen gestures. I
83.19 heard the name of Mr. Brocklehurst pro-
83.20 nounced by some lips; at which Miss Miller
83.21 shook her head disapprovingly; but she made
83.22 no great effort to check the general wrath:
83.23 doubtless she shared in it.
83.24 A clock in the school-room struck nine;
83.25 Miss Miller left her circle, and standing in the
83.26 middle of the room, cried: --
83.27 "Silence! To your seats!"
83.28 Discipline prevailed: in five minutes the
84.01 confused throng was resolved into order, and
84.02 comparative silence quelled the Babel clamour
84.03 of tongues. The upper teachers now punc-
84.04 tually resumed their posts; but still, all seemed
84.05 to wait. Ranged on benches down the sides
84.06 of the room, the eighty girls sat motionless
84.07 and erect: a quaint assemblage they appeared,
84.08 all with plain locks combed from their faces,
84.09 not a curl visible; in brown dresses, made high
84.10 and surrounded by a narrow tucker about the
84.11 throat, with little pockets of holland / shaped
84.12 something like a Highlander's purse / tied in
84.13 front of their frocks, and destined to serve the
84.14 purpose of a work-bag: all too wearing wool-

84.15 len stockings and country-made shoes, fastened
84.16 with brass buckles. Above twenty of those
84.17 clad in this costume were full-grown girls; or
84.18 rather young women: it suited them ill,
84.19 and gave an air of oddity even to the pret-
84.20 tiest.
84.21 I was still looking at them, and also at in-
84.22 tervals examining the teachers -- none of whom
84.23 precisely pleased me; for the stout one was a
84.24 little coarse, the dark one not a little fierce,
84.25 the foreigner harsh and grotesque, and Miss
84.26 Miller, poor thing! looked purple, weather--
84.27 beaten, and over-worked -- when, as my eye
84.28 wandered from face to face, the whole school
85.01 rose simultaneously, as if moved by a common
85.02 spring.
85.03 What was the matter? I had heard no
85.04 order given: I was puzzled. Ere I had ga-
85.05 thered my wits, the classes were again seated:
85.06 but as all eyes were now turned to one point,
85.07 mine followed the general direction, and en-
85.08 countered the personage who had received me
85.09 last night. She stood at the bottom of the
85.10 long room, on the hearth; for there was a fire
85.11 at each end: she surveyed the two rows of
85.12 girls silently and gravely. Miss Miller ap-
85.13 proaching, seemed to ask her a question, and
85.14 having received her answer, went back to her
85.15 place, and said aloud, --
85.16 "Monitor of the first class, fetch the
85.17 globes!"
85.18 While the direction was being executed, the
85.19 lady consulted moved slowly up the room. I
85.20 suppose I have a considerable organ of Vene-
85.21 ration, for I retain yet the sense of admiring
85.22 awe with which my eyes tracked her steps.
85.23 Seen now, in broad daylight, she looked tall,
85.24 fair, and shapely; brown eyes, with a benig-
85.25 nant light in their irids, and a fine pencilling
85.26 of long lashes round, relieved the whiteness
85.27 of her large front; on each of her temples her
85.28 hair, of a very dark brown, was clustered in
86.01 round curls, according to the fashion of those
86.02 times, when neither smooth bands nor long
86.03 ringlets were in vogue; her dress, also in the
86.04 mode of the day, was of purple cloth, relieved
86.05 by a sort of Spanish trimming of black velvet;
86.06 a gold watch / watches were not so common
86.07 then as now / shone at her girdle. Let the
86.08 reader add, to complete the picture, refined
86.09 features; a complexion, if pale, clear; and a
86.10 stately air and carriage, and he will have, at
86.11 least as clearly as words can give it, a correct
86.12 idea of the exterior of Miss Temple, -- Maria
86.13 Temple, as I afterwards saw the name written
86.14 in a prayer-book entrusted to me to carry to
86.15 church.
86.16 The superintendent of Lowood / for such
86.17 was this lady / having taken her seat before a
86.18 pair of globes placed on one of the tables,
86.19 summoned the first class round her, and com-
86.20 menced giving a lesson in geography; the
86.21 lower classes were called by the teachers:
86.22 repetitions in history, grammar, &c. went on
86.23 for an hour; writing and arithmetic succeeded,
86.24 and music lessons were given by Miss Temple
86.25 to some of the elder girls. The duration of
86.26 each lesson was measured by the clock, which
86.27 at last struck twelve. The superintendent
86.28 rose: --
87.01 "I have a word to address to the pupils,"
87.02 said she.
87.03 The tumult of cessation from lessons was
87.04 already breaking forth, but it sank at her
87.05 voice. She went on: --
87.06 "You had this morning a breakfast which
87.07 you could not eat; you must be hungry: -- I
87.08 have ordered that a lunch of bread and cheese
87.09 shall be served to all."
87.10 The teachers looked at her with a sort of
87.11 surprise.
87.12 "It is to be done on my responsibility," she
87.13 added, in an explanatory tone to them, and
87.14 immediately afterwards left the room.
87.15 The bread and cheese was presently brought
87.16 in and distributed, to the high delight and re-
87.17 freshment of the whole school. The order
87.18 was now given "To the garden!" Each put
87.19 on a coarse straw bonnet, with strings of
87.20 coloured calico, and a cloak of grey frieze. I
87.21 was similarly equipped, and, following the
87.22 stream, I made my way into the open air.
87.23 The garden was a wide enclosure, surrounded
87.24 with walls so high as to exclude every glimpse
87.25 of prospect; a covered verandah ran down
87.26 one side, and broad walks bordered a middle
87.27 space divided into scores of little beds: these
87.28 beds were assigned as gardens for the pupils
88.01 to cultivate, and each bed had an owner.
88.02 When full of flowers they would, doubtless,
88.03 look pretty; but now, at the latter end of
88.04 January, all was wintry blight and brown decay.
88.05 I shuddered as I stood and looked round me:
88.06 it was an inclement day for out-door exercise;
88.07 not positively rainy, but darkened by a drizz-
88.08 ling yellow fog; all underfoot was still soaking
88.09 wet with the floods of yesterday. The stronger
88.10 among the girls ran about and engaged in ac-
88.11 tive games, but sundry pale and thin ones
88.12 herded together for shelter and warmth in the
88.13 varandah; and amongst these as the dense

88.14 mist penetrated to their shivering frames, I
88.15 heard frequently the sound of a hollow cough.
88.16 As yet I had spoken to no one, nor did any-
88.17 body seem to take notice of me; I stood lonely
88.18 enough: but to that feeling of isolation I was
88.19 accustomed; it did not oppress me much. I
88.20 leant against a pillar of the verandah, drew my
88.21 gray mantle close about me, and trying to for-
88.22 get the cold which nipped me without, and the
88.23 unsatisfied hunger which gnawed me within,
88.24 delivered myself up to the employment of
88.25 watching and thinking. My reflections were
88.26 too undefined and fragmentary to merit record:
88.27 I hardly yet knew where I was; Gateshead
88.28 and my past life seemed floated away to an
89.01 immeasurable distance; the present was vague
89.02 and strange, and of the future I could form no
89.03 conjecture. I looked round the convent-like
89.04 garden, and then up at the house; a large
89.05 building, half of which seemed gray and old,
89.06 the other half quite new. The new part, con-
89.07 taining the school-room and dormitory, was lit
89.08 by mullioned and latticed windows, which gave
89.09 it a church-like aspect; a stone tablet over the
89.10 door, bore this inscription: --
89.11 "Lowood Institution. -- This portion was re-
89.12 built A.D. -- -- , by Naomi Brocklehurst, of
89.13 Brocklehurst Hall, in this county." "Let
89.14 your light so shine before men that they may
89.15 see your good works, and glorify your Father
89.16 which is in heaven." -- St. Matt. 5.16.
89.17 I read these words over and over again: I
89.18 felt that an explanation belonged to them, and
89.19 was unable fully to penetrate their import.
89.20 I was still pondering the signification of "In-
89.21 stitution," and endeavouring to make out a
89.22 connection between the first words and the
89.23 verse of scripture, when the sound of a cough
89.24 close behind me, made me turn my head. I
89.25 saw a girl sitting on a stone bench near; she
89.26 was bent over a book, on the perusal of which
89.27 she seemed intent: from where I stood I could
89.28 see the title -- it was "Rasselas;" a name that
90.01 struck me as strange, and consequently attrac-
90.02 tive. In turning a leaf she happened to look
90.03 up, and I said to her directly: --
90.04 "Is your book interesting?" I had already
90.05 formed the intention of asking her to lend it to
90.06 me some day.
90.07 "I like it," she answered, after a pause of a
90.08 second or two, during which she examined me.
90.09 "What is it about?" I continued. I hardly
90.10 know where I found the hardihood thus to
90.11 open a conversation with a stranger; the step
90.12 was contrary to my nature and habits: but I
90.13 think her occupation touched a cord of sympa-
90.14 thy somewhere; for I too liked reading, though
90.15 of a frivolous and childish kind; I could not
90.16 digest or comprehend the serious or substantial.
90.17 "You may look at it," replied the girl,
90.18 offering me the book.
90.19 I did so; a brief examination convinced me
90.20 that the contents were less taking than the
90.21 title: "Rasselas" looked dull to my trifling
90.22 taste; I saw nothing about fairies, nothing
90.23 about genii; no bright variety seemed spread
90.24 over the closely-printed pages. I returned it
90.25 to her; she received it quietly, and without
90.26 saying anything she was about to relapse into
90.27 her former studious mood: again I ventured to
90.28 disturb her: --
91.01 "Can you tell me what the writing on that
91.02 stone over the door, means? what is Lowood
91.03 Institution?"
91.04 "This house where you are come to live."
91.05 "And why do they call it Institution? Is it
91.06 in any way different from other schools?"
91.07 "It is partly a charity-school: you and I,
91.08 and all the rest of us, are charity-children. I
91.09 suppose you are an orphan: are not either
91.10 your father or your mother dead?"
91.11 "Both died before I can remember."
91.12 "Well, all the girls here have lost either one
91.13 or both parents, and this is called an institution
91.14 for educating orphans."
91.15 "Do we pay no money? Do they keep us
91.16 for nothing?"
91.17 "We pay, or our friends pay, fifteen pounds
91.18 a year for each."
91.19 "Then why do they call us charity-children?"
91.20 "Because fifteen pounds is not enough for
91.21 board and teaching, and the deficiency is sup-
91.22 plied by subscription."
91.23 "Who subscribes?"
91.24 "Different benevolent-minded ladies and
91.25 gentlemen in this neighbourhood and in Lon-
91.26 don."
91.27 "Who was Naomi Brocklehurst?"
91.28 "The lady who built the new part of this
92.01 house as that tablet records, and whose son
92.02 overlooks and directs everything here."
92.03 "Why?"
92.04 "Because he is treasurer and manager of
92.05 the establishment."
92.06 "Then this house does not belong to that tall
92.07 lady who wears a watch, and who said we were
92.08 to have some bread and cheese?"
92.09 "To Miss Temple? Oh, no! I wish it did:
92.10 she has to answer to Mr. Brocklehurst for all
92.11 she does. Mr. Brocklehurst buys all our food
92.12 and all our clothes."

92.13 "Does he live here?"
92.14 "No -- two miles off, at a large hall."
92.15 "Is he a good man?"
92.16 "He is a clergyman, and is said to do a great
92.17 deal of good."
92.18 "Did you say that tall lady was called Miss
92.19 Temple?"
92.20 "Yes."
92.21 "And what are the other teachers called?"
92.22 "The one with red cheeks is called Miss
92.23 Smith; she attends to the work, and cuts out
92.24 -- for we make our own clothes, our frocks, and
92.25 pelisses, and everything; the little one with
92.26 black hair is Miss Scatcherd; she teaches
92.27 history and grammar, and hears the second
92.28 class repetitions; and the one who wears a
93.01 shawl, and has a pocket-handkerchief tied to
93.02 her side with a yellow riband, is Madame
93.03 Pierrot: she comes from Lisle, in France, and
93.04 teaches French."
93.05 "Do you like the teachers?"
93.06 "Well enough."
93.07 "Do you like the little black one, and the
93.08 Madame -- ? -- I cannot pronounce her
93.09 name as you do."
93.10 "Miss Scatcherd is hasty -- you must take
93.11 care not to offend her; Madame Pierrot is
93.12 not a bad sort of person."
93.13 "But Miss Temple is the best -- isn't she?"
93.14 "Miss Temple is very good, and very clever;
93.15 she is above the rest, because she knows far
93.16 more than they do."
93.17 "Have you been long here?"
93.18 "Two years."
93.19 "Are you an orphan?"
93.20 "My mother is dead."
93.21 "Are you happy here?"
93.22 "You ask rather too many questions. I
93.23 have given you answers enough for the pre-
93.24 sent: now I want to read."
93.25 But at that moment the summons sounded
93.26 for dinner: all re-entered the house. The
93.27 odour which now filled the refectory was
93.28 scarcely more appetizing than that which had
94.01 regaled our nostrils at breakfast: the dinner
94.02 was served in two huge tin-plated vessels,
94.03 whence rose a strong steam redolent of rancid
94.04 fat. I found the mess to consist of indifferent
94.05 potatoes and strange shreds of rusty meat,
94.06 mixed and cooked together. Of this prepara-
94.07 tion a tolerably abundant plateful was appor-
94.08 tioned to each pupil. I ate what I could, and
94.09 wondered within myself whether every day's
94.10 fare would be like this.
94.11 After dinner, we immediately adjourned to
94.12 the school-room: lessons recommenced, and
94.13 were continued till five o'clock.
94.14 The only marked event of the afternoon
94.15 was, that I saw the girl with whom I had con-
94.16 versed in the verandah, dismissed in disgrace,
94.17 by Miss Scatcherd, from a history class, and
94.18 sent to stand in the middle of the large school--
94.19 room. The punishment seemed to me in a
94.20 high degree ignominious, especially for so
94.21 great a girl -- she looked thirteen or upwards.
94.22 I expected she would show signs of great dis-
94.23 tress and shame; but to my surprise she
94.24 neither wept nor blushed: composed, though
94.25 grave, she stood, the central mark of all eyes.
94.26 "How can she bear it so quietly -- so firmly?"
94.27 I asked of myself. "Were I in her place, it
94.28 seems to me I should wish the earth to open
95.01 and swallow me up. She looks as if she were
95.02 thinking of something beyond her punishment
95.03 -- beyond her situation: of something not
95.04 round her nor before her. I have heard of
95.05 day-dreams -- is she in a day-dream now? Her
95.06 eyes are fixed on the floor, but I am sure they
95.07 do not see it -- her sight seems turned in, gone
95.08 down into her heart: she is looking at what
95.09 she can remember, I believe; not at what is
95.10 really present. I wonder what sort of a girl
95.11 she is -- whether good or naughty."
95.12 Soon after five P.M. we had another meal,
95.13 consisting of a small mug of coffee, and half a
95.14 slice of brown bread. I devoured my bread
95.15 and drank my coffee with relish; but I should
95.16 have been glad of as much more -- I was still
95.17 hungry. Half an hour's recreation succeeded,
95.18 then study; then the glass of water and the
95.19 piece of oat-cake, prayers, and bed. Such was
95.20 my first day at Lowood.
96.01 [Vol. 1 Chapter 6]
96.02 The next day commenced as before, getting up
96.03 and dressing by rushlight; but this morning
96.04 we were obliged to dispense with the ceremony
96.05 of washing: the water in the pitchers was
96.06 frozen. A change had taken place in the
96.07 weather the preceding evening, and a keen
96.08 north-east wind, whistling through the crevices
96.09 of our bed-room windows all night long, had
96.10 made us shiver in our beds, and turned the
96.11 contents of the ewers to ice.
96.12 Before the long hour and a half of prayers
96.13 and Bible reading was over, I felt ready to
96.14 perish with cold. Breakfast-time came at last,
96.15 and this morning the porridge was not burnt;
96.16 the quality was eatable, the quantity small:
96.17 how small my portion seemed! I wished it had
96.18 been doubled.
96.19 In the course of the day I was enrolled a

96.20 member of the fourth class, and regular tasks
97.01 and occupations were assigned me: hitherto,
97.02 I had only been a spectator of the proceedings
97.03 at Lowood, I was now to become an actor
97.04 therein. At first, being little accustomed to
97.05 learn by heart, the lessons appeared to me
97.06 both long and difficult: the frequent change
97.07 from task to task, too, bewildered me; and
97.08 I was glad, when, about three o'clock in the
97.09 afternoon, Miss Smith put into my hands a
97.10 border of muslin two yards long, together with
97.11 needle, thimble, &c., and sent me to sit in a
97.12 quiet corner of the school-room, with directions
97.13 to hem the same. At that hour most of the
97.14 others were sewing likewise; but one class
97.15 still stood round Miss Scatcherd's chair read-
97.16 ing, and as all was quiet, the subject of their
97.17 lessons could be heard, together with the man-
97.18 ner in which each girl acquitted herself, and
97.19 the animadversions or commendations of Miss
97.20 Scatcherd on the performance. It was English
97.21 history: among the readers, I observed my
97.22 acquaintance of the verandah; at the com-
97.23 mencement of the lesson, her place had been
97.24 at the top of the class, but for some error of
97.25 pronunciation or some inattention to stops, she
97.26 was suddenly sent to the very bottom. Even
97.27 in that obscure position, Miss Scatcherd con-
97.28 tinued to make her an object of constant notice:
98.01 she was continually addressing to her such
98.02 phrases as the following: --
98.03 "Burns, /such it seems was her name: the
98.04 girls here, were all called by their surnames,
98.05 as boys are elsewhere/; Burns, you are standing
98.06 on the side of your shoe, turn your toes out
98.07 immediately." "Burns, you poke your chin
98.08 most unpleasantly, draw it in." "Burns, I in-
98.09 sist on your holding your head up: I will not
98.10 have you before me in that attitude," &c. &c.
98.11 A chapter having been read through twice,
98.12 the books were closed and the girls examined.
98.13 The lesson had comprised part of the reign of
98.14 Charles 1., and there were sundry questions
98.15 about tonnage and poundage, and ship-money,
98.16 which most of them appeared unable to answer;
98.17 still, every little difficulty was solved instantly
98.18 when it reached Burns: her memory seemed
98.19 to have retained the substance of the whole
98.20 lesson, and she was ready with answers on
98.21 every point. I kept expecting that Miss
98.22 Scatcherd would praise her attention; but, in-
98.23 stead of that, she suddenly cried out: --
98.24 "You dirty, disagreeable girl! you have
98.25 never cleaned your nails this morning!"
98.26 Burns made no answer: I wondered at her
98.27 silence.
98.28 "Why," thought I, "does she not explain
99.01 that she could neither clean her nails nor wash
99.02 her face, as the water was frozen?"
99.03 My attention was now called off by Miss
99.04 Smith, desiring me to hold a skein of thread:
99.05 while she was winding it, she talked to me from
99.06 time to time, asking, whether I had ever been
99.07 at school before, whether I could mark,
99.08 stitch, knit, &c.; till she dismissed me, I could
99.09 not pursue my observations on Miss Scatcherd's
99.10 movements. When I returned to my seat, that
99.11 lady was just delivering an order, of which
99.12 I did not catch the import; but Burns imme-
99.13 diately left the class, and, going into the small
99.14 inner room where the books were kept, re-
99.15 turned in half a minute, carrying in her hand
99.16 a bundle of twigs tied together at one end.
99.17 This ominous tool she presented to Miss Scat-
99.18 cherd with a respectful courtesy; then she
99.19 quietly, and without being told, unloosed her
99.20 pinafore, and the teacher instantly and sharply
99.21 inflicted on her neck a dozen strokes with the
99.22 bunch of twigs. Not a tear rose to Burns's
99.23 eye; and while I paused from my sewing, be-
99.24 cause my fingers quivered at this spectacle with
99.25 a sentiment of unavailing and impotent anger,
99.26 not a feature of her pensive face altered its
99.27 ordinary expression.
100.01 "Hardened girl!" exclaimed Miss Scat-
100.02 cherd, "nothing can correct you of your
100.03 slatternly habits: carry the rod away."
100.04 Burns obeyed: I looked at her narrowly as
100.05 she emerged from the book-closet; she was just
100.06 putting back her handkerchief into her pocket,
100.07 and the trace of a tear glistened on her thin cheek.
100.08 The play-hour in the evening I thought the
100.09 pleasantest fraction of the day at Lowood: the
100.10 bit of bread, the draught of coffee swallowed
100.11 at five o'clock had revived vitality, if it had not
100.12 satisfied hunger; the long restraint of the day
100.13 was slackened; the school-room felt warmer
100.14 than in the morning: its fires being allowed to
100.15 burn a little more brightly to supply, in some
100.16 measure, the place of candles, not yet intro-
100.17 duced; the ruddy gloaming, the licensed uproar,
100.18 the confusion of many voices gave one a wel-
100.19 come sense of liberty.
100.20 On the evening of the day on which I had
100.21 seen Miss Scatcherd flog her pupil, Burns, I
100.22 wandered as usual among the forms and tables
100.23 and laughing groups without a companion, yet
100.24 not feeling lonely: when I passed the windows,
100.25 I now and then lifted a blind and looked out;
100.26 it snowed fast, a drift was already forming
100.27 against the lower panes; putting my ear close

101.01 to the window, I could distinguish from the
101.02 gleeful tumult within, the disconsolate moan of
101.03 the wind outside.
101.04 Probably, if I had lately left a good home
101.05 and kind parents, this would have been the
101.06 hour when I should most keenly have regretted
101.07 the separation: that wind would then have
101.08 saddened my heart; this obscure chaos would
101.09 have disturbed my peace: as it was I derived
101.10 from both a strange excitement, and reckless
101.11 and feverish, I wished the wind to howl more
101.12 wildly, the gloom to deepen to darkness, and
101.13 the confusion to rise to clamour.
101.14 Jumping over forms, and creeping under
101.15 tables, I made my way to one of the fire-places:
101.16 there, kneeling by the high wire fender, I found
101.17 Burns, absorbed, silent, abstracted from all
101.18 round her by the companionship of a book,
101.19 which she read by the dim glare of the embers.
101.20 "Is it still Rasselas?" I asked, coming be-
101.21 hind her.
101.22 "Yes," she said, "and I have just finished it."
101.23 And in five minutes more she shut it up. I
101.24 was glad of this.
101.25 "Now," thought I, "I can perhaps get her
101.26 to talk." I sat down by her on the floor.
101.27 "What is your name besides Burns?"
101.28 "Helen."
102.01 "Do you come a long way from here?"
102.02 "I come from a place further north; quite
102.03 on the borders of Scotland."
102.04 "Will you ever go back?"
102.05 "I hope so; but nobody can be sure of the
102.06 future."
102.07 "You must wish to leave Lowood?"
102.08 "No: why should I? I was sent to Lowood
102.09 to get an education; and it would be of no use
102.10 going away until I have attained that object."
102.11 "But that teacher, Miss Scatcherd, is so
102.12 cruel to you?"
102.13 "Cruel? Not at all! She is severe: she
102.14 dislikes my faults."
102.15 "And if I were in your place I should dis-
102.16 like her; I should resist her; if she struck me
102.17 with that rod, I should get it from her hand;
102.18 I should break it under her nose."
102.19 "Probably you would do nothing of the
102.20 sort: but if you did, Mr. Brocklehurst would
102.21 expel you from the school; that would be a
102.22 great grief to your relations. It is far better
102.23 to endure patiently a smart which nobody feels
102.24 but yourself, than to commit a hasty action
102.25 whose evil consequences will extend to all
102.26 connected with you -- and, besides, the Bible
102.27 bids us return good for evil."
102.28 "But then it seems disgraceful to be flogged,
103.01 and to be sent to stand in the middle of a room
103.02 full of people; and you are such a great girl:
103.03 I am far younger than you, and I could not
103.04 bear it."
103.05 "Yet it would be your duty to bear it, if you
103.06 could not avoid it: it is weak and silly to say
103.07 you cannot bear what it is your fate to be
103.08 required to bear."
103.09 I heard her with wonder: I could not com-
103.10 prehend this doctrine of endurance; and still
103.11 less could I understand or sympathize with the
103.12 forbearance she expressed for her chastiser.
103.13 Still I felt that Helen Burns considered things
103.14 by a light invisible to my eyes. I suspected
103.15 she might be right and I wrong; but I would
103.16 not ponder the matter deeply: like Felix, I
103.17 put it off to a more convenient season.
103.18 "You say you have faults, Helen: what are
103.19 they? To me you seem very good."
103.20 "Then learn from me, not to judge by ap-
103.21 pearances: I am, as Miss Scatcherd said, slat-
103.22 ternly; I seldom put, and never keep, things in
103.23 order; I am careless; I forget rules; I read
103.24 when I should learn my lessons; I have no
103.25 method; and sometimes I say, like you, I can-
103.26 not bear to be subjected to systematic arrange-
103.27 ments. This is all very provoking to Miss
104.01 Scatcherd, who is naturally neat, punctual, and
104.02 particular."
104.03 "And cross and cruel," I added; but Helen
104.04 Burns would not admit my addition: she kept
104.05 silence.
104.06 "Is Miss Temple as severe to you as Miss
104.07 Scatcherd?"
104.08 At the utterance of Miss Temple's name, a
104.09 soft smile flitted over her grave face.
104.10 "Miss Temple is full of goodness; it pains
104.11 her to be severe to any one, even the worst in
104.12 the school: she sees my errors, and tells me of
104.13 them gently; and, if I do anything worthy of
104.14 praise, she gives me my meed liberally. One
104.15 strong proof of my wretchedly defective nature
104.16 is, that even her expostulations, so mild, so
104.17 rational, have not influence to cure me of my
104.18 faults; and even her praise, though I value it
104.19 most highly, cannot stimulate me to continued
104.20 care and foresight."
104.21 "That is curious," said I: "it is so easy to
104.22 be careful."
104.23 "For you I have no doubt it is. I observed
104.24 you in your class this morning, and saw you
104.25 were closely attentive: your thoughts never
104.26 seemed to wander while Miss Miller explained
104.27 the lesson and questioned you. Now, mine
105.01 continually rove away: when I should be lis-

105.02 tening to Miss Scatcherd, and collecting all she
105.03 says with assiduity, often I lose the very sound
105.04 of her voice; I fall into a sort of dream. Some-
105.05 times I think I am in Northumberland, and
105.06 that the noises I hear round me are the bub-
105.07 bling of a little brook which runs through
105.08 Deepden, near our house; -- then, when it comes
105.09 to my turn to reply, I have to be wakened; and,
105.10 having heard nothing of what was read for lis-
105.11 tening to the visionary brook, I have no an-
105.12 swer ready."
105.13 "Yet how well you replied this afternoon!"
105.14 "It was mere chance: the subject on which
105.15 we had been reading had interested me. This
105.16 afternoon, instead of dreaming of Deepden, I
105.17 was wondering how a man who wished to do
105.18 right could act so unjustly and unwisely as
105.19 Charles the First sometimes did; and I thought
105.20 what a pity it was that, with his integrity and
105.21 conscientiousness, he could see no farther than
105.22 the prerogatives of the crown. If he had but
105.23 been able to look to a distance, and see how
105.24 what they call the spirit of the age was tend-
105.25 ing! Still, I like Charles -- I respect him -- I
105.26 pity him, poor murdered king! Yes, his ene-
105.27 mies were the worst: they shed blood they had
105.28 no right to shed. How dared they kill him!"
106.01 Helen was talking to herself now: she had
106.02 forgotten I could not very well understand her
106.03 -- that I was ignorant, or nearly so, of the sub-
106.04 ject she discussed. I recalled her to my level.
106.05 "And when Miss Temple teaches you, do
106.06 your thoughts wander then?"
106.07 "No, certainly, not often; because Miss
106.08 Temple has generally something to say which
106.09 is newer than my own reflections: her lan-
106.10 guage is singularly agreeable to me, and the in-
106.11 formation she communicates is often just what
106.12 I wished to gain."
106.13 "Well, then, with Miss Temple you are
106.14 good?"
106.15 "Yes, in a passive way: I make no effort;
106.16 I follow as inclination guides me. There is no
106.17 merit in such goodness."
106.18 "A great deal: you are good to those who
106.19 are good to you. It is all I ever desire to be.
106.20 If people were always kind and obedient to
106.21 those who are cruel and unjust, the wicked
106.22 people would have it all their own way: they
106.23 would never feel afraid, and so they would
106.24 never alter, but would grow worse and worse.
106.25 When we are struck at without a reason, we
106.26 should strike back again very hard; I am sure
106.27 we should -- so hard as to teach the person who
106.28 struck us never to do it again."
107.01 "You will change your mind, I hope, when
107.02 you grow older: as yet you are but a little un-
107.03 taught girl."
107.04 "But I feel this, Helen: I must dislike those
107.05 who, whatever I do to please them, persist in
107.06 disliking me; I must resist those who punish
107.07 me unjustly. It is as natural as that I should
107.08 love those who show me affection, or submit
107.09 to punishment when I feel it is deserved."
107.10 "Heathens and savage tribes hold that
107.11 doctrine; but Christians and civilized nations
107.12 disown it."
107.13 "How? I don't understand."
107.14 "It is not violence that best overcomes hate
107.15 -- nor vengeance that most certainly heals in-
107.16 jury."
107.17 "What then?"
107.18 "Read the New Testament, and observe
107.19 what Christ says, and how he acts -- make his
107.20 word your rule, and his conduct your example."
107.21 "What does he say?"
107.22 "Love your enemies; bless them that curse
107.23 you; do good to them that hate you and de-
107.24 spitefully use you."
107.25 "Then I should love Mrs. Reed, which I
107.26 cannot do; I should bless her son John, which
107.27 is impossible."
107.28 In her turn, Helen Burns asked me to ex-
108.01 plain; and I proceeded forthwith to pour out,
108.02 in my own way, the tale of my sufferings and
108.03 resentments. Bitter and truculent when ex-
108.04 cited, I spoke as I felt, without reserve or
108.05 softening.
108.06 Helen heard me patiently to the end: I ex-
108.07 pected she would then make a remark, but she
108.08 said nothing.
108.09 "Well," I asked impatiently, "is not Mrs.
108.10 Reed a hard-hearted, bad woman?"
108.11 "She has been unkind to you, no doubt;
108.12 because, you see, she dislikes your cast of cha-
108.13 racter, as Miss Scatcherd does mine; but how
108.14 minutely you remember all she has done and
108.15 said to you! What a singularly deep impres-
108.16 sion her injustice seems to have made on your
108.17 heart! No ill usage so brands its record on
108.18 my feelings. Would you not be happier if you
108.19 tried to forget her severity, together with the
108.20 passionate emotions it excited? Life appears
108.21 to me too short to be spent in nursing animo-
108.22 sity, or registering wrongs. We are, and must
108.23 be, one and all, burdened with faults in this
108.24 world: but the time will soon come when, I
108.25 trust, we shall put them off in putting off our
108.26 corruptible bodies; when debasement and sin
108.27 will fall from us with this cumbrous frame of
108.28 flesh, and only the spark of the spirit will re-

109.01 main, -- the impalpable principle of life and
109.02 thought, pure as when it left the Creator to
109.03 inspire the creature: whence it came it will
109.04 return; perhaps again to be communicated to
109.05 some being higher than man -- perhaps to pass
109.06 through gradations of glory, from the pale
109.07 human soul to brighten to the seraph! Surely
109.08 it will never, on the contrary, be suffered to
109.09 degenerate from man to fiend? No; I cannot
109.10 believe that: I hold another creed; which no
109.11 one ever taught me, and which I seldom men-
109.12 tion; but in which I delight, and to which I
109.13 cling; for it extends hope to all: it makes
109.14 Eternity a rest -- a mighty home, not a terror
109.15 and an abyss. Besides, with this creed, I can
109.16 so clearly distinguish between the criminal and
109.17 his crime; I can so sincerely forgive the first
109.18 while I abhor the last: with this creed revenge
109.19 never worries my heart, degradation never too
109.20 deeply disgusts me, injustice never crushes me
109.21 too low: I live in calm, looking to the end."
109.22 Helen's head, always drooping, sank a little
109.23 lower as she finished this sentence. I saw by
109.24 her look she wished no longer to talk to me,
109.25 but rather to converse with her own thoughts.
109.26 She was not allowed much time for medita-
109.27 tion: a monitor, a great rough girl, presently
110.01 came up, exclaiming in a strong Cumberland
110.02 accent: --
110.03 "Helen Burns, if you don't go and put your
110.04 drawer in order, and fold up your work this
110.05 minute, I'll tell Miss Scatcherd to come and
110.06 look at it!"
110.07 Helen sighed as her reverie fled, and getting
110.08 up, obeyed the monitor without reply as with-
110.09 out delay.
111.01 [Vol. 1 Chapter 7]
111.02 My first quarter at Lowood seemed an age;
111.03 and not the golden age either: it comprised
111.04 an irksome struggle with difficulties in ha-
111.05 bituating myself to new rules and unwonted
111.06 tasks. The fear of failure in these points
111.07 harassed me worse than the physical hard-
111.08 ships of my lot; though these were no trifles.
111.09 During January, February, and part of
111.10 March, the deep snows, and after their melt-
111.11 ing, the almost impassable roads prevented
111.12 our stirring beyond the garden walls, except
111.13 to go to church; but within these limits we
111.14 had to pass an hour every day in the open
111.15 air. Our clothing was insufficient to protect
111.16 us from the severe cold: we had no boots,
111.17 the snow got into our shoes and melted there;
111.18 our ungloved hands became numbed and
111.19 covered with chilblains, as were our feet: I
111.20 remember well the distracting irritation I
111.21 endured from this cause, every evening when
112.01 my feet inflamed; and the torture of thrusting
112.02 the swelled, raw, and stiff toes into my shoes
112.03 in the morning. Then the scanty supply of
112.04 food was distressing: with the keen appetites
112.05 of growing children, we had scarcely sufficient
112.06 to keep alive a delicate invalid. From this
112.07 deficiency of nourishment resulted an abuse,
112.08 which pressed hardly on the younger pupils:
112.09 whenever the famished great girls had an
112.10 opportunity, they would coax or menace the
112.11 little ones out of their portion. Many a time
112.12 I have shared between two claimants the
112.13 precious morsel of brown bread distributed
112.14 at tea-time; and after relinquishing to a third,
112.15 half the contents of my mug of coffee, I have
112.16 swallowed the remainder with an accompani-
112.17 ment of secret tears, forced from me by the
112.18 exigency of hunger.
112.19 Sundays were dreary days in that wintry
112.20 season. We had to walk two miles to Brockle-
112.21 bridge church, where our patron officiated.
112.22 We set out cold, we arrived at church colder:
112.23 during the morning service we became almost
112.24 paralyzed. It was too far to return to dinner,
112.25 and an allowance of cold meat and bread, in
112.26 the same penurious proportion observed in our
112.27 ordinary meals, was served round between the
112.28 services.
113.01 At the close of the afternoon service we
113.02 returned by an exposed and hilly road, where
113.03 the bitter winter wind, blowing over a range
113.04 of snowy summits to the north, almost flayed
113.05 the skin from our faces.
113.06 I can remember Miss Temple walking
113.07 lightly and rapidly along our drooping line,
113.08 her plaid cloak, which the frosty wind flut-
113.09 tered, gathered close about her, and encourag-
113.10 ing us, by precept and example, to keep up
113.11 our spirits, and march forward, as she said,
113.12 "like stalwart soldiers." The other teachers,
113.13 poor things, were generally themselves too
113.14 much dejected to attempt the task of cheering
113.15 others.
113.16 How we longed for the light and heat of
113.17 a blazing fire when we got back! But, to
113.18 the little ones at least, this was denied: each
113.19 hearth in the school-room was immediately
113.20 surrounded by a double row of great girls, and
113.21 behind them the younger children crouched
113.22 in groups, wrapping their starved arms in their
113.23 pinafores.
113.24 A little solace came at tea time, in the
113.25 shape of a double ration of bread -- a whole,
113.26 instead of a half-slice -- with the delicious ad-

113.27 dition of a thin scrape of butter: it was the
113.28 hebdomadal treat to which we all looked
114.01 forward from Sabbath to Sabbath. I gene-
114.02 rally contrived to reserve a moiety of this
114.03 bounteous repast for myself; but the re-
114.04 mainder I was invariably obliged to part
114.05 with.
114.06 The Sunday evening was spent in repeating,
114.07 by heart, the Church Catechism, and the fifth,
114.08 sixth, and seventh chapters of St. Matthew;
114.09 and in listening to a long sermon, read by
114.10 Miss Miller, whose irrepressible yawns at-
114.11 tested her weariness. A frequent interlude
114.12 of these performances was the enactment of
114.13 the part of Eutychus by some half dozen of
114.14 little girls; who, overpowered with sleep,
114.15 would fall down, if not out of the third loft,
114.16 yet off the fourth form, and be taken up half
114.17 dead. The remedy was, to thrust them forward
114.18 into the centre of the school-room, and oblige
114.19 them to stand there till the sermon was
114.20 finished. Sometimes their feet failed them,
114.21 and they sank together in a heap; they were
114.22 then propped up with the monitor's high
114.23 stools.
114.24 I have not yet alluded to the visits of Mr.
114.25 Brocklehurst; and indeed that gentleman was
114.26 from home during the greater part of the first
114.27 month after my arrival; perhaps prolonging
114.28 his stay with his friend the archdeacon: his
115.01 absence was a relief to me. I need not say
115.02 that I had my own reasons for dreading his
115.03 coming: but come he did at last.
115.04 One afternoon /I had then been three weeks
115.05 at Lowood/, as I was sitting with a slate in
115.06 my hand, puzzling over a sum in long division,
115.07 my eyes, raised in abstraction to the window,
115.08 caught sight of a figure just passing: I re-
115.09 cognised almost instinctively that gaunt out-
115.10 line; and when, two minutes after, all the
115.11 school, teachers included, rose en masse, it was
115.12 not necessary for me to look up in order to
115.13 ascertain whose entrance they thus greeted.
115.14 A long stride measured the school-room, and
115.15 presently beside Miss Temple, who herself
115.16 had risen, stood the same black column which
115.17 had frowned on me so ominously from the
115.18 hearth-rug of Gateshead. I now glanced
115.19 sideways at this piece of architecture. Yes,
115.20 I was right: it was Mr. Brocklehurst, but-
115.21 toned up in a surtout, and looking longer,
115.22 narrower, and more rigid than ever.
115.23 I had my own reasons for being dismayed at
115.24 this apparition: too well I remembered the
115.25 perfidious hints given by Mrs. Reed about my
115.26 disposition, &c.; the promise pledged by Mr.
115.27 Brocklehurst to apprise Miss Temple and the
115.28 teachers of my vicious nature. All along I had
116.01 been dreading the fulfilment of this promise, --
116.02 I had been looking out daily for the "Coming
116.03 Man," whose information respecting my past
116.04 life and conversation was to brand me as a bad
116.05 child for ever: now there he was. He stood
116.06 at Miss Temple's side; he was speaking low
116.07 in her ear: I did not doubt he was making
116.08 disclosures of my villany; and I watched her
116.09 eye with painful anxiety, expecting every mo-
116.10 ment to see its dark orb turn on me a glance
116.11 of repugnance and contempt. I listened too;
116.12 and as I happened to be seated quite at the
116.13 top of the room, I caught most of what he
116.14 said: its import relieved me from immediate
116.15 apprehension.
116.16 "I suppose, Miss Temple, the thread I
116.17 bought at Lowton will do; it struck me that
116.18 it would be just of the quality for the calico
116.19 chemises, and I sorted the needles to match.
116.20 You may tell Miss Smith that I forgot to make
116.21 a memorandum of the darning needles, but she
116.22 shall have some papers sent in next week; and
116.23 she is not, on any account, to give out more
116.24 than one at a time to each pupil: if they have
116.25 more, they are apt to be careless and lose them.
116.26 And, oh, ma'am! I wish the woollen stockings
116.27 were better looked to! -- when I was here last,
116.28 I went into the kitchen-garden and examined
117.01 the clothes drying on the line; there was a
117.02 quantity of black hose in a very bad state of
117.03 repair: from the size of the holes in them
117.04 I was sure they had not been well mended
117.05 from time to time."
117.06 He paused.
117.07 "Your directions shall be attended to, sir,"
117.08 said Miss Temple.
117.09 "And, ma'am," he continued, "the laund-
117.10 dress tells me some of the girls have two clean
117.11 tuckers in the week; it is too much: the rules
117.12 limit them to one."
117.13 "I think I can explain that circumstance,
117.14 sir. Agnes and Catherine Johnstone were in-
117.15 vited to take tea with some friends at Lowton
117.16 last Thursday, and I gave them leave to put
117.17 on clean tuckers for the occasion."
117.18 Mr. Brocklehurst nodded.
117.19 "Well, for once it may pass; but please not
117.20 to let the circumstance occur too often. And
117.21 there is another thing which surprised me:
117.22 I find, in settling accounts with the house--
117.23 keeper, that a lunch, consisting of bread and
117.24 cheese, has twice been served out to the girls
117.25 during the past fortnight. How is this? I

117.26 look over the regulations, and I find no such
117.27 meal as lunch mentioned. Who introduced
117.28 this innovation? and by what authority?"
118.01 "I must be responsible for the circumstance,
118.02 sir," replied Miss Temple: "the breakfast was
118.03 so ill prepared that the pupils could not pos-
118.04 sibly eat it; and I dared not allow them to re-
118.05 main fasting till dinner time."
118.06 "Madam, allow me an instant. -- You are
118.07 aware that my plan in bringing up these girls
118.08 is, not to accustom them to habits of luxury
118.09 and indulgence, but to render them hardy,
118.10 patient, self-denying. Should any little acci-
118.11 dental disappointment of the appetite occur,
118.12 such as the spoiling of a meal, the under or
118.13 the over dressing of a dish, the incident ought
118.14 not to be neutralized by replacing with some-
118.15 thing more delicate the comfort lost, thus pam-
118.16 pering the body and obviating the aim of this
118.17 institution; it ought to be improved to the
118.18 spiritual edification of the pupils, by encourag-
118.19 ing them to evince fortitude under the tem-
118.20 porary privation. A brief address on those
118.21 occasions would not be mistimed, wherein a
118.22 judicious instructor would take the opportunity
118.23 of referring to the sufferings of the primitive
118.24 Christians; to the torments of martyrs, to the
118.25 exhortations of our blessed Lord himself, call-
118.26 ing upon his disciples to take up their cross
118.27 and follow him; to his warnings that man shall
118.28 not live by bread alone, but by every word that
119.01 proceedeth out of the mouth of God; to his
119.02 divine consolations, `if ye suffer hunger or
119.03 thirst for my sake, happy are ye.` Oh, madam,
119.04 when you put bread and cheese, instead of
119.05 burnt porridge into these children's mouths,
119.06 you may indeed feed their vile bodies, but you
119.07 little think how you starve their immortal
119.08 souls!"
119.09 Mr. Brocklehurst again paused -- perhaps
119.10 overcome by his feelings. Miss Temple had
119.11 looked down when he first began to speak to
119.12 her; but she now gazed straight before her,
119.13 and her face, naturally pale as marble, appeared
119.14 to be assuming also the coldness and fixity of
119.15 that material; especially her mouth closed as
119.16 if it would have required a sculptor's chisel to
119.17 open it, and her brow settled gradually into
119.18 petrified severity.
119.19 Meantime, Mr. Brocklehurst, standing on
119.20 the hearth with his hands behind his back,
119.21 majestically surveyed the whole school. Sud-
119.22 denly his eye gave a blink, as if it had met
119.23 something that either dazzled or shocked its
119.24 pupil; turning, he said in more rapid accents
119.25 than he had hitherto used: --
119.26 "Miss Temple, Miss Temple, what -- what is
119.27 that girl with curled hair? Red hair, ma'am,
119.28 curled -- curled all over?" And extending his
120.01 cane he pointed to the awful object, his hand
120.02 shaking as he did so.
120.03 "It is Julia Severn," replied Miss Temple,
120.04 very quietly.
120.05 "Julia Severn, ma'am! And why has she,
120.06 or any other, curled hair? why, in defiance
120.07 of every precept and principle of this house,
120.08 does she conform to the world so openly -- here
120.09 in an evangelical, charitable establishment -- as
120.10 to wear her hair one mass of curls?"
120.11 "Julia's hair curls naturally," returned Miss
120.12 Temple, still more quietly.
120.13 "Naturally! Yes, but we are not to con-
120.14 form to nature: I wish these girls to be the
120.15 children of Grace: and why that abundance?
120.16 I have again and again intimated that I desire
120.17 the hair to be arranged closely, modestly,
120.18 plainly. Miss Temple, that girl's hair must
120.19 be cut off entirely; I will send a barber to-
120.20 morrow: and I see others who have far too
120.21 much of the excrescence -- that tall girl, tell her
120.22 to turn round. Tell all the first form to rise
120.23 up and direct their faces to the wall."
120.24 Miss Temple passed her handkerchief over
120.25 her lips, as if to smooth away the involuntary
120.26 smile that curled them; she gave the order,
120.27 however, and when the first class could take
120.28 in what was required of them, they obeyed.
121.01 Leaning a little back on my bench, I could see
121.02 the looks and grimaces with which they com-
121.03 mented on this manoeuvre: it was a pity Mr.
121.04 Brocklehurst could not see them too; he would
121.05 perhaps have felt that, whatever he might do
121.06 with the outside of the cup and platter, the
121.07 inside was further beyond his interference than
121.08 he imagined.
121.09 He scrutinized the reverse of these living
121.10 medals some five minutes, then pronounced
121.11 sentence. These words fell like the knell of
121.12 doom: --
121.13 "All those top-knots must be cut off."
121.14 Miss Temple seemed to remonstrate.
121.15 "Madam," he pursued, "I have a Master
121.16 to serve whose kingdom is not of this world:
121.17 my mission is to mortify in these girls the lusts
121.18 of the flesh; to teach them to clothe them-
121.19 selves with shame-facedness and sobriety, not
121.20 with braided hair and costly apparel; and each
121.21 of the young persons before us has a string of
121.22 hair twisted in plaits which vanity itself might
121.23 have woven: these, I repeat, must be cut off;
121.24 think of the time wasted, of -- "

121.25 Mr. Brocklehurst was here interrupted:
121.26 three other visitors, ladies, now entered the
121.27 room. They ought to have come a little
121.28 sooner to have heard his lecture on dress, for
122.01 they were splendidly attired in velvet, silk, and
122.02 furs. The two younger of the trio /fine girls
122.03 of sixteen and seventeen/ had gray beaver
122.04 hats, then in fashion, shaded with ostrich
122.05 plumes, and from under the brim of this grace-
122.06 ful head-dress fell a profusion of light tresses,
122.07 elaborately curled; the elder lady was enve-
122.08 loped in a costly velvet shawl, trimmed with
122.09 ermine, and she wore a false front of French
122.10 curls.
122.11 These ladies were deferentially received by
122.12 Miss Temple, as Mrs. and the Misses Brockle-
122.13 hurst, and conducted to seats of honour at the
122.14 top of the room. It seems they had come in
122.15 the carriage with their reverend relative, and
122.16 had been conducting a rummaging scrutiny
122.17 of the rooms up stairs, while he transacted
122.18 business with the housekeeper, questioned the
122.19 laundress, and lectured the superintendent.
122.20 They now proceeded to address divers remarks
122.21 and reproofs to Miss Smith, who was charged
122.22 with the care of the linen and the inspection
122.23 of the dormitories: but I had no time to listen
122.24 to what they said; other matters called off and
122.25 enchained my attention.
122.26 Hitherto, while gathering up the discourse
122.27 of Mr. Brocklehurst and Miss Temple, I had
122.28 not, at the same time, neglected precautions to
123.01 secure my personal safety; which I thought
123.02 would be effected, if I could only elude obser-
123.03 vation. To this end, I had sat well back on
123.04 the form, and while seeming to be busy with
123.05 my sum, had held my slate in such a manner
123.06 as to conceal my face: I might have escaped
123.07 notice, had not my treacherous slate somehow
123.08 happened to slip from my hand, and falling
123.09 with an obtrusive crash, directly drawn every
123.10 eye upon me; I knew it was all over now, and,
123.11 as I stooped to pick up the two great fragments of
123.12 slate, I rallied my forces for the worst. It
123.13 came.
123.14 "A careless girl!" said Mr. Brocklehurst,
123.15 and immediately after -- "It is the new pupil,
123.16 I perceive." And before I could draw breath,
123.17 "I must not forget I have a word to say
123.18 respecting her." Then aloud: how loud it
123.19 seemed to me! "Let the child who broke
123.20 her slate, come forward!"
123.21 Of my own accord, I could not have stirred;
123.22 I was paralyzed: but the two great girls who
123.23 sat on each side of me, set me on my legs and
123.24 pushed me towards the dread judge, and then
123.25 Miss Temple gently assisted me to his very
123.26 feet, and I caught her whispered counsel:
123.27 "Don't be afraid, Jane, I saw it was an acci-
123.28 dent; you shall not be punished."
124.01 The kind whisper went to my heart like a
124.02 dagger.
124.03 "Another minute, and she will despise me
124.04 for a hypocrite," thought I; and an impulse
124.05 of fury against Reed, Brocklehurst, and Co.,
124.06 bounded in my pulses at the conviction. I was
124.07 no Helen Burns.
124.08 "Fetch that stool," said Mr. Brocklehurst,
124.09 pointing to a very high one from which a
124.10 monitor had just risen: it was brought.
124.11 "Place the child upon it."
124.12 And I was placed there, by whom I don't
124.13 know: I was in no condition to note particu-
124.14 lars; I was only aware that they had hoisted
124.15 me up to the height of Mr. Brocklehurst's
124.16 nose, that he was within a yard of me, and that
124.17 a spread of shot orange and purple silk pelisses,
124.18 and a cloud of silvery plumage extended and
124.19 waved below me.
124.20 Mr. Brocklehurst hemmed.
124.21 "Ladies," said he, turning to his family;
124.22 "Miss Temple, teachers, and children, you all
124.23 see this girl?"
124.24 Of course they did; for I felt their eyes
124.25 directed like burning-glasses against my
124.26 scorched skin.
124.27 "You see she is yet young; you observe
124.28 she possesses the ordinary form of childhood;
125.01 God has graciously given her the shape that
125.02 He has given to all of us; no signal deformity
125.03 points her out as a marked character. who
125.04 would think that the Evil One had already
125.05 found a servant and agent in her? Yet such,
125.06 I grieve to say, is the case."
125.07 A pause -- in which I began to steady the
125.08 palsy of my nerves, and to feel that the Rubi-
125.09 con was passed; and that the trial, no longer
125.10 to be shirked, must be firmly sustained.
125.11 "My dear children," pursued the black
125.12 marble clergyman, with pathos, "this is a sad,
125.13 a melancholy occasion; for it becomes my duty
125.14 to warn you, that this girl, who might be one
125.15 of God's own lambs, is a little castaway: not
125.16 a member of the true flock, but evidently an
125.17 interloper and an alien. You must be on your
125.18 guard against her; you must shun her ex-
125.19 ample: if necessary, avoid her company,
125.20 exclude her from your sports, and shut her out
125.21 from your converse. Teachers, you must
125.22 watch her: keep your eyes on her movements,
125.23 weigh well her words, scrutinize her actions,

354

125.24 punish her body to save her soul; if, indeed,
125.25 such salvaton be possible, for /my tongue
125.26 falters while I tell it/ this girl, this child, the
125.27 native of a Christian land, worse than many a
125.28 little heathen who says its prayers to Brahma
126.01 and kneels before Juggernaut -- this girl is -- a
126.02 liar!"
126.03 Now came a pause of ten minutes; during
126.04 which I, by this time in perfect possession of
126.05 my wits, observed all the female Brocklehursts
126.06 produce their pocket-handkerchiefs and apply
126.07 them to their optics, while the elderly lady
126.08 swayed herself to and fro, and the two younger
126.09 ones whispered, "How shocking!"
126.10 Mr. Brocklehurst resumed.
126.11 "This I learned from her benefactress; from
126.12 the pious and charitable lady who adopted her
126.13 in her orphan state, reared her as her own
126.14 daughter, and whose kindness, whose gene-
126.15 rosity, the unhappy girl repaid by an ingra-
126.16 titude so bad, so dreadful, that at last her
126.17 excellent patroness was obliged to separate
126.18 her from her own young ones, fearful lest her
126.19 vicious example should contaminate their
125.20 purity: she has sent her here to be healed,
126.21 even as the Jews of old sent their diseased to
126.22 the troubled pool of Bethesda; and, teachers,
126.23 superintendent, I beg of you not to allow the
126.24 waters to stagnate round her."
125.25 With this sublime conclusion, Mr. Brockle-
126.26 hurst adjusted the top button of his surtout,
126.27 muttered something to his family, who rose,
125.28 bowed to Miss Temple, and then all the great
127.01 people sailed in state from the room. Turning
127.02 at the door, my judge said: --
127.03 "Let her stand half an hour longer on that
127.04 stool, and let no one speak to her during the
127.05 remainder of the day."
127.06 There I was, then, mounted aloft; I, who
127.07 had said I would not bear the shame of standing
127.08 on my natural feet in the middle of the room,
127.09 was now exposed to general view on a pedestal
127.10 of infamy. what my sensations were, no lan-
127.11 guage can describe; but just as they all rose,
127.12 stifling my breath and constricting my throat,
127.13 a girl came up and passed me: in passing,
127.14 she lifted her eyes. what a strange light
127.15 inspired them! what an extraordinary sensa-
127.16 tion that ray sent through me! How the new
127.17 feeling bore me up! It was as if a martyr, a
127.18 hero, had passed a slave or victim, and im-
127.19 parted strength in the transit. I mastered the
127.20 rising hysteria, lifted up my head, and took a
127.21 firm stand on the stool. Helen Burns asked
127.22 some slight question about her work of Miss
127.23 Smith, was chidden for the triviality of the
127.24 inquiry, returned to her place, and smiled at
127.25 me as she again went by. What a smile! I
127.26 remember it now, and I know that it was the
127.27 effluence of fine intellect, of true courage; it
127.28 lit up her marked lineaments, her thin face,
128.01 her sunken gray eye, like a reflection from the
128.02 aspect of an angel. Yet at that moment
128.03 Helen Burns wore on her arm "the untidy
128.04 badge;" scarcely an hour ago I had heard her
128.05 condemned by Miss Scatcherd to a dinner of
128.06 bread and water on the morrow, because she
128.07 had blotted an exercise in copying it out.
128.08 Such is the imperfect nature of man! such
128.09 spots are there on the disc of the clearest
128.10 planet; and eyes like Miss Scatcherd's can
128.11 only see those minute defects, and are blind to
128.12 the full brightness of the orb.
129.01 [Vol. 1 Chapter 8]
129.02 Ere the half-hour ended, five o'clock struck;
129.03 school was dismissed, and all were gone into
129.04 the refectory to tea. I now ventured to
129.05 descend: it was deep dusk: I retired into a
129.06 corner and sat down on the floor. The spell
129.07 by which I had been so far supported began
129.08 to dissolve; reaction took place, and soon, so
129.09 overwhelming was the grief that seized me, I
129.10 sank prostrate with my face to the ground.
129.11 Now I wept: Helen Burns was not here;
129.12 nothing sustained me; left to myself I aban-
129.13 doned myself, and my tears watered the
129.14 boards. I had meant to be so good, and to
129.15 do so much at Lowood; to make so many
129.16 friends, to earn respect, and win affection.
129.17 Already I had made visible progress: that
129.18 very morning I had reached the head of my
129.19 class; Miss Miller had praised my warmly;
130.01 Miss Temple had smiled approbation; she
130.02 had promised to teach me drawing, and to let
130.03 me learn French, if I continued to make similar
130.04 improvement two months longer: and then I
130.05 was well received by my fellow-pupils; treated
130.06 as an equal by those of my own age, and not
130.07 molested by any: now, here I lay again
130.08 crushed and trodden on; and could I ever
130.09 rise more.
130.10 "Never," I thought; and ardently I wished
130.11 to die. while sobbing out this wish in broken
130.12 accents, some one approached: I started up --
130.13 again Helen Burns was near me; the fading
130.14 fires just showed her coming up the long,
130.15 vacant room; she brought my coffee and bread.
130.16 "Come, eat something," she said; but I put
130.17 both away from me, feeling as if a drop or a
130.18 crumb would have choked me in my present
130.19 condition. Helen regarded me, probably with

130.20 surprise: I could not now abate my agitation.
130.21 though I tried hard; I continued to weep aloud.
130.22 She sat down on the ground near me, embraced
130.23 her knees with her arms, and rested her head
130.24 upon them; in that attitude she remained silent
130.25 as an Indian. I was the first who spoke: --
130.26 "Helen, why do you stay with a girl whom
130.27 everybody believes to be a liar?"
130.28 "Everybody, Jane? Why, there are only
131.01 eighty people who have heard you called so,
131.02 and the world contains hundreds of mil-
131.03 lions."
131.04 "But what have I to do with millions? The
131.05 eighty I know despise me."
131.06 "Jane, you are mistaken: probably not one
131.07 in the school either despises or dislikes you:
131.08 many, I am sure, pity you much."
131.09 "How can they pity me after what Mr.
131.10 Brocklehurst said?"
131.11 "Mr. Brocklehurst is not a god; nor is he
131.12 even a great and admired man: he is little
131.13 liked here; he never took steps to make him-
131.14 self liked. Had he treated you as an especial
131.15 favourite, you would have found enemies, de-
131.16 clared or covert, all around you; as it is, the
131.17 greater number would offer you sympathy if
131.18 they dared. Teachers and pupils may look
131.19 coldly on you for a day or two, but friendly
131.20 feelings are concealed in their hearts; and if
131.21 you persevere in doing well, these feelings will
131.22 ere long appear so much the more evidently
131.23 for their temporary suppression. Besides,
131.24 Jane," -- she paused.
131.25 "Well, Helen?" said I, putting my hand
131.26 into hers: she chafed my fingers gently to
131.27 warm them, and went on: --
131.28 "If all the world hated you, and believed
132.01 you wicked, while your own conscience ap-
132.02 proved you, and absolved you from guilt, you
132.03 would not be without friends."
132.04 "No; I know I should think well of my-
132.05 self; but that is not enough: if others don't
132.06 love me, I would rather die than live -- I can-
132.07 not bear to be solitary and hated, Helen. Look
132.08 here; to gain some real affection from you, or
132.09 Miss Temple, or any other whom I truly love,
132.10 I would willingly submit to have the bone of
132.11 my arm broken, or to let a bull toss me, or to
132.12 stand behind a kicking horse, and let it dash
132.13 its hoof at my chest, --"
132.14 "Hush, Jane! you think too much of the
132.15 love of human beings; you are too impulsive,
132.16 too vehement: the sovereign hand that created
132.17 your frame, and put life into it, has provided
132.18 you with other resources than your feeble self,
132.19 or than creatures feeble as you. Besides this
132.20 earth, and besides the race of men, there is an
132.21 invisible world and a kingdom of spirits: that
132.22 world is round us, for it is everywhere; and
132.23 those spirits watch us, for they are commis-
132.24 sioned to guard us; and if we were dying in
132.25 pain and shame, if scorn smote us on all sides,
132.26 and hatred crushed us, angels see our tortures,
132.27 recognise our innocence /if innocent we be: as
132.28 I know you are of this charge which Mr.
133.01 Brocklehurst has weakly and pompously re-
133.02 peated at second hand from Mrs. Reed; for I
133.03 read a sincere nature in your ardent eyes and
133.04 on your clear front/, and God waits only the
133.05 separation of spirit from flesh to crown us with
173.06 a full reward. Why, then, should we ever
133.07 sink overwhelmed with distress, when life is so
133.08 soon over, and death is so certain an entrance
133.09 to happiness: to glory?"
133.10 I was silent: Helen had calmed me; but in
133.11 the tranquillity she imparted there was an
133.12 alloy of inexpressible sadness. I felt the im-
133.13 pression of woe as she spoke, but I could
133.14 not tell whence it came; and when, having
133.15 done speaking, she breathed a little fast and
133.16 coughed a short cough, I momentarily forgot
133.17 my own sorrows to yield to a vague concern
133.18 for her.
133.19 Resting my head on Helen's shoulder, I put
173.20 my arms round her waist; she drew me to her,
133.21 and we reposed in silence. We had not sat
133.22 long thus, when another person came in. Some
133.23 heavy clouds, swept from the sky by a rising
133.24 wind, had left the moon bare; and her light,
133.25 streaming in through a window near, shone
133.26 full both on us and on the approaching figure,
133.27 which we at once recognised as Miss Temple.
133.28 "I came on purpose to find you, Jane Eyre,"
134.01 said she; "I want you in my room; and as
134.02 Helen Burns is with you, she may come too."
134.03 We went; following the superintendent's
134.04 guidance, we had to thread some intricate pass-
134.05 ages, and mount a staircase before we reached
134.06 her apartment; it contained a good fire, and
134.07 looked cheerful. Miss Temple told Helen
134.08 Burns to be seated in a low arm-chair on one
134.09 side of the hearth, and herself taking another,
134.10 she called me to her side.
134.11 "Is it all over?" she asked, looking down at
134.12 my face. "Have you cried your grief away?"
134.13 "I am afraid I never shall do that."
134.14 "Why?"
134.15 "Because I have been wrongly accused; and
134.16 you, ma'am, and everybody else will now think
134.17 me wicked."
134.18 "We shall think you what you prove your-

134.19 self to be, my child. Continue to act as a good
134.20 girl, and you will satisfy me."
134.21 "Shall I, Miss Temple?"
134.22 "You will," said she passing her arm round
134.23 me. "And now tell me who is the lady whom
134.24 Mr. Brocklehurst called your benefactress?"
134.25 "Mrs. Reed, my uncle's wife. My uncle is
134.26 dead, and he left me to her care."
134.27 "Did she not, then, adopt you of her own
134.28 accord?"
135.01 "No, ma'am; she was sorry to have to do it:
135.02 but my uncle, as I have often heard the ser-
135.03 vants say, got her to promise, before he died,
135.04 that she would always keep me."
135.05 "Well now, Jane, you know, or at least I
135.06 will tell you, that when a criminal is accused,
135.07 he is always allowed to speak in his own
135.08 defence. You have been charged with false-
135.09 hood: defend yourself to me as well as you can.
135.10 Say whatever your memory suggests as true;
135.11 but add nothing and exaggerate nothing."
135.12 I resolved in the depth of my heart that I
135.13 would be most moderate: most correct; and,
135.14 having reflected a few minutes in order to
135.15 arrange coherently what I had to say, I told
135.16 her all the story of my sad childhood. Ex-
135.17 hausted by emotion, my language was more
135.18 subdued than it generally was when it deve-
135.19 loped that sad theme; and mindful of Helen's
135.20 warnings against the indulgence of resentment,
135.21 I infused into the narrative far less of gall and
135.22 wormwood than ordinary. Thus restrained
135.23 and simplified, it sounded more credible: I
135.24 felt as I went on that Miss Temple fully be-
135.25 lieved me.
135.26 In the course of the tale I had mentioned
135.27 Mr. Lloyd as having come to see me after the
135.28 fit: for I never forgot the, to me, frightful
136.01 episode of the red room; in detailing which,
136.02 my excitement was sure, in some degree, to
136.03 break bounds; for nothing could soften in my
136.04 recollection the spasm of agony which clutched
136.05 my heart when Mrs. Reed spurned my wild
136.06 supplication for pardon, and locked me a second
136.07 time in the dark and haunted chamber.
136.08 I had finished: Miss Temple regarded me a
136.09 few minutes in silence; she then said: --
136.10 "I know something of Mr. Lloyd; I shall
136.11 write to him; if his reply agrees with your
136.12 statement, you shall be publicly cleared from
136.13 every imputation: to me, Jane, you are clear
136.14 now."
136.15 She kissed me, and still keeping me at her
136.16 side /where I was well contented to stand, for
136.17 I derived a child's pleasure from the con-
136.18 templation of her face, her dress, her one or
136.19 two ornaments, her white forehead, her clus-
136.20 tered and shining curls, and beaming dark
136.21 eyes/, she proceeded to address Helen Burns.
136.22 "How are you to-night, Helen? Have
136.23 you coughed much to-day?"
136.24 "Not quite so much I think, ma'am."
136.25 "And the pain in your chest?"
136.26 "It is a little better."
136.27 Miss Temple got up, took her hand and ex-
136.28 amined her pulse; then she returned to her
137.01 own seat: as she resumed it, I heard her sigh
137.02 low. She was pensive a few minutes, then
137.03 rousing herself, she said cheerfully: --
137.04 "But you two are my visitors to-night; I
137.05 must treat you as such." She rang her bell.
137.06 "Barbara," she said to the servant who
137.07 answered it, "I have not yet had tea; bring
137.08 the tray, and place cups for these two young
137.09 ladies."
137.10 And a tray was soon brought. How pretty
137.11 to my eyes, did the china cups and bright
137.12 teapot look, placed on the little round table
137.13 near the fire! How fragrant was the steam
137.14 of the beverage, and the scent of the toast!
137.15 of which, however, I, to my dismay /for I was
137.16 beginning to be hungry/, discerned only a
137.17 very small portion: Miss Temple discerned it
137.18 too: --
137.19 "Barbara," said she, "can you not bring a
137.20 little more bread and butter? There is not
137.21 enough for three."
137.22 Barbara went out: she returned soon: --
137.23 "Madam, Mrs. Harden says she has sent
137.24 up the usual quantity."
137.25 Mrs. Harden, be it observed, was the house-
137.26 keeper; a woman after Mr. Brocklehurst's
137.27 own heart, made up of equal parts whalebone
137.28 and iron.
138.01 "Oh, very well!" returned Miss Temple;
138.02 "we must make it do, Barbara, I suppose."
138.03 And as the girl withdrew, she added, smiling,
138.04 "Fortunately, I have it in my power to supply
138.05 deficiencies for this once."
138.06 Having invited Helen and me to approach
138.07 the table, and placed before each of us a cup
138.08 of tea with one delicious but thin morsel
138.09 of toast, she got up, unlocked a drawer, and
138.10 taking from it a parcel wrapped in paper,
138.11 disclosed presently to our eyes a good-sized
138.12 seed-cake.
138.13 "I meant to give each of you some of this
138.14 to take with you," said she; "but as there is
138.15 so little toast you must have it now," and she
138.16 proceeded to cut slices with a generous hand.
138.17 We feasted that evening as on nectar and

138.18 ambrosia; and not the least delight of the
138.19 entertainment was the smile of gratification
138.20 with which our hostess regarded us, as we
138.21 satisfied our famished appetites on the deli-
138.22 cate fare she liberally supplied. Tea over and
138.23 the tray removed, she again summoned us to
138.24 the fire; we sat one on each side of her, and
138.25 now a conversation followed between her and
138.26 Helen, which it was indeed a privilege to be
138.27 admitted to hear.
138.28 Miss Temple had always something of
139.01 serenity in her air, of state in her mien, of
139.02 refined propriety in her language, which pre-
139.03 cluded deviation into the ardent, the excited,
139.04 the eager: something which chastened the
139.05 pleasure of those who looked on her and
139.06 listened to her, by a controlling sense of awe;
139.07 and such was my feeling now: but as to
139.08 Helen Burns, I was struck with wonder.
139.09 The refreshing meal, the brilliant fire, the
139.10 presence and kindness of her beloved instruc-
139.11 tress, or, perhaps more than all these, some-
139.12 thing in her own unique mind, had roused her
139.13 powers within her. They woke, they kindled:
139.14 first, they glowed in the bright tint of her
139.15 cheek, which till this hour I had never seen
139.16 but pale and bloodless; then they shone in
139.17 the liquid lustre of her eyes, which had sud-
139.18 denly acquired a beauty more singular than
139.19 that of Miss Temple's -- a beauty neither of
139.20 fine colour nor long eyelash, nor pencilled
139.21 brow, but of meaning, of movement, of ra-
139.22 diance. Then her soul sat on her lips, and
139.23 language flowed, from what source I cannot
139.24 tell: has a girl of fourteen a heart large
139.25 enough, vigorous enough to hold the swelling
139.26 spring of pure, full, fervid eloquence? Such
139.27 was the characteristic of Helen's discourse on
139.28 that, to me, memorable evening; her spirit
140.01 seemed hastening to live within a very brief
140.02 span as much as many live during a pro-
140.03 tracted existence.
140.04 They conversed of things I had never heard
140.05 of; of nations and times past; of countries
140.06 far away: of secrets of nature discovered or
140.07 guessed at: they spoke of books: how many
140.08 they had read! What stores of knowledge
140.09 they possessed! Then they seemed so familiar
140.10 with French names and French authors: but
140.11 my amazement reached its climax when Miss
140.12 Temple asked Helen if she sometimes snatched
140.13 a moment to recall the Latin her father had
140.14 taught her, and taking a book from a shelf,
140.15 bade her read and construe a page of
140.16 "Virgil"; and Helen obeyed, my organ of
140.17 veneration expanding at every sounding line.
140.18 She had scarcely finished ere the bell an-
140.19 nounced bed-time: no delay could be ad-
140.20 mitted; Miss Temple embraced us both, say-
140.21 ing, as she drew us to her heart: --
140.22 "God bless you, my children!"
140.23 Helen she held a little longer than me:
140.24 she let her go more reluctantly; it was Helen
140.25 her eye followed to the door; it was for her
140.26 she a second time breathed a sad sigh; for
140.27 her she wiped a tear from her cheek.
140.28 On reaching the bed-room, we heard the
141.01 voice of Miss Scatcherd: she was examining
141.02 drawers; she had just pulled out Helen
141.03 Burns's, and when we entered Helen was
141.04 greeted with a sharp reprimand, and told that
141.05 to-morrow she should have half a dozen of
141.06 untidily folded articles pinned to her shoulder.
141.07 "My things were indeed in shameful dis-
141.08 order," murmured Helen to me, in a low
141.09 voice, "I intended to have arranged them, but
141.10 I forgot."
141.11 Next morning, Miss Scatcherd wrote in
141.12 conspicuous characters on a piece of paste-
141.13 board the word "Slattern," and bound it
141.14 like a phylactery round Helen's large, mild,
141.15 intelligent, and benign-looking forehead. She
141.16 wore it till evening, patient, unresentful, re-
141.17 garding it as a deserved punishment. The
141.18 moment Miss Scatcherd withdrew after after-
141.19 noon-school, I ran to Helen, tore it off, and
141.20 thrust it into the fire: the fury of which she
141.21 was incapable had been burning in my soul
141.22 all day, and tears, hot and large, had con-
141.23 tinually been scalding my cheek; for the
141.24 spectacle of her sad resignation gave me an
141.25 intolerable pain at the heart.
141.26 About a week subsequently to the incidents
141.27 above narrated, Miss Temple, who had written
141.28 to Mr. Lloyd, received his answer: it ap-
142.01 peared that what he said went to corroborate
142.02 my account. Miss Temple, having assembled
142.03 the whole school, announced that inquiry had
142.04 been made into the charges alleged against
142.05 Jane Eyre, and that she was most happy to
142.06 be able to pronounce her completely cleared
142.07 from every imputation. The teachers then
142.08 shook hands with me and kissed me, and a
142.09 murmur of pleasure ran through the ranks of
142.10 my companions.
142.11 Thus relieved of a grievous load, I from
142.12 that hour set to work afresh, resolved to
142.13 pioneer my way through every difficulty: I
142.14 toiled hard, and my success was proportionate
142.15 to my efforts; my memory, not naturally
142.16 tenacious, improved with practice; exercise

356

142.17 sharpened my wits; in a few weeks I was
142.18 promoted to a higher class; in less than two
142.19 months I was allowed to commence French
142.20 and drawing. I learned the first two tenses
142.21 of the verb Etre, and sketched my first cottage
142.22 /whose walls, by-the-by, outrivalled in slope
142.23 those of the leaning tower of Pisa/, on the
142.24 same day. That night, on going to bed, I
142.25 forgot to prepare in imagination the Barme-
142.26 cide supper of hot roast potatoes, or white
142.27 bread and new milk, with which I was wont
142.28 to amuse my inward cravings: I feasted in-
143.01 stead on the spectacle of ideal drawings, which
143.02 I saw in the dark; all the work of my own
143.03 hands: freely pencilled houses and trees, pic-
143.04 turesque rocks and ruins, Cuyp-like groups
143.05 of cattle, sweet paintings of butterflies hover-
143.06 ing over unblown roses, of birds picking at
143.07 ripe cherries, of wrens' nests enclosing pearl-
143.08 like eggs, wreathed about with young ivy
143.09 sprays. I examined, too, in thought, the
143.10 possibility of my ever being able to translate
143.11 currently a certain little French story-book
143.12 which Madam Pierrot had that day shewn
143.13 me; nor was that problem solved to my
143.14 satisfaction ere I fell sweetly asleep.
143.15 Well has Solomon said: -- "Better is a
143.16 dinner of herbs where love is, than a stalled
143.17 ox and hatred therewith."
143.18 I would not now have exchanged Lowood
143.19 with all its privations, for Gateshead and its
143.20 daily luxuries.
144.01 [Vol. 1 Chapter 9]
144.02 But the privations, or rather the hardships, of
144.03 Lowood lessened. Spring drew on: she was
144.04 indeed already come; the frosts of winter had
144.05 ceased; its snows were melted; its cutting
144.06 winds ameliorated. My wretched feet, flayed
144.07 and swollen to lameness by the sharp air of
144.08 January, began to heal and subside under the
144.09 gentler breathings of April; the nights and
144.10 mornings no longer by their Canadian tem-
144.11 perature froze the very blood in our veins;
144.12 we could now endure the play-hour passed
144.13 in the garden: sometimes on a sunny day it
144.14 began even to be pleasant and genial, and a
144.15 greenness grew over those brown beds which,
144.16 freshening daily, suggested the thought that
144.17 Hope traversed them at night, and left each
144.18 morning brighter traces of her steps. Flowers
144.19 peeped out amongst the leaves; snow-drops,
145.01 crocuses, purple auriculas, and golden-eyed
145.02 pansies. On Thursday afternoons /half holi-
145.03 days/ we now took walks, and found still
145.04 sweeter flowers opening by the way-side,
145.05 under the hedges.
145.06 I discovered, too, that a great pleasure, an
145.07 enjoyment which the horizon only bounded,
145.08 lay all outside the high and spike-guarded
145.09 walls of our garden: this pleasure consisted in
145.10 a prospect of noble summits girdling a great
145.11 hill-hollow, rich in verdure and shadow; in a
145.12 bright beck, full of dark stones and sparkling
145.13 eddies. How different had this scene looked
145.14 when I viewed it laid out beneath the iron sky
145.15 of winter, stiffened in frost, shrouded with
145.16 snow! when mists as chill as death wan-
145.17 dered to the impulse of east winds along those
145.18 purple peaks, and rolled down `ing` and holm
145.19 till they blended with the frozen fog of the
145.20 beck! That beck itself was then a torrent,
145.21 turbid and curbless: it tore asunder the wood,
145.22 and sent a raving sound through the air, often
145.23 thickened with wild rain or whirling sleet;
145.24 and for the forest on its banks, that showed
145.25 only ranks of skeletons.
145.26 April advanced to May: a bright, serene
145.27 May it was; days of blue sky, placid sun-
145.28 shine, and soft western or southern gales filled
146.01 up its duration. And now vegetation matured
146.02 with vigour; Lowood shook loose its tresses;
146.03 it became all green, all flowery; its great elm,
146.04 ash, and oak skeletons were restored to ma-
146.05 jestic life; woodland plants sprang up pro-
146.06 fusely in its recesses; unnumbered varieties of
146.07 moss filled its hollows, and it made a strange
146.08 ground-sunshine out of the wealth of its wild
146.09 primrose plants: I have seen their pale gold
146.10 gleam in overshadowed spots like scatterings
146.11 of the sweetest lustre. All this I enjoyed often
146.12 and fully, free, unwatched, and almost alone:
146.13 for this unwonted liberty and pleasure, there
146.14 was a cause, to which it now becomes my task
146.15 to avert.
146.16 Have I not described a pleasant site for a
146.17 dwelling, when I speak of it as bosomed in
146.18 hill and wood, and rising from the verge of a
146.19 stream? Assuredly, pleasant enough: but
146.20 whether healthy or not is another question.
146.21 That forest-dell, where Lowood lay, was the
146.22 cradle of fog and fog-bred pestilence; which,
146.23 quickening with the quickening spring, crept
146.24 into the Orphan Asylum, breathed typhus
146.25 through its crowded school-room and dormi-
146.26 tory, and ,ere May arrived, transformed the
146.27 seminary into an hospital.
146.28 Semi-starvation and neglected colds had
147.01 predisposed most of the pupils to receive
147.02 infection: forty-five out of the eighty girls
147.03 lay ill at one time. Classes were broken up,
147.04 rules relaxed. The few who continued well

147.05 were allowed almost unlimited license; be-
147.06 cause the medical attendant insisted on the
147.07 necessity of frequent exercise to keep them in
147.08 health: and had it been otherwise, no one
147.09 had leisure to watch or restrain them. Miss
147.10 Temple's whole attention was absorbed by the
147.11 patients: she lived in the sick-room; never
147.12 quitting it except to snatch a few hours' rest at
147.13 night. The teachers were fully occupied with
147.14 packing up and making other necessary pre-
147.15 parations for the departure of those girls who
147.16 were fortunate enough to have friends and
147.17 relations able and willing to remove them from
147.18 the seat of contagion. Many, already smitten,
147.19 went home only to die: some died at the
147.20 school, and were buried quietly and quickly;
147.21 the nature of the malady forbidding delay.
147.22 While disease had thus become an inha-
147.23 bitant of Lowood, and death its frequent
147.24 visitor; while there was gloom and fear
147.25 within its walls; while its rooms and passages
147.26 steamed with hospital smells: the drug and
147.27 the pastille striving vainly to overcome the
147.28 effluvia of mortality; that bright May shone
148.01 unclouded over the bold hills and beautiful
148.02 woodland out of doors. Its garden, too, glowed
148.03 with flowers: hollyhocks had sprung up tall
148.04 as trees, lilies had opened, dahlias and roses
148.05 were in bloom; the borders of the little beds
148.06 were gay with pink thrift and crimson double--
148.07 daisies; the sweet-briars gave out, morning
148.08 and evening, their scent of spice and apples;
148.09 and these fragrant treasures were all useless
148.10 for most of the inmates of Lowood: except
148.11 to furnish now and then a handful of herbs
148.12 and blossoms to put in a coffin.
148.13 But I, and the rest who continued well,
148.14 enjoyed fully the beauties of the scene and
148.15 season: they let us ramble in the wood, like
148.16 gipsies, from morning till night; we did what
148.17 we liked, went where we liked: we lived
148.18 better too. Mr. Brocklehurst and his family
148.19 never came near Lowood now: household
148.20 matters were not scrutinized into; the cross
148.21 housekeeper was gone, driven away by the
148.22 fear of infection; her successor, who had been
148.23 matron at Lowton Dispensary, unused to
148.24 the ways of her new abode, provided with
148.25 comparative liberality. Besides, there were
148.26 fewer to feed: the sick could eat little; our
148.27 breakfast-basons were better filled: when there
148.28 was no time to prepare a regular dinner, which
149.01 often happened, she would give us a large
149.02 piece of cold pie, or a thick slice of bread
149.03 and cheese, and this we carried away with us
149.04 to the wood, where we each chose the spot we
149.05 liked best, and dined sumptuously.
149.06 My favourite seat was a smooth and broad
149.07 stone, rising white and dry from the very
149.08 middle of the beck, and only to be got at by
149.09 wading through the water; a feat I accom-
149.10 plished barefoot. The stone was just broad
149.11 enough to accommodate, comfortably, another
149.12 girl and me, at that time my chosen comrade
149.13 -- one Mary Ann Wilson; a shrewd obser-
149.14 vant personage, whose society I took pleasure
149.15 in, partly because she was witty and original,
149.16 and partly because she had a manner which
149.17 set me at my ease. Some years older than I,
149.18 she knew more of the world, and could tell
149.19 me many things I liked to hear: with her my
149.20 curiosity found gratification: to my faults also
149.21 she gave ample indulgence; never imposing
149.22 curb or rein on anything I said. She had a
149.23 turn for narrative, I for analysis; she liked to
149.24 inform, I to question; so we got on swim-
149.25 mingly together, deriving much entertainment,
149.26 if not much improvement, from our mutual
149.27 intercourse.
149.28 And where, meantime, was Helen Burns?
150.01 Why did I not spend these sweet days of liberty
150.02 with her? Had I forgotten her; or was I so
150.03 worthless as to have grown tired of her pure
150.04 society? Surely the Mary Ann Wilson I have
150.05 mentioned was inferior to my first acquain-
150.06 tance: she could only tell me amusing stories,
150.07 and reciprocate any racy and pungent gossip
150.08 I chose to indulge in; while, if I have spoken
150.09 truth of Helen, she was qualified to give those
150.10 who enjoyed the privilege of her converse, a
150.11 taste of far higher things.
150.12 True, reader; and I knew and felt this: and
150.13 though I am a defective being, with many
150.14 faults and few redeeming points, yet I never
150.15 tired of Helen Burns; nor ever ceased to cher-
150.16 ish for her a sentiment of attachment, as strong,
150.17 tender, and respectful as any that ever ani-
150.18 mated my heart. How could it be otherwise,
150.19 when Helen, at all times and under all circum-
150.20 stances, evinced for me a quiet and faithful
150.21 friendship, which ill-humour never soured nor
150.22 irritation ever troubled? But Helen was ill at
150.23 present: for some weeks she had been removed
150.24 from my sight to I knew not what room up-
150.25 stairs. She was not, I was told, in the hospital
150.26 portion of the house with the fever patients;
150.27 for her complaint was consumption, not typhus:
150.28 and by consumption I, in my ignorance, under-
151.01 stood something mild, which time and care
151.02 would be sure to alleviate.
151.03 I was confirmed in this idea by the fact of

151.04 her once or twice coming down stairs on very
151.05 warm sunny afternoons, and being taken by
151.06 Miss Temple into the garden: but, on these
151.07 occasions, I was not allowed to go and speak
151.08 to her; I only saw her from the school-room
151.09 window, and then not distinctly; for she was
151.10 much wrapped up, and sat at a distance under
151.11 the verandah.
151.12 One evening in the beginning of June, I had
151.13 stayed out very late with Mary Ann in the
151.14 wood; we had, as usual, separated ourselves
151.15 from the others, and had wandered far: so far
151.16 that we lost our way, and had to ask it at a
151.17 lonely cottage, where a man and woman lived,
151.18 who looked after a herd of half-wild swine that
151.19 fed on the mast in the wood. When we got back,
151.20 it was after moon-rise: a pony, which we knew
151.21 to be the surgeon's, was standing at the garden
151.22 door. Mary Ann remarked that she supposed
151.23 some one must be very ill, as Mr. Bates had
151.24 been sent for at that time of the evening. She
151.25 went into the house; I stayed behind a few
151.26 minutes to plant in my garden a handful of roots
151.27 I had dug up in the forest, and which I feared
151.28 would wither if I left them till morning. This
152.01 done, I lingered yet a little longer: the flowers
152.02 smelt so sweet as the due fell; it was such a
152.03 pleasant evening, so serene, so warm; the still
152.04 glowing west promised so fairly another fine
152.05 day on the morrow; the moon rose with such
152.06 majesty in the grave east. I was noting these
152.07 things and enjoying them as a child might
152.08 when it entered my mind as it had never done
152.09 before: --
152.10 "How sad to be lying now on a sickbed,
152.11 and to be in danger of dying! This world is
152.12 pleasant -- it would be dreary to be called from
152.13 it, and to have to go who knows where?"
152.14 And then my mind made its first earnest
152.15 effort to comprehend what had been infused
152.16 into it concerning heaven and hell: and for
152.17 the first time it recoiled, baffled; and for the
152.18 first time glancing behind, on each side, and
152.19 before it, it saw all round an unfathomed gulf:
152.20 it felt the one point where it stood -- the pre-
152.21 sent; all the rest was formless cloud and
152.22 vacant depth: and it shuddered at the thought
152.23 of tottering, and plunging amid that chaos.
152.24 While pondering this new idea, I heard the
152.25 front door open; Mr. Bates came out, and with
152.26 him was a nurse. After she had seen him
152.27 mount his horse and depart, she was about to
152.28 close the door, but I ran up to her.
153.01 "How is Helen Burns?"
153.02 "Very poorly," was the answer.
153.03 "Is it her Mr. Bates has been to see?" "Yes."
153.04 "And what does he say about her?"
153.05 "He says she'll not be here long."
153.06 This phrase uttered in my hearing yesterday,
153.07 would have only conveyed the notion that she
153.08 was about to be removed to Northumberland,
153.09 to her own home. I should not have suspected
153.10 that it meant she was dying; but I knew
153.11 instantly now: it opened clear on my compre-
153.12 hension that Helen Burns was numbering her
153.13 last days in this world, and that she was going
153.14 to be taken to the region of spirits, if such
153.15 region there were. I experienced a shock of
153.16 horror, then a strong thrill of grief, then a
153.17 desire -- a necessity to see her; and I asked in
153.18 what room she lay.
153.19 "She is in Miss Temple's room," said the
153.20 nurse.
153.21 "May I go up and speak to her?"
153.22 "Oh, no, child! It is not likely; and now
153.23 it is time for you to come in; you'll catch the
153.24 fever if you stop out when the dew is falling."
153.25 The nurse closed the front door; I went in
153.26 by the side entrance which led to the school--
153.27 room: I was just in time; it was nine o'clock,
154.01 and Miss Miller was calling the pupils to go
154.02 to bed.
154.03 It might be two hours later, probably near
154.04 eleven, when I -- not having been able to fall
154.05 asleep, and deeming, from the perfect silence
154.06 of the dormitory, that my companions were all
154.07 wrapt in profound repose -- rose softly, put on
154.08 my frock over my night-dress, and, without
154.09 shoes, crept from the apartment, and set off in
154.10 quest of Miss Temple's room. It was quite at
154.11 the other end of the house; but I knew my
154.12 way; and the light of the unclouded summer
154.13 moon, entering here and there at passage win-
154.14 dows, enabled me to find it without difficulty.
154.15 An odour of camphor and burnt vinegar warned
154.16 me when I came near the fever room; and I
154.17 passed its door quickly, fearful lest the nurse
154.18 who sat up all night should hear me. I dreaded
154.19 being discovered and sent back; for I must
154.20 see Helen, -- I must embrace her before she
154.21 died, -- I must give her one last kiss, exchange
154.22 with her one last word.
154.23 Having descended a staircase, traversed a
154.24 portion of the house below, and succeeded in
154.25 opening and shutting, without noise, two doors,
154.26 I reached another flight of steps; these I
154.27 mounted, and then just opposite to me was
154.28 Miss Temple's room. A light shone through
155.01 the key-hole, and from under the door: a pro-
155.02 found stillness pervaded the vicinity. Coming
155.03 near, I found the door slightly ajar; probably
155.04 to admit some fresh air into the close abode of
155.05 sickness. Indisposed to hesitate, and full of
155.06 impatient impulses -- soul and senses quivering
155.07 with keen throes -- I put it back and looked
155.08 in. My eye sought Helen, and feared to find
155.09 death.
155.10 Close by Miss Temple's bed, and half covered
155.11 with its white curtains, there stood a little crib.
155.12 I saw the outline of a form under the clothes,
155.13 but the face was hid by the hangings: the
155.14 nurse I had spoken to in the garden sat in an
155.15 easy chair, asleep; an unsnuffed candle burnt
155.16 dimly on the table. Miss Temple was not to
155.17 be seen: I knew afterwards that she had been
155.18 called to a delirious patient in the fever-room.
155.19 I advanced; then paused by the crib side: my
155.20 hand was on the curtain, but I preferred speak-
155.21 ing before I withdrew it. I still recoiled at the
155.22 dread of seeing a corpse.
155.23 "Helen!" I whispered softly; "are you
155.24 awake?"
155.25 She stirred, herself put back the curtain, and
155.26 I saw her face, pale, wasted, but quite com-
155.27 posed: she looked so little changed that my
155.28 fear was instantly dissipated.
156.01 "Can it be you, Jane?" she asked in her
156.02 own gentle voice.
156.03 "Oh!" I thought, "she is not going to die;
156.04 they are mistaken: she could not speak and
156.05 look so calmly if she were."
156.06 I got on to her crib and kissed her: her
156.07 forehead was cold, and her cheek both cold and
156.08 thin, and so were her hand and wrist; but she
156.09 smiled as of old.
156.10 "Why are you come here, Jane? It is past
156.11 eleven o'clock: I heard it strike some minutes
156.12 since."
156.13 "I came to see you, Helen: I heard you
156.14 were very ill, and I could not sleep till I had
156.15 spoken to you."
156.16 "You came to bid me good-bye, then: you
156.17 are just in time probably."
156.18 "Are you going somewhere, Helen? Are
156.19 you going home?"
156.20 "Yes; to my long home -- my last home."
156.21 "No, no, Helen!" I stopped, distressed.
156.22 While I tried to devour my tears, a fit of
156.23 coughing seized Helen; it did not, however,
156.24 wake the nurse; when it was over, she lay
156.25 some minutes exhausted; then she whis-
156.26 pered: --
156.27 "Jane, your little feet are bare; lie down
156.28 and cover yourself with my quilt."
157.01 I did so: she put her arm over me, and I
157.02 nestled close to her. After a long silence, she
157.03 resumed; still whispering: --
157.04 "I am very happy, Jane; and when you
157.05 hear that I am dead you must be sure and not
157.06 grieve: there is nothing to grieve about. We
157.07 all must die one day, and the illness which is
157.08 removing me is not painful; it is gentle and
157.09 gradual: my mind is at rest. I leave no one
157.10 to regret me much: I have only a father; and
157.11 he is lately married, and will not miss me. By
157.12 dying young I shall escape great sufferings.
157.13 I had not qualities or talents to make my way
157.14 very well in the world: I would have been
157.15 continually at fault."
157.16 "But where are you going to, Helen? Can
157.17 you see? Do you know?"
157.18 "I believe; I have faith: I am going to
157.19 God."
157.20 "Where is God? What is God?"
157.21 "My Maker and yours; who will never
157.22 destroy what he created. I rely implicitly on
157.23 his power, and confide wholly in his goodness:
157.24 I count the hours till that eventful one arrives
157.25 which shall restore me to him, reveal him to
157.26 me."
157.27 "You are sure, then, Helen, that there is
158.01 such a place as heaven; and that our souls can
158.02 get to it when we die?"
158.03 "I am sure there is a future state; I believe
158.04 God is good: I can resign my immortal part
158.05 to him without any misgiving. God is my
158.06 father; God is my friend: I love him; I be-
158.07 lieve he loves me."
158.08 "And shall I see you again, Helen, when I
158.09 die?"
158.10 "You will come to the same region of hap-
158.11 piness: be received by the same mighty, uni-
158.12 versal Parent, no doubt, dear Jane."
158.13 Again I questioned; but this time only in
158.14 thought. "Where is that region? Does it
158.15 exist?" And I clasped my arms closer round
158.16 Helen: she seemed dearer to me than ever; I
158.17 felt as if I could not let her go; I lay with my
158.18 face hidden on her neck. Presently she said
158.19 in the sweetest tone; --
158.20 "How comfortable I am! That last fit of
158.21 coughing has tired me a little; I feel as if I
158.22 could sleep: but don't leave me, Jane; I like
158.23 to have you near me."
158.24 "I'll stay with you, dear Helen: no one
158.25 shall take me away."
158.26 "Are you warm, darling?"
158.27 "Yes."
159.01 "Good-night, Jane."
159.02 "Good-night, Helen."
159.03 She kissed me, and I her; and we both soon
159.04 slumbered.

159.05   When I awoke it was day: an unusual
159.06 movement roused me; I looked up; I was in
159.07 somebody's arms; the nurse held me; she was
159.08 carrying me through the passage back to the
159.09 dormitory. I was not reprimanded for leaving
159.10 my bed; people had something else to think
159.11 about: no explanation was afforded then to my
159.12 many questions; but a day or two afterwards
159.13 I learned that Miss Temple, on returning to
159.14 her own room at dawn, had found me laid in
159.15 a little crib; my face against Helen Burn's
159.16 shoulder, my arms round her neck. I was
159.17 asleep, and Helen was -- dead.
159.18   Her grave is in Brocklebridge churchyard:
159.19 for fifteen years after her death it was only
159.20 covered by a grassy mound; but now a gray
159.21 marble tablet marks the spot, inscribed with
159.22 her name, and the word "Resurgam."
160.01 [Vol. 1 Chapter 10]
160.02   Hitherto I have recorded in detail the events
160.03 of my insignificant existence: to the first ten
160.04 years of my life, I have given almost as many
160.05 chapters. But this is not to be a regular auto-
160.06 biography: I am only bound to invoke me-
160.07 mory where I know her responses will possess
160.08 some degree of interest; therefore I now pass
160.09 a space of eight years almost in silence: a few
160.10 lines only are necessary to keep up the links
160.11 of connection.
160.12   When the typhus fever had fulfilled its mis-
160.13 sion of devastation at Lowood, it gradually dis-
160.14 appeared from thence; but not till its virulence
160.15 and the number of its victims had drawn public
160.16 attention on the school. Inquiry was made
160.17 into the origin of the scourge, and by degrees
160.18 various facts came out which excited public
160.19 indignation in a high degree. The unhealthy
160.20 nature of the site; the quantity and quality of
161.01 the children's food; the brackish, fetid water
161.02 used in its preparation; the pupils' wretched
161.03 clothing and accommodations: all these things
161.04 were discovered; and the discovery produced
161.05 a result mortifying to Mr. Brocklehurst, but
161.06 beneficial to the institution.
161.07   Several wealthy and benevolent individuals
161.08 in the county subscribed largely for the erec-
161.09 tion of a more convenient building in a better
161.10 situation; new regulations were made; im-
161.11 provements in diet and clothing introduced;
161.12 the funds of the school were entrusted to the
161.13 management of a committee. Mr. Brockle-
161.14 hurst, who, from his wealth and family con-
161.15 nections, could not be overlooked, still retained
161.16 the post of treasurer; but he was aided in the
161.17 discharge of his duties by gentlemen of rather
161.18 more enlarged and sympathizing minds: his
161.19 office of inspector, too, was shared by those
161.20 who knew how to combine reason with strict-
161.21 ness, comfort with economy, compassion with
161.22 uprightness. The school, thus improved, be-
161.23 came in time a truly useful and noble institu-
161.24 tion. I remained an inmate of its walls, after
161.25 its regeneration, for eight years: six as pupil,
161.26 and two as teacher; and in both capacities I
161.27 bear my testimony to its value and importance.
161.28   During these eight years my life was uniform:
162.01 but not unhappy, because it was not inactive.
162.02 I had the means of an excellent education
162.03 placed within my reach; a fondness for some
162.04 of my studies, and a desire to excel in all, to-
162.05 gether with a great delight in pleasing my
162.06 teachers, especially such as I loved, urged me
162.07 on: I availed myself fully of the advantages
162.08 offered me. In time I rose to be the first girl
162.09 of the first class; then I was invested with the
162.10 office of teacher; which I discharged with zeal
162.11 for two years: but at the end of that time I
162.12 altered.
162.13   Miss Temple, through all changes, had thus
162.14 far continued superintendent of the seminary:
162.15 to her instruction I owed the best part of my
162.16 acquirements; her friendship and society had
162.17 been my continual solace; she had stood in
162.18 the stead of mother, governess, and latterly,
162.19 companion. At this period she married, re-
162.20 moved with her husband /a clergyman, an
162.21 excellent man, almost worthy of such a wife/
162.22 to a distant county, and consequently was lost
162.23 to me.
162.24   From the day she left I was no longer the
162.25 same: with her was gone every settled feeling
162.26 every association that had made Lowood in
162.27 some degree a home to me. I had imbibed
162.28 from her something of her nature and much
163.01 of her habits: more harmonious thoughts;
163.02 what seemed better regulated feelings had be-
163.03 come the inmates of my mind. I had given
163.04 in allegiance to duty and order; I was quiet;
163.05 I believed I was content: to the eyes of others,
163.06 usually even to my own, I appeared a disci-
163.07 plined and subdued character.
163.08   But destiny, in the shape of the Rev. Mr.
163.09 Nasmyth, came between me and Miss Temple:
163.10 I saw her in her travelling dress step into a
163.11 post-chaise, shortly after the marriage cere-
163.12 mony, I watched the chaise mount the hill and
163.13 disappear beyond its brow; and then retired
163.14 to my own room; and there spent in solitude
163.15 the greatest part of the half-holiday granted in
163.16 honour of the occasion.
163.17   I walked about the chamber most of the

163.18 time. I imagined myself only to be regretting
163.19 my loss and thinking how to repair it; but
163.20 when my reflections were concluded, and I
163.21 looked up and found that the afternoon was
163.22 gone, and evening far advanced, another dis-
163.23 covery dawned on me: namely, that in the
163.24 interval I had undergone a transforming pro-
163.25 cess; that my mind had put off all it had bor-
163.26 rowed of Miss Temple -- or rather that she had
163.27 taken with her the serene atmosphere I had
163.28 been breathing in her vicinity -- and that now
164.01 I was left in my natural element; and begin-
164.02 ning to feel the stirring of old emotions. It
164.03 did not seem as if a prop were withdrawn, but
164.04 rather as if a motive were gone: it was not
164.05 the power to be tranquil which had failed me,
164.06 but the reason for tranquillity was no more.
164.07 My world had for some years been in Lowood:
164.08 my experience had been of its rules and sys-
164.09 tems; now I remembered that the real world
164.10 was wide, and that a varied field of hopes and
164.11 fears, of sensations and excitements, awaited
164.12 those who had courage to go forth into its
164.13 expanse to seek real knowledge of life amidst
164.14 its perils.
164.15   I went to my window, opened it, and looked
164.16 out. There were the two wings of the build-
164.17 ing; there was the garden; there were the
164.18 skirts of Lowood; there was the hilly hori-
164.19 zon. My eye passed all other objects to rest
164.20 on those most remote, the blue peaks: it was
164.21 those I longed to surmount; all within their
164.22 boundary of rock and heath seemed prison-
164.23 ground, exile limits. I traced the white road
164.24 winding round the base of one mountain, and
164.25 vanishing in a gorge between two: how I
164.26 longed to follow it further! I recalled the
164.27 time when I had travelled that very road in a
164.28 coach; I remembered descending that hill at
165.01 twilight: an age seemed to have elapsed since
165.02 the day which brought me first to Lowood;
165.03 and I had never quitted it since. My vaca-
165.04 tions had all been spent at school: Mrs. Reed
165.05 had never sent for me to Gateshead; neither
165.06 she nor any of her family had ever been to
165.07 visit me. I had had no communication by
165.08 letter or message with the outer world: school--
165.09 rules, school-duties, school-habits and notions,
165.10 and voices, and faces, and phrases, and cos-
165.11 tumes, and preferences, and antipathies: such
165.12 was what I knew of existence. And now I
165.13 felt that it was not enough: I tired of the rou-
165.14 tine of eight years in one afternoon. I desired
165.15 liberty; for liberty I gasped; for liberty I
165.16 uttered a prayer; it seemed scattered on the
165.17 wind faintly blowing. I abandoned it,
165.18 and framed a humbler supplication; for change,
165.19 stimulus: that petition, too, seemed swept off
165.20 into vague space; "Then," I cried, half des-
165.21 perate, "Grant me at least a new servitude!"
165.22   Here, a bell, ringing the hour of supper,
165.23 called me down stairs.
165.24   I was not free to resume the interrupted
165.25 chain of my reflections till bed-time: even
165.26 then a teacher who occupied the same room
165.27 with me kept me from the subject to which I
165.28 longed to recur, by a prolonged effusion of
166.01 small talk. How I wished sleep would silence
166.02 her! It seemed as if, could I but go back to
166.03 the idea which had last entered my mind as I
166.04 stood at the window, some inventive sugges-
166.05 tion would rise for my relief.
166.06   Miss Gryce snored at last: she was a heavy
166.07 welshwoman, and till now her habitual nasal
166.08 strains had never been regarded by me in any
166.09 other light than as a nuisance: to-night I
166.10 hailed the first deep notes with satisfaction;
166.11 I was debarrassed of interruption; my half--
166.12 effaced thought instantly revived.
166.13   "A new servitude! There is something in
166.14 that," I soliloquized /mentally, be it under-
166.15 stood; I did not talk aloud/. "I know there
166.16 is, because it does not sound too sweet; it is
166.17 not like such words as Liberty, Excitement,
166.18 Enjoyment: delightful sounds truly; but no
166.19 more than sounds for me; and so hollow and
166.20 fleeting that it is mere waste of time to listen to
166.21 them. But Servitude! That must be matter
166.22 of fact. Any one may serve: I have served
166.23 here eight years; now all I want is to serve
166.24 elsewhere. Can I not get so much of my own
166.25 will? Is not the thing feasible? Yes -- yes --
166.26 the end is not so difficult; if I had only a
166.27 brain active enough to ferret out the means of
166.28 attaining it."
167.01   I sat up in bed by way of arousing this said
167.02 brain: it was a chilly night; I covered my
167.03 shoulders with a shawl, and then I proceeded
167.04 to think again with all my might.
167.05   "What do I want? A new place, in a new
167.06 house, amongst new faces, under new circum-
167.07 stances: I want this because it is of no use
167.08 wanting anything better. How do people do
167.09 to get a new place? They apply to friends, I
167.10 suppose: I have no friends. There are many
167.11 others who have no friends, who must look
167.12 about for themselves and be their own helpers;
167.13 and what is their resource?"
167.14   I could not tell: nothing answered me; I
167.15 then ordered my brain to find a response, and
167.16 quickly. It worked and worked faster: I felt

167.17 the pulses throb in my head and temples; but
167.18 for nearly an hour it worked in chaos, and no
167.19 result came of its efforts. Feverish with vain
167.20 labour, I got up and took a turn in the room;
167.21 undrew the curtain, noted a star or two, shi-
167.22 vered with cold, and again crept to bed.
167.23 A kind fairy, in my absence, had surely
167.24 dropped the required suggestion on my pillow
167.25 for as I lay down it came quietly and naturally
167.26 to my mind: -- "Those who want situations
167.27 advertise; you must advertise in the --shire
167.28 Herald."
168.01 "How? I know nothing about advertising."
168.02 Replies rose smooth and prompt now: --
168.03 "You must inclose the advertisement and
168.04 the money to pay for it under a cover directed
168.05 to the Editor of the Herald; you must put it,
168.06 the first opportunity you have, into the post at
168.07 Lowton; answers must be addressed to J.E.
168.08 at the post-office there: you can go and inquire
168.09 in about a week after you send your letter, if
168.10 any are come, and act accordingly."
168.11 This scheme I went over twice, thrice; it
168.12 was then digested in my mind: I had it in a
168.13 clear practical form; I felt satisfied, and fell
168.14 asleep.
168.15 With earliest day, I was up: I had my adver-
168.16 tisement written, enclosed, and directed before
168.17 the bell rang to rouse the school; it ran thus: --
168.18 "A young lady accustomed to tuition /had I
168.19 not been a teacher two years?/ is desirous of
168.20 meeting with a situation in a private family
168.21 where the children are under fourteen /I
168.22 thought that as I was barely eighteen, it would
168.23 not do to undertake the guidance of pupils
168.24 nearer my own age/. She is qualified to teach
168.25 the usual branches of a good English educa-
168.26 tion, together with French, Drawing, and Music
168.27 /in those days, reader, this now narrow cata-
168.28 logue of accomplishments, would have been
169.01 held tolerably comprehensive/. Address J.E.
169.02 Post-office, Lowton, --shire."
169.03 This document remained locked in my drawer
169.04 all day: after tea, I asked leave of the new
169.05 Superintendent to go to Lowton, in order to
169.06 perform some small commissions for myself
169.07 and one or two of my fellow-teachers; per-
169.08 mission was readily granted; I went. It was
169.09 a walk of two miles, and the evening was wet,
169.10 but the days were still long; I visited a shop
169.11 or two, slipped the letter into the post-office,
169.12 and came back through heavy rain, with
169.13 streaming garments, but with a relieved heart.
169.14 The succeeding week seemed long: it came
169.15 to an end at last, however, like all sublunary
169.16 things, and once more, towards the close of a
169.17 pleasant autumn day, I found myself afoot on
169.18 the road to Lowton. A picturesque track it
169.19 was, by the way; lying along the side of the
169.20 beck and through the sweetest curves of the
169.21 dale: but that day I thought more of the
169.22 letters, that might or might not be awaiting
169.23 me at the little burgh whither I was bound,
169.24 than of the charms of lea and water.
169.25 My ostensible errand on this occasion was
169.26 to get measured for a pair of shoes; so I dis-
169.27 charged that business first, and when it was
169.28 done, I stepped across the clean and quiet
170.01 little street from the shoemaker's to the post--
170.02 office: it was kept by an old dame, who wore
170.03 horn spectacles on her nose, and black mittens
170.04 on her hands.
170.05 "Are there any letters for J.E.?" I asked.
170.06 She peered at me over her spectacles, and
170.07 then she opened a drawer and fumbled among
170.08 its contents for a long time; so long that my
170.09 hopes began to falter. At last, having held a
170.10 document before her glasses for nearly five
170.11 minutes, she presented it across the counter;
170.12 accompanying the act by another inquisitive
170.13 and mistrustful glance -- it was for J.E.
170.14 "Is there only one?" I demanded.
170.15 "There are no more," said she; and I put
170.16 it in my pocket and turned my face homeward:
170.17 I could not open it then; rules obliged me to
170.18 be back by eight, and it was already half-past
170.19 seven.
170.20 Various duties awaited me on my arrival: I
170.21 had to sit with the girls during their hour of
170.22 study; then it was my turn to read prayers; to
170.23 see them to bed: afterwards I supped with the
170.24 other teachers. Even when we finally retired
170.25 for the night, the inevitable Miss Gryce was
170.26 still my companion: we had only a short end
170.27 of candle in our candlestick, and I dreaded lest
170.28 she should talk till it was all burnt out; for-
171.01 tunately, however, the heavy supper she had
171.02 eaten produced a soporific effect: she was
171.03 already snoring, before I had finished undress-
171.04 ing. There still remained an inch of candle:
171.05 I now took out my letter; the seal was an
171.06 initial F.; I broke it; the contents were brief.
171.07 "If J.E., who advertised in the --shire
171.08 Herald of last Thursday, possesses the acquire-
171.09 ments mentioned; and if she is in a position
171.10 to give satisfactory references as to character
171.11 and competency; a situation can be offered
171.12 her where there is but one pupil, a little girl,
171.13 under ten years of age; and where the salary
171.14 is thirty pounds per annum. J.E. is requested
171.15 to send references, name, address, and all par-

171.16 ticulars to the direction: --
171.17 "Mrs. Fairfax, Thornfield, near Millcote,
171.18 --shire."
171.19 I examined the document long: the writing
171.20 was old fashioned and rather uncertain, like
171.21 that of an elderly lady. This circumstance was
171.22 satisfactory: a private fear had haunted me,
171.23 that in thus acting for myself, and by my own
171.24 guidance, I ran the risk of getting into some
171.25 scrape; and above all things, I wished the
171.26 result of my endeavours to be respectable, pro-
171.27 per, en regle. I now felt that an elderly lady
171.28 was no bad ingredient in the business I had on
172.01 hands. Mrs. Fairfax! I saw her in a black
172.02 gown and widow's cap; frigid, perhaps, but
172.03 not uncivil: a model of elderly English re-
172.04 spectability. Thornfield! that, doubtless was
172.05 the name of her house: a neat, orderly spot,
172.06 I was sure; though I failed in my efforts to
172.07 conceive a correct plan of the premises. Mill-
172.08 cote, --shire: I brushed up my recollections
172.09 of the map of England; yes, I saw it; both
172.10 the shire and the town. --shire was seventy
172.11 miles nearer London than the remote county
172.12 where I now resided: that was a recommenda-
172.13 tion to me. I longed to go where there was
172.14 life and movement: Millcote was a large ma-
172.15 nufacturing town on the banks of the A--;
172.16 a busy place enough, doubtless: so much the
172.17 better, it would be a complete change at least.
172.18 Not that my fancy was much captivated by the
172.19 idea of long chimneys and clouds of smoke --
172.20 "but," I argued, "Thornfield will, probably,
172.21 be a good way from the town."
172.22 Here the socket of the candle dropped, and
172.23 the wick went out.
172.24 Next day new steps were to be taken: my
172.25 plans could no longer be confined to my own
172.26 breast; I must impart them in order to achieve
172.27 their success. Having sought and obtained
172.28 an audience of the Superintendent, during the
173.01 noontide recreation, I told her I had a pros-
173.02 pect of getting a new situation where the salary
173.03 would be double what I now received /for, at
173.04 Lowood, I only got 15l. per annum/; and re-
173.05 quested she would break the matter for me to
173.06 Mr. Brocklehurst or some of the committee,
173.07 and ascertain whether they would permit me
173.08 to mention them as references. She obligingly
173.09 consented to act as mediatrix in the matter.
173.10 The next day she laid the affair before Mr.
173.11 Brocklehurst; who said that Mrs. Reed must
173.12 be written to, as she was my natural guardian.
173.13 A note was accordingly addressed to that lady,
173.14 who returned for answer, that "I might do as
173.15 I pleased: she had long relinquished all inter-
173.16 ference in my affairs." This note went the
173.17 round of the committee, and at last, after what
173.18 appeared to me most tedious delay, formal
173.19 leave was given me to better my condition if
173.20 I could; and an assurance added, that as I had
173.21 always conducted myself well, both as teacher
173.22 and pupil, at Lowood, a testimonial of cha-
173.23 racter and capacity signed by the inspectors of
173.24 that institution, should forthwith be furnished
173.25 me.
173.26 This testimonial I accordingly received in
173.27 about a week; forwarded a copy of it to Mrs.
173.28 Fairfax, and got that lady's reply, stating that
174.01 she was satisfied, and fixing that day fortnight
174.02 as the period for my assuming the post of
174.03 governess in her house.
174.04 I now busied myself in preparations: the
174.05 fortnight passed rapidly. I had not a very
174.06 large wardrobe, though it was adequate to my
174.07 wants; and the last day sufficed to pack my
174.08 trunk, -- the same I had brought with me eight
174.09 years ago from Gateshead.
174.10 The box was corded, the card nailed on. In
174.11 half an hour the carrier was to call for it to
174.12 take it to Lowton; whither I myself was to
174.13 repair at an early hour the next morning to
174.14 meet the coach. I had brushed my black stuff
174.15 travelling dress, prepared my bonnet, gloves,
174.16 and muff; sought in all my drawers to see that
174.17 no article was left behind; and now, having
174.18 nothing more to do, I sat down and tried to
174.19 rest. I could not; though I had been on foot
174.20 all day, I could not now repose an instant;
174.21 I was too much excited. A phase of my life
174.22 was closing to-night, a new one opening to-
174.23 morrow: impossible to slumber in the interval;
174.24 I must watch feverishly while the change was
174.25 being accomplished.
174.26 "Miss," said a servant who met me in
174.27 the lobby, where I was wandering like a
174.28 troubled spirit, "a person below wishes to see
174.29 you."
175.01 "The carrier, no doubt," I thought, and
175.02 ran down stairs without inquiry. I was pass-
175.03 ing the back parlour, or teacher's sitting--
175.04 room, the door of which was half open, to go
175.05 to the kitchen, when some one ran out: --
175.06 "It's her, I am sure! -- I could have told
175.07 her anywhere!" cried the individual who
175.08 stopped my progress and took my hand.
175.09 I looked: I saw a woman attired like a
175.10 well-dressed servant, matronly, yet still young;
175.11 very good looking, with black hair and eyes,
175.12 and lively complexion.
175.13 "Well, who is it?" she asked in a voice and

175.14 with a smile I half recognised; "you've not
175.15 quite forgotten me, I think, Miss Jane?"
175.16 In another second I was embracing and
175.17 kissing her rapturously: "Bessie! Bessie!
175.18 Bessie!" that was all I said; whereat she
175.19 half laughed, half cried, and we both went
175.20 into the parlour. By the fire stood a little
175.21 fellow of three years old, in plaid frock and
175.22 trousers.
175.23 "That is my little boy," said Bessie, directly.
175.24 "Then you are married, Bessie?"
175.25 "Yes: nearly five years since, to Robert
175.26 Leaven, the coachman; and I've a little girl
175.27 besides Bobby there, that I've christened
175.28 Jane."
176.01 "And you don't live at Gateshead?"
176.02 "I live at the Lodge: the old porter has
176.03 left."
176.04 "Well, and how do they all get on? Tell
176.05 me everything about them, Bessie: but sit
176.06 down first; and, Bobby, come and sit on my
176.07 knee, will you?" but Bobby preferred sidling
176.08 over to his mother.
176.09 "You're not grown so very tall, Miss Jane,
176.10 nor so very stout," continued Mrs. Leaven.
176.11 "I dare say they've not kept you too well
176.12 at school: Miss Reed is the head and
176.13 shoulders taller than you are; and Miss
176.14 Georgiana would make two of you in
176.15 breadth."
176.16 "Georgiana is handsome, I suppose, Bes-
176.17 sie?"
176.18 "Very. She went to London last winter
176.19 with her mama, and there everybody admired
176.20 her, and a young lord fell in love with her:
176.21 but his relations were against the match;
176.22 and -- what do you think? -- he and Miss
176.23 Georgiana made it up to run away: but they
176.24 were found out and stopped. It was Miss
176.25 Reed that found them out: I believe she was
176.26 envious; and now she and her sister lead
176.27 a cat and dog life together; they are always
176.28 quarrelling."
177.01 "Well, and what of John Reed?"
177.02 "Oh, he is not doing so well as his mama
177.03 could wish. He went to college, and he got
177.04 -- plucked, I think they call it: and then
177.05 his uncles wanted him to be a barrister, and
177.06 study the law: but he is such a dissipated
177.07 young man, they will never make much of
177.08 him, I think."
177.09 "What does he look like?"
177.10 "He is very tall: some people call him a
177.11 fine looking young man; but he has such
177.12 thick lips."
177.13 "And Mrs. Reed?"
177.14 "Missis looks stout and well enough in the
177.15 face, but I think she's not quite easy in her
177.16 mind: Mr. John's conduct does not please her
177.17 -- he spends a deal of money."
177.18 "Did she send you here, Bessie?"
177.19 "No, indeed: but I have long wanted to
177.20 see you, and when I heard that there had
177.21 been a letter from you, and that you were
177.22 going to another part of the country, I
177.23 thought I'd just set off, and get a look at
177.24 you before you were quite out of my reach."
177.25 "I am afraid you are disappointed in me,
177.26 Bessie." I said this laughing: I perceived
177.27 that Bessie's glance, though it expressed re-
177.28 gard, did in no shape denote admiration.
178.01 "No, Miss Jane, not exactly: you are
178.02 genteel enough; you look like a lady, and
178.03 it is as much as ever I expected of you: you
178.04 were no beauty as a child."
178.05 I smiled at Bessie's frank answer: I felt
178.06 that it was correct, but I confess I was not
178.07 quite indifferent to its import: at eighteen
178.08 most people wish to please, and the con-
178.09 viction that they have not an exterior likely
178.10 to second that desire brings anything but
178.11 gratification."
178.12 "I daresay you are clever, though," con-
178.13 tinued Bessie, by way of solace. "What can
178.14 you do? Can you play on the piano?"
178.15 "A little."
178.16 There was one in the room; Bessie went
178.17 and opened it, and then asked me to sit down
178.18 and give her a tune: I played a waltz or two
178.19 and she was charmed.
178.20 "The Miss Reeds could not play as well!"
178.21 said she exultingly. "I always said you would
178.22 surpass them in learning: and can you
178.23 draw?"
178.24 "That is one of my paintings over the chim-
178.25 ney-piece." It was a landscape in water
178.26 colours, of which I had made a present to the
178.27 Superintendent in acknowledgment of her
178.28 obliging mediation with the committee on
179.01 my behalf; and which she had framed and
179.02 glazed.
179.04 "Well, that is beautiful, Miss Jane! It is
179.05 as fine a picture as any Miss Reed's drawing-
179.05 master could paint, let alone the young ladies
179.06 themselves; who could not come near it: and
179.07 have you learnt French?"
179.08 "Yes, Bessie, I can both read it and speak
179.09 it."
179.10 "And you can work on muslin and canvass?"
179.11 "I can."
179.12 "Oh, you are quite a lady, Miss Jane! I

179.13 knew you would be: you will get on whether
179.14 your relations notice you or not. There was
179.15 something I wanted to ask you. -- Have you
179.16 ever heard anything from your father's kins-
179.17 folk, the Eyres?"
179.18 "Never in my life."
179.19 "Well, you know Missis always said they
179.20 were poor and quite despicable: and they may
179.21 be poor; but I believe they are as much gentry
179.22 as the Reeds are; for one day, nearly seven
179.23 years ago, a Mr. Eyre came to Gateshead and
179.24 wanted to see you; Missis said you were at
179.25 school fifty miles off; he seemed so much dis-
179.26 appointed, for he could not stay: he was going
179.27 on a voyage to a foreign country, and the ship
179.28 was to sail from London in a day or two. He
180.01 looked quite a gentleman, and I believe he was
180.02 your father's brother."
180.03 "What foreign country was he going to,
180.04 Bessie?"
180.05 "An island thousands of miles off, where
180.06 they make wine -- the butler did tell me -- "
180.07 "Madeira?" I suggested.
180.08 "Yes, that is it -- that is the very word."
180.09 "So he went?"
180.10 "Yes; he did not stay many minutes in the
180.11 house: Missis was very high with him; she
180.12 called him afterwards a 'sneaking tradesman.'
180.13 My Robert believes he was a wine-merchant."
180.14 "Very likely," I returned; "or perhaps
180.15 clerk or agent to a wine-merchant."
180.16 Bessie and I conversed about old times an
180.17 hour longer, and then she was obliged to leave
180.18 me: I saw her again for a few minutes the
180.19 next morning at Lowton, while I was waiting
180.20 for the coach. We parted finally at the door
180.21 of the Brocklehurst Arms there: each went
180.22 her separate way; she set off for the brow of
180.23 Lowood Fell to meet the conveyance which
180.24 was to take her back to Gateshead, I mounted
180.25 the vehicle which was to bear me to new duties
180.26 and a new life in the unknown environs of
180.27 Millcote.
181.01 [Vol. 1 Chapter 11]
181.02 A new chapter in a novel is something like a
181.03 new scene in a play; and when I draw up the
181.04 curtain this time, reader, you must fancy you
181.05 see a room in the George Inn at Millcote, with
181.06 such large figured papering on the walls as
181.07 inn rooms have; such a carpet, such furniture,
181.08 such ornaments on the mantel-piece, such
181.09 prints; including a portrait of George the
181.10 Third, and another of the Prince of Wales,
181.11 and a representation of the death of Wolfe.
181.12 All this is visible to you by the light of an
181.13 oil-lamp hanging from the ceiling, and by that
181.14 of an excellent fire, near which I sit in my
181.15 cloak and bonnet; my muff and umbrella lie
181.16 on the table, and I am warming away the
181.17 numbness and chill contracted by sixteen
181.18 hours' exposure to the rawness of an October
181.19 day: I left Lowton at four o'clock P.M., and
181.20 the Millcote town clock is now just striking
181.21 eight.
182.01 Reader, though I look comfortably accom-
182.02 modated, I am not very tranquil in my mind
182.03 I thought when the coach stopped here there
182.04 would be some one to meet me; I looked
182.05 anxiously round as I descended the wooden
182.06 steps the "boots" placed for my convenience,
182.07 expecting to hear my name pronounced, and
182.08 to see some description of carriage waiting to
182.09 convey me to Thornfield. Nothing of the sort
182.10 was visible; and when I asked a waiter if any
182.11 one had been to inquire after a Miss Eyre, I
182.12 was answered in the negative; so I had no
182.13 resource but to request to be shown into a
182.14 private room: and here I am waiting, while
182.15 all sorts of doubts and fears are troubling my
182.16 thoughts.
182.17 It is a very strange sensation to inexpe-
182.18 rienced youth to feel itself quite alone in the
182.19 world: cut adrift from every connection; un-
182.20 certain whether the port to which it is bound
182.21 can be reached, and prevented by many im-
182.22 pediments from returning to that it has quitted.
182.23 The charm of adventure sweetens that sensa-
182.24 tion, the glow of pride warms it; but then the
182.25 throb of fear disturbs it; and fear with me
182.26 became predominant, when half an hour elapsed
182.27 and still I was alone. I bethought myself to
182.28 ring the bell.
183.01 "Is there a place in this neighbourhood
183.02 called Thornfield?" I asked of the waiter who
183.03 answered the summons.
183.04 "Thornfield? I don't know, ma'am; I'll
183.05 inquire at the bar." He vanished, but reap-
183.06 peared instantly: --
183.07 "Is your name Eyre, Miss?"
183.08 "Yes."
183.09 "Person here waiting for you."
183.10 I jumped up, took my muff and umbrella,
183.11 and hastened into the inn-passage: a man was
183.12 standing by the open door, and in the lamp-
183.13 lit street, I dimly saw a one-horse conveyance.
183.14 "This will be your luggage, I suppose?"
183.15 said the man rather abruptly when he saw me,
183.16 pointing to my trunk in the passage.
183.17 "Yes." He hoisted it on to the vehicle,
183.18 which was a sort of car, and then I got in:
183.19 before he shut me up, I asked him how far it

183.20 was to Thornfield.
183.21 "A matter of six miles."
183.22 "How long shall we be before we get
183.23 there?"
183.24 "Happen an hour and a half."
183.25 He fastened the car door, climbed to his
183.26 own seat outside, and we set off. Our pro-
183.27 gress was leisurely, and gave me ample time
183.28 to reflect: I was content to be at length so
184.01 near the end of my journey; and as I leaned
184.02 back in the comfortable though not elegant
184.03 conveyance, I meditated much at my ease.
184.04 "I suppose," thought I, "judging from the
184.05 plainness of the servant and carriage, Mrs.
184.06 Fairfax is not a very dashing person: so much
184.07 the better; I never lived amongst fine people
184.08 but once, and I was very miserable with them.
184.09 I wonder if she lives alone except this little
184.10 girl; if so, and if she is in any degree ami-
184.11 able, I shall surely be able to get on with her;
184.12 I will do my best: it is a pity that doing one's
184.13 best does not always answer. At Lowood,
184.14 indeed, I took that resolution, kept it, and
184.15 succeeded in pleasing; but with Mrs. Reed, I
184.16 remember my best was always spurned with
184.17 scorn. I pray God Mrs. Fairfax may not
184.18 turn out a second Mrs. Reed; but if she does,
184.19 I am not bound to stay with her! let the
184.20 worst come to the worst, I can advertise again.
184.21 How far are we on our road now, I wonder?"
184.22 I let down the window and looked out:
184.23 Millcote was behind us; judging by the num-
184.24 ber of its lights, it seemed a place of con-
184.25 siderable magnitude, much larger than Low-
184.26 ton. We were now, as far as I could see, on
184.27 a sort of common; but there were houses
184.28 scattered all over the district; I felt we were
185.01 in a different region to Lowood, more popu-
185.02 lous, less picturesque; more stirring, less
185.03 romantic.
185.04 The roads were heavy, the night misty; my
185.05 conductor let his horse walk all the way, and
185.06 the hour and a half extended, I verily believe,
185.07 to two hours; at last he turned in his seat and
185.08 said: --
185.09 "You're noan so far fro' Thornfield now."
185.10 Again I looked out: we were passing a
185.11 church: I saw its low broad tower against the
185.12 sky, and its bell was tolling a quarter; I saw
185.13 a narrow galaxy of lights too, on a hill-side,
185.14 marking a village or hamlet. About ten
185.15 minutes after, the driver got down and opened
185.16 a pair of gates: we passed through, and they
185.17 clashed to behind us. We now slowly as-
185.18 cended a drive, and came upon the long front
185.19 of a house: candle-light gleamed from one
185.20 curtained bow-window; all the rest were dark.
185.21 The car stopped at the front door; it was
185.22 opened by a maid-servant; I alighted and
185.23 went in.
185.24 "Will you walk this way, ma'am," said the
185.25 girl; and I followed her across a square hall
185.26 with high doors all round: she ushered me
185.27 into a room whose double illumination of fire
186.01 and candle at first dazzled me, contrasting as
186.02 it did with the darkness to which my eyes had
186.03 been for two hours inured; when I could see,
186.04 however, a cozy and agreeable picture pre-
186.05 sented itself to my view.
186.06 A snug, small room; a round table by a
186.07 cheerful fire; an arm-chair high-backed and
186.08 old-fashioned, wherein sat the neatest imagin-
186.09 able little old lady, in widow's cap, black
186.10 silk gown and snowy muslin apron: exactly
186.11 like what I had fancied Mrs. Fairfax, only
186.12 less stately and milder looking. She was
186.13 occupied in knitting; a large cat sat demurely
186.14 at her feet; nothing in short was wanting to
186.15 complete the beau-ideal of domestic comfort.
186.16 A more reassuring introduction for a new
186.17 governess could scarcely be conceived: there
186.18 was no grandeur to overwhelm, no stateliness
186.19 to embarrass; and then, as I entered, the old
186.20 lady got up, and promptly and kindly came
186.21 forward to meet me.
186.22 "How do you do, my dear? I am afraid
186.23 you have had a tedious ride; John drives so
186.24 slowly: you must be cold, come to the fire."
186.25 "Mrs. Fairfax, I suppose?" said I.
186.26 "Yes, you are right: do sit down."
186.27 She conducted me to her own chair, and
187.01 then began to remove my shawl and untie my
187.02 bonnet-strings; I begged she would not give
187.03 herself so much trouble.
187.04 "Oh, it is no trouble; I dare say your own
187.05 hands are almost numbed with cold. Leah,
187.06 make a little hot negus and cut a sandwich or
187.07 two: here are the keys of the store-room."
187.08 And she produced from her pocket a most
187.09 housewifely bunch of keys, and delivered them
187.10 to the servant.
187.11 "Now, then, draw nearer to the fire;" she
187.12 continued. "You've brought your luggage
187.13 with you, haven't you, my dear?"
187.14 "Yes, ma'am."
187.15 "I'll see it carried into your room," she
187.16 said, and bustled out.
187.17 "She treats me like a visitor," thought I.
187.18 "I little expected such a reception; I antici-
187.19 pated only coldness and stiffness: this is not
187.20 like what I have heard of the treatment of

187.21 governesses; but I must not exult too soon."
187.22 She returned; with her own hands cleared
187.23 her knitting apparatus and a book or two
187.24 from the table, to make room for the tray
187.25 which Leah now brought, and then herself
187.26 handed me the refreshments. I felt rather
187.27 confused at being the object of more attention
187.28 than I had ever before received, and that, too,
188.01 shewn by my employer and superior; but as
188.02 she did not herself seem to consider she was
188.03 doing anything out of her place, I thought it
188.04 better to take her civilities quietly.
188.05 "Shall I have the pleasure of seeing Miss
188.06 Fairfax to-night?" I asked, when I had par-
188.07 taken of what she offered me.
188.08 "What did you say, my dear? I am a little
188.09 deaf," returned the good lady, approaching her
188.10 ear to my mouth.
188.11 I repeated the question more distinctly.
188.12 "Miss Fairfax? Oh, you mean Miss
188.13 Varens! Varens is the name of your future
188.14 pupil."
188.15 "Indeed! Then she is not your daughter?"
188.16 "No, -- I have no family."
188.17 I should have followed up my first inquiry,
188.18 by asking in what way Miss Varens was con-
188.19 nected with her; but I recollected it was not
188.20 polite to ask too many questions: besides, I
188.21 was sure to hear in time.
188.22 "I am so glad --" she continued, as she sat
188.23 down opposite to me, and took the cat on her
188.24 knee: "I am so glad you are come; it will be
188.25 quite pleasant living here now with a com-
188.26 panion. To be sure it is pleasant at any time;
188.27 for Thornfield is a fine old hall, rather ne-
188.28 glected of late years perhaps, but still it is
189.01 a respectable place; yet you know in winter
189.02 time, one feels dreary quite alone, in the best
189.03 quarters. I say alone -- Leah is a nice girl
189.04 to be sure, and John and his wife are very
189.05 decent people; but then you see they are only
189.06 servants, and one can't converse with them on
189.07 terms of equality: one must keep them at due
189.08 distance, for fear of losing one's authority.
189.09 I'm sure last winter /it was a very severe one,
189.10 if you recollect, and when it did not snow,
189.11 it rained and blew/, not a creature but the
189.12 butcher and postman came to the house, from
189.13 November till February; and I really got quite
189.14 melancholy with sitting night after night alone;
189.15 don't think the poor girl liked the task much:
189.16 she felt it confining. In spring and summer
189.17 one got on better: sunshine and long days
189.18 make such a difference; and then just at the
189.19 commencement of this autumn, little Adela
189.20 Varens came and her nurse: a child makes a
189.21 house alive all at once; and now you are here
189.22 I shall be quite gay."
189.23 My heart really warmed to the worthy lady
189.24 as I heard her talk; and I drew my chair a
189.25 little nearer to her, and expressed my sincere
189.26 wish that she might find my company as agree-
189.27 able as she anticipated.
190.01 "But I'll not keep you sitting up late to--
190.02 night," said she; "it is on the stroke of twelve
190.03 now, and you have been travelling all day:
190.04 you must feel tired. If you have got your feet
190.05 well warmed, I'll shew you your bed-room.
190.06 I've had the room next to mine prepared for
190.07 you; it is only a small apartment, but I
190.08 thought you would like it better than one of
190.09 the large front chambers: to be sure they
190.10 have finer furniture, but they are so dreary
190.11 and solitary, I never sleep in them myself."
190.12 I thanked her for her considerate choice,
190.13 and as I really felt fatigued with my long
190.14 journey, expressed my readiness to retire. She
190.15 took her candle, and I followed her from the
190.16 room. First she went to see if the hall-door
190.17 was fastened; having taken the key from the
190.18 lock, she led the way up stairs. The steps and
190.19 banisters were of oak; the staircase window
190.20 was high and latticed: both it and the long
190.21 gallery into which the bed-room doors opened,
190.22 looked as if they belonged to a church rather
190.23 than a house. A very chill and vault-like air
190.24 pervaded the stairs and gallery, suggesting
190.25 cheerless ideas of space and solitude; and I
190.26 was glad when finally ushered into my chamber,
190.27 to find it of small dimensions and furnished in
190.28 ordinary modern style.
191.01 When Mrs. Fairfax had bidden me a kind
191.02 good-night, and I had fastened my door, gazed
191.03 leisurely round, and in some measure effaced
191.04 the eerie impression made by that wide hall,
191.05 that dark and spacious staircase, and that long,
191.06 cold gallery, by the livelier aspect of my little
191.07 room, I remembered that after a day of bodily
191.08 fatigue and mental anxiety, I was now at last
191.09 in safe haven. The impulse of gratitude
191.10 swelled my heart, and I knelt down at the
191.11 bed-side and offered up thanks where thanks
191.12 were due; not forgetting, ere I rose, to implore
191.13 aid on my further path, and the power of
191.14 meriting the kindness which seemed so frankly
191.15 offered me before it was earned. My couch
191.16 had no thorns in it that night; my solitary
191.17 room no fears. At once weary and content, I
191.18 slept soon and soundly: when I awoke it was
191.19 broad day.
191.20 The chamber looked such a bright little

362

191.21 place to me as the sun shone in between the
191.22 gay blue chintz window curtains, showing
191.23 papered walls and a carpeted floor, so unlike
191.24 the bare planks and stained plaster of Lowood,
191.25 that my spirits rose at the view. Externals have
191.26 a great effect on the young: I thought that a
191.27 fairer era of life was beginning for me, -- one
191.28 that was to have its flowers and pleasures, as
192.01 well as its thorns and toils. My faculties,
192.02 roused by the change of scene, the new field
192.03 offered to hope, seemed all astir. I cannot
192.04 precisely define what they expected, but it
192.05 was something pleasant: not perhaps that day
192.06 or that month, but at an indefinite future
192.07 period.
192.08 I rose; I dressed myself with care: obliged
192.09 to be plain -- for I had no article of attire that
192.10 was not made with extreme simplicity -- I was
192.11 still by nature solicitous to be neat. It was not
192.12 my habit to be disregardful of appearance, or
192.13 careless of the impression I made: on the
192.14 contrary, I ever wished to look as well as I
192.15 could, and to please as much as my want of
192.16 beauty would permit. I sometimes regretted
192.17 that I was not handsomer: I sometimes wished
192.18 to have rosy cheeks, a straight nose, and small
192.19 cherry mouth; I desired to be tall, stately, and
192.20 finely developed in figure; I felt it a misfor-
192.21 tune that I was so little, so pale, and had
192.22 features so irregular and so marked. And
192.23 why had I these aspirations and these regrets?
192.24 It would be difficult to say: I could not then
192.25 distinctly say it to myself; yet I had a reason,
192.26 and a logical, natural reason too. However,
192.27 when I had brushed my hair very smooth, and
192.28 put on my black frock -- which, Quaker-like as
193.01 it was, at least had the merit of fitting to a
193.02 nicety -- and adjusted my clean white tucker, I
193.03 thought I should do respectably enough to
193.04 appear before Mrs. Fairfax; and that my new
193.05 pupil would not at least recoil from me with
193.06 antipathy. Having opened my chamber win-
193.07 dow, and seen that I left all things straight
193.08 and neat on the toilet table, I ventured
193.09 forth.
193.10 Traversing the long and matted gallery, I
193.11 descended the slippery steps of oak; then I
193.12 gained the hall: I halted there a minute; I
193.13 looked at some pictures on the walls /one I
193.14 remember represented a grim man in a cuirass,
193.15 and one a lady with powdered hair and a
193.16 pearl necklace/, at a bronze lamp pendent from
193.17 the ceiling, at a great clock whose case was of
193.18 oak curiously carved, and ebon black with
193.19 time and rubbing. Everything appeared very
193.20 stately and imposing to me: but then I was
193.21 so little accustomed to grandeur. The hall--
193.22 door, which was half of glass, stood open; I
193.23 stepped over the threshold. It was a fine
193.24 autumn morning; the early sun shone se-
193.25 renely on embrowned groves and still green
193.26 fields: advancing on to the lawn, I looked up
193.27 and surveyed the front of the mansion. It
193.28 was three stories high, of proportions not
194.01 vast, though considerable; a gentleman's
194.02 manor-house, not a nobleman's seat: battle-
194.03 ments round the top gave it a picturesque
194.04 look. Its gray front stood out well from the
194.05 back ground of a rookery, whose cawing
194.06 tenants were now on the wing: they flew over
194.07 the lawn and grounds to alight in a great
194.08 meadow, from which these were separated by
194.09 a sunk fence, and where an array of mighty
194.10 old thorn trees, strong, knotty, and broad as
194.11 oaks, at once explained the etymology of the
194.12 mansion's designation. Farther off were hills:
194.13 not so lofty as those round Lowood, nor so
194.14 craggy, nor so like barriers of separation from
194.15 the living world; but yet quiet and lonely
194.16 hills enough, and seeming to embrace Thorn-
194.17 field with a seclusion I had not expected to
194.18 find existent so near the stirring locality of
194.19 Millcote. A little hamlet, whose roofs were
194.20 blent with trees, straggled up the side of one
194.21 of these hills; the church of the district stood
194.22 nearer Thornfield: its old tower-top looked
194.23 over a knoll between the house and gates.
194.24 I was yet enjoying the calm prospect and
194.25 pleasant fresh air, yet listening with delight to
194.26 the cawing of the rooks, yet surveying the
194.27 wide, hoary front of the hall, and thinking
194.28 what a great place it was for one lonely little
195.01 dame like Mrs. Fairfax to inhabit, when that
195.02 lady appeared at the door.
195.03 "What! out already?" said she. "I see you
195.04 are an early riser." I went up to her, and was
195.05 received with an affable kiss and shake of the
195.06 hand.
195.07 "How do you like Thornfield?" she asked.
195.08 I told her I liked it very much.
195.09 "Yes," she said, "it is a pretty place; but
195.10 I fear it will be getting out of order, unless
195.11 Mr. Rochester should take it into his head to
195.12 come and reside here permanently; or, at least,
195.13 visit it rather oftener: great houses and fine
195.14 grounds require the presence of the pro-
195.15 prietor."
195.16 "Mr. Rochester!" I exclaimed. "Who is
195.17 he?"
195.18 "The owner of Thornfield," she responded
195.19 quietly. "Did you not know he was called

195.20 Rochester?"
195.21 Of course I did not -- I had never heard of
195.22 him before; but the old lady seemed to regard
195.23 his existence as a universally understood fact,
195.24 with which everybody must be acquainted by
195.25 instinct.
195.26 "I thought," I continued, "Thornfield be-
195.27 longed to you."
195.28 "To me? Bless you child what an idea!
196.01 To me? I am only the housekeeper -- the
196.02 manager. To be sure I am distantly related
196.03 to the Rochesters by the mother's side; or, at
196.04 least, my husband was: he was a clergyman,
196.05 incumbent of Hay -- that little village yonder
196.06 on the hill -- and that church near the gates was
196.07 his. The present Mr. Rochester's mother was
196.08 a Fairfax, and second cousin to my husband;
196.09 but I never presume on the connection -- in
196.10 fact, it is nothing to me; I consider myself
196.11 quite in the light of an ordinary housekeeper:
196.12 my employer is always civil, and I expect
196.13 nothing more."
196.14 "And the little girl -- my pupil?"
196.15 "She is Mr. Rochester's ward; he commis-
196.16 sioned me to find a governess for her. He
196.17 intends to have her brought up in --shire,
196.18 I believe. Here she comes, with her `bonne,`
196.19 as she calls her nurse." The enigma then was
196.20 explained: this affable and kind little widow
196.21 was no great dame, but a dependant like my-
196.22 self. I did not like her the worse for that; on
196.23 the contrary, I felt better pleased than ever.
196.24 The equality between her and me was real;
196.25 not the mere result of condescension on her
196.26 part: so much the better -- my position was all
196.27 the freer.
196.28 As I was meditating on this discovery, a
197.01 little girl, followed by her attendant, came
197.02 running up the lawn. I looked at my pupil,
197.03 who did not at first appear to notice me: she
197.04 was quite a child, perhaps seven or eight years
197.05 old, slightly built, with a pale small-featured
197.06 face, and a redundancy of hair falling in curls
197.07 to her waist.
197.08 "Good-morning, Miss Adela," said Mrs.
197.09 Fairfax. "Come and speak to the lady who
197.10 is to teach you, and to make you a clever
197.11 woman some day." She approached.
197.12 "C'est la ma gouvernante?" said she,
197.13 pointing to me, and addressing her nurse; who
197.14 answered:
197.15 "Mais oui, certainement."
197.16 "Are they foreigners?" I inquired, amazed
197.17 at hearing the French language.
197.18 "The nurse is a foreigner, and Adela was
197.19 born on the continent; and, I believe, never
197.20 left it till within six months ago. When she
197.21 first came here she could speak no English;
197.22 now she can make shift to talk it a little: I
197.23 don't understand her, she mixes it so with
197.24 French; but you will make out her meaning
197.25 very well, I daresay."
197.26 Fortunately I had had the advantage of
197.27 being taught French by a French lady; and
197.28 as I had always made a point of conversing
198.01 with Madame Pierrot, as often as I could, and
198.02 had, besides, during the last seven years, learnt
198.03 a portion of French by heart daily -- applying
198.04 myself to take pains with my accent, and imi-
198.05 tating as closely as possible the pronunciation
198.06 of my teacher -- I had acquired a certain degree
198.07 of readiness and correctness in the language,
198.08 and was not likely to be much at a loss with
198.09 Mademoiselle Adela. She came and shook
198.10 hands with me when she heard that I was her
198.11 governess; and as I led her into breakfast, I
198.12 addressed some phrases to her in her own
198.13 tongue: she replied briefly at first, but after
198.14 we were seated at the table, and she had
198.15 examined me some ten minutes with her large
198.16 hazel eyes, she suddenly commenced chatter-
198.17 ing fluently.
198.18 "Ah!" cried she, in French, "you speak
198.19 my language as well as Mr. Rochester does:
198.20 I can talk to you as I can to him, and so can
198.21 Sophie. She will be glad: nobody here un-
198.22 derstands her: Madame Fairfax is all English.
198.23 Sophie is my nurse; she came with me over
198.24 the sea in a great ship with a chimney that
198.25 smoked -- how it did smoke! -- and I was sick,
198.26 and so was Sophie, and so was Mr. Rochester.
198.27 Mr. Rochester lay down on a sofa in a pretty
198.28 room called the salon, and Sophie and I had
199.01 little beds in another place. I nearly fell out
199.02 of mine; it was like a shelf. And, Mademoi-
199.03 selle -- what is your name?"
199.04 "Eyre -- Jane Eyre."
199.05 "Aire? Bah! I cannot say it. Well: our
199.06 ship stopped in the morning, before it was
199.07 quite daylight, at a great city -- a huge city,
199.08 with very dark houses and all smoky; not at
199.09 all like the pretty clean town I came from;
199.10 and Mr. Rochester carried me in his arms
199.11 over a plank to the land, and Sophie came
199.12 after, and we all got into a coach, which took
199.13 us to a beautiful large house, larger than this
199.14 and finer, called an hotel. We stayed there
199.15 nearly a week: I and Sophie used to walk
199.16 every day in a great green place full of
199.17 trees, called the Park; and there were many
199.18 children there besides me, and a pond with

199.19 beautiful birds in it, that I fed with crumbs."
199.20   "Can you understand her when she runs on
199.21 so fast?" asked Mrs. Fairfax.
199.22   I understood her very well, for I had been
199.23 accustomed to the fluent tongue of Madame
199.24 Pierrot.
199.25   "I wish," continued the good lady, "you
199.26 would ask her a question or two about her
199.27 parents: I wonder if she remembers them?"
199.28   ""Adele," I inquired, "with whom did you
200.01 live when you were in that pretty clean town
200.02 you spoke of?"
200.03   "I lived long ago with mama; but she is
200.04 gone to the Holy Virgin. Mama used to
200.05 teach me to dance and sing, and to say verses.
200.06 A great many gentlemen and ladies came to
200.07 see mama, and I used to dance before them,
200.08 or to sit on their knees and sing to them: I
200.09 liked it. Shall I let you hear me sing now?"
200.10   She had finished her breakfast, so I per-
200.11 mitted her to give a specimen of her accom-
200.12 plishments. Descending from her chair, she
200.13 came and placed herself on my knee; then,
200.14 folding her little hands demurely before her,
200.15 shaking back her curls and lifting her eyes to
200.16 the ceiling, she commenced singing a song
200.17 from some opera. It was the strain of a for-
200.18 saken lady, who, after bewailing the perfidy of
200.19 her lover, calls pride to her aid; desires her
200.20 attendant to deck her in her brightest jewels
200.21 and richest robes, and resolves to meet the
200.22 false one that night at a ball, and prove to him
200.23 by the gaiety of her demeanor how little his
200.24 desertion has affected her.
200.25   The subject seemed strangely chosen for an
200.26 infant singer; but I suppose the point of the
200.27 exhibition lay in hearing the notes of love
200.28 and jealousy warbled with the lisp of child-
201.01 hood; and in very bad taste that point was: at
201.02 least I thought so.
201.03   Adele sang the canzonette tunefully enough,
201.04 and with the naivete of her age. This
201.05 achieved, she jumped from my knee and said,
201.06 "Now, mademoiselle, I will repeat you some
201.07 poetry."
201.08   Assuming an attitude, she began "La Ligue
201.09 des Rats; fable de La Fountaine." She then
201.10 declaimed the little piece with an attention to
201.11 punctuation and emphasis, a flexibility of voice
201.12 and an appropriateness of gesture, very un-
201.13 usual indeed at her age; and which proved she
201.14 had been carefully trained.
201.15   "Was it your mama who taught you that
201.16 piece?" I asked.
201.17   "Yes, and she just used to say it in this way:
201.18 `Qu'avez vous donc? lui dit un de ces rats;
201.19 parlez!` She made me lift my hand -- so -- to
201.20 remind me to raise my voice at the question.
201.21 Now shall I dance for you?"
201.22   "No, that will do: but after your mama
201.23 went to the Holy Virgin, as you say, with
201.24 whom did you live then?"
201.25   "With Madame Frederic and her husband:
201.26 she took care of me, but she is nothing related
201.27 to me. I think she is poor, for she had not
201.28 so fine a house as mama. I was not long
202.01 there; Mr. Rochester asked me if I would
202.02 like to go and live with him in England, and
202.03 I said yes; for I knew Mr. Rochester before
202.04 I knew Madame Frederic, and he was always
202.05 kind to me and gave me pretty dresses and
202.06 toys: but you see he has not kept his word,
202.07 for he has brought me to England, and now
202.08 he is gone back again himself, and I never see
202.09 him."
202.10   After breakfast, Adele and I withdrew to
202.11 the library; which room, it appears, Mr.
202.12 Rochester had directed should be used as the
202.13 school-room. Most of the books were locked
202.14 up behind glass doors; but there was one
202.15 book-case left open containing everything
202.16 that could be needed in the way of elementary
202.17 works and several volumes of light literature,
202.18 poetry, biography, travels, a few romances, &c.
202.19 I suppose he had considered that these were
202.20 all the governess would require for her private
202.21 perusal; and, indeed, they contented me amply
202.22 for the present; compared with the scanty
202.23 pickings I had now and then been able to
202.24 glean at Lowood, they seemed to offer an
202.25 abundant harvest of entertainment and infor-
202.26 mation. In this room, too, there was a cabinet
202.27 piano, quite new and of superior tone; also an
202.28 easel for painting, and a pair of globes.
203.01   I found my pupil sufficiently docile, though
203.02 disinclined to apply: she had not been used to
203.03 regular occupation of any kind. I felt it
203.04 would be injudicious to confine her too much
203.05 at first; so, when I had talked to her a great
203.06 deal, and got her to learn a little, and when
203.07 the morning had advanced to noon, I allowed
203.08 her to return to her nurse. I then proposed
203.09 to occupy myself till dinner-time in drawing
203.10 some little sketches for her use.
203.11   As I was going up stairs to fetch my port-
203.12 folio and pencils, Mrs. Fairfax called to me:
203.13 "Your morning school-hours are over now, I
203.14 suppose," said she. She was in a room the
203.15 folding-doors of which stood open: I went in
203.16 when she addressed me. It was a large,
203.17 stately apartment, with purple chairs and cur-

203.18 tains, a Turkey carpet, walnut-panelled walls,
203.19 one vast window rich in stained glass, and a
203.20 lofty ceiling, nobly moulded. Mrs. Fairfax
203.21 was dusting some vases of fine purple spar,
203.22 which stood on a side-board.
203.23   "What a beautiful room!" I exclaimed, as
203.24 I looked round; for I had never before seen
203.25 any half so imposing.
203.26   "Yes; this is the dining-room. I have just
203.27 opened the window, to let in a little air and
203.28 sunshine; for everything gets so damp in
204.01 apartments that are seldom inhabited: the
204.02 drawing-room yonder feels like a vault."
204.03   She pointed to a wide arch corresponding to
204.04 the window, and hung like it with a Tyrian--
204.05 dyed curtain, now looped up. Mounting to it
204.06 by two broad steps and looking through, I
204.07 thought I caught a glimpse of a fairy place: so
204.08 bright to my novice-eyes appeared the view
204.09 beyond. Yet it was merely a very pretty
204.10 drawing-room, and within it a boudoir, both
204.11 spread with white carpets, on which seemed
204.12 laid brilliant garlands of flowers; both ceiled
204.13 with snowy mouldings of white grapes and
204.14 vine-leaves, beneath which glowed in rich
204.15 contrast crimson couches and ottomans; while
204.16 the ornaments on the pale Parian mantel-piece
204.17 were of sparkling Bohemian glass, ruby red;
204.18 and between the windows large mirrors re-
204.19 peated the general blending of snow and fire.
204.20   "In what order you keep these rooms, Mrs.
204.21 Fairfax!" said I. "No dust, no canvass cover-
204.22 ings: except that the air feels chilly, one
204.23 would think they were inhabited daily."
204.24   "Why, Miss Eyre, though Mr. Rochester's
204.25 visits here are rare, they are always sudden
204.26 and unexpected; and as I observed that it put
204.27 him out to find everything swathed up, and to
204.28 have a bustle of arrangement on his arrival,
205.01 I thought it best to keep the rooms in readi-
205.02 ness."
205.03   "Is Mr. Rochester an exacting, fastidious
205.04 sort of man?"
205.05   "Not particularly so; but he has a gentle-
205.06 man's tastes and habits, and he expects to
205.07 have things managed in conformity to them."
205.08   "Do you like him? Is he generally
205.09 liked?"
205.10   "Oh, yes; the family have always been
205.11 respected here. Almost all the land in this
205.12 neighbourhood, as far as you can see, has
205.13 belonged to the Rochesters time out of mind."
205.14   "Well, but, leaving his land out of the
205.15 question, do you like him? Is he liked for
205.16 himself?"
205.17   "I have no cause to do otherwise than like
205.18 him; and I believe he is considered a just and
205.19 liberal landlord by his tenants: but he has
205.20 never lived much amongst them."
205.21   "But has he no peculiarities? What, in
205.22 short, is his character?"
205.23   "Oh! his character is unimpeachable, I
205.24 suppose. He is rather peculiar, perhaps: he
205.25 has travelled a great deal, and seen a great
205.26 deal of the world, I should think. I dare say
205.27 he is clever: but I never had much conversa-
205.28 tion with him."
206.01   "In what way is he peculiar?"
206.02   "I don't know -- it is not easy to describe --
206.03 nothing striking, but you feel it when he
206.04 speaks to you: you cannot be always sure
206.05 whether he is in jest or earnest, whether he is
206.06 pleased or the contrary; you don't thoroughly
206.07 understand him, in short -- at least, I don't: but
206.08 it is of no consequence, he is a very good
206.09 master."
206.10   This was all the account I got from Mrs.
206.11 Fairfax, of her employer and mine. There
206.12 are people who seem to have no notion of
206.13 sketching a character, or observing and de-
206.14 scribing salient points, either in persons or
206.15 things: the good lady evidently belonged to
206.16 this class; my queries puzzled, but did not
206.17 draw her out. Mr. Rochester was Mr. Roches-
206.18 ter in her eyes; a gentleman, a landed proprie-
206.19 tor -- nothing more: she inquired and searched
206.20 no further, and evidently wondered at my
206.21 wish to gain a more definite notion of his
206.22 identity.
206.23   When we left the dining-room, she proposed
206.24 to show me over the rest of the house; and
206.25 I followed her up stairs and down stairs, ad-
206.26 miring as I went: for all was well arranged
206.27 and handsome. The large front chambers I
206.28 thought especially grand; and some of the
207.01 third story rooms, though dark and low, were
207.02 interesting from their air of antiquity. The
207.03 furniture once appropriated to the lower apart-
207.04 ments had from time to time been removed
207.05 here, as fashions changed; and the imperfect
207.06 light entering by their narrow casements
207.07 showed bedsteads of a hundred years old:
207.08 chests in oak or walnut, looking, with their
207.09 strange carvings of palm branches and cherubs'
207.10 heads, like types of the Hebrew ark; rows of
207.11 venerable chairs, high-backed and narrow;
207.12 stools still more antiquated, on whose cushioned
207.13 tops were yet apparent traces of half-effaced
207.14 embroideries, wrought by fingers that for two
207.15 generations had been coffin-dust. All these
207.16 relics gave to the third story of Thornfield-Hall

207.17 the aspect of a home of the past: a shrine of
207.18 memory. I liked the hush, the gloom, the
207.19 quaintness of these retreats in the day; but
207.20 I by no means coveted a night's repose on one
207.21 of those wide and heavy beds: shut in, some
207.22 of them with doors of oak; shaded, others with
207.23 wrought old English hangings crusted with
207.24 thick work, portraying effigies of strange
207.25 flowers, and strange birds, and strangest
207.26 human beings, -- all which would have looked
207.27 strange, indeed, by the pallid gleam of moon--
207.28 light.
208.01 "Do the servants sleep in these rooms?" I
208.02 asked.
208.03 "No; they occupy a range of smaller
208.04 apartments to the back; no one ever sleeps
208.05 here: one would almost say that, if there
208.06 were a ghost at Thornfield-Hall, this would
208.07 be its haunt."
208.08 "So I think: you have no ghost then?"
208.09 "None that I ever heard of," returned
208.10 Mrs. Fairfax, smiling.
208.11 "Nor any traditions of one? no legends or
208.12 ghost stories?"
208.13 "I believe not. And yet it is said, the
208.14 Rochesters have been rather a violent than a
208.15 quiet race in their time: perhaps, though, that
208.16 is the reason they rest tranquilly in their
208.17 graves now."
208.18 "Yes -- 'after life's fitful fever they sleep
208.19 well,'" I muttered. "Where are you going
208.20 now, Mrs. Fairfax?" for she was moving
208.21 away.
208.22 "On to the leads; will you come and see
208.23 the view from thence?" I followed still, up a
208.24 very narrow staircase to the attics, and thence
208.25 by a ladder and through a trap-door to the
208.26 roof of the hall. I was now on a level with
208.27 the crow-colony, and could see into their
208.28 nests. Leaning over the battlements and look-
209.01 ing far down, I surveyed the grounds laid out
209.02 like a map: the bright and velvet lawn
209.03 closely girdling the gray base of the mansion;
209.04 the field, wide as a park, dotted with its
209.05 ancient timber; the wood, dun and sere,
209.06 divided by a path visibly overgrown, greener
209.07 with moss than the trees were with foliage;
209.08 the church at the gates, the road, the tranquil
209.09 hills all reposing in the autumn day's sun;
209.10 the horizon bounded by a propitious sky
209.11 azure, marbled with pearly white. No fea-
209.12 ture in the scene was extraordinary, but all
209.13 was pleasing. when I turned from it and
209.14 repassed the trap-door, I could scarcely see
209.15 my way down the ladder; the attic seemed
209.16 black as a vault compared with that arch of
209.17 blue air to which I had been looking up, and
209.18 to that sunlit scene of grove, pasture and
209.19 green hill of which the hall was the centre,
209.20 and over which I had been gazing with
209.21 delight.
209.22 Mrs. Fairfax stayed behind a moment to
209.23 fasten the trap-door; I, by dint of groping,
209.24 found the outlet from the attic, and proceeded
209.25 to descend the narrow garret staircase. I
209.26 lingered in the long passage to which this
209.27 led, separating the front and back rooms of
209.28 the third story: narrow, low, and dim, with
210.01 only one little window at the far end, and look-
210.02 ing, with its two rows of small black doors
210.03 all shut, like a corridor in some Bluebeard's
210.04 castle.
210.05 while I paced softly on, the last sound I
210.06 expected to hear in so still a region, a laugh,
210.07 struck my ear. It was a curious laugh; dis-
210.08 tinct, formal, mirthless. I stopped: the sound
210.09 ceased, only for an instant; it began again,
210.10 louder: for at first, though distinct, it was very
210.11 low. It passed off in a clamorous peal that
210.12 seemed to wake an echo in every lonely
210.13 chamber; though it originated but in one, and
210.14 I could have pointed out the door whence the
210.15 accents issued.
210.16 "Mrs. Fairfax!" I called out: for I now
210.17 heard her descending the great stairs. "Did
210.18 you hear that loud laugh? who is it?"
210.19 "Some of the servants very likely," she
210.20 answered: "perhaps Grace Poole."
210.21 "Did you hear it?" I again inquired.
210.22 "Yes, plainly: I often hear her; she
210.23 sews in one of these rooms. Sometimes
210.24 Leah is with her: they are frequently noisy
210.25 together."
210.26 The laugh was repeated in its low, syllabic
210.27 tone, and terminated in an odd murmur.
210.28 "Grace!" exclaimed Mrs. Fairfax.
211.01 I really did not expect any Grace to an-
211.02 swer; for the laugh was as tragic, as preter-
211.03 natural a laugh as any I ever heard; and, but
211.04 that it was high noon, and that no circum-
211.05 stance of ghostliness accompanied the curious
211.06 cachination; but that neither scene nor
211.07 season favoured fear, I should have been
211.08 superstitiously afraid. However, the event
211.09 showed me I was a fool for entertaining a
211.10 sense even of surprise.
211.11 The door nearest me opened, and a servant
211.12 came out, -- a woman of between thirty and
211.13 forty; a set, square-made figure, red-haired,
211.14 and with a hard, plain face: any apparition
211.15 less romantic or less ghostly could scarcely be

211.16 conceived.
211.17 "Too much noise, Grace," said Mrs. Fair-
211.18 fax. "Remember directions!" Grace curt-
211.19 seyed silently and went in.
211.20 "She is a person we have to sew and assist
211.21 Leah in her housemaid's work," continued
211.22 the widow; "not altogether unobjectionable
211.23 in some points, but she does well enough.
211.24 By-the-by, how have you got on with your new
211.25 pupil this morning?"
211.26 The conversation, thus turned on Adele,
211.27 continued till we reached the light and cheer-
212.01 ful region below. Adele came running to
212.02 meet us in the hall, exclaiming: --
212.03 "Mesdames, vous etes servies!" adding
212.04 "J'ai bien faim, moi!"
212.05 We found dinner ready, and waiting for us
212.06 in Mrs. Fairfax's room.
213.01 [Vol. 1 Chapter 12]
213.02 The promise of a smooth career, which my
213.03 first calm introduction to Thornfield-Hall
213.04 seemed to pledge, was not belied on a longer
213.05 acquaintance with the place and its inmates.
213.06 Mrs. Fairfax turned out to be what she
213.07 appeared, a placid-tempered, kind-natured
213.08 woman, of competent education and average
213.09 intelligence. My pupil was a lively child, who
213.10 had been spoilt and indulged, and therefore
213.11 was sometimes wayward; but as she was
213.12 committed entirely to my care, and no inju-
213.13 dicious interference from any quarter ever
213.14 thwarted my plans for her improvement, she
213.15 soon forget her little freaks, and became obe-
213.16 dient and teachable. She had no great talents,
213.17 no marked traits of character, no peculiar de-
213.18 velopment of feeling or taste which raised
213.19 her one inch above the ordinary level of child-
213.20 hood; but neither had she any deficiency or
214.01 vice which sunk her below it. She made
214.02 reasonable progress, entertained for me a vi-
214.03 vacious, though perhaps not very profound
214.04 affection, and by her simplicity, gay prattle,
214.05 and efforts to please, inspired me, in return,
214.06 with a degree of attachment sufficient to make
214.07 us both content in each other's society.
214.08 This par parenthese, will be thought cool
214.09 language by persons who entertain solemn
214.10 doctrines about the angelic nature of children,
214.11 and the duty of those charged with their edu-
214.12 cation to conceive for them an idolatrous
214.13 devotion: but I am not writing to flatter
214.14 parental egotism, to echo cant, or prop up
214.15 humbug; I am merely telling the truth. I
214.16 felt a conscientious solicitude for Adele's well-
214.17 fare and progress, and a quiet liking to her
214.18 little self; just as I cherished towards Mrs.
214.19 Fairfax a thankfulness for her kindness, and a
214.20 pleasure in her society proportionate to the
214.21 tranquil regard she had for me, and the mode-
214.22 ration of her mind and character.
214.23 Anybody may blame me who likes, when I
214.24 add further, that, now and then, when I took
214.25 a walk by myself in the grounds; when I went
214.26 down to the gates and looked through them
214.27 along the road; or when, while Adele played
214.28 with her nurse, and Mrs. Fairfax made jellies
215.01 in the store-room, I climbed the three stair--
215.02 cases, raised the trap-door of the attic, and
215.03 having reached the leads, looked out afar over
215.04 sequestered field and hill, and along dim sky--
215.05 line: that then I longed for a power of vision
215.06 which might overpass that limit; which might
215.07 reach the busy world, towns, regions full of
215.08 life I had heard of but never seen: that then
215.09 I desired more of practical experience than I
215.10 possessed; more of intercourse with my kind,
215.11 of acquaintance with variety of character, than
215.12 was here within my reach. I valued what
215.13 was good in Mrs. Fairfax, and what was good
215.14 in Adele; but I believed in the existence of
215.15 other and more vivid kinds of goodness, and
215.16 what I believed in I wished to behold.
215.17 Who blames me? Many no doubt; and I
215.18 shall be called discontented. I could not help
215.19 it: the restlessness was in my nature; it agi-
215.20 tated me to pain sometimes. Then my sole
215.21 relief was to walk along the corridor of the
215.22 third story, backwards and forwards, safe in
215.23 the silence and solitude of the spot, and allow
215.24 my mind's eye to dwell on whatever bright
215.25 visions rose before it -- and certainly they were
215.26 many and glowing; to let my heart be heaved
215.27 by the exultant movement which, while it
215.28 swelled it in trouble, expanded it with life; and,
216.01 best of all, to open my inward ear to a tale
216.02 that was never ended -- a tale my imagination
216.03 created, and narrated continuously; quickened
216.04 with all of incident, life, fire, feeling, that I
216.05 desired and had not in my actual existence.
216.06 It is in vain to say human beings ought to
216.07 be satisfied with tranquillity: they must have
216.08 action; and they will make it if they cannot
216.09 find it. Millions are condemned to a stiller
216.10 doom than mine, and millions are in silent
216.11 revolt against their lot. Nobody knows how
216.12 many rebellions besides political rebellions
216.13 ferment in the masses of life which people
216.14 earth. Women are supposed to be very calm
216.15 generally: but women feel just as men feel;
216.16 they need exercise for their faculties, and a
216.17 field for their efforts as much as their brothers

216.18 do; they suffer from too rigid a restraint, too
216.19 absolute a stagnation, precisely as men would
216.20 suffer; and it is narrow-minded in their more
216.21 privileged fellow-creatures to say that they
216.22 ought to confine themselves to making pud-
216.23 dings and knitting stockings, to playing on
216.24 the piano and embroidering bags. It is
216.25 thoughtless to condemn them, or laugh at
216.26 them, if they seek to do more or learn more
216.27 than custom has pronounced necessary for
216.28 their sex.
217.01   When thus alone, I not unfrequently heard
217.02 Grace Poole's laugh: the same peal, the same
217.03 low, slow ha! ha! which, when first heard,
217.04 had thrilled me: I heard too, her eccentric
217.05 murmurs; stranger than her laugh. There
217.06 were days when she was quite silent; but there
217.07 were others when I could not account for the
217.08 sounds she made. Sometimes I saw her: she
217.09 would come out of her room with a basin, or
217.10 a plate, or a tray in her hand, go down to the
217.11 kitchen and shortly return, generally /oh,
217.12 romantic reader, forgive me for telling the
217.13 plain truth!/ bearing a pot of porter. Her
217.14 appearance always acted as a damper to the
217.15 curiosity raised by her oral oddities: hard--
217.16 featured and staid, she had no point to which
217.17 interest could attach. I made some attempts
217.18 to draw her into conversation, but she seemed
217.19 a person of few words: a monosyllabic reply
217.20 usually cut short every effort of that sort.
217.21   The other members of the household, viz.
217.22 John and his wife, Leah the housemaid, and
217.23 Sophie the French nurse, were decent people;
217.24 but in no respect remarkable: with Sophie I
217.25 used to talk French, and sometimes I asked
217.26 her questions about her native country; but
217.27 she was not of a descriptive or narrative turn,
217.28 and generally gave such vapid and confused
218.01 answers as were calculated rather to check
218.02 than encourage inquiry.
218.03   October, November, December passed away.
218.04 One afternoon in January, Mrs. Fairfax had
218.05 begged a holiday for Adele, because she had a
218.06 cold; and, as Adele seconded the request with
218.07 an ardour that reminded me how precious
218.08 occasional holidays had been to me in my
218.09 own childhood, I accorded it; deeming that I
218.10 did well in shewing pliability on the point.
218.11 It was a fine, calm day, though very cold; I
218.12 was tired of sitting still in the library through
218.13 a whole long morning: Mrs. Fairfax had just
218.14 written a letter which was waiting to be posted,
218.15 so I put on my bonnet and cloak and volun-
218.16 teered to carry it to Hay; -- the distance, two
218.17 miles, would be a pleasant winter afternoon
218.18 walk. Having seen Adele comfortably seated
218.19 in her little chair by Mrs. Fairfax's parlour
218.20 fireside, and given her her best wax doll
218.21 /which I usually kept enveloped in silver
218.22 paper in a drawer/ to play with, and a story--
218.23 book for change of amusement; and having re-
218.24 plied to her "Revenez bientot ma bonne amie,
218.25 ma chere Mdlle. Jeannette," with a kiss, I
218.26 set out.
218.27   The ground was hard, the air was still, my
218.28 road was lonely; I walked fast till I got warm,
219.01 and then I walked slowly to enjoy and analyze
219.02 the species of pleasure brooding for me in the
219.03 hour and situation. It was three o'clock;
219.04 the church bell tolled as I passed under the
219.05 belfry: the charm of the hour lay in its ap-
219.06 proaching dimness, in the low-gliding and
219.07 pale-beaming sun. I was a mile from Thorn-
219.08 field, in a lane noted for wild roses in summer,
219.09 for nuts and blackberries in autumn, and even
219.10 now possessing a few coral treasures in hips
219.11 and haws; but whose best winter delight lay in
219.12 its utter solitude and leafless repose. If a
219.13 breath of air stirred, it made no sound here;
219.14 for there was not a holly, not an evergreen to
219.15 rustle, and the stripped hawthorn and hazel
219.16 bushes were as still as the white, worn stones
219.17 which causewayed the middle of the path.
219.18 Far and wide, on each side, there were only
219.19 fields, where no cattle now browsed; and the
219.20 little brown birds which stirred occasionally in
219.21 the hedge, looked like single russet leaves that
219.22 had forgotten to drop.
219.23   This lane inclined up-hill all the way to
219.24 Hay: having reached the middle, I sat down
219.25 on a stile which led thence into a field. Ga-
219.26 thering my mantle about me, and sheltering
219.27 my hands in my muff, I did not feel the cold,
219.28 though it froze keenly; as was attested by a
220.01 sheet of ice covering the causeway, where a
220.02 little brooklet, now congealed, had overflowed
220.03 after a rapid thaw some days since. From my
220.04 seat I could look down on Thornfield: the
220.05 gray and battlemented hall was the principal
220.06 object in the vale below me; its woods and
220.07 dark rookery rose against the west. I lingered
220.08 till the sun went down amongst the trees, and
220.09 sank crimson and clear behind them. I then
220.10 turned eastward.
220.11   On the hill-top above me sat the rising
220.12 moon; pale yet as a cloud, but brightening
220.13 momently: she looked over Hay, which, half
220.14 lost in trees, sent up a blue smoke from its
220.15 few chimneys; it was yet a mile distant, but
220.16 in the absolute hush I could hear plainly its

220.17 thin murmurs of life. My ear too felt the
220.18 flow of currents; in what dales and depths I
220.19 could not tell: but there were many hills
220.20 beyond Hay, and doubtless many becks
220.21 threading their passes. That evening calm
220.22 betrayed alike the tinkle of the nearest
220.23 streams, the sough of the most remote.
220.24   A rude noise broke on these fine ripplings
220.25 and whisperings, at once so far away and so
220.26 clear: a positive tramp, tramp; a metallic
220.27 clatter, which effaced the soft wave-wander-
220.28 ings; as, in a picture, the solid mass of a crag,
221.01 or the rough boles of a great oak, drawn in
221.02 dark and strong on the foreground, efface the
221.03 aerial distance of azure hill, sunny horizon
221.04 and blended clouds, where tint melts into tint.
221.05   The din was on the causeway: a horse was
221.06 coming; the windings of the lane yet hid it,
221.07 but it approached. I was just leaving the stile;
221.08 yet as the path was narrow, I sat still to let
221.09 it go by. In those days I was young, and all
221.10 sorts of fancies bright and dark tenanted my
221.11 mind: the memories of nursery stories were
221.12 there amongst other rubbish; and when they
221.13 recurred, maturing youth added to them a
221.14 vigour and vividness beyond what childhood
221.15 could give. As this horse approached, and as
221.16 I watched for it to appear through the dusk,
221.17 I remembered certain of Bessie's tales wherein
221.18 figured a North-of-England spirit, called a
221.19 "Gytrash;" which, in the form of horse, mule,
221.20 or large dog, haunted solitary ways, and some-
221.21 times came upon belated travellers, as this
221.22 horse was now coming upon me.
221.23   It was very near, but not yet in sight; when,
221.24 in addition to the tramp, tramp, I heard a rush
221.25 under the hedge, and close down by the hazel
221.26 stems glided a great dog, whose black and
221.27 white colour made him a distinct object
221.28 against the trees. It was exactly one mask of
222.01 Bessie's Gytrash, -- a lion-like creature with
222.02 long hair and a huge head: it passed me,
222.03 however, quietly enough; not staying to look
222.04 up, with strange pretercanine eyes, in my
222.05 face, as I half expected it would. The horse
222.06 followed, -- a tall steed, and on its back a
222.07 rider. The man, the human being, broke the
222.08 spell at once. Nothing ever rode the Gytrash:
222.09 it was always alone; and goblins, to my
222.10 notions, though they might tenant the dumb
222.11 carcasses of beasts, could scarce covet shelter
222.12 in the common-place human form. No Gy-
222.13 trash was this, -- only a traveller taking the
222.14 short cut to Millcote. He passed, and I went
222.15 on; a few steps, and I turned: a sliding sound
222.16 and an exclamation of "What the deuce is to
222.17 do now?" and a clattering tumble, arrested
222.18 my attention. Man and horse were down;
222.19 they had slipped on the sheet of ice which
222.20 glazed the causeway. The dog came bounding
222.21 back, and seeing his master in a predicament,
222.22 and hearing the horse groan, barked till the
222.23 evening hills echoed the sound; which was
222.24 deep in proportion to his magnitude. He
222.25 snuffed round the prostrate group, and then
222.26 he ran up to me; it was all he could do, --
222.27 there was no other help at hand to summon.
222.28 I obeyed him, and walked down to the tra-
223.01 veller, by this time struggling himself free of
223.02 his steed. His efforts were so vigorous, I
223.03 thought he could not be much hurt; but I
223.04 asked him the question: --
223.05 "Are you injured, sir?"
223.06 I think he was swearing, but am not certain;
223.07 however, he was pronouncing some formula
223.08 which prevented him from replying to me
223.09 directly.
223.10 "Can I do anything?" I asked again.
223.11 "You must just stand on one side," he
223.12 answered as he rose, first to his knees, and
223.13 then to his feet. I did; whereupon began a
223.14 heaving, stamping, clattering process, accom-
223.15 panied by a barking and baying which removed
223.16 me effectually some yards distance; but I
223.17 would not be driven quite away till I saw the
223.18 event. This was finally fortunate; the horse
223.19 was re-established, and the dog was silenced
223.20 with a "Down Pilot!" The traveller now,
223.21 stooping, felt his foot and leg, as if trying
223.22 whether they were sound; apparently some-
223.23 thing ailed them, for he halted to the stile
223.24 whence I had just risen, and sat down.
223.25 I was in the mood for being useful, or at
223.26 least officious, I think, for I now drew near
223.27 him again.
223.28 "If you are hurt, and want help, sir, I can
224.01 fetch some one, either from Thornfield-Hall or
224.02 from Hay."
224.03 "Thank you; I shall do: I have no broken
224.04 bones, -- only a sprain;" and again he stood
224.05 up and tried his foot, but the result extorted
224.06 an involuntary "Ugh!"
224.07 Something of daylight still lingered, and
224.08 the moon was waxing bright; I could see
224.09 him plainly. His figure was enveloped in a
224.10 riding cloak, fur collared, and steel clasped;
224.11 its details were not apparent, but I traced the
224.12 general points of middle height, and con-
224.13 siderable breadth of chest. He had a dark
224.14 face, with stern features and a heavy brow;
224.15 his eyes and gathered eyebrows looked ireful

224.16 and thwarted just now; he was past youth,
224.17 but had not reached middle age: perhaps he
224.18 might be thirty-five. I felt no fear of him,
224.19 and but little shyness. Had he been a hand-
224.20 some, heroic-looking young gentleman, I
224.21 should not have dared to stand thus questioning
224.22 him against his will, and offering my services
224.23 unasked. I had hardly ever seen a handsome
224.24 youth: never in my life spoken to one. I had
224.25 a theoretical reverence and homage for beauty,
224.26 elegance, gallantry, fascination; but had I met
224.27 those qualities incarnate in masculine shape, I
224.28 should have known instinctively that they
225.01 neither had nor could have sympathy with
225.02 anything in me, and should have shunned
225.03 them as one would fire, lightning, or anything
225.04 else that is bright but antipathetic.
225.05   If even this stranger had smiled and been
225.06 good-humoured to me when I addressed him;
225.07 if he had put off my offer of assistance gaily
225.08 and with thanks, I should have gone on my
225.09 way and not felt any vocation to renew in-
225.10 quiries: but the frown, the roughness of the
225.11 traveller set me at my ease: I retained my
225.12 station when he waved to me to go, and an-
225.13 nounced: --
225.14   "I cannot think of leaving you, sir, at so
225.15 late an hour, in this solitary lane, till I see you
225.16 are fit to mount your horse."
225.17   He looked at me when I said this: he had
225.18 hardly turned his eyes in my direction before.
225.19   "I should think you ought to be at home
225.20 yourself," said he, "if you have a home in this
225.21 neighbourhood: where do you come from?"
225.22   "From just below; and I am not at all
225.23 afraid of being out late when it is moonlight:
225.24 I will run over to Hay for you with pleasure,
225.25 if you wish it -- indeed, I am going there to
225.26 post a letter."
225.27   "You live just below -- do you mean at
226.01 that house with the battlements?" pointing to
226.02 Thornfield-Hall, on which the moon cast a
226.03 hoary gleam, bringing it out distinct and pale
226.04 from the woods, that, by contrast with the
226.05 western sky, now seemed one mass of shadow.
226.06   "Yes, sir."
226.07   "Whose house is it?"
226.08   "Mr. Rochester's."
226.09   "Do you know Mr. Rochester?"
226.10   "No, I have never seen him."
226.11   "He is not resident then?"
226.12   "No."
226.13   "Can you tell me where he is?"
226.14   "I cannot."
226.15   "You are not a servant at the hall, of
226.16 course. You are --." He stopped, ran
226.17 his eye over my dress, which, as usual, was
226.18 quite simple: a black merino cloak, a black
226.19 beaver bonnet; neither of them half fine
226.20 enough for a lady's maid. He seemed puzzled
226.21 to decide what I was: I helped him.
226.22   "I am the governess."
226.23   "Ah, the governess!" he repeated; "deuce
226.24 take me, if I had not forgotten! the go-
226.25 verness!" and again my raiment underwent
226.26 scrutiny. In two minutes he rose from the
226.27 stile: his face expressed pain when he tried to
226.28 move.
227.01   "I cannot commission you to fetch help," he
227.02 said; "but you may help me a little yourself,
227.03 if you will be so kind."
227.04   "Yes, sir."
227.05   "You have not an umbrella that I can use
227.06 as a stick?"
227.07   "No."
227.08   "Try to get hold of my horse's bridle and
227.09 lead him to me: you are not afraid?"
227.10   I should have been afraid to touch a horse
227.11 when alone, but when told to do it, I was dis-
227.12 posed to obey. I put down my muff on the
227.13 stile, and went up to the tall steed; I en-
227.14 deavoured to catch the bridle, but it was a
227.15 spirited thing, and would not let me come
227.16 near its head; I made effort on effort, though
227.17 in vain: meantime, I was mortally afraid of
227.18 its trampling fore feet. The traveller waited
227.19 and watched for some time, and at last he
227.20 laughed.
227.21   "I see," he said, "the mountain will never
227.22 be brought to Mahomet, so all you can do is
227.23 to aid Mahomet to go to the mountain; I must
227.24 beg of you to come here."
227.25   I came -- "Excuse me;" he continued, "ne-
227.26 cessity compels me to make you useful." He
227.27 laid a heavy hand on my shoulder, and leaning
227.28 on me with some stress, limped to his horse.
228.01 Having once caught the bridle, he mastered it
228.02 directly, and sprang to his saddle; grimacing
228.03 grimly as he made the effort, for it wrenched
228.04 his sprain.
228.04   "Now," said he, releasing his under lip
228.05 from a hard bite, "just hand me my whip; it
228.06 lies there under the hedge."
228.07   I sought it and found it.
228.08   "Thank you; now make haste with the
228.09 letter to Hay, and return as fast as you can."
228.10   A touch of a spurred heel made his horse
228.11 first start and rear, and then bound away; the
228.12 dog rushed in his traces: all three vanished
228.13   "Like heath that in the wilderness
228.14   The wild wind whirls away."

228.15   I took up my muff and walked on. The
228.16 incident had occurred and was gone for me:
228.17 it was an incident of no moment, no romance,
228.18 no interest in a sense; yet it marked with
228.19 change one single hour of a monotonous life.
228.20 My help had been needed and claimed; I had
228.21 given it: I was pleased to have done some-
228.22 thing; trivial, transitory though the deed was,
228.23 it was yet an active thing, and I was weary of
228.24 an existence all passive. The new face, too,
228.25 was like a new picture introduced to the gal-
228.26 lery of memory; and it was dissimilar to all
228.27 others hanging there: firstly, because it
228.28 was masculine; and secondly, because it was
229.01 dark, strong, and stern. I had it still before
229.02 me when I entered Hay, and slipped the letter
229.03 into the post-office; I saw it as I walked fast
229.04 down hill all the way home. When I came
229.05 to the stile I stopped a minute, looked round
229.06 and listened; with an idea that a horse's hoofs
229.07 might ring on the causeway again, and that
229.08 a rider in a cloak, and a Gytrash-like New-
229.09 foundland dog, might be again apparent: I
229.10 saw only the hedge and a pollard willow before
229.11 me, rising up still and straight to meet the
229.12 moonbeams; I heard only the faintest waft
229.13 of wind, roaming fitful among the trees round
229.14 Thornfield, a mile distant; and when I glanced
229.15 down in the direction of the murmur, my eye,
229.16 traversing the hall-front, caught a light kind-
229.17 ling in a window: it reminded me that I was
229.18 late, and I hurried on.
229.19   I did not like re-entering Thornfield. To
229.20 pass its threshold was to return to stagnation:
229.21 to cross the silent hall, to ascend the darksome
229.22 staircase, to seek my own lonely little room,
229.23 and then to meet tranquil Mrs. Fairfax, and
229.24 spend the long winter evening with her, and
229.25 her only, was to quell wholly the faint ex-
229.26 citement wakened by my walk, -- to slip again
229.27 over my faculties the viewless fetters of an uni-
229.28 form and too still existence; of an existence
230.01 whose very privileges of security and ease I
230.02 was becoming incapable of appreciating. What
230.03 good it would have done me at that time to
230.04 have been tossed in the storms of an uncertain
230.05 struggling life, and to have been taught by
230.06 rough and bitter experience to long for the
230.07 calm amidst which I now repined! Yes, just
230.08 as much good as it would do a man tired of
230.09 sitting still in a "too easy chair" to take a
230.10 long walk: and just as natural was the wish
230.11 to stir, under my circumstances, as it would
230.12 be under his.
230.13   I lingered at the gates; I lingered on the
230.14 lawn; I paced backwards and forwards on the
230.15 pavement: the shutters of the glass door were
230.16 closed; I could not see into the interior; and
230.17 both my eyes and spirit seemed drawn from
230.18 the gloomy house -- from the gray hollow filled
230.19 with rayless cells, as it appeared to me -- to that
230.20 sky expanded before me, -- a blue sea absolved
230.21 from taint of cloud; the moon ascending it in
230.22 solemn march; her orb seeming to look up
230.23 as she left the hill tops, from behind which she
230.24 had come, far and farther below her, and as-
230.25 pired to the zenith, midnight-dark in its fathom-
230.26 less depth and measureless distance: and for
230.27 those trembling stars that followed her course,
230.28 they made my heart tremble, my veins glow
231.01 when I viewed them. Little things recall us
231.02 to earth: the clock struck in the hall; that
231.03 sufficed; I turned from moon and stars, opened
231.04 a side-door and went in.
231.05   The hall was not dark, nor yet was it lit,
231.06 only by the high-hung bronze lamp: a warm
231.07 glow suffused both it and the lower steps of
231.08 the oak staircase. This ruddy shine issued
231.09 from the great dining-room, whose two-leaved
231.10 door stood open and showed a genial fire in
231.11 the grate, glancing on marble hearth and brass
231.12 fire-irons, and revealing purple draperies and
231.13 polished furniture in the most pleasant ra-
231.14 diance. It revealed, too, a group near the
231.15 mantelpiece: I had scarcely caught it, and
231.16 scarcely become aware of a cheerful mingling
231.17 of voices, amongst which I seemed to dis-
231.18 tinguish the tones of Adele, when the door
231.19 closed.
231.20   I hastened to Mrs. Fairfax's room: there
231.21 was a fire there, too; but no candle, and no
231.22 Mrs. Fairfax. Instead, all alone, sitting up-
231.23 right on the rug, and gazing with gravity at
231.24 the blaze, I beheld a great black and white
231.25 long-haired dog, just like the Gytrash of the
231.26 lane. It was so like it that I went forward
231.27 and said --
231.28   "Pilot," and the thing got up and came to
232.01 me and snuffed me. I caressed him, and he
232.02 wagged his great tail: but he looked an eerie
232.03 creature to be alone with, and I could not tell
232.04 whence he had come. I rang the bell, for I
232.05 wanted a candle; and I wanted, too, to get an
232.06 account of this visitant. Leah entered.
232.07   "What dog is this?"
232.08   "He came with master."
232.09   "With whom?"
232.10   "With master -- Mr. Rochester -- he is just
232.11 arrived."
232.12   "Indeed! and is Mrs. Fairfax with him?"
232.13   "Yes, and Miss Adela; they are in the

232.14 dining-room, and John is gone for a surgeon:
232.15 for master has had an accident; his horse fell
232.16 and his ankle is sprained."
232.17 "Did the horse fall in Hay-lane?"
232.18 "Yes, coming down hill; it slipped on some
232.19 ice."
232.20 "Ah! Bring me a candle, will you, Leah?"
232.21 Leah brought it; she entered, followed by
232.22 Mrs. Fairfax, who repeated the news; adding
232.23 that Mr. Carter the surgeon was come and
232.24 was now with Mr. Rochester: then she hur-
232.25 ried out to give orders about tea, and I went
232.26 up stairs to take off my things.
233.01 [Vol. 1 Chapter 13]
233.02 Mr. Rochester, it seems, by the surgeon's
233.03 orders, went to bed early that night; nor did
233.04 he rise soon next morning. When he did
233.05 come down, it was to attend to business: his
233.06 agent and some of his tenants were arrived,
233.07 and waiting to speak with him.
233.08 Adele and I had now to vacate the library:
233.09 it would be in daily requisition as a reception--
233.10 room for callers. A fire was lit in an apart-
233.11 ment up stairs, and there I carried our books,
233.12 and arranged it for the future school-room. I
233.13 discerned in the course of the morning that
233.14 Thornfield-Hall was a changed place: no
233.15 longer silent as a church, it echoed every hour
233.16 or two to a knock at the door or a clang of
233.17 the bell; steps, too, often traversed the hall,
233.18 and new voices spoke in different keys below:
233.19 a rill from the outer world was flowing through
234.01 it; it had a master: for my part, I liked it
234.02 better.
234.03 Adele was not easy to teach that day; she
234.04 could not apply: she kept running to the door
234.05 and looking over the banisters to see if she
234.06 could get a glimpse of Mr. Rochester; then
234.07 she coined pretexts to go down stairs, in order,
234.08 as I shrewdly suspected, to vist the library,
234.09 where I knew she was not wanted; then,
234.10 when I got a little angry, and made her sit
234.11 still, she continued to talk incessantly of her
234.12 "ami, Monsieur Edouard Fairfax de Rochester,"
234.13 as she dubbed him /I had not before heard his
234.14 prenomens/, and to conjecture what presents
234.15 he had brought her: for it appears he had
234.16 intimated the night before that when his lug-
234.17 gage came from Millcote, there would be found
234.18 amongst it a little box in whose contents she
234.19 had an interest.
234.20 "Et cela doit signifier," said she, "qu'il y
234.21 aura la dedans un cadeau pour moi, et peut etre
234.22 pour vous aussi, mademoiselle. Monsieur a
234.23 parle de vous: il m'a demande le nom de ma
234.24 gouvernante, et si elle n'etait pas une petite
234.25 personne, assez mince et un peu pale. J'ai dit
234.26 qu'oui: car c'est vrai, n'est-ce pas, made-
234.27 moiselle?"
234.28 I and my pupil dined as usual in Mrs.
235.01 Fairfax's parlour; the afternoon was wild and
235.02 snowy, and we passed it in the school-room.
235.03 At dark I allowed Adele to put away books
235.04 and work, and to run down stairs; for, from
235.05 the comparative silence below, and from the
235.06 cessation of appeals to the door-bell, I conjec-
235.07 tured that Mr. Rochester was now at liberty.
235.08 Left alone, I walked to the window; but nothing
235.09 was to be seen thence: twilight and snow--
235.10 flakes together thickened the air, and hid the
235.11 very shrubs on the lawn. I let down the cur-
235.12 tain and went back to the fireside.
235.13 In the clear embers I was tracing a view,
235.14 not unlike a picture I remembered to have
235.15 seen of the castle of Heidelberg, on the Rhine,
235.16 when Mrs. Fairfax came in: breaking up by
235.17 her entrance the fiery mosaic I had been
235.18 piecing together, and scattering too some
235.19 heavy, unwelcome thoughts that were begin-
235.20 ning to throng on my solitude.
235.21 "Mr. Rochester would be glad if you and
235.22 your pupil would take tea with him in the
235.23 drawing-room this evening," said she: "he
235.24 has been so much engaged all day that he
235.25 could not ask to see you before."
235.26 "when is his tea-time?" I inquired.
235.27 "Oh, at six o'clock: he keeps early hours
235.28 in the country. You had better change your
236.01 frock now; I will go with you and fasten it.
236.02 Here is a candle."
236.03 "Is it necessary to change my frock?"
236.04 "Yes, you had better: I always dress for the
236.05 evening when Mr. Rochester is here."
236.06 This additional ceremony seemed somewhat
236.07 stately: however, I repaired to my room, and,
236.08 with Mrs. Fairfax's aid, replaced my black
236.09 stuff dress by one of black silk; the best and
236.10 the only additional one I had, except one of
236.11 light gray, which, in my Lowood notions of
236.12 the toilette, I thought too fine to be worn,
236.13 except on first-rate occasions.
236.14 "You want a brooch," said Mrs. Fairfax.
236.15 I had a single little pearl ornament which
236.16 Miss Temple gave me as a parting keepsake:
236.17 I put it on, and then we went down stairs.
236.18 Unused as I was to strangers, it was rather a
236.19 trial to appear thus formally summoned in
236.20 Mr. Rochester's presence. I let Mrs. Fairfax
236.21 precede me into the dining-room, and kept
236.22 in her shade as we crossed that apartment;
236.23 and, passing the arch, whose curtain was now

236.24 dropped, entered the elegant recess beyond.
236.25 Two wax candles stood lighted on the table,
236.26 and two on the mantelpiece; basking in the
236.27 light and heat of a superb fire, lay Pilot --
236.28 Adele knelt near him. Half reclined on a
237.01 couch appeared Mr. Rochester, his foot sup-
237.02 ported by the cushion; he was looking at
237.03 Adele and the dog: the fire shone full on his
237.04 face. I knew my traveller with his broad and
237.05 jetty eyebrows; his square forehead, made
237.06 squarer by the horizontal sweep of his black
237.07 hair. I recognised his decisive nose, more
237.08 remarkable for character than beauty; his full
237.09 nostrils, denoting, I thought, choler; his grim
237.10 mouth, chin, and jaw -- yes, all three were
237.11 very grim, and no mistake. His shape, now
237.12 divested of cloak, I perceived harmonized in
237.13 squareness with his physiognomy: I suppose
237.14 it was a good figure in the athletic sense of
237.15 the term -- broad chested and thin flanked;
237.16 though neither tall nor graceful.
237.17 Mr. Rochester must have been aware of the
237.18 entrance of Mrs. Fairfax and myself; but
237.19 it appeared he was not in the mood to
237.20 notice us, for he never lifted his head as we
237.21 approached.
237.22 "Here is Miss Eyre, sir," said Mrs. Fair-
237.23 fax, in her quiet way. He bowed; still not
237.24 taking his eyes from the group of the dog and
237.25 child.
237.26 "Let Miss Eyre be seated," said he: and
237.27 there was something in the forced stiff bow,
237.28 in the impatient yet formal tone, which
238.01 seemed further to express, "what the deuce is
238.02 it to me whether Miss Eyre be there or not?
238.03 At this moment I am not disposed to accost
238.04 her."
238.05 I sat down quite disembarrassed. A recep-
238.06 tion of finished politeness would probably have
238.07 confused me: I could not have returned or
238.08 repaid it by answering grace and elegance on
238.09 my part; but harsh caprice laid me under no
238.10 obligation; on the contrary, a decent quies-
238.11 cence, under the freak of manner, gave me
238.12 the advantage. Besides, the eccentricity of
238.13 the proceeding was piquant: I felt interested
238.14 to see how he would go on.
238.15 He went on as a statue would: that is, he
238.16 neither spoke nor moved. Mrs. Fairfax
238.17 seemed to think it necessary that some one
238.18 should be amiable, and she began to talk.
238.19 Kindly, as usual -- and, as usual, rather trite --
238.20 she condoled with him on the pressure of
238.21 business he had had all day; on the annoy-
238.22 ance it must have been to him with that pain-
238.23 ful sprain: then she commenced his patience
238.24 and perseverance in going through with it.
238.25 "Madam, I should like some tea," was the
238.26 sole rejoinder she got. She hastened to ring
238.27 the bell; and, when the tray came, she pro-
238.28 ceeded to arrange the cups, spoons, &c., with
239.01 assiduous celerity. I and Adele went to the
239.02 table; but the master did not leave his couch.
239.03 "will you hand Mr. Rochester's cup?" said
239.04 Mrs. Fairfax to me; "Adele might perhaps
239.05 spill it."
239.06 I did as requested. As he took the cup
239.07 from my hand, Adele, thinking the moment
239.08 propitious for making a request in my favour,
239.09 cried out: --
239.10 "N'est-ce pas, Monsieur, qu'il y a un cadeau
239.11 pour Mademoiselle Eyre, dans votre petit
239.12 coffre?"
239.13 "who talks of cadeaux?" said he gruffly:
239.14 "did you expect a present, Miss Eyre? Are
239.15 you fond of presents?" and he searched my
239.16 face with eyes that I saw were dark, irate, and
239.17 piercing.
239.18 "I hardly know, sir; I have little expe-
239.19 rience of them: they are generally thought
239.20 pleasing things."
239.21 "Generally thought? But what do you
239.22 think?"
239.23 "I should be obliged to take time, sir, before
239.24 I could give you an answer worthy of your ac-
239.25 ceptance: a present has many faces to it, has
239.26 it not? and one should consider all, before
239.27 pronouncing an opinion as to its nature."
239.28 "Miss Eyre, you are not so unsophisticated
240.01 as Adele: she demands a 'cadeau,' clamor-
240.02 ously the moment she sees me; you beat
240.03 about the bush."
240.04 "Because I have less confidence in my
240.05 deserts than Adele has: she can prefer the
240.06 claim of old acquaintance, and the right too of
240.07 custom; for she says you have always been in
240.08 the habit of giving her playthings; but if I
240.09 had to make out a case I should be puzzled,
240.10 since I am a stranger and have done nothing
240.11 to entitle me to an acknowledgment."
240.12 "Oh, don't fall back on over-modesty! I
240.13 have examined Adele, and find you have taken
240.14 great pains with her: she is not bright, she
240.15 has no talents; yet in a short time she has
240.16 made much improvement."
240.17 "Sir, you have now given me my 'cadeau';
240.18 I am obliged to you: it is the meed teachers
240.19 most covet; praise of their pupil's progress."
240.20 "Humph!" said Mr. Rochester, and he
240.21 took his tea in silence.
240.22 "Come to the fire," said the master, when

240.23 the tray was taken away and Mrs. Fairfax
240.24 had settled into a corner with her knitting;
240.25 while Adele was leading me by the hand
240.26 round the room, showing me the beautiful
240.27 books and ornaments on the consoles and
240.28 chiffonieres. We obeyed, as in duty bound;
241.01 Adele wanted to take a seat on my knee, but
241.02 she was ordered to amuse herself with
241.03 Pilot.
241.04 "You have been resident in my house three
241.05 months?"
241.06 "Yes, sir."
241.07 "And you came from --?"
241.08 "From Lowood school in --shire."
241.09 "Ah! a charitable concern. -- How long
241.10 were you there?"
241.11 "Eight years."
241.12 "Eight years! you must be tenacious of
241.13 life. I thought half the time in such a place
241.14 would have done up any constitution! No
241.15 wonder you have rather the look of another
241.16 world. I marvelled where you had got that
241.17 sort of face. when you came on me in Hay
241.18 Lane last night, I thought unaccountably of
241.19 fairy tales, and had half a mind to demand
241.20 whether you had bewitched my horse: I am
241.21 not sure yet. who are your parents?"
241.22 "I have none."
241.23 "Nor ever had, I suppose: do you remem-
241.24 ber them?"
241.25 "No."
241.26 "I thought not. And so you were wait-
241.27 ing for your people when you sat on that
241.28 stile?"
242.01 "For whom, sir?"
242.02 "For the men in green: it was a proper
242.03 moonlight evening for them. Did I break
242.04 through one of your rings, that you spread that
242.05 damned ice on the causeway?"
242.06 I shook my head. "The men in green all
242.07 forsook England a hundred years ago," said
242.08 I, speaking as seriously as he had done. "And
242.09 not even in Hay Lane or the fields about it
242.10 could you find a trace of them. I don't think
242.11 either summer or harvest, or winter moon, will
242.12 ever shine on their revels more."
242.13 Mrs. Fairfax had dropped her knitting, and
242.14 with raised eyebrows, seemed wondering what
242.15 sort of talk this was.
242.16 "well," resumed Mr. Rochester, "if you
242.17 disown parents, you must have some sort of
242.18 kinsfolk: uncles and aunts?"
242.19 "No; none that I ever saw."
242.20 "And your home?"
242.21 "I have none."
242.22 "where do your brothers and sisters live?"
242.23 "I have no brothers or sisters."
242.24 "who recommended you to come here?"
242.25 "I advertised, and Mrs. Fairfax answered
242.26 my advertisement."
242.27 "Yes," said the good lady, who now knew
242.28 what ground we were upon, "and I am daily
243.01 thankful for the choice Providence led me to
243.02 make. Miss Eyre has been an invaluable
243.03 companion to me, and a kind and careful
243.04 teacher to Adele."
243.05 "Don't trouble yourself to give her a cha-
243.06 racter," returned Mr. Rochester: "eulogiums
243.07 will not bias me; I shall judge for myself.
243.08 She began by felling my horse."
243.09 "Sir?" said Mrs. Fairfax.
243.10 "I have to thank her for this sprain."
243.11 The widow looked bewildered.
243.12 "Miss Eyre, have you ever lived in a town?"
243.13 "No, sir."
243.14 "Have you seen much society?"
243.15 "None but the pupils and teachers of
243.16 Lowood; and now the inmates of Thorn-
243.17 field."
243.18 "Have you read much?"
243.19 "Only such books as came in my way; and
243.20 they have not been numerous or very learned."
243.21 "You have lived the life of a nun: no doubt
243.22 you are well drilled in religious forms; --
243.23 brocklehurst, who I understand directs Lo-
243.24 wood, is a parson, is he not?"
243.25 "Yes, sir."
243.26 "And you girls probably worshipped him
243.27 as a convent full of religieuses would worship
243.28 their director."
244.01 "Oh, no."
244.02 "You are very cool! No! What! a no-
244.03 vice not worship her priest? That sounds
244.04 blasphemous."
244.05 "I disliked Mr. Brocklehurst; and I was
244.06 not alone in the feeling. He is a harsh man;
244.07 at once pompous and meddling: he cut off
244.08 our hair; and for economy's sake, bought us
244.09 bad needles and thread, with which we could
244.10 hardly sew."
244.11 "That was very false economy," remarked
244.12 Mrs. Fairfax, who now again caught the drift
244.13 of the dialogue.
244.14 "And was that the head and front of his
244.15 offending?" demanded Mr. Rochester.
244.16 "He starved us when he had the sole
244.17 superintendence of the provision department,
244.18 before the committee was appointed; and he
244.19 bored us with long lectures once a week, and
244.20 with evening readings from books of his own
244.21 inditing, about sudden deaths and judgments,

244.22 which made us afraid to go to bed."
244.23 "What age were you when you went to
244.24 Lowood?"
244.25 "About ten."
244.26 "And you stayed there eight years: you
244.27 are now, then, eighteen?"
244.28 I assented.
245.01 "Arithmetic, you see, is useful: without its
245.02 aid, I should have guessed your age. It is a point difficult to
245.03 fix where the features and countenance are
245.04 so much at variance as in your case. And
245.05 now, what did you learn at Lowood? Can
245.06 you play?"
245.07 "A little."
245.08 "Of course: that is the established answer.
245.09 Go into the library -- I mean, if you please. --
245.10 /Excuse my tone of command; I am used to
245.11 say `Do this,` and it is done: I cannot alter
245.12 my customary habits for one new inmate./ --
245.13 Go, then, into the library; take a candle with
245.14 you; leave the door open; sit down to the
245.15 piano, and play a tune."
245.16 I departed, obeying his directions.
245.17 "Enough!" he called out in a few minutes.
245.18 "You play a little, I see; like any other
245.19 English school-girl: perhaps rather better
245.20 than some, but not well."
245.21 I closed the piano, and returned. Mr.
245.22 Rochester continued.
245.23 "Adele showed me some sketches this
245.24 morning, which she said were yours. I don't
245.25 know whether they were entirely of your
245.26 doing: probably a master aided you?"
245.27 "No, indeed!" I interjected.
246.01 "Ah! that pricks pride. Well, fetch me
246.02 your portfolio, if you can vouch for its contents
246.03 being original; but don't pass your word un-
246.04 less you are certain: I can recognise patch-
246.05 work."
246.06 "Then I will say nothing, and you shall
246.07 judge for yourself, sir."
246.08 I brought the portfolio from the library.
246.09 "Approach the table," said he; and I
246.10 wheeled it to his couch. Adele and Mrs.
246.11 Fairfax drew near to see the pictures.
246.12 "No crowding," said Mr. Rochester: "take
246.13 the drawings from my hand as I finish with
246.14 them; but don't push your faces up to mine."
246.15 He deliberately scrutinized each sketch and
246.16 painting. Three he laid aside; the others,
246.17 when he had examined them, he swept from
246.18 him.
246.19 "Take them off to the other table, Mrs.
246.20 Fairfax," said he, "and look at them with
246.21 Adele; -- you" /glancing at me/ "resume your
246.22 seat, and answer my questions. I perceive these
246.23 pictures were done by one hand: was that hand
246.24 yours?"
246.25 "Yes."
246.26 "And when did you find time to do them?
246.27 They have taken much time, and some
246.28 thought."
247.01 "I did them in the last two vacations I
247.02 spent at Lowood, when I had no other occu-
247.03 pation."
247.04 "where did you get your copies?"
247.05 "Out of my head."
247.06 "That head I see now on your shoulders?"
247.07 "Yes, sir."
247.08 "Has it other furniture of the same kind
247.09 within?"
247.10 "I should think it may have: I should hope
247.11 -- better."
247.12 He spread the pictures before him, and
247.13 again surveyed them alternately.
247.14 while he is so occupied, I will tell you,
247.15 reader, what they are: and first, I must pre-
247.16 mise that they are nothing wonderful. The
247.17 subjects had indeed risen vividly on my mind.
247.18 As I saw them with the spiritual eye, before I
247.19 attempted to embody them, they were striking;
247.20 but my hand would not second my fancy, and
247.21 in each case it had wrought out but a pale por-
247.22 trait of the thing I had conceived.
247.23 The pictures were in water colours. The
247.24 first represented clouds low and livid, rolling
247.25 over a swollen sea: all the distanceclipse; so, too, was the foregro
247.26 the nearest billows, for there was no land.
247.27 One gleam of light lifted into relief a half--
248.01 submerged mast, on which sat a cormorant,
248.02 dark and large, with wings flecked with foam;
248.03 its beak held a gold bracelet, set with gems,
248.04 that I had touched with as brilliant tints as
248.05 my palette could yield, and as glittering dis-
248.06 tinctness as my pencil could impart. Sink-
248.07 ing below the bird and mast, a drowned corpse
248.08 glanced through the green water; a fair arm
248.09 was the only limb clearly visible, whence the
248.10 bracelet had been washed or torn.
248.11 The second picture contained for foreground
248.12 only the dim peak of a hill, with grass and
248.13 some leaves slanting as if by a breeze. Beyond
248.14 and above spread an expanse of sky, dark blue
248.15 as at twilight: rising into the sky, was a
248.16 woman's shape to the bust, portrayed in tints
248.17 as dusk and soft as I could combine. The
248.18 dim forehead was crowned with a star; the
248.19 lineaments below were seen as through the
248.20 suffusion of vapour; the eyes shone dark and
248.21 wild; the hair streamed shadowy, like a beam-
248.22 less cloud torn by storm or by electric travail.

248.23 On the neck lay a pale reflection like moon--
248.24 light; the same faint lustre touched the train
248.25 of thin clouds from which rose and bowed this
248.26 vision of the Evening Star.
248.27 The third showed the pinnacle of an ice-
248.28 berg piercing a polar winter sky: a muster of
249.01 northern lights reared their dim lances, close
249.02 serried, along the horizon. Throwing these
249.03 into distance, rose, in the foreground, a head, --
249.04 a colossal head, inclined towards the iceberg,
249.05 and resting against it. Two thin hands, joined
249.06 under the forehead, and supporting it, drew
249.07 up before the lower features a sable veil; a
249.08 brow quite bloodless, white as bone, and an
249.09 eye hollow and fixed, blank of meaning but
249.10 for the glassiness of despair, alone were visible.
249.11 Above the temples, amidst wreathed turban
249.12 folds of black drapery, vague in its character
249.13 and consistency as cloud, gleamed a ring of
249.14 white flame, gemmed with sparkles of a more
249.15 lurid tinge. This pale crescent was "The like-
249.16 ness of a Kingly Crown;" what it diademed
249.17 was "the shape which shape had none."
249.18 "Were you happy when you painted these
249.19 pictures?" asked Mr. Rochester, presently.
249.20 "I was absorbed, sir: yes, and I was happy.
249.21 To paint them, in short, was to enjoy one of
249.22 the keenest pleasures I have ever known."
249.23 "That is not saying much. Your pleasures,
249.24 by your own account, have been few; but I
249.25 daresay you did exist in a kind of artist's
249.26 dreamland while you blent and arranged these
249.27 strange tints. Did you sit at them long each
249.28 day?"
250.01 "I had nothing else to do, because it was
250.02 the vacation, and I sat at them from morning
250.03 till noon, and from noon till night: the length
250.04 of the midsummer days favoured my inclina-
250.05 tion to apply."
250.06 "And you felt self-satisfied with the result
250.07 of your ardent labours?"
250.08 "Far from it. I was tormented by the
250.09 contrast between my idea and my handiwork:
250.10 in each case I had imagined something which
250.11 I was quite powerless to realize."
250.12 "Not quite: -- you have secured the shadow
250.13 of your thought; but no more, probably. You
250.14 had not enough of the artist's skill and science
250.15 to give it full being: yet the drawings are, for
250.16 a school girl, peculiar. As to the thoughts,
250.17 they are elfish. These eyes in the Evening
250.18 Star you must have seen in a dream. How
250.19 could you make them look so clear, and yet
250.20 not at all brilliant? for the planet above quells
250.21 their rays. And what meaning is that in
250.22 their solemn depth? And who taught you to
250.23 paint wind? There is a high gale in that sky,
250.24 and on this hill-top. Where did you see Lat-
250.25 mos? For that is Latmos. There, -- put the
250.26 drawings away!"
250.27 I had scarce tied the strings of the port-
250.28 folio, when, looking at his watch, he said
250.29 abruptly --
251.01 "It is nine o'clock: what are you about,
251.02 Miss Eyre, to let Adele sit up so long? Take
251.03 her to bed."
251.04 Adele went to kiss him before quitting the
251.05 room: he endured the caress, but scarcely
251.06 seemed to relish it more than Pilot would
251.07 have done, nor so much.
251.08 "I wish you all good-night, now," said he,
251.09 making a movement of the hand towards the
251.10 door, in token that he was tired of our com-
251.11 pany, and wished to dismiss us. Mrs. Fairfax
251.12 folded up her knitting: I took my portfolio:
251.13 we curtseyed to him, received a frigid bow in
251.14 return, and so withdrew.
251.15 "You said Mr. Rochester was not strik-
251.16 ingly peculiar, Mrs. Fairfax," I observed, when
251.17 I rejoined her in her room, after putting Adele
251.18 to bed.
251.19 "Well, is he?"
251.20 "I think so: he is very changeful and
251.21 abrupt."
251.22 "True: no doubt he may appear so to a
251.23 stranger, but I am so accustomed to his
251.24 manner, I never think of it; and then, if he
251.25 has peculiarities of temper, allowance should
251.26 be made."
251.27 "Why?"
251.28 "Partly, because it is his nature -- and we
252.01 can none of us help our nature; and partly,
252.02 he has painful thoughts, no doubt, to harass
252.03 him, and make his spirits unequal."
252.04 "What about?"
252.05 "Family troubles, for one thing."
252.06 "But he has no family."
252.07 "Not now; but he has had -- or, at least,
252.08 relatives. He lost his elder brother a few
252.09 years since."
252.10 "His elder brother?"
252.11 "Yes. The present Mr. Rochester has not
252.12 been very long in possession of the property:
252.13 only about nine years."
252.14 "Nine years is a tolerable time. Was he
252.15 so very fond of his brother as to be still
252.16 inconsolable for his loss?"
252.17 "Why, no -- perhaps not. I believe there
252.18 were some misunderstandings between them.
252.19 Mr. Rowland Rochester was not quite just to
252.20 Mr. Edward; and perhaps he prejudiced his

252.21 father against him. The old gentleman was
252.22 fond of money, and anxious to keep the family
252.23 estate together. He did not like to diminish
252.24 the property by division, and yet he was
252.25 anxious that Mr. Edward should have wealth,
252.26 too, to keep up the consequence of the name;
252.27 and soon after he was of age, some steps were
252.28 taken that were not quite fair, and made a
253.01 great deal of mischief. Old Mr. Rochester
253.02 and Mr. Rowland combined to bring Mr. Ed-
253.03 ward into what he considered a painful posi-
253.04 tion, for the sake of making his fortune: what
253.05 the precise nature of that position was I never
253.06 clearly knew, but his spirit could not brook
253.07 what he had to suffer in it. He is not very
253.08 forgiving: he broke with his family, and now
253.09 for many years he has led an unsettled kind
253.10 of life. I don't think he has ever been re-
253.11 sident at Thornfield for a fortnight together,
253.12 since the death of his brother without a will,
253.13 left him master of the estate: and, indeed, no
253.14 wonder he shuns the old place."
253.15 "Why should he shun it?"
253.16 The answer was evasive -- I should have
253.17 liked something clearer; but Mrs. Fairfax
253.18 either could not, or would not, give me more
253.19 explicit information of the origin and nature
253.20 of Mr. Rochester's trials. She averred they
253.21 were a mystery to herself, and that what she
253.22 knew was chiefly from conjecture. It was
253.23 evident, indeed, that she wished me to drop
253.24 the subject; which I did accordingly.
254.01 [Vol. 1 Chapter 14]
254.02 For several subsequent days I saw little of
254.03 Mr. Rochester. In the mornings he seemed
254.04 much engaged with business, and in the after-
254.05 noon, gentlemen from Millcote or the neigh-
254.06 bourhood called, and sometimes stayed to dine
254.07 with him, when his sprain was well enough
254.08 to admit of horse exercise, he rode out a good
254.09 deal; probably to return these visits, as he
254.10 generally did not come back till late at night.
254.11 During this interval, even Adele was seldom
254.12 sent for to his presence, and all my acquaint-
254.13 ance with him was confined to an occasional
254.14 rencontre in the hall, on the stairs, or in the
254.15 gallery; when he would sometimes pass me
254.16 haughtily and coldly, just acknowledging my
254.17 presence by a distant nod or a cool glance,
254.18 and sometimes bow and smile with gentle-
254.19 manlike affability. His changes of mood did
254.20 not offend me, because I saw that I had
255.01 nothing to do with their alternation; the ebb
255.02 and flow depended on causes quite discon-
255.03 nected with me.
255.04 One day he had had company to dinner,
255.05 and had sent for my portfolio; in order, doubt-
255.06 less, to exhibit its contents: the gentlemen
255.07 went away early, to attend a public meeting at
255.08 Millcote, as Mrs. Fairfax informed me; but the
255.09 night being wet and inclement, Mr. Rochester
255.10 did not accompany them. Soon after they
255.11 were gone, he rang the bell: a message came
255.12 that I and Adele were to go down stairs. I
255.13 brushed Adele's hair and made her neat, and
255.14 having ascertained that I was myself in my
255.15 usual Quaker trim, where there was nothing to
255.16 retouch -- all being too close and plain, braided
255.17 locks included, to admit of disarrangement --
255.18 we descended; Adele wondering whether the
255.19 petit coffre was at length come: for owing to
255.20 some mistake, its arrival had hitherto been de-
255.21 layed. She was gratified: there stood, a
255.22 little carton, on the table when we entered the
255.23 dining-room. She appeared to know it by
255.24 instinct.
255.25 "Ma boite! ma boite!" exclaimed she, run-
255.26 ning towards it.
255.27 "Yes -- there is your `boite' at last: take it
255.28 into a corner, you genuine daughter of Paris,
256.01 and amuse yourself with disembowelling it,"
256.02 said the deep and rather sarcastic voice of Mr.
256.03 Rochester, proceeding from the depths of an
256.04 immense easy-chair at the fire-side. "And
256.05 mind," he continued, "don't bother me with
256.06 any details of the anatomical process, or any
256.07 notice of the condition of the entrails: let your
256.08 operation be conducted in silence -- tiens-toi
256.09 tranquille, enfant; comprenus-tu?"
256.10 Adele seemed scarcely to need the warning;
256.11 she had already retired to a sofa with her trea-
256.12 sure, and was busy untying the cord which
256.13 secured the lid. Having removed this impedi-
256.14 ment, and lifted certain silvery envelopes of
256.15 tissue paper, she merely exclaimed: --
256.16 "Oh, Ciel! Que c'est beau!" and then re-
256.17 mained absorbed in ecstatic contemplation.
256.18 "Is Miss Eyre, there?" now demanded the
256.19 master, half rising from his seat to look round
256.20 to the door, near which I still stood.
256.21 "Ah! well; come forward: be seated here."
256.22 He drew a chair near his own. "I am not
256.23 fond of the prattle of children," he continued;
256.24 "for, old bachelor as I am, I have no pleasant
256.25 associations connected with their lisp. It would
256.26 be intolerable to me to pass a whole evening
256.27 tete a tete with a brat. Don't draw that chair
256.28 further off, Miss Eyre; sit down exactly where
257.01 I placed it -- if you please, that is. Confound
257.02 these civilities! I continually forget them.
257.03 Nor do I particularly affect simple-minded old

257.04 ladies. By-the-by, I must have in mine; it
257.05 won't do to neglect her: she is a Fairfax, or
257.06 wed to one; and blood is said to be thicker
257.07 than water."
257.08 He rang and despatched an invitation to
257.09 Mrs. Fairfax, who soon arrived, knitting--
257.10 basket in hand.
257.11 "Good-evening, madam; I sent to you for
257.12 a charitable purpose: I have forbidden Adele
257.13 to talk to me about her presents, and she is
257.14 bursting with repletion; have the goodness
257.15 to serve her as auditress and interlocutrice:
257.16 it will be one of the most benevolent acts you
257.17 ever performed."
257.18 Adele, indeed, no sooner saw Mrs. Fairfax,
257.19 than she summoned her to her sofa, and there
257.20 quickly filled her lap with the porcelain, the
257.21 ivory, the waxen contents of her "boite;"
257.22 pouring out, meantime, explanations and rap-
257.23 tures in such broken English as she was mis-
257.24 tress of.
257.25 "Now I have performed the part of a good
257.26 host," pursued Mr. Rochester; "put my guests
257.27 into the way of amusing each other, I ought
257.28 to be at liberty to attend to my own pleasure.
258.01 Miss Eyre, draw your chair still a little fur-
258.02 ther forward: you are yet too far back; I
258.03 cannot see you without disturbing my position
258.04 in this comfortable chair, which I have no
258.05 mind to do."
258.06 I did as I was bid; though I would much
258.07 rather have remained somewhat in the shade:
258.08 but Mr. Rochester had such a direct way of
258.09 giving orders, it seemed a matter of course to
258.10 obey him promptly.
258.11 We were, as I have said, in the dining--
258.12 room: the lustre, which had been lit for dinner,
258.13 filled the room with a festal breadth of light;
258.14 the large fire was all red and clear; the purple
258.15 curtains hung rich and ample before the lofty
258.16 window and loftier arch: everything was still,
258.17 save the subdued chat of Adele /she dared not
258.18 speak loud/, and, filling up each pause, the
258.19 beating of winter rain against the panes.
258.20 Mr. Rochester, as he sat in his damask--
258.21 covered chair, looked different to what I had
258.22 seen him look before, -- not quite so stern;
258.23 much less gloomy. There was a smile on his
258.24 lips, and his eyes sparkled, whether with wine
258.25 or not, I am not sure; but I think it very
258.26 probable. He was, in short, in his after--
258.27 dinner-mood; more expanded and genial, and
258.28 also more self-indulgent than the frigid and
259.01 rigid temper of the morning: still, he looked
259.02 preciously grim, cushioning his massive head
259.03 against the swelling back of his chair, and
259.04 receiving the light of the fire on his granite--
259.05 hewn features, and in his great, dark eyes -- for
259.06 he had great, dark eyes, and very fine ones,
259.07 too: not without a certain change in their
259.08 depths sometimes, which, if it was not softness,
259.09 reminded you, at least, of that feeling.
259.10 He had been looking two minutes at the
259.11 fire, and I had been looking the same length
259.12 of time at him, when, turning suddenly, he
259.13 caught my gaze fastened on his physiognomy.
259.14 "You examine me, Miss Eyre," said he:
259.15 "do you think me handsome?"
259.16 I should, if I had deliberated, have replied
259.17 to this question by something conventionally
259.18 vague and polite; but the answer somehow
259.19 slipped from my tongue before I was aware: --
259.20 "No, sir."
259.21 "Ah! By my word! there is something
259.22 singular about you," said he: "you have the
259.23 air of a little nonnette; quaint, quiet, grave,
259.24 and simple, as you sit with your hands before
259.25 you, and your eyes generally bent on the
259.26 carpet /except, by-the-by, when they are di-
259.27 rected piercingly at my face; as just now, for
260.01 instance/; and when one asks you a question,
260.02 or makes a remark to which you are obliged
260.03 to reply, you rap out a round rejoinder, which,
260.04 if not blunt, is at least brusque. What do you
260.05 mean by it?"
260.06 "Sir, I was too plain: I beg your pardon.
260.07 I ought to have replied that it was not easy to
260.08 appearances; that tastes differ; that beauty is
260.09 of little consequence, or something of that
260.10 sort."
260.11 "You ought to have replied no such thing.
260.12 Beauty of little consequence, indeed! And
260.13 so, under pretence of softening the previous
260.14 outrage, of stroking and soothing me into
260.15 placidity, you stick a sly penknife under my
260.16 ear! Go on: what fault do you find with me,
260.17 pray? I suppose I have all my limbs and all
260.18 my features like any other man?"
260.19 "Mr. Rochester, allow me to disown my
260.20 first answer: I intended no pointed repartee:
260.21 it was only a blunder."
260.22 "Just so: I think so: and you shall be
260.23 answerable for it. Criticize me: does my
260.24 forehead not please you?"
260.25 He lifted up the sable waves of hair which
260.26 lay horizontally over his brow, and showed a
261.01 solid enough mass of intellectual organs; but
261.02 an abrupt deficiency where the suave sign of
261.03 benevolence should have risen.
261.04 "Now, ma'am, am I a fool?"
261.05 "Far from it sir. You would, perhaps,

261.06 think me rude if I inquired in return whether
261.07 you are a philanthropist?
261.08 "There again! Another stick of the pen-
261.09 knife, when she pretended to pat my head:
261.10 and that is because I said I did not like the
261.11 society of children and old women /low be it
261.12 spoken!/. No, young lady, I am not a
261.13 general philanthropist; but I bear a con-
261.14 science:" and he pointed to the prominences
261.15 which are said to indicate that faculty -- and
261.16 which, fortunately for him, were sufficiently
261.17 conspicuous; giving, indeed, a marked breadth
261.18 to the upper part of his head: "and besides,
261.19 I once had a kind of rude tenderness of heart.
261.20 when I was as old as you, I was a feeling
261.21 fellow enough; partial to the unfledged, un-
261.22 fostered, and unlucky; but fortune has knocked
261.23 me about since: she has even kneaded me
261.24 with her knuckles, and now I flatter myself
261.25 I am hard and tough as an Indian-rubber
261.26 ball; pervious, though, through a chink or
261.27 two still, and with one sentient point in the
262.01 middle of the lump. Yes: does that leave
262.02 hope for me?"
262.03 "Hope for what, sir?"
262.04 "Of my final re-transformation from Indian--
262.05 rubber back to flesh?"
262.06 "Decidedly he has had too much wine,"
262.07 I thought; and I did not know what answer
262.08 to make to his queer question: how could
262.09 I tell whether he was capable of being re--
262.10 transformed?
262.11 "You look very much puzzled, Miss Eyre;
262.12 and though you are not pretty any more than
262.13 I am handsome, yet a puzzled air becomes
262.14 you; besides, it is convenient, for it keeps those
262.15 searching eyes of yours away from my phy-
262.16 siognomy, and busies them with the worsted
262.17 flowers of the rug; so puzzle on. Young
262.18 lady, I am disposed to be gregarious and
262.19 communicative to-night."
262.20 with this announcement he rose from his
262.21 chair, and stood, leaning his arm on the marble
262.22 mantel-piece: in that attitude his shape was
262.23 seen plainly as well as his face; his unusual
262.24 breadth of chest, disproportionate almost to
262.25 his length of limb. I am sure most people
262.26 would have thought him an ugly man; yet
262.27 there was so much unconscious pride in his
263.01 port; so much ease in his demeanor; such a
263.02 look of complete indifference to his own ex-
263.03 ternal appearance; so haughty a reliance on
263.04 the power of other qualities, intrinsic or ad-
263.05 ventitious, to atone for the lack of mere per-
263.06 sonal attractiveness, that in looking at him,
263.07 one inevitable shared the indifference; and
263.08 even in a blind, imperfect sense, put faith in
263.09 the confidence.
263.10 "I am disposed to be gregarious and com-
263.11 municative to-night," he repeated; "and that
263.12 is why I sent for you: the fire and the change-
263.13 lier were not sufficient company for me; nor
263.14 would Pilot have been, for none of these can
263.15 talk. Adele is a degree better, but still far
263.16 below the mark; Mrs. Fairfax ditto; you, I
263.17 am persuaded, can suit me if you will: you
263.18 puzzled me the first evening I invited you
263.19 down here. I have almost forgotten you
263.20 since: other ideas have driven yours from my
263.21 head; but to-night I am resolved to be at
263.22 ease; to dismiss what importunes, and recall
263.23 what pleases. It would please me now to
263.24 draw you out: to learn more of you -- therefore
263.25 speak."
263.26 Instead of speaking, I smiled: and not a
263.27 very complacent or submissive smile either.
263.28 "Speak," he urged.
264.01 "What about, sir?"
264.02 "Whatever you like. I leave both the
264.03 choice of subject and the manner of treating
264.04 it, entirely to yourself."
264.05 Accordingly I sat and said nothing: "If he
264.06 expects me to talk for the mere sake of
264.07 talking and showing off, he will find he has
264.08 addressed himself to the wrong person," I
264.09 thought.
264.10 "You are dumb, Miss Eyre."
264.11 I was dumb still. He bent his head a little
264.12 towards me and with a single hasty glance
264.13 seemed to dive into my eyes.
264.14 "Stubborn?" he said, "and annoyed. Ah,
264.15 it is consistent. I put my request in an absurd,
264.16 almost insolent form. Miss Eyre, I beg your
264.17 pardon. The fact is, once for all, I don't wish
264.18 to treat you like an inferior: that is /correcting
264.19 himself/, I claim only such superiority as must
264.20 result from twenty years' difference in age and
264.21 a century's advance in experience. This is
264.22 legitimate, et j'y tiens, as Adele would say;
264.23 and it is by virtue of this superiority and this
264.24 alone that I desire you to have the goodness to
264.25 talk to me a little now, and divert my thoughts,
264.26 which are galled with dwelling on one point:
264.27 cankering as a rusty nail."
264.28 He had deigned an explanation; almost an
265.01 apology: I did not feel insensible to his con-
265.02 descension, and would not seem so.
265.03 "I am willing to amuse you if I can, sir:
265.04 quite willing; but I cannot introduce a topic,
265.05 because how do I know what will interest
265.06 you? Ask me questions, and I will do my

265.07 best to answer them."
265.08 "Then, in the first place, do you agree with
265.09 me that I have a right to be a little masterful,
265.10 abrupt; perhaps exacting, sometimes, on the
265.11 grounds I stated: namely, that I am old enough
265.12 to be your father, and that I have battled
265.13 through a varied experience with many men
265.14 of many nations, and roamed over half the
265.15 globe, while you have lived quietly with one
265.16 set of people in one house?"
265.17 "Do as you please, sir."
265.18 "That is no answer; or rather it is a very
265.19 irritating, because a very evasive one -- reply
265.20 clearly."
265.21 "I don't think, sir, you have a right to com-
265.22 mand me, merely because you are older than
265.23 I, or because you have seen more of the world
265.24 than I have -- your claim to superiority depends
265.25 on the use you have made of your time and
265.26 experience."
265.27 "Humph! Promptly spoken. But I won't
265.28 allow that, seeing that it would never suit my
266.01 case; and I have made an indifferent, not to say
266.02 a bad use of both advantages. Leaving supe-
266.03 riority out of the question then, you must still
266.04 agree to receive my orders now and then,
266.05 without being piqued or hurt by the tone of
266.06 command -- will you?"
266.07 I smiled: I thought to myself Mr. Ro-
266.08 chester is peculiar -- he seems to forget that he
266.09 pays me 30l. per annum for receiving his
266.10 orders.
266.11 "The smile is very well," said he, catching
266.12 instantly the passing expression; "but speak
266.13 too."
266.14 "I was thinking, sir, that very few masters
266.15 would trouble themselves to inquire whether
266.16 or not their paid subordinates were piqued and
266.17 hurt by their orders."
266.18 "Paid subordinates! What, you are my
266.19 paid subordinate, are you? Oh yes, I had
266.20 forgotten the salary! Well then, on that mer-
266.21 cenary ground, will you agree to let me hector
266.22 a little?"
266.23 "No, sir, not on that ground: but, on the
266.24 ground that you did forget it, and that you
266.25 care whether or not a dependant is comfort-
266.26 able in his dependency, I agree heartily."
266.27 "And will you consent to dispense with a
266.28 great many conventional forms and phrases,
267.01 without thinking that the omission arises from
267.02 insolence?"
267.03 "I am sure, sir, I should never mistake in-
267.04 formality for insolence: one I rather like, the
267.05 other nothing free-born would submit to, even
267.06 for a salary."
267.07 "Humbug! Most things free-born will
267.08 submit to anything for a salary; therefore
267.09 keep to yourself, and don't venture on gene-
267.10 ralities of which you are intensely ignorant.
267.11 However, I mentally shake hands with you
267.12 for your answer, despite its inaccuracy; and as
267.13 much for the manner in which it was said, as
267.14 for the substance of the speech: the manner
267.15 was frank and sincere; one does not often see
267.16 such a manner: no, on the contrary, affecta-
267.17 tion, or coldness, or stupid, coarse-minded
267.18 misapprehension of one's meaning are the
267.19 usual rewards of candour. Not three in three
267.20 thousand raw school-girl-governesses would
267.21 have answered me as you have just done. But
267.22 I don't mean to flatter you: if you are cast in
267.23 a different mould to the majority, it is no merit
267.24 of yours: Nature did it. And then, after all,
267.25 I go too fast in my conclusions: for what I
267.26 yet know, you may be no better than the rest;
267.27 you may have intolerable defects to counter--
267.28 balance your few good points."
268.01 "And so may you," I thought. My eye
268.02 met his as the idea crossed my mind: he
268.03 seemed to read the glance, answering as if
268.04 its import had been spoken as well as imag-
268.05 ined: --
268.06 "Yes, yes, you are right," said he; "I have
268.07 plenty of faults of my own: I know it, and I
268.08 don't wish to palliate them, I assure you.
268.09 God wot I need not be too severe about others;
268.10 I have a past existence, a series of deeds, a
268.11 colour of life to contemplate within my own
268.12 breast, which might well call my sneers and
268.13 censures from my neighbours to myself: I
268.14 started, or rather /for like other defaulters,
268.15 I like to lay half the blame on ill fortune and
268.16 adverse circumstances/ was thrust on to a
268.17 wrong tack at the age of one and twenty, and
268.18 have never recovered the right course since:
268.19 but I might have been very different; I might
268.20 have been as good as you, -- wiser, -- almost as
268.21 stainless. I envy you your peace of mind, your
268.22 clean conscience, your unpolluted memory.
268.23 Little girl, a memory without blot or con-
268.24 tamination must be an exquisite treasure: -- an
268.25 inexhaustible source of pure refreshment: is it
268.26 not?"
268.27 "How was your memory when you were
268.28 eighteen, sir?"
269.01 "All right then; limpid, salubrious: no
269.02 gush of bilge water had turned it to fetid
269.03 puddle. I was your equal at eighteen -- quite
269.04 your equal. Nature meant me to be, on the
269.05 whole, a good man, Miss Eyre: one of the

269.06 better end; and you see I am not so. You
269.07 would say you don't see it: at least I flatter
269.08 myself I read as much in your eye /beware,
269.09 by-the-by, what you express with that organ,
269.10 I am quick at interpreting its language/.
269.11 Then take my word for it, -- I am not a villain:
269.12 you are not to suppose that -- not to attri-
269.13 bute to me any such bad eminence; but,
269.14 owing, I verily believe, rather to circum-
269.15 stances than to my natural bent, I am a trite
269.16 common-place sinner, hackneyed in all the
269.17 poor petty dissipations with which the rich and
269.18 worthless try to put on life. Do you wonder
269.19 that I avow this to you? Know, that in the
269.20 course of your future life you will often find
269.21 yourself elected the involuntary confidant of
269.22 your acquaintances' secrets: people will in-
269.23 stinctively find out, as I have done, that it is
269.24 not your forte to talk of yourself, but to listen
269.25 while others talk of themselves; they will feel,
269.26 too, that you listen with no malevolent scorn
269.27 of their indiscretion, but with a kind of innate
269.28 sympathy; not the less comforting and en-
270.01 couraging because it is very unobtrusive in its
270.02 manifestations."
270.03 "How do you know? -- how can you guess
270.04 all this, sir?"
270.05 "I know it well; therefore I proceed al-
270.06 most as freely as if I were writing my thoughts
270.07 in a diary. You would say, I should have
270.08 been superior to circumstances: so I should --
270.09 so I should; but you see I was not. When
270.10 fate wronged me, I had not the wisdom to
270.11 remain cool: I turned desperate; then I
270.12 degenerated. Now, when any vicious simple-
270.13 ton excites my disgust by his paltry ribaldry,
270.14 I cannot flatter myself that I am better than
270.15 he: I am forced to confess that he and I are
270.16 on a level. I wish I had stood firm -- God
270.17 knows I do! Dread remorse when you are
270.18 tempted to err, Miss Eyre: remorse is the
270.19 poison of life."
270.20 "Repentance is said to be its cure, sir."
270.21 "It is not a cure. Reformation may be
270.22 its cure; and I could reform -- I have strength
270.23 yet for that -- if -- but where is the use of think-
270.24 ing of it, hampered, burdened, cursed as I am?
270.25 Besides, since happiness is irrevocably denied
270.26 me, I have a right to get pleasure out of life:
270.27 and I will get it, cost what it may."
270.28 "Then you will degenerate still more, sir."
271.01 "Possibly: yet why should I, if I can get
271.02 sweet, fresh pleasure? And I may get it as
271.03 sweet and fresh as the wild honey the bee
271.04 gathers on the moor."
271.05 "It will sting -- it will taste bitter, sir."
271.06 "How do you know? -- you never tried it.
271.07 How very serious -- how very solemn you look;
271.08 and you are as ignorant of the matter as this
271.09 cameo head /taking one from the mantel-piece/!
271.10 You have no right to preach to me; you neo-
271.11 phyte, that have not passed the porch of life,
271.12 and are absolutely unacquainted with its mys-
271.13 teries."
271.14 "I only remind you of your own words, sir:
271.15 you said error brought remorse, and you pro-
271.16 nounced remorse the poison of existence."
271.17 "And who talks of error now? I scarcely
271.18 think the notion that flittered across my brain
271.19 was an error. I believe it was an inspiration
271.20 rather than a temptation: it was very genial,
271.21 very soothing, -- I know that. Here it comes
271.22 again! It is no devil, I assure you: or if it
271.23 be, it has put on the robes of an angel of light.
271.24 I think I must admit so fair a guest when it
271.25 asks entrance to my heart."
271.26 "Distrust it, sir; it is not a true angel."
271.27 "Once more, how do you know? By what
271.28 instinct do you pretend to distinguish between
272.01 a fallen seraph of the abyss, and a messenger
272.02 from the eternal throne -- between a guide and
272.03 a seducer?"
272.04 "I judged by your countenance, sir; which
272.05 was troubled: when you said the suggestion
272.06 had returned upon you. I feel sure it will
272.07 work you more misery if you listen to it."
272.08 "Not at all -- it bears the most gracious
272.09 message in the world: for the rest, you are
272.10 not my conscience-keeper, so don't make your-
272.11 self uneasy. Here, come in, bonny wan-
272.12 derer!"
272.13 He said this as if he spoke to a vision, view-
272.14 less to any eye but his own; then folding his
272.15 arms, which he had half extended, on his chest,
272.16 he seemed to enclose in their embrace the
272.17 invisible being.
272.18 "Now," he continued, again addressing me,
272.19 "I have received the pilgrim -- a disguised
272.20 deity, as I verily believe. Already it has done
272.21 me good: my heart was a sort of charnel; it
272.22 will now be a shrine."
272.23 "To speak truth, sir, I don't understand
272.24 you at all: I cannot keep up the conversation,
272.25 because it has got out of my depth. Only one
272.26 thing I know: you said you were not as good
272.27 as you should like to be, and that you regretted
272.28 your own imperfection -- one thing I can com-
273.01 prehend: you intimated that to have a sullied
273.02 memory was a perpetual bane. It seems to
273.03 me, that if you tried hard, you would in time
273.04 find it possible to become what you yourself

273.05 would approve; and that if from this day you
273.06 began with resolution to correct your thoughts
273.07 and actions, you would in a few years have
273.08 laid up a new and stainless store of recollec-
273.09 tions, to which you might revert with pleasure."
273.10 "Justly thought; rightly said, Miss Eyre;
273.11 and at this moment, I am paving hell with
273.12 energy."
273.13 "Sir?"
273.14 "I am laying down good intentions, which
273.15 I believe durable as flint. Certainly, my asso-
273.16 ciates and pursuits shall be other than they
273.17 have been."
273.18 "And better?"
273.19 "And better -- so much better as pure ore is
273.20 than foul dross. You seem to doubt me; I
273.21 don't doubt myself: I know what my aim is,
273.22 what my motives are; and at this moment I
273.23 pass a law, unalterable as that of the Medes
273.24 and Persians, that both are right."
273.25 "They cannot be, sir, if they require a new
273.26 statute to legalize them."
273.27 "They are, Miss Eyre, though they abso-
273.28 lutely require a new statute: unheard-of com-
274.01 binations of circumstances demand unheard--
274.02 of rules."
274.03 "That sounds a dangerous maxim, sir; be-
274.04 cause one can see at once that it is liable to
274.05 abuse."
274.06 "Sententious sage! so it is: but I swear by
274.07 my household gods not to abuse it."
274.08 "You are human and fallible."
274.09 "I am; so are you -- what then?"
274.10 "The human and fallible should not arrogate
274.11 a power with which the devine and perfect
274.12 alone can be safely entrusted."
274.13 "What power?"
274.14 "That of saying of any strange, unsanctioned
274.15 line of action, -- `Let it be right.`"
274.16 "`Let it be right` -- the very words: you
274.17 have pronounced them."
274.18 "May it be right then," I said, as I rose;
274.19 deeming it useless to continue a discourse
274.20 which was all darkness to me; and, besides,
274.21 sensible that the character of my interlocutor
274.22 was beyond my penetration: at least, beyond
274.23 its present reach; and feeling the uncertainty,
274.24 the vague sense of insecurity, which accom-
274.25 panies a conviction of ignorance.
274.26 "Where are you going?"
274.27 "To put Adele to bed: it is past her bed-
274.28 time."
275.01 "You are afraid of me, because I talk like a
275.02 Sphynx."
275.03 "Your language is enigmatical, sir: but
275.04 though I am bewildered, I am certainly not
275.05 afraid."
275.06 "You are afraid -- your self-love dreads a
275.07 blunder."
275.08 "In that sense I do feel apprehensive -- I
275.09 have no wish to talk nonsense."
275.10 "If you did, it would be in such a grave,
275.11 quiet manner, I should mistake it for sense.
275.12 Do you never laugh, Miss Eyre? Don't
275.13 trouble yourself to answer -- I see, you laugh
275.14 rarely; but you can laugh very merrily: believe
275.15 me, you are not naturally austere, any more
275.16 than I am naturally vicious. The Lowood
275.17 constraint still clings to you somewhat; con-
275.18 trolling your features, muffling your voice, and
275.19 restricting your limbs; and you fear in the
275.20 presence of a man and a brother -- or father,
275.21 or master, or what you will -- to smile too gaily,
275.22 speak too freely, or move too quickly: but in
275.23 time, I think you will learn to be natural with
275.24 me, as I find it impossible to be conventional
275.25 with you; and then your looks and movements
275.26 will have more vivacity and variety than they
275.27 dare offer now. I see, at intervals, the glance
275.28 of a curious sort of bird through the close-
276.01 set bars of a cage: a vivid, restless, resolute
276.02 captive is there; were it but free, it would soar
276.03 cloud-high. You are still bent on going?"
276.04 "It has struck nine, sir."
276.05 "Never mind, -- wait a minute: Adele is
276.06 not ready to go to bed yet. My position,
276.07 Miss Eyre, with my back to the fire, and my
276.08 face to the room, favours observation. While
276.09 talking to you, I have also occasionally watched
276.10 Adele; /I have my own reasons for thinking
276.11 her a curious study, -- reasons that I may, nay
276.12 that I shall, impart to you some day;/ she
276.13 pulled out of her box, about ten minutes ago,
276.14 a little pink silk frock; rapture lit her face as
276.15 she unfolded it: coquetry runs in her blood,
276.16 blends with her brains, and seasons the marrow
276.17 of her bones. `Il faut que je l'essaie!` cried
276.18 she; `et a l'instant meme!` and she rushed
276.19 out of the room. She is now with Sophie,
276.20 undergoing a robing process: in a few minutes
276.21 she will re-enter; and I know what I shall
276.22 see, -- a miniature of Celine Varens, as she used
276.23 to appear on the boards at the rising of -- --:
276.24 but never mind that. However, my ten-
276.25 derest feelings are about to receive a shock:
276.26 such is my presentiment; stay now, to see
276.27 whether it will be realized."
276.28 Ere long, Adele's little foot was heard
277.01 tripping across the hall. She entered, trans-
277.02 formed as her guardian had predicted. A dress
277.03 of rose-coloured satin, very short, and as full

277.04 in the skirt as it could be gathered, replaced
277.05 the brown frock she had previously worn; a
277.06 wreath of rosebuds circled her forehead; her
277.07 feet were dressed in silk stockings and small
277.08 white satin sandals.
277.09 "Est-ce que ma robe va bien?" cried she,
277.10 bounding forwards; "et mes souliers? et mes
277.11 bas? Tenez, je crois que je vais danser!"
277.12 And spreading out her dress, she chasseed
277.13 across the room; till having reached Mr.
277.14 Rochester, she wheeled lightly round before
277.15 him on tip-toe, then dropped on one knee at
277.16 his feet, exclaiming:
277.17 "Monsieur, je vous remercie mille fois de
277.18 votre bonte;" then rising, she added, "C'est
277.19 comme cela que maman faisait, n'est-ce pas,
277.20 Monsieur?"
277.21 "Pre-cise-ly!" was the answer; "and
277.22 `comme cela,` she charmed my English gold
277.23 out of my British breeches' pocket. I have
277.24 been green, too, Miss Eyre, -- ay, grass green:
277.25 not a more vernal tint freshens you now than
277.26 once freshened me. My Spring is gone,
277.27 however: but it has left me that French
277.28 floweret on my hands; which, in some moods,
278.01 I would fain be rid of. Not valuing now the
278.02 root whence it sprang; having found that it
278.03 was of a sort which nothing but gold dust
278.04 could manure, I have but half a liking to
278.05 the blossom: especially when it looks so
278.06 artificial, as just now. I keep it and rear it
278.07 rather on the Roman Catholic principle of ex-
278.08 piating numerous sins, great or small, by one
278.09 good work. I'll explain all this some day.
278.10 Good-night."
279.01 [Vol. 1 Chapter 15]
279.02 Mr. Rochester did, on a future occasion,
279.03 explain it.
279.04 It was one afternoon, when he chanced to
279.05 meet me and Adele in the grounds; and
279.06 while she played with Pilot and her shuttle-
279.07 cock, he asked me to walk up and down a
279.08 long beech avenue within sight of her.
279.09 He then said that she was the daughter of a
279.10 French opera dancer, Celine Varens; towards
279.11 whom he had once cherished what he called a
279.12 "grande passion." This passion Celine had
279.13 professed to return with even superior ardour.
279.14 He thought himself her idol; ugly as he was:
279.15 he believed, as he said, that she preferred his
279.16 "taille d'athlete" to the elegance of the Apollo
279.17 Belvidere.
279.18 "And, Miss Eyre, so much was I flattered
279.19 by this preference of the Gallic sylph for her
279.20 British gnome, that I installed her in an hotel;
280.01 gave her a complete establishment of servants,
280.02 a carriage, cashmeres, diamonds, dentelles, &c.
280.03 In short, I began the process of ruining my-
280.04 self in the received style; like any other
280.05 spoonie. I had not, it seems, the originality
280.06 to chalk out a new road to shame and de-
280.07 struction, but trode the old track with stupid
280.08 exactness not to deviate an inch from the
280.09 beaten centre. I had -- as I deserved to have --
280.10 the fate of all other spoonies. Happening to
280.11 call one evening, when Celine did not expect
280.12 me, I found her out; but it was a warm night,
280.13 and I was tired with strolling through Paris, so
280.14 I sat down in her boudoir; happy to breathe
280.15 the air consecrated so lately by her presence.
280.16 No, -- I exaggerate; I never thought there
280.17 was any consecrating virtue about her: it was
280.18 rather a sort of pastile perfume she had left;
280.19 a scent of musk and amber, than an odour of
280.20 sanctity. I was just beginning to stifle with
280.21 the fumes of conservatory flowers and sprin-
280.22 kled essences, when I bethought myself to open
280.23 the window and step out on to the balcony.
280.24 It was moonlight, and gas-light besides, and
280.25 very still and serene. The balcony was fur-
280.26 nished with a chair or two; I sat down, took
280.27 out a cigar, -- I will take one now, if you will
280.28 excuse me."
281.01 Here ensued a pause, filled up by the pro-
281.02 ducing and lighting of a cigar; having placed
281.03 it to his lips and breathed a trail of Havannah
281.04 incense on the freezing and sunless air, he
281.05 went on: --
281.06 "I liked bonbons too, in those days, Miss
281.07 Eyre, and I was croquant --/overlook the bar-
281.08 barism/ croquant chocolate comfits, and smok-
281.09 ing alternately, watching meantime the equi-
281.10 pages that rolled along the fashionable streets
281.11 towards the neighbouring opera-house, when
281.12 in an elegant close carriage drawn by a beau-
281.13 tiful pair of English horses, and distinctly seen
281.14 in the brilliant city-night, I recognised the
281.15 `voiture` I had given Celine. She was re-
281.16 turning: of course my heart thumped with
281.17 impatience against the iron rails I leant upon.
281.18 The carriage stopped, as I had expected, at
281.19 the hotel door; my flame /that is the very
281.20 word for an opera inammorata/ alighted:
281.21 though muffled in a cloak -- an unnecessary
281.22 incumbrance, by-the-bye, on so warm a June
281.23 evening -- I knew her instantly by her little
281.24 foot, seen peeping from the skirt of her dress,
281.25 as she skipped from the carriage-step. Bend-
281.26 ing over the balcony I was about to murmur,
281.27 `Mon ange` -- in a tone, of course, which
281.28 should be audible to the ear of love alone --

282.01 when a figure jumped from the carriage after
282.02 her; cloaked also; but that was a spurred heel
282.03 which had rung on the pavement, and that
282.04 was a hatted head which now passed under
282.05 the arched porte cochere of the hotel.
282.06 "You never felt jealousy, did you, Miss
282.07 Eyre? Of course not: I need not ask you;
282.08 because you never felt love. You have both
282.09 sentiments yet to experience: your soul sleeps;
282.10 the shock is yet to be given which shall waken
282.11 it. You think all existence lapses in as quiet
282.12 a flow as that in which your youth has
282.13 hitherto slid away. Floating on with closed
282.14 eyes and muffled ears, you neither see the
282.15 rocks bristling not far off in the bed of the
282.16 flood, nor hear the breakers boil at their base.
282.17 But I tell you -- and you may mark my words
282.18 -- you will come some day to a craggy pass of
282.19 the channel, where the whole of life's stream
282.20 will be broken up into whirl and tumult, foam
282.21 and noise: either you will be dashed to atoms
282.22 on crag points, or lifted up and borne on by
282.23 some master wave into a calmer current -- as I
282.24 am now.
282.25 "I like this day: I like that sky of steel; I
282.26 like the sternness and stillness of the world
282.27 under this frost. I like Thornfield; its anti-
282.28 quity; its retirement; its old crow-trees and
283.01 thorn-trees; its gray facade, and lines of dark
283.02 windows reflecting that metal welkin: and yet
283.03 how long have I abhorred the very thought
283.04 of it; shunned it like a great plague-house!
283.05 How I do still abhor -- "
283.06 He ground his teeth and was silent: he ar-
283.07 rested his step and struck his boot against the
283.08 hard ground. Some hated thought seemed to
283.09 have him in its grip, and to hold him so tightly
283.10 that he could not advance.
283.11 We were ascending the avenue when he thus
283.12 paused; the hall was before us. Lifting his eye
283.13 to its battlements, he cast over them a glare
283.14 such as I never saw before or since. Pain,
283.15 shame, ire -- impatience, disgust, detestation --
283.16 seemed momentarily to hold a quivering con-
283.17 flict in the large pupil dilating under his ebon
283.18 eyebrow. Wild was the wrestle which should
283.19 be paramount; but another feeling rose and
283.20 triumphed: something hard and cynical; self--
283.21 willed and resolute: it settled his passion and
283.22 petrified his countenance: he went on: --
283.23 "During the moment I was silent, Miss
283.24 Eyre, I was arranging a point with my destiny.
283.25 She stood there, by that beech-trunk -- a hag
283.26 like one of those who appeared to Macbeth
283.27 on the heath of Forres. `You like Thorn-
283.28 field?` she said, lifting her finger; and then
284.01 she wrote in the air a memento, which ran
284.02 in lurid hieroglyphics all along the house--
284.03 front, between the upper and lower row of
284.04 windows. `Like it if you can!` `Like it if
284.05 you dare!`
284.06 "`I will like it,` said I. `I dare like it;
284.07 and /he subjoined moodily/ I will keep my
284.08 word: I will break obstacles to happiness, to
284.09 goodness -- yes, goodness; I wish to be a better
284.10 man than I have been; than I am -- as Job's
284.11 leviathan broke the spear and dart and the
284.12 habergeon, hinderances which others count
284.13 as iron and brass, I will esteem but straw and
284.14 rotten wood."
284.15 Adele here ran before him with her shuttle-
284.16 cock. "Away!" he cried harshly; "keep at a
284.17 distance, child; or go in to Sophie!" Con-
284.18 tinuing then to pursue his walk in silence, I
284.19 ventured to recall him to the point whence he
284.20 had abruptly diverged: --
284.21 "Did you leave the balcony, sir," I asked,
284.22 "when Mdlle. Varens entered?"
284.23 I almost expected a rebuff for this hardly
284.24 well-timed question: but, on the contrary,
284.25 waking out of his scowling abstraction, he
284.26 turned his eyes towards me, and the shade
284.27 seemed to clear off his brow.
284.28 "Oh, I had forgotten Celine! Well, to re-
285.01 sume. When I saw my charmer thus come in
285.02 accompanied by a cavalier, I seemed to hear a
285.03 hiss, and the green snake of jealousy, rising on
285.04 undulating coils from the moonlit balcony,
285.05 glided within my waistcoat and ate its way in
285.06 two minutes to my heart's core. Strange!"
285.07 he exclaimed, suddenly starting again from
285.08 the point. "Strange that I should choose you
285.09 for the confidant of all this, young lady: pass-
285.10 ing strange that you should listen to me
285.11 quietly, as if it were the most usual thing in
285.12 the world for a man like me to tell stories of
285.13 his opera-mistresses to a quaint, inexperienced
285.14 girl like you! But the last singularity ex-
285.15 plains the first, as I intimated once before:
285.16 you, with your gravity, considerateness, and
285.17 caution were made to be the recipient of
285.18 secrets. Besides, I know what sort of a mind
285.19 I have placed in communication with my own;
285.20 I know it is one not liable to take infection: it
285.21 is a peculiar mind; it is an unique one. Hap-
285.22 pily I do not mean to harm it: but if I did,
285.23 it would not take harm from me. The more
285.24 you and I converse, the better; for while I
285.25 cannot blight you, you may refresh me."
285.26 After this digression he proceeded: --
285.27 "I remained in the balcony. `They will

285.28 come to her boudoir no doubt,` thought I: `let
286.01 me prepare an ambush.` So putting my hand
286.02 in through the open window, I drew the cur-
286.03 tain over it, leaving only an opening through
286.04 which I could take observations; then I closed
286.05 the casement, all but a chink just wide enough
286.06 to furnish an outlet to `lovers` whispered vows:
286.07 then I stole back to my chair; and as I re-
286.08 sumed it the pair came in. My eye was
286.09 quickly at the aperture. Celine's chamber--
286.10 maid entered, lit a lamp, left it on the table
286.11 and withdrew. The couple were thus revealed
286.12 to me clearly: both removed their cloaks, and
286.13 there was `the Varens` shining in satin and
286.14 jewels, -- my gifts of course, -- and there was her
286.15 companion in an officer's uniform; and I knew
286.16 him for a young roue of a vicomte -- a brainless
286.17 and vicious youth whom I had sometimes met
286.18 in society, and had never thought of hating
286.19 because I despised him so absolutely. On re-
286.20 cognising him, the fang of the snake, -- jealousy,
286.21 was instantly broken; because at the same mo-
286.22 ment my love for Celine sank under an ex-
286.23 tinguisher. A woman who could betray me
286.24 for such a rival was not worth contending for:
286.25 she deserved only scorn; less, however, than I,
286.26 who had been her dupe."
286.27 They began to talk; their conversation eased
286.28 me completely: frivolous, mercenary, heart-
287.01 less, and senseless, it was rather calculated to
287.02 weary than enrage a listener. A card of mine
287.03 lay on the table; this being perceived brought
287.04 my name under discussion. Neither of them
287.05 possessed energy or wit to belabour me soundly;
287.06 but they insulted me as coarsely as they could
287.07 in their little way: especially Celine; who even
287.08 waxed rather brilliant on my personal defects
287.09 -- deformities she termed them. Now it had
287.10 been her custom to launch out into fervent
287.11 admiration of what she called by `beaute
287.12 male;` wherein she differed diametrically from
287.13 you, who told me point blank at the second
287.14 interview, that you did not think me hand-
287.15 some. The contrast struck me at the time,
287.16 and --"
287.17 Adele here came running up again.
287.18 "Monsieur, John has just been to say that
287.19 your agent has called and wishes to see you."
287.20 "Ah! in that case I must abridge. Opening
287.21 the window, I walked in upon them; liberated
287.22 Celine from my protection; gave her notice
287.23 to vacate her hotel; offered her a purse for
287.24 immediate exigencies; disregarded screams,
287.25 hysterics, prayers, protestations, convulsions;
287.26 made an appointment with the Vicomte for
287.27 a meeting at the bois de Boulogne. Next
287.28 morning I had the pleasure of encountering
288.01 him; left a bullet in one of his poor, etiolated
288.02 arms, feeble as the wing of a chicken in the
288.03 pip, and then thought I had done with the
288.04 whole crew. But unluckily the Varens, six
288.05 months before, had given me this fillette Adele;
288.06 who she affirmed was my daughter, and per-
288.07 haps she may be; though I see no proofs of
288.08 such grim paternity written in her counte-
288.09 nance: Pilot is more like me than she. Some
288.10 years after I had broken with the mother, she
288.11 abandoned her child and ran away to Italy
288.12 with a musician, or singer. I acknowledged
288.13 no natural claim on Adele's part to be sup-
288.14 ported by me; nor do I now acknowledge
288.15 any, for I am not her father; but hearing that
288.16 she was quite destitute, I e'en took the poor
288.17 thing out of the slime and mud of Paris, and
288.18 transplanted it here, to grow up clean in the
288.19 wholesome soil of an English country garden.
288.20 Mrs. Fairfax found you to train it; but now
288.21 you know that it is the illegitimate offspring of
288.22 a French opera-girl, you will perhaps think
288.23 differently of your post and protegee: you will
288.24 be coming to me some day with notice that
288.25 you have found another place -- that you beg
288.26 me to look out for a new governess, &c. -- eh?`
288.27 "No -- Adele is not answerable for either
288.28 her mother's faults or yours: I have a regard
289.01 for her, and now that I know she is, in a sense,
289.02 parentless -- forsaken by her mother and dis-
289.03 owned by you, sir, -- I shall cling closer to her
289.04 than before. How could I possibly prefer the
289.05 spoilt pet of a wealthy family, who would
289.06 hate her governess as a nuisance, to a lonely
289.07 little orphan, who leans towards her as a
289.08 friend?"
289.09 "Oh, that is the light in which you view
289.10 it! Well, I must go in now; and you too: it
289.11 darkens."
289.12 But I stayed out a few minutes longer with
289.13 Adele and Pilot -- ran a race with her, and
289.14 played a game of battledore and shuttlecock.
289.15 When we went in and I had removed her
289.16 bonnet and coat, I took her on my knee; kept
289.17 her there an hour, allowing her to prattle as
289.18 she liked: not rebuking even some little free-
289.19 doms and trivialities into which she was apt
289.20 to stray when much noticed; and which be-
289.21 trayed in her a superficiality of character,
289.22 inherited probably from her mother, hardly
289.23 congenial to an English mind. Still she had
289.24 her merits; and I was disposed to appreciate
289.25 all that was good in her to the utmost. I
289.26 sought in her countenance and features a like-

374

289.27 ness to Mr. Rochester, but found none: no
289.28 trait, no turn of expression announced rela-
290.01 tionship. It was a pity: if she could but have
290.02 been proved to resemble him, he would have
290.03 thought more of her.
290.04   It was not till after I had withdrawn to my
290.05 own chamber for the night, that I steadily
290.06 reviewed the tale Mr. Rochester had told me.
290.07 As he had said, there was probably nothing at
290.08 all extraordinary in the substance of the nar-
290.09 rative itself: a wealthy Englishman's passion
290.10 for a French dancer, and her treachery to him
290.11 were every-day matters enough, no doubt, in
290.12 society; but there was something decidedly
290.13 strange in the paroxysm of emotion which had
290.14 suddenly seized him, when he was in the act
290.15 of expressing the present contentment of his
290.16 mood, and his newly revived pleasure in the
290.17 old Hall and its environs. I meditated won-
290.18 deringly on this incident: but gradually quit-
290.19 ting it, as I found it for the present inexpli-
290.20 cable, I turned to the consideration of my
290.21 master's manner to myself. The confidence
290.22 he had thought fit to repose in me seemed a
290.23 tribute to my discretion: I regarded and ac-
290.24 cepted it as such. His deportment had now
290.25 for some weeks been more uniform towards
290.26 me than at the first. I never seemed in his
290.27 way; he did not take fits of chilling hauteur:
290.28 when he met me unexpectedly, the encounter
291.01 seemed welcome; he had always a word and
291.02 sometimes a smile for me: when summoned
291.03 by formal invitation to his presence, I was
291.04 honoured by a cordiality of reception that
291.05 made me feel I really possessed the power to
291.06 amuse him, and that these evening conferences
291.07 were sought as much for his pleasure as for
291.08 my benefit.
291.09   I, indeed, talked comparatively little; but I
291.10 heard him talk with relish. It was his nature
291.11 to be communicative; he liked to open to a
291.12 mind unacquainted with the world, glimpses of
291.13 its scenes and ways /I do not mean its corrupt
291.14 scenes and wicked ways, but such as derived
291.15 their interest from the great scale on which
291.16 they were acted, the strange novelty by which
291.17 they were characterized/; and I had a keen
291.18 delight in receiving the new ideas he offered,
291.19 in imagining the new pictures he portrayed, and
291.20 following him in thought through the new
291.21 regions he disclosed, never startled or troubled
291.22 by one noxious allusion.
291.23   The ease of his manner freed me from pain-
291.24 ful restraint: the friendly frankness, as correct
291.25 as cordial, with which he treated me, drew me
291.26 to him. I felt at times, as if he were my rela-
291.27 tion, rather than my master: yet he was
291.28 imperious sometimes still; but I did not mind
292.01 that; I saw it was his way. So happy, so
292.02 gratified did I become with this new interest
292.03 added to life, that I ceased to pine after kin-
292.04 dred: my thin crescent-destiny seemed to
292.05 enlarge; the blanks of existence were filled
292.06 up; my bodily health improved; I gathered
292.07 flesh and strength.
292.08   And was Mr. Rochester now ugly in my
292.09 eyes? No, reader: gratitude, and many asso-
292.10 ciations, all pleasurable and genial, made his
292.11 face the object I best liked to see; his presence
292.12 in a room was more cheering than the bright-
292.13 est fire. Yet I had not forgotten his faults:
292.14 indeed, I could not, for he brought them
292.15 frequently before me. He was proud, sar-
292.16 donic, harsh to inferiority of every description:
292.17 in my secret soul I knew that his great kind-
292.18 ness to me was balanced by unjust severity to
292.19 many others. He was moody, too; unaccount-
292.20 ably so: I more than once, when sent for to
292.21 read to him, found him sitting in his library
292.22 alone, with his head bent on his folded arms;
292.23 and, when he looked up, a morose, almost a
292.24 malignant, scowl blackened his features. But
292.25 I believed that his moodiness, his harshness,
292.26 and his former faults of morality /I say former,
292.27 for now he seemed corrected of them/ had
292.28 their source in some cruel cross of fate. I
293.01 believed he was naturally a man of better
293.02 tendencies, higher principles, and purer tastes
293.03 than such as circumstances had developed,
293.04 education instilled, or destiny encouraged. I
293.05 thought there were excellent materials in him;
293.06 though for the present they hung together
293.07 somewhat spoiled and tangled. I cannot
293.08 deny that I grieved for his grief, whatever that
293.09 was, and would have given much to assuage it.
293.10   Though I had now extinguished my candle
293.11 and was laid down in bed, I could not sleep,
293.12 for thinking of his look when he paused in
293.13 the avenue, and told how his destiny had risen
293.14 up before him and dared him to be happy at
293.15 Thornfield.
293.16   "Why not?" I asked myself: "what alien-
293.17 ates him from the house? Will he leave it
293.18 again soon? Mrs. Fairfax said he seldom
293.19 stayed here longer than a fortnight at a time;
293.20 and he has now been resident eight weeks.
293.21 If he does go, the change will be doleful.
293.22 Suppose he should be absent, spring, summer,
293.23 and autumn: how joyless sunshine and fine
293.24 days will seem!"
293.25   I hardly know whether I had slept or not

293.26 after this musing; at any rate I started wide
293.27 awake on hearing a vague murmur, peculiar
293.28 and lugubrious, which sounded, I thought, just
294.01 above me. I wished I had kept my candle
294.02 burning: the night was drearily dark; my
294.03 spirits were depressed. I rose and sat up in
294.04 bed, listening. The sound was hushed.
294.05   I tried again to sleep; but my heart beat
294.06 anxiously: my inward tranquillity was broken.
294.07 The clock, far down in the hall, struck two.
294.08 Just then it seemed my chamber-door was
294.09 touched; as if fingers had swept the panels in
294.10 groping a way along the dark gallery outside.
294.11 I said, "Who is there?" Nothing answered.
294.12 I was chilled with fear.
294.13   All at once I remembered that it might be
294.14 Pilot; who, when the kitchen-door chanced to
294.15 be left open, not unfrequently found his way
294.16 up to the threshold of Mr. Rochester's cham-
294.17 ber: I had seen him lying there myself, in the
294.18 mornings. The idea calmed me somewhat: I
294.19 lay down. Silence composes the nerves; and
294.20 as an unbroken hush now reigned again
294.21 through the whole house, I began to feel the
294.22 return of slumber. But it was not fated that
294.23 I should sleep that night. A dream had
294.24 scarcely approached my ear, when it fled
294.25 affrighted, scared by a marrow-freezing in-
294.26 cident enough.
294.27   This was a demoniac laugh -- low, suppressed,
294.28 and deep -- uttered, as it seemed, at the very
295.01 key-hole of my chamber-door. The head of
295.02 my bed was near the door, and I thought at
295.03 first, the goblin-laughter stood at my bedside --
295.04 or rather, crouched by my pillow: but I rose,
295.05 looked round, and could see nothing; while,
295.06 as I still gazed, the unnatural sound was
295.07 reiterated: and I knew it came from behind
295.08 the panels. My first impulse was to rise and
295.09 fasten the bolt; my next, again to cry out,
295.10 "Who is there?"
295.11   Something gurgled and moaned. Ere long,
295.12 steps retreated up the gallery towards the
295.13 third story staircase: a door had lately been
295.14 made to shut in that staircase: I heard it open
295.15 and close, and all was still.
295.16   "Was that Grace Poole? and is she pos-
295.17 sessed with a devil?" thought I. Impossible
295.18 now to remain longer by myself: I must go
295.19 to Mrs. Fairfax. I hurried on my frock and
295.20 shawl; I withdrew the bolt and opened the
295.21 door with a trembling hand. There was a
295.22 candle burning just outside, left on the mat-
295.23 ting in the gallery. I was surprised at this
295.24 circumstance: but still more was I amazed to
295.25 perceive the air quite dim, as if filled with
295.26 smoke; and, while looking to the right hand
295.27 and left, to find whence these blue wreaths
296.01 issued, I became further aware of a strong
296.02 smell of burning.
296.03   Something creaked: it was a door ajar; and
296.04 that door was Mr. Rochester's, and the smoke
296.05 rushed in a cloud from thence. I thought no
296.06 more of Mrs. Fairfax; I thought no more of
296.07 Grace Poole or the laugh: in an instant, I
296.08 was within the chamber. Tongues of flame
296.09 darted round the bed: the curtains were on
296.10 fire. In the midst of blaze and vapour, Mr.
296.11 Rochester lay stretched motionless, in deep
296.12 sleep.
296.13   "Wake! wake!" I cried -- I shook him, but
296.14 he only murmured and turned: the smoke
296.15 had stupified him. Not a moment could be
296.16 lost: the very sheets were kindling. I rushed
296.17 to his basin and ewer; fortunately, one was
296.18 wide and the other deep, and both were filled
296.19 with water, I heaved them up, deluged the
296.20 bed and its occupant, flew back to my own
296.21 room, brought my own water-jug, baptized
296.22 the couch afresh, and by God's aid, succeeded
296.23 in extinguishing the flames which were de-
296.24 vouring it.
296.25   The hiss of the quenched element, the
296.26 breakage of a pitcher which I flung from my
296.27 hand when I had emptied it, and above all,
297.01 the splash of the shower-bath I had libe-
297.02 rally bestowed, roused Mr. Rochester at last.
297.03 Though it was now dark, I knew he was
297.04 awake; because I heard him fulminating
297.05 strange anathemas at finding himself lying in
297.06 a pool of water.
297.07   "Is there a flood?" he cried.
297.08   "No, sir," I answered; "but there has been
297.09 a fire: get up, do, you are quenched now; I
297.10 will fetch you a candle."
297.11   "In the name of all the elves in Christen-
297.12 dom, is that Jane Eyre?" he demanded.
297.13 "What have you done with me, witch, sor-
297.14 ceress? who is in the room besides you?
297.15 Have you plotted to drown me?"
297.16   "I will fetch you a candle, sir; and in
297.17 Heaven's name, get up. Somebody has plotted
297.18 something: you cannot too soon find out who
297.19 and what it is."
297.20   "There -- I am up now; but at your peril
297.21 you fetch a candle yet: wait two minutes till I
297.22 get into some dry garments, if any dry there
297.23 be -- yes, here is my dressing-gown, now
297.24 run!"
297.25   I did run; I brought the candle which still
297.26 remained in the gallery. He took it from my

297.27 hand, held it up, and surveyed the bed, all
298.01 blackened and scorched, the sheets drenched
298.02 the carpet round swimming in water.
298.03 "What is it? and who did it?" he asked.
298.04 I briefly related to him what had trans-
298.05 pired: the strange laugh I had heard in the
298.06 gallery; the step ascending to the third story;
298.07 the smoke, -- the smell of fire which had con-
298.08 ducted me to his room; in what state I had
298.09 found matters there, and how I had deluged
298.10 him with all the water I could lay hands on.
298.11 He listened very gravely; his face, as I
298.12 went on, expressed more concern then aston-
298.13 ishment: he did not immediately speak when
298.14 I had concluded.
298.15 "Shall I call Mrs. Fairfax?" I asked.
298.16 "Mrs. Fairfax? No: -- what the deuce
298.17 would you call her for? what can she do?
298.18 Let her sleep unmolested."
298.19 "Then I will fetch Leah, and wake John
298.20 and his wife."
298.21 "Not at all: just be still. You have a
298.22 shawl on; if you are not warm enough, you
298.23 may take my cloak yonder; wrap it about
298.24 you, and sit down in the arm-chair: there, -- I
298.25 will put it on. Now place your feet on the
298.26 stool, to keep them out of the wet. I am
298.27 going to leave you a few minutes. I shall
299.01 take the candle. Remain where you are till I
299.02 return; be as still as a mouse. I must pay a
299.03 visit to the second story. Don't move, re-
299.04 member, or call any one."
299.05 He went: I watched the light withdraw.
299.06 He passed up the gallery very softly, unclosed
299.07 the staircase door with as little noise as pos-
299.08 sible, shut it after him, and the last ray
299.09 vanished. I was left in total darkness. I
299.10 listened for some noise, but heard nothing. A
299.11 very long time elapsed. I grew weary: it
299.12 was cold, in spite of the cloak; and then I did
299.13 not see the use of staying, as I was not to
299.14 rouse the house. I was on the point of risk-
299.15 ing Mr. Rochester's displeasure, by disobeying
299.16 his orders, when the light once more gleamed
299.17 dimly on the gallery-wall, and I heard his
299.18 unshod feet tread the matting. "I hope it is
299.19 he," thought I, "and not something worse."
299.20 He re-entered, pale and very gloomy. "I
299.21 have found it all out," said he, setting his
299.22 candle down on the wash-stand; it is as I
299.23 thought."
299.24 "How, sir?"
299.25 He made no reply, but stood with his arms
299.26 folded, looking on the ground. At the end
299.27 of a few minutes he inquired in rather a
299.28 peculiar tone: --
300.01 "I forget whether you said you saw any-
300.02 thing when you opened your chamber door."
300.03 "No, sir, only the candlestick on the
300.04 ground."
300.05 "But you heard an odd laugh? You have
300.06 heard that laugh before I should think, or
300.07 something like it?"
300.08 "Yes, sir: there is a woman who sews here
300.09 called Grace Poole, -- she laughs in that way.
300.10 She is a singular person."
300.11 "Just so. Grace Poole -- you have guessed
300.12 it. She is, as you say, singular, -- very. Well,
300.13 I shall reflect on the subject. Meantime, I
300.14 am glad that you are the only person, besides
300.15 myself, acquainted with the precise details of
300.16 to-night's incident. You are no talking fool:
300.17 say nothing about it. I will account for this
300.18 state of affairs /pointing to the bed/: and now
300.19 return to your own room. I shall do very
300.20 well on the sofa in the library for the rest of
300.21 the night. It is near four: -- in two hours the
300.22 servants will be up."
300.23 "Good-night, then, sir," said I, departing.
300.24 He seemed surprised -- very inconsistently
300.25 so, as he had just told me to go.
300.26 "What!" he exclaimed, "are you quitting
300.27 me already: and in that way?"
300.28 "You said I might go, sir."
301.01 "But not without taking leave; not without a
301.02 word or two of acknowledgment and good will:
301.03 not, in short, in that brief, dry fashion. Why,
301.04 you have saved my life! -- snatched me from a
301.05 horrible and excruciating death! -- and you
301.06 walk past me as if we were mutual strangers!
301.07 At least shake hands."
301.08 He held out his hand; I gave him mine:
301.09 he took it first in one, then in both his own.
301.10 "You have saved my life: I have a pleasure
301.11 in owing you so immense a debt. I cannot
301.12 say more. Nothing else that has being would
301.13 have been tolerable to me in the character of
301.14 creditor for such an obligation: but you; it is
301.15 different; -- I feel your benefits no burden,
301.16 Jane."
301.17 He paused; gazed at me: words almost
301.18 visible trembled on his lips, -- but his voice was
301.19 checked.
301.20 "Good-night again, sir. There is no debt,
301.21 benefit, burden, obligation, in the case."
301.22 "I knew," he continued, "you would do
301.23 me good in some way, at some time; -- I saw it
301.24 in your eyes when I first beheld you: their
301.25 expression and smile did not -- /again he
301.26 stopped/ -- did not /he proceeded hastily/ strike
301.27 delight to my very inmost heart so for nothing.

301.28 People talk of natural sympathies; I have
302.01 heard of good genii: -- there are grains of
302.02 truth in the wildest fable. My cherished pre-
302.03 server, good-night!" Strange energy was in his voice; strange
302.04 fire in his look.
302.05 "I am glad I happened to be awake," I
302.06 said; and then I was going.
302.07 "What! you will go?"
302.08 "I am cold, sir."
302.09 "Cold? Yes, -- and standing in a pool!
302.10 Go, then, Jane; go!" But he still retained
302.11 my hand, and I could not free it. I bethought
302.12 myself of an expedient.
302.13 "I think I hear Mrs. Fairfax move, sir,"
302.14 said I.
302.15 "Well, leave me:" he relaxed his fingers,
302.16 and I was gone.
302.17 I regained my couch, but never thought of
302.18 sleep. Till morning dawned I was tossed on
302.19 a buoyant but unquiet sea, where billows of
302.20 trouble rolled under surges of joy. I thought
302.21 sometimes I saw beyond its wild waters a
302.22 shore, sweet as the hills of Beulah; and now
302.23 and then a freshening gale wakened by hope,
302.24 bore my spirit triumphantly towards the
302.25 bourne: but I could not reach it, even in
302.26 fancy, -- a counteracting breeze blew off land,
303.01 and continually drove me back. Sense would
303.02 resist delirium: judgment would warn passion.
303.03 Too feverish to rest, I rose as soon as day
303.04 dawned.
303.05 [END OF VOL. 1]
305.01 [Jane Eyre.
305.02 Vol. 2 Chapter 1]
305.03 I both wished and feared to see Mr. Rochester
305.04 on the day which followed this sleepless night:
305.05 I wanted to hear his voice again, yet feared to
305.06 meet his eye. During the early part of the
305.07 morning, I momentarily expected his coming:
305.08 he was not in the frequent habit of entering
305.09 the school-room; but he did step in for a few
305.10 minutes sometimes, and I had the impression
305.11 that he was sure to visit it that day.
305.12 But the morning passed just as usual:
305.13 nothing happened to interrupt the quiet course
305.14 of Adele's studies; only, soon after breakfast, I
305.15 heard some bustle in the neighbourhood of Mr.
305.16 Rochester's chamber, Mrs. Fairfax's voice,
305.17 and Leah's, and the cook's -- that is, John's
305.18 wife -- and even John's own gruff tones. There
305.19 were exclamations of "what a mercy master
305.20 was not burnt in his bed!" "It is always
306.01 dangerous to keep a candle lit at night."
306.02 "How providential that he had presence of
306.03 mind to think of the water-jug!" "I wonder
306.04 he waked nobody!" "It is to be hoped he
306.05 will not take cold with sleeping on the library
306.06 sofa," &c.
306.07 To much confabulation succeeded a sound
306.08 of scrubbing and setting to rights; and when I
306.09 passed the room, in going down stairs to dinner,
306.10 I saw through the open door that all was again
306.11 restored to complete order: only the bed was
306.12 stripped of its hangings. Leah stood up in
306.13 the window-seat, rubbing the panes of glass
306.14 dimmed with smoke. I was about to address
306.15 her; for I wished to know what account had
306.16 been given of the affair: but, on advancing, I
306.17 saw a second person in the chamber -- a
306.18 woman sitting on a chair by the bed-side, and
306.19 sewing rings to new curtains. That woman
306.20 was no other than Grace Poole.
306.21 There she sat, staid and taciturn-looking, as
306.22 usual, in her brown stuff gown, her check
306.23 apron, white handkerchief, and cap. She was
306.24 intent on her work, in which her whole
306.25 thoughts seemed absorbed: on her hard fore-
306.26 head, and in her common-place features, was
306.27 nothing either of the paleness or desperation
306.28 one would have expected to see marking the
307.01 countenance of a woman who had attempted
307.02 murder; and whose intended victim had fol-
307.03 lowed her last night to her lair, and /as I
307.04 believe/ charged her with the crime she
307.05 wished to perpetrate. I was amazed -- con-
307.06 founded. She looked up while I still gazed at
307.07 her: no start, no increase or failure of colour
307.08 betrayed emotion, consciousness of guilt, or
307.09 fear of detection. She said, "Good-morning,
307.10 Miss," in her usual phlegmatic and brief
307.11 manner; and taking up another ring and more
307.12 tape, went on with her sewing.
307.13 "I will put her to some test," thought I:
307.14 "such absolute impenetrability is past com-
307.15 prehension."
307.16 "Good-morning, Grace," I said. "Has
307.17 anything happened here? I thought I heard
307.18 the servants all talking together a while ago."
307.19 "Only master had been reading in his bed
307.20 last night; he fell asleep with his candle lit,
307.21 and the curtains got on fire: but, fortunately,
307.22 he awoke before the bed-clothes or the wood-
307.23 work caught, and contrived to quench the flame
307.24 with the water in the ewer."
307.25 "A strange affair!" I said, in a low voice:
307.26 then, looking at her fixedly, -- "Did Mr.
307.27 Rochester wake nobody? Did no one hear
307.28 him move?"
308.01 She again raised her eyes to me; and this
308.02 time there was something of consciousness in
308.03 their expression. She seemed to examine me

308.04 warily; then she answered, --
308.05 "The servants sleep so far off, you know,
308.06 Miss, they would not be likely to hear. Mrs.
308.07 Fairfax's room and yours are the nearest to
308.08 master's; but Mrs. Fairfax said she heard
308.09 nothing: when people get elderly, they often
308.10 sleep heavy." She paused, and then added,
308.11 with a sort of assumed indifference, but still in
308.12 a marked and significant tone, "But you are
308.13 young, Miss; and I should say a light sleeper:
308.14 perhaps you may have heard a noise?"
308.15 "I did," said I, dropping my voice, so that
308.16 Leah, who was still polishing the panes, could
308.17 not hear me, "and at first I thought it was
308.18 Pilot: but Pilot cannot laugh; and I am cer-
308.19 tain I heard a laugh, and a strange one."
308.20 She took a new needleful of thread, waxed
308.21 it carefully, threaded her needle with a steady
308.22 hand, and then observed, with perfect com-
308.23 posure, --
308.24 "It is hardly likely master would laugh, I
308.25 should think, Miss, when he was in such
308.26 danger: you must have been dreaming."
308.27 "I was not dreaming," I said, with some
308.28 warmth: for her brazen coolness provoked me.
309.01 Again she looked at me; and with the same
309.02 scrutinizing and conscious eye.
309.03 "Have you told master that you heard a
309.04 laugh?" she inquired.
309.05 "I have not had the opportunity of speak-
309.06 ing to him this morning."
309.07 "You did not think of opening your door
309.08 and looking out into the gallery?" she further
309.09 asked.
309.10 She appeared to be cross-questioning me;
309.11 attempting to draw from me information un-
309.12 awares: the idea struck me that if she dis-
309.13 covered I knew or suspected her guilt, she would
309.14 be playing off some of her malignant pranks
309.15 on me; I thought it advisable to be on my
309.16 guard.
309.17 "On the contrary," said I, "I bolted my
309.18 door."
309.19 "Then you are not in the habit of bolting
309.20 your door every night before you get into
309.21 bed?"
309.22 "Fiend! she wants to know my habits
309.23 that she may lay her plans accordingly!" In-
309.24 dignation again prevailed over prudence; I
309.25 replied sharply: "Hitherto I have often
309.26 omitted to fasten the bolt: I did not think it
309.27 necessary. I was not aware any danger or
309.28 annoyance was to be dreaded at Thornfield--
310.01 Hall: but in future /and I laid marked stress
310.02 on the words/ I shall take good care to make
310.03 all secure before I venture to lie down."
310.04 "It will be wise so to do," was her answer:
310.05 "this neighbourhood is as quiet as any I know,
310.06 and I never heard of the Hall being attempted
310.07 by robbers since it was a house; though there
310.08 are hundreds of pounds' worth of plate in the
310.09 plate-closet, as is well known. And you see, for
310.10 such a large house, there are very few servants,
310.11 because master has never lived here much;
310.12 and when he does come, being a bachelor, he
310.13 needs little waiting on: but I always think it
310.14 best to err on the safe side; a door is soon
310.15 fastened, and it is as well to have a drawn bolt
310.16 between one and any mischief that may be
310.17 about. A deal of people, Miss, are for trust-
310.18 ing all to Providence; but I say Providence
310.19 will not dispense with the means, though he
310.20 often blesses them when they are used dis-
310.21 creetly." And here she closed her harangue:
310.22 a long one for her, and uttered with the de-
310.23 mureness of a Quakeress.
310.24 I still stood absolutely dumbfoundered at
310.25 what appeared to me her miraculous self-pos-
310.26 session and most inscrutable hypocrisy; when
310.27 the cook entered.
310.28 "Mrs. Poole," said she, addressing Grace,
311.01 "the servants' dinner will soon be ready: will
311.02 you come down?"
311.03 "No; just put my pint of porter and bit of
311.04 pudding on a tray, and I'll carry it up stairs."
311.05 "You'll have some meat?"
311.06 "Just a morsel, and a taste of cheese, that's
311.07 all."
311.08 "And the sago?"
311.09 "Never mind it, at present: I shall be
311.10 coming down before tea time: I'll make it
311.11 myself."
311.12 The cook here turned to me, saying that
311.13 Mrs. Fairfax was waiting for me: so I de-
311.14 parted.
311.15 I hardly heard Mrs. Fairfax's account of the
311.16 curtain conflagration during dinner, so much
311.17 was I occupied in puzzling my brains over the
311.18 enigmatical character of Grace Poole; and still
311.19 more in pondering the problem of her position
311.20 at Thornfield: in questioning why she had not
311.21 been given into custody that morning; or at
311.22 the very least dismissed from her master's ser-
311.23 vice. He had almost as much as declared his
311.24 conviction of her criminality last night: what
311.25 mysterious cause withheld him from accusing
311.26 her? Why had he enjoined me too to secresy?
311.27 It was strange: a bold, vindictive, and haughty
311.28 gentleman seemed somehow in the power of
312.01 one of the meanest of his dependants; so much
312.02 in her power, that even when she lifted her

312.03 hand against his life, he dared not openly
312.04 charge her with the attempt, much less punish
312.05 her for it.
312.06 Had Grace been young and handsome, I
312.07 should have been tempted to think that ten-
312.08 derer feelings than prudence or fear influenced
312.09 Mr. Rochester in her behalf; but hard-favoured
312.10 and matronly as she was, the idea could not
312.11 be admitted. "Yet," I reflected, "she has
312.12 been young once; her youth would be con-
312.13 temporary with her master's: Mrs. Fairfax
312.14 told me once, she had lived here many years.
312.15 I don't think she can ever have been pretty;
312.16 but for aught I know she may possess origi-
312.17 nality and strength of character to compen-
312.18 sate for the want of personal advantages.
312.19 Mr. Rochester is an amateur of the decided
312.20 and eccentric: Grace is eccentric at least.
312.21 what if a former caprice /a freak very possible
312.22 to a nature so sudden and headstrong as his/
312.23 has delivered him into her power, and she
312.24 now exercises over his actions a secret influ-
312.25 ence, the result of his own indiscretion, which
312.26 he cannot shake off and dare not disregard?"
312.27 But, having reached this point of conjecture,
312.28 Mrs. Poole's square, flat figure, and uncomely,
313.01 dry, even coarse face, recurred so distinctly to
313.02 my mind's eye, that I thought "No; impos-
313.03 sible! my supposition cannot be correct. Yet,"
313.04 suggested the secret voice which talks to us in
313.05 our hearts, "you are not beautiful either,
313.06 and perhaps Mr. Rochester approves you: at
313.07 any rate you have often felt as if he did; and
313.08 last night -- remember his words; remember
313.09 his look; remember his voice!"
313.10 I well remembered all: language, glance, and
313.11 tone seemed at the moment vividly renewed.
313.12 I was now in the school-room; Adele was
313.13 drawing; I bent over her and directed her
313.14 pencil. She looked up with a sort of start.
313.15 "Qu'avez-vous, mademoiselle?" said she;
313.16 "Vos doigts tremblent comme le feuille, et vos
313.17 joues sont rouges: mais, rouges comme des
313.18 cerises!"
313.19 "I am hot, Adele, with stooping!" She
313.20 went on sketching, I went on thinking.
313.21 I hastened to drive from my mind the
313.22 hateful notion I had been conceiving respect-
313.23 ing Grace Poole: it disgusted me. I compared
313.24 myself with her, and found we were different.
313.25 Bessie Leaven had said I was quite a lady; and
313.26 she spoke truth: I was a lady. And now I
313.27 looked much better than I did when Bessie
313.28 saw me: I had more colour and more flesh;
314.01 more life, more vivacity; because I had brighter
314.02 hopes and keener enjoyments.
314.03 "Evening approaches," said I, as I looked
314.04 towards the window. "I have never heard
314.05 Mr. Rochester's voice or step in the house to-
314.06 day; but surely I shall see him before night: I
314.07 feared the meeting in the morning; now I
314.08 desire it, because expectation has been so long
314.09 baffled that it is grown impatient."
314.10 When dusk actually closed, and when Adele
314.11 left me to go and play in the nursery with
314.12 Sophie, I did most keenly desire it. I listened
314.13 for the bell to ring below; I listened for Leah
314.14 coming up with a message; I fancied some-
314.15 times I heard Mr. Rochester's own tread, and
314.16 I turned to the door, expecting it to open and
314.17 admit him. The door remained shut: dark-
314.18 ness only came in through the window. Still
314.19 it was not late: he often sent for me at seven
314.20 and eight o'clock, and it was yet but six.
314.21 Surely I should not be wholly disappointed
314.22 to-night, when I had so many things to say to
314.23 him! I wanted again to introduce the subject
314.24 of Grace Poole, and to hear what he would
314.25 answer; I wanted to ask him plainly if he
314.26 really believed it was she who had made last
314.27 night's hideous attempt; and if so, why he
314.28 kept her wickedness a secret. It little mattered
315.01 whether my curiosity irritated him; I knew
315.02 the pleasure of vexing and soothing him by
315.03 turns; it was one I chiefly delighted in, and
315.04 a sure instinct always prevented me from
315.05 going too far: beyond the verge of provocation
315.06 I never ventured; on the extreme brink I liked
315.07 well to try my skill. Retaining every minute
315.08 form of respect, every propriety of my station,
315.09 I could still meet him in argument without
315.10 fear or uneasy restraint: this suited both him
315.11 and me.
315.12 A tread creaked on the stairs at last; Leah
315.13 made her appearance: but it was only to in-
315.14 timate that tea was ready in Mrs. Fairfax's
315.15 room. Thither I repaired, glad at least to go
315.16 down stairs; for that brought me, I imagined,
315.17 nearer to Mr. Rochester's presence.
315.18 "You must want your tea," said the good
315.19 lady as I joined her; "you ate so little at
315.20 dinner. I am afraid," she continued, "you
315.21 are not well to-day: you look flushed and
315.22 feverish."
315.23 "Oh, quite well! I never felt better."
315.24 "Then you must prove it by evincing a
315.25 good appetite; will you fill the tea-pot while
315.26 I knit off this needle?" Having completed
315.27 her task, she rose to draw down the blind
315.28 which she had hitherto kept up; by way, I
316.01 suppose, of making the most of daylight:

316.02 though dusk was now fast deepening into total
316.03 obscurity.
316.04 "It is fair to-night," said she, as she looked
316.05 through the panes, "though not starlight;
316.06 Mr. Rochester has, on the whole, had a favour-
316.07 able day for his journey."
316.08 "Journey! -- Is Mr. Rochester gone any-
316.09 where? I did not know he was out."
316.10 "Oh, he set off the moment he had break-
316.11 fasted! He is gone to the Leas; Mr. Esh-
316.12 ton's place, ten miles on the other side Mill-
316.13 cote; I believe there is quite a party assem-
316.14 bled there; Lord Ingram, Sir George Lynn,
316.15 Colonel Dent, and others."
316.16 "Do you expect him back to-night?"
316.17 "No -- nor to-morrow either; I should think
316.18 he is very likely to stay a week or more:
316.19 when these fine, fashionable people get to-
316.20 gether, they are so surrounded by elegance
316.21 and gaiety; so well provided with all that can
316.22 please and entertain, they are in no hurry to
316.23 separate. Gentlemen, especially, are often in
316.24 request on such occasions; and Mr. Rochester
316.25 is so talented and so lively in society, that I
316.26 believe he is a general favourite: the ladies
316.27 are very fond of him; though you would not
316.28 think his appearance calculated to recommend
317.01 him particularly in their eyes: but I suppose
317.02 his acquirements and abilities, perhaps his
317.03 wealth and good blood, make amends for any
317.04 little fault of look."
317.05 "Are there ladies at the Leas?"
317.06 "There are Mrs. Eshton and her three
317.07 daughters -- very elegant young ladies, indeed;
317.08 and there are the honourable Blanche and
317.09 Mary Ingram; most beautiful women, I sup-
317.10 pose: indeed I have seen Blanche, six or seven
317.11 years since, when she was a girl of eighteen.
317.12 She came here to a Christmas ball and party
317.13 Mr. Rochester gave. You should have seen
317.14 the dining-room that day -- how richly it was
317.15 decorated, how brilliantly lit up! I should
317.16 think there were fifty ladies and gentlemen
317.17 present -- all of the first county-families; and
317.18 Miss Ingram was considered the belle of the
317.19 evening."
317.20 "You saw her, you say, Mrs. Fairfax: what
317.21 was she like?"
317.22 "Yes, I saw her. The dining-room doors
317.23 were thrown open; and, as it was Christmas--
317.24 time, the servants were allowed to assemble in
317.25 the hall, to hear some of the ladies sing and
317.26 play. Mr. Rochester would have me to come
317.27 in, and I sat down in a quiet corner and
317.28 watched them. I never saw a more splendid
318.01 scene: the ladies were magnificently dressed;
318.02 most of them -- at least most of the younger
318.03 ones -- looked handsome; but Miss Ingram
318.04 was certainly the queen."
318.05 "And what was she like?"
318.06 "Tall, fine bust, sloping shoulders; long,
318.07 graceful neck: olive complexion, dark and
318.08 clear; noble features; eyes rather like Mr.
318.09 Rochester's: large and black, and as brilliant
318.10 as her jewels. And then she had such a fine
318.11 head of hair; raven-black, and so becomingly
318.12 arranged: a crown of thick plaits behind, and
318.13 in front the longest, and glossiest curls I
318.14 ever saw. She was dressed in pure white;
318.15 an amber-coloured scarf was passed over her
318.16 shoulder and across her breast, tied at the side,
318.17 and descending in long, fringed ends below
318.18 her knee. She wore an amber-coloured flower,
318.19 too, in her hair: it contrasted well with the
318.20 jetty mass of her curls."
318.21 "She was greatly admired of course?"
318.22 "Yes, indeed: and not only for her beauty,
318.23 but for her accomplishments. She was one of
318.24 the ladies who sang: a gentleman accompanied
318.25 her on the piano. She and Mr. Rochester
318.26 sang a duet."
318.27 "Mr. Rochester? I was not aware he could
318.28 sing."
319.01 "Oh! he has a fine bass voice, and an
319.02 excellent taste for music."
319.03 "And Miss Ingram: what sort of a voice
319.04 had she?"
319.05 "A very rich and powerful one: she sang
319.06 delightfully; it was a treat to listen to her; --
319.07 and she played afterwards. I am no judge of
319.08 music, but Mr. Rochester is; and I heard him
319.09 say her execution was remarkably good."
319.10 "And this beautiful and accomplished lady
319.11 is not yet married?"
319.12 "It appears not: I fancy neither she nor
319.13 her sister have very large fortunes. Old Lord
319.14 Ingram's estates were chiefly entailed, and the
319.15 eldest son came in for everything almost."
319.16 "But I wonder no wealthy nobleman or
319.17 gentleman has taken a fancy to her: Mr.
319.18 Rochester, for instance. He is rich, is he
319.19 not?"
319.20 "Oh! yes. But you see there is a consider-
319.21 able difference in age: Mr. Rochester is near
319.22 forty; she is but twenty-five."
319.23 "What of that? More unequal matches are
319.24 made every day."
319.25 "True: yet I should scarcely fancy Mr.
319.26 Rochester would entertain an idea of the sort.
319.27 -- but you eat nothing: you have scarcely
319.28 tasted since you began tea."

320.01 "No: I am too thirsty to eat. Will you
320.02 let me have another cup?"
320.03 I was about again to revert to the proba-
320.04 bility of a union between Mr. Rochester and
320.05 the beautiful Blanche: but Adele came in,
320.06 and the conversation was turned into another
320.07 channel.
320.08 When once more alone, I reviewed the
320.09 information I had got; looked into my heart,
320.10 examined its thoughts and feelings, and endea-
320.11 voured to bring back with a strict hand such
320.12 as had been straying through imagination's
320.13 boundless and trackless waste, into the safe
320.14 fold of common sense.
320.15 Arraigned at my own bar, Memory having
320.16 given her evidence of the hopes, wishes, senti-
320.17 ments I had been cherishing since last night --
320.18 of the general state of mind in which I
320.19 had indulged for nearly a fortnight past; Reason
320.20 having come forward and told in her own
320.21 quiet way, a plain, unvarnished tale, showing
320.22 how I had rejected the real, and rabidly de-
320.23 voured the ideal; -- I pronounced judgment to
320.24 this effect: --
320.25 That a greater fool than Jane Eyre had
320.26 never breathed the breath of life: that a more
320.27 fantastic idiot had never surfeited herself on
320.28 sweet lies, and swallowed poison as if it were
320.29 nectar.
321.01 "You," I said, "a favourite with Mr.
321.02 Rochester? You gifted with the power of
321.03 pleasing him? You of importance to him in
321.04 any way? Go! your folly sickens me. And
321.05 you have derived pleasure from occasional
321.06 tokens of preference -- equivocal tokens, shown
321.07 by a gentleman of family, and a man of the
321.08 world, to a dependant and a novice. How
321.09 dare you? Poor stupid dupe! -- Could not
321.10 even self-interest make you wiser? You re-
321.11 peated to yourself this morning the brief scene
321.12 of last night? -- Cover your face and be
321.13 ashamed! He said something in praise of
321.14 your eyes, did he? Blind puppy! Open
321.15 their blear lids and look on your own ac-
321.16 cursed senselessness! It does good to no
321.17 woman to be flattered by her superior, who
321.18 cannot possibly intend to marry her; and it is
321.19 madness in all women to let a secret love
321.20 kindle within them, which, if unreturned and
321.21 unknown, must devour the life that feeds it:
321.22 and, if discovered and responded to, must lead,
321.23 ignis-fatuus-like, into miry wilds whence there
321.24 is no extrication.
321.25 "Listen, then, Jane Eyre, to your sentence:
321.26 to-morrow, place the glass before you, and
321.27 draw in chalk your own picture, faithfully;
321.28 without softening one defect: omit no harsh
322.01 line, smooth away no displeasing irregularity;
322.02 write under it, 'Portrait of a Governess, dis-
322.03 connected, poor, and plain.'
322.04 "Afterwards, take a piece of smooth ivory
322.05 -- you have one prepared in your drawing--
322.06 box: take your palette, mix your freshest,
322.07 finest, clearest tints; choose your most deli-
322.08 cate camel-hair pencils; delineate carefully
322.09 the loveliest face you can imagine; paint it in
322.10 your softest shades and sweetest hues, accord-
322.11 ing to the description given by Mrs. Fairfax
322.12 of Blanche Ingram: remember the raven
322.13 ringlets, the oriental eye; -- what! you revert
322.14 to Mr. Rochester as a model! Order! No
322.15 snivel! -- no sentiment! -- no regret! I will
322.16 endure only sense and resolution. Recall the
322.17 august and harmonious lineaments, the Gre-
322.18 cian neck and bust: let the round and dazzling
322.19 arm be visible, and the delicate hand; omit
322.20 neither diamond ring nor gold bracelet; por-
322.21 tray faithfully the attire, aerial lace and glis-
322.22 tening satin, graceful scarf and golden rose:
322.23 call it 'Blanche, an accomplished lady of
322.24 rank.'
322.25 "Whenever, in future, you should chance
322.26 to fancy Mr. Rochester thinks well of you,
322.27 take out these two pictures and compare
322.28 them: say, 'Mr. Rochester might probably
323.01 win that noble lady's love, if he chose to strive
323.02 for it; is it likely he would waste a serious
323.03 thought on this indigent and insignificant
323.04 plebeian?'"
323.05 "I'll do it," I resolved: and having framed
323.06 this determination, I grew calm, and fell
323.07 asleep.
323.08 I kept my word. An hour or two sufficed
323.09 to sketch my own portrait in crayons; and in
323.10 less than a fortnight I had completed an ivory
323.11 minature of an imaginary Blanche Ingram.
323.12 It looked a lovely face enough, and when
323.13 compared with the real head in chalk, the
323.14 contrast was as great as self-control could
323.15 desire. I derived benefit from the task: it
323.16 had kept my head and hands employed, and
323.17 had given force and fixedness to the new im-
323.18 pressions I wished to stamp indelibly on my
323.19 heart.
323.20 Ere long, I had reason to congratulate my-
323.21 self on the course of wholesome discipline to
323.22 which I had thus forced my feelings to submit:
323.23 thanks to it, I was able to meet subsequent oc-
323.24 currences with a decent calm; which, had they
323.25 found me unprepared, I should probably have
323.26 been unequal to maintain, even externally.

378

324.01 [Vol. 2 Chapter 2]
324.02 A week passed, and no news arrived of Mr.
324.03 Rochester: ten days; and still he did not
324.04 come. Mrs. Fairfax said she should not be
324.05 surprised if he were to go straight from the
324.06 Leas to London, and thence to the continent,
324.07 and not show his face again at Thornfield for
324.08 a year to come: he had not unfrequently
324.09 quitted it in a manner quite as abrupt and
324.10 unexpected. When I heard this I was begin-
324.11 ning to feel a strange chill and failing at the
324.12 heart. I was actually permitting myself to
324.13 experience a sickening sense of disappoint-
324.14 ment: but rallying my wits, and recollecting
324.15 my principles, I at once called my sensations
324.16 to order; and it was wonderful how I got over
324.17 the temporary blunder -- How I cleared up the
324.18 mistake of supposing Mr. Rochester's move-
324.19 ments a matter in which I had any cause to
324.20 take a vital interest. Not that I humbled
325.01 myself by a slavish notion of inferiority: on
325.02 the contrary, I just said: --
325.03 "You have nothing to do with the master
325.04 of Thornfield, further than to receive the
325.05 salary he gives you for teaching his protegee,
325.06 and be grateful for such respectful and kind
325.07 treatment as, if you do your duty, you have a
325.08 right to expect at his hands. Be sure that is
325.09 the only tie he seriously acknowledges be-
325.10 tween you and him: so don't make him the
325.11 object of your fine feelings, your raptures,
325.12 agonies, and so forth. He is not of your
325.13 order: keep to your caste; and be too self--
325.14 respecting to lavish the love of the whole
325.15 heart, soul, and strength, where such a gift is
325.16 not wanted and would be despised."
325.17 I went on with my day's business tranquilly;
325.18 but ever and anon, vague suggestions kept
325.19 wandering across my brain of reasons why I
325.20 should quit Thornfield; and I kept involunta-
325.21 rily framing advertisements and pondering con-
325.22 jectures about new situations; these thoughts
325.23 I did not think it necessary to check; they
325.24 might germinate and bear fruit if they could.
325.25 Mr. Rochester had been absent upwards of
325.26 a fortnight, when the post brought Mrs. Fair-
325.27 fax a letter.
325.28 "It is from the master," said she, as she
326.01 looked at the direction. "Now I suppose we
326.02 shall know whether we are to expect his re-
326.03 turn or not."
326.04 And while she broke the seal and perused
326.05 the document, I went on taking my coffee:
326.06 /we were at breakfast/ it was hot, and I attri-
326.07 buted to that circumstance a fiery glow which
326.08 suddenly rose to my face. why my hand
326.09 shook, and why I involuntarily spilt half the
326.10 contents of my cup into my saucer, I did not
326.11 choose to consider.
326.12 but we run a chance of being busy enough
326.13 now: for a little while at least," said Mrs.
326.14 Fairfax, still holding the note before her spec-
326.15 tacles.
326.16 Ere I permitted myself to request an ex-
326.17 planation, I tied the string of Adele's pinafore
326.18 which happened to be loose: having helped her
326.19 also to another bun and refilled her mug with
326.20 milk, I said, nonchalantly: --
326.21 "Mr. Rochester is not likely to return soon,
326.22 I suppose?"
326.23 "Indeed, he is -- in three days, he says; that
326.24 will be next Thursday; and not alone either. I
326.25 don't know how many of the fine people at
326.26 the Leas are coming with him: he sends
326.27 directions for all the best bed-rooms to be
327.01 prepared; and the library and drawing-rooms
327.02 are to be cleaned out; and I am to get more
327.03 kitchen hands from the George Inn, at Mill-
327.04 cote, and from wherever else I can; and the
327.05 ladies will bring their maids and the gentle-
327.06 men their valets: so we shall have a full
327.07 house of it." And Mrs. Fairfax swallowed
327.08 her breakfast and hastened away to commence
327.09 operations.
327.10 The three days were, as she had foretold,
327.11 busy enough. I had thought all the rooms
327.12 at Thornfield beautifully clean and well-ar-
327.13 ranged: but it appears I was mistaken. Three
327.14 women were got to help; and such scrubbing,
327.15 such brushing, such washing of paint and
327.16 beating of carpets, such taking down and
327.17 putting up of pictures, such polishing of
327.18 mirrors and lustres, such lighting of fires in
327.19 bedrooms, such airing of sheets and feather-
327.20 beds on hearths, I never beheld, either before
327.21 or since. Adele ran quite wild in the midst of
327.22 it: the preparations for company and the
327.23 prospect of their arrival, seemed to throw her
327.24 into ecstasies. She would have Sophie to look
327.25 over all her "toilettes" as she called frocks;
327.26 to furbish up any that were "passees," and to
327.27 air and arrange the new. For herself, she did
327.28 nothing but caper about in the front chambers,
328.01 jump on and off the bedsteads, and lie on the
328.02 mattresses and piled-up bolsters and pillows
328.03 before the enormous fires roaring in the chim-
328.04 neys. From school duties she was exonerated:
328.05 Mrs. Fairfax has pressed me into her service,
328.06 and I was all day in the store-room, helping
328.07 /or hindering/ her and the cook; learning to
328.08 make custards and cheesecakes and French

328.09 pastry, to truss game and garnish dessert--
328.10 dishes.
328.11 The party were expected to arrive on Thurs-
328.12 day afternoon, in time for dinner at six.
328.13 During the intervening period I had no time
328.14 to nurse chimeras; and I believe I was as
328.15 active and gay as anybody -- Adele excepted.
328.16 Still, now and then, I received a damping
328.17 check to my cheerfulness; and was, in spite of
328.18 myself, thrown back on the region of doubts
328.19 and portents, and dark conjectures. This was
328.20 when I chanced to see the third story staircase
328.21 door /which of late had always been kept
328.22 locked/ open slowly, and give passage to the
328.23 form of Grace Poole, in prim cap, white apron,
328.24 and handkerchief; when I watched her glide
328.25 along the gallery, her quiet tread muffled in a
328.26 list slipper; when I saw her look into the
328.27 bustling, topsy-turvy bed-rooms, -- just say a
328.28 word, perhaps, to the charwoman about the
329.01 proper way to polish a grate, or clean a marble
329.02 mantel-piece, or take stains from papered walls,
329.03 and then pass on. She would thus descend to
329.04 the kitchen once a day, eat her dinner, smoke
329.05 a moderate pipe on the hearth, and go back,
329.06 carrying her pot of porter with her, for her
329.07 private solace, in her own gloomy upper
329.08 haunt. Only one hour in the twenty-four did
329.09 she pass with her fellow-servants below; all
329.10 the rest of her time was spent in some low--
329.11 ceiled, oaken chamber of the second story:
329.12 there she sat and sewed -- and probably laughed
329.13 drearily to herself, -- as companionless as a
329.14 prisoner in his dungeon.
329.15 The strangest thing of all was, that not a
329.16 soul in the house, except me, noticed her
329.17 habits, or seemed to marvel at them: no one
329.18 discussed her position or employment; no one
329.19 pitied her solitude or isolation. I once, indeed,
329.20 overheard part of a dialogue between Leah and
329.21 one of the charwomen, of which Grace formed
329.22 the subject. Leah had been saying something
329.23 I had not caught, and the charwoman re-
329.24 marked: --
329.25 "She gets good wages, I guess?"
329.26 "Yes," said Leah; "I wish I had as good;
329.27 not that mine are to complain of, -- there's no
329.28 stinginess at Thornfield; but they're not one--
330.01 fifth of the sum Mrs. Poole receives. And she
330.02 is laying by: she goes every quarter to the
330.03 bank at Millcote. I should not wonder but
330.04 she has saved enough to keep her independent
330.05 if she liked to leave; but I suppose she's got
330.06 used to the place; and then she's not forty yet,
330.07 and strong and able for anything. It is too
330.08 soon for her to give up business."
330.09 "She is a good hand, I daresay," said the
330.10 charwoman.
330.11 "Ah! -- she understands what she has to do,
330.12 -- nobody better," rejoined Leah, significantly;
330.13 "and it is not every one could fill her shoes:
330.14 not for all the money she gets."
330.15 "That it is not!" was the reply. "I wonder
330.16 whether master --"
330.17 The charwoman was going on; but here
330.18 Leah turned and perceived me, and she in-
330.19 stantly gave her companion a nudge.
330.20 "Doesn't she know?" I heard the woman
330.21 whisper.
330.22 Leah shook her head, and the conversation
330.23 was of course dropped. All I had gathered from
330.24 it amounted to this, -- that there was a mystery
330.25 at Thornfield; and that from participation in
330.26 that mystery, I was purposely excluded.
330.27 Thursday came: all work had been com-
330.28 pleted the previous evening; carpets were laid
331.01 down, bed-hangings festooned, radiant white
331.02 counterpanes spread, toilet tables arranged, fur-
331.03 niture rubbed, flowers piled in vases: both
331.04 chambers and saloons looked as fresh and bright
331.05 as hands could make them. The hall, too, was
331.06 scoured; and the great carved clock, as well as
331.07 the steps and banisters of the staircase, were
331.08 polished to the brightness of glass: in the
331.09 dining-room, the sideboard flashed resplendent
331.10 with plate; in the drawing-room and boudoir,
331.11 vases of exotics bloomed on all sides.
331.12 Afternoon arrived: Mrs. Fairfax assumed
331.13 her best black satin gown, her gloves, and her
331.14 gold watch; for it was her part to receive the
331.15 company, -- to conduct the ladies to their rooms,
331.16 &c. Adele, too, would be dressed: though I
331.17 thought she had little chance of being intro-
331.18 duced to the party that day at least. However,
331.19 to please her, I allowed Sophie to apparel her
331.20 in one of her short, full muslin frocks. For
331.21 myself, I had no need to make any change;
331.22 I should not be called upon to quit my sanc-
331.23 tum of the school-room; for a sanctum it was
331.24 now become to me, -- "a very pleasant refuge
331.25 in time of trouble."
331.26 It had been a mild, serene spring day: one
331.27 of those days which towards the end of March
331.28 or the beginning of April, rise shining over
332.01 the earth as heralds of summer. It was draw-
332.02 ing to an end now; but the evening was even
332.03 warm, and I sat at work in the school-room
332.04 with the window open.
332.05 "It gets late," said Mrs. Fairfax, entering
332.06 in rustling state. "I am glad I ordered
332.07 dinner an hour after the time Mr. Rochester

332.08 mentioned; for it is past six now. I have sent
332.09 John down to the gates to see if there is any-
332.10 thing on the road: one can see a long way
332.11 from thence in the direction of Millcote."
332.12 She went to the window. "Here he is!" said
332.13 she. "Well John," /leaning out/ "any news?"
332.14 "They're coming, ma'am," was the answer.
332.15 "They'll be here in ten minutes."
332.16 Adèle flew to the window. I followed; taking
332.17 care to stand on one side, so that, screened by
332.18 the curtain, I could see without being seen.
332.19 The ten minutes John had given seemed
332.20 very long, but at last wheels were heard; four
332.21 equestrians galloped up the drive, and after
332.22 them came two open carriages. Fluttering
332.23 veils and waving plumes filled the vehicles;
332.24 two of the cavaliers were young, dashing look-
332.25 ing gentlemen; the third was Mr. Rochester
332.26 on his black horse, Mesrour; Pilot bounding
332.27 before him: at his side rode a lady, and he and
332.28 she were the first of the party. Her purple
333.01 riding-habit almost swept the ground, her veil
333.02 streamed long on the breeze; mingling with its
333.03 transparent folds, and gleaming through them,
333.04 shone rich raven ringlets.
333.05 "Miss Ingram!" exclaimed Mrs. Fairfax,
333.06 and away she hurried to her post below.
333.07 The cavalcade, following the sweep of the
333.08 drive, quickly turned the angle of the house,
333.09 and I lost sight of it. Adèle now petitioned
333.10 to go down; but I took her on my knee and
333.11 gave her to understand that she must not on
333.12 any account think of venturing in sight of the
333.13 ladies, either now or at any other time, unless
333.14 expressly sent for: that Mr. Rochester would
333.15 be very angry, &c. "Some natural tears she
333.16 shed" on being told this; but as I began to
333.17 look very grave, she consented at last to wipe
333.18 them.
333.19 A joyous stir was now audible in the hall:
333.20 gentlemen's deep tones, and ladies' silvery ac-
333.21 cents blent harmoniously together, and distin-
333.22 guishable above all, though not loud, was the
333.23 sonorous voice of the master of Thornfield
333.24 Hall, welcoming his fair and gallant guests
333.25 under its roof. Then light steps ascended the
333.26 stairs; and there was a tripping through the
333.27 gallery, and soft, cheerful laughs, and opening
333.28 and closing doors, and, for a time, a hush.
334.01 "Elles changent de toilettes," said Adèle;
334.02 who, listening attentively, had followed every
334.03 movement; and she sighed.
334.04 "Chez maman," said she, "quand il y avait
334.05 du monde, je les suivais partout, au salon et a
334.06 leurs chambres; souvent je regardais les femmes
334.07 de chambre coiffer et habiller les dames, et
334.08 c'était si amusant: comme cela on apprend."
334.09 "Don't you feel hungry, Adèle?"
334.10 "Mais oui, mademoiselle: voila cinq ou six
334.11 heures que nous n'avons pas mangé."
334.12 "Well now, while the ladies are in their
334.13 rooms, I will venture down and get you some-
334.14 thing to eat."
334.15 And issuing from my asylum with precau-
334.16 tion, I sought a back-stairs which conducted
334.17 directly to the kitchen. All in that region
334.18 was fire and commotion; the soup and fish
334.19 were in the last stage of projection, and the
334.20 cook hung over her crucibles in a frame of
334.21 mind and body threatening spontaneous com-
334.22 bustion. In the servants' hall two coachmen
334.23 and three gentlemen's gentlemen stood or sat
334.24 round the fire; the Abigails I suppose were
334.25 up-stairs with their mistresses; the new ser-
334.26 vants that had been hired from Millcote, were
334.27 bustling about everywhere. Threading this
334.28 chaos, I at last reached the larder; there I
335.01 took possession of a cold chicken, a roll of
335.02 bread, some tarts, a plate or two and a knife
335.03 and fork: with this booty I made a hasty
335.04 retreat. I had regained the gallery, and was
335.05 just shutting the back-door behind me, when
335.06 an accelerated hum warned me that the ladies
335.07 were about to issue from their chambers. I
335.08 could not proceed to the school-room without
335.09 passing some of their doors, and running the
335.10 risk of being surprised with my cargo of
335.11 victualage; so I stood still at this end, which,
335.12 being windowless, was dark: quite dark now,
335.13 for the sun was set and twilight gathering.
335.14 Presently the chambers gave up their fair
335.15 tenants one after another: each came out
335.16 gaily and airily, with dress that gleamed lus-
335.17 trous through the dusk. For a moment they
335.18 stood grouped together at the other extremity
335.19 of the gallery, conversing in a key of sweet
335.20 subdued vivacity: they then descended the
335.21 staircase almost as noiselessly as a bright mist
335.22 rolls down a hill. Their collective appearance
335.23 had left on me an impression of high-born ele-
335.24 gance, such as I had never before received.
335.25 I found Adèle peeping through the school-
335.26 room door, which she held ajar. "What beau-
335.27 tiful ladies!" cried she in English. "Oh, I
335.28 wish I might go to them! Do you think Mr.
336.01 Rochester will send for us by-and-by, after
336.02 dinner?"
336.03 "No, indeed, I don't; Mr. Rochester has
336.04 something else to think about. Never mind
336.05 the ladies to-night; perhaps you will see them
336.06 to-morrow: here is your dinner."
336.07 She was really hungry, so the chicken and
336.08 tarts served to divert her attention for a time.
336.09 It was well I secured this forage; or both she,
336.10 I and Sophie, to whom I conveyed a share of
336.11 our repast, would have run a chance of getting
336.12 no dinner at all: every one down stairs was
336.13 too much engaged to think of us. The dessert
336.14 was not carried out till after nine, and at ten,
336.15 footmen were still running to and fro with
336.16 trays and coffee-cups. I allowed Adèle to sit
336.17 up much later than usual; for she declared she
336.18 could not possibly go to sleep while the doors
336.19 kept opening and shutting below, and people
336.20 bustling about. Besides, she added, a mes-
336.21 sage might possibly come from Mr. Rochester
336.22 when she was undressed; "et alors quel dom-
336.23 mage!"
336.24 I told her stories as long as she would listen
336.25 to them; and then for a change I took her out
336.26 into the gallery. The hall lamp was now lit,
336.27 and it amused her to look over the balustrade
336.28 and watch the servants passing backwards and
337.01 forwards. when the evening was far ad-
337.02 vanced, a sound of music issued from the
337.03 drawing-room, whither the piano had been
337.04 removed; Adèle and I sat down on the top step
337.05 of the stairs to listen. Presently a voice blent
337.06 with the rich tones of the instrument; it was a
337.07 lady who sang, and very sweet her notes were.
337.08 The solo over, a duet followed, and then a
337.09 glee: a joyous conversational murmur filled
337.10 up the intervals. I listened long: suddenly
337.11 I discovered that my ear was wholly intent on
337.12 analyzing the mingled sounds, and trying to
337.13 discriminate amidst the confusion of accents
337.14 those of Mr. Rochester; and when it caught
337.15 them, which it soon did, it found a further
337.16 task in framing the tones, rendered by dis-
337.17 tance inarticulate, into words.
337.18 The clock struck eleven. I looked at Adèle,
337.19 whose head leant against my shoulder; her
337.20 eyes were waxing heavy, so I took her up in
337.21 my arms and carried her off to bed. It was
337.22 near one before the gentlemen and ladies
337.23 sought their chambers.
337.24 The next day was as fine as its predecessor;
337.25 it was devoted by the party to an excursion to
337.26 some site in the neighbourhood. They set out
337.27 early in the forenoon, some on horseback, the
337.28 rest in carriages; I witnessed both the depar-
338.01 ture and the return. Miss Ingram, as before,
338.02 was the only lady equestrian; and as before,
338.03 Mr. Rochester galloped at her side; the two
338.04 rode a little apart from the rest. I pointed out
338.05 this circumstance to Mrs. Fairfax, who was
338.06 standing at the window with me: --
338.07 "You said it was not likely they should
338.08 think of being married," said I, "but you see
338.09 Mr. Rochester evidently prefers her to any of
338.10 the other ladies."
338.11 "Yes; I daresay: no doubt he admires
338.12 her."
338.13 "And she him," I added; "look how she
338.14 leans her head towards him as if she were con-
338.15 versing confidentially! I wish I could see
338.16 her face; I have never had a glimpse of it
338.17 yet."
338.18 "You will see her this evening," answered
338.19 Mrs. Fairfax. "I happened to remark to
338.20 Mr. Rochester how much Adèle wished to
338.21 be introduced to the ladies, and he said:
338.22 'Oh! let her come into the drawing-room
338.23 after dinner; and request Miss Eyre to ac-
338.24 company her.'
338.25 "Yes -- he said that from mere politeness:
338.26 I need not go, I am sure," I answered.
338.27 "well -- I observed to him that as you
338.28 were unused to company, I did not think you
339.01 would like appearing before so gay a party --
339.02 all strangers; and he replied, in his quick
339.03 way: 'Nonsense! If she objects, tell her it
339.04 is my particular wish; and if she resists, say I
339.05 shall come and fetch her in case of contumacy.'"
339.06 "I will not give him that trouble;" I an-
339.07 swered. "I will go, if no better may be: but
339.08 I don't like it. Shall you be there, Mrs.
339.09 Fairfax?"
339.10 plea. I'll tell you how to manage so as to
339.11 avoid the embarrassment of making a formal
339.12 entrance, which is the most disagreeable part
339.13 of the business. You must go into the draw-
339.14 ing-room while it is empty, before the ladies
339.15 leave the dinner-table; choose your seat in any
339.16 quiet nook you like; you need not stay long
339.17 after the gentlemen come in, unless you please:
339.18 just let Mr. Rochester see you are there and
339.19 then slip away -- nobody will notice you."
339.20 "will these people remain long, do you
339.21 think?"
339.22 "Perhaps two or three weeks; certainly not
339.23 more. After the Easter recess, Sir George
339.24 Lynn, who was lately elected member for
339.25 Millcote, will have to go up to town and take
339.26 his seat; I dare say Mr. Rochester will ac-
339.27 company him: it surprises me that he has
340.01 already made so protracted a stay at Thorn-
340.02 field.
340.03 It was with some trepidation that I per-
340.04 ceived the hour approach when I was to
340.05 repair with my charge to the drawing-room.
340.06 Adèle had been in a state of ecstasy all day,

340.07 after hearing she was to be presented to the
340.08 ladies in the evening; and it was not till
340.09 Sophie commenced the operation of dressing
340.10 her, that she sobered down. Then the im-
340.11 portance of the process quickly steadied her;
340.12 and by the time she had her curls arranged
340.13 in well-smoothed, drooping clusters, her pink
340.14 satin frock put on, her long sash tied, and her
340.15 lace mittens adjusted, she looked as grave as
340.16 any judge. No need to warn her not to dis-
340.17 arrange her attire: when she was dressed, she
340.18 sat demurely down in her little chair, taking
340.19 care previously to lift up the satin skirt for
340.20 fear she should crease it, and assured me she
340.21 would not stir thence till I was ready. This I
340.22 quickly was: my best dress /the silver-gray
340.23 one, purchased for Miss Temple's wedding,
340.24 and never worn since/ was soon put on; my
340.25 hair was soon smoothed; my sole ornament,
340.26 the pearl brooch, soon assumed. We descended.
340.27 Fortunately there was another entrance to
340.28 the drawing-room than that through the saloon
341.01 where they were all seated at dinner. We found
341.02 the apartment vacant; a large fire burning
341.03 silently on the marble hearth, and wax candles
341.04 shining in bright solitude, amid the exquisite
341.05 flowers with which the tables were adorned.
341.06 The crimson curtain hung before the arch:
341.07 slight as was the separation this drapery
341.08 formed from the party in the adjoining saloon,
341.09 they spoke in so low a key that nothing of
341.10 their conversation could be distinguished be-
341.11 yond a soothing murmur.
341.12 Adele, who appeared to be still under the
341.13 influence of a most solemnizing impression,
341.14 sat down without a word on the footstool I
341.15 pointed out to her. I retired to a window seat,
341.16 and taking a book from a table near, en-
341.17 deavoured to read. Adele brought her stool to
341.18 my feet; ere long she touched my knee.
341.19 "What is it, Adele?"
341.20 "Est-ce je ne puis pas prendre une
341.21 seule de ces fleurs magnifiques, mademoiselle?
341.22 Seulement pour compléter ma toilette."
341.23 "You think too much of your `toilette,'
341.24 Adele: but you may have a flower." And I
341.25 took a rose from a vase and fastened it in her
341.26 sash. She sighed a sigh of ineffable satisfac-
341.27 tion, as if her cup of happiness were now full.
341.28 I turned my face away to conceal a smile I
342.01 could not suppress: there was something ludi-
342.02 crous as well as painful in the little Parisienne's
342.03 earnest and innate devotion to matters of dress.
342.04 A soft sound of rising now became audible;
342.05 the curtain was swept back from the arch;
342.06 through it appeared the dining-room, with its
342.07 lit lustre pouring down light on the silver and
342.08 glass of a magnificent dessert-service covering
342.09 a long table; a band of ladies stood in the
342.10 opening; they entered, and the curtain fell
342.11 behind them.
342.12 There were but eight; yet somehow as they
342.13 flocked in, they gave the impression of a much
342.14 larger number. Some of them were very tall;
342.15 many were dressed in white; and all had a
342.16 sweeping amplitude of array that seemed to
342.17 magnify their persons as a mist magnifies the
342.18 moon. I rose and curtseyed to them; one or
342.19 two bent their heads in return; the others
342.20 only stared at me.
342.21 They dispersed about the room; reminding
342.22 me, by the lightness and buoyancy of their
342.23 movements, of a flock of white plumy birds.
342.24 Some of them threw themselves in half--
342.25 reclining positions on the sofas and ottomans;
342.26 some bent over the tables and examined the
342.27 flowers and books; the rest gathered in a
342.28 group round the fire: all talked in a low but
343.01 clear tone which seemed habitual to them. I
343.02 knew their names afterwards, and may as well
343.03 mention them now.
343.04 First, there was Mrs. Eshton and two of
343.05 her daughters. She had evidently been a
343.06 handsome woman, and was well preserved
343.07 still. Of her daughters, the eldest, Amy, was
343.08 rather little; naive, and child-like in face and
343.09 manner, and piquant in form: her white
343.10 muslin dress and blue sash became her well.
343.11 The second, Louisa, was taller and more
343.12 elegant in figure; with a very pretty face, of
343.13 that order the French term "minois chiffoné:"
343.14 both sisters were fair as lilies.
343.15 Lady Lynn was a large and stout personage
343.16 of about forty; very erect, very haughty--
343.17 looking, richly dressed in a satin robe of
343.18 changeful sheen: her dark hair shone glossily
343.19 under the shade of an azure plume, and within
343.20 the circlet of a band of gems.
343.21 Mrs. Colonel Dent was less showy; but, I
343.22 thought more lady-like. She had a slight
343.23 figure, a pale, gentle face, and fair hair. Her
343.24 black satin dress, her scarf of rich foreign
343.25 lace, and her pearl ornaments, pleased me
343.26 better than the rainbow of radiance of the titled
343.27 dame.
343.28 But the three most distinguished -- partly
344.01 perhaps, because the tallest figures of the band
344.02 -- were the Dowager Lady Ingram and her
344.03 daughters, Blanche and Mary. They were
344.04 all three of the loftiest stature of woman.
344.05 The Dowager might be between forty and fifty:

344.06 her shape was still fine; her hair /by candle
344.07 light at least/ still black; her teeth, too, were
344.08 still apparently perfect. Most people would
344.09 have termed her a splendid woman of her age:
344.10 and so she was, no doubt, physically speaking;
344.11 but then there was an expression of almost
344.12 insupportable haughtiness in her bearing and
344.13 countenance. She had Roman features and
344.14 a double chin, disappearing into a throat like
344.15 a pillar: these features appeared to me not
344.16 only inflated and darkened, but even fur-
344.17 rowed with pride; and the chin was sustained
344.18 by the same principle, in a position of almost
344.19 preternatural erectness. She had, likewise, a
344.20 fierce and a hard eye: it reminded me of Mrs.
344.21 Reed's; she mouthed her words in speaking;
344.22 her voice was deep, its inflections very pompous,
344.23 very dogmatical, -- very intolerable, in short.
344.24 A crimson velvet robe, and a shawl turban of
344.25 some gold-wrought Indian fabric, invested her
344.26 /I suppose she thought/ with a truly imperial
344.27 dignity.
344.28 Blanche and Mary were of equal stature, --
345.01 straight and tall as poplars. Mary was too
345.02 slim for her height; but Blanche was moulded
345.03 like a Dian. I regarded her, of course, with
345.04 special interest. First, I wished to see whether
345.05 her appearance accorded with Mrs. Fairfax's
345.06 description; secondly, whether it at all re-
345.07 sembled the fancy miniature I had painted of
345.08 her; and thirdly -- it will out! -- whether it
345.09 were such as I should fancy likely to suit
345.10 Mr. Rochester's taste.
345.11 As far as person went, she answered point
345.12 for point, both to my picture and Mrs. Fair-
345.13 fax's description. The noble bust, the sloping
345.14 shoulders, the graceful neck, the dark eyes
345.15 and black ringlets were all there: -- but her
345.16 face? -- Her face was like her mother's; a
345.17 youthful unfurrowed likeness: the same low
345.18 brow, the same high features, the same pride.
345.19 It was not, however, so saturnine a pride: she
345.20 laughed continually; her laugh was satirical,
345.21 and so was the habitual expression of her
345.22 arched and haughty lip.
345.23 Genius is said to be self-conscious: I cannot
345.24 tell whether Miss Ingram was a genius, but
345.25 she was self-conscious -- remarkably self-con-
345.26 scious indeed. She entered into a discourse
345.27 on botany with the gentle Mrs. Dent. It
345.28 seems Mrs. Dent had not studied that science:
346.01 though, as she said, she liked flowers, "espe-
346.02 cially wild ones;" Miss Ingram had, and she
346.03 ran over its vocabulary with an air. I pre-
346.04 sently perceived she was /what is vernacularly
346.05 termed/ trailing Mrs. Dent; that is, playing on
346.06 her ignorance: her trail might be clever, but
346.07 it was decidedly not good-natured. She play-
346.08 ed: her execution was brilliant; she sang: her
346.09 voice was fine; she talked French apart to her
346.10 mama; and she talked it well, with fluency
346.11 and with a good accent.
346.12 Mary had a milder and more open counte-
346.13 nance than Blanche; softer features too, and a
346.14 skin some shades fairer /Miss Ingram was
346.15 dark as a Spaniard/ -- but Mary was deficient
346.16 in life: her face lacked expression, her eye lus-
346.17 tre; she had nothing to say, and having once
346.18 taken her seat, remained fixed like a statue in
346.19 its niche. The sisters were both attired in
346.20 spotless white.
346.21 And did I now think Miss Ingram such a
346.22 choice as Mr. Rochester would be likely to
346.23 make? I could not tell -- I did not know his
346.24 taste in female beauty. If he liked the majes-
346.25 tic, she was the very type of majesty: then
346.26 she was accomplished, sprightly. Most gen-
346.27 tlemen would admire her, I thought; and that
346.28 he did admire her, I already seemed to have
347.01 obtained proof: o remove the last shade of
347.02 doubt, it remained but to see them together.
347.03 You are not to suppose, reader, that Adele
347.04 has all this time been sitting motionless on the
347.05 stool at my feet: no; when the ladies entered,
347.06 she rose, advanced to meet them, made a
347.07 stately reverence, and said, with gravity, --
347.08 "Bon jour, mesdames."
347.09 And Miss Ingram had looked down at her
347.10 with a mocking air, and exclaimed, "Oh,
347.11 what a little puppet!"
347.12 Lady Lynn had remarked, "It is Mr.
347.13 Rochester's ward, I suppose -- the little French
347.14 girl he was speaking of."
347.15 Mrs. Dent had kindly taken her hand, and
347.16 given her a kiss. Amy and Louisa Eshton
347.17 had cried out simultaneously, --
347.18 "What a love of a child!"
347.19 And then they had called her to a sofa,
347.20 where she now sat, ensconced between them,
347.21 chattering alternately in French and broken
347.22 English; absorbing not only the young ladies'
347.23 attention, but that of Mrs. Eshton and Lady
347.24 Lynn, and getting spoilt to her heart's con-
347.25 tent.
347.26 At last coffee is brought in, and the gentle-
347.27 men are summoned. I sit in the shade -- if any
347.28 shade there be in this brilliantly-lit apartment;
348.01 the window-curtain half hides me. Again the
348.02 arch yawns: they come. The collective ap-
348.03 pearance of the gentlemen, like that of the
348.04 ladies, is very imposing: they are all cos-

348.05 tumed in black; most of them are tall, some
348.06 young. Henry and Frederick Lynn are very
348.07 dashing sparks, indeed; and Colonel Dent is a
348.08 fine soldierly man. Mr. Eshton, the magistrate
348.09 of the district, is gentleman-like: his hair is quite
348.10 white, his eyebrows and whiskers still dark,
348.11 which gives him something of the appearance
348.12 of a "pere noble de theatre." Lord Ingram,
348.13 like his sisters, is very tall; like them, also,
348.14 he is handsome; but he shares Mary's apa-
348.15 thetic and listless look: he seems to have
348.16 more length of limb than vivacity of blood or
348.17 vigour of brain.
348.18   And where is Mr. Rochester?
348.19   He comes in last: I am not looking at the
348.20 arch, yet I see him enter. I try to concen-
348.21 trate my attention on these netting-needles, on
348.22 the meshes of the purse I am forming -- I wish
348.23 to think only of the work I have in my hands,
348.24 to see only the silver beads and silk threads that
348.25 lie in my lap; whereas, I distinctly behold his
348.26 figure, and I inevitably recall the moment
348.27 when I last saw it: just after I had rendered
348.28 him, what he deemed, an essential service -- and
349.01 he, holding my hand, and looking down on
349.02 my face, surveyed me with eyes that revealed
349.03 a heart full and eager to overflow; in whose
349.04 emotions I had a part. How near had I
349.05 approached him at that moment! What had
349.06 occurred since, calculated to change his and
349.07 my relative positions? Yet now, how distant,
349.08 how far estranged we were! So far estranged,
349.09 that I did not expect him to come and speak
349.10 to me. I did not wonder, when, without look-
349.11 ing at me, he took a seat at the other side of
349.12 the room, and began conversing with some of
349.13 the ladies.
349.14   No sooner did I see that his attention was
349.15 riveted on them, and that I might gaze without
349.16 being observed, than my eyes were drawn
349.17 involuntarily to his face: I could not keep
349.18 their lids under control: they would rise, and
349.19 the irids would fix on him. I looked, and had
349.20 an acute pleasure in looking, -- a precious, yet
349.21 poignant pleasure; pure gold, with a steely
349.22 point of agony: a pleasure like what the thirst--
349.23 perishing man might feel who knows the well
349.24 to which he has crept is poisoned, yet stoops
349.25 and drinks devine draughts nevertheless.
349.26   Most true is it that "beauty is in the eye
349.27 of the gazer." My master's colourless, olive
349.28 face, square, massive brow, broad and jetty
350.01 eyebrows, deep eyes, strong features, firm,
350.02 grim mouth, -- all energy, decision, will, -- were
350.03 not beautiful, according to rule; but they were
350.04 more than beautiful to me: they were full of
350.05 an interest, an influence that quite mastered
350.06 me, -- that took my feelings from my own
350.07 power and fettered them in his. I had not
350.08 intended to love him: the reader knows I had
350.09 wrought hard to extirpate from my soul the
350.10 germs of love there detected; and now, at the
350.11 first renewed view of him, they spontaneously
350.12 revived, green and strong! He made me love
350.13 him without looking at me.
350.14   I compared him with his guests. What was
350.15 the gallant grace of the Lynns, the languid
350.16 elegance of Lord Ingram, -- even the military
350.17 distinction of Colonel Dent, contrasted with
350.18 his look of native pith and genuine power? I
350.19 had no sympathy in their appearance, their
350.20 expression: yet I could imagine that most
350.21 observers would call them attractive, hand-
350.22 some, imposing; while they would pronounce
350.23 Mr. Rochester at once harsh-featured and
350.24 melancholy-looking. I saw them smile, laugh
350.25 -- it was nothing: the light of the candles had
350.26 as much soul in it as their smile; the tinkle of
350.27 the bell as much significance as their laugh.
350.28 I saw Mr. Rochester smile: -- his stern features
351.01 softened; his eye grew both brilliant and
351.02 gentle, its ray both searching and sweet. He
351.03 was talking, at the moment, to Louisa and
351.04 Amy Eshton. I wondered to see them receive
351.05 with calm that look which seemed to me so
351.06 penetrating: I expected their eyes to fall,
351.07 their colour to rise under it; yet I was glad
351.08 when I found they were in no sense moved.
351.09 "He is not to them what he is to me," I
351.10 thought; "he is not of their kind. I believe
351.11 he is of mine; -- I am sure he is, -- I feel
351.12 akin to him, -- I understand the language of
351.13 his countenance and movements: though rank
351.14 and wealth sever us widely, I have something
351.15 in my brain and heart, in my blood and nerves,
351.16 that assimilates me mentally to him. Did I
351.17 say, a few days since, that I had nothing to do
351.18 with him but to receive my salary at his hands?
351.19 Did I forbid myself to think of him in any
351.20 other light than as a paymaster? Blasphemy
351.21 against nature! Every good, true, vigorous
351.22 feeling I have, gathers impulsively round him.
351.23 I know I must conceal my sentiments: I must
351.24 smother hope; I must remember that he can-
351.25 not care much for me. For when I say that I
351.26 am of his kind, I do not mean that I have his
351.27 force to influence, and his spell to attract: I
351.28 mean only that I have certain tastes and
352.01 feelings in common with him. I must, then,
352.02 repeat continually that we are for ever sun-
352.03 dered: -- and yet, while I breathe and think, I

352.04 must love him.
352.05   Coffee is handed. The ladies, since the gen-
352.06 tlemen entered, have become lively as larks:
352.07 conversation waxes brisk and merry. Colonel
352.08 Dent and Mr. Eshton argue on politics;
352.09 their wives listen. The two proud dowagers,
352.10 Lady Lynn and Lady Ingram, confabulate
352.11 together. Sir George -- whom, by-the-by, I
352.12 have forgotten to describe, -- a very big, and
352.13 very fresh-looking country gentleman, stands
352.14 before their sofa, coffee-cup in hand, and
352.15 occasionally puts in a word. Mr. Frederick
352.16 Lynn has taken a seat beside Mary Ingram,
352.17 and is showing her the engravings of a splendid
352.18 volume: she looks, smiles now and then, but
352.19 apparently says little. The tall and phleg-
352.20 matic Lord Ingram leans with folded arms on
352.21 the chair-back of the little and lively Amy
352.22 Eshton; she glances up at him, and chatters
352.23 like a wren: she likes him better than she
352.24 does Mr. Rochester. Henry Lynn has taken
352.25 possession of an ottoman at the feet of Louisa;
352.26 Adele shares it with him: he is trying to
352.27 talk French with her, and Louisa laughs at his
352.28 blunders. with whom will Blanche Ingram
353.01 pair? She is standing alone at the table,
353.02 bending gracefully over an album. She seems
353.03 waiting to be sought; but she will not wait too
353.04 long: she herself selects a mate.
353.05   Mr. Rochester, having quitted the Eshtons,
353.06 stands on the hearth as solitary as she stands
353.07 by the table; she confronts him, taking her
353.08 station on the opposite side of the mantel--
353.09 piece.
353.10 "Mr. Rochester, I thought you were not
353.11 fond of children?"
353.12 "Nor am I."
353.13 "Then, what induced you to take charge of
353.14 such a little doll as that? /pointing to Adele/.
353.15 where did you pick her up?"
353.16 "I did not pick her up, she was left on my
353.17 hands."
353.18 "You should have sent her to school."
353.19 "I could not afford it: schools are so
353.20 dear."
353.21 "why, I suppose you have a governess for
353.22 her: I saw a person with her just now -- is she
353.23 gone? Oh, no! there she is still behind the
353.24 window-curtain. You pay her, of course; I
353.25 should think it quite as expensive, -- more so;
353.26 for you have them both to keep in addition."
353.27   I feared -- or should I say, hoped? -- the al-
353.28 lusion to me would make Mr. Rochester glance
354.01 my way; and I involuntarily shrank further
354.02 into the shade: but he never turned his
354.03 eyes.
354.04 "I have not considered the subject," said he
354.05 indifferently, looking straight before him.
354.06 "No -- you men never do consider economy
354.07 and common sense. You should hear mama on
354.08 the chapter of governesses: Mary and I have
354.09 had, I should think, a dozen at least in our
354.10 day; half of them detestable and the rest ridi-
354.11 culous, and all incubi -- were they not, mama?"
354.12 "Did you speak, my own?"
354.13   The young lady thus claimed as the dow-
354.14 ager's special property, reiterate her question
354.15 with an explanation.
354.16 "My dearest, don't mention governesses:
354.17 the word makes me nervous. I have suffered
354.18 martyrdom from their incompetency and
354.19 caprice: I thank Heaven I have now done
354.20 with them!"
354.21   Mrs. Dent here bent over to the pious lady,
354.22 and whispered something in her ear: I sup-
354.23 pose from the answer elicited, it was a re-
354.24 minder that one of the anathematized race was
354.25 present.
354.26 "Tant pis!" said her ladyship, "I hope it
354.27 may do her good!" Then, in a lower tone,
354.28 but still loud enough for me to hear. "I
355.01 noticed her: I am a judge of physiognomy, and
355.02 in hers I see all the faults of her class."
355.03 "what are they, madam?" inquired Mr.
355.04 Rochester aloud.
355.05 "I will tell you in your private ear," replied
355.06 she, wagging her turban three times with por-
355.07 tentous significancy.
355.08 "But my curiosity will be past its appetite:
355.09 it craves food now."
355.10 "Ask Blanche: she is nearer you than I."
355.11 "Oh, don't refer him to me, mama! I have
355.12 just one word to say of the whole tribe: they
355.13 are a nuisance. Not that I ever suffered much
355.14 from them: I took care to turn the tables.
355.15 what tricks Theodore and I used to play on our
355.16 Miss Wilsons, and Mrs. Greys, and Madame
355.17 Jouberts! Mary was always too sleepy to join
355.18 in a plot with spirit. The best fun was with
355.19 Madame Joubert: Miss Wilson was a poor
355.20 sickly thing, lachrymose and low-spirited: not
355.21 worth the trouble of vanquishing, in short; and
355.22 Mrs. Grey was coarse and insensible: no blow
355.23 took effect on her. But poor Madame Jou-
355.24 bert! I see her yet in her raging passions,
355.25 when we had driven her to extremities -- spilt
355.26 our tea, crumbled our bread and butter, tossed
355.27 our books up to the ceiling, and played a cha-
355.28 rivari with the ruler and desk, the fender and
356.01 fire-irons. Theodore, do you remember those
356.02 merry days?"

356.03 "Yaas, to be sure I do," drawled Lord
356.04 Ingram: "and the poor old stick used to cry
356.05 out `Oh you villains childs!` -- and then we ser-
356.06 monized her on the presumption of attempting
356.07 to teach such clever blades as we were, when
356.08 she was herself so ignorant."
356.09 "We did: and Tedo, you know, I helped
356.10 you in prosecuting /or persecuting/ your tutor,
356.11 whey-faced Mr. Vining -- the parson in the pip,
356.12 as we used to call him. He and Miss Wilson
356.13 took the liberty of falling in love with each
356.14 other -- at least Tedo and I thought so: we sur-
356.15 prised sundry tender glances and sighs which
356.16 we interpreted as tokens of `la belle passion,`
356.17 and I promise you the public soon had the
356.18 benefit of our discovery: we employed it as a
356.19 sort of lever to hoist our dead-weights from
356.20 the house. Dear mama there, as soon as she
356.21 got an inkling of the business, found out that
356.22 it was of an immoral tendency. Did you not,
356.23 my lady-mother?"
356.24 "Certainly, my best. And I was quite right;
356.25 depend on that: there are a thousand reasons
356.26 why liaisons between governesses and tutors
356.27 should never be tolerated a moment in any
356.28 well-regulated house; firstly --"
357.01 "Oh gracious, mama! Spare us the enu-
357.02 meration! Au reste, we all know them: dan-
357.03 ger of bad example to innocence of childhood;
357.04 distractions and consequent neglect of duty on
357.05 the part of the attached mutual alliance and
357.06 reliance; confidence thence resulting -- inso-
357.07 lence accompanying -- mutiny and general
357.08 blow-up. Am I right, Baroness Ingram of
357.09 Ingram Park?"
357.10 "My lily-flower, you are right now, as
357.11 always."
357.12 "Then no more need be said: change the
357.13 subject."
357.14 Amy Eshton, not hearing or not needing
357.15 this dictum, joined in with her soft, infantine
357.16 tone: "Louisa and I used to quiz our govern-
357.17 ness too; but she was such a good creature, she
357.18 would bear anything: nothing put her out.
357.19 She was never cross with us; was she, Louisa?"
357.20 "No, never: we might do what we pleased;
357.21 ransack her desk and her workbox, and turn
357.22 her drawers inside out; and she was so good--
357.23 natured, she would give us anything we asked
357.24 for."
357.25 "I suppose now," said Miss Ingram, curl-
357.26 ing her lip sarcastically, we shall have an
357.27 abstract of the memoirs of all the governesses
357.28 extant: in order to avert such a visitation, I
358.01 again move the introduction of a new topic.
358.02 Mr. Rochester, do you second my motion?"
358.03 "Madam, I support you on this point as on
358.04 every other."
358.05 "Then on me be the onus of bringing it
358.06 forward. Signior Eduardo, are you in voice
358.07 to-night?"
358.08 "Donna Bianca, if you command it, I will
358.09 be."
358.10 "Then Signior, I lay on you my sovereign
358.11 behest to furbish up your lungs and other
358.12 vocal organs, as they will be wanted on my
358.13 royal service."
358.14 "Who would not be the Rizzio of so divine
358.15 a Mary?"
358.16 "A fig for Rizzio!" cried she, tossing her
358.17 head with all its curls, as she moved to the
358.18 piano. "It is my opinion the fiddler David
358.19 must have been an insipid sort of fellow: I
358.20 like black Bothwell better: to my mind a
358.21 man is nothing without a spice of the devil in
358.22 him; and history may say what it will of
358.23 James Hepburn, but I have a notion, he was
358.24 just the sort of wild, fierce, bandit-hero whom
358.25 I could have consented to gift with my hand."
358.26 "Gentlemen, you hear! Now which of
358.27 you most resembles Bothwell?" cried Mr.
358.28 Rochester.
359.01 "I should say the preference lies with you,"
359.02 responded Colonel Dent.
359.03 "On my honour, I am much obliged to
359.04 you," was the reply.
359.05 Miss Ingram, who had now seated herself
359.06 with proud grace at the piano, spreading out
359.07 her snowy robes in queenly amplitude, com-
359.08 menced a brilliant prelude; talking meantime.
359.09 She appeared to be on her high horse to-night
359.10 both her words and her air seemed intended
359.11 to excite not only the admiration, but the
359.12 amazement of her auditors: she was evidently
359.13 bent on striking them as something very dash-
359.14 ing and daring indeed.
359.15 "Oh, I am so sick of the young men of the
359.16 present day!" exclaimed she, rattling away at
359.17 the instrument. "Poor, puny things not fit
359.18 to stir a step beyond papa's park-gates: nor to
359.19 go even so far beyond mama's permission and
359.20 guardianship! Creatures so absorbed in care
359.21 about their pretty faces and their white hands,
359.22 and their small feet; as if a man had anything
359.23 to do with beauty! As if loveliness were not
359.24 the special prerogative of woman -- her legiti-
359.25 mate appanage and heritage! I grant an
359.26 ugly woman is a blot on the fair face of crea-
359.27 tion; but as to the gentlemen, let them be soli-
359.28 citous to possess only strength and valour: Let
360.01 their motto be: -- Hunt, shoot, and fight: the

360.02 rest is not worth a filip. Such should be my
360.03 device, were I a man."
360.04 "Whenever I marry," she continued, after
360.05 a pause which none interrupted, "I am re-
360.06 solved my husband shall not be a rival, but a
360.07 foil to me. I will suffer no competitor near the
360.08 throne; I shall exact an undivided homage: his
360.09 devotions shall not be shared between me and
360.10 the shape he sees in his mirror. Mr. Roches-
360.11 ter, now sing, and I will play for you."
360.12 "I am all obedience," was the response.
360.13 "Here then is a Corsair-song. Know that
360.14 I doat on Corsairs; and for that reason, sing it
360.15 `con spirito.` "
360.16 "Commands from Miss Ingram's lips would
360.17 put spirit into a mug of milk and water."
360.18 "Take care, then: if you don't please me, I
360.19 will shame you by showing how such things
360.20 should be done."
360.21 "That is offering a premium on incapacity:
360.22 I shall now endeavour to fail."
360.23 "Gardez-vous en bien! If you err wilfully,
360.24 I shall devise a proportionate punishment."
360.25 "Miss Ingram ought to be clement, for she
360.26 has it in her power to inflict a chastisement
360.27 beyond mortal endurance."
360.28 "Ha! explain!" commanded the lady.
361.01 "Pardon, me, madam: no need of explana-
361.02 tion; your own fine sense must inform you
361.03 that one of your frowns would be a sufficient
361.04 substitute for capital punishment."
361.05 "Sing!" said she, and again touching the
361.06 piano, she commenced an accompaniment in
361.07 spirited style.
361.08 "Now is my time to slip away," thought I:
361.09 but the tones that then severed the air arrested
361.10 me. Mrs. Fairfax had said Mr. Rochester
361.11 possessed a fine voice: he did -- a mellow,
361.12 powerful bass, into which he threw his own
361.13 feeling, his own force; finding a way through
361.14 the ear to the heart, and there waking sen-
361.15 sation strangely. I waited till the last deep
361.16 and full vibration had expired -- till the tide
361.17 of talk, checked an instant, had resumed its
361.18 flow; I then quitted my sheltered corner and
361.19 made my exit by the side-door, which was
361.20 fortunately near. Thence a narrow passage
361.21 led into the hall: in crossing it, I perceived
361.22 my sandal was loose; I stopped to tie it, kneel-
361.23 ing down for that purpose on the mat at the
361.24 foot of the staircase. I heard the dining-room
361.25 door unclose; a gentleman came out; rising
361.26 hastily, I stood face to face with him: it was
361.27 Mr. Rochester.
361.28 "How do you do?" he asked.
362.01 "I am very well, sir."
362.02 "Why did you not come and speak to me
362.03 in the room?"
362.04 I thought I might have retorted the ques-
362.05 tion on him who put it: but I would not take
362.06 that freedom. I answered: --
362.07 "I did not wish to disturb you, as you
362.08 seemed engaged, sir."
362.09 "What have you been doing during my
362.10 absence?"
362.11 "Nothing particular; teaching Adele as
362.12 usual."
362.13 "And getting a good deal paler than you
362.14 were -- as I saw at first sight. What is the
362.15 matter?"
362.16 "Nothing at all, sir."
362.17 "Did you take any cold that night you half
362.18 drowned me?"
362.19 "Not the least."
362.20 "Return to the drawing-room: you are
362.21 deserting too early."
362.22 "I am tired, sir."
362.23 He looked at me for a minute.
362.24 "And a little depressed," he said. "What
362.25 about? Tell me."
362.26 "Nothing -- nothing, sir. I am not de-
362.27 pressed."
362.28 "But I affirm that you are: so much de-
363.01 pressed that a few more words would bring
363.02 tears to your eyes -- indeed, they are there now,
363.03 shining and swimming; and a bead has slipped
363.04 from the lash and fallen on to the flag. If I
363.05 had time, and was not in mortal dread of some
363.06 prating prig of a servant passing, I would
363.07 know what all this means. Well, to-night I
363.08 excuse you; but understand that so long as my
363.09 visitors stay, I expect you to appear in the
363.10 drawing-room every evening; it is my wish;
363.11 don't neglect it. Now go, and send Sophie for
363.12 Adele. Good-night, my --" He stopped,
363.13 bit his lip, and abruptly left me.
364.01 [Vol. 2 Chapter 3]
364.02 Merry days were these at Thornfield-Hall;
364.03 and busy days too: how different from the
364.04 first three months of stillness, monotony, and
364.05 solitude I had passed beneath its roof! All
364.06 sad feelings seemed now driven from the
364.07 house, all gloomy associations forgotten: there
364.08 was life everywhere, movement all day long.
364.09 You could not now traverse the gallery, once
364.10 so hushed, nor enter the front chamber, once
364.11 so tenantless, without encountering a smart
364.12 lady's maid or a dandy valet.
364.13 The kitchen, the butler's pantry, the ser-
364.14 vant's hall, the entrance hall, were equally
364.15 alive; and the saloons were only left void and

364.16 still, when the blue sky and halcyon sunshine
364.17 of the genial spring weather called their occu-
364.18 pants out into the grounds. Even when that
364.19 weather was broken, and continuous rain set
364.20 in for some days, no damp seemed cast over
365.01 enjoyment: in-door amusements only became
365.02 more lively and varied, in consequence of the
365.03 stop put to out-door gaiety.
365.04 I wondered what they were going to do the
365.05 first evening a change of entertainment was
365.06 proposed: they spoke of "playing charades,"
365.07 but in my ignorance I did not understand the
365.08 term. The servants were called in, the dining--
365.09 room tables wheeled away, the lights other--
365.10 wise disposed, the chairs placed in a semicircle
365.11 opposite the arch. While Mr. Rochester and
365.12 the other gentlemen directed these alterations,
365.13 the ladies were running up and down stairs
365.14 ringing for their maids. Mrs. Fairfax was
365.15 summoned to give information respecting the
365.16 resources of the house in shawls, dresses,
365.17 draperies of any kind; and certain ward--
365.18 robes of the third story were ransacked, and
365.19 their contents, in the shape of brocaded and
365.20 hooped petticoats, satin sacques, black modes,
365.21 lace lappets, &c., were brought down in arm-
365.22 fuls by the Abigails; then a selection was
365.23 made, and such things as were chosen were
365.24 carried to the boudoir within the drawing--
365.25 room.
365.26 Meantime, Mr. Rochester had again sum-
365.27 moned the ladies round him, and was selecting
365.28 certain of their number to be of his party.
366.01 "Miss Ingram is mine, of course," said he:
366.02 afterwards he named the two Misses Eshton,
366.03 and Mrs. Dent. He looked at me: I hap-
366.04 pened to be near him, as I had been fastening
366.05 the clasp of Mrs. Dent's bracelet, which had
366.06 got loose.
366.07 "Will you play?" he asked. I shook my
366.08 head. He did not insist, which I rather feared
366.09 he would have done: he allowed me to return
366.10 quietly to my usual seat.
366.11 He and his aids now withdrew behind the
366.12 curtain: the other party, which was headed
366.13 by Colonel Dent, sat down on the crescent of
366.14 chairs. One of the gentlemen, Mr. Eshton,
366.15 observing me, seemed to propose that I should
366.16 be asked to join them; but Lady Ingram
366.17 instantly negatived the notion.
366.18 "No," I heard her say: "she looks too
366.19 stupid for any game of the sort."
366.20 Ere long, a bell tinkled, and the curtain
366.21 drew up. Within the arch, the bulky figure
366.22 of Sir George Lynn, whom Mr. Rochester
366.23 had likewise chosen, was seen enveloped in
366.24 a white sheet: before him, on a table, lay
366.25 open a large book; and at his side stood Amy
366.26 Eshton, draped in Mr. Rochester's cloak, and
366.27 holding a book in her hand. Somebody, un-
366.28 seen, rung the bell merrily; then Adele /who
367.01 had insisted on being one of her guardian's
367.02 party/ bounded forward, scattering round her
367.03 the contents of a basket of flowers she carried
367.04 on her arm. Then appeared the magnificent
367.05 figure of Miss Ingram, clad in white, a long
367.06 veil on her head, and a wreath of roses round
367.07 her brow: by her side walked Mr. Rochester,
367.08 and together they drew near the table. They
367.09 knelt; while Mrs. Dent and Louisa Eshton,
367.10 dressed also in white, took up their stations
367.11 behind them. A ceremony followed, in dumb
367.12 show, in which it was easy to recognise the
367.13 pantomime of a marriage. At its termination,
367.14 Colonel Dent and his party consulted in whis-
367.15 pers for two minutes, then the Colonel called
367.16 out, --
367.17 "Bride!" Mr. Rochester bowed, and the
367.18 curtain fell.
367.19 A considerable interval elapsed before it
367.20 again rose. Its second rising displayed a
367.21 more elaborately prepared scene than the last.
367.22 The drawing-room, as I have before observed,
367.23 was raised two steps above the dining-room,
367.24 and on the top of the upper step, placed a
367.25 yard to two back within the room, appeared a
367.26 large marble basin, which I recognised as an
367.27 ornament of the conservatory -- where it usually
367.28 stood surrounded by exotics, and tenanted by
368.01 gold fish -- and whence it must have been
368.02 transported with some trouble, on account of
368.03 its size and weight.
368.04 Seated on the carpet, by the side of this
368.05 basin, was seen Mr. Rochester, costumed in
368.06 shawls, with a turban on his head. His dark
368.07 eyes and swarth skin and Paynim features
368.08 suited the costume exactly: he looked the very
368.09 model of an eastern emir; an agent or a victim
368.10 of the bowstring. Presently advanced into
368.11 view Miss Ingram. She, too, was attired in
368.12 oriental fashion: a crimson scarf tied sash--
368.13 like round the waist; an embroidered hand-
368.14 kerchief knotted about her temples; her beau-
368.15 tifully-moulded arms bare, one of them up-
368.16 raised in the act of supporting a pitcher, poised
368.17 gracefully on her head. Both her cast of
368.18 form and feature, her complexion and her
368.19 general air, suggested the idea of some Israel-
368.20 itish princess of the patriarchal days; and such
368.21 was doubtless the character she intended to re-
368.22 present.

368.23 She approached the basin, and bent over it
368.24 as if to fill her pitcher; she again lifted it to
368.25 her head. The personage on the well-brink
368.26 now seemed to accost her; to make some re-
368.27 quest: -- "She hasted, let down her pitcher on
368.28 her hand and gave him to drink." From the
369.01 bosom of his robe, he then produced a casket,
369.02 opened it and showed magnificent bracelets
369.03 and earrings; she acted astonishment and ad-
369.04 miration; kneeling, he laid the treasure at her
369.05 feet; incredulity and delight were expressed
369.06 by her looks and gestures; the stranger fast-
369.07 ened the bracelets on her arms, and the rings
369.08 in her ears. It was Eliezer and Rebecca: the
369.09 camels only were wanting.
369.10 The divining party again laid their heads
369.11 together: apparently they could not agree
369.12 about the word or syllable this scene illustrated.
369.13 Colonel Dent, their spokesman, demanded
369.14 "the tableau of the whole;" whereupon the
369.15 curtain again descended.
369.16 On its third rising only a portion of the
369.17 drawing-room was disclosed; the rest being
369.18 concealed by a screen, hung with some sort of
369.19 dark and coarse drapery. The marble basin
369.20 was removed; in its place stood a deal table
369.21 and a kitchen chair: these objects were visible
369.22 by a very dim light proceeding from a horn
369.23 lantern, the wax candles being all extinguished.
369.24 Amidst this sordid scene, sat a man with
369.25 his clenched hands resting on his knees, and
369.26 his eyes bent on the ground. I knew Mr.
369.27 Rochester; though the begrimed face, the dis-
369.28 ordered dress /his coat hanging loose from
370.01 one arm, as if it had been almost torn from
370.02 his back in a scuffle/, the desperate and scowl-
370.03 ing countenance, the rough, bristling hair
370.04 might well have disguised him. As he moved,
370.05 a chain clanked: to his wrist were attached
370.06 fetters.
370.07 "Bridewell!" exclaimed Colonel Dent, and
370.08 the charade was solved.
370.09 A sufficient interval having elapsed for the
370.10 performers to resume their ordinary costume,
370.11 they re-entered the dining-room. Mr. Ro-
370.12 chester led in Miss Ingram; she was com-
370.13 plimenting him on his acting.
370.14 "Do you know," said she, "that, of the
370.15 three characters, I liked you in the last best?
370.16 Oh, had you but lived a few years earlier,
370.17 what a gallant gentleman-highwayman you
370.18 would have made!"
370.19 "Is all the soot washed from my face?" he
370.20 asked, turning it towards her.
370.21 "Alas! yes; the more's the pity! Nothing
370.22 could be more becoming to your complexion
370.23 than that ruffian's rouge."
370.24 "You would like a hero of the road then?"
370.25 "An English hero of the road would be the
370.26 next best thing to an Italian bandit; and that
370.27 could only be surpassed by a Levantine
370.28 pirate."
371.01 "Well, whatever I am, remember you are
371.02 my wife; we were married an hour since, in
371.03 the presence of all these witnesses." She gig-
371.04 gled, and her colour rose.
371.05 "Now, Dent," continued Mr. Rochester,
371.06 "it is your turn." And as the other party
371.07 withdrew, he and his band took the vacated
371.08 seats. Miss Ingram placed herself at her
371.09 leader's right hand; the other diviners filled
371.10 the chairs on each side of him and her. I did
371.11 not now watch the actors; I no longer waited
371.12 with interest for the curtain to rise; my at-
371.13 tention was absorbed by the spectators; my
371.14 eyes, erewhile fixed on the arch, were now
371.15 irresistibly attracted to the semicircle of chairs.
371.16 What charade Colonel Dent and his party
371.17 played, what word they chose, how they ac-
371.18 quitted themselves, I no longer remember;
371.19 but I still see the consultation which followed
371.20 each scene: I see Mr. Rochester turn to Miss
371.21 Ingram, and Miss Ingram to him; I see her
371.22 incline her head towards him, till the jetty
371.23 curls almost touch his shoulder and wave
371.24 against his cheek; I hear their mutual whis-
371.25 perings; I recall their interchanged glances;
371.26 and something even of the feeling roused by
371.27 the spectacle returns in memory at this mo-
371.28 ment.
372.01 I have told you, reader, that I had learnt to
372.02 love Mr. Rochester: I could not unlove him
372.03 now, merely because I found that he had
372.04 ceased to notice me -- because I might pass
372.05 hours in his presence, and he would never
372.06 once turn his eyes in my direction -- because I
372.07 saw all his attentions appropriated by a great
372.08 lady, who scorned to touch me with the hem
372.09 of her robes as she passed; who, if ever her
372.10 dark and imperious eye fell on me by chance,
372.11 would withdraw it instantly as from an object
372.12 too mean to merit observation. I could not
372.13 unlove him, because I felt sure he would soon
372.14 marry this very lady -- because I read daily in
372.15 her a proud security in his intentions respect-
372.16 ing her -- because I witnessed hourly in him a
372.17 style of courtship which, if careless and choos-
372.18 ing rather to be sought than to seek, was yet,
372.19 in its very carelessness, captivating, and in its
372.20 very pride, irresistible.
372.21 There was nothing to cool or banish love in

372.22 these circumstances; though much to create
372.23 despair. Much too, you will think, reader, to
372.24 engender jealousy: if a woman, in my position,
372.25 could presume to be jealous of a woman in
372.26 Miss Ingram's. But I was not jealous: or very
372.27 rarely; -- the nature of the pain I suffered
372.28 could not be explained by that word. Miss
373.01 Ingram was a mark beneath jealousy: she
373.02 was too inferior to excite the feeling. Pardon
373.03 the seeming paradox: I mean what I say. She
373.04 was very showy, but she was not genuine: she
373.05 had a fine person, many brilliant attainments;
373.06 but her mind was poor, her heart barren by
373.07 nature: nothing bloomed spontaneously on
373.08 that soil; no unforced natural fruit delighted
373.09 by its freshness. She was not good; she was
373.10 not original: she used to repeat sounding
373.11 phrases from books; she never offered, nor had,
373.12 an opinion of her own. She advocated a
373.13 high tone of sentiment; but she did not know
373.14 the sensations of sympathy and pity; tender-
373.15 ness and truth were not in her. Too often she
373.16 betrayed this, by the undue vent she gave to a
373.17 spiteful antipathy she had conceived against
373.18 little Adele: pushing her away with some con-
373.19 tumelious epithet if she happened to approach
373.20 her; sometimes ordering her from the room,
373.21 and always treating her with coldness and
373.22 acrimony. Other eyes besides mine watched
373.23 these manifestations of character -- watched
373.24 them closely, keenly, shrewdly. Yes: the future
373.25 bridegroom, Mr. Rochester himself, exer-
373.26 cised over his intended a ceaseless surveillance:
373.27 and it was from this sagacity -- this guard-
373.28 edness of his -- this perfect, clear conscious-
374.01 ness of his fair one's defects -- this obvious
374.02 absence of passion in his sentiments towards
374.03 her, that my ever-torturing pain arose.
374.04 I saw he was going to marry her, for family,
374.06 perhaps political reasons; because her rank
374.06 and connexions suited him; I felt he had not
374.07 given her his love, and that her qualifications
374.08 were ill adapted to win from him that trea-
374.09 sure. This was the point -- this was where the
374.10 nerve was touched and teazed -- this was where
374.11 the fever was sustained and fed: she could not
374.12 charm him.
374.13 If she had managed the victory at once,
374.14 and he had yielded and sincerely laid his heart
374.15 at her feet, I should have covered my face,
374.16 turned to the wall, and /figuratively/ have died
374.17 to them. If Miss Ingram had been a good
374.18 and noble woman, endowed with force, fervour,
374.19 kindness, sense, I should have had one vital
374.20 struggle with two tigers -- jealousy and de-
374.21 spair: then, my heart torn out and devoured,
374.22 I should have admired her -- acknowledged her
374.23 excellence, and been quiet for the rest of my
374.24 days: and the more absolute her superiority,
374.25 the deeper would have been my admiration --
374.26 the more truly tranquil my quiescence. But as
374.27 matters really stood, to watch Miss Ingram's
374.28 efforts at fascinating Mr. Rochester; to witness
375.01 their repeated failure -- herself unconscious that
375.02 they did fail; vainly fancying that each shaft
375.03 launched, hit the mark, and infatuatedly plum-
375.04 ing herself on success, when her pride and
375.05 self-complacency repelled further and further
375.06 what she wished to allure -- to witness this, was
375.07 to be at once under ceaseless excitation and
375.08 ruthless restraint.
375.09 Because, when she failed, I saw how she
375.10 might have succeeded. Arrows that continu-
375.11 ally glanced off from Mr. Rochester's breast
375.12 and fell harmless at his feet, might, I knew,
375.13 if shot by a surer hand, have quivered keen in
375.14 his proud heart -- have called love into his stern
375.15 eye, and softness into his sardonic face: or,
375.16 better still, without weapons a silent conquest
375.17 might have been won.
375.18 "Why can she not influence him more,
375.19 when she is privileged to draw so near to him?"
375.20 I asked myself. "Surely she cannot truly
375.21 like him; or not like him with true affection!
375.22 If she did, she need not coin her smiles so
375.23 lavishly; flash her glances so unremittingly;
375.24 manufacture airs so elaborate, graces so mul-
375.25 tituainous. I seems to me, that she might,
375.26 by merely sitting quietly at his side, saying
375.27 little and looking less, get nigher his heart. I
375.28 have seen in his face a far different expression
376.01 from that which hardens it now while she is so
376.02 vivaciously accosting him; but then it came of
376.03 itself: it was not elicited by meretricious arts
376.04 and calculated manoeuvres; and one had but
376.05 to accept it -- to answer what he asked without
376.06 pretension, to address him when needful with-
376.07 out grimace -- and it increased and grew kinder
376.08 and more genial, and warmed one like a fos-
376.09 tering sunbeam. How will she manage to
376.10 please him when they are married? I do
376.11 not think she will manage it: and yet it might
376.12 be managed; and his wife might, I verily be-
376.13 lieve, be the very happiest woman the sun
376.14 shines on."
376.15 I have not yet said anything condemnatory
376.16 of Mr. Rochester's project of marrying for
376.17 interest and connexions. It surprised me
376.18 when I first discovered that such was his in-
376.19 tention: I had thought him a man unlikely to
376.20 be influenced by motives so common-place in

376.21 his choice of a wife; but the longer I considered
376.22 the position, education, &c. of the parties, the
376.23 less I felt justified in judging and blaming
376.24 either him or Miss Ingram, for acting in con-
376.25 formity to ideas and principles instilled into
376.26 them, doubtless, from their childhood. All
376.27 their class held these principles: I supposed,
376.28 then, they had reasons for holding them such
377.01 as I could not fathom. It seemed to me that,
377.02 were I a gentleman like him, I would take to
377.03 my bosom only such a wife as I could love;
377.04 but the very obviousness of the advantages to
377.05 the husband's own happiness, offered by this
377.06 plan, convinced me that there must be argu-
377.07 ments against its general adoption of which I
377.08 was quite ignorant: otherwise I felt sure all the
377.09 world would act as I wished to act.
377.10 But in other points, as well as this, I was
377.11 growing very lenient to my master: I was for-
377.12 getting all his faults, for which I had once
377.13 kept a sharp look-out. It had formerly been
377.14 my endeavour to study all sides of his charac-
377.15 ter: to take the bad with the good; and from
377.16 the just weighing of both, to form an equitable
377.17 judgment. Now I saw no bad. The sarcasm
377.18 that had repelled, the harshness that had
377.19 startled me once, were only like keen condi-
377.20 ments in a choice dish: their presence was
377.21 pungent, but their absence would be felt as com-
377.22 paratively insipid. And as for the vague some-
377.23 thing -- was it a sinister or a sorrowful, a
377.24 designing or a desponding expression? -- that
377.25 opened upon a careful observer, now and then,
377.26 in his eye, and closed again before one could
377.27 fathom the strange depth partially disclosed;
377.28 that something which used to make me fear
378.01 and shrink, as if I had been wandering
378.02 amongst volcanic-looking hills, and had sud-
378.03 denly felt the ground quiver, and seen it gape:
378.04 that something, I, at intervals, beheld still; and
378.05 with throbbing heart, but not with palsied
378.06 nerves. Instead of wishing to shun, I longed
378.07 only to dare -- to divine it; and I thought Miss
378.08 Ingram happy, because one day she might
378.09 look into the abyss at her leisure, explore its
378.10 secrets and analyze their nature.
378.11 Meantime, while I thought only of my
378.12 master and his future bride -- saw only them,
378.13 heard only their discourse, and considered only
378.14 their movements of importance -- the rest of the
378.15 party were occupied with their own separate
378.16 interests and pleasures. The ladies Lynn and
378.17 Ingram continued to consort in solemn con-
378.18 ferences; where they nodded their two turbans
378.19 at each other, and held up their four hands in
378.20 confronting gestures of surprise, or mystery, or
378.21 horror, according to the theme on which their
378.22 gossip ran, like a pair of magnified puppets.
378.23 Mild Mrs. Dent talked with good-natured
378.24 Mrs. Eshton; and the two sometimes bestowed
378.25 a courteous word or smile on me. Sir George
378.26 Lynn, Colonel Dent, and Mr. Eshton, dis-
378.27 cussed politics, or county affairs, or justice
378.28 business. Lord Ingram flirted with Amy
379.01 Eshton; Louisa played and sang to and with
379.02 one of the Messrs. Lynn; and Mary Ingram
379.03 listened languidly to the gallant speeches of
379.04 the other. Sometimes all, as with one consent,
379.05 suspended their by-play to observe and listen
379.06 to the principal actors: for, after all, Mr. Ro-
379.07 chester, and -- because closely connected with
379.08 him -- Miss Ingram, were the life and soul of
379.09 the party. If he was absent from the room
379.10 an hour, a perceptible dulness seemed to steal
379.11 over the spirits of his guests; and his re--
379.12 entrance was sure to give a fresh impulse to
379.13 the vivacity of conversation.
379.14 The want of his animating influence appeared
379.15 to be peculiarly felt one day that he had been
379.16 summoned to Millcote on business, and was
379.17 not likely to return till late. The afternoon
379.18 was wet: a walk the party had proposed to
379.19 take to see a gipsy camp, lately pitched on
379.20 a common beyond Hay, was consequently de-
379.21 ferred. Some of the gentlemen were gone to
379.22 the stables: the younger ones, together with
379.23 the younger ladies, were playing billiards in
379.24 the billiard-room. The dowagers Ingram and
379.25 Lynn sought solace in a quiet game at cards.
379.26 Blanche Ingram, after having repelled, by
379.27 supercilious taciturnity, some efforts of Mrs.
379.28 Dent and Mrs. Eshton to draw her into con-
380.01 versation, had first murmured over some sen-
380.02 timental tunes and airs on the piano, and then,
380.03 having fetched a novel from the library, had
380.04 flung herself in haughty listlessness on a sofa,
380.05 and prepared to beguile, by the spell of fiction,
380.06 the tedious hours of absence. The room and
380.07 the house were silent: only now and then the
380.08 merriment of the billiard players was heard
380.09 from above.
380.10 It was verging on dusk, and the clock had
380.11 already given warning of the hour to dress for
380.12 dinner, when little Adele, who knelt by me in
380.13 the drawing-room window seat, exclaimed: --
380.14 "Voila Monsieur Rochester, qui revient!"
380.15 I turned, and Miss Ingram darted forwards
380.16 from her sofa: the others, too, looked up from
380.17 their several occupations; for at the same time
380.18 a crunching of wheels, and a splashing tramp
380.19 of horse-hoofs became audible on the wet

380.20 gravel. A post-chaise was approaching.
380.21 "what can possess him to come home in
380.22 that style?" said Miss Ingram. "he rode
380.23 Mesrour /the black horse/ did he not, when
380.24 he went out? and Pilot was with him: -- what
380.25 has he done with the animals?"
380.26 As she said this, she approached her tall
380.27 person and ample garments so near the window,
380.28 that I was obliged to bend back almost to the
381.01 breaking of my spine: in her eagerness she
381.02 did not observe me at first, but when she did,
381.03 she curled her lip and moved to another case-
381.04 ment. The post-chaise stopped; the driver
381.05 rang the door-bell, and a gentleman alighted,
381.06 attired in travelling garb; but it was not Mr.
381.07 Rochester; it was a tall fashionable-looking
381.08 man, a stranger.
381.09 "Provoking!" exclaimed Miss Ingram:
381.10 "you tiresome monkey!" /apostrophizing
381.11 Adele/ "who perched you up in the window
381.12 to give false intelligence?" and she cast on me
381.13 an angry glance, as if I were in fault.
381.14 Some parleying was audible in the hall, and
381.15 soon the new comer entered. He bowed to
381.16 Lady Ingram, as deeming her the eldest lady
381.17 present.
381.18 "It appears I come at an inopportune time,
381.19 madam," said he, "when my friend, Mr.
381.20 Rochester, is from home; but I arrive from a
381.21 very long journey, and I think I may presume
381.22 so far on old and intimate acquaintance as to
381.23 instal myself here till he returns."
381.24 His manner was polite; his accent, in speak-
381.25 ing, struck me as being somewhat unusual, --
381.26 not precisely foreign, but still not altogether
381.27 English: his age might be about Mr. Ro-
381.28 chester's, -- between thirty and forty; his com-
382.01 plexion was singularly sallow: otherwise he
382.02 was a fine-looking man, at first sight espe-
382.03 cially. On closer examination, you detected
382.04 something in his face that displeased: or rather,
382.05 that failed to please. His features were regu-
382.06 lar, but too relaxed: his eye was large and
382.07 well cut, but the life looking out of it was a
382.08 tame, vacant life -- at least so I thought.
382.09 The sound of the dressing-bell dispersed the
382.10 party. It was not till after dinner that I saw
382.11 him again: he then seemed quite at his ease.
382.12 But I liked his physiognomy even less than
382.13 before: it struck me as being, at the same
382.14 time, unsettled and inanimate. His eye wan-
382.15 dered, and had no meaning in its wandering:
382.16 this gave him an odd look, such as I never
382.17 remembered to have seen. For a handsome
382.18 and not an unamiable-looking man, he repelled
382.19 me exceedingly: there was no power in that
382.20 smooth-skinned face of a full oval shape; no
382.21 firmness in that aquiline nose, and small,
382.22 cherry mouth; there was no thought on the
382.23 low, even forehead; no command on that
382.24 blank, brown eye.
382.25 As I sat in my usual nook, and looked at
382.26 him with the light of the girandoles on the
382.27 mantel-piece beaming full over him -- for he
382.28 occupied an arm-chair, drawn close to the fire,
383.01 and kept shrinking still nearer, as if he were
383.02 cold -- I compared him with Mr. Rochester. I
383.03 think /with deference be it spoken/ the contrast
383.04 could not be much greater between a sleek
383.05 gander and a fierce falcon: between a meek
383.06 sheep and the rough-coated keen-eyed dog, its
383.07 guardian.
383.08 He had spoken of Mr. Rochester as an old
383.09 friend. A curious friendship theirs must have
383.10 been: a pointed illustration, indeed, of the old
383.11 adage that "extremes meet."
383.12 Two or three of the gentlemen sat near
383.13 him, and I caught at times scraps of their
383.14 conversation across the room. At first I could
383.15 not make much sense of what I heard; for the
383.16 discourse of Louisa Eshton and Mary Ingram,
383.17 who sat nearer to me, confused the frag-
383.18 mentary sentences that reached me at inter-
383.19 vals. These last were discussing the stranger:
383.20 they both called him "a beautiful man."
383.21 Louisa said he was "a love of a creature," and
383.22 she "adored him"; and Mary instanced his
383.23 "pretty little mouth, and nice nose," as her
383.24 ideal of the charming.
383.25 "And what a sweet-tempered forehead he
383.26 has? cried Louisa, -- "so smooth -- none of
383.27 those frowning irregularities I dislike so
383.28 much: and such a placid eye and smile!"
384.01 And then, to my great relief, Mr. Henry
384.02 Lynn summoned them to the other side of the
384.03 room, to settle some point about the deferred
384.04 excursion to Hay Common.
384.05 I was now able to concentrate my attention
384.06 on the group by the fire, and I presently
384.07 gathered that the new comer was called Mr.
384.08 Mason: then I learnt that he was but just
384.09 arrived in England, and that he came from
384.10 some hot country; which was the reason,
384.11 doubtless, his face was so sallow, and that he
384.12 sat so near the hearth, and wore a surtout in
384.13 the house. Presently the words Jamaica,
384.14 Kingston, Spanish Town, indicated the West
384.15 Indies as his residence; and it was with no
384.16 little surprise I gathered, ere long, that he
384.17 had there first seen and become acquainted
384.18 with Mr. Rochester. He spoke of his friend's

384.19 dislike of the burning heats, the hurricanes,
384.20 and rainy seasons of that region. I knew Mr.
384.21 Rochester had been a traveller: Mrs. Fairfax
384.22 had said so: but I thought the continent of
384.23 Europe had bounded his wanderings: till
384.24 now I had never heard a hint given of visits to
384.25 more distant snores.
384.26 I was pondering these things, when an inci-
384.27 dent, and a somewhat unexpected one, broke
384.28 the thread of my musings. Mr. Mason, shiver-
385.01 ing as some one chanced to open the door,
385.02 asked for more coal to be put on the fire, which
385.03 had burnt out its flame, though its mass of cinder
385.04 still shone hot and red. The footman who
385.05 brought the coal, in going out, stopped near
385.06 Mr. Eshton's chair, and said something to
385.07 him in a low voice, of which I heard only
385.08 the words, "old woman" -- "quite trouble-
385.09 some."
385.10 "Tell her she shall be put in the stocks, if
385.11 she does not take herself off," replied the
385.12 magistrate.
385.13 "No -- stop!" interrupted Colonel Dent.
385.14 "Don't send her away, Eshton; we might
385.15 turn the thing to account: better consult the
385.16 ladies." And speaking aloud, he continued,
385.17 "Ladies, you talked of going to Hay Com-
385.18 mon to visit the gipsy camp; Sam, here, says
385.19 that one of the old Mother Bunches is in the
385.20 servants' hall at this moment, and insists upon
385.21 being brought in before `the quality,' to tell
385.22 them their fortunes. Would you like to see
385.23 her?"
385.24 "Surely, Colonel," cried Lady Ingram,
385.25 "you would not encourage such a low impos-
385.26 tor? Dismiss her, by all means, at once!"
385.27 "But I cannot persuade her to go away,
385.28 my lady," said the footman; "nor can any
386.01 of the servants: Mrs. Fairfax is with her just
386.02 now, entreating her to be gone; but she has
386.03 taken a chair in the chimney-corner, and says
386.04 nothing shall stir her from it till she gets leave
386.05 to come in here."
386.06 "what does she want?" asked Mrs.
386.07 Eshton.
386.08 "`To tell the gentry their fortunes,' she
386.09 says, ma'am: and she swears she must and
386.10 will do it."
386.11 "what is she like?" inquired the Misses
386.12 Eshton in a breath.
386.13 "A shockingly ugly old creature, Miss;
386.14 almost as black as a crock."
386.15 "why, she's a real sorceress!" cried
386.16 Frederick Lynn. "Let us have her in, of
386.17 course."
386.18 "To be sure," rejoined his brother; "it
386.19 would be a thousand pities to throw away
386.20 such a chance of fun."
386.21 "My dear boys, what are you thinking
386.22 about?" exclaimed Lady Lynn.
386.23 "I cannot possibly countenance any such
386.24 inconsistent proceeding," chimed in the Dow-
386.25 ager Ingram.
386.26 "Indeed, mama, but you can -- and will," pro-
386.27 nounced the haughty voice of Blanche, as she
386.28 turned round on the piano-stool; where till
387.01 now she has sat silent, apparently examining
387.02 sundry sheets of music. "I have a curiosity
387.03 to hear my fortune told: therefore, Sam, order
387.04 the beldame forwards."
387.05 "My darling Blanche! recollect --"
387.06 "I do -- I recollect all you can suggest; and
387.07 I must have my will -- quick, Sam!"
387.08 "Yes -- yes -- yes!" cried all the juveniles,
387.09 both ladies and gentlemen. "Let her come --
387.10 it will be excellent sport!"
387.11 The footman still lingered. "She looks
387.12 such a rough one," said he.
387.13 "Go!" ejaculated Miss Ingram, and the
387.14 man went.
387.15 Excitement instantly seized the whole party:
387.16 a running fire of raillery and jests was pro-
387.17 ceeding when Sam returned.
387.18 "She won't come now," said he. "She
387.19 says its not her mission to appear before the
387.20 `vulgar herd' /them's her words/. I must
387.21 show her into a room by herself, and then
387.22 those who wish to consult her must go to her
387.23 one by one."
387.24 "You see now, my queenly Blanche," began
387.25 Lady Ingram, "she encroaches. Be advised,
387.26 my angel-girl -- and --"
387.27 "Show her into the library, of course,"
387.28 cut in the "angel girl." "It is not my mission
388.01 to listen to her before the vulgar herd either:
388.02 I mean to have her all to myself. Is there a
388.03 fire in the library?"
388.04 "Yes, ma'am -- but she looks such a tinkler."
388.05 "Cease that chatter, blockhead! and do my
388.06 bidding."
388.07 Again Sam vanished; and mystery, anima-
388.08 tion, expectation rose to full flow once more.
388.09 "She's ready now," said the footman, as he
388.10 re-appeared. "She wishes to know who will
388.11 be her first visitor."
388.12 "I think I had better just look in upon her
388.13 before any of the ladies go," said Colonel Dent.
388.14 "Tell her, Sam, a gentleman is coming."
388.15 Sam went and returned.
388.16 "She says, sir, that she'll have no gentle-
388.17 men; they need not trouble themselves to

388.18 come near her: nor," he added, with difficulty
388.19 suppressing a titter, "any ladies either, except
388.20 the young and single."
388.21 "By Jove, she has taste!" exclaimed Henry
388.22 Lynn.
388.23 Miss Ingram rose solemnly: "I go first,"
388.24 she said, in a tone which might have befitted
388.25 the leader of a forlorn hope, mounting a breach
388.26 in the van of his men.
388.27 "Oh, my best! oh, my dearest! pause --
388.28 reflect!" was her mama's cry; but she swept
389.01 past her in stately silence, passed through the
389.02 door which Colonel Dent held open, and we
389.03 heard her enter the library.
389.04 A comparative silence ensued. Lady In-
389.05 gram thought it "le cas" to wring her hands:
389.06 which she did accordingly. Miss Mary de-
389.07 clared she felt, for her part, she never dared
389.08 venture. Amy and Louisa Eshton tittered un-
389.09 der their breath, and looked a little frightened.
389.10 The minutes passed very slowly: fifteen were
389.11 counted before the library-door again opened.
389.12 Miss Ingram returned to us through the arch.
389.13 Would she laugh? Would she take it as
389.14 a joke? All eyes met her with a glance of
389.15 eager curiosity, and she met all eyes with one
389.16 of rebuff and coldness; she looked neither
389.17 flurried nor merry; she walked stiffly to her
389.18 seat, and took it in silence.
389.19 "Well, Blanche?" said Lord Ingram.
389.20 "What did she say, sister?" asked Mary.
389.21 "What did you think? How do you feel?
389.22 Is she a real fortune-teller?" demanded the
389.23 Misses Eshton.
389.24 "Now, now, good people," returned Miss
389.25 Ingram, "don't press upon me. Really your
389.26 organs of wonder and credulity are easily ex-
389.27 cited: you seem by the importance you all --
389.28 my good mama included -- ascribe to this mat-
390.01 ter -- absolutely to believe we have a genuine
390.02 witch in the house, who is in close alliance
390.03 with the old gentleman. I have seen a gipsy--
390.04 vagabond; she has practised in hackneyed
390.05 fashion the science of palmistry, and told me
390.06 what such people usually tell. My whim is
390.07 gratified; and now I think Mr. Eshton will do
390.08 well to put the hag in the stocks to-morrow
390.09 morning, as he threatened."
390.10 Miss Ingram took a book, leant back in her
390.11 chair, and so declined further conversation.
390.12 I watched her for nearly half an hour: during
390.13 all that time she never turned a page, and her
390.14 face grew momently darker, more dissatisfied,
390.15 and more sourly expressive of disappointment.
390.16 She had obviously not heard anything to her
390.17 advantage; and it seemed to me, from her pro-
390.18 longed fit of gloom and taciturnity, that she
390.19 herself, notwithstanding her professed indif-
390.20 ference, attached undue importance to what-
390.21 ever revelations had been made her.
390.22 Meantime, Mary Ingram, Amy and Louisa
390.23 Eshton, declared they dared not go alone; and
390.24 yet they all wished to go. A negociation was
390.25 opened through the medium of the ambas-
390.26 sador, Sam; and after much pacing to and
390.27 fro, till, I think, the said Sam's calves must
390.28 have ached with the exercise, permission was
391.01 at last, with great difficulty, extorted from the
391.02 rigorous Sybil, for the three to wait upon her
391.03 in a body.
391.04 Their visit was not so still as Miss Ingram's
391.05 had been: we heard hysterical giggling and
391.06 little shrieks proceeding from the library; and
391.07 at the end of about twenty minutes they burst
391.08 the door open, and came running across the
391.09 hall, as if they were half-scared out of their
391.10 wits.
391.11 "I'm sure she is something not right!"
391.12 they cried, one and all. "She told us such
391.13 things! She knows all about us!" and they
391.14 sank breathless into the various seats the
391.15 gentlemen hastened to bring them.
391.16 Pressed for further explanation, they de-
391.17 clared she had told them of things they had
391.18 said and done when they were mere children;
391.19 described books and ornaments they had in
391.20 their boudoirs at home: keepsakes that dif-
391.21 ferent relations had presented to them. They
391.22 affirmed that she had even divined their
391.23 thoughts, and had whispered in the ear of
391.24 each the name of the person she liked best in
391.25 the world, and informed them of what they
391.26 most wished for.
391.27 Here the gentlemen interposed with earnest
392.01 petitions to be further enlightened on these
392.02 two last-named points; but they got only
392.03 blushes, ejaculations, tremors, and titters, in
392.04 return for their importunity. The matrons,
392.05 meantime, offered vinaigarettes and wielded
392.06 fans; and again and again reiterated the ex-
392.07 pression of their concern that their warning
392.08 had not been taken in time; and the elder
392.09 gentlemen laughed, and the younger urged
392.10 their services on the agitated fair ones.
392.11 In the midst of the tumult, and while my
392.12 eyes and ears were fully engaged in the scene
392.13 before me, I heard a hem close at my elbow:
392.14 I turned, and saw Sam.
392.15 "If you please, Miss, the gipsy declares
392.16 that there is another young single lady in the
392.17 room who has not been to her yet, and she

392.18 swears she will not go till she has seen all. I
392.19 thought it must be you: there is no one else
392.20 for it. What shall I tell her?"
392.21 "Oh, I will go by all means," I answered;
392.22 and I was glad of the unexpected opportunity
392.23 to gratify my much-excited curiosity. I slip-
392.24 ped out of the room, unobserved by any eye --
392.25 for the company were gathered in one mass
392.26 about the trembling trio just returned -- and I
392.27 closed the door quietly behind me.
393.01 "If you like, Miss," said Sam, "I'll wait in
393.02 the hall for you; and if she frightens you, just
393.03 call and I'll come in."
393.04 "No, Sam, return to the kitchen: I am not
393.05 in the least afraid." Nor was I; but I was a
393.06 good deal interested and excited.
394.01 [Vol. 2 Chapter 4]
394.02 The Library looked tranquil enough as I
394.03 entered it, and the Sybil -- if Sybil she were,
394.04 was seated snugly enough in an easy chair
394.05 at the chimney-corner. She had on a red
394.06 cloak and a black bonnet: or rather, a broad--
394.07 brimmed gipsy hat, tied down with a striped
394.08 handkerchief under her chin. An extinguished
394.09 candle stood on the table; she was bending
394.10 over the fire, and seemed reading in a little
394.11 black book, like a prayer-book, by the light
394.12 of the blaze: she muttered the words to her-
394.13 self, as most old women do, while she read;
394.14 she did not desist immediately on my entrance:
394.15 it appeared she wished to finish a paragraph.
394.16 I stood on the rug and warmed my hands,
394.17 which were rather cold with sitting at a dis-
394.18 tance from the drawing-room fire. I felt now
394.19 as composed as ever I did in my life: there
394.20 was nothing indeed in the gipsy's appearance to
395.01 trouble one's calm. She shut her book and
395.02 slowly looked up; her hat-brim partially
395.03 shaded her face, yet I could see, as she raised
395.04 it, that it was a strange one. It looked all
395.05 brown and black: elf-locks bristled out from
395.06 beneath a white band which passed under her
395.07 chin, and came half over her cheeks or rather
395.08 jaws; her eye confronted me at once, with a
395.09 bold and direct gaze.
395.10 "Well, and you want your fortune told?"
395.11 she said in a voice as decided as her glance,
395.12 as harsh as her features.
395.13 "I don't care about it, mother; you may
395.14 please yourself: but I ought to warn you, I
395.15 have no faith."
395.16 "It's like your impudence to say so: I ex-
395.17 pected it of you; I heard it in your step as
395.18 you crossed the threshold."
395.19 "Did you? You've a quick ear."
395.20 "I have; and a quick eye, and a quick
395.21 brain."
395.22 "You need them all in your trade."
395.23 "I do; especially when I've customers like
395.24 you to deal with. Why don't you tremble?"
395.25 "I'm not cold."
395.26 "Why don't you turn pale?"
395.27 "I am not sick."
395.28 "Why don't you consult my art?"
396.01 "I'm not silly."
396.02 The old crone "nichered" a laugh under her
396.03 bonnet and bandage: she then drew out a
396.04 short black pipe, and lighting it, began to
396.05 smoke. Having indulged awhile in this seda-
396.06 tive, she raised her bent body, took the pipe
396.07 from her lips, and while gazing steadily at the
396.08 fire, said very deliberately: --
396.09 "You are cold; you are sick; and you are
396.10 silly."
396.11 "Prove it," I rejoined.
396.12 "I will; in few words. You are cold, be-
396.13 cause you are alone: no contact strikes the fire
396.14 from you that is in you. You are sick; be-
396.15 cause the best of feelings, the highest and the
396.16 sweetest given to man, keeps far away from
396.17 you. You are silly, because, suffer as you may,
396.18 you will not beckon it to approach; nor will
396.19 you stir one step to meet it where it waits
396.20 you."
396.21 She again put her short, black pipe to her
396.22 lips and renewed her smoking with vigour.
396.23 "You might say all that to almost any one
396.24 who, you knew, lived as a solitary dependant
396.25 in a great house."
396.26 "I might say it to almost any one; but
396.27 would it be true of almost any one?"
396.28 "In my circumstances?"
397.01 "Yes; just so, in your circumstances: but
397.02 find me another precisely placed as you are."
397.03 "It would be easy to find you thousands."
397.04 "You could scarcely find me one. If you
397.05 knew it, you are peculiarly situated: very near
397.06 happiness; yes; within reach of it. The ma-
397.07 terials are all prepared; there only wants a
397.08 movement to combine them. Chance laid them
397.09 somwhere apart; let them be once approached
397.10 and bliss results."
397.11 "I don't understand enigmas. I never could
397.12 guess a riddle in my life."
397.13 "If you wish me to speak more plainly,
397.14 show me your palm."
397.15 "And I must cross it with silver, I suppose?"
397.16 "To be sure."
397.17 I gave her a shilling: she put it into an old
397.18 stocking-foot which she took out of her pocket,
397.19 and having tied it round and returned it, she

397.20 told me to hold out my hand. I did. She
397.21 approached her face to the palm, and pored
397.22 over it without touching it.
397.23 "It is too fine," said she. "I can make
397.24 nothing of such a hand as that; almost with-
397.25 out lines: besides, what is in a palm? Destiny
397.26 is not written there."
397.27 "I believe you," said I.
397.28 "No," she continued, "it is in the face: on
398.01 the forehead, about the eyes, in the eyes them-
398.02 selves, in the lines of the mouth. Kneel, and
398.03 lift up your head."
398.04 "Ah! now you are coming to reality," I
398.05 said as I obeyed her. "I shall begin to put
398.06 some faith in you presently."
398.07 I knelt within half a yard of her. She stirred
398.08 the fire, so that a ripple of light broke from
398.09 the disturbed coal: the glare, however, as she
398.10 sat, only threw her face into deeper shadow:
398.11 mine, it illumined.
398.12 "I wonder with what feelings you came to
398.13 me to-night," she said, when she had examined
398.14 me awhile. "I wonder what thoughts are
398.15 busy in your heart during all the hours you
398.16 sit in yonder room with the fine people flitting
398.17 before you like shapes in a magic-lantern:
398.18 just as little sympathetic communion passing
398.19 between you and them, as if they were really
398.20 mere shadows of human forms and not the
398.21 actual substance."
398.22 "I feel tired often, sleepy sometimes; but
398.23 seldom sad."
398.24 "Then you have some secret hope to buoy
398.25 you up and please you with whispers of the
398.26 future?"
398.27 "Not I. The utmost I hope is, to save
398.28 money enough out of my earnings to set up
399.01 a school some day in a little house rented by
399.02 myself."
399.03 "A mean nutriment for the spirit to exist
399.04 on: and sitting in that window-seat /you see
399.05 I know your habits/ --."
399.06 "You have learned them from the servants."
399.07 "Ah! you think yourself sharp. Well --
399.08 perhaps I have: to speak truth, I have an ac-
399.09 quaintance with one of them -- Mrs. Poole --"
399.10 I started to my feet when I heard the
399.11 name.
399.12 "You have -- have you?" thought I; "there
399.13 is diablerie in the business after all, then!"
399.14 "Don't be alarmed," continued the strange
399.15 being; "She's a safe hand, is Mrs. Poole:
399.16 close and quiet; any one may repose confi-
399.17 dence in her. But, as I was saying: sitting in
399.18 that window-seat, do you think of nothing but
399.19 your future school? Have you no present in-
399.20 terest in any of the company who occupy the
399.21 sofas and chairs before you? Is there not one
399.22 face you study? One figure whose move-
399.23 ments you follow with, at least, curiosity?"
399.24 "I like to observe all the faces, and all the
399.25 figures."
399.26 "But do you never single one from the
399.27 rest -- or it may be, two?"
399.28 "I do frequently; when the gestures or
400.01 looks of a pair seem telling a tale: it amuses
400.02 me to watch them."
400.03 "What tale do you like best to hear?"
400.04 "Oh, I have not much choice! They
400.05 generally run on the same theme -- courtship;
400.06 and promise to end in the same catastrophe --
400.07 marriage."
400.08 "And do you like that monotonous theme?"
400.09 "Positively, I don't care about it: it is
400.10 nothing to me."
400.11 "Nothing to you? When a lady, young and
400.12 full of life and health, charming with beauty
400.13 and endowed with the gifts of rank and for-
400.14 tune, sits and smiles in the eyes of a gentle-
400.15 man you --"
400.16 "I what?"
400.17 "You know -- and, perhaps, think well of."
400.18 "I don't know the gentlemen here. I have
400.19 scarcely interchanged a syllable with one of
400.20 them; and as to thinking well of them, I con-
400.21 sider some respectable and stately, and middle--
400.22 aged, and others young, dashing, handsome
400.23 and lively: but certainly they are all at liberty
400.24 to be the recipients of whose smiles they please,
400.25 without my feeling disposed to consider the
400.26 transaction of any moment to me."
400.27 "You don't know the gentlemen here?
400.28 You have not exchanged a syllable with one
401.01 of them? Will you say that of the master of
401.02 the house?"
401.03 "He is not at home."
401.04 "A profound remark! A most ingenious
401.05 quibble! He went to Millcote this morning,
401.06 and will be back here to-night, or to-morrow:
401.07 does that circumstance exclude him from the
401.08 list of your acquaintance -- blot him, as it were,
401.09 out of existence?"
401.10 "No: but I can scarcely see what Mr. Ro-
401.11 chester has to do with the theme you had in-
401.12 troduced."
401.13 "I was talking of ladies smiling in the eyes
401.14 of gentlemen; and of late so many smiles have
401.15 been shed into Mr. Rochester's eyes that they
401.16 overflow like two cups filled above the brim:
401.17 have you never remarked that?"
401.18 "Mr. Rochester has a right to enjoy the
401.19 society of guests."
401.20 "No question about his right: but have you
401.21 never observed that, of all the tales told here
401.22 about matrimony, Mr. Rochester has been
401.23 favoured with the most lively and the most
401.24 continuous?"
401.25 "The eagerness of a listener quickens the
401.26 tongue of a narrator." I said this rather to
401.27 myself than to the gipsy; whose strange talk,
402.01 voice, manner, had by this time wrapped me in
402.02 a kind of dream. One unexpected sentence
402.03 came from her lips after another, till I got
402.04 involved in a web of mystification; and won-
402.05 dered what unseen spirit had been sitting for
402.06 weeks by my heart watching its workings, and
402.07 taking record of every pulse.
402.08 "Eagerness of a listener!" repeated she:
402.09 "yes; Mr. Rochester has sat by the hour, his
402.10 ear inclined to the fascinating lips that took
402.11 such delight in their task of communicating;
402.12 and Mr. Rochester was so willing to receive,
402.13 and looked so grateful for the pastime given
402.14 him: you have noticed this?"
402.15 "Grateful! I cannot remember detecting
402.16 gratitude in his face."
402.17 "Detecting! You have analyzed, then.
402.18 And what did you detect, if not gratitude?"
402.19 I said nothing.
402.20 "You have seen love: have you not? -- and,
402.21 looking forward, you have seen him married,
402.22 and beheld his bride happy?"
402.23 "Humph! Not exactly. Your witch's
402.24 skill is rather at fault sometimes."
402.25 "What the devil have you seen, then?"
402.26 "Never mind: I came here to inquire, not
402.27 to confess. Is it known that Mr. Rochester is
402.28 to be married?"
403.01 "Yes; and to the beautiful Miss Ingram."
403.02 "Shortly?"
403.03 "Appearances would warrant that conclu-
403.04 sion; and, no doubt /though, with an audacity
403.05 that wants chastising out of you, you seem to
403.06 question it/, they will be a superlatively happy
403.07 pair. He must love such a handsome, noble,
403.08 witty, accomplished lady; and probably she
403.09 loves him: or, if not his person, at least his
403.10 purse. I know she considers the Rochester
403.11 estate eligible to the last degree: though /God
403.12 pardon me!/ I told her something on that
403.13 point about an hour ago, which made her look
403.14 wondrous grave: the corners of her mouth fell
403.15 half an inch. I would advise her blackavised
403.16 suitor to look out: if another comes, with a
403.17 longer or clearer rent-roll, -- he's dished -- "
403.18 "But, mother, I did not come to hear Mr.
403.19 Rochester's fortune: I came to hear my own;
403.20 and you have told me nothing of it."
403.21 "Your fortune is yet doubtful: when I
403.22 examined your face, one trait contradicted
403.23 another. Chance has meted you a measure of
403.24 happiness: that I know. I knew it before I
403.25 came here this evening. She has laid it care-
403.26 fully on one side for you. I saw her do it. It
403.27 depends on yourself to stretch out your hand,
403.28 and take it up: but whether you will do so,
404.01 is, the problem I study. Kneel again on the
404.02 rug."
404.03 "Don't keep me long; the fire scorches me."
404.04 I knelt. She did not stoop towards me, but
404.05 only gazed, leaning back in her chair. She
404.06 began muttering:
404.07 "The flame flickers in the eye; the eye
404.08 shines like dew; it looks soft and full of feel-
404.09 ing; it smiles at my jargon: it is susceptible;
404.10 impression follows impression through its clear
404.11 sphere; where it ceases to smile, it is sad; an
404.12 unconscious lassitude weighs on the lid: that
404.13 signifies melancholy resulting from loneliness.
404.14 It turns from me; it will not suffer farther
404.15 scrutiny; it seems to deny, by a mocking
404.16 glance, the truth of the discoveries I have
404.17 already made, -- to disown the charge both of
404.18 sensibility and chagrin: its pride and reserve
404.19 only confirm me in my opinion. The eye is
404.20 favourable.
404.21 "As to the mouth, it delights at times in
404.22 laughter: it is disposed to impart all that the
404.23 brain conceives; though I dare say it would
404.24 be silent on much the heart experiences.
404.25 Mobile and flexible, it was never intended to
404.26 be compressed in the eternal silence of soli-
404.27 tude: it is a mouth which should speak much
404.28 and smile often, and have human affection
405.01 for its interlocutor. That feature too is pro-
405.02 pitious.
405.03 "I see no enemy to a fortunate issue but in
405.04 the brow; and that brow professes to say, --
405.05 `I can live alone, if self-respect and circum-
405.06 stances require me so to do. I need not sell
405.07 my soul to buy bliss. I have an inward trea-
405.08 sure, born with me, which can keep me alive if
405.09 all extraneous delights should be withheld;
405.10 or offered only at a price I cannot afford to
405.11 give.` The forehead declares, `Reason sits
405.12 firm and holds the reins, and she will not let
405.13 the feelings burst away and hurry her to wild
405.14 chasms. The passions may rage furiously,
405.15 like true heathens, as they are; and the desires
405.16 may imagine all sorts of vain things: but judg-
405.17 ment shall still have the last word in every
405.18 argument, and the casting vote in every deci-

405.19 sion. Strong wind, earthquake-shock, and
405.20 fire may pass by: I shall follow the guiding
405.21 but of that still small voice which interprets
405.22 the dictates of conscience.`
405.23 "Well said, forehead; your declaration
405.24 shall be respected. I have formed my plans
405.25 -- right plans I deem them -- and in them I
405.26 have attended to the claims of conscience, the
405.27 counsels of reason. I know how soon youth
405.28 would fade and bloom perish, if, in the cup of
406.01 bliss offered, but one dreg of shame, or one
406.02 flavour of remorse were detected; and I do
406.03 not want sacrifice, sorrow, dissolution -- such
406.04 is not my taste. I wish to foster, not to blight --
406.05 to earn gratitude, not to wring tears of blood
406.06 -- no, nor of brine: my harvest must be in
406.07 smiles, in endearments, in sweet. -- That will do.
406.08 I think I rave in a kind of exquisite delirium.
406.09 I should wish now to protract this moment ad
406.10 infinitum; but I dare not. So far I have
406.11 governed myself thoroughly. I have acted as
406.12 I inwardly swore I would act; but farther
406.13 might try me beyond my strength. Rise,
406.14 Miss Eyre: leave me; `the play is played
406.15 out.` "
406.16 where was I? Did I wake or sleep? Had
406.17 I been dreaming? Did I dream still? The
406.18 old woman's voice had changed: her accent,
406.19 her gesture, and all were familiar to me as my
406.20 own face in the glass -- as the speech of my own
406.21 tongue. I got up, but did not go. I looked:
406.22 I stirred the fire, and I looked again: but she
406.23 drew her bonnet and her bandage closer about
406.24 her face, and again beckoned me to depart.
406.25 The flame illuminated her hand stretched out:
406.26 roused now, and on the alert for discoveries, I
406.27 at once noticed that hand. It was no more
406.28 the withered limb of eld than my own: it was
407.01 a rounded supple member, with smooth fingers,
407.02 symmetrically turned; a broad ring flashed
407.03 on the little finger, and stooping forward, I
407.04 looked at it, and saw a gem I had seen a
407.05 hundred times before. Again I looked at the
407.06 face; which was no longer turned from me
407.07 -- on the contrary, the bonnet was doffed, the
407.08 bandage displaced, the head advanced.
407.09 "Well, Jane, do you know me?" asked
407.10 the familiar voice.
407.11 "Only take off the red cloak, sir, and
407.12 then -- "
407.13 "But the string is in a knot -- help me."
407.14 "Break it, sir."
407.15 "There then -- `Off, ye lendings!` " And
407.16 Mr. Rochester stepped out of his disguise.
407.17 "Now, sir, what a strange idea!"
407.18 "But well carried out, eh? Don't you
407.19 think so?"
407.20 "With the ladies you must have managed
407.21 well."
407.22 "But not with you?"
407.23 "You did not act the character of a gipsy
407.24 with me."
407.25 "what character did I act? My own?"
407.26 "No; some unaccountable one. In short,
407.27 I believe you have been trying to draw me
407.28 out -- or in: you have been talking nonsense to
407.29 make me talk nonsense. It is scarcely fair, sir."
408.01 "Do you forgive me, Jane?"
408.02 "I cannot tell till I have thought it all
408.03 over. If, on reflection, I find I have fallen
408.04 into no great absurdity, I shall try to forgive
408.05 you: but it was not right."
408.06 "Oh! you have been very correct -- very
408.07 careful, very sensible."
408.08 I reflected, and thought, on the whole, I
408.09 had. It was a comfort: but, indeed, I had
408.10 been on my guard almost from the beginning
408.11 of the interview. Something of masquerade I
408.12 suspected. I knew gipsies and fortune-tellers
408.13 did not express themselves as this seeming old
408.14 woman had expressed herself: besides, I had
408.15 noted her feigned voice, her anxiety to conceal
408.16 her features. But my mind had been running
408.17 on Grace Poole -- that living enigma, that mys-
408.18 tery of mysteries, as I considered her: I had
408.19 never thought of Mr. Rochester.
408.20 "Well," said he, "what are you musing
408.21 about? What does that grave smile sig-
408.22 nify?" "wonder and self-congratulation, sir. I
408.23 have your permission to retire now, I suppose?"
408.24 "No: stay a moment; and tell me what
408.25 the people in the drawing-room yonder are
408.26 doing."
408.27 "Discussing the gipsy, I daresay."
409.01 "Sit down! -- Let me hear what they said
409.02 about me."
409.03 "I had better not stay long, sir: it must be
409.04 near eleven o'clock. Oh! are you aware, Mr.
409.05 Rochester, that a stranger has arrived here
409.06 since you left this morning?"
409.07 "A stranger! -- no: who can it be? I
409.08 expected no one: is he gone?"
409.09 "No: he said he had known you long, and
409.10 that he could take the liberty of installing
409.11 himself here till you returned."
409.12 "The devil he did! Did he give his
409.13 name?"
409.14 "His name is Mason, sir; and he comes
409.15 from the West Indies: from Spanish Town, in
409.16 Jamaica, I think."
409.17 Mr. Rochester was standing near me: he

409.18 had taken my hand, as if to lead me to a
409.19 chair. As I spoke, he gave my wrist a con-
409.20 vulsive grip; the smile on his lips froze: ap-
409.21 parently a spasm caught his breath.
409.22 "Mason! -- the West Indies!" he said, in
409.23 the tone one might fancy a speaking automaton
409.24 to enounce its single words; "Mason! -- the
409.25 west Indies!" he reiterated; and he went
409.26 over the syllables three times, growing, in the
409.27 intervals of speaking, whiter than ashes: he
409.28 hardly seemed to know what he was doing.
410.01 "Do you feel ill, sir?" I inquired.
410.02 "Jane, I've got a blow: -- I've got a blow,
410.03 Jane!" he staggered.
410.04 "Oh! -- lean on me, sir."
410.05 "Jane, you offered me your shoulder once
410.06 before; let me have it now."
410.07 "Yes, sir, yes; and my arm."
410.08 He sat down, and made me sit beside him.
410.09 Holding my hand in both his own, he chafed
410.10 it; gazing on me, at the same time with the
410.11 most troubled and dreary look.
410.12 "My little friend!" said he, "I wish I were
410.13 in a quiet island with only you; and trouble,
410.14 and danger, and hideous recollections removed
410.15 from me."
410.16 "Can I help you, sir? -- I'd give my life to
410.17 serve you."
410.18 "Jane, if aid is wanted, I'll seek it at your
410.19 hands: I promise you that."
410.20 "Thank you, sir: tell me what to do, -- I'll
410.21 try, at least, to do it."
410.22 "fetch me now, Jane, a glass of wine from
410.23 the dining-room: they will be at supper there;
410.24 and tell me if Mason is with them, and what
410.25 he is doing."
410.26 I went. I found all the party in the dining-
410.27 room at supper, as Mr. Rochester had said;
410.28 they were not seated at table, -- the supper was
411.01 arranged on the sideboard; each had taken
411.02 what he chose, and they stood about here and
411.03 there in groups, their plates and glasses in
411.04 their hands. Every one seemed in high glee;
411.05 laughter and conversation were general and
411.06 animated. Mr. Mason stood near the fire,
411.07 talking to Colonel and Mrs. Dent, and ap-
411.08 peared as merry as any of them. I filled a
411.09 wine-glass /I saw Miss Ingram watch me
411.10 frowningly as I did so: she thought I was
411.11 taking a liberty, I dare say/, and I returned
411.12 to the library.
411.13 Mr. Rochester's extreme pallor had disap-
411.14 peared, and he looked once more firm and
411.15 stern. He took the glass from my hand.
411.16 "Here is to your health, ministrant spirit!"
411.17 he said: he swallowed the contents and re-
411.18 turned it to me. "what are they doing,
411.19 Jane?"
411.20 "Laughing and talking, sir."
411.21 "They don't look grave and mysterious, as
411.22 if they had heard something strange?"
411.23 "Not at all: -- they are full of jests and
411.24 gaiety."
411.25 "And Mason?"
411.26 "He was laughing too."
411.27 "If all these people came in a body and
411.28 spat at me, what would you do, Jane?"
412.01 "Turn them out of the room, sir, if I could."
412.02 He half smiled. "But if I were to go to
412.03 them, and they only looked at me coldly, and
412.04 whispered sneeringly amongst each other, and
412.05 then dropt off and left me one by one, what
412.06 then? would you go with them?"
412.07 "I rather think not, sir: I should have more
412.08 pleasure in staying with you."
412.09 "To comfort me?"
412.10 "Yes, sir, to comfort you, as well as I
412.11 could."
412.12 "And if they laid you under a ban for ad-
412.13 hering to me?"
412.14 "I, probably, should know nothing about
412.15 their ban; and if I did, I should care nothing
412.16 about it."
412.17 "Then, you could dare censure for my
412.18 sake?"
412.19 "I could dare it for the sake of any friend
412.20 who deserved my adherence; as you, I am
412.21 sure do."
412.22 "Go back now into the room; step quietly
412.23 up to Mason, and whisper in his ear that Mr.
412.24 Rochester is come and wishes to see him:
412.25 show him in here, and then leave me."
412.26 "Yes, sir."
412.27 I did his behest. The company all stared
412.28 at me as I passed straight among them. I
413.01 sought Mr. Mason, delivered the message, and
413.02 preceded him from the room: I ushered him
413.03 into the library, and then I went up stairs.
413.04 At a late hour, after I had been in bed some
413.05 time, I heard the visitors repair to their cham-
413.06 bers: I distinguished Mr. Rochester's voice,
413.07 and heard him say, "This way, Mason; this
413.08 is your room."
413.09 He spoke cheerfully: the gay tones set my
413.10 heart at ease. I was soon asleep.
414.01 [Vol. 2 Chapter 5]
414.02 I had forgotten to draw my curtain, which
414.03 I usually did; and also to let down my
414.04 window-blind. The consequence was, that
414.05 when the moon, which was full and bright
414.06 /for the night was fine/ came in her course to

414.07 that space in the sky opposite my casement,
414.08 and looked in at me through the unveiled
414.09 panes, her glorious gaze roused me. Awaking
414.10 in the dead of night, I opened my eyes on her
414.11 disk -- silver-white and crystal-clear. It was
414.12 beautiful, but too solemn: I half rose, and
414.13 stretched my arm to draw the curtain.
414.14   Good God! What a cry!
414.15   The night -- its silence -- its rest, was rent in
414.16 twain by a savage, a sharp, a shrilly sound
414.17 that ran from end to end of Thornfield-Hall.
414.18   My pulse stopped: my heart stood still;
414.19 my stretched arm was paralyzed. The cry
414.20 died, and was not renewed. Indeed, whatever
415.01 being uttered that fearful shriek could not
415.02 soon repeat it: not the widest-winged condor
415.03 on the Andes could, twice in succession, send
415.04 out such a yell from the cloud shrouding his
415.05 eyrie. The thing delivering such utterance
415.06 must rest ere it could repeat the effort.
415.07   It came out of the third story; for it passed
415.08 overhead. And overhead -- yes, in the room just
415.09 above my chamber-ceiling -- I now heard a
415.10 struggle: a deadly one it seemed from the
415.11 noise; and a half-smothered voice shouted: --
415.12 "Help! help! help!" three times rapidly.
415.13 "Will no one come?" it cried; and then
415.14 while the staggering and stamping went on
415.15 wildly, I distinguished through plank and
415.16 plaster: --
415.17 "Rochester! Rochester! for God's sake,
415.18 come!"
415.19   A chamber-door opened: some one ran, or
415.20 rushed, along the gallery. Another step stamp-
415.21 ed on the flooring above, and something fell;
415.22 and there was silence.
415.23   I had put on some clothes, though horror
415.24 shook all my limbs: I issued from my apart-
415.25 ment. The sleepers were all aroused: ejacu-
415.26 lations, terrified murmurs sounded in every
415.27 room; door after door unclosed; one looked
415.28 out and another looked out; the gallery filled.
416.01 Gentlemen and ladies alike had quitted their
416.02 beds; and "Oh! what is it?" -- "Who is
416.03 hurt?" -- "What has happened?" -- "Fetch a
416.04 light!" -- "Is it fire?" -- "Are there robbers?"
416.05 -- "Where shall we run?" was demanded
416.06 confusedly on all hands. But for the moon-
416.07 light they would have been in complete dark-
416.08 ness. They ran to and fro; they crowded
416.09 together: some sobbed, some stumbled: the
416.10 confusion was inextricable.
416.11 "Where the devil is Rochester?" cried
416.12 Colonel Dent. "I cannot find him in his
416.13 bed."
416.14 "Here! here!" was shouted in return. "Be
416.15 composed, all of you: I'm coming."
416.16   And the door at the end of the gallery
416.17 opened, and Mr. Rochester advanced with a
416.18 candle: he had just descended from the upper
416.19 story. One of the ladies ran to him directly;
416.20 she seized his arm: it was Miss Ingram.
416.21 "What awful event has taken place?" said
416.22 she. "Speak! let us know the worst at
416.23 once!"
416.24 "But don't pull me down or strangle me,"
416.25 he replied: for the Misses Eshton were cling-
416.26 ing about him now; and the two dowagers, in
416.27 vast white wrappers, were bearing down on
416.28 him like ships in full sail.
417.01 "All's right! -- all's right!" he cried. "It's
417.02 a mere rehearsal of much ado about nothing.
417.03 Ladies, keep off; or I shall wax dangerous."
417.04   And dangerous he looked: his black eyes
417.05 darted sparks. Calming himself by an effort
417.06 he added: --
417.07 "A servant has had the nightmare; that is
417.08 all. She's an excitable, nervous person: she
417.09 construed her dream into an apparition, or
417.10 something of that sort, no doubt; and has
417.11 taken a fit with fright. Now, then, I must
417.12 see you all back into your rooms; for, till the
417.13 house is settled, she cannot be looked after.
417.14 Gentlemen, have the goodness to set the ladies
417.15 the example. Miss Ingram, I am sure you
417.16 will not fail in evincing superiority to idle
417.17 terrors. Amy and Louisa, return to your
417.18 nests like a pair of doves, as you are. Mes-
417.19 dames," /to the dowagers/ "you will take cold
417.20 to a dead certainty, if you stay in this chill
417.21 gallery any longer."
417.22   And so, by dint of alternate coaxing and
417.23 commanding, he contrived to get them all
417.24 once more enclosed in their separate dormi-
417.25 tories. I did not wait to be ordered back to
417.26 mine; but retreated unnoticed: as unnoticed I
417.27 had left it.
417.28   Not, however, to go to bed: on the contrary,
418.01 I began and dressed myself carefully. The
418.02 sounds I had heard after the scream, and the
418.03 words that had been uttered, had probably
418.04 been heard only by me; for they had pro-
418.05 ceeded from the room above mine: but they
418.06 assured me that it was not a servant's dream
418.07 which had thus struck horror through the
418.08 house; and that the explanation Mr. Rochester
418.09 had given was merely an invention framed to
418.10 pacify his guests. I dressed, then, to be ready
418.11 for emergencies. When dressed, I sat a long
418.12 time by the window, looking out over the
418.13 silent grounds and silvered fields, and waiting

418.14 for I knew not what. It seemed to me that
418.15 some event must follow the strange cry,
418.16 struggle, and call.
418.17   No: stillness returned: each murmur and
418.18 movement ceased gradually, and in about an
418.19 hour Thornfield-Hall was again as hushed as
418.20 a desert. It seemed that sleep and night had
418.21 resumed their empire. Meantime the moon
418.22 declined: she was about to set. Not liking
418.23 to sit in the cold and darkness, I thought I
418.24 would lie down on my bed, dressed as I was.
418.25 I left the window, and moved with little noise
418.26 across the carpet; as I stooped to take off my
418.27 shoes, a cautious hand tapped low at the
418.28 door.
419.01 "Am I wanted?" I asked.
419.02 "Are you up?" asked the voice I expected
419.03 to hear, viz., my master's.
419.04 "Yes, sir."
419.05 "And dressed?"
419.06 "Yes."
419.07 "Come out, then, quietly."
419.08   I obeyed. Mr. Rochester stood in the gal-
419.09 lery, holding a light.
419.10 "I want you," he said: "come this way:
419.11 take your time, and make no noise."
419.12   My slippers were thin: I could walk the
419.13 matted floor as softly as a cat. He glided up
419.14 the gallery and up the stairs, and stopped in
419.15 the dark, low corridor of the fateful third
419.16 story: I had followed and stood at his side.
419.17 "Have you a sponge in your room?" he
419.18 asked in a whisper.
419.19 "Yes, sir."
419.20 "Have you any salts -- volatile salts?"
419.21 "Yes."
419.22 "Go back and fetch both."
419.23   I returned, sought the sponge on the wash-
419.24 stand, the salts in my drawer, and once more
419.25 retraced my steps. He still waited; he held
419.26 a key in his hand: approaching one of the
419.27 small, black doors, he put it in the lock; he
419.28 paused and addressed me again.
420.01 "You don't turn sick at the sight of blood?"
420.02 "I think I shall not: I have never been
420.03 tried yet."
420.04   I felt a thrill while I answered him; but no
420.05 coldness, and no faintness.
420.06 "Just give me your hand," he said; "it will
420.07 not do to risk a fainting fit."
420.08   I put my fingers into his. "Warm and
420.09 steady," was his remark: he turned the key
420.10 and opened the door.
420.11   I saw a room I remembered to have seen
420.12 before; the day Mrs. Fairfax showed me over
420.13 the house: it was hung with tapestry; but the
420.14 tapestry was now looped up in one part, and
420.15 there was a door apparent, which had then
420.16 been concealed. This door was open; a light
420.17 shone out of the room within: I heard thence
420.18 a snarling, snatching sound, almost like a dog
420.19 quarrelling. Mr. Rochester, putting down his
420.20 candle, said to me, "wait a minute," and he
420.21 went forward to the inner apartment. A
420.22 shout of laughter greeted his entrance; noisy
420.23 at first, and terminating in Grace Poole's own
420.24 goblin ha! ha! She then was there. He
420.25 made some sort of arrangement, without
420.26 speaking: though I heard a low voice ad-
420.27 dress him: he came out and closed the door
420.28 behind him.
421.01 "Here, Jane!" he said; and I walked
421.02 round to the other side of a large bed, which
421.03 with its drawn curtains concealed a consider-
421.04 able portion of the chamber. An easy-chair
421.05 was near the bed-head: a man sat in it,
421.06 dressed with the exception of his coat; he was
421.07 still; his head leant back; his eyes were
421.08 closed. Mr. Rochester held the candle over
421.09 him; I recognised in his pale and seemingly
421.10 lifeless face -- the stranger, Mason: I saw too
421.11 that his linen on one side, and one arm, was
421.12 almost soaked in blood.
421.13 "Hold the candle," said Mr. Rochester,
421.14 and I took it; he fetched a basin of water
421.15 from the wash-stand: "Hold that," said he. I
421.16 obeyed. He took the sponge, dipped it in
421.17 and moistened the corpse-like face: he asked
421.18 for my smelling-bottle, and applied it to
421.19 the nostrils. Mr. Mason shortly unclosed his
421.20 eyes; he groaned. Mr. Rochester opened the
421.21 shirt of the wounded man, whose arm and
421.22 shoulder were bandaged: he sponged away
421.23 blood, trickling fast down.
421.24 "Is there immediate danger?" murmured
421.25 Mr. Mason.
421.26 "Pooh! No -- a mere scratch. Don't be
421.27 so overcome, man: bear up! I'll fetch a
421.28 surgeon for you now, myself: you'll be able to
422.01 be removed by morning, I hope. Jane --" he
422.02 continued.
422.03 "Sir?"
422.04 "I shall have to leave you in this room with
422.05 this gentleman, for an hour, or perhaps two
422.06 hours; you will sponge the blood as I do
422.07 when it returns: if he feels faint, you will put
422.08 the glass of water on that stand to his lips,
422.09 and your salts to his nose. You will not speak
422.10 to him on any pretext -- and -- Richard -- it will
422.11 be at the peril of your life if you speak to her:
422.12 open your lips -- agitate yourself -- and I'll not

422.13 answer for the consequences."
422.14   Again the poor man groaned: he looked
422.15 as if he dared not move: fear, either of
422.16 death or of something else, appeared almost to
422.17 paralyze him. Mr. Rochester put the now
422.18 bloody sponge into my hand, and I proceeded
422.19 to use it as he had done. He watched me a
422.20 second, then saying, "Remember! -- No con-
422.21 versation," he left the room. I experienced a
422.22 strange feeling as the key grated in the lock,
422.23 and the sound of his retreating step ceased to
422.24 be heard.
422.25   Here then I was in the third story, fastened
422.26 into one of its mystic cells; night around me;
422.27 a pale and bloody spectacle under my eyes and
422.28 hands; a murderess hardly separated from me
423.01 by a single door: yes -- that was appalling --
423.02 the rest I could bear; but I shuddered at the
423.03 thought of Grace Poole bursting out upon me.
423.04   I must keep to my post, however. I must
423.05 watch this ghastly countenance -- these blue,
423.06 still lips forbidden to unclose -- these eyes now
423.07 shut, now opening, now wandering through
423.08 the room, now fixing on me, and ever glazed
423.09 with the dulness of horror. I must dip my
423.10 hand again and again in the basin of blood
423.11 and water, and wipe away the trickling gore.
423.12 I must see the light of the unsnuffed candle
423.13 wane on my employment; the shadows darken
423.14 on the wrought, antique tapestry round me,
423.15 and grow black under the hangings of the
423.16 vast old bed, and quiver strangely over the
423.17 doors of a great cabinet opposite -- whose front,
423.18 divided into twelve panels, bore in grim design,
423.19 the heads of the twelve apostles, each inclosed
423.20 in its separate panel as in a frame; while above
423.21 them at the top rose an ebon crucifix and a
423.22 dying Christ.
423.23   According as the shifting obscurity and
423.24 flickering gleam hovered here or glanced
423.25 there, it was now the bearded physician,
423.26 Luke, that bent his brow; now St. John's long
423.27 hair that waved; and anon the devilish face of
423.28 Judas, that grew out of the panel and seemed
424.01 gathering life and threatening a revelation of
424.02 the arch-traitor -- of Satan himself -- in his sub-
424.03 ordinate's form.
424.04   Amidst all this, I had to listen as well as
424.05 watch: to listen for the movements of the wild
424.06 beast or the fiend in yonder side den. But
424.07 since Mr. Rochester's visit it seemed spell-
424.08 bound: all the night I heard but three sounds
424.09 at three long intervals, -- a step creak, a mo-
424.10 mentary renewal of the snarling, canine noise,
424.11 and a deep human groan.
424.12   Then my own thoughts worried me. What
424.13 crime was this, that lived incarnate in this
424.14 sequestered mansion, and could neither be ex-
424.15 pelled or subdued by the owner? -- What
424.16 mystery, that broke out, now in fire and now
424.17 in blood, at the deadest hours of night? -- what
424.18 creature was it, that, masked in an ordinary
424.19 woman's face and shape, uttered the voice,
424.20 now of a mocking demon, and anon of a car-
424.21 rion-seeking bird of prey?
424.22   And this man I bent over -- this common--
424.23 place, quiet stranger -- how had he become
424.24 involved in the web of horror? and why had
424.25 the Fury flown at him? what made him seek
424.26 this quarter of the house at an untimely season,
424.27 when he should have been asleep in bed? I
424.28 had heard Mr. Rochester assign him an apart-
425.01 ment below --what brought him here? And
425.02 why, now, was he so tame under the violence
425.03 or treachery done him? Why did he so quietly
425.04 submit to the concealment Mr. Rochester en-
425.05 forced? why did Mr. Rochester enforce this
425.06 concealment? His guest had been outraged,
425.07 his own life on a former occasion had been
425.08 hideously plotted against; and both attempts
425.09 he smothered in secresy and sank in ob-
425.10 livion! Lastly, I saw Mr. Mason was sub-
425.11 missive to Mr. Rochester; that the impetuous
425.12 will of the latter held complete sway over the
425.13 inertness of the former: the few words which
425.14 had passed between them assured me of this.
425.15 It was evident that in their former intercourse,
425.16 the passive disposition of the one had been
425.17 habitually influenced by the active energy of
425.18 the other: whence then had arisen Mr. Roches-
425.19 ter's dismay when he heard of Mr. Mason's
425.20 arrival? Why had the mere name of this
425.21 unresisting individual -- whom his word now
425.22 sufficed to control like a child -- fallen on him,
425.23 a few hours since, as a thunderbolt might fall
425.24 on an oak?
425.25   Oh! I could not forget his look and his
425.26 paleness when he whispered: "Jane, I have
425.27 got a blow -- I have got a blow, Jane." I
425.28 could not forget how the arm had trembled
426.01 which he rested on my shoulder: and it
426.02 was no light matter which could thus bow the
426.03 resolute spirit and thrill the vigorous frame of
426.04 Fairfax Rochester.
426.05   "When will he come? when will he
426.06 come?" I cried inwardly, as the night lingered
426.07 and lingered -- as my bleeding patient drooped,
426.08 moaned, sickened: and neither day nor aid
426.09 arrived. I had, again and again, held the
426.10 water to Mason's white lips; again and again
426.11 offered him the stimulating salts: my efforts

426.12 seemed ineffectual: either bodily or mental
426.13 suffering, or loss of blood, or all three com-
426.14 bined, were fast prostrating his strength. He
426.15 moaned so, and looked so weak, wild, and
426.16 lost, I feared he was dying; and I might not
426.17 even speak to him!
426.18   The candle, wasted at last, went out; as it
426.19 expired, I perceived streaks of grey light
426.20 edging the window curtains: dawn was then
426.21 approaching. Presently I heard Pilot bark far
426.22 below, out of his distant kennel in the court--
426.23 yard: hope revived. Nor was it unwarranted:
426.24 in five minutes more the grating key, the yield-
426.25 ing lock, warned me my watch was relieved.
426.26 It could not have lasted more than two hours:
426.27 many a week has seemed shorter.
427.01   Mr. Rochester entered, and with him the
427.02 surgeon he had been to fetch.
427.03   "Now, Carter, be on the alert," he said to
427.04 this last: "I give you but half an hour for
427.05 dressing the wound, fastening the bandages,
427.06 getting the patient down stairs and all."
427.07   "But is he fit to move, sir?"
427.08   "No doubt of it; it is nothing serious: he
427.09 is nervous, his spirits must be kept up. Come,
427.10 set to work."
427.11   Mr. Rochester drew back the thick curtain,
427.12 drew up the holland blind, let in all the day-
427.13 light he could; and I was surprised and cheered
427.14 to see how far dawn was advanced: what rosy
427.15 streaks were beginning to brighten the east.
427.16 Then he approached Mason, whom the sur-
427.17 geon was already handling.
427.18   "Now, my good fellow, how are you?" he asked.
427.19   "She's done for me, I fear," was the faint
427.20 reply.
427.21   "Not a whit! -- courage! This day fort--
427.22 night you'll hardly be a pin the worse of it:
427.23 you've lost a little blood; that's all. Carter,
427.24 assure him there's no danger."
427.25   "I can do that conscientiously," said Carter,
427.26 who had now undone the bandages; "only I
427.27 wish I could have got here sooner: he would
428.01 not have bled so much -- but how is this? The
428.02 flesh on the shoulder is torn as well as cut.
428.03 This wound was not done with a knife: there
428.04 have been teeth here?"
428.05   "She bit me," he murmured. "She wor-
428.06 ried me like a tigress, when Rochester got the
428.07 knife from her."
428.08   "You should not have yielded: you should
428.09 have grappled with her at once," said Mr.
428.10 Rochester.
428.11   "But under such circumstances, what could
428.12 one do?" returned Mason. "Oh, it was fright-
428.13 ful!" he added, shuddering. "And I did not
428.14 expect it: she looked so quiet at first."
428.15   "I warned you," was his friend's answer;
428.16 "I said -- be on your guard when you go near
428.17 her. Besides, you might have waited till to--
428.18 morrow, and had me with you: it was mere
428.19 folly to attempt the interview to-night, and
428.20 alone."
428.21   "I thought I could have done some good."
428.22   "You thought! you thought! Yes; it
428.23 makes me impatient to hear you: but, how-
428.24 ever, you have suffered, and are likely to suffer
428.25 enough for not taking my advice; so I'll say
428.26 no more. Carter -- hurry! -- hurry! The sun
428.27 will soon rise, and I must have him off."
428.28   "Directly, sir; the shoulder is just ban-
429.01 daged. I must look to this other wound in the
429.02 arm: she has had her teeth here too, I think."
429.03   "She sucked the blood: she said she'd drain
429.04 my heart," said Mason.
429.05   I saw Mr. Rochester shudder: a singularly
429.06 marked expression of disgust, horror, hatred
429.07 warped his countenance almost to distortion;
429.08 but he only said: --
429.09   "Come, be silent, Richard, and never mind
429.10 her gibberish: don't repeat it."
429.11   "I wish I could forget it," was the answer.
429.12   "You will when you are out of the country:
429.13 when you get back to Spanish Town, you may
429.14 think of her as dead and buried -- or rather
429.15 you need not think of her at all."
429.16   "Impossible to forget this night!"
429.17   "It is not impossible: have some energy,
429.18 man. You thought you were as dead as a
429.19 herring two hours since, and you are all alive
429.20 and talking now. There! -- Carter has done
429.21 with you or nearly so; I'll make you decent
429.22 in a trice. Jane," /he turned to me for the
429.23 first time since his re-entrance/ "take this
429.24 key: go down into my bed-room, and walk
429.25 straight forward into my dressing-room; open
429.26 the top drawer of the wardrobe and take out a
429.27 clean shirt and neck-handkerchief: bring them
429.28 here; and be nimble."
430.01   I went; sought the repository he had men-
430.02 tioned, found the articles named, and returned
430.03 with them.
430.04   "Now," said he, "go to the other side of
430.05 the bed while I order his toilet; but don't
430.06 leave the room: you may be wanted again."
430.07   I retired as directed.
430.08   "Was anybody stirring below when you
430.09 went down, Jane?" inquired Mr. Rochester,
430.10 presently.
430.11   "No, sir; all was very still."
430.12   "We shall get you off cannily, Dick: and

430.13 it will be better, both for your sake, and for
430.14 that of the poor creature in yonder. I have
430.15 striven long to avoid exposure, and I should
430.16 not like it to come at last. Here, Carter,
430.17 help him on with his waistcoat. where did
430.18 you leave your furred cloak? You can't
430.19 travel a mile without that, I know, in this
430.20 damned cold climate. In your room? -- Jane,
430.21 run down to Mr. Mason's room, -- the one
430.22 next mine, -- and fetch a cloak you will see
430.23 there."
430.24 Again I ran, and again returned, bearing an
430.25 immense mantle lined and edged with fur.
430.26 "Now I've another errand for you," said
430.27 my untiring master; "you must away to my
430.28 room again. what a mercy you are shod
431.01 with velvet, Jane! -- a clod-hopping messenger
431.02 would never do at this juncture. You must
431.03 open the middle drawer of my toilet-table and
431.04 take out a little phial and a little glass you
431.05 will find there, -- quick!"
431.06 I flew thither and back, bringing the desired
431.07 vessels.
431.08 "That's well! Now, doctor, I shall take
431.09 the liberty of administering a dose myself; on
431.10 my own responsibility. I got this cordial at
431.11 Rome, of an Italian charlatan -- a fellow you
431.12 would have kicked, Carter. It is not a thing
431.13 to be used indiscriminately, but it is good upon
431.14 occasion: as now, for instance. Jane, a little
431.15 water."
431.16 He held out the tiny glass, and I half filled
431.17 it from the water bottle on the wash-stand.
431.18 "That will do: -- now wet the lip of the
431.19 phial."
431.20 I did so: he measured twelve drops of a
431.21 crimson liquid, and presented it to Mason.
431.22 "Drink, Richard: it will give you the heart
431.23 you lack, for an hour or so."
431.24 "But will it hurt me? -- is it inflammatory?"
431.25 "Drink! drink!"
431.26 Mr. Mason obeyed, because it was evidently
431.27 useless to resist. He was dressed now: he
431.28 still looked pale, but he was no longer gory
432.01 and sullied. Mr. Rochester let him sit three
432.02 minutes after he had swallowed the liquid; he
432.03 then took his arm: --
432.04 "Now I am sure you can get on your feet,"
432.05 he said: -- "try."
432.06 The patient rose.
432.07 "Carter, take him under the other shoulder.
432.08 Be of good cheer, Richard; step out: --
432.09 that's it!"
432.10 "I do feel better," remarked Mr. Mason.
432.11 "I am sure you do. Now, Jane, trip on
432.12 before us away to the backstairs; unbolt the
432.13 side passage door, and tell the driver of the
432.14 post-chaise you will see in the yard -- or just
432.15 outside, for I told him not to drive his rattling
432.16 wheels over the pavement -- to be ready; we are
432.17 coming: and Jane, if any one is about, come
432.18 to the foot of the stairs and hem."
432.19 It was by this time half-past five, and the
432.20 sun was on the point of rising; but I found the
432.21 kitchen still dark and silent. The side-passage
432.22 door was fastened; I opened it with as little
432.23 noise as possible: all the yard was quiet; but
432.24 the gates stood wide open, and there was a
432.25 post-chaise, with horses ready harnessed, and
432.26 driver seated on the box, stationed outside. I
432.27 approached him, and said the gentlemen were
432.28 coming; he nodded: then I looked carefully
433.01 round and listened. The stillness of early
433.02 morning slumbered everywhere; the curtains
433.03 were yet drawn over the servants' chamber
433.04 windows; little birds were just twittering in the
433.05 blossom-blanched orchard trees, whose boughs
433.06 drooped like white garlands over the wall
433.07 enclosing one side of the yard; the carriage
433.08 horses stamped from time to time in their
433.09 closed stables: all else was still.
433.10 The gentlemen now appeared. Mason, sup-
433.11 ported by Mr. Rochester and the surgeon,
433.12 seemed to walk with tolerable ease: they
433.13 assisted him into the chaise; Carter fol-
433.14 lowed.
433.15 "Take care of him," said Mr. Rochester to
433.16 the latter, "and keep him at your house till he
433.17 is quite well: I shall ride over in a day or two
433.18 to see how he gets on. Richard, how is it
433.19 with you?"
433.20 "The fresh air revives me, Fairfax."
433.21 "Leave the window open on his side, Car-
433.22 ter; there is no wind -- good-bye, Dick."
433.23 "Fairfax --"
433.24 "Well, what is it?"
433.25 "Let her be taken care of; let her be treated
433.26 as tenderly as may be: let her -- " he stop-
433.27 ped and burst into tears.
433.28 "I do my best; and have done it, and will
434.01 do it," was the answer: he shut up the chaise
434.02 door, and the vehicle drove away.
434.03 "Yet would to God there was an end of all
434.04 this!" added Mr. Rochester, as he closed and
434.05 barred the heavy yard-gates. This done, he
434.06 moved with slow step and abstracted air,
434.07 towards a door in the wall bordering the
434.08 orchard. I, supposing he had done with me,
434.09 prepared to return to the house; again, how-
434.10 ever, I heard him call "Jane!" He had
434.11 opened the portal and stood at it, waiting

434.12 for me.
434.13 "Come where there is some freshness, for a
434.14 few moments," he said; "that house is a mere
434.15 dungeon; don't you feel it so?"
434.16 "It seems to me a splendid mansion, sir."
434.17 "The glamour of inexperience is over your
434.18 eyes," he answered; "and you see it through
434.19 a charmed medium: you cannot discern that
434.20 the gilding is slime and the silk draperies cob-
434.21 webs; that the marble is sordid slate, and the
434.22 polished woods mere refuse chips and scaly
434.23 bark. Now here /he pointed to the leafy en-
434.24 closure we had entered/ all is real, sweet, and
434.25 pure."
434.26 He strayed down a walk edged with box;
434.27 with apple trees, pear trees, and cherry trees
434.28 on one side, and a border on the other, full of
435.01 all sorts of old-fashioned flowers, stocks, sweet-
435.02 williams, primroses, pansies, mingled with
435.03 southernwood, sweet-briar, and various fra-
435.04 grant herbs. They were fresh now as a suc-
435.05 cession of April showers and gleams, followed
435.06 by a lovely spring morning, could make them:
435.07 the sun was just entering the dappled east,
435.08 and his light illumined the wreathed and
435.09 dewy orchard trees and shone down the quiet
435.10 walks under them.
435.11 "Jane, will you have a flower?"
435.12 He gathered a half-blown rose, the first on
435.13 the bush, and offered it to me.
435.14 "Thank you, sir."
435.15 "Do you like this sunrise, Jane? That
435.16 sky with its high and light clouds which are
435.17 sure to melt away as the day waxes warm --
435.18 this placid and balmy atmosphere?"
435.19 "I do, very much."
435.20 "You have passed a strange night, Jane."
435.21 "Yes, sir."
435.22 "And it has made you look pale -- were you
435.23 afraid when I left you alone with Mason?"
435.24 "I was afraid of some one coming out of the
435.25 inner room."
435.26 "But I had fastened the door -- I had the
435.27 key in my pocket: I should have been a care-
435.28 less shepherd if I had left a lamb -- my pet
436.01 lamb -- so near a wolf's den, unguarded: you
436.02 were safe."
436.03 "Will Grace Poole live here still, sir?"
436.04 "Oh, yes! don't trouble your head about
436.05 her -- put the thing out of your thoughts."
436.06 "Yet it seems to me your life is hardly
436.07 secure while she stays."
436.08 "Never fear -- I will take care of myself."
436.09 "Is the danger you apprehended last night
436.10 gone by now, sir?"
436.11 "I cannot vouch for that till Mason is out
436.12 of England: nor even then. To live, for me,
436.13 Jane, is to stand on a crater-crust which may
436.14 crack and spue fire any day."
436.15 "But Mr. Mason seems a man easily led.
436.16 Your influence, sir, is evidently potent with
436.17 him: he will never set you at defiance, or wil-
436.18 fully injure you."
436.19 "Oh, no! Mason will not defy me; nor
436.20 knowing it, will he hurt me -- but, uninten-
436.21 tionally, he might in a moment, by one care-
436.22 less word, deprive me, if not of life, yet for
436.23 ever of happiness."
436.24 "Tell him to be cautious, sir: let him know
436.25 what you fear, and show him how to avert the
436.26 danger."
436.27 He laughed sardonically, hastily took my
436.28 hand, and as hastily threw it from him.
437.01 "If I could do that, simpleton, where would
437.02 the danger be? Annihilated in a moment.
437.03 Ever since I have known Mason, I have only
437.04 had to say to him 'Do that,' and the thing has
437.05 been done. But I cannot give him orders in
437.06 this case: I cannot say 'Beware of harming
437.07 me, Richard;' for it is imperative that I
437.08 should keep him ignorant that harm to me is
437.09 possible. Now you look puzzled; and I will
437.10 puzzle you farther. You are my little friend,
437.11 are you not?"
437.12 "I like to serve you, sir, and to obey you in
437.13 all that is right."
437.14 "Precisely: I see you do. I see genuine
437.15 contentment in your gait and mien, your eye
437.16 and face, when you are helping me and pleas-
437.17 ing me -- working for me, and with me, in, as
437.18 you characteristically say, 'all that is right:' for
437.19 if I bid you do what you thought wrong, there
437.20 would be no light-footed running, no neat--
437.21 handed alacrity, no lively glance and animated
437.22 complexion. My friend would then turn to
437.23 me, quiet and pale, and would say, 'No, sir;
437.24 that is impossible: I cannot do it, because it is
437.25 wrong;' and would become immutable as a
437.26 fixed star. well, you too have power over
437.27 me, and may injure me: yet I dare not show
437.28 you where I am vulnerable lest, faithful and
438.01 friendly as you are, you should transfix me at
438.02 once."
438.03 "If you have no more to fear from Mr.
438.04 Mason than you have from me, sir, you are
438.05 very safe."
438.06 "God grant it may be so! Here, Jane, is
438.07 an arbour; sit down."
438.08 The arbour was an arch in the wall, lined
438.09 with ivy; it contained a rustic seat. Mr.
438.10 Rochester took it, leaving room, however, for

438.11 me: but I stood before him.
438.12 "Sit," he said; "the bench is long enough
438.13 for two. You don't hesitate to take a place at
438.14 my side, do you? Is that wrong, Jane?"
438.15 I answered him by assuming it: to refuse
438.16 would, I felt, have been unwise.
438.17 "Now, my little friend, while the sun drinks
438.18 the dew -- while all the flowers in this old
438.19 garden awake and expand, and the birds fetch
438.20 their young ones' breakfast out of the Thorn-
438.21 field, and the early bees do their first spell of
438.22 work -- I'll put a case to you; which you must
438.23 endeavour to suppose your own: but first, look
438.24 at me, and tell me you are at ease, and not
438.25 fearing that I err in detaining you, or that you
438.26 err in staying."
438.27 "No, sir; I am content."
438.28 "well then, Jane, call to aid your fancy: --
439.01 suppose you were no longer a girl well reared
439.02 and disciplined, but a wild boy indulged from
439.03 childhood upwards; imagine yourself in a
439.04 remote foreign land; conceive that you there
439.05 commit a capital error, no matter of what
439.06 nature or from what motives, but one whose
439.07 consequences must follow you through life and
439.08 taint all your existence. Mind, I don't say a
439.09 crime; I am not speaking of shedding of blood
439.10 or any other guilty act, which might make the
439.11 perpetrator amenable to the law: my word is
439.12 error. The results of what you have done
439.13 become in time to you utterly insupportable;
439.14 you take measures to obtain relief: unusual
439.15 measures, but neither unlawful nor culpable.
439.16 Still you are miserable; for hope has quitted
439.17 you on the very confines of life: your sun at
439.18 noon darkens in an eclipse, which you feel will
439.19 not leave it till the time of setting. Bitter and
439.20 base associations have become the sole food
439.21 of your memory: you wander here and there,
439.22 seeking rest in exile: happiness in pleasure --
439.23 I mean in heartless, sensual pleasure -- such as
439.24 dulls intellect and blights feeling. Heart-
439.25 weary and soul-withered, you come home after
439.26 years of voluntary banishment; you make
439.27 a new acquaintance -- how or where no matter:
439.28 you find in this stranger much of the good
440.01 and bright qualities which you have sought for
440.02 twenty years, and never before encountered;
440.03 and they are all fresh, healthy, without soil and
440.04 without taint. Such society revives, regene-
440.05 rates: you feel better days come back -- higher
440.06 wishes, purer feelings; you desire to recom-
440.07 mence your life, and to spend what remains
440.08 to you of days in a way more worthy of an
440.09 immortal being. To attain this end, are you
440.10 justified in overleaping an obstacle of custom
440.11 -- a mere conventional impediment, which
440.12 neither your conscience sanctifies nor your
440.13 judgment approves?"
440.14 He paused for an answer: and what was I
440.15 to say? Oh, for some good spirit to suggest
440.16 a judicious and satisfactory response! Vain
440.17 aspiration! The west wind whispered in the
440.18 ivy round me; but no gentle Ariel borrowed
440.19 its breath as a medium of speech: the birds
440.20 sang in the tree-tops; but their song, however
440.21 sweet, was inarticulate.
440.22 Again Mr. Rochester propounded his query:
440.23 "Is the wandering and sinful, but now rest--
440.24 seeking and repentant man, justified in daring
440.25 the world's opinion, in order to attach to him
440.26 for ever, this gentle, gracious, genial stranger;
440.27 thereby securing his own peace of mind and
440.28 regeneration of life?"
441.01 "Sir," I answered, "a Wanderer's repose
441.02 or a Sinner's reformation should never depend
441.03 on a fellow-creature. Men and women die;
441.04 philosophers falter in wisdom, and Christians
441.05 in goodness: if any one you know has suf-
441.06 fered and erred, let him look higher than
441.07 his equals for strength to amend, and solace
441.08 to heal."
441.09 "But the instrument -- the instrument!
441.10 God, who does the work, ordains the instru-
441.11 ment. I have myself -- I tell it you without
441.12 parable -- been a worldly, dissipated, restless
441.13 man; and I believe I have found the in-
441.14 strument for my cure, in --"
441.15 He paused: the birds went on carolling,
441.16 the leaves lightly rustling. I almost wondered
441.17 they did not check their songs and whispers
441.18 to catch the suspended revelation: but they
441.19 would have had to wait many minutes -- so
441.20 long was the silence protracted. At last I
441.21 looked up at the tardy speaker: he was look-
441.22 ing eagerly at me.
441.23 "Little friend," said he, in quite a changed
441.24 tone -- while his face changed too; losing all
441.25 its softness and gravity, and becoming harsh
441.26 and sarcastic, -- "you have noticed my tender
441.27 penchant for Miss Ingram: don't you think
442.01 if I married her she would regenerate me with
442.02 a vengeance!"
442.03 He got up instantly, went quite to the other
442.04 end of the walk, and when he came back he
442.05 was humming a tune.
442.06 "Jane, Jane," said he, stopping before me,
442.07 "you are quite pale with your vigils: don't
442.08 you curse me for disturbing your rest?"
442.09 "Curse you? No, sir."
442.10 "Shake hands in confirmation of the word.

442.11 what cold fingers! They were warmer last
442.12 night when I touched them at the door of the
442.13 mysterious chamber. Jane, when will you
442.14 watch with me again?"
442.15 "Whenever I can be useful, sir."
442.16 "For instance, the night before I am mar-
442.17 ried? I am sure I shall not be able to sleep.
442.18 will you promise to sit up with me to bear me
442.19 company? To you I can talk of my lovely
442.20 one: for now you have seen her and know
442.21 her."
442.22 "Yes, sir."
442.23 "She's a rare one, is she not, Jane?"
442.24 "Yes, sir."
442.25 "A strapper -- a real strapper, Jane: big,
442.26 brown, and buxom; with hair just such as the
442.27 ladies of Carthage must have had. Bless me!
443.01 there's Dent and Lynn in the stables! Go in
443.02 by the shrubbery, through that wicket."
443.03 As I went one way, he went another, and
443.04 I heard him in the yard, saying cheeringly: --
443.05 "Mason got the start of you all this morn-
443.06 ing; he was gone before sunrise: I rose at
443.07 four to see him off."
444.01 [Vol. 2 Chapter 6]
444.02 Presentiments are strange things! and so are
444.03 sympathies; and so are signs: and the three
444.04 combined make one mystery to which human-
444.05 ity has not yet found the key. I never laughed
444.06 at presentiments in my life; because I have had
444.07 strange ones of my own. Sympathies, I believe,
444.08 exist: /for instance, between far-distant, long--
444.09 absent, wholly estranged relatives; asserting,
444.10 notwithstanding their alienation, the unity of
444.11 the source to which each traces his origin/
444.12 whose workings baffle moral comprehension.
444.13 And signs, for aught we know, may be but the
444.14 sympathies of Nature with man.
444.15 when I was a little girl, only six years old,
444.16 I, one night, heard Bessie Leaven say to
444.17 Martha Abbott that she had been dreaming
444.18 about a little child; and that to dream of chil-
444.19 dren was a sure sign of trouble, either to one's
444.20 self or one's kin. The saying might have
445.01 worn out of my memory, had not a circum-
445.02 stance immediately followed which served in-
445.03 delibly to fix it there. The next day Bessie
445.04 was sent for home to the deathbed of her
445.05 little sister.
445.06 Of late I had often recalled this saying and
445.07 this incident; for during the past week scarcely
445.08 a night had gone over my couch that had not
445.09 brought with it a dream of an infant: which I
445.10 sometimes hushed in my arms, sometimes
445.11 dandled on my knee, sometimes watched play-
445.12 ing with daisies on a lawn; or again, dabbling
445.13 its hands in running water. It was a wailing
445.14 child this night, and a laughing one the next:
445.15 now it nestled close to me, and now it ran from
445.16 me; but whatever mood the apparition evinced,
445.17 whatever aspect it wore, it failed not for seven
445.18 successive nights to meet me the moment I
445.19 entered the land of slumber.
445.20 I did not like this iteration of one idea -- this
445.21 strange recurrence of one image; and I grew
445.22 nervous as bed-time approached, and the hour
445.23 of the vision drew near. It was from com-
445.24 panionship with this baby-phantom I had been
445.25 roused on that moonlight night when I heard
445.26 the cry; and it was on the afternoon of the day
445.27 following I was summoned down stairs by a
445.28 message that some one wanted me in Mrs.
446.01 Fairfax's room. On repairing thither, I
446.02 found a man waiting for me, having the ap-
446.03 pearance of a gentleman's servant: he was
446.04 dressed in deep mourning, and the hat he
446.05 held in his hand was surrounded with a crape
446.06 band.
446.07 "I daresay you hardly remember me, Miss,"
446.08 he said, rising as I entered; "but my name is
446.09 Leaven: I lived coachman with Mrs. Reed
446.10 when you were at Gateshead eight or nine
446.11 years since, and I live there still."
446.12 "Oh, Robert! how do you do? I remem-
446.13 ber you very well: you used to give me a ride
446.14 sometimes on Miss Georgiana's bay pony.
446.15 And how is Bessie? You are married to
446.16 Bessie?"
446.17 "Yes, Miss: my wife is very hearty, thank
446.18 you; she brought me another little one about
446.19 two months since -- we have three now -- and
446.20 both mother and child are thriving."
446.21 "And are the family well at the House,
446.22 Robert?"
446.23 "I am sorry I can't give you better news of
446.24 them, Miss: they are very badly at present --
446.25 in great trouble."
446.26 "I hope no one is dead," I said, glancing at
446.27 his black dress. He too looked down at the
446.28 crape round his hat and replied: --
447.01 "Mr. John died yesterday was a week, at
447.02 his chambers in London."
447.03 "Mr. John?"
447.04 "Yes."
447.05 "And how does his mother bear it?"
447.06 "Why you see, Miss Eyre, it is not a com-
447.07 mon mishap: his life has been very wild: these
447.08 last three years he gave himself up to strange
447.09 ways; and his death was shocking."
447.10 "I heard from Bessie he was not doing
447.11 well."

447.12 "Doing well! He could not do worse: he
447.13 ruined his health and his estate amongst the
447.14 worst men and the worst women. He got into
447.15 debt and into jail: his mother helped him out
447.16 twice, but as soon as he was free he returned
447.17 to his old companions and habits. His head
447.18 was too strong: the knaves he lived amongst
447.19 fooled him beyond anything I ever heard.
447.20 He came down to Gateshead about three
447.21 weeks ago and wanted Missis to give up all to
447.22 him. Missis refused: her means have long
447.23 been much reduced by his extravagance; so he
447.24 went back again, and the next news was that
447.25 he was dead. How he died, God knows! -- they
447.26 say he killed himself."
447.27 I was silent: the tidings were frightful.
447.28 Robert Leaven resumed: --
448.01 "Missis had been out of health herself for
448.02 some time: she had got very stout, but was not
448.03 strong with it; and the loss of money and fear
448.04 of poverty were quite breaking her down.
448.05 The information about Mr. John's death and
448.06 the manner of it came too suddenly: it brought
448.07 on a stroke. She was three days without
448.08 speaking; but last Tuesday she seemed rather
448.09 better: she appeared as if she wanted to say
448.10 something, and kept making signs to my wife
448.11 and mumbling. It was only yesterday morn-
448.12 ing, however, that Bessie understood she was
448.13 pronouncing your name; and at last she made
448.14 out the words, `Bring Jane -- fetch Jane Eyre:
448.15 I want to speak to her.' Bessie is not sure
448.16 whether she is in her right mind, or means
448.17 anything by the words; but she told Miss Reed
448.18 and Miss Georgiana, and advised them to send
448.19 for you. The young ladies put it off at first:
448.20 but their mother grew so restless and said,
448.21 `Jane, Jane,' so many times, that at last they
448.22 consented. I left Gateshead yesterday; and if
448.23 you can get ready, Miss, I should like to take
448.24 you back with me early to-morrow morning."
448.25 "Yes, Robert, I shall be ready: it seems to
448.26 me that I ought to go."
448.27 "I think so too, Miss. Bessie said she was
448.28 sure you would not refuse: but I suppose
449.01 you will have to ask leave before you can get
449.02 off?"
449.03 "Yes; and I will do it now;" and having
449.04 directed him to the servants' hall, and recom-
449.05 mended him to the care of John's wife, and
449.06 the attentions of John himself, I went in search
449.07 of Mr. Rochester.
449.08 He was not in any of the lower rooms; he
449.09 was not in the yard, the stables, or the grounds.
449.10 I asked Mrs. Fairfax if she had seen him; --
449.11 yes: she believed he was playing billiards with
449.12 Miss Ingram. To the billiard-room I has-
449.13 tened: the click of balls and the hum of voices
449.14 resounded thence; Mr. Rochester, Miss In-
449.15 gram, the two Misses Eshton, and their
449.16 admirers, were all busied in the game. It
449.17 required some courage to disturb so interesting
449.18 a party; my errand, however, was one I could
449.19 not defer, so I approached the master where
449.20 he stood at Miss Ingram's side. She turned
449.21 as I drew near, and looked at me haughtily:
449.22 her eyes seemed to demand, "What can the
449.23 creeping creature want now?" and when I
449.24 said, in a low voice, "Mr. Rochester," she
449.25 made a movement as if tempted to order me
449.26 away. I remember her appearance at the
449.27 moment, -- it was very graceful and very strik-
449.28 ing: she wore a morning robe of sky-blue
450.01 crape; a gauzy azure scarf was twisted in her
450.02 hair. She had been all animation with the
450.03 game, and irritated pride did not lower the
450.04 expression of her haught lineaments.
450.05 "Does that person want you?" she inquired
450.06 of Mr. Rochester; and Mr. Rochester turned
450.07 to see who the "person" was. He made a
450.08 curious grimace, -- one of his strange and equi-
450.09 vocal demonstrations, -- threw down his cue and
450.10 followed me from the room.
450.11 "Well, Jane?" he said, as he rested his
450.12 back against the school-room door, which he
450.13 had shut.
450.14 "If you please, sir, I want leave of absence
450.15 for a week or two."
450.16 "What to do? -- Where to go?"
450.17 "To see a sick lady who has sent for me."
450.18 "What sick lady? -- Where does she live?"
450.19 "At Gateshead, in --shire."
450.20 "--shire? That is a hundred miles off!
450.21 who may she be that sends for people to see
450.22 her that distance?"
450.23 "Her name is Reed, sir, -- Mrs. Reed."
450.24 "Reed of Gateshead? There was a Reed
450.25 of Gateshead, a magistrate."
450.26 "It is his widow, sir."
450.27 "And what have you to do with her? How
450.28 do you know her?"
451.01 "Mr. Reed was my uncle, -- my mother's
451.02 brother."
451.03 "The deuce he was! You never told me
451.04 that before: you always said you had no rela-
451.05 tions."
451.06 "None that would own me, sir, Mr. Reed
451.07 is dead, and his wife cast me off."
451.08 "Why?"
451.09 "Because I was poor, and burdensome, and
451.10 she disliked me."

451.11 "But Reed left children? -- you must have
451.12 cousins? Sir George Lynn was talking of a
451.13 Reed of Gateshead, yesterday -- who, he said,
451.14 was one of the veriest rascals on town; and
451.15 Ingram was mentioning a Georgiana Reed of
451.16 the same place, who was much admired for her
451.17 beauty, a season or two ago, in London.
451.18 "John Reed is dead, too, sir: he ruined
451.19 himself and half-ruined his family, and is sup-
451.20 posed to have committed suicide. The news so
451.21 shocked his mother that it brought on an apo-
451.22 plectic attack."
451.23 "And what good can you do her? Non-
451.24 sense, Jane! I would never think of running
451.25 a hundred miles to see an old lady who will,
451.26 perhaps, be dead before you reach her: besides,
451.27 you say she cast you off."
452.01 "Yes, sir, but that is long ago; and when
452.02 her circumstances were very different: I could
452.03 not be easy to neglect her wishes now."
452.04 "How long will you stay?"
452.05 "As short a time as possible, sir."
452.06 "Promise me only to stay a week --"
452.07 "I had better not pass my word: I might
452.08 be obliged to break it."
452.09 "At all events you will come back: you will
452.10 not be induced under any pretext to take up a
452.11 permanent residence with her?"
452.12 "Oh, no! I shall certainly return if all be
452.13 well."
452.14 "And who goes with you? You don't
452.15 travel a hundred miles alone?"
452.16 "No, sir, she has sent her coachman."
452.17 "A person to be trusted?"
452.18 "Yes, sir, he has lived ten years in the
452.19 family."
452.20 Mr. Rochester meditated. "When do you
452.21 wish to go?"
452.22 "Early to-morrow morning, sir."
452.23 "Well, you must have some money; you
452.24 can't travel without money, and I dare say you
452.25 have not much: I have given you no salary
452.26 yet. How much have you in the world,
452.27 Jane?" he asked, smiling.
452.28 I drew out my purse; a meagre thing it
453.01 was. "Five shillings, sir." He took the
453.02 purse, poured the hoard into his palm and
453.03 chuckled over it as if its scantiness pleased
453.04 him. Soon he produced his pocket-book:
453.05 "Here," said he, offering me a note: it was
453.06 fifty pounds, and he owed me but fifteen,
453.07 I told him I had no change.
453.08 "I don't want change: you know that.
453.09 Take your wages."
453.10 I declined accepting more than was my due.
453.11 He scowled at first; then, as if recollecting
453.12 something, he said: --
453.13 "Right, right! better not give you all
453.14 now: you would, perhaps, stay away three
453.15 months if you had fifty pounds. There are
453.16 ten: is it not plenty?"
453.17 "Yes, sir, but now you owe me five."
453.18 "Come back for it then: I am your banker
453.19 for forty pounds."
453.20 "Mr. Rochester, I may as well mention
453.21 another matter of business to you while I have
453.22 the opportunity."
453.23 "Matter of business? I'm curious to hear
453.24 it."
453.25 "You have as good as informed me, sir,
453.26 that you are going shortly to be married?"
453.27 "Yes: what then?"
453.28 "In that case, sir, Adele ought to go to
454.01 school: I am sure you will perceive the neces-
454.02 sity of it."
454.03 "To get her out of my bride's way; who
454.04 might otherwise walk over her rather too
454.05 emphatically. There's sense in the sugges-
454.06 tion; not a doubt of it: Adele, as you say,
454.07 must go to school; and you, of course, must
454.08 march straight to -- the devil?"
454.09 "I hope not, sir: but I must seek another
454.10 situation somewhere."
454.11 "In course!" he exclaimed, with a twang
454.12 of voice and a distortion of features equally
454.13 fantastic and ludicrous. He looked at me
454.14 some minutes,
454.15 "And old Madam Reed, or the Misses,
454.16 her daughters, will be solicited by you to seek
454.17 a place, I suppose?"
454.18 "No, sir; I am not on such terms with my
454.19 relatives as would justify me in asking favours
454.20 of them -- but I shall advertise."
454.21 "You shall walk up the pyramids of
454.22 Egypt!" he growled. "At your peril you
454.23 advertise! I wish I had only offered you a
454.24 sovereign instead of ten pounds. Give me
454.25 back nine pounds, Jane; I've a use for it."
454.26 "And so have I sir," I returned, putting
454.27 my hands and my purse behind me. "I
454.28 could not spare the money on any account."
455.01 "Little niggard!" said he, "refusing me a
455.02 pecuniary request! Give me five pounds,
455.03 Jane."
455.04 "Not five shillings, sir; nor five pence."
455.05 "Just let me look at the cash."
455.06 "No, sir; you are not to be trusted."
455.07 "Jane!"
455.08 "Sir?"
455.09 "Promise me one thing."
455.10 "I'll promise you anything, sir, that I think

393

455.11 I am likely to perform."
455.12 "Not to advertise: and to trust this quest
455.13 of a situation to me. I'll find you one in
455.14 time."
455.15 "I shall be glad so to do, sir, if you, in your
455.16 turn, will promise that I and Adele shall be
455.17 both safe out of the house before your bride
455.18 enters it."
455.19 "Very well! very well! I'll pledge my
455.20 word on it. You go to-morrow, then?"
455.21 "Yes, sir; early."
455.22 "Shall you come down to the drawing-room
455.23 after dinner?"
455.24 "No, sir, I must prepare for the journey."
455.25 "Then you and I must bid good-bye for a
455.26 little while?"
455.27 "I suppose so, sir."
455.28 "And how do people perform that cere-
456.01 mony of parting, Jane? Teach me; I'm not
456.02 quite up to it."
456.03 "They say, Farewell; or any other form they
456.04 prefer."
456.05 "Then say it."
456.06 "Farewell, Mr. Rochester, for the present."
456.07 "What must I say?"
456.08 "The same, if you like, sir."
456.09 "Farewell, Miss Eyre, for the present: is
456.10 that all?"
456.11 "Yes."
456.12 "It seems stingy, to my notions, and dry,
456.13 and unfriendly. I should like something else:
456.14 a little addition to the rite. If one shook
456.15 hands, for instance; but no, -- that would not
456.16 content me either. So you'll do no more
456.17 than say Farewell, Jane?"
456.18 "It is enough, sir: as much good-will may
456.19 be conveyed in one hearty word as in many."
456.20 "Very likely; but it is blank and cool --
456.21 'farewell.'"
456.22 "How long is he going to stand with his
456.23 back against the door?" I asked myself; "I
456.24 want to commence my packing." The dinner-
456.25 bell rang, and suddenly away he bolted, with-
456.26 out another syllable: I saw him no more
456.27 during the day, and was off before he had risen
456.28 in the morning.
457.01 I reached the lodge at Gateshead about
457.02 five o'clock in the afternoon of the first of
457.03 May: I stepped in there before going up to
457.04 the hall. It was very clean and neat: the
457.05 ornamental windows were hung with little
457.06 white curtains; the floor was spotless; the
457.07 grate and fire-irons were burnished bright,
457.08 and the fire burnt clear. Bessie sat on the
457.09 hearth, nursing her last-born, and Robert and
457.10 his sister played quietly in a corner.
457.11 "Bless you! -- I knew you would come!"
457.12 exclaimed Mrs. Leaven, as I entered.
457.13 "Yes, Bessie," said I, after I had kissed
457.14 her; "and I trust I am not too late. How is
457.15 Mrs. Reed? -- Alive still, I hope."
457.16 "Yes, she is alive; and more sensible and
457.17 collected than she was. The doctor says she
457.18 may linger a week or two yet; but he hardly
457.19 thinks she will finally recover."
457.20 "Has she mentioned me lately?"
457.21 "She was talking of you only this morning,
457.22 and wishing you would come: but she is
457.23 sleeping now; or was ten minutes ago, when I
457.24 was up at the house. She generally lies in a
457.25 kind of lethargy all the afternoon, and wakes
457.26 up about six or seven. Will you rest yourself
457.27 here an hour, Miss, and then I will go up
457.28 with you?"
458.01 Robert here entered, and Bessie laid her
458.02 sleeping child in the cradle and went to
458.03 welcome him: afterwards she insisted on my
458.04 taking off my bonnet and having some tea; for
458.05 she said I looked pale and tired. I was glad
458.06 to accept her hospitality; and I submitted to
458.07 be relieved of my travelling garb just as pas-
458.08 sively as I used to let her undress me when a
458.09 child.
458.10 Old times crowded fast back on me as I
458.11 watched her bustling about -- setting out the
458.12 tea-tray with her best china, cutting bread
458.13 and butter, toasting a tea-cake, and, between
458.14 whiles, giving little Robert or Jane an occa-
458.15 sional tap or push, just as she used to give
458.16 me in former days. Bessie had retained her
458.17 quick temper as well as her light foot and
458.18 good looks.
458.19 Tea ready, I was going to approach the
458.20 table; but she desired me to sit still, quite in
458.21 her old, peremptory tones. I must be served
458.22 at the fire-side, she said; and she placed before
458.23 me a little round stand with my cup and a
458.24 plate of toast, absolutely as she used to ac-
458.25 commodate me with some privately purloined
458.26 dainty on a nursery chair: and I smiled and
458.27 obeyed her as in bygone days.
458.28 She wanted to know if I was happy at
459.01 Thornfield-Hall, and what sort of a person
459.02 the mistress was; and when I told her there
459.03 was only a master, whether he was a nice
459.04 gentleman, and if I liked him. I told her he
459.05 was rather an ugly man, but quite a gentleman;
459.06 and that he treated me kindly, and I was
459.07 content. Then I went on to describe to her the
459.08 gay company that had lately been staying at the
459.09 house; and to these details Bessie listened with

459.10 interest: they were precisely of the kind she
459.11 relished.
459.12 In such conversation an hour was soon
459.13 gone: Bessie restored to me my bonnet, &c.
459.14 and, accompanied by her, I quitted the lodge
459.15 for the hall. It was also accompanied by her
459.16 that I had, nearly nine years ago, walked down
459.17 the path I was now ascending. On a dark,
459.18 misty, raw morning in January, I had left a hos-
459.19 tile roof with a desperate and embittered heart --
459.20 a sense of outlawry and almost of reprobation --
459.21 to seek the chilly harbourage of Lowood: that
459.22 bourne so far away and unexplored. The
459.23 same hostile roof now again rose before me:
459.24 my prospects were doubtful yet; and I had
459.25 yet an aching heart. I still felt as a wanderer
459.26 on the face of the earth; but I experienced
459.27 firmer trust in myself and my own powers,
459.28 and less withering dread of oppression. The
460.01 gaping wound of my wrongs, too, was now
460.02 quite healed; and the flame of resentment
460.03 extinguished.
460.04 "You shall go into the breakfast-room first,"
460.05 said Bessie, as she preceded me through the
460.06 hall; "the young ladies will be there."
460.07 In another moment I was within that apart-
460.08 ment. There was every article of furniture
460.09 looking just as it did on the morning I was
460.10 first introduced to Mr. Brocklehurst: the very
460.11 rug he had stood upon still covered the hearth.
460.12 Glancing at the book-cases, I thought I could
460.13 distinguish the two volumes of Bewick's British
460.14 Birds occupying their old place on the third
460.15 shelf, and Gulliver's Travels and the Arabian
460.16 Nights ranged just above. The inanimate
460.17 objects were not changed: but the living things
460.18 had altered past recognition.
460.19 Two young ladies appeared before me;
460.20 one very tall, almost as tall as Miss Ingram, --
460.21 very thin too, with a sallow face and severe
460.22 mien. There was something ascetic in her
460.23 look, which was augmented by the extreme
460.24 plainness of a straight-skirted, black, stuff dress,
460.25 a starched linen collar, hair combed away
460.26 from the temples, and the nun-like ornament
460.27 of a string of ebony beads and a crucifix.
460.28 This I felt sure was Eliza, though I could
461.01 trace little resemblance to her former self in
461.02 that elongated and colourless visage.
461.03 The other was as certainly Georgiana: but
461.04 not the Georgiana I remembered -- the slim
461.05 and fairy-like girl of eleven. This was a full--
461.06 blown, very plump damsel, fair as wax-work,
461.07 with handsome and regular features, languish-
461.08 ing blue eyes, and ringleted yellow hair. The
461.09 hue of her dress was black too; but its fashion
461.10 was so different from her sister's -- so much
461.11 more flowing and becoming -- it looked as stylish
461.12 as the other's looked puritanical.
461.13 In each of the sisters there was one trait
461.14 of the mother -- and only one: the thin and
461.15 pallid elder daughter had her parent's Cairn-
461.16 gorm eye: the blooming and luxuriant younger
461.17 girl had her contour of jaw and chin, -- perhaps
461.18 a little softened, but still imparting an inde-
461.19 scribable hardness to the countenance, otherwise
461.20 so voluptuous and buxom.
461.21 Both ladies, as I advanced, rose to welcome
461.22 me, and both addressed me by the name of
461.23 "Miss Eyre." Eliza's greeting was delivered
461.24 in a short, abrupt voice, without a smile; and
461.25 then she sat down again, fixed her eyes on
461.26 the fire, and seemed to forget me. Georgiana
461.27 added to her "How d'ye do?" several common--
461.28 places about my journey, the weather and
462.01 so on, uttered in rather a drawling tone; and
462.02 accompanied by sundry side-glances that mea-
462.03 sured me from head to foot -- now traversing
462.04 the folds of my drab merino pelisse, and now
462.05 lingering on the plain trimming of my cottage
462.06 bonnet. Young ladies have a remarkable
462.07 way of letting you know that they think you a
462.08 "quiz," without actually saying the words. A
462.09 certain superciliousness of look, coolness of
462.10 manner, nonchalance of tone, express fully
462.11 their sentiments on the point, without com-
462.12 mitting them by any positive rudeness in word
462.13 or deed.
462.14 A sneer, however, whether covert or open,
462.15 had now no longer that power over me it once
462.16 possessed: as I sat between my cousins, I was
462.17 surprised to find how easy I felt under the
462.18 total neglect of the one and the semi-sarcastic
462.19 attentions of the other -- Eliza did not mortify,
462.20 nor Georgiana ruffle me. The fact was, I had
462.21 other things to think about; within the last
462.22 few months feelings had been stirred in me so
462.23 much more potent than any they could raise --
462.24 pains and pleasures so much more acute and
462.25 exquisite had been excited, than any it was
462.26 in their power to inflict or bestow -- that their
462.27 airs gave me no concern either for good or
462.28 bad.
463.01 "How is Mrs. Reed?" I asked soon, look-
463.02 ing calmly at Georgiana; who thought fit to
463.03 bridle at the direct address, as if it were an un-
463.04 expected liberty.
463.05 "Mrs. Reed? Ah! mama you mean; she
463.06 is extremely poorly: I doubt if you can see
463.07 her to-night."
463.08 "If," said I, "you would just step up stairs

463.09 and tell her I am come, I should be much obliged to you."
463.10 Georgiana almost started, and she opened
463.11 her blue eyes wild and wide. "I know she
463.12 had a particular wish to see me," I added,
463.13 "and I would not defer attending to her desire
463.14 longer than is absolutely necessary."
463.15 "Mama dislikes being disturbed in an even-
463.16 ing," remarked Eliza. I soon rose, quietly
463.17 took off my bonnet and gloves, uninvited, and
463.18 said I would just step out to Bessie -- who was,
463.19 I dared say, in the kitchen -- and ask her to
463.20 ascertain whether Mrs. Reed was disposed to
463.21 receive me or not to-night. I went, and hav-
463.22 ing found Bessie and despatched her on my
463.23 errand, I proceeded to take further measures.
463.24 It had heretofore been my habit always to
463.25 shrink from arrogance: received as I had
463.26 been to-day, I should, a year ago, have re-
463.27 solved to quit Gateshead the very next morn-
464.01 ing; now, it was disclosed to me all at once,
464.02 that that would be a foolish plan. I had taken
464.03 a journey of a hundred miles to see my aunt,
464.04 and I must stay with her till she was better -- or
464.05 dead: as to her daughters' pride or folly, I
464.06 must put it on one side: make myself indepen-
464.07 dent of it. So I addressed the housekeeper;
464.08 asked her to show me a room, told her I
464.09 should probably be a visitor here for a week
464.10 or two, had my trunk conveyed to my chamber,
464.11 and followed it thither myself: I met Bessie
464.12 on the landing.
464.13 "Missis is awake," said she; "I have told
464.14 her you are here: come and let us see if she
464.15 will know you."
464.16 I did not need to be guided to the well--
464.17 known room: to which I had so often been
464.18 summoned for chastisement or reprimand in
464.19 former days. I hastened before Bessie, I
464.20 softly opened the door: a shaded light stood
464.21 on the table, for it was now getting dark.
464.22 There was the great four-post bed with amber
464.23 hangings as of old: there the toilet-table, the
464.24 arm-chair, and the footstool: at which I had a
464.25 hundred times been sentenced to kneel, to ask
464.26 pardon for offences, by me, uncommitted. I
464.27 looked into a certain corner near, half-expect-
464.28 ing to see the slim outline of a once-dreaded
465.01 switch; which used to lurk there, waiting to
465.02 leap out imp-like and lace my quivering palm
465.03 or shrinking neck. I approached the bed; I
465.04 opened the curtains and leant over the high--
465.05 piled pillows.
465.06 Well did I remember Mrs. Reed's face, and
465.07 I eagerly sought the familiar image. It is a
465.08 happy thing that time quells the longings of
465.09 vengeance, and hushes the promptings of rage
465.10 and aversion: I had left this woman in bitter-
465.11 ness and hate, and I came back to her now
465.12 with no other emotion than a sort of ruth for
465.13 her great sufferings, and a strong yearning to
465.14 forget and forgive all injuries -- to be reconciled,
465.15 and clasp hands in amity.
465.16 The well-known face was there: stern, re-
465.17 lentless as ever -- there was that peculiar eye
465.18 which nothing could melt; and the somewhat
465.19 raised, imperious, despotic eyebrow. How
465.20 often had it lowered on me menace and hate!
465.21 and how the recollection of childhood's terrors
465.22 and sorrows revived as I traced its harsh line
465.23 now! And yet I stooped down and kissed
465.24 her: she looked at me.
465.25 "Is this Jane Eyre?" she said.
465.26 "Yes, aunt Reed. How are you, dear
465.27 aunt?"
465.28 I had once vowed that I would never call
466.01 her aunt again: I thought it no sin to forget
466.02 and break that vow, now. My fingers had
466.03 fastened on her hand which lay outside the
466.04 sheet: had she pressed mine kindly, I should at
466.05 that moment have experienced true pleasure.
466.06 But unimpressionable natures are not so soon
466.07 softened, nor are natural antipathies so readily
466.08 eradicated: Mrs. Reed took her hand away, and
466.09 turning her face rather from me, she remarked
466.10 that the night was warm. Again she regarded
466.11 me, so icily, I felt at once that her opinion of
466.12 me -- her feeling towards me -- was unchanged,
466.13 and unchangeable. I knew by her stony eye --
466.14 opaque to tenderness, indissoluble to tears --
466.15 that she was resolved to consider me bad to
466.16 the last; because to believe me good, would
466.17 give her no generous pleasure: only a sense of
466.18 mortification.
466.19 I felt pain, and then I felt ire; and then I
466.20 felt a determination to subdue her -- to be her
466.21 mistress in spite both of her nature and her
466.22 will. My tears had risen, just as in childhood:
466.23 I ordered them back to their source. I brought
466.24 a chair to the bed-head: I sat down and leaned
466.25 over the pillow.
466.26 "You sent for me," I said, "and I am here;
466.27 and it is my intention to stay till I see how you
466.28 get on."
467.01 "Oh, of course! You have seen my
467.02 daughters?"
467.03 "Yes."
467.04 "Well, you may tell them I wish you to
467.05 stay, till I can talk some things over with you I
467.06 have on my mind: to-night it is too late, and I
467.07 have a difficulty in recalling them. But there was
467.08 something I wished to say -- let me see --"

467.09 The wandering look and changed utterance
467.10 told what wreck had taken place in her once--
467.11 vigorous frame. Turning restlessly, she drew the
467.12 bed-clothes round her; my elbow, resting on a
467.13 corner of the quilt, fixed it down: she was at
467.14 once irritated.
467.15 "Sit up!" said she; "don't annoy me with
467.16 holding the clothes fast -- are you Jane Eyre?"
467.17 "I am Jane Eyre."
467.18 "I have had more trouble with that child
467.19 than any one would believe. Such a burden to
467.20 be left on my hands -- and so much annoyance
467.21 as she caused me, daily and hourly, with her
467.22 incomprehensible disposition, and her sudden
467.23 starts of temper, and her continual, unnatural
467.24 watchings of one's movements! I declare she
467.25 talked to me once like something mad, or like a
467.26 fiend -- no child ever spoke or looked as she
467.27 did; I was glad to get her away from the
467.28 house. What did they do with her at Lowood?"
468.01 The fever broke out there, and many of the
468.02 pupils died. She, however, did not die: but I
468.03 said she did -- I wish she had died!"
468.04 "A strange wish, Mrs. Reed: why do you
468.05 hate her so?"
468.06 "I had a dislike to her mother always; for
468.07 she was my husband's only sister, and a
468.08 great favourite with him: he opposed the
468.09 family's disowning her when she made her
468.10 low marriage; and when news came of her
468.11 death, he wept like a simpleton. He would
468.12 send for the baby; though I entreated him
468.13 rather to put it out to nurse and pay for its
468.14 maintenance. I hated it the first time I set
468.15 my eyes on it -- a sickly, whining, pining thing!
468.16 It would wail in its cradle all night long -- not
468.17 screaming heartily like any other child, but
468.18 whimpering and moaning. Reed pitied it; and
468.19 he used to nurse it and notice it as if it had
468.20 been his own: more, indeed, than he ever
468.21 noticed his own at that age. He would try to
468.22 make my children friendly to the little beg-
468.23 gar: the darlings could not bear it, and he
468.24 was angry with them when they showed their
468.25 dislike. In his last illness, he had it brought
468.26 continually to his bedside; and but an hour
468.27 before he died, he bound me by vow to keep
468.28 the creature. I would as soon have been
469.01 charged with a pauper brat out of a work--
469.02 house: but he was weak, naturally weak.
469.03 John does not at all resemble his father, and I
469.04 am glad of it: John is like me and like my
469.05 brothers -- he is quite a Gibson. Oh, I wish
469.06 he would cease tormenting me with letters for
469.07 money! I have no more money to give him:
469.08 we are getting poor. I must send away half
469.09 the servants and shut up part of the house; or
469.10 let it off. I can never submit to do that -- yet
469.11 how are we to get on? Two-thirds of my
469.12 income goes in paying the interest of mort-
469.13 gages. John gambles dreadfully, and always
469.14 loses -- poor boy! He is beset by sharpers:
469.15 John is sunk and degraded -- his look is
469.16 frightful -- I feel ashamed for him when I see
469.17 him."
469.18 She was getting much excited. "I think I
469.19 had better leave her now," said I to Bessie, who
469.20 stood on the other side of the bed.
469.21 "Perhaps you had, Miss: but she often talks
469.22 in this way towards night -- in the morning she
469.23 is calmer."
469.24 I rose. "Stop!" exclaimed Mrs. Reed,
469.25 "There is another thing I wished to say. He
469.26 threatens me -- he continually threatens me
469.27 with his own death, or mine: and I dream
469.28 sometimes that I see him laid out with a great
470.01 wound in his throat, or with a swollen and
470.02 blackened face. I am come to a strange pass:
470.03 I have heavy troubles. What is to be done?
470.04 How is the money to be had?"
470.05 Bessie now endeavoured to persuade her to
470.06 take a sedative draught: she succeeded with
470.07 difficulty. Soon after, Mrs. Reed grew more
470.08 composed, and sank into a dozing state. I then
470.09 left her.
470.10 More than ten days elapsed before I had
470.11 again any conversation with her. She continued
470.12 either delirious or lethargic; and the doctor
470.13 forbade everything which could painfully excite
470.14 her. Meantime, I got on as well as I could
470.15 with Georgiana and Eliza. They were very
470.16 cold, indeed, at first. Eliza would sit half the
470.17 day sewing, reading, or writing, and scarcely
470.18 utter a word either to me or her sister.
470.19 Georgiana would chatter nonsense to her
470.20 canary bird by the hour, and take no notice of
470.21 me. But I was determined not to seem at a
470.22 loss for occupation or amusement: I had
470.23 brought my drawing materials with me, and
470.24 they served me for both.
470.25 Provided with a case of pencils, and some
470.26 sheets of paper, I used to take a seat apart
470.27 from them, near the window, and busy myself
470.28 in sketching fancy vignettes, representing any
471.01 scene that happened momentarily to shape
471.02 itself in the ever-shifting kaleidoscope of ima-
471.03 gination: a glimpse of sea between two
471.04 rocks; the rising moon, and a ship crossing
471.05 its disk; a group of reeds and water-flags,
471.06 and a naiad's head, crowned with lotus-flowers,
471.07 rising out of them; an elf sitting in a hedge--

471.08 sparrow's nest, under a wreath of hawthorn--
471.09 bloom.
471.10 One morning I fell to sketching a face:
471.11 what sort of a face it was to be, I did not care
471.12 or know. I took a soft black pencil, gave it
471.13 a broad point, and worked away. Soon I
471.14 had traced on the paper a broad and promi-
471.15 nent forehead, and a square lower outline of
471.16 visage: that contour gave me pleasure; my
471.17 fingers proceeded actively to fill it with fea-
471.18 tures. Strongly-marked horizontal eyebrows
471.19 must be traced under that brow; then followed,
471.20 naturally, a well-defined nose, with a straight
471.21 ridge and full nostrils; then a flexible-looking
471.22 mouth, by no means narrow; then a firm chin,
471.23 with a decided cleft down the middle of it: of
471.24 course, some black whiskers were wanted, and
471.25 some jetty hair, tufted on the temples, and
471.26 waved above the forehead. Now for the eyes:
471.27 I had left them to the last, because they
471.28 required the most careful working. I drew
472.01 them large; I shaped them well: the eye-
472.02 lashes I traced long and sombre; the irids
472.03 lustrous and large. "Good! but not quite
472.04 the thing," I thought, as I surveyed the
472.05 effect: "They want more force and spirit;"
472.06 and I wrought the shades blacker, that the
472.07 lights might flash more brilliantly -- a happy
472.08 touch or two secured success. There, I had a
472.09 friend's face under my gaze; and what did it
472.10 signify that those young ladies turned their
472.11 backs on me? I looked at it; I smiled at the
472.12 speaking likeness: I was absorbed and content.
472.13 "Is that a portrait of some one you know?"
472.14 asked Eliza, who had approached me unno-
472.15 ticed. I responded that it was merely a fancy
472.16 head, and hurried it beneath the other sheets.
472.17 Of course, I lied: it was, in fact, a very faith-
472.18 ful representation of Mr. Rochester. But
472.19 what was that to her; or to any one but my-
472.20 self? Georgiana also advanced to look. The
472.21 other drawings pleased her much, but she
472.22 called that "an ugly man." They both
472.23 seemed surprised at my skill. I offered to
472.24 sketch their portraits; and each, in turn, sat
472.25 for a pencil outline. Then Georgiana pro-
472.26 duced her album. I promised to contribute a
472.27 water-colour drawing: this put her at once
472.28 into good humour. She proposed a walk in
473.01 the grounds. Before we had been out two
473.02 hours, we were deep in a confidential conver-
473.03 sation: she had favoured me with a descrip-
473.04 tion of the brilliant winter she had spent in
473.05 London two seasons ago -- of the admiration
473.06 she had there excited -- the attention she had
473.07 received; and I even got hints of the titled
473.08 conquest she had made. In the course of the
473.09 afternoon and evening these hints were en-
473.10 larged on: various soft conversations were
473.11 reported, and sentimental scenes represented;
473.12 and, in short, a volume of a novel of fashion-
473.13 able life was that day improvised by her for
473.14 my benefit. The communications were re-
473.15 newed from day to day: they always ran on
473.16 the same theme -- herself, her loves, and woes.
473.17 It was strange she never once adverted either
473.18 to her mother's illness, or her brother's death,
473.19 or the present gloomy state of the family pros-
473.20 pects. Her mind seemed wholly taken up with
473.21 reminiscences of past gaiety, and aspirations
473.22 after dissipations to come. She passed about
473.23 five minutes each day in her mother's sick--
473.24 room, and no more.
473.25 Eliza still spoke little: she had evidently no
473.26 time to talk. I never saw a busier person
473.27 than she seemed to be; yet it was difficult to
473.28 say what she did: or rather, to discover any
474.01 result of her diligence. She had an alarum
474.02 to call her up early. I know not how she
474.03 occupied herself before breakfast, but after
474.04 that meal she divided her time into regular
474.05 portions; and each hour had its allotted task.
474.06 Three times a day she studied a little book,
474.07 which I found, on inspection, was a Common
474.08 Prayer Book. I asked her once what was the
474.09 great attraction of that volume, and she said
474.10 "the Rubric." Three hours she gave to
474.11 stitching, with gold thread, the border of a
474.12 square crimson cloth, almost large enough for
474.13 a carpet. In answer to my inquiries after the
474.14 use of this article, she informed me it was a
474.15 covering for the altar of a new church lately
474.16 erected near Gateshead. Two hours she devoted
474.17 to her diary; two to working by herself in
474.18 the kitchen-garden; and one to the regulation
474.19 of her accounts. She seemed to want no
474.20 company; no conversation. I believe she was
474.21 happy in her way: this routine sufficed to her;
474.22 and nothing annoyed her so much as the
474.23 occurrence of any incident which forced her to
474.24 vary its clock-working regularity.
474.25 She told me one evening, when more dis-
474.26 posed to be communicative than usual, that
474.27 John's conduct, and the threatened ruin of the
474.28 family, had been a source of profound affliction
475.01 to her: but she had now, she said, settled her
475.02 mind, and formed her resolution. Her own
475.03 fortune she had taken care to secure; and
475.04 when her mother died, -- and it was wholly
475.05 improbable, she tranquilly remarked, that she
475.06 should either recover or linger long, -- she

475.07 would execute a long-cherished project: seek
475.08 a retirement where punctual habits would be
475.09 permanently secured from disturbance, and
475.10 place safe barriers between herself and a
475.11 frivolous world. I asked if Georgiana would
475.12 accompany her.
475.13 "Of course not. Georgiana and she had
475.14 nothing in common: they never had had. She
475.15 would not be burdened with her society for
475.16 any consideration. Georgiana should take her
475.17 own course; and she, Eliza, would take hers."
475.18 Georgiana, when not unburdening her heart
475.19 to me, spent most of her time in lying on the
475.20 sofa, fretting about the dulness of the house,
475.21 and wishing over and over again that her
475.22 aunt Gibson would send her an invitation up
475.23 to town. "It would be so much better," she
475.24 said, "if she could only get out of the way for
475.25 a month or two, till all was over. I did not
475.26 ask what she meant by "all being over," but I
475.27 suppose she referred to the expected decease
475.28 of her mother, and the gloomy sequel of
476.01 funeral rites. Eliza generally took no more
476.02 notice of her sister's indolence and complaints
476.03 than if no such murmuring, lounging object
476.04 had been before her. One day, however, as
476.05 she put away her account-book, and unfolded
476.06 her embroidery, she suddenly took her up
476.07 thus: --
476.08 "Georgiana, a more vain and absurd animal
476.09 than you, was certainly never allowed to cum-
476.10 ber the earth. You had no right to be born;
476.11 for you make no use of life. Instead of living
476.12 for, in, and with yourself, as a reasonable being
476.13 ought, you seek only to fasten your feebleness
476.14 on some other person's strength: if no one
476.15 can be found willing to burden her or him-
476.16 self with such a fat, weak, puffy, useless thing,
476.17 you cry out that you are ill-treated, neglected,
476.18 miserable. Then, too, existence for you must
476.19 be a scene of continual change and excitement,
476.20 or else the world is a dungeon: you must be
476.21 admired, you must be courted, you must be
476.22 flattered -- you must have music, dancing, and
476.23 society -- or you languish, you die away. Have
476.24 you no sense to devise a system which will make
476.25 you independent of all efforts, and all wills, but
476.26 your own? Take one day; share it into sec-
476.27 tions; to each section apportion its task: leave
476.28 no stray unemployed quarters of an hour, ten
477.01 minutes, five minutes, -- include all; do each
477.02 piece of business in its turn with method, with
477.03 rigid regularity. The day will close almost
477.04 before you are aware it has begun; and you
477.05 are indebted to no one for helping you to get
477.06 rid of one vacant moment: you have had
477.07 to seek no one's company, conversation, sym-
477.08 pathy, forbearance: you have lived, in short,
477.09 as an independent being ought to do. Take
477.10 this advice: the first and last I shall offer you;
477.11 then you will not want me or any one else,
477.12 happen what may. Neglect it -- go on as here-
477.13 tofore, craving, whining, and idling -- and suffer
477.14 the results of your idiocy: however bad and
477.15 insufferable they may be. I tell you this
477.16 plainly; and listen: for though I shall no
477.17 more repeat what I am now about to say,
477.18 I shall steadily act on it. After my mother's
477.19 death, I wash my hands of you: from the
477.20 day her coffin is carried to the vault in Gates-
477.21 head church, you and I will be as separate
477.22 as if we had never known each other. You
477.23 need not think that because we chanced to
477.24 be born of the same parents, I shall suffer
477.25 you to fasten me down by even the feeblest
477.26 claim: I can tell you this -- if the whole human
477.27 race, ourselves excepted, were swept away,
477.28 and we two stood alone on the earth, I would
478.01 leave you in the old world, and betake myself
478.02 to the new."
478.03 She closed her lips.
478.04 "You might have spared yourself the trouble
478.05 of delivering that tirade," answered Georgiana.
478.06 "Everybody knows you are the most selfish,
478.07 heartless creature in existence; and I know
478.08 your spiteful hatred towards me: I have had
478.09 a specimen of it before in the trick you played
478.10 me about Lord Edwin Vere: you could not
478.11 bear me to be raised above you, to have a
478.12 title, to be received into circles where you
478.13 dare not show your face, and so you acted
478.14 the spy and informer, and ruined my pros-
478.15 pects for ever." Georgiana took out her
478.16 handkerchief and blew her nose for an hour
478.17 afterwards; Eliza sat cold, impassible, and
478.18 assiduously industrious.
478.19 True, generous feeling is made small ac-
478.20 count of by some: but here were two natures
478.21 rendered, the one intolerably acrid, the other
478.22 despicably savourless for the want of it. Feel-
478.23 ing without judgment is a washy draught
478.24 indeed; but judgment untempered by feeling
478.25 is too bitter and husky a morsel for human
478.26 deglutition.
478.27 It was a wet and windy afternoon: Geor-
478.28 giana had fallen asleep on the sofa over the
479.01 perusal of a novel; Eliza was gone to attend
479.02 a saint's-day service at the new church -- for
479.03 in matters of religion she was a rigid formalist:
479.04 no weather ever prevented the punctual dis-
479.05 charge of what she considered her devotional

479.06 duties; fair or foul, she went to church thrice
479.07 every Sunday, and as often on week-days as
479.08 there were prayers.
479.09   I bethought myself to go up stairs and
479.10 see how the dying woman sped, who lay there
479.11 almost unheeded: the very servants paid her
479.12 but a remittent attention; the hired nurse,
479.13 being little looked after, would slip out of
479.14 the room whenever she could. Bessie was
479.15 faithful; but she had her own family to mind,
479.16 and could only come occasionally to the Hall.
479.17 I found the sick-room unwatched, as I had
479.18 expected: no nurse was there; the patient lay
479.19 still, and seemingly lethargic; her livid face
479.20 sunk in the pillows. The fire was dying in
479.21 the grate. I renewed the fuel, re-arranged
479.22 the bed-clothes, gazed awhile on her who
479.23 could not now gaze on me, and then I moved
479.24 away to the window.
479.25   The rain beat strongly against the panes,
479.26 the wind blew tempestuously: "One lies
479.27 there," I thought, "who will soon be beyond
479.28 the war of earthly elements. Whither will
480.01 that spirit -- now struggling to quit its material
480.02 tenement -- flit when at length released?"
480.03   In pondering the great mystery, I thought
480.04 of Helen Burns: recalled her dying words --
480.05 her faith -- her doctrine of the equality of dis-
480.06 embodied souls. I was still listening in thought
480.07 to her well-remembered tones -- still picturing
480.08 her pale and spiritual aspect, her wasted face
480.09 and sublime gaze, as she lay on her placid
480.10 deathbed, and whispered her longing to be
480.11 restored to her divine Father's bosom - when a
480.12 feeble voice murmured from the couch behind:
480.13   "who is that?"
480.14   I knew Mrs. Reed had not spoken for days:
480.15 was she reviving? I went up to her.
480.16   "It is I, aunt Reed."
480.17   "Who -- I?" was her answer. "who are
480.18 you?" looking at me with surprise and a
480.19 sort of alarm, but still not wildly. "You are
480.20 quite a stranger to me -- where is Bessie?"
480.21   "She is at the lodge, aunt."
480.22   "Aunt!" she repeated. "who calls me
480.23 Aunt? You are not one of the Gibsons; and
480.24 yet I know you -- that face, and the eyes and
480.25 forehead are quite familiar to me: you are
480.26 like -- why, you are like Jane Eyre!"
480.27   I said nothing: I was afraid of occasioning
480.28 some shock by declaring my identity.
481.01   "Yet," said she, "I am afraid it is a mistake:
481.02 my thoughts deceive me. I wished to see
481.03 Jane Eyre, and I fancy a likeness where none
481.04 exists: besides, in eight years she must be so
481.05 changed." I now gently assured her that I
481.06 was the person she supposed and desired me
481.07 to be: and seeing that I was understood, and
481.08 that her senses were quite collected, I explained
481.09 how Bessie had sent her husband to fetch me
481.10 from Thornfield.
481.11   "I am very ill, I know," she said ere long.
481.12 "I was trying to turn myself a few minutes
481.13 since, and find I cannot move a limb. It is as
481.14 well I should ease my mind before I die: what
481.15 we think little of in health, burdens us at such
481.16 an hour as the present is to me. Is the nurse
481.17 here? or is there no one in the room but you?"
481.18   I assured her we were alone.
481.19   "Well, I have twice done you a wrong
481.20 which I regret now. One was in breaking the
481.21 promise which I gave my husband to bring
481.22 you up as my own child; the other --" she
481.23 stopped. "After all, it is of no great import-
481.24 ance perhaps," she murmured to herself: "and
481.25 then I may get better; and to humble myself so
481.26 to her is painful."
481.27   She made an effort to alter her position, but
481.28 failed: her face changed; she seemed to expe-
482.01 rience some inward sensation -- the percursor,
482.02 perhaps, of the last pang.
482.03   "Well: I must get it over. Eternity is
482.04 before me: I had better tell her. -- Go to my
482.05 dressing-case, open it, and take out a letter you
482.06 will see there."
482.07   I obeyed her directions. "Read the letter,"
482.08 she said.
482.09   It was short, and thus conceived: --
482.10 "Madam,
482.11   "Will you have the goodness to send me
482.12 the address of my niece, Jane Eyre, and to
482.13 tell me how she is: it is my intention to
482.14 write shortly and desire her to come to me at
482.15 Madeira. Providence has blessed my endea-
482.16 vours to secure a competency; and as I am
482.17 unmarried and childless, I wish to adopt her
482.18 during my life, and bequeath her at my death
482.19 whatever I may have to leave.
482.20   "I am, Madam, &c. &c.
482.21   "John Eyre, Madeira."
482.22   It was dated three years back.
482.23   "Why did I never hear of this?" I asked.
482.24   "Because I disliked you too fixedly and
482.25 thoroughly ever to lend a hand in lifting you
482.26 to prosperity. I could not forget your con-
483.01 duct to me, Jane -- the fury with which you
483.02 once turned on me; the tone in which you
483.03 declared you abhorred me the worst of any-
483.04 body in the world; the unchildlike look and
483.05 voice with which you affirmed that the very
483.06 thought of me made you sick, and asserted

483.07 that I had treated you with miserable cruelty.
483.08 I could not forget my own sensations when
483.09 you thus started up and poured out the venom
483.10 of your mind: I felt fear, as if an animal that
483.11 I had struck or pushed had looked up at me
483.12 with human eyes and cursed me in a man's
483.13 voice. -- Bring me some water! Oh, make
483.14 haste!"
483.15   "Dear Mrs. Reed," said I, as I offered her
483.16 the draught she required, "think no more of
483.17 all this, let it pass away from your mind.
483.18 Forgive me for my passionate language: I was
483.19 a child then; eight, nine years have passed
483.20 since that day."
483.21   She heeded nothing of what I said; but
483.22 when she had tasted the water and drawn
483.23 breath, she went on thus: --
483.24   "I tell you I could not forget it; and I took
483.25 my revenge: for you to be adopted by your
483.26 uncle, and placed in a state of ease and comfort
483.27 was what I could not endure. I wrote to him;
483.28 I said I was sorry for his disappointment, but
484.01 Jane Eyre was dead: she had died of typhus
484.02 fever at Lowood. Now act as you please:
484.03 write and contradict my assertion -- expose my
484.04 falsehood as soon as you like. You were born,
484.05 I think, to be my torment: my last hour is
484.06 racked by the recollection of a deed, which,
484.07 but for you, I should never have been tempted
484.08 to commit."
484.09   "If you could but be persuaded to think no
484.10 more of it, aunt, and to regard me with kind-
484.11 ness and forgiveness --"
484.12   "You have a very bad disposition," said she,
484.13 "and one to this day I feel it impossible to
484.14 understand: how for nine years you could be
484.15 patient and quiescent under any treatment, and
484.16 in the tenth break out all fire and violence, I
484.17 can never comprehend."
484.18   "My disposition is not so bad as you think:
484.19 I am passionate, but not vindictive. Many a
484.20 time, as a little child, I should have been glad
484.21 to love you if you would have let me; and I
484.22 long earnestly to be reconciled to you now:
484.23 kiss me, aunt."
484.24   I approached my cheek to her lips: she
484.25 would not touch it. She said I oppressed her
484.26 by leaning over the bed; and again demanded
484.27 water. As I laid her down -- for I raised her
484.28 and supported her on my arm while she drank --
485.01 I covered her ice-cold and clammy hand with
485.02 mine: the feeble fingers shrank from my touch
485.03 -- the glazing eyes shunned my gaze.
485.04   "Love me, then, or hate me, as you will,"
485.05 I said at last, "you have my full and free
485.06 forgiveness: ask now for God's; and be at
485.07 peace."
485.08   Poor, suffering woman! it was too late for her
485.09 to make now the effort to change her habitual
485.10 frame of mind: living, she had ever hated me
485.11 -- dying, she must hate me still.
485.12   The nurse now entered, and Bessie followed.
485.13 I yet lingered half an hour longer, hoping to
485.14 see some sign of amity: but she gave none.
485.15 She was fast relapsing into stupor; nor did
485.16 her mind again rally: at twelve o'clock that
485.17 night she died. I was not present to close her
485.18 eyes; nor were either of her daughters. They
485.19 came to tell us the next morning that all was
485.20 over. She was by that time laid out. Eliza
485.21 and I went to look at her: Georgiana, who
485.22 had burst out into loud weeping, said she
485.23 dared not go. There was stretched Sarah
485.24 Reed's once robust and active frame, rigid
485.25 and still: her eye of flint was covered with its
485.26 cold lid; her brow and strong traits wore yet
485.27 the impress of her inexorable soul. A strange
485.28 and solemn object was that corpse to me. I
486.01 gazed on it with gloom and pain: nothing soft,
486.02 nothing sweet, nothing pitying, or hopeful, or
486.03 subduing, did it inspire; only a grating anguish
486.04 for her woes -- not my loss -- and a sombre tear-
486.05 less dismay at the fearfulness of death in such a
486.06 form.
486.07   Eliza surveyed her parent calmly. After a
486.08 silence of some minutes she observed: --
486.09   "With her constitution she should have lived
486.10 to a good old age: her life was shortened by
486.11 trouble." And then a spasm constricted her
486.12 mouth for an instant: as it passed away she
486.13 turned and left the room, and so did I. Neither
486.14 of us had dropt a tear.
487.01 [Vol. 2 Chapter 7]
487.02   Mr. Rochester had given me but one week's
487.03 leave of absence: yet a month elapsed be-
487.04 fore I quitted Gateshead. I wished to leave
487.05 immediately after the funeral; but Georgiana
487.06 entreated me to stay till she could get off to
487.07 London: whither she was now at last invited
487.08 by her uncle, Mr. Gibson; who had come
487.09 down to direct his sister's interment, and settle
487.10 the family affairs. Georgiana said she dreaded
487.11 being left alone with Eliza; from her she got
487.12 neither sympathy in her dejection, support in
487.13 her fears, nor aid in her preparations; so I
487.14 bore with her feeble-minded wailings, and sel-
487.15 fish lamentations, as well as I could, and did my
487.16 best in sewing for her and packing her dresses.
487.17 It is true, that while I worked, she would
487.18 idle; and I thought to myself, "If you and I
487.19 were destined to live always together, cousin,

487.20 we would commence matters on a different
488.01 footing. I should not settle tamely down into
488.02 being the forbearing party; I should assign you
488.03 your share of labour, and compel you to accom-
488.04 plish it, or else it should be left undone: I
488.05 should insist, also, on your keeping some of those
488.06 drawling, half-insincere complaints hushed in
488.07 your own breast. It is only because our con-
488.08 nection happens to be very transitory, and
488.09 comes at a peculiarly mournful season, that I
488.10 consent thus to render it so patient and compliant
488.11 on my part."
488.12 At last I saw Georgiana off; but now it
488.13 was Eliza's turn to request me to stay another
488.14 week. Her plans required all her time and
488.15 attention, she said: she was about to de-
488.16 part for some unknown bourne; and all day
488.17 long she stayed in her own room, her door
488.18 bolted within, filling trunks, emptying drawers,
488.19 burning papers, and holding no communication
488.20 with any one. She wished me to look after the
488.21 house, to see callers, and answer notes of con-
488.22 dolence.
488.23 One morning, she told me I was at liberty.
488.24 "And,," she added, "I am obliged to you for
488.25 your valuable services and discreet conduct.
488.26 There is some difference between living with
488.27 such a one as you, and with Georgiana: you
488.28 perform your own part in life, and burden no
489.01 one. To-morrow," she continued, "I set out
489.02 for the continent. I shall take up my abode
489.03 in a religious house, near Lisle — a nunnery
489.04 you would call it: there I shall be quiet and
489.05 unmolested. I shall devote myself for a time
489.06 to the examination of the Roman Catholic
489.07 dogmas, and to a careful study of the work-
489.08 ings of their system: if I find it to be, as I
489.09 half suspect it is, the one best calculated to
489.10 ensure the doing of all things decently and in
489.11 order, I shall embrace the tenets of Rome and
489.12 probably take the veil."
489.13 I neither expressed surprise at this reso-
489.14 lution nor attempted to dissuade her from it.
489.15 "The vocation will fit you to a hair," I thought:
489.16 "much good may it do you!"
489.17 When we parted, she said: "Good-bye,
489.18 cousin Jane Eyre; I wish you well: you have
489.19 some sense."
489.20 I then returned: "You are not without
489.21 sense, cousin Eliza; but what you have, I sup-
489.22 pose in another year will be walled up alive in
489.23 a French convent. However, it is not my busi-
489.24 ness, and so it suits you -- I don't much care."
489.25 "You are in the right," said she: and with
489.26 these words we each went our separate way.
489.27 As I shall not have occasion to refer either to
489.28 her or her sister again, I may as well mention
490.01 here, that Georgiana made an advantageous
490.02 match with a wealthy worn-out man of fashion;
490.03 and that Eliza actually took the veil, and is at
490.04 this day superior of the convent where she
490.05 passed the period of her novitiate: and which
490.06 she endowed with her fortune.
490.07 How people feel when they are returning
490.08 home from an absence, long or short, I did not
490.09 know: I had never experienced the sensation.
490.10 I had known what it was to come back to
490.11 Gateshead when a child, after a long walk --
490.12 to be scolded for looking cold or gloomy; and
490.13 later, what it was to come back from church
490.14 to Lowood -- to long for a plenteous meal and a
490.15 good fire, and to be unable to get either.
490.16 Neither of these returnings were very pleasant
490.17 or desirable: no magnet drew me to a given
490.18 point, increasing in its strength of attraction
490.19 the nearer I came. The return to Thornfield
490.20 was yet to be tried.
490.21 My journey seemed tedious -- very tedious:
490.22 fifty miles one day, a night spent at an inn;
490.23 fifty miles the next day. During the first
490.24 twelve hours I thought of Mrs. Reed in her
490.25 last moments: I saw her disfigured and dis-
490.26 coloured face, and heard her strangely altered
490.27 voice. I mused on the funeral day, the coffin,
490.28 the hearse, the black train of tenants and ser-
491.01 vants -- few was the number of relatives -- the
491.02 gaping vault, the silent church, the solemn ser-
491.03 vice. Then I thought of Eliza and Georgiana:
491.04 I beheld one the cynosure of a ball-room, the
491.05 other the inmate of a convent cell; and I dwelt
491.06 on and analyzed their separate peculiarities of
491.07 person and character. The evening arrival at
491.08 the great town of ---- scattered these thoughts;
491.09 night gave them quite another turn: laid down
491.10 on my traveller's bed, I left reminiscence for
491.11 anticipation.
491.12 I was going back to Thornfield: but how
491.13 long was I to stay there? Not long; of that I
491.14 was sure. I had heard from Mrs. Fairfax in
491.15 the interim of my absence: the party at the
491.16 hall was dispersed; Mr. Rochester had left for
491.17 London three weeks ago, but he was then ex-
491.18 pected to return in a fortnight. Mrs. Fairfax
491.19 surmised that he was gone to make arrange-
491.20 ments for his wedding, as he had talked of
491.21 purchasing a new carriage: she said the idea
491.22 of his marrying Miss Ingram still seemed
491.23 strange to her; but from what everybody said,
491.24 and from what she had herself seen, she could
491.25 no longer doubt that the event would shortly
491.26 take place. "You would be strangely in-

491.27 credulous if you did doubt it," was my mental
491.28 comment. "I don't doubt it."
492.01 The question followed, "Where was I to
492.02 go?" I dreamt of Miss Ingram all the night:
492.03 in a vivid morning dream I saw her closing
492.04 the gates of Thornfield against me and point-
492.05 ing me out another road; and Mr. Rochester
492.06 looked on with his arms folded -- smiling sar-
492.07 donically, as it seemed, at both her and me.
492.08 I had not notified to Mrs. Fairfax the exact
492.09 day of my return; for I did not wish either car
492.10 or carriage to meet me at Millcote. I proposed
492.11 to walk the distance quietly by myself; and
492.12 very quietly, after leaving my box in the
492.13 ostler's care, did I slip away from the George
492.14 Inn, about six o'clock of a June evening, and
492.15 take the old road to Thornfield: a road which
492.16 lay chiefly through fields, and was now little
492.17 frequented.
492.18 It was not a bright or splendid summer
492.19 evening, though fair and soft: the hay-makers
492.20 were at work all along the road; and the sky,
492.21 though far from cloudless, was such as pro-
492.22 mised well for the future: its blue -- where
492.23 blue was visible -- was mild and settled, and
492.24 its cloud strata high and thin. The west,
492.25 too, was warm: no watery gleam chilled it -- it
492.26 seemed as if there was a fire lit, an altar burn-
492.27 ing behind its screen of marbled vapour, and
492.28 out of apertures shone a golden redness.
493.01 I felt glad as the road shortened before me:
493.02 so glad that I stopped once to ask myself
493.03 what that joy meant: and to remind reason
493.04 that it was not to my home I was going, or to
493.05 a permanent resting-place, or to a place where
493.06 fond friends looked out for me and waited my
493.07 arrival. "Mrs. Fairfax will smile you a calm
493.08 welcome, to be sure," said I; "and little
493.09 Adele will clap her hands and jump to see
493.10 you: but you know very well you are think-
493.11 ing of another than they; and that he is not
493.12 thinking of you."
493.13 But what is so headstrong as youth? What
493.14 so blind as inexperience? These affirmed that
493.15 it was pleasure enough to have the privilege
493.16 of again looking on Mr. Rochester, whether
493.17 he looked on me or not; and they added --
493.18 "Hasten! hasten! be with him while you
493.19 may: but a few more days or weeks, at most,
493.20 and you are parted with him for ever!" And
493.21 then I strangled a new-born agony -- a de-
493.22 formed thing which I could not persuade my-
493.23 self to own and rear -- and ran on.
493.24 They are making hay, too, in Thornfield
493.25 meadows: or rather, the labourers are just
493.26 quitting their work, and returning home with
493.27 their rakes on their shoulders: now, at the
493.28 hour I arrive. I have but a field or two to
494.01 traverse, and then I shall cross the road and
494.02 reach the gates. How full the hedges are of
494.03 roses! But I have no time to gather any; I
494.04 want to be at the house. I passed a tall briar,
494.05 shooting leafy and flowery branches across the
494.06 path; I see the narrow stile with stone steps;
494.07 and I see -- Mr. Rochester sitting there, a book
494.08 and a pencil in his hand: he is writing.
494.09 Well, he is not a ghost; yet every nerve I
494.10 have is unstrung: for a moment I am beyond
494.11 my own mastery. What does it mean? I
494.12 did not think I should tremble in this way
494.13 when I saw him -- or lose my voice or the
494.14 power of motion in his presence. I will go
494.15 back as soon as I can stir: I need not make
494.16 an absolute fool of myself. I know another
494.17 way to the house. It does not signify if I
494.18 knew twenty ways; for he has seen me.
494.19 "Hillo!" he cries; and he puts up his
494.20 book and his pencil. "There you are! Come
494.21 on, if you please."
494.22 I suppose I do come on; though in what
494.23 fashion I know not: being scarcely cognizant
494.24 of my movements, and solicitous only to appear
494.25 calm; and, above all, to control the working
494.26 muscles of my face -- which I feel rebel inso-
494.27 lently against my will, and struggle to express
494.28 what I had resolved to conceal. But I have a
495.01 veil -- it is down: I may make shift yet to
495.02 behave with decent composure.
495.03 "And this is Jane Eyre? Are you coming
495.04 from Millcote, and on foot? Yes -- just one of
495.05 your tricks: not to send for a carriage, and
495.06 come clattering over street and road like a
495.07 common mortal, but to steal into the vicinage
495.08 of your home along with twilight, just as if
495.09 you were a dream or a shade. What the
495.10 deuce have you done with yourself this last
495.11 month?"
495.12 "I have been with my aunt, sir, who is
495.13 dead."
495.14 "A true Janian reply! Good angels be my
495.15 guard! She comes from the other world --
495.16 from the abode of people who are dead; and
495.17 tells me so when she meets me alone here in
495.18 the gloaming! If I dared, I'd touch you, to see
495.19 if you are substance or shadow, you elf! -- but
495.20 I'd as soon offer to take hold of a blue ignis
495.21 fatuus light in a marsh. Truant! truant!" he
495.22 added, when he had paused an instant. "Absent
495.23 from me a whole month: and forgetting me
495.24 quite, I'll be sworn!"
495.25 I knew there would be pleasure in meeting

495.26 my master again; even though broken by the
495.27 fear that he was so soon to cease to be my
495.28 master, and by the knowledge that I was
496.01 nothing to him: but there was ever in Mr.
496.02 Rochester /so at least I thought/ such a wealth
496.03 of the power of communicating happiness, that
496.04 to taste but of the crumps he scattered to
496.05 stray and stranger birds like me, was to feast
496.06 genially. His last words were balm: they
496.07 seemed to imply that it imported something to
496.08 him whether I forgot him or not. And he had
496.09 spoken of Thornfield as my home -- would that
496.10 it were my home!
496.11 He did not leave the stile, and I hardly
496.12 liked to ask to go by. I inquired soon if he
496.13 had not been to London.
496.14 "Yes: I suppose you found that out by
496.15 second-sight."
496.16 "Mrs. Fairfax told me in a letter."
496.17 "And did she inform you what I went to
496.18 do?"
496.19 "Oh, yes, sir! Everybody knew your
496.20 errand."
496.21 "You must see the carriage, Jane, and tell
496.22 me if you don't think it will suit Mrs. Roches-
496.23 ter exactly; and whether she won't look like
496.24 Queen Boadicea, leaning back against those
496.25 purple cushions. I wish, Jane, I were a trifle
496.26 better adapted to match with her externally.
496.27 Tell me now, fairy as you are, -- can't you give
497.01 me a charm, or a philter, or something of that
497.02 sort, to make me a handsome man?"
497.03 "It would be past the power of magic, sir;"
497.04 and, in thought, I added, "A loving eye is all
497.05 the charm needed: to such you are handsome
497.06 enough; or rather, your sternness has a power
497.07 beyond beauty."
497.08 Mr. Rochester had sometimes read my un-
497.09 spoken thoughts with an acumen to me incom-
497.10 prehensible: in the present instance he took no
497.11 notice of my abrupt vocal response; but he
497.12 smiled at me with a certain smile he had of his
497.13 own, and which he used but on rare occasions.
497.14 He seemed to think it too good for common
497.15 purposes: it was the real sunshine of feeling --
497.16 he shed it over me now.
497.17 "Pass, Janet," said he, making room for
497.18 me to cross the stile: "go up home, and stay
497.19 your weary little wandering feet at a friend's
497.20 threshold."
497.21 All I had now to do was to obey him in
497.22 silence: no need for me to colloquize further.
497.23 I got over the stile without a word, and meant
497.24 to leave him calmly. An impulse held me
497.25 fast, -- a force turned me round. I said -- or
497.26 something in me said for me, and in spite of
497.27 me: --
497.28 "Thank you, Mr. Rochester, for your great
498.01 kindness. I am strangely glad to get back
498.02 again to you; and wherever you are is my
498.03 home, -- my only home."
498.04 I walked on so fast that even he could
498.05 hardly have overtaken me had he tried.
498.06 Little Adele was half wild with delight when
498.07 she saw me. Mrs. Fairfax received me with
498.08 her usual plain friendliness. Leah smiled; and
498.09 even Sophie did me "bon soir" with glee.
498.10 This was very pleasant: there is no happiness
498.11 like that of being loved by your fellow-crea-
498.12 tures, and feeling that your presence is an
498.13 addition to their comfort.
498.14 I, that evening, shut my eyes resolutely
498.15 against the future: I stopped my ears against
498.16 the voice that kept warning me of near sepa-
498.17 ration and coming grief. When tea was over,
498.18 and Mrs. Fairfax had taken her knitting, and
498.19 I had assumed a low seat near her, and Adele,
498.20 kneeling on the carpet, had nestled close up to
498.21 me, and a sense of mutual affection seemed to
498.22 surround us with a ring of golden peace, I
498.23 uttered a silent prayer that we might not be
498.24 parted far or soon; but when, as we thus sat,
498.25 Mr. Rochester entered, unannounced, and look-
498.26 ing at us, seemed to take pleasure in the
498.27 spectacle of a group so amicable -- when he
498.28 said he supposed the old lady was all right now
499.01 that she had got her adopted daughter back
499.02 again, and added that he saw Adele was
499.03 "prete a croquer sa petite maman Anglaise" --
499.04 I half ventured to hope that he would, even
499.05 after his marriage, keep us together somewhere
499.06 under the shelter of his protection, and not
499.07 quite exiled from the sunshine of his presence.
499.08 A fortnight of dubious calm succeeded my
499.09 return to Thornfield-Hall. Nothing was said
499.10 of the master's marriage, and I saw no pre-
499.11 paration going on for such an event. Almost
499.12 every day I asked Mrs. Fairfax if she had yet
499.13 heard anything decided: her answer was
499.14 always in the negative. Once, she said, she had
499.15 actually put the question to Mr. Rochester as
499.16 to when he was going to bring his bride home;
499.17 but he had answered her only by a joke, and
499.18 one of his queer looks, and she could not tell
499.19 what to make of him.
499.20 One thing specially surprised me, and that
499.21 was, there was no journeyings backward and
499.22 forward, no visits to Ingram Park: to be sure
499.23 it was twenty miles off, on the borders of an-
499.24 other county; but what was that distance to
499.25 an ardent lover? To so practised and inde-

499.26 fatigable a horseman as Mr. Rochester, it
499.27 would be but a morning's ride. I began to
499.28 cherish hopes I had no right to conceive: that
500.01 the match was broken off; that rumour had
500.02 been mistaken; that one or both parties had
500.03 changed their minds. I used to look at my
500.04 master's face to see if it were sad or fierce; but
500.05 I could not remember the time when it had
500.06 been so uniformly clear of clouds or evil feel-
500.07 ings. If, in the moments I and my pupil
500.08 spent with him, I lacked spirits and sank into
500.09 inevitable dejection, he became even gay.
500.10 Never had he called me more frequently to his
500.11 presence; never been kinder to me when there
500.12 -- and, alas! never had I loved him so well.
501.01 [Vol. 2 Chapter 6]
501.02 A splendid Midsummer shone over England:
501.03 skies so pure, suns so radiant as were then seen
501.04 in long succession, seldom favour, even singly,
501.05 our wave-girt land. It was as if a band of
501.06 Italian days had come from the South, like a
501.07 flock of glorious passenger birds, and lighted
501.08 to rest them on the cliffs of Albion. The hay
501.09 was all got in; the fields round Thornfield
501.10 were green and shorn; the roads white and
501.11 baked; the trees were in their dark prime:
501.12 hedge and wood, full-leaved and deeply tinted,
501.13 contrasted well with the sunny hue of the
501.14 clear meadows between.
501.15 On Midsummer-eve, Adele, weary with
501.16 gathering wild strawberries in Hay-Lane half
501.17 the day, had gone to bed with the sun. I
501.18 watched her drop asleep, and when I left her I
501.19 sought the garden.
501.20 It was now the sweetest hour of the twenty--
502.01 four: -- "Day its fervid fires had wasted," and
502.02 dew fell cool on panting plain and scorched sum-
502.03 mit. Where the sun had gone down in simple
502.04 state -- pure of the pomp of clouds -- spread
502.05 a solemn purple, burning with the light of red
502.06 jewel and furnace flame at one point, on one
502.07 hill-peak, and extending high and wide, soft
502.08 and still softer, over half heaven. The east
502.09 had its own charm of fine, deep blue, and its
502.10 own modest gem, a rising and solitary star:
502.11 soon it would boast the moon; but she was
502.12 yet beneath the horizon.
502.13 I walked awhile on the pavement; but a
502.14 subtle, well-known scent -- that of a cigar -- stole
502.15 from some window; I saw the library case-
502.16 ment open a handbreadth; I knew I might
502.17 be watched thence; so I went apart into the
502.18 orchard. No nook in the grounds more shel-
502.19 tered and more Eden-like; it was full of trees,
502.20 it bloomed with flowers: a very high wall
502.21 shut it out from the court, on one side; on the
502.22 other, a beech avenue screened it from the
502.23 lawn. At the bottom was a sunk fence; its sole
502.24 separation from lonely fields: a winding walk,
502.25 bordered with laurels and terminating in a
502.26 giant horse-chestnut, circled at the base by a
502.27 seat, led down to the fence. Here one could
502.28 wander unseen. While such honey-dew fell,
503.01 such silence reigned, such gloaming gathered,
503.02 I felt as if I could haunt such shade for ever:
503.03 but in threading the flower and fruit-parterres
503.04 at the upper part of the enclosure, enticed
503.05 there by the light the now-rising moon casts on
503.06 this more open quarter, my step is stayed --
503.07 not by sound, not by sight, but once more by a
503.08 warning fragrance.
503.09 Sweet-briar and southernwood, jasmine, pink,
503.10 and rose have long been yielding their even-
503.11 ing sacrifice of incense: this new scent is
503.12 neither of shrub nor flower; it is -- I know it
503.13 well -- it is Mr. Rochester's cigar. I look
503.14 round and I listen. I see trees laden with
503.15 ripening fruit. I hear a nightingale warbling
503.16 in a wood half a mile off; no moving form is
503.17 visible, no coming step audible; but that per-
503.18 fume increases: I must flee. I make for the
503.19 wicket leading to the shrubbery, and I see
503.20 Mr. Rochester entering. I step aside into the
503.21 ivy recess; he will not stay long: he will soon
503.22 return whence he came, and if I sit still he will
503.23 never see me.
503.24 But no -- eventide is as pleasant to him as
503.25 to me, and this antique garden as attractive;
503.26 and he strolls on, now lifting the gooseberry-
503.27 tree branches to look at the fruit, large as
503.28 plums, with which they are laden; now taking
504.01 a ripe cherry from the wall; now stooping
504.02 towards a knot of flowers, either to inhale
504.03 their fragrance or to admire the dew-beads
504.04 on their petals. A great moth goes humming
504.05 by me; it alights on a plant at Mr. Roches-
504.06 ter's foot: he sees it, and bends to examine it.
504.07 "Now, he has his back towards me," thought
504.08 I, "and he is occupied too; perhaps, if I walk
504.09 softly, I can slip away unnoticed."
504.10 I trod on an edging of turf that the crackle
504.11 of the pebbly gravel might not betray me:
504.12 he was standing among the beds at a yard
504.13 or two distant from where I had to pass; the
504.14 moth apparently engaged him. "I shall get by
504.15 very well," I meditated. As I crossed his sha-
504.16 dow, thrown long over the garden by the moon,
504.17 not yet risen high, he said quietly without
504.18 turning: --
504.19 "Jane, come and look at this fellow."
504.20 I had made no noise: he had not eyes

504.21 behind -- could his shadow feel? I started at
504.22 first, and then I approached him.
504.23 "Look at his wings," said he," he reminds
504.24 me rather of a West Indian insect; one does
504.25 not often see so large and gay a night-rover in
504.26 England: there! he is flown."
504.27 The moth roamed away; I was sheepishly
504.28 retreating also: but Mr. Rochester followed
505.01 me, and when we reached the wicket, he
505.02 said: --
505.03 "Turn back: on so lovely a night it is
505.04 a shame to sit in the house; and surely no
505.05 one can wish to go to bed while sunset is thus
505.06 at meeting with moonrise."
505.07 It is one of my faults, that though my tongue
505.08 is sometimes prompt enough at an answer,
505.09 there are times when it sadly fails me in fram-
505.10 ing an excuse; and always the lapse occurs
505.11 at some crisis, when a facile word or plausible
505.12 pretext is specially wanted to get me out
505.13 of painful embarrassment. I did not like to
505.14 walk at this hour alone with Mr. Rochester in
505.15 the shadowy orchard; but I could not find a
505.16 reason to allege for leaving him. I followed
505.17 with lagging step, and thoughts busily bent
505.18 on discovering a means of extrication; but he
505.19 himself looked so composed and so grave also,
505.20 I became ashamed of feeling any confusion:
505.21 the evil -- if evil existent or prospective there
505.22 was -- seemed to lie with me only; his mind
505.23 was unconscious and quiet.
505.24 "Jane," he recommenced, as we entered the
505.25 laurel-walk, and slowly strayed down in the
505.26 direction of the sunk fence and the horse--
505.27 chestnut, "Thornfield is a pleasant place in
505.28 summer, is it not?"
506.01 "Yes, sir."
506.02 "You must have become in some degree
506.03 attached to the house, -- you, who have an eye
506.04 for natural beauties, and a good deal of the
506.05 organ of Adhesiveness?"
506.06 "I am attached to it, indeed."
506.07 "And though I don't comprehend now it
506.08 is, I perceive you have acquired a degree of
506.09 regard for that foolish little child Adele, too;
506.10 and even for simple dame Fairfax?"
506.11 "Yes, sir; in different ways, I have an af-
506.12 fection for both."
506.13 "And would be sorry to part with them?"
506.14 "Yes."
506.15 "Pity!" he said, and sighed and paused.
506.16 "It is always the way of events in this life,"
506.17 he continued presently: "no sooner have you
506.18 got settled in a pleasant resting-place, than
506.19 a voice calls out to you to rise and move on,
506.20 for the hour of repose is expired."
506.21 "Must I move on, sir?" I asked. "Must
506.22 I leave Thornfield?"
506.23 "I believe you must, Jane. I am sorry,
506.24 Janet, but I believe indeed you must."
506.25 This was a blow: but I did not let it pros-
506.26 trate me.
506.27 "Well, sir, I shall be ready when the order
506.28 to march comes."
507.01 "It is come now -- I must give it to-night."
507.02 "Then you are going to be married, sir?"
507.03 "Ex-act-ly -- pre-cise-ly: with your usual
507.04 acuteness, you have hit the nail straight on the
507.05 head."
507.06 "Soon, sir?"
507.07 "Very soon, my -- -- that is, Miss Eyre:
507.08 and you'll remember, Jane, the first time I, or
507.09 Rumour, plainly intimated to you that it was
507.10 my intention to put my old bachelor's neck
507.11 into the sacred noose, to enter into the holy
507.12 estate of matrimony -- to take Miss Ingram to
507.13 my bosom, in short, (she's an extensive armful:
507.14 but that's not to the point -- one can't have too
507.15 much of such a very excellent thing as my
507.16 beautiful Blanche(: well, as I was saying --
507.17 listen to me, Jane! You're not turning your
507.18 head to look after more moths, are you? That
507.19 was only a lady-clock, child, "flying away
507.20 home." I wish to remind you that it was you
507.21 who first said to me with that discretion, I
507.22 respect in you -- with that foresight, prudence,
507.23 and humility which befit your responsible and
507.24 dependent position -- that in case I married Miss
507.25 Ingram, both you and little Adele had better
507.26 trot forthwith. I pass over the sort of slur
507.27 conveyed in this suggestion on the character of
507.28 my beloved; indeed, when you are far away,
508.01 Janet, I'll try to forget it: I shall notice only
508.02 its wisdom; which is such that I have made it
508.03 my law of action. Adele must go to school;
508.04 and you, Miss Eyre, must get a new situation."
508.05 "Yes, sir, I will advertise immediately: and
508.06 meantime, I suppose -- --" I was going to
508.07 say, "I suppose I may stay here, till I find
508.08 another shelter to betake myself to:" but I
508.09 stopped, feeling it would not do to risk a long
508.10 sentence, for my voice was not quite under
508.11 command.
508.12 "In about a month I hope to be a bride-
508.13 groom," continued Mr. Rochester; "and in
508.14 the interim, I shall myself look out for em-
508.15 ployment and an asylum for you."
508.16 "Thank you, sir; I am sorry to give -- --"
508.17 "Oh, no need to apologize! I consider
508.18 that when a dependant does her duty as well
508.19 as you have done yours, she has a sort of claim

508.20 upon her employer for any little assistance he
508.21 can conveniently render her; indeed I have
508.22 already, through my future mother-in-law,
508.23 heard of a place that I think will suit: it is to
508.24 undertake the education of the five daughters
508.25 of Mrs. Dionysius O'Gall of Bitternutt Lodge,
508.26 Connaught, Ireland. You'll like Ireland, I
508.27 think: they're such warm-hearted people
508.28 there, they say."
509.01 "It is a long way off, sir."
509.02 "No matter -- a girl of your sense will not
509.03 object to the voyage or the distance."
509.04 "Not the voyage, but the distance: and then
509.05 the sea is a barrier -- --"
509.06 "From what, Jane?"
509.07 "From England and from Thornfield:
509.08 and -- --"
509.09 "Well?"
509.10 "From you, sir."
509.11 I said this almost involuntarily; and with as
509.12 little sanction of free will, my tears gushed
509.13 out. I did not cry so as to be heard, however;
509.14 I avoided sobbing. The thought of Mrs.
509.15 O'Gall and Bitternutt Lodge struck cold to
509.16 my heart; and colder the thought of all the
509.17 brine and foam, destined, as it seemed, to rush
509.18 between me and the master at whose side I
509.19 now walked; and coldest the remembrance of
509.20 the wider ocean -- wealth, caste, custom inter-
509.21 vened between me and what I naturally and
509.22 inevitably loved."
509.23 "It is a long way," I again said.
509.24 "It is to be sure; and when you get to
509.25 Bitternutt Lodge, Connaught, Ireland, I shall
509.26 never see you again, Jane: that's morally cer-
509.27 tain. I never go over to Ireland, not having
509.28 myself much of a fancy for the country.
510.01 We have been good friends, Jane; have we
510.02 not?"
510.03 "Yes, sir."
510.04 "And when friends are on the eve of sepa-
510.05 ration, they like to spend the little time that
510.06 remains to them close to each other. Come --
510.07 we'll talk over the voyage and the parting
510.08 quietly, half an hour or so, while the stars
510.09 enter into their shining life up in heaven
510.10 yonder: here is the chestnut tree; here is the
510.11 bench at its old roots. Come, we will sit there
510.12 in peace to-night, though we should never
510.13 more be destined to sit there together." He
510.14 seated me and himself.
510.15 "It is a long way to Ireland, Janet, and I
510.16 am sorry to send my little friend on such
510.17 weary travels: but if I can't do better, how
510.18 is it to be helped? Are you anything akin to
510.19 me, do you think, Jane?"
510.20 I could risk no sort of answer by this time:
510.21 my heart was full.
510.22 "Because," he said, "I sometimes have a
510.23 queer feeling with regard to you -- especially
510.24 when you are near me, as now: it is as if I
510.25 had a string somewhere under my left ribs,
510.26 tightly and inextricably knotted to a similar
510.27 string situated in the corresponding quarter
510.28 of your little frame. And if that boisterous
511.01 channel, and a two hundred miles or so of land
511.02 come broad between us, I am afraid that cord
511.03 of communion will be snapt; and then I've a
511.04 nervous notion I should take to bleeding in-
511.05 wardly. As for you, -- you'd forget me."
511.06 "That I never should, sir: you know -- --"
511.07 impossible to proceed.
511.08 "Jane, do you hear that nightingale singing
511.09 in the wood? -- Listen!"
511.10 In listening, I sobbed convulsively; for I
511.11 could repress what I endured no longer; I was
511.12 obliged to yield, and I was shaken from head
511.13 to foot with acute distress. When I did speak,
511.14 it was only to express an impetuous wish that
511.15 I had never been born, or never come to
511.16 Thornfield.
511.17 "Because you are sorry to leave it?"
511.18 The vehemence of emotion, stirred by grief
511.19 and love within me, was claiming mastery, and
511.20 struggling for full sway; and asserting a right
511.21 to predominate: to overcome, to live, rise, and
511.22 reign at last; yes, -- and to speak.
511.23 "I grieve to leave Thornfield: I love Thorn-
511.24 field: -- I love it, because I have lived in it a
511.25 full and delightful life, -- momentarily at least.
511.26 I have not been trampled on. I have not been
511.27 petrified. I have not been buried with inferior
511.28 minds, and excluded from every glimpse of
512.01 communion with what is bright, and energetic,
512.02 and high. I have talked, face to face, with
512.03 what I reverence; with what I delight in, --
512.04 with an original, a vigorous, an expanded
512.05 mind. I have known you, Mr. Rochester;
512.06 and it strikes me with terror and anguish to
512.07 feel I absolutely must be torn from you for
512.08 ever. I see the necessity of departure; and it
512.09 is like looking on the necessity of death."
512.10 "Where do you see the necessity?" he
512.11 asked, suddenly.
512.12 "Where? You, sir, have placed it before
512.13 me."
512.14 "In what shape?"
512.15 "In the shape of Miss Ingram; a noble and
512.16 beautiful woman, -- your bride."
512.17 "My bride! what bride? I have no
512.18 bride!"

512.19 "But you will have."
512.20 "Yes; -- I will! -- I will!" He set his teeth.
512.21 "Then I must go: -- you have said it your-
512.22 self."
512.23 "No: you must stay! I swear it -- and the
512.24 oath shall be kept."
512.25 "I tell you I must go!" I retorted, roused
512.26 to something like passion. "Do you think I
512.27 can stay to become nothing to you? Do you
512.28 think I am an automaton? -- a machine without
513.01 feelings? and can bear to have my morsel of
513.02 bread snatched from my lips, and my drop of
513.03 living water dashed from my cup? Do you
513.04 think, because I am poor, obscure, plain, and
513.05 little, I am soulless and heartless? -- You
513.06 think wrong! -- I have as much soul as you, --
513.07 and full as much heart! And if God had gifted
513.08 me with some beauty, and much wealth, I
513.09 should have made it as hard for you to leave
513.10 me, as it is now for me to leave you. I am
513.11 not talking to you now through the medium
513.12 of custom, conventionalities, nor even of mortal
513.13 flesh: -- it is my spirit that addresses your
513.14 spirit; just as if both had passed through the
513.15 grave, and we stood at God's feet, equal, -- as
513.16 we are!"
513.17 "As we are!" repeated Mr. Rochester --
513.18 "so," he added, enclosing me in his arms,
513.19 gathering me to his breast, pressing his lips
513.20 on my lips: "so, Jane!"
513.21 "Yes, so, sir," I rejoined: "and yet not
513.22 so; for you are a married man -- or as good
513.23 as a married man, and wed to one inferior
513.24 to you -- to one with whom you have no sym-
513.25 pathy -- whom I do not believe you truly love;
513.26 for I have seen and heard you sneer at her.
513.27 I would scorn such a union: therefore I am
513.28 better than you -- let me go!"
514.01 "Where, Jane? To Ireland?"
514.02 "Yes -- to Ireland. I have spoken my mind,
514.03 and can go anywhere now."
514.04 "Jane, be still; don't struggle so, like a
514.05 wild, frantic bird that is rending its own plu-
514.06 mage in its desperation."
514.07 "I am no bird; and no net ensnares me:
514.08 I am a free human being with an independent
514.09 will; which I now exert to leave you."
514.10 Another effort set me at liberty, and I stood
514.11 erect before him.
514.12 "And your will shall decide your destiny,"
514.13 he said: "I offer you my hand, my heart, and
514.14 a share of all my possessions."
514.15 "You play a farce, which I merely laugh
514.16 at."
514.17 "I ask you to pass through life at my side --
514.18 to be my second self, and best earthly com-
514.19 panion."
514.20 "For that fate you have already made your
514.21 choice, and must abide by it."
514.22 "Jane, be still a few moments; you are
514.23 over-excited: I will be still too."
514.24 A waft of wind came sweeping down the
514.25 laurel-walk, and trembled through the boughs
514.26 of the chestnut: it wandered away -- away --
514.27 to an indefinite distance -- it died. The night-
514.28 ingale's song was then the only voice of the
515.01 hour: in listening to it, I again wept. Mr.
515.02 Rochester sat quiet, looking at me gently
515.03 and seriously. Some time passed before he
515.04 spoke; he at last said: --
515.05 "Come to my side, Jane, and let us explain
515.06 and understand one another."
515.07 "I will never again come to your side:
515.08 I am torn away now, and cannot return."
515.09 "But, Jane, I summon you as my wife: it is
515.10 you only I intend to marry."
515.11 I was silent: I thought he mocked me.
515.12 "Come, Jane -- come hither."
515.13 "Your bride stands between us."
515.14 He rose, and with a stride reached me.
515.15 "My bride is here," he said, again drawing
515.16 me to him, "because my equal is here, and my
515.17 likeness. Jane, will you marry me?"
515.18 Still I did not answer, and still I writhed
515.19 myself from his grasp: for I was still incre-
515.20 dulous.
515.21 "Do you doubt me, Jane?"
515.22 "Entirely."
515.23 "You have no faith in me?"
515.24 "Not a whit."
515.25 "Am I a liar in your eyes?" he asked
515.26 passionately. "Little sceptic, you shall be
515.27 convinced. What love have I for Miss
515.28 Ingram? None: and that you know. What
516.01 love has she for me? None; as I have taken
516.02 pains to prove: I caused a rumour to reach
516.03 her that my fortune was not a third of what
516.04 was supposed, and after that I presented
516.05 myself to see the result; it was coldness both
516.06 from her and her mother. I would not -- I
516.07 could not -- marry Miss Ingram. You -- you
516.08 strange -- you almost unearthly thing! -- I love
516.09 as my own flesh. You -- poor and obscure, and
516.10 small and plain as you are -- I entreat to ac-
516.11 cept me as a husband."
516.12 "What me!" I ejaculated: beginning in his
516.13 earnestness -- and especially in his incivility -
516.14 to credit his sincerity: "me, who have not
516.15 a friend in the world but you -- if you are
516.16 my friend: not a shilling but what you have
516.17 given me?"

516.18 "You, Jane. I must have you for my own
516.19 -- entirely my own. Will you be mine? Say
516.20 yes, quickly."
516.21 "Mr. Rochester, let me look at your face:
516.22 turn to the moonlight."
516.23 "Why?"
516.24 "Because I want to read your countenance;
516.25 turn!"
516.26 "There: you will find it scarcely more legible
516.27 than a crumpled, scratched page. Read on:
516.28 only make haste, for I suffer."
517.01 His face was very much agitated and very
517.02 much flushed, and there were strong workings
517.03 in the features, and strange gleams in the
517.04 eyes.
517.05 "Oh, Jane, you torture me!" he exclaimed.
517.06 "With that searching and yet faithful and gene-
517.07 rous look, you torture me!"
517.08 "How can I do that? If you are true, and
517.09 your offer real, my only feelings to you must
517.10 be gratitude and devotion -- they cannot tor-
517.11 ture."
517.12 "Gratitude!" he ejaculated; and added
517.13 wildly -- "Jane, accept me quickly. Say, Ed-
517.14 ward -- give me my name -- Edward -- I will
517.15 marry you."
517.16 "Are you in earnest? -- Do you truly love
517.17 me? -- Do you sincerely wish me to be your
517.18 wife?"
517.19 "I do; and if an oath is necessary to satisfy
517.20 you, I swear it."
517.21 "Then, sir, I will marry you."
517.22 "Edward -- my little wife!"
517.23 "Dear Edward!"
517.24 "Come to me -- come to me entirely now,"
517.25 said he: and added, in his deepest tone, speak-
517.26 ing in my ear as his cheek was laid on mine,
517.27 "Make my happiness -- I will make yours."
517.28 "God pardon me!" he subjoined ere long;
518.01 "and man meddle not with me: I have her,
518.02 and will hold her."
518.03 "There is no one to meddle, sir. I have no
518.04 kindred to interfere."
518.05 "No -- that is the best of it," he said. And
518.06 if I had loved him less I should have thought
518.07 his accent and look of exultation savage: but,
518.08 sitting by him, roused from the nightmare of
518.09 parting -- called to the paradise of union -- I
518.10 thought only of the bliss given me to drink in
518.11 so abundant a flow. Again and again he said,
518.12 "Are you happy, Jane?" And again and
518.13 again I answered, "Yes." After which he
518.14 murmured, "It will atone -- it will atone.
518.15 Have I not found her friendless, and cold, and
518.16 comfortless? Will I not guard, and cherish,
518.17 and solace her? Is there not love in my
518.18 heart, and constancy in my resolves? It will
518.19 expiate at God's tribunal. I know my Maker
518.20 sanctions what I do. For the world's judg-
518.21 ment -- I wash my hands thereof. For man's
518.22 opinion -- I defy it."
518.23 But what had befallen the night? The
518.24 moon was not yet set, and we were all in
518.25 shadow: I could scarcely see my master's face,
518.26 near as I was. And what ailed the chestnut
518.27 tree? it writhed and groaned; while wind
518.28 roared in the laurel walk, and came sweeping
518.29 over us.
519.01 "We must go in," said Mr. Rochester:
519.02 "the weather changes. I could have sat with
519.03 thee till morning, Jane."
519.04 "And so," thought I, "could I with you." I
519.05 should have said so, perhaps, but a livid, vivid
519.06 spark leapt out of a cloud at which I was look-
519.07 ing, and there was a crack, a crash, and a close
519.08 rattling peal; and I thought only of hiding my
519.09 dazzled eyes against Mr. Rochester's shoulder.
519.10 The rain rushed down. He hurried me up
519.11 the walk, through the grounds, and into the
519.12 house; but we were quite wet before we could
519.13 pass the threshold. He was taking off my
519.14 shawl in the hall, and shaking the water
519.15 out of my loosened hair, when Mrs. Fairfax
519.16 emerged from her room. I did not observe
519.17 her at first, nor did Mr. Rochester. The
519.18 lamp was lit. The clock was on the stroke of
519.19 twelve.
519.20 "Hasten to take off your wet things," said
519.21 he; "and before you go, good-night -- good--
519.22 night, my darling!"
519.23 He kissed me repeatedly. When I looked
519.24 up, on leaving his arms, there stood the widow,
519.25 pale, grave, and amazed. I only smiled at
519.26 her, and ran up stairs. "Explanation will do
519.27 for another time," thought I. Still, when I
519.28 reached my chamber, I felt a pang at the idea
520.01 she should even temporarily misconstrue what
520.02 she had seen. But joy soon effaced every
520.03 other feeling; and loud as the wind blew,
520.04 near and deep as the thunder crashed, fierce
520.05 and frequent as the lightning gleamed, cata-
520.06 ract-like as the rain fell during a storm of two
520.07 hours' duration, I experienced no fear, and
520.08 little awe. Mr. Rochester came thrice to my
520.09 door in the course of it, to ask if I was safe
520.10 and tranquil: and that was comfort, that was
520.11 strength for anything.
520.12 Before I left my bed in the morning, little
520.13 Adele came running in to tell me that the
520.14 great horse-chestnut at the bottom of the or-
520.15 chard had been struck by lightning in the

520.16 night, and half of it split away.
521.01 [Vol. 2 Chapter 9]
521.02   As I rose and dressed, I thought over what
521.03 had happened, and wondered if it were a
521.04 dream. I could not be certain of the reality
521.05 till I had seen Mr. Rochester again, and heard
521.06 him renew his words of love and promise.
521.07   While arranging my hair, I looked at my
521.08 face in the glass, and felt it was no longer
521.09 plain: there was hope in its aspect, and life
521.10 in its colour; and my eyes seemed as if they
521.11 had beheld the fount of fruition, and borrowed
521.12 beams from the lustrous ripple. I had often
521.13 been unwilling to look at my master, because
521.14 I feared he could not be pleased at my look;
521.15 but I was sure I might lift my face to his now,
521.16 and not cool his affection by its expression. I
521.17 took a plain but clean and light summer dress
521.18 from my drawer and put it on: it seemed no
521.19 attire had ever so well become me; because
521.20 none had I ever worn in so blissful a mood.
522.01   I was not surprised, when I ran down into
522.02 the hall, to see that a brilliant June morn-
522.03 ing had succeeded to the tempest of the night;
522.04 and to feel, through the open glass door, the
522.05 breathing of a fresh and fragrant breeze.
522.06 Nature must be gladsome when I was so
522.07 happy. A beggar-woman and her little boy --
522.08 pale, ragged objects both -- were coming up
522.09 the walk, and I ran down and gave them all
522.10 the money I happened to have in my purse --
522.11 some three or four shillings: good or bad, they
522.12 must partake of my jubilee. The rooks cawed,
522.13 and blither birds sang; but nothing was so
522.14 merry or so musical as my own rejoicing heart.
522.15   Mrs. Fairfax surprised me by looking out
522.16 of the window with a sad countenance, and
522.17 saying gravely: -- "Miss Eyre, will you come
522.18 to breakfast?" During the meal she was quiet
522.19 and cool: but I could not undeceive her then.
522.20 I must wait for my master to give explanations;
522.21 and so must she. I ate what I could, and then
522.22 I hastened up stairs. I met Adele leaving the
522.23 school-room.
522.24   "Where are you going? It is time for les-
522.25 sons."
522.26   "Mr. Rochester has sent me away to the
522.27 nursery."
522.28   "Where is he?"
523.01   "In there," pointing to the apartment
523.02 she had left; and I went in, and there he
523.03 stood.
523.04   "Come and bid me good-morning," said he.
523.05 I gladly advanced; and it was not merely a
523.06 cold word now, or even a shake of the hand
523.07 that I received, but an embrace and a kiss. It
523.08 seemed natural: it seemed genial to be so
523.09 well-loved, so caressed by him.
523.10   "Jane, you look blooming, and smiling, and
523.11 pretty," said he: "truly pretty this morning.
523.12 Is this my pale, little elf? Is this my mustard--
523.13 seed? This little sunny-faced girl with the
523.14 dimpled cheek and rosy lips; the satin-smooth
523.15 hazel hair, and radiant hazel eyes?" /I had
523.16 green eyes, reader; but you must excuse the
523.17 mistake: for him they were new-dyed, I sup-
523.18 pose./
523.19   "It is Jane Eyre, sir."
523.20   "Soon to be Jane Rochester," he added: "in
523.21 four weeks, Janet; not a day more. Do you
523.22 hear that?"
523.23   I did, and I could not quite comprehend it: it
523.24 made me giddy. The feeling, the announce-
523.25 ment sent through me, was something stronger
523.26 than was consistent with joy -- something that
523.27 smote and stunned: it was, I think, almost
523.28 fear.
524.01   "You blushed, and now you are white,
524.02 Jane: what is that for?"
524.03   "Because you gave me a new name -- Jane
524.04 Rochester; and it seems so strange."
524.05   "Yes; Mrs. Rochester," said he; "young
524.06 Mrs. Rochester -- Fairfax Rochester's girl--
524.07 bride."
524.08   "It can never be, sir: it does not sound
524.09 likely. Human beings never enjoy complete
524.10 happiness in this world. I was not born for a
524.11 different destiny to the rest of my species: to
524.12 imagine such a lot befalling me is a fairy tale --
524.13 a day-dream."
524.14   "Which I can and will realize. I shall
524.15 begin to-day. This morning I wrote to my
524.16 banker in London to send me certain jewels
524.17 he has in his keeping, -- heir-looms for the
524.18 ladies of Thornfield. In a day or two I hope
524.19 to pour them into your lap: for every privi-
524.20 lege, every attention shall be yours, that I would
524.21 accord a peer's daughter, if about to marry
524.22 her."
524.23   "Oh, sir! -- never mind jewels! I don't
524.24 like to hear them spoken of. Jewels for Jane
524.25 Eyre sounds unnatural and strange: I would
524.26 rather not have them."
524.27   "I will myself put the diamond chain round
524.28 your neck, and the circlet on your forehead, --
525.01 which it will become: for nature, at least, has
525.02 stamped her patent of nobility on this brow,
525.03 Jane; and I will clasp the bracelets on these
525.04 fine wrists, and load these fairy-like fingers
525.05 with rings."
525.06   "No, no, sir! think of other subjects, and

525.07 speak of other things, and in another strain.
525.08 Don't address me as if I were a beauty; I am
525.09 your plain, Quakerish governess."
525.10   "You are a beauty, in my eyes; and a
525.11 beauty just after the desire of my heart, --
525.12 delicate and aerial."
525.13   "Puny and insignificant, you mean. You
525.14 are dreaming, sir -- or you are sneering. For
525.15 God's sake don't be ironical!"
525.16   "I will make the world acknowledge you a
525.17 beauty, too," he went on, while I really
525.18 became uneasy at the strain he had adopted;
525.19 because I felt he was either deluding himself,
525.20 or trying to delude me. "I will attire my
525.21 Jane in satin and lace, and she shall have
525.22 roses in her hair; and I will cover the head
525.23 I love best with a priceless veil."
525.24   "And then you won't know me, sir; and I
525.25 shall not be your Jane Eyre any longer, but
525.26 an ape in a harlequin's jacket, -- a jay in
525.27 borrowed plumes. I would as soon see you,
525.28 Mr. Rochester, tricked out in stage-trappings,
526.01 as myself clad in a court-lady's robe; and I
526.02 don't call you handsome, sir, though I love
526.03 you most dearly: far too dearly to flatter you.
526.04 Don't flatter me."
526.05   He pursued his theme, however, without
526.06 noticing my deprecation. "This very day I
526.07 shall take you in the carriage to Millcote, and
526.08 you must choose some dresses for yourself. I
526.09 told you we shall be married in four weeks.
526.10 The wedding is to take place quietly, in the
526.11 church down below yonder; and then I shall
526.12 waft you away at once to town. After a brief
526.13 stay there, I shall bear my treasure to regions
526.14 nearer the sun: to French vineyards and
526.15 Italian plains; and she shall see whatever is
526.16 famous in old story and in modern record: she
526.17 shall taste, too, of the life of cities; and she
526.18 shall learn to value herself by just comparison
526.19 with others."
526.20   "Shall I travel? -- and with you, sir?"
526.21   "You shall sojourn at Paris, Rome, and
526.22 Naples: at Florence, Venice, and Vienna:
526.23 all the ground I have wandered over shall
526.24 be re-trodden by you: wherever I stamped
526.25 my hoof, your sylph's foot shall step also.
526.26 Ten years since, I flew through Europe half
526.27 mad; with disgust, hate, and rage, as my
526.28 companions: now I shall revisit it healed
527.01 and cleansed, with a very angel as my com-
527.02 forter."
527.03   I laughed at him as he said this. "I am
527.04 not an angel," I asserted; "and I will not be
527.05 one till I die: I will be myself. Mr. Rochester,
527.06 you must neither expect nor exact anything ce-
527.07 lestial of me -- for you will not get it, any more
527.08 than I shall get it of you; which I do not at
527.09 all anticipate."
527.10   "What do you anticipate of me?"
527.11   "For a little while you will perhaps be as
527.12 you are now, -- a very little while; and then
527.13 you will turn cool; and then you will be
527.14 capricious; and then you will be stern, and I
527.15 shall have much ado to please you: but when
527.16 you get well used to me, you will perhaps like
527.17 me again, -- like me, I say, not love me. I
527.18 suppose your love will effervesce in six months,
527.19 or less. I have observed in books written by
527.20 men, that period assigned as the farthest to
527.21 which a husband's ardour extends. Yet, after
527.22 all, as a friend and companion, I hope never
527.23 to become quite distasteful to my dear master."
527.24   "Distasteful! and like you again! I think
527.25 I shall like you again and yet again: and I
527.26 will make you confess I do not only like, but
527.27 love you -- with truth, fervour, constancy.""
527.28   "Yet are you not capricious, sir?"
528.01   "To women who please me only by their
528.02 faces, I am the very devil when I find out they
528.03 have neither souls nor hearts -- when they open
528.04 to me a prospective of flatness, triviality, and
528.05 perhaps imbecility, coarseness, and ill-temper:
528.06 but to the clear eye and eloquent tongue, to
528.07 the soul made of fire, and the character that
528.08 bends but does not break -- at once supple and
528.09 stable, tractable and consistent -- I am ever ten-
528.10 der and true."
528.11   "Had you ever experience of such a charac-
528.12 ter, sir? Did you ever love such an one?"
528.13   "I love it now."
528.14   "But before me: if I, indeed, in any respect
528.15 come up to that difficult standard?"
528.16   "I never met your likeness. Jane: you
528.17 please me, and you master me -- you seem to
528.18 submit, and I like the sense of pliancy you
528.19 impart; and while I am twining the soft,
528.20 silken skein round my finger, it sends a thrill
528.21 up my arm to my heart. I am influenced --
528.22 conquered; and the influence is sweeter than
528.23 I can express; and the conquest I undergo has
528.24 a witchery beyond any triumph I can win.
528.25 Why do you smile, Jane? What does that
528.26 inexplicable, that uncanny turn of countenance
528.27 mean?"
528.28   "I was thinking, sir /you will excuse the
529.01 idea; it was involuntary/, I was thinking of
529.02 Hercules and Samson with their charmers -- --"
529.03   "You were, you little elfish ----"
529.04   "Hush, sir! You don't talk very wisely just
529.05 now; any more than those gentlemen acted

529.06 very wisely. However, had they been married,
529.07 they would no doubt by their severity as hus-
529.08 bands have made up for their softness as
529.09 suitors; and so will you, I fear. I wonder how
529.10 you will answer me a year hence, should I ask
529.11 a favour it does not suit your convenience or
529.12 pleasure to grant."
529.13 "Ask me something now, Janet -- the least
529.14 thing: I desire to be entreated ----"
529.15 "Indeed, I will, sir; I have my petition all
529.16 ready."
529.17 "Speak! But if you look up and smile
529.18 with that countenance, I shall swear concession
529.19 before I know to what, and that will make a fool
529.20 of me."
529.21 "Not at all, sir; I ask only this: don't send
529.22 for the jewels, and don't crown me with roses:
529.23 you might as well put a border of gold lace
529.24 round that plain pocket handkerchief you have
529.25 there."
529.26 "I might as well `gild refined gold.` I
529.27 know it: your request is granted then -- for the
529.28 time. I will remand the order I despatched
530.01 to my banker. But you have not yet asked for
530.02 anything; you have prayed a gift to be with-
530.03 drawn: try again."
530.04 "Well, then, sir; have the goodness to gra-
530.05 tify my curiosity, which is much piqued on one
530.06 point."
530.07 He looked disturbed. "What? what?" he
530.08 said hastily. "Curiosity is a dangerous peti-
530.09 tioner: it is well I have not taken a vow to ac-
530.10 cord every request ----"
530.11 "But there can be no danger in complying
530.12 with this, sir."
530.13 "Utter it, Jane: but I wish that instead of a
530.14 mere inquiry into, perhaps, a secret, it was a
530.15 wish for half my estate."
530.16 "Now, king Ahasuerus! What do I want
530.17 with half your estate? Do you think I am a
530.18 Jew-usurer, seeking good investment in land?
530.19 I would much rather have all your confidence.
530.20 You will not exclude me from your confidence,
530.21 if you admit me to your heart?"
530.22 "You are welcome to all of my confidence
530.23 that is worth having, Jane: but for God's sake,
530.24 don't desire a useless burden! Don't long for
530.25 poison -- don't turn out a downright Eve on my
530.26 hands!"
530.27 "Why not, sir? You have just been telling
531.01 me how much you like to be conquered, and
531.02 how pleasant overpersuasion is to you. Don't
531.03 you think I had better take advantage of the
531.04 confession, and begin and coax, and entreat --
531.05 even cry and be sulky if necessary -- for the
531.06 sake of a mere essay of my power?"
531.07 "I dare you to any such experiment. En-
531.08 croach, presume, and the game is up."
531.09 "Is it, sir? You soon give in. How stern
531.10 you look now! Your eyebrows have become
531.11 as thick as my finger, and your forehead re-
531.12 sembles, what, in some very astonishing poetry,
531.13 I once saw styled, `a blue-piled thunderloft.`
531.14 That will be your married look, sir, I sup-
531.15 pose?"
531.16 "If that will by your married look, I, as a
531.17 Christian, will soon give up the notion of con-
531.18 sorting with a mere sprite or salamander.
531.19 But what had you to ask, thing? -- out with
531.20 it!"
531.21 "There, you are less than civil now; and I
531.22 like rudeness a great deal better than flattery.
531.23 I had rather be a thing than an angel. This
531.24 is what I have to ask, -- why did you take
531.25 such pains to make me believe you wished to
531.26 marry Miss Ingram?"
531.27 "Is that all? Thank God, it is no worse!"
531.28 And now he unknit his black brows; looked
532.01 down, smiling at me, and stroked my hair, as
532.02 if well pleased at seeing a danger averted.
532.03 "I think I may confess," he continued, even
532.04 although I should make you a little indignant,
532.05 Jane -- and I have seen what a fire-spirit you
532.06 can be when you are indignant. You glowed
532.07 in the cool moonlight last night, when you
532.08 mutinied against fate, and claimed your rank
532.09 as my equal. Janet, by-the-by, it was you
532.10 who made me the offer."
532.11 "Of course I did. But to the point if you
532.12 please, sir -- Miss Ingram?"
532.13 "Well, I feigned courtship of Miss Ingram,
532.14 because I wished to render you as madly in
532.15 love with me as I was with you; and I knew
532.16 jealousy would be the best ally I could call in
532.17 for the furtherance of that end."
532.18 "Excellent! -- Now you are small -- not one
532.19 whit bigger than the end of my little finger.
532.20 It was a burning shame, and a scandalous dis-
532.21 grace to act in that way. Did you think
532.22 nothing of Miss Ingram's feelings, sir?"
532.23 "Her feelings are concentrated in one --
532.24 pride; and that needs humbling. Were you
532.25 jealous, Jane?"
532.26 "Never mind, Mr. Rochester: it is in no
532.27 way interesting to you to know that. An-
532.28 swer me truly once more. Do you think
533.01 Miss Ingram will not suffer from your dis-
533.02 honest coquetry? Won't she feel forsaken
533.03 and deserted?"
533.04 "Impossible! -- when I told you how she,
533.05 on the contrary, deserted me: the idea of my

533.06 insolvency cooled, or rather extinguished, her
533.07 flame in a moment."
533.08 "You have a curious, designing mind, Mr.
533.09 Rochester. I am afraid your principles on
533.10 some points are eccentric."
533.11 "My principles were never trained, Jane:
533.12 they may have grown a little awry for want of
533.13 attention."
533.14 "Once again, seriously; may I enjoy the
533.15 great good that has been vouchsated to me,
533.16 without fearing that any one else is suffer-
533.17 ing the bitter pain I myself felt a while
533.18 ago?"
533.19 "That you may, my good little girl: there
533.20 is not another being in the world has the same
533.21 pure love for me as yourself -- for I lay that
533.22 pleasant unction to my soul, Jane, a belief in
533.23 your affection."
533.24 I turned my lips to the hand that lay on my
533.25 shoulder. I loved him very much -- more than
533.26 I could trust myself to say -- more than words
533.27 had power to express.
533.28 "Ask something more," he said presently;
534.01 "it is my delight to be entreated, and to
534.02 yield."
534.03 I was again ready with my request. "Com-
534.04 municate your intentions to Mrs. Fairfax, sir:
534.05 she saw me with you last night in the hall, and
534.06 she was shocked. Give her some explanation
534.07 before I see her again. It pains me to be mis-
534.08 judged by so good a woman."
534.09 "Go to your room, and put on your bonnet,"
534.10 he replied. "I mean you to accompany me to
534.11 Millcote this morning; and while you prepare
534.12 for the drive, I will enlighten the old lady's
534.13 understanding. Did she think, Janet, you had
534.14 given the world for love, and considered it well
534.15 lost?"
534.16 "I believe she thought I had forgotten my
534.17 station; and yours, sir."
534.18 "Station! station! -- your station is in my
534.19 heart, and on the necks of those who would
534.20 insult you, now or hereafter. -- Go."
534.21 I was soon dressed; and when I heard Mr.
534.22 Rochester quit Mrs. Fairfax's parlour, I hurried
534.23 down to it. The old lady had been reading
534.24 her morning portion of Scripture -- the lesson
534.25 for the day; her Bible lay open before
534.26 her, and her spectacles were upon it. Her
534.27 occupation, suspended by Mr. Rochester's
534.28 announcement, seemed now forgotten; her
535.01 eyes, fixed on the blank wall opposite, ex-
535.02 pressed the surprise of a quiet mind, stirred by
535.03 unwonted tidings. Seeing me, she roused
535.04 herself: she made a sort of effort to smile, and
535.05 framed a few words of congratulation; but the
535.06 smile expired, and the sentence was aban-
535.07 doned unfinished. She put up her spectacles,
535.08 shut the Bible, and pushed her chair back from
535.09 the table.
535.10 "I feel so astonished," she began, "I hardly
535.11 know what to say to you, Miss Eyre. I have
535.12 surely not been dreaming, have I? Some-
535.13 times I half fall asleep when I am sitting
535.14 alone, and fancy things that have never hap-
535.15 pened. It has seemed to me more than once,
535.16 when I have been in a doze, that my dear
535.17 husband, who died fifteen years since, has
535.18 come in and sat down beside me; and that I
535.19 have even heard him call me by my name,
535.20 Alice, as he used to do. Now, can you tell me
535.21 whether it is actually true that Mr. Rochester
535.22 has asked you to marry him? Don't laugh
535.23 at me. But I really thought he came in here
535.24 five minutes ago, and said, that in a month you
535.25 would be his wife."
535.26 "He has said the same thing to me," I
535.27 replied.
536.01 "He has! Do you believe him? Have you
536.02 accepted him?"
536.03 "Yes."
536.04 She looked at me bewildered.
536.05 "I could never have thought it. He is a
536.06 proud man: all the Rochesters were proud:
536.07 and his father, at least, liked money. He, too,
536.08 has always been called careful. He means to
536.09 marry you?"
536.10 "He tells me so."
536.11 She surveyed my whole person: in her eyes
536.12 I read that they had there found no charm
536.13 powerful enough to solve the enigma.
536.14 "It passes me!" she continued: "but no
536.15 doubt it is true since you say so. How it will
536.16 answer, I cannot tell: I really don't know.
536.17 Equality of position and fortune is often ad-
536.18 visable in such cases; and there are twenty
536.19 years of difference in your ages. He might
536.20 almost be your father."
536.21 "No, indeed, Mrs. Fairfax!" exclaimed I,
536.22 nettled; "he is nothing like my father! No
536.23 one, who saw us together, would suppose it
536.24 for an instant. Mr. Rochester looks as young,
536.25 and is as young as some men at five-and--
536.26 twenty."
536.27 "Is it really for love he is going to marry
536.28 you?" she asked.
537.01 I was so hurt by her coldness and scepticism,
537.02 that the tears rose to my eyes.
537.03 "I am sorry to grieve you," pursued the
537.04 widow; "but you are so young, and so little
537.05 acquainted with men, I wished to put you on

537.06 your guard. It is an old saying that `all is not
537.07 gold that glitters`; and in this case I do fear
537.08 there will be something found to be different to
537.09 what either you or I expect."
537.10 "Why? -- am I a monster?" I said: "Is it
537.11 impossible that Mr. Rochester should have a
537.12 sincere affection for me?"
537.13 "No: you are very well; and much im-
537.14 proved of late; and Mr. Rochester, I daresay,
537.15 is fond of you. I have always noticed that you
537.16 were a sort of pet of his. There are times
537.17 when, for your sake, I have been a little uneasy
537.18 at his marked preference, and have wished to
537.19 put you on your guard: but I did not like to
537.20 suggest even the possibility of wrong. I knew
537.21 such an idea would shock, perhaps offend you;
537.22 and you were so discreet, and so thoroughly
537.23 modest and sensible, I hoped you might be
537.24 trusted to protect yourself. Last night I cannot
537.25 tell you what I suffered when I sought all over
537.26 the house, and could find you nowhere, nor the
537.27 master either; and then, at twelve o`clock, saw
537.28 you come in with him."
538.01 "Well, never mind that now," I inter-
538.02 rupted, impatiently: "it is enough that all was
538.03 right."
538.04 "I hope all will be right in the end," she
538.05 said: "but, believe me, you cannot be too care-
538.06 ful. Try and keep Mr. Rochester at a distance:
538.07 distrust yourself as well as him. Gentlemen in
538.08 his station are not accustomed to marry their
538.09 governesses."
538.10 I was growing truly irritated: happily, Adele
538.11 ran in.
538.12 "Let me go, -- let me go to Millcote too!"
538.13 she cried. "Mr. Rochester won`t: though
538.14 there is so much room in the new carriage.
538.15 Beg him to let me go, mademoiselle."
538.16 "That I will, Adele;" and I hastened away
538.17 with her, glad to quit my gloomy monitress.
538.18 The carriage was ready: they were bringing it
538.19 round to the front, and my master was pacing
538.20 the pavement, Pilot following him backwards
538.21 and forwards.
538.22 "Adele may accompany us, may she not,
538.23 sir?"
538.24 "I told her no. I`ll have no brats! -- I`ll
538.25 have only you."
538.26 "Do let her go, Mr. Rochester, if you please:
538.27 it would be better."
538.28 "Not it: she will be a restraint."
539.01 He was quite peremptory, both in look and
539.02 voice. The chill of Mrs. Fairfax`s warnings,
539.03 and the damp of her doubts, were upon me:
539.04 something of unsubstantiality and uncertainty
539.05 had beset my hopes. I half lost the sense of
539.06 power over him. I was about mechanically to
539.07 obey him, without further remonstrance; but
539.08 as he helped me into the carriage, he looked
539.09 at my face.
539.10 "What is the matter?" he asked: "all the
539.11 sunshine is gone. Do you really wish the
539.12 bairn to go? Will it annoy you if she is left
539.13 behind?"
539.14 "I would far rather she went, sir."
539.15 "Then off for your bonnet, and back, like a
539.16 flash of lightning!" cried he to Adele.
539.17 She obeyed him with what speed she
539.18 might.
539.19 "After all, a single morning`s interruption
539.20 will not matter much," said he, "when I mean
539.21 shortly to claim you -- your thoughts, conversa-
539.22 tion, and company -- for life."
539.23 Adele, when lifted in, commenced kissing
539.24 me, by way of expressing her gratitude for
539.25 my intercession: she was instantly stowed
539.26 away into a corner on the other side of
539.27 him. She then peeped round to where I sat;
539.28 so stern a neighbour was too restrictive: to
540.01 him, in his present fractious mood, she dared
540.02 whisper no observations, nor ask of him any
540.03 information.
540.04 "Let her come to me," I entreated; "she
540.05 will, perhaps, trouble you, sir: there is plenty
540.06 of room on this side."
540.07 He handed her over as if she had been
540.08 a lap-dog; "I`ll send her to school yet," he
540.09 said, but now he was smiling.
540.10 Adele heard him, and asked if she was
540.11 to go to school "sans mademoiselle?"
540.12 "Yes," he replied, "absolutely sans made-
540.13 moiselle; for I am to take mademoiselle to
540.14 the moon, and there I shall seek a cave in one
540.15 of the white valleys among the volcano-tops,
540.16 and mademoiselle shall live with me there,
540.17 and only me."
540.18 "She will have nothing to eat: you will
540.19 starve her," observed Adele.
540.20 "I shall gather manna for her morning
540.21 and night: the plains and hill-sides in the
540.22 moon are bleached with manna, Adele."
540.23 "She will want to warm herself: what will
540.24 she do for a fire?"
540.25 "Fire rises out of the lunar mountains:
540.26 when she is cold, I`ll carry her up to a peak
540.27 and lay her down on the edge of a crater."
540.28 "Oh, qu`elle y sera mal -- peu comfortable!
541.01 And her clothes, they will wear out: how can
541.02 she get new ones?"
541.03 Mr. Rochester professed to be puzzled.
541.04 "Hem!" said he. "What would you do,

541.05 Adele? Cudgel your brains for an expedient.
541.06 How would a white or a pink cloud answer
541.07 for a gown, do you think? And one would
541.08 cut a pretty enough scarf out of a rainbow."
541.09 "She is far better as she is," concluded
541.10 Adele, after musing some time: "besides, she
541.11 would get tired of living with only you in the
541.12 moon. If I were mademoiselle, I would never
541.13 consent to go with you."
541.14 "She has consented: she has pledged her
541.15 word."
541.16 "But you can`t get her there: there is
541.17 no road to the moon: it is all air; and neither
541.18 you nor she can fly."
541.19 "Adele, look at that field." We were now
541.20 outside Thornfield gates, and bowling lightly
541.21 along the smooth road to Millcote, where the
541.22 dust was well laid by the thunder-storm, and
541.23 where the low hedges and lofty timber trees
541.24 on each side glistening green, and rain--
541.25 refreshed.
541.26 "In that field, Adele, I was walking late
541.27 one evening about a fortnight since -- the even-
541.28 ing of the day you helped me to make hay
542.01 in the orchard meadows; and as I was tired
542.02 with raking swaths, I sat down to rest me
542.03 on a stile; and there I took out a little book
542.04 and a pencil, and began to write about a mis-
542.05 fortune that befell me long ago, and a wish
542.06 I had for happy days to come: I was writing
542.07 away very fast, though daylight was fading
542.08 from the leaf, when something came up the
542.09 path and stopped two yards off me. I looked
542.10 at it. It was a little thing with a veil of gos-
542.11 samer on its head. I beckoned it to come
542.12 near me: it stood soon at my knee. I never
542.13 spoke to it, and it never spoke to me, in words:
542.14 but I read its eyes, and it read mine; and our
542.15 speechless colloquy was to this effect: --
542.16 "It was a fairy, and come from Elf-land, it
542.17 said; and its errand was to make me happy:
542.18 I must go with it out of the common world
542.19 to a lonely place -- such as the moon, for in-
542.20 stance -- and it nodded its head towards her
542.21 horn, rising over Hay-hill: it told me of the
542.22 alabaster cave and silver vale where we might
542.23 live. I said I should like to go; but re-
542.24 minded it, as you did me, that I had no
542.25 wings to fly.
542.26 "`Oh,` returned the fairy, `that does not
542.27 signify! Here is a talisman will remove all
542.28 difficulties;` and she held out a pretty gold
543.01 ring. `Put it,` she said, `on the fourth finger
543.02 of my left hand, and I am yours, and you
543.03 are mine; and we shall leave earth, and make
543.04 our own heaven yonder.` She nodded again
543.05 at the moon. The ring, Adele, is in my
543.06 breeches-pocket, under the disguise of a so-
543.07 vereign: but I mean soon to change it to
543.08 a ring again."
543.09 "But what has mademoiselle to do with
543.10 it? I don`t care for the fairy: you said it
543.11 was mademoiselle you would take to the
543.12 moon -- --?"
543.13 "Mademoiselle is a fairy," he said, whispering
543.14 mysteriously. Whereupon I told her not to
543.15 mind his badinage; and she, on her part, evinced
543.16 a fund of genuine French scepticism: denomi-
543.17 nating Mr. Rochester "un vrai menteur," and
543.18 assuring him that she made no account whatever
543.19 of his "Contes de fée," and that "du rest, il
543.20 n`y avait pas de fées, et quand même il y en
543.21 avait:" she was sure they would never appear
543.22 to him, nor ever give him rings, or offer to live
543.23 with him in the moon.
543.24 The hour spent at Millcote was a somewhat
543.25 harassing one to me. Mr. Rochester obliged
543.26 me to go to a certain silk warehouse: there I
543.27 was ordered to choose half a dozen dresses. I
543.28 hated the business, I begged leave to defer it:
544.01 no -- it should be gone through with now. By
544.02 dint of entreaties expressed in energetic whis-
544.03 pers, I reduced the half-dozen to two: these,
544.04 however, he vowed he would select himself.
544.05 With anxiety I watched his eye rove over the
544.06 gay stores: he fixed on a rich silk of the most
544.07 brilliant amethyst dye, and a superb pink satin.
544.08 I told him in a new series of whispers, that he
544.09 might as well buy me a gold gown and a silver
544.10 bonnet at once: I should certainly never ven-
544.11 ture to wear his choice. With infinite difficulty,
544.12 for he was stubborn as a stone, I persuaded
544.13 him to make an exchange in favour of a sober
544.14 black satin and a pearl-grey silk. "It might
544.15 pass for the present," he said; "but he would
544.16 yet see me glittering like a parterre."
544.17 Glad was I to get him out of the silk ware-
544.18 house, and then out of a jeweller`s shop: the
544.19 more he bought me, the more my cheek
544.20 burned with a sense of annoyance and degra-
544.21 dation. As we re-entered the carriage, and I
544.22 sat back feverish and fagged, I remembered
544.23 what in the hurry of events, dark and bright,
544.24 I had wholly forgotten -- the letter of my
544.25 uncle, John Eyre, to Mrs. Reed: his intention
544.26 to adopt me and make me his testatrix. "It
544.27 would, indeed, be a relief," I thought, "if I
544.28 had ever so small an independency; I never
545.01 can bear being dressed like a doll by Mr.
545.02 Rochester, or sitting like a second Danae with
545.03 the golden shower falling daily round me. I

545.04 will write to Madeira the moment I get home,
545.05 and tell my uncle John I am going to be
545.06 married, and to whom: if I had but a prospect
545.07 of one day bringing Mr. Rochester an acces-
545.08 sion of fortune, I could better endure to be
545.09 kept by him now." And somewhat relieved
545.10 by this idea /which I failed not to execute
545.11 that day/, I ventured once more to meet my
545.12 master's and lover's eye; which most perti-
545.13 naciously sought mine, though I averted both
545.14 face and gaze. He smiled; and I thought his
545.15 smile was such as a sultan might, in a blissful
545.16 and fond moment, bestow on a slave his gold
545.17 and gems had enriched: I crushed his hand,
545.18 which was ever hunting mine, vigorously, and
545.19 thrust it back to him red with the passionate
545.20 pressure ----
545.21 "You need not look in that way," I said:
545.22 "if you do, I'll wear nothing but my old
545.23 Lowood frocks to the end of the chapter. I'll be
545.24 married in this lilac gingham -- you may make
545.25 a dressing-gown for yourself out of the pearl--
545.26 grey silk, and an infinite series of waistcoats
545.27 out of the black satin."
545.28 He chuckled; he rubbed his hands: "Oh,
546.01 it is rich to see and hear her!" he exclaimed.
546.02 "Is she original? Is she piquant? I would
546.03 not exchange this one little English girl for
546.04 the grand Turk's whole seraglio; gazelle-eyes,
546.05 houri forms and all!"
546.06 The eastern allusion bit me again: "I'll not
546.07 stand you an inch in the stead of a seraglio," I
546.08 said; "so don't consider me an equivalent for
546.09 one; if you have a fancy for anything in that
546.10 line, away with you, sir, to the bazars of Stam-
546.11 boul without delay; and lay out in extensive
546.12 slave-purchases some of that spare cash you
546.13 seem at a loss to spend satisfactorily here."
546.14 "And what will you do, Janet, while I am
546.15 bargaining for so many tons of flesh and such
546.16 an assortment of black eyes?"
546.17 "I'll be preparing myself to go out as a
546.18 missionary to preach liberty to them that are
546.19 enslaved -- your harem inmates amongst the
546.20 rest. I'll get admitted there, and I'll stir up
546.21 mutiny; and you, three-tailed bashaw as you
546.22 are, sir, shall in a trice find yourself fettered
546.23 amongst our hands: nor will I, for one, con-
546.24 sent to cut your bonds till you have signed a
546.25 charter, the most literal that despot ever yet
546.26 conferred."
546.27 "I would consent to be at your mercy,
546.28 Jane."
547.01 "I would have no mercy, Mr. Rochester, if
547.02 you supplicated for it with an eye like that.
547.03 While you looked so, I should be certain that
547.04 whatever charter you might grant under coer-
547.05 cion, your first act, when released, would be to
547.06 violate its conditions."
547.07 "Why, Jane, what would you have? I
547.08 fear you will compel me to go through a
547.09 private marriage ceremony, besides that per-
547.10 formed at the altar. You will stipulate, I
547.11 see, for peculiar terms -- what will they
547.12 be?"
547.13 "I only want an easy mind, sir; not
547.14 crushed by crowded obligations. Do you re-
547.15 member what you said of Celine Varens? --
547.16 of the diamonds, the cashmeres you gave her?
547.17 I will not be your English Celine Varens. I
547.18 shall continue to act as Adele's governess: by
547.19 that I shall earn my board and lodging, and
547.20 thirty pounds a year besides. I'll furnish my
547.21 own wardrobe out of that money, and you shall
547.22 give me nothing but ----"
547.23 "Well, but what?"
547.24 "Your regard: and if I give you mine in re-
547.25 turn, that debt will be quit."
547.26 "Well, for cool native impudence, and pure
547.27 innate pride, you haven't your equal," said he.
547.28 We were now approaching Thornfield. "Will
548.01 it please you to dine with me to-day?" he
548.02 asked, as we re-entered the gates.
548.03 "No, thank you, sir."
548.04 "And what for, `no thank you'? if one may
548.05 inquire."
548.06 "I never have dined with you, sir; and I
548.07 see no reason why I should now: till ----"
548.08 "Till what? You delight in half phrases."
548.09 "Till I can't help it."
548.10 "Do you suppose I eat like an ogre, or a
548.11 ghoul, that you dread being the companion of
548.12 my repast?"
548.13 "I have formed no supposition on the sub-
548.14 ject, sir; but I want to go on as usual for
548.15 another month."
548.16 "You will give up your governessing slavery
548.17 at once."
548.18 "Indeed! begging your pardon, sir, I shall
548.19 not. I shall just go on with it as usual. I
548.20 shall keep out of your way all day, as I have
548.21 been accustomed to do: you may send for
548.22 me in the evening, when you feel disposed to
548.23 see me, and I'll come then; but at no other
548.24 time."
548.25 "I want a smoke, Jane, or a pinch of snuff,
548.26 to comfort me under all this `pour me donner
548.27 une contenance,' as Adele would say; and un-
548.28 fortunately I have neither my cigar-case, nor
549.01 my snuff-box. But listen -- whisper -- it is your
549.02 time now, little tyrant, but it will be mine

549.03 presently: and when once I have fairly seized
549.04 you, to have and to hold, I'll just -- figuratively
549.05 speaking -- attach you to a chain like this
549.06 /touching his watch-guard/. Yes, bonny wee
549.07 thing, I'll wear you in my bosom, lest my
549.08 jewel I should tyne."
549.09 He said this as he helped me to alight from
549.10 the carriage; and while he afterwards lifted out
549.11 Adele, I entered the house, and made good my
549.12 retreat up stairs.
549.13 He duly summoned me to his presence in
549.14 the evening. I had prepared an occupation
549.15 for him; for I was determined not to spend
549.16 the whole time in a tete a-tete conversation;
549.17 I remembered his fine voice; I knew he
549.18 liked to sing -- good singers generally do.
549.19 I was no vocalist myself, and in his fasti-
549.20 dious judgment, no musician, either; but I
549.21 delighted in listening when the performance
549.22 was good. No sooner had twilight, that hour
549.23 of romance, began to lower her blue and starry
549.24 banner over the lattice, than I rose, opened
549.25 the piano, and entreated him, for the love of
549.26 heaven, to give me a song. He said I was a
549.27 capricious witch, and that he would rather
550.01 sing another time; but I averred that no time
550.02 was like the present.
550.03 "Did I like his voice?" he asked.
550.04 "Very much," I was not fond of pampering
550.05 that susceptible vanity of his; but for once,
550.06 and from motives of expediency, I would e'en
550.07 soothe and stimulate it.
550.08 "Then, Jane, you must play the accom-
550.09 paniment."
550.10 "Very well, sir, I will try."
550.11 I did try, but was presently swept off the
550.12 stool and denominated, "a little bungler."
550.13 Being pushed unceremoniously to one side --
550.14 which was precisely what I wished -- he usurped
550.15 my place, and proceeded to accompany him-
550.16 self: for he could play as well as sing. I hied
550.17 me to the window-recess; and while I sat there
550.18 and looked out on the still trees and dim
550.19 lawn, to a sweet air was sung in mellow tones,
550.20 the following strain:
550.21 The truest love that ever heart
550.22 Felt at its kindled core,
550.23 Did through each vein, in quickened start,
550.24 The tide of being pour.
550.25 Her coming was my hope each day,
550.26 Her parting was my pain;
550.27 The chance that did her steps delay,
550.28 Was ice in every vein.
551.01 I dreamed it would be nameless bliss,
551.02 As I loved, loved to be;
551.03 And to this object did I press
551.04 As blind as eagerly.
551.05 But wide as pathless was the space
551.06 That lay, our lives, between,
551.07 And dangerous as the foamy race
551.08 Of ocean-surges green.
551.09 And haunted as a robber-path
551.10 Through wilderness or wood;
551.11 For Might and Right, and woe and Wrath,
551.12 Between our spirits stood.
551.13 I dangers dared; I hind'rance scorned;
551.14 I omens did defy:
551.15 Whatever menaced, harassed, warned,
551.16 I passed impetuous by.
551.17 On sped my rainbow, fast as light;
551.18 I flew as in a dream;
551.19 For glorious rose upon my sight
551.20 That child of Shower and Gleam.
551.21 Still bright on clouds of suffering dim
551.22 Shines that soft, solemn joy;
551.23 Nor care I now, how dense and grim
551.24 Disasters gather nigh:
551.25 I care not in this moment sweet,
551.26 Though all I have rushed o'er
551.27 Should come on pinion, strong and fleet,
551.28 Proclaiming vengeance sore:
552.01 Though haughty Hate should strike me down,
552.02 Right, bar approach to me,
552.03 And grinding Might, with furious frown,
552.04 Swear endless enmity.
552.05 My love has placed her little hand
552.06 With noble faith in mine,
552.07 And vowed that wedlock's sacred band
552.08 Our natures shall entwine.
552.09 My love has sworn, with sealing kiss,
552.10 With me to live -- to die;
552.11 I have at last my nameless bliss:
552.12 As I love -- loved am I!
552.13 He rose and came towards me, and I saw
552.14 his face all kindled, and his full falcon-eye
552.15 flashing, and tenderness and passion in every
552.16 lineament. I quailed momentarily -- then I
552.17 rallied. Soft scene, daring demonstration, I
552.18 would not have; and I stood in peril of both:
552.19 a weapon of defence must be prepared -- I
552.20 whetted my tongue: as he reached me, I
552.21 asked with asperity, "whom he was going to
552.22 marry now?"
552.23 "That was a strange question to be put by
552.24 his darling Jane."
552.25 "Indeed! I considered it a very natural
552.26 and necessary one: he had talked of his future
552.27 wife dying with him. What did he mean by
553.01 such a pagan idea? I had no intention of
553.02 dying with him -- he might depend on that."
553.03 "Oh, all he longed, all he prayed for, was

553.04 that I might live with him! Death was not for
553.05 such as I."
553.06 "Indeed it was: I had as good a right to die
553.07 when my time came as he had: but I should
553.08 bide that time, and not be hurried away in a
553.09 suttee."
553.10 "Would I forgive him for the selfish idea,
553.11 and prove my pardon by a reconciling kiss?"
553.12 "No: I would rather be excused."
553.13 Here I heard myself apostrophized as a
553.14 "hard little thing;" and it was added, "any
553.15 other woman would have been melted to mar-
553.16 row at hearing such stanzas crooned in her
553.17 praise."
553.18 I assured him I was naturally hard -- very
553.19 flinty, and that he would often find me so; and
553.20 that, moreover, I was determined to show him
553.21 divers rugged points in my character before the
553.22 ensuing four weeks elapsed: he should know
553.23 fully what sort of a bargain he had made, while
553.24 there was yet time to rescind it.
553.25 "Would I be quiet, and talk rationally?"
553.26 "I would be quiet if he liked; and as to
553.27 talking rationally, I flattered myself I was doing
553.28 that now."
554.01 He fretted, pished and pshawed. "Very
554.02 good," I thought; "you may fume and fidget
554.03 as you please: but this is the best plan to
554.04 pursue with you, I am certain. I like you
554.05 more than I can say; but I'll not sink into a
554.06 bathos of sentiment: and with this needle of
554.07 repartee I'll keep you from the edge of the
554.08 gulph too; and, moreover, maintain by its
554.09 pungent aid that distance between you and
554.10 myself most conducive to our real mutual
554.11 advantage."
554.12 From less to more, I worked him up to con-
554.13 siderable irritation; then, after he had retired,
554.14 in dudgeon, quite to the other end of the
554.15 room, I got up, and saying, "I wish you good--
554.16 night, sir," in my natural and wonted respect-
554.17 ful manner, I slipped out by the side-door and
554.18 got away.
554.19 The system thus entered on, I pursued
554.20 during the whole season of probation; and
554.21 with the best success. He was kept, to be
554.22 sure, rather cross and crusty: but on the whole
554.23 I could see he was excellently entertained; and
554.24 that a lamb-like submission and turtle-dove
554.25 sensibility, while fostering his despotism more,
554.26 would have pleased his judgment, satisfied his
554.27 common-sense, and even suited his taste, less.
554.28 In other people's presence I was, as formerly,
555.01 deferential and quiet; any other line of conduct
555.02 being uncalled-for: it was only in the evening
555.03 conferences I thus thwarted and afflicted him.
555.04 He continued to send for him punctually at the
555.05 moment the clock struck seven; though when
555.06 I appeared before him now, he had no such
555.07 honeyed terms as "love" and "darling" on
555.08 his lips: the best words at my service were
555.09 "provoking puppet," "malicious elf," "sprite,"
555.10 "changeling," &c. For caresses too, I now got
555.11 grimaces; for a pressure of the hand, a pinch
555.12 on the arm; for a kiss on the cheek, a severe
555.13 tweak of the ear. It was all right: at present
555.14 I decidedly preferred these fierce favours to
555.15 anything more tender. Mrs. Fairfax, I saw
555.16 approved me: her anxiety on my account
555.17 vanished; therefore I was certain I did well.
555.18 Meantime, Mr. Rochester affirmed I was wear-
555.19 ing him to skin and bone, and threatened
555.20 awful vengeance for my present conduct at
555.21 some period fast coming. I laughed in my
555.22 sleeve at his menaces: "I can keep you in
555.23 reasonable check now," I reflected; "and I
555.24 don't doubt to be able to do it hereafter: if
555.25 one expedient loses its virtue, another must be
555.26 devised."
555.27 Yet after all my task was not an easy one;
555.28 often I would rather have pleased than teased
556.01 him. My future husband was becoming to me
556.02 my whole world; and more than the world:
556.03 almost my hope of heaven. He stood between
556.04 me and every thought of religion, as an eclipse
556.05 intervenes between man and the broad sun. I
556.06 could not, in those days, see God for his crea-
556.07 ture: of whom I had made an idol.
557.01 [Vol. 2 Chapter 10]
557.02 The month of courtship had wasted: its very
557.03 last hours were being numbered. There was
557.04 no putting off the day that advanced -- the
557.05 bridal day; and all preparations for its arrival
557.06 were complete. I, at least, had nothing more
557.07 to do: there were my trunks, packed, locked,
557.08 corded, ranged in a row along the wall of my
557.09 little chamber; to-morrow, at this time, they
557.10 would be far on their road to London: and so
557.11 should I /D. V./, -- or rather, not I, but one
557.12 Jane Rochester, a person whom as yet I knew
557.13 not. The cards of address alone remained to nail
557.14 on: they lay, four little squares, on the drawer.
557.15 Mr. Rochester had himself written the direction,
557.16 "Mrs. Rochester, -- Hotel, London," on each:
557.17 I could not persuade myself to affix them, or
557.18 to have them affixed. Mrs. Rochester! She
558.01 did not exist: she would not be born till
558.02 to-morrow, some time after eight o'clock A.M.;
558.03 and I would wait to be assured she had come
558.04 into the world alive, before I assigned to her
558.05 all that property. It was enough that in

558.06 yonder closet, opposite my dressing-table, gar-
558.07 ments said to be hers had already displaced
558.08 my black stuff Lowood frock and straw
558.09 bonnet: for not to me appertained that suit of
558.10 wedding raiment; the pearl-coloured robe, the
558.11 vapoury veil, pendent from the usurped port-
558.12 manteau. I shut the closet, to conceal the
558.13 strange, wraith-like apparel it contained;
558.14 which, at this evening hour -- nine o'clock --
558.15 gave out certainly a most ghostly shimmer
558.16 through the shadow of my apartment. "I
558.17 will leave you by yourself, white dream," I
558.18 said. "I am feverish: I hear the wind blow-
558.19 ing; I will go out of doors and feel it."
558.20 It was not only the hurry of preparation
558.21 that made me feverish; not only the antici-
558.22 pation of the great change -- the new life which
558.23 was to commence to-morrow: both these
558.24 circumstances had their share, doubtless, in
558.25 producing that restless, excited mood which
559.01 hurried me forth at this late hour into the
559.02 darkening grounds; but a third cause influ-
559.03 enced my mind more than they.
559.04 I had at heart a strange and anxious thought.
559.05 Something had happened which I could not
559.06 comprehend; no one knew of or had seen the
559.07 event but myself: it had taken place the
559.08 preceding night. Mr. Rochester that night
559.09 was absent from home; nor was he yet re-
559.10 turned: business had called him to a small
559.11 estate of two or three farms he possessed thirty
559.12 miles off -- business it was requisite he should
559.13 settle in person, previously to his meditated
559.14 departure from England. I waited now his
559.15 return; eager to disburthen my mind, and to
559.16 seek of him the solution of the enigma that
559.17 perplexed me. Stay till he comes reader;
559.18 and, when I disclose my secret to him, you
559.19 shall share the confidence.
559.20 I sought the orchard: driven to its shelter
559.21 by the wind, which all day had blown strong
559.22 and full from the south; without, however,
559.23 bringing a speck of rain. Instead of subsiding
559.24 as night drew on, it seemed to augment its
559.25 rush and deepen its roar: the trees blew
560.01 steadfastly one way, never writhing round, and
560.02 scarcely tossing back their boughs once in an
560.03 hour; so continuous was the strain bending
560.04 their branchy heads northward -- the clouds
560.05 drifted from pole to pole, fast following, mass
560.06 on mass: no glimpse of blue sky had been
560.07 visible that July day.
560.08 It was not without a certain wild pleasure I
560.09 ran before the wind delivering my trouble of
560.10 mind to the measureless air-torrent thundering
560.11 through space. Descending the laurel-walk,
560.12 I faced the wreck of the chestnut tree; it
560.13 stood up, black and riven: the trunk, split
560.14 down the centre, gasped ghastly. The cloven
560.15 halves were not broken from each other; for
560.16 the firm base and strong roots kept them un-
560.17 sundered below; though community of vitality
560.18 was destroyed -- the sap could flow no more:
560.19 their great boughs on each side were dead,
560.20 and next winter's tempests would be sure to
560.21 fell one or both to earth: as yet, however, they
560.22 might be said to form one tree -- a ruin; but an
560.23 entire ruin.
560.24 "You did right to hold fast to each other,"
560.25 I said: as if the monster-splinters were living
561.01 things, and could hear me. "I think, scathed
561.02 as you look, and charred and scorched, there
561.03 must be a little sense of life in you yet; rising
561.04 out of that adhesion at the faithful, honest
561.05 roots: you will never have green leaves more --
561.06 never more see birds making nests and singing
561.07 idyls in your boughs; the time of pleasure
561.08 and love is over with you; but you are not
561.09 desolate: each of you has a comrade to sym-
561.10 pathize with him in his decay." As I looked
561.11 up at them, the moon appeared momentarily
561.12 in that part of the sky which filled their fis-
561.13 sure: her disk was blood-red and half over--
561.14 cast: she seemed to throw on me one be-
561.15 wildered, dreary glance, and buried herself
561.16 again instantly in the deep drift of cloud.
561.17 The wind fell, for a second, round Thornfield;
561.18 but far away over wood and water, poured a
561.19 wild, melancholy wail: it was sad to listen to,
561.20 and I ran off again.
561.21 Here and there I strayed through the or-
561.22 chard, gathered up the apples with which the
561.23 grass round the tree roots was thickly strewn:
561.24 then I employed myself in dividing the ripe
561.25 from the unripe; I carried them into the house
562.01 and put them away in the store-room. Then
562.02 I repaired to the library to ascertain whether
562.03 the fire was lit; for, though summer, I knew
562.04 on such a gloomy evening, Mr. Rochester
562.05 would like to see a cheerful hearth when he
562.06 came in: yes, the fire had been kindled some
562.07 time, and burnt well. I placed his arm-chair by
562.08 the chimney-corner: I wheeled the table near
562.09 it: I let down the curtain, and had the candles
562.10 brought in ready for lighting. More restless
562.11 than ever, when I had completed these ar-
562.12 rangements I could not sit still, nor even re-
562.13 main in the house: a little time-piece in the
562.14 room and the old clock in the hall simulta-
562.15 neously struck ten.
562.16 "How late it grows!" I said: "I will run

562.17 down to the gates: it is moonlight at inter-
562.18 vals; I can see a good way on the road. He
562.19 may be coming now, and to meet him will save
562.20 some minutes of suspense."
562.21 The wind roared high in the great trees
562.22 which embowered the gates; but the road as far
562.23 as I could see, to the right hand and the left,
562.24 was all still and solitary: save for the shadows
562.25 of clouds crossing it at intervals, as the moon
563.01 looked out, it was but a long pale line, unvaried
563.02 by one moving speck.
563.03 A puerile tear dimmed my eye while I looked
563.04 -- a tear of disappointment and impatience:
563.05 ashamed of it, I wiped it away. I lingered;
563.06 the moon shut herself wholly within her cham-
563.07 ber, and drew close her curtain of dense cloud:
563.08 the night grew dark; rain came driving fast on
563.09 the gale.
563.10 "I wish he would come! I wish he would
563.11 come!" I exclaimed, seized with hypochon-
563.12 driac foreboding. I had expected his arrival
563.13 before tea; now it was dark: what could keep
563.14 him? Had an accident happened? The event
563.15 of last night again recurred to me. I inter-
563.16 preted it as a warning of disaster. I feared
563.17 my hopes were too bright to be realized; and I
563.18 had enjoyed so much bliss lately that I ima-
563.19 gined my fortune had passed its meridian, and
563.20 must now decline.
563.21 "Well, I cannot return to the house," I
563.22 thought; "I cannot sit by the fireside, while
563.23 he is abroad in inclement weather: better tire
563.24 my limbs than strain my heart; I will go
563.25 forward and meet him."
564.01 I set out; I walked fast, but not far: ere
564.02 I had measured a quarter of a mile, I heard
564.03 the tramp of hoofs; a horseman came on,
564.04 full gallop; a dog ran by his side. Away with
564.05 evil presentiment! It was he: here he was,
564.06 mounted on Mesrour, followed by Pilot. He
564.07 saw me; for the moon had opened a blue
564.08 field in the sky, and rode in it watery bright:
564.09 he took his hat off, and waved it round his
564.10 head. I now ran to meet him.
564.11 "There!" he exclaimed, as he stretched out
564.12 his hand and bent from the saddle: "You
564.13 can't do without me, that is evident. Step
564.14 on my boot-toe; give me both hands:
564.15 mount!"
564.16 I obeyed; joy made me agile: I sprang up
564.17 before him. A hearty kissing I got for a
564.18 welcome: and some boastful triumph; which
564.19 I swallowed as well as I could. He checked
564.20 himself in his exultation to demand, "But
564.21 is there anything the matter, Janet, that you
564.22 come to meet me at such an hour? Is there
564.23 anything wrong?"
564.24 "No; but I thought you would never come.
565.01 I could not bear to wait in the house for you,
565.02 especially with this rain and wind."
565.03 "Rain and wind, indeed! Yes, you are
565.04 dripping like a mermaid; pull my cloak round
565.05 you: but I think you are feverish, Jane; both
565.06 your cheek and hand are burning hot. I ask
565.07 again, is there anything the matter?"
565.08 "Nothing, now: I am neither afraid nor
565.09 unhappy."
565.10 "Then you have been both?"
565.11 "Rather: but I'll tell you all about it by--
565.12 and-by, sir; and I dare say you will only laugh
565.13 at me for my pains."
565.14 "I'll laugh at you heartily when to-morrow
565.15 is past; till then I dare not: my prize is not
565.16 certain. This is you; who have been as slip-
565.17 pery as an eel this last month, and as thorny
565.18 as a briar-rose? I could not lay a finger
565.19 anywhere but I was pricked; and now I seem
565.20 to have gathered up a stray lamb in my arms:
565.21 you wandered out of the fold to seek your
565.22 shepherd, did you, Jane?"
565.23 "I wanted you: but don't boast. Here we
565.24 are at Thornfield: now let me get down."
565.25 He landed on the pavement. As John
566.01 took his horse, and he followed me into the hall,
566.02 he told me to make haste and put something
566.03 dry on, and then to return to him in the
566.04 library; and he stopped me, as I made for the
566.05 staircase, to extort a promise that I would not
566.06 be long; nor was I long; in five minutes I
566.07 rejoined him. I found him at supper.
566.08 "Take a seat, and bear me company, Jane:
566.09 please God, it is the last meal but one you will
566.10 eat at Thornfield-Hall for a long time."
566.11 I sat down near him; but told him I could
566.12 not eat.
566.13 "Is it because you have the prospect of a
566.14 journey before you, Jane? Is is the thoughts
566.15 of going to London that takes away your appe-
566.16 tite?"
566.17 "I cannot see my prospects clearly to--
566.18 night, sir; and I hardly know what thoughts
566.19 I have in my head. Everything in life seems
566.20 unreal."
566.21 "Except me: I am substantial enough: --
566.22 touch me."
566.23 "You, sir, are the most phantom-like of all:
566.24 you are a mere dream."
566.25 He held out his hand, laughing: "Is that a
567.01 dream?" said he, placing it close to my eyes.
567.02 He had a rounded, muscular, and vigorous
567.03 hand, as well as a long, strong arm.

567.04 "Yes; though I touch it, it is a dream,"
567.05 said I, as I put it down from before my face.
567.06 "Sir, have you finished supper?"
567.07 "Yes, Jane."
567.08 I rang the bell, and ordered away the tray.
567.09 When we were again alone, I stirred the fire,
567.10 and then took a low seat at my master's knee.
567.11 "It is near midnight," I said.
567.12 "Yes: but remember, Jane, you promised
567.13 to wake with me the night before my wedding."
567.14 "I did; and I will keep my promise, for an
567.15 hour or two at least: I have no wish to go
567.16 to bed."
567.17 "Are all your arrangements complete?"
567.18 "All, sir."
567.19 "And on my part, likewise," he returned.
567.20 "I have settled everything; and we shall leave
567.21 Thornfield to-morrow, within half an hour after
567.22 our return from church."
567.23 "Very well, sir."
567.24 "With what an extraordinary smile you
568.01 uttered that word -- 'very well,' Jane! what
568.02 a bright spot of colour you have on each
568.03 cheek! and how strangely your eyes glitter!
568.04 Are you well?"
568.05 "I believe I am."
568.06 "Believe! What is the matter? -- Tell me
568.07 what you feel."
568.08 "I could not, sir: no words could tell you
568.09 what I feel. I wish this present hour would
568.10 never end: who knows with what fate the
568.11 next may come charged?"
568.12 "This is hypochondria, Jane. You have
568.13 been over-excited, or over-fatigued."
568.14 "Do you, sir, feel calm and happy?"
568.15 "Calm? -- no: but happy -- to the heart's core."
568.16 I looked up at him to read the signs of bliss
568.17 in his face: it was ardent and flushed.
568.18 "Give me your confidence, Jane," he said:
568.19 "relieve your mind of any weight that oppresses
568.20 it, by imparting it to me. What do you fear?
568.21 -- that I shall not prove a good husband?"
568.22 "It is the idea farthest from my thoughts."
568.23 "Are you apprehensive of the new sphere
568.24 you are about to enter? -- of the new life into
568.25 which you are passing?"
569.01 "No."
569.02 "You puzzle me, Jane: your look and tone
569.03 of sorrowful audacity perplex and pain me. I
569.04 want an explanation."
569.05 "Then, sir, -- listen. You were from home
569.06 last night?"
569.07 "I was: I know that; and you hinted a
569.08 while ago at something which had happened
569.09 in my absence: -- nothing, probably, of conse-
569.10 quence; but, in short, it has disturbed you.
569.11 Let me hear it. Mrs. Fairfax has said some-
569.12 thing, perhaps? or you have overheard the
569.13 servants talk? -- your sensitive self-respect has
569.14 been wounded?"
569.15 "No, sir." It struck twelve -- I waited till
569.16 the time-piece had concluded its silver chime,
569.17 and the clock its hoarse, vibrating stroke, and
569.18 then I proceeded.
569.19 "All day, yesterday, I was very busy, and
569.20 very happy in my ceaseless bustle; for I am
569.21 not, as you seem to think, troubled by any
569.22 haunting fears about the new sphere, et cetera:
569.23 I think it a glorious thing to have the hope of
569.24 living with you, because I love you. No,
569.25 sir, don't caress me now -- let me talk undis-
570.01 turbed. Yesterday I trusted well in Provi-
570.02 dence, and believed that events were working
570.03 together for your good and mine: it was a
570.04 fine day, if you recollect -- the calmness of the
570.05 air and sky forbade apprehensions respecting
570.06 your safety or comfort on your journey. I
570.07 walked a little while on the pavement after
570.08 tea, thinking of you; and I beheld you in
570.09 imagination so near me, I scarcely missed
570.10 your actual presence. I thought of the life that
570.11 lay before me -- your life, sir -- an existence
570.12 more expansive and stirring than my own: as
570.13 much more so as the depths of the sea to
570.14 which the brook runs, are than the shallows
570.15 of its own strait channel. I wondered why
570.16 moralists call this world a dreary wilderness:
570.17 for me it blossomed like a rose. Just at sunset,
570.18 the air turned cold and the sky cloudy: I
570.19 went in. Sophie called me up stairs to look at
570.20 my wedding-dress, which they had just brought;
570.21 and under it in the box I found your present --
570.22 the veil which, in your princely extravagance,
570.23 you sent for from London: resolved, I suppose
570.24 since I would not have jewels, to cheat me into
570.25 accepting something as costly. I smiled as I
571.01 unfolded it, and devised how I would tease
571.02 you about your aristocratic tastes, and your
571.03 efforts to masque your plebeian bride in the
571.04 attributes of a peeress. I thought how I would
571.05 carry down to you the square of unembroidered
571.06 blonde I had myself prepared as a covering for
571.07 my low-born head, and ask if that was not
571.08 good enough for a woman who could bring
571.09 her husband neither fortune, beauty, nor con-
571.10 nections. I saw plainly how you would look;
571.11 and heard your impetuous republican answers,
571.12 and your haughty disavowal of any necessity
571.13 on your part to augment your wealth, or ele-
571.14 vate your standing, by marrying either a purse
571.15 or a coronet."

571.16   "How well you read me, you witch!" inter-
571.17 posed Mr. Rochester: "but what did you find
571.18 in the veil besides its embroidery? Did you
571.19 find poison, or a dagger, that you look so
571.20 mournful now?

571.21   "No, no, sir; besides the delicacy and rich-
571.22 ness of the fabric, I found nothing save Fair-
571.23 fax Rochester's pride; and that did not scare
571.24 me, because I am used to the sight of the
571.25 demon. But, sir, as it grew dark, the wind
572.01 rose; it blew yesterday evening, not as it blows
572.02 now -- wild and high -- but "with a sullen, moan-
572.03 ing sound" far more eerie. I wished you were
572.04 at home. I came into this room, and the sight
572.05 of the empty chair and fireless hearth chilled
572.06 me. For some time after I went to bed, I
572.07 could not sleep -- a sense of anxious excitement
572.08 distressed me. The gale still rising, seemed to
572.09 my ear to muffle a mournful under-sound;
572.10 whether in the house or abroad I could not at
572.11 first tell, but it recurred, doubtful yet doleful at
572.12 every lull: at last I made out it must be some
572.13 dog howling at a distance. I was glad when it
572.14 ceased. On sleeping, I continued in dreams
572.15 the idea of a dark and gusty night. I con-
572.16 tinued also the wish to be with you, and expe-
572.17 rienced a strange, regretful consciousness of
572.18 some barrier dividing us. During all my first
572.19 sleep, I was following the windings of an un-
572.20 known road; total obscurity environed me; rain
572.21 pelted me; I was burdened with the charge of a
572.22 little child: a very small creature, too young and
572.23 feeble to walk, and which shivered in my cold
572.24 arms, and wailed piteously in my ear. I
572.25 thought, sir, that you were on the road a long
573.01 way before me; and I strained every nerve to
573.02 overtake you, and made effort on effort to
573.03 utter your name and entreat you to stop --
573.04 but my movements were fettered; and my
573.05 voice still died away inarticulate; while you,
573.06 I felt, withdrew farther and farther every
573.07 moment."

573.08   "And these dreams weigh on your spirits
573.09 now, Jane, when I am close to you? Little
573.10 nervous subject! Forget visionary woe, and
573.11 think only of real happiness! You say you
573.12 love me, Janet: yes -- I will not forget that;
573.13 and you cannot deny it. Those words did not
573.14 die inarticulate on your lips. I heard them
573.15 clear and soft: a thought too solemn perhaps,
573.16 but sweet as music -- `I think it is a glorious
573.17 thing to have the hope of living with you, Ed-
573.18 ward, because I love you.` -- Do you love me
573.19 Jane? repeat it."

573.20   "I do, sir. -- I do, with my whole heart."
573.21   "Well," he said, after some minutes' silence,
573.22 "it is strange: but that sentence has pene-
573.23 trated my breast painfully. Why? I think
573.24 because you said it with such an earnest, reli-
573.25 gious energy; and because your upward gaze
574.01 at me now is the very sublime of faith, truth,
574.02 and devotion: it is too much as if some spirit
574.03 were near me. Look wicked, Jane; as you
574.04 know well how to look; coin one of your wild,
574.05 shy, provoking smiles; tell me you hate me --
574.06 teaze me, vex me; do anything but move
574.07 me: I would rather be incensed than sad-
574.08 dened."

574.09   "I will teaze you and vex you to your heart's
574.10 content, when I have finished my tale: but
574.11 hear me to the end."

574.12   "I thought, Jane, you had told me all. I
574.13 thought I had found the source of your melan-
574.14 choly in a dream!"

574.15   I shook my head. "What! is there more?
574.16 But I will not believe it to be anything im-
574.17 portant. I warn you of incredulity before
574.18 hand. Go on."

574.19   The disquietude of his air, the somewhat
574.20 apprehensive impatience of his manner, sur-
574.21 prised me: but I proceeded.

574.22   "I dreamt another dream, sir: that Thorn-
574.23 field-Hall was a dreary ruin, the retreat of
574.24 bats and owls. I thought that of all the
574.25 stately front nothing remained but a shell-like
575.01 wall, very high and very fragile-looking. I
575.02 wandered, on a moonlight night, through the
575.03 grass-grown enclosure within: here I stum-
575.04 bled over a marble hearth, and there over a
575.05 fallen fragment of cornice. Wrapped up in a
575.06 shawl, I still carried the unknown little child:
575.07 I might not lay it down anywhere, however
575.08 tired were my arms -- however much its weight
575.09 impeded my progress, I must retain it. I
575.10 heard the gallop of a horse at a distance on
575.11 the road: I was sure it was you; and you were
575.12 departing for many years, and for a distant
575.13 country. I climbed the thin wall with frantic
575.14 perilous haste, eager to catch one glimpse of
575.15 you from the top: the stones rolled from
575.16 under my feet, the ivy branches I grasped
575.17 gave way, the child clung round my neck in
575.18 terror, and almost strangled me: at last I
575.19 gained the summit. I saw you like a speck
575.20 on a white track, lessening every moment.
575.21 The blast blew so strong I could not stand. I
575.22 sat down on the narrow ledge; I hushed the
575.23 scared infant in my lap: you turned an angle
575.24 of the road; I bent forward to take a last
576.01 look; the wall crumbled; I was shaken; the
576.02 child rolled from my knee; I lost my balance,

576.03 fell, and woke."

576.04   "Now, Jane, that is all."

576.05   "All the preface, sir; the tale is yet to
576.06 come. On waking, a gleam dazzled my
576.07 eyes: I thought -- oh, it is daylight! But
576.08 I was mistaken: it was only candle-light.
576.09 Sophie, I supposed, had come in. There was
576.10 a light on the dressing-table, and the door of
576.11 the closet, where, before going to bed, I had
576.12 hung my wedding-dress and veil, stood open:
576.13 I heard a rustling there. I asked, `Sophie,
576.14 what are you doing?" No one answered; but
576.15 a form emerged from the closet: it took the
576.16 light, held it aloft and surveyed the garments
576.17 pendant from the portmanteau. `Sophie!
576.18 Sophie!` I again cried: and still it was silent.
576.19 I had risen up in bed, I bent forward: first,
576.20 surprise, then bewilderment, came over me;
576.21 and then my blood crept cold through my
576.22 veins. Mr. Rochester, this was not Sophie, it
576.23 was not Leah, it was not Mrs. Fairfax: it was
576.24 not -- no, I was sure of it, and am still -- it
577.01 was not even that strange woman, Grace
577.02 Poole."

577.03   "It must have been one of them," interrupted
577.04 my master.

577.05   "No, sir, I solemnly assure you to the con-
577.06 trary. The shape standing before me had never
577.07 crossed my eyes within the precincts of Thorn-
577.08 field-Hall before; the height, the contour were
577.09 new to me."

577.10   "Describe it, Jane."

577.11   "It seemed, sir, a woman, tall and large, with
577.12 thick and dark hair hanging long down her
577.13 back. I know not what dress she had on: it
577.14 was white and straight; but whether gown,
577.15 sheet, or shroud, I cannot tell."

577.16   "Did you see her face?"

577.17   "Not at first. But presently she took my
577.18 veil from its place; she held it up, gazed at it
577.19 long, and then she threw it over her own head,
577.20 and turned to the mirror. At that moment I
577.21 saw the reflection of the visage and features
577.22 quite distinctly in the dark oblong glass."

577.23   "And how were they?"

577.24   "Fearful and ghastly to me -- oh, sir, I never
578.01 saw a face like it! It was a discoloured face --
578.02 it was a savage face. -- I wish I could forget the
578.03 roll of the red eyes and the fearful blackened
578.04 inflation of the lineaments!"

578.05   "Ghosts are usually pale, Jane."

578.06   "This, sir, was purple: the lips were swelled
578.07 and dark; the brow furrowed; the black eye-
578.08 brows widely raised over the blood-shot eyes.
578.09 Shall I tell you of what it reminded me?"

578.10   "You may."

578.11   "Of the foul German spectre -- the Vampyre."

578.12   "Ah! -- what did it do?"

578.13   "Sir, it removed my veil from its gaunt head,
578.14 rent it in two parts, and flinging both on the
578.15 floor, trampled on them."

578.16   "Afterwards?"

578.17   "It drew aside the window-curtain and
578.18 looked out: perhaps it saw dawn approaching,
578.19 for, taking the candle, it retreated to the door.
578.20 Just at my bedside, the figure stopped: the
578.21 fiery eye glared upon me -- she thrust up her
578.22 candle close to my face, and extinguished it
578.23 under my eyes. I was aware her lurid visage
578.24 flamed over mine, and I lost consciousness:
579.01 for the second time in my life -- only the second
579.02 time -- I became insensible from terror."

579.03   "Who was with you when you revived?"

579.04   "No one, sir; but the broad day. I rose,
579.05 bathed my head and face in water, drank a
579.06 long draught; felt that though enfeebled I
579.07 was not ill, and determined that to none but
579.08 you would I impart this vision. Now, sir,
579.09 tell me who and what that woman was?"

579.10   "The creature of an over-stimulated brain;
579.11 that is certain. I must be careful of you, my
579.12 treasure: nerves like yours were not made for
579.13 rough handling."

579.14   "Sir, depend on it, my nerves were not in
579.15 fault; the thing was real: the transaction ac-
579.16 tually took place."

579.17   "And your previous dreams: were they real
579.18 too? Is Thornfield-Hall a ruin? Am I
579.19 severed from you by insuperable obstacles?
579.20 Am I leaving you without a tear -- without a
579.21 kiss -- without a word?"

579.22   "Not yet."

579.23   "Am I about to do it? -- Why the day is
579.24 already commenced which is to bind us in-
580.01 dissolubly; and when we are once united, there
580.02 shall be no recurrence of these mental terrors:
580.03 I guarantee that."

580.04   "Mental terrors, sir! I wish I could be-
580.05 lieve them to be only such: I wish it more
580.06 now than ever; since even you cannot explain
580.07 to me the mystery of that awful visitant."

580.08   "And since I cannot do it, Jane, it must
580.09 have been unreal."

580.10   "But, sir, when I said so to myself on rising
580.11 this morning, and when I looked round the
580.12 room to gather courage and comfort from the
580.13 cheerful aspect of each familiar object in full
580.14 daylight, there -- on the carpet -- I saw what
580.15 gave the distinct lie to my hypothesis, -- the
580.16 veil, torn from top to bottom in two halves!"

580.17   I felt Mr. Rochester start and shudder; he

580.18 hastily flung his arms round me: "Thank
580.19 God!" he exclaimed, "that if anything malig-
580.20 nant did come near you last night, it was only
580.21 the veil that was harmed. -- Oh, to think what
580.22 might have happened!"
580.23 He drew his breath short, and strained
580.24 me so close to him, I could scarcely pant.
581.01 After some minutes' silence, he continued,
581.02 cheerily: --
581.03 "Now, Janet, I'll explain to you all about
581.04 it. It was half dream, half reality: a woman
581.05 did, I doubt not, enter your room: and that
581.06 woman was -- must have been -- Grace Poole.
581.07 You call her a strange being yourself: from all
581.08 you know, you have reason so to call her --
581.09 what did she do to me? what to Mason? In
581.10 a state between sleeping and waking, you
581.11 noticed her entrance and her actions; but
581.12 feverish, almost delirious as you were, you
581.13 ascribed to her a goblin appearance different
581.14 from her own: the long dishevelled hair, the
581.15 swelled black face, the exaggerated stature,
581.16 were figments of imagination, results of night-
581.17 mare: the spiteful tearing of the veil was real:
581.18 and it is like her. I see you would ask why I
581.19 keep such a woman in my house: when we
581.20 have been married a year and a day, I will tell
581.21 you; but not now. Are you satisfied, Jane?
581.22 Do you accept my solution of the mys-
581.23 tery?"
581.24 I reflected, and in truth it appeared to me
582.01 the only possible one: satisfied I was not; but
582.02 to please him I endeavoured to appear so --
582.03 relieved, I certainly did feel; so I answered
582.04 him with a contented smile. And now, as it
582.05 was long past one, I prepared to leave him.
582.06 "Does not Sophie sleep with Adele in the
582.07 nursery?" he asked, as I lit my candle.
582.08 "Yes, sir."
582.09 "And there is room enough in Adele's little
582.10 bed for you. You must share it with her to--
582.11 night, Jane: it is no wonder that the incident
582.12 you have related should make you nervous,
582.13 and I would rather you did not sleep alone:
582.14 promise me to go to the nursery."
582.15 "I shall be very glad to do so, sir."
582.16 "And fasten the door securely on the in-
582.17 side. Wake Sophie when you go up stairs,
582.18 under pretence of requesting her to rouse you
582.19 in good time to-morrow; for you must be
582.20 dressed and have finished breakfast before
582.21 eight. And now, no more sombre thoughts:
582.22 chase dull care away, Janet. Don't you hear to
582.23 what soft whispers the wind has fallen? and
582.24 there is no more beating of rain against the
583.01 window-panes: look here -- /he lifted up the
583.02 curtain/ it is a lovely night!"
583.03 It was. Half heaven was pure and stainless:
583.04 the clouds, now trooping before the wind, which
583.05 had shifted to the west, were filing off east-
583.06 ward in long, silvered columns. The moon
583.07 shone peacefully.
583.08 "Well," said Mr. Rochester, gazing in-
583.09 quiringly into my eyes, "how is my Janet
583.10 now?"
583.11 "The night is serene, sir; and so am I."
583.12 "And you will not dream of separation and
583.13 sorrow to-night; but of happy love and blissful
583.14 union."
583.15 This prediction was but half fulfilled: I did
583.16 not indeed dream of sorrow, but as little did I
583.17 dream of joy; for I never slept at all. With
583.18 little Adele in my arms, I watched the slumber
583.19 of childhood -- so tranquil, so passionless, so
583.20 innocent -- and waited for the coming day: all
583.21 my life was awake and astir in my frame:
583.22 and as soon as the sun rose, I rose too. I re-
583.23 member Adele clung to me as I left her: I
583.24 remember I kissed her as I loosened her little
584.01 hands from my neck; and I cried over her
584.02 with strange emotion, and quitted her because
584.03 I feared my sobs would break her still sound
584.04 repose. She seemed the emblem of my past
584.05 life; and he, I was now to array myself to meet,
584.06 the dread, but adored, type of my unknown
584.07 future day.
585.01 [Vol. 2 Chapter 11]
585.02 Sophie came at seven to dress me; she was
585.03 very long indeed in accomplishing her task; so
585.04 long that Mr. Rochester, grown, I suppose,
585.05 impatient of my delay, sent up to ask why I did
585.06 not come. She was just fastening my veil /the
585.07 plain square of blond after all/ to my hair with
585.08 a brooch; I hurried from under her hands as
585.09 soon as I could.
585.10 "Stop!" she cried in French. "Look at
585.11 yourself in the mirror: you have not taken one
585.12 peep."
585.13 So I turned at the door: I saw a robed and
585.14 veiled figure, so unlike my usual self that it
585.15 seemed almost the image of a stranger.
585.16 "Jane!" called a voice, and I hastened down.
585.17 I was received at the foot of the stairs by
585.18 Mr. Rochester.
586.01 "Lingerer," he said, "my brain is on fire
586.02 with impatience; and you tarry so long!"
586.03 He took me into the dining-room, surveyed
586.04 me keenly all over, pronounced me "fair as a
586.05 lily, and not only the pride of his life, but the
586.06 desire of his eyes," and then telling me he
586.07 would give me but ten minutes to eat some

586.08 breakfast, he rang the bell. One of his lately
586.09 hired servants, a footman, answered it.
586.10 "Is John getting the carriage ready?"
586.11 "Yes, sir."
586.12 "Is the luggage brought down?"
586.13 "They are bringing it down, sir."
586.14 "Go you to the church: see if Mr. Wood
586.15 /the clergyman/ and the clerk are there: return
586.16 and tell me."
586.17 The church, as the reader knows, was but
586.18 just beyond the gates; the footman soon re-
586.19 turned.
586.20 "Mr. Wood is in the vestry, sir, putting on
586.21 his surplice."
586.22 "And the carriage?"
586.23 "The horses are harnessing."
586.24 "We shall not want it to go to church; but
586.25 it must be ready the moment we return: all
587.01 the boxes and luggage arranged and strapped
587.02 on, and the coachman in his seat."
587.03 "Yes, sir."
587.04 "Jane, are you ready?"
587.05 I rose. There were no groomsmen, no
587.06 bridesmaids, no relatives to wait for or marshal:
587.07 none but Mr. Rochester and I. Mrs. Fairfax
587.08 stood in the hall as we passed. I would fain
587.09 have spoken to her, but my hand was held by
587.10 a grasp of iron: I was hurried along by a stride
587.11 I could hardly follow; and to look at Mr.
587.12 Rochester's face was to feel that not a second
587.13 of delay would be tolerated for any purpose.
587.14 I wonder what other bridegroom ever looked
587.15 as he did -- so bent up to a purpose, so grimly
587.16 resolute: or who, under such steadfast brows,
587.17 ever revealed such flaming and flashing
587.18 eyes.
587.19 I know not whether the day was fair or
587.20 foul; in descending the drive, I gazed neither
587.21 on sky nor earth: my heart was with my eyes;
587.22 and both seemed migrated into Mr. Rochester's
587.23 frame. I wanted to see the invisible thing on
587.24 which, as we went along, he appeared to fasten
587.25 a glance fierce and fell. I wanted to feel the
588.01 thoughts whose force he seemed breasting and
588.02 resisting.
588.03 At the churchyard wicket he stopped: he
588.04 discovered I was quite out of breath. "Am I
588.05 cruel in my love?" he said. "Delay an in-
588.06 stant: lean on me, Jane."
588.07 And now I can recall the picture of the
588.08 gray old house of God rising calm before me,
588.09 of a rook wheeling round the steeple, of a
588.10 ruddy morning sky beyond. I remember
588.11 something, too, of the green grave-mounds;
588.12 and I have not forgotten, either, two figures of
588.13 strangers, straying amongst the low hillocks,
588.14 and reading the mementoes graven on the few
588.15 mossy head-stones. I noticed them, because,
588.16 as they saw us, they passed round to the back
588.17 of the church; and I doubted not they were
588.18 going to enter by the side-aisle door, and wit-
588.19 ness the ceremony. By Mr. Rochester they
588.20 were not observed; he was earnestly looking
588.21 at my face, from which the blood had, I dare
588.22 say, momentarily fled: for I felt my forehead
588.23 dewy, and my cheeks and lips cold. When I
588.24 rallied, which I soon did, he walked gently with
588.25 me up the path to the porch.
589.01 We entered the quiet and humble temple;
589.02 the priest waited in his white surplice at the
589.03 lowly altar, the clerk beside him. All was
589.04 still: two shadows only moved in a remote
589.05 corner. My conjecture had been correct: the
589.06 strangers had slipped in before us, and they
589.07 now stood by the vault of the Rochesters,
589.08 their backs towards us, viewing through the
589.09 rails the old, time-stained marble tomb, where
589.10 a kneeling angel guarded the remains of
589.11 Damer de Rochester, slain at Marston Moor
589.12 in the time of the civil wars; and of Elizabeth,
589.13 his wife.
589.14 Our place was taken at the communion--
589.15 rails. Hearing a cautious step behind me, I
589.16 glanced over my shoulder: one of the stran-
589.17 gers -- a gentleman, evidently -- was advancing
589.18 up the chancel. The service began. The
589.19 explanation of the intent of matrimony was
589.20 gone through; and then the clergyman came
589.21 a step further forward, and bending slightly
589.22 towards Mr. Rochester, went on.
589.23 "I require and charge you both / as ye will
589.24 answer at the dreadful day of judgment, when
589.25 the secrets of all hearts shall be disclosed/,
590.01 that if either of you know any impediment
590.02 why ye may not lawfully be joined together in
590.03 matrimony, ye do now confess it; for be ye
590.04 well assured that so many as are coupled
590.05 together otherwise than God's word doth
590.06 allow, are not joined together by God, neither
590.07 is their matrimony lawful."
590.08 He paused, as the custom is. When is
590.09 the pause after that sentence ever broken by
590.10 reply? Not, perhaps, once in a hundred
590.11 years. And the clergyman, who had not lifted
590.12 his eyes from his book, and had held his
590.13 breath but for a moment, was proceeding: his
590.14 hand was already stretched towards Mr. Ro-
590.15 chester, as his lips unclosed to ask, "Wilt
590.16 thou have this woman for thy wedded wife?"
590.17 -- when a distinct and near voice said: --
590.18 "The marriage cannot go on: I declare the

410

590.19 existence of an impediment."
590.20 The clergyman looked up at the speaker,
590.21 and stood mute; the clerk did the same; Mr.
590.22 Rochester moved slightly, as if an earthquake
590.23 had rolled under his feet: taking a firmer
590.24 footing, and not turning his head or eyes, he
590.25 said, "Proceed."
591.01 Profound silence fell when he had uttered
591.02 that word, with deep but low intonation. Pre-
591.03 sently Mr. Wood said: --
591.04 "I cannot proceed without some investiga-
591.05 tion into what has been asserted, and evidence
591.06 of its truth or falsehood."
591.07 "The ceremony is quite broken off," sub-
591.08 joined the voice behind us. "I am in a con-
591.09 dition to prove my allegation: an insuperable
591.10 impediment to this marriage exists."
591.11 Mr. Rochester heard, but heeded not: he
591.12 stood stubborn and rigid: making no move-
591.13 ment, but to possess himself of my hand.
591.14 what a hot and strong grasp he had!" -- and
591.15 how like quarried marble was his pale, firm,
591.16 massive front at this moment! How his
591.17 eye shone, still watchful, and yet wild be-
591.18 neath!
591.19 Mr. Wood seemed at a loss. "What is
591.20 the nature of the impediment?" he asked.
591.21 "Perhaps it may be got over -- explained
591.22 away?"
591.23 "Hardly," was the answer: "I have called
591.24 it insuperable, and I speak advisedly."
591.25 The speaker came forwards, and leaned on
592.01 the rails. He continued, uttering each word
592.02 distinctly, calmly, steadily, but not loudly.
592.03 "It simply consists in the existence of a
592.04 previous marriage: Mr. Rochester has a wife
592.05 now living."
592.06 My nerves vibrated to those low-spoken
592.07 words as they had never vibrated to thunder --
592.08 my blood felt frost or fire: but I was collected,
592.09 and in no danger of swooning. I looked at
592.10 Mr. Rochester: I made him look at me. His
592.11 whole face was colourless rock: his eye was
592.12 both spark and flint. He disavowed nothing:
592.13 he seemed as if he would defy all things.
592.14 without speaking; without smiling; without
592.15 seeming to recognise in me a human being, he
592.16 only twined my waist with his arm, and riveted
592.17 me to his side.
592.18 "Who are you?" he asked of the intruder.
592.19 "My name is Briggs -- a solicitor of ------
592.20 street, London."
592.21 "And you would thrust on me a wife?"
592.22 "I would remind you of your lady's ex-
592.23 istence, sir: which the law recognises, if you
592.24 do not."
593.01 "Favour me with an account of her -- with
593.02 her name, her parentage, her place of
593.03 abode."
593.04 "Certainly." Mr. Briggs calmly took a
593.05 paper from his pocket, and read out in a sort of
593.06 official, nasal voice: --
593.07 "'I affirm and can prove that on the 20th of
593.08 October, A.D. ----, / date of fifteen years
593.09 back/ Edward Fairfax Rochester of Thornfield--
593.10 Hall, in the county of ----, and of Fern-
593.11 dean Manor, in ----shire, England, was
593.12 married to my sister, Bertha Antoinetta Ma-
593.13 son, daughter of Jonas Mason, merchant,
593.14 and of Antoinetta his wife, a Creole -- at ------
593.15 church, Spanish-Town, Jamaica. The record
593.16 of the marriage will be found in the register
593.17 of that church -- a copy of it is now in my pos-
593.18 session. Signed, Richard Mason'"
593.19 "That -- if a genuine document -- may prove I
593.20 have been married, but it does not prove that
593.21 the woman mentioned therein as my wife is still
593.22 living."
593.23 "She was living three months ago," re-
593.24 turned the lawyer.
593.25 "How do you know?"
594.01 "I have a witness to the fact; whose testi-
594.02 mony even you, sir, will scarcely controvert."
594.03 "Produce him -- or go to hell."
594.04 "I will produce him first -- he is on the
594.05 spot: Mr. Mason, have the goodness to step
594.06 forward."
594.07 Mr. Rochester, on hearing the name, set his
594.08 teeth; he experienced, too, a sort of strong con-
594.09 vulsive quiver; near to him as I was, I felt
594.10 the spasmodic movement of fury or despair
594.11 run through his frame. The second stranger,
594.12 who had hitherto lingered in the background,
594.13 now drew near; a pale face looked over the
594.14 solicitor's shoulder -- yes, it was Mason him-
594.15 self. Mr. Rochester turned and glared at him.
594.16 His eye, as I have often said, was a black
594.17 eye: it had now a tawny, nay a bloody light in
594.18 its gloom; and his face flushed -- olive cheek,
594.19 and hueless forehead received a glow, as from
594.20 spreading, ascending heart-fire; and he stirred,
594.21 lifted his strong arm -- he could have struck
594.22 Mason -- dashed him on the church-floor --
594.23 shocked by ruthless blow the breath from his
594.24 body -- but Mason shrank away, and cried
594.25 faintly, "Good God!" Contempt fell cool on
595.01 Mr. Rochester -- his passion died as if a blight
595.02 had shrivelled it up: he only asked, "What
595.03 have you to say?"
595.04 An inaudible reply escaped Mason's white
595.05 lips.

595.06 "The devil is in it if you cannot answer
595.07 distinctly. I again demand, what have you to
595.08 say?"
595.09 "Sir -- sir --" interrupted the clergyman,
595.10 "do not forget you are in a sacred place."
595.11 Then addressing Mason, he inquired gently,
595.12 "Are you aware, sir, whether or not this gentle-
595.13 man's wife is still living?"
595.14 "Courage," urged the lawyer, -- "speak out."
595.15 "She is now living at Thornfield-Hall,"
595.16 said Mason, in more articulate tones: "I saw
595.17 her there last April. I am her brother."
595.18 "At Thornfield-Hall!" ejaculated the cler-
595.19 gyman. "Impossible! I am an old resident
595.20 in this neighbourhood, sir, and I never heard
595.21 of a Mrs. Rochester at Thornfield-Hall."
595.22 I saw a grim smile contort Mr. Rochester's
595.23 lip and he muttered: --
595.24 "No -- by God! I took care that none should
595.25 hear of it -- or of her under that name." He
596.01 mused -- for ten minutes he held counsel with
596.02 himself: he formed his resolve, and announced
596.03 it: --
596.04 "Enough -- all shall bolt out at once, like
596.05 the bullet from the barrel. -- Wood, close your
596.06 book and take off your surplice; John Green,
596.07 /to the clerk/ leave the church: there will be
596.08 no wedding to-day:" the man obeyed.
596.09 Mr. Rochester continued, hardily and reck-
596.10 lessly: "Bigamy is an ugly word! -- I meant,
596.11 however, to be a bigamist: but fate has out--
596.12 manoeuvered me; or Providence has checked
596.13 me, -- perhaps the last. I am little better than
596.14 a devil at this moment; and, as my pastor
596.15 there would tell me, deserve no doubt the
596.16 sternest judgments of God, -- even to the
596.17 quenchless fire and deathless worm. Gentle-
596.18 men, my plan is broken up! -- what this lawyer
596.19 and his client say is true: I have been mar-
596.20 ried; the woman to whom I was married
596.21 lives! You say you never heard of a Mrs.
596.22 Rochester at the house up yonder, Wood:
596.23 but I daresay you have many a time inclined
596.24 your ear to gossip about the mysterious lunatic
596.25 kept there under watch and ward. Some
597.01 have whispered to you that she is my bastard
597.02 half-sister: some, my cast-off mistress; I now
597.03 inform you that she is my wife, whom I mar-
597.04 ried fifteen years ago, -- Bertha Mason by
597.05 name; sister of this resolute personage, who is
597.06 now, with his quivering limbs and white cheeks,
597.07 showing you what a stout heart men may
597.08 bear. Cheer up, Dick! -- never fear me! -- I'd
597.09 almost as soon strike a woman as you. Bertha
597.10 Mason is mad; and she came of a mad family;
597.11 -- idiots and maniacs through three genera-
597.12 tions! Her mother, the Creole, was both a
597.13 mad woman and a drunkard! -- as I found out
597.14 after I had wed the daughter: for they were
597.15 silent on family secrets before. Bertha, like a
597.16 dutiful child, copied her parent in both points.
597.17 I had a charming partner -- pure, wise, modest:
597.18 you can fancy I was a happy man. -- I went
597.19 through rich scenes! Oh! my experience has
597.20 been heavenly, if you only knew it! But I owe
597.21 you no further explanation. Briggs, Wood,
597.22 Mason, -- I invite you all to come up to the
597.23 house and visit Mrs. Poole's patient, and my
597.24 wife! -- You shall see what sort of a being I
597.25 was cheated into espousing, and judge whether
598.01 or not I had a right to break the compact, and
598.02 seek sympathy with something at least human.
598.03 This girl," he continued, looking at me, "knew
598.04 no more than you, Wood, of the disgusting
598.05 secret: she thought all was fair and legal; and
598.06 never dreamt she was going to be entrapped
598.07 into a feigned union with a defrauded wretch,
598.08 already bound to a bad, mad, and embruted
598.09 partner! Come, all of you, follow!"
598.10 Still holding me fast, he left the church:
598.11 the three gentlemen came after. At the front
598.12 door of the hall we found the carriage.
598.13 "Take it back to the coach-house, John,"
598.14 said Mr. Rochester, coolly; "it will not be
598.15 wanted to-day."
598.16 At our entrance, Mrs. Fairfax, Adele,
598.17 Sophie, Leah, advanced to meet and greet us.
598.18 "To the right about -- every soul!" cried
598.19 the master: "away with your congratulations!
598.20 Who wants them? -- Not I! -- they are fifteen
598.21 years too late!"
598.22 He passed on and ascended the stairs, still
598.23 holding my hand, and still beckoning the
598.24 gentlemen to follow him; which they did.
598.25 We mounted the first staircase, passed up the
599.01 gallery, proceeded to the third story: the low,
599.02 black door, opened by Mr. Rochester's master
599.03 key, admitted us to the tapestried room, with
599.04 its great bed, and its pictorial cabinet.
599.05 "You know this place, Mason," said our
599.06 guide; "she bit and stabbed you here."
599.07 He lifted the hangings from the wall, un-
599.08 covering the second door: this, too, he opened.
599.09 In a room without a window, there burnt a
599.10 fire, guarded by a high and strong fender, and a
599.11 lamp suspended from the ceiling by a chain.
599.12 Grace Poole bent over the fire, apparently
599.13 cooking something in a saucepan. In the
599.14 deep shade, at the further end of the room, a
599.15 figure ran backwards and forwards. What it
599.16 was, whether beast or human being, one could

599.17 not, at first sight, tell: it grovelled, seemingly
599.18 on all fours; it snatched and growled like some
599.19 strange wild animal: but it was covered with
599.20 clothing; and a quantity of dark, grizzled hair,
599.21 wild as a mane, hid its head and face.
599.22 "Good-morning, Mrs. Poole!" said Mr.
599.23 Rochester. "How are you? and how is your
599.24 charge to-day?"
599.25 "We're tolerable, sir, I thank you," replied
600.01 Grace, lifting the boiling mess carefully on to
600.02 the hob: "rather snappish, but not 'rageous."
600.03 A fierce cry seemed to give the lie to her
600.04 favourable report: the clothed hyena rose up,
600.05 and stood tall on its hind feet.
600.06 "Ah, sir, she sees you!" exclaimed Grace:
600.07 "you'd better not stay."
600.08 "Only a few moments, Grace: you must
600.09 allow me a few moments."
600.10 "Take care then, sir! -- for God's sake, take
600.11 care!"
600.12 The maniac bellowed: she parted her shaggy
600.13 locks from her visage, and gazed wildly at her
600.14 visitors. I recognised well that purple face, --
600.15 those bloated features. Mrs. Poole advanced.
600.16 "Keep out of the way," said Mr. Rochester,
600.17 thrusting her aside: "she has no knife now, I
600.18 suppose? and I'm on my guard."
600.19 "One never knows what she has, sir: she is
600.20 so cunning: it is not in mortal discretion to
600.21 fathom her craft."
600.22 "We had better leave her," whispered
600.23 Mason.
600.24 "Go to the devil!" was his brother-in-law's
600.25 recommendation.
601.01 "'Ware!" cried Grace. The three gentle-
601.02 men retreated simultaneously. Mr. Rochester
601.03 flung me behind him: the lunatic sprang and
601.04 grappled his throat viciously, and laid her teeth
601.05 to his cheek: they struggled. She was a big
601.06 woman, in stature almost equalling her hus-
601.07 band, and corpulent besides: she showed virile
601.08 force in the contest -- more than once she
601.09 almost throttled him, athletic as he was. He
601.10 could have settled her with a well-planted
601.11 blow; but he would not strike: he would only
601.12 wrestle. At last he mastered her arms;
601.13 Grace Poole gave him a cord, and he pinioned
601.14 them behind her: with more rope, which was
601.15 at hand, he bound her to a chair. The opera-
601.16 tion was performed amidst the fiercest yells,
601.17 and the most convulsive plunges. Mr.
601.18 Rochester then turned to the spectators: he
601.19 looked at them with a smile both acrid and
601.20 desolate.
601.21 "That is my wife," said he. "Such is the
601.22 sole conjugal embrace I am ever to know --
601.23 such are the endearments which are to solace
601.24 my leisure hours! And this is what I wished
601.25 to have /laying his hand on my shoulder/:
602.01 this young girl, who stands so grave and quiet
602.02 at the mouth of hell, looking collectedly at the
602.03 gambols of a demon. I wanted her just as a
602.04 change after that fierce ragout. Wood and
602.05 Briggs, look at the difference! Compare these
602.06 these clear eyes with the red balls yonder --
602.07 this face with that mask -- this form with that
602.08 bulk; then judge me, priest of the Gospel and
602.09 man of the law, and remember, with what judg-
602.10 ment ye judge ye shall be judged! Off with
602.11 you now. I must shut up my prize."
602.12 We all withdrew. Mr. Rochester stayed a
602.13 moment behind us, to give some further
602.14 orders to Grace Poole. The solicitor addressed
602.15 me as he descended the stair.
602.16 "You, madam," said he, "are cleared from
602.17 all blame: your uncle will be glad to hear it
602.18 -- if, indeed, be should he still living -- when
602.19 Mr. Mason returns to Madeira."
602.20 "My uncle! what of him? Do you know
602.21 him?"
602.22 "Mr. Mason does: Mr. Eyre has been
602.23 the Funchal correspondent of his house for
602.24 some years. When your uncle received your
602.25 letter intimating the contemplating union be-
603.01 tween yourself and Mr. Rochester, Mr.
603.02 Mason, who was staying at Madeira to recruit
603.03 his health, on his way back to Jamaica, hap-
603.04 pened to be with him. Mr. Eyre mentioned
603.05 the intelligence; for he knew that my client
603.06 here was acquainted with a gentleman of the
603.07 name of Rochester. Mr. Mason, astonished
603.08 and distressed as you may suppose, revealed
603.09 the real state of matters. Your uncle, I am
603.10 sorry to say, is now on a sick bed; from
603.11 which, considering the nature of his disease
603.12 -- decline -- and the stage it has reached, it
603.13 is unlikely he will ever rise. He could not
603.14 then hasten to England himself, to extricate
603.15 you from the snare into which you had fallen,
603.16 but he implored Mr. Mason to lose no time in
603.17 taking steps to prevent the false marriage.
603.18 He referred him to me for assistance. I used
603.19 all despatch, and am thankful I was not too
603.20 late: as you, doubtless, must be also. Were I
603.21 not morally certain that your uncle will be
603.22 dead ere you reach Madeira, I would advise
603.23 you to accompany Mr. Mason back: but as it
603.24 is, I think you had better remain in England
603.25 till you can hear further, either from or of Mr.
604.01 Eyre. Have we anything else to stay for?"
604.02 he inquired of Mr. Mason.

604.03 "No, no -- let us be gone," was the anxious
604.04 reply; and without waiting to take leave of
604.05 Mr. Rochester, they made their exit at the
604.06 hall door. The clergyman stayed to exchange
604.07 a few sentences, either of admonition or re-
604.08 proof, with his haughty parishioner: this duty
604.09 done, he too departed.
604.10 I heard him go as I stood at the half open
604.11 door of my own room, to which I had now
604.12 withdrawn. The house cleared, I shut myself
604.13 in, fastened the bolt that none might intrude,
604.14 and proceeded -- not to weep, not to mourn, I
604.15 was yet too calm for that, but -- mechanically to
604.16 take off the wedding dress, and replace it by the
604.17 stuff gown I had worn yesterday, as I thought,
604.18 for the last time. I then sat down: I felt
604.19 weak and tired. I leaned my arms on a
604.20 table, and my head dropped on them. And
604.21 now I thought: till now I had only heard,
604.22 seen, moved -- followed up and down where
604.23 I was led or dragged -- watched event rush on
604.24 event, disclosure open beyond disclosure: but
604.25 now, I thought.
605.01 The morning had been a quiet morning
605.02 enough -- all except the brief scene with the
605.03 lunatic: the transaction in the church had not
605.04 been noisy; there was no explosion of passion,
605.05 no loud altercation, no dispute, no defiance or
605.06 challenge, no tears, no sobs: a few words had
605.07 been spoken, a calmly pronounced objection
605.08 to the marriage made; some stern, short ques-
605.09 tions put by Mr. Rochester; answers, expla-
605.10 nations given, evidence adduced; an open ad-
605.11 mission of the truth had been uttered by my
605.12 master; then the living proof had been seen;
605.13 the intruders were gone, and all was over.
605.14 I was in my own room as usual -- just myself,
605.15 without obvious change: nothing had smitten
605.16 me, or scathed me, or maimed me. And yet,
605.17 where was the Jane Eyre of yesterday? -- where
605.18 was her life? -- where were her prospects?
605.19 Jane Eyre, who had been an ardent, ex-
605.20 pectant woman -- almost a bride -- was a cold,
605.21 solitary girl again: her life was pale; her pros-
605.22 pects were desolate. A Christmas frost had
605.23 come at midsummer; a white December storm
605.24 had whirled over June; ice glazed the ripe
605.25 apples, drifts crushed the blowing roses; on
606.01 hay-field and corn-field lay a frozen shroud:
606.02 lanes which last night blushed full of flowers,
606.03 to-day were pathless with untrodden snow;
606.04 and the woods, which twelve hours since waved
606.05 leafy and fragrant as groves between the
606.06 tropics, now spread, waste, wild, and white
606.07 as pine-forests in wintry Norway. My hopes
606.08 were all dead -- struck with a subtle doom,
606.09 such as, in one night, fell on all the first-born
606.10 in the land of Egypt. I looked on my che-
606.11 rished wishes, yesterday so blooming and
606.12 glowing; they lay stark, chill, livid corpses
606.13 that could never revive. I looked at my love:
606.14 that feeling which was my master's -- which he
606.15 had created; it shivered in my heart, like a
606.16 suffering child in a cold cradle; sickness and
606.17 anguish had seized it; it could not seek Mr.
606.18 Rochester's arms -- it could not derive warmth
606.19 from his breast. Oh, never more could it turn
606.20 to him; for faith was blighted -- confidence
606.21 destroyed! Mr. Rochester was not to me
606.22 what he had been; for he was not what I
606.23 had thought him. I would not ascribe vice
606.24 to him; I would not say he had betrayed me:
606.25 but the attribute of stainless truth was gone
607.01 from his idea; and from his presence I must
607.02 go: that I perceived well. When -- how --
607.03 whither, I could not yet discern: but he himself
607.04 I doubted not, would hurry me from Thorn-
607.05 field. Real affection, it seemed, he could not
607.06 have for me; it had been only fitful passion:
607.07 that was balked; he would want me no more.
607.08 I should fear even to cross his path now: my
607.09 view must be hateful to him. Oh, how blind
607.10 had been my eyes! How weak my conduct!
607.11 My eyes were covered and closed: eddying
607.12 darkness seemed to swim round me, and re-
607.13 flection came in as black and confused a flow.
607.14 Self-abandoned, relaxed, and effortless, I seemed
607.15 to have laid me down in the dried-up bed of
607.16 a great river; I heard a flood loosened in
607.17 remote mountains, and felt the torrent come:
607.18 to rise I had no will, to flee I had no
607.19 strength. I lay faint; longing to be dead.
607.20 One idea only still throbbed life-like within
607.21 me -- a remembrance of God: it begot an un-
607.22 uttered prayer: these words went wandering
607.23 up and down in my rayless mind, as something
607.24 that should be whispered; but no energy was
607.25 found to express them: --
608.01 "Be not far from me, for trouble is near:
608.02 there is none to help."
608.03 It was near: and as I had lifted no peti-
608.04 tion to Heaven to avert it -- as I had neither
608.05 joined my hands, nor bent my knees, nor
608.06 moved my lips -- it came: in full, heavy swing
608.07 the torrent poured over me. The whole con-
608.08 sciousness of my life lorn, my love lost, my
608.09 hope quenched, my faith death-struck, swayed
608.10 full and mighty above me in one sullen mass.
608.11 That bitter hour cannot be described: in truth,
608.12 "the waters came into my soul; I sank in deep
608.13 mire: I felt no standing; I came into deep

608.14 waters; the floods overflowed me."
608.15 [END OF VOL. 2]
609.01 Vol. 3 Chapter 1]
609.02 Some time in the afternoon I raised my head, and
609.03 looking round and seeing the western sun gilding
609.04 the sign of its decline on the wall, I asked, "What
609.05 am I to do?"
609.06 But the answer my mind gave -- "Leave Thorn-
609.07 field at once" -- was so prompt, so dread, that I
609.08 stopped my ears: I said, I could not bear such
609.09 words now. "That I am not Edward Rochester's
609.10 bride, is the least part of my woe," I alleged:
609.11 "that I have wakened out of most glorious dreams,
609.12 and found them all void and vain, is a horror I
609.13 could bear and master; but that I must leave him
609.14 decidedly, instantly, entirely, is intolerable. I
609.15 cannot do it."
609.16 But, then, a voice within me averred that I
609.17 could do it; and foretold that I should do it. I
609.18 wrestled with my own resolution: I wanted to be
610.01 weak that I might avoid the awful passage of further
610.02 suffering I saw laid out for me; and conscience,
610.03 turned tyrant, held passion by the throat, told her,
610.04 tauntingly, she had yet but dipped her dainty
610.05 foot in the slough, and swore that with that arm
610.06 of iron, he would thrust her down to unsounded
610.07 depths of agony.
610.08 "Let me be torn away, then!" I cried, "Let
610.09 another help me!"
610.10 "No; you shall tear yourself away, none shall
610.11 help you: you shall, yourself, pluck out your
610.12 right eye; yourself cut off your right hand: your
610.13 heart shall be the victim; and you, the priest, to
610.14 transfix it."
610.15 I rose up suddenly, terror-struck at the solitude
610.16 which so ruthless a judge haunted, -- at the silence
610.17 which so awful a voice filled. My head swam as I
610.18 stood erect: I perceived that I was sickening
610.19 from excitement and inanition: neither meat nor
610.20 drink had passed my lips that day, for I had taken
610.21 no breakfast. And, with a strange pang, I now
610.22 reflected that, long as I had been shut up here, no
610.23 message had been sent to ask how I was, or to
610.24 invite me to come down: not even little Adele
610.25 had tapped at the door; not even Mrs. Fairfax
610.26 had sought me. "Friends always forget those
610.27 whom fortune forsakes," I murmured, as I un-
610.28 drew the bolt and passed out. I stumbled over
611.01 an obstacle: my head was still dizzy, my sight
611.02 was dim, and my limbs were feeble. I could not
611.03 soon recover myself. I fell, but not on to the
611.04 ground: an out-stretched arm caught me; I looked
611.05 up -- I was supported by Mr. Rochester, who sat
611.06 in a chair across my chamber threshold.
611.07 "You come out at last," he said. "Well, I
611.08 have been waiting for you long, and listening: yet
611.09 not one movement have I heard, nor one sob:
611.10 five minutes more of that death-like hush, and I
611.11 should have forced the lock like a burglar. So,
611.12 you shun me? -- you shut yourself up and grieve
611.13 alone! I would rather you had come and up-
611.14 braided me with vehemence. You are passionate:
611.15 I expected a scene of some kind. I was prepared
611.16 for the hot rain of tears; only I wanted them to be
611.17 shed on my breast: now a senseless floor has
611.18 received them, or your drenched handkerchief.
611.19 But I err: you have not wept at all! I see a
611.20 white cheek and a faded eye, but no trace of tears.
611.21 I suppose, then, your heart has been weeping
611.22 blood!
611.23 "Well, Jane; not a word of reproach? No-
611.24 thing bitter -- nothing poignant? Nothing to cut
611.25 a feeling or sting a passion? You sit quietly
611.26 where I have placed you, and regard me with a
611.27 weary, passive look.
611.28 "Jane, I never meant to wound you thus. If
612.01 the man who had but one little ewe lamb that was
612.02 dear to him as a daughter, that ate of his bread
612.03 and drank of his cup, and lay in his bosom, had
612.04 by some mistake slaughtered it at the shambles,
612.05 he would not have rued his bloody blunder more
612.06 than I now rue mine. Will you ever forgive
612.07 me?"
612.08 Reader! -- I forgave him at the moment, and on
612.09 the spot. There was such deep remorse in his
612.10 eye, such true pity in his tone, such manly energy
612.11 in his manner; and, besides, there was such un-
612.12 changed love in his whole look and mein -- I for-
612.13 gave him all: yet not in words, not outwardly;
612.14 only at my heart's core.
612.15 "You know I am a scoundrel, Jane?" ere long
612.16 he inquired wistfully -- wondering, I suppose, at my
612.17 continued silence and tameness: the result rather
612.18 of weakness than of will.
612.19 "Yes, sir."
612.20 "Then tell me so roundly and sharply -- don't
612.21 spare me."
612.22 "I cannot: I am tired and sick. I want some
612.23 water." He heaved a sort of shuddering sigh and
612.24 taking me in his arms, carried me down stairs.
612.25 At first I did not know to what room he had borne
612.26 me; all was cloudy to my glazed sight: presently
612.27 I felt the reviving warmth of a fire; for, summer
612.28 as it was, I had become icy cold in my chamber.
613.01 He put wine to my lips; I tasted it and revived;
613.02 then I ate something he offered me, and was soon
613.03 myself. I was in the library -- sitting in his chair
613.04 -- he was quite near. "If I could go out of life
613.05 now, without too sharp a pang, it would be well
613.06 for me," I thought; "then I should not have to
613.07 make the effort of cracking my heart-strings in
613.08 rending them from among Mr. Rochester's. I
613.09 must leave him, it appears. I do not want to
613.10 leave him -- I cannot leave him."
613.11 "How are you now, Jane?"
613.12 "Much better, sir: I shall be well soon."
613.13 "Taste the wine again, Jane."
613.14 I obeyed him; then he put the glass on the
613.15 table, stood before me, and looked at me atten-
613.16 tively. Suddenly he turned away, with an inarti-
613.17 culate exclamation, full of passionate emotion of
613.18 some kind: he walked fast through the room and
613.19 came back: he stooped towards me as if to kiss
613.20 me; but I remembered caresses were now forbid-
613.21 den. I turned my face away, and put his aside.
613.22 "What! -- How is this?" he exclaimed hastily,
613.23 "Oh, I know! you won't kiss the husband of
613.24 Bertha Mason? You consider my arms filled, and
613.25 my embraces appropriated?"
613.26 "At any rate, there is neither room nor claim
613.27 for me, sir."
613.28 "Why, Jane? I will spare you the trouble of
614.01 much talking: I will answer for you -- because I
614.02 have a wife already, you would reply. -- I guess
614.03 rightly?"
614.04 "Yes."
614.05 "If you think so, you must have a strange opi-
614.06 nion of me: you must regard me as a plotting
614.07 profligate -- a base and low rake who has been
614.08 simulating disinterested love in order to draw you
614.09 into a snare deliberately laid, and strip you of
614.10 honour, and rob you of self-respect. What do you
614.11 say to that? I see you can say nothing: in the
614.12 first place, you are faint, still, and have enough to
614.13 do to draw your breath; in the second place, you
614.14 cannot yet accustom yourself to accuse and revile
614.15 me; and, besides, the flood-gates of tears are
614.16 opened, and they would rush out if you spoke
614.17 much; and you have no desire to expostulate, to
614.18 upbraid, to make a scene: you are thinking how to
614.19 act -- talking, you consider, is of no use. I know
614.20 you -- I am on my guard."
614.21 "Sir, I do not wish to act against you," I said;
614.22 and my unsteady voice warned me to curtail my
614.23 sentence.
614.24 "Not in your sense of the word but in mine,
614.25 you are scheming to destroy me. You have as
614.26 good as said that I am a married man -- as a mar-
614.27 ried man you will shun me, keep out of my way:
614.28 just now you have refused to kiss me. You intend
615.01 to make yourself a complete stranger to me; to
615.02 live under this roof only as Adele's governess: if
615.03 ever I say a friendly word to you; if ever a
615.04 friendly feeling inclines you again to me, you will
615.05 say, -- `That man had nearly made me his mistress:
615.06 I must be ice and rock to him;` and ice and rock
615.07 you will accordingly become."
615.08 I cleared and steadied my voice to reply: "All
615.09 is changed about me, sir; I must change too --
615.10 there is no doubt of that; and, to avoid fluctua-
615.11 tions of feeling, and continual combats with recol-
615.12 lections and associations, there is only one way --
615.13 Adele must have a new governess, sir."
615.14 "Oh, Adele will go to school -- I have settled
615.15 that already: nor do I mean to torment you with
615.16 the hideous associations and recollections of
615.17 Thornfield Hall -- this accursed place -- this tent of
615.18 Achan -- this insolent vault, offering the ghastli-
615.19 ness of living death to the light of the open sky --
615.20 this narrow stone hell, with its one real fiend,
615.21 worse than a legion of such as we imagine. -- Jane,
615.22 you shall not stay here, nor will I. I was wrong
615.23 ever to bring you to Thornfield Hall, knowing as
615.24 I did how it was haunted. I charged them to con-
615.25 ceal from you, before I ever saw you, all know-
615.26 ledge of the curse of the place; merely because I
615.27 feared Adele never would have a governess to stay
615.28 if she knew with what inmate she was housed, and
616.01 my plans would not permit me to remove the
616.02 maniac elsewhere -- though I possess an old house,
616.03 Ferndean Manor, even more retired and hidden
616.04 than this, where I could have lodged her safely
616.05 enough, had not a scruple about the unhealthiness
616.06 of the situation, in the heart of a wood, made my
616.07 conscience recoil from the arrangement. Probably
616.08 those damp walls would soon have eased me of
616.09 her charge: but to each villain his own vice; and
616.10 mine is not a tendency to indirect assassination,
616.11 even of what I most hate.
616.12 "Concealing the mad-woman's neighbourhood
616.13 from you, however, was something like covering a
616.14 child with a cloak, and laying it down near a upas-
616.15 tree: that demon's vicinage is poisoned, and always
616.16 was. But I'll shut up Thornfield Hall: I'll nail
616.17 up the front door, and board the lower windows;
616.18 I'll give Mrs. Poole two hundred a year to live
616.19 here with my wife, as you term that fearful hag:
616.20 Grace will do much for money, and she shall have
616.21 her son, the keeper at Grimsby Retreat, to bear
616.22 her company and be at hand to give her aid in the
616.23 paroxysms, when my wife is prompted by her
616.24 familiar to burn people in their beds at night, to
616.25 stab them, to bite their flesh from their bones, and
616.26 so on" --
616.27 "Sir," I interrupted him, "you are inexorable
616.28 for that unfortunate lady: you speak of her with
617.01 hate -- with vindictive antipathy. It is cruel -- she
617.02 cannot help being mad."
617.03 "Jane, my little darling, /so I will call you, for
617.04 so you are/, you don't know what you are talking
617.05 about; you misjudge me again: it is not because
617.06 she is mad I hate her. If you were mad, do you

617.07 think I should hate you?"
617.08 "I do indeed, sir."
617.09 "Then you are mistaken, and you know nothing
617.10 about me, and nothing about the sort of love of
617.11 which I am capable. Every atom of your flesh is
617.12 as dear to me as my own: in pain and sickness it
617.13 would still be dear. Your mind is my treasure,
617.14 and if it were broken, it would be my treasure still:
617.15 if you raved, my arms should confine you, and not
617.16 a straight waistcoat -- your grasp, even in fury, would
617.17 have a charm for me: if you flew at me as wildly
617.18 as that woman did this morning, I should receive
617.19 you in an embrace, at least as fond as it would be
617.20 restrictive. I should not shrink from you with
617.21 disgust as I did from her: in your quiet moments
617.22 you should have no watcher and no nurse but
617.23 me; and I could hang over you with untiring
617.24 tenderness, though you gave me no smile in return;
617.25 and never weary of gazing into your eyes, though
617.26 they had no longer a ray of recognition for me. --
617.27 But why do I follow that train of ideas? I was
617.28 talking of removing you from Thornfield. All,
618.01 you know, is prepared for prompt departure: to--
618.02 morrow you shall go. I only ask you to endure
618.03 one more night under this roof, Jane; and then,
618.04 farewell to its miseries and terrors for ever! I
618.05 have a place to repair to, which will be a secure
618.06 sanctuary from hateful reminiscences, from un-
618.07 welcome intrusion -- even from falsehood and
618.08 slander."
618.09 "And take Adele with you, sir," I interrupted;
618.10 "she will be a companion for you."
618.11 "What do you mean, Jane? I told you I
618.12 would send Adele to school: and what do I want
618.13 with a child for a companion? and not my own
618.14 child, -- a French dancer's bastard. Why do you
618.15 importune me about her? I say, why do you
618.16 assign Adele to me for a companion?"
618.17 "You spoke of a retirement, sir; and retirement
618.18 and solitude are dull: too dull for you."
618.19 "Solitude! solitude!" he reiterated, with irri-
618.20 tation. "I see I must come to an explanation.
618.21 I don't know what sphynx-like expression is form-
618.22 ing in your countenance. You are to share my
618.23 solitude. Do you understand?"
618.24 I shook my head: it required a degree of cou-
618.25 rage, excited as he was becoming, even to risk
618.26 that mute sign of dissent. He had been walking
618.27 fast about the room, and he stopped, as if suddenly
618.28 rooted to one spot. He looked at me long and
619.01 hard: I turned my eyes from him, fixed them on
619.02 the fire, and tried to assume and maintain a quiet,
619.03 collected aspect.
619.04 "Now for the hitch in Jane's character," he
619.05 said at last, speaking more calmly than from his
619.06 look I had expected him to speak. "The reel of
619.07 silk has run smoothly enough so far; but I always
619.08 knew there would come a knot and a puzzle: here
619.09 it is. Now for vexation, and exasperation, and
619.10 endless trouble! By God! I long to exert a frac-
619.11 tion of Samson's strength, and break the entan-
619.12 glement like tow!"
619.13 He recommenced his walk: but soon again
619.14 stopped, and this time just before me.
619.15 "Jane! will you hear reason?" /he stooped and
619.16 approached his lips to my ear/ "because, if you
619.17 won't, I'll try violence." His voice was hoarse;
619.18 his look that of a man who is just about to burst
619.19 an insufferable bond and plunge headlong into
619.20 wild licence. I saw that in another moment, and
619.21 with one impetus of frenzy more, I should be able
619.22 to do nothing with him. The present -- the pass-
619.23 ing second of time -- was all I had in which to
619.24 control and restrain him: a movement of repulsion,
619.25 flight, fear, would have sealed my doom, -- and
619.26 his. But I was not afraid: not in the least. I
619.27 felt an inward power, a sense of influence, which
619.28 supported me. The crisis was perilous; but not
620.01 without its charm: such as the Indian, perhaps,
620.02 feels when he slips over the rapid in his canoe.
620.03 I took hold of his clenched hand; loosened the
620.04 contorted fingers; and said to him, soothingly, --
620.05 "Sit down; I'll talk to you as long as you like,
620.06 and hear all you have to say, whether reasonable
620.07 or unreasonable."
620.08 He sat down: but he did not get leave to speak
620.09 directly. I had been struggling with tears for
620.10 some time: I had taken great pains to repress
620.11 them, because I knew he would not like to see
620.12 me weep. Now, however, I considered it well to
620.13 let them flow as freely and as long as they liked.
620.14 If the flood annoyed him, so much the better.
620.15 So I gave way and cried heartily.
620.16 Soon I heard him earnestly entreating me to be
620.17 composed. I said I could not while he was in
620.18 such a passion.
620.19 "But I am not angry, Jane: I only love you
620.20 too well; and you had steeled your little pale
620.21 face with such a resolute, frozen look, I could
620.22 not endure it. Hush, now, and wipe your
620.23 eyes."
620.24 His softened voice announced that he was sub-
620.25 dued; so I, in my turn, became calm. Now he
620.26 made an effort to rest his head on my shoulder:
620.27 but I would not permit it. Then he would draw
620.28 me to him: no.
621.01 "Jane! Jane!" he said -- in such an accent of
621.02 bitter sadness, it thrilled along every nerve I had;
621.03 "you don't love me, then? It was only my
621.04 station, and the rank of my wife, that you valued?
621.05 Now that you think me disqualified to become

621.06 your husband, you recoil from my touch as if I
621.07 were some toad or ape."
621.08 These words cut me: yet what could I do or
621.09 say? I ought probably to have done or said
621.10 nothing: but I was so tortured by a sense of
621.11 remorse at thus hurting his feelings, I could
621.12 not control the wish to drop balm where I had
621.13 wounded.
621.14 "I do love you," I said, "more than ever: but
621.15 I must not show or indulge the feeling; and this
621.16 is the last time I must express it."
621.17 "The last time, Jane! What! do you think
621.18 you can live with me, and see me daily, and yet,
621.19 if you still love me, be always cold and dis-
621.20 tant?"
621.21 "No, sir; that I am certain I could not; and
621.22 therefore I see there is but one way: but you will
621.23 be furious if I mention it."
621.24 "Oh, mention it! If I storm, you have the art
621.25 of weeping."
621.26 "Mr. Rochester, I must leave you."
621.27 "For how long, Jane? For a few minutes,
621.28 while you smooth your hair -- which is somewhat
622.01 dishevelled; and bathe your face -- which looks
622.02 feverish?"
622.03 "I must leave Adele and Thornfield. I must
622.04 part with you for my whole life: I must begin a
622.05 new existence amongst strange faces and strange
622.06 scenes."
622.07 "Of course: I told you you should. I pass
622.08 over the madness about parting from me. You
622.09 mean you must become a part of me. As to the
622.10 new existence, it is all right: you shall yet be my
622.11 wife: I am not married. You shall be Mrs.
622.12 Rochester -- both virtually and nominally. I shall
622.13 keep only to you so long as you and I live. You
622.14 shall go to a place I have in the south of France:
622.15 a white-walled villa on the shores of the Mediter-
622.16 ranean. There you shall live a happy, and
622.17 guarded, and most innocent life. Never fear that
622.18 I wish to lure you into error -- to make you my
622.19 mistress. Why do you shake your head? Jane,
622.20 you must be reasonable; or in truth I shall again
622.21 become frantic."
622.22 His voice and hand quivered; his large nostrils
622.23 dilated; his eye blazed: still, I dared to speak: --
622.24 "Sir, your wife is living: that is a fact ac-
622.25 knowledged this morning by yourself. If I lived
622.26 with you as you desire, I should then be your
622.27 mistress: to say otherwise is sophistical -- is
622.28 false."
623.01 "Jane, I am not a gentle-tempered man -- you
623.02 forget that: I am not long-enduring; I am not
623.03 cool and dispassionate. Out of pity to me and
623.04 yourself, put your finger on my pulse, feel how it
623.05 throbs, and -- beware!"
623.06 He bared his wrist, and offered it to me: the
623.07 blood was forsaking his cheek and lips, they were
623.08 growing livid; I was distressed on all hands. To
623.09 agitate him thus deeply, by a resistance he so
623.10 abhorred, was cruel: to yield was out of the ques-
623.11 tion. I did what human beings do instinctively
623.12 when they are driven to utter extremity -- looked
623.13 for aid to one higher than man: the words "God
623.14 help me!" burst involuntarily from my lips.
623.15 "I am a fool!" cried Mr. Rochester, suddenly.
623.16 "I keep telling her I am not married, and do not
623.17 explain to her why. I forget she knows nothing
623.18 of the character of that woman, or of the circum-
623.19 stances attending my infernal union with her.
623.20 Oh, I am certain Jane will agree with me in
623.21 opinion, when she knows all that I know! Just
623.22 put your hand in mine, Janet -- that I may have
623.23 the evidence of touch as well as sight, to prove
623.24 you are near me -- and I will in a few words show
623.25 you the real state of the case. Can you listen to
623.26 me?"
623.27 "Yes, sir; for hours if you will."
623.28 "I ask only minutes. Jane, did you ever hear,
624.01 or know, that I was not the eldest son of my house:
624.02 that I had once a brother older than I?"
624.03 "I remember Mrs. Fairfax told me so once."
624.04 "And did you ever hear that my father was an
624.05 avaricious, grasping man?"
624.06 "I have understood something to that effect."
624.07 "Well, Jane, being so, it was his resolution to
624.08 keep the property together; he could not bear
624.09 the idea of dividing his estate and leaving me a
624.10 fair portion: all, he resolved, should go to my
624.11 brother, Russell. Yet as little could he endure
624.12 that a son of his should be a poor man. I must
624.13 be provided for by a wealthy marriage. He sought
624.14 me a partner betimes. Mr. Mason, a West India
624.15 planter and merchant, was his old acquaintance.
624.16 He was certain his possessions were real and vast:
624.17 he made inquiries. Mr. Mason, he found, had a
624.18 son and daughter; and he learned from him that
624.19 he could and would give the latter a fortune of
624.20 thirty thousand pounds: that sufficed. When I
624.21 left college, I was sent out to Jamaica, to espouse
624.22 a bride already courted for me. My father said
624.23 nothing about her money; but he told me Miss
624.24 Mason was the boast of Spanish Town for her
624.25 beauty: and this was no lie. I found her a fine
624.26 woman, in the style of Blanche Ingram; tall, dark,
624.27 and majestic. Her family wished to secure me,
624.28 because I was of a good race; and so did she.
625.01 They showed her to me in parties, splendidly
625.02 dressed. I seldom saw her alone, and had very
625.03 little private conversation with her. She flattered
625.04 me, and lavishly displayed for my pleasure her

625.05 charms and accomplishments. All the men in her
625.06 circle seemed to admire her and envy me. I was
625.07 dazzled, stimulated: my senses were excited; and
625.08 being ignorant, raw, and inexperienced, I thought
625.09 I loved her. There is no folly so besotted that
625.10 the idiotic rivalries of society, the prurience, the
625.11 rashness, the blindness of youth, will not hurry a
625.12 man to its commission. Her relatives encouraged
625.13 me; competitors piqued me; she allured me: a
625.14 marriage was achieved almost before I knew where
625.15 I was. Oh, I have no respect for myself when I
625.16 think of that act! -- an agony of inward contempt
625.17 masters me. I never loved, I never esteemed, I
625.18 did not even know her. I was not sure of the
625.19 existence of one virtue in her nature: I had
625.20 marked neither modesty, nor benevolence, nor
625.21 candour, nor refinement in her mind or manners --
625.22 and, I married her: -- gross, grovelling, mole-eyed
625.23 blockhead that I was! with less sin I might have
625.24 -- but let me remember to whom I am speaking.
625.25 "My bride's mother I had never seen: I under-
625.26 stood she was dead. The honey-moon over, I
625.27 learned my mistake; she was only mad, and shut
625.28 up in a lunatic asylum. There was a younger
626.01 brother, too; a complete dumb idiot. The elder
626.02 one, whom you have seen / and whom I cannot
626.03 hate, whilst I abhor all his kindred, because he has
626.04 some grains of affection in his feeble mind; shown
626.05 in the continued interest he takes in his wretched
626.06 sister, and also in a dog-like attachment he once
626.07 bore me/, will probably be in the same state one
626.08 day. My father, and my brother Russell, knew
626.09 all this; but they thought only of the thirty thou-
626.10 sand pounds, and joined in the plot against me.
626.11 "These were vile discoveries; but, except for
626.12 the treachery of concealment, I should have made
626.13 them no subject of reproach to my wife: even
626.14 when I found her nature wholly alien to mine,
626.15 her tastes obnoxious to me; her cast of mind com-
626.16 mon, low, narrow, and singularly incapable of
626.17 being led to anything higher, expanded to any-
626.18 thing larger -- when I found that I could not pass
626.19 a single evening, nor even a single hour of the
626.20 day with her in comfort; that kindly conversation
626.21 could not be sustained between us, because, what-
626.22 ever topic I started, immediately received from
626.23 her a turn at once coarse and trite, perverse and
626.24 imbecile -- when I perceived that I should never
626.25 have a quiet or settle household, because no ser-
626.26 vant would bear the continued outbreaks of her
626.27 violent and unreasonable temper, or the vexations
626.28 of her absurd, contradictory, exacting orders --
627.01 even then I restrained myself: I eschewed up-
627.02 braiding, I curtailed remonstrance; I tried to
627.03 devour my repentance and disgust in secret; I
627.04 repressed the deep antipathy I felt.
627.05 "Jane, I will not trouble you with abominable
627.06 details: some strong words shall express what I
627.07 have to say. I lived with that woman up-stairs
627.08 four years, and before that time she had tried me
627.09 indeed: her character ripened and developed with
627.10 frightful rapidity; her vices sprang up fast and
627.11 rank: they were so strong, only cruelty could
627.12 check them; and I would not use cruelty. What a
627.13 pigmy intellect she had -- and what giant propensi-
627.14 ties! How fearful were the curses those propen-
627.15 sities entailed on me! Bertha Mason, -- the true
627.16 daughter of an infamous mother, -- dragged me
627.17 through all the hideous and degrading agonies
627.18 which must attend a man bound to a wife at once
627.19 intemperate and unchaste.
627.20 "My brother in the interval was dead; and at
627.21 the end of the four years my father died too. I
627.22 was rich enough now -- yet poor to hideous indi-
627.23 gence: a nature the most gross, impure, depraved
627.24 I ever saw, was associated with mine, and called
627.25 by the law and by society a part of me. And I
627.26 could not rid myself of it by any legal proceedings:
627.27 for the doctors now discovered that my wife was
627.28 mad -- her excesses had prematurely developed
628.01 the germs of insanity: -- Jane, you don't like my
628.02 narrative; you look almost sick -- shall I defer the
628.03 rest to another day?"
628.04 "No, sir, finish it now: I pity you -- I do
628.05 earnestly pity you."
628.06 "Pity, Jane, from some people is a noxious and
628.07 insulting sort of tribute, which one is justified in
628.08 hurling back in the teeth of those who offer it; but
628.09 that is the sort of pity native to callous, selfish hearts:
628.10 it is a hybrid, egotistical pain at hearing of woes,
628.11 crossed with ignorant contempt for those who have
628.12 endured them. But that is not your pity, Jane: it
628.13 is not the feeling of which your whole face is full
628.14 at this moment -- with which your eyes are now
628.15 almost overflowing -- with which your heart is
628.16 heaving -- with which your hand is trembling in
628.17 mine. Your pity, my darling, is the suffering
628.18 mother of love: its anguish is the very natal pang
628.19 of the divine passion. I accept it, Jane; let the
628.20 daughter have free advent -- my arms wait to
628.21 receive her."
628.22 "Now, sir, proceed: what did you do when
628.23 you found she was mad?"
628.24 "Jane -- I approached the verge of despair: a
628.25 remnant of self-respect was all that intervened
628.26 between me and the gulf. In the eyes of the
628.27 world, I was doubtless covered with grimy dis-
628.28 honour: but I resolved to be clean in my own
629.01 sight -- and to the last I repudiated the contami-
629.02 nation of her crimes, and wrenched myself from
629.03 connexion with her mental defects. Still, society

629.04 associated my name and person with hers; I yet
629.05 saw her and heard her daily: something of her
629.06 breath /faugh!/ mixed with the air I breathed;
629.07 and besides, I remembered I had once been her
629.08 husband -- the recollection was then, and is now,
629.09 inexpressibly odious to me: moreover, I knew
629.10 that while she lived I could never be the husband
629.11 of another and better wife; and, though five years
629.12 my senior, /her family and my father had lied to
629.13 me even in the particular of her age/, she was
629.14 likely to live as long as I, being as robust in frame
629.15 as she was infirm in mind. Thus, at the age of
629.16 twenty-six, I was hopeless.
629.17 "One night I had been awakened by her yells
629.18 -- /since the medical men had pronounced her
629.19 mad, she had of course been shut up/ -- it was a
629.20 fiery West-Indian night; one of the description
629.21 that frequently precede the hurricanes of those
629.22 climates; being unable to sleep in bed, I got up
629.23 and opened the window. The air was like sul-
629.24 phur-steams -- I could find no refreshment any-
629.25 where. Mosquitoes came buzzing in and hummed
629.26 sullenly round the room; the sea, which I could
629.27 hear from thence, rumbled dull like an earthquake
629.28 -- black clouds were coasting up over it; the moon
630.01 was setting in the waves, broad and red, like a hot
630.02 cannon-ball -- she threw her bloody glance
630.03 over a world quivering with the ferment of tem-
630.04 pest. I was physically influenced by the atmo-
630.05 sphere and scene, and my ears were filled with the
630.06 curses the maniac still shrieked out; wherein she
630.07 momentarily mingled my name with such a tone
630.08 of demon-hate, with such language! -- no professed
630.09 harlot ever had a fouler vocabulary than she:
630.10 though two rooms off, I heard every word -- the
630.11 thin partitions of the West-India house opposing
630.12 but slight obstruction to her wolfish cries.
630.13 "'This life,' said I at last, 'is hell! this is the air
630.14 -- those are the sounds of the bottomless pit! I
630.15 have a right to deliver myself from it if I can. The
630.16 sufferings of this mortal state will leave me with
630.17 the heavy flesh that now cumbers my soul. Of the
630.18 fanatic's burning eternity I have no fear: there is
630.19 not a future state worse than this present one -- let
630.20 me break away, and go home to God!'
630.21 "I said this while I knelt down at, and unlocked
630.22 a trunk which contained a brace of loaded pistols:
630.23 I meant to shoot myself. I only entertained the
630.24 intention for a moment; for, not being insane, the
630.25 crisis of exquisite and unalloyed despair which had
630.26 originated the wish and design of self-destruction,
630.27 was past in a second.
630.28 "A wind fresh from Europe blew over the ocean
631.01 and rushed through the open casement: the
631.02 storm broke, streamed, thundered, blazed, and the
631.03 air grew pure. I then framed and fixed a resolu-
631.04 tion. While I walked under the dripping orange--
631.05 trees of my wet garden, and amongst its drenched
631.06 pomegranates and pine-apples, and while the reful-
631.07 gent dawn of the tropics kindled round me -- I
631.08 reasoned thus, Jane: -- and now listen; for it was
631.09 true Wisdom that consoled me in that hour, and
631.10 showed me the right path to follow.
631.11 "The sweet wind from Europe was still whis-
631.12 pering in the refreshed leaves, and the Atlantic was
631.13 thundering in glorious liberty; my heart, dried
631.14 up and scorched for a long time, swelled to the
631.15 tone, and filled with living blood -- my being
631.16 longed for renewal -- my soul thirsted for a pure
631.17 draught. I saw Hope revive -- and felt Regenera-
631.18 tion possible. From a flowery arch at the bottom
631.19 of my garden I gazed over the sea -- bluer than the
631.20 sky: the old world was beyond; clear prospects
631.21 opened thus: --
631.22 "'Go,' said Hope, 'and live again in Europe:
631.23 there it is not known what a sullied name you
631.24 bear, nor what a filthy burden is bound to you.
631.25 You may take the maniac with you to England;
631.26 confine her with due attendance and precautions
631.27 at Thornfield: then travel yourself to what clime
631.28 you will, and form what new tie you like. That
632.01 woman, who has so abused your long-suffering --
632.02 so sullied your name; so outraged your honour;
632.03 so blighted your youth -- is not your wife; nor are
632.04 you her husband. See that she is cared for as her
632.05 condition demands, and you have done all that
632.06 God and humanity require of you. Let her
632.07 identity, her connection with yourself, be buried
632.08 in oblivion: you are bound to impart them to no
632.09 living being. Place her in safety and comfort:
632.10 shelter her degradation with secrecy, and leave
632.11 her.'
632.12 "I acted precisely on this suggestion. My
632.13 father and brother had not made my marriage
632.14 known to their acquaintance; because, in the
632.15 very first letter I wrote to apprise them of the
632.16 union -- having already begun to experience ex-
632.17 treme disgust of its consequences; and from the
632.18 family character and constitution, seeing a hideous
632.19 future opening to me -- I added an urgent charge
632.20 to keep it secret: and very soon, the infamous
632.21 conduct of the wife my father had selected for
632.22 me, was such as to make him blush to own her as
632.23 his daughter-in-law. Far from desiring to publish
632.24 the connection, he became as anxious to conceal
632.25 it as myself.
632.26 "To England, then, I conveyed her; a fearful
632.27 voyage I had with such a monster in the vessel.
632.28 Glad was I when I at last got her to Thornfield,
633.01 and saw her safely lodged in that third story
633.02 room, of whose secret inner cabinet she has now

633.03 for ten years made a wild beast's den -- a goblin's
633.04 cell. I had some trouble in finding an attendant
633.05 for her; as it was necessary to select one on
633.06 whose fidelity dependence could be placed; for
633.07 her ravings would inevitably betray my secret:
633.08 besides, she had lucid intervals of days -- sometimes
633.09 weeks -- which she filled up with abuse for me. At
633.10 last I hired Grace Poole, from the Grimsby Re-
633.11 treat. She and the surgeon, Carter /who dressed
633.12 Mason's wounds that night he was stabbed and
633.13 worried/, are the only two I have ever admitted to
633.14 my confidence. Mrs. Fairfax may indeed have
633.15 suspected something; but she could have gained
633.16 no precise knowledge as to facts. Grace has, on
633.17 the whole, proved a good keeper: though, owing
633.18 partly to a fault of her own, of which it appears
633.19 nothing can cure her, and which is incident to
633.20 her harassing profession, her vigilance has been
633.21 more than once lulled and baffled. The lunatic
633.22 is both cunning and malignant; she has never
633.23 failed to take advantage of her guardian's tem-
633.24 porary lapses; once to secret the knife with
633.25 which she stabbed her brother, and twice to pos-
633.26 sess herself of the key of her cell, and issue
633.27 therefrom in the night-time. On the first of
633.28 these occasions, she perpetrated the attempt to
634.01 burn me in my bed; on the second, she paid that
634.02 ghastly visit to you. I thank Providence, who
634.03 watched over you, that she then spent her fury
634.04 on your wedding apparel; which perhaps brought
634.05 back vague reminiscences of her own bridal days:
634.06 but on what might have happened, I cannot en-
634.07 dure to reflect. When I think of the thing which
634.08 flew at my throat this morning, hanging its black
634.09 and scarlet visage over the nest of my dove, my
634.10 blood curdles ----"
634.11 "And what, sir," I asked, while he paused,
634.12 "did you do when you had settled her here?
634.13 where did you go?"
634.14 "What did I do, Jane? I transformed myself
634.15 into a Will-o'-the-wisp. Where did I go? I pur-
634.16 sued wanderings as wild as those of the March-
634.17 spirit. I sought the Continent, and went devious
634.18 through all its lands. My fixed desire was to
634.19 seek and find a good and intelligent woman,
634.20 whom I could love: a contrast to the fury I left
634.21 at Thornfield ----"
634.22 "But you could not marry, sir."
634.23 "I had determined, and was convinced, that, I
634.24 could and ought. It was not my original inten-
634.25 tion to deceive, as I have deceived you. I meant
634.26 to tell my tale plainly, and make my proposals
634.27 openly: and it appeared to me so absolutely
634.28 rational that I should be considered free to love
635.01 and be loved, I never doubted some woman
635.02 might be found willing and able to understand
635.03 my case and accept me, in spite of the curse with
635.04 which I was burdened."
635.05 "Well, sir?"
635.06 "When you are inquisitive, Jane, you always
635.07 make me smile. You open your eyes like an
635.08 eager bird, and make every now and then a rest-
635.09 less movement; as if answers in speech did not
635.10 flow fast enough for you, and you wanted to read
635.11 the tablet of one's heart. But before I go on, tell
635.12 me what you mean by your 'well, sir?' It is
635.13 a small phrase very frequent with you; and which
635.14 many a time has drawn me on and on through
635.15 interminable talk: I don't very well know why."
635.16 "I mean, -- What next? How did you pro-
635.17 ceed? What came of such an event?"
635.18 "Precisely: and what do you wish to know
635.19 now?"
635.20 "Whether you found any one you liked:
635.21 whether you asked her to marry you; and what
635.22 she said."
635.23 "I can tell you whether I found any one I
635.24 liked, and whether I asked her to marry me: but
635.25 what she said is yet to be recorded in the book
635.26 of Fate. For ten long years I roved about, living
635.27 first in one capital, then another: sometimes in
635.28 St. Petersburg; oftener in Paris; occasionally in
636.01 Rome, Naples, and Florence. Provided with
636.02 plenty of money, and the passport of an old name,
636.03 I could choose my own society: no circles were
636.04 closed against me. I sought my ideal of a woman
636.05 amongst English ladies, French countesses, Italian
636.06 signoras, and German grafinnen. I could not
636.07 find her. Sometimes, for a fleeting moment, I
636.08 thought I caught a glance, heard a tone, beheld a
636.09 form, which announced the realization of my
636.10 dream: but I was presently undeceived. You
636.11 are not to suppose that I desired perfection, either
636.12 of mind or person. I longed only for what suited
636.13 me -- for the antipodes of the Creole: and I
636.14 longed vainly. Amongst them all I found not
636.15 one, whom, had I been ever so free, I -- warned as
636.16 I was of the risks, the horrors, the loathings of
636.17 incongruous unions -- would have asked to marry
636.18 me. Disappointment made me reckless. I tried
636.19 dissipation -- never debauchery: that I hated, and
636.20 hate. That was my Indian Messalina's attribute:
636.21 rooted disgust at it and her restrained me much,
636.22 even in pleasure. Any enjoyment that bordered
636.23 on riot seemed to approach me to her and her
636.24 vices, and I eschewed it.
636.25 "Yet I could not live alone: so I tried the
636.26 companionship of mistresses. The first I chose
636.27 was Celine Varens -- another of those steps which
636.28 make a man spurn himself when he recalls them.
637.01 You already know what she was, and how my

637.02 liaison with her terminated. She had two suc-
637.03 cessors: an Italian, Giacinta, and a German, Clara;
637.04 both considered singularly handsome. What was
637.05 their beauty to me in a few weeks? Giacinta
637.06 was unprincipled and violent: I tired of her in
637.07 three months. Clara was honest and quiet; but
637.08 heavy, mindless, unimpressible: not one whit to
637.09 my taste. I was glad to give her a sufficient sum
637.10 to set her up in a good line of business, and so
637.11 get decently rid of her. But, Jane, I see by your
637.12 face you are not forming a very favourable opinion
637.13 of me just now. You think me an unfeeling,
637.14 loose-principled rake: don't you?"
637.15 "I don't like you so well as I have done some-
637.16 times, indeed, sir. Did it not seem to you in the
637.17 least wrong to live in that way: first with one
637.18 mistress and then another? You talk of it as a
637.19 mere matter of course."
637.20 "It was with me; and I did not like it. It
637.21 was a grovelling fashion of existence: I should
637.22 never like to return to it. Hiring a mistress is
637.23 the next worst thing to buying a slave: both are
637.24 often by nature, and always by position, inferior:
637.25 and to live familiarly with inferiors is degrading.
637.26 I now hate the recollection of the time I passed
637.27 with Celine, Giacinta, and Clara."
637.28 I felt the truth of these words; and I drew
638.01 from them the certain inference, that if I were so
638.02 far to forget myself and all the teaching that had
638.03 ever been instilled into me, as -- under any pre-
638.04 text -- with any justification -- through any temp-
638.05 tation -- to become the successor of these poor
638.06 girls, he would one day regard me with the same
638.07 feeling which now in his mind desecrated their
638.08 memory. I did not give utterance to this con-
638.09 viction: it was enough to feel it. I impressed it
638.10 on my heart, that it might remain there to serve
638.11 me as aid in the time of trial.
638.12 "Now, Jane, why don't you say 'well, sir?'
638.13 I have not done. You are looking grave. You
638.14 disapprove of me still, I see. But let me come to
638.15 the point. Last January, rid of all mistresses --
638.16 in a harsh, bitter, frame of mind, the result of a
638.17 useless, roving, lonely life -- corroded with disap-
638.18 pointment, sourly disposed against all men, and
638.19 especially against all womankind /for I began to
638.20 regard the notion of any intellectual, faithful, loving
638.21 woman as a mere dream/, recalled by business, I
638.22 came back to England.
638.23 "On a frosty winter afternoon, I rode in sight
638.24 of Thornfield Hall. Abhorred spot! I expected
638.25 no peace -- no pleasure there. On a style in Hay-
638.26 lane I saw a quiet little figure sitting by itself. I
638.27 passed it as negligently as I did the pollard willow
638.28 opposite to it: I had no presentiment of what it
639.01 would be to me; no inward warning that the
639.02 arbitress of my life -- my genius for good or evil --
639.03 waited there in humble guise. I did not know
639.04 it, even when, on the occasion of Mesrour's acci-
639.05 dent, it came up and gravely offered me help.
639.06 Childish and slender creature! It seemed as if
639.07 a linnet had hopped to my foot and proposed to
639.08 bear me on its tiny wing. I was surly; but the
639.09 thing would not go: it stood by me with strange
639.10 perseverance, and looked and spoke with a sort of
639.11 authority. I must be aided, and by that hand:
639.12 and aided I was.
639.13 "When once I had pressed the frail shoulder,
639.14 something new -- a fresh sap and sense -- stole into
639.15 my frame. It was well I had learnt that this elf
639.16 must return to me -- that it belonged to my house
639.17 down below -- or I could not have felt it pass
639.18 away from under my hand, and seen it vanish
639.19 behind the dim hedge, without singular regret.
639.20 I heard you come home that night, Jane: though
639.21 probably you were not aware that I thought of
639.22 you, or watched for you. The next day I ob-
639.23 served you -- myself unseen -- for half an hour,
639.24 while you played with Adele in the gallery. It
639.25 was a snowy day, I recollect, and you could not
639.26 go out of doors. I was in my room; the door
639.27 was ajar: I could both listen and watch. Adele
639.28 claimed your outward attention for a while; yet
640.01 I fancied your thoughts were elsewhere: but you
640.02 were very patient with her, my little Jane; you
640.03 talked to her and amused her a long time. When
640.04 at last she left you, you lapsed at once into deep
640.05 reverie: you betook yourself slowly to pace the
640.06 gallery. Now and then, in passing a casement,
640.07 you glanced out at the thick-falling snow; you
640.08 listened to the sobbing wind, and again you paced
640.09 gently on, and dreamed. I think those day-
640.10 visions were not dark: there was a pleasurable
640.11 illumination in your eye occasionally, a soft
640.12 excitement in your aspect, which told of no bitter,
640.13 bilious, hypochondriac brooding: your look re-
640.14 vealed rather the sweet musings of youth, when
640.15 its spirit follows on willing wings the flight of
640.16 Hope, up and on to an ideal heaven. The voice
640.17 of Mrs. Fairfax, speaking to a servant in the hall,
640.18 wakened you: and how curiously you smiled to
640.19 and at yourself, Janet! There was much sense
640.20 in your smile: it was very shrewd, and seemed to
640.21 make light of your own abstraction. It seemed
640.22 to say -- 'My fine visions are all very well, but I
640.23 must not forget they are absolutely unreal. I
640.24 have a rosy sky, and a green flowery Eden in my
640.25 brain; but without, I am perfectly aware, lies at
640.26 my feet a rough tract to travel, and around me
640.27 gather black tempests to encounter. 'You ran
640.28 down stairs and demanded of Mrs. Fairfax some

641.01 occupation: the weekly house-accounts to make
641.02 up, or something of that sort, I think it was.
641.03 I was vexed with you for getting out of my
641.04 sight.
641.05   "Impatiently I waited for evening, when I
641.06 might summon you to my presence. An unusual
641.07 -- to me -- a perfectly new character I suspected
641.08 was yours: I desired to search it deeper, and know
641.09 it better. You entered the room with a look and
641.10 air at once shy and independent; you were quaintly
641.11 dressed -- much as you are now. I made you talk:
641.12 ere long I found you full of strange contrasts.
641.13 Your garb and manner were restricted by rule;
641.14 your air was often diffident, and altogether that of
641.15 one refined by nature, but absolutely unused to
641.16 society, and a good deal afraid of making herself
641.17 disadvantageously conspicuous by some solecism
641.18 or blunder; yet, when addressed, you lifted a
641.19 keen, a daring, and a glowing eye to your inter-
641.20 locutor's face: there was penetration and power in
641.21 each glance you gave; when plied by close ques-
641.22 tions, you found ready and round answers. Very
641.23 soon, you seemed to get used to me -- I believe you
641.24 felt the existence of sympathy between you and
641.25 your grim and cross master, Jane; for it was
641.26 astonishing to see how quickly a certain pleasant
641.27 ease tranquillized your manner: snarl as I would,
641.28 you showed no surprise, fear, annoyance, or dis-
642.01 pleasure at my moroseness; you watched me, and
642.02 now and then smiled at me with a simple yet
642.03 sagacious grace I cannot describe. I was at once
642.04 content and stimulated with what I saw: I liked
642.05 what I had seen, and wished to see more. Yet,
642.06 for a long time, I treated you distantly, and sought
642.07 your company rarely. I was an intellectual epi-
642.08 cure, and wished to prolong the gratification of
642.09 making this novel and piquant acquaintance: be-
642.10 sides, I was for a while troubled with a haunting
642.11 fear that if I handled the flower freely its bloom
642.12 would fade -- the sweet charm of freshness would
642.13 leave it. I did not then know that it was no tran-
642.14 sitory blossom; but rather the radiant resemblance
642.15 of one, cut in an indestructible gem. Moreoover,
642.16 I wished to see whether you would seek me if I
642.17 shunned you -- but you did not; you kept in the
642.18 school-room as still as your own desk and easel:
642.19 if by chance I met you, you passed me as soon,
642.20 and with as little token of recognition, as was con-
642.21 sistent with respect. Your habitual expression in
642.22 those days, Jane, was a thoughtful look; not
642.23 despondent, for you were not sickly; but not
642.24 buoyant, for you had little hope, and no actual
642.25 pleasure. I wondered what you thought of me -- or
642.26 if you ever thought of me: to find this out, I
642.27 resumed my notice of you. There was something
642.28 glad in your glance, and genial in your manner,
643.01 when you conversed: I saw you had a social heart;
643.02 it was the silent school-room -- it was the tedium
643.03 of your life that made you mournful. I permitted
643.04 myself the delight of being kind to you; kindness
643.05 stirred emotion soon: your face became soft in
643.06 expression, your tones gentle; I liked my name
643.07 pronounced by your lips in a grateful, happy
643.08 accent. I used to enjoy a chance meeting with
643.09 you, Jane, at this time: there was a curious
643.10 hesitation in your manner; you glanced at me
643.11 with a slight trouble -- a hovering doubt: you did
643.12 not know what my caprice might be -- whether I
643.13 was going to play the master and be stern, or the
643.14 friend and be benignant. I was now too fond of
643.15 you often to simulate the first whim; and, when I
643.16 stretched my hand out cordially, such bloom and
643.17 light and bliss rose to your young, wistful features,
643.18 I had much ado often to avoid straining you then
643.19 and there to my heart."
643.20   "Don't talk any more of those days, sir," I
643.21 interrupted, furtively dashing away some tears
643.22 from my eyes; his language was torture to me; for
643.23 I knew what I must do -- and do soon -- and all
643.24 these reminiscences, and these revelations of his
643.25 feelings only made my work more difficult.
643.26   "No, Jane," he returned: "what necessity is
643.27 there to dwell on the Past, when the Present is
643.28 so much surer -- the Future so much brighter?"
644.01   I shuddered to hear the infatuated assertion.
644.02   "You see now how the case stands -- do you
644.03 not?" he continued. "After a youth and man-
644.04 hood passed half in unutterable misery and half
644.05 in dreary solitude, I have for the first time found
644.06 what I can truly love -- I have found you. You
644.07 are my sympathy -- my better self -- my good angel
644.08 -- I am bound to you with a strong attachment.
644.09 I think you good, gifted, lovely: a fervent, a
644.10 solemn passion is conceived in my heart; it
644.11 leans to you, draws you to my centre and spring
644.12 of life, wraps my existence about you -- and, kind-
644.13 ling in pure, powerful flame, fuses you and me
644.14 in one.
644.15   "It was because I felt and knew this, that I
644.16 resolved to marry you. To tell me that I had
644.17 already a wife is empty mockery: you know now
644.18 that I had but a hideous demon. I was wrong to
644.19 attempt to deceive you; but I feared a stubbornness
644.20 that exists in your character. I feared early
644.21 instilled prejudice: I wanted to have you safe
644.22 before hazarding confidences. This was cowardly:
644.23 I should have appealed to your nobleness and
644.24 magnanimity at first, as I do now -- opened to you
644.25 plainly my life of agony -- described to you my
644.26 hunger and thirst after a higher and worthier exis-
644.27 tence -- shown to you, not my resolution /that word

644.28 is weak/ but my resistless bent to love faithfully and
645.01 well, where I am faithfully and well loved in
645.02 return. Then I should have asked you to accept my
645.03 pledge of fidelity, and to give me yours: Jane --
645.04 give it me now."
645.05   A pause.
645.06   "Why are you silent, Jane?"
645.07   I was experiencing an ordeal: a hand of fiery
645.08 iron grasped my vitals. Terrible moment: full
645.09 of struggle, blackness, burning! Not a human
645.10 being that ever lived could wish to be loved better
645.11 than I was loved; and him who thus loved me I
645.12 absolutely worshipped: and I must renounce love
645.13 and idol. One drear word comprised my intoler-
645.14 able duty -- "Depart!"
645.15   "Jane, you understand what I want of you?
645.16 Just this promise -- `I will be yours, Mr. Ro-
645.17 chester.'"
645.18   "Mr. Rochester, I will not be yours."
645.19   Another long silence.
645.20   "Jane!" recommenced he, with a gentleness
645.21 that broke me down with grief, and turned me
645.22 stone-cold with ominous terror -- for this still voice
645.23 was the pant of a lion rising -- "Jane, do you
645.24 mean to go one way in the world, and to let me
645.25 go another?"
645.26   "I do."
645.27   "Jane," /bending towards and embracing me/
645.28 "do you mean it now?"
646.01   "I do."
646.02   "And now?" softly kissing my forehead and
646.03 cheek.
646.04   "I do --" extricating myself from restraint ra-
646.05 pidly and completely.
646.06   "Oh, Jane, this is bitter! This -- this is wicked.
646.07 It would not be wicked to love me."
646.08   "It would to obey you."
646.09   A wild look raised his brows -- crossed his fea-
646.10 tures: he rose; but he forbore yet. I laid my
646.11 hand on the back of a chair for support: I shook,
646.12 I feared -- but I resolved.
646.13   "One instant, Jane. Give one glance to my
646.14 horrible life when you are gone. All happiness
646.15 will be torn away with you. What then is left?
646.16 For a wife I have but the maniac up-stairs: as well
646.17 might you refer me to some corpse in yonder church--
646.18 yard. What shall I do, Jane? Where turn for a
646.19 companion, and for some hope?"
646.20   "Do as I do: trust in God and yourself. Be-
646.21 lieve in Heaven. Hope to meet again there."
646.22   "Then you will not yield?"
646.23   "No."
646.24   "Then you condemn me to live wretched, and
646.25 to die accursed?" His voice rose.
646.26   "I advise you to live sinless; and I wish you to
646.27 die tranquil."
646.28   "Then you snatch love and innocence from
647.01 me? You fling me back on lust for a passion --
647.02 vice for an occupation?"
647.03   "Mr. Rochester, I no more assign this fate to
647.04 you than I grasp at it for myself. We were born
647.05 to strive and endure -- you as well as I: do so.
647.06 You will forget me before I forget you."
647.07   "You make me a liar by such language: you
647.08 sully my honour. I declare I could not change:
647.09 you tell me to my face I shall change soon. And
647.10 what a distortion in your judgment, what a per-
647.11 versity in your ideas, is proved by your conduct!
647.12 Is it better to drive a fellow-creature to despair
647.13 than to transgress a mere human law -- no man
647.14 being injured by the breach? for you have
647.15 neither relatives nor acquaintances whom you
647.16 need fear to offend by living with me."
647.17   This was true: and while he spoke my very
647.18 Conscience and Reason turned traitors against me,
647.19 and charged me with crime in resisting him. They
647.20 spoke almost as loud as Feeling: and that
647.21 clamoured wildly. "Oh comply!" it said.
647.22 "Think of his misery; think of his danger -- look
647.23 at his state when left alone; remember his head-
647.24 long nature; consider the recklessness following
647.25 on despair -- soothe him; save him; love him;
647.26 tell him you love him and will be his. Who in
647.27 the world cares for you? or who will be injured
647.28 by what you do?"
648.01   Still indomitable was the reply -- "I care for
648.02 myself. The more solitary, the more friendless,
648.03 the more unsustained I am, the more I will respect
648.04 myself. I will keep the law given by God; sanc-
648.05 tioned by man. I will hold to the principles
648.06 received by me when I was sane, and not mad --
648.07 as I am now. Laws and principles are not for
648.08 the times when there is no temptation: they are
648.09 for such moments as this, when body and soul
648.10 rise in mutiny against their rigour; stringent are
648.11 they; inviolate they shall be. If at my individual
648.12 convenience I might break them, what would be
648.13 their worth? They have a worth -- so I have
648.14 always believed; and if I cannot believe it now,
648.15 it is because I am insane -- quite insane: with my
648.16 veins running fire, and my heart beating faster
648.17 than I can count its throbs. Preconceived
648.18 opinions, foregone determinations, are all I have
648.19 at this hour to stand by: there I plant my
648.20 foot."
648.21   I did. Mr. Rochester, reading my counte-
648.22 nance, saw I had done so. His fury was wrought
648.23 to the highest: he must yield to it for a moment,
648.24 whatever followed; he crossed the floor and
648.25 seized my arm, and grasped my waist. He
648.26 seemed to devour me with his flaming glance:

648.27 physically, I felt, at the moment, powerless as
648.28 stubble exposed to the draught and glow of a
649.01 furnace -- mentally, I still possessed my soul, and
649.02 with it the certainty of ultimate safety. The
649.03 soul, fortunately, has an interpreter -- often an
649.04 unconscious, but still a truthful interpreter -- in the
649.05 eye. My eye rose to his; and while I looked in
649.06 his fierce face, I gave an involuntary sigh: his
649.07 gripe was painful, and my over-tasked strength
649.08 almost exhaused.
649.09   "Never," said he, as he ground his teeth,
649.10 "never was anything at once so frail and so
649.11 indomitable. A mere reed she feels in my hand!
649.12 /and he shook me with the force of his hold./ I
649.13 could bend her with my finger and thumb: and
649.14 what good would it do if I bent, if I uptore, if
649.15 I crushed her? Consider that eye: consider the
649.16 resolute, wild, free thing looking out of it, defy-
649.17 ing me, with more than courage -- with a stern
649.18 triumph. Whatever I do with its cage, I cannot
649.19 get at it -- the savage, beautiful creature! If I
649.20 tear, if I rend the slight prison, my outrage will
649.21 only let the captive loose. Conqueror I might
649.22 be of the house; but the inmate would escape to
649.23 heaven before I could call myself possessor of its
649.24 clay dwelling-place. And it is you, spirit -- with
649.25 will and energy, and virtue and purity -- that I
649.26 want: not alone your brittle frame. Of yourself,
649.27 you could come with soft flight and nestle against
649.28 my heart, if you would: seized against your will,
650.01 you will elude the grasp like an essence -- you will
650.02 vanish ere I inhale your fragrance. Oh! come,
650.03 Jane, come!"
650.04   As he said this, he released me from his clutch,
650.05 and only looked at me. The look was far worse to
650.06 resist than the frantic strain: only an idiot, how-
650.07 ever, would have succumbed now. I had dared
650.08 and baffled his fury; I must elude his sorrow:
650.09 I retired to the door.
650.10   "You are going, Jane?"
650.11   "I am going, sir:"
650.12   "You are leaving me?"
650.13   "Yes."
650.14   "You will not come? -- You will not be my
650.15 comforter, my rescuer? -- My deep love, my wild
650.16 woe, my frantic prayer, are all nothing to you?"
650.17   What unutterable pathos was in his voice!
650.18 How hard it was to reiterate firmly, "I am going."
650.19   "Jane!"
650.20   "Mr. Rochester!"
650.21   "Withdraw, then -- I consent -- but remember,
650.22 you leave me here in anguish. Go up to your
650.23 own room; think over all I have said, and, Jane,
650.24 cast a glance on my sufferings -- think of me."
650.25   He turned away; he threw himself on his face
650.26 on the sofa. "Oh, Jane! my hope -- my love -- my
650.27 life!" broke in anguish from his lips. Then
650.28 came a deep, strong sob.
651.01   I had already gained the door: but, reader, I
651.02 walked back -- walked back as determinedly as I
651.03 had retreated. I knelt down by him; I turned
651.04 his face from the cushion to me; I kissed his
651.05 cheek; I smoothed his hair with my hand.
651.06   "God bless you, my dear master!" I said.
651.07 "God keep you from harm and wrong -- direct
651.08 you, solace you -- reward you well for your past
651.09 kindness to me."
651.10   "Little Jane's love would have been my best
651.11 reward," he answered: "without it, my heart is
651.12 broken. But Jane will give me her love: yes --
651.13 nobly, generously."
651.14   Up the blood rushed to his face; forth flashed
651.15 the fire from his eyes; erect he sprang; he held
651.16 his arms out; but I evaded the embrace, and at
651.17 once quitted the room.
651.18   "Farewell!" was the cry of my heart, as
651.19 I left him. Despair added, -- "Farewell, for
651.20 ever!"
651.21   - - - - -
651.22   That night I never thought to sleep: but a
651.23 slumber fell on me as soon as I lay down in bed.
651.24 I was transported in thought to the scenes of
651.25 childhood: I dreamt I lay in the red-room at
651.26 Gateshead; that the night was dark, and my
651.27 mind impressed with strange fears. The light that
651.28 long ago had struck me into syncope, recalled in
652.01 this vision, seemed gliding to mount the wall,
652.02 and tremblingly to pause in the centre of the
652.03 obscured ceiling. I lifted up my head to look:
652.04 the roof resolved to clouds, high and dim; the
652.05 gleam was such as the moon imparts to vapours,
652.06 she is about to sever. I watched her come --
652.07 watched with the strangest anticipation; as though
652.08 some word of doom were to be written on her
652.09 disk. She broke forth as never moon yet burst
652.10 from cloud: a hand first penetrated the sable
652.11 folds and waved them away; then, not a moon,
652.12 but a white human form shone in the azure, in-
652.13 clining a glorious brow earthward. It gazed and
652.14 gazed on me. It spoke to my spirit: immeasure-
652.15 ably distant was the tone, yet so near, it whispered
652.16 in my heart ---
652.17   "My daughter, flee temptation!"
652.18   "Mother, I will."
652.19   So I answered after I had waked from the
652.20 trance-like dream. It was yet night, but July
652.21 nights are short: soon after midnight, dawn
652.22 comes. "It cannot be too early to commence the
652.23 task I have to fulfil," thought I. I rose: I was
652.24 dressed; for I had taken off nothing but my shoes.
652.25 I knew where to find in my drawers some linen,

652.26 a locket, a ring. In seeking these articles, I
652.27 encountered the beads of a pearl necklace Mr.
652.28 Rochester had forced me to accept a few days
653.01 ago. I left that; it was not mine: it was the
653.02 visionary bride's, who had melted in air. The
653.03 other articles I made up in a parcel; my purse,
653.04 containing twenty shillings /it was all I had/, I
653.05 put in my pocket: I tied on my straw bonnet,
653.06 pinned my shawl, took the parcel and my slippers,
653.07 which I would not put on yet, and stole from my
653.08 room.
653.09   "Farewell, kind Mrs. Fairfax!" I whispered,
653.10 as I glided past her door. "Farewell, my dar-
653.11 ling Adele!" I said, as I glanced towards the
653.12 nursery. No thought could be admitted of
653.13 entering to embrace her. I had to deceive
653.14 a fine ear: for aught I knew, it might now be
653.15 listening.
653.16   I would have got past Mr. Rochester's chamber
653.17 without a pause; but my heart momentarily stop-
653.18 ping its beat at that threshold, my foot was forced
653.19 to stop also. No sleep was there: the inmate
653.20 was walking restlessly from wall to wall; and
653.21 again and again he sighed while I listened. There
653.22 was a heaven -- a temporary heaven -- in this room
653.23 for me, if I chose: I had but to go in and to
653.24 say --
653.25   "Mr. Rochester, I will love you and live with
653.26 you through life till death," and a fount of rap-
653.27 ture would spring to my lips. I thought of
653.28 this.
654.01   That kind master, who could not sleep now,
654.02 was waiting with impatience for day. He would
654.03 send for me in the morning; I should be gone.
654.04 He would have me sought for: vainly. He would
654.05 feel himself forsaken; his love rejected: he would
654.06 suffer; perhaps grow desperate. I thought of this
654.07 too. My hand moved towards the lock: I caught
654.08 it back, and glided on.
654.09   Drearily I wound my way down stairs: I knew
654.10 what I had to do, and I did it mechanically. I
654.11 sought the key of the side-door in the kitchen:
654.12 I sought, too, a phial of oil and a feather; I oiled
654.13 the key and the lock. I got some water, I got
654.14 some bread: for perhaps I should have to walk
654.15 far; and my strength, sorely shaken of late, must
654.16 not break down. All this I did without one
654.17 sound. I opened the door, passed out, shut it
654.18 softly. Dim dawn glimmered in the yard. The
654.19 great gates were closed and locked; but a wicket
654.20 in one of them was only latched. Through that
654.21 I departed: it, too, I shut; and now I was out of
654.22 Thornfield.
654.23   A mile off, beyond the fields, lay a road which
654.24 stretched in the contrary direction to Millcote;
654.25 a road I had never travelled, but often noticed,
654.26 and wondered where it led: thither I bent my
654.27 steps. No reflection was to be allowed now: not
654.28 one glance was to be cast back; not even one
655.01 forward. Not one thought was to be given either
655.02 to the past or the future. The first was a page
655.03 so heavenly sweet -- so deadly sad -- that to read one
655.04 line of it would dissolve my courage and break
655.05 down my energy. The last was an awful blank:
655.06 something like the world when the deluge was
655.07 gone by.
655.08   I skirted fields, and hedges, and lanes, till after
655.09 sunrise. I believe it was a lovely summer morn-
655.10 ing: I know my shoes, which I had put on when
655.11 I left the house, were soon wet with dew. But
655.12 I looked neither to rising sun, nor smiling sky,
655.13 nor wakening nature. He who is taken out to
655.14 pass through a fair scene to the scaffold, thinks
655.15 not of the flowers that smile on his road, but of
655.16 the block and axe-edge; of the disseverment of
655.17 bone and vein; of the grave gaping at the end:
655.18 and I thought of drear flight and homeless wan-
655.19 dering -- and, oh! with agony I thought of what
655.20 I left. I could not help it. I thought of him
655.21 now -- in his room -- watching the sunrise; hoping
655.22 I should soon come to say I would stay with him,
655.23 and be his. I longed to be his; I panted to re-
655.24 turn: it was not too late; I could yet spare him
655.25 the bitter pang of bereavement. As yet my flight,
655.26 I was sure, was undiscovered. I could go back
655.27 and be his comforter -- his pride; his redeemer
655.28 from misery; perhaps from ruin. Oh, that fear
656.01 of his self-abandonment -- far worse than my
656.02 abandonment -- how it goaded me! It was a
656.03 barbed arrow-head in my breast; it tore me when
656.04 I tried to extract it; it sickened me when Re-
656.05 membrance thrust it further in. Birds began
656.06 singing in brake and copse: birds were faithful
656.07 to their mates; birds were emblems of love.
656.08 What was I? In the midst of my pain of heart,
656.09 and frantic effort of principle, I abhorred myself.
656.10 I had no solace from self-approbation: none even
656.11 from self-respect. I had injured -- wounded -- left
656.12 my master. I was hateful in my own eyes. Still
656.13 I could not turn, nor retrace one step. God
656.14 must have led me on. As to my own will or
656.15 conscience, impassioned grief had trampled one
656.16 and stifled the other. I was weeping wildly as
656.17 I walked along my solitary way: fast, fast I went
656.18 like one delirious. A weakness, beginning in-
656.19 wardly, extending to the limbs, seized me, and
656.20 I fell: I lay on the ground some minutes, press-
656.21 ing my face to the wet turf. I had some fear -- or
656.22 hope -- that here I should die: but I was soon up;
656.23 crawling forwards on my hands and knees, and then
656.24 again raised to my feet -- as eager and as determined

656.25   as ever to reach the road.
656.26   When I got there I was forced to sit to rest
656.27   me under the hedge; and while I sat, I heard
656.28   wheels, and saw a coach come on. I stood up
657.01   and lifted my hand; it stopped. I asked where it
657.02   was going: the driver named a place a long way
657.03   off, and where I was sure Mr. Rochester had no
657.04   connexions. I asked for what sum he would take
657.05   me there; he said thirty shillings; I answered I
657.06   had but twenty; well, he would try to make it do.
657.07   He further gave me leave to get into the inside, as
657.08   the vehicle was empty: I entered, was shut in, and
657.09   it rolled on its way.
657.10   Gentle reader, may you never feel what I then
657.11   felt! May your eyes never shed such stormy,
657.12   scalding, heart-wrung tears as poured from mine.
657.13   May you never appeal to Heaven in prayers so
657.14   hopeless and so agonized as in that hour left my
657.15   lips: for never may you, like me, dread to be the
657.16   instrument of evil to what you wholly love.
658.01   [Vol. 3 Chapter 2]
658.02   Two days are passed. It is a summer evening;
658.03   the coachman has set me down at a place called
658.04   Whitcross: he could take me no farther for the
658.05   sum I had given, and I was not possessed of another
658.06   shilling in the world. The coach is a mile off by
658.07   this time; I am alone. At this moment I discover
658.08   that I forgot to take my parcel out of the pocket
658.09   of the coach, where I had placed it for safety;
658.10   there it remains, there it must remain; and now
658.11   I am absolutely destitute.
658.12   Whitcross is no town, nor even a hamlet; it is
658.13   but a stone pillar set up where four roads meet:
658.14   white-washed, I suppose, to be more obvious at a
658.15   distance and in darkness. Four arms spring
658.16   from its summit: the nearest town to which these
658.17   point is, according to the inscription, distant ten
658.18   miles; the farthest, above twenty. From the
658.19   well-known names of these towns I learn in what
658.20   county I have lighted; a north-midland shire,
658.21   dusk with moorland, ridged with mountain: this
659.01   I see. There are great moors behind and on
659.02   each hand of me; there are waves of mountains
659.03   far beyond that deep valley at my feet. The
659.04   population here must be thin, and I see no pas-
659.05   sengers on these roads: they stretch out east,
659.06   west, north, and south -- white, broad, lonely; they
659.07   are all cut in the moor, and the heather grows
659.08   deep and wild to their very verge. Yet a chance
659.09   traveller might pass by; and I wish no eye to see
659.10   me now: strangers would wonder what I am
659.11   doing, lingering here at the sign-post, evidently
659.12   objectless and lost. I might be questioned: I
659.13   could give no answer but what would sound
659.14   incredible, and excite suspicion. Not a tie holds
659.15   me to human society at this moment -- not a
659.16   charm or hope calls me where my fellow-creatures
659.17   are -- none that saw me would have a kind thought
659.18   or a good wish for me. I have no relative but the
659.19   universal mother, Nature: I will seek her breast
659.20   and ask repose.
659.21   I struck straight into the heath: I held on to a
659.22   hollow I saw deeply furrowing the brown moor-
659.23   side; I waded, knee-deep in its dark growth; I
659.24   turned with its turnings, and finding a moss--
659.25   blackened granite crag in a hidden angle, I sat
659.26   down under it. High banks of moor were about
659.27   me; the crag protected my head: the sky was
659.28   over that.
660.01   Some time passed before I felt tranquil even
660.02   here: I had a vague dread that wild cattle might
660.03   be near, or that some sportsman or poacher might
660.04   discover me. If a gust of wind swept the waste,
660.05   I looked up, fearing it was the rush of a bull; if
660.06   a plover whistled, I imagined it a man. Find-
660.07   ing my apprehensions unfounded, however, and
660.08   calmed by the deep silence that reigned as even-
660.09   ing declined to night-fall, I took confidence. As
660.10   yet I had not thought; I had only listened,
660.11   watched, dreaded: now I regained the faculty of
660.12   reflection.
660.13   What was I to do? where to go? Oh, in-
660.14   tolerable questions, when I could do nothing and
660.15   go nowhere! -- when a long way must yet be
660.16   measured by my weary, trembling limbs, before
660.17   I could reach human habitation -- when cold
660.18   charity must be entreated before I could get a
660.19   lodging: reluctant sympathy importuned: almost
660.20   certain repulse incurred: before my tale could be
660.21   listened to, or one of my wants relieved!
660.22   I touched the heath: it was dry, and yet warm
660.23   with the heat of the summer-day. I looked at
660.24   the sky; it was pure: a kindly star twinkled just
660.25   above the chasm ridge. The dew fell, but with
660.26   propitious softness; no breeze whispered. Nature
660.27   seemed to me benign and good: I thought she
660.28   loved me, outcast as I was; and I, who from
661.01   man could anticipate only mistrust, rejection,
661.02   insult, clung to her with filial fondness. To-
661.03   night, at least, I would be her guest -- as I was her
661.04   child: my mother would lodge me without
661.05   money and without price. I had one morsel of
661.06   bread yet: the remnant of a roll I had bought in
661.07   a town we passed through at noon with a stray
661.08   penny -- my last coin. I saw ripe bilberries
661.09   gleaming here and there, like jet beads in the
661.10   heath: I gathered a handful and ate them with
661.11   the bread. My hunger, sharp before, was, if not
661.12   satisfied, appeased by this hermit's meal. I said
661.13   my evening prayers at its conclusion, and then
661.14   chose my couch.

661.15   Beside the crag, the heath was very deep:
661.16   when I lay down my feet were buried in it; rising
661.17   high on each side, it left only a narrow space for
661.18   the night-air to invade. I folded my shawl
661.19   double, and spread it over me for a coverlet; a
661.20   low, mossy swell was my pillow. Thus lodged, I
661.21   was not, at least at the commencement of the
661.22   night, cold.
661.23   My rest might have been blissful enough, only
661.24   a sad heart broke it. It plained of its gaping
661.25   wounds, its inward bleeding, its riven chords.
661.26   It trembled for Mr. Rochester and his doom: it
661.27   bemoaned him with bitter pity; it demanded him
661.28   with ceaseless longing: and, impotent as a bird
662.01   with both wings broken, it still quivered its shat-
662.02   tered pinions in vain attempts to seek him.
662.03   Worn out with this torture of thought, I rose to
662.04   my knees. Night was come, and her planets
662.05   were risen: a safe, still night; too serene for the
662.06   companionship of fear. We know that God is
662.07   everywhere; but certainly we feel His presence
662.08   most when His works are on the grandest scale
662.09   spread before us: and it is in the unclouded night--
662.10   sky, where His worlds wheel their silent course,
662.11   that we read clearest His infinitude, His omnipo-
662.12   tence, His omnipresence. I had risen to my
662.13   knees to pray for Mr. Rochester. Looking up,
662.14   I, with tear-dimmed eyes, saw the mighty milky--
662.15   way. Remembering what it was -- what countless
662.16   systems there swept space like a soft trace of
662.17   light -- I felt the might and strength of God.
662.18   Sure was I of His efficiency to save what He
662.19   had made: convinced I grew that neither earth
662.20   should perish, nor one of the souls it treasured.
662.21   I turned my prayer to thanksgiving: the Source
662.22   of Life was also the Saviour of spirits. Mr.
662.23   Rochester was safe: he was God's, and by God
662.24   would he be guarded. I again nestled to the
662.25   breast of the hill; and ere long, in sleep, forgot
662.26   sorrow.
662.27   But next day, Want came to me, pale and bare.
662.28   Long after the little birds had left their nests;
663.01   long after bees had come in the sweet prime of
663.02   day to gather the heath honey before the dew was
663.03   dried -- when the long morning shadows were cur-
663.04   tailed, and the sun filled earth and sky -- I got up,
663.05   and I looked round me.
663.06   What a still, hot, perfect day! What a golden
663.07   desert this spreading moor! Everywhere sun-
663.08   shine. I wished I could live in it and on it. I
663.09   saw a lizard run over the crag; I saw a bee busy
663.10   amongst the sweet bilberries. I would fain at the
663.11   moment have become bee or lizard, that I might
663.12   have found fitting nutriment, permanent shelter
663.13   here. But I was a human being, and had a human
663.14   being's wants: I must not linger where there was
663.15   nothing to supply them. I rose; I looked back
663.16   at the bed I had left. Hopeless of the future, I
663.17   wished but this -- that my Maker had that night
663.18   thought good to require my soul of me while I
663.19   slept; and that this weary frame, absolved by
663.20   death from further conflict with fate, had now but
663.21   to decay quietly, and mingle in peace with the
663.22   soil of this wilderness. Life, however, was yet
663.23   in my possession; with all its requirements, and
663.24   pains, and responsibilities. The burden must be
663.25   carried; the want provided for; the suffering
663.26   endured; the responsibility fulfilled. I set out.
663.27   Whitcross regained, I followed a road which
663.28   led from the sun, now fervent and high. By no
664.01   other circumstance had I will to decide my choice.
664.02   I walked a long time, and when I thought I had
664.03   nearly done enough, and might conscientiously
664.04   yield to the fatigue that almost overpowered me --
664.05   might relax this forced action, and, sitting down
664.06   on a stone I saw near, submit resistlessly to the
664.07   apathy that clogged heart and limb -- I heard a
664.08   bell chime -- a church bell.
664.09   I turned in the direction of the sound, and
664.10   there, amongst the romantic hills, whose changes
664.11   and aspect I had ceased to note an hour ago, I
664.12   saw a hamlet and a spire. All the valley at my
664.13   right hand was full of pasture-fields, and corn--
664.14   fields, and wood; and a glittering stream ran
664.15   zig-zag through the varied shades of green, the
664.16   mellowing grain, the sombre wood-land, the clear
664.17   and sunny lea. Recalled by the rumbling of
664.18   wheels to the road before me, I saw a heavily--
664.19   laden waggon labouring up the hill; and not far
664.20   beyond were two cows and their drover. Human
664.21   life and human labour were near. I must struggle
664.22   on: strive to live and bend to toil like the rest.
664.23   About two o'clock, P.M., I entered the village.
664.24   At the bottom of its one street, there was a little
664.25   shop with some cakes of bread in the window.
664.26   I coveted a cake of bread. With that refresh-
664.27   ment I could perhaps regain a degree of energy;
664.28   without it, it would be difficult to proceed. The
665.01   wish to have some strength and some vigour re-
665.02   turned to me as soon as I was amongst my fellow--
665.03   beings. I felt it would be degrading to faint with
665.04   hunger on the causeway of a hamlet. Had I
665.05   nothing about me I could offer in exchange for
665.06   one of these rolls? I considered. I had a small
665.07   silk handkerchief tied round my throat; I had
665.08   my gloves. I could hardly tell how men and
665.09   women in extremities of destitution proceeded.
665.10   I did not know whether either of these articles
665.11   would be accepted: probably they would not; but
665.12   I must try.
665.13   I entered the shop: a woman was there. See-

665.14 ing a respectably-dressed person, a lady as she
665.15 supposed, she came forward with civility. How
665.16 could she serve me? I was seized with shame:
665.17 my tongue would not utter the request I had
665.18 prepared. I dared not offer her the half-worn
665.19 gloves, the creased handkerchief: besides, I felt
665.20 it would be absurd. I only begged permission to
665.21 sit down a moment, as I was tired. Disappointed
665.22 in the expectation of a customer, she coolly ac-
665.23 ceded to my request. She pointed to a seat; I
665.24 sank into it. I felt sorely urged to weep; but
665.25 conscious how unseasonable such a manifestation
665.26 would be, I restrained it. Soon I asked her, "if
665.27 there were any dressmaker or plain-work-woman
665.28 in the village?"
666.01 "Yes; two or three. Quite as many as there
666.02 was employment for."
666.03 I reflected. I was driven to the point now.
666.04 I was brought face to face with Necessity. I
666.05 stood in the position of one without a resource:
666.06 without a friend; without a coin. I must do
666.07 something. What? I must apply somewhere.
666.08 Where?"
666.09 "Did she know of any place in the neighbour-
666.10 hood where a servant was wanted?"
666.11 "Nay; she couldn't say."
666.12 "What was the chief trade in this place? what
666.13 did most of the people do?"
666.14 "Some were farm labourers; a good deal
666.15 worked at Mr. Oliver's needle-factory, and at the
666.16 foundry."
666.17 "Did Mr. Oliver employ women?"
666.18 "Nay; it was men's work."
666.19 "And what do the women do?"
666.20 "I knawn't," was the answer. "Some does
666.21 one thing, and some another. Poor folk mun get
666.22 on as they can."
666.23 She seemed to be tired of my questions: and,
666.24 indeed, what claim had I to importune her? A
666.25 neighbour or two came in; my chair was evidently
666.26 wanted. I took leave.
666.27 I passed up the street, looking as I went at all
666.28 the houses to the right hand and to the left: but
667.01 I could discover no pretext, nor see an induce-
667.02 ment, to enter any. I rambled round the hamlet,
667.03 going sometimes to a little distance and returning
667.04 again, for an hour or more. Much exhausted,
667.05 and suffering greatly now for want of food, I
667.06 turned aside into a lane and sat down under the
667.07 hedge. Ere many minutes had elapsed, I was
667.08 again on my feet, however, and again searching
667.09 something -- a resource, or at least an informant.
667.10 A pretty little house stood at the top of the lane,
667.11 with a garden before it; exquisitely neat, and
667.12 brilliantly blooming. I stopped at it. What
667.13 business had I to approach the white door, or
667.14 touch the glittering knocker? In what way
667.15 could it possibly be the interest of the inhabitants
667.16 of that dwelling to serve me? Yet I drew near
667.17 and knocked. A mild-looking, cleanly-attired
667.18 young woman opened the door. In such a voice
667.19 as might be expected from a hopeless heart and
667.20 fainting frame -- a voice wretchedly low and
667.21 faltering -- I asked if a servant was wanted
667.22 here?
667.23 "No," said she: "we do not keep a servant."
667.24 "Can you tell me where I could get employ-
667.25 ment of any kind?" I continued. "I am a
667.26 stranger, without acquaintance, in this place. I
667.27 want some work: no matter what."
667.28 But it was not her business to think for me, or
668.01 to seek a place for me: besides, in her eyes, how
668.02 doubtful must have appeared my character, po-
668.03 sition, tale. She shook her head, she "was sorry
668.04 she could give me no information," and the white
668.05 door closed, quite gently and civilly: but it shut
668.06 me out. If she had held it open a little longer, I
668.07 believe I should have begged a piece of bread; for
668.08 I was now brought low.
668.09 I could not bear to return to the sordid village;
668.10 where, besides, no prospect of aid was visible. I
668.11 should have longed rather to deviate to a wood
668.12 I saw not far off, which appeared in its thick
668.13 shade to offer inviting shelter; but I was so sick,
668.14 so weak, so gnawed with nature's cravings, in-
668.15 stinct kept me roaming round abodes where there
668.16 was a chance of food. Solitude would be no soli-
668.17 tude -- rest no rest -- while the vulture, hunger,
668.18 thus sunk beak and talons in my side.
668.19 I drew near houses; I left them, and came back
668.20 again, and again I wandered away: always re-
668.21 pelled by the consciousness of having no claim to
668.22 ask -- no right to expect interest in my isolated
668.23 lot. Meantime, the afternoon advanced, while I
668.24 thus wandered about like a lost and starving dog.
668.25 In crossing a field, I saw the church-spire before
668.26 me: I hastened towards it. Near the church-
668.27 yard, and in the middle of a garden, stood a well-
668.28 built though small house, which I had no doubt
669.01 was the parsonage. I remembered that strangers
669.02 who arrive at a place where they have no friends,
669.03 and who want employment, sometimes apply to
669.04 the clergyman for introduction and aid. It is
669.05 the clergyman's function to help -- at least with
669.06 advice -- those who wish to help themselves. I
669.07 seemed to have something like a right to seek
669.08 counsel here. Renewing then, my courage, and
669.09 gathering my feeble remains of strength, I pushed
669.10 on. I reached the house, and knocked at the
669.11 kitchen-door. An old woman opened: I asked
669.12 was this the parsonage?

669.13 "Yes."
669.14 "Was the clergyman in?"
669.15 "No."
669.16 "Would he be in soon?"
669.17 "No, he was gone from home."
669.18 "To a distance?"
669.19 "Not so far -- happen three mile. He had
669.20 been called away by the sudden death of his
669.21 father: he was at Marsh End now, and would
669.22 very likely stay there a fortnight longer."
669.23 "Was there any lady of the house?"
669.24 "Nay, there was naught but her, and she was
669.25 housekeeper;" and of her, reader, I could not
669.26 bear to ask the relief for want of which I was
669.27 sinking; I could not yet beg; and again I crawled
669.28 away.
670.01 Once more I took off my handkerchief -- once
670.02 more I thought of the cakes of bread in the little
670.03 shop. Oh, for but a crust! for but one mouthful
670.04 to allay the pang of famine! Instinctively I
670.05 turned my face again to the village: I found the
670.06 shop again, and I went in; and though others
670.07 were there besides the woman, I ventured the
670.08 request, "would she give me a roll for this
670.09 handkerchief?"
670.10 She looked at me with evident suspicion:
670.11 "Nay, she never sold stuff i' that way."
670.12 Almost desperate, I asked for half a cake; she
670.13 again refused. "How could she tell where I had
670.14 got the handkerchief," she said.
670.15 "Would she take my gloves?"
670.16 "No! what could she do with them?"
670.17 Reader, it is not pleasant to dwell on these
670.18 details. Some say there is enjoyment in looking
670.19 back to painful experience past; but at this day I
670.20 can scarcely bear to review the times to which I
670.21 allude: the moral degradation, blent with the
670.22 physical suffering, form too distressing a recollec-
670.23 tion ever to be willingly dwelt on. I blamed
670.24 none of those who repulsed me. I felt it was
670.25 what was to be expected, and what could not be
670.26 helped: an ordinary beggar is frequently an
670.27 object of suspicion; a well-dressed beggar in-
670.28 evitably so. To be sure, what I begged was
671.01 employment: but whose business was it to pro-
671.02 vide me with employment? Not, certainly that
671.03 of persons who saw me then for the first time,
671.04 and who knew nothing about my character. And
671.05 as to the woman who would not take my hand-
671.06 kerchief in exchange for her bread, why, she
671.07 was right; if the offer appeared to her sinister, or
671.08 the exchange unprofitable. Let me condense
671.09 now. I am sick of the subject.
671.10 A little before dark I passed a farm-house, at
671.11 the open door of which the farmer was sitting,
671.12 eating his supper of bread and cheese: I stopped
671.13 and said: --
671.14 "Will you give me a piece of bread? for I am
671.15 very hungry." He cast on me a glance of surprise;
671.16 but without answering, he cut a thick slice from
671.17 his loaf, and gave it to me. I imagine he did not
671.18 think I was a beggar, but only an eccentric sort of
671.19 lady, who had taken a fancy to his brown loaf. As
671.20 soon as I was out of sight of his house, I sat down
671.21 and ate it.
671.22 I could not hope to get a lodging under a roof,
671.23 and sought it in the wood I have before alluded
671.24 to. But my night was wretched, my rest broken:
671.25 the ground was damp, the air cold: besides, in-
671.26 truders passed near me more than once, and I
671.27 had again and again to change my quarters: no
671.28 sense of safety or tranquillity befriended me.
672.01 Towards morning it rained; the whole of the
672.02 following day was wet. Do not ask me, reader,
672.03 to give a minute account of that day; as before, I
672.04 sought work; as before, I was repulsed; as before,
672.05 I starved; but once did food pass my lips. At the
672.06 door of a cottage I saw a little girl about to
672.07 throw a mess of cold porridge into a pig-trough.
672.08 "Will you give me that?" I asked.
672.09 She stared at me. "Mother!" she exclaimed;
672.10 "there is a woman wants me to give her these
672.11 porridge."
672.12 "Well, lass," replied a voice within, "give it
672.13 her if she's a beggar. T' pig doesn't want it."
672.14 The girl emptied the stiffened mould into my
672.15 hand, and I devoured it ravenously.
672.16 As the wet twilight deepened, I stopped in a
672.17 solitary bridle-path, which I had been pursuing an
672.18 hour or more.
672.19 "My strength is quite failing me," I said, in
672.20 soliloquy. "I feel I cannot go much further.
672.21 Shall I be an outcast again this night? While
672.22 the rain descends so, must I lay my head on the
672.23 cold drenched ground! I fear I cannot do
672.24 otherwise: for who will receive me? But it will
672.25 be very dreadful: with this feeling of hunger,
672.26 faintness, chill, and this sense of desolation -- this
672.27 total prostration of hope. In all likelihood,
672.28 though, I should die before morning. And why
673.01 cannot I reconcile myself to the prospect of
673.02 death? Why do I struggle to retain a valueless
673.03 life? Because I know, or believe, Mr. Rochester
673.04 is still living: and then, to die of want and cold,
673.05 is a fate to which nature cannot submit passively.
673.06 Oh, Providence! sustain me a little longer! Aid
673.07 -- direct me!"
673.08 My glazed eye wandered over the dim and
673.09 misty landscape. I saw I had strayed far from
673.10 the village: it was quite out of sight. The very
673.11 cultivation surrounding it had disappeared. I

673.12 had, by cross-ways and by-paths, once more
673.13 drawn near the tract of moorland; and now,
673.14 only a few fields, almost as wild and unproductive
673.15 as the heath from which they were scarcely re-
673.16 claimed, lay between me and the dusky hill.
673.17 "Well, I would rather die yonder than in a
673.18 street, or on a frequented road," I reflected.
673.19 "And far better that crows and ravens -- if any
673.20 ravens there be in these regions -- should pick my
673.21 flesh from my bones, than that they should be
673.22 prisoned in a workhouse coffin, and moulder in a
673.23 pauper's grave."
673.24 To the hill, then, I turned. I reached it. It
673.25 remained now only to find a hollow where I
673.26 could lie down, and feel at least hidden, if not
673.27 secure: but all the surface of the waste looked
673.28 level. It showed no variation but of tint: green,
673.29 where rush and moss overgrew the marshes; black,
674.01 where the dry soil bore only heath. Dark as it was
674.02 getting, I could still see these changes; though
674.03 but as mere alternations of light and shade: for
674.04 colour had faded with the daylight.
674.05 My eye still roved over the sullen swell, and along
674.06 the moor-edge, vanishing amidst the wildest
674.07 scenery; when, at one dim point, far in among
674.08 the marshes and the ridges, a light sprang up.
674.09 "That is an ignis fatuus," was my first thought;
674.10 and I expected it would soon vanish. It burnt
674.11 on, however, quite steadily; neither receding nor
674.12 advancing. "Is it then a bonfire just kindled?" I
674.13 questioned. I watched to see whether it would
674.14 spread: but no; as it did not diminish, so it did
674.15 not enlarge. "It may be a candle in a house," I
674.16 then conjectured; "but if so, I can never reach
674.17 it. It is much too far away: and were it within
674.18 a yard of me, what would it avail? I should
674.19 but knock at the door to have it shut in my face."
674.20 And I sank down where I stood, and hid my
674.21 face against the ground. I lay still a while: the
674.22 night-wind swept over the hill and over me, and
674.23 died moaning in the distance; the rain fell fast,
674.24 wetting me afresh to the skin. Could I but have
674.25 stiffened to the still frost -- the friendly numbness
674.26 of death -- it might have pelted on: I should not
674.27 have felt it; but my yet living flesh shuddered to
674.28 its chilling influence. I rose ere long.
675.01 The light was yet there; shining dim, but con-
675.02 stant, through the rain. I tried to walk again: I
675.03 dragged my exhausted limbs slowly towards it.
675.04 It led me aslant over the hill, through a wide bog;
675.05 which would have been impassable in winter, and
675.06 was splashy and shaking even now, in the height
675.07 of summer. Here I fell twice; but as often I rose
675.08 and rallied my faculties. This light was my for-
675.09 lorn hope: I must gain it.
675.10 Having crossed the marsh, I saw a trace of
675.11 white over the moor. I approached it; it was a
675.12 road or a track: it led straight up to the light,
675.13 which now beamed from a sort of knoll, amidst a
675.14 clump of trees -- firs, apparently, from what I could
675.15 distinguish of the character of their forms and
675.16 foliage through the gloom. My star vanished as
675.17 I drew near: some obstacle had intervened be-
675.18 tween me and it. I put out my hand to feel the
675.19 dark mass before me; I discriminated the rough
675.20 stones of a low wall -- above it, something like
675.21 palisades, and within, a high and prickly hedge.
675.22 I groped on. Again a whitish object gleamed
675.23 before me: it was a gate -- a wicket; it moved on
675.24 its hinges as I touched it. On each side stood a
675.25 sable bush -- holly or yew.
675.26 Entering the gate and passing the shrubs, the
675.27 silhouette of a house rose to view; black, low, and
675.28 rather long: but the guiding light shone nowhere.
676.01 All was obscurity. Were the inmates retired to
676.02 rest? I feared it must be so. In seeking the
676.03 door, I turned an angle: there shot out the friendly
676.04 gleam again, from the lozenged panes of a very
676.05 small latticed window, within a foot of the ground;
676.06 made still smaller by the growth of ivy or some
676.07 other creeping plant, whose leaves clustered thick
676.08 over the portion of the house wall in which it
676.09 was set. The aperture was so screened and
676.10 narrow, that curtain or shutter had been deemed
676.11 unnecessary; and when I stooped down and put
676.12 aside the spray of foliage shooting over it, I
676.13 could see all within. I could see clearly a room
676.14 with a sanded floor, clean scoured; a dresser of
676.15 walnut, with pewter plates ranged in rows, reflect-
676.16 ing the redness and radiance of a glowing peat-
676.17 fire. I could see a clock, a white deal table, some
676.18 chairs. The candle, whose ray had been my
676.19 beacon, burnt on the table; and by its light an
676.20 elderly woman, somewhat rough-looking, but
676.21 scrupulously clean, like all about her, was knitting
676.22 a stocking.
676.23 I noticed these objects cursorily only -- in them
676.24 there was nothing extraordinary. A group of
676.25 more interest appeared near the hearth, sitting
676.26 still amidst the rosy peace and warmth suffusing
676.27 it. Two young, graceful women -- ladies in every
676.28 point -- sat, one in a low rocking-chair, the other
677.01 on a lower stool; both wore deep mourning of
677.02 crape and bombazeen, which sombre garb singu-
677.03 larly set off very fair necks and faces: a large old
677.04 pointer dog rested its massive head on the knee of
677.05 one girl -- in the lap of the other was cushioned a
677.06 black cat.
677.07 A strange place was this humble kitchen for
677.08 such occupants! Who were they? They could
677.09 not be the daughters of the elderly person at the

677.10 table; for she looked like a rustic, and they were
677.11 all delicacy and cultivation. I had nowhere seen
677.12 such faces as theirs: and yet, as I gazed on them,
677.13 I seemed intimate with every lineament. I cannot
677.14 call them handsome -- they were too pale and grave
677.15 for the word: as they each bent over a book, they
677.16 looked thoughtful almost to severity. A stand
677.17 between them supported a second candle and two
677.18 great volumes, to which they frequently referred;
677.19 comparing them seemingly with the smaller books
677.20 they held in their hands, like people consulting a
677.21 dictionary to aid them in the task of translation.
677.22 This scene was as silent as if all the figures had
677.23 been shadows, and the fire-lit apartment a picture:
677.24 so hushed was it, I could hear the cinders fall
677.25 from the grate, the clock tick in its obscure cor-
677.26 ner; and I even fancied I could distinguish the
677.27 click-click of the woman's knitting-needles. When,
678.01 therefore, a voice broke the strange stillness at last,
678.02 it was audible enough to me.
678.03 "Listen, Diana," said one of the absorbed stu-
678.04 dents; "Franz and old Daniel are together in the
678.05 night-time, and Franz is telling a dream from
678.06 which he has wakened in terror -- listen!" And
678.07 in a low voice she read something, of which not
678.08 one word was intelligible to me; for it was in an
678.09 unknown tongue -- neither French nor Latin.
678.10 whether it were Greek or German I could not
678.11 tell.
678.12 "That is strong," she said, when she had finished:
678.13 "I relish it." The other girl, who had lifted her
678.14 head to to listen to her sister, repeated, while she
678.15 gazed at the fire, a line of what had been read. At
678.16 a later day, I knew the language and the book;
678.17 therefore I will here quote the line: though, when
678.18 I first heard it, it was only like a stroke on sound-
678.19 ing brass to me -- conveying no meaning: --
678.20 "'Da trat hervor Einer, anzusehen wie die
678.21 Sternen Nacht.' Good! good!" she exclaimed,
678.22 while her dark and deep eye sparkled. "There
678.23 you have a dim and mighty archangel fitly set
678.24 before you! The line is worth a hundred pages
678.25 of fustian. 'Ich wage die Gedanken in der
678.26 Schale meines Zornes und die Werke mit dem
678.27 Gewichte meines Grimms.' I like it!"
679.01 Both were again silent.
679.02 "Is there any country where they talk i' that
679.03 way?" asked the old woman, looking up from her
679.04 knitting.
679.05 "Yes, Hannah -- a far larger country than Eng-
679.06 land; where they talk in no other way."
679.07 "Well, for sure case, I know't how they can
679.08 understand t' one t' other: and if either o' ye went
679.09 there, ye could tell what they said, I guess?"
679.10 "We could probably tell something of what
679.11 they said, but not all -- for we are not as clever as
679.12 you think us, Hannah. We don't speak German,
679.13 and we cannot read it without a dictionary to help
679.14 us."
679.15 "And what good does it do you?"
679.16 "We mean to teach it some time -- or at least
679.17 the elements, as they say; and then we shall get
679.18 more money than we do now."
679.19 "Varry like: but give ower studying; ye've
679.20 done enough for to-night."
679.21 "I think we have: at least, I'm tired. Mary,
679.22 are you?"
679.23 "Mortally: after all, it's tough work fagging
679.24 away at a language with no master but a lexicon."
679.25 "It is: especially such a language as this crab-
679.26 bed but glorious Deutsch. I wonder when St.
679.27 John will come home."
679.28 "Surely he will not be long now: it is just ten"
680.01 /looking at a little gold watch she drew from her
680.02 girdle/. "It rains fast. Hannah, will you have
680.03 the goodness to look at the fire in the parlour?"
680.04 The woman rose; she opened a door, through
680.05 which I dimly saw a passage: soon I heard her
680.06 stir a fire in an inner room; she presently came
680.07 back.
680.08 "Ah, childer!" said she, "it fair troubles me
680.09 to go into yond' room now: it looks so lonesome
680.10 wi' the chair empty and set back in a corner."
680.11 She wiped her eyes with her apron: the two
680.12 girls, grave before, looked sad now.
680.13 "But he is in a better place," continued
680.14 Hannah: "we shouldn't wish him here again.
680.15 And then, nobody need to have a quieter death
680.16 nor he had."
680.17 "You say he never mentioned us?" inquired
680.18 one of the ladies.
680.19 "He hadn't time, bairn: he was gone in a
680.20 minute -- was your father. He had been a bit
680.21 ailing like the day before, but naught to signify;
680.22 and when Mr. St. John asked if he would like
680.23 either o' ye to be sent for, he fair laughed at him.
680.24 He began again with a bit of a heaviness in his
680.25 head the next day -- that is, a fortnight sin' -- and
680.26 he went to sleep and niver wakened: he wor
680.27 a'most stark when your brother went into t' chamber
680.28 and fand him. Ah, childer! that's t' last o' t' old
681.01 stock -- for ye and Mr. St. John is like of a different
681.02 soart to them 'at's gone; for all your mother wor
681.03 mich i' your way; and a'most as book-learned.
681.04 She wor the pictur' o' ye, Mary: Diana is more
681.05 like your father."
681.06 I thought them so similar I could not tell where
681.07 the old servant /for such I now concluded her to
681.08 be/ saw the difference. Both were fair com-
681.09 plexioned and slenderly made; both possessed
681.10 faces full of distinction and intelligence. One, to

681.11 be sure, had hair a shade darker than the other,
681.12 and there was a difference in their style of wear-
681.13 ing it: Mary's pale brown locks were parted and
681.14 braided smooth; Diana's duskier tresses covered
681.15 her neck with thick curls. The clock struck ten.
681.16 "Ye'll want your supper, I'm sure," observed
681.17 Hannah; "and so will Mr. St. John when he
681.18 comes in."
681.19 And she proceeded to prepare the meal. The
681.20 ladies rose: they seemed about to withdraw to
681.21 the parlour. Till this moment, I had been so
681.22 intent on watching them, their appearance and
681.23 conversation had excited in me so keen an in-
681.24 terest, I had half-forgotten my own wretched
681.25 position: now it recurred to me. More desolate,
681.26 more desperate than ever, it seemed from contrast.
681.27 And how impossible did it appear to touch the
681.28 inmates of this house with concern on my behalf:
682.01 to make them believe in the truth of my wants
682.02 and woes -- to induce them to vouchsafe a rest for
682.03 my wanderings! As I groped out the door, and
682.04 knocked at it hesitatingly, I felt that last idea to
682.05 be indeed a mere chimera. Hannah opened.
682.06 "What do you want?" she inquired, in a voice
682.07 of surprise, as she surveyed me by the light of the
682.08 candle she held.
682.09 "May I speak to your mistresses?" I said.
682.10 "You had better tell me what you have to say
682.11 to them. Where do you come from?"
682.12 "I am a stranger."
682.13 "What is your business here at this hour?"
682.14 "I want a night's shelter in an out-house or
682.15 anywhere, and a morsel of bread to eat."
682.16 Distrust, the very feeling I dreaded, appeared
682.17 in Hannah's face. "I'll give you a piece of
682.18 bread," she said, after a pause; "but we can't
682.19 take in a vagrant to lodge. It isn't likely."
682.20 "Do let me speak to your mistresses."
682.21 "No; not I. What can they do for you?
682.22 You should not be roving about now: it looks
682.23 very ill."
682.24 "But where shall I go if you drive me away?
682.25 What shall I do?"
682.26 "Oh, I'll warrant you know where to go, and
682.27 what to do. Mind you don't do wrong, that's all.
682.28 Here is a penny; now go ----"
683.01 "A penny cannot feed me, and I have no
683.02 strength to go farther. Don't shut the door: -- oh,
683.03 don't, for God's sake!"
683.04 "I must; the rain is driving in ----"
683.05 "Tell the young ladies. -- Let me see them -- "
683.06 "Indeed, I will not. You are not what you
683.07 ought to be, or you wouldn't make such a noise.
683.08 Move off!"
683.09 "But I must die if I am turned away."
683.10 "Not you. I'm fear'd you have some ill plans
683.11 agate, that bring you about folk's houses at this time
683.12 o' night. If you've any followers -- housebreakers
683.13 or such like -- anywhere near, you may tell them
683.14 we are not by ourselves in the house: we have a
683.15 gentleman, and dogs, and guns." Here the honest
683.16 but inflexible servant clapped the door to and
683.17 bolted it within.
683.18 This was the climax. A pang of exquisite
683.19 suffering -- a throe of true despair -- rent and heaved
683.20 my heart. Worn out, indeed, I was; not another
683.21 step could I stir. I sank on the wet door-step:
683.22 I groaned -- I wrung my hands -- I wept in utter
683.23 anguish. Oh, this spectre of death! Oh, this
683.24 last hour, approaching in such horror! Alas, this
683.25 isolation -- this banishment from my kind! Not
683.26 only the anchor of home, but the footing of forti-
683.27 tude was gone -- at least for a moment: but the last
683.28 I soon endeavoured to regain.
684.01 "I can but die," I said, "and I believe in God.
684.02 Let me try to wait His will in silence."
684.03 These words I not only thought but uttered;
684.04 and thrusting back all my misery into my heart, I
684.05 made an effort to compel it to remain there --
684.06 dumb and still.
684.07 "All men must die," said a voice quite close at
684.08 hand; "but all are not condemned to meet a
684.09 lingering and premature doom, such as yours
684.10 would be if you perished here of want."
684.11 "Who or what speaks?" I asked, terrified at
684.12 the unexpected sound, and incapable now of
684.13 deriving from any occurrence a hope of aid. A
684.14 form was near -- what form, the pitch-dark night
684.15 and my enfeebled vision prevented me from dis-
684.16 tinguishing. With a loud, long knock, the new
684.17 comer appealed to the door.
684.18 "Is it you, Mr. St. John?" cried Hannah.
684.19 "Yes -- yes; open quickly."
684.20 "Well, how wet and cold you must be, such a
684.21 wild night as it is! Come in -- your sisters are
684.22 quite uneasy about you, and I believe there are
684.23 bad folks about. There has been a beggar-woman
684.24 -- I declare she is not gone yet! -- laid down there.
684.25 Get up! for shame! Move off, I say!"
684.26 "Hush, Hannah! I have a word to say to the
684.27 woman. You have done your duty in excluding,
684.28 now let me do mine in admitting her. I was
685.01 near, and listened to both you and her. I think
685.02 this is a peculiar case -- I must at least examine
685.03 into it. Young woman, rise, and pass before me
685.04 into the house."
685.05 With difficulty I obeyed him. Presently I
685.06 stood within that clean, bright kitchen -- on the very
685.07 hearth -- trembling, sickening; conscious of an as-
685.08 pect in the last degree ghastly, wild, and weather--
685.09 beaten. The two ladies, their brother, Mr. St.

685.10 John, the old servant, were all gazing at me.
685.11 "St. John, who is it?" I heard one ask.
685.12 "I cannot tell: I found her at the door," was
685.13 the reply.
685.14 "She does look white," said Hannah.
685.15 "As white as clay or death," was responded.
685.16 "She will fall: let her sit."
685.17 And indeed my head swam: I dropped; but a
685.18 chair received me. I still possessed my senses;
685.19 though just now I could not speak.
685.20 "Perhaps a little water would restore her.
685.21 Hannah, fetch some. But she is worn to nothing.
685.22 How very thin, and how very bloodless!"
685.23 "A mere spectre!"
685.24 "Is she ill, or only famished?"
685.25 "Famished, I think. Hannah, is that milk?
685.26 Give it me, and a piece of bread."
685.27 Diana /I knew her by the long curls which I
685.28 saw drooping between me and the fire as she bent
686.01 over me/ broke some bread, dipped it in milk, and
686.02 put it to my lips. Her face was near mine: I saw
686.03 there was pity in it, and I felt sympathy in her
686.04 hurried breathing. In her simple words, too, the
686.05 same balm-like emotion spoke: "Try to eat."
686.06 "Yes -- try," repeated Mary gently; and Mary's
686.07 hand removed my sodden bonnet and lifted my
686.08 head. I tasted what they offered me: feebly at
686.09 first, eagerly soon.
686.10 "Not too much at first -- restrain her," said the
686.11 brother; "she has had enough." And he with-
686.12 drew the cup of milk and the plate of bread.
686.13 "A little more, St. John -- look at the avidity in
686.14 her eyes."
686.15 "No more at present, sister. Try if she can
686.16 speak now -- ask her her name."
686.17 I felt I could speak, and I answered -- "My name
686.18 is Jane Elliott." Anxious as ever to avoid dis-
686.19 covery, I had before resolved to assume an alias.
686.20 "And where do you live? Where are your
686.21 friends?"
686.22 I was silent.
686.23 "Can we send for any one you know?"
686.24 I shook my head.
686.25 "What account can you give of yourself?"
686.26 Somehow, now that I had once crossed the
686.27 threshold of this house, and once was brought face
686.28 to face with its owners, I felt no longer outcast,
687.01 vagrant, and disowned by the wide world. I
687.02 dared to put off the mendicant -- to resume my
687.03 natural manner and character. I began once more
687.04 to know myself; and when Mr. St. John demanded
687.05 an account -- which at present I was far too weak
687.06 to render -- I said after a brief pause, --
687.07 "Sir, I can give you no details to-night."
687.08 "But what, then," said he, "do you expect me
687.09 to do for you?"
687.10 "Nothing," I replied. My strength sufficed for
687.11 but short answers. Diana took the word: --
687.12 "Do you mean," she asked, "that we have now
687.13 given you what aid you require; and that we may
687.14 dismiss you to the moor and the rainy night?"
687.15 I looked at her. She had, I thought, a remarkable
687.16 countenance; instinct both with power and good-
687.17 ness. I took sudden courage. Answering her
687.18 compassionate gaze with a smile, I said: "I will
687.19 trust you. If I were a masterless and stray dog, I
687.20 know that you would not turn me from your hearth
687.21 to-night: as it is, I really have no fear. Do with
687.22 me and for me as you like; but excuse me from
687.23 much discourse -- my breath is short -- I feel a
687.24 spasm when I speak." All three surveyed me, and
687.25 all three were silent.
687.26 "Hannah," said Mr. St. John, at last, "let her
687.27 sit there at present, and ask her no questions; in
687.28 ten minutes more, give her the remainder of that
688.01 milk and bread. Mary and Diana, let us go into
688.02 the parlour and talk the matter over."
688.03 They withdrew. Very soon one of the ladies
688.04 returned -- I could not tell which. A kind of plea-
688.05 sant stupor was stealing over me as I sat by the
688.06 genial fire. In an under tone she gave some direc-
688.07 tions to Hannah. Ere long, with the servant's aid,
688.08 I contrived to mount a staircase: my dripping
688.09 clothes were removed; soon, a warm, dry bed
688.10 received me. I thanked God -- experienced amidst
688.11 unutterable exhaustion a glow of grateful joy -- and
688.12 slept.
689.01 [Vol. 3 Chapter 3]
689.02 The recollection of about three days and nights
689.03 succeeding this is very dim in my mind. I
689.04 can recall some sensations felt in that interval;
689.05 but few thoughts framed, and no actions per-
689.06 formed. I knew I was in a small room, and in a
689.07 narrow bed. To that bed I seemed to have
689.08 grown: I lay on it motionless as a stone; and to
689.09 have torn me from it would have been almost to
689.10 kill me. I took no note of the lapse of time -- of
689.11 the change from morning to noon, from noon to
689.12 evening. I observed when any one entered or
689.13 left the apartment; I could even tell who they
689.14 were; I could understand what was said when
689.15 the speaker stood near to me; but I could not an-
689.16 swer: to open my lips or move my limbs was
689.17 equally impossible. Hannah, the servant, was my
689.18 most frequent visitor. Her coming disturbed me.
689.19 I had a feeling that she wished me away; that
689.20 she did not understand me or my circumstances;
690.01 that she was prejudiced against me. Diana and
690.02 Mary appeared in the chamber once or twice a day.
690.03 They would whisper sentences of this sort at my
690.04 bed-side: --

690.05 "It is very well we took her in."
690.06 "Yes; she would certainly have been found
690.07 dead at the door in the morning, had she been
690.08 left out all night. I wonder what she has gone
690.09 through?"
690.10 "Strange hardships, I imagine -- poor, emaciated,
690.11 pallid wanderer!"
690.12 "She is not an uneducated person, I should
690.13 think, by her manner of speaking; her accent was
690.14 quite pure; and the clothes she took off, though
690.15 splashed and wet, were little worn and fine."
690.16 "She has a peculiar face; fleshless and haggard
690.17 as it is, I rather like it; and when in good health
690.18 and animated, I can fancy her physiognomy would
690.19 be agreeable."
690.20 Never once in their dialogues did I hear a
690.21 syllable of regret at the hospitality they had ex-
690.22 tended to me; or of suspicion of, or aversion to,
690.23 myself. I was comforted.
690.24 Mr. St. John came but once: he looked at me,
690.25 and said my state of lethargy was the result of
690.26 reaction from excessive and protracted fatigue.
690.27 He pronounced it needless to send for a doctor:
690.28 nature, he was sure, would manage best, left to
691.01 herself. He said every nerve had been over--
691.02 strained in some way, and the whole system must
691.03 sleep torpid awhile. There was no disease. He
691.04 imagined my recovery would be rapid enough
691.05 when once commenced. These opinions he de-
691.06 livered in a few words, in a quiet, low voice; and
691.07 added, after a pause, in the tone of a man little
691.08 accustomed to expansive comment, "rather an
691.09 unusual physiognomy; certainly, not indicative of
691.10 vulgarity or degradation."
691.11 "Far otherwise," responded Diana. "To speak
691.12 truth, St. John, my heart rather warms to the
691.13 poor little soul. I wish we may be able to benefit
691.14 her permanently."
691.15 "That is hardly likely," was the reply. "You
691.16 will find she is some young lady who has had a
691.17 misunderstanding with her friends, and has pro-
691.18 bably injudiciously left them. We may, perhaps,
691.19 succeed in restoring her to them, if she is not ob-
691.20 stinate: but I trace lines of force in her face which
691.21 make me skeptical of her tractability." He stood
691.22 considering me some minutes; then added, "She
691.23 looks sensible, but not at all handsome."
691.24 "She is so ill, St. John."
691.25 "Ill or well, she would always be plain. The
691.26 grace and harmony of beauty are quite wanting in
691.27 those features."
691.28 On the third day, I was better; on the fourth,
692.01 I could speak, move, rise in bed, and turn.
692.02 Hannah had brought me some gruel and dry
692.03 toast, about, as I supposed, the dinner hour. I
692.04 had eaten with relish: the food was good -- void
692.05 of the feverish flavour which had hitherto poisoned
692.06 what I had swallowed. When she left me, I felt
692.07 comparatively strong and revived; ere long satiety
692.08 of repose, and desire for action stirred me. I
692.09 wished to rise; but what could I put on? Only
692.10 my damp and bemired apparel; in which I had
692.11 slept on the ground and fallen in the marsh. I
692.12 felt ashamed to appear before my benefactors so
692.13 clad. I was spared the humiliation.
692.14 On a chair by the bed-side were all my own
692.15 things, clean and dry. My black silk frock hung
692.16 against the wall. The traces of the bog were
692.17 removed from it; the creases left by the wet
692.18 smoothed out: it was quite decent. My very
692.19 shoes and stockings were purified and rendered
692.20 presentable. There were the means of washing
692.21 in the room, and a comb and brush to smooth my
692.22 hair. After a weary process, and resting every
692.23 five minutes, I succeeded in dressing myself. My
692.24 clothes hung loose on me; for I was much wasted,
692.25 but I covered deficiencies with a shawl, and once
692.26 more, clean and respectable-looking -- no speck of
692.27 the dirt, no trace of the disorder I so hated, and
692.28 which seemed so to degrade me, left -- I crept
693.01 down a stone staircase, with the aid of the ban-
693.02 nisters, to a narrow, long passage, and found my
693.03 way presently to the kitchen.
693.04 It was full of the fragrance of new bread, and
693.05 the warmth of a generous fire. Hannah was
693.06 baking. Prejudices, it is well known, are most
693.07 difficult to eradicate from the heart whose soil has
693.08 never been loosened or fertilized by education:
693.09 they grow there, firm as weeds among stones.
693.10 Hannah had been cold and stiff, indeed, at the
693.11 first: latterly, she had begun to relent a little;
693.12 and when she saw me come in tidy and well--
693.13 dressed, she even smiled.
693.14 "What, you have got up?" she said. "You are
693.15 better, then. You may sit you down in my chair
693.16 on the hearthstone, if you will."
693.17 She pointed to the rocking chair: I took it.
693.18 She bustled about, examining me every now and
693.19 then with the corner of her eye. Turning to me,
693.20 as she took some loaves from the oven, she asked,
693.21 bluntly --
693.22 "Did you ever go a-begging afore you came
693.23 here?"
693.24 I was indignant for a moment: but remember-
693.25 ing that anger was out of the question, and that I
693.26 had indeed appeared as a beggar to her, I answered
693.27 quietly; but still not without a certain marked
693.28 firmness, --
694.01 "You are mistaken in supposing me a beggar.
694.02 I am no beggar; any more than yourself or your
694.03 young ladies."

694.04 After a pause, she said, "I dunnut understand
694.05 that: you've like no house, nor no brass, I
694.06 guess?"
694.07 "The want of house or brass /by which I sup-
694.08 pose you mean money/ does not make a beggar in
694.09 your sense of the word."
694.10 "Are you book-learned?" she inquired, pre-
694.11 sently.
694.12 "Yes, very."
694.13 "But you've never been to boarding-school?"
694.14 "I was at boarding-school eight years."
694.15 She opened her eyes wide. "Whatever cannot
694.16 ye keep yourseln for, then?"
694.17 "I have kept myself; and, I trust, shall keep
694.18 myself again. What are you going to do with
694.19 these gooseberries?" I inquired, as she brought
694.20 out a basket of the fruit.
694.21 "Mak'em into pies."
694.22 "Give them to me and I'll pick them."
694.23 "Nay; I dunnut want ye to do nought."
694.24 "But I must do something. Let me have
694.25 them."
694.26 She consented; and she even brought me a
694.27 clean towel to spread over my dress, "lest," as
694.28 she said, "I should mucky it."
695.01 "Ye've not been used to sarvant's wark, I see
695.02 by your hands," she remarked. "Happen ye've
695.03 been a dressmaker?"
695.04 "No, you are wrong. And, now, never mind
695.05 what I have been: don't trouble your head fur-
695.06 ther about me; but tell me the name of the house
695.07 where we are."
695.08 "Some calls it Marsh-End, and some calls it
695.09 Moor House."
695.10 "And the gentleman who lives her is called
695.11 Mr. St. John?"
695.12 "Nay; he doesn't live here: he is only staying
695.13 awhile. When he is at home, he is in his own
695.14 parish at Morton."
695.15 "That village a few miles off?"
695.16 "Aye."
695.17 "And what is he?"
695.18 "He is a parson."
695.19 I remembered the answer of the old house-
695.20 keeper at the parsonage, when I had asked to see
695.21 the clergyman. "This, then, was his father's
695.22 residence?"
695.23 "Aye; old Mr. Rivers lived here, and his
695.24 father, and grandfather, and gurt / great/ grand-
695.25 father afore him."
695.26 "The name, then, of the gentleman, is Mr. St.
695.27 John Rivers?"
695.28 "Aye; St. John is like his kirstened name."
696.01 "And his sisters are called Diana and Mary
696.02 Rivers?"
696.03 "Yes."
696.04 "Their father is dead?"
696.05 "Dead three weeks sin', of a stroke."
696.06 "They have no mother?"
696.07 "The mistress has been dead this mony a
696.08 year."
696.09 "Have you lived with the family long?"
696.10 "I've lived here thirty year. I nursed them
696.11 all three."
696.12 "That proves you must have been an honest
696.13 and faithful servant. I will say so much for you,
696.14 though you have had the incivility to call me a
696.15 beggar."
696.16 She again regarded me with a surprised stare.
696.17 "I believe," she said, "I was quite mistaken in
696.18 my thoughts of you: but there is so mony cheats
696.19 goes about, you mun forgie me."
696.20 "And though," I continued, rather severely,
696.21 "you wished to turn me from the door, on a
696.22 night when you should not have shut out a
696.23 dog."
696.24 "Well, it was hard: but what can a body do?
696.25 I thought more o' th' childer nor of mysel: poor
696.26 things! They've like nobody to tak' care on 'em
696.27 but me. I'm like to look sharpish."
696.28 I maintained a grave silence for some minutes.
697.01 "You munnut think to hardly of me," she
697.02 again remarked.
697.03 "But I do think hardly of you," I said; "and
697.04 I'll tell you why -- not so much because you refused
697.05 to give me shelter, or regarded me as an impostor,
697.06 as because you just now made it a species of re-
697.07 proach that I had no "brass," and no house. Some
697.08 of the best people that ever lived have been as
697.09 destitute as I am; and if you are a Christian, you
697.10 ought not to consider poverty a crime."
697.11 "No more I ought," said she: "Mr. St. John
697.12 tells me so too; and I see I wor wrang -- but I've
697.13 clear a different notion on you now to what I had.
697.14 You look a raight down dacent little crater."
697.15 "That will do -- I forgive you now. Shake
697.16 hands."
697.17 She put her floury and horny hand into mine;
697.18 another and heartier smile illumined her rough
697.19 face: and from that moment we were friends.
697.20 Hannah was evidently fond of talking. While
697.21 I picked the fruit, and she made the paste for the
697.22 pies, she proceeded to give me sundry details
697.23 about her deceased master and mistress, and "the
697.24 childer," as she called the young people.
697.25 Old Mr. Rivers, she said, was a plain man
697.26 enough; but a gentleman, and of as ancient a family
697.27 as could be found. Marsh-End had belonged to
697.28 the Rivers' ever since it was a house: and it was,
698.01 she affirmed, "aboon two hundred year old -- for
698.02 all it looked but a small, humble place, naught to

698.03 compare wi' Mr. Oliver's grand hall down i' Mor-
698.04 ton Vale. But she could remember Bill Oliver's
698.05 father a journeyman needle-maker; and th' Rivers'
698.06 wor gentry i' th' owd days o' th' Henrys, as ony-
698.07 body might see by looking into th' registers i'
698.08 Morton Church vestry." Still, she allowed, "the
698.09 owd maister was like other folk -- naught mich out
698.10 o' t' common way: stark mad o' shooting, and
698.11 farming, and sich like." The mistress was differ-
698.12 ent. She was a great reader, and studied a deal;
698.13 and the "bairns" had taken after her. There was
698.14 nothing like them in these parts, nor ever had been:
698.15 they had liked learning, all three, almost from
698.16 the time they could speak; and they had always
698.17 been "of a mak' of their own." Mr. St. John,
698.18 when he grew up, would go to college and be a
698.19 parson; as soon as they left school, the girls
698.20 would seek places as governesses: for they had
698.21 told her their father had some years ago lost a
698.22 great deal of money, by a man he has trusted turn-
698.23 ing bankrupt; and as he was now not rich enough
698.24 to give them fortunes, they must provide for
698.25 themselves. They had lived very little at home
698.26 for a long while, and were only come now to stay
698.27 a few weeks on account of their father's death:
698.28 but they did so like Marsh-End and Morton, and
699.01 all these moors and hills about. They had been
699.02 in London, and many other grand towns; but they
699.03 always said there was no place like home: and
699.04 then they were so agreeable with each other --
699.05 never fell out nor "threaped." She did not know
699.06 where there was such a family for being united.
699.07   Having finished my task of gooseberry picking,
699.08 I asked where the two ladies and their brother
699.09 were now.
699.10   "Gone over to Morton for a walk; but they
699.11 would be back in half an hour to tea."
699.12   They returned within the time Hannah had
699.13 allotted them: they entered by the kitchen door.
699.14 Mr. St. John, when he saw me, merely bowed and
699.15 passed through; the two ladies stopped: Mary,
699.16 in a few words, kindly and calmly expressed the
699.17 pleasure she felt in seeing me well enough to be
699.18 able to come down; Diana took my hand: she
699.19 shook her head at me.
699.20   "You should have waited for my leave to
699.21 descend," she said. "You still look very pale --
699.22 and so thin! Poor child! -- poor girl!"
699.23   Diana had a voice toned, to my ear, like the
699.24 cooing of a dove. She possessed eyes whose gaze
699.25 I delighted to encounter. Her whole face seemed
699.26 to me full of charm. Mary's countenance was
699.27 equally intelligent -- her features equally pretty:
699.28 but her expression was more reserved; and her
700.01 manners, though gentle, more distant. Diana
700.02 looked and spoke with a certain authority: she
700.03 had a will evidently. It was my nature to feel
700.04 pleasure in yielding to an authority supported like
700.05 hers; and to bend, where my conscience and self--
700.06 respect permitted, to an active will.
700.07   "And what business have you here?" she con-
700.08 tinued. "It is not your place. Mary and I sit
700.09 in the kitchen sometimes, because at home we
700.10 like to be free, even to license -- but you are a
700.11 visitor, and must go into the parlour."
700.12   "I am very well here."
700.13   "Not at all -- with Hannah bustling about and
700.14 covering you with flour."
700.15   "Besides, the fire is too hot for you," interposed
700.16 Mary.
700.17   "To be sure," added her sister. "Come, you
700.18 must be obedient." And still holding my hand,
700.19 she made me rise, and led me into the inner
700.20 room.
700.21   "Sit there," she said, placing me on the sofa,
700.22 "while we take our things off and get the tea
700.23 ready: it is another privilege we exercise in our
700.24 little moorland home -- to prepare our own meals
700.25 when we are so inclined; or when Hannah is
700.26 baking, brewing, washing, or ironing,"
700.27   She closed the door, leaving me solus with Mr.
700.28 St. John, who sat opposite; a book or newspaper
701.01 in his hand. I examined, first, the parlour, and
701.02 then its occupant.
701.03   The parlour was rather a small room, very
701.04 plainly furnished; yet comfortable, because clean
701.05 and neat. The old-fashioned chairs were very
701.06 bright, and the walnut-wood table was like a look-
701.07 ing-glass. A few strange, antique portraits of the
701.08 men and women of other days decorated the
701.09 stained walls; a cupboard with glass doors con-
701.10 tained some books and an ancient set of china.
701.11 There was no superfluous ornament in the room --
701.12 not one modern piece of furniture, save a brace of
701.13 work-boxes and a lady's desk in rosewood, which
701.14 stood on a side-table: every thing -- including the
701.15 carpet and curtains -- looked at once well worn
701.16 and well saved.
701.17   Mr. St. John -- sitting as still as one of the
701.18 dusky pictures on the walls; keeping his eyes
701.19 fixed on the page he perused, and his lips mutely
701.20 sealed -- was easy enough to examine. Had he been
701.21 a statue instead of a man, he could not have been
701.22 easier. He was young -- perhaps from twenty--
701.23 eight to thirty -- tall, slender; his face riveted the
701.24 eye: it was like a Greek face, very pure in out-
701.25 line; quite a straight, classic nose; quite an Athe-
701.26 nian mouth and chin. It is seldom, indeed, an
701.27 English face comes so near the antique models as
701.28 did his. He might well be a little shocked at the
702.01 irregularity of my lineaments, his own being so

702.02 harmonious. His eyes were large and blue, with
702.03 brown lashes; his high forehead, colourless as
702.04 ivory, was partially streaked over by careless locks
702.05 of fair hair.
702.06   This is a gentle delineation, is it not, reader?
702.07 Yet he whom it describes scarcely impressed one
702.08 with the idea of a gentle, a yielding, an impres-
702.09 sible, or even of a placid nature. Quiescent as
702.10 he now sat, there was something about his nostril,
702.11 his mouth, his brow, which, to my perceptions,
702.12 indicated elements within either restless, or hard,
702.13 or eager. He did not speak to me one word nor
702.14 even direct to me one glance, till his sisters re-
702.15 turned. Diana, as she passed in and out, in the
702.16 course of preparing tea, brought me a little cake,
702.17 baked on the top of the oven.
702.18   "Eat that now," she said: "you must be
702.19 hungry. Hannah says you have had nothing but
702.20 some gruel since breakfast."
702.21   I did not refuse it, for my appetite was awakened
702.22 and keen. Mr. Rivers now closed his book, ap-
702.23 proached the table, and, as he took a seat, fixed
702.24 his blue, pictorial-looking eyes full on me. There
702.25 was an unceremonious directness, a searching, de-
702.26 cided steadfastness in his gaze now, which told
702.27 that intention, and not diffidence, had hitherto
702.28 kept it averted from the stranger.
703.01   "You are very hungry," he said.
703.02   "I am, sir." It is my way -- it always was my
703.03 way, by instinct -- ever to meet the brief with bre-
703.04 vity, the direct with plainness."
703.05   "It is well for you that a low fever has forced
703.06 you to abstain for the last three days: there
703.07 would have been danger in yielding to the cravings
703.08 of your appetite at first. Now you may eat;
703.09 though still not immoderately."
703.10   "I trust I shall not eat long at your expense,
703.11 sir," was my very clumsily-contrived, unpolished
703.12 answer.
703.13   "No," he said, coolly: "when you have in-
703.14 dicated to us the residence of your friends, we
703.15 can write to them, and you may be restored to
703.16 home."
703.17   "That, I must plainly tell you, it is out of my
703.18 power to do; being absolutely without home and
703.19 friends."
703.20   The three looked at me: but not distrustfully.
703.21 I felt there was no suspicion in their glances:
703.22 there was more of curiosity. I speak particularly
703.23 of the young ladies. St. John's eyes, though
703.24 clear enough in a literal sense, in a figurative one
703.25 were difficult to fathom. He seemed to use them
703.26 rather as instruments to search other people's
703.27 thoughts, than as agents to reveal his own: the
703.28 which combination of keenness and reserve was
704.01 considerably more calculated to embarrass then to
704.02 encourage.
704.03   "Do you mean to say," he asked, "that you
704.04 are completely isolated from every connection?"
704.05   "I do. Not a tie links me to any living thing:
704.06 not a claim do I possess to admittance under any
704.07 roof in England."
704.08   "A most singular position at your age!"
704.09   Here I saw his glance directed to my hands,
704.10 which were folded on the table before me. I
704.11 wondered what he sought there: his words soon
704.12 explained the quest.
704.13   "You have never been married? You are a
704.14 spinster?"
704.15   Diana laughed. "Why, she can't be above
704.16 seventeen or eighteen years old, St. John," said
704.17 she.
704.18   "I am near nineteen: but I am not married.
704.19 No."
704.20   I felt a burning glow mount to my face; for
704.21 bitter and agitating recollections were awakened
704.22 by the allusion to marriage. They all saw the
704.23 embarrassment, and the emotion. Diana and
704.24 Mary relieved me by turning their eyes elsewhere
704.25 than to my crimsoned visage; but the colder and
704.26 sterner brother continued to gaze, till the trouble
704.27 he had excited forced out tears as well as
704.28 colour.
705.01   "Where did you last reside?" he now
705.02 asked.
705.03   "You are too inquisitive, St. John," murmured
705.04 Mary, in a low voice; but he leaned over the
705.05 table and required an answer, by a second firm and
705.06 piercing look.
705.07   "The name of the place where, and of the
705.08 person with whom I lived, is my secret," I re-
705.09 plied, concisely.
705.10   "Which, if you like, you have, in my opinion,
705.11 a right to keep, both from St. John and every
705.12 other questioner," remarked Diana.
705.13   "Yet if I know nothing about you or your
705.14 history, I cannot help you," he said. "And you
705.15 need help: do you not?"
705.16   "I need it, and I seek it; so far, sir, that some
705.17 true philanthropist will put me in the way of get-
705.18 ting work which I can do, and the remuneration
705.19 for which will keep me: if but in the barest neces-
705.20 saries of life."
705.21   "I know not whether I am a true philanthropist;
705.22 yet I am willing to aid you to the utmost of my
705.23 power, in a purpose so honest. First, then, tell
705.24 me what you have been accustomed to do, and
705.25 what you can do."
705.26   I had now swallowed my tea. I was mightily
705.27 refreshed by the beverage; as much so as a
705.28 giant with wine: it gave new tone to my unstrung

706.01 nerves, and enabled me to address this pene-
706.02 trating young judge steadily.
706.03 "Mr. Rivers," I said, turning to him, and look-
706.04 ing at him, as he looked at me, openly and without
706.05 diffidence, "you and your sisters have done me a
706.06 great service -- the greatest man can do his fellow--
706.07 being: you have rescued me, by your noble hospi-
706.08 tality, from death. This benefit conferred gives
706.09 you an unlimited claim on my gratitude; and a
706.10 claim, to a certain extent, on my confidence. I
706.11 will tell you as much of the history of the wanderer
706.12 you have harboured, as I can tell without compro-
706.13 mising my own peace of mind -- my own security,
706.14 moral and physical, and that of others.
706.15 "I am an orphan; the daughter of a clergy-
706.16 man. My parents died before I could know
706.17 them. I was brought up a dependant; educated
706.18 in a charitable institution. I will even tell you the
706.19 name of the establishment, where I passed six
706.20 years as a pupil, and two as a teacher -- Lowood
706.21 Orphan Asylum, ----shire: you will have heard
706.22 of it, Mr. Rivers? -- the Rev. Robert Brocklehurst
706.23 is the treasurer."
706.24 "I have heard of Mr. Brocklehurst, and I have
706.25 seen the school."
706.26 "I left Lowood nearly a year since to become a
706.27 private governess. I obtained a good situation,
706.28 and was happy. This place I was obliged to leave
707.01 four days before I came here. The reason of my
707.02 departure I cannot and ought not to explain: it
707.03 would be useless -- dangerous; and would sound
707.04 incredible. No blame attached to me: I am as
707.05 free from culpability as any one of you three.
707.06 Miserable I am, and must be for a time; for the
707.07 catastrophe which drove me from a house I had
707.08 found a paradise was of a strange and direful
707.09 nature. I observed but two points in planning
707.10 my departure -- speed, secrecy: to secure these, I
707.11 had to leave behind me everything I possessed,
707.12 except a small parcel; which, in my hurry and
707.13 trouble of mind, I forgot to take out of the coach
707.14 that brought me to Whitcross. To this neighbour-
707.15 hood, then, I came, quite destitute. I slept two
707.16 nights in the open air, and wandered about two
707.17 days without crossing a threshold: but twice in
707.18 that space of time did I taste food; and it was
707.19 when brought by hunger, exhaustion, and despair,
707.20 almost to the last gasp, that you, Mr. Rivers, for-
707.21 bade me to perish of want at your door, and took
707.22 me under the shelter of your roof. I know all
707.23 your sisters have done for me since -- for I have
707.24 not been insensible during my seeming torpor --
707.25 and I owe to their spontaneous, genuine, genial
707.26 compassion, as large a debt as to your evangelical
707.27 charity."
707.28 "Don't make her talk any more now, St. John,"
708.01 said Diana, as I paused; "she is evidently not yet
708.02 fit for excitement. Come to the sofa, and sit down
708.03 now, Miss Elliott."
708.04 I gave an involuntary half-start at hearing the
708.05 alias: I had forgotten my new name. Mr. Rivers,
708.06 whom nothing seemed to escape, noticed it at once.
708.07 "You said your name was Jane Elliott?" he
708.08 observed.
708.09 "I did say so; and it is the name by which I
708.10 think it expedient to be called at present but it
708.11 is not my real name, and when I hear it, it sounds
708.12 strange to me."
708.13 "Your real name you will not give?"
708.14 "No: I fear discovery above all things; and
708.15 whatever disclosure would lead to it I avoid."
708.16 "You are quite right, I am sure," said Diana.
708.17 "Now, do, brother, let her be at peace a while."
708.18 But when St. John had mused a few moments,
708.19 he recommenced, as imperturbably, and with as
708.20 much acumen as ever.
708.21 "You would not like to be long dependent on
708.22 our hospitality -- you would wish, I see, to dispense
708.23 as soon as may be with my sisters' compassion;
708.24 and, above all, with my charity /I am quite sensible
708.25 of the distinction drawn, nor do I resent it -- it is
708.26 just/: you desire to be independent of us?"
708.27 "I do: I have already said so. Show me how
708.28 to work, or how to seek work: that is all I now
709.01 ask; then let me go, if it be but to the meanest
709.02 cottage -- but till then, allow me to stay here: I
709.03 dread another essay of the horrors of homeless
709.04 destitution."
709.05 "Indeed, you shall stay here," said Diana, put-
709.06 ting her white hand on my head. "You shall,"
709.07 repeated Mary, in the tone of undemonstrative
709.08 sincerity, which seemed natural to her.
709.09 "My sisters, you see, have a pleasure in keep-
709.10 ing you," said Mr. St. John, "as they would have
709.11 a pleasure in keeping and cherishing a half-frozen
709.12 bird, some wintry wind might have driven through
709.13 their casement. I feel more inclination to put
709.14 you in the way of keeping yourself; and shall
709.15 endeavour to do so: but observe, my sphere is
709.16 narrow. I am but the incumbent of a poor country
709.17 parish: my aid must be of the humblest sort.
709.18 And if you are inclined to despise the day of small
709.19 things, seek some more efficient succour than such
709.20 as I can offer."
709.21 "She has already said that she is willing to do
709.22 anything honest she can do," answered Diana, for
709.23 me; "and you know, St. John, she has no choice
709.24 of helpers: she is forced to put up with such
709.25 crusty people as you."
709.26 "I will be a dressmaker: I will be a plain-work--
709.27 woman; I will be a servant, a nurse-girl, if I can

709.28 be no better," I answered.
710.01 "Right," said Mr. St. John, quite coolly. "If
710.02 such is your spirit, I promise to aid you; in my
710.03 own time and way."
710.04 He now resumed the book with which he had
710.05 been occupied before tea. I soon withdrew; for I
710.06 had talked as much, and sat up as long, as my
710.07 present strength would permit.
711.01 [Vol. 3 Chapter 4]
711.02 The more I knew of the inmates of Moor-House,
711.03 the better I liked them. In a few days I had so
711.04 far recovered my health that I could sit up all
711.05 day, and walk out sometimes. I could join with
711.06 Diana and Mary in all their occupations; converse
711.07 with them as much as they wished, and aid them
711.08 when and where they would allow me. There was
711.09 a reviving pleasure in this intercourse, of a kind
711.10 now tasted by me for the first time -- the pleasure
711.11 arising from perfect congeniality of tastes, senti-
711.12 ments, and principles.
711.13 I liked to read what they liked to read: what
711.14 they enjoyed, delighted me; what they approved,
711.15 I reverenced. They loved their sequestered home.
711.16 I, too, in the gray, small, antique structure, with
711.17 its low roof, its latticed casements, its mouldering
711.18 walls, its avenue of aged firs -- all grown aslant
711.19 under the stress of mountain winds; its garden,
711.20 dark with yew and holly -- and where no flowers
712.01 but of the hardiest species would bloom -- found a
712.02 charm, both potent and permanent. They clung
712.03 to the purple moors behind and around their
712.04 dwelling -- to the hollow vale into which the pebbly
712.05 bridal-path leading from their gate descended;
712.06 and which wound between fern-banks first, and
712.07 then amongst a few of the wildest little pasture--
712.08 fields that ever bordered a wilderness of heath, or
712.09 gave sustenance to a flock of gray moorland sheep,
712.10 with their little mossy-faced lambs: -- they clung
712.11 to this scene, I say, with a perfect enthusiasm of
712.12 attachment. I could comprehend the feeling, and
712.13 share both its strength and truth. I saw the fasci-
712.14 nation of the locality. I felt the consecration of
712.15 its loneliness: my eye feasted on the outline of
712.16 swell and sweep -- on the wild colouring commu-
712.17 nicated to ridge and dell, by moss, by heath-bell,
712.18 by flower-sprinkled turf, by brilliant bracken, and
712.19 mellow granite crag. These details were just to
712.20 me what they were to them -- so many pure and
712.21 sweet sources of pleasure. The strong blast and
712.22 the soft breeze; the rough and the halcyon day;
712.23 the hours of sunrise and sunset; the moonlight
712.24 and the clouded night, developed for me, in these
712.25 regions, the same attraction as for them -- wound
712.26 round my faculties the same spell that entranced
712.27 theirs.
712.28 In-doors we agreed equally well. They were
713.01 both more accomplished and better read than I
713.02 was: but with eagerness I followed in the path of
713.03 knowledge they had trodden before me. I de-
713.04 voured the books they lent me: then it was full
713.05 satisfaction to discuss with them in the evening
713.06 what I had perused during the day. Thought
713.07 fitted thought; opinion met opinion: we coin-
713.08 cided, in short, perfectly.
713.09 If in our trio there was a superior and a leader,
713.10 it was Diana. Physically, she far excelled me: I
713.11 she was handsome; she was vigorous. In her
713.12 animal spirits, there was an affluence of life, and
713.13 certainty of flow, such as excited my wonder,
713.14 while it baffled my comprehension. I could talk
713.15 a while when the evening commenced: but the
713.16 first gush of vivacity and fluency gone, I was fain
713.17 to sit on a stool at Diana's feet, to rest my head
713.18 on her knee, and listen alternately to her and
713.19 Mary; while they sounded thoroughly the topic
713.20 on which I had but touched. Diana offered to
713.21 teach me German. I liked to learn of her: I
713.22 saw the part of instructress pleased and suited
713.23 her; that of scholar pleased and suited me no
713.24 less. Our natures dovetailed: mutual affection
713.25 -- of the strongest kind -- was the result. They
713.26 discovered I could draw: their pencils and colour--
713.27 boxes were immediately at my service. My skill,
714.01 greater in this one point than theirs, surprised
714.02 and charmed them. Mary would sit and watch
714.03 me by the hour together: then she would take
714.04 lessons; and a docile, intelligent, assiduous pupil,
714.05 she made. Thus occupied, and mutually enter-
714.06 tained, days passed like hours, and weeks like
714.07 days.
714.08 As to Mr. St. John, the intimacy which had
714.09 arisen so naturally and rapidly between me and
714.10 his sisters, did not extend to him. One reason of
714.11 the distance yet observed between us was, that he
714.12 was comparatively seldom at home: a large pro-
714.13 portion of his time appeared devoted to visiting
714.14 the sick and poor among the scattered population
714.15 of his parish.
714.16 No weather seemed to hinder him in these
714.17 pastoral excursions: rain or fair, he would, when
714.18 his hours of morning study were over, take his
714.19 hat, and, followed by his father's old pointer,
714.20 Carlo, go out on his mission of love or duty -- I
714.21 scarcely know in which light he regarded it.
714.22 Sometimes, when the day was very unfavourable,
714.23 his sisters would expostulate. He would then say,
714.24 with a peculiar smile, more solemn than cheerful, --
714.25 "And if I let a gust of wind or a sprinkling of
714.26 rain turn me aside from these easy tasks, what
714.27 preparation would such sloth be for the future I
714.28 propose to myself?"

714.28 Diana and Mary's general answer to this ques-
715.01 tion was a sigh, and some minutes of apparently
715.02 mournful meditation.
715.03 But besides his frequent absences, there was
715.04 another barrier to friendship with him: he seemed
715.05 of a reserved, an abstracted, and even of a brood-
715.06 ing nature. Zealous in his ministerial labours,
715.07 blameless in his life and habits, he yet did not
715.08 appear to enjoy that mental serenity, that inward
715.09 content, which should be the reward of every
715.10 sincere Christian and practical philanthropist.
715.11 Often, of an evening, when he sat at the window,
715.12 his desk and papers before him, he would cease
715.13 reading or writing, rest his chin on his hand, and
715.14 deliver himself up to I know not what course of
715.15 thought: but that it was perturbed and exciting
715.16 might be seen in the frequent flash and changeful
715.17 dilation of his eye.
715.18 I think, moreover, that Nature was not to him
715.19 that treasury of delight it was to his sisters. He
715.20 expressed once, and but once in my hearing, a
715.21 strong sense of rugged charm of the hills, and
715.22 an inborn affection for the dark roof and hoary
715.23 walls he called his home: but there was more of
715.24 gloom than pleasure in the tone and words in
715.25 which the sentiment was manifested; and never
715.26 did he seem to roam the moors for the sake of their
715.27 soothing silence -- never seek out or dwell upon the
715.28 thousand peaceful delights they could yield.
716.01 Incommunicative as he was, some time elapsed
716.02 before I had an opportunity of gauging his mind.
716.03 I first got an idea of its calibre when I heard him
716.04 preach in his own church at Morton. I wish I
716.05 could describe that sermon: but it is past my
716.06 power. I cannot even render faithfully the effect
716.07 it produced on me.
716.08 It began calm -- and indeed, as far as delivery
716.09 and pitch of voice went, it was calm to the end:
716.10 an earnestly felt, yet strictly restrained zeal breathed
716.11 soon in the distinct accents, and prompted the
716.12 nervous language. This grew to force -- com-
716.13 pressed, condensed, controlled. The heart was
716.14 thrilled, the mind astonished, by the power of the
716.15 preacher: neither were softened. Throughout
716.16 there was a strange bitterness; an absence of con-
716.17 solatory gentleness: stern allusions to Calvinistic
716.18 doctrines -- election, predestination, reprobation --
716.19 were frequent; and each reference to these points
716.20 sounded like a sentence pronounced for doom.
716.21 When he had done, instead of feeling better,
716.22 calmer, more enlightened by his discourse, I ex-
716.23 perienced an inexpressible sadness; for it seemed
716.24 to me -- I know not whether equally so to others --
716.25 that the eloquence to which I had been listening
716.26 had sprung from a depth where lay turbid dregs of
716.27 disappointment -- where moved troubling impulses
716.28 of insatiate yearnings and disquieting aspirations.
717.01 I was sure St. John Rivers -- pure-lived, conscien-
717.02 tious, zealous as he was -- had not yet found that
717.03 peace of God which passeth all understanding: he
717.04 had no more found it, I thought, than had I; with
717.05 my concealed and racking regrets for my broken
717.06 idol and lost elysium -- regrets to which I have
717.07 latterly avoided referring; but which possessed me
717.08 and tyrannized over me ruthlessly.
717.09 Meantime a month was gone. Diana and Mary
717.10 were soon to leave Moor-House, and return to the
717.11 far different life and scene which awaited them, as
717.12 governesses in a large, fashionable, south-of-Eng-
717.13 land city; where each held a situation in families,
717.14 by whose wealthy and haughty members they were
717.15 regarded only as humble dependants, and who
717.16 neither knew nor sought one of their innate ex-
717.17 cellences, and appreciated only their acquired
717.18 accomplishments as they appreciated the skill of
717.19 their cook, or the taste of their waiting-woman.
717.20 Mr. St. John had said nothing to me yet about the
717.21 employment he had promised to obtain for me: yet
717.22 it became urgent that I should have a vocation
717.23 of some kind. One morning, being left alone
717.24 with him a few minutes in the parlour, I ventured
717.25 to approach the window-recess -- which his table,
717.26 chair, and desk consecrated as a kind of study -- and
717.27 I was going to speak; though not very well know-
717.28 ing in what words to frame my inquiry -- for it is at
718.01 all times difficult to break the ice of reserve glass-
718.02 ing over such natures as his -- when he saved me
718.03 the trouble, by being the first to commence a
718.04 dialogue.
718.05 Looking up as I drew near -- "You have a ques-
718.06 tion to ask of me?" he said.
718.07 "Yes; I wish to know whether you have heard
718.08 of any service I can offer myself to undertake."
718.09 "I found or devised something for you three
718.10 weeks ago; but as you seemed both useful and
718.11 happy here -- as my sisters had evidently become
718.12 attached to you, and your society gave them un-
718.13 usual pleasure -- I deemed it inexpedient to break
718.14 in on your mutual comfort, till their approaching
718.15 departure from Marsh-End should render yours
718.16 necessary."
718.17 "And they will go in three days now?" I said.
718.18 "Yes; and when they go, I shall return to the
718.19 parsonage at Morton: Hannah will accompany
718.20 me; and this old house will be shut up."
718.21 I waited a few moments, expecting he would go
718.22 on with the subject first broached; but he seemed
718.23 to have entered another train of reflection: his
718.24 look denoted abstraction from me and my business.
718.25 I was obliged to recall him to a theme which was
718.26 of necessity one of close and anxious interest to
718.27 me.
718.28 "What is the employment you had in view,
719.01 Mr. Rivers? I hope this delay will not have in-
719.02 creased the difficulty of securing it."
719.03 "Oh, no; since it is an employment which
719.04 depends only on me to give, and you to accept."
719.05 He again paused: there seemed a reluctance to
719.06 continue. I grew impatient: a restless movement
719.07 or two, and an eager and exacting glance fastened
719.08 on his face, conveyed the feeling to him as effec-
719.09 tually as words could have done, and with less
719.10 trouble.
719.11 "You need be in no hurry to hear," he said:
719.12 "let me frankly tell you, I have nothing eligible or
719.13 profitable to suggest. Before I explain, recall, if
719.14 you please, my notice, clearly given, that if I helped
719.15 you, it must be as the blind man would help the
719.16 lame. I am poor; for I find that, when I have
719.17 paid my father's debts, all the patrimony remaining
719.18 to me will be this crumbling grange, the row of
719.19 scathed firs behind, and the patch of moorish soil,
719.20 with the yew-trees and holly-bushes in front. I
719.21 am obscure: Rivers is an old name; but of the
719.22 three sole descendants of the race, two earn the
719.23 dependant's crust among strangers, and the third
719.24 considers himself an alien from his native country
719.25 -- not only for life, but in death. Yes, and deems,
719.26 and is bound to deem, himself honoured by the lot;
719.27 and aspires but after the day when the cross of
719.28 separation from fleshly ties shall be laid on his
720.01 shoulders, and when the Head of that church--
720.02 militant of whose humblest members he is one,
720.03 shall give the word, `Rise, follow me!'"
720.04 St. John said these words as he pronounced his
720.05 sermons, with a quiet, deep voice; with an unflushed
720.06 cheek, and a coruscating radiance of glance. He
720.07 resumed: --
720.08 "And since I am myself poor and obscure, I can
720.09 offer you but a service of poverty and obscurity.
720.10 You may even think it degrading -- for I see now
720.11 your habits have been what the world calls refined:
720.12 your tastes lean to the ideal; and your society has
720.13 at least been amongst the educated -- but I con-
720.14 sider that no service degrades which can better our
720.15 race. I hold that the more arid and unreclaimed
720.16 the soil where the Christian labourer's task of til-
720.17 lage is appointed him -- the scantier the meed his
720.18 toil brings -- the higher the honour. His, under
720.19 such circumstances, is the destiny of the pioneer:
720.20 and the first pioneers of the Gospel were the
720.21 Apostles -- their captain was Jesus, the Redeemer,
720.22 himself."
720.23 "Well?" I said, as he again paused -- "proceed."
720.24 He looked at me before he proceeded: indeed,
720.25 he seemed leisurely to read my face, as if its
720.26 features and lines were characters on a page. The
720.27 conclusions drawn from this scrutiny he partially
720.28 expressed in his succeeding observations.
721.01 "I believe you will accept the post I offer you,"
721.02 said he; "and hold it for a while: not permanently,
721.03 though: any more than I could permanently keep
721.04 the narrow and narrowing -- the tranquil, hidden
721.05 office of English country incumbent: for in your
721.06 nature is an alloy as detrimental to repose as that
721.07 in mine; though of a different kind."
721.08 "Do explain," I urged, when he halted once
721.09 more.
721.10 "I will; and you shall hear how poor the pro-
721.11 posal is -- how trivial -- how cramping. I shall not
721.12 stay long at Morton, now that my father is dead,
721.13 and that I am my own master. I shall leave the
721.14 place probably in the course of a twelvemonth:
721.15 but while I do stay, I will exert myself to the
721.16 utmost for its improvement. Morton, when I
721.17 came to it two years ago, had no school: the chil-
721.18 dren of the poor were excluded from every hope of
721.19 progress. I established one for boys: I mean now
721.20 to open a second school for girls. I have hired a
721.21 building for the purpose, with a cottage of two
721.22 rooms attached to it for the mistress's house. Her
721.23 salary will be thirty pounds a year: her house is
721.24 already furnished, very simply, but sufficiently, by
721.25 the kindness of a lady, Miss Oliver; the only daugh-
721.26 ter of the sole rich man in my parish -- Mr. Oliver,
721.27 the proprietor of a needle-factory and iron-foundry
721.28 in the valley. The same lady pays for the education
722.01 and clothing of an orphan from the workhouse; on
722.02 condition that she shall aid the mistress in such
722.03 menial offices connected with her own house and
722.04 the school, as her occupation of teaching will pre-
722.05 vent her having time to discharge in person. Will
722.06 you be this mistress?"
722.07 He put the question rather hurriedly; he seemed
722.08 half to expect an indignant, or at least a disdainful
722.09 rejection of the offer: not knowing all my thoughts
722.10 and feelings, though guessing some, he could not
722.11 tell in what light the lot would appear to me. In
722.12 truth it was humble -- but then it was sheltered,
722.13 and I wanted a safe asylum: it was plodding -- but
722.14 then, compared with that of a governess in a rich
722.15 house, it was independent; and the fear of servi-
722.16 tude with strangers entered my soul like iron: it
722.17 was not ignoble -- not unworthy -- not mentally de-
722.18 grading. I made my decision.
722.19 "I thank you for the proposal, Mr. Rivers; and
722.20 I accept it with all my heart."
722.21 "But you comprehend me?" he said. "It is
722.22 a village-school: your scholars will be only poor
722.23 girls -- cottagers' children -- at the best, farmers'
722.24 daughters. Knitting, sewing, reading, writing,
722.25 cyphering, will be all you will have to teach.

426

722.26 what will you do with your accomplishments?
722.27 what, with the largest portion of your mind --
722.28 sentiments -- tastes?"
723.01 "Save them till they are wanted. They will
723.02 keep."
723.03 "You know what you undertake, then?"
723.04 "I do."
723.05 He now smiled: and not a bitter or a sad
723.06 smile; but one well pleased and deeply gratified.
723.07 "And when will you commence the exercise of
723.08 your function?"
723.09 "I will go to my house to-morrow; and open
723.10 the school, if you like, next week."
723.11 "Very well: so be it."
723.12 He rose and walked through the room. Stand-
723.13 ing still, he again looked at me. He shook his
723.14 head.
723.15 "what do you disapprove of, Mr. Rivers?" I
723.16 asked.
723.17 "You will not stay at Morton long: no, no!"
723.18 "Why? What is your reason for saying
723.19 so?"
723.20 "I read it in your eye: it is not of that
723.21 description which promises the maintenance of an
723.22 even tenor in life."
723.23 "I am not ambitious."
723.24 He started at the word "ambitious." He re-
723.25 peated, "No. What made you think of ambition?
723.26 who is ambitious? I know I am: but how did
723.27 you find it out?"
723.28 "I was speaking of myself."
724.01 "well, if you are not ambitious, you are -- --."
724.02 He paused.
724.03 "what?"
724.04 "I was going to say, impassioned: but perhaps
724.05 you would have misunderstood the word, and been
724.06 displeased. I mean, that human affections and
724.07 sympathies have a most powerful hold on you. I
724.08 am sure you cannot long be content to pass your
724.09 leisure in solitude, and to devote your working
724.10 hours to a monotonous labour wholly void of
724.11 stimulus; any more than I can be content," he
724.12 added, with emphasis, "to live here buried in
724.13 morass, pent in with mountain -- my nature, that
724.14 God gave me, contravened; my faculties, heaven--
724.15 bestowed, paralyzed -- made useless. You hear
724.16 now how I contradict myself. I, who preached
724.17 contentment with a humble lot, and justified the
724.18 vocation even of hewers of wood, and drawers of
724.19 water, in God's service -- I, his ordained minister,
724.20 almost rave in my restlessness. well, propensi-
724.21 ties and principles must be reconciled by some
724.22 means."
724.23 He left the room. In this brief hour I had
724.24 learnt more of him than in the whole previous
724.25 month: yet still he puzzled me.
724.26 Diana and Mary Rivers became more sad
724.27 and silent as the day approached for leaving
724.28 their brother, and their home. They both tried
725.01 to appear as usual; but the sorrow they had to
725.02 struggle against was one that could not be entirely
725.03 conquered or concealed. Diana intimated that
725.04 this would be a different parting from any they
725.05 had ever yet known. It would probably, as far as
725.06 St. John was concerned, be a parting for years:
725.07 it might be a parting for life.
725.08 "He will sacrifice all to his long-framed re-
725.09 solves," she said: "natural affection and feelings
725.10 more potent still. St. John looks quiet, Jane;
725.11 but he hides a fever in his vitals. You would
725.12 think him gentle, yet in some things he is in-
725.13 exorable as death; and the worst of it is, my
725.14 conscience will hardly permit me to dissuade him
725.15 from his severe decision: certainly, I cannot
725.16 for a moment blame him for it. It is right, noble,
725.17 Christian: yet it breaks my heart." And the
725.18 tears gushed to her fine eyes. Mary bent her
725.19 head low over her work.
725.20 "We are now without father: we shall soon be
725.21 without home and brother," she murmured.
725.22 At that moment a little accident supervened,
725.23 which seemed decreed by fate, purposely to prove
725.24 the truth of the adage, that "misfortunes never
725.25 come singly;" and to add to their distresses the
725.26 vexing one of the slip between the cup and the
725.27 lip. St. John passed the window reading a letter.
725.28 He entered.
726.01 "Our uncle John is dead," said he.
726.02 Both the sisters seemed struck: not shocked or
726.03 appalled: the tidings appeared in their eyes rather
726.04 momentous than afflicting.
726.05 "Dead?" repeated Diana.
726.06 "Yes."
726.07 She riveted a searching gaze on her brother's face.
726.08 "And what then?" she demanded, in a low voice.
726.09 "what then, Die?" he replied, maintaining
726.10 a marble immobility of feature. "What then?
726.11 why -- nothing. Read."
726.12 He threw the letter into her lap. She glanced
726.13 over it, and handed it to Mary. Mary perused
726.14 it in silence, and returned it to her brother.
726.15 All three looked at each other, and all three
726.16 smiled -- a dreary, pensive smile enough.
726.17 "Amen! we can yet live," said Diana, at last.
726.18 "At any rate, it makes us no worse off than we
726.19 were before," remarked Mary.
726.20 "Only it forces rather strongly on the mind
726.21 the picture of what might have been," said Mr.
726.22 Rivers; "and contrasts it somewhat too vividly
726.23 with what is."
726.24 He folded the letter, locked it in his desk, and

726.25 again went out.
726.26 For some minutes no one spoke. Diana then
726.27 turned to me.
726.28 "Jane, you will wonder at us and our mys-
727.01 teries," she said; "and think us hard-hearted
727.02 beings not to be more moved at the death of so
727.03 near a relation as an uncle; but we have never
727.04 seen him or known him. He was my mother's
727.05 brother. My father and he quarrelled long ago.
727.06 It was by his advice that my father risked most
727.07 of his property in the speculation that ruined him.
727.08 Mutual recriminations passed between them: they
727.09 parted in anger, and were never reconciled. My
727.10 uncle engaged afterwards in more prosperous
727.11 undertakings: it appears he realized a fortune of
727.12 twenty thousand pounds. He was never married,
727.13 and had no near kindred but ourselves, and one
727.14 other person, not more closely related than we.
727.15 My father always cherished the idea that he would
727.16 atone for his error, by leaving his possessions to
727.17 us; that letter informs us that he has bequeathed
727.18 every penny to the other relation, with the ex-
727.19 ception of thirty guineas, to be divided between
727.20 St. John, Diana, and Mary Rivers, for the pur-
727.21 chase of three mourning rings. He had a right,
727.22 of course, to do as he pleased: and yet a mo-
727.23 mentary damp is cast on the spirits by the receipt
727.24 of such news. Mary and I would have esteemed
727.25 ourselves rich with a thousand pounds each; and
727.26 to St. John such a sum would have been valuable,
727.27 for the good it would have enabled him to do."
727.28 This explanation given, the subject was dropped,
728.01 and no further reference made to it, by either Mr.
728.02 Rivers or his sisters. The next day, I left Marsh
728.03 End for Morton. The day after, Diana and Mary
728.04 quitted it for distant B--. In a week, Mr. Rivers
728.05 and Hannah repaired to the parsonage: and so
728.06 the old grange was abandoned.
729.01 [Vol. 3 Chapter 5]
729.02 My home, then, -- when I at last find a home, -- is
729.03 a cottage: a little room with white-washed walls,
729.04 and a sanded floor; containing four painted chairs
729.05 and a table, a clock, a cupboard, with two or
729.06 three plates and dishes, and a set of tea-things in
729.07 delf. Above, a chamber of the same dimensions
729.08 as the kitchen, with a deal bedstead, and chest of
729.09 drawers; small, yet too large to be filled with my
729.10 scanty wardrobe: though the kindness of my
729.11 gentle and generous friends has increased that,
729.12 by a modest stock of such things as are ne-
729.13 cessary.
729.14 It is evening. I have dismissed, with the fee
729.15 of an orange, the little orphan who serves me as
729.16 a handmaid. I am sitting alone on the hearth.
729.17 This morning, the village school opened. I had
729.18 read: none write or cypher. Several knit, and
729.19 a few sew a little. They speak with the broadest
730.01 accent of the district. At present, they and I
730.02 have a difficulty in understanding each other's
730.03 language. Some of them are unmannered, rough,
730.04 intractable, as well as ignorant; but others are
730.05 docile, have a wish to learn, and evince a dispo-
730.06 sition that pleases me. I must not forget that
730.07 these coarsely-clad little peasants are of flesh and
730.08 blood as good as the scions of gentlest genealogy;
730.09 and that the germs of native excellence, refine-
730.10 ment, intelligence, kind feeling, are as likely to
730.11 exist in their hearts as in those of the best-born.
730.12 My duty will be to develop these germs: surely
730.13 I shall find some happiness in discharging that
730.14 office. Much enjoyment I do not expect in the
730.15 life opening before me: yet it will, doubtless, if I
730.16 regulate my mind, and exert my powers as I
730.17 ought, yield me enough to live on from day to
730.18 day.
730.19 was I very gleeful, settled, content, during the
730.20 hours I passed in yonder bare, humble school--
730.21 room this morning and afternoon? not to deceive
730.22 myself, I must reply -- No: I felt desolate to a
730.23 degree. I felt -- yes, idiot that I am -- I felt de-
730.24 graded. I doubted I had taken a step which sank
730.25 instead of raising me in the scale of social existence.
730.26 I was weakly dismayed at the ignorance, the
730.27 poverty, the coarseness of all I heard and saw
730.28 round me. But let me not hate and despise my-
731.01 self too much for these feelings: I know them to
731.02 be wrong -- that is a great step gained; I shall
731.03 strive to overcome them. To-morrow, I trust, I
731.04 shall get the better of them partially; and in a few
731.05 weeks, perhaps, they will be quite subdued. In a
731.06 few months, it is possible, the happiness of seeing
731.07 progress, and a change for the better in my scholars,
731.08 may substitute gratification for disgust.
731.09 Meantime, let me ask myself one question --
731.10 which is better? -- To have surrendered to tempta-
731.11 tion; listened to passion; made no painful effort
731.12 -- no struggle; -- but to have sunk down in the
731.13 silken snare; fallen asleep on the flowers covering
731.14 it; wakened in a southern clime, amongst the
731.15 luxuries of a pleasure-villa: to have been now living
731.16 in France, Mr. Rochester's mistress; delirious with
731.17 his love half my time -- for he would -- oh, yes, he
731.18 would have loved me well for a while. He did love
731.19 me -- no one will ever love me so again. I shall
731.20 never more know the sweet homage given to
731.21 beauty, youth, and grace -- for never to any one else
731.22 shall I seem to possess these charms. He was
731.23 fond and proud of me -- it is what no man besides
731.24 will ever be. -- But where am I wandering, and
731.25 what am I saying; and, above all, feeling? Whe-
731.26 ther is it better, I ask, to be a slave in a fool's

731.27 paradise at Marseilles -- fevered with delusive bliss
731.28 one hour -- suffocating with the bitterest tears of
732.01 remorse and shame the next -- or to be a village--
732.02 schoolmistress, free and honest, in a breezy moun-
732.03 tain nook in the healthy heart of England?
732.04 Yes; I feel now that I was right when I adhered
732.05 to principle and law, and scorned and crushed the
732.06 insane promptings of a frenzied moment. God
732.07 directed me to a correct choice: I thank His pro-
732.08 vidence for the guidance!
732.09 Having brought my eventide musings to this
732.10 point, I rose, went to my door, and looked at the
732.11 sunset of the harvest-day, and at the quiet fields
732.12 before my cottage; which, with the school, was
732.13 distant half a mile from the village. The birds
732.14 were singing their last strains --
732.15 "The air was mild; the dew was balm."
732.16 while I looked, I thought myself happy, and was
732.17 surprised to find myself ere long weeping -- and
732.18 why? For the doom which had reft me from
732.19 adhesion to my master: for him I was no more to
732.20 see; for the desperate grief and fatal fury -- conse-
732.21 quences of my departure -- which might now, per-
732.22 haps, be dragging him from the path of right, too
732.23 far to leave hope of ultimate restoration thither.
732.24 At this thought, I turned my face aside from the
732.25 lovely sky of eve and lonely vale of Morton -- I
732.26 say lonely, for in that bend of it visible to me, there
732.27 was no building apparent save the church and the
732.28 parsonage, half-hid in trees; and, quite at the
733.01 extremity, the roof of Vale-Hall, where the rich
733.02 Mr. Oliver and his daughter lived. I hid my eyes,
733.03 and leant my head against the stone frame of my
733.04 door; but soon a slight noise near the wicket which
733.05 shut in my tiny garden from the meadow beyond
733.06 it, made me look up. A dog -- old Carlo, Mr.
733.07 Rivers' pointer, as I saw in a moment -- was pushing
733.08 the gate with his nose, and St. John himself leant
733.09 upon it with folded arms; his brow knit, his gaze,
733.10 grave almost to displeasure, fixed on me. I asked
733.11 him to come in.
733.12 "No, I cannot stay: I have only brought you a
733.13 little parcel my sisters left for you. I think it con-
733.14 tains a colour-box, pencils, and paper."
733.15 I approached to take it: a welcome gift it was.
733.16 He examined my face, I thought, with austerity,
733.17 as I came near: the traces of tears were doubtless
733.18 very visible upon it.
733.19 "Have you found your first day's work harder
733.20 than you expected?" he asked.
733.21 "Oh, no! On the contrary, I think in time I
733.22 shall get on with my scholars very well."
733.23 "But perhaps your accommodations -- your cot-
733.24 tage -- your furniture -- have disappointed your
733.25 expectations? They are, in truth, scanty enough;
733.26 but" -- -- I interrupted: --
733.27 "My cottage is clean and weather-proof; my
733.28 furniture sufficient and commodious. All I see
734.01 has made me thankful, not despondent. I am not
734.02 absolutely such a fool and sensualist as to regret
734.03 the absence of a carpet, a sofa, and silver-plate:
734.04 besides, five weeks ago I had nothing -- I was an
734.05 outcast, a beggar, a vagrant; now I have acquaint-
734.06 ance, a home, a business. I wonder at the good-
734.07 ness of God; the generosity of my friends; the
734.08 bounty of my lot. I do not repine."
734.09 "But you feel solitude an oppression? The
734.10 little house there behind you is dark and empty."
734.11 "I have hardly had time yet to yield to a sense of
734.12 tranquillity, much less to grow impatient under
734.13 one of loneliness."
734.14 "Very well; I hope you feel the content you
734.15 express: at any rate, your good sense will tell you
734.16 that it is too soon yet to yield to the vacillating
734.17 fears of Lot's wife. What you had left before I
734.18 saw you, of course I do not know; but I counsel
734.19 you to resist, firmly, every temptation which would
734.20 incline you to look back: pursue your present
734.21 career steadily, for some months at least."
734.22 "It is what I mean to do," I answered. St.
734.23 John continued:
734.24 "It is hard work to control the workings of
734.25 inclination, and turn the bent of nature: but that
734.26 it may be done, I know from experience. God
734.27 has given us, in a measure, the power to make
734.28 our own fate; and when our energies seem to
735.01 demand a sustenance they cannot get -- when our
735.02 will strains after a path we may not follow -- we
735.03 need neither starve from inanition, nor stand still
735.04 in despair: we have but to seek another nourish-
735.05 ment for the mind, as strong as the forbidden
735.06 food it longed to taste -- and perhaps purer; and
735.07 to hew out for the adventurous foot a road as
735.08 direct and broad as the one Fortune has blocked
735.09 up against us, if rougher than it.
735.10 "A year ago, I was myself intensely miserable,
735.11 because I thought I had made a mistake in enter-
735.12 ing the ministry: its uniform duties wearied me
735.13 to death. I burnt for the more active life of the
735.14 world -- for the more exciting toils of a literary
735.15 career -- for the destiny of an artist, author, orator;
735.16 anything rather than that of a priest: yes, the
735.17 heart of a politician, of a soldier, of a votary of
735.18 glory, a lover of renown, a luster after power,
735.19 beat under my curate's surplice. I considered;
735.20 my life was so wretched, it must be changed, or I
735.21 must die. After a season of darkness and strug-
735.22 gling, light broke and relief fell: my cramped
735.23 existence all at once spread out to a plain without
735.24 bounds -- my powers heard a call from heaven to
735.25 rise, gather their full strength, spread their wings

735.26 and mount beyond ken. God had an errand for
735.27 me; to bear which afar, to deliver it well, skill
735.28 and strength, courage and eloquence, the best
736.01 qualifications of soldier, statesman, and orator,
736.02 were all needed: for these all centre in the good
736.03 missionary.
736.04 "A missionary I resolved to be. From that
736.05 moment my state of mind changed: the fetters
736.06 dissolved and dropped from every faculty, leaving
736.07 nothing of bondage but its galling soreness -- which
736.08 time only can heal. My father, indeed, opposed
736.09 the determination; but since his death, I have not
736.10 a legitimate obstacle to contend with: some affairs
736.11 settled, a successor for Morton provided, and en-
736.12 tanglement or two of the feelings broken through
736.13 or cut asunder -- a last conflict with human weak-
736.14 ness, in which I know I shall overcome, because
736.15 I have vowed that I will overcome -- and I leave
736.16 Europe for the East."
736.17 He said this in his peculiar, subdued, yet em-
736.18 phatic voice; looking, when he had ceased speak-
736.19 ing, not at me, but at the setting sun: at which I
736.20 looked too. Both he and I had our backs towards
736.21 the path leading up the field to the wicket. We
736.22 had heard no step on that grass-grown track; the
736.23 water running in the vale was the one lulling
736.24 sound of the hour and scene: we might well then
736.25 start, when a gay voice, sweet as a silver bell, ex-
736.26 claimed: --
736.27 "Good-evening, Mr. Rivers. And good-even-
736.28 ing, old Carlo. Your dog is quicker to recognise
737.01 his friends than you are, sir: he pricked his ears
737.02 and wagged his tail when I was at the bottom of
737.03 the field, and you have your back towards me
737.04 now."
737.05 It was true. Though Mr. Rivers had started
737.06 at the first of those musical accents, as if a
737.07 thunderbolt had split a cloud over his head, he
737.08 stood yet, at the close of the sentence, in the
737.09 same attitude in which the speaker had surprised
737.10 him: his arm resting on the gate, his face directed
737.11 towards the west. He turned at last, with mea-
737.12 sured deliberation. A vision, as it seemed to me,
737.13 had risen at his side. There appeared, within
737.14 three feet of him, a form clad in pure white -- a
737.15 youthful, graceful form: full; yet fine in contour;
737.16 and when, after bending to caress Carlo, it lifted
737.17 up its head, and threw back a long veil, there
737.18 bloomed under his glance a face of perfect beauty.
737.19 Perfect beauty is a strong expression; but I do
737.20 not retrace or qualify it: as sweet features as
737.21 ever the temperate clime of Albion moulded; as
737.22 pure hues of rose and lily as ever her humid
737.23 gales and vapoury skies generated and screened,
737.24 justified, in this instance, the term. No charm
737.25 was wanting, no defect was perceptible: the
737.26 young girl had regular and delicate lineaments;
737.27 eyes shaped and coloured as we see them in
737.28 lovely pictures, large, and dark, and full; the
738.01 long and shadowy eyelash which encircles a fine
738.02 eye with so soft a fascination; the pencilled brow
738.03 which gives such clearness; the white, smooth
738.04 forehead, which adds such repose to the livelier
738.05 beauties of tint and ray; the cheek, oval, fresh
738.06 and smooth; the lips, fresh too, ruddy, healthy,
738.07 sweetly formed; the even and gleaming teeth
738.08 without flaw; the small, dimpled chin; the orna-
738.09 ment of rich, plenteous tresses, -- all advantages, in
738.10 short, which combined, realize the ideal of beauty,
738.11 were fully hers. I wondered, as I looked at this
738.12 fair creature: I admired her with my whole heart.
738.13 Nature had surely formed her in a partial mood;
738.14 and, forgetting her usual stinted step-mother dole
738.15 of gifts, had endowed this, her darling, with a
738.16 grandame's bounty.
738.17 What did St. John Rivers think of this earthly
738.18 angel? I naturally asked myself that question as
738.19 I saw him turn to her and look at her; and, as
738.20 naturally, I sought the answer to the inquiry in
738.21 his countenance. He had already withdrawn his
738.22 eye from the Peri, and was looking at a humble
738.23 tuft of daisies which grew by the wicket.
738.24 "A lovely evening; but late for you to be out
738.25 alone," he said, as he crushed the snowy heads of
738.26 the closed flowers with his foot.
738.27 "Oh, I only came home from S---- /she men-
738.28 tioned the name of a large town some twenty
739.01 miles distant/ this afternoon. Papa told me you
739.02 had opened your school, and that the new mistress
739.03 was come; and so I put on my bonnet after tea,
739.04 and ran up the valley to see her: this is she?"
739.05 pointing to me.
739.06 "It is," said St. John.
739.07 "Do you think you shall like Morton?" she
739.08 asked of me, with a direct and naive simplicity of
739.09 tone and manner, pleasing, if child-like.
739.10 "I hope I shall. I have many inducements to
739.11 do so."
739.12 "Did you find your scholars as attentive as you
739.13 expected?"
739.14 "Quite"
739.15 "Do you like your house?"
739.16 "Very much."
739.17 "Have I furnished it nicely?"
739.18 "Very nicely, indeed."
739.19 "And made a good choice of an attendant for
739.20 you in Alice Wood?"
739.21 "You have, indeed. She is teachable and
739.22 handy." /This, then, I thought, is Miss Oliver,
739.23 the heiress: favoured, it seems, in the gifts of
739.24 fortune, as well as in those of nature! what

739.25 happy combination of the planets presided over
739.26 her birth, I wonder?/
739.27 "I shall come up and help you to teach some-
739.28 times," she added. "It will be a change for me
740.01 to visit you now and then; and I like a change.
740.02 Mr. Rivers, I have been so gay during my stay at
740.03 S----. Last night, or rather this morning, I was
740.04 dancing till two o'clock. The ----th regiment are
740.05 stationed there, since the riots; and the officers are
740.06 the most agreeable men in the world: they put all
740.07 our young knife-grinders and scissor merchants to
740.08 shame."
740.09 It seemed to me that Mr. St. John's under lip
740.10 protruded, and his upper lip curled a moment.
740.11 His mouth certainly looked a good deal compress-
740.12 ed, and the lower part of his face unusually stern
740.13 and square, as the laughing girl gave him this in-
740.14 formation. He lifted his gaze, too, from the
740.15 daisies, and turned it on her. An unsmiling, a
740.16 searching, a meaning gaze it was. She answered
740.17 it with a second laugh: and laughter well be-
740.18 came her youth, her roses, her dimples, her bright
740.19 eyes.
740.20 As he stood, mute and grave, she again fell to
740.21 caressing Carlo. "Poor Carlo loves me," said she.
740.22 "He is not stern and distant to his friends; and if
740.23 he could speak, he would not be silent."
740.24 As she patted the dog's head, bending with
740.25 native grace before his young and austere master,
740.26 I saw a glow rise to that master's face. I saw his
740.27 solemn eye melt with sudden fire, and flicker with
740.28 resistless emotion. Flushed and kindled thus, he
741.01 looked nearly as beautiful for a man as she for a
741.02 woman. His chest heaved once, as if his large
741.03 heart, weary of despotic constriction, had expanded,
741.04 despite the will, and made a vigorous bound for the
741.05 attainment of liberty. But he curbed it, I think,
741.06 as a resolute rider would curb a rearing steed. He
741.07 responded neither by word nor movement to the
741.08 gentle advances made him.
741.09 "Papa says you never come to see us now,"
741.10 continued Miss Oliver, looking up. "You are
741.11 quite a stranger at Vale-Hall. He is alone this
741.12 evening, and not very well: will you return with
741.13 me and visit him?"
741.14 "It is not a seasonable hour to intrude on Mr.
741.15 Oliver," answered St. John.
741.16 "Not a seasonable hour! But, I declare, it is.
741.17 It is just the hour when papa most wants company:
741.18 when the works are closed, and he has no business
741.19 to occupy him. Now, Mr. Rivers, do come. why
741.20 are you so very shy, and so very sombre?" She
741.21 filled up the hiatus his silence left by a reply of her
741.22 own.
741.23 "I forgot!" she exclaimed, shaking her beautiful
741.24 curled head, as if shocked at herself. "I am so
741.25 giddy and thoughtless! Do excuse me. It had
741.26 slipped my memory that you have good reasons to
741.27 be indisposed for joining in my chatter. Diana
741.28 and Mary have left you, and Moor-House is shut
742.01 up, and you are so lonely. I am sure I pity you.
742.02 Do come and see papa."
742.03 "Not to-night, Miss Rosamond, not to-night."
742.04 Mr. St. John spoke almost like an automaton:
742.05 himself only knew the effort it cost him thus to
742.06 refuse.
742.07 "Well, if you are so obstinate, I will leave you;
742.08 for I dare not stay any longer: the dew begins to
742.09 fall. Good-evening!"
742.10 She held out her hand. He just touched it.
742.11 "Good-evening!" he repeated, in a voice low and
742.12 hollow as an echo. She turned; but in a moment
742.13 returned.
742.14 "Are you well?" she asked. Well might she
742.15 put the question: his face was blanched as her
742.16 gown.
742.17 "Quite well," he enunciated; and, with a bow,
742.18 he left the gate. She went one way; he another.
742.19 She turned twice to gaze after him, as she tripped
742.20 fairy-like down the field; he, as he strode firmly
742.21 across, never turned at all.
742.22 This spectacle of another's suffering and sacri-
742.23 fice, rapt my thoughts from exclusive meditation
742.24 on my own. Diana Rivers had designated her
742.25 brother "inexorable as death." She had not ex-
742.26 aggerated.
743.01 [Vol. 3 Chapter 6]
743.02 I continued the labours of the village-school
743.03 as actively and faithfully as I could. It was
743.04 truly hard work at first. Some time elapsed
743.05 before, with all my efforts, I could comprehend
743.06 my scholars and their nature. wholly untaught,
743.07 with faculties quite torpid, they seemed to me
743.08 hopelessly dull; and, at first sight, all dull
743.09 alike: but I soon found I was mistaken. There
743.10 was a difference amongst them as amongst the
743.11 educated; and when I got to know them, and
743.12 they me, this difference rapidly developed itself.
743.13 Their amazement at me, my language, my rules
743.14 and ways, once subsided, I found some of these
743.15 heavy-looking, gaping rustics wake up into sharp--
743.16 witted girls enough. Many showed themselves
743.17 obliging, and amiable too; and I discovered
743.18 amongst them not a few examples of natural
743.19 politeness, and innate self--respect, as well as of
743.20 excellent capacity, that won both my good-will
744.01 and my admiration. These soon took a pleasure
744.02 in doing their work well; in keeping their per-
744.03 sons neat; in learning their tasks regularly; in
744.04 acquiring quiet and orderly manners. The rapid-
744.05 ity of their progress, in some instances, was even

744.06 surprising; and an honest and happy pride I
744.07 took in it: besides, I began personally to like
744.08 some of the best girls; and they liked me. I
744.09 had amongst my scholars several farmers' daugh-
744.10 ters: young women grown, almost. These could
744.11 already read, write, and sew; and to them I
744.12 taught the elements of grammar, geography, his-
744.13 tory, and the finer kinds of needlework. I found
744.14 estimable characters amongst them -- characters
744.15 desirous of information, and disposed for im-
744.16 provement -- with whom I passed many a pleasant
744.17 evening hour in their own homes. Their parents
744.18 then /the farmer and his wife/ loaded me with
744.19 attentions. There was an enjoyment in accept-
744.20 ing their simple kindness, and in repaying it by
744.21 a consideration -- a scrupulous regard to their feel-
744.22 ings -- to which they were not, perhaps, at all
744.23 times accustomed, and which both charmed and
744.24 benefited them; because, while it elevated them
744.25 in their own eyes, it made them emulous to merit
744.26 the deferential treatment they received.
744.27 I felt I became a favourite in the neighbour-
744.28 hood. Whenever I went out, I heard on all
745.01 sides cordial salutations, and was welcomed with
745.02 friendly smiles. To live amidst general regard,
745.03 though it be but the regard of working-people,
745.04 is like "sitting in sunshine, calm and sweet:"
745.05 serene inward feelings bud and bloom under the
745.06 ray. At this period of my life, my heart far
745.07 oftener swelled with thankfulness than sank with
745.08 dejection: and yet, reader, to tell you all, in the
745.09 midst of this calm, this useful existence -- after a
745.10 day passed in honourable exertion amongst my
745.11 scholars, and evening spent in drawing or reading
745.12 contentedly alone -- I used to rush into strange
745.13 dreams at night: dreams many-coloured, agi-
745.14 tated, full of the ideal, the stirring, the stormy --
745.15 dreams where, amidst unusual scenes, charged
745.16 with adventure, with agitating risk and romantic
745.17 chance, I still again and again met Mr. Rochester,
745.18 always at some exciting crisis; and then the sense
745.19 of being in his arms, hearing his voice, meeting
745.20 his eye, touching his hand and cheek, loving him,
745.21 being loved by him -- the hope of passing a life-
745.22 time at his side, would be renewed, with all its
745.23 first force and fire. Then I awoke. Then I
745.24 recalled where I was, and how situated. Then
745.25 I rose up on my curtainless bed, trembling and
745.26 quivering; and then the still, dark night wit-
745.27 nessed the convulsion of despair, and heard the
745.28 burst of passion. By nine o'clock the next
746.01 morning, I was punctually opening the school;
746.02 tranquil, settled, prepared for the steady duties
746.03 of the day.
746.04 Rosamond Oliver kept her word in coming
746.05 to visit me. Her call at the school was gene-
746.06 rally made in the course of her morning ride.
746.07 She would canter up to the door on her pony,
746.08 followed by a mounted livery servant. Any-
746.09 thing more exquisite than her appearance, in
746.10 her purple habit, with her Amazon's cap of
746.11 black velvet placed gracefully above the long
746.12 curls that kissed her cheek and floated to her
746.13 shoulders, can scarcely be imagined: and it was
746.14 thus she would enter the rustic building, and
746.15 glide through the dazzled ranks of the village
746.16 children. She generally came at the hour
746.17 when Mr. Rivers was engaged in giving his
746.18 daily catechising lesson. Keenly, I fear, did
746.19 the eye of the visitress pierce the young pas-
746.20 tor's heart. A sort of instinct seemed to warn
746.21 him of her entrance, even when he did not see
746.22 it; and when he was looking quite away from
746.23 the door, if she appeared at it, his cheek would
746.24 glow, and his marble-seeming features, though
746.25 they refused to relax, changed indescribably;
746.26 and in their very quiescence became expressive
746.27 of a repressed fervour, stronger than working
746.28 muscle or darting glance could indicate.
747.01 Of course, she knew her power: indeed, he did
747.02 not, because he could not, conceal it from her. In
747.03 spite of his Christian stoicism, when she went up
747.04 and addressed him, and smiled gaily, encourage-
747.05 ingly, even fondly in his face, his hand would
747.06 tremble, and his eye burn. He seemed to say,
747.07 with his sad and resolute look, if he did not say it
747.08 with his lips, "I love you, and I know you prefer
747.09 me. It is not despair of success that keeps me
747.10 dumb. If I offered my heart, I believe you would
747.11 accept it. But that heart is already laid on a
747.12 sacred altar: the fire is arranged round it. It
747.13 will soon be no more than a sacrifice consumed."
747.14 And then she would pout like a disappointed
747.15 child; a pensive cloud would soften her radiant
747.16 vivacity; she would withdraw her hand hastily
747.17 from his, and turn in transient petulance from his
747.18 aspect, at once so heroic and so martyr-like. St.
747.19 John, no doubt, would have given the world to
747.20 follow, recall, retain her, when she thus left him:
747.21 but he would not give one chance of Heaven; nor
747.22 relinquish, for the elysium of her love, one hope
747.23 of the true, eternal Paradise. Besides, he could
747.24 not bound all that he had in his nature -- the rover,
747.25 the aspirant, the poet, the priest -- in the limits
747.26 of a single passion. He could not -- he would not
747.27 -- renounce his wild field of mission warfare for
747.28 the parlours and the peace of Vale-Hall. I learnt
748.01 so much from himself, in an inroad I once, despite
748.02 his reserve, had the daring to make on his con-
748.03 fidence.
748.04 Miss Oliver already honoured me with frequent

748.05 visits to my cottage. I had learnt her whole
748.06 character; which was without mystery or dis-
748.07 guise: she was coquettish, but not heartless; ex-
748.08 acting, but not worthlessly selfish. She had been
748.09 indulged from her birth, but was not absolutely
748.10 spoilt. She was hasty, but good-humoured; vain
748.11 /she could not help it, when every glance in
748.12 the glass showed her such a flush of loveliness/,
748.13 but not affected; liberal-handed; innocent of
748.14 the pride of wealth; ingenuous; sufficiently
748.15 intelligent; gay, lively, and unthinking: she
748.16 was very charming, in short, even to a cool
748.17 observer of her own sex like me; but she was not
748.18 profoundly interesting or thoroughly impressive.
748.19 A very different sort of mind was hers from that,
748.20 for instance, of the sisters of St. John. Still, I
748.21 liked her almost as I liked my pupil Adele:
748.22 except that, for a child whom we have watched
748.23 over and taught, a closer affection is engendered
748.24 than we can give an equally attractive adult
748.25 acquaintance.
748.26 She had taken an amiable caprice to me. She
748.27 said I was like Mr. Rivers /only, certainly, she
748.28 allowed, "not one-tenth so handsome; though I
749.01 was a nice neat little soul enough, but he was an
749.02 angel"/. I was, however, good, clever, composed,
749.03 and firm, like him. I was a lusus naturae, she
749.04 affirmed, as a village-schoolmistress: she was sure
749.05 my previous history, if known, would make a
749.06 delightful romance.
749.07 One evening, while, with her usual child-like
749.08 activity, and thoughtless yet not offensive inqui-
749.09 sitiveness, she was rummaging the cupboard and
749.10 the table-drawer of my little kitchen, she dis-
749.11 covered first two French books, a volume of Schil-
749.12 ler, a German grammar and dictionary; and then
749.13 my drawing-materials and some sketches, includ-
749.14 ing a pencil-head of a pretty, little cherub-like girl,
749.15 one of my scholars, and sundry views from nature,
749.16 taken in the Vale of Morton and on the surround-
749.17 ing moors. She was first transfixed with surprise,
749.18 and then electrified with delight.
749.19 "Had I done these pictures? Did I know
749.20 French and German? what a love -- what a
749.21 miracle I was! I drew better than her master in
749.22 the first school in S----. would I sketch a por-
749.23 trait of her, to show to papa?"
749.24 "With pleasure," I replied; and I felt a thrill
749.25 of artist-delight at the idea of copying from so
749.26 perfect and radiant a model. She had then on a
749.27 dark-blue silk dress; her arms and her neck were
749.28 bare; her only ornament was her chestnut tresses,
750.01 which waved over her shoulders with all the wild
750.02 grace of natural curls. I took a sheet of fine card-
750.03 board, and drew a careful outline. I promised
750.04 myself the pleasure of colouring it; and, as it was
750.05 getting late then, I told her she must come and
750.06 sit another day.
750.07 She made such a report of me to her father,
750.08 that Mr. Oliver himself accompanied her next
750.09 evening -- a tall, massive-featured, middle-aged,
750.10 and gray-headed man, at whose side his lovely
750.11 daughter looked like a bright flower near a hoary
750.12 turret. He appeared a taciturn, and perhaps a
750.13 proud personage; but he was very kind to me.
750.14 The sketch of Rosamond's portrait pleased him
750.15 highly: he said I must make a finished picture of
750.16 it. He insisted, too, on my coming the next day
750.17 to spend the evening at Vale-Hall.
750.18 I went. I found it a large, handsome resi-
750.19 dence, shewing abundant evidences of wealth in
750.20 the proprietor. Rosamond was full of glee and
750.21 pleasure all the time I stayed. Her father was
750.22 affable; and when he entered into conversation
750.23 with me after tea, he expressed in strong terms
750.24 his approbation of what I had done in Morton
750.25 school; and said he only feared, from what he
750.26 saw and heard, I was too good for the place, and
750.27 would soon quit it for one more suitable.
750.28 "Indeed!" cried Rosamond, "she is clever
751.01 enough to be a governess in a high family,
751.02 papa."
751.03 I thought -- I would far rather be where I am
751.04 than in any high family in the land. Mr.
751.05 Oliver spoke of Mr. Rivers -- of the Rivers
751.06 family -- with great respect. He said it was a
751.07 very old name in that neighbourhood; that the
751.08 ancestors of the house were wealthy; that all
751.09 Morton had once belonged to them; that even
751.10 now he considered the representative of that
751.11 house might, if he liked, make an alliance with
751.12 the best. He accounted it a pity that so fine
751.13 and talented a young man should have formed
751.14 the design of going out as a missionary; it was
751.15 quite throwing a valuable life away. It appeared,
751.16 then, that her father would throw no obstacle
751.17 in the way of Rosamond's union with St. John.
751.18 Mr. Oliver evidently regarded the young
751.19 clergyman's good birth, old name, and sacred
751.20 profession, as sufficient compensation for the want
751.21 of fortune.
751.22 It was the fifth of November, and a holiday.
751.23 My little servant, after helping me to clean my
751.24 house, was gone, well satisfied with the fee of a
751.25 penny for her aid. All about me was spotless
751.26 and bright -- scoured floor, polished grate, and
751.27 well rubbed chairs. I had also made myself
752.01 neat, and had now the afternoon before me to
752.02 spend as I would.
752.03 The translation of a few pages of German
752.04 occupied an hour; then I got my palette and

752.05 pencils, and fell to the more soothing, because
752.06 easier occupation, of completing Rosamond
752.07 Oliver's miniature. The head was finished
752.08 already: there was but the background to tint,
752.09 and the drapery to shade off; a touch of car-
752.10 mine, too, to add to the ripe lips -- a soft curl
752.11 here and there to the tresses -- a deeper tinge to
752.12 the shadow of the lash under the azured eyelid.
752.13 I was absorbed in the execution of these nice
752.14 details, when, after one rapid tap, my door
752.15 unclosed, admitting St. John Rivers.
752.16 "I am come to see how you are spending
752.17 your holiday," he said. "Not, I hope in
752.18 thought? No, that is well: while you draw
752.19 you will not feel lonely. You see, I mistrust
752.20 you still: though you have borne up wonder-
752.21 fully so far. I have brought you a book for even-
752.22 ing solace," and he laid on the table a new publi-
752.23 cation -- a poem: one of those genuine productions
752.24 so often vouchsafed to the fortunate public of those
752.25 days -- the golden age of modern literature.
752.26 Alas! the readers of our era are less favoured.
752.27 But, courage! I will not pause either to accuse
753.01 or repine. I know poetry is not dead, nor
753.02 genius lost; nor has Mammon gained power
753.03 over either, to bind or slay: they will both assert
753.04 their existence, their presence, their liberty, and
753.05 strength again one day. Powerful angels, safe in
753.06 heaven! they smile when sordid souls triumph,
753.07 and feeble ones weep over their destruction.
753.08 Poetry destroyed? Genius banished? No!
753.09 Mediocrity, no: do not let envy prompt you
753.10 to the thought. No; they not only live, but
753.11 reign, and redeem: and without their divine
753.12 influence spread everywhere, you would be in hell
753.13 -- the hell of your own meanness.
753.14 while I was eagerly glancing at the bright
753.15 pages of Marmion /for Marmion it was/, St. John
753.16 stooped to examine my drawing. His tall figure
753.17 sprang erect again with a start: he said nothing.
753.18 I looked up at him: he shunned my eye. I knew
753.19 his thoughts well, and could read his heart
753.20 plainly; at the moment I felt calmer and cooler
753.21 than he: I had then temporarily the advantage of
753.22 him; and I conceived an inclination to do him
753.23 some good, if I could.
753.24 "with all his firmness and self-control," thought
753.25 I, "he tasks himself too far: locks every feeling
753.26 and pang within -- expresses, confesses, imparts
753.27 nothing. I am sure it would benefit him to talk
753.28 a little about this sweet Rosamond, whom he
754.01 thinks he ought not to marry: I will make him
754.02 talk."
754.03 I said first: "Take a chair, Mr. Rivers." But
754.04 he answered, as he always did, that he could not
754.05 stay. "Very well," I responded, mentally, "stand
754.06 if you like; but you shall not go just yet, I am
754.07 determined: solitude is at least as bad for you as
754.08 it is for me. I'll try if I cannot discover the
754.09 secret spring of your confidence, and find an
754.10 aperture in that marble breast through which I
754.11 can shed one drop of the balm of sympathy."
754.12 "Is this portrait like?" I asked, bluntly.
754.13 "Like! Like whom? I did not observe it
754.14 closely."
754.15 "You did, Mr. Rivers."
754.16 He almost started at my sudden and strange
754.17 abruptness: he looked at me astonished. "Oh,
754.18 that is nothing yet," I muttered within. "I
754.19 don't mean to be baffled by a little stiffness
754.20 on your part; I'm prepared to go to considerable
754.21 lengths." I continued, "You observed it closely
754.22 and distinctly: but I have no objection to your
754.23 looking at it again," and I rose and placed it in his
754.24 hand
754.25 "A well-executed picture," he said; "very soft,
754.26 clear colouring; very graceful and correct drawing."
754.27 "Yes, yes; I know all that. But what of the
754.28 resemblance? Who is it like?"
755.01 Mastering some hesitation, he answered, "Miss
755.02 Oliver, I presume."
755.03 "Of course. And now, sir, to reward you for
755.04 the accurate guess, I will promise to paint you a
755.05 careful and faithful duplicate of the very pic-
755.06 ture, provided you admit that the gift would be
755.07 acceptable to you. I don't wish to throw away
755.08 my time and trouble on an offering you would
755.09 deem worthless."
755.10 He continued to gaze at the picture: the
755.11 longer he looked, the firmer he held it, the more
755.12 he seemed to covet it. "It is like!" he murmured;
755.13 "the eye is well managed: the colour, light, ex-
755.14 pression, are perfect. It smiles!"
755.15 "would it comfort, or would it wound you
755.16 to have a similar painting? Tell me that.
755.17 when you are at Madagascar, or at the Cape,
755.18 or in India, would it be a consolation to have
755.19 that memento in your possession? or would the
755.20 sight of it bring recollections calculated to ener-
755.21 vate and distress?"
755.22 He now furtively raised his eyes: he glanced at
755.23 me, irresolute, disturbed: he again surveyed the
755.24 picture.
755.25 "That I should like to have it, is certain:
755.26 whether it would be judicious or wise is another
755.27 question."
755.28 Since I had ascertained that Rosamond really
756.01 preferred him, and that her father was not likely
756.02 to oppose the match, I -- less exalted in my views
756.03 than St. John -- had been strongly disposed in my
756.04 own heart to advocate their union. It seemed to

756.05 me that, should he become the possessor of Mr.
756.06 Oliver's large fortune, he might do as much good
756.07 with it as if he went and laid his genius out
756.08 to wither, and his strength to waste, under
756.09 a tropical sun. With this persuasion I now
756.10 answered: --
756.11 "As far as I can see, it would be wiser and
756.12 more judicious if you were to take to yourself the
756.13 original at once."
756.14 By this time he had sat down: he had laid
756.15 the picture on the table before him, and, with his
756.16 brow supported on both hands, hung fondly
756.17 over it. I discerned he was now neither angry
756.18 nor shocked at my audacity. I saw even that
756.19 to be thus frankly addressed on a subject he had
756.20 deemed unapproachable -- to hear it thus freely
756.21 handled -- was beginning to be felt by him as a
756.22 new pleasure -- an unhoped-for relief. Reserved
756.23 people often really need the frank discussion of
756.24 their sentiments and griefs more than the expan-
756.25 sive. The sternest-seeming stoic is human after
756.26 all; and to "burst" with boldness and good will
756.27 into "the silent sea" of their souls, is often to
756.28 confer on them the first of obligations.
757.01 "She likes you, I am sure," said I, as I stood
757.02 behind his chair, "and her father respects you.
757.03 Moreover, she is a sweet girl -- rather thought-
757.04 less; but you would have sufficient thought for
757.05 both yourself and her. You ought to marry
757.06 her."
757.07 "Does she like me?" he asked.
757.08 "Certainly; better than she likes any one
757.09 else. She talks of you continually: there is no
757.10 subject she enjoys so much, or touches upon so
757.11 often."
757.12 "It is very pleasant to hear this," he said -- "very:
757.13 go on for another quarter of an hour." And he
757.14 actually took out his watch and laid it upon the
757.15 table to measure the time.
757.16 "But where is the use of going on," I asked,
757.17 "when you are probably preparing some iron blow
757.18 of contradiction, or forging a fresh chain to fetter
757.19 your heart?"
757.20 "Don't imagine such hard things. Fancy me
757.21 yielding and melting, as I am doing: human love
757.22 rising like a freshly opened fountain in my mind,
757.23 and overflowing with sweet inundation all the field
757.24 I have so carefully, and with such labour prepared
757.25 -- so assiduously sown with the seeds of good in-
757.26 tentions, of self-denying plans. And now it is
757.27 deluged with a nectarous flood -- the young germs
757.28 swamped -- delicious poison cankering them: now
758.01 I see myself stretched on an ottoman in the draw-
758.02 ing-room at Vale-Hall, at my bride Rosamond Oli-
758.03 ver's feet: she is talking to me with her sweet voice
758.04 -- gazing down on me with those eyes your skilful
758.05 hand has copied so well -- smiling at me with these
758.06 coral lips. She is mine -- I am hers -- this pre-
758.07 sent life and passing world suffice to me. Hush!
758.08 say nothing -- my heart is full of delight -- my
758.09 senses are entranced -- let the time I marked pass
758.10 in peace."
758.11 I humoured him: the watch ticked on: he
758.12 breathed fast and low: I stood silent. Amidst
758.13 this hush the quarter sped: he replaced the watch,
758.14 laid the picture down, rose, and stood on the
758.15 hearth.
758.16 "Now," said he, "that little space was given
758.17 to delirium and delusion. I rested my temples
758.18 on the breast of temptation, and put my neck
758.19 voluntarily under her yoke of flowers; I tasted
758.20 her cup. The pillow was burning: there is an
758.21 asp in the garland: the wine has a bitter taste:
758.22 her promises are hollow -- her offers false: I see
758.23 and know all this."
758.24 I gazed at him in wonder.
758.25 "It is strange," pursued he, "that while I
758.26 love Rosamond Oliver so wildly -- with all the
758.27 intensity, indeed, of a first passion, the object
758.28 of which is exquisitely beautiful, graceful, and
759.01 fascinating -- I experience at the same time a
759.02 calm, unwarped consciousness, that she would
759.03 not make me a good wife; that she is not the
759.04 partner suited to me; that I should discover
759.05 this within a year after marriage; and that to
759.06 twelve months' rapture would succeed a lifetime
759.07 of regret. This I know."
759.08 "Strange, indeed!" I could not help ejacu-
759.09 lating.
759.10 "While something in me," he went on, "is
759.11 acutely sensible to her charms, something else
759.12 is as deeply impressed with her defects: they
759.13 are such that she could sympathize in nothing I
759.14 aspired to -- co-operate in nothing I undertook.
759.15 Rosamond a sufferer, a labourer, a female
759.16 apostle? Rosamond a missionary's wife? No!"
759.17 "But you need not be a missionary. You
759.18 might relinquish that scheme."
759.19 "Relinquish! what! my vocation? My
759.20 great work? My foundation laid on earth for
759.21 a mansion in heaven? My hopes of being
759.22 numbered in the band who have merged all
759.23 ambitions in the glorious one of bettering their
759.24 race -- of carrying knowledge into the realms of
759.25 ignorance -- of substituting peace for war -- free-
759.26 dom for bondage -- religion for superstition -- the
759.27 hope of heaven for the fear of hell? Must I
759.28 relinquish that? It is dearer than the blood in
760.01 my veins. It is what I have to look forward to,
760.02 and to live for."
760.03 After a considerable pause, I said -- "And

760.04 Miss Oliver? Are her disappointment and
760.05 sorrow of no interest to you?"
760.06 "Miss Oliver is ever surrounded by suitors
760.07 and flatterers: in less than a month, my image
760.08 will be effaced from her heart. She will forget
760.09 me; and will marry, probably, some one who
760.10 will make her far happier than I should do."
760.11 "You speak coolly enough; but you suffer
760.12 in the conflict. You are wasting away."
760.13 "No. If I get a little thin, it is with an-
760.14 xiety about my prospects, yet unsettled -- my
760.15 departure, continually procrastinated. Only
760.16 this morning, I received intelligence that the
760.17 successor, whose arrival I have been so long
760.18 expecting, cannot be ready to replace me for
760.19 three months to come yet: and perhaps the three
760.20 months may extend to six."
760.21 "You tremble and become flushed whenever
760.22 Miss Oliver enters the school-room."
760.23 Again the surprised expression crossed his
760.24 face. He had not imagined that a woman
760.25 would dare to speak so to a man. For me, I
760.26 felt at home in this sort of discourse. I could
760.27 never rest in communication with strong, dis-
760.28 creet, and refined minds, whether male or female,
761.01 till I had passed the outworks of conventional
761.02 reserve, and crossed the threshold of confidence,
761.03 and won a place by their heart's very hearth-
761.04 stone.
761.05 "You are original," said he, "and not timid.
761.06 There is something brave in your spirit, as well as
761.07 penetrating in your eye: but allow me to assure
761.08 you that you partially misinterpret my emotions.
761.09 You think them more profound and potent than
761.10 they are. You give me a larger allowance of
761.11 sympathy than I have a just claim to. When
761.12 I colour, and when I shake before Miss Oliver,
761.13 I do not pity myself. I scorn the weakness.
761.14 I know it is ignoble; a mere fever of the flesh:
761.15 not, I declare, a convulsion of the soul. That
761.16 is just as fixed as a rock, firm set in the depths
761.17 of a restless sea. Know me to be what I am --
761.18 a cold, hard man."
761.19 I smiled incredulously.
761.20 "You have taken my confidence by storm,"
761.21 he continued; "and now it is much at your ser-
761.22 vice. I am simply, in my original state -- stripped
761.23 of that blood-bleached robe with which Chris-
761.24 tianity covers human deformity -- a cold, hard,
761.25 ambitious man. Natural affection only, of all
761.26 the sentiments, has permanent power over me.
761.27 Reason, and not Feeling, is my guide: my
761.28 ambition is unlimited; my desire to rise higher,
762.01 to do more than others, insatiable. I honour
762.02 endurance, perseverance, industry, talent; because
762.03 these are the means by which men achieve great
762.04 ends, and mount to lofty eminence. I watch
762.05 your career with interest, because I consider
762.06 you a specimen of a diligent, orderly, energetic
762.07 woman: not because I deeply compassionate
762.08 what you have gone through, or what you still
762.09 suffer."
762.10 "You would describe yourself as a mere pagan
762.11 philosopher," I said.
762.12 "No. There is this difference between me
762.13 and deistic philosophers: I believe; and I
762.14 believe the Gospel. You missed your epithet.
762.15 I am not a pagan, but a Christian philosopher
762.16 -- a follower of the sect of Jesus. As his
762.17 disciple, I adopt his pure, his merciful, his be-
762.18 nignant doctrines. I advocate them: I am sworn
762.19 to spread them. Won in youth to religion, she
762.20 has cultivated my original qualities thus: -- From
762.21 the minute germ, natural affection, she has deve-
762.22 loped the overshadowing tree, philanthropy. From
762.23 the wild, stringy root of human uprightness, she
762.24 has reared a due sense of the Divine justice. Of
762.25 the ambition to win power and renown for my
762.26 wretched self, she has formed the ambition to
762.27 spread my Master's kingdom; to achieve victories
762.28 for the standard of the cross. So much has religion
763.01 done for me; turning the original materials to the
763.02 best account; pruning and training nature. But
763.03 she could not eradicate nature: nor will it be
763.04 eradicated "till this mortal shall put on immor-
763.05 tality."
763.06 Having said this, he took his hat, which lay on
763.07 the table beside my palette. Once more he looked
763.08 at the portrait.
763.09 "She is lovely," he murmured. "She is well
763.10 named the Rose of the world, indeed!"
763.11 "And may I not paint one like it for you?"
763.12 "Cui bono? No."
763.13 He drew over the picture the sheet of thin paper
763.14 on which I was accustomed to rest my hand in
763.15 painting to prevent the card-board from being
763.16 sullied. What he suddenly saw on this blank
763.17 paper, it was impossible for me to tell: but some-
763.18 thing had caught his eye. He took it up with a
763.19 snatch; he looked at the edge; then shot a glance
763.20 at me, inexpressibly peculiar, and quite incom-
763.21 prehensible: a glance that seemed to take and
763.22 make note of every point in my shape, face, and
763.23 dress; for it traversed all, quick, keen as lightning.
763.24 His lips parted, as if to speak: but he checked the
763.25 coming sentence, whatever it was.
763.26 "What is the matter?" I asked.
763.27 "Nothing in the world," was the reply; and,
763.28 replacing the paper, I saw him dexterously tear a
764.01 narrow slip from the margin. It disappeared in
764.02 his glove; and, with one hasty nod and "good--

764.03 afternoon," he vanished.
764.04 "Well!" I exclaimed, using an expression of
764.05 the district; "that caps the globe, however!"
764.06 I, in my turn, scrutinized the paper; but saw
764.07 nothing on it, save a few dingy stains of paint,
764.08 where I had tried the tint in my pencil. I pon-
764.09 dered the mystery a minute or two; but finding it
764.10 insolvable, and being certain it could not be of
764.11 much moment, I dismissed, and soon forgot it.
765.01 [Vol. 3 Chapter 7]
765.02 When Mr. St. John went, it was beginning to
765.03 snow: the whirling storm continued all night.
765.04 The next day a keen wind brought fresh and
765.05 blinding falls: by twilight the valley was drifted
765.06 up and almost impassable. I had closed my shutter,
765.07 laid a mat to the door to prevent the snow from
765.08 blowing in under it, trimmed my fire, and after
765.09 sitting nearly an hour on the hearth listening to
765.10 the muffled fury of the tempest, I lit a candle, took
765.11 down Marmion, and beginning --
765.12 "Day set on Norham's castled steep,
765.13 And Tweed's fair river broad and deep,
765.14 And Cheviot mountains lone;
765.15 The massive towers, the donjon keep,
765.16 The flanking walls that round them sweet
765.17 In yellow lustre shone."
765.18 I soon forgot storm in music.
765.19 I heard a noise: the wind, I thought, shook the
766.01 door. No; it was St. John Rivers, who, lifting
766.02 the latch, came in out of the frozen hurricane -- the
766.03 howling darkness -- and stood before me; the cloak
766.04 that covered his tall figure all white as a glacier.
766.05 I was almost in consternation; so little had I ex-
766.06 pected any guest from the blocked-up vale that
766.07 night.
766.08 "Any ill news?" I demanded. "Has anything
766.09 happened?"
766.10 "No. How very easily alarmed you are!" he
766.11 answered, removing his cloak and hanging it up
766.12 against the door; towards which he again coolly
766.13 pushed the mat which his entrance had deranged.
766.14 He stamped the snow from his boots.
766.15 "I shall sully the purity of your floor," said he,
766.16 "but you must excuse me for once." Then he
766.17 approached the fire: "I have had hard work to
766.18 get here, I assure you," he observed, as he warmed
766.19 his hands over the flame. "One drift took me up
766.20 to the waist: happily the snow is quite soft yet."
766.21 "But why are you come?" I could not forbear
766.22 saying.
766.23 "Rather an inhospitable question to put to
766.24 a visitor; but since you ask it, I answer, simply
766.25 to have a little talk with you; I got tired of my
766.26 mute books and empty rooms. Besides, since
766.27 yesterday, I have experienced the excitement of a
767.01 person to whom a tale has been half-told, and who
767.02 is impatient to hear the sequel."
767.03 He sat down. I recalled his singular conduct
767.04 of yesterday, and really I began to fear his wits
767.05 were touched. If he were insane, however, his
767.06 was a very cool and collected insanity: I had never
767.07 seen that handsome-featured face of his, look more
767.08 like chiselled marble than it did just now; as he put
767.09 aside his snow-wet hair from his forehead and let
767.10 the fire-light shine free on his pale brow and cheek
767.11 as pale: where it grieved me to discover the hollow
767.12 trace of care or sorrow now so plainly graved. I
767.13 waited, expecting he would say something I could
767.14 at least comprehend; but his hand was now at his
767.15 chin, his finger on his lip: he was thinking. It
767.16 struck me that his hand looked wasted like his face.
767.17 A perhaps uncalled-for gush of pity came over my
767.18 heart: I was moved to say: --
767.19 "I wish Diana or Mary would come and live
767.20 with you: it is too bad that you should be quite
767.21 alone; and you are recklessly rash about your own
767.22 health."
767.23 "Not at all," said he: "I care for myself when
767.24 necessary: I am well now. What do you see amiss
767.25 in me?"
767.26 This was said with a careless, abstracted indif-
767.27 ference, which showed that my solicitude was, at
768.01 least in his opinion, wholly superfluous. I was
768.02 silenced.
768.03 He still slowly moved his finger over his upper
768.04 lip, and still his eye dwelt dreamily on the glowing
768.05 grate: thinking it urgent to say something, I asked
768.06 him presently if he felt any cold draught from the
768.07 door, which was behind him.
768.08 "No, no;" he responded, shortly and somewhat
768.09 testily.
768.10 "Well," I reflected, "if you won't talk, you
768.11 may be still: I'll let you alone now, and return to
768.12 my book."
768.13 So I snuffed the candle, and resumed the perusal
768.14 of Marmion. He soon stirred; my eye was in-
768.15 stantly drawn to his movements: he only took out
768.16 a morocco pocket-book, thence produced a letter,
768.17 which he read in silence, folded it, put it back, re-
768.18 lapsed into meditation. It was vain to try to read
768.19 with such an inscrutable fixture before me; nor
768.20 could I, in my impatience, consent to be dumb:
768.21 he might rebuff me if he liked, but talk I would.
768.22 "Have you heard from Diana and Mary
768.23 lately?"
768.24 "Not since the letter I showed you a week
768.25 ago."
768.26 "There has not been any change made about
768.27 your own arrangements? You will not be sum-
768.28 moned to leave England sooner than you ex-
768.29 pected?"

769.01 "I fear not, indeed: such chance is too good to
769.02 befall me." Baffled so far, I changed my ground --
769.03 I bethought myself to talk about the school and my
769.04 scholars.
769.05 "Mary Garrett's mother is better, and Mary
769.06 came back to the school this morning, and I shall
769.07 have four new girls next week from the Foundry
769.08 Close -- they would have come to-day but for the
769.09 snow."
769.10 "Indeed!"
769.11 "Mr. Oliver pays for two."
769.12 "Does he?"
769.13 "He means to give the whole school a treat at
769.14 Christmas."
769.15 "I know."
769.16 "Was it at your suggestion?"
769.17 "No."
769.18 "Whose then?"
769.19 "His daughter's, I think."
769.20 "It is like her: she is so good-natured."
769.21 "Yes."
769.22 Again came the blank of a pause: the clock
769.23 struck eight strokes. It aroused him; he uncross-
769.24 ed his legs, sat erect, turned to me.
769.25 "Leave your book a moment, and come a little
769.26 nearer the fire," he said.
769.27 Wondering, and of my wonder finding no end,
769.28 I complied.
770.01 "Half and hour ago," he pursued, "I spoke of
770.02 my impatience to hear the sequel of a tale: on re-
770.03 flection, I find the matter will be better managed
770.04 by my assuming the narrator's part, and converting
770.05 you into a listener. Before commencing, it is but
770.06 fair to warn you that the story will sound some-
770.07 what hackneyed in your ears: but stale details
770.08 often regain a degree of freshness when they pass
770.09 through new lips. For the rest, whether trite or
770.10 novel, it is short.
770.11 "Twenty years ago, a poor curate -- never mind
770.12 the name at this moment -- fell in love with a rich
770.13 man's daughter: she fell in love with him, and mar-
770.14 ried him, against the advice of all her friends; who
770.15 consequently disowned her immediately after the
770.16 wedding. Before two years passed, the rash pair
770.17 were both dead, and laid quietly side by side under
770.18 one slab. /I have seen their grave; it formed part of
770.19 the pavement of a huge churchyard surrounding
770.20 the grim, soot-black old cathedral of an overgrown
770.21 manufacturing town in ----shire./ They left a
770.22 daughter, which, at its very birth, Charity re-
770.23 ceived in her lap -- cold as that of the snow-drift
770.24 I almost stuck fast in to-night. Charity carried
770.25 the friendless thing to the house of its rich, ma-
770.26 ternal relations; it was reared by an aunt-in-law,
770.27 called /I come to names now/ Mrs. Reed of Gates-
770.28 head -- you start -- did you hear a noise? I dare-say
771.01 it is only a rat scrambling along the rafters of
771.02 the adjoining schoolroom: it was a barn before I
771.03 had it repaired and altered, and barns are gene-
771.04 rally haunted by rats. To proceed. Mrs. Reed
771.05 kept the orphan ten years: whether it was happy
771.06 or not with her, I cannot say, never having been
771.07 told; but at the end of that time she transferred
771.08 it to a place you know -- being no other than
771.09 Lowood school, where you so long resided your-
771.10 self. It seems her career there was very honour-
771.11 able: from a pupil, she became a teacher, like
771.12 yourself -- really it strikes me there are parallel
771.13 points in her history and yours -- she left it to be a
771.14 governess: there, again, your fates were analogous;
771.15 she undertook the education of the ward of a cer-
771.16 tain Mr. Rochester."
771.17 "Mr. Rivers!" I interrupted.
771.18 "I can guess your feelings," he said, "but re-
771.19 strain them for a while: I have nearly finished;
771.20 hear me to the end. Of Mr. Rochester's character
771.21 I know nothing, but the one fact that he professed
771.22 to offer honourable marriage to this young girl,
771.23 and that at the very altar she discovered he had
771.24 a wife yet alive, though a lunatic. What his sub-
771.25 sequent conduct and proposals were is a matter of
771.26 pure conjecture; but when an event transpired
771.27 which rendered inquiry after the governess neces-
771.28 sary, it was discovered she was gone -- no one could
772.01 tell when, where, or how. She had left Thorn-
772.02 field-Hall in the night; every research after her
772.03 course had been vain: the country had been
772.04 scoured far and wide; no vestige of information
772.05 could be gathered respecting her. Yet that she
772.06 should be found is become a matter of serious ur-
772.07 gency: advertisements have been put in all the
772.08 papers; I myself have received a letter from one
772.09 Mr. Briggs, a solicitor, communicating the details
772.10 I have just imparted. Is it not an odd tale?"
772.11 "Just tell me this," said I, "and since you know
772.12 so much, you surely can tell it me -- what of Mr.
772.13 Rochester? How and where is he? what is he
772.14 doing? Is he well?"
772.15 "I am ignorant of all concerning Mr. Rochester:
772.16 the letter never mentions him but to narrate the
772.17 fraudulent and illegal attempt I have adverted to.
772.18 You should rather ask the name of the governess --
772.19 the nature of the event which requires her appear-
772.20 ance."
772.21 "Did no one go to Thornfield-Hall then? Did
772.22 no one see Mr. Rochester?"
772.23 "I suppose not."
772.24 "But they wrote to him?"
772.25 "Of course."
772.26 "And what did he say? Who has his letters?"
772.27 "Mr. Briggs intimates that the answer to his application

773.01 was not from Mr. Rochester but from a
773.02 lady: it is signed `Alice Fairfax.``
773.03 I felt cold and dismayed: my worst fears then
773.04 were probably true: he had in all probability left
773.05 England and rushed in reckless desperation to some
773.06 former haunt on the continent. And what opiate
773.07 for his severe sufferings -- what object for his strong
773.08 passions -- had he sought there? I dared not
773.09 answer the question. Oh, my poor master -- once
773.10 almost my husband -- whom I had often called
773.11 "my dear Edward!"
773.12 "He must have been a bad man," observed Mr.
773.13 Rivers.
773.14 "You don't know him -- don't pronounce an
773.15 opinion upon him," I said, with warmth.
773.16 "Very well," he answered, quietly: "and indeed
773.17 my head is otherwise occupied than with him: I
773.18 have my tale to finish. Since you won't ask the
773.19 governess's name, I must tell it of my own accord
773.20 -- stay -- I have it here -- it is always more satisfac-
773.21 tory to see important points written down, fairly
773.22 committed to black and white."
773.23 And the pocket-book was again deliberately
773.24 produced, opened, sought through; from one of
773.25 its compartments was extracted a shabby slip of
773.26 paper, hastily torn off: I recognised in its texture
773.27 and its stains of ultra-marine, and lake, and vermilion,
774.01 the ravished margin of the portrait-cover.
774.02 He got up, held it close to my eyes: and I read,
774.03 traced in Indian ink, in my own handwriting, the
774.04 words "Jane Eyre" -- the work doubtless of some
774.05 moment of abstraction.
774.06 "Briggs wrote to me of a Jane Eyre:" he said,
774.07 "the advertisements demanded a Jane Eyre: I
774.08 knew a Jane Elliot. -- I confess I had my suspi-
774.09 cions, but it was only yesterday afternoon they
774.10 were at once resolved into certainty. You own
774.11 the name and renounce the alias?"
774.12 "Yes -- yes -- but where is Mr. Briggs? He
774.13 perhaps knows more of Mr. Rochester than you
774.14 do."
774.15 "Briggs is in London; I should doubt his
774.16 knowing anything at all about Mr. Rochester;
774.17 it is not in Mr. Rochester he is interested.
774.18 Meantime, you forget essential points in pur-
774.19 suing trifles: you do not inquire why Mr.
774.20 Briggs sought after you -- what he wanted with
774.21 you."
774.22 "Well, what did he want?"
774.23 "Merely to tell you that your uncle, Mr. Eyre
774.24 of Madeira, is dead; that he has left you all his
774.25 property, and that you are now rich -- merely that
774.26 -- nothing more."
774.27 "I! rich?"
774.28 "Yes, you, rich -- quite an heiress."
775.01 Silence succeeded.
775.02 "You must prove your identity of course,"
775.03 resumed St. John, presently: "a step which will
775.04 offer no difficulties; you can then enter on im-
775.05 mediate possession. Your fortune is vested in the
775.06 English funds; Briggs has the will and the neces-
775.07 sary documents."
775.08 Here was a new card turned up! It is a
775.09 fine thing, reader, to be lifted in a moment
775.10 from indigence to wealth -- a very fine thing:
775.11 but not a matter one can comprehend, or con-
775.12 sequently enjoy, all at once. And then there
775.13 are other chances in life far more thrilling
775.14 and rapture-giving: this is solid, an affair of
775.15 the actual world, nothing ideal about it: all its
775.16 associations are solid and sober, and its mani-
775.17 festations are the same. One does not jump,
775.18 and spring, and shout hurrah! at hearing one
775.19 has got a fortune; one begins to consider respon-
775.20 sibilities, and to ponder business; on a base of
775.21 steady satisfaction rise certain grave cares -- and
775.22 we contain ourselves, and brood over our bliss with
775.23 a solemn brow.
775.24 Besides, the words Legacy, Bequest, go side
775.25 by side with the words Death, Funeral. My
775.26 uncle I had heard was dead -- my only relative;
775.27 ever since being made aware of his existence,
775.28 I had cherished the hope of one day seeing
776.01 him: now, I never should. And then this
776.02 money came only to me: not to me and a re-
776.03 joicing family, but to my isolated self. It was
776.04 a grand boon doubtless; and independence would
776.05 be glorious -- yes, I felt that -- that thought swelled
776.06 "You unbend your forehead at last," said
776.07 Mr. Rivers: "I thought Medusa had looked
776.08 at you, and that you were turning to stone --
776.09 perhaps now you will ask how much you are
776.10 worth?"
776.11 "How much am I worth?"
776.12 "Oh, a trifle! Nothing of course to speak
776.13 of -- twenty thousand pounds, I think they say --
776.14 but what is that?"
776.15 "Twenty thousand pounds!"
776.16 Here was a new stunner -- I had been calculat-
776.17 ing on four of five thousand. This news actually
776.18 took my breath for a moment: Mr. St. John,
776.19 whom I had never heard laugh before, laughed
776.20 now.
776.21 "Well," said he, "if you had committed a mur-
776.22 der, and I had told you your crime was discovered,
776.23 you could scarcely look more aghast."
776.24 "It is a large sum -- don't you think there is a
776.25 mistake?"
776.26 "No mistake at all."
777.01 "Perhaps you have read the figures wrong -- it
777.02 may be 2000?"

777.03 "It is written in letters, not figures, -- twenty
777.04 thousand."
777.05 I again felt rather like an individual of but
777.06 average gastronomical powers, sitting down to
777.07 feast alone at a table spread with provisions for
777.08 a hundred. Mr. Rivers rose now and put his
777.09 cloak on.
777.10 "If it were not such a very wild night," he said,
777.11 "I would send Hannah down to keep you com-
777.12 pany: you look too desperately miserable to be
777.13 left alone. But Hannah, poor woman! could not
777.14 stride the drifts so well as I: her legs are not quite
777.15 so long; so I must e'en leave you to your sorrows.
777.16 Good-night."
777.17 He was lifting the latch: a sudden thought
777.18 occurred to me.
777.19 "Stop one minute!" I cried.
777.20 "Well?"
777.21 "It puzzles me to know why Mr. Briggs wrote
777.22 to you about me; or how he knew you, or could
777.23 fancy that you, living in such an out-of-the-way
777.24 place, had the power to aid in my discovery."
777.25 "Oh! I am a clergyman," he said; "and the
777.26 Again the latch rattled.
778.01 "No: that does not satisfy me!" I exclaimed:
778.02 and, indeed, there was something in the hasty and
778.03 unexplanatory reply, which, instead of allaying,
778.04 piqued my curiosity more than ever.
778.05 "It is a very strange piece of business," I added:
778.06 "I must know more about it."
778.07 "Another time."
778.08 "No: to-night! -- to-night!" and as he turned
778.09 form the door, I placed myself between it and him.
778.10 He looked rather embarrassed.
778.11 "You certainly shall not go till you have told
778.12 me all!" I said.
778.13 "I would rather not, just now."
778.14 "You shall! -- you must!"
778.15 "I would rather Diana or Mary informed you."
778.16 Of course these objections wrought my eager-
778.17 ness to a climax: gratified it must be, and that
778.18 without delay; and I told him so.
778.19 "But I apprised you that I was a hard man,"
778.20 said he; "difficult to persuade."
778.21 "And I am a hard woman, -- impossible to put
778.22 off."
778.23 "And then," he pursued, "I am cold: no fer-
778.24 vour infects me."
778.25 "Whereas I am hot, and fire dissolves ice.
778.26 The blaze there has thawed all the snow from
778.27 your cloak; by the same token, it has streamed
778.28 on to my floor, and made it like a trampled
779.01 street. As you hope ever to be forgiven, Mr.
779.02 Rivers, the high crime and misdemeanor of
779.03 spoiling a sanded kitchen, tell me what I wish
779.04 to know."
779.05 "Well, then," he said, "I yield; if not to your
779.06 earnestness, to yor perseverance: as stone is
779.07 worn by continual dropping. Besides, you must
779.08 know some day, -- as well now as later. Your
779.09 name is Jane Eyre?"
779.10 "Of course: that was all settled before."
779.11 "You are not, perhaps, aware that I am your
779.12 namesake? -- that I was christened St. John Eyre
779.13 Rivers?"
779.14 "No, indeed! I remember now seeing the
779.15 letter E comprised in your initials written in
779.16 books you have at different times lent me; but I
779.17 never asked for what name it stood. But what
779.18 then? Surely ---- "
779.19 I stopped: I could not trust myself to enter-
779.20 tain, much less to express, the thought that
779.21 rushed upon me -- that embodied itself, -- that, in
779.22 a second, stood out a strong, solid probability.
779.23 Circumstances knit themselves, fitted themselves,
779.24 shot into order: the chain that had been lying
779.25 hitherto a formless lump of links, was drawn out
779.26 straight, -- every ring was perfect, the connection
779.27 complete. I knew, by instinct, how the matter
779.28 stood, before St. John had said another word: but
780.01 I cannot expect the reader to have the same
780.02 intuitive perception, so I must repeat his explana-
780.03 tion.
780.04 "My mother's name was Eyre: she had two
780.05 brothers; one a clergyman, who married Miss
780.06 Jane Reed, of Gateshead; the other, John Eyre,
780.07 Esq., merchant, late of Funchal, Madeira. Mr.
780.08 Briggs, being Mr. Eyre's solicitor, wrote to us last
780.09 August to inform us of our uncle's death; and to
780.10 say that he had left his property to his brother the
780.11 clergyman's orphan daughter; overlooking us, in
780.12 consequence of a quarrel, never forgiven, between
780.13 him and my father. He wrote again a few weeks
780.14 since, to intimate that the heiress was lost; and
780.15 asking if we knew anything of her. A name
780.16 casually written on a slip of paper has enabled
780.17 me to find her out. You know the rest." Again
780.18 he was going, but I set my back against the door.
780.19 "Do let me speak," I said; "let me have one
780.20 moment to draw breath and reflect." I paused --
780.21 he stood before me, hat in hand, looking composed
780.22 enough. I resumed:
780.23 "Your mother was my father's sister."
780.24 "Yes."
780.25 "My aunt, consequently?"
780.26 He bowed.
780.27 "My uncle John was your uncle John? You,
781.01 Diana and Mary, are his sister's children; as I am
781.02 his brother's child?"
781.03 "Undeniably."
781.04 "You three, then, are my cousins: half our

781.05 blood on each side flows from the same source?"
781.06 "We are cousins; yes."
781.07 I surveyed him. It seemed I had found a
781.08 brother: one I could be proud of, -- one I could
781.09 love; and two sisters, whose qualities were such,
781.10 that, when I knew them but as mere strangers,
781.11 they had inspired me with genuine affection and
781.12 admiration. The two girls, on whom, kneeling
781.13 down on the wet ground, and looking through
781.14 the low, latticed window of Moor-House kitchen,
781.15 I had gazed with so bitter a mixture of interest
781.16 and despair, were my near kinswomen; and the
781.17 young and stately gentleman who had found me
781.18 almost dying at his threshold, was my blood rela-
781.19 tion. Glorious discovery to a lonely wretch!
781.20 This was wealth indeed! -- wealth to the heart! --
781.21 a mine of pure, genial affections. This was a
781.22 blessing, bright, vivid, and exhilarating! -- not
781.23 like the ponderous gift of gold: rich and welcome
781.24 enough in its way, but sobering from its weight.
781.25 I now clapped my hands in sudden joy -- my pulse
781.26 bounded, my veins thrilled.
781.27 "Oh, I am glad! -- I am glad!" I exclaimed.
782.01 St. John smiled. "Did I not say you neglected
782.02 essential points to pursue trifles?" he asked.
782.03 "You were serious when I told you you had got
782.04 a fortune; and now, for a matter of no moment,
782.05 you are excited."
782.06 "What can you mean? It may be of no
782.07 moment to you: you have sisters, and don't
782.08 care for a cousin; but I had nobody; and now
782.09 three relations, -- or two, if you don't choose to
782.10 be counted, -- are born into my world, full grown.
782.11 I say again, I am glad!"
782.12 I walked fast through the room: I stopped, half
782.13 suffocated with the thoughts that rose faster than I
782.14 could receive, comprehend, settle them: -- thoughts
782.15 of what might, could, would, and should be, and
782.16 that ere long. I looked at the blank wall: it
782.17 seemed a sky, thick with ascending stars, -- every
782.18 one lit me to a purpose or delight. Those who
782.19 had saved my life, whom, till this hour, I had loved
782.20 barrenly, I could now benefit. They were under
782.21 a yoke: I could free them: they were scattered, --
782.22 I could reunite them -- the independence, the
782.23 affluence which was mine, might be theirs too.
782.24 Were we not four? Twenty thousand pounds
782.25 shared equally, would be five thousand each, --
782.26 enough and to spare: justice would be done, --
782.27 mutual happiness secured. Now the wealth did
783.01 not weigh on me: now it was not a mere bequest
783.02 of coin, -- it was a legacy of life, hope, enjoy-
783.03 ment.
783.04 How I looked while these ideas were taking my
783.05 spirit by storm, I cannot tell; but I perceived
783.06 soon that Mr. Rivers had placed a chair behind
783.07 me, and was gently attempting to make me sit
783.08 down on it. He also advised me to be composed.
783.09 I scorned the insinuation of helplessness and dis-
783.10 traction, shook off his hand, and began to walk
783.11 about again.
783.12 "Write to Diana and Mary to-morrow," I said,
783.13 "and tell them to come home directly; Diana
783.14 said they would both consider themselves rich with
783.15 a thousand pounds, so with five thousand, they will
783.16 do very well."
783.17 "Tell me where I can get you a glass of water,"
783.18 said St. John: "you must really make an effort to
783.19 tranquillize your feelings."
783.20 "Nonsense! and what sort of an effect will the
783.21 bequest have on you? will it keep you in Eng-
783.22 land, induce you to marry Miss Oliver, and settle
783.23 down like an ordinary mortal?"
783.24 "You wander: your head becomes confused.
783.25 I have been too abrupt in communicating the
783.26 news: it has excited you beyond your strength."
783.27 "Mr. Rivers! you quite put me out of patience;
784.01 I am rational enough; it is you who misunder-
784.02 stand; or rather, who affect to misunderstand."
784.03 "Perhaps if you explained yourself a little more
784.04 fully, I should comprehend better."
784.05 "Explain! what is there to explain? You
784.06 cannot fail to see that twenty thousand pounds, the
784.07 sum in question, divided equally between the
784.08 nephew and three nieces of our uncle, will give
784.09 five thousand to each? What I want is, that you
784.10 should write to your sisters and tell them of the
784.11 fortune that has accrued to them."
784.12 "To you, you mean."
784.13 "I have intimated my view of the case: I am
784.14 incapable of taking any other. I am not brutally
784.15 selfish, blindly unjust, or fiendishly ungrateful.
784.16 Besides, I am resolved I will have a home and
784.17 connexions. I like Moor-House, and I will live
784.18 at Moor-House; I like Diana and Mary, and I
784.19 will attach myself for life to Diana and Mary. It
784.20 would please and benefit me to have five thousand
784.21 pounds; it would torment and oppress me to have
784.22 twenty thousand; which, moreover, could never be
784.23 mine in justice, though it might in law. I abandon
784.24 to you, then, what is absolutely superfluous to me.
784.25 Let there be no opposition, and no discussion
784.26 about it; let us agree amongst each other, and
784.27 decide the point at once."
784.28 "This is acting on first impulses; you must
785.01 take days to consider such a matter, ere your word
785.02 can be regarded as valid."
785.03 "Oh! if all you doubt is my sincerity, I am
785.04 easy: you see the justice of the case?"
785.05 "I do see a certain justice; but it is contrary to
785.06 all custom. Besides, the entire fortune is your

785.07 right: my uncle gained it by his own efforts; he
785.08 was free to leave it to whom he would: he left it
785.09 to you. After all, justice permits you to keep it:
785.10 you may, with a clear conscience, consider it abso-
785.11 lutely your own."
785.12 "With me," said I, "it is fully as much a matter
785.13 of feeling as of conscience: I must indulge my
785.14 feelings; I so seldom have had an opportunity of
785.15 doing so. Were you to argue, object, and annoy
785.16 me for a year, I could not forego the delicious
785.17 pleasure of which I have caught a glimpse -- that
785.18 of repaying, in part, a mighty obligation, and
785.19 winning to myself life-long friends."
785.20 "You think so now," rejoined St. John; "be-
785.21 cause you do not know what it is to possess, nor
785.22 consequently to enjoy wealth: you cannot form a
785.23 notion of the importance twenty thousand pounds
785.24 would give you; of the place it would enable you
785.25 to take in society; of the prospects it would open
785.26 to you: you cannot ---- "
785.27 "And you," I interrupted, "cannot at all imagine
785.28 the craving I have for fraternal and sisterly love.
786.01 I never had a home, I never had brothers or sisters;
786.02 I must and will have them now: you are not
786.03 reluctant to admit me and own me, are you?"
786.04 "Jane: I will be your brother -- my sisters
786.05 will be your sisters -- without stipulating for the
786.06 sacrifice of your just rights."
786.07 "Brother? Yes; at the distance of a thou-
786.08 sand leagues! Sisters? Yes; slaving amongst
786.09 strangers! I, wealthy -- gorged with gold I never
786.10 earned and do not merit! You, pennyless!
786.11 Famous equality and fraternization! Close union!
786.12 Intimate attachment!"
786.13 "But, Jane, your aspirations after family ties
786.14 and domestic happiness may be realized other-
786.15 wise than by the means you contemplate: you
786.16 may marry."
786.17 "Nonsense, again! Marry! I don't want to
786.18 marry, and never shall marry."
786.19 "That is saying too much: such hazardous
786.20 affirmations are a proof of the excitement under
786.21 which you labour."
786.22 "It is not saying too much: I know what I
786.23 feel, and how averse are my inclinations to the
786.24 bare thought of marriage. No one would take
786.25 me for love; and I will not be regarded in the
786.26 light of a mere money-speculation. And I do
786.27 not want a stranger -- unsympathizing, alien, diffe-
786.28 rent from me; I want my kindred: those with
787.01 whom I have full fellow-feeling. Say again you
787.02 will be my brother: when you uttered the words
787.03 I was satisfied, happy; repeat them, if you can
787.04 repeat them sincerely."
787.05 "I think I can. I know I have always
787.06 loved my own sisters; and I know on what my
787.07 affection for them is grounded, -- respect for their
787.08 worth, and admiration of their talents. You too
787.09 have principle and mind: your tastes and habits
787.10 resemble Diana's and Mary's; your presence is
787.11 always agreeable to me; in your conversation I
787.12 have already for some time found a salutary solace.
787.13 I feel I can easily and naturally make room in my
787.14 heart for you, as my third and youngest sister."
787.15 "Thank you: that contents me for to-night.
787.16 Now you had better go; for if you stay longer,
787.17 you will perhaps irritate me afresh by some mis-
787.18 trustful scruple."
787.19 "And the school, Miss Eyre? It must now
787.20 be shut up, I suppose?"
787.21 "No. I will retain my post of mistress till you
787.22 get a substitute."
787.23 He smiled approbation: we shook hands, and
787.24 he took leave.
787.25 I need not narrate in detail the further struggles
787.26 I had, and arguments I used, to get matters re-
787.27 garding the legacy settled as I wished. My task
787.28 was a very hard one: but, as I was absolutely
788.01 resolved -- as my cousins saw at length that my
788.02 mind was really and immutably fixed on making
788.03 a just division of the property -- as they must in
788.04 their own hearts have felt the equity of the inten-
788.05 tion; and must, besides, have been innately con-
788.06 scious that in my place they would have done
788.07 precisely what I wished to do -- they yielded at
788.08 length so far as to consent to put the affair to
788.09 arbitration. The judges chosen were Mr. Oliver
788.10 and an able lawyer: both coincided in my
788.11 opinion: I carried my point. The instruments
788.12 of transfer were drawn out: St. John, Diana,
788.13 Mary, and I, each became possessed of a com-
788.14 petency.
789.01 [Vol. 3 Chapter 8]
789.02 It was near Christmas by the time all was settled:
789.03 the season of general holiday approached. I now
789.04 closed Morton school; taking care that the part-
789.05 ing should not be barren on my side. Good
789.06 fortune opens the hand as well as the heart won-
789.07 derfully; and to give somewhat when we have
789.08 largely received, is but to afford a vent to the
789.09 unusual ebullition of the sensations. I had long
789.10 felt with pleasure that many of my rustic scholars
789.11 liked me, and when we parted, that consciousness
789.12 was confirmed: they manifested their affection
789.13 plainly and strongly. Deep was my gratification
789.14 to find I had really a place in their unsophisticated
789.15 hearts: I promised them that never a week should
789.16 pass in future that I did not visit them, and give
789.17 them an hour's teaching in their school.
789.18 Mr. Rivers came up, as -- having seen the
789.19 classes, now numbering sixty girls, file out before

790.01 me, and locked the door -- I stood with the key
790.02 in my hand, exchanging a few words of special
790.03 farewell with some half-dozen of my best scholars:
790.04 as decent, respectable, modest, and well-informed
790.05 young women as could be found in the ranks of
790.06 the British peasantry. And that is saying a great
790.07 deal; for after all, the British peasantry are the
790.08 best taught, best mannered, most self-respecting
790.09 of any in Europe: since those days I have seen
790.10 paysannes and Bäuerinnen; and the best of them
790.11 seemed to me ignorant, coarse, and besotted, com-
790.12 pared with my Morton girls.
790.13 "Do you consider you have got your reward for
790.14 a season of exertion?" asked Mr. Rivers when
790.15 they were gone. "Does not the consciousness of
790.16 having done some real good in your day and gene-
790.17 ration give pleasure?"
790.18 "Doubtless."
790.19 "And you have only toiled a few months!
790.20 Would not a life devoted to the task of regenerat-
790.21 ing your race be well spent?"
790.22 "Yes," I said; "but I could not go on for ever
790.23 so: I want to enjoy my own faculties as well as to
790.24 cultivate those of other people. I must enjoy them
790.25 now: don't recall either my mind or body to the
790.26 school; I am out of it and disposed for full holi-
790.27 day.
790.28 He looked grave. "What now? What sudden
791.01 eagerness is this you evince? what are you going
791.02 to do?"
791.03 "To be active: as active as I can. And first I
791.04 must beg you to set Hannah at liberty, and get
791.05 somebody else to wait on you."
791.06 "Do you want her?"
791.07 "Yes, to go with me to Moor-House: Diana
791.08 and Mary will be at home in a week, and I want
791.09 to have everything in order against their arrival."
791.10 "I understand: I thought you were for flying
791.11 off on some excursion. It is better so: Hannah
791.12 shall go with you."
791.13 "Tell her to be ready by to-morrow then; and
791.14 here is the school-room key: I will give you the
791.15 key of my cottage in the morning."
791.16 He took it. "You give it up very gleefully,"
791.17 said he: "I don't quite understand your light--
791.18 heartedness; because I cannot tell what employ-
791.19 ment you propose to yourself as a substitute for
791.20 the one you are relinquishing. What aim, what
791.21 purpose, what ambition in life have you now?"
791.22 "My first aim will be to clean down /do you
791.23 comprehend the full force of the expression?/ to
791.24 clean down Moor-House from chamber to cellar;
791.25 my next to rub it up with bees-wax, oil, and an
791.26 indefinite number of cloths, till it glitters again;
791.27 my third, to arrange every chair, table, bed, carpet,
791.28 with mathematical precision; afterwards I shall go
792.01 near to ruin you in coals and peat to keep up good
792.02 fires in every room; and lastly, the two days pre-
792.03 ceding that on which your sisters are expected,
792.04 will be devoted by Hannah and me to such a beat-
792.05 ing of eggs, sorting of currants, grating of spices,
792.06 compounding of Christmas cakes, chopping up of
792.07 materials for mince-pies, and solemnizing of other
792.08 culinary rites, as words can convey but an inade-
792.09 quate notion of to the uninitiated like you. My
792.10 purpose, in short, is to have all things in an abso-
792.11 lutely perfect state of readiness for Diana and
792.12 Mary, before next Thursday; and my ambition is
792.13 to give them a beau-ideal of a welcome when they
792.14 come."
792.15 St. John smiled slightly: still he was dissatis-
792.16 fied.
792.17 "It is all very well for the present," said he:
792.18 "but seriously, I trust that when the first flush of
792.19 vivacity is over, you will look a little higher than
792.20 domestic endearments and household joys."
792.21 "The best things the world has!" I interrupted.
792.22 "No, Jane, no: this world is not the scene of
792.23 fruition; do not attempt to make it so: nor of rest;
792.24 do not turn slothful."
792.25 "I mean, on the contrary, to be busy."
792.26 "Jane, I excuse you for the present: two
792.27 months' grace I allow you for the full enjoyment
792.28 of your new position, and for pleasing yourself
793.01 with this late-found charm of relationship; but
793.02 then, I hope you will begin to look beyond Moor--
793.03 House and Morton, and sisterly society, and the
793.04 selfish calm and sensual comfort of civilized
793.05 affluence. I hope your energies will then once
793.06 more trouble you with their strength."
793.07 I looked at him with surprise. "St. John,"
793.08 I said, "I think you are almost wicked to talk so.
793.09 I am disposed to be as content as a queen, and
793.10 you try to stir me up to restlessness! To what
793.11 end?"
793.12 "To the end of turning to profit the talents
793.13 which God has committed to your keeping; and
793.14 of which he will surely one day demand a strict
793.15 account. Jane, I shall watch you closely and
793.16 anxiously -- I warn you of that. And try to restrain
793.17 the disproportionate fervour with which you throw
793.18 yourself into common-place home pleasure. Don't
793.19 cling so tenaciously to ties of the flesh; save your
793.20 constancy and ardour for an adequate cause; for-
793.21 bear to waste them on trite transient objects. Do
793.22 you hear, Jane?"
793.23 "Yes; just as if you were speaking Greek. I
793.24 feel I have adequate cause to be happy, and I will
793.25 be happy. Good-bye!"
793.26 Happy at Moor-House I was, and hard I
793.27 worked; and so did Hannah: she was charmed

793.28 to see how jovial I could be amidst the bustle of
794.01 a house turned topsy-turvy -- how I could brush,
794.02 and dust, and clean, and cook. And really after a
794.03 day or two of confusion worse confounded, it was
794.04 delightful, by degrees, to invoke order from the
794.05 chaos ourselves had made. I had previously taken
794.06 a journey to S----, to purchase some new furni-
794.07 ture: my cousins having given me carte blanche
794.08 to effect what alterations I pleased, and a sum
794.09 having been set aside for that purpose. The ordi-
794.10 nary sitting-room and bed-rooms I left much as
794.11 they were: for I knew Diana and Mary would de-
794.12 rive more pleasure from seeing again the old
794.13 homely tables, and chairs, and beds, than from the
794.14 spectacle of the smartest innovations. Still some
794.15 novelty was necessary, to give to their return the
794.16 piquancy of which I wished it to be invested.
794.17 Dark handsome new carpets and curtains, an
794.18 arrangement of some carefully selected antique
794.19 ornaments in porcelain and bronze, new coverings,
794.20 and mirrors, and dressing-cases for the toilet tables,
794.21 answered the end: they looked fresh without
794.22 being glaring. A spare parlour and bed-room I
794.23 refurnished entirely, with old mahogany and crim-
794.24 son upholstery: I laid canvass on the passage, and
794.25 carpets on the stairs. When all was finished, I
794.26 thought Moor-House as complete a model of
794.27 bright modest snugness within, as it was, at this
795.01 season, a specimen of wintry waste and desert
795.02 dreariness without.
795.03 The eventful Thursday at length came. They
795.04 were expected about dark, and ere dusk, fires were
795.05 lit up stairs and below; the kitchen was in perfect
795.06 trim; Hannah and I were dressed and all was in
795.07 readiness.
795.08 St. John arrived first. I had entreated him to
795.09 keep quite clear of the house till everything
795.10 was arranged: and, indeed, the bare idea of the
795.11 commotion, at once sordid and trivial, going on
795.12 within its walls sufficed to scare him to estrange-
795.13 ment. He found me in the kitchen, watching
795.14 the progress of certain cakes for tea, then baking.
795.15 Approaching the hearth, he asked, "If I was at
795.16 last satisfied with house-maid's work?" I an-
795.17 swered by inviting him to accompany me on a
795.18 general inspection of the result of my labours.
795.19 With some difficulty, I got him to make the tour
795.20 of the house. He just looked in at the doors I
795.21 opened; and when he had wandered up stairs and
795.22 down stairs, he said I must have gone through a
795.23 great deal of fatigue and trouble to have effected
795.24 such considerable changes in so short a time: but
795.25 not a syllable did he utter indicating pleasure in
795.26 the improved aspect of his abode.
795.27 This silence damped me. I thought perhaps
796.01 the alterations had disturbed some old associations
796.02 he valued. I inquired whether this was the case:
796.03 no doubt in a somewhat crest-fallen tone.
796.04 "Not at all; he had, on the contrary, re-
796.05 marked that I had scrupulously respected every
796.06 association: he feared, indeed, I must have be-
796.07 stowed more thought on the matter than it was
796.08 worth. How many minutes, for instance, had I
796.09 devoted to studying the arrangement of this very
796.10 room? -- By-the-bye, could I tell him where such
796.11 a book was?"
796.12 I showed him the volume on the shelf: he took
796.13 it down and withdrawing to his accustomed window
796.14 recess, he began to read it.
796.15 Now, I did not like this, reader. St. John
796.16 was a good man; but I began to feel he had
796.17 spoken truth of himself, when he said he was hard
796.18 and cold. The humanities and amenities of life
796.19 had no attraction for him -- its peaceful enjoyments
796.20 no charm. Literally, he lived only to aspire --
796.21 after what was good and great, certainly: but still
796.22 he would never rest; nor approve of others rest-
796.23 ing round him. As I looked at the lofty forehead,
796.24 still and pale as a white stone -- at his fine linea-
796.25 ments fixed in study -- I comprehended all at once
796.26 that he would hardly make a good husband: that
796.27 it would be a trying thing to be his wife. I un-
796.28 derstood, as by inspiration, the nature of his love
797.01 for Miss Oliver; I agreed with him that it was but
797.02 a love of the senses. I comprehended how he
797.03 should despise himself for the feverish influence it
797.04 exercised over him; how he should wish to stifle
797.05 and destroy it; how he should mistrust its ever
797.06 conducing permanently to his happiness, or hers.
797.07 I saw he was of the material from which nature
797.08 hews her heroes -- Christian and Pagan -- her law-
797.09 givers, her statesmen, her conquerors: a steadfast
797.10 bulwark for great interests to rest upon; but, at the
797.11 fireside, too often a cold cumbrous column, gloomy
797.12 and out of place.
797.13 "This parlour is not his sphere," I reflected:
797.14 "the Himalayan ridge, or Caffre bush, even the
797.15 plague-cursed Guinea coast swamp, would suit
797.16 him better. Well may he eschew the calm of
797.17 domestic life; it is not his element: there his
797.18 faculties stagnate -- they cannot develope or ap-
797.19 pear to advantage. It is in scenes of strife and
797.20 danger -- where courage is proved, and energy ex-
797.21 ercised, and fortitude tasked -- that he will speak
797.22 and move, the leader and superior. A merry
797.23 child would have the advantage of him on this
797.24 hearth. He is right to choose a missionary's
797.25 career -- I see it now."
797.26 "They are coming! they are coming!" cried
797.27 Hannah, throwing open the parlour door. At the
797.28 same moment old Carlo barked joyfully. Out I

798.01 ran. It was now dark; but a rumbling of wheels
798.02 was audible. Hannah soon had a lantern lit. The
798.03 vehicle had stopped at the wicket; the driver opened
798.04 the door: first one well-known form, then another,
798.05 stepped out. In a minute I had my face under
798.06 their bonnets, in contact, first with Mary's soft
798.07 cheek, then with Diana's flowing curls. They
798.08 laughed -- kissed me -- then Hannah: patted Carlo,
798.09 who was half wild with delight, asked eagerly if
798.10 all was well; and being assured in the affirmative,
798.11 hastened into the house.
798.12 They were stiff with their long and jolting drive
798.13 from Whitcross, and chilled with the frosty night
798.14 air; but their pleasant countenances expanded
798.15 to the cheering fire light. While the driver and
798.16 Hannah brought in the boxes, they demanded St.
798.17 John. At this moment he advanced from the
798.18 parlour. They both threw their arms round his
798.19 neck at once. He gave each one quiet kiss, said
798.20 in a low tone a few words of welcome, stood
798.21 a while to be talked to, and then, intimating that
798.22 he supposed they would soon rejoin him in the
798.23 parlour, withdrew there as to a place of refuge.
798.24 I had lit their candles to go up stairs, but Diana
798.25 had first to give hospitable orders respecting the
798.26 driver; this done, both followed me. They were
798.27 delighted with the renovation and decoration of
798.28 their rooms; with the new drapery, and fresh
799.01 carpets, and rich tinted china vases: they ex-
799.02 pressed their gratification ungrudgingly. I had
799.03 the pleasure of feeling that my arrangements met
799.04 their wishes exactly; and that what I had done
799.05 added a vivid charm to their joyous return home.
799.06 Sweet was that evening. My cousins, full of
799.07 exhilaration, were so eloquent in narrative and
799.08 comment, that their fluency covered St. John's
799.09 taciturnity: he was sincerely glad to see his sis-
799.10 ters; but in their glow of fervour and flow of joy
799.11 he could not sympathize. The event of the day --
799.12 that is, the return of Diana and Mary -- pleased
799.13 him; but the accompaniments of that event, the
799.14 glad tumult, the garrulous glee of reception, irked
799.15 him: I saw he wished the calmer morrow was
799.16 come. In the very meridian of the night's enjoy-
799.17 ment, about an hour after tea, a rap was heard at
799.18 the door. Hannah entered with the intimation
799.19 that "a poor lad was come, at that unlikely time,
799.20 to fetch Mr. Rivers to see his mother, who was
799.21 drawing away."
799.22 "Where does she live, Hannah?"
799.23 "Clear up at Whitcross Brow, almost four miles
799.24 off; and moor and moss all the way."
799.25 "Tell him I will go."
799.26 "I'm sure, sir, you had better not. It's the
799.27 worst road to travel after dark that can be: there's
799.28 no track at all over the bog. And then it is such
800.01 a bitter night -- the keenest wind you ever felt.
800.02 You had better send word, sir, that you will be
800.03 there in the morning."
800.04 But he was already in the passage, putting on
800.05 his cloak; and without one objection, one mur-
800.06 mur, he departed. It was then nine o'clock: he
800.07 did not return till midnight. Starved and tired
800.08 enough he was: but he looked happier than when
800.09 he set out. He had performed an act of duty;
800.10 made an exertion; felt his own strength to do
800.11 and deny, and was on better terms with himself.
800.12 I am afraid the whole of the ensuing week tried
800.13 his patience. It was Christmas week: we took to
800.14 no settled employment, but spent it in a sort of
800.15 merry domestic dissipation. The air of the moors,
800.16 the freedom of home, the dawn of prosperity,
800.17 acted on Diana and Mary's spirits like some life--
800.18 giving elixir: they were gay from morning till
800.19 noon, and from noon till night. They could al-
800.20 ways talk; and their discourse, witty, pithy,
800.21 original, had such charms for me, that I preferred
800.22 listening to, and sharing in it, to doing anything
800.23 else. St. John did not rebuke our vivacity; but
800.24 he escaped from it: he was seldom in the house:
800.25 his parish was large, the population scattered, and
800.26 he found daily business in visiting the sick and
800.27 poor in its different districts.
800.28 One morning, at breakfast, Diana, after looking
801.01 a little pensive for some minutes, asked him, "If
801.02 his plans were yet unchanged?"
801.03 "Unchanged and unchangeable," was the reply.
801.04 And he proceeded to inform us that his departure
801.05 from England was now definitively fixed for the
801.06 ensuing year.
801.07 "And Rosamond Oliver?" suggested Mary:
801.08 the words seeming to escape her lips involun-
801.09 tarily; for no sooner had she uttered them, than
801.10 she made a gesture as if wishing to recall them.
801.11 St. John had a book in his hand -- it was his un-
801.12 social custom to read at meals -- he closed it, and
801.13 looked up.
801.14 "Rosamond Oliver," said he, "is about to be
801.15 married to Mr. Granby; one of the best connected
801.16 and most estimable residents in S----, grandson
801.17 and heir to Sir Frederic Granby: I had the intel-
801.18 ligence from her father yesterday."
801.19 His sisters looked at each other, and at me; we
801.20 all three looked at him: he was serene as glass.
801.21 "The match must have been got up hastily,"
801.22 said Diana: "they cannot have known each
801.23 other long."
801.24 "But two months: they met in October at
801.25 the county ball at S----. But where there
801.26 are no obstacles to a union, as in the present
801.27 case, where the connection is in every point

801.28 desirable, delays are unnecessary: they will be
802.01 married as soon as S---- Place, which Sir Fre-
802.02 deric gives up to them, can be refitted for their
802.03 reception."
802.04 The first time I found St. John alone after this
802.05 communication, I felt tempted to inquire if the
802.06 event distressed him: but he seemed so little
802.07 to need sympathy, that, so far from venturing
802.08 to offer him more, I experienced some shame
802.09 at the recollection of what I had already hazarded.
802.10 Besides, I was out of practice in talking to him:
802.11 his reserve was again frozen over, and my frank-
802.12 ness was congealed beneath it. He had not
802.13 kept his promise of treating me like his sisters;
802.14 he continually made little, chilling differences
802.15 between us, which did not at all tend to the
802.16 development of cordiality: in short, now that I
802.17 was acknowledged his kinswoman, and lived
802.18 under the same roof with him, I felt the distance
802.19 between us to be far greater than when he had
802.20 known me only as the village schoolmistress.
802.21 when I remembered how far I had once been
802.22 admitted to his confidence, I could hardly com-
802.23 prehend his present frigidity.
802.24 Such being the case, I felt not a little surprised
802.25 when he raised his head suddenly from the desk
802.26 over which he was stooping, and said: --
802.27 "You see, Jane, the battle is fought and the
802.28 victory won."
803.01 Startled at being thus addressed, I did not
803.02 immediately reply: after a moment's hesitation I
803.03 answered: --
803.04 "But are you sure, you are not in the position
803.05 of those conquerors whose triumphs have cost
803.06 them too dear? Would not such another ruin
803.07 you?"
803.08 "I think not; and if I were, it does not
803.09 much signify: I shall never be called upon to
803.10 contend for such another. The event of the con-
803.11 flict is decisive: my way is now clear; I thank
803.12 God for it!" So saying, he returned to his
803.13 papers and his silence.
803.14 As our mutual happiness /i.e. Diana's, Mary's,
803.15 and mine/ settled into a quieter character, and we
803.16 resumed our usual habits and regular studies,
803.17 St. John stayed more at home: he sat with us in
803.18 the same room, sometimes for hours together.
803.19 While Mary drew, Diana pursued a course of
803.20 Encyclopaedic reading she had /to my awe and
803.21 amazement/ undertaken, and I fagged away at
803.22 German, he pondered a mystic lore of his own:
803.23 that of some Eastern tongue, the acquisition of
803.24 which he thought necessary to his plans.
803.25 Thus engaged, he appeared, sitting in his own
803.26 recess, quiet and absorbed enough; but that blue
803.27 eye of his had a habit of leaving the outlandish--
803.28 looking grammar, and wandering over, and some-times
804.01 fixing upon us, his fellow-students, with
804.02 a curious intensity of observation: if caught, it
804.03 could be instantly withdrawn; yet ever and anon,
804.04 it returned searchingly to our table. I wondered
804.05 what it meant: I wondered, too, at the punctual
804.06 satisfaction he never failed to exhibit on an occa-
804.07 sion that seemed to me of small moment, namely,
804.08 -- my weekly visit to Morton school; and still
804.09 more was I puzzled when, if the day was unfa-
804.10 vourable, if there was snow, or rain, or high
804.11 wind, and his sisters urged me not to go, he
804.12 would invariably make light of their solicitude,
804.13 and encourage me to accomplish the task without
804.14 regard to the elements.
804.15 "Jane is not such a weakling as you would
804.16 make her," he would say: "she can bear a
804.17 mountain blast, or a shower, or a few flakes of
804.18 snow, as well as any of us. Her constitution is
804.19 both sound and elastic; -- better calculated to
804.20 endure variations of climate than many more
804.21 robust."
804.22 And when I returned, sometimes a good deal
804.23 tired, and not a little weather-beaten, I never
804.24 dared complain, because I saw that to murmur
804.25 would be to vex him: on all occasions fortitude
804.26 pleased him; the reverse was a special annoy-
804.27 ance.
804.28 One afternoon, however, I got leave to stay at
805.01 home, because I really had a cold. His sisters
805.02 were gone to Morton in my stead: I sat reading
805.03 Schiller; he, deciphering his crabbed Oriental
805.04 scrolls. As I exchanged a translation for an
805.05 exercise, I happened to look his way: there I
805.06 found myself under the influence of the ever--
805.07 watchful blue eye. How long it had been
805.08 searching me through and through, and over
805.09 and over, I cannot tell: so keen was it, and yet
805.10 so cold, I felt for the moment superstitious --
805.11 as if I were sitting in the room with some-
805.12 thing uncanny.
805.13 "Jane, what are you doing?"
805.14 "Learning German."
805.15 "I want you to give up German, and learn
805.16 Hindostanee."
805.17 "You are not in earnest?"
805.18 "In such earnest that I must have it so: and I
805.19 will tell you why."
805.20 He then went on to explain that Hindostanee
805.21 was the language he was himself at present study-
805.22 ing: that, as he advanced, he was apt to forget the
805.23 commencement; that it would assist him greatly
805.24 to have a pupil with whom he might again and
805.25 again go over the elements, and so fix them
805.26 thoroughly in his mind; that his choice had hovered

805.27 for some time between me and his sisters; but that
805.28 he had fixed on me, because he saw I could sit at
806.01 a task the longest of the three. Would I do him
806.02 this favour? I should not, perhaps, have to make
806.03 the sacrifice long; as it wanted now barely three
806.04 months to his departure.
806.05 St. John was not a man to be lightly refused:
806.06 you felt that every impression made on him, either
806.07 for pain or pleasure, was deep-graved and perma-
806.08 nent. I consented. When Diana and Mary re-
806.09 turned, the former found her scholar transferred
806.10 from her to her brother: she laughed; and both
806.11 she and Mary agreed that St. John should never
806.12 have persuaded them to such a step. He answered,
806.13 quietly: --
806.14 "I knew it."
806.15 I found him a very patient, very forbearing, and
806.16 yet an exacting master: he expected me to do a
806.17 great deal; and when I fulfilled his expectations
806.18 he, in his own way, fully testified his approbation.
806.19 By degrees, he acquired a certain influence over
806.20 me that took away my liberty of mind: his praise
806.21 and notice were more restraining than his indif-
806.22 ference. I could no longer talk or laugh freely
806.23 when he was by; because a tiresomely importunate
806.24 instinct reminded me that vivacity /at least in me/
806.25 was distasteful to him. I was so fully aware that
806.26 only serious moods and occupations were accept-
806.27 able, that in his presence every effort to sustain or
806.28 follow any other became vain: I fell under a
807.01 freezing spell. When he said "go," I went;
807.02 "come," I came; "do this," I did it. But I did
807.03 not love my servitude: I wished, many a time, he
807.04 had continued to neglect me.
807.05 One evening when, at bed-time, his sisters and
807.06 I stood round him, bidding him good-night, he
807.07 kissed each of them, as was his custom; and, as
807.08 was equally his custom, he gave me his hand.
807.09 Diana, who chanced to be in a frolicksome humour
807.10 /she was not painfully controlled by his will; for
807.11 hers, in another way, was as strong/, exclaimed: --
807.12 "St. John! you used to call Jane your third
807.13 sister, but you don't treat her a such: you should
807.14 kiss her too."
807.15 She pushed me towards him. I thought Diana
807.16 very provoking, and felt uncomfortably confused;
807.17 and while I was thus thinking and feeling, St.
807.18 John bent his head, his Greek face was brought to
807.19 a level with mine, his eyes questioned my eyes
807.20 piercingly -- he kissed me. There are no such
807.21 things as marble kisses, or ice kisses, or I should
807.22 say, my ecclesiastical cousin's salute belonged to
807.23 one of these classes; but there may be experiment
807.24 kisses, and his was an experiment kiss. When
807.25 given, he viewed me to learn the result; it was
807.26 not striking: I am sure I did not blush; perhaps
807.27 I might have turned a little pale, for I felt as if
807.28 this kiss were a seal affixed to my fetters. He
808.01 never omitted the ceremony afterwards, and the
808.02 gravity and quiescence with which I underwent
808.03 it, seemed to invest it for him with a certain
808.04 charm.
808.05 As for me, I daily wished more to please him:
808.06 but to do so, I felt daily more and more that I
808.07 must disown half my nature, stifle half my facul-
808.08 ties, wrest my tastes from their original bent, force
808.09 myself to the adoption of pursuits for which I had
808.10 no natural vocation. He wanted to train me to an
808.11 elevation I could never reach; it racked me hourly
808.12 to aspire to the standard he uplifted. The thing
808.13 was as impossible as to mould my irregular fea-
808.14 tures to his correct and classic pattern, to give to
808.15 my changeable green eyes the sea-blue tint and
808.16 solemn lustre of his own.
808.17 Not his ascendancy alone, however, held me in
808.18 thrall at present. Of late it had been easy enough
808.19 for me to look sad: a cankering evil sat at my
808.20 heart and drained my happiness at its source -- the
808.21 evil of suspense.
808.22 Perhaps you think I had forgotten Mr. Rochester,
808.23 reader, amidst these changes of place and fortune.
808.24 Not for a moment. His idea was still with me;
808.25 because it was not a vapour sunshine could dis-
808.26 perse; nor a sand-traced effigy storms could wash
808.27 away: it was a name graven on a tablet, fated to
808.28 last as long as the marble it inscribed. The craving
809.01 to know what had become of him followed me
809.02 everywhere; when I was at Morton, I re-entered
809.03 my cottage every evening to think of that; and
809.04 now at Moor-House, I sought my bed-room each
809.05 night to brood over it.
809.06 In the course of my necessary correspondence
809.07 with Mr. Briggs about the will, I had inquired if
809.08 he knew anything of Mr. Rochester's present resi-
809.09 dence and state of health: but, as St. John
809.10 conjectured, he was quite ignorant of all concern-
809.11 ing him. I then wrote to Mrs. Fairfax, entreating
809.12 information on the subject. I had calculated with
809.13 certain, on this step answering my end: I felt
809.14 sure it would elicit an early answer. I was
809.15 astonished when a fortnight passed without reply;
809.16 but, when two months wore away, and day after
809.17 day the post arrived and brought nothing for me,
809.18 I fell a prey to the keenest anxiety.
809.19 I wrote again: there was a chance of my first
809.20 letter having missed. Renewed hope followed
809.21 renewed effort: it shone like the former for some
809.22 weeks, then, like it, it faded, flickered: not a line,
809.23 not a word reached me. When half a year wasted
809.24 in vain expectancy, my hope died out; and then
809.25 I felt dark indeed.

809.26 A fine spring shone round me, which I could
809.27 not enjoy. Summer approached; Diana tried
810.01 to cheer me: she said I looked ill, and wished
810.02 to accompany me to the sea-side. This St. John
810.03 opposed; he said I did not want dissipation, I
810.04 wanted employment: my present life was too
810.05 purposeless, I required an aim; and, I suppose, by
810.06 way of supplying deficiencies, he prolonged still
810.07 further my lessons in Hindostanee, and grew more
810.08 urgent in requiring their accomplishment: and I,
810.09 like a fool, never thought of resisting him -- I
810.10 could not resist him.
810.11 One day I had come to my studies in lower
810.12 spirits than usual; the ebb was occasioned by
810.13 poignantly felt disappointment: Hannah had told
810.14 me in the morning there was a letter for me, and
810.15 when I went down to take it, almost certain that
810.16 the long looked-for tidings were vouchsafed me at
810.17 last, I found only an unimportant note from Mr.
810.18 Briggs on business. The bitter check had wrung
810.19 from me some tears; and now as I sat poring
810.20 over the crabbed characters and flourishing tropes
810.21 of an Indian scribe, my eyes filled again.
810.22 St. John called me to his side to read; in
810.23 attempting to do this my voice failed me: words
810.24 were lost in sobs. He and I were the only occu-
810.25 pants of the parlour: Diana was practising her
810.26 music in the drawing-room, Mary was gardening
810.27 -- it was a very fine May-Day, clear, sunny, and
811.01 breezy. My companion expressed no surprise at
811.02 this emotion, nor did he question me as to its
811.03 cause; he only said: --
811.04 "We will wait a few minutes, Jane, till you are
811.05 more composed." And while I smothered the
811.06 paroxysm with all haste, he sat calm and patient,
811.07 leaning on his desk and looking like a physician
811.08 watching with the eye of science an expected and
811.09 fully-understood crisis in a patient's malady.
811.10 Having stifled my sobs, wiped my eyes, and mut-
811.11 tered something about not being very well that
811.12 morning, I resumed my task, and succeeded in
811.13 completing it. St. John put away my books and
811.14 his, locked his desk, and said: --
811.15 "Now, Jane, you shall take a walk; and with
811.16 me."
811.17 "I will call Diana and Mary."
811.18 "No. I want only one companion this morn-
811.19 ing, and that must be you: put on your things;
811.20 go out by the kitchen door; take the road towards
811.21 the head of Marsh-Glen: I will join you in a
811.22 moment."
811.23 I know no medium: I never in my life have
811.24 known any medium in my dealings with positive,
811.25 hard characters, antagonistic to my own, between
811.26 absolute submission and determined revolt. I
811.27 have always faithfully observed the one, up to the
811.28 very moment of bursting, sometimes with volcanic
812.01 vehemence, into the other; and as neither present
812.02 circumstances warranted, nor my present mood
812.03 inclined me to mutiny, I observed careful obe-
812.04 dience to St. John's directions; and in ten minutes
812.05 I was treading the wild track of the glen, side by
812.06 side with him.
812.07 The breeze was from the west: it came over
812.08 the hills, sweet with scents of heath and rush;
812.09 the sky was of stainless blue; the stream descend-
812.10 ing the ravine, swelled with past spring rains,
812.11 poured along plentiful and clear, catching golden
812.12 gleams from the sun, and sapphire tints from the
812.13 firmament. As we advanced and left the track,
812.14 we trod a soft turf, mossy fine and emerald green,
812.15 minutely enamelled with a tiny white flower, and
812.16 spangled with a star-like yellow blossom: the
812.17 hills, meantime, shut us quite in; for the glen,
812.18 towards its head, wound to their very core.
812.19 "Let us rest here," said St. John, as we reached
812.20 the first stragglers of a battalion of rocks, guarding
812.21 a sort of pass, beyond which the beck rushed
812.22 down a waterfall; and where, still a little fur-
812.23 ther, the mountain shook off turf and flower, had
812.24 only heath for raiment, and crag for gem -- where
812.25 it exaggerated the wild to the savage, and ex-
812.26 changed the fresh for the frowning -- where it
812.27 guarded the forlorn hope of solitude, and a last
812.28 refuge for silence.
813.01 I took a seat: St. John stood near me. He
813.02 looked up the pass and down the hollow; his
813.03 glance wandered away with the stream, and re-
813.04 turned to traverse the unclouded heaven which
813.05 coloured it: he removed his hat, let the breeze
813.06 stir his hair and kiss his brow. He seemed in
813.07 communion with the genius of the haunt: with
813.08 his eye he bade farewell to something.
813.09 "And I shall see it again," he said aloud, "in
813.10 dreams, when I sleep by the Ganges: and again,
813.11 in a more remote hour -- when another slumber
813.12 overcomes me -- on the shore of a darker stream."
813.13 Strange words of a strange love! An austere
813.14 patriot's passion for his fatherland! He sat down;
813.15 for half an hour we never spoke; neither he to me
813.16 nor I to him: that interval past, he recom-
813.17 menced: --
813.18 "Jane, I go in six weeks; I have taken my
813.19 berth in an East Indiaman which sails on the
813.20 twentieth of June."
813.21 "God will protect you; for you have undertaken
813.22 his work," I answered.
813.23 "Yes," said he, "there is my glory and joy.
813.24 I am the servant of an infallible master. I am not
813.25 going out under human guidance, subject to the
813.26 defective laws and erring control of my feeble fel-

813.27 low-worms: my king, my lawgiver, my captain, is
813.28 the All-perfect. It seems strange to me that all
814.01 round me do not burn to enlist under the same
814.02 banner, -- to join in the same enterprise."
814.03 "All have not your powers; and it would be
814.04 folly for the feeble to wish to march with the
814.05 strong."
814.06 "I do not speak to the feeble, or think of them:
814.07 I address only such as are worthy of the work, and
814.08 competent to accomplish it."
814.09 "Those are few in number, and difficult to dis-
814.10 cover."
814.11 "You say truly: but when found, it is right to
814.12 stir them up -- to urge and exhort them to the
814.13 effort -- to show them what their gifts are, and why
814.14 they were given -- to speak Heaven's message in
814.15 their ear, -- to offer them, direct from God, a place
814.16 in the ranks of his chosen."
814.17 "If they are really qualified for the task, will
814.18 not their own hearts be the first to inform them
814.19 of it?"
814.20 I felt as if an awful charm was framing round
814.21 and gathering over me: I trembled to hear some
814.22 fatal word spoken which would at once declare and
814.23 rivet the spell.
814.24 "And what does your heart say?" demanded
814.25 St. John.
814.26 "My heart is mute, -- my heart is mute," I
814.27 answered, struck and thrilled.
814.28 "Then I must speak for it," continued the deep,
815.01 relentless voice. "Jane, come with me to India:
815.02 come as my help-meet and fellow-labourer."
815.03 The glen and sky spun round: the hills heaved!
815.04 It was as if I had heard a summons from Heaven --
815.05 as if a visionary messenger, like him of Macedonia,
815.06 had enounced, "Come over and help us!" But
815.07 I was no apostle, -- I could not behold the herald,
815.08 -- I could not receive his call.
815.09 "Oh, St. John!" I cried, "have some mercy!"
815.10 I appealed to one who, in the discharge of what
815.11 he believed his duty, knew neither mercy nor
815.12 remorse. He continued: --
815.13 "God and nature intended you for a mission-
815.14 ary's wife. It is not personal, but mental endow-
815.15 ments they have given you: you are formed for
815.16 labour, not for love. A missionary's wife you must
815.17 -- shall be. You shall be mine: I claim you -- not
815.18 for my pleasure, but for my Sovereign's service."
815.19 "I am not fit for it: I have no vocation," I
815.20 said.
815.21 He had calculated on these first objections: he
815.22 was not irritated by them. Indeed, as he leaned
815.23 back against the crag behind him, folded his arms
815.24 on his chest, and fixed his countenance, I saw he
815.25 was prepared for a long and trying opposition, and
815.26 had taken in a stock of patience to last him to its
815.27 close -- resolved, however, that that close should be
815.28 conquest for him.
816.01 "Humility, Jane," said he, "is the ground-
816.02 work of Christian virtues: you say right that you
816.03 are not fit for the work. Who is fit for it? Or
816.04 who, that ever was truly called, believed himself
816.05 worthy of the summons? I, for instance, am but
816.06 dust and ashes. With St. Paul, I acknowledge
816.07 myself the chiefest of sinners: but I do not suffer
816.08 this sense of my personal vileness to daunt me. I
816.09 know my Leader: that He is just as well as
816.10 mighty; and while he has chosen a feeble instru-
816.11 ment to perform a great task, He will, from the
816.12 boundless stores of His providence, supply the
816.13 inadequacy of the means to the end. Think like
816.14 me, Jane -- trust like me. It is the Rock of Ages
816.15 I ask you to lean on: do not doubt but it will bear
816.16 the weight of your human weakness."
816.17 "I do not understand a missionary life: I have
816.18 never studied missionary labours."
816.19 "There, I, humble as I am, can give you the
816.20 aid you want: I can set you your task from hour
816.21 to hour; stand by you always; help you from
816.22 moment to moment. This I could do in the
816.23 beginning: soon /for I know your powers/ you
816.24 would be as strong and apt as myself, and would
816.25 not require my help."
816.26 "But my powers -- where are they for this
816.27 undertaking? I do not feel them. Nothing
816.28 speaks or stirs in me while you talk. I am sen-sible
817.01 of no light kindling -- no life quickening --
817.02 no voice counselling or cheering. Oh, I wish I
817.03 could make you see how much my mind is at
817.04 this moment like a rayless dungeon, with one
817.05 shrinking fear fettered in its depths -- the fear of
817.06 being persuaded by you to attempt what I cannot
817.07 accomplish!"
817.08 "I have an answer for you -- hear it. I have
817.09 watched you ever since we first met. I have
817.10 made you my study for ten months. I have
817.11 proved you in that time by sundry tests: and
817.12 what have I seen and elicited? In the village
817.13 school I found you could perform well, punctu-
817.14 ally, uprightly, labour uncongenial to your habits
817.15 and inclinations; I saw you could perform it with
817.16 capacity and tact: you could win while you con-
817.17 trolled. In the calm with which you learnt you
817.18 had become suddenly rich, I read a mind clear of
817.19 the vice of Demas: -- lucre had no undue power
817.20 over you. In the resolute readiness with which
817.21 you cut your wealth into four shares, keeping but
817.22 one to yourself, and relinquishing the three others
817.23 to the claim of abstract justice, I recognised a soul
817.24 that revelled in the flame and excitement of sacri-
817.25 fice. In the tractability with which, at my wish,

817.26 you forsook a study in which you were interested,
817.27 and adopted another, because it interested me; in
817.28 the untiring assiduity with which you have since
818.01 persevered in it -- in the unflagging energy and
818.02 unshaken temper with which you have met its
818.03 difficulties -- I acknowledge the complement of
818.04 the qualities I seek. Jane, you are docile, dili-
818.05 gent, disinterested, faithful, constant, and coura-
818.06 geous; very gentle, and very heroic: cease to
818.07 mistrust yourself -- I can trust you unreservedly.
818.08 As a conductress of Indian schools, and a helper
818.09 amongst Indian women, your assistance will be to
818.10 me invaluable."
818.11 My iron shroud contracted round me: persua-
818.12 sion advanced with slow sure step. Shut my eyes
818.13 as I would, these last words of his succeeded in
818.14 making the way, which had seemed blocked up,
818.15 comparatively clear. My work, which had ap-
818.16 peared so vague, so hopelessly diffuse, condensed
818.17 itself as he proceeded, and assumed a definite form
818.18 under his shaping hand. He waited for an answer.
818.19 I demanded a quarter of an hour to think, before
818.20 I again hazarded a reply.
818.21 "Very willingly," he rejoined: and rising, he
818.22 strode a little distance up the pass, threw himself
818.23 down on a swell of heath, and there lay still.
818.24 "I can do what he wants me to do: I am
818.25 forced to see and acknowledge that," I meditated
818.26 -- "That is, if life be spared me. But I feel
818.27 mine is not the existence to be long protracted
818.28 under an Indian sun. -- what then? He does not
819.01 care for that: when my time came to die he
819.02 would resign me, in all serenity and sanctity, to
819.03 the God who gave me. The case is very plain
819.04 before me. In leaving England, I should leave
819.05 a loved and empty land -- Mr. Rochester is not
819.06 there: and if he were, what is, what can that
819.07 ever be to me? My business is to live without
819.08 him now: nothing so absurd, so weak as to drag
819.09 on from day to day, as if I were waiting some
819.10 impossible change in circumstances, which might
819.11 reunite me to him. Of course /as St. John once
819.12 said/ I must seek another interest in life to replace
819.13 the one lost: is not the occupation he now offers
819.14 me truly the most glorious man can adopt or God
819.15 assign? Is it not, by its noble cares and sublime
819.16 results, the one best calculated to fill the void left
819.17 by uptorn affections and demolished hopes? I
819.18 believe I must say, yes -- and yet I shudder.
819.19 Alas! If I join St. John, I abandon half my-
819.20 self: if I go to India, I go to premature death.
819.21 And now will the interval between leaving Eng-
819.22 land for India, and India for the grave, be filled?
819.23 Oh, I know well! That, too, is very clear to
819.24 my vision. By straining to satisfy St. John till
819.25 my sinews ache, I shall satisfy him -- to the finest
819.26 central point and farthest outward circle of his
819.27 expectations. If I do go with him -- if I do make
820.01 the sacrifice he urges, I will make it absolutely:
820.02 I will throw all on the altar -- heart, vitals, the
820.03 entire victim. He will never love me; but he
820.04 shall approve me: I will show him energies he
820.05 has not yet seen, resources he has never sus-
820.06 pected. Yes: I can work as hard as he can;
820.07 and with as little grudging.
820.08 "Consent, then, to his demand is possible: but
820.09 for one item -- one dreadful item. It is -- that he
820.10 asks me to be his wife, and has no more of a
820.11 husband's heart for me than that frowning giant
820.12 of a rock, down which the stream is foaming in
820.13 yonder gorge. He prizes me as a soldier would
820.14 a good weapon; and that is all. Unmarried to
820.15 him, this would never grieve me; but can I let
820.16 him complete his calculations -- coolly put into
820.17 practice his plans -- go through the wedding cere-
820.18 mony? Can I receive from him the bridal ring,
820.19 endure all the forms of love /which I doubt not
820.20 he would scrupulously observe/ and know that
820.21 the spirit was quite absent? Can I bear the
820.22 consciousness that every endearment he bestows
820.23 is a sacrifice made on principle? No: such a
820.24 martyrdom would be monstrous. I will never
820.25 undergo it: As his sister, I might accompany
820.26 him -- not as his wife: I will tell him so."
820.27 I looked towards the knoll: there he lay, still as
821.01 a prostrate column; his face turned to me: his eye
821.02 beaming watchful, and keen. He started to his
821.03 feet, and approached me.
821.04 "I am ready to go to India, if I may go free."
821.05 "Your answer requires a commentary," he said;
821.06 "it is not clear."
821.07 "You have hitherto been my adopted brother:
821.08 I, your adopted sister; let us continue as such:
821.09 you and I had better not marry."
821.10 He shook his head. "Adopted fraternity will
821.11 not do in this case. If you were my real sister it
821.12 would be different: I should take you, and seek
821.13 no wife. But, as it is, either our union must be
821.14 consecrated and sealed by marriage, or it cannot
821.15 exist: practical obstacles oppose themselves to any
821.16 other plan. Do you not see it, Jane? Consider
821.17 a moment -- your strong sense will guide you."
821.18 I did consider: and still my sense, such as it
821.19 was, directed me only to the fact that we did not
821.20 love each other as man and wife should; and
821.21 therefore it inferred we ought not to marry. I said
821.22 so. "St. John," I returned, "I regard you as a
821.23 brother -- you, me as a sister: so let us continue."
821.24 "We cannot -- we cannot," he answered, with
821.25 short, sharp determination: "it would not do.
821.26 You have said you will go with me to India: re-

821.27 member -- you have said that."
821.28 "Conditionally."
822.01 well -- well. To the main point -- the de-
822.02 parture with me from England, the co-operation
822.03 with me in my future labors -- you do not object.
822.04 You have already as good as put your hand to the
822.05 plough: you are too consistent to withdraw it.
822.06 You have but one end to keep in view -- how the
822.07 work you have undertaken can best be done.
822.08 Simplify yor complicated interests, feelings,
822.09 thoughts, wishes, aims; merge all considerations in
822.10 one purpose: that of fulfilling with effect -- with
822.11 power -- the mission of your great Master. To do
822.12 so, you must have a coadjutor -- not a brother;
822.13 that is a loose tie: but a husband. I, too, do not
822.14 want a sister: a sister might any day be taken from
822.15 me. I want a wife: the sole helpmeet I can
822.16 influence efficiently in life, and retain absolutely
822.17 till death."
822.18 I shuddered as he spoke: I felt his influence in
822.19 my marrow -- his hold on my limbs.
822.20 "Seek one elsewhere than in me, St. John:
822.21 seek one fitted to you."
822.22 "One fitted to my purpose, you mean -- fitted to
822.23 my vocation. Again I tell you it is not the insig-
822.24 nificant private individual -- the mere man, with
822.25 the man's selfish senses -- I wish to mate; it is the
822.26 missionary."
822.27 'And I will give the missionary my energies --
822.28 it is all he wants -- but not myself: that would be
823.01 only adding the husk and shell to the kernel. For
823.02 them he has no use; I retain them."
823.03 "You cannot -- you ought not. Do you think
823.04 God will be satisfied with half an oblation? Will
823.05 He accept a mutilated sacrifice? It is the cause of
823.06 God I advocate: it is under his standard I enlist
823.07 you. I cannot accept on his behalf a divided
823.08 allegiance: it must be entire."
823.09 "Oh! I will give my heart to God," I said, "You
823.10 do not want it."
823.11 I will not swear, reader, that there was not some-
823.12 thing of repressed sarcasm both in the tone in
823.13 which I uttered this sentence, and in the feeling
823.14 that accompanied it. I had silently feared St. John
823.15 till now, because I had not understood him. He
823.16 had held me in awe, because he had held me in
823.17 doubt. How much of him was saint, how much
823.18 mortal, I could not heretofore tell; but revelations
823.19 were being made in this conference: the analysis
823.20 of his nature was proceeding before my eyes. I
823.21 saw his fallibilities: I comprehended them. I un-
823.22 derstood that, sitting there where I did, on the
823.23 bank of heath, and with that handsome form before
823.24 me, I sat at the feet of a man, erring as I. The
823.25 veil fell from his hardness and despotism. Having
823.26 felt in him the presence of these qualities, I felt
823.27 his imperfection, and took courage. I was with an
824.01 equal -- one with whom I might argue -- one whom,
824.02 if I saw good, I might resist.
824.03 He was silent after I had uttered the last sen-
824.04 tence, and I presently risked an upward glance at
824.05 his countenance. His eye, bent on me, expressed
824.06 at once stern surprise and keen inquiry. "Is she
824.07 sarcastic, and sarcastic to me!" it seemed to say.
824.08 "What does this signify?"
824.09 "Do not let us forget that this is a solemn
824.10 matter," he said, ere long; "one of which we may
824.11 neither think nor talk lightly without sin. I trust,
824.12 Jane, you are in earnest when you say you will
824.13 give your heart to God: it is all I want. Once
824.14 wrench your heart from man, and fix it on your
824.15 Maker, the advancement of that Maker's spiritual
824.16 kingdom on earth will be your chief delight and
824.17 endeavour: you will be ready to do at once what-
824.18 ever furthers that end. You will see what impetus
824.19 would be given to your efforts and mine by our
824.20 physical and mental union in marriage: the only
824.21 union that gives a character permanent con-
824.22 formity to the destinies and designs of human
824.23 beings: and, passing over all minor caprices -- all
824.24 trivial difficulties and delicacies of feeling -- all
824.25 scruple about the degree, kind, strength, or tender-
824.26 ness of mere personal inclination -- you will hasten
824.27 to enter into that union at once."
825.01 "Shall I?" I said, briefly; and I looked at his
825.02 features, beautiful in their harmony, but strangely
825.03 formidable in their still severity: at his brow, com-
825.04 manding but not open; at his eyes, bright and
825.05 deep, and searching, but never soft; at his tall,
825.06 imposing figure; and fancied myself in idea his
825.07 wife. Oh! it would never do! As his curate,
825.08 his comrade, all would be right: I would cross
825.09 oceans with him in that capacity; toil under
825.10 eastern suns, in Asian deserts with him in that
825.11 office; admire and emulate his courage, and devo-
825.12 tion, and vigour; accommodate quietly to his
825.13 masterhood; smile undisturbed at his ineradicable
825.14 ambition; discriminate the Christian from the
825.15 man: profoundly esteem the one, and freely for-
825.16 give the other. I should suffer often, no doubt,
825.17 attached to him only in this capacity: my body
825.18 would be under rather a stringent yoke, but my
825.19 heart and mind would be free. I should still have
825.20 my unblighted self to turn to: my natural unen-
825.21 slaved feelings with which to communicate in
825.22 moments of loneliness. There would be recesses in
825.23 my mind which would be only mine, to which he
825.24 never came; and sentiments growing there fresh
825.25 and sheltered, which his austerity could never
825.26 blight, nor his measured warrior-march trample
825.27 down: but as his wife -- at his side always, and

825.28 always restrained, and always checked -- forced to
826.01 keep the fire of my nature continually low, to com-
826.02 pel it to burn inwardly and never utter a cry,
826.03 though the imprisoned flame consumed vital after
826.04 vital -- this would be unendurable.
826.05 "St. John!" I exclaimed, when I had got so far
826.06 in my meditation.
826.07 "Well?" he answered icily.
826.08 "I repeat: I freely consent to go with you as
826.09 your fellow-missionary; but not as your wife; I
826.10 cannot marry you and become a part of you."
826.11 "A part of me you must become," he answered
826.12 steadily; "otherwise the whole bargain is void.
826.13 How can I, a man not yet thirty, take out with me
826.14 to India a girl of nineteen, unless she be married
826.15 to me? How can we be for ever together -- some-
826.16 times in solitudes, sometimes amidst savage tribes
826.17 -- and unwed?"
826.18 "Very well," I said, shortly; "under the cir-
826.19 cumstances, quite as well as if I were either your
826.20 real sister; or a man and a clergyman like your-
826.21 self."
826.22 "It is known that your are not my sister. I can-
826.23 not introduce you as such: to attempt it would be
826.24 to fasten injurious suspicions on us both. And
826.25 for the rest, though you have a man's vigorous
826.26 brain, you have a woman's heart, and -- it would
826.27 not do."
826.28 "It would do," I affirmed with some disdain,
827.01 "perfectly well. I have a woman's heart; but not
827.02 where you are concerned: for you I have only a
827.03 comrade's constancy; a fellow-soldier's frankness,
827.04 fidelity, fraternity, if you like; a neophyte's respect
827.05 and submission to his hierophant: nothing more
827.06 -- don't fear."
827.07 "It is what I want," he said, speaking to him-
827.08 self; "it is just what I want. And there are
827.09 obstacles in the way: they must be hewn down.
827.10 Jane, you would not repent marrying me; be cer-
827.11 tain of that; we must be married. I repeat it:
827.12 there is no other way; and undoubtedly enough
827.13 of love would follow upon marriage to render the
827.14 union right even in your eyes."
827.15 "I scorn your idea of love," I could not help
827.16 saying; as I rose up and stood before him, leaning
827.17 my back against the rock. "I scorn the counter-
827.18 feit sentiment you offer: yes, St. John, and I scorn
827.19 you when you offer it."
827.20 He looked at me fixedly: compressing his well--
827.21 cut lips while he did so. Whether he was incensed
827.22 or surprised, or what, it was not easy to tell: he
827.23 could command his countenance thoroughly.
827.24 "I scarcely expected to hear that expression
827.25 from you," he said: "I think I have done and
827.26 uttered nothing to deserve scorn."
827.27 I was touched by his gentle tone, and overawed
827.28 by his high, calm mien.
828.01 "Forgive me the words, St. John: but it is your
828.02 own fault that I have been roused to speak so un-
828.03 guardedly. You have introduced a topic on which
828.04 our natures are at variance -- a topic we should
828.05 never discuss: the very name of love is an apple
828.06 of discord between us -- if the reality were required
828.07 what should we do? How should we feel? My
828.08 dear cousin, abandon your scheme of marriage --
828.09 forget it."
828.10 "No," said he; "it is a long-cherished scheme,
828.11 and the only one which can secure my great end:
828.12 but I shall urge you no further at present. To--
828.13 morrow I leave home for Cambridge: I have many
828.14 friends there to whom I should wish to say fare-
828.15 well. I shall be absent a fortnight -- take that
828.16 space of time to consider my offer: and do not
828.17 forget that if you reject it, it is not me you deny,
828.18 but God. Through my means, He opens to you
828.19 a noble career: as my wife only can you enter
828.20 upon it. Refuse to be my wife, and you limit
828.21 yourself for ever to a track of selfish ease and barren
828.22 obscurity. Tremble, lest in that case you should
828.23 be numbered with those who have denied the faith
828.24 and are worse than infidels!"
828.25 He had done. Turning from me, he once
828.26 more --
828.27 "Looked to river, looked to hill:" But this time his feelings were a
829.01 heart: I was not worthy to hear them uttered. As
829.02 I walked by his side homeward, I read well in his
829.03 iron silence all he felt towards me: the disappoint-
829.04 ment of an austere and despotic nature, which has
829.05 met resistance where it expected submission -- the
829.06 disapprobation of a cool, inflexible judgment,
829.07 which has detected in another feelings and views
829.08 in which it has no power to sympathize: in short,
829.09 as a man, he would have wished to coerce me into
829.10 obedience: it was only as a sincere Christian he
829.11 bore so patiently with my perversity, and allowed
829.12 so long a space for reflection and repentance.
829.13 That night, after he had kissed his sisters, he
829.14 thought proper to forget even to shake hands with
829.15 me; but left the room in silence. I -- who, though
829.16 I had no love, had much friendship for him -- was
829.17 hurt by the marked omission: so much hurt that
829.18 tears started to my eyes.
829.19 "I see you and St. John have been quarrelling,
829.20 Jane," said Diana, "during your walk on the moor.
829.21 But go after him; he is now lingering in the pass-
829.22 age, expecting you -- he will make it up."
829.23 I have not much pride under such circum-
829.24 stances: I would always rather be happy than dig-
829.25 nified; and I ran after him -- he stood at the foot
829.26 of the stairs.
829.27 "Good-night, St. John," said I.

829.28   "Good-night, Jane," he replied, calmly.
830.01   "Then shake hands," I added.
830.02 What a cold, loose touch he impressed on my
830.03 fingers! He was deeply displeased by what had
830.04 occurred that day: cordiality would not warm, nor
830.05 tears move him. No happy reconciliation was to
830.06 be had with him -- no cheering smile or generous
830.07 word: but still the Christian was patient and
830.08 placid; and when I asked him if he forgave me,
830.09 he answered that he was not in the habit of
830.10 cherishing the remembrance of vexation; that he
830.11 had nothing to forgive; not having been of-
830.12 fended.
830.13   And with that answer, he left me. I would
830.14 much rather he had knocked me down.
831.01 [Vol. 3 Chapter 9]
831.02 He did not leave for Cambridge the next day, as
831.03 he had said he would. He deferred his departure
831.04 a whole week; and during that time he made me
831.05 feel what severe punishment a good, yet stern, a
831.06 conscientious, yet implacable man can inflict on
831.07 one who has offended him. Without one overt
831.08 act of hostility, one upbraiding word, he contrived
831.09 to impress me momently with the conviction that
831.10 I was put beyond the pale of his favour.
831.11   Not that St. John harboured a spirit of unchris-
831.12 tian vindictiveness -- not that he would have in-
831.13 jured a hair of my head, if it had been fully in his
831.14 power to do so. Both by nature and principle he
831.15 was superior to the mean gratification of ven-
831.16 geance: he had forgiven me for saying I scorned
831.17 him and his love, but he had not forgotten the
831.18 words; and as long as he and I lived he never
831.19 would forget them. I saw by his look, when he
832.01 turned to me, that they were always written on
832.02 the air between me and him; whenever I spoke,
832.03 they sounded in my voice to his ear; and their
832.04 echo toned every answer he gave me.
832.05 He did not abstain from conversing with me:
832.06 he even called me as usual each morning to join
832.07 him at his desk; and I fear the corrupt man within
832.08 him had a pleasure unimparted to, and unshared
832.09 by, the pure Christian, in evincing with what skill
832.10 he could, while acting and speaking apparently just
832.11 as usual, extract from every deed and every phrase
832.12 the spirit of interest and approval which had for-
832.13 merly communicated a certain austere charm to
832.14 his language and manner. To me, he was in
832.15 reality become no longer flesh, but marble: his eye
832.16 was a cold, bright, blue gem; his tongue, a speak-
832.17 ing instrument -- nothing more.
832.18   All this was torture to me -- refined, lingering
832.19 torture. It kept up a slow fire of indignation,
832.20 and a trembling trouble of grief, which harassed
832.21 and crushed me altogether. I felt how -- if I were
832.22 his wife -- this good man, pure as the deep sunless
832.23 source, could soon kill me: without drawing from
832.24 my veins a single drop of blood, or receiving on
832.25 his own crystal conscience the faintest stain of
832.26 crime. Especially I felt this, when I made any
832.27 attempt to propitiate him. No ruth met my ruth.
832.28 He experienced no suffering from estrangement --
833.01 no yearning after reconciliation; and though, more
833.02 than once, my fast falling tears blistered the page
833.03 over which we both bent, they produced no more
833.04 effect on him than if his heart had been really a
833.05 matter of stone or metal. To his sisters, mean-
833.06 time, he was somewhat kinder than usual: as if
833.07 afraid that mere coldness would not sufficiently
833.08 convince me how completely I was banished and
833.09 banned, he added the force of contrast: and this I
833.10 am sure he did, not by malice, but on principle.
833.11   The night before he left home, happening to
833.12 see him walking in the garden about sunset, and
833.13 remembering, as I looked at him, that this man,
833.14 alienated as he now was, had once saved my life,
833.15 and that we were near relations, I was moved to
833.16 make a last attempt to regain his friendship. I
833.17 went out and approached him, as he stood leaning
833.18 over the little gate: I spoke to the point at once.
833.19   "St. John, I am unhappy, because you are still
833.20 angry with me. Let us be friends."
833.21   "I hope we are friends," was the unmoved
833.22 reply; while he still watched the rising of the
833.23 moon, which he had been contemplating as I
833.24 approached.
833.25   "No, St. John, we are not friends as we were.
833.26 You know that."
833.27   "Are we not? That is wrong. For my part,
833.28 I wish you no ill and all good."
834.01 I believe you, St. John; for I am sure you
834.02 are incapable of wishing any one ill: but, as I
834.03 am your kinswoman, I should desire somewhat
834.04 more of affection than that sort of general philan-
834.05 thropy you extend to mere strangers."
834.06   "Of course," he said "Your wish is reason-
834.07 able; and I am far from regarding you as a
834.08 stranger."
834.09   This, spoken in a cool, tranquil tone, was mor-
834.10 tifying and baffling enough. Had I attended to
834.11 the suggestions of pride and ire, I should imme-
834.12 diately have left him: but something worked
834.13 within me more strongly than those feelings could.
834.14 I deeply venerated my cousin's talent and princi-
834.15 ple. His friendship was of value to me: to lose it
834.16 tried me severely. I would not so soon relinquish
834.17 the attempt to reconquer it.
834.18   "Must we part in this way, St. John? And
834.19 when you go to India, will you leave me so, with-
834.20 out a kinder word than you have spoken?"
834.21   He now turned quite from the moon, and faced

834.22 me.
834.23   "When I go to India, Jane, will I leave you?
834.24 what! do you not go to India?"
834.25   "You said I could not, unless I married you."
834.26   "And you will not marry me? You adhere to
834.27 that resolution?"
834.28   Reader, do you know, as I do, what terror those
835.01 cold people can put into the ice of their questions?
835.02 How much of the fall of the avalanche is in their
835.03 anger? of the breaking up of the frozen sea in
835.04 their displeasure?
835.05   "No, St. John, I will not marry you. I adhere
835.06 to my resolution."
835.07   The avalanche had shaken and slid a little
835.08 forward; but it did not yet crash down.
835.09   "Once more, why this refusal?" he asked.
835.10   "Formerly," I answered, "because you did
835.11 not love me; now, I reply, because you almost
835.12 hate me. If I were to marry you, you would
835.13 kill me. You are killing me now."
835.14   His lips and cheeks turned white -- quite
835.15 white.
835.16   "I should kill you -- I am killing you? Your
835.17 words are such as ought not to be used: violent,
835.18 unfeminine, and untrue. They betray an unfor-
835.19 tunate state of mind: they merit severe reproof:
835.20 they would seem inexcusable; but that it is the
835.21 duty of man to forgive his fellow, even until
835.22 seventy-and-seven times."
835.23   I had finished the business now, while
835.24 earnestly wishing to erase from his mind the
835.25 trace of my former offence, I had stamped on that
835.26 tenacious surface, another and far deeper im-
835.27 pression: I had burnt it in.
835.28   "Now you will indeed hate me," I said. "It
836.01 is useless to attempt to conciliate you: I see I
836.02 have made an eternal enemy of you."
836.03   A fresh wrong did these words inflict: the
836.04 worse, because they touched on the truth. That
836.05 bloodless lip quivered to a temporary spasm.
836.06 I knew the steely ire I had whetted. I was
836.07 heart-wrung.
836.08   "You utterly misinterpret my words," I said,
836.09 at once seizing his hand: "I have no inten-
836.10 tion to grieve or pain you -- indeed, I have
836.11 not."
836.12   Most bitterly he smiled -- most decidedly he
836.13 withdrew his hand from mine. "And now you
836.14 recall your promise, and will not go to India at
836.15 all, I presume?" said he, after a considerable
836.16 pause.
836.17   "Yes I will, as your assistant," I answered.
836.18   A very long silence succeeded. What struggle
836.19 there was in him between Nature and Grace
836.20 in this interval, I cannot tell: only singular
836.21 gleams scintillated in his eyes, and strange
836.22 shadows passed over his face. He spoke at
836.23 last.
836.24   "I before proved to you the absurdity of a
836.25 single woman of your age proposing to accom-
836.26 pany abroad a single man of mine. I proved it
836.27 to you in such terms, as, I should have thought,
836.28 would have prevented your ever again alluding to
837.01 the plan. That you have done so, I regret -- for
837.02 your sake."
837.03   I interrupted him. Anything like a tangible
837.04 reproach gave me courage at once. "Keep to
837.05 common sense, St. John: you are verging on
837.06 nonsense. You pretend to be shocked by what
837.07 I have said. You are not really shocked; for,
837.08 with your superior mind, you cannot be either
837.09 so dull or so conceited as to misunderstand my
837.10 meaning. I say again, I will be your curate, if
837.11 you like, but never your wife."
837.12   Again he turned lividly pale; but, as before,
837.13 controlled his passion perfectly. He answered
837.14 emphatically, but calmly: --
837.15   "A female curate, who is not my wife, would
837.16 never suit me. With me, then, it seems, you
837.17 cannot go: but if you are sincere in your offer,
837.18 I will, while in town, speak to a married mis-
837.19 sionary, whose wife needs a coadjutor. Your
837.20 own fortune will make you independent of the
837.21 Society's aid; and thus you may still be spared
837.22 the dishonour of breaking your promise, and
837.23 deserting the band you engaged to join."
837.24   Now I never had, as the reader knows, either
837.25 given any formal promise, or entered into any
837.26 engagement; and this language was all much
837.27 too hard, and much too despotic for the occasion.
837.28 I replied: --
838.01   "There is no dishonour, no breach of pro-
838.02 mise; no desertion in the case. I am not under
838.03 the slightest obligation to go to India: especially
838.04 with strangers. With you, I would have ven-
838.05 tured much; because I admire, confide in, and,
838.06 as a sister, I love you: but I am convinced that,
838.07 go when and with whom I would, I should not
838.08 live long in that climate."
838.09   "Ah! you are afraid of yourself," he said,
838.10 curling his lip.
838.11   "I am. God did not give me my life to throw
838.12 away; and to do as you wish me, would, I begin
838.13 to think, be almost equivalent to committing
838.14 suicide. Moreover, before I definitively resolve
838.15 on quitting England, I will know for certain,
838.16 whether I cannot be of greater use by remaining
838.17 in it than by leaving it."
838.18   "What do you mean?"
838.19   "It would be fruitless to attempt to explain:
838.20 but there is a point on which I have long endured

838.21 painful doubt; and I can go nowhere till by some
838.22 means that doubt is removed."
838.23 "I know where your heart turns, and to what
838.24 it clings. The interest you cherish is lawless and
838.25 unconsecrated. Long since you ought to have
838.26 crushed it: now you should blush to allude to it.
838.27 You think of Mr. Rochester?"
838.28 It was true. I confessed it by silence.
839.01 "Are you going to seek Mr. Rochester?"
839.02 "I must find out what is become of him."
839.03 "It remains for me, then," he said, "to re-
839.04 member you in my prayers; and to entreat God
839.05 for you, in all earnestness, that you may not in-
839.06 deed become a castaway. I had thought I re-
839.07 cognised in you one of the chosen. But God
839.08 sees not as man sees: His will be done."
839.09 He opened the gate, passed through it, and
839.10 strayed away down the glen. He was soon out of
839.11 sight.
839.12 On re-entering the parlour, I found Diana
839.13 standing at the window, looking very thoughtful.
839.14 Diana was a great deal taller than I: she put her
839.15 hand on my shoulder, and, stooping, examined
839.16 my face.
839.17 "Jane," she said, "you are always agitated and
839.18 pale now. I am sure there is something the mat-
839.19 ter. Tell me what business St. John and you
839.20 have on hands. I have watched you this half hour
839.21 from the window: you must forgive my being
839.22 such a spy, but for a long time I have fancied I
839.23 hardly know what. St. John is a strange being
839.24 --"
839.25 She paused -- I did not speak: soon she re-
839.26 sumed: --
839.27 "That brother of mine cherishes peculiar views
840.01 of some sort respecting you, I am sure: he has
840.02 long distinguished you by a notice and interest he
840.03 never showed to any one else -- to what end? I
840.04 wish he loved you -- does he, Jane?"
840.05 I put her cool hand to my hot forehead: "No,
840.06 Die, not one whit."
840.07 "Then why does he follow you so with his
840.08 eyes -- and get you so frequently alone with him,
840.09 and keep you so continually at his side? Mary
840.10 and I had both concluded he wished you to marry
840.11 him."
840.12 "He does -- he has asked me to be his wife."
840.13 Diana clapped her hands. "That is just what
840.14 we hoped and thought! And you will marry
840.15 him, Jane, won't you? And then he will stay in
840.16 England."
840.17 "Far from that, Diana; his sole idea in propos-
840.18 ing to me is to procure a fitting fellow-labourer in
840.19 his Indian toils."
840.20 "What! He wishes you to go to India?"
840.21 "Yes."
840.22 "Madness!" she exclaimed. "You would not
840.23 live three months there, I am certain. You never
840.24 shall go: you have not consented -- have you,
840.25 Jane?"
840.26 "I have refused to marry him -- "
840.27 "And have consequently displeased him?" she
840.28 suggested.
841.01 "Deeply: he will never forgive me, I fear: yet
841.02 I offered to accompany him as his sister."
841.03 "It was frantic folly to do so, Jane. Think of
841.04 the task you undertook -- one of incessant fatigue:
841.05 where fatigue kills even the strong; and you are
841.06 weak. St. John -- you know him -- would urge
841.07 you to impossibilities: with him there would be
841.08 no permission to rest during the hot hours; and
841.09 unfortunately, I have noticed, whatever he exacts,
841.10 you force yourself to perform. I am astonished
841.11 you found courage to refuse his hand. You do
841.12 not love him then, Jane?"
841.13 "Not as a husband."
841.14 "Yet he is a handsome fellow."
841.15 "And I am so plain you see, Die. We should
841.16 never suit."
841.17 "Plain! You? Not at all. You are much
841.18 too pretty, as well as too good, to be grilled alive
841.19 in Calcutta." And again she earnestly conjured
841.20 me to give up all thoughts of going out with her
841.21 brother.
841.22 "I must, indeed," I said; "for when just now
841.23 I repeated the offer of serving him for a deacon,
841.24 he expressed himself shocked at my want of de-
841.25 cency. He seemed to think I had committed an
841.26 impropriety in proposing to accompany him un-
841.27 married: as if I had not from the first hoped to
842.01 find in him a brother; and habitually regarded
842.02 him as such."
842.03 "What makes you say he does not love you,
842.04 Jane?"
842.05 "You should hear himself on the subject. He
842.06 has again and again explained that it is not him-
842.07 self, but his office he wishes to mate. He has told
842.08 me I am formed for labour -- not for love: which
842.09 is true, no doubt. But, in my opinion, if I am not
842.10 formed for love, it follows that I am not formed
842.11 for marriage. Would it not be strange, Die, to be
842.12 chained for life to a man who regarded one but as
842.13 a useful tool?"
842.14 "Insupportable -- unnatural -- out of the ques-
842.15 tion!"
842.16 "And then," I continued, "though I have only
842.17 sisterly affection for him now, yet, if forced to be
842.18 his wife, I can imagine the possibility of conceiv-
842.19 ing an inevitable, strange, torturing kind of love
842.20 for him: because he is so talented; and there is
842.21 often a certain heroic grandeur in his look, manner,

842.22 and conversation. In that case, my lot would be-
842.23 come unspeakably wretched. He would not want
842.24 me to love him; and if I showed the feeling, he
842.25 would make me sensible that it was a superfluity,
842.26 unrequired by him, unbecoming in me. I know
842.27 he would."
843.01 "And yet, St. John is a good man," said Diana.
843.02 "He is a good and a great man: but he forgets,
843.03 pitilessly, the feelings and claims of little people,
843.04 in pursuing his own large views. It is better, there-
843.05 fore, for the insignificant to keep out of his way; lest,
843.06 in his progress, he should trample them down.
843.07 Here he comes! I will leave you, Diana." And I hast-
843.08 ened up stairs, as I saw him entering the garden.
843.09 But I was forced to meet him again at supper.
843.10 During that meal he appeared just as composed as
843.11 usual. I had thought he would hardly speak to
843.12 me, and I was certain he had given up the pursuit
843.13 of his matrimonial scheme: the sequel showed I
843.14 was mistaken on both points. He addressed me
843.15 precisely in his ordinary manner; or what had, of
843.16 late, been his ordinary manner: one scrupulously
843.17 polite. No doubt he had invoked the help of the
843.18 Holy Spirit to subdue the anger I had roused in
843.19 him, and now believed he had forgiven me once
843.20 more.
843.21 For the evening reading before prayers, he
843.22 selected the twenty-first chapter of Revelations.
843.23 It was at all times pleasant to listen, while from his
843.24 lips fell the words of the Bible: never did his fine
843.25 voice sound at once so sweet and full -- never did
843.26 his manner become so impressive in its noble sim-
843.27 plicity, as when he delivered the oracles of God;
843.28 and to-night that voice took a more solemn tone --
844.01 that manner a more thrilling meaning -- as he sat
844.02 in the midst of his house hold circle (the May moon
844.03 shining in through the uncurtained window, and
844.04 rendering almost unnecessary the light of the
844.05 candle on the table/: as he sat there, bending over
844.06 the great old Bible, and described from its page
844.07 the vision of the new heaven and the new earth --
844.08 told how God would come to dwell with men,
844.09 how he would wipe away all tears from their eyes,
844.10 and promised that there should be no more death,
844.11 neither sorrow nor crying, nor any more pain, be-
844.12 cause the former things were passed away.
844.13 The succeeding words thrilled me strangely as he
844.14 spoke them: especially as I felt, by the slight, in-
844.15 describable alteration in sound, that in uttering
844.16 them, his eye had turned on me.
844.17 "He that overcometh shall inherit all things;
844.18 and I will be his God, and he shall be my son.
844.19 But," was slowly, distinctly read, the "fearful, the
844.20 unbelieving, &c., shall have their part in the lake
844.21 which burneth with fire and brimstone, which is
844.22 the second death."
844.23 Henceforward, I knew what fate St. John feared
844.24 for me.
844.25 A calm, subdued triumph, blent with a longing
844.26 earnestness, marked his enunciation of the last
844.27 glorious verses of that chapter. The reader be-
844.28 lieved his name was already written in the Lamb's
845.01 book of life, and he yearned after the hour which
845.02 should admit him to the city to which the kings of
845.03 the earth bring their glory and honour; which
845.04 has no need of sun or moon to shine in it, because
845.05 the glory of God lightens it, and the Lamb is the
845.06 light thereof.
845.07 In the prayer following the chapter, all his
845.08 energy gathered -- all his stern zeal woke: he was
845.09 in deep earnest, wrestling with God, and resolved
845.10 on a conquest. He supplicated strength for the
845.11 weak-hearted; guidance for wanderers from the
845.12 fold: a return, even at the eleventh hour, for
845.13 those whom the temptations of the world and
845.14 the flesh were luring from the narrow path. He
845.15 asked, he urged, he claimed the boon of a brand
845.16 snatched from the burning. Earnestness is ever
845.17 deeply solemn: first, as I listened to that prayer,
845.18 I wondered at his; then, when it continued and
845.19 rose, I was touched by it, and at last awed. He
845.20 felt the greatness and goodness of his purpose so
845.21 sincerely: others who heard him plead for it,
845.22 could not but feel it too.
845.23 The prayer over, we took leave of him: he
845.24 was to go at a very early hour in the morning.
845.25 Diana and Mary having kissed him, left the room
845.26 -- in compliance, I think, with a whispered hint
845.27 from him: I tendered my hand, and wished him
845.28 a pleasant journey.
846.01 "Thank you, Jane. As I said, I shall return
846.02 from Cambridge in a fortnight: that space, then,
846.03 is yet left you for reflection. If I listened to
846.04 human pride, I should say no more to you of
846.05 marriage with me; but I listen to my duty, and
846.06 keep steadily in view my first aim -- to do all
846.07 things to the glory of God. My Master was
846.08 long-suffering: so will I be. I cannot give you
846.09 up to perdition as a vessel of wrath: repent --
846.10 resolve; while there is yet time. Remember,
846.11 we are bid to work while it is day -- warned that
846.12 `the night cometh when no man shall work.`
846.13 Remember the fate of Dives, who had his good
846.14 things in this life. God give you strength to
846.15 choose that better part which shall not be taken
846.16 from you!"
846.17 He laid his hand on my head as he uttered the
846.18 last words. He had spoken earnestly, mildly:
846.19 his look was not, indeed, that of a lover beholding
846.20 his mistress; but it was that of a pastor recalling
846.21 his wandering sheep -- or better, of a guardian

846.22 angel watching the soul for which he is respon-
846.23 sible. All men of talent, whether they be men
846.24 of feeling or not; whether they be zealots, or
846.25 aspirants, or despots -- provided only they be sin-
846.26 cere -- have their sublime moments: when they
846.27 subdue and rule. I felt veneration for St. John
846.28 -- veneration so strong that its impetus thrust me
847.01 at once to the point I had so long shunned. I
847.02 was tempted to cease struggling with him -- to
847.03 rush down the torrent of his will into the gulf
847.04 of his existence, and there lose my own. I was
847.05 almost as hard beset by him now as I had been
847.06 once before, in a different way, by another. I
847.07 was a fool both times. To have yielded then
847.08 would have been an error of principle; to have
847.09 yielded now would have been an error of judg-
847.10 ment. So I think at this hour, when I look
847.11 back to the crisis through the quiet medium of
847.12 time: I was unconcious of folly at the instant.
847.13 I stood motionless under my hierophant's touch.
847.14 My refusals were forgotten -- my fears overcome --
847.15 my wrestlings paralyzed. The Impossible -- i.e.
847.16 my marriage with St. John -- was fast becoming
847.17 the Possible. All was changing utterly, with a
847.18 sudden sweep. Religion called -- Angels beckoned
847.19 -- God commanded -- life rolled together like a
847.20 scroll -- death's gates opening, shewed eternity be-
847.21 yond: it seemed, that for safety and bliss there,
847.22 all here might be sacrificed in a second. The
847.23 dim room was full of visions.
847.24 "Could you decide now?" asked the missionary.
847.25 The inquiry was put in gentle tones: he drew me
847.26 to him as gently. Oh, that gentleness! how far
847.27 more potent is it than force! I could resist St.
847.28 John's wrath: I grew pliant as a reed under his
848.01 kindness. Yet I knew all the time, if I yielded
848.02 now, I should not the less be made to repent, some
848.03 day, of my former rebellion. His nature was not
848.04 changed by one hour of solemn prayer: it was
848.05 only elevated.
848.06 "I could decide if I were but certain," I an-
848.07 swered: "were I but convinced that it is God's
848.08 will I should marry you, I could vow to marry you
848.09 here and now -- come afterwards what would!"
848.10 "My prayers are heard!" ejaculated St. John.
848.11 He pressed his hand firmer on my head, as if he
848.12 claimed me: he surrounded me with his arm, almost
848.13 as if he loved me /I say almost -- I knew the dif-
848.14 ference -- for I had felt what it was to be loved;
848.15 but, like him, I had now put love out of the ques-
848.16 tion, and thought only of duty/: I contended with
848.17 my inward dimness of vision, before which clouds
848.18 yet rolled. I sincerely, deeply, fervently longed
848.19 to do what was right; and only that. "Shew me,
848.20 shew me the path!" I entreated of Heaven. I was
848.21 excited more than I had ever been; and whether
848.22 what followed was the effect of excitement, the
848.23 reader shall judge.
848.24 All the house was still; for I believe all, except
848.25 St. John and myself, were now retired to rest.
848.26 The one candle was dying out: the room was full
848.27 of moonlight. My heart beat fast and thick: I
848.28 heard its throb. Suddenly it stood still to an inexpresible
849.01 feeling that thrilled it through, and
849.02 passed at once to my head and extremities. The
849.03 feeling was not like an electric shock; but it was
849.04 quite as sharp, as strange, as startling: it acted on
849.05 my senses as if their utmost activity hitherto had
849.06 been but torpor; from which they were now sum-
849.07 moned, and forced to wake. They rose expectant:
849.08 eye and ear waited, while the flesh quivered on
849.09 my bones.
849.10 "What have you heard? What do you see?"
849.11 asked St. John. I saw nothing: but I heard a
849.12 voice somewhere cry --
849.13 "Jane! Jane! Jane!" nothing more.
849.14 "Oh, God! what is it?" I gasped.
849.15 I might have said, "Where is it?" for it did not
849.16 seem in the room -- nor in the house -- nor in the
849.17 garden: it did not come out of the air -- nor from
849.18 under the earth -- nor from overhead. I had heard
849.19 it -- where, or whence, for ever impossible to know!
849.20 And it was the voice of a human being -- a known,
849.21 loved, well-remembered voice -- that of Edward
849.22 Fairfax Rochester; and it spoke in pain and woe
849.23 wildly, eerily, urgently.
849.24 "I am coming!" I cried. "Wait for me! Oh,
849.25 I will come!" I flew to the door, and looked into
849.26 the passage: it was dark. I ran out into the gar-
849.27 den: it was void.
849.28 "Where are you?" I exclaimed.
850.01 The hills beyond Marsh-Glen sent the answer
850.02 faintly back -- "Where are you?" I listened. The
850.03 wind sighed low in the firs: all was moorland lone-
850.04 liness and midnight hush.
850.05 "Down superstition!" I commented, as that
850.06 spectre rose up black by the black yew at the gate.
850.07 "This is not thy deception, nor thy witchcraft: it
850.08 is the work of nature. She was roused, and did --
850.09 no miracle -- but her best."
850.10 I broke from St. John; who had followed, and
850.11 would have detained me. It was my turn to
850.12 assume ascendancy. My powers were in play, and
850.13 in force. I told him to forbear question or remark;
850.14 I desired him to leave me: I must, and would be
850.15 alone. He obeyed at once. Where there is
850.16 energy to command well enough, obedience never
850.17 fails. I mounted to my chamber; locked myself
850.18 in; fell on my knees; and prayed in my way -- a
850.19 different way to St. John's, but effective in its own
850.20 fashion. I seemed to penetrate very near a Mighty
850.21 Spirit; and my soul rushed out in gratitude at His
850.22 feet. I rose from the thanksgiving -- took a resolve
850.23 -- and lay down, unscared, enlightened -- eager but
850.24 for the daylight.
851.01 [Vol. 3 Chapter 10]
851.02 The daylight came. I rose at dawn. I busied
851.03 myself for an hour or two with arranging my
851.04 things in my chamber, drawers and wardrobe,
851.05 in the order wherein I should wish to leave them
851.06 during a brief absence. Meantime, I heard St.
851.07 John quit his room. He stopped at my door: I
851.08 feared he would knock -- no, but a slip of paper
851.09 was passed under the door. I took it up. I
851.10 bore these words --
851.11 "You left me too suddenly last night. Had
851.12 you stayed but a little longer, you would have
851.13 laid your hand on the Christian's cross and the
851.14 angel's crown. I shall expect your clear decision
851.15 when I return this day fortnight. Meantime,
851.16 watch and pray that you enter not into temptation:
851.17 the spirit, I trust, is willing, but the flesh, I see,
851.18 is weak. I shall pray for you hourly. -- Yours,
851.19 St. John,"
852.01 "My spirit," I answered, mentally, "is willing
852.02 to do what is right; and my flesh, I hope, is
852.03 strong enough to accomplish the will of Heaven,
852.04 when once that will is distinctly known to me.
852.05 At any rate, it shall be strong enough to search --
852.06 inquire -- to grope an outlet from this cloud of
852.07 doubt, and find the open day of certainty."
852.08 It was the first of June; yet the morning was
852.09 overcast and chilly: rain beat fast on my casement.
852.10 I heard the front-door open, and St. John pass
852.11 out. Looking through the window, I saw him
852.12 traverse the garden. He took the way over the
852.13 misty moors in the direction of Whitcross -- there
852.14 he would meet the coach.
852.15 "In a few more hours I shall succeed you in
852.16 that track, cousin," thought I: "I too have a
852.17 coach to meet at Whitcross. I too have some to see
852.18 and ask after in England, before I depart for ever."
852.19 It wanted yet two hours of breakfast-time. I
852.20 filled the interval in walking softly about my room,
852.21 and pondering the visitation which had given my
852.22 plans their present bent. I recalled that inward
852.23 sensation I had experienced: for I could recall it,
852.24 with all its unspeakable strangeness. I recalled
852.25 the voice I had heard; again I questioned whence
852.26 it came, as vainly as before: it seemed in me -- not
852.27 in the external world. I asked, was it a mere
852.28 nervous impression -- a delusion? I could not
853.01 conceive or believe: it was more like an inspiration.
853.02 The wondrous shock of feeling had come like the
853.03 earthquake which shook the foundations of Paul
853.04 and Silas's prison: it had opened the doors of the
853.05 soul's cell, and its bands -- it had wakened
853.06 it out of its sleep, whence it sprang trembling,
853.07 listening, aghast; then vibrated thrice a cry on my
853.08 startled ear, and in my quaking heart, and through
853.09 my spirit; which neither feared nor shook, but
853.10 exulted as if in joy over the success of one effort
853.11 it had been privileged to make, independent of
853.12 the cumbrous body.
853.13 "Ere many days," I said, as I terminated my
853.14 musings, "I will know something of him whose
853.15 voice seemed last night to summon me. Letters
853.16 have proved of no avail -- personal inquiry shall
853.17 replace them."
853.18 At breakfast, I announced to Diana and Mary
853.19 that I was going a journey, and should be absent
853.20 at least four days.
853.21 "Alone, Jane?" they asked.
853.22 "Yes; it was to see, or hear news of, a friend
853.23 about whom I had for some time been uneasy."
853.24 They might have said, as I have no doubt they
853.25 thought, that they had believed me to be without
853.26 any friends save them: for, indeed, I had often
853.27 said so; but with their true, natural delicacy, they
853.28 abstained from comment: except that Diana asked
854.01 me if I was sure I was well enough to travel. I
854.02 looked very pale, she observed. I replied, that no-
854.03 thing ailed me save anxiety of mind, which I hoped
854.04 soon to alleviate.
854.05 It was easy to make my further arrangements;
854.06 for I was troubled with no inquiries -- no surmises.
854.07 Having once explained to them that I could not
854.08 now be explicit about my plans, they kindly and
854.09 wisely acquiesced in the silence with which I pur-
854.10 sued them; according to me the privilege of free
854.11 action I should, under similar circumstances, have
854.12 accorded them.
854.13 I left Moor-House at three o'clock P.M., and
854.14 soon after four, I stood at the foot of the sign-post
854.15 of Whitcross, waiting the arrival of the coach
854.16 which was to take me to distant Thornfield.
854.17 Amidst the silence of those solitary roads and desert
854.18 hills, I heard it approach from a great distance.
854.19 It was the same vehicle whence, a year ago, I had
854.20 alighted on summer evening on this very spot --
854.21 how desolate, and hopeless, and objectless! It
854.22 stopped as I beckoned. I entered -- not now obliged
854.23 to part with my whole fortune as the price of its
854.24 accommodation. Once more on the road to Thorn-
854.25 field, I felt like the messenger-pigeon flying home.
854.26 It was a journey of six-and-thirty hours. I had
854.27 set out from Whitcross on a Tuesday afternoon,
854.28 and early on the succeeding Thursday morning the
855.01 coach stopped to water the horses at a wayside inn,
855.02 situated in the midst of scenery whose green hedges
855.03 and large fields, and low pastoral hills, /how mild of
855.04 feature and verdant of hue compared with the

855.05 stern north-midland moors of Morton!/ met my
855.06 eye like the lineaments of a once familiar face.
855.07 Yes, I knew the character of this landscape: I was
855.08 sure we were near my bourne.
855.09 "How far is Thornfield-Hall from here?" I
855.10 asked of the ostler.
855.11 "Just two miles, ma'am, across the fields."
855.12 "My journey is closed," I thought to myself.
855.13 I got out of the coach, gave a box I had into the
855.14 ostler's charge, to be kept till I called for it; paid
855.15 my fare; satisfied the coachman, and was going:
855.16 the brightening day gleamed on the sign of the inn,
855.17 and I read in gilt letters, "The Rochester Arms."
855.18 My heart leapt up: I was already on my master's
855.19 very lands. It fell again: the thought struck it: --
855.20 "Your master himself may be beyond the British
855.21 Channel, for aught you know: and then, if he is
855.22 at Thornfield-Hall, towards which you hasten, who
855.23 besides him is there? His lunatic wife; and you
855.24 have nothing to do with him: you dare not speak
855.25 to him or seek his presence. You have lost your
855.26 labour -- you had better go no farther," urged the
855.27 monitor. "Ask information of the people at the
855.28 inn; they can give you all you seek: they can
856.01 solve your doubts at once. Go up to that man,
856.02 and inquire if Mr. Rochester be at home."
856.03 The suggestion was sensible; and yet I could
856.04 not force myself to act on it. I so dreaded a reply
856.05 that would crush me with despair. To prolong
856.06 doubt was to prolong hope. I might yet once more
856.07 see the Hall under the ray of her star. There
856.08 was the stile before me -- the very fields through
856.09 which I had hurried, blind, deaf, distracted, with
856.10 a revengeful fury tracking and scourging me, on
856.11 the morning I fled from Thornfield: ere I well
856.12 knew what course I had resolved to take, I was in
856.13 the midst of them. How fast I walked! How I
856.14 ran sometimes! How I looked forward to catch
856.15 the first view of the well-known woods! with
856.16 what feelings I welcomed single trees I knew, and
856.17 familiar glimpses of meadow and hill between
856.18 them!
856.19 At last the woods rose; the rookery clustered
856.20 dark; a loud cawing broke the morning stillness.
856.21 Strange delight inspired me: on I hastened. An-
856.22 other field crossed -- a lane threaded -- and there
856.23 were the court-yard walls -- the back-offices: the
856.24 house itself, the rookery still hid. "My first view
856.25 of it shall be in front," I determined, "where its
856.26 bold battlements will strike the eye nobly at once,
856.27 and where I can single out my master's very win-
856.28 dow: perhaps he will be standing at it -- he rises
857.01 early: perhaps he is now walking in the orchard,
857.02 or on the pavement in front. Could I but see him!
857.03 -- but a moment! Surely, in that case, I should not
857.04 be so mad as to run to him? I cannot tell -- I am
857.05 not certain. And if I did -- what then? God bless
857.06 him! what then? who would be hurt by my
857.07 once more tasting the life his glance can give me?
857.08 -- I rave: perhaps at this moment he is watching
857.09 the sun rise over the Pyrenees, or on the tideless
857.10 sea of the south."
857.11 I had coasted along the lower wall of the orchard
857.12 -- turned its angle: there was a gate just there,
857.13 opening into the meadow, between two stone pil-
857.14 lars, crowned by stone balls. From behind one
857.15 pillar, I could peep round quietly at full front
857.16 of the mansion. I advanced my head with pre-
857.17 caution, desirous to ascertain if any bedroom
857.18 window-blinds were yet drawn up: battlements,
857.19 windows, long front -- all from this sheltered station
857.20 were at my command.
857.21 The crows sailing overhead perhaps watched me
857.22 while I took this survey. I wonder what they
857.23 thought: they must have considered I was very
857.24 careful and timid at first, and that gradually I grew
857.25 very bold and reckless. A peep, and then a long
857.26 spectacle; and then a departure from my niche and a
857.27 straying out into the meadow; and a sudden stop
857.28 full in front of the great mansion, and a protracted,
858.01 hardy gaze towards it. "what affectation of diffi-
858.02 dence was this at first!" they might have demanded,
858.03 "what stupid regardlessness now?"
858.04 Hear an illustration, reader.
858.05 A lover finds his mistress asleep on a mossy
858.06 bank; he wishes to catch a glimpse of her fair
858.07 face without waking her. He steals softly over the
858.08 grass, careful to make no sound; he pauses -- fan-
858.09 cying she has stirred: he withdraws; not for worlds
858.10 would he be seen. All is still: he again advances:
858.11 he bends above her; a light veil rests on her fea-
858.12 tures: he lifts it, bends lower; now his eyes anti-
858.13 cipate the vision of beauty -- warm, and blooming,
858.14 and lovely, in rest. How hurried was their first
858.15 glance! But how they fix! How he starts! How
858.16 he suddenly and vehemently clasps in both arms
858.17 the form he dared not, a moment since, touch with
858.18 his finger! How he calls aloud a name, and drops
858.19 his burden, and gazes on it wildly! He thus grasps
858.20 and cries, and gazes, because he no longer fears to
858.21 waken by any sound he can utter -- by any move-
858.22 ment he can make. He thought his love slept
858.23 sweetly: he finds she is stone-dead.
858.24 I looked with timorous joy towards a stately
858.25 house: I saw a blackened ruin.
858.26 No need to cower behind a gate-post, indeed! --
858.27 to peep up at chamber lattices, fearing life was astir
858.28 behind them! No need to listen for doors opening
859.01 -- to fancy steps on the pavement of the gravel--
859.02 walk! The lawn, the grounds were trodden and
859.03 waste: the portal yawned void. The front was, as

859.04 I had once seen it in a dream, but a shell-like wall,
859.05 very high and very fragile looking, perforated with
859.06 paneless windows: no roof, no battlements, no
859.07 chimneys -- all had crashed in.
859.08 And there was the silence of death about it:
859.09 the solitude of a lonesome wild. No wonder that
859.10 letters addressed to people here had never received
859.11 an answer: as well despatch epistles to a vault in
859.12 a church-aisle. The grim blackness of the stones
859.13 told by what fate the Hall had fallen -- by confla-
859.14 gration: but how kindled? What story belonged
859.15 to this disaster? What loss, besides mortar, and
859.16 marble, and wood-work, had followed upon it?
859.17 Had life been wrecked, as well as property? If
859.18 so, whose? Dreadful question: there was no one
859.19 here to answer it -- not even dumb sign, mute
859.20 token.
859.21 In wandering round the shattered walls and
859.22 through the devastated interior, I gathered evidence
859.23 that the calamity was not of late occurrence.
859.24 Winter snows, I thought, had drifted through that
859.25 void arch, winter rains beaten in at those hollow
859.26 casements; for, amidst the drenched piles of rub-
859.27 bish, spring had cherished vegetation: grass and
859.28 weed grew here and there between the stones and
860.01 fallen rafters. And oh! where, meantime, was the
860.02 hapless owner of this wreck? In what land?
860.03 Under what auspices? My eye involuntarily wan-
860.04 dered to the gray church tower near the gates, and
860.05 I asked, "Is he with Damer de Rochester, sharing
860.06 the shelter of his narrow marble house?"
860.07 Some answer must be had to these questions.
860.08 I could find it nowhere but at the inn, and thither,
860.09 ere long, I returned. The host himself brought
860.10 my breakfast into the parlour. I requested him to
860.11 shut the door and sit down: I had some questions
860.12 to ask him. But when he complied, I scarcely
860.13 knew how to begin; such horror had I of the
860.14 possible answers. And yet the spectacle of deso-
860.15 lation I had just left, prepared me in a measure
860.16 for a tale of misery. The host was a respectable--
860.17 looking, middle-aged man.
860.18 "You know Thornfield Hall, of course?" I
860.19 managed to say at last.
860.20 "Yes, ma'am; I lived there once."
860.21 "Did you?" Not in my time, I thought: you
860.22 are a stranger to me.
860.23 "I was the late Mr. Rochester's butler," he
860.24 added.
860.25 The late! I seemed to have received with full
860.26 force the blow I had been trying to evade.
860.27 "The late!" I gasped. "Is he dead?"
860.28 "I mean the present gentleman, Mr. Edward's
861.01 father," he explained. I breathed again: my blood
861.02 resumed its flow. Fully assured by these words
861.03 that Mr. Edward -- my Mr. Rochester /God bless
861.04 him, wherever he was!/ -- was at least alive: was,
861.05 in short, "the present gentleman." Gladdening
861.06 words! It seemed I could hear all that was to
861.07 come -- whatever the disclosures might be -- with
861.08 comparative tranquillity. Since he was not in the
861.09 grave, I could bear, I thought, to learn that he
861.10 was at the Antipodes.
861.11 "Is Mr. Rochester living at Thornfield-Hall
861.12 now?" I asked, knowing, of course, what the an-
861.13 swer would be, but yet desirous of deferring the
861.14 direct question as to where he really was.
861.15 "No, ma'am -- oh, no! No one is living there.
861.16 I suppose you are a stranger in these parts, or you
861.17 would have heard what happened last autumn. --
861.18 Thornfield-Hall is quite a ruin: it was burnt down
861.19 just about harvest time. A dreadful calamity!
861.20 such an immense quantity of valuable property
861.21 destroyed: hardly any of the furniture could be
861.22 saved. The fire broke out at dead of night, and
861.23 before the engines arrived from Millcote, the build-
861.24 ing was one mass of flame. It was a terrible
861.25 spectacle: I witnessed it myself."
861.26 "At dead of night!" I muttered. Yes, that was
861.27 ever the hour of fatality at Thornfield. "Was it
861.28 known how it originated?" I demanded.
862.01 "They guessed, ma'am: they guessed. Indeed,
862.02 I should say it was ascertained beyond a doubt.
862.03 You are not perhaps aware," he continued, edging
862.04 his chair a little nearer the table, and speaking low,
862.05 "that there was a lady, -- a -- a lunatic, kept in the
862.06 house?"
862.07 "I have heard something of it."
862.08 "She was kept in very close confinement, ma'am:
862.09 people even for some years was not absolutely cer-
862.10 tain of her existence. No one saw her: they only
862.11 knew by rumour that such a person was at the
862.12 Hall; and who or what she was it was difficult to
862.13 conjecture. They said Mr. Edward had brought
862.14 her from abroad; and some believed she had been
862.15 his mistress. But a queer thing happened a year
862.16 since -- a very queer thing."
862.17 I feared now to hear my own story. I endea-
862.18 voured to recall him to the main fact.
862.19 "And this lady?"
862.20 "This lady, ma'am," he answered, "turned out
862.21 to be Mr. Rochester's wife! The discovery was
862.22 brought about in the strangest way. There was a
862.23 young lady, a governess at the Hall, that Mr. Ro-
862.24 chester fell in --"
862.25 "But the fire," I suggested.
862.26 "I'm coming to that, ma'am -- that Mr. Edward
862.27 fell in love with. The servants say they never saw
862.28 anybody so much in love as he was: he was after
863.01 her continually. They used to watch him -- servants
863.02 will, you know, ma'am -- and he set store on her

863.03 past everything: for all, nobody but him thought
863.04 her so very handsome. She was a little small
863.05 thing, they say, almost like a child. I never saw
863.06 herself; but I've heard Leah, the housemaid, tell
863.07 of her. Leah liked her well enough. Mr. Ro-
863.08 chester was about forty, and this governess not
863.09 twenty; and, you see, when gentlemen of his age
863.10 fall in love with girls, they are often like as if they
863.11 were bewitched: well, he would marry her."
863.12 "You shall tell me this part of the story another
863.13 time," I said; "but now I have a particular reason
863.14 for wishing to hear all about the fire. Was it sus-
863.15 pected that this lunatic, Mrs. Rochester, had any
863.16 hand in it?"
863.17 "You've hit it, ma'am: it's quite certain that it
863.18 was her, and nobody but her, that set it going.
863.19 She had a woman to take care of her called Mrs.
863.20 Poole -- an able woman in her line, and very trust-
863.21 worthy, but for one fault -- a fault common to a
863.22 deal of them nurses and matrons -- she kept a pri-
863.23 vate bottle of gin by her, and now and then took a
863.24 drop over much. It's excusable, for she had a
863.25 hard life of it: but still it was dangerous; for,
863.26 when Mrs. Poole was fast asleep, after the gin and
863.27 water, the mad lady, who was as cunning as a witch,
863.28 would take the keys out of her pocket, let herself
864.01 out of her chamber, and go roaming about the
864.02 house, doing any wild mischief that came into her
864.03 head. They say she had nearly burnt her husband
864.04 in his bed once: but I don't know about that.
864.05 However, on this night, she set fire first to the
864.06 hangings of the room next her own; and then she
864.07 got down to a lower story, and made her way to
864.08 the chamber that had been the governess's -- /she
864.09 was like as if she knew somehow how matters had
864.10 gone on, and had a spite at her/ -- and she kindled
864.11 the bed there: but there was nobody sleeping in
864.12 it, fortunately. The governess had run away two
864.13 months before; and for all Mr. Rochester sought
864.14 her as if she had been the most precious thing he
864.15 had in the world, he never could hear a word of
864.16 her; and he grew savage -- quite savage on his
864.17 disappointment: he never was a wild man, but he
864.18 got dangerous after he lost her. He would be alone,
864.19 too. He sent Mrs. Fairfax, the housekeeper, away
864.20 to her friends at a distance; but he did it hand-
864.21 somely, for he settled an annuity on her for life:
864.22 and she deserved it -- she was a very good woman.
864.23 Miss Adele, a ward he had, was put to school. He
864.24 broke off acquaintance with all the gentry, and
864.25 shut himself up, like a hermit, at the Hall."
864.26 "What! did he not leave England!"
864.27 "Leave England? Bless you, no! He would
864.28 not cross the door-stones of the house; except at
865.01 night, when he walked just like a ghost about the
865.02 grounds and in the orchard as if he had lost his
865.03 senses -- which it is my opinion he had; for a more
865.04 spirited, bolder, keener gentleman than he was be-
865.05 fore that midge of a governess crossed him, you
865.06 never saw, ma'am. He was not a man given to
865.07 wine, or cards, or racing, as some are, and he was
865.08 not so very handsome; but he had a courage and
865.09 a will of his own, if ever man had. I knew him
865.10 from a boy, you see: and for my part I have often
865.11 wished that Miss Eyre had been sunk in the sea
865.12 before she came to Thornfield-Hall."
865.13 "Then Mr. Rochester was at home when the fire
865.14 broke out?"
865.15 "Yes, indeed was he; and he went up to the
865.16 attics when all was burning above and below, and
865.17 got the servants out of their beds and helped them
865.18 down himself -- and went back to get his mad wife
865.19 out of her cell. And then they called out to him
865.20 that she was on the roof; where she was standing,
865.21 waving her arms, above the battlements, and shout-
865.22 ing out till they could hear her a mile off: I saw
865.23 her and heard her with my own eyes. She was a
865.24 big woman, and had long, black hair: we could
865.25 see it streaming against the flames as she stood.
865.26 I witnessed, and several more witnessed Mr. Ro-
865.27 chester ascend through the skylight on to the
865.28 roof: we heard him call "Bertha!" we saw
866.01 him approach her; and then, ma'am, she yelled,
866.02 and gave a spring, and the next minute she lay
866.03 smashed on the pavement."
866.04 "Dead?"
866.05 "Dead? Ay, dead as the stones on which her
866.06 brains and blood were scattered."
866.07 "Good God!"
866.08 "You may well say so, ma'am: it was fright-
866.09 ful!"
866.10 He shuddered.
866.11 "And afterwards?" I urged.
866.12 "Well, ma'am, afterwards the house was burnt
866.13 to the ground: there are only some bits of walls
866.14 standing now."
866.15 "Were any other lives lost?"
866.16 "No -- perhaps it would have been better if there
866.17 had."
866.18 "What do you mean?"
866.19 "Poor Mr. Edward!" he ejaculated, "I little
866.20 thought ever to have seen it! Some say it was a
866.21 just judgment on him for keeping his first mar-
866.22 riage secret, and wanting to take another wife
866.23 while he had one living: but I pity him, for my
866.24 part."
866.25 "You said he was alive?" I exclaimed.
866.26 "Yes, yes: he is alive; but many think he had
866.27 better be dead."
866.28 "Why? How?" My blood was again run-
866.29 ning cold.

867.01 "Where is he?" I demanded. "Is he in Eng-
867.02 land?"
867.03 "Ay -- ay -- he's in England; he can't get out
867.04 of England, I fancy -- he's a fixture now."
867.05 What agony was this! And the man seemed
867.06 resolved to protract it.
867.07 "He is stone-blind," he said at last. "Yes --
867.08 he is stone-blind -- is Mr. Edward."
867.09 I had dreaded worse. I had dreaded he was
867.10 mad. I summoned strength to ask what had
867.11 caused this calamity.
867.12 "It was all his own courage, and a body may
867.13 say, his kindness, in a way, ma'am: he wouldn't
867.14 leave the house till every one else was out before
867.15 him. As he came down the great staircase at
867.16 last, after Mrs. Rochester had flung herself from
867.17 the battlements, there was a great crash -- all fell.
867.18 He was taken out from under the ruins, alive, but
867.19 sadly hurt: a beam had fallen in such a way as to
867.20 protect him partly; but one eye was knocked out,
867.21 and one hand so crushed that Mr. Carter, the sur-
867.22 geon, had to amputate it directly. The other eye
867.23 inflamed: he lost the sight of that also. He is
867.24 now helpless, indeed -- blind and a cripple."
867.25 "Where is he? Where does he now live?"
867.26 "At Ferndean, a manor-house on a farm he has,
867.27 about thirty miles off: quite a desolate spot."
867.28 "Who is with him?"
868.01 "Old John and his wife: he would have none
868.02 else. He is quite broken down, they say."
868.03 "Have you any sort of conveyance?"
868.04 "We have a chaise, ma'am, a very handsome
868.05 chaise."
868.06 "Let it be got ready instantly; and if your
868.07 post-boy can drive me to Ferndean before dark
868.08 this day, I'll pay both you and him twice the hire
868.09 you usually demand."
869.01 [Vol. 3 Chapter 11]
869.02 The manor-house of Ferndean was a building of
869.03 considerable antiquity, moderate size, and no archi-
869.04 tectural pretensions, deep buried in a wood. I had
869.05 heard of it before. Mr. Rochester often spoke of
869.06 it, and sometimes went there. His father had pur-
869.07 chased the estate for the sake of the game covers.
869.08 He would have let the house; but could find no
869.09 tenant, in consequence of its ineligible and insa-
869.10 lubrious site. Ferndean then remained uninhabited
869.11 and unfurnished; with the exception of some two
869.12 or three rooms fitted up for the accommodation of
869.13 the squire when he went there in the season to
869.14 shoot.
869.15 To this house I came, just ere dark, on an even-
869.16 ing marked by the characteristics of sad sky, cold
869.17 gale, and continued small, penetrating rain. The
869.18 last mile I performed on foot, having dismissed the
869.19 chaise and driver with the double remuneration I
869.20 had promised. Even when within a very short
870.01 distance of the manor-house, you could see no-
870.02 thing of it; so thick and dark grew the timber of
870.03 the gloomy wood about it. Iron gates between
870.04 granite pillars showed me where to enter, and
870.05 passing through them, I found myself at once in
870.06 the twilight of close-ranked trees. There was a
870.07 grass-grown track descending the forest-aisle, be-
870.08 tween hoar and knotty shafts and under branched
870.09 arches. I followed it, expecting soon to reach the
870.10 dwelling; but it streached on and on, it wound far
870.11 and farther: no sign of habitation or grounds was
870.12 visible.
870.13 I thought I had taken a wrong direction and
870.14 lost my way. The darkness of natural as well as
870.15 of sylvan dusk gathered over me: I looked round
870.16 in search of another road. There was none: all
870.17 was interwoven stem, columnar trunk, dense, sum-
870.18 mer foliage -- no opening anywhere.
870.19 I proceeded: at last my way opened, the trees
870.20 thinned a little; presently I beheld a railing, then
870.21 the house -- scarce, by this dim light, distinguish-
870.22 able from the trees; so dank and green were its
870.23 decaying walls. Entering a portal, fastened only
870.24 by a latch, I stood amidst a space of enclosed
870.25 ground, from which the wood swept away in a
870.26 semicircle. There were no flowers, no garden--
870.27 beds; only a broad gravel-walk girdling a grass--
870.28 plat, and this set in the heavy frame of the forest.
871.01 The house presented two pointed gables in its
871.02 front; the windows were latticed and narrow: the
871.03 front-door was narrow too, one step led up to it.
871.04 The whole looked, as the host of the Rochester
871.05 arms had said, "quite a desolate spot." It was
871.06 as still as a church on a week-day: the pattering
871.07 rain on the forest leaves was the only sound audi-
871.08 ble in its vicinage.
871.09 "Can there be life here?" I asked.
871.10 Yes: life of some kind there was; for I heard a
871.11 movement -- that narrow front-door was unclosing,
871.12 and some shape was about to issue from the grange.
871.13 It opened slowly: a figure came out into the
871.14 twilight and stood on the step; a man without a
871.15 hat: he stretched forth his hand as if to feel whe-
871.16 ther it rained. Dusk as it was, I had recognised
871.17 him -- it was my master, Edward Fairfax Roches-
871.18 ter, and no other.
871.19 I stayed my step, almost my breath, and stood
871.20 to watch him -- to examine him, myself unseen, and
871.21 alas! to him invisible. It was a sudden meeting,
871.22 and one in which rapture was kept well in check
871.23 by pain. I had no difficulty in restraining my
871.24 voice from exclamation, my step from hasty ad-
871.25 vance.
871.26 His form was of the same strong and stalwart

871.27 contour as ever: his port was still erect, his hair
871.28 was still raven-black; nor were his features altered
872.01 or sunk: not in one year's space, by any sorrow,
872.02 could his athletic strength be quelled, or his vigorous
872.03 prime blighted. But in his countenance, I saw a
872.04 change: that looked desperate and brooding --
872.05 that reminded me of some wronged and fettered
872.06 wild beast or bird, dangerous to approach in his
872.07 sullen woe. The caged eagle, whose gold-ringed
872.08 eyes cruelty has extinguished, might look as looked
872.09 that sightless Samson.
872.10   And, reader, do you think I feared him in his
872.11 blind ferocity? -- if you do, you little know me. A
872.12 soft hope blent with my sorrow that soon I should
872.13 dare to drop a kiss on that brow of rock, and on
872.14 those lips so sternly sealed beneath it: but not yet.
872.15 I would not accost him yet.
872.16   He descended the one step, and advanced slowly
872.17 and gropingly towards the grass-plat, where was
872.18 his daring stride now? Then he paused, as if
872.19 he knew not which way to turn. He lifted his
872.20 hand and opened his eyelids; gazed blank, and
872.21 with a straining effort, on the sky, and towards the
872.22 amphitheatre of trees: one saw that all to him
872.23 was void darkness. He stretched his right hand
872.24 /the left arm, the mutilated one, he kept hidden in
872.25 his bosom/; he seemed to wish by touch to gain
872.26 an idea of what lay around him: he met but va-
872.27 cancy still; for the trees were some yards off where
872.28 he stood. He relinquished the endeavour, folded
873.01 his arms, and stood quiet and mute in the rain,
873.02 now falling fast on his uncovered head. At this
873.03 moment John approached him from some quarter.
873.04   "Will you take my arm, sir?" he said, "there
873.05 is a heavy shower coming on: had you not better
873.06 go in?"
873.07   "Let me alone," was the answer.
873.08   John withdrew, without having observed me.
873.09 Mr. Rochester now tried to walk about: vainly, --
873.10 all was too uncertain, He groped his way back to
873.11 the house, and re-entering it, closed the door.
873.12   I now drew near and knocked: John's wife
873.13 opened for me. "Mary," I said, "how are you?"
873.14   She started as if she had seen a ghost: I calmed
873.15 her. To her hurried "Is it really you, Miss, come
873.16 at this late hour to this 'only place?" I answered
873.17 by taking her hand; and then I followed her into
873.18 the kitchen, where John now sat by a good fire.
873.19 I explained to them, in few words, that I had heard
873.20 all which had happened since I left Thornfield, and
873.21 that I was come to see Mr. Rochester. I asked
873.22 John to go down to the turnpike-house, where I
873.23 had dismissed the chaise, and bring my trunk,
873.24 which I had left there: and then, while I removed
873.25 my bonnet and shawl, I questioned Mary as to
873.26 whether I could be accommodated at the Manor
873.27 House for the night; and finding that arrangements
873.28 to that effect, though difficult, would not be impos-sible,
874.01 I informed her I should stay. Just at this
874.02 moment the parlour-bell rang.
874.03   "When you go in," said I, "tell your master
874.04 that a person wishes to speak to him, but do not
874.05 give my name."
874.06   "I don't think he will see you," she answered;
874.07 "he refuses everybody."
874.08   When she returned, I inquired what he had
874.09 said.
874.10   "You are to send in your name and your busi-
874.11 ness," she replied. She then proceeded to fill a
874.12 glass with water, and place it on a tray, together
874.13 with candles.
874.14   "Is that what he rang for?" I asked.
874.15   "Yes: he always has candles brought in at dark,
874.16 though he is blind."
874.17   "Give the tray to me, I will carry it in."
874.18   I took it from her hand: she pointed me out the
874.19 parlour door. The tray shook as I held it; the
874.20 water spilt from the glass; my heart struck my
874.21 ribs loud and fast. Mary opened the door for me,
874.22 and shut it behind me.
874.23   This parlour looked gloomy: a neglected handful
874.24 of fire burnt low in the grate; and, leaning over
874.25 it, with his head supported against the high, old-
874.26 fashioned mantel-piece, appeared the blind tenant
874.27 of the room. His old dog, Pilot, lay on one side,
875.01 removed out of the way, and coiled up as if afraid
875.02 of being inadvertently trodden upon. Pilot pricked
875.03 up his ears when I came in; then he jumped up
875.04 with a yelp and a whine, and bounded towards
875.05 me: he almost knocked the tray from my hands.
875.06 I set it on the table; then patted him, and said
875.07 softly, "Lie down!" Mr. Rochester turned me-
875.08 chanically to see what the commotion was: but as
875.09 he saw nothing, he returned and sighed.
875.10   "Give me the water, Mary," he said.
875.11   I approached him with the now only half-filled
875.12 glass: Pilot followed me, still excited.
875.13   "What is the matter?" he inquired.
875.14   "Down, Pilot?" I again said. He checked the
875.15 water on its way to his lips, and seemed to listen:
875.16 he drank, and put the glass down. "This is you,
875.17 Mary, is it not?"
875.18   "Mary is in the kitchen," I answered.
875.19   He put out his hand with a quick gesture, but
875.20 not seeing where I stood, he did not touch me.
875.21 "Who is this? Who is this?" he demanded, try-
875.22 ing, as it seemed, to see with those sightless eyes --
875.23 unavailing and distressing attempt! "Answer
875.24 me -- speak again!" he ordered, imperiously and
875.25 aloud.
875.26   "Will you have a little more water, sir? I spilt

875.27 half of what was in the glass," I said.
875.28   "Who is it? What is it? Who speaks?"
876.01   "Pilot knows me, and John and Mary know I
876.02 am here. I came only this evening," I answered.
876.03   "Great God! -- what delusion has come over
876.04 me? what sweet madness has seized me?"
876.05   "No delusion -- no madness: your mind, sir, is
876.06 too strong for delusion, your health too sound for
876.07 frenzy."
876.08   "And where is the speaker? Is it only a voice?
876.09 Oh! I cannot see, but I must feel, or my heart will
876.10 stop and my brain burst. Whatever -- whoever you
876.11 are -- be perceptible to the touch or I cannot live!"
876.12   He groped: I arrested his wandering hand, and
876.13 prisoned it in both mine.
876.14   "Her very fingers!" he cried; "her small,
876.15 slight fingers! If so, there must be more of her."
876.16   The muscular hand broke from my custody;
876.17 my arm was seized, my shoulder -- neck -- waist -- I
876.18 was entwined and gathered to him.
876.19   "Is it Jane? What is it? This is her shape --
876.20 this is her size -- "
876.21   "And this her voice," I added. "She is all here:
876.22 her heart, too. God bless you, sir! I am glad to
876.23 be so near you again."
876.24   "Jane Eyre! -- Jane Eyre," was all he said.
876.25   "My dear master," I answered, "I am Jane
876.26 Eyre: I have found you out -- I am come back
876.27 to you."
876.28   "In truth? -- in the flesh? My living Jane?"
877.01   "You touch me, sir, -- you hold me, and fast
877.02 enough: I am not cold like a corpse, nor vacant
877.03 like air, am I?"
877.04   "My living darling! These are certainly her
877.05 limbs, and these her features: but I cannot be so
877.06 blest after all my misery. It is a dream: such
877.07 dreams as I have had at night when I have clasped
877.08 her once more to my heart, as I do now; and
877.09 kissed her, as thus -- and felt that she loved me,
877.10 and trusted that she would not leave me."
877.11   "Which I never will, sir, from this day."
877.12   "Never will, says the vision? But I always
877.13 woke and found it an empty mockery; and I was
877.14 desolate and abandoned -- my life dark, lonely,
877.15 hopeless -- my soul athirst and forbidden to drink
877.16 -- my heart famished and never to be fed.
877.17 Gentle, soft dream, nestling in my arms now,
877.18 you will fly, too; as your sisters have all fled be-
877.19 fore you: but kiss me before you go -- embrace
877.20 me, Jane."
877.21   "There, sir -- and there!"
877.22   I pressed my lips to his once brilliant and now
877.23 rayless eyes -- I swept his hair from his brow,
877.24 and kissed that too. He suddenly seemed to rouse
877.25 himself: the conviction of the reality of all this
877.26 seized him.
877.27   "It is you -- is it Jane? You are come back to
877.28 me then?"
878.01   "I am."
878.02   "And you do not lie dead in some ditch, under
878.03 some stream? And you are not a pining outcast
878.04 amongst strangers?"
878.05   "No, sir; I am an independent woman now."
878.06   "Independent! What do you mean, Jane?"
878.07   "My uncle in Madeira is dead, and he left me
878.08 five thousand pounds."
878.09   "Ah, this is practical -- this is real!" he cried:
878.10 "I should never dream that. Besides, there is
878.11 that peculiar voice of hers, so animating and
878.12 piquant, as well as soft: it cheers my withered
878.13 heart; it puts life into it. -- What Janet! Are
878.14 you an independent woman? A rich woman?"
878.15   "Quite rich, sir. If you won't let me live with
878.16 you, I can build a house of my own close up to
878.17 your door, and you may come and sit in my parlour
878.18 when you want company of an evening."
878.19   "But as you are rich, Jane, you have now, no
878.20 doubt, friends who will look after you, and not
878.21 suffer you to devote yourself to a blind lameter
878.22 like me?"
878.23   "I told you I am independent, sir, as well as
878.24 rich: I am my own mistress."
878.25   "And you will stay with me?"
878.26   "Certainly -- unless you object. I will be your
878.27 neighbour, your nurse, your housekeeper. I find
878.28 you lonely: I will be your companion -- to read to
879.01 you, to walk with you, to sit with you, to wait on
879.02 you, to be eyes and hands to you. Cease to look
879.03 so melancholy, my dear master; you shall not be
879.04 left desolate, so long as I live."
879.05   He replied not: he seemed serious -- abstracted;
879.06 he sighed; he half-opened his lips as if to speak:
879.07 he closed them again. I felt a little embarrassed.
879.08 Perhaps I had too rashly overleaped convention-
879.09 alities; and he, like St. John, saw impropriety in
879.10 my inconsiderateness. I had indeed made my
879.11 proposal from the idea that he wished and would
879.12 ask me to be his wife: an expectation, not the less
879.13 certain because unexpressed, had buoyed me up,
879.14 that he would claim me at once as his own. But
879.15 no hint to that effect escaping him and his counte-
879.16 nance becoming more overcast, I suddenly re-
879.17 membered that I might have been all wrong, and
879.18 was perhaps playing the fool unwittingly; and I
879.19 began gently to withdraw myself from his arms --
879.20 but he eagerly snatched me closer.
879.21   "No -- no -- Jane; you must not go. No -- I
879.22 have touched you, heard you, felt the comfort of
879.23 your presence -- the sweetness of your consolation:
879.24 I cannot give up these joys. I have little left in
879.25 myself -- I must have you. The world may laugh

879.26 -- may call me absurd, selfish -- but it does not
879.27 signify. My very soul demands you: it will be
880.01 satisfied: or it will take deadly vengeance on its
880.02 frame."
880.03 "Well, sir, I will stay with you: I have said
880.04 so."
880.05 "Yes -- but you understand one thing by staying
880.06 with me; and I understand another. You, per-
880.07 haps, could make up your mind to be about my
880.08 hand and chair -- to wait on me as a kind little
880.09 nurse /for you have an affectionate heart and a
880.10 generous spirit, which prompt you to make sacri-
880.11 fices for those you pity/, and that ought to suffice
880.12 for me no doubt. I suppose I should now enter-
880.13 tain none but fatherly feelings for you: do you
880.14 think so? Come -- tell me."
880.15 "I will think what you like, sir: I am content
880.16 to be only your nurse, if you think it best."
880.17 "But you cannot always be my nurse, Janet:
880.18 you are young -- you must marry one day."
880.19 "I don't care about being married."
880.20 "You should care, Janet: if I were what I once
880.21 was, I would try to make you care -- but -- a sight-
880.22 less block!"
880.23 He relapsed again into gloom. I, on the con-
880.24 trary, became more cheerful, and took fresh
880.25 courage: these last words gave me an insight as to
880.26 where the difficulty lay; and as it was no difficulty
880.27 with me, I felt quite relieved from my previous
881.01 embarrassment. I resumed a livelier vein of con-
881.02 versation.
881.03 "It is time some one undertook to rehumanize
881.04 you," said I, parting his thick and long uncut
881.05 locks; "for I see you are being metamorphosed
881.06 into a lion, or something of that sort. You have a
881.07 `faux air' of Nebuchadnezzar in the fields about
881.08 you, that is certain: your hair reminds me of
881.09 eagles' feathers; whether your nails are grown like
881.10 birds' claws or not, I have not yet noticed."
881.11 "On this arm, I have neither hand nor nails,"
881.12 he said, drawing the mutilate limb from his
881.13 breast, and shewing it to me. "It is a mere stump
881.14 -- a ghastly sight! Don't you think so, Jane?"
881.15 "It is a pity to see it; and a pity to see your
881.16 eyes -- and the scar of fire on your forehead: and
881.17 the worst of it is, one is in danger of loving you
881.18 too well for all this; and making too much of
881.19 you."
881.20 "I thought you would be revolted, Jane, when
881.21 you saw my arm, and my cicatrized visage."
881.22 "Did you? Don't tell me so -- lest I should
881.23 say something disparaging to your judgment.
881.24 Now, let me leave you an instant, to make a better
881.25 fire, and have the hearth swept up. Can you tell
881.26 when there is a good fire?"
881.27 "Yes; with the right eye I see a glow -- a ruddy
881.28 haze."
882.01 "And you see the candles?"
882.02 "Very dimly -- each is a luminous cloud."
882.03 "Can you see me?"
882.04 "No, my fairy: but I am only too thankful too
882.05 hear and feel you."
882.06 "When do you take supper?"
882.07 "I never take supper."
882.08 "But you shall have some to-night. I am
882.09 hungry: so are you, I dare say, only you forget."
882.10 Summoning Mary, I soon had the room in more
882.11 cheerful order: I prepared him, likewise, a com-
882.12 fortable repast. My spirits were excited, and with
882.13 pleasure and ease I talked to him during supper,
882.14 and for a long time after. There was no harassing
882.15 restraint, no repressing of glee and vivacity with
882.16 him; for with him I was at perfect ease, because
882.17 I knew I suited him: all I said or did seemed
882.18 either to console or revive him. Delightful con-
882.19 sciousness! It brought to life and light my whole
882.20 nature: in his presence I thoroughly lived; and
882.21 he lived in mine. Blind as he was, smiles played
882.22 over his face, joy dawned on his forehead: his
882.23 lineaments softened and warmed.
882.24 After supper, he began to ask me many ques-
882.25 tions, of where I had been, what I had been doing,
882.26 how I had found him out; but I gave him only
882.27 very partial replies: it was too late to enter into
882.28 particulars that night. Besides, I wished to touch
883.01 no deep-thrilling chord -- to open no fresh well of
883.02 emotion in his heart: my sole present aim was to
883.03 cheer him. Cheered, as I have said, he was: and
883.04 yet but by fits. If a moment's silence broke the
883.05 conversation, he would turn restless, touch me,
883.06 then say, "Jane."
883.07 "You are altogether a human being, Jane? You
883.08 are certain of that?"
883.09 "I conscientiously believe so, Mr. Rochester."
883.10 "Yet how, on this dark and doleful evening,
883.11 could you so suddenly rise on my lone hearth? I
883.12 stretched my hand to take a glass of water from a
883.13 hireling, and it was given me by you: I asked a
883.14 question, expecting John's wife to answer me, and
883.15 your voice spoke at my ear."
883.16 "Because I had come in, in Mary's stead, with
883.17 the tray."
883.18 "And there is enchantment in the very hour I
883.19 am now spending with you. Who can tell what a
883.20 dark, dreary, hopeless life I have dragged on for
883.21 months past? Doing nothing, expecting nothing;
883.22 merging night in day; feeling but the sensation of
883.23 cold when I let the fire go out, of hunger when I
883.24 forgot to eat: and then a ceaseless sorrow, and,
883.25 at times, a very delirium of desire to behold
883.26 my Jane again. Yes: for her restoration I longed

883.27 far more than for that of my lost sight. How can
884.01 it be that Jane is with me, and says she loves me?
884.02 Will she not depart as suddenly as she came? To--
884.03 morrow I fear I shall find her no more."
884.04 A common-place, practical reply, out of the train
884.05 of his own disturbed ideas, was, I was sure, the
884.06 best and most re-assuring for him in this frame of
884.07 mind. I passed my finger over his eyebrows, and
884.08 remarked that they were scorched, and that I
884.09 would apply something which should make them
884.10 grow as broad and black as ever.
884.11 "Where is the use of doing me good in any
884.12 way, beneficent spirit, when, at some fatal
884.13 moment, you will again desert me -- passing like
884.14 a shadow, whither and how, to me unknown;
884.15 and for me, remaining afterwards undiscover-
884.16 able?"
884.17 "Have you a pocket-comb about you, sir?"
884.18 "What for, Jane?"
884.19 "Just to comb out this shaggy black mane. I
884.20 find you rather alarming, when I examine you
884.21 close at hand: you talk of my being a fairy; but
884.22 I am sure, you are more like a brownie."
884.23 "Am I hideous, Jane?"
884.24 "Very, sir: you always were, you know."
884.25 "Humph! The wickedness has not been taken
884.26 out of you, wherever you have sojourned."
884.27 "Yet I have been with good people; far better
884.28 than you: a hundred times better people; possessed
885.01 of ideas and views you never entertained in your
885.02 life: quite more refined and exalted."
885.03 "Who the deuce have you been with?"
885.04 "If you twist in that way, you will make me
885.05 pull the hair out of your head; and then I think
885.06 you will cease to entertain doubts of my substan-
885.07 tiality."
885.08 "Who have you been with, Jane?"
885.09 "You shall not get it out of me to-night, sir;
885.10 you must wait till to-morrow: to leave my tale
885.11 half-told, will, you know, be a sort of security that
885.12 I shall appear at your breakfast-table to finish it.
885.13 By-the-bye, I must mind not to rise on your hearth
885.14 with only a glass of water, then: I must bring an
885.15 egg at the least, to say nothing of fried ham."
885.16 "You mocking changeling -- fairy-born and
885.17 human-bred! You make me feel as I have not felt
885.18 these twelve months. If Saul could have had you
885.19 for his David, the evil spirit would have been exor-
885.20 cised without the aid of the harp."
885.21 "There, sir, you are read up and made decent.
885.22 Now I'll leave you: I have been travelling these last
885.23 three days, and I believe I am tired. Good-night!"
885.24 "Just one word, Jane: were there only ladies in
885.25 the house where you have been?"
885.26 I laughed and made my escape, still laughing as
885.27 I ran up stairs. "A good idea!" I thought, with
886.01 glee. "I see I have the means of fretting him out
886.02 of his melancholy for some time to come."
886.03 Very early the next morning, I heard him up
886.04 and astir, wandering from one room to another.
886.05 As soon as Mary came down, I heard the question:
886.06 "Is Miss Eyre here?" Then: "Which room did
886.07 you put her into? Was it dry? Is she up? Go
886.08 and ask if she wants anything; and when she will
886.09 come down."
886.10 I came down as soon as I thought there was a
886.11 prospect of breakfast. Entering the room very
886.12 softly, I had a view of him before he discovered
886.13 my presence. It was mournful, indeed, to witness
886.14 the subjugation of that vigorous spirit to a corpo-
886.15 real infirmity. He sat in his chair, -- still, but not
886.16 at rest: expectant evidently; the lines of now
886.17 habitual sadness marking his strong features. His
886.18 countenance reminded one of a lamp quenched,
886.19 waiting to be re-lit -- and alas! it was not himself
886.20 that could now kindle the lustre of animated ex-
886.21 pression: he was dependent on another for that
886.22 office! I had meant to be gay and careless, but the
886.23 powerlessness of the strong man touched my heart
886.24 to the quick: still I accosted him with what vivacity
886.25 I could: --
886.26 "It is a bright, sunny morning, sir," I said.
886.27 "The rain is over and gone, and there is a tender
886.28 shining after it: you shall have a walk soon."
887.01 I had wakened the glow: his features beamed.
887.02 "Oh, you are indeed there, my sky-lark! Come
887.03 to me. You are not gone: not vanished? I heard
887.04 one of your kind an hour ago, singing high over
887.05 the wood: but its song had no music for me, any
887.06 more than the rising sun had rays. All the melody
887.07 on earth is concentrated in my Jane's tongue to
887.08 my ear: /I am glad it is not naturally a silent one/,
887.09 all the sunshine I can feel is in her presence."
887.10 The water stood in my eyes to hear this avowal
887.11 of his dependence: just as if a royal eagle, chained
887.12 to a perch, should be forced to entreat a sparrow to
887.13 become its purveyor. But I would not be lachry-
887.14 mose: I dashed off the salt-drops, and busied my-
887.15 self with preparing breakfast.
887.16 Most of the morning was spent in the open air.
887.17 I led him out of the wet and wild wood into some
887.18 cheerful fields: I described to him how brilliantly
887.19 green they were; how the flowers and hedges
887.20 looked refreshed; how sparkling blue was the
887.21 sky. I sought a seat for him in a hidden and
887.22 lovely spot: a dry stump of a tree; nor did I
887.23 refuse to let him, when seated, place me on his
887.24 knee: why should I, when both he and I were
887.25 happier near than apart? Pilot lay beside us: all
887.26 was quiet. He broke out suddenly while clasping
887.27 me in his arms: --

887.28 "Cruel, cruel deserter! Oh, Jane, what did I
888.01 feel when I discovered you had fled from Thorn-
888.02 field, and when I could nowhere find you; and,
888.03 after examining your apartment, ascertained that
888.04 you had taken no money, nor anything which
888.05 could serve as an equivalent! A pearl necklace I
888.06 had given you lay untouched in its little casket;
888.07 your trunks were left corded and locked as they
888.08 had been prepared for the bridal tour. What
888.09 could my darling do, I asked, left destitute and
888.10 pennyless? And what did she do? Let me hear
888.11 now."
888.12   Thus urged, I began the narrative of my expe-
888.13 rience for the last year. I softened considerably
888.14 what related to the three days of wandering and
888.15 starvation, because to have told him all would
888.16 have been to inflict unnecessary pain: the little I
888.17 did say lacerated his faithful heart deeper than I
888.18 wished.
888.19   I should not have left him thus, he said, with-
888.20 out any means of making my way: I should have
888.21 told him my intention. I should have confided in
888.22 him: he would never have forced me to be his
888.23 mistress. Violent as he had seemed in his despair,
888.24 he, in truth, loved me far too well and too tenderly
888.25 to constitute himself my tyrant: he would have
888.26 given me half his fortune, without demanding so
888.27 much as a kiss in return, rather than I should have
888.28 flung myself friendless on the wide world. I had
889.01 endured, he was certain, more than I had con-
889.02 fessed to him.
889.03   "Well, whatever my sufferings had been they
889.04 were very short," I answered: and then I pro-
889.05 ceeded to tell him how I had been received at
889.06 Moor-House, how I had obtained the office of
889.07 school-mistress, &c. The accession of fortune, the
889.08 discovery of my relations, followed in due order.
889.09 Of course, St. John Rivers' name came in fre-
889.10 quently in the progress of my tale. When I had
889.11 done, that name was immediately taken up.
889.12   "This St. John, then, is your cousin?"
889.13   "Yes."
889.14   "You have spoken of him often: did you like
889.15 him?"
889.16   "He was a very good man, sir; I could not
889.17 help liking him."
889.18   "A good man? Does that mean a respectable,
889.19 well-conducted man of fifty? Or what does it
889.20 mean?"
889.21   "St. John was only twenty-nine, sir."
889.22   "`Jeune encore,` as the French say. Is he a
889.23 person of low stature, phlegmatic, and plain? A
889.24 person whose goodness consists rather in his guilt-
889.25 lessness of vice, than in his prowess in virtue?"
889.26   "He is untiringly active. Great and exalted
889.27 deeds are what he lives to perform."
889.28   "But his brain? That is probably rather soft?
890.01 He means well: but you shrug your shoulders to
890.02 hear him talk?"
890.03   "He talks little, sir: what he does say is ever
890.04 to the point. His brain is first rate, I should
890.05 think: not impressible, but vigorous."
890.06   "Is he an able man, then?"
890.07   "Truly able."
890.08   "A thoroughly educated man?"
890.09   "St. John is an accomplished and profound
890.10 scholar."
890.11   "His manners, I think, you said are not to your
890.12 taste? --priggish and parsonic?"
890.13   "I never mentioned his manners; but, unless
890.14 I had a very bad taste, they must suit it: they
890.15 are polished, calm, and gentlemanlike."
890.16   "His appearance, -- I forget what description
890.17 you gave of his appearance; -- sort of raw curate,
890.18 half strangled with his white neck-cloth, and stilt-
890.19 ed up on his thick-soled highlow, eh?"
890.20   "St. John dresses well. He is a handsome
890.21 man: tall, fair, with blue eyes, and a Grecian
890.22 profile."
890.23   /Aside./ "Damn him!" -- /To me./ "Did you
890.24 like him, Jane?"
890.25   "Yes, Mr. Rochester, I liked him: but you
890.26 asked me that before."
890.27   I perceived, of course, the drift of my interlo-
890.28 cutor. Jealousy had got hold of him: she stung
891.01 him; but the sting was salutary: it gave him
891.02 respite from the gnawing fang of melancholy.
891.03 I would not, therefore, immediately charm the
891.04 snake.
891.05   "Perhaps you would rather not sit any longer
891.06 on my knee, Miss Eyre?" was the next somewhat
891.07 unexpected observation.
891.08   "Why not, Mr. Rochester?"
891.09   "The picture you have just drawn is suggestive
891.10 of a rather too overwhelming contrast. Your words
891.11 have delineated very prettily a graceful Apollo: he
891.12 is present to your imagination, -- tall, fair, blue--
891.13 eyed, and with a Grecian profile. Your eyes dwell
891.14 on a Vulcan, -- a real blacksmith, brown, broad--
891.15 shouldered; and blind and lame into the bar-
891.16 gain."
891.17   "I never thought of it, before; but you certainly
891.18 are rather like Vulcan, sir."
891.19   "Well, -- you can leave me, ma'am: but before
891.20 you go /and he retained me by a firmer grasp than
891.21 ever/, you will be pleased just to answer me a ques-
891.22 tion or two." He paused.
891.23   "What questions, Mr. Rochester?"
891.24   Then followed this cross-examination: --
891.25   "St. John made you school-mistress of Morton
891.26 before he knew you were his cousin?"

891.27   "Yes."
892.01   "You would often see him? He would visit the
892.02 school sometimes?"
892.03   "Daily."
892.04   "He would approve of your plans, Jane? I
892.05 know they would be clever, for you are a talented
892.06 creature?"
892.07   "He approved of them -- yes."
892.08   "He would discover many things in you he
892.09 could not have expected to find? Some of your
892.10 accomplishments are not ordinary."
892.11   "I don't know about that."
892.12   "You had a little cottage near the school, you
892.13 say: did he ever come there to see you?"
892.14   "Now and then."
892.15   "Of an evening?"
892.16   "Once or twice."
892.17   A pause.
892.18   "How long did you reside with him and his
892.19 sisters after the cousinship was discovered?"
892.20   "Five months."
892.21   "Did Rivers spend much time with the ladies
892.22 of his family?"
892.23   "Yes; the back parlour was both his study and
892.24 ours: he sat near the window, and we by the table."
892.25   "Did he study much?"
892.26   "A good deal."
892.27   "What?"
893.01   "Hindostanee."
893.02   "And what did you do meantime?"
893.03   "I learnt German, at first."
893.04   "Did he teach you?"
893.05   "He did not understand German."
893.06   "Did he teach you nothing?"
893.07   "A little Hindostanee."
893.08   "Rivers taught you Hindostanee?"
893.09   "Yes, sir."
893.10   "And his sisters also?"
893.11   "No."
893.12   "Only you?"
893.13   "Only me."
893.14   "Did you ask to learn?"
893.15   "No."
893.16   "He wished to teach you?"
893.17   "Yes."
893.18   A second pause.
893.19   "Why did he wish it? Of what use could
893.20 Hindostanee be to you?"
893.21   "He intended me to go with him to India."
893.22   "Ah! here I reach the root of the matter. He
893.23 wanted you to marry him?"
893.24   "He asked me to marry him."
893.25   "That is a fiction -- an impudent invention to
893.26 vex me."
893.27   "I beg your pardon, it is the literal truth: he
894.01 asked me more than once, and was as stiff about
894.02 urging his point as ever you could be."
894.03   "Miss Eyre, I repeat it, you can leave me. How
894.04 often am I to say the same thing? Why do you
894.05 remain pertinaciously perched on my knee, when
894.06 I have given you notice to quit?"
894.07   "Because I am comfortable there."
894.08   "No, Jane, you are not comfortable there, be-
894.09 cause your heart is not with me: it is with this
894.10 cousin -- this St. John. Oh, till this moment, I
894.11 thought my little Jane was all mine! I had
894.12 a belief she loved me even when she left me: that
894.13 was an atom of sweet in much bitter. Long as
894.14 we have been parted, hot tears as I have wept over our
894.15 separation, I never thought that while I was
894.16 mourning her, she was loving another! But it is
894.17 useless grieving. Jane, leave me: go and marry
894.18 Rivers."
894.19   "Shake me off, then, sir -- push me away, for
894.20 I'll not leave you of my own accord."
894.21   "Jane, I ever like your tone of voice: it still
894.22 renews hope, it sounds so truthful. When I hear
894.23 it, it carries me back a year. I forget that you
894.24 have formed a new tie. But I am not a fool --
894.25 go -- ."
894.26   "Where must I go, sir?"
894.27   "Your own way -- with the husband you have
894.28 chosen."
895.01   "Who is that?"
895.02   "You know -- this St. John Rivers."
895.03   "He is not my husband, nor ever will be. He
895.04 does not love me: I do not love him. He loves
895.05 /as he can love, and that is not as you love/ a
895.06 beautiful young lady called Rosamond. He wanted
895.07 to marry me only because he thought I should
895.08 make a suitable missionary's wife, which she would
895.09 not have done. He is good and great, but severe;
895.10 and, for me, cold as an iceberg. He is not like
895.11 you, sir: I am not happy at his side, nor near him,
895.12 nor with him. He has no indulgence for me -- no
895.13 fondness. He sees nothing attractive in me: not
895.14 even youth -- only a few useful mental points. --
895.15 Then must I leave you, sir, to go to him?"
895.16   I shuddered involuntarily, and clung instinct-
895.17 ively closer to my blind but beloved master. He
895.18 smiled.
895.19   "What, Jane! Is this true? Is such really the
895.20 state of matters between you and Rivers?"
895.21   "Absolutely, sir. Oh, you need not be jealous!
895.22 I wanted to tease you a little to make you less sad:
895.23 I thought anger would be better than grief. But
895.24 if you wish me to love you, could you but see how
895.25 much I do love you, you would be proud and con-
895.26 tent. All my heart is yours, sir: it belongs to you;
895.27 and with you it would remain, were fate to exile the
895.28 rest of me from your presence for ever."

896.01   Again, as he kissed me, painful thoughts dark-
896.02 ened his aspect.
896.03   "My seared vision! My crippled strength!" he
896.04 murmured regretfully.
896.05   I caressed, in order to soothe him. I knew of
896.06 what he was thinking, and wanted to speak for
896.07 him; but dared not. As he turned aside his face
896.08 a minute, I saw a tear slide from under the sealed
896.09 eyelid, and trickle down the manly cheek. My
896.10 heart swelled.
896.11   "I am no better than the old lightning-struck
896.12 chestnut tree in Thornfield orchard;" he remarked,
896.13 ere long. "And what right would that ruin have
896.14 to bid a budding woodbine cover its decay with
896.15 freshness?"
896.16   "You are no ruin, sir -- no lightning-struck tree:
896.17 you are green and vigorous. Plants will grow
896.18 about your roots, whether you ask them or not, be-
896.19 cause they take delight in your bountiful shadow;
896.20 and as they grow they will lean towards you, and
896.21 wind round you, because your strength offers them
896.22 so safe a prop."
896.23   Again he smiled: I gave him comfort.
896.24   "You speak of friends, Jane?" he asked.
896.25   "Yes; of friends," I answered rather hesita-
896.26 tingly: for I knew I meant more than friends, but
896.27 could not tell what other word to employ. He
896.28 helped me.
897.01   "Ah! Jane. But I want a wife."
897.02   "Do you, sir?"
897.03   "Yes: is it news to you?"
897.04   "Of course: you said nothing about it before."
897.05   "Is it unwelcome news?"
897.06   "That depends on circumstances, sir -- on your
897.07 choice."
897.08   "Which you shall make for me, Jane. I will
897.09 abide by your decision."
897.10   "Choose then, sir -- her who loves you best."
897.11   "I will at least choose -- her I love best. Jane,
897.12 will you marry me?"
897.13   "Yes, sir."
897.14   "A poor blind man, whom you will have to lead
897.15 about by the hand?"
897.16   "Yes, sir."
897.17   "A crippled man, twenty years older than you,
897.18 whom you will have to wait on?"
897.19   "Yes, sir."
897.20   "Truly, Jane?"
897.21   "Most truly, sir."
897.22   "Oh! my darling! God bless you and reward
897.23 you!"
897.24   "Mr. Rochester, if ever I did a good deed in
897.25 my life -- if ever I thought a good thought -- if ever
897.26 I prayed a sincere and blameless prayer -- if ever I
897.27 wished a righteous wish, -- I am rewarded now. To
898.01 be your wife is, for me, to be as happy as I can be
898.02 on earth."
898.03   "Because you delight in sacrifice!"
898.04   "Sacrifice! What do I sacrifice? Famine for
898.05 food, expectation for content. To be privileged to
898.06 put my arms round what I value -- to press my lips
898.07 to what I love -- to repose on what I trust: is that
898.08 to make a sacrifice? If so, then certainly I delight
898.09 in sacrifice."
898.10   "And to bear with my infirmities, Jane: to over-
898.11 look my deficiencies."
898.12   "Which are none, sir, to me. I love you better
898.13 now, when I can really be useful to you, than I did
898.14 in your state of proud independence, when you
898.15 disdained every part but that of the giver and pro-
898.16 tector."
898.17   "Hitherto I have hated to be helped -- to be led:
898.18 henceforth, I feel, I shall hate it no more. I did
898.19 not like to put my hand into a hireling's, but it is
898.20 pleasant to feel it circled by Jane's little fingers. I
898.21 preferred utter loneliness to the constant attendance
898.22 of servants; but Jane's soft ministry will be a per-
898.23 petual joy. Jane suits me: do I suit her?"
898.24   "To the finest fibre of my nature, sir."
898.25   "The case being so, we have nothing in the
898.26 world to wait for: we must be married instantly."
898.27   He looked and spoke with eagerness: his old
898.28 impetuosity was rising.
899.01   "We must become one flesh without any delay,
899.02 Jane: there is but the licence to get -- then we
899.03 marry."
899.04   "Mr. Rochester, I have just discovered the sun
899.05 is far declined from its meridian, and Pilot is
899.06 actually gone home to his dinner. Let me look at
899.07 your watch."
899.08   "Fasten it into your girdle, Janet, and keep it
899.09 henceforward: I have no use for it."
899.10   "It is nearly four o'clock in the afternon, sir.
899.11 Don't you feel hungry?"
899.12   "The third day from this must be our wedding--
899.13 day, Jane. Never mind fine clothes and jewels,
899.14 now: all that is not worth a fillip."
899.15   "The sun has dried up all the rain-drops, sir.
899.16 The breeze is still: it is quite hot."
899.17   "Do you know, Jane, I have your little pearl
899.18 necklace at this moment fastened round my bronze
899.19 scrag under my cravat? I have worn it since the
899.20 day I lost my only treasure: as a memento
899.21 of her."
899.22   "We will go home through the wood: that will
899.23 be the shadiest way."
899.24   He pursued his own thoughts without heed-
899.25 ing me.
899.26   "Jane! you think me, I daresay, an irreligious
899.27 dog: but my heart swells with gratitude to the
899.28 beneficent God of this earth just now. He sees

900.01 not as man sees, but far clearer: judges not as
900.02 man judges, but far more wisely. I did wrong: I
900.03 would have sullied my innocent flower -- breathed
900.04 guilt on its purity: the Omnipotent snatched it
900.05 from me. I, in my stiff-necked rebellion, almost
900.06 cursed the dispensation: instead of bending to
900.07 the decree, I defied it. Divine justice pursued
900.08 its course; disasters came thick on me: I was
900.09 forced to pass through the valley of the shadow of
900.10 death. His chastisements are mighty; and one
900.11 smote me which has humbled me for ever. You
900.12 know I was proud of my strength: but what is it
900.13 now, when I must give it over to foreign guidance,
900.14 as a child does its weakness? Of late, Jane --
900.15 only -- only of late -- I began to see and acknow-
900.16 ledge the hand of God in my doom. I began
900.17 to experience remorse, repentance; the wish for
900.18 reconcilement to my Maker. I began sometimes
900.19 to pray: very brief prayers they were, but very
900.20 sincere.
900.21   "Some days since: nay, I can number them --
900.22 four; it was last Monday night, a singular mood
900.23 came over me: one in which grief replaced frenzy
900.24 -- sorrow, sullenness. I had long had the impres-
900.25 sion that since I could nowhere find you, you must
900.26 be dead. Late that night -- perhaps it might be
900.27 between eleven and twelve o'clock -- ere I retired
900.28 to my dreary rest, I supplicated God, that, if it
901.01 seemed good to Him, I might soon be taken
901.02 from this life, and admitted to that world to
901.03 come, where there was still hope of rejoining
901.04 Jane.
901.05   "I was in my own room, and sitting by the
901.06 window, which was open: it soothed me to feel
901.07 the balmy night-air; though I could see no stars
901.08 and only by a vague, luminous haze, knew
901.09 the presence of a moon. I longed for thee,
901.10 Janet! Oh, I longed for thee both with soul and
901.11 flesh! I asked of God, at once in anguish and
901.12 humility, if I had not been long enough desolate,
901.13 afflicted, tormented; and might not soon taste
901.14 bliss and peace once more. That I merited all I
901.15 endured, I acknowledge -- that I could scarcely
901.16 endure more, I pleaded; and the alpha and omega
901.17 of my heart's wishes broke involuntarily from my
901.18 lips, in the words -- "Jane! Jane! Jane!"
901.19   "Did you speak these words aloud?"
901.20   "I did, Jane. If any listener had heard me,
901.21 he would have thought me mad: I pronounced
901.22 them with such frantic energy."
901.23   "And it was last Monday night: somewhere
901.24 near midnight?"
901.25   "Yes; but the time is of no consequence:
901.26 what followed is the strange point. You will
901.27 think me superstitious -- some superstition I have
902.01 in my blood, and always had: nevertheless, this
902.02 is true -- true at least it is that I heard what I
902.03 now relate.
902.04   "As I exclaimed 'Jane! Jane! Jane!' a
902.05 voice -- I cannot tell whence the voice came, but
902.06 I know whose voice it was -- replied, 'I am com-
902.07 ing: wait for me;' and a moment after, went
902.08 whispering on the wind, the words -- 'where are
902.09 you?'
902.10   "I'll tell you, if I can, the idea, the picture
902.11 these words opened to my mind: yet it is difficult
902.12 to express what I want to express. Ferndean is
902.13 buried, as you can see, in a heavy wood, where sound
902.14 falls dull, and dies unreverberating. 'Where are
902.15 you?' seemed spoken amongst mountains; for I
902.16 heard a hill-sent echo repeat the words. Cooler
902.17 and fresher at the moment the gale seemed to visit
902.18 my brow: I could have deemed that in some
902.19 wild, lone scene, I and Jane were meeting. In
902.20 spirit, I believe, we must have met. You no doubt
902.21 were, at that hour, in unconcious sleep, Jane:
902.22 perhaps your soul wandered from its cell to com-
902.23 fort mine; for those were your accents -- as certain
902.24 as I live -- they were yours!"
902.25   Reader, it was on Monday night -- near midnight
902.26 -- that I too had received the mysterious summons:
902.27 those were the very words by which I replied to
903.01 it. I listened to Mr. Rochester's narrative; but
903.02 made no disclosure in return. The coincidence
903.03 struck me as too awful and inexplicable to be com-
903.04 municated or discussed. If I told anything, my tale
903.05 would be such as must necessarily make a profound
903.06 impression on the mind of my hearer; and that
903.07 mind, yet from its sufferings too prone to gloom,
903.08 needed not the deeper shade of the supernatural.
903.09 I kept these things, then, and pondered them
903.10 in my heart.
903.11   "You cannot now wonder," continued my master,
903.12 "that when you rose upon me so unexpectedy
903.13 last night, I had difficulty in believing you any
903.14 other than a mere voice and vision: something
903.15 that would melt to silence and annihilation, as
903.16 the midnight whisper and mountain echo had
903.17 melted before. Now, I thank God! I know it to
903.18 be otherwise. Yes, I thank God!"
903.19   He put me off his knee, rose, and reverently lift-
903.20 ing his hat from his brow, and bending his sight-
903.21 less eyes to the earth, he stood in mute devotion.
903.22 Only the last words of the worship were audible.
903.23   "I thank my Maker, that in the midst of
903.24 judgment he has remembered mercy. I humbly
903.25 entreat my Redeemer to give me strength to
903.26 lead henceforth a purer life than I have done
903.27 hitherto!"
904.01   Then he stretched his hand out to be led. I
904.02 took that dear hand, held it a moment to my lips,

904.03   then let it pass round my shoulder: being so much
904.04   lower of stature than he, I served both for his
904.05   prop and guide. we entered the wood, and wended
904.06   homeward.
905.01   [Vol. 3 Chapter 12]
905.02   CONCLUSION.
905.03   Reader, I married him. A quiet wedding we had:
905.04   he and I, the parson and clerk, were alone present.
905.05   when we got back from church, I went into the
905.06   kitchen of the manor-house, where Mary was
905.07   cooking the dinner, and John cleaning the knives,
905.08   and I said: --
905.09   "Mary, I have been married to Mr. Rochester
905.10   this morning." The housekeeper and her husband
905.11   were both of that decent phlegmatic order of people,
905.12   to whom one may at any time safely communicate a
905.13   remarkable piece of news without incurring the
905.14   danger of having one's ears pierced by some shrill
905.15   ejaculation, and subsequently stunned by a torrent
905.16   of wordy wonderment. Mary did look up, and
905.17   she did stare at me: the ladle with which she was
905.18   basting a pair of chickens roasting at the fire, did
905.19   for some three minutes hang suspended in air; and
905.20   for the same space of time John's knives also had
906.01   rest from the polishing process: but Mary, bending
906.02   again over the roast, said only --
906.03   "Have you, miss? well, for sure!"
906.04   out with the master, but I didn't know you were
906.05   gone to church to be wed;" and she basted away.
906.06   John, when I turned to him, was grinning from
906.07   ear to ear.
906.08   "I telled Mary how it would be," he said: "I
906.09   knew what Mr. Edward" [John was an old servant,
906.10   and had known his master when he was the cadet
906.11   of the house, therefore, he often gave him his
906.12   christian name] -- "I knew what Mr. Edward would
906.13   do; and I was certain he would not wait long neither:
906.14   and he's done right, for aught I know. I wish you
906.15   joy, miss!" and he politely pulled his forelock.
906.16   "Thank you, John. Mr. Rochester told me to
906.17   give you and Mary this. "I put into his hand a
906.18   five-pound note. Without waiting to hear more, I
906.19   left the kitchen. In passing the door of that sanc-
906.20   tum some time after, I caught the words, --
906.21   "She'll happen do better for him nor ony o't'
906.22   grand ladies." And again, "If she ben't one o'
906.23   th' handsomest, she's noan faal and varry good-
906.24   natured; and i' his een she's fair beautiful, onybody
906.25   may see that."
906.26   I wrote to Moor-House and to Cambridge im-
906.27   mediately, to say what I had done: fully explaining
907.01   also why I had thus acted. Diana and Mary ap-
907.02   proved the step unreservedly. Diana announced
907.03   that she would just give me time to get over the
907.04   honey-moon, and then she would come and see me.
907.05   "She had better not wait till then, Jane," said
907.06   Mr. Rochester, when I read her letter to him; "if
907.07   she does, she will be too late, for our honey-moon
907.08   will shine our life-long: its beams will only fade
907.09   over your grave or mine."
907.10   How St. John received the news, I don't know;
907.11   he never answered the letter in which I communi-
907.12   cated it: yet six months after, he wrote to me; with-
907.13   out, however, mentioning Mr. Rochester's name, or
907.14   alluding to my marriage. His letter was then
907.15   calm; and, though very serious, kind. He has
907.16   maintained a regular, though not frequent corre-
907.17   spondence ever since: he hopes I am happy, and
907.18   trusts I am not of those who live without God in
907.19   the world, and only mind earthly things.
907.20   You have not quite forgotten little Adele, have
907.21   you, reader? I had not; I soon asked and obtained
907.22   leave of Mr. Rochester, to go and see her at the
907.23   school where he had placed her. Her frantic joy
907.24   at beholding me again moved me much. She
907.25   looked pale and thin: she said she was not happy.
907.26   I found the rules of the establishment were too
907.27   strict, its course of study too severe, for a child of
907.28   her age: I took her home with me. I meant to
908.01   become her governess once more; but I soon found
908.02   this impracticable; my time and cares were now
908.03   required by another -- my husband needed them
908.04   all. So I sought out a school conducted on a
908.05   more indulgent system; and near enough to permit
908.06   of my visiting her often, and bringing her home
908.07   sometimes. I took care she should never want for
908.08   anything that could contribute to her comfort: she
908.09   soon settled in her new abode, became very happy
908.10   there, and made fair progress in her studies. As
908.11   she grew up, a sound English education corrected
908.12   in a great measure her French defects; and when
908.13   she left school, I found in her a pleasing and
908.14   obliging companion: docile, good-tempered and
908.15   well-principled. By her grateful attention to me
908.16   and mine, she has long since well repaid any
908.17   little kindness I ever had it in my power to offer
908.18   her.
908.19   My tale draws to its close: one word respecting
908.20   my experience of married life, and one brief glance
908.21   at the fortunes of those whose names have most
908.22   frequently recurred in this narrative, and I have
908.23   done.
908.24   I have now been married ten years. I know
908.25   what it is to live entirely for and with what I love
908.26   best on earth. I hold myself supremely blest --
908.27   blest beyond what language can express; because
908.28   I am my husband's life as fully as he is mine. No
909.01   woman was ever nearer to her mate than I am:
909.02   ever more absolutely bone of his bone, and flesh of
909.03   his flesh. I know no weariness of my Edward's
909.04   society: he knows none of mine, any more than

909.05   we each do of the pulsation of the heart that beats
909.06   in our separate bosoms; consequently, we are ever
909.07   together. To be together is for us to be at once
909.08   as free as in solitude, as gay as in company. We
909.09   talk, I believe, all day long: to talk to each other
909.10   is but a more animated and an audible thinking.
909.11   All my confidence is bestowed on him, all his
909.12   confidence is devoted to me; we are precisely
909.13   suited in character -- perfect concord is the result.
909.14   Mr. Rochester continued blind the first two years
909.15   of our union: perhaps it was that circumstance
909.16   that drew us so very near -- that knit us so very
909.17   close; for I was then his vision, as I am still his
909.18   right hand. Literally, I was [what he often called
909.19   me] the apple of his eye. He saw nature -- he saw
909.20   books through me; and never did I weary of gazing
909.21   on his behalf, and of putting into words the effect
909.22   of field, tree, town, river, cloud, sunbeam -- of the
909.23   landscape before us; of the weather round us --
909.24   and impressing by sound on his ear what light
909.25   could no longer stamp on his eye. Never did I
909.26   weary of reading to him; never did I weary of
909.27   conducting him where he wished to go: of doing
909.28   for him what he wished to be done. And there
910.01   was a pleasure in my services, most full, most ex-
910.02   quisite, even though sad -- because he claimed these
910.03   services without painful shame or damping humi-
910.04   liation. He loved me so truly, that he knew no
910.05   reluctance in profiting by my attendance: he felt
910.06   I loved him so fondly, that to yield that attendance
910.07   was to indulge my sweetest wishes.
910.08   One morning at the end of the two years, as I
910.09   was writing a letter to his dictation, he came and
910.10   bent over me, and said --
910.11   "Jane, have you a glittering ornament round
910.12   your neck?"
910.13   I had a gold watch-chain: I answered "Yes."
910.14   "And have you a pale blue dress on?"
910.15   I had. He informed me then, that for some
910.16   time he had fancied the obscurity clouding one eye
910.17   was becoming less dense; and that now he was
910.18   sure of it.
910.19   He and I went up to London. He had the ad-
910.20   vice of an eminent oculist; and he eventually reco-
910.21   vered the sight of that one eye. He cannot now
910.22   see very distinctly: he cannot read or write much;
910.23   but he can find his way without being led by the
910.24   hand: the sky is no longer a blank to him -- the
910.25   earth no longer a void. When his first-born was
910.26   put into his arms, he could see that the boy had
910.27   inherited his own eyes, as they once were -- large
910.28   brilliant, and black. On that occasion, he again,
911.01   with a full heart, acknowledged that God had tem-
911.02   pered judgment with mercy.
911.03   My Edward and I, then, are happy: and the
911.04   more so, because those we most love are happy
911.05   likewise. Diana and Mary Rivers are both mar-
911.06   ried: alternately, once every year, they come to
911.07   see us, and we go to see them. Diana's husband
911.08   is a captain in the navy; a gallant officer, and a
911.09   good man. Mary's is a clergyman: a college
911.10   friend of her brother's; and, from his attainments
911.11   and principles, worthy of the connexion. Both
911.12   Captain Fitzjames and Mr. Wharton love their
911.13   wives, and are loved by them.
911.14   As to St. John Rivers, he left England: he
911.15   went to India. He entered on the path he had
911.16   marked for himself; he pursues it still. A more re-
911.17   solute, indefatigable pioneer never wrought amidst
911.18   rocks and dangers. Firm, faithful, and devoted;
911.19   full of energy, and zeal, and truth, he labours for
911.20   his race: he clears their painful way to improve-
911.21   ment; he hews down like a giant the prejudices of
911.22   creed and caste that encumber it. He may be
911.23   stern; he may be exacting; he may be ambitious
911.24   yet; but his is the sternness of the warrior
911.25   Greatheart, who guards his pilgrim-convoy from
911.26   the onslaught of Apollyon. His is the exaction of
911.27   the apostle, who speaks but for Christ, when he
911.28   says -- "whosoever will come after me, let him
912.01   deny himself, and take up his cross and follow
912.02   me." His is the ambition of the high master-
912.03   spirit, which aims to fill a place in the first rank of
912.04   those who are redeemed from the earth -- who
912.05   stand without fault before the throne of God; who
912.06   share the last mighty victories of the Lamb; who
912.07   are called, and chosen, and faithful.
912.08   St. John is unmarried: he never will marry now.
912.09   Himself has hitherto sufficed to the toil; and the
912.10   toil drawn near its close: his glorious sun hastens
912.11   to its setting. The last letter I received from him
912.12   drew from my eyes human tears, and yet filled my
912.13   heart with Divine joy: he anticipated his sure
912.14   reward, his incorruptible crown. I know that a
912.15   stranger's hand will write to me next, to say that
912.16   the good and faithful servant has been called at
912.17   length into the joy of his Lord. And why weep
912.18   for this? No fear of death will darken St. John's
912.19   last hour: his mind will be unclouded; his heart
912.20   will be undaunted; his hope will be sure; his faith
912.21   steadfast. His own words are a pledge of this: --
912.22   "My Master," he says, "has forewarned me.
912.23   Daily he announces more distinctly, -- 'Surely I
912.24   come quickly;' and hourly I more eagerly respond,
912.25   -- 'Amen; even so come, Lord Jesus!'"
912.26   [FINIS.]